Mastering™ Visual C++® 6

Michael J. Young

SYBEX®

San Francisco • Paris • Düsseldorf • Soest

Associate Publisher: Gary Masters

Contracts and Licensing Manager: Kristine Plachy

Acquisitions & Developmental Editors: Suzanne Rotondo and Peter Kuhns

Editor: Mark Woodworth

Project Editor: Raquel Baker

Technical Editors: Dale Wright and Brian Donaldson

Book Designer: Catalin Dulfu

Graphic Illustrator: Tony Jonick

Electronic Publishing Specialist: Cynthia Johnsen

Production Coordinators: Charles Mathews and Blythe Woolston

Indexer: Ted Laux

Companion CD: Ginger Warner

Cover Designer: Design Site

Cover Photographer: David Bishop

Screen reproductions produced with Collage Complete.

Collage Complete is a trademark of Inner Media Inc.

SYBEX is a registered trademark of SYBEX, Inc.

Mastering is a trademark of SYBEX Inc.

TRADEMARKS: SYBEX has attempted throughout this book to distinguish proprietary trademarks from descriptive terms by following the capitalization style used by the manufacturer.

The CD Interface music is from GIRA Sound AURIA Music Library ©GIRA Sound 1996.

Library of Congress Card Number: 98-85538

ISBN: 0-7821-2273-6

Manufactured in the United States of America

10 9 8 7 6 5 4 3 2

MFC Classes Discussed in the Book

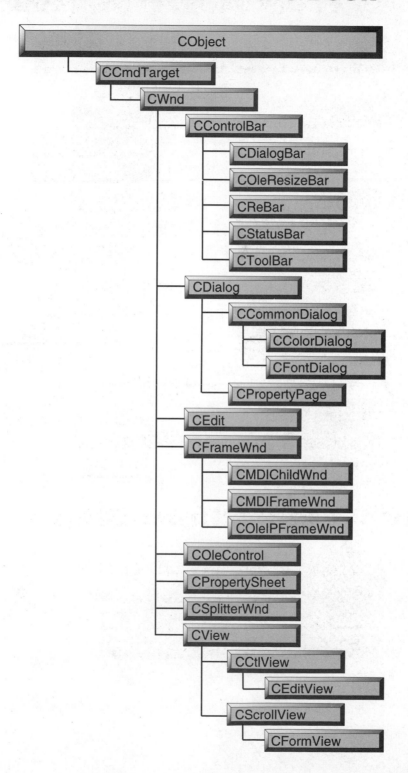

Mastering Visual C++ 6

CONTENTS AT A GLANCE

TABLE OF CONTENTS

INTRODUCTION

Microsoft Visual C++ has always been one of the most comprehensive and sophisticated software development environments available. It has consistently provided a high level of programming power and convenience, while offering a diverse set of tools designed to suit almost every programming style. And Visual C++ version 6 adds significantly to the already impressive array of features. New features include easier application coding, building, and debugging; greater support for ActiveX and Internet technologies; additional database development options; and new application architectures and user-interface elements, such as Microsoft Internet Explorer 4 style controls.

Learning to use Visual C++, however, can be a daunting task. The purpose of this book is to provide you with a single, comprehensive, step-by-step guide to Visual C++. It's designed to be read through from the beginning and to give you a broad general understanding of the product, enabling you to choose the specific tools you need for particular programming tasks and allowing you to find all the information you need to use these tools. The book, however, provides much more than an overview or introduction. The detailed discussions and the tutorial exercises are designed to give you a solid understanding of the key programming tools and techniques, as well as to supply you with the tools and techniques that will help you become proficient in developing your programs.

How, you might ask, can a single book serve as a comprehensive guide to such an enormous product? *Mastering Visual C++ 6* does this in two ways. First, it focuses on the *newer* software technologies (for example, C++, Windows' graphical interface programming, the Microsoft Foundation Classes, and the Wizard code generators), assuming that you have some knowledge of the older technologies (such as C, procedural character-mode programming, and the standard C runtime libraries). Second, the book contains many "pointers" to the comprehensive online documentation provided with Visual C++. Rather than attempting to discuss every detail of every feature—for example, every parameter passed to every function in a particular group—the book provides an in-depth discussion of the key features and then points you to the exact location in the documentation where you can find additional details.

An Overview of the Book

Part I of the book (Chapters 1 and 2) explains how to install and set up both Visual C++ and the companion CD included with this book, and it provides a general description of the components of the Visual C++ product. Part I also introduces you to the basic techniques required to write and build programs using the Visual C++ integrated development environment, the Developer Studio. You'll learn just enough about the Developer Studio to be able to write and test simple example programs as you work through Part II.

Part II (Chapters 3 through 8) offers an introduction to the C++ programming language. These chapters are designed to help you make the transition from C to C++ programming, and they focus on the C++ features used by the Microsoft Foundation Classes. You'll learn just enough C++ programming to be able to understand the C++ techniques given in the coverage of the Microsoft Foundation Classes in Part III.

Part III (Chapters 9 through 25) forms the heart of the book. It explains how to write programs for the graphical user interface of Microsoft Windows 95 or later or Windows NT. (If you have the RISC edition of Visual C++, you can use these techniques to develop for Windows NT on PowerPC, Alpha, or MIPS systems, as well as Intel systems. If you have the Macintosh cross-development edition of Visual C++, you can also develop for the Macintosh or Power Macintosh.) Part III shows you how to use the Developer Studio and the most advanced development tools that it provides, such as the Microsoft Foundation Classes, the Wizard code-generating tools, and the resource editors. Chiefly because of the comparative simplicity of programming with these tools, Part III is able to cover not only the basics of Windows programming, but also many relatively advanced topics, such as implementing split window views, displaying status bars and docking toolbars, writing MDI (multiple document interface) applications, using drawing functions and bitmaps, print previewing, running multiple threads of execution, exchanging data with OLE (object linking and embedding), and creating and using ActiveX controls.

The Companion CD

The compact disc accompanying this book includes all the source files you need to build the example programs in this book, plus the executable files for these programs so that you can run them immediately. Chapter 1 describes the contents of this companion CD and explains how to install and use it.

What Is Required

The book *doesn't* require knowledge of either the C++ language or Windows' graphical interface programming. The book assumes, however, that you have a basic knowledge of the C language. C++ concepts are frequently explained in terms of—or are contrasted with—C language concepts. If you need to learn or review C, you might consult one of the following books, which are among the many good C programming titles: *The C Programming Language* by Kernighan and Ritchie (Prentice-Hall), and *C: A Reference Manual* by Harbison and Steele (Prentice-Hall).

Conventions

The book contains many notes, which are labeled "Note," "Tip," or "Warning." Such notes emphasize important points or expand on topics in the main text. Notes are an integral part of the discussions, and you should read them as you proceed through the text.

The book also contains sidebars, which have titles and are presented in shaded boxes. The sidebars are typically much longer than the notes and provide additional information that's important but not essential for understanding the primary chapter topics. You can therefore safely skip a sidebar or peruse it before or after reading the main text. In some chapters, the sidebars develop a connected thread of topics, so it's best to read them in order.

Finally, the book contains many references to the Visual C++ online help. Chapters 1 and 2 explain how to interpret these references and how to access the online help.

How to Contact the Author

You can send me e-mail at `mjy@compuserve.com`. I welcome your comments
and feedback. Although my schedule seldom permits me to answer questions
that require research (as many of them do), if you have a question I can readily
answer, I'm happy to share what I know. You're also invited to visit my Web site
at `http://ourworld.compuserve.com/homepages/mjy/`. There, you'll find
book corrections, reader questions and answers, programming tips, descriptions of some of my other books, and additional information.

PART I

Introduction to Microsoft Visual C++ 6

CHAPTER
ONE

1

Setting Up the Software

- Installing Microsoft Visual C++ 6

- What's included in Visual C++ 6

- Using the companion CD

This chapter describes how to install Microsoft Visual C++ 6 and provides an overview of the Visual C++ components to help you choose the appropriate installation options and to introduce you to the product. The chapter concludes with instructions for using the companion CD provided with this book.

Installing Microsoft Visual C++ 6

To use Visual C++ 6, you must be running Windows 95 or a later version, or Windows NT version 4.0 or later (see the Visual C++ 6 documentation for additional requirements). To install Visual C++ on your hard disk, insert the product CD into your CD-ROM drive (if there are several CDs, insert the first one). If the CD Autorun feature is enabled on your computer, the Setup program will automatically begin running after a few seconds. If this doesn't happen, run the Setup.exe program in the root folder of the CD. Then simply enter the requested information, and Setup will install Visual C++ 6 on your hard disk.

NOTE   Throughout this book, *Windows 95* refers to Windows 95 or a later version, *Windows NT* refers to Windows NT version 4.0 or later, and *Windows* refers to either system.

The particular Setup options and components that you see depend on whether you have the Visual Studio 6 product (which includes Visual Basic 6, Visual C++ 6, Visual J++ 6, and other development environments) or you have just Visual C++ 6. The available options and components also depend on which version of Visual Studio 6 or Visual C++ 6 you have—Standard, Professional, or Enterprise.

The Setup program will give you the opportunity to customize your installation by choosing individual components from a series of dialog boxes. For example, if you're installing the Visual Studio 6.0 Enterprise Edition, the Setup program displays the "Visual Studio 6.0 Enterprise - Custom" dialog box shown in Figure 1.1. The components listed in this dialog box include all the major development environments provided with Visual Studio 6.0 (Microsoft Visual Basic 6.0, Microsoft Visual C++ 6.0, and so on), plus the following common tools and accessories that you can use with one or more of the development environments:

- ActiveX

- Data Access

- Enterprise Tools

- Graphics

- Tools

Check the box next to each component that you want to include in your installation, and clear the check mark from each component you want to exclude. Click the Select All button if you want to include all the components.

FIGURE 1.1:

The first custom-installation dialog box displayed by the Setup program for Visual Studio 6.0 Enterprise Edition

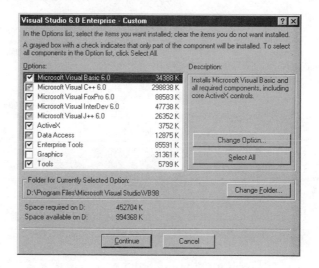

Each of the main Visual Studio components shown in Figure 1.1 consists of a collection of subcomponents, which you can choose individually (except ActiveX, which has no subcomponents). A check mark in a dimmed box indicates that the component will be installed but *not* all its subcomponents. To specify which subcomponents are installed if a component is checked, highlight the component by clicking on it, click the Change Option… button, and then select the subcomponents you want in the dialog box that appears. For example, if you highlight Microsoft Visual C++ 6.0 and click Change Option…, the Visual Studio Setup program will display the dialog box shown in Figure 1.2. This dialog box lists the installable subcomponents that are specific to Visual C++, namely:

- VC++ Developer Studio

- VC++ Runtime Libraries

- VC++ MFC and Template Libraries

- VC++ Build Tools

Many of the subcomponents consist of further subcomponents. You use a sub-component dialog box in the same way as the main Visual Studio component dialog box.

FIGURE 1.2:

The dialog box displayed by the Setup program for Visual Studio 6.0 Enterprise Edition, if you highlight the Microsoft Visual C++ 6.0 component and click the Change Option… button

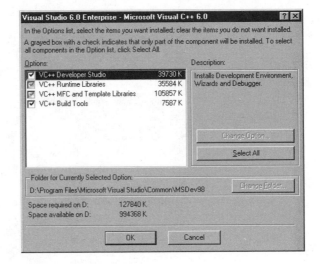

Throughout the remainder of the chapter, all installable components and sub-components will be referred to simply as *components*. The Visual C++ 6.0 components listed above—as well as the common tool and accessory components listed previously—are described in the following section. You might want to read that section before you make your installation choices and complete the installation.

TIP   You can rerun the Setup program at any time to remove components or to include additional ones.

Installing the Visual C++ Online Help

Be sure to install the Visual C++ online help. The book contains *many* references to online help topics, and Chapter 2 (the section "Accessing the Online Help") explains how to use it. To install the online help, follow the instructions provided with your Visual Studio or Visual C++ product. For example, if you have the Visual Studio 6.0 Enterprise Edition, you install the online help by running the Setup program on the MSDN Library CD 1.

What's Included in Visual C++ 6

This section describes each of the Visual C++ components, as well as the common tools and accessories, that you can install with the Setup program. This information indicates which components are required for working with this book. It will help you decide which components you want to install. It will also provide you with an overview of the Visual C++ product and indicate where each component is discussed in this book or in the Visual C++ online help.

NOTE   You might not have all the components discussed here. The particular components available depend on which edition of Visual C++ 6 you have—Standard, Professional, or Enterprise. For example, as you might guess, the Enterprise Features component is included only with the Enterprise Edition.

VC++ Developer Studio

The Developer Studio is the core of the Visual C++ product. It's an integrated application that provides a complete set of programming tools. The Developer Studio includes a project manager for keeping track of your program source files and build options, a text editor for entering program source code, and a set of resource editors for designing program resources, such as menus, dialog boxes, and icons. It also provides programming *wizards* (*AppWizard* and *ClassWizard*), which help you to generate the basic source code for your programs, define C++ classes, handle Windows messages, and perform other tasks. You can build and execute your programs from within the Developer Studio, which automatically runs the optimizing compiler, the incremental linker, and any other required build tools. You can also debug programs using the integrated debugger, and you can view and manage program symbols and C++ classes using the ClassView window. Finally, you can access the Visual C++ online help by choosing commands on the Help menu of the Developer Studio. You'll definitely need to install the Developer Studio to work through the chapters in this book.

The wizards and the resource editors are introduced in Chapter 9, and the other development tools and the online help are introduced in Chapter 2.

VC++ Runtime Libraries

The Visual C++ runtime libraries provide standard functions such as `strcpy` and `sprintf`, which you can call from either C or C++ programs. If you perform a custom installation of Visual C++, the Setup program lets you select the specific library version or versions that you want to copy to your hard disk (static, shared, or single-threaded). You can also opt to copy the runtime library source code. For the purpose of working with this book, you should install the static or shared runtime library (or both); you won't need the source code.

The runtime library functions are discussed throughout the book. Note that the Microsoft Foundation Classes library is *not* part of this component.

VC++ MFC and Template Libraries

The Microsoft Foundation Classes (the MFC) is an extensive C++ class library designed for creating Windows GUI (graphical user interface) programs. The MFC simplifies writing these programs, and it provides many high-level features that can save you considerable coding effort. Although you can build Windows GUI programs in C or C++ *without* using the MFC, this book (in Part III) teaches Windows GUI programming *with* the MFC, so be sure to install it for working with the book.

You can also install the Microsoft Active Template Library (ATL), which is a set of template-based C++ classes that facilitate creating ActiveX controls and other types of COM (Component Object Model) objects. The ATL provides an *alternative* to using the MFC to create COM objects. Objects created using the ATL tend to be smaller and faster than those created using the MFC. However, the ATL doesn't provide the extensive set of built-in features or the ease of programming that the MFC offers. Because this book takes the MFC approach, it doesn't cover the ATL, and you don't need to install the ATL for using the book.

For information on the ATL, see the following topic in the Visual C++ online help: *Visual C++ Documentation, Reference, Microsoft Foundation Class Library and Templates, Active Template Library*.

NOTE The book contains many references to topics in the Visual C++ online help. The Contents tab of the online help window displays the complete help contents in a hierarchical graph. The help citations in this book describe each topic by giving all the headings—from the highest to the lowest level—under which the topic appears in this graph. Accessing the Visual C++ online help is discussed in the section "Accessing the Online Help" in Chapter 2. The headings given in this book are those found in the online help of Visual Studio 6.0 Enterprise Edition (and the top level heading, "MSDN Library Visual Studio 6.0," is omitted because *all* topics fall under this heading). The headings in your Visual Studio or Visual C++ product might be slightly different.

VC++ Build Tools

This component of Visual C++ consists of the optimizing C/C++ compiler, the incremental linker, the resource compiler (for preparing program resources such as menus and dialog boxes), and the other tools required to generate 32-bit Windows programs. You generally run these tools *through* the Microsoft Developer Studio. You'll need these tools to perform the tasks discussed in this book. These tools are used and explained throughout the entire book.

ActiveX

This component installs ActiveX controls that you can add to the Windows programs you create using the Microsoft Foundation Classes library. ActiveX controls are reusable software components that can perform a wide variety of tasks. You don't need to install this component for working with this book. In Chapter 25 you'll learn how to create and use your own ActiveX controls in Visual C++.

Data Access

The Data Access component includes database drivers, controls, and other tools that are used by Visual C++, and that allow you to develop Windows database programs. Although database programming isn't covered in this book, you must select those Data Access subcomponents that are initially selected because they form an essential part of Visual C++ (if you deselect any of them, Setup displays a warning). For information on writing database applications, see the following online help topics: *Visual C++ Documentation, Using Visual C++, Visual C++ Tutorials, Enroll and DAOEnrol: Database Applications*, and *Visual C++ Documentation, Using Visual C++, Visual C++ Programmer's Guide, Adding Program Functionality, Overviews, Overviews: Adding Program Functionality, Databases: Overview*.

Enterprise Tools

This component consists of the following enterprise tools:

- Microsoft Visual SourceSafe 6.0 Client
- Application Performance Explorer
- Repository
- Visual Component Manager
- Self-installing .exe redistributable files
- Visual Basic Enterprise Components
- VC++ Enterprise Tools
- Microsoft Visual Modeler
- Visual Studio Analyzer

Enterprise programming is beyond the scope of this book, and you don't need any of these tools to perform the tasks discussed. For information on the enterprise features see the Visual C++ help topic *Visual C++ Documentation, What's New in Visual C++?, Visual C++ Editions, Enterprise Edition*, and also look up the individual enterprise tools in the online help.

Graphics

This component consists of graphics elements (metafiles, bitmaps, cursors, and icons) as well as video clips that you can add to your programs. You don't need to install any of these elements for working with this book, though you might find them useful for enhancing the example programs and developing programs of your own.

Tools

The Tools component of Visual C++ comprises the following supplemental development tools:

- API Text Viewer
- MS Info
- MFC Trace Utility
- Spy++
- Win 32 SDK Tools
- OLE/Com Object Viewer
- ActiveX Control Test Container
- VC Error Lookup

These tools aren't discussed in the book, and none of them is required to create the example programs presented, although the ActiveX Control Test Container can be quite useful for developing ActiveX controls as described in Chapter 25. For information, look up the individual tools in the Visual C++ online help.

Using the Companion CD

The companion CD provided with this book contains the following files:

- All the source code files required to prepare the example programs given in the book. These files include the numbered listings printed in the book (such as Listing 9.1), project files for building each program using the Developer Studio (as explained in Chapter 2), plus all auxiliary files needed to generate the programs (for example, resource, icon, and bitmap files). For each example program, the book names the companion-CD subfolder that contains all its source files, which is known as the *project folder*. All the project folders are contained within the \Examples folder on the CD.

- The executable program file for each example program, so that you can immediately run the program without having to process its source code. The project folder for each program on the CD includes both the release program version (in the \Release subfolder) and the Debug version (in the \Debug subfolder). Chapter 2 explains these two program versions.

- The code listings from the introduction to C++ given in Part II of the book (which are not part of complete programs). These listings are all contained in the \Cpp subfolder of the \Examples folder on the companion CD folder.

Because the files on the CD are *not* compressed, you can directly read the source files, open the project files in the Developer Studio, or run the executable files. If, however, you want to modify a program's source code and rebuild the program, *you must copy all the program's source files to your hard disk.* You can use your favorite method for copying these files (such as dragging and dropping the folder icon in Windows 95 Explorer), but be sure to copy the *entire project folder* (for example, the \BitDemo folder for the BitDemo program), *together with any subfolders contained within the project folder* (such as the \Debug, \Release, and \Res subfolders within \BitDemo). Also, you can change the name of the project folder (for example, you could rename the \BitDemo folder \MyBitDemo), but don't change the names of the subfolders (these names are stored in the project file for the program). If you want to modify a project, you must also turn off the read-only attribute for all the files contained in the project folder on your hard disk. For tips on turning off the read-only attribute, and for additional information on using the companion CD, see the file Readme.txt in the CD's root folder.

Summary

This chapter explained how to install the Microsoft Visual C++ 6 product and provided an overview of the components of Visual C++. It also explained how to use the companion CD included with the book. The next chapter introduces the Microsoft Developer Studio, by showing you how to use the tools it provides to create a simple *console* (that is, character-mode) program.

CHAPTER

TWO

2

Creating a Program Using the Microsoft Developer Studio

- Creating the project

- Creating and editing the program source file

- Changing project settings

- Building the program

- Running the program

- Debugging the program

The Microsoft Developer Studio is an integrated application that serves as the primary interface for accessing the development tools provided by Microsoft Visual C++. You can use it to manage programming projects, to create and edit program source files, to design program resources (such as menus, dialog boxes, and icons), and even to generate some of the basic program source code (by means of the *wizards*). You can build and debug your programs directly within the Developer Studio. You can also examine and manage program symbols and C++ classes, and you can access the Visual C++ online help, using commands on the Help menu. This chapter will introduce you to all these basic facilities and tools except the resource editors and the wizards, which are used for creating Windows GUI (graphical user interface) programs and are discussed in Part III.

In this chapter, you'll create a very simple *console* (that is, character-mode) program. The knowledge you gain here will allow you to enter and run the example code—as well as to create simple test programs—while you're reading through the introduction to the C++ language given in Part II of the book. Part III provides detailed information on using the Developer Studio to create Windows GUI programs. For further instructions on creating console programs, see the following two Visual C++ online help topics: *Visual C++ Documentation, Using Visual C++, Visual C++ Programmer's Guide, Beginning Your Program, Creating a Console Program*, and *Platform SDK, Windows Base Services, Files and I/O, Consoles and Character-Mode Support*.

Creating the Project

To run the Developer Studio, choose the Microsoft Visual C++ 6 command on the Programs submenu of your Windows Start menu, which will look something like this:

Once the Developer Studio begins running, the first step is to create a *project* for the program you're about to write. A Visual C++ project stores all the information required to build a particular program. This information includes the names and relationships of the program source files; a list of the required library files; and a list of all options for the compiler, linker, and other tools used in building the program.

In this chapter, you'll write an example C++ program named Greet. To create a project for this program, perform the following steps:

1. Choose the File ➤ New... menu command in the Developer Studio, or simply press Ctrl+N. The New dialog box will appear.

2. Open the Projects tab of the New dialog box (if it's not already open), so that you can create a new project.

NOTE

When you create the new project, the Developer Studio automatically creates a *project workspace* and adds the new project to it. A project workspace is capable of storing one or more individual projects. All the example programs in this book use a project workspace that contains only a single project. For more complex undertakings, you can add additional projects to a project workspace, which allows you to open and work with several projects at the same time.

---

3. In the list of project types, select the "Win32 Console Application" item. A *console* application is a 32-bit character-mode program. Like a 16-bit MS-DOS program, it can be run either in a simple window on the Windows desktop or using the full screen. A console program can be written using many of the basic techniques that are commonly used to write character-mode programs for MS-DOS or Unix. Specifically, you can display output and read input using simple stream-mode library functions such as `printf` and `gets` or—in C++ programs—the member functions of the `iostream` class library. The example programs given in Part II of the book use the `iostream` functions and are written as console applications so that you can concentrate on learning C++ without bothering with the complexities of programming for the Windows GUI. In Part III you'll choose the "MFC AppWizard (exe)" project type to write Windows GUI applications using the Microsoft Foundation Classes and the Visual C++ Wizards.

NOTE   For an explanation of the different project types, see the following topic in the online help: *Visual C++ Documentation*, *Using Visual C++*, *Visual C++ User's Guide*, *Working with Projects*, *Overview: Working with Projects*, *Project Types*.

4. Enter Greet into the Project Name: text box. This will cause the Developer Studio to assign the name Greet to the new project (as well as to the project workspace that contains this project).

5. In the Location: text box, specify the path of the folder that is to contain the project files, which is known as the *project folder*. If you wish, you can simply accept the default folder path that is initially contained in this box (the default project folder is given the same name as the project workspace, Greet). Click the button with the ellipsis (...) if you want to search for a different location for the project folder. If the specified project folder doesn't exist, the Developer Studio will create it (it will also create one or more subfolders within the project folder to store output files, as explained later).

6. To complete the Projects tab of the New dialog box, make sure that the Win32 item is checked in the Platforms: area. Unless you have installed a cross-development edition of Visual C++ (such as Microsoft Visual C++ Cross-Development Edition for Macintosh), Win32 will be the only option in this area. *Win32* is the 32-bit API (application programming interface) for both GUI and console programs written for Windows 95 and Windows NT. Selecting the Win32 platform means that the program will be supported by Win32, that it can call the Win32 functions, and that it will be able to run as a 32-bit program on Windows 95 as well as Windows NT. The completed Projects tab is shown in Figure 2.1.

NOTE   Because you didn't previously open an existing project workspace, you can't select the Add To Current Workspace option. You can select only the Create New Workspace option.

FIGURE 2.1:

The completed Projects tab of the New dialog box for creating the Greet example program

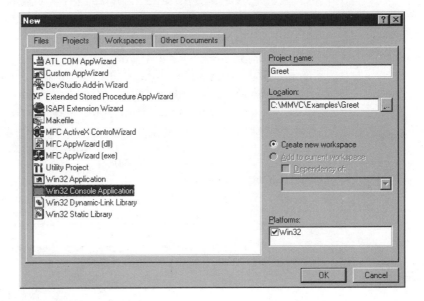

16-Bit vs. 32-Bit Programs

Programs written for MS-DOS and for Windows through version 3.x are *16-bit programs*, meaning that they run in a processor mode that uses 16-bit-wide registers. The primary implications of running in a 16-bit mode are that the size of an integer is 16 bits, and a memory location is addressed using a 16-bit segment address (or segment selector) *plus* a 16-bit offset.

Win32 programs developed with Visual C++ 6 are *32-bit programs*, meaning that they run in a processor mode that uses 32-bit-wide registers. The primary implications of running in a 32-bit mode are that the size of an integer is 32 bits, and a memory location is addressed using a *single* 32-bit address (this is known as a *flat* memory addressing model, and it allows a program to theoretically address up to 4GB of virtual memory).

Using Visual C++ 6, you can develop only 32-bit applications. To develop 16-bit applications (for Windows 3.1 or MS-DOS), you'll need a 16-bit version of Visual C++ or a 16-bit development environment by another vendor.

Note that for compatibility you can run 16-bit MS-DOS and Windows 3.1 programs under Windows 95 or Windows NT, though they can't take full advantage of the system.

7. Click the OK button in the New dialog box. The Developer Studio will now display the Win32 Console Application wizard, which consists of only a single dialog box.

8. In the Win32 Console Application dialog box, select the An Empty Project option as shown in Figure 2.2. This option creates a project without adding any source code files to it. It's recommended for this exercise so that you can learn how to create your own source code files. Later, you can save time by choosing the options A Simple Application or A "Hello, World!" Application, which create initial source code files for you. Or you can choose the An Application That Supports MFC option so that you can use the MFC classes that are compatible with console programs (such as the CString class, and the collection classes discussed in Chapter 11).

FIGURE 2.2:

The completed Win32 Console Application dialog box

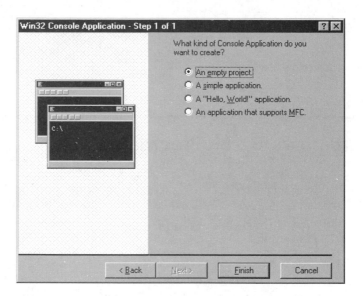

9. Click the Finish button at the bottom of the Win32 Console Application dialog box, and the New Project Information dialog box will appear, which displays basic information on the new project that will be created. See Figure 2.3.

10. Click the OK button at the bottom of the New Project Information dialog box.

The New Project Information
dialog box for the Greet
project

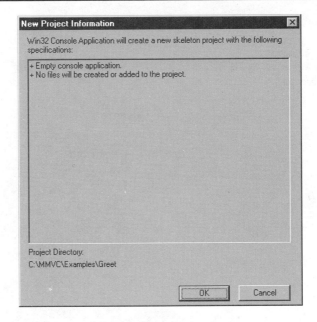

The Developer Studio will now create and open a new project workspace, named Greet, which contains a single project, also named Greet. Information on the project will be displayed within the Workspace window, shown in Figure 2.4. If the Workspace window isn't visible, display it by choosing the View ➢ Workspace menu option or by pressing Alt+0. The Workspace window consists of two tabs, ClassView and FileView, which display different types of information on the project; they will be explained later in the chapter. (When you create a Windows GUI program, as discussed in Chapter 9, the Workspace window will include an additional tab, ResourceView.)

NOTE   Because the arrangement of toolbars and windows in the Developer Studio is highly customizable, what you see might be quite a bit different than what's shown in Figure 2.4.

FIGURE 2.4:

Information on the newly created Greet project displayed within the Workspace window of the Developer Studio

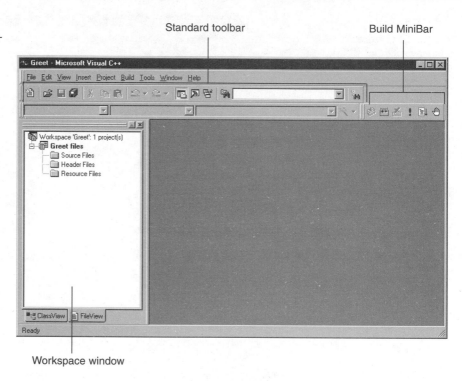

Standard toolbar   Build MiniBar

Workspace window

You can close the Greet project if you wish by choosing the File ➢ Close Workspace menu command. You can later reopen the project by choosing the File ➢ Open Workspace... menu command and selecting the Greet project workspace file, Greet.dsw, in the Open Workspace dialog box. Alternatively, if you've worked with the Greet project recently, you can quickly open it by choosing the Greet item on the File ➢ Recent Workspaces submenu.

Creating and Editing the Program Source File

The next step is to create the program source file, Greet.cpp. To do this, choose the File ➢ New... menu command in the Developer Studio. This time, open the Files tab and select the "C++ Source File" item from the list of file types. Then, enter the source file name, Greet.cpp, into the File Name: text box, and make sure that the Add To Project box is checked. The list under the Add To Project check box will already contain the name of the project, Greet, and the Location: text box will contain the full path of the project folder you specified when you created the project; leave both of these items as they are. The completed dialog box is shown in Figure 2.5. Click the OK button when you're done.

FIGURE 2.5:

The completed Files tab of the New dialog box

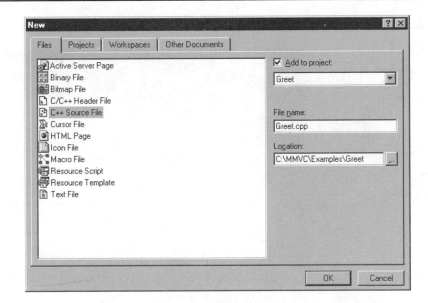

The Developer Studio will now create a new empty source file named Greet.cpp. It will add this file to the Greet project and it will open it in a text-editor window. Type into this window the C++ source code contained in Listing 2.1. The result is shown in Figure 2.6.

Listing 2.1

```cpp
// Greet.cpp: The C++ source code for the Greet program.

#include <iostream.h>

char Name [16];

void main ()
    {
    cout << "enter your name: ";
```

```
cin.getline (Name, sizeof (Name));
cout << "\ngreetings, " << Name << "\n";

cout << "\nPress Enter to continue...";
cin.get ();
}
```

FIGURE 2.6:

Adding the Greet program source file, Greet.cpp, to the Greet project

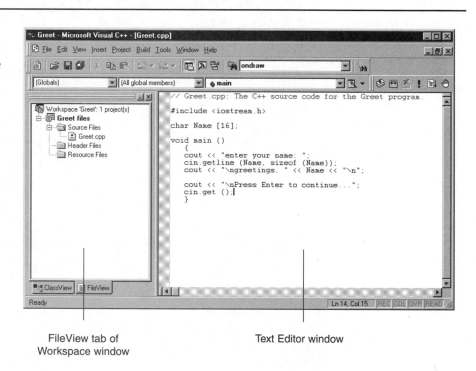

FileView tab of
Workspace window

Text Editor window

Many of the Developer Studio editing commands will already be familiar to you if you've used other Windows text editors or development environments. Table 2.1 summarizes most of the important editing keystrokes. Note that these are the default keystrokes; you can modify any of them. To see a complete list of Visual C++ keyboard commands, which reflects any modifications that have been made, choose the Help ➤ Keyboard Map... menu command. For a full description of the editing commands, operations you can perform with the mouse, and ways to customize the editor, see the following online help topic: *Visual C++ Documentation, Using Visual C++, Visual C++ User's Guide, Text Editor.*

TABLE 2.1: Useful Default Keystrokes for Developer Studio Text Editor

Move Insertion Point	Keystroke
One character back	←
One character forward	→
One line up	↑
One line down	↓
One word forward	Ctrl+→
One word back	Ctrl+←
To first character in line	Home
To column 1	Home, and then Home
One screen up	PgUp
One screen down	PgDn
To beginning of file	Ctrl+Home
To end of file	Ctrl+End
To matching brace	Place insertion point in front of brace and press Ctrl+]
To a specific line or other target	Ctrl+G

Scroll Window	Keystroke
Up one line	Ctrl+↑
Down one line	Ctrl+↓

Select	Keystroke
Text	Shift + one of the movement keystrokes given above
Columns of text	Ctrl+Shift+F8 to enter column select mode, and then movement keystrokes given above
End column select mode	Ctrl+Shift+F8 again, or Esc
Select entire file	Ctrl+A

Continued on next page

TABLE 2.1 CONTINUED: Useful Default Keystrokes for Developer Studio Text Editor

Copy, Cut, Paste, and Delete Text	Keystroke
Copy selected text to Clipboard (Copy)	Ctrl+C
Copy seleCopy selected text to Clipboard and delete it (Cut)	Ctrl+X
Copy current line to Clipboard and delete it (Cut Line)	Ctrl+L
Paste text from Clipboard (Paste)	Ctrl+V
Delete selected text	Del
Delete character to right of insertion point	Del
Delete character to left of insertion point	Backspace
Delete word to left of insertion point	Ctrl+Backspace
Delete current line	Ctrl+Shift+L

Tabs	Keystroke
Insert tab character (or spaces)	Tab
Move to previous tab position	Shift+Tab
Move several lines one tab to right	Select lines and then press Tab
Move several lines one tab to left	Select lines and then press Shift+Tab
Toggle display of tab characters (as » characters) and spaces (as dots)	Ctrl+Shift+8

Miscellaneous Editing Operations	Keystroke
Change selection to uppercase	Ctrl+Shift+U
Change selection to lowercase	Ctrl+U
Toggle between insert and overwrite modes	Ins
Swap current and previous lines	Alt+Shift+T

Continued on next page

TABLE 2.1 CONTINUED: Useful Default Keystrokes for Developer Studio Text Editor

Undo/Redo	Keystroke
Undo previous edit	Ctrl+Z
Redo previous edit	Ctrl+Y

Find	Keystroke
Find text using Find list on Standard toolbar	Ctrl+D, enter text, then press Enter or F3
Open Find dialog box	Ctrl+F
Find next occurrence	F3
Find previous occurrence	Shift+F3
Find next occurrence of selected text or word under insertion point	Ctrl+F3
Find previous occurrence of selected text or word under insertion point	Ctrl+Shift+F3
Perform forward incremental search	Press Ctrl+I and then begin typing search text
Perform backward incremental search	Press Ctrl+Shift+I and then begin typing search text
Find and replace text	Ctrl+H
Find next build error	F4
Find previous build error	Shift+F4
Find matching brace	Place insertion point in front of brace and press Ctrl+]

Bookmarks	Keystroke
Toggle bookmark on/off	Ctrl+F2
Go to next bookmark	F2
Go to previous bookmark	Shift+F2
Clear all bookmarks	Ctrl+Shift+F2
Open Bookmark dialog box to create, remove, or go to *named* bookmarks	Alt+F2

Continued on next page

TABLE 2.1 CONTINUED: Useful Default Keystrokes for Developer Studio Text Editor

Windows	Keystroke
Go to next window	Ctrl+F6
Go to previous window	Ctrl+Shift+F6
Close active window	Ctrl+F4

When you've finished typing in the source code, save your work by choosing the File ➢ Save menu command, or by clicking the Save button on the Standard toolbar:

The Greet program uses the C++ **iostream** library. This library provides a comprehensive collection of predefined classes, which console programs written in C++ can use for performing basic input and output. C++ classes are explained in Chapter 4, and the **iostream** library is described in the following online help topic: *Visual C++ Documentation, Reference, C/C++ Language and C++ Libraries, iostream Library Reference.*

TIP

Copies of the Greet source code file (Greet.cpp) and project files (the project workspace file Greet.dsw and other files used by the Developer Studio) are included in the \Greet companion-CD folder. However, you'll probably find it more instructional to create your own project and manually type in the source code.

The program includes the Iostream.h header file, which contains declarations that are required for using the **iostream** library. The statement

```
cout << "enter your name: ";
```

displays the string "enter your name: " within the console window. This expression generates output using the **cout** *object*; objects are explained in Chapter 4. The << operator in this expression is said to be *overloaded*, signifying that it has a special meaning within this context. Overloaded operators are explained in Chapter 6.

The statement

```
cin.getline (Name, sizeof (Name));
```

then reads the characters that the user types, and stores them in the character array Name. The first parameter passed to getline is the receiving buffer, and the second parameter is the size of this buffer; getline is known as a *member function* of the cin object (member functions are also explained in Chapter 4).

The statement

```
cout << "\ngreetings, " << Name << "\n";
```

then displays (at the start of a new line in the window) the string "greetings, ", followed by the characters that the user entered, which are now stored in Name, followed by a new line. This statement uses the cout object.

The last two statements cause the program to pause until the user presses the Enter key:

```
cout << "\nPress Enter to continue...";
cin.get ();
```

The member function get reads a single character. Note that both getline and get wait until the user presses the Enter key before reading the input.

NOTE

Pausing until the user presses Enter at the end of the program allows the user to contemplate the program output before the program window is closed. This code isn't necessary if the program is run through the Developer Studio (as described later), because the window remains open after the program exits, until the user presses any key. However, the code *is* necessary if the program is run outside the Developer Studio or if it's run through the Developer Studio debugger, because in these cases the program window is automatically closed as soon as the program exits.

Using FileView and ClassView

If you click the FileView tab at the bottom of the Workspace window, the names of the project workspace and project (both Greet) and the source file belonging in the project (Greet.cpp) will be displayed in a hierarchical graph. To see the name of the source file, you'll need to expand the graph. You can expand (or collapse) a branch of the graph by clicking the + (or –) symbol to the left of the node at the top of the branch:

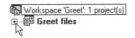

The expanded graph was shown in Figure 2.6.

You can open a source file (or display it if it's already open) by double-clicking the name of the file within the FileView graph. For projects that have several source files—such as those you'll see later in the book—FileView is much more useful than it is for a project with only a single source file like Greet.

If you click the ClassView tab at the bottom of the Workspace window, a graph will appear that lists all the global symbols defined in the Greet program:

If you double-click a symbol in the ClassView graph (such as main or Name for the Greet program), the Developer Studio will display the source file in which the symbol is defined and will place the insertion point on the definition. For a C++ program that contains classes, the ClassView tab also displays all the classes and class members defined in the program (as explained in the section "Viewing and Managing Classes Using ClassView" in Chapter 5).

Accessing the Online Help

Chapter 1 discussed installing the Visual C++ online help and explained how to interpret the many references to online help topics included in the book. In Visual C++ 6, online help is displayed in a separate program window. To locate one of the topics mentioned in this book, choose the Help ➤ Contents menu command in the Developer Studio. This will open the online help window and display the Contents tab. The online help window for Visual Studio 6.0 Enterprise Edition is shown in Figure 2.7.

FIGURE 2.7:

The online help window for Visual Studio 6.0 Enterprise Edition, with the Contents tab displayed

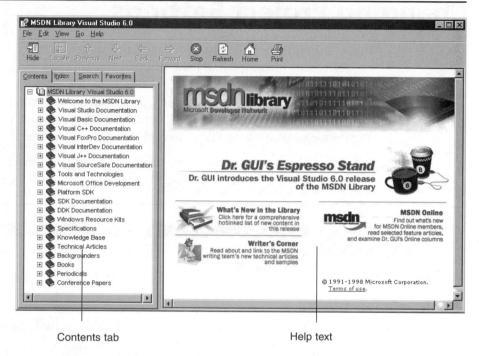

Contents tab   Help text

The Contents tab displays the online help topics in a hierarchical graph (similar to the FileView and ClassView graphs). To expand (or collapse) a branch of the graph, click on the + (or –) symbol to the left of the node at the top of the branch. The nodes at the lowest level of the graph represent individual help articles (they don't have + or – symbols). If you click one of these nodes, the corresponding help text will be displayed within the pane on the right side of the online help window.

Help article — click to display text

For more information on accessing the Visual C++ online help, see the online help topic *Welcome to the MSDN Library, MSDN Library Help*.

Changing Project Settings

Before building the program, you'll change a project setting that affects the way the source file is compiled. If the Greet project isn't open, open it now by choosing the File ➢ Open Workspace... menu command and selecting the Greet project workspace file, Greet.dsw, in the Open Workspace dialog box. Alternatively, if you've worked with the Greet project recently, you can quickly open it by choosing the Greet item on the File ➢ Recent Workspaces submenu.

To change the setting, choose the Project ➢ Settings... menu command or press Alt+F7. The Project Settings dialog box will appear, as shown in Figure 2.8.

FIGURE 2.8:

The Project Settings dialog box as it's first displayed

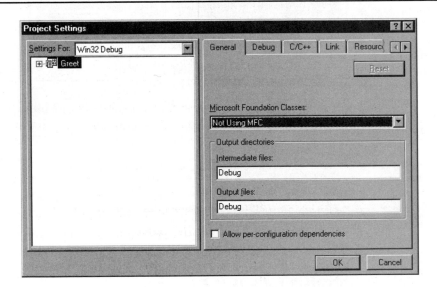

The Settings For: list in the Project Settings dialog box contains a list of the project *configurations* for the Greet program. A configuration generates a particular version of the program. All configurations generally build the program from the same set of source code files; however, each configuration builds the program using a unique set of compiler, linker, and other build tool settings.

The new project you just created has two configurations: a configuration named Win32 Debug that generates the *debug* version of the program, and a configuration named Win32 Release that generates the *release* version of the program.

The debug configuration contains settings that allow the program to be debugged with the integrated debugger; normally, you use this configuration while you're developing and testing the program. The release configuration contains settings that produce the final, fully optimized version of the program. Note that you can add or remove configurations by choosing the Build ➢ Configurations... menu command.

You can change the settings for a particular configuration by choosing the configuration name in the Settings For: list. Or, you can change the settings for all project configurations by choosing the All Configurations item. Once you've chosen a particular configuration, or all configurations, you can specify which project files will be affected by the settings you make. To apply the settings to the entire project, select the project name in the hierarchical graph in the left pane of the Project Settings dialog box. To apply the settings to one or more individual project files, select the file or files in the graph. As usual, to expand or collapse a branch of the graph, click the + or – symbol in the node at the top of the branch. To select a single node or file, click on it; to select additional nodes or files, press Ctrl while you click each one. Selecting a node applies the settings to all files contained in that branch of the graph. For example, selecting the node labeled Source Files applies the settings to *all* source files in the project (though in the Greet project there's only one). To make the settings, you must first choose the appropriate settings category by opening one of the tabs in the Project Settings dialog box (General, Debug, C/C++, and so on). Note that some tabs, such as Link, appear only when you've selected the name of an entire project in the left pane, because the settings they contain affect the creation of the executable file for the project, *not* the processing of individual source files.

To gain some practice in changing settings, first select the Win32 Debug configuration in the Settings For: list so that the change you make will affect the processing of files only when you build the debug version of your program. In the graph, click the name of the project, Greet, to apply the setting change to the entire project. Next, open the C/C++ tab to access the compiler settings. Then, make sure that the General category is selected in the Category: list near the top of the dialog box. Finally, check the Warnings As Errors check box. Choosing this option causes the compiler to treat a warning message (for example, a warning that a local parameter is unused) as an error; accordingly, when a warning condition occurs, the build process stops and you can immediately tend to the problem. The completed Project Settings dialog box is shown in Figure 2.9. Click the OK button at the bottom of this dialog box to save your change (the settings you make are permanently saved within the project, until you explicitly change them).

FIGURE 2.9:

The completed Project Settings dialog box

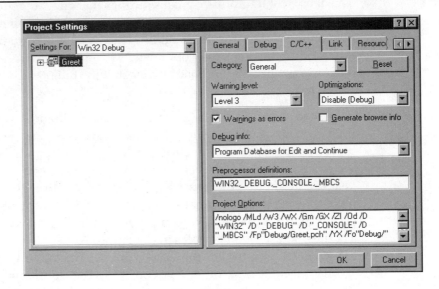

For information on the other settings you can change in the Project Settings dialog box, click the ? button in the upper-right corner of the dialog box, and then click the control used to make the setting. Also, see the following topic in the Visual C++ online help: *Visual C++ Documentation, Using Visual C++, Visual C++ Programmer's Guide, Compiling and Linking, Details, Project Settings Dialog Box.*

NOTE You may have noticed that the Project Settings dialog box *doesn't* include settings for C/C++ memory models. A pleasant consequence of generating 32-bit programs is that you no longer have to worry about memory models. All pointers are simple 32-bit values, with no distinction between near and far pointers, and no need for different memory-addressing models.

Building the Program

The next step is to build the debug version of the Greet program. If it's not already open, open the Greet project via the File ➤ Open Workspace... menu command.

When you issue the build command, the Developer Studio always builds the program using *active* project configuration. You must therefore make sure that Win32 Debug is the current active configuration for the Greet project. To do this, choose the Build ➤ Set Active Configuration… menu command, be sure that the Win32 Debug item is selected in the Set Active Project Configuration dialog box, and click the OK button. Alternatively, you can check that the Win32 Debug item is selected in the Select Active Configuration list on the Build toolbar:

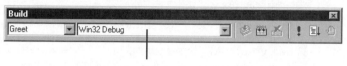

Set Active Configuration list

If the Build toolbar isn't displayed, click on the menu bar or on a toolbar with the right mouse button, and choose the Build option from the pop-up menu that appears.

To build the program, choose the Build ➤ Build Greet.exe menu command, or press F7, or click the Build button on the Build toolbar or Build MiniBar:

NOTE   If a program consists of several source files, the Developer Studio normally processes only the files that have changed since the last time you built the program. If, however, you've changed one or more project settings, a message box will appear indicating that the project settings have changed; if you click the Yes button in this box, all affected program files will be rebuilt. You can also force the Developer Studio to rebuild *all* files in the project by choosing the Build ➤ Rebuild All menu command.

While it's building the program, the Developer Studio displays the results of each step of the build process within the Output window. If the Output window isn't visible, choose the View ➤ Output menu command or press Alt+2. Also, to see the output from the build process, the Build tab must be opened within the Output window (the other Output window tabs allow you to view the output from other development tools). Any error or warning messages will appear within the Output window, and when the build has completed (successfully or unsuccessfully), the Developer Studio will beep and display the total number of errors and warnings in this window.

If an error or warning message is displayed in the Output window, you can locate the source line that caused the problem by simply double-clicking on the line that contains the message in the Output window. Alternatively, you can press F4 to view the *next* error that occurred when building the program, and you can press Shift+F4 to view the *previous* error. You might want to introduce an error into the Greet.cpp file and rebuild the program to experiment with these features.

When you build the program, Visual C++ creates a subfolder, \Greet\Debug, to store the program output files (Greet.obj, Greet.exe, and others). If you later build the release configuration, Visual C++ will create a separate subfolder, \Greet\Release, for storing the output files for the release version of the program. Accordingly, the output files for the different program configurations don't overwrite each other. Note that you can change the names of these folders by choosing the Project ➢ Settings... menu command and opening the General tab in the Project Settings dialog box; here you can specify a separate folder both for the intermediate output files (for example, Greet.obj) and for the final output files (for example, Greet.exe). Note that if you delete the folder name from one of the text boxes used to specify the output folders, the corresponding output files will be placed directly within the project folder.

You can stop the build process before it has completed by clicking the Stop Build button on the Build toolbar or Build MiniBar:

Running the Program

After the program has been built successfully, you can run it directly from the Developer Studio by choosing the Build ➢ Execute Greet.exe menu command or by pressing Ctrl+F5. You can also run the program outside the Developer Studio by using any of the standard Windows methods to run the Greet executable file, Greet.exe. The program will run within a *console* window, which has the same appearance as the window used to run MS-DOS programs within Windows. And, as with an MS-DOS program, you can toggle the program display between a window and the full screen by pressing Alt+Enter. Figure 2.10 shows the Greet window after the program has displayed the text entered by the user.

FIGURE 2.10:

The Greet program

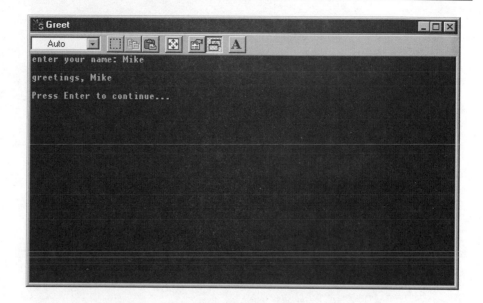

```
enter your name: Mike

greetings, Mike

Press Enter to continue...
```

If you run the Greet program from the MS-DOS Prompt, the Greet program output will appear within the MS-DOS Prompt window. Greet *won't* create a separate console window.

A Shortcut

In this chapter, you created a project, created a source file (Greet.cpp) and added it to the project, and then built the program. This procedure was given so that you could learn how to create and work with Visual C++ projects. However, if you're writing a console application that consists of a single C or C++ source file, you can use the following quick method instead.

Continued on next page

1. If a project is currently open, close it by choosing the File ≻ Close Workspace menu command.

2. Click the New Text File button on the Standard toolbar to create a new C or C++ source code file.

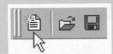

3. Enter the source code and save the file under the desired name (for example, Test.c or Test.cpp).

4. Click the Build button on the Build toolbar or Build MiniBar:

The Developer Studio will display a message box asking whether you want to create a default project workspace. Click the Yes button.

The Developer Studio will then create a project workspace containing a single project; both the workspace and the project will have the same name as the source file (for example, Test). It will place the project workspace file (for example, Test.dsw) in the folder in which you saved the source file, and that folder will become the project folder. The initial project settings will be appropriate for creating a Win32 console application. The Developer Studio will create both a debug configuration (Win32 Debug) and a release configuration (Win32 Release), and it will activate and build the debug configuration.

Debugging the Program

One of the most useful features of the Microsoft Developer Studio is the integrated debugger, which allows you to debug your programs quickly and easily while you're developing them. This section presents a simple exercise using the Greet program to introduce you to this debugger.

Table 2.2 summarizes most of the important default debugging keystrokes (like the editing keystrokes, they can be modified). For a complete description of all the debugger commands and features, see the following topic in the Visual C++ online help: *Visual C++ Documentation, Using Visual C++, Visual C++ User's Guide, Debugger*.

TABLE 2.2 Summary of Default Keystrokes for the Developer Studio Debugger

Debugging Action	Keystroke
Add or remove a breakpoint on the line containing the insertion point	F9
Remove all breakpoints	Ctrl+Shift+F9
Start program execution, or resume program execution from current statement	F5
Restart program execution from beginning	Ctrl+Shift+F5
Execute next statement; include statements within functions (step into)	F11
Execute next statement; skip statements within functions (step over)	F10
Run program until reaching first statement outside of current function (step out)	Shift+F11
Run program, and then break at position of insertion point (run to cursor)	Ctrl+F10
Jump to position of insertion point, without executing intermediate statements	Ctrl+Shift+F10
Open QuickWatch dialog box to quickly view or modify a variable or expression	Shift+F9
Open Breakpoints dialog box to set breakpoints	Ctrl+B
End debugging session	Shift+F5

Here's a simple exercise to help you get started with the Developer Studio debugger:

1. If it's not already open, open the Greet project by choosing the File ➢ Open Workspace... menu command and then selecting the Greet project workspace file, Greet.dsw.

2. Make sure that the Win32 Debug configuration is the active project configuration. To do this, choose the Build ➢ Set Active Configuration... menu command, make sure that the Win32 Debug item is selected in the Set Active Project Configuration dialog box, and click the OK button. Alternatively, you can check that the Win32 Debug item is selected in the Select Active Configuration list on the Build toolbar. The debugger always runs the executable file generated from the current active configuration.

3. If it's not already open, open the program source file by double-clicking the Greet.cpp file name in the FileView tab of the Workspace window:

Notice how the FileView tab affords you easy access to the program source files. (You could also have opened this file using the traditional method of choosing the File ➤ Open... menu command or clicking the Open button on the Standard toolbar.)

4. Place the insertion point on the first line within the main function of Greet.cpp,

```
cout << "enter your name: ";
```

and press F9 or click the Insert/Remove Breakpoint button on the Build toolbar or Build MiniBar:

This will place a *breakpoint* on the line; as a result, when you run the program in the debugger, the program will stop running immediately before executing the code in this line. To indicate the presence of the breakpoint, Visual C++ displays a dot in the left margin next to the line (the default color of this dot is red, though you can change its color by choosing the Tools ➤ Options... menu command and opening the Format tab). Note that if you press F9 or click the Insert/Remove Breakpoint button again, while the insertion point is still on the line, the breakpoint is removed.

5. Choose the Build ➤ Start Debug ➤ Go menu command, or press F5, or click the Go button on the Build toolbar or Build MiniBar:

This begins running the program within the debugger. The Greet program window will appear on the screen. The Greet program, however, will stop running immediately before it executes the line containing the breakpoint, control will return to the debugger, and the Developer Studio window will become active (depending on how the windows are arranged on your screen, the Developer Studio window may cover the Greet program window partially or completely). Note that the breakpoint line is now marked with an arrow in the left margin to indicate that it's the *next* line that will be executed; the next line to be executed is known as the *current line* (the default color of the arrow is yellow). The Developer Studio should now appear as shown in Figure 2.11.

FIGURE 2.11:

Running the Greet program in the Developer Studio integrated debugger; the program is stopped at the breakpoint line (the first line of main)

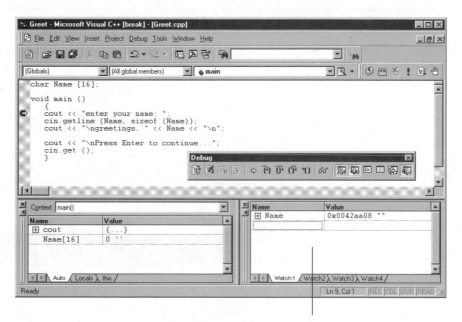

Watch window

6. The Watch window should now be open on the screen (Figure 2.11 shows this window in the lower-right corner of the Developer Studio work area). If it isn't open, choose the View ➢ Debug Windows ➢ Watch menu command, or press Alt+3, or click the Watch button on the Debug toolbar (which is normally displayed temporarily when you run the debugger):

7.   You'll now begin monitoring the contents of the variable Name, the global character array defined in Greet.cpp. To do this, click within the outlined rectangular area at the top of the Watch window, type Name, and press Enter. The Watch window will now display the address of the Name variable, but won't immediately display the values of the array elements. To view the elements, click the + symbol to the left of the word Name in the Watch window (or place the insertion point on the top line and press Enter). The members of the array will now be displayed, as shown in Figure 2.12. Notice that because Name is a global C++ variable, it's initialized with 0 values.

FIGURE 2.12:

The Watch window displaying the Name array

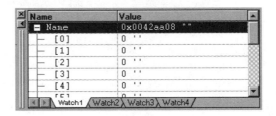

8.   You'll now begin single-stepping through the code (that is, executing the code one line at a time). To start, press F10 or click the Step Over button on the Debug toolbar

to execute the current line. The string displayed by this line ("enter your name: ") *doesn't* yet appear in the Greet window because it's held in a buffer and won't be written to the window until the input statement in the second line of code is executed. Notice that the second line has now become the current line.

9. Press F10 or click the Step Over button again to execute the second line of code. When the program executes this line (`cin.get (Name, sizeof (Name));`), it pauses until you enter a name (you won't be able to resume the Greet program from the debugger until this line has completed executing). Therefore, you must now switch to the Greet program window, enter some text, and press Enter. After you press Enter, control returns to the debugger. Notice that the third line of code has now become the current line. Also, observe in the Watch window that `Name` now contains the string that you just typed.

10. The Watch window also allows you to *alter* the value of a variable. To demonstrate this, double-click one of the array member values in the Watch window, type a new number, and press Enter.

11. Choose the Debug ➤ Go menu command, or press F5, or click the Go button to resume execution of the program. Because there are no further breakpoints in the code, the program will finish executing normally. The program will display the `Name` string, as you just altered it, within the Greet window. After you press Enter, the Greet window will be closed and control will return to the debugger, which will display a message indicating that the program has exited. This message—along with previous messages from the debugger—appears in the Debug tab of the Output window. If the Output window isn't visible, you can display it by choosing the View ➤ Output menu command, or by pressing Alt+2.

Once you've finished developing a program, and have debugged and tested it, you'll probably want to generate the *release* version, which will be fully optimized and will typically be smaller. To do this, choose the Build ➤ Set Active Configuration... menu command, select the *Project* - Win32 Release item (where *Project* is the name of the project), and click the OK button. Alternatively, you can select the Win32 Release item in the Set Active Configuration list on the Build toolbar. Then, build the program using this configuration by choosing the Build ➤ Build *Program* menu command (where *Program* is the name of the executable program file), or pressing F7, or clicking the Build button on the Build toolbar or Build MiniBar.

Summary

In this chapter, you learned how to use the Microsoft Developer Studio to perform the following tasks:

- Create a *project*, which stores all the information required to build a program
- Add a source file to a project
- Enter and edit program code in a source file
- View program files and symbols using the FileView and ClassView tabs of the Developer Studio Workspace window
- Access the Visual C++ online help
- Change the settings that affect the way a program is built
- Build a program
- Run a program
- Debug a program

You can use the simple Greet program that you created in this chapter while you're working through the introduction to C++ in Part II of the book. Whenever you want to enter some example code, or test some code of your own, you can open the Greet project and modify the Greet.cpp source file. You can then rebuild the program and run it, and the program output will appear in a console window on the Windows desktop.

PART II

Introduction to C++

CHAPTER

THREE

3

Moving to C++

- Converting from C to C++

- New features of C++

This chapter is designed to help you make the transition from C programming to C++ programming. It begins by showing you how to convert your existing C programs, as well as your C programming habits, to C++. It then shows you how to take advantage of some of the convenient new features of C++. The chapter, however, stops short of presenting C++ classes or any of the features that require classes; this is postponed until Chapter 4. It might take you a while to master the effective use of classes and restructure your programs to take advantage of them. Meanwhile, the information given here will allow you to get started quickly by using C++ as simply an enhanced version of C.

NOTE　As mentioned in the Introduction, this part—as well as the remainder of the book—assumes that you possess a rudimentary knowledge of the C language (if you need to learn C, see the Introduction for reading suggestions). Accordingly, it focuses on the unique features of C++ that aren't provided by C, and it often explains C++ concepts in terms of related C language concepts. Although the concepts and techniques presented here apply equally to writing Windows GUI (graphical user interface) programs as well as Windows console programs, for the sake of simplicity the code examples are written as console programs. If you want to experiment with a particular C++ feature, you can run the Visual C++ Developer Studio and open the Greet project you created in Chapter 2. You can then enter the example code—or your own code—into the Greet.cpp source file and build the program as explained in Chapter 2. Note that the source file for each of the numbered listings given in this part of the book (such as Listing 4.1) is contained in the \Cpp companion-CD directory.

Converting from C to C++

If you've written a C program, you've probably already written your first C++ program! With few exceptions, C++ is a superset of C; that is, C++ supports almost all the features of the C language *in addition to* the many new features that it offers. Therefore, to get started with C++, you can simply compile your existing C programs, as well as the new programs you write, using the C++ compiler rather than the C compiler. You can then gradually begin adding to your code various features that are unique to C++.

To begin using the C++ compiler, you need only name your source file with the .cpp or .cxx extension, rather than the .c extension. There are, however, several programming practices permitted in most versions of C that won't compile using the C++ compiler, or that will compile with C++ but with altered meanings. The following is a description of some of the most important C constructs that *don't* work with C++:

- C++ has many more reserved keywords than C; these are words that you *can't* use as identifiers in your programs. The following is a list of the reserved keywords used in Visual C++. This list includes the C keywords, plus many additional ones unique to C++:

auto	else	new	this
bad_cast	enum	operator	throw
bad_typeid	except	private	true
bool	explicit	protected	try
break	extern	public	type_info
case	false	register	typedef
catch	finally	reinterpret_	typeid
char	float	cast	typename
class	for	return	union
const	friend	short	unsigned
const_cast	goto	signed	using
continue	if	sizeof	virtual
default	inline	static	void
delete	int	static_cast	volatile
do	long	struct	while
double	mutable	switch	
dynamic_cast	namespace	template	

- The following are the Microsoft-specific keywords used in Visual C++:

__asm	__finally	__leave	__try
__based	__inline	__multiple_	__uuidof
__cdecl	__int8	inheritance	__virtual_
__declspec	__int16	__single_	inheritance
__except	__int32	inheritance	
__fastcall	__int64	__stdcall	

- In C, you're permitted to call a function that isn't preceded by the function declaration or definition (though doing so might generate a warning message). In C++, however, the function declaration or definition *must* precede any call to the function within the source file (otherwise, the compiler will generate an *undeclared identifier* error).

NOTE

Throughout this book, the term *function declaration* refers to a declaration that specifies only the function name, the return type, and the types of the parameters, while the term *function definition* refers to a declaration that includes the complete function code. Note that both these items can be described using the general term *declaration*; a declaration simply associates a name with a type.

- In C, you can declare a function that takes one or more parameters without listing these parameters, as in the following declaration:

```
int FuncX ();  /* this C function actually takes
                    several parameters */
```

In C++, however, such a declaration can be used only for a function that has no parameters.

- In C, you can use the "old style" function definition syntax, in which the types of the parameters *follow* the parameter list; for example:

```
int FuncX (A, B)    /* OK in C; an ERROR in C++ */
int A;
int B;
    {
    /* code for FuncX */
    return 0;
    }
```

In C++, however, this style *isn't* permitted.

- In some versions of C, you can declare a global data object more than once in a given program, without using the `extern` specifier. In C++, however, you can declare a global data object only once without the `extern` specifier, to define the data item; all other declarations of the item must include the `extern` keyword to make the item accessible within a given scope. (The term *scope* refers to the portion of the program text in which a particular name can be used.)

- In C (as defined by the ANSI standard), you can assign a void pointer to *any* pointer type; for example, the following code assigns a void pointer to an int pointer:

```
int A;
int *PInt;
void *PVoid = &A;

PInt = PVoid;   /* OK in C; an ERROR in C++ */
```

In C++, however, the assignment to PInt would generate an error, because the C++ compiler *won't* automatically convert a void pointer to another pointer type in an assignment expression. You could, however, use a cast operation to make the assignment:

```
PInt = (int *)PVoid;   /* OK in C and C++ */
```

- In C, a struct, union, or enum tag can be identical to a typedef name within the same scope. For example, the following code would compile successfully in C:

```
/* this code is OK in C, but erroneous in C++: */

typedef int TypeA;
struct TypeA
    {
    int I;
    char C;
    double D;
    };

typedef int TypeB;
union TypeB
    {
    int I;
    char C;
    double D;
    };

typedef int TypeC;
enum TypeC {Red, Green, Blue};
```

The C compiler is able to distinguish between the duplicate names because the structure, union, or enumeration is always referred to using the `struct`, `union`, or `enum` prefix, as in the following example:

```
/* this code is OK in C, but erroneous in C++: */

typedef int TypeA;
struct TypeA
  {
  int I;
  char C;
  double D;
  };

TypeA X;         /* creates an int */
struct TypeA Y;  /* creates a TypeA structure */

sizeof (TypeA);         /* yields size of an int */
sizeof (struct TypeA);  /* yields size of a TypeA
                           structure */
```

In C++, however, a `struct`, `union`, `enum`, or `class` tag (which in C++ is usually called a *name* rather than a *tag*) must be *different* from any `typedef` name within the same scope. (A `class` is unique to C++; classes will be explained in Chapter 4.) The reason is that the definition creates a new type that you can refer to using the name alone; you aren't required to use the `struct`, `union`, `enum`, or `class` prefix (though you can use it if you wish). This feature is illustrated in the following C++ code:

```
/* this code is erroneous in C, but OK in C++: */

struct TypeA
  {
  int I;
  char C;
  double D;
  };

struct TypeA X; /* creates a TypeA structure */
TypeA Y;        /* also creates a TypeA structure */

sizeof (struct TypeA); /* yields the size of the TypeA
                          structure */
sizeof (TypeA);        /* also yields the size of the
                          TypeA structure */
```

Therefore, if you created a `typedef` with the same name, the C++ compiler wouldn't always be able to distinguish the two types, as shown in the following erroneous code:

```
typedef int TypeA;
struct TypeA /* C++ ERROR: redefinition of TypeA */
    {
    int I;
    char C;
    double D;
    };

TypeA X;        /* should this create an int or a TypeA
                   structure? */
sizeof (TypeA); /* should this yield the size of an int
                   or the size of a TypeA structure? */
```

- The following incompatibility is related to the previous one: in C, if a `struct`, `union`, or `enum` tag is the same as a `typedef` name in an outer scope, you can still refer to the `typedef` within the inner scope (that is, the `typedef` *isn't* hidden). In C++, however, the `typedef` name would be hidden. The following code illustrates the difference:

```
typedef int TypeA;

void main ()
    {
    struct TypeA
        {
        int I;
        char C;
        double D;
        };

    TypeA X;  /* in C, X is an int;
                 in C++, X is a TypeA structure */

    sizeof (TypeA);  /* in C, yields the size of an int;
                        in C++, yields the size of a TypeA
                        struct */

    }
```

- There are two additional differences in values returned by the `sizeof` operator. First, in C, `sizeof ('x')` equals `sizeof (int)`, but in C++ it equals `sizeof (char)`. Second, assume that you've defined the enumeration

  ```
  enum E {X, Y, Z};
  ```

  In C, `sizeof (X)` equals `sizeof (int)`, but in C++ it equals `sizeof (E)`, which isn't necessarily equal to `sizeof (int)`.

Dealing with Incompatible Constructs   You'll have to remove any of these incompatible constructs from an existing C program so that the code will compile—and have the same meaning—when using the C++ compiler. The C++ compiler will flag any of these incompatibilities except the last two (specifically, the differences in values supplied by the `sizeof` operator), which don't generate compiler errors and *change the meaning* of the program. They're exceptions to the general rule that if a program compiles successfully under either the C compiler or the C++ compiler, then it will have the same meaning in either language.

New Features of C++

This section describes several of the useful new features of C++ that don't pertain to classes. After reading this section, you might conclude that these features alone justify changing from C to C++. Some of these features are also provided by recent versions of C—specifically, the new comment style, inline functions, and constant types (though there may be syntactic differences from C++). The other features described here are unique to C++.

Comments

As an alternative to the standard comment delimiters (/* and */), you can mark a single-line comment in a C++ program using the `//` character pair. All characters following the `//`, *through the end of the line*, are part of the comment and are ignored by the compiler.

```
void main ()  // this is a single-line comment
   {
/* you can still use the traditional comment delimiters, which
   are useful for marking comments that encompass more than
   one line ... */

   // statements ...

   }
```

Declaration Statements

In C, you must declare a local variable (that is, a variable defined within a function) at the beginning of a block, before any program statement. In C++, however, a declaration of a local variable is considered a normal program statement; you can therefore place it at any position where a statement can occur, provided that the declaration occurs before the variable is first referenced.

NOTE
> A *block* is a section of code that's delimited with the { and } characters. A variable defined within a given block can be referenced only within that block or within a nested block (unless it's hidden by an identically named variable within the nested block). That is, the block defines the *scope* of the variable.

Accordingly, in C++ you can make your code easier to read and maintain by placing the declaration for a variable immediately before the code that uses it, as in the following example:

```
void main ()
   {

   // other statements ...

   int Count = 0;
   while (++Count <= 100)
      {

      // loop statements ...

      }

   // other statements ...

   }
```

You can even declare a variable *within* a for statement:

```
// other statements ...

for (int i = 0; i < MAXLINES; ++i)
   {

   // other statements ...
```

```
    int Length = GetLineLength (i);
    if (Length == 0)
       break;

    // other statements ...

    }
if (i < MAXLINES)
    // then a 0 length line was encountered
```

In the above code, the declaration of the loop counter i within the for statement is considered to be *outside* the block that immediately follows the for statement; it can therefore be referenced after the for block. The variable Length, however, is declared *within* the for block, and can therefore be referenced only within this block.

If the declaration contains an initialization, the data item is initialized when the flow of program control reaches the declaration statement. Thus, in the example above, i is created and initialized *once* whenever control reaches the for statement; Length, however, is created and initialized with each iteration of the for loop.

NOTE   If a local variable is declared as `static`, it's created and initialized only once—the *first* time program control reaches the declaration statement.

Note that if a variable declaration contains an initialization, you must make sure that the declaration statement can't be skipped, as in the following switch construct, which generates a C++ compiler error:

```
switch (Code)
   {
   case 1:
      // ...
      break;

   case 2:
      int Count = 0;   // ERROR
      // ...
      break;

   case 3:
      // ...
      break;
   }
```

The compiler generates an error for the following reason: Count is initialized only if the `case` 2 branch of the `switch` statement receives control. If the `case` 3 branch received control and accessed Count, the variable would be uninitialized. (The `case` 3 branch has access to Count because the declaration precedes it within the same block. The compiler will generate an error even if the code in this branch doesn't actually reference Count; the fact that it *could* reference it is sufficient.) To eliminate this error, you could place the code for the `case` 2 branch within its own block, as follows:

```
case 2:
    {
    int Count = 0;
    // ...
    break;
    }
```

In this version of the `switch` statement, Count can be referenced only within the `case` 2 branch, after it has been initialized. Alternatively, you could eliminate the initialization from the declaration, and could *assign* Count its initial value:

```
case 2:
    int Count;
    Count = 0;
    // ...
    break;
```

The Scope Resolution Operator

When you declare a variable in an inner scope that has the same name as a variable in an outer scope, the variable in the inner scope *hides* the one in the outer scope; that is, within the inner scope, the variable name refers to a different entity. For example, in the following code the `int` A declared within FuncB hides the `double` A declared outside the function, causing the assignment within the function to change the value of the `int` variable rather than the `double` variable:

```
double A;

void main ()
    {
    int A;

    A = 5;     // assigns 5 to int A

    }
```

In C++, however, you can access a global variable (that is, one declared outside any function), even if it's hidden by a local variable with the same name. To do this, you preface the variable name with the *scope resolution operator*, ::, as illustrated in the following code:

```
double A;  // global variable A

void main ()
   {
   int A;     // local variable A

   A = 5;     // assigns 5 to local int A
   ::A = 2.5  // assigns 2.5 to global double A

   }
```

Note that you can use the scope resolution operator to access only a global variable. You *can't* use it to access a local variable declared within an enclosing block, as attempted in the following erroneous code:

```
void FuncX (int Code)
   {
   double A;

   if (Code == 1)
      {
      int A;

      // attempt to access double A in enclosing block:
      ::A = 2.5;  // ERROR: ::A specifies global A, which is an
                  // error if there is no variable A declared at
                  // global level
      // ...
      }
   // ...
   }
```

You can also use the scope resolution operator to access a global type or enumeration that's hidden by a local type or enumeration with the same name, as shown in the following example:

```
#include <iostream.h>

typedef int A;
enum {Red, White, Blue};
```

```
void main ()
  {
  typedef double A;
  enum {Blue, White, Red};

  cout << sizeof (A) << '\n';    // prints size of a double
  cout << sizeof (::A) << '\n';  // prints size of an int

  cout << (int)Blue << '\n';     // prints 0
  cout << (int)::Blue << '\n';   // prints 2
  }
```

NOTE In the next two chapters, you'll learn several additional uses for the scope resolution operator. These uses pertain to C++ classes.

Inline Functions

If you declare a function using the `inline` keyword, as in this example,

```
inline int FuncA (int X)
  {
  // function code ...
  }
```

the compiler will attempt to replace all calls to the function with the actual function code. Replacing a function call with a copy of the function code is known as *inline expansion* or *inlining*.

NOTE The `inline` directive, which is equivalent to the Microsoft-specific `__inline` directive, doesn't guarantee that the function will be expanded inline. The compiler might need to generate a conventional function call in certain situations—for example, if the function is recursive (that is, it calls itself), or if the function is called through a function pointer. You can force the compiler to expand a function inline, unless it's *impossible* to do so, by using the Microsoft-specific `__forceinline` directive rather than `inline`. For more information on inlining and on using these directives, see the online help topic *Visual C++ Documentation, Reference, C/C++ Language and C++ Libraries, C++ Language Reference, Declarations, Specifiers, Function Specifiers*.

The definition of an inline function (that is, the declaration that includes the complete function code) must be present within every source file in which the function is called (the compiler must have immediate access to the code so that it can perform the inline expansion). The easiest way to ensure that an identical copy of the definition is available to each calling module is to define the function within a header file that you include within each source file. Unlike a non-inline function, if you change an inline function, all source files that call it must be recompiled.

NOTE   You can customize the way Microsoft Visual C++ handles inline functions for a project by choosing the Project ➢ Settings... menu command (explained in Chapter 2). In the Project Settings dialog box, choose the C/C++ tab and select the Optimizations item in the Category: list. You can then choose the desired inline function option in the Inline Function Expansion: list. For an explanation of the different options, see the following topic in the Visual C++ online help: *Visual C++ Documentation*, *Using Visual C++*, *Visual C++ Programmer's Guide*, *Compiling and Linking*, *Details*, *Compiler Reference*, *IO options (Optimize Code)*, */Ob (Inline Function Expansion)*.

Making a function inline doesn't change its meaning; it merely affects the speed and size of the resulting code, generally increasing both. Accordingly, you might want to use the `inline` specifier when defining a *small* function that's called from relatively few places within your code, especially if it's called repeatedly within a loop.

An inline function is similar to a macro defined using the `#define` preprocessor directive. For example, the following inline function for returning the absolute value of an integer:

```
inline int Abs (int N) {return N < 0 ? -N : N;}
```

is similar to the macro

```
#define ABS(N) ((N) < 0 ? -(N) : (N))
```

Calls to the inline function, however, are processed by the compiler, while calls to the macro are expanded by the preprocessor, which performs simple text substitution. Consequently, the inline function has two important advantages over the macro. First, when the function is called, the compiler checks the type of the parameter it's passed (to make sure that it's an integer or a value that can be converted to an integer). Second, if an expression is passed to the function, it is evaluated only once. In contrast, if an expression is passed to the macro, it's evaluated twice, possibly causing unexpected side effects. For example, the following macro call would decrement I twice (probably not the expected or desired result!):

```
ABS (--I);
```

The macro does have an advantage over the inline function: you can pass it any appropriate data type and the macro will return the same type (for example, a `long`, `int`, or `double`). Although you can pass any numeric type to the inline function, the value will be converted to an `int` and the function will return an `int`, resulting in possible truncation or loss of precision. However, as you'll see later in the chapter (under "Overloaded Functions"), in C++ you can overcome this limitation by defining several versions of the same function, one for each parameter type or set of types you want to pass to the function.

NOTE   See Chapter 4 for a description of inline member functions belonging to classes.

Default Function Parameters

In C++ you can save some programming effort by defining default parameter values when you declare a function. For example, the following declaration defines default values for the second and third parameters:

```
void ShowMessage (char *Text, int Length = -1, int Color = 0);
```

(In this hypothetical function, a Length value of –1 causes the function to calculate the length of the text, and a Color value of 0 displays the text in black letters.)

If you define a default value for a given parameter, you must define default values for all subsequent parameters (that is, all parameters to its right). For example, you *couldn't* declare a function as follows:

```
void ShowMessage (char *Text, int Length = -1, int Color);
// ERROR: missing default value for parameter 3
```

When you call a function, a default parameter works as follows: if you specify the parameter value, the compiler passes this value to the function; if you omit the parameter, the compiler passes the default parameter value. For example, when calling the ShowMessage function, you could specify one, two, or three parameters:

```
ShowMessage ("Hello");      // same as ShowMessage ("Hello",-1, 0);
ShowMessage ("Hello", 5);   // same as ShowMessage ("Hello", 5, 0);
ShowMessage ("Hello", 5, 8);
```

If you omit a default parameter when calling a function, you must also omit any parameters to its right (which will also have default values). For example, you *couldn't* call ShowMessage as follows:

```
ShowMessage ("Hello", ,8);  // ERROR: syntax error
```

When defining a default value, you can use an expression containing global variables or function calls (the expression *can't* contain local variables). For example, the following declaration is permissible (assuming that the code is placed *outside* a function):

```
// at global level:
int Palette = 1;
int GetColor (int Pal);
void ShowMessage (char *Text, int Length = -1,
                  int Color = GetColor (Palette));
```

You can define default parameters in a function declaration or definition. However, once you've defined a default parameter, you can't define it again in a subsequent function declaration or definition within the same scope (even if you assign it the same value). For example, the following code generates an error:

```
void ShowMessage (char *Text, int Length = -1, int Color = 0);

void main ()
   {

   // function code ...

   }

void ShowMessage (char *Text, int Length = -1, int Color = 0)
// ERROR: redefinition of default parameters 2 and 3
   {

   // function code ...

   }
```

You can, however, *add* one or more default parameters in a subsequent declaration or definition within the same scope, as in the following example:

```
void ShowMessage (char *Text, int Length = -1, int Color = 0);

// later in source file:

void ShowMessage (char *Text = "", int Length, int Color);
// OK: ADDS a default parameter value
```

Reference Types

A variable declared as a *reference* serves as an alias for another variable. You declare a reference using the & operator, as in the following example:

```
int Count = 0;
int &RefCount = Count;
```

In this example, RefCount is declared as a reference to an int, and is initialized so that it refers specifically to the int variable Count. This definition causes RefCount to become an alias for Count; that is, both RefCount and Count refer to the *same* memory location. The two variables will always have the same value, and an assignment made to one variable will affect the value of the other variable, as shown in the following code:

```
int Count = 0;
int &RefCount = Count;

// here, Count and RefCount both equal 0

RefCount = 1;

// here, Count and RefCount both equal 1

++Count;

// here, Count and RefCount both equal 2
```

NOTE   White space immediately before or after the & operator isn't significant. Therefore, you could declare RefCount as int& RefCount, as int & RefCount, as int &RefCount, or even as int&RefCount (though the last form isn't very readable).

When you define a variable as a reference, you *must* initialize it, and you must initialize it with a variable of the declared type. Once you've performed this one-time initialization, you can't make a reference variable refer to a different variable. Also, you can't initialize a reference variable using a constant value (such as 5 or 'a'), unless you've declared the variable as a reference to a `const` type (which will be explained in the section "Constant Types"):

```
int &RInt = 5;  // ERROR
```

NOTE   With a nonreference variable, an initialization in the variable definition is similar to a subsequent assignment expression that changes the value of the variable. With a reference variable, however, these two uses for the = operator are quite different. A reference initialization specifies the variable for which the reference will be an alias; in other words, the initialization specifies *which memory location* the reference variable will represent. A subsequent assignment expression *changes the value* of this memory location.

A reference variable is very different from a pointer. A pointer refers to a memory location that contains the address of the target memory location. A reference variable, however, refers directly to the target memory location (just like the variable that was used to initialize it). Figure 3.1 illustrates the differences between a variable, a reference to the variable, and a pointer to the variable; this figure assumes that the following declarations have been made:

```
int Count = 0;
int &RefCount = Count;
int *PtrCount = &Count;
```

Note that the pointer in the code above, `PtrCount`, could also be declared and initialized as follows:

```
int *PtrCount = &RefCount;  // equivalent to:
                            // int *PtrCount = &Count;
```

Because `Count` and `RefCount` refer to the same memory location, using the address operator (&) on either of them yields the same result. When in doubt about the behavior of a reference variable, remember that it almost always behaves exactly like the variable that was used to initialize it.

FIGURE 3.1:

A variable, a reference to a variable, and a pointer to a variable

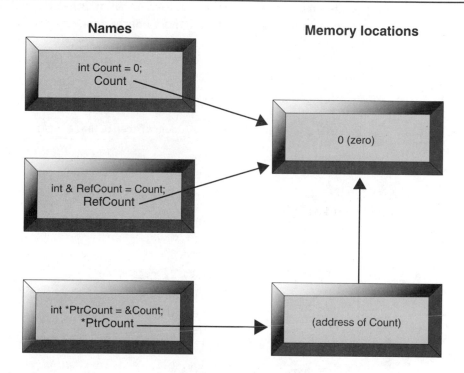

Names   **Memory locations**

int Count = 0;
Count

0 (zero)

int & RefCount = Count;
RefCount

int *PtrCount = &Count;
*PtrCount

(address of Count)

References and Functions

You can also declare function parameters, as well as function return types, as references. For example, the following function has a parameter that's a reference to an int:

```
void FuncA (int &Parm);
```

When this function is called, it must be passed an int variable; this variable is used to initialize the reference parameter Parm. Within the function code, Parm is an alias for the variable passed in the call, and any change made to Parm is also made to the original passed variable. Thus, a reference parameter provides a way to pass a parameter to a function by reference rather than by value (in C and C++, nonreference parameters are passed *by value*, meaning that the function receives a private *copy* of the original variable). The following code shows the difference between a reference parameter and a nonreference parameter:

```
void FuncA (int &Parm)  // reference parameter
   {
   ++Parm;
   }

void FuncB (int Parm)    // nonreference parameter
   {
   ++Parm;
   }

void main ()
   {
   int N = 0;

   FuncA (N);   // N passed by reference

   // here, N equals 1

   FuncB (N);   // N passed by value

   // here, N still equals 1
   }
```

As you can see in this example, both FuncA and FuncB increment the value of the parameter Parm. However, only FuncA, which receives the parameter as a reference, affects the value of the variable N that's passed from the calling function. Note that you can't pass a constant (such as 5) to a reference parameter unless the parameter is declared as a reference to a const type, as will be explained in the section "Constants and Functions":

```
void FuncA (int &RInt);

void main ()
   {
   FuncA (5);   // ERROR: can't initialize reference using
                // constant expression
   // ...
   }
```

If a large variable is passed to a function (for example, a big structure), using a reference parameter can make the function call more efficient. For a nonreference parameter, the entire contents of the variable is copied into the parameter; for a reference parameter, the parameter is merely initialized so that it refers directly to the original variable, and no separate copy of this variable is created.

As in C, you can use a pointer parameter to achieve the same basic advantages offered by a reference parameter (namely, the ability to alter the variable passed by the calling program, and the elimination of the copy operation). Reference parameters, however, can be manipulated using a simpler syntax, which is the same as that used for ordinary variables.

You can declare a function that *returns* a reference type by using the & operator, as in the following example:

```
int & GetIndex ();
```

This declaration means that a call to GetIndex produces a temporary alias for some existing integer variable (the particular variable depends on the return statement within the function). Accordingly, you can place a call to GetIndex at any position within an expression where you could place an integer variable; the following are valid examples:

```
int N;

N = GetIndex ();   // copies value from the int variable
GetIndex () = 5;   // assigns 5 to the int variable
++GetIndex ();      // increments the int variable
```

The code below shows how GetIndex might be implemented and indicates the effects of calling the function:

```
int Index = 0;

int & GetIndex ()
   {
   return Index;
   }

void main ()
   {
   int N;

   // here Index equals 0
```

```
N = GetIndex ();
// here Index equals 0 and N equals 0

GetIndex () = 5;
// here Index equals 5

++GetIndex ();
// here Index equals 6
}
```

A function that has a reference return type must return a variable of the appropriate type (the function can return a constant, such as 5, only if it has been declared to return a reference to a const, as will be explained in the section "Constants and Functions"). The variable that's returned is used to initialize a temporary reference variable that is conceptually produced by the function call. In other words, assuming that Index and GetIndex are defined as shown above, the statement

```
++GetIndex ();   // function call conceptually produces a
                 // temporary reference variable that is an alias
                 // for Index
```

is equivalent to the code

```
int &Temp = Index;   // declare and initialize an actual temporary
                     // reference variable
++Temp;
```

Both examples increment the value of Index.

Because a reference produced by a function call is used *after* the function has returned, the function *shouldn't* return reference to a variable that's destroyed when the function exits; specifically, it shouldn't return a reference to an automatic variable or a parameter, as shown in the following dangerous code:

```
int &BadIdea1 ()
  {
  int i;

  return i;
  }

int &BadIdea2 (int Parm)
  {
  return Parm;
  }
```

This code doesn't generate compiler errors; however, the result of using the reference furnished by one of these functions is unpredictable. A function that has a reference return type can safely return a global variable, a static variable, or a dynamically allocated variable (dynamic variables will be explained in the section "The new and delete Operators").

In contrast, a function that returns a nonreference type can safely return an automatic variable or parameter, because the function call creates a *separate copy* of the variable's contents rather than merely generating a reference to the variable. For this same reason, however, a function that returns a nonreference type is less efficient than a function that returns a reference, especially if it returns a large data object.

NOTE   See Chapter 6 for further examples of passing and returning references from functions.

Constant Types

You can define a variable for storing a constant value, using the const keyword as in the following example:

```
const int MaxLines = 100;
```

NOTE   Because its value can't be changed, a const object is sometimes called a *named constant* rather than a *constant variable* (the term *variable* is actually a misnomer).

When you define a const variable, you must initialize it. This one-time initialization is your only opportunity to set the variable's value; you *can't* change its value using an assignment. The following code illustrates legal and illegal operations with a const type:

```
const double CD = 2.5;
double D;

D = CD;     // OK to read const type

CD = 5.0;   // ERROR: cannot assign new value to const type

++CD;       // ERROR: cannot change value of const type
```

You can initialize a const variable, using either a constant expression (such as 5 or 'a') or a variable. For example, the following const declarations are all valid (the first two initialize using constant expressions and the second two initialize using variables):

```
void Func (int Parm)
   {
   int I = 3;

   const int CI1 = 5;
   const int CI2 = 2 * sizeof (float);
   const int CI3 = I;
   const int CI4 = Parm;
   }
```

If a const variable has been initialized using a constant integer expression (such as 10 or sizeof (double) * 2), you can use it to dimension an array. If, however, you've initialized a const variable with an expression containing another variable, you *can't* use it to dimension an array. (This would be an invalid method for dynamically creating an array whose size is determined at runtime; see the last section in the chapter for a discussion on the correct method for allocating a dynamic array.) For example:

```
void Func (int Parm)
   {
   const int CI1 = 100;
   const int CI2 = Parm;

   char Buf1 [CI1];  // valid
   char Buf2 [CI2];  // ERROR: constant expression required
   }
```

You can use a const variable in the same way that a symbolic constant defined with the #define preprocessor directive is traditionally used in a C program. (Remember, however, that if you use a const variable where a constant expression is required, you must initialize the const variable with a constant expression.) Like a #define constant, a const variable can be defined within a header file that's included within one or more of the source files that compose a program. (Unlike a nonconstant variable, a constant variable is, by default, *local* to the file in which it's defined; it can therefore be defined within more than one source file without causing an error when the program is linked.)

NOTE   A `const` variable has the advantage over a `#define` constant that it can be referenced using a symbolic debugger.

Constants and Pointers

You can use the `const` keyword when declaring a pointer, in several ways.

First, you can define a pointer to a constant type—for example, a pointer to a `const int`:

```
const int *PCInt;
```

You can freely change the value of such a pointer, but not the value of the variable that it points to—for example:

```
const int A = 1;
int B = 2;

const int *PCInt;   // no need to initialize; PCInt is not a const
PCInt = &A;

*PCInt = 5;         // ERROR: can't change variable pointed to

PCInt = &B;         // OK to change PCInt itself
```

Note that `PCInt` can be assigned the address of either a constant or a nonconstant `int` variable. However, even if `PCInt` is assigned the address of a nonconstant variable, it can't be used to change this variable (in this case, the pointer serves as a read-only way to access a read-write variable).

Second, you can define a constant pointer to a nonconstant variable, as in this example:

```
int N;
int *const CPInt = &N;
```

Since this pointer is a constant, it must be initialized when it's defined, and it can't subsequently be assigned a different address. The pointer, however, can be used to change the value of the variable it points to, as demonstrated in the following code:

```
int A = 1;
int B = 2;

int *const CPInt = &A;   // must initialize CPInt

*CPInt = 5;              // OK to change variable pointed to

CPInt = &B;              // ERROR: can't change const pointer
```

Third, you can define a constant pointer to a constant object. In this case, you must initialize the pointer when defining it, and you can't change either the value of the pointer itself or the value of the variable that it points to.

Note, finally, that you *can't* assign the address of a constant variable to a pointer to a nonconstant variable; doing so would provide a sneaky way of changing a constant variable, as shown in the following code:

```
const int N = 1;
int *PInt;

PInt = &N;  // ERROR: can't assign the address of a const int to
            // a pointer to a nonconst int

*PInt = 2;  // if assignment had been allowed, this statement
            // would change a constant variable!
```

Constants and References

You can also define a reference to a constant object. You can initialize this type of reference using a constant variable:

```
const int A = 1;
const int &RCIntA = A;
```

or you can initialize it using a nonconstant variable:

```
int B;
const int &RCIntB = B;
```

In either case, you *can't* use the reference to change the value of the variable it refers to:

```
const int A = 1;
const int &RCIntA = A;

int B;
const int &RCIntB = B;

RCIntA = 5;  // ERROR: can't change value of reference to const
RCIntB = 10; // ERROR: can't change value of reference to const
```

If you initialize a reference to a `const` type using a nonconstant variable, the reference serves as a read-only alias for that variable. (This is a rare case in which a reference behaves differently from the variable it refers to.)

You can also initialize a reference to a `const` using a constant expression (recall that it's illegal to initialize a reference to a nonconstant variable with a constant expression)—for example:

```
const int &RCInt = 5;  // valid initialization
```

In this definition, the compiler (conceptually if not actually) creates a temporary `const int` variable containing the value 5, and then initializes PCInt so that it's an alias for this temporary variable.

Note that it's meaningless (though legal) to define a reference variable that's constant itself, since all reference variables are automatically constant (recall that once a reference is initialized, you can't make it refer to a different variable):

```
int N;

int &const RCInt = N;  // legal but senseless
```

Finally, you can't use a constant variable to initialize a reference to a nonconstant type, because doing so would provide an indirect way to change the constant variable:

```
const int CInt = 1;

int &RInt = CInt;  // ERROR

RInt = 5;          // if initialization had been allowed, this
                   // statement would change a const variable!
```

Constants and Functions

You can also declare function parameters, as well as function return types, using the const keyword.

Declaring a parameter as a const simply means that the function can't change the value of its parameter; this information probably isn't of much interest to the programmer calling the function, because it's merely an implementation detail with no effect outside the function:

```
void FuncA (const int N);  // FuncA can't change N; so what?
```

If a parameter is a *pointer* or *reference*, the function can normally change the value of the variable that's passed:

```
FuncA (int *PInt);
FuncB (int &RInt);

void main ()
   {
   int N = 1;

   FuncA (&N);  // FuncA can change value of N
   FuncB (N);   // FuncB can change value of N

   // ...
   }
```

If, however, a variable is a pointer or reference to a const type, the function *can't* change the value of the variable that's passed; this information is usually of considerable interest to the programmer calling the function, because it guarantees that the function won't have the side effect of changing the value of a variable. For example:

```
FuncA (const int *PInt);
FuncB (const int &RInt);

void main ()
   {
   int N = 1;

   FuncA (&N);  // FuncA CAN'T change value of N
   FuncB (N);   // FuncB CAN'T change value of N

   // ...
   }
```

Furthermore, if a parameter is a pointer or reference to a `const`, you can pass the function a constant variable. (If the parameter is a pointer or reference to a nonconstant type, passing a constant variable is illegal because it would permit the constant variable to be changed.) For example, if N were declared as

```
const int N = 1;
```

you could legally pass the address of N to FuncA or pass N to FuncB, as in the code above.

Additionally, if a parameter is declared as a reference to a constant, you can pass the function a constant expression (recall that this is illegal for a parameter that's a reference to a nonconstant):

```
void FuncA (const int &RInt);

void main ()
    {
    FuncA (5);  // legal

    // ...
    }
```

If a function returns a fundamental type (such as `int` or `double`), adding `const` to the definition of the function return type doesn't have much significance, because you can't change such a return value anyway (that is, it's not an *lvalue*). For example:

```
const int Func ();  // so what? return value isn't an lvalue and
                    // therefore can't be changed anyway
```

If, however, a function returns a pointer or reference to some type, adding the keyword `const` to the declaration means that the calling function can't use the return value to alter the variable that's pointed to or referenced; for example:

```
const int *FuncA ()
    {
    static int Protected = 1;
    ++Protected;

    return &Protected;
    }
```

```
const int &FuncB ()
   {
   static int Safe = 100;
   --Safe;

   return Safe;
   }

void main (int Parm)
   {
   int N;

   N = *FuncA ();  // legal: N gets a copy of Protected
   N = FuncB ();    // legal: N gets a copy of Safe

   *FuncA () = 5;  // ERROR: attempt to change const type
   ++FuncB ();      // ERROR: attempt to change const type
   }
```

Note that both FuncA and FuncB change the value of an internal data item; however, because of the const keyword in the declarations, they prevent the calling function from changing the data items.

Overloaded Functions

In C++ you can use the *same name* to define more than one function within a program, provided that each function differs from all other identically named functions in the number or type of parameters. For example, you could declare two different versions of the function Abs, one for obtaining the absolute value of an int and the other for obtaining the absolute value of a double, as follows:

```
int Abs (int N)
   {
   return N < 0 ? -N : N;
   }

double Abs (double N)
   {
   return N < 0.0 ? -N : N;
   }
```

When such identically named functions are declared within the same scope, they're known as *overloaded functions*. The compiler automatically calls the appropriate version of an overloaded function, based on the type of the parameter or parameters passed in the actual function call, as shown in the following code:

```
int Abs (int N);        // both versions of Abs declared in file
double Abs (double N);  // scope

void main ()
   {
   int I;
   double D;

   I = Abs (5);       // calls 'int Abs (int N)'
   D = Abs (-2.5);    // calls 'double Abs (double N)'

   // ...

   }
```

Two overloaded functions must differ in one or both of the following ways:

- The functions have different numbers of parameters.

- The type of one or more parameters is different.

As you can see in the example above, overloaded functions can return different types. However, you may not define two overloaded functions that differ *only* in their return types, as shown in the following erroneous code:

```
int Abs (int N)
   {
   return N < 0 ? -N : N;
   }

double Abs (int N)  // ERROR: an overloaded function that differs
                    // only by return type
   {
   return (double)(N < 0 ? -N : N);
   }
```

Also, if two parameters are identical except that only one of them is a `const` or a reference type, they're considered to be the same type when overloaded functions are defined. For example, you *can't* define overloaded functions as follows:

```
int Abs (int N);
int Abs (const int N);  // ERROR: parameter lists too similar
```

The compiler doesn't allow these overloaded functions, because both `int` and `const int` are initialized using the same set of types; if you passed one of these types when calling the function, the compiler would be unable to determine which overloaded function to call. Likewise, you can't define overloaded functions like this,

```
int Abs (int N);
int Abs (int &N);  // ERROR: parameter lists too similar
```

because both functions could be passed an `int` variable.

If you pass an argument to an overloaded function that doesn't match the argument type defined by any of the function versions, the compiler will attempt to convert the argument to one of the defined types. As necessary, the compiler will perform standard conversions (for example, `int` to `long`) as well as user-defined conversions (which are described in Chapter 6). If the type can't be converted, the compiler generates an error. Also, if the compiler is able to convert the parameters you pass so that they match the types defined for more than one overloaded function, it calls the function that matches most closely; if all functions match equally closely, it generates an error (the function call in this case being ambiguous). For details on the rather complex criteria that the compiler uses for comparing type matches, see the following topic in the Visual C++ online help: *Visual C++ Documentation, Reference, C/C++ Language and C++ Libraries, C++ Language Reference, Overloading.*

Default function parameters can also result in ambiguous overloaded function calls. Consider, for example, the following overloaded functions:

```
void Display (char *Buffer);
void Display (char *Buffer, int Length = 32);
```

The following call would generate an error, because the parameter list would match *both* overloaded functions:

```
Display ("Hello");  // ERROR: ambiguous call!
```

Note that the compiler doesn't generate an error when the above overloaded functions are defined. Rather, it flags an error only when an overloaded function is actually called ambiguously.

NOTE   See Chapter 4 for information on overloading member functions of a C++ class (specifically, constructors), and Chapter 6 for a discussion on overloading standard C operators. Also, Chapter 7 shows how to define function *templates* as an alternative—and often simpler—way to handle different data types.

The *new* and *delete* Operators

You can use the C++ new and delete operators to allocate and release blocks of memory. The area of memory from which these blocks are allocated is known in C++ as the *free store*. When using new, you specify a data type; new then allocates a block of memory large enough to hold an object of the specified type, and it returns the address of the block as a pointer to the specified type. You can allocate a block of memory for storing an object of a built-in type such as a char, int, or double, as in the following code:

```
char *PChar;            // declare pointers
int *PInt;
double *PDouble;

PChar = new char;       // allocate memory objects
PInt = new int;
PDouble = new double;

*PChar = 'a';           // assign values
*PInt = 5;
*PDouble = 2.25;
```

More commonly, you use new to allocate memory for a user-defined type, such as a struct:

```
struct Node
    {
    char *Name;
    int Value;
    Node *Next;
    };
```

```
// ...

Node *PNode;              // declare a pointer

PNode = new Node;         // allocate memory

PNode->Name = "hello";   // assign values
PNode->Value = 1;
PNode->Next = 0;
```

If the new operator is unable to allocate the requested memory, it returns the value 0. Ideally, therefore, you should check the pointer before using it:

```
PNode = new Node;
if (PNode == 0)
   // handle error condition...
else
   // use PNode...
```

In Chapter 8, you'll learn another way to handle such errors.

When you've finished using a memory block allocated through the new operator, you can release the memory by using the delete operator on a pointer containing the address of the block. For example, the following statements would release the memory blocks allocated in the previous examples:

```
delete PChar;
delete PInt;
delete PDouble;
delete PNode;
```

TIP

Be sure not to invoke the delete operator more than once using the same address. Deleting a pointer containing 0, however, is always harmless. It's a good idea, therefore, to set a pointer variable to 0 immediately after using the delete operator on it.

The new and delete operators are useful for dynamically creating memory objects, especially when the number or size of the objects is unknown at compile time. Also, unlike a global or local named object that you've defined, you can precisely control the lifetime of an object created with new. A globally defined object always lasts the entire duration of the program, and a locally defined object always lasts until program control leaves the block in which it's defined; an object created with new, however, can be allocated at any point in the program, and it can be released at any point in the program by using delete.

The new and delete operators are generally more useful than the traditional malloc family of memory allocation functions provided by the runtime library. Unlike malloc, the new operator automatically determines the correct size for the object and returns a pointer of the correct type. Also, as you'll learn in Chapter 4, when used for a class object, new automatically calls the class *constructor* (which is the class initialization function) and delete automatically calls the class *destructor* (if one has been defined).

NOTE
You can *overload* the new and delete operators to provide custom memory management for your program. For a general discussion on operator overloading, see Chapter 6. For information specifically on overloading new and delete, see the following online help topic: *Visual C++ Documentation, Reference, C/C++ Language and C++ Libraries, C++ Language Reference, Special Member Functions, The new and delete Operators.*

Allocating Arrays with *new*

To allocate an array with new, you specify the base type (that is, the type of the array elements) and indicate the number of elements within [] characters, as in the following examples:

```
void Func (int Size)
   {
   char *String = new char [25];   // array of 25 chars

   int *ArrayInt = new int [Size]; // array of 'Size' ints

   double *ArrayDouble;
   ArrayDouble = new double [32];  // array of 32 doubles

   // ...
   }
```

When you allocate an array, new returns the address of the first array element. Notice that you can specify the number of elements in the array using a variable, which would be illegal in the declaration of an array variable.

When you invoke `delete` to free an array, you must include a pair of empty []characters to indicate that you're releasing an array rather than a single object of the base type. For example, the following statements would release the arrays allocated in the previous example:

```
delete [] String;
delete [] ArrayInt;
delete [] ArrayDouble;
```

Initializing Allocations

A memory block allocated with new *isn't* automatically initialized to 0. However, when you use new to allocate a memory object of a built-in type (such as a char), you can explicitly initialize the object with a constant of the appropriate type, using the following syntax:

```
char *PChar = new char ('a'); // initialize char with 'a'
int *PInt = new int (3);      // initialize int with 3
```

You can also initialize an object of a user-defined type (such as a `struct`) with an existing object of the same type:

```
struct Node
   {
   char *String;
   int Value;
   Node *Next;
   };

void Func ()
   {
   Node NodeA = {"hello", 1, 0};

   Node *PNode = new Node (NodeA);
   }
```

The contents of NodeA will be copied—field by field—into the new object allocated by the new operator.

NOTE   You can't initialize an array of a built-in type within a **new** statement (you have to write code to initialize it *after* the **new** statement). As you'll learn in Chapter 4, however, you can write a special function known as a *class constructor* for initializing an array of a user-defined type when it's allocated with **new**.

Summary

In this chapter, you learned how to translate your C programs to C++, and how to begin writing new programs in C++. The chapter also described many of the new features provided by C++ that don't depend on classes. The following is a brief summary of the main topics:

- With only a few exceptions, C++ is a superset of the C language. You can therefore make the move to C++ by compiling your existing C programs—as well as the new programs you write—using the C++ compiler rather than the C compiler. You can then gradually add unique C++ features to your code.

- To use the C++ compiler, name your source file with the .cpp or .cxx extension.

- There are, however, several constructs that you might need to update when you port your C program to C++. Almost all of these constructs represent obsolete C programming practices and will be flagged by the C++ compiler.

- In C++, you can mark a single-line comment using the // characters.

- In C++, you can declare a local variable at any position in the code before it's referenced. You *don't* need to place all local declarations at the beginning of a block.

- You can reference a global variable that's hidden by an identically named local variable, by prefacing the name of the global variable with the *scope resolution operator*, ::.

- If you declare a function using the `inline` keyword, the compiler will replace all calls to the function with a copy of the actual function code (whenever possible).

- When you declare or define a function, you can assign a default value to one or more of the parameters. If you omit a parameter with a default value when you call the function, the compiler will automatically pass the default value.

- You can use the & character to define a *reference* variable, which serves as an alias for another variable. You can also define function parameters and function return types as references.

- You can create a variable for storing a constant value by using the `const` keyword in the definition. A pointer or reference to a `const` type can be used as a read-only means of accessing a variable. A function parameter declared as a pointer or reference to `const` guarantees that the function can't change the value of the variable that's passed.

- You can declare more than one function using the same name, provided that each function differs in the number or type of parameters. When such functions occur within the same scope, they're said to be *overloaded*. When you call an overloaded function, the compiler calls the function version that matches the number and types of the parameters that you pass.

- You can allocate and free blocks of memory from the free store using the C++ `new` and `delete` operators. These operators are well adapted to the needs of C++ programs, especially programs that use classes.

The next chapter introduces the central new feature of C++: classes.

CHAPTER

FOUR

Defining C++ Classes

■ Defining a class

■ Creating a class instance

■ Accessing class members

■ Encapsulation

■ Constructors and destructors

■ Inline member functions

■ The this pointer

■ Static class members

4

This chapter introduces C++ classes. When you define a class, you create a new data type, which you can use much like one of the built-in C++ data types. A class, however, contains code as well as data. A class allows you to encapsulate all the code and data you need to manage a particular kind of program item, such as a window on the screen, a figure that the program draws, a device connected to a computer, or a task run by an operating system. This chapter describes the basic techniques for creating and using individual classes. In the next chapter, you'll learn how to define and use hierarchies of related classes.

Defining a Class

A C++ class is somewhat similar to a standard C structure, though the features of C++ classes go far beyond those provided by C structures. To understand C++ classes, it's useful to start by considering how structures are used in the C language.

A C structure allows you to group a set of related data items. As a simple example, if your C program draws a rectangle on the screen, you might find it convenient to store the coordinates of the rectangle within a structure defined as follows:

```
struct Rectangle
{
    int Left;
    int Top;
    int Right;
    int Bottom;
};
```

You could then define a function for drawing the rectangle, as in the following example:

```
void DrawRectangle (struct Rectangle *Rect)
    {
    Line (Rect->Left, Rect->Top, Rect->Right, Rect->Top);
    Line (Rect->Right, Rect->Top, Rect->Right, Rect->Bottom);
    Line (Rect->Right, Rect->Bottom, Rect->Left, Rect->Bottom);
    Line (Rect->Left, Rect->Bottom, Rect->Left, Rect->Top);
    }
```

In this example, `Line` is a hypothetical function that draws a line from the point given by the first two coordinates to the point given by the second two coordinates. Such a function might be defined elsewhere in the program or obtained from a function library.

Finally, to draw a rectangle at a particular position, you'd define and initialize a variable of type `Rectangle` and then pass this variable to the function `DrawRectangle`:

```
struct Rectangle Rect = {25, 25, 100, 100};

DrawRectangle (&Rect);
```

A C++ class, unlike a C structure, defines not only a collection of data items, but also the functions that operate on these data items. Thus, in C++ you could combine both the coordinates of the rectangle *and* the function for drawing the rectangle within a single class definition, as in the following example:

```
class CRectangle
{
    int Left;
    int Top;
    int Right;
    int Bottom;

    void Draw (void)
        {
        Line (Left, Top, Right, Top);
        Line (Right, Top, Right, Bottom);
        Line (Right, Bottom, Left, Bottom);
        Line (Left, Bottom, Left, Top);
        }
};
```

Data items defined within a class are known as *data members* or *member variables*, and functions defined within a class are known as *member functions*. In this class example, the data members are `Left`, `Top`, `Right`, and `Bottom`, and the member function is `Draw`. Notice that a member function can refer directly to any of the data members of the same class, without using any special syntax.

Creating a Class Instance

In C, providing a structure definition such as

```
struct Rectangle
{
    int Left;
    int Top;
    int Right;
    int Bottom;
};
```

tells the compiler the form of the structure, but doesn't actually reserve memory or create a variable that you can use for storing data. To reserve memory and create a variable, you must provide a definition, such as the following:

```
struct Rectangle Rect;
```

In the same manner, defining a class, such as the class CRectangle shown in the previous sections, provides the compiler with a blueprint of the class, but doesn't actually reserve memory. As with a structure, you must define a data item, such as the following:

```
CRectangle Rect;
```

This definition creates an *instance* of the CRectangle class. An instance of a class is also known as an *object*; throughout the book, the terms *class instance* and *object* will be used synonymously. The class instance, Rect, occupies its own block of memory and can be used for storing data and performing operations on that data. As with a variable of a built-in type, an object will remain in existence until its definition goes out of scope (for example, if it's defined within a function, it will be destroyed when the function returns).

NOTE   Just as with C structures, the definition of a class must precede the definition and use of a class instance within the source file.

You can also create an instance of a class using the C++ new operator, as in the following statement:

```
CRectangle *PRect = new CRectangle;
```

This statement allocates a block of memory large enough to hold an instance of the class, and returns a pointer to this object. The object will remain allocated until you explicitly free it using the `delete` operator (as explained in Chapter 3 for built-in types):

```
delete PRectangle;
```

You can create any number of instances of a given class.

TIP

In creating a class instance, you're not required to preface the name of the class with the word `class`. In C++, a class definition creates a new data type, which can be referred to using the class name alone.

Accessing Class Members

After you've created a class instance, you access the data members and member functions using a syntax similar to that used for C structures. However, with the current definition of the `CRectangle` class, the program *wouldn't* be able to access any of its members. The reason is that—by default—all data members and member functions belonging to a class are *private*, meaning that they can be used only within member functions of the class itself. Thus, it's legal for the function `Draw` to access the data members `Top`, `Left`, `Right`, and `Bottom`, because `Draw` is a member function of the class. However, it would be illegal for the other parts of the program, such as the function `main`, to access the data members or call the member function `Draw`.

Fortunately, you can use the `public` *access specifier* to make one or more members *public*, rendering these members accessible to all other functions in the program (functions defined either within classes or outside classes). For example, in the following version of the `CRectangle` class, all members are made public:

```
class CRectangle
{
public:
    int Left;
    int Top;
    int Right;
    int Bottom;
```

```
void Draw (void)
   {
   Line (Left, Top, Right, Top);
   Line (Right, Top, Right, Bottom);
   Line (Right, Bottom, Left, Bottom);
   Line (Left, Bottom, Left, Top);
   }
};
```

The access specifier applies to *all* members that come after it in the class definition (until another access specifier is encountered, as will be explained later).

Now that all members of CRectangle have been made public, they can be accessed using the dot operator (.), in the same way that fields of a C structure are accessed. For example:

```
CRectangle Rect;      // define a CRectangle object

Rect.Left = 5;        // assign values to the data members to
Rect.Top = 10;        // specify the rectangle coordinates
Rect.Right = 100;
Rect.Bottom = 150;


Rect.Draw ();         // draw the rectangle
```

Alternatively, you could dynamically create a class instance with the new operator, and then use a pointer to the instance to access the data members, as in the following code:

```
CRectangle *PRect = new CRectangle;

PRect->Left = 5;
PRect->Top = 10;
PRect->Right = 100;
PRect->Bottom = 150;

PRect->Draw ();
```

Encapsulation

According to the principle of *encapsulation*, the internal data structures used in implementing a class shouldn't be directly accessible to the user of the class (the advantages of encapsulation are discussed later). The current version of the CRectangle class, however, clearly violates this principle since the user can directly read or modify any of the data members.

To achieve greater encapsulation, CRectangle should be defined following the usual C++ custom of providing public access to the generally useful member functions (so far, only Draw), but denying access to the internal data members used by these functions (Left, Top, Right, and Bottom):

```
class CRectangle
{
private:
    int Left;
    int Top;
    int Right;
    int Bottom;

public:
    void Draw (void)
        {
        Line (Left, Top, Right, Top);
        Line (Right, Top, Right, Bottom);
        Line (Right, Bottom, Left, Bottom);
        Line (Left, Bottom, Left, Top);
        }
};
```

The private access specifier makes the members that follow it private, so that they can't be accessed except by member functions of the class. Like the public access specifier discussed previously, the private specifier affects all declarations that come after it, until another specifier is encountered. Therefore, this definition makes Left, Top, Right, and Bottom private, and it makes Draw public. (Note that the private specifier isn't actually required at the beginning of the class definition, because class members are private by default; including the private specifier, however, makes this fact explicit to the reader of the program.)

C++ provides a third access specifier, **protected**. The explanation of this specifier is postponed until Chapter 5, because it requires an understanding of inheritance.

The following code illustrates legal and illegal accesses to members of the current version of the CRectangle class:

```
void main ()
    {
    CRectangle Rect;     // define a CRectangle object

    Rect.Left = 5;       // ERROR: can't access private member
    Rect.Top = 10;       // ERROR
    Rect.Right = 100;    // ERROR
    Rect.Bottom = 150;   // ERROR

    Rect.Draw ();        // OK (but coordinates are undefined)
    }
```

Now that the user of the class is denied direct access to the data members, the class must provide an alternative means for the user to specify the coordinates of the rectangle before the rectangle is drawn. A good way to do this is to provide a public member function that receives the desired coordinate values and uses these values to set the data members; the following is an example:

```
void SetCoord (int L, int T, int R, int B)
    {
    L = __min (__max (0,L), 80);
    T = __min (__max (0,T), 25);
    R = __min (__max (0,R), 80);
    B = __min (__max (0,B), 25);
    R = __max (R,L);
    B = __max (B,T);
    Left = L; Top = T; Right = R; Bottom = B;
    }
```

This function should be added to the public section of the CRectangle class definition, so that it can be called by any function in the program. Notice that before assigning the parameters to the data members of the class, SetCoord adjusts the parameters, if necessary, to make sure that they're within the ranges of valid values; it also makes sure that the right coordinate is greater than the left, and the bottom greater than the top. (The macros __max and __min are provided by the C++ runtime library; to use them in your program, you must include the Stdlib.h header file.)

You could now use the CRectangle class to draw a rectangle as follows:

```
void main ()
  {
  // ...

  CRectangle Rect;

  Rect.SetCoord (25,25,100,100);   // set rectangle coordinates
  Rect.Draw ();                    // draw the rectangle

  // ...
  };
```

Later in the chapter (in the section "Constructors"), you'll learn how to initialize data members at the same time that you create an instance of the class.

You might also want to add a member function that permits other parts of the program to *obtain* the current values of the rectangle coordinates. The following is an example of such a function:

```
void GetCoord (int *L, int *T, int *R, int *B)
  {
  *L = Left;
  *T = Top;
  *R = Right;
  *B = Bottom;
  }
```

This function should also be added to the public section of the class definition. The following is the complete CRectangle class definition, including both new member functions, SetCoord and GetCoord:

```
#include <Stdlib.h>

class CRectangle
  {
private:
    int Left;
    int Top;
    int Right;
    int Bottom;
```

```cpp
public:
    void Draw (void)
        {
        Line (Left, Top, Right, Top);
        Line (Right, Top, Right, Bottom);
        Line (Right, Bottom, Left, Bottom);
        Line (Left, Bottom, Left, Top);
        }
    void GetCoord (int *L, int *T, int *R, int *B)
        {
        *L = Left;
        *T = Top;
        *R = Right;
        *B = Bottom;
        }
    void SetCoord (int L, int T, int R, int B)
        {
        L = __min (__max (0,L), 80);
        T = __min (__max (0,T), 25);
        R = __min (__max (0,R), 80);
        B = __min (__max (0,B), 25);
        R = __max (R,L);
        B = __max (B,T);
        Left = L; Top = T; Right = R; Bottom = B;
        }
};
```

By means of the SetCoord and GetCoord member functions, the CRectangle class now provides access to its private data members, but—in the spirit of encapsulation—only through a clearly defined interface that carefully checks the validity of the new assigned values and adjusts these values if necessary.

The Benefits of Encapsulation

One obvious benefit of encapsulation is that it allows the designer of the class to check the validity of any value that's assigned to a data member, and thus helps prevent programming errors.

Another advantage of controlling access to internal data structures is that the author of the class can freely change the design of these data structures, without disturbing the other parts of the program that use the class (as long as the calling protocol of the public member functions remains the same). As a simple example, the author of the CRectangle class might decide to store the coordinates of the top and left of the rectangle, together with the width and height of the rectangle rather than the right and bottom coordinates. In this case, the data members might be defined as follows:

```
private:
    int Left;
    int Top;
    int Width;
    int Height;
```

As long as the calling protocols for the SetCoord and GetCoord functions remained the same, this internal change wouldn't affect other portions of the program, nor any other program that used the CRectangle class. (Of course, these two functions would have to be changed internally to convert between coordinate values and the values for width and height.) Encapsulation would thus prevent the user of the class from creating dependencies on specific internal data representations.

Constructors and Destructors

This section discusses two special types of member functions that you can define for a class: *constructors* and *destructors*.

Constructors

The current version of the CRectangle class allows you to initialize the data members by calling the SetCoord member function. As an alternative way of initializing data members, you can define a special member function known as a *constructor*. A constructor is called automatically whenever an instance of the class is created; it can initialize data members and perform any other initialization tasks required to prepare the class object for use.

A constructor has the same name as the class itself. When you define a constructor, you can't specify a return value, not even void (a constructor never returns a value). A constructor may, however, take any number of parameters (zero or more). For example, the following version of the CRectangle class has a constructor that takes four parameters, which are used to initialize the data members:

```
class CRectangle
{
private:
    int Left;
    int Top;
    int Right;
    int Bottom;

public:
    // constructor:
    CRectangle (int L, int T, int R, int B)
        {
        SetCoord (L, T, R, B);
        }

// definitions of other member functions ...

};
```

> **NOTE**   If you want to be able to create instances of a class, you must make the constructor a *public* member function. (If you use the class only for deriving other classes, you can make the constructor a *protected* member, as explained in Chapter 5.)

Recall that the SetCoord member function checks the validity of its parameters and assigns the parameter values to the private data members that store the coordinates of the rectangle.

When you define an object, you pass the parameter values to the constructor using a syntax similar to a normal function call:

```
CRectangle Rect (25, 25, 100, 100);
```

This definition creates an instance of the CRectangle class and invokes the class's constructor, passing it the specified parameter values.

You also pass the parameter values to the constructor when you create a class instance using the new operator:

```
CRectangle *PRect = new CRectangle (25, 25, 100, 100);
```

The new operator automatically invokes the constructor for the object that it creates. (This is an important advantage of using new rather than other memory-allocation methods, such as the malloc function.)

With the constructor in place, you can create a CRectangle object and draw a rectangle in only two statements (rather than the three statements shown previously, in the section "Encapsulation"):

```
void main ()
    {
    CRectangle Rect (25,25,100,100); // create object and specify
                                     // rectangle dimensions
    Rect.Draw ();                    // draw the rectangle
    };
```

Default Constructors

A constructor that takes no parameters is known as a *default constructor*. A default constructor typically initializes data members by assigning them default values. For example, the following version of the CRectangle class has a default constructor that initializes all data members to 0:

```
class CRectangle
{
private:
    int Left;
    int Top;
    int Right;
    int Bottom;
public:
    CRectangle ()
        {
        Left = Top = Right = Bottom = 0;
        }

// definitions of other member functions ...

};
```

NOTE A constructor with one or more parameters, all of which have default values, is also considered to be a default constructor, because it *can* be invoked without passing parameters (see the section "Default Function Parameters" in Chapter 3).

If you *don't* define a constructor for a particular class, the compiler will generate a default constructor for you. Such a compiler-generated constructor won't assign initial values to the class's data members; therefore, if you want to explicitly initialize data members or perform any other initialization tasks, you must define your own constructor.

If a class has a default constructor (either an explicitly defined one or a compiler-generated one), you can define a class object without passing parameters; for example:

```
CRectangle Rect;
```

If you don't pass parameters to a constructor, however, *don't be tempted to include empty parentheses* in the object definition. Doing so will actually declare a function that returns a class type rather than defining an instance of a class:

```
CRectangle Rect ();  // declares a function that takes no
                     // parameters and returns a CRectangle
                     // object
```

(If you make this mistake, the compiler won't generate an error until you attempt to use Rect as if it were a class instance.)

See Chapter 6 for an explanation of the special properties of constructors that take a *single* parameter (in the section "Using Copy and Conversion Constructors").

Overloaded Constructors

Just as you can overload a global function (as explained in Chapter 3), you can also overload the class constructor or any other member function of a class except the destructor. (You can't overload the destructor because it never takes parameters, as explained later.) In fact, overloaded constructors are quite common; they provide alternative ways to initialize a newly created class object. For example, the following definition of CRectangle provides overloaded constructors that allow you either to specify the initial values of the data members, or to simply accept default initial values:

```
class CRectangle
{
private:
    int Left;
    int Top;
    int Right;
    int Bottom;
```

```
public:
    // default constructor:
    CRectangle ()
        {
        Left = Top = Right = Bottom = 0;
        }

    // constructor with parms:
    CRectangle (int L, int T, int R, int B)
        {
        SetCoord (L, T, R, B);
        }

// definitions of other member functions ...

};
```

The following code demonstrates the use of the overloaded CRectangle constructors:

```
void main ()
    {
    // create an object using default constructor:
    CRectangle Rect1;

    // create an object, specifying initial values:
    CRectangle Rect2 (25, 25, 100, 100);

    // ...

    }
```

NOTE

If you define a constructor for a class, the compiler *won't* create a default constructor for you. If, therefore, you define one or more constructors, but you don't include a default constructor among them, the class *won't have* a default constructor. As you'll see later in the chapter, using a class that doesn't have a default constructor can cause errors in certain situations.

Member Initialization in Constructors

You aren't permitted to initialize a data member of a class when you define it. Thus, the following class definition generates errors:

```
class C
{
private:
    int N = 0;              // ERROR
    const int CInt = 5;   // ERROR
    int &RInt = N;         // ERROR

// ...

};
```

It doesn't make sense to initialize a data member within a class definition, because the class definition merely indicates the *type* of each data member and doesn't actually reserve memory. Rather, you want to initialize the data members each time you create a specific *instance* of the class. The logical place to initialize data members, therefore, is within the class constructor. The example `CRectangle` class constructor initializes the data members by using *assignment* expressions. However, certain data types—specifically, constants and references—*can't* be assigned values. To solve this problem, C++ provides a special constructor feature known as a *member initializer list* that allows you to *initialize* (rather than *assign* a value to) one or more data members.

A member initializer list is placed immediately after the parameter list in the constructor definition; it consists of a colon, followed by one or more *member initializers*, separated with commas. A member initializer consists of the name of a data member followed by the initial value in parentheses. For example, the constructor in the following class has a member initializer list that contains a member initializer for each data member:

```
class C
{
private:
    int N;
    const int CInt;
    int &RInt;
    // ...
```

```
public:
   C (int Parm) : N (Parm), CInt (5), RInt (N)
      {
      // constructor code ...
      }

   // ...
};
```

To illustrate the effect of this member initializer list, the following definition would create an object in which the data members N and CInt are initialized to 0 and 5, and the data member RInt is initialized so that it refers to N:

```
C CObject (0);
```

const Objects and const Member Functions

As explained in Chapter 3, adding the keyword const to a variable definition means that you can't change the value of the variable. Likewise, adding const to the definition of a class object means that you can't change the value of any data member belonging to that class. Consider, for example, the following class:

```
class CTest
{
public:
   int A;
   int B;
   CTest (int AVal, int BVal)
      {
      A = AVal;
      B = BVal;
      }
};
```

The statement:

```
const CTest Test (1, 2);
```

would create a constant object of this class and would initialize both data members. This is the last time, however, that any data member can be assigned a value. Because of the const keyword, the following assignment would be illegal:

```
Test.A = 3;   // ERROR: can't change a data member of a
              // const object!
```

Continued on next page

There's another ramification of declaring an object using the **const** keyword. To illustrate it, consider declaring a **const** object of the **CRectangle** class given in this chapter:

```
const CRectangle Rect (5, 5, 25, 25);
```

Even though the **CRectangle** member function **GetCoord** doesn't change any data member, the compiler *won't* allow the program to call it for a **const** object:

```
int L, T, R, B;
Rect.GetCoord (&L, &T, &R, &B); // ERROR
```

Because a normal member function *can* change the value of one or more data members, the compiler doesn't allow you to call a member function of a **const** object (it would be difficult or impossible for the compiler to check whether a member function actually modifies data members—the function implementation might even be located in a separate source code file).

To allow calling **GetCoord** for a **const** object, you have to include the keyword **const** in the function definition:

```
class CRectangle
{

// ...

    void GetCoord (int *L, int *T, int *R, int *B) const
        {
        *L = Left;
        *T = Top;
        *R = Right;
        *B = Bottom;
        }

// ...

};
```

Continued on next page

The **const** keyword in the **GetCoord** definition means that the function *can't* change any data member; if it attempts to do so, the compiler will generate an error when it compiles the function code. **GetCoord** can now be called for a **const CRectangle** object:

```
const CRectangle Rect (5, 5, 25, 25);

int L, T, R, B;
Rect.GetCoord (&L, &T, &R, &B); // legal now that
                                // GetCoord is a const
                                // member function
```

You could also declare the **Draw** member function as **const**, because it likewise doesn't modify a data member. It might be a good idea to declare as **const** any member function that doesn't change a data member, so that the user of the class will be free to call the function for **const** objects (obviously, a function like **CRectangle::SetCoord** can't be declared as **const**).

Initializing Member Objects   You can define a data member that's an object of another class; that is, you can embed an object of one class within an object of another class. Such a data member is known as a *member object*. You can initialize a member object by passing the required parameters to the object's constructor within the member initializer list of the constructor of the containing class. For example, the class **CContainer** in the following code contains a member object of class **CEmbedded**, which is initialized within the **CContainer** constructor:

```
class CEmbedded
{
  // ...

public:
    CEmbedded (int Parm1, int Parm2)
       {
       // ...
       }

    // ...

  };
```

```
class CContainer
{
private:
  CEmbedded Embedded;

public:
  CContainer (int P1, int P2, int P3) : Embedded (P1, P2)
    {

    // constructor code ...

    }

  // ...
};
```

If you *don't* initialize a member object in the member initializer list of the constructor (or if the constructor is a compiler-generated default constructor), the compiler will automatically invoke the member object's default constructor, if one is available (recall that not every class has a default constructor); if a default constructor isn't available, a compiler error will result.

NOTE   As you'll see in Chapter 5, you can also use the member initializer list within a constructor of a derived class to pass values to a constructor belonging to a base class.

Destructors

You can also define a special member function known as a *destructor*, which is called automatically whenever a class object is destroyed. The name of the destructor is the same as the name of the class, prefaced with the ~ character. Like a constructor, the destructor must be defined with no return type (not even void); unlike a constructor, however, it can't accept parameters. For example, if a class is named CMessage, its destructor would be defined as follows:

```
~CMessage ()
  {

  // destructor code ...

  }
```

A destructor can perform any tasks required before an object is destroyed. For example, the constructor for the following class (CMessage) allocates a block of memory for storing a message string; the destructor releases this memory immediately before a class instance is destroyed:

```
#include <string.h>

class CMessage
{
private:
   char *Buffer;  // stores message string

public:
   CMessage ()
      {
      Buffer = new char ('\0');  // initialize Buffer to
                                 // empty string
      }

   ~CMessage ()                  // class destructor
      {
      delete [] Buffer;          // free the memory
      }

   void Display ()
      {

      // code for displaying contents of Buffer ...

      }
   void Set (char *String)       // store a new message string
      {
      delete [] Buffer;
      Buffer = new char [strlen (String) + 1];
      strcpy (Buffer, String);
      }
};
```

When Constructors and Destructors Are Called

In general, a constructor is called when an object is created, and a destructor is called when an object is destroyed. The following list explains exactly when constructors and destructors are called for specific types of objects:

- For an object defined globally (that is, outside any function), the constructor is called when the program first begins running, before main (or WinMain for a Windows GUI program) receives control. The destructor is called when the program ends.

- For an object defined locally (that is, within a function), the constructor is called whenever the flow of control reaches the object definition, and the destructor is called when control passes out of the block in which the object is defined (that is, when the object goes out of scope).

- For an object defined locally using the static keyword, the constructor is called when control *first* reaches the object definition, and the destructor is called when the program ends.

- For an object created dynamically using the new operator, the constructor is called when the object is created, and the destructor is called when the object is explicitly destroyed using the delete operator (if you don't explicitly destroy the object, the destructor will never be called).

Arrays of Objects

You can define an array of objects, as in the following example:

```
CRectangle RectTable [10];
```

CRectangle is the class shown in the previous examples. You can also create an array of objects dynamically:

```
CRectangle *PRectTable = new CRectangle [10];
```

In either case, when the array is created, the compiler calls the default constructor for each element in the array, and when the array's destroyed, the compiler calls the destructor for each element (assuming that a destructor has been defined for the class). If the class doesn't have a default constructor, a compiler error results.

If you *define* a named array of objects (as in the first example), you can initialize each element of the array by passing the desired values to a constructor; this technique is described in Chapter 6 (in the section "Initializing Arrays").

If, however, you've dynamically created an array using new, you can't supply initializers for specific elements; rather, the compiler always calls the default constructor for each element. Also, for a dynamically created array, you must include the [] characters when destroying the array with the **delete** operator:

```
delete [] PRectTable;
```

If you omit the [] characters, the compiler will call the destructor only for the *first* array element.

NOTE   The constructors for elements of an array are called in the order of increasing addresses. The destructors are called in the reverse order.

Inline Member Functions

In each of the example classes given so far in this chapter, the member functions are fully defined *within* the body of the class definition. As an alternative, you can *declare* a member function within the class, and *define* the function outside the class. For instance, if the CRectangle member functions are defined outside the class definition, the class could be defined as follows:

```
class CRectangle
{
private:
    int Left;
    int Top;
    int Right;
    int Bottom;

public:
    CRectangle ();
    CRectangle (int L, int T, int R, int B);
    void Draw (void);
    void GetCoord (int *L, int *T, int *R, int *B);
    void SetCoord (int L, int T, int R, int B);
};
```

When you define a member function outside the class definition, you must preface the name of the function with the name of the class followed by the scope resolution operator (::). For example, the CRectangle member functions could be defined outside the class definition as follows:

```cpp
#include <Stdlib.h>

CRectangle::CRectangle ()
    {
    Left = Top = Right = Bottom = 0;
    }

CRectangle::CRectangle (int L, int T, int R, int B)
    {
    SetCoord (L,T,R,B);
    }

void CRectangle::Draw (void)
    {
    Line (Left, Top, Right, Top);
    Line (Right, Top, Right, Bottom);
    Line (Right, Bottom, Left, Bottom);
    Line (Left, Bottom, Left, Top);
    }

void CRectangle::GetCoord (int *L, int *T, int *R, int *B)
    {
    *L = Left;
    *T = Top;
    *R = Right;
    *B = Bottom;
    }

void CRectangle::SetCoord (int L, int T, int R, int B)
    {
    L = __min (__max (0,L), 80);
    T = __min (__max (0,T), 25);
    R = __min (__max (0,R), 80);
    B = __min (__max (0,B), 25);
    R = __max (R,L);
    B = __max (B,T);
    Left = L; Top = T; Right = R; Bottom = B;
    }
```

There's an important difference between a function defined within the body of the class and one defined outside the class: a function that's defined within a class is treated as an inline function, while a function defined outside the class is—by default—treated as a non-inline function (see the description of inline functions in Chapter 3). Accordingly, you might want to define very short functions within the body of the class and define longer functions outside the class. As an example, for the CRectangle class, the constructors and the GetCoord function (the shortest member functions) might be defined within the class as inline functions, and Draw and SetCoord (the two longest functions) might be defined outside the class as non-inline functions; see the complete CRectangle listing, Listing 4.1, at the end of the next section.

You can *force* the compiler to treat a function defined outside the class definition as inline, by using the inline keyword as explained in Chapter 3. For instance, you could make the function CRectangle::GetCoord inline by declaring it within the CRectangle class definition as follows,

```
void inline GetCoord (int *L, int *T, int *R, int *B);
```

and then by defining it outside the class definition, as follows:

```
void inline CRectangle::GetCoord (int *L, int *T, int *R, int *B)
   {
   *L = Left;
   *T = Top;
   *R = Right;
   *B = Bottom;
   }
```

Organizing the Source Files

If a program consists of more than one C++ source file, you generally place the class definition—together with the definitions of any inline member functions defined outside the class—within a single header file (an .h file). You then include this header within any C++ source code file that uses the class. This arrangement ensures that the class definition, plus the code for any inline function, is available whenever the class is referenced or a member function is called. Recall from Chapter 3 that the compiler must have access to the inline function code whenever it encounters a call to the function.

Also, you generally place the definitions of any non-inline member functions within a separate C++ source code file, which is commonly known as the class *implementation* file. You must link the compiled version of the implementation file with your program (for example, by simply including the .cpp implementation file in the list of files in a Visual C++ project). Note that placing the definition of the non-inline functions within the header file rather than within a separate .cpp implementation file would result in a "symbol redefinition" Link error if you included the header in more than one source file.

To illustrate, Listings 4.1 and 4.2 give the complete source code for the latest version of the CRectangle class. The definition of the CRectangle class is placed in a file named CRect.h (the class header file), and the definitions of the non-inline member functions are placed in the file CRect.cpp (the class implementation file).

Listing 4.1

```cpp
// CRect.h: CRectangle header file

class CRectangle
{
private:
    int Left;
    int Top;
    int Right;
    int Bottom;

public:
    CRectangle ()
       {
       Left = Top = Right = Bottom = 0;
       }
    CRectangle (int L, int T, int R, int B)
       {
       SetCoord (L, T, R, B);
       }
    void Draw (void);
    void GetCoord (int *L, int *T, int *R, int *B)
       {
       *L = Left;
       *T = Top;
       *R = Right;
```

```
    *B = Bottom;
    }
  void SetCoord (int L, int T, int R, int B);
};
```

Listing 4.2

```
// CRect.cpp: CRectangle implementation file

#include "crect.h"
#include <stdlib.h>

void Line (int X1, int Y1, int X2, int Y2);

void CRectangle::Draw (void)
  {
  Line (Left, Top, Right, Top);
  Line (Right, Top, Right, Bottom);
  Line (Right, Bottom, Left, Bottom);
  Line (Left, Bottom, Left, Top);
  }

void CRectangle::SetCoord (int L, int T, int R, int B)
  {
  L = __min (__max (0,L), 80);
  T = __min (__max (0,T), 25);
  R = __min (__max (0,R), 80);
  B = __min (__max (0,B), 25);
  R = __max (R,L);
  B = __max (B,T);
  Left = L; Top = T; Right = R; Bottom = B;
  }
```

Recall that the CRectangle class assumes that the Line function is defined within another module. CRect.h must be included within any C++ file that references the CRectangle class (including CRect.cpp!), and the compiled version of CRect.cpp must be linked with the program.

The *this* Pointer

When you reference a data member of a class from code that's *outside* the class, you always specify a particular instance of the class in the expression. The compiler therefore knows which copy of the data member to access. Assume, for example, that CTest is a class containing a data member N; the following code would first print the copy of N belonging to the CTest object Test1, and would then print the copy of N belonging to the CTest object *PTest2:

```
CTest Test1;
CTest *PTest2 = new CTest;

// ...

cout << Test1.N << '\n';
cout << PTest2->N << '\n';
```

When you reference a data member *inside* a member function of a class, however, you *don't* specify a particular class instance:

```
class CTest
{
public:
   int N;

   int GetN ()
      {
      return N;   // N referenced WITHOUT specifying an object
      }
}
```

Therefore, how does the compiler determine which copy of N is being referenced within a member function? To do this, the compiler actually passes to the member function a hidden pointer to the object referenced in the function call. The function implicitly uses this hidden pointer to access the correct copy of a data member. For instance, in the call:

```
Test.GetN ();
```

the compiler passes GetN a hidden pointer to the object Test. GetN implicitly uses this pointer to access the copy of N that belongs to the object Test.

You can directly access this hidden pointer using the C++ keyword `this`. In other words, within a member function, `this` is a predefined pointer containing the address of the object referenced in the function call (sometimes called the *current* object). Thus, `GetN` could be rewritten as follows:

```
int GetN ()
   {
   return this->N;  // equivalent to 'return N;'
   }
```

Prefacing the name of a data member with the expression `this->` is valid but serves no purpose, because the use of the `this` pointer is implicit in a simple reference to the data member. Later in the book, however, you'll see several practical uses for `this`.

If you need to access a global data item or function that has the same name as a data member or member function, you must preface the name with the scope resolution operator, `::`. For example,

```
int N = 0;  // global N

class CTest
{
public:
   int N;    // data member N

   int Demo ()
      {
      cout << ::N << '\0'; // prints global N
      cout << N << '\0';    // accesses data member N using 'this'
      }
}
```

Static Class Members

Normally, each instance of a class has its own private copy of a data member that belongs to the class. If, however, you declare a data member using the `static` keyword, then a *single copy* of that data item will exist regardless of how many instances of the class have been created (even if *no* class instance has been created). For example, the following class defines the static data item Count:

```
class CTest
{
public:
    static int Count;

// remainder of class definition ...

}
```

No matter how many instances of CTest are created, there will be exactly one copy of Count.

In addition to declaring the static data member within the class, you must also define and initialize it *outside* the class, as a global data item. Because the definition of a static data member occurs outside the class, you must specify the class in which it is declared using the scope resolution operator (CTest::, in this example). For instance, you could define and initialize Count as follows:

```
// outside of any class or function:
int CTest::Count = 0;
```

Because a static data member exists independently of any class object, you can access it using the class name and the scope resolution operator *without reference to* a class instance, as shown in the following example:

```
void main ()
    {
    CTest::Count = 1;

    // ...
    }
```

You can think of a static data member as a hybrid between a global variable and a normal data member belonging to a class. Like a global variable, it's defined and initialized outside a function, and it represents a single memory location that persists during the entire course of the program. Like a normal data member, however, it's declared within a class, and access to it can be controlled (that is, it can be made public, private, or protected).

You can also define a member function using the `static` keyword, as in the following example:

```
class CTest
{

// ...

static int GetCount ()
   {
   // function code ...
   }

// ...

}
```

A static member function has the following properties:

- Code outside the class can call the function using the class name and the scope resolution operator, without reference to a class instance (a class instance doesn't even need to exist), as in the following example:

```
void main ()
   {
   int Count = CTest::GetCount ();

   // ...
   }
```

- A static member function can directly reference only static data members or static member functions that belong to its class. (Because it can be called without reference to a class instance, a static member function doesn't have a `this` pointer containing the address of an object. Nonstatic data members are allocated only when an object is created.)

Static data members and member functions can be used to maintain a data item that applies to a class in general, or a data item shared by all instances of a class. The following program illustrates using static members to maintain a count of the current number of instances of a class:

```cpp
#include <iostream.h>

class CTest
{
private:
   static int Count;

public:
   CTest ()
      {
      ++Count;
      }
   ~CTest ()
      {
      --Count;
      }
   static int GetCount ()
      {
      return Count;
      };
};

int CTest::Count = 0;

void main ()
   {
   cout << CTest::GetCount () << " objects exist\n";

   CTest Test1;
   CTest *PTest2 = new CTest;

   cout << CTest::GetCount () << " objects exist\n";

   delete PTest2;

   cout << CTest::GetCount () << " objects exist\n";
   }
```

This program prints the following:

```
0 objects exist
2 objects exist
1 objects exist
```

Summary

In this chapter, you learned how to define a class, how to create a class instance, and how to access the data and functions belonging to a class. You also learned about several special types of class members: constructors, destructors, inline member functions, and static members. The following are some of the specific concepts discussed:

- A class is somewhat similar to a structure in C. However, a class can contain both data items (known as *data members* or *member variables*) and functions (known as *member functions*) that operate on the data items.

- A class definition creates a new type. To use the class, you must create an actual data item belonging to this type. Such a data item is known as an *instance* of the class or a class *object*.

- You can create a class object by defining it the same way you would define a variable of a built-in type. Alternatively, you can use the new and delete operators to dynamically create and destroy a class object.

- You access the members of a class using the . or -> operators in the same way that you access the elements of a C structure. You can control access to class members by using the public or private *access specifiers* (by default, a member is private).

- According to the principle of *encapsulation*, you should use access specifiers to prevent the user from directly accessing data members employed internally by the class. You can provide a member function that changes a data member *after* it tests the validity of the value that the user supplies.

- A *constructor* is a special member function that's automatically called whenever you create an instance of the class. You typically use it to initialize data members or perform any other tasks required to prepare the class for use. A constructor can be defined to take any number of parameters; a *default constructor* is one that takes no parameters.

- A *destructor* is a special member function that's automatically called whenever a class object is destroyed. It can be used either to release memory allocated by the class object or to perform other cleanup tasks.

- A member function can be defined within the body of the class, or it can merely be declared within the class and defined outside it.

- A member function defined within the class is automatically treated as an inline function. A member function defined outside the class is treated as an inline function only if it's declared using the `inline` keyword.

- Within a member function, the C++ keyword `this` contains the address of the object referenced in the call to the function (that is, the particular object for which the member function was called).

- If a data member is defined using the `static` keyword, only a single copy of the data member exists, regardless of the number of class instances created. A static data member can be accessed using the class name and the scope resolution operator, without reference to a particular class instance.

- A member function defined using the `static` keyword can be called using the class name and the scope resolution operator, without reference to a specific object. It can directly reference only static data members or static member functions that belong to its class.

In the next chapter, you'll learn how to *derive* a new class from an existing one, so that you can adapt the class for managing new types of objects.

CHAPTER

FIVE

5

Deriving C++ Classes

- Deriving classes

- Creating hierarchies of classes

- Using virtual functions

In the previous chapter, you learned how to define independent classes. In this chapter, you'll learn how to define classes derived from other classes. Deriving classes allows you to reuse the code and data structures belonging to existing classes, as well as to customize and extend existing classes for specific purposes.

You'll also learn how to define and use *virtual* member functions. Such functions allow you to modify the behavior of existing classes and to write simple, elegant routines that can manage a variety of different program objects.

Deriving Classes

Suppose you've already written and tested the CRectangle class described in the previous chapter and are using this class in your program. You now decide that in addition to displaying open rectangles, you'd like to display solid blocks (that is, rectangles filled with solid colors). To do this, you could define a new class, perhaps named CBlock. The CBlock class would contain most of the features of CRectangle, plus some additional facilities required for filling the rectangles once they've been drawn.

If you made CBlock an entirely new class, you'd duplicate much of what you already wrote for the CRectangle class. Fortunately, C++ lets you avoid duplicating code and data by *deriving* a new class from an existing class. When you derive a new class, it *inherits* all the data members and member functions belonging to the existing class.

For example, you could define the class CBlock as follows:

```
class CBlock : public CRectangle
{
};
```

The expression : public CRectangle causes the CBlock class to be derived from the CRectangle class. Because CBlock is derived from CRectangle, it inherits all the data members and member functions belonging to CRectangle. In other words, though the CBlock class definition is empty, the CBlock class automatically possesses the GetCoord, SetCoord, and Draw member functions, as well as the Left, Top, Right, and Bottom data members that were defined for CRectangle. CRectangle is known as the *base* class, and CBlock as the *derived* class.

In general, you should include the keyword `public` in the first line of the derived class definition, as shown in the example. This keyword causes all members that are public in the base class to remain public in the derived class.

Once you've created a derived class, the next step is to add any new members that are required to meet the specific needs of the new class. For example, you might expand the CBlock definition as follows:

```
class CBlock : public CRectangle
{
private:
    int FillColor;  // stores the color used to fill the block

public:
    void Draw (void)
        {
        int L, T, R, B;

        CRectangle::Draw ();
        GetCoord (&L, &T, &R, &B);
        Fill ((L + R) / 2, (T + B) / 2, FillColor);
        }
    void SetColor (int Color)
        {
        FillColor = __max (0, Color);
        }
};
```

In addition to its inherited members, CBlock now has a new private data member, FillColor (which stores a code for the color used to fill the block), and a new public member function, SetColor (which assigns a color value to FillColor). CBlock also has a *new version* of the Draw member function, which draws a simple rectangle and then fills the inside of the rectangle with a solid color.

The CBlock class actually has *two* versions of the Draw function: one that it has inherited and one that it has explicitly defined. If you call Draw for a CBlock object, however, the version of the function defined within `CBlock` overrides the version defined within `CRectangle`, as shown in the following code:

```
CBlock Block;

// ...

Block.Draw ();   // calls the version of Draw defined within the
                 // CBlock class because Block is of type CBlock
```

NOTE   Later in the chapter (in the section "Using Virtual Functions") you'll learn a more powerful way to write an overriding member function.

The `CBlock` version of `Draw` begins by calling the `CRectangle` version of `Draw` to draw a simple rectangle:

```
CRectangle::Draw ();
```

The scope resolution expression (`CRectangle::`) preceding the call to `Draw` forces the compiler to call the version of the `Draw` function belonging to the `CRectangle` class. If the scope resolution expression were not included, the compiler would generate a recursive call to the version of `Draw` defined for the current class, `CBlock`. (Again, the version of the function defined within the current class overrides the inherited version.)

Next, the `Draw` function calls the inherited member function `GetCoord` to obtain the current values of the rectangle coordinates, and then it calls the function `Fill` to paint the inside of the rectangle with the current color value:

```
GetCoord (&L, &T, &R, &B);
Fill ((L + R) / 2, (T + B) / 2, FillColor);
```

`Fill` is a hypothetical function that fills a bordered area. The first two parameters give the coordinates of a point within the border, while the third parameter gives the value of the color to be used for painting the area. Such a function might be defined elsewhere in your program or obtained from a function library.

The following code draws a block using the `CBlock` class:

```
CBlock Block;                   // create an instance of CBlock

Block.SetCoord (25,25,100,100); // set coordinates of block
Block.SetColor (5);             // set color of block
Block.Draw ();                  // call version of Draw defined
                                // for CBlock class
```

Providing Constructors for Derived Classes

Notice that the code for drawing a block using CBlock must call two member functions (SetCoord and SetColor) to set the values of the data members before calling Draw to draw the block. To make CBlock easier to use, you could add the following constructor, which would set the values of all data members when an instance of the class is created:

```
CBlock (int L, int T, int R, int B, int Color)
   : CRectangle (L, T, R, B)
   {
   SetColor (Color);
   }
```

The member initializer list in this constructor calls the constructor belonging to the base class (CRectangle), passing it the values to be assigned to the data members defined within the base class. (The member initializer list can be used to initialize a base class, as well as data members, as described in Chapter 4 in the section "Member Initialization in Constructors.") The body of the CBlock constructor then calls SetColor to set the value of the FillColor data member. With this constructor in place, you could now create a CBlock object and draw a block with only two statements:

```
CBlock Block (25, 25, 100, 100, 5);
Block.Draw ();
```

You could also add the following default constructor, which would assign 0 to all data members:

```
CBlock ()
   {
   FillColor = 0;
   }
```

Because this constructor *doesn't* explicitly initialize the base class (the member initializer list is empty), the compiler *automatically* calls the base class's default constructor (CRectangle::CRectangle ()), which sets all the data members defined within the base class to 0. (If the base class lacked a default constructor, a compiler error would result.)

The CBlock default constructor allows you to create an object with all data members set to 0, without passing any values or calling any member functions:

```
CBlock Block;  // create a CBlock object with all data members
               // set to 0
```

See Listing 5.1, the complete listing for the CBlock class, including the two new constructors, at the end of the next section.

Order of Construction and Destruction

When you create an instance of a derived class, the compiler calls constructors in the following order:

1. The constructor of the base class.

2. The constructors for any member objects (that is, data members that are class objects). These constructors are called in the order in which the objects are defined within the class definition.

3. The class's own constructor.

Destructors, where defined, are called in the exact reverse order.

Thus, when the body of a particular constructor is executed, you know that the base class and any member objects have already been initialized and may safely be used. Likewise, when the body of a particular destructor is executed, you know that the base class and any member objects haven't yet been destroyed and can still be used.

Accessing Inherited Members

Even though CBlock has inherited the data members Left, Top, Right, and Bottom from its base class, it *isn't* allowed to access them directly, because they're defined as private in the base class. Rather, it must use the public function, GetCoord, in the same manner as any other part of the program. This restriction leads to code in the Draw member function of CBlock that's somewhat awkward and inefficient. As an alternative, you could make the CRectangle data members *protected* rather than private by using the protected access specifier in place of the private specifier, as shown in Listing 5.1.

Listing 5.1

```
// CRect1.h: CRectangle header file

class CRectangle
{
protected:
    int Left;
    int Top;
    int Right;
    int Bottom;

public:
    CRectangle ()
        {
        Left = Top = Right = Bottom = 0;
        }
    CRectangle (int L, int T, int R, int B)
        {
        SetCoord (L, T, R, B);
        }
    void Draw (void);
    void GetCoord (int *L, int *T, int *R, int *B)
        {
        *L = Left;
        *T = Top;
        *R = Right;
        *B = Bottom;
        }
    void SetCoord (int L, int T, int R, int B);
};
```

(Recall that this version of CRectangle assumes that the Draw and SetCoord member functions are defined outside the class.) Like a private member, a protected member can't be accessed from outside the class; thus, the following type of access is still illegal:

```
void main ()
    {
    CRectangle Rect;

    Rect.Left = 10; // ERROR: cannot access protected data member

    }
```

However, unlike a private member, a protected member *can* be directly accessed from within a class that's *derived* from the class in which the member is defined. Thus, the `Draw` member function of the `CBlock` class can now be rewritten to directly access the data members defined in `CRectangle`, making the code two lines shorter and slightly more efficient. The complete revised definition of `CBlock` is given in Listing 5.2.

Listing 5.2

```
// CBlock.h: CBlock header file

#include "crect1.h"
#include <stdlib.h>

void Fill (int X, int Y, int Color);

class CBlock : public CRectangle
{
protected:
    int FillColor;

public:
    CBlock ()
        {
        FillColor = 0;
        }
    CBlock (int L, int T, int R, int B, int Color)
        : CRectangle (L, T, R, B)
        {
        SetColor (Color);
        }
    void Draw (void)
        {
        CRectangle::Draw ();
        Fill ((Left + Right) / 2, (Top + Bottom) / 2, FillColor);
        }
    void SetColor (int Color)
        {
        FillColor = __max (0, Color);
        }
};
```

Notice that CBlock makes the data member that it defines (FillColor) protected rather than private, so that it can be accessed from any class derived from CBlock (as discussed in the next section).

You can allow code within another class or within a global function to access the private or protected data members of your class by declaring the other class or function as a *friend* of your class. For an explanation of this technique, see the section "Overloading the Assignment Operator" in Chapter 6.

Public and Private Derivation

If you derive a class using the **public** keyword,

```
class CBlock : public CRectangle
{
// class definition ...
}
```

then all public members of the base class become public members of the derived class, and all protected members of the base class become protected members of the derived class.

If, however, you derive a class using the **private** keyword,

```
class CBlock : private CRectangle
{
// class definition ...
}
```

then all public and protected members of the base class become private members of the derived class. (If you specify neither the **public** nor the **private** keyword in the derivation, then by default the class is derived privately.)

With either type of derivation, private members in the base class are always inaccessible in the derived class (that is, though they're inherited by the derived class, and are therefore a part of any instance of the derived class, they can't be directly accessed within the derived class code).

In C++, you almost always derive classes publicly; hence, you'll see public derivations in all the examples given in this book.

Creating Hierarchies of Classes

A derived class can serve as a base for yet another derived class. You can thus create hierarchies of related classes. For example, you might derive a class from CBlock, named CRoundBlock, for creating a rounded block (that is, a block with rounded corners), as follows:

```
class CRoundBlock : public CBlock
{
protected:
   int Radius;

public:
   CRoundBlock ()
      {
      int Radius = 0;
      }
   CRoundBlock (int L, int T, int R, int B, int Color, int Rad)
      : CBlock (L, T, R, B, Color)
      {
      SetRadius (Rad);
      }
   void Draw (void)
      {
      // draw a rounded, open rectangle (use Radius) ...

      // now fill the rectangle with color:
      Fill ((Left + Right) / 2, (Top + Bottom) / 2, FillColor);
      }
   void SetRadius (int Rad)
      {
      Radius = __max (0, Rad);
      }
};
```

NOTE   The class **CRoundBlock** is said to be derived *directly* from **CBlock**, which is known as its *direct base*, and it's said to be derived *indirectly* from **CRectangle**, which is known as its *indirect base*.

CRoundBlock inherits all members of the CBlock class, including the members that CBlock inherits from CRectangle. CRoundBlock defines an additional data member, Radius, which stores the radius of the rounded corners, and it defines a new version of the Draw function, which draws a solid rectangle with rounded corners. CRoundBlock also provides a public member function, SetRadius, for setting the value of its data member Radius, and it provides both a default constructor that sets all data members to 0 and a constructor that initializes all data members with specific values.

The following code creates an instance of RoundBlock, initializing all data members, and then draws a rounded block:

```
CRoundBlock RoundBlock (10, 15, 50, 75, 5, 3);

RoundBlock.Draw ();
```

Figure 5.1 illustrates the hierarchy of example classes, while Figure 5.2 shows the figures drawn by each of these classes.

FIGURE 5.1:

The hierarchy of example classes

CRectangle

members defined in CRectangle

CBlock

members defined in CRectangle

members defined in CBlock

CRoundBlock

members defined in CRectangle

members defined in CBlock

members defined in CRoundBlock

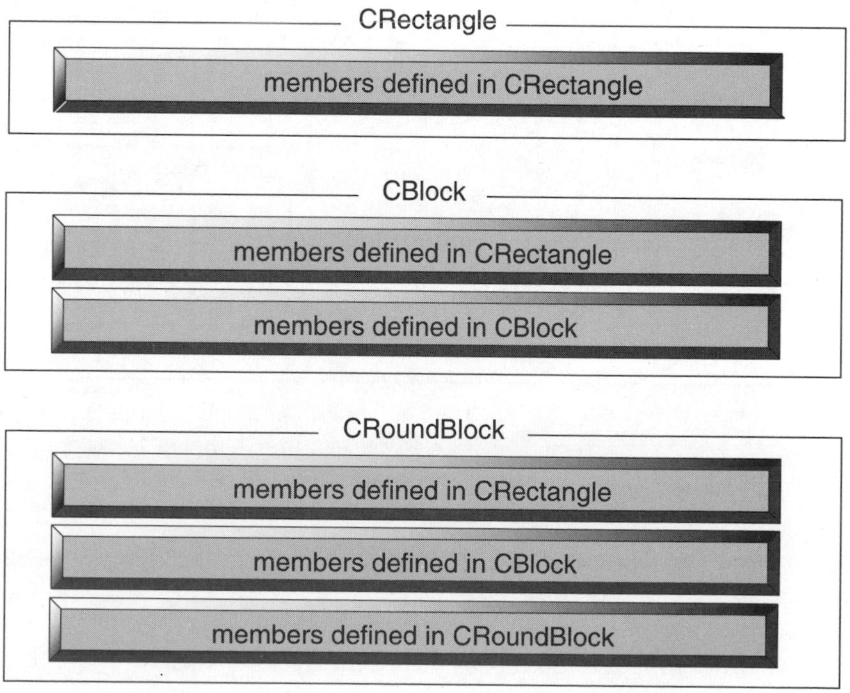

FIGURE 5.2:

The figures drawn by the example classes

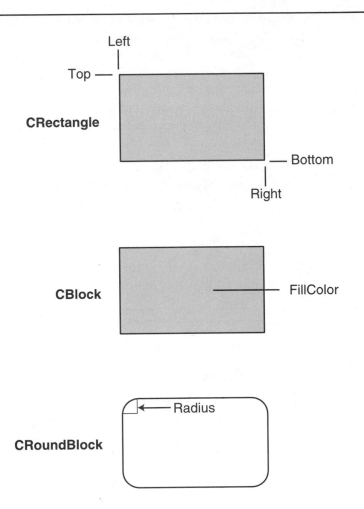

> **NOTE**   The CRoundBlock data member Radius is made protected so that it can be accessed by any class derived from CRoundBlock, but not by code outside the class hierarchy.

Commercial class libraries, such as the Microsoft Foundation Classes and the standard iostream class library, consist primarily of tree-like hierarchies of related classes. In such hierarchies, a single class often serves as the base for several derived classes (hence the tree-like structure). (Both of these class libraries are included with Microsoft Visual C++. The Microsoft Foundation Classes, or MFC, are discussed in Part III of the book.)

Also, as exemplified in the iostream library, it's possible for a class to be derived from more than one base class. This is known as *multiple inheritance*.

The Advantages of Inheritance

As you can see from the simple examples given, inheritance allows you to reuse code you've already written and data structures you've already designed. It thus prevents code and data duplication.

A related advantage of inheritance is that it can make your programs easier to maintain, since the code and data that handle a given task are generally contained within a single, easily located class definition in your code, rather than being scattered throughout the program.

Also, the hierarchies of classes you can define in C++ effectively model many real-world relationships. For example, deriving the CBlock class from the CRectangle class reflects the fact that a block is a *type of* rectangle (namely, one that's filled with color), and deriving the CRoundBlock class from CBlock reflects the fact that a rounded block is a *type* of block. As another example, the hierarchy of classes in the Microsoft Foundation Classes library closely models the relationships among the Windows items that these classes manage.

Viewing and Managing Classes Using ClassView

The ClassView graph was introduced in Chapter 2 (in the section "Using File-View and ClassView"). You display this graph by opening the ClassView tab of the Workspace window in the Developer Studio (see Figure 2.4). In Chapter 2, you saw that the ClassView graph displays all the global symbols defined in your program, and it allows you to rapidly find a symbol definition by double-clicking the symbol in the graph.

In a C++ program that defines classes, the ClassView graph also displays each class together with its data members and member functions. If, for example, you included in a program the three classes presented in this chapter (CRectangle, CBlock, and CRoundBlock), the ClassView view would display these classes as shown in Figure 5.3.

FIGURE 5.3:

The CRectangle, CBlock, and CRoundBlock classes displayed in the Developer Studio ClassView graph

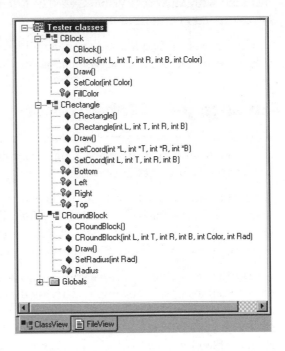

If you double-click a class, class member, or global symbol within the ClassView graph, the Developer Studio will display the source file containing the definition of the item, and it will place the insertion point on the definition. You can also perform a variety of operations by clicking a class or class member name with the right mouse button and selecting a command from the shortcut menu that appears. The following are among the operations you can perform:

- You can go to the item's definition or declaration.

- For a class, you can have the Developer Studio assist you in adding a member function or member variable (that is, a data member) to the class. (If, however, you're defining a message-handling function for a Windows program, you should use the Visual C++ ClassWizard, as described in Chapter 10.)

- You can search for references to the item.

- For a class, you can find all derived and base classes.

- For a class, you can add the class to the Developer Studio *Gallery*, which you can use to store reusable software components and insert them into your programs. For information on the Gallery, see the following Visual C++ online help topic: *Visual C++ Documentation, Using Visual C++, Visual C++ Programmer's Guide, Adding Program Functionality, Overviews, MFC: Overview, Reusing Code: Overview.*

- For a member function, you can find functions that call the member function, as well as functions that are called by the member function.

- For a member function, you can set a breakpoint.

- You can delete a member function.

- If you right-click the name of the project at the top of the list of classes, you can choose the New Class... command for assistance in defining a new class.

For some of these operations, you need to generate *browse* information for the program, as explained in the following online help topic: *Visual C++ Documentation, Using Visual C++, Visual C++ Programmer's Guide, Adding Program Functionality, How Do I..., Class Browsing Tasks.* Finally, for more information on using ClassView, see *Visual C++ Documentation, Using Visual C++, Visual C++ User's Guide, Working with Classes, Classview.*

Using Virtual Functions

Virtual functions can be a bit difficult to understand at first. Learning about them, however, is well worth the effort. Not only do they form an important tool for object-oriented programming, but also they're used extensively in class libraries such as the Microsoft Foundation Classes. As you'll learn in this section, virtual functions allow you to write simple, general-purpose routines for manipulating a variety of object types. They also allow you to easily modify the behavior of existing base classes, even if you lack access to the source code for these classes.

To get a general idea of what virtual functions are, consider once more the CRectangle and CBlock example classes that have been presented. Recall that CBlock is derived from CRectangle; that is, CRectangle is the base class, and CBlock is the derived class.

As you saw earlier, both of these classes define a member function named Draw. Say that you've declared an instance of each class:

```
CRectangle Rect;
CBlock Block;
```

Given these declarations, the statement

```
Rect.Draw ();
```

will clearly call the version of Draw defined within the CRectangle class, and the statement

```
Block.Draw ();
```

will clearly call the version of Draw defined within the CBlock class. In both statements, the compiler has no trouble determining which version of the function to call, since the call statement includes a reference to an instance of a specific class.

In C++, however, it's common to use a pointer to a base class to hold *either* the address of an instance of the base class *or* the address of an instance of a derived class. For example, consider the following CRectangle pointer:

```
CRectangle *PRect;
```

C++ allows you to assign this pointer the address of a CRectangle instance *or* an instance of a class derived (directly or indirectly) from CRectangle, without using a cast operation. For example, both of the assignment statements in the following code are legal:

```
CRectangle *PRect; // declare a pointer to CRectangle

CRectangle Rect;   // create an instance of the CRectangle class
CBlock Block;      // create an instance of the CBlock class

PRect = &Rect;     // legal: assign address of CRectangle
                   // instance to pointer
PRect = &Block;    // also legal: assign address of CBlock
                   // instance to pointer
```

Assignments to Base Class Pointers

C++ allows you to freely assign the address of a derived class to a base class pointer because it's *safe* to use such a pointer. The base class pointer can be used to access only members defined within the base class. All these members are also defined within the derived class (by inheritance); therefore, if the pointer contains the address of a derived class object, any member that can be referenced with the pointer will be defined.

Although you can force the compiler to assign the address of a base class to a derived class pointer by means of a cast operation, such a pointer *isn't* safe, because the pointer could be used to access members that aren't defined in the object referenced (a base class *doesn't* always have all the members defined in a derived class).

A problem arises, however, if you call the Draw member function using the PRect pointer. The compiler can't know in advance which type of object PRect will point to when the program actually runs; therefore, it always generates a call to the version of Draw that's defined within the CRectangle class, since PRect is declared as a pointer to CRectangle.

For example, say that PRect points to Rect, which is an instance of the CRectangle class:

```
CRectangle *PRect;
CRectangle Rect;

// ...

PRect = &Rect;
```

In this case, using PRect to call the Draw member function will invoke the version of Draw defined within CRectangle, exactly as desired:

```
PRect->Draw ();
```

Assume, however, that PRect points to an instance of the CBlock class:

```
CRectangle *PRect;
CBlock Block;

// ...

PRect = &Block;
```

If you now use this pointer to call Draw,

```
PRect->Draw ();
```

the program will *still* call the version of Draw defined within CRectangle. The result is that the *wrong version* of the Draw member function is called, producing an open rectangle rather than the desired filled block.

The solution to this problem is to make Draw a *virtual* function. Defining Draw as virtual ensures that the correct version of the function will be called when the program is run, even if the function is called using a base class pointer. To make Draw a virtual function, you include the virtual keyword in the declaration of Draw within the base class, CRectangle, as follows:

```
class CRectangle
{

// other declarations ...

public:
    virtual void Draw (void);

// other declarations ...

}
```

Note that you can't include the virtual keyword in the definition of Draw, which occurs outside the class definition.

You can also include the virtual keyword in the declaration of Draw within the derived class CBlock, though it isn't necessary to do so:

```
class CBlock : public CRectangle
{

// other declarations ...

public:
    virtual void Draw (void);

// other declarations ...

}
```

(If a function is declared as virtual in a base class, a function with the same name, return type, and parameters that is declared in a derived class is automatically considered to be virtual. You therefore don't need to repeat the `virtual` keyword in each derived class, though doing so might make the program easier to read and understand.)

If Draw is a defined as a virtual function and your program calls Draw using the PRect pointer,

```
CRectangle *PRect;

// ...

PRect->Draw ();
```

the compiler *doesn't* automatically generate a call to the version of Draw defined within CRectangle. Rather, it generates special code that calls the *correct* version of Draw when the program is run. Thus, the following statements will result in calling the version of Draw defined within CRectangle:

```
CRectangle *PRect;
CRectangle Rect;

// ...

PRect = &Rect;
PRect->Draw ();
```

while the following statements will result in calling the version of Draw defined within CBlock:

```
CRectangle *PRect;
CBlock Block;

// ...

PRect = &Block;
PRect->Draw ();
```

Since the actual function address isn't determined until the program is run, this calling mechanism is known as *late binding* or *dynamic binding*. The standard function-calling mechanism, in which the compiler knows in advance the exact target address of the call, is termed *early binding* or *static binding*.

TIP For a virtual function, the program must store the address of the correct version of the function within each object. (More accurately, it stores the address of a *table* of virtual function addresses.) In addition to requiring additional storage, the virtual function-calling mechanism is less direct and therefore slightly slower than a standard function call. Therefore, you shouldn't make a member function virtual unless late binding is required.

The next two sections illustrate two different ways that you can use virtual functions in a program.

Polymorphism

Virtual functions support an important feature of object-oriented programming: *polymorphism*. Polymorphism is the ability to use a single instruction to perform one of a variety of different actions, where the actual action performed depends on the specific kind of object involved. As an example of how a virtual function supports polymorphism, if you've defined **Draw** as a virtual member function, you can use a *single* function call such as

```
PRect->Draw ();
```

to draw a rectangle, a block, or a rounded block; the specific action performed depends on the class of the object currently pointed to by **PRect**.

Using Virtual Functions to Handle Class Objects

Virtual functions allow you to write simple, general-purpose routines that can automatically handle a variety of different object types. For example, suppose that you're writing a drawing program that allows the user to draw rectangles, blocks, or rounded blocks. Each time the user draws one of these figures, the program invokes the new operator to dynamically create an object of the appropriate class (CRectangle, CBlock, or CRoundBlock) to manage the new figure. Because CBlock and CRoundBlock are both derived from CRectangle, you can conveniently store the pointers to all the objects within a single array of CRectangle pointers, as in the following code:

```
const int MAXFIGS = 100;
CRectangle *PFigure [MAXFIGS];
int Count = 0;

// ...

// the user draws a block:
PFigure [Count++] = new CBlock (10, 15, 25, 30, 5);

// ...

// the user draws a rectangle:
PFigure [Count++] = new CRectangle (5, 8, 19, 23);

// ...

// the user draws a rounded block:
PFigure [Count++] = new CRoundBlock (27, 33, 43, 56, 10, 5);
```

Suppose now that you're writing a routine that redraws all the objects on the screen. If Draw *weren't* a virtual function, for each element in the array you'd somehow have to determine the type of the figure and then call the appropriate version of Draw. For instance, you might add a data member named Type to the CRectangle class, which would store a code indicating the object's class:

```
// NOT RECOMMENDED:

class CRectangle
{
// other definitions ...

public:
    int Type;  // inherited by all derived classes; stores a code
               // indicating the object's class: RECT, BLOCK, or
               // ROUNDBLOCK
}
```

(This example assumes that the three symbolic constants RECT, BLOCK, and ROUNDBLOCK have been defined previously in the program.)

You could then use the Type member to determine the type of each figure in the array and call the appropriate version of Draw:

```
// ugly code; NOT RECOMMENDED:

for (int i = 0; i < Count; ++i)
    switch (PFigure [i]->Type)
        {
        case RECT:
            PFigure [i]->Draw ();
            break;

        case BLOCK:
            ((CBlock *)PFigure [i])->Draw ();
            break;

        case ROUNDBLOCK:
            ((CRoundBlock *)PFigure [i])->Draw ();
            break;
        }
```

Not only is this code cumbersome, but also it would require you to add a new case branch whenever you modify the program to support a new type of figure (that is, whenever you add a class for a new figure to the hierarchy).

If, however, you declare the Draw function virtual (by adding the virtual keyword to its declaration in CRectangle), the program would *automatically* call the appropriate version of Draw for the current object type. Redrawing the figures could then be accomplished with the following code:

```
for (int i = 0; i < Count; ++i)
    PFigure [i]->Draw ();
```

This code is much simpler and more elegant, plus you *don't* need to modify it if you add a class to the hierarchy to support another type of figure.

An actual drawing program, of course, would probably support many more kinds of figures. You can use this same general approach, however, as long as all the classes for managing specific figures are derived from a common base class. The MiniDraw program given in Part III of the book illustrates this method.

Using Virtual Functions to Modify Base Classes

A virtual function can also be used to modify the behavior of a base class, without changing the base class code. For example, assume that you've been given the following class for displaying a message box (perhaps as part of a commercial class library):

```
class CMessageBox
{
protected:
    char *Message;

    virtual void DrawBackground (int L, int T, int R, int B);
    // paints a WHITE background in message box

public:
    CMessageBox ()
        {
        Message = new char ('\0');
        }
    ~CMessageBox ()
        {
        delete [] Message;
        }
    void Display ()
        {
        DrawBackground (0, 0, 35, 25);

        // code for displaying Msg string ...

        }
    void Set (char *Msg);
};
```

The public member function Set allows you to assign a message string, and the public member function Display displays the message within a box on the screen. Notice that Display erases the background by calling another member function, DrawBackground, passing it the dimensions of the message box; this function paints the background using a solid white color. DrawBackground is intended to be used internally by the class; it *isn't* intended to be called from outside the class, and it's therefore declared as a protected member.

DrawBackground is also declared as a virtual function. Accordingly, if you derive your own class from CMessageBox, which includes your own version of Draw-Background, your version of the function will override the version defined within CMessageBox, even when this function is called from within a CMessageBox member function. For example, you could derive the following class from CMessageBox:

```
class CMyMessageBox : public CMessageBox
{
protected:
    virtual void DrawBackground (int L, int T, int R, int B)
        {
        // paint a BLUE background in message box ...
        }
};
```

Notice that the overriding version of DrawBackground draws a blue background rather than a white background. Thus, the following code would create an object and display a message box with a blue background:

```
CMyMessageBox MyMessageBox;

MyMessageBox.Set ("hello");
MyMessageBox.Display ();
```

By providing DrawBackground as a separate virtual function, the CMessageBox class allows you to change the behavior of the class (namely, the color or pattern that's drawn as the background within the box), without modifying the CMessage-Box source code (you don't even need to see the source code). As you'll learn in Part III of this book, many of the classes defined in the MFC provide virtual functions that you can override in your derived classes, enabling you to easily modify the behavior of the MFC classes.

How Overriding Works

The chapter introduced virtual functions by explaining that if you call a virtual function using a pointer to a class object, the function call will be interpreted according to the actual type of the object rather than the type of the pointer. How does this property apply to a virtual function called from within a member function of a base class, as described in this section?

Recall from Chapter 4 that when a class member is referenced from within a member function, it's implicitly referenced using the **this** pointer. Thus, the **Display** member function of **CMessageBox** could be written in the following equivalent way:

```
class CMessageBox
{

// other declarations ...

public:
    void Display ()
        {
        this->DrawBackground (0, 0, 35, 25);

        // ...

        }

// other declarations...

};
```

If **DrawBackground** *weren't* virtual, the function call in **Display** would invoke the version of **DrawBackground** defined within **CMessageBox** (because within **CMessageBox**, **this** is a pointer to a **CMessageBox** object). However, if **DrawBackground** *is* virtual, the function call would invoke the version of **DrawBackground** defined within the current object's class. Thus, if **Display** is called for a **CMyMessageBox** object,

```
CMyMessageBox MyMessageBox;

// ...

MyMessageBox.Display ();
```

the overriding version of **DrawBackground** defined within **CMyMessageBox** would be called.

Summary

This chapter introduced the basic techniques for deriving new classes from existing classes, as well as for creating hierarchies of related classes. It also explained virtual functions and described several ways to use them. The following are the basic concepts and techniques presented:

- You can *derive* a new class from an existing class by specifying the name of the existing class in the definition of the new class. The existing class is known as the *base* class and the new class as the *derived* class.

- The derived class *inherits* all the members of the base class. You can add new members to the derived class to adapt it for its purpose.

- A constructor for a derived class can explicitly initialize its base class by passing parameters to the base class constructor. If the derived class constructor *doesn't* explicitly initialize its base class, the compiler automatically calls the default constructor for the base class.

- If a data member in a base class is declared using the `protected` access specifier, the member can be accessed from within a derived class, but it *can't* be accessed from other functions in the program.

- A derived class can serve as the base for another class, allowing you to create multilevel hierarchies of related classes.

- Inheritance (that is, the ability to derive one class from another) allows you to reuse code and data structures you've already written for a class. It can also make your program easier to maintain and at the same time help you model the relationships among the real-world items that your program manages.

- Each class in a hierarchy of derived classes can have its own version of a particular member function. If this function is declared as `virtual`, calling the function will automatically invoke the version of the function that's defined for the current object type, even if the function is called through a base-class type pointer.

- Virtual functions support *polymorphism*, which is the ability to use a single instruction to perform one of a variety of different actions, the particular action depending on the type of object involved.

- Virtual functions allow you to write simple, general-purpose routines that can handle a variety of different—but related—objects.

- Virtual functions also allow you to override the default behavior of a base class, without modifying the base class source code.

In the next chapter, you'll learn about several additional C++ features that pertain to classes.

Overloading, Copying, and Converting

- Overloading operators

- Using copy and conversion constructors

This chapter describes several ways in which you can customize the behavior of the classes you create. Specifically, you'll learn how to *overload* standard C++ operators to specify the way they work with objects belonging to your class. You'll also learn how to define special constructors that affect the way a class object is initialized with another object of the same type (a *copy constructor*) or the way another data type is converted to a class object (a *conversion constructor*).

Overloading Operators

The C++ operators work in predefined ways when used with the built-in data types. For example, when the + operator is used with two `int` variables, it performs an integer addition, and when + is used with two `double` variables, it performs a floating-point addition operation. C++ also allows you to use standard operators with objects of classes, provided that you've defined the exact action that a given operator is to perform. Defining the way that an operator works with objects of a particular class is known as *overloading* the operator.

For example, suppose that you've defined the class `CCurrency` for storing and manipulating monetary amounts:

```
class CCurrency
{
private:
   long Dollars;
   int Cents;

public:
   CCurrency ()
      {
      Dollars = Cents = 0;
      }
   CCurrency (long Dol, int Cen)
      {
      SetAmount (Dol, Cen);
      }
   void GetAmount (long *PDol, int *PCen)
```

```
        {
        *PDol = Dollars;
        *PCen = Cents;
        }
    void PrintAmount ()
        {
        cout.fill ('0');
        cout.width (1);
        cout << '$' << Dollars << '.';
        cout.width (2);
        cout << Cents << '\n';
        }
    void SetAmount (long Dol, int Cen)
        {
        // adjust for cent amounts >= 100:
        Dollars = Dol + Cen / 100;
        Cents = Cen % 100;
        }
    };
```

The CCurrency class stores monetary amounts as integer values, so that these amounts can be manipulated using fast, accurate integer operations. The class provides a default constructor that sets the dollar and cent values both to 0, and it provides a constructor that allows you to specify initial dollar and cent amounts. It also provides a separate member function (SetAmount) for setting the monetary amount, plus member functions for obtaining the amount (GetAmount) and printing the amount (PrintAmount). (Note that rather than storing the monetary amount in a single long integer as the total number of cents, it stores the number of dollars in a long member and the number of cents in a separate int member so that it can manage larger monetary amounts. As a result, it can handle a dollar value up to the maximum value of a long, which in Visual C++ is 2,147,483,647.)

NOTE   Although under Visual C++ 6, the size of an int happens to be the same as the size of a long (both are 4 bytes long), Dollars is explicitly declared long so that it can contain the largest supported integer value under any compiler.

Instead of providing member functions for performing arithmetic operations on the monetary amounts, you can overload standard C++ operators so that you may perform arithmetic using expressions just like those used with built-in data types. To overload an operator, you define a member function that's named by using the `operator` keyword, followed by the operator itself. For example, you could overload the + operator by adding the following member function to the `CCurrency` class definition:

```
class CCurrency
{

// other declarations ...

public:
   CCurrency operator+ (CCurrency Curr)
      {
      CCurrency Temp (Dollars + Curr.Dollars,
                      Cents + Curr.Cents);
      return Temp;
      }

// other declarations ...

};
```

An operator function should be defined as *public* so that the operator can be used by other functions in the program. Once this function is defined, you can use the + operator as follows:

```
CCurrency Amount1 (12, 95);
CCurrency Amount2 (4, 38);
CCurrency Total;

Total = Amount1 + Amount2;
```

The C++ compiler interprets the expression `Amount1 + Amount2` as

```
Amount1.operator+ (Amount2);
```

The `operator+` function creates a temporary `CCurrency` object (`Temp`) containing the sum of the amounts stored in the two classes appearing in the addition expression. It then returns the temporary object. In the addition expression above, the returned object is assigned to the `CCurrency` object `Total`. (As you'll see later in the chapter, this assignment causes the compiler to perform a member-by-member copy operation.)

Like the standard + operator, an expression containing more than one overloaded + operator is evaluated from left to right. For example, the following program uses the overloaded + operator to add the values stored in three CCurrency objects:

```
void main ()
    {
    CCurrency Advertising (235, 42);
    CCurrency Rent (823, 68);
    CCurrency Entertainment (1024, 32);
    CCurrency Overhead;

    Overhead = Advertising + Rent + Entertainment;
    Overhead.PrintAmount ();
    }
```

The operator+ function could be simplified by replacing the explicit temporary CCurrency object with an implicit temporary object:

```
CCurrency operator+ (CCurrency Curr)
    {
    return CCurrency (Dollars + Curr.Dollars, Cents + Curr.Cents);
    }
```

When you call a class constructor within an expression, the compiler creates a temporary class object. The operator+ function immediately returns the contents of this temporary object. (The section "Writing Copy Constructors," later in the chapter, explains how class objects are returned from functions.)

You could also make the operator+ function more efficient by passing it a *reference* to a CCurrency object rather than an object itself. (As explained in Chapter 3, passing a reference eliminates the need to copy the object into a local parameter; this is especially important for large objects.) The following is the final version of the operator+ function:

```
CCurrency operator+ (const CCurrency &Curr)
    {
    return CCurrency (Dollars + Curr.Dollars, Cents + Curr.Cents);
    }
```

(As was also explained in Chapter 3, using the const keyword when declaring the parameter guarantees that the function won't change the value of the parameter.)

Defining Additional Operator Functions

Like other functions in C++, operator functions can be overloaded to provide several ways to use the operator. For example, you might want to be able to use the + operator to add a CCurrency object to a constant int or long value. (With the operator function that has already been defined, both operands must be CCurrency objects.) To do this, you could add the following member function to the CCurrency class:

```
CCurrency operator+ (long Dol)
    {
    return CCurrency (Dollars + Dol, Cents);
    }
```

Adding this function would allow you to use the + operator as follows:

```
CCurrency Advertising (235, 42);
```

```
// ...
```

```
Advertising = Advertising + 100;
```

The compiler would interpret the expression Advertising + 100 as

```
Advertising.operator+ (100)
```

and it would therefore call the newly defined version of operator+. You *can't,* however, put the integer constant first, because the compiler would be forced to interpret the expression 100 + Advertising as

```
100.operator+ (Advertising)   // nonsense!
```

To circumvent this limitation, you can write a *nonmember* operator function whose first parameter is a long:

```
// defined globally:
```

```
CCurrency operator+ (long Dol, const CCurrency &Curr)
    {
    return CCurrency (Dol + Curr.Dollars, Curr.Cents);
    }
```

There's a problem with this function, however; because it's *not* a member of CCurrency, it can't normally access the private data members of this class (namely, Dollars and Cents). To grant it access to the private members of

CCurrency, you must make it a *friend* of the CCurrency class, by declaring it within the CCurrency class definition using the friend keyword:

```
class CCurrency
{

// other declarations ...

    friend CCurrency operator+ (long Dol, const CCurrency &Curr);

// other declarations ...

};
```

Even though a friend function isn't a member of a class, it can access any of the private or protected members of the class that declares it a friend.

Once this new operator function has been defined, you could use the + operator as follows:

```
CCurrency Advertising (235, 42);

// ...

Advertising = 100 + Advertising;
```

The compiler would now interpret the expression 100 + Advertising as:

```
operator+ (100, Advertising)
```

and it would therefore call the *friend* version of the operator function.

Note that you *could* have defined nonmember friend functions rather than member functions for the first two versions of operator+ (though there's no particular advantage in doing so):

```
friend CCurrency operator+ (const CCurrency &Curr1,
                            const CCurrency &Curr2);
friend CCurrency operator+ (const CCurrency &Curr, long Dol);
```

A nonmember function that overloads an operator must take at least one parameter that is a class object. (Thus, you can't use an operator function to change the standard meaning of a C++ operator that occurs in an expression containing only built-in types.)

Friend Classes

In a class definition, you can also declare another *class* as a friend, as in the following example:

```
class A
{
// ...

    friend class FriendOfA;

// ...
};
```

Because of this friend declaration, any member function of class FriendOfA can access the private and protected members of class A.

The following is the complete definition of the CCurrency class and the non-member operator+ function:

```
#include <iostream.h>

class CCurrency
{
private:
    long Dollars;
    int Cents;

public:
    CCurrency ()
        {
        Dollars = Cents = 0;
        }
    CCurrency (long Dol, int Cen)
        {
        SetAmount (Dol, Cen);
        }
    void GetAmount (long *PDol, int *PCen)
        {
        *PDol = Dollars;
        *PCen = Cents;
        }
```

```
void PrintAmount ()
   {
   cout.fill ('0');
   cout.width (1);
   cout << '$' << Dollars << '.';
   cout.width (2);
   cout << Cents << '\n';
   }
void SetAmount (long Dol, int Cen)
   {
   // adjust for cent amounts >= 100:
   Dollars = Dol + Cen / 100;
   Cents = Cen % 100;
   }
CCurrency operator+ (const CCurrency &Curr)
   {
   return CCurrency (Dollars + Curr.Dollars,
                     Cents + Curr.Cents);
   }
CCurrency operator+ (long Dol)
   {
   return CCurrency (Dollars + Dol, Cents);
   }
friend CCurrency operator+ (long Dol, const CCurrency &Curr);
};

CCurrency operator+ (long Dol, const CCurrency &Curr)
   {
   return CCurrency (Dol + Curr.Dollars, Curr.Cents);
   }
```

The following program demonstrates the use of all three of the operator functions that have been defined:

```
void main ()
   {
   CCurrency Advertising (235, 42);
   CCurrency Rent (823, 68);
   CCurrency Entertainment (1024, 32);
   CCurrency Overhead;

   Overhead = Advertising + Rent + Entertainment;
   Overhead.PrintAmount ();
```

```
Overhead = Overhead + 100;
Overhead.PrintAmount ();

Overhead = 100 + Overhead;
Overhead.PrintAmount ();
}
```

This program would print the values:

```
$2083.42
$2183.42
$2283.42
```

In conclusion, defining three versions of the `operator+` function makes it possible to use the + operator with two objects, or with an object and a constant, or with a constant and an object. (The fourth possible combination, two constants, would cause the + operator to have its standard meaning.) Later in the chapter, in the section "Writing Conversion Constructors," you'll learn how to write a special constructor that allows you to eliminate the two versions of the `operator+` function that are members of the `CCurrency` class.

Enhancing *CCurrency*

You could enhance the `CCurrency` class by adding support for negative monetary amounts (currently, the class behaves unpredictably if you assign a negative amount) and by overloading other operators. You could define operator functions for the – operator (for subtracting two objects, or an object and a constant), the * operator (for multiplying an object by a constant), and the / operator (for dividing an object by a constant).

When defining these operators, avoid the temptation to convert the dollar-and-cent values to a single `long` value (storing the total number of cents). Doing so would simplify the arithmetic routines but would risk causing overflows (or it would reduce the maximum dollar amount the class can manage).

General Guidelines for Overloading Operators

You can overload almost any of the existing binary and unary C++ operators; the overloadable operators are listed next. When you overload an operator for a class, you define the *meaning* of the operator when it's used in an expression containing at least one class object. You can't, however, change the *syntax* of the operator; specifically, you can't change the operator's precedence, its associativity (the way it groups), or the number of operands that it takes. Also, you can't redefine the standard meaning of an operator when it's used in an expression containing only built-in types.

```
+    -    *    /    %    ^    &    |    ~    !    =    <    >
+=   -=   *=   /=   %=   ^=   &=   |=   <<   >>   >>=  <<=  ==
!=   <=   >=   &&   ||   ++   --   ,    ->*  ->   ()   []
new  delete
```

You've already seen an example of overloading a binary operator. You can overload a unary operator using a member function that takes *no* parameters, such as

```
// defined within CCurrency class definition:
CCurrency operator- ()  // unary - (negation) operator
   {
   return CCurrency (-Dollars, Cents);
   }
```

or you can overload a unary operator using a nonmember friend function that takes one parameter,

```
// defined globally:
CCurrency operator- (CCurrency &Curr)
   {
   return CCurrency (-Curr.Dollars, Curr.Cents);
   }
```

(These examples assume that the sign of the monetary amount is maintained in the Dollars member; for example, that –$5.75 would be stored as –5 in Dollars and +75 in Cents.)

The examples given here illustrate the general procedures for overloading an operator. However, when overloading certain operators (such as ++), you must observe special guidelines. The guidelines for overloading the assignment operator (=) are discussed in the next section. For a discussion of the procedures for overloading other specific operators, see the following topic in the Visual C++ online help: *Visual C++ Documentation, Reference, C/C++ Language and C++ Libraries, C++ Language Reference, Overloading.*

NOTE   The operators overloaded by the Microsoft Foundation Classes are discussed in Part III of the book. For an explanation of the operators overloaded by the iostream class library (such as <<, which you've seen many times), see the following online help topic: *Visual C++ Documentation, Reference, C/C++ Language and C++ Libraries, iostream Library Reference.*

Overloading the Assignment Operator

C++ allows you to assign a class object to another object of the same class. By default, the compiler handles the assignment by generating a data-member by data-member copy operation. For example, if you made the following assignment,

```
CCurrency Money1 (12, 95);
CCurrency Money2;

Money2 = Money1;
```

the compiler would copy Money1.Dollars to Money2.Dollars, and Money1.Cents to Money2.Cents (the same way that recent versions of C handle assignments of one struct to another). You can also create a temporary class object and assign it to a declared object, as a convenient way to reinitialize an existing object; for example:

```
CCurrency Money (85, 25);    // create an object

Money.PrintAmount ();        // display it

Money = CCurrency (24, 65); // now create a temporary object and
                            // assign it to existing object
```

If the default assignment operation isn't suitable for a class you have written, then you should overload the = operator, thereby specifying a custom assignment operation. For example, consider the following class, CMessage, which is designed for storing and displaying messages:

```
#include <string.h>
#include <iostream.h>

class CMessage
{
private:
    char *Buffer;  // stores message string

public:
    CMessage ()
        {
        Buffer = new char ('\0');  // initialize Buffer to
                                    // empty string

        }
    ~CMessage ()
```

```
      {
      delete [] Buffer;              // free the memory
      }
    void Display ()
      {
      cout << Buffer << '\n';     // display the message
      }
    void Set (char *String)       // store a new message string
      {
      delete [] Buffer;
      Buffer = new char [strlen (String) + 1];
      strcpy (Buffer, String);
      }
  };
```

If you were to assign one CMessage object to another CMessage object, then the Buffer data member of *both* objects would point to the *same* block of memory. If you then called the Set member function to change the message stored by one object, this block of memory would be released, leaving the Buffer member of the other object pointing to unpredictable data. (The same thing would happen if one object were destroyed before the other object, because the destructor also releases the block of memory pointed to by Buffer.)

To provide a suitable routine for assigning one CMessage object to another, you could add the following operator function to the class definition:

```
class CMessage
{
// other declarations:

public:
    void operator= (const CMessage &Message)
      {
      delete [] Buffer;
      Buffer = new char [strlen (Message.Buffer) + 1];
      strcpy (Buffer, Message.Buffer);
      }

// other declarations:
}
```

Rather than simply copying the *address* of the memory block (stored in Buffer) from the source object to the destination object, the overloaded = operator creates an entirely new block of memory for the destination object, and then copies the string into this memory. Thus, each object has its own copy of the string.

You could then safely assign one **CMessage** object to another, as in the following program:

```
void main ()
   {
   CMessage Message1;
   Message1.Set ("initial Message1 message");
   Message1.Display ();

   CMessage Message2;
   Message2.Set ("initial Message2 message");
   Message2.Display ();

   Message1 = Message2;
   Message1.Display ();
   }
```

This program would print the following:

```
initial Message1 message
initial Message2 message
initial Message2 message
```

NOTE　You must use a *member* function to overload the = operator. (You can't use a non-member friend function.)

The way the **operator=** function is written, you can include only a *single* assignment operator in an expression. If, however, the function returns a reference to the destination **CMessage** object, as follows:

```
CMessage & operator= (const CMessage &Message)
   {
   delete [] Buffer;
   Buffer = new char [strlen (Message.Buffer) + 1];
   strcpy (Buffer, Message.Buffer);
   return *this;
   }
```

then you can string assignment operators together (as you can with the standard = operator). For example:

```
void main ()
   {
   CMessage Message1;
   CMessage Message2;
   CMessage Message3;
```

```
Message1.Set ("hello");

Message3 = Message2 = Message1;
}
```

The compiler evaluates a series of assignments moving from right to left. In this example, it first invokes the `operator=` function to assign `Message1` to `Message2`. The operator function returns a reference to `Message2` (which now contains a copy of the string "hello"). The compiler then invokes the operator function to assign the `Message2` reference to `Message3`. The final result is that all three `CMessage` objects have separate copies of the string "hello". (Note that the `operator=` function *could* return a `CMessage` object rather than a *reference* to a `CMessage` object; however, doing so would generate an unnecessary copy operation and would therefore be slightly less efficient.)

As a final refinement, the `operator=` function should make sure that it hasn't inadvertently been called to assign an object to itself (doing so would cause the function to delete `Buffer` and then try to copy a string from it). If an object is being assigned to itself, the address of the source object (`&Message`) would be the same as the address of the current object (`this`). If the function detects a self-assignment, it returns immediately since no copy operation is needed:

```
CMessage & operator= (const CMessage &Message)
   {
   if (&Message == this)
      return *this;
   delete [] Buffer;
   Buffer = new char [strlen (Message.Buffer) + 1];
   strcpy (Buffer, Message.Buffer);
   return *this;
   }
```

The following is the complete listing of the `CMessage` class, including the final version of the `operator=` function:

```
#include <string.h>
#include <iostream.h>

class CMessage
{
private:
   char *Buffer;  // stores message string
```

```
public:
   CMessage ()
      {
      Buffer = new char ('\0');   // initialize Buffer to
                                   // empty string

      }
   ~CMessage ()
      {
      delete [] Buffer;           // free the memory
      }
   void Display ()
      {
      cout << Buffer << '\n';     // display the message
      }
   void Set (char *String)        // store a new message string
      {
      delete [] Buffer;
      Buffer = new char [strlen (String) + 1];
      strcpy (Buffer, String);
      }
   CMessage & operator= (const CMessage &Message)
      {
      if (&Message == this)
         return *this;
      delete [] Buffer;
      Buffer = new char [strlen (Message.Buffer) + 1];
      strcpy (Buffer, Message.Buffer);
      return *this;
      }
};
```

Using Copy and Conversion Constructors

This section discusses the special properties of constructors that take a single parameter (including constructors that have additional parameters with default values and that therefore *can* be called with a single parameter). If the single (or first) parameter is a reference to the same type as the class, then the constructor is known as a *copy constructor*, and if the parameter is a different type, then the constructor is known as a *conversion constructor*.

The special features of each of these two types of constructors will be discussed separately. First, however, you should be aware of one general feature of constructors that take a single parameter: such constructors allow you to initialize an object using an equals sign in the definition rather than the conventional constructor syntax. For example, if the class CTest has the constructor

```
CTest (int Parm)
    {
    // constructor code ...
    }
```

then you can create an object using the statement

```
CTest Test (5);
```

or the equivalent statement

```
CTest Test = 5;
```

The use of the equals sign is merely an alternative syntax for passing a single value to the constructor; it's an initialization, *not* an assignment. Because it's not an assignment, overloading the = operator has *no effect* on the operation.

Writing Copy Constructors

A copy constructor for a class is one that takes a single parameter that's a reference to the class type, as in the following example:

```
class CTest
{
// ...

public:
    CTest (const CTest &Test)
        {
        // use Test members to initialize new CTest object ...
        }

// ...
}
```

(Later in this section, you'll see why the parameter must be a *reference* to an object rather than an actual object.)

If you don't define a copy constructor for a class, the compiler implicitly generates one for you. The compiler-generated constructor initializes the new object by performing a member-by-member copy operation from the existing object that's passed as a parameter. Accordingly, you can always initialize an object using an object of the same type, even if you haven't defined a copy constructor for the class. For example, even though the CCurrency class presented earlier doesn't include a copy constructor, the following initializations are legal:

```
CCurrency Money1 (95, 34);

CCurrency Money2 (Money1);
CCurrency Money3 = Money1;
```

The initializations of Money2 and Money3 both invoke the compiler-generated copy constructor. As a result of these initializations, the objects Money2 and Money3 would both contain the same values as Money1 (that is, Dollars would equal 95, and Cents 34).

If the member-by-member copy operation performed by the compiler-generated copy constructor is unsuitable for a class you've written, and if you want to be able to initialize new objects with existing objects of the same type, you should define your own copy constructor. For example, the CMessage class presented earlier in the chapter *shouldn't* be initialized using a simple memberwise copy operation (because it has a data member that is a pointer to a block of memory, as explained previously). You could add the following copy constructor to this class:

```
class CMessage
{
// ...

public:
    CMessage (const CMessage &Message)
        {
        Buffer = new char [strlen (Message.Buffer) + 1];
        strcpy (Buffer, Message.Buffer);
        }

// ...
};
```

This copy constructor would allow you to safely initialize objects, as shown in the following code:

```
CMessage Message1;
Message1.Set ("hello");

CMessage Message2 (Message1);  // uses copy constructor
CMessage Message3 = Message1;  // uses copy constructor
```

The compiler also automatically invokes a class's copy constructor in the following two circumstances: when you pass a class object as a function parameter, and when a function returns a class object. Consider, for example, the following operator function:

```
CCurrency operator+ (CCurrency Curr)
    {
    return CCurrency (Dollars + Curr.Dollars, Cents + Curr.Cents);
    }
```

The parameter Curr is a CCurrency object; each time the function is called, Curr must be created and *initialized* using the object that's passed to the function. To initialize the parameter, the compiler invokes the copy constructor (either one you've defined or a compiler-generated one).

NOTE

Because the compiler invokes the copy constructor whenever you pass a class object to a function, you can't pass a class object as the first parameter to the copy constructor function—rather, you must pass a *reference* to a class object. Passing an actual class object (assuming the compiler permitted it) would cause an infinite recursion.

Because the return type of the function is a CCurrency object, when you call the function, the compiler generates a temporary CCurrency object, and it uses the value specified in the return statement to initialize this temporary object. Again, the compiler invokes the copy constructor to perform the initialization.

TIP

You can eliminate the overhead of invoking the copy constructor by passing and returning *references* to objects, if possible, rather than actual objects. (The **operator+** function shown above *doesn't* return a reference to the temporary CCurrency object, because it's bad programming practice to return a reference to an object that no longer exists after the function returns.)

Writing Conversion Constructors

A class conversion constructor is one that takes a single parameter of a type other than the class type. Such a constructor typically initializes a new object using data from an existing variable or object of another type. For example, you could add the following conversion constructor to the CCurrency class to permit initializing an object using a dollar-and-cent amount stored in a single floating-point number:

```
class CCurrency
{

// ...

public:
  // ...

  CCurrency (double DolAndCen)
    {
    Dollars = long (DolAndCen);
    Cents = int ((DolAndCen - Dollars) * 100.0 + 0.5);
    }

// ...
};
```

Notice that the constructor rounds the cent value stored in the DolAndCen parameter to the nearest whole number of cents. Notice, also, that the constructor explicitly converts values to standard types, using an alternative syntax that's permitted in C++, rather that the traditional *cast* notation. For example, it uses the expression long (DolAndCen) rather than the traditional notation (long)DolAndCen. (You can, of course, continue to use casts in C++, though the new syntax may be slightly easier to read for some expressions.)

This conversion constructor allows you to initialize CCurrency objects as follows:

```
CCurrency Bucks1 (29.63);
CCurrency Bucks2 = 43.247; // would be rounded to 43.25
CCurrency Bucks3 (2.0e9);  // close to max dollar value
CCurrency *Bucks = new CCurrency (534.85);
```

The CCurrency class definition given previously included the following constructor:

```
CCurrency (long Dol, int Cen)
    {
    SetAmount (Dol, Cen);
    }
```

This constructor could be changed to a conversion constructor by simply adding a default value to the second parameter:

```
CCurrency (long Dol, int Cen = 0)
    {
    SetAmount (Dol, Cen);
    }
```

Since this constructor can now accept a single parameter, you can use it to initialize CCurrency objects by specifying only the number of dollars:

```
// set Dollars to 25 and Cents to 0:
CCurrency Dough = 25L;
CCurrency *PDough = new CCurrency (25L);
```

An L is appended to each integer constant to make it a long value. If the L weren't included, the constant would be considered an int, and the compiler wouldn't know whether to convert the int to a double so that it could call the constructor that takes a double, or whether to convert it to a long so that it could call the constructor that takes a long. Such a situation is known as an *ambiguous call* to an overloaded function, and it generates a compiler error. (Converting an int to a double and converting an int to a long are both *standard conversions*. Although int and long have the same size under Visual C++ 6, they're nevertheless considered to be distinct types requiring a conversion.)

As another example, you could add the following conversion constructor to the CMessage class:

```
class CMessage
{
// ...

public:
    // ...

    CMessage (const char *String)
```

```
        {
        Buffer = new char [strlen (String) + 1];
        strcpy (Buffer, String);
        }

    // ...
    };
```

You could now initialize objects using a single string:

```
CMessage Note = "do it now";
CMessage *PNote = new CMessage ("remember!");
```

Implicit Use of Conversion Constructors

In addition to using a conversion constructor when you explicitly create a class object and initialize it with a single value of another type, the compiler also invokes an appropriate conversion constructor if it needs to convert a data item of another type to a class object. In other words, a class conversion constructor tells the compiler how to convert an object or variable of another type to an object of the class type. For example, the two CCurrency conversion constructors allow you to assign either a double value or a long value to an existing CCurrency object:

```
CCurrency Bucks;

Bucks = 29.95;
Bucks = 35L;
```

In both assignments, the compiler *first* converts the constant to a CCurrency object using the appropriate conversion constructor, and *then* assigns this object to the CCurrency object Bucks. (As explained, the L is required in the second assignment to avoid an ambiguous call to the conversion constructor.)

As another example, assume that a function takes a CCurrency parameter,

```
void Insert (CCurrency Dinero);
```

Because of the two conversion constructors defined for CCurrency, you could pass this function either a double or a long value, as well as a CCurrency object. The compiler would call the appropriate conversion constructor to convert the value to a CCurrency object.

An important benefit of writing conversion constructors is that they can greatly extend the use of overloaded operators you've defined for the class, as well as free you from the need to write a separate operator function for each anticipated combination of operands. For example, the CCurrency class presently has three operator+ functions:

```
class CCurrency
{
// ...

public:
    // ...

    CCurrency operator+ (const CCurrency &Curr)
        {
        return CCurrency (Dollars + Curr.Dollars,
                          Cents + Curr.Cents);
        }
    CCurrency operator+ (long Dol)
        {
        return CCurrency (Dollars + Dol, Cents);
        }
    friend CCurrency operator+ (long Dol, const CCurrency &Curr);

// ...
};
```

Given that CCurrency now has a conversion constructor that converts a long value to a class object (CCurrency (long Dol, int Cen = 0)), you could eliminate the two member operator+ functions and rewrite the nonmember function as follows:

```
class CCurrency
{
// ...

public:
    // ...

    friend CCurrency operator+ (const CCurrency &Curr1,
                                const CCurrency &Curr2);

// ...
};

CCurrency operator+ (const CCurrency &Curr1,
                     const CCurrency &Curr2)
```

```
    {
    return CCurrency (Curr1.Dollars + Curr2.Dollars,
                      Curr1.Cents + Curr2.Cents);
    }
```

This single operator function can handle the following + operations:

```
CCurrency Bucks1 (39, 95);
CCurrency Bucks2 (149, 85);
CCurrency Bucks3;

Bucks3 = Bucks1 + Bucks2;
Bucks3 = Bucks1 + 10L;
Bucks3 = 15L + Bucks1;
```

In the second two addition expressions, the compiler first converts the long constant to a CCurrency object (using the appropriate conversion constructor), and *then* invokes the operator+ friend function to add the two objects.

Furthermore, because CCurrency now has a conversion constructor that takes a *double* parameter, the single operator function can also handle floating-point values:

```
CCurrency Bucks1 (39, 95);
CCurrency Bucks2 (149, 85);
CCurrency Bucks3;

Bucks3 = Bucks1 + 29.51;
Bucks3 = 87.64 + Bucks1;
```

The following listings, Listing 6.1 and Listing 6.2, show the complete final versions of the CCurrency and CMessage classes, including the new copy and conversion constructors:

Listing 6.1

```
// CCurr.h: CCurrency header file

#include <string.h>
#include <iostream.h>

class CCurrency
{
private:
    long Dollars;
    int Cents;
```

```
public:
   CCurrency ()                         // default constructor
      {
      Dollars = Cents = 0;
      }
   CCurrency (long Dol, int Cen = 0)  // conversion constructor
      {
      SetAmount (Dol, Cen);
      }
   CCurrency (double DolAndCen)         // conversion constructor
      {
      Dollars = long (DolAndCen);
      Cents = int ((DolAndCen - Dollars) * 100.0 + 0.5);
      }
   void GetAmount (long *PDol, int *PCen)
      {
      *PDol = Dollars;
      *PCen = Cents;
      }
   void PrintAmount ()
      {
      cout.fill ('0');
      cout.width (1);
      cout << '$' << Dollars << '.';
      cout.width (2);
      cout << Cents << '\n';
      }
   void SetAmount (long Dol, int Cen)
      {
      Dollars = Dol + Cen / 100;
      Cents = Cen % 100;
      }
   friend CCurrency operator+ (const CCurrency &Curr1,
                               const CCurrency &Curr2);
};

CCurrency operator+ (const CCurrency &Curr1, const CCurrency &Curr2)
   {
   return CCurrency (Curr1.Dollars + Curr2.Dollars,
                     Curr1.Cents + Curr2.Cents);
   }
```

Listing 6.2

```
// CMess.h: CMessage header file

#include <string.h>
#include <iostream.h>

class CMessage
{
private:
   char *Buffer;

public:
   CMessage ()                          // default constructor
      {
      Buffer = new char ('\0');
      }
   CMessage (const CMessage &Message)  // copy constructor
      {
      Buffer = new char [strlen (Message.Buffer) + 1];
      strcpy (Buffer, Message.Buffer);
      }
   CMessage (const char *String)        // conversion constructor
      {
      Buffer = new char [strlen (String) + 1];
      strcpy (Buffer, String);
      }
   ~CMessage ()
      {
      delete [] Buffer;
      }
   void Display ()
      {
      cout << Buffer << '\n';
      }
   void Set (char *String)
      {
      delete [] Buffer;
      Buffer = new char [strlen (String) + 1];
      strcpy (Buffer, String);
      }
```

```
CMessage & operator= (const CMessage &Message)
    {
    if (&Message == this)
        return *this;
    delete [] Buffer;
    Buffer = new char [strlen (Message.Buffer) + 1];
    strcpy (Buffer, Message.Buffer);
    return *this;
    }
};
```

> **NOTE** As explained in this section, a class conversion constructor tells the compiler how to convert another data type to a class object. You can also write a *conversion function* that tells the compiler how to convert a class object to another data type. A conversion function is defined as a member function and is quite similar to an operator function used to overload a standard operator. Conversion functions are less common than conversion constructors, however, and must be defined judiciously to avoid introducing ambiguities. For information on defining them, see the following Visual C++ online help topic: *Visual C++ Documentation, Reference, C/C++ Language and C++ Libraries, C++ Language Reference, Special Member Functions, Conversions*.

Initializing Arrays

Arrays of objects were first described in Chapter 4. To initialize any type of array, you must use the standard array initialization syntax (inherited from the C language), as shown in the following example:

```
int Table [5] = {1, 2, 3, 4, 5};
```

A limitation of this syntax is that if you're initializing an array of objects, you can assign only a *single* value to each element—you *can't* pass a series of values to a constructor. Copy constructors and conversion constructors, however, allow you to initialize objects using single values and are therefore useful for initializing arrays of objects. As an example, the following array of CCurrency objects is initialized using a variety of methods:

```
CCurrency Money (95, 34);

CCurrency MoneyTable [5] =
```

```
{
Money,
CCurrency (15, 94),
10L,
12.23,
};
```

The first element (MoneyTable [0]) is initialized using an existing CCurrency object, by means of the copy constructor. The second element is initialized by invoking a constructor to create a temporary CCurrency object; this object is then used to initialize the array element, also by means of the copy constructor. The third element is initialized using a long constant, by means of the conversion constructor that takes a long parameter, and the fourth element is initialized using a double constant, by means of the conversion constructor that takes a double parameter. The last array element *isn't* explicitly initialized; therefore, the compiler calls the default CCurrency constructor for this element.

As mentioned in Chapter 3, you *can't* explicitly initialize an array of objects that is created dynamically using the new operator. Rather, the compiler calls the default constructor for each element.

Summary

This chapter focused on the techniques for writing special functions that customize the behavior of class objects. It included the following points:

- An *operator function* allows you to *overload* a standard C++ operator. That is, it defines the way that the operator works with objects of a specific class.

- An operator function can be either a member function of a class or a nonmember function. If it's a nonmember function, it's usually declared (within the class) as a *friend*, which permits it to directly access the private and protected data members of the class.

- A *copy constructor* for a class is one that takes a single parameter that's a reference to an existing object of the same class. If you don't define a copy constructor, the compiler generates one for you, which initializes the new object by simply copying each data member from the existing object. If this behavior isn't suitable for your class, you should define your own copy constructor.

- The compiler calls the copy constructor when you pass a class object as a function parameter, or when a function returns a class object.

- A *conversion constructor* for a class is one that takes a single parameter of a type other than the class type. It can be used to initialize a new object using an existing variable or object of another type. The compiler also automatically calls the conversion constructor if it needs to convert a variable or object of the other type to a class object.

Many of the features of classes that have been described in this part of the book have a common purpose: to allow you to use class types in the same way that you use built-in types. In other words, C++ supports user-defined types (that is, classes) almost to the degree that it supports built-in types. To elaborate, you can do the following with classes:

- You can declare objects of a class in the same way that you declare variables of a built-in type. Furthermore, these objects obey the standard scope rules that apply to variables.

- As with variables of built-in types, you can initialize class objects when you define them.

- You can use standard C++ operators with class objects, as well as with variables of built-in types.

- The compiler will perform automatic conversions to and from class types, in the same way that it performs standard conversions among built-in types.

Because the compiler is unfamiliar with the details of a type that you define, to permit it to fully support this type, you must tell it the following:

- How to initialize the type (you specify this information by writing a copy constructor)

- How to use standard operators with objects of the type (by overloading operators)

- How to convert the type to or from other types (by writing conversion constructors and conversion functions)

CHAPTER

SEVEN

7

Using C++ Templates

- Defining function templates

- Defining class templates

C++ templates allow you to easily generate families of functions or classes that can operate on a variety of different data types, freeing you from the need to create a separate function or class for each type. Using templates, you have the convenience of writing a single generic function or class definition, which the compiler automatically translates into a specific version of the function or class for each of the different data types that your program actually uses.

The chapter first describes writing templates for functions, and then writing templates for classes.

Defining Function Templates

With C++ function templates, you can write a single general function definition that can be used with a variety of data types.

Recall from Chapter 3 (the section "Overloaded Functions") that if you want to use a function with a variety of data types, you can define a separate overloaded version of the function for each type. Using the example from Chapter 3, if you need a function that can return the absolute value of either an int or a double value, you could write the following two overloaded function definitions:

```
int Abs (int N)
   {
   return N < 0 ? -N : N;
   }


double Abs (double N)
   {
   return N < 0.0 ? -N : N;
   }
```

Using a C++ template, however, you can write a *single* definition that automatically handles values of type int, type double, or any other appropriate type. Such a template could be defined as follows:

```
template <class T> T Abs (T N)
   {
   return N < 0 ? -N : N;
   }
```

In this template definition, T is a *type parameter*. It stands for the type of the variable or constant that's passed in a call to the function. If the program calls Abs and passes an `int` value, for example,

```
cout << "absolute value of -5 is " << Abs (-5);
```

then the compiler will automatically generate a version of the function in which T is replaced with `int`, and it will insert into the code a call to this function version. The generated function would be equivalent to a function explicitly defined as follows:

```
int Abs (int N)
    {
    return N < 0 ? -N : N;
    }
```

Likewise, if the program calls Abs and passes a `double` value, for example,

```
double D = -2.54;
cout << "absolute value of D is " << Abs (D);
```

then the compiler will generate a version of the function in which T is replaced with `double`, and it will insert into the code a call to this function. This version of the function would be equivalent to

```
double Abs (double N)
    {
    return N < 0 ? -N : N;
    }
```

In the same way, the compiler will generate an additional version of the function for each call that passes a new numeric type, such as `short` or `float`. Generating a new version of the function is known as *instantiating* the function template (that is, creating a specific *instance* of the function).

When you define a template, you must include the keywords `template` and `class`, as well as the angle brackets, exactly as shown in the example above. You can substitute any valid name for the type parameter T, and, as you'll see shortly, you can include more than one type parameter within the angle brackets.

NOTE   Don't confuse a normal *function parameter* with a *type parameter* in a function template. A function parameter represents a value that will be passed to a function at *runtime*. A type parameter, however, represents the type of a parameter passed to a function, and is fully resolved at *compile* time. Note also that in the context of a template definition, the keyword `class` within the angle brackets doesn't refer specifically to a `class` data type, but rather to *whatever* data type is actually passed in a call to the function (whether a built-in type or a programmer-defined type).

The template definition itself doesn't cause the compiler to generate code. The compiler generates function code only when it encounters an actual call to the function (accordingly, if the source lines within a function template contain errors, the compiler won't flag them unless there's a call to the function within the same source file). The first function call that's passed a given data type causes the compiler to generate the code for the corresponding version of the function. Subsequent calls passed this same data type *don't* generate additional copies of the function; rather, they produce calls to the original copy. (The compiler will, however, generate a new function version if the type in a function call doesn't match the type in a previous call *exactly*. Consider, for example, that the program passes a `long` to a template function and the compiler has generated the corresponding function version. If the program then passes an `int`, the compiler will generate an entirely new function version to process the `int`; it *won't* perform the standard `int` to `long` conversion so that it can use the first version.)

One advantage of using templates, rather than overloaded functions, is that with a template you don't need to anticipate which function versions are going to be called by a given program. Rather, you simply include a single template definition and the compiler will automatically generate and store only those function versions actually called.

The following is another example of a function template:

```
template <class T> T Max (T A, T B)
    {
    return  A > B ? A : B;
    }
```

This template generates functions that return the larger of two values of the same type. Because both parameters are defined to be of type T, in a call to the function both parameters passed must be of exactly the same type (otherwise the compiler wouldn't know whether T is to be the type of the first parameter or the type of the second parameter; recall that the meaning of T is determined by the type of parameter passed). Thus, the following function calls are legal:

```
cout << "The greater of 10 and 5 is " << Max (10, 5) << '\n';
cout << "The greater of 'A' and 'M' is " << Max ('A', 'M')
     << '\n';
cout << "The greater of 2.5 and 2.6 is " << Max (2.5, 2.6)
     << '\n';
```

while the following call is illegal:

```
cout << "The greater of 15.5 and 10 is " << Max (15.5, 10)
     << '\n'; // ERROR!
```

Notice that the compiler *doesn't* convert the second parameter from int to double in order to make the parameters have the same type (though this is a standard conversion).

To be able to pass two different types, you could define the function template as follows:

```
template <class Type1, class Type2> Type1 Max (Type1 A, Type2 B)
   {
   return  Type1 (A > B ? A : B);
   }
```

With this template, Type1 stands for the type of the value passed as the first parameter, and Type2 stands for the type of the value passed as the second parameter. With the new version of the template, the following statement is now legal and will print the value 15.5:

```
cout << "The greater of 15.5 and 10 is " << Max (15.5, 10)
     << '\n'; // now legal
```

In the new definition of Max, notice that a type parameter, Type1, appears within the body of the function, where it's used to convert the return value—if necessary—to the type of the first function parameter:

```
return Type1 (A > B ? A : B);
```

In general, you can use a type parameter at any place within the code where you can normally use a type name in C++.

Because the return type is converted to the type of the first parameter, if you reverse the order of the parameters from the previous example,

```
cout << "The greater of 15.5 and 10 is " << Max (10, 15.5)
    << '\n';
```

the program will truncate the result of the comparison, 15.5, and will print 15.

Note that every type parameter appearing inside the <> characters must also appear in the function parameter list. Thus, the following template definition is illegal:

```
// ERROR: function parameter list must include Type2 as a
// parameter type:
template <class Type1, class Type2> Type1 Max (Type1 A, Type1 B)
    {
    return  A > B ? A : B;
    }
```

With this definition, when the compiler encounters a call to the function, it wouldn't be able to determine the meaning of Type2 (this is an error even though Type2 is never used).

Overriding Templates

Each version of a function generated from a template contains the same basic code; the only feature of the function that changes is the meaning of the type parameter or parameters. You can, however, provide special processing for a specific parameter type or specific parameter types. To do this, you simply define a normal C++ function that has the same name as the function template but uses specific types rather than type parameters. The normal function *overrides* the function template—that is, if you pass parameters of the types specified in the normal function, the compiler will call this function rather than generating a function based on the template.

As an example, you could define a version of the Max function that would work with instances of the CCurrency class that was given in Chapter 6 (in the section "Overloading Operators"). Recall that a CCurrency object stores a monetary amount as the number of dollars and the number of cents. Obviously, the code defined in the Max template wouldn't be suitable for comparing the monetary values stored in two CCurrency objects. You could therefore include the following version of Max in your program *in addition* to the Max template given previously:

```
CCurrency Max (CCurrency A, CCurrency B)
    {
    long DollarsA, DollarsB;
    int CentsA, CentsB;

    A.GetAmount (&DollarsA, &CentsA);
    B.GetAmount (&DollarsB, &CentsB);

    if (DollarsA > DollarsB || DollarsA == DollarsB
       && CentsA > CentsB)
       return A;
    else
       return B;
    }
```

If your program then called Max, passing two CCurrency objects, the compiler would invoke the function above rather than instantiating a function from the Max template. The following is an example:

```
CCurrency Bucks1 (29, 95);
CCurrency Bucks2 (31, 47);

Max (Bucks1, Bucks2).PrintAmount ();
```

This code would print the following:

```
$31.47
```

TIP

Rather than writing an overriding version of Max for comparing two CCurrency objects, you could overload the > operator for the CCurrency class so that it would properly compare the sizes of the monetary values stored in two objects. The Max template given here, which uses the > operator, would then work properly with CCurrency objects. For a description of operator overloading, see Chapter 6.

Defining Class Templates

In Chapter 5, you saw how deriving a new class from an existing one allows you to reuse code and avoid unnecessarily duplicating your coding effort. Consider, however, that you've designed a class for storing a list of up to 100 integer values; the basic definition of this class might look something like the following:

```
class IntList
{
public:
   IntList ();

   int SetItem (int Index, const int &Item);
   int GetItem (int Index, int &Item);

private:
   int Buffer [100];
};
```

The integers are stored in the private array `Buffer`, and the default constructor could be written to initialize all values in this array to 0. The `SetItem` and `GetItem` member functions would be used to assign or obtain the values at specific positions in the list.

Suppose that you now wanted a similar class for storing a list of `double` values or a list of structures, or suppose that you wanted to be able to store 250 items rather than only 100. In any of these cases, you'd normally have to define an entirely new class. *Deriving* a new class from `IntList` wouldn't help, because you aren't simply adding a few new features—rather, you're changing the basic types or constants on which the class is built.

To save coding effort, you can write a single *class template*, which you can use to automatically generate an entire family of related classes for storing various data types and various numbers of items. The following is a simple version of such a class:

```
template <class T, int I> class CList
{
public:
   int SetItem (int Index, const T &Item);
   int GetItem (int Index, T &Item);

private:
   T Buffer [I];
};
```

In this definition, T is a type parameter and I is a constant parameter (more specifically, in this example it's a constant int parameter). As you'll see shortly, you specify the actual values of T and I when you create a specific instance of the class. In a class template, you can include any number of type or constant parameters in the list within the <> characters (the list must contain at least one parameter). A constant parameter can be of any valid type (not just int as in the example). Within the class definition, you can use a type parameter at any place within the code where you can normally use a type specification, and you can use a constant parameter at any place within the code where you can normally use a constant expression of the specified type (which in this example is int).

The SetItem member function could be defined as follows:

```
template <class T, int I> int CList <T, I>::SetItem
   (int Index, const T &Item)
   {
   if (Index < 0 || Index > I - 1)
      return 0; // error
   Buffer [Index] = Item;
   return 1;    // successful
   }
```

Notice that the function returns 1 if successful, or 0 if the specified index value is invalid.

As illustrated in this example, the implementation of a member function of a class template that's outside the class template definition must include the following two elements (in addition to the elements normally included in a member function definition):

1. The definition must begin with the keyword template followed by the same parameter list (within the <> characters) that precedes the class template definition (in this example, template <class T, int I>).

2. The name of the class preceding the scope resolution operator must be followed by a list of the names of the template parameters (in this example, CList <T, I>). This parameter list is necessary to fully specify the type of the class to which the function belongs.

TIP

Although a member function of a class template can be defined outside the template definition, you should include the definition within every source file that calls it so that the compiler can generate the function source code from the definition. In a multisource file program, you might simply include both the template definition and the definitions of all its member functions within a single header file that's included in each of the source files (with member functions of a class template, including the function definition in several source files *doesn't* cause a "multiply defined symbol" Link error).

Likewise, the `GetItem` member function could be defined as follows:

```
template <class T, int I> int CList <T, I>::GetItem
    (int Index, T &Item)
    {
    if (Index < 0 || Index > I - 1)
        return 0;
    Item = Buffer [Index];
    return 1;
    }
```

NOTE

In the class template definition, `I` can be used to dimension an array because it's a template *constant parameter* rather than a normal parameter or variable (which can't be used to dimension an array, because C++ doesn't allow you to dynamically dimension an array at runtime). The value of a constant parameter is fully resolved at compile time, so at runtime it becomes a constant.

Creating an Object Based on a Template

When you create an object based on a class template, you must specify the values of the template parameters. For example, you could create an instance of the `CList` class template, which could be used for storing a list of up to 100 integer values (like the example nontemplate class given previously), as follows:

```
CList <int, 100> IntList;
```

This declaration would make `IntList` an instance of a version of the `CList` class in which every occurrence of the T parameter is replaced with `int` and every occurrence of the I parameter is replaced with the constant 100. As a result, in this object `Buffer` would be defined as an array of 100 `int` values, and the `Set-Item` and `GetItem` member functions would receive references to `int` values (as the second parameters).

Note that according to the template parameter list in the `CList` template definition,

```
<class T, int I>
```

when you create an object you must assign the first template parameter a valid type specification, and you must assign the second template parameter a constant `int` value (or other value that can be converted to an `int`) or a `const int` variable that has been initialized with a constant expression (you can't pass the second parameter a non-`const` variable or a `const` variable that has been initialized with another variable).

Once you've created an object and specified any types in the parameter list, the compiler fully enforces those types when you subsequently access a data member or call a member function. Thus, in the `IntList` example object you'd have to pass two `int` values to the `SetItem` member function:

```
IntList.SetItem (0, 5);  // assign an integer to first list item
```

To create an object for storing a list of strings, you could define an instance of `CList` as follows:

```
CList <char *, 25> StringList;
```

To assign a string to an item in the list, you'd then pass a character pointer to the second `SetItem` parameter:

```
StringList.SetItem (0, "Mike"); // assign a string to first list
                                // item
```

You could create an object for storing a list of `double` values as follows:

```
CList <double, 25> *DoubleList;
DoubleList = new CList <double, 25>;
```

Notice that when specifying the type of the `DoubleList` pointer, as well as when supplying the type to the new operator, the template parameter list (`<double, 25>`) must be included with the template name. The template parameter list is an integral part of the type specification. (A template name alone doesn't represent a specific type; rather, it represents a *family* of types. To represent a specific type, you must add a parameter list.)

You could even create an object for storing objects of a user-defined type—a structure, union, or class—provided that the user-defined type is defined globally (that is, outside any function). For example, the following code creates an object for storing structures:

```
// define the Record structure at global level:
struct Record
    {
    char Name [25];
    char Phone [15];
    };

void main ()
    {
    // create an object for storing a list of up to 50 Record
    // structures:
    CList <Record, 50> RecordList;

    // create and initialize an instance of the Record structure:
    Record Rec =
        {
        "John",
        "287-981-0119"
        };

    // copy the contents of Rec to the first list item:
    RecordList.SetItem (0, Rec);

    // remainder of main code ...

    }
```

TIP

As with a function template, the compiler *doesn't* generate the code for a member function of a class template until the function is actually called (and it generates a different version of the code for each object that's assigned a unique set of template parameters). You can, however, use *explicit instantiation* to force the compiler to generate code for all member functions of a class or for a specific member function, without actually calling any member function. This is useful for creating a library (.lib) file containing member functions generated from class templates. For information on explicit instantiation, see the following topic in the online help: *Visual C++ Documentation, Reference, C/C++ Language and C++ Libraries, C++ Language Reference, Declarations, Template Specifications, Explicit Instantiation.*

Adding Constructors to the Function Template

It would be convenient to add a constructor to the CList template to initialize the items in the list. The constructor must receive a parameter of type T that it can use to initialize Buffer (the constructor can't simply initialize the Buffer elements with a default value such as 0, because the data type of the elements is unknown). For example, the constructor could be declared within the public section of the CList definition as follows:

```
// within public section of CList definition:
CList (T InitValue);
```

The constructor could be implemented as follows:

```
// outside of CList definition:
template <class T, int I> CList <T, I>::CList (T InitValue)
   {
   for (int N = 0; N < I; ++N)
      Buffer [N] = InitValue;
   }
```

(Alternatively, you could define the constructor entirely within the template definition.)

Notice that the template parameter list (<I, I>) isn't included with the occurrence of CList that *follows* the scope resolution operator (the designers of C++ apparently felt that repeating the parameter list would be redundant). With this constructor in place, you could create an object for storing integers and simultaneously initialize all list items to 0, as follows:

```
CList <int, 100> IntList (0);
```

Likewise, the following code would create and initialize an object for storing a list of Record structures:

```
// 'Record' definition at global level:
struct Record
   {
   char Name [25];
   char Phone [15];
   };

// ...

Record Rec = {"", ""};
CList <Record, 50> RecordList (Rec);
```

In the newly created object, each item in the list would contain a Record structure in which both fields hold a null string.

CList should also have a default constructor (that is, one with no parameters) so that an object can be created *without* initializing the list. Recall that when you define a constructor that has one or more parameters, the compiler no longer automatically generates a default constructor. You can, however, explicitly add a do-nothing default constructor to the CList definition, as follows:

```
CList () {};
```

You define a *destructor* for a class template using a syntax similar to that for a constructor. For example, a destructor for the CList class template would be declared within the template definition as

```
~CList ();
```

and it would be implemented as follows:

```
template <class T, int I> CList <T, I>::~CList ()
    {
    // code for destructor ...
    }
```

(Alternatively, you could define the destructor entirely within the template definition.)

NOTE   The Microsoft Foundation Classes (MFC) provides a set of templates for creating objects that store collections of various types of data objects. Chapter 11 describes the use of one of these templates, CTypedPtrArray.

Listing 7.1 provides the final definition of the CList class and its member functions.

Listing 7.1

```cpp
// CList.h: CList template header file

template <class T, int I> class CList
{
public:
   CList () {};
   CList (T InitValue);

   int SetItem (int Index, const T &Item);
   int GetItem (int Index, T &Item);

private:
   T Buffer [I];
};

template <class T, int I> CList <T, I>::CList (T InitValue)
   {
   for (int N = 0; N < I; ++N)
      Buffer [N] = InitValue;
   }

template <class T, int I> int CList <T, I>::SetItem
   (int Index, const T &Item)
   {
   if (Index < 0 || Index > I - 1)
      return 0;
   Buffer [Index] = Item;
   return 1;
   }

template <class T, int I> int CList <T, I>::GetItem
   (int Index, T &Item)
   {
   if (Index < 0 || Index > I - 1)
      return 0;
   Item = Buffer [Index];
   return 1;
   }
```

Summary

This chapter introduced a relatively new addition to the C++ language: templates. The following are the primary features of templates that were discussed:

- A template is a special type of function or class definition that allows you to generate an entire family of related functions or classes, each of which is suited for working with a specific kind of data.

- A function template defines a generic function that will accept parameters of a variety of different types. When the compiler encounters a call to the function, it automatically generates a version of the function that works properly with the data types passed in the call.

- Defining a single function template provides a convenient alternative to defining a set of overloaded functions.

- In a function template definition, *type parameters* represent the types of the data items passed in a call to the function.

- If you want to provide custom processing for a specific type of data, you can define a normal function that has the same name as the function template but uses specific types rather than type parameters. If the function is called with these types, the normal function will override the function template.

- You can define a single class template to generate an entire family of related classes for operating on different types of data.

- In a class template definition, you can use *constant parameters* as well as *type parameters,* rather than specific constants or types.

- When you create an object based on the template, you supply the values of the constant and type parameters. The compiler then generates an instance of a version of the class that uses the specified constants and types.

In the next chapter, you'll learn about another relatively new addition to the C++ language: exception handling.

CHAPTER
EIGHT

Handling Exceptions in C++

- Handling thrown exceptions

- Handling Win32 exceptions

An *exception* is an interruption in the normal flow of program control in response to an unexpected or abnormal event. An exception can originate from a hardware error, such as an attempt to divide a number by zero or to access an invalid memory address. An exception can also be generated by a software routine—such as a library function or a Win32 API function—when it encounters a situation that prevents it from completing its task (for example, it's passed an invalid pointer or handle). Finally, you can generate exceptions yourself in the C++ code that you write.

The C++ language, as implemented in Visual C++ 6, provides a simple, comprehensive mechanism that allows you to handle any of these types of exceptions. If you *don't* provide a handler for a particular exception, a default exception handler will typically display an error message and terminate your program. Using the C++ exception-handling mechanism, however, you can choose exactly which exceptions you want to handle yourself. For an exception that you handle, either you can remedy the problem and allow the program to continue running, or you can perform any required clean-up tasks and terminate the program gracefully.

The chapter begins by explaining how to handle exceptions generated by C++ code—that is, exceptions generated through the C++ throw keyword. It then shows how to extend the C++ exception facility to handle *Win32 exceptions*, which are generated by hardware events or by Win32 API functions (a *Win32 API function* is one that's provided by the underlying Windows system, as explained in Chapter 9). Be aware that, like templates, the C++ exception-handling mechanism is still evolving and is subject to change.

Handling Thrown Exceptions

This section explains how to handle exceptions generated within C++ code through use of the C++ throw keyword. (Generating an exception is also known as *raising* or *throwing* an exception.) A C++ exception is thrown by means of a statement consisting of the throw keyword followed by some value; the value can be a constant, a variable, or an object (that is, an instance of a class, structure, or union). The purpose of the value is to supply information about the exception that can be used by the exception handler. For example, the following code throws an exception if a memory allocation fails, and it supplies a string with this exception that describes the error:

```
char *Buffer = new char [1000];
if (Buffer == 0)
    throw "out of memory";
```

If this exception is thrown and the program *doesn't* provide a handler for it, the exception mechanism calls the runtime library function terminate, which displays the message "abnormal program termination" in a dialog box and stops the program.

To handle such an exception, you must provide a try block and a catch block, as in the following example:

```
try
    {
    // statements ...

    char *Buffer = new char [1000];
    if (Buffer == 0)
        throw "out of memory";    // generate an exception

    // statements ...
    }
catch (char *ErrorMsg)
    {                              // handle the exception
    cout << ErrorMsg << '\n';

    // handle error and resume program execution or
    // call 'exit' to quit program

    }
// execution continues here ...
```

If an exception is thrown anywhere within the block of code following the try keyword (or in any function that it calls, directly or indirectly), control will immediately pass out of this block, and, if there's an appropriate catch block following the try block, control will enter the catch block, which will handle the exception. A catch block is preceded by the catch keyword together with a declaration in parentheses. If the type specified in this declaration matches the type of the value given in the throw statement that generated the exception, control will pass into the block following the catch keyword (this is what was meant by an *appropriate* catch block). If the types *don't* match, the program will look for another handler (as described later in the chapter). When the code in the catch block has finished executing, control passes to the first statement following the block (unless, of course, the catch block contains a return statement or a call to a function such as exit), and the program resumes running normally. The presence of the try and catch statements thus prevents the default exception handler from terminating the program.

To use the C++ exception-handling mechanism, the Enable Exception Handling setting must be enabled for the project configuration. When you create a new project, this setting is enabled for both configurations by default. To change the setting, choose the Project ➢ Settings… menu command, open the C/C++ tab in the Project Settings dialog box, and choose the C++ Language item in the Category: list. You can then check or clear the Enable Exception Handling check box.

A try block is also known as a *guarded section* of code. If *no* exception is thrown in the try block, the catch block is skipped and control passes directly to the first statement beyond it.

In the example above, the throw statement includes a string ("out of memory") that has the data type char *. Because the type given in the catch declaration is also char *, the block of code that follows catch will receive control if the exception is thrown.

Notice that the catch declaration actually declares a char * parameter, ErrorMsg. This parameter allows the catch block to access the value given in the throw statement. The mechanism is quite similar to passing a parameter to a function. To understand it, think of the throw statement:

```
throw "out of memory";
```

as a call to a function in which the value ("out of memory") is passed to the function. Then, think of the catch block as the function that is called and the declaration, (char *ErrorMsg), as the function's formal parameter declaration. Like a function parameter, ErrorMsg can be accessed only within the catch block.

Note that a catch declaration *can* include merely a type, without a parameter:

```
catch (char *)
   {
   // can't access the value specified in the throw statement
   }
```

In this case, the `catch` block would still receive control in response to the `throw "out of memory`; statement, but it wouldn't be able to access the `char *` value that was thrown.

If the `catch` declaration specified a different type, such as an `int`,

```
catch (int ErrorCode)
    {
    // would NOT receive control in response to the statement
    //    throw "out of memory";
    }
```

it *wouldn't* receive control in response to the exception that was thrown.

You can handle several different types of exceptions by including more than one `catch` block following the `try` block. For example, the following code would be able to handle a `char *` exception *or* an `int` exception:

```
try
    {
    // ...

    throw "string"; // this exception would be handled by the
                    // first catch block

    // ...

    throw 5;        // this exception would be handled by the
                    // second catch block

    }
catch (char *ErrorMsg)
    {
    // handle any 'char *' exception ...
    }
catch (int ErrorCode)
    {
    // handle any 'int' exception ...
    }
```

If a catch declaration contains an ellipsis (that is, three period characters, . . .) rather than a type specification,

```
catch (...)
   {
   // will receive control in response to any type of exception
   }
```

then the catch block will receive control in response to *any type* of exception that's thrown in the preceding try block. Because it has no parameter, however, it can't access the value that was supplied when the exception was thrown. If there is more than one catch block, the catch with the ellipsis must be placed *last*. (The program searches through the catch blocks in the order they appear in the code, and activates the first one that matches the type of the exception. Because the ellipsis catch block is last, if there's a catch block that exactly matches the type of the exception, it—rather than the general-purpose code in the ellipsis catch block—will receive control.)

NOTE For a detailed list of the rules that the exception mechanism uses to match types between **throw** statements and **catch** blocks, see the following topic in the online help: *Visual C++ Documentation, Using Visual C++, Visual C++ Programmer's Guide, Adding Program Functionality, Details, Exception Handling Topics (General), Exception Handling Topics (C++), C++ Exception Examples, Catchable Types.*

The example program ExcTypes.cpp, shown in Listing 8.1, allows the user to trigger various types of exceptions, and shows the flow of program control when an exception is thrown (this program is designed to be built as a console application, as described in Chapter 2):

Listing 8.1

```
// ExcTypes.cpp: Example program illustrating the throwing and
// handling of different types of exceptions.

#include <iostream.h>

class CExcept
```

```
{
public:
    CExcept (int ExCode)
        {
        m_ExCode = ExCode;
        }
    int GetExCode ()
        {
        return m_ExCode;
        }
private:
    int m_ExCode;
};


void main ()
    {
    char Ch;

    try
        {
        cout << "at beginning of try block" << '\n';

        cout << "throw 'char *' exception? (y/n): "; cin >> Ch;
        if (Ch == 'y' || Ch == 'Y')
            throw "error description";

        cout << "throw 'int' exception? (y/n): "; cin >> Ch;
        if (Ch == 'y' || Ch == 'Y')
            throw 1;

        cout << "throw 'class CExcept' exception? (y/n): ";
        cin >> Ch;
        if (Ch == 'y' || Ch == 'Y')
            throw CExcept (5);

        cout << "throw 'double' exception? (y/n): "; cin >> Ch;
        if (Ch == 'y' || Ch == 'Y')
            throw 3.1416;
```

```
    cout << "at end of try block (no exceptions thrown)"
        << '\n';
    }
catch (char *ErrorMsg)
    {
    cout << "'char *' exception thrown; exception message: "
        << ErrorMsg << '\n';
    }
catch (int ErrorCode)
    {
    cout << "'int' exception thrown; exception code: "
        << ErrorCode << '\n';
    }
catch (CExcept Except)
    {
    cout << "'class CExcept' exception thrown; code: "
        << Except.GetExCode () << '\n';
    }
catch (...)
    {
    cout << "unknown type of exception thrown" << '\n';
    }
cout << "after last catch block" << '\n';
}
```

This program provides a special catch handler for each type of exception that can be thrown in the try block except for the double exception, which causes control to pass to the general exception-handling code in the catch (...) block.

If the user chooses to throw the class CExcept exception, the program creates a temporary CExcept object, passing an integer to the CExcept constructor. The resulting object is then thrown,

```
    throw CExcept (5);
```

causing the object to be copied into the Except parameter in the CExcept catch block. Throwing a class object provides a highly effective and versatile way to process an exception. You can include extensive error information in a class object and provide member functions for supplying this information to the catch block as well as for handling the error condition.

When you run the example program, notice that as soon as any exception is thrown, no further statements are executed within the try block. Notice also that after the code in a catch block is executed, control passes immediately to the statement following the last catch block and the program finishes running normally.

Writing the Catch Code

When you write the code for a catch block, you must choose the best way to handle the particular exception raised. The actions you take can be influenced by the general type of the exception as well as by the information supplied through the catch parameter. The following is a summary of three general, alternative ways that a catch block might handle an exception:

- **Continue the program**   If the problem isn't too severe, the catch block might notify the user of the problem and perhaps prompt the user for information, remedy the error situation, and then allow control to pass out of the catch block, causing the program to continue running with the statement immediately following the last catch block. The catch block must be sure to delete any program resources (such as memory blocks or file handles) that would have been deleted by the code in the try block if it hadn't been interrupted by the exception. As you'll see in the next section, "Placing Exception Handlers," the program will automatically delete any local parameters, variables, or objects that were created in the try block and were still within scope when the exception occurred.

NOTE   With the C++ exception-handling mechanism, you *don't* have the option of continuing program execution with the statement immediately following the statement that caused the exception. You can resume the program only at the point beyond the last catch handler. The C++ exception model is thus termed *nonresumable*.

- **Terminate the program**   If the problem is severe, the catch handler can perform any required final clean-up tasks (such as closing file handles), notify the user of the error, and then call a runtime library function such as exit to terminate the program.

- **Leave the exception unhandled**   The catch block may decide not to handle a particular exception. To do this, it can use the throw keyword without specifying a value:

```
throw;
```

This statement generates an exception with the *same* type and value as the original exception that caused the catch block to receive control. Control will immediately branch out of the catch block and the program will look for another exception handler (or call terminate if none is found), as described later in the chapter (in the section "Nesting Exception Handlers"). Note that you can use the catch keyword without a type *only* within a catch block or in a function called by one.

Placing Exception Handlers

In the examples given so far in this chapter, exceptions have been generated by throw statements placed directly within try blocks. A throw statement, however, can be within a function that's called directly or indirectly by the try block, and control will still jump to the adjoining catch block (unless the throw statement is within a *nested* try block, as described in the next section).

An exception can be thrown by a function that you've written as part of your program (where you've included an explicit *throw* statement), or it can be generated by a library function that's called by your program. For example, as you'll see in Chapter 9, many of the Microsoft Foundation Classes (MFC) functions throw specific types of exceptions when they encounter errors.

NOTE   You can have the C++ **new** operator throw an exception (with an object of the predefined **xalloc** class) rather than return 0 if the allocation fails. For instructions on doing this, see the following topic in the online help: *Visual C++ Documentation*, *Reference*, *C/C++ Language and C++ Libraries*, *C++ Language Reference*, *Special Member Functions*, *The new and delete Operators*, *Handling Insufficient Memory Conditions*. Note that in a program written with the Microsoft Foundation Classes, a **new** error automatically throws an exception rather than returning 0 (for more information, see the sidebar on MFC exceptions near the end of Chapter 9).

You should place your try and catch blocks at the most advantageous level within your program. Including a large amount of code within a single try block will reduce the number of exception handlers you need to write. For example, you could even place your entire program within a single try block and write a single general-purpose exception handler:

```
void main ()
    {
    try
        {
        // all program code is within or is called from this block
        }
```

```
catch (...)
   {
   // single, general-purpose exception-handling routine...
   }
}
```

One problem with placing a large amount of code in a try block, however, is that it would be difficult (or impossible in the example above) to resume the program execution after an exception occurs. The larger the amount of code that's in a try block, the larger will be the amount of code—possibly vital code—that might be skipped if an exception occurs.

Placing a small amount of code within a try block will necessitate writing more exception handlers, but will allow you to provide highly specific handling for each kind of exception. It will also make it easier to recover from an exception and keep the program running.

Destruction of Objects

When an exception is thrown in a try block, control immediately passes out of one or more blocks of code (it always passes out of the try block; it may also pass out of blocks nested within the try block, out of functions called from the try block, and out of blocks nested within these functions). Accordingly, the C++ exception mechanism must destroy all automatic variables, automatic objects, or function parameters that were declared within any of these blocks (recall that automatic variables and objects as well as parameters are destroyed when they go out of scope; that is, when control leaves the { } delimited block in which they're declared).

To destroy these objects, the exception mechanism adjusts the stack and invokes any destructors that have been defined for automatic objects; the destructors are called in the reverse order in which the objects were created. This process is known as *unwinding the stack*, and it takes place immediately after the formal parameter to the catch block has been initialized but before the code within the catch block begins executing.

NOTE If an exception occurs while the catch parameter is being initialized or during the unwinding of the stack, the exception mechanism immediately calls the termi-nate function without attempting to find another exception handler.

In unwinding the stack, the program *doesn't* destroy `static` variables or objects, because they'll be destroyed—as usual—when the program exits. Nor does it destroy variables or objects created dynamically with the `new` operator; these must be explicitly destroyed using the `delete` keyword (if the code that normally deletes them is skipped when an exception occurs, you must be sure to delete them within the `catch` block).

In the example program Unwind.cpp, shown in Listing 8.2, an exception is thrown in a function that's called from a `try` block. This code illustrates the destruction of objects that occurs during the unwinding of the stack in response to an exception.

Listing 8.2

```cpp
// Unwind.cpp: Example program illustrating the destruction of
// objects during the unwinding of the stack caused by an
// exception.

#include <iostream.h>

class CA
{
public:
    CA ()
        {
        cout << "class CA constructor called" << '\n';
        }
    ~CA ()
        {
        cout << "class CA destructor called" << '\n';
        }
};

class CB
{
public:
    CB ()
        {
        cout << "class CB constructor called" << '\n';
        }
    ~CB ()
```

```
        {
        cout << "class CB destructor called" << '\n';
        }
};

class CC
{
public:
    CC ()
        {
        cout << "class CC constructor called" << '\n';
        }
    ~CC ()
        {
        cout << "class CC destructor called" << '\n';
        }
};

CC *PCC = 0;   // define global pointer to class CC

void Func ()
    {
    CB B;   // define an instance of class CB

    PCC = new CC;   // dynamically create an instance of class CC

    throw "exception message";

    cout << "you'll never see this!";

    delete PCC;
    }

void main ()
    {
    cout << "beginning of main ()" << '\n';
    try
        {
        CA A;   // define an instance of class CA

        Func ();
```

```
        cout << "end of try block" << '\n';
        }
    catch (char * ErrorMsg)
        {
        cout << ErrorMsg << '\n';

        delete PCC;
        }
    cout << "end of main ()" << '\n';
    }
```

The output of this program is as follows:
```
beginning of main ()
class CA constructor called
class CB constructor called
class CC constructor called
class CB destructor called
class CA destructor called
exception message
class CC destructor called
end of main ()
```

Between the beginning of the `try` block and the point in the `try` block where the exception is thrown, the example program creates three objects (one instance of each of the three classes CA, CB, and CC). The instances of classes CA and CB are declared as automatic objects. Because the blocks in which these two objects are defined are exited when the exception occurs, the objects are both destroyed—and their destructors are called—before the `catch` block receives control. Notice that they're destroyed in the opposite order in which they were created.

However, because the CC object is dynamically created using new, it *isn't* automatically deleted when the exception is thrown. Notice that because the code that normally deletes the CC object (the last statement in Func) is skipped when the exception occurs, the `catch` block explicitly deletes this object.

Nesting Exception Handlers

At the time an exception is thrown, the flow of program control may have entered two or more nested `try` blocks. Consider, for example, the following code:

```
void Func ()
    {
    try
```

```
      {
      // ...
      throw "help!";
      // ...
      }
   catch (char * Msg)
      {
      // ...
      }
   catch (...)
      {
      // ...
      }
   }

void main ()
   {
   // other statements ...
   try
      {
      // ...
      Func ();
      // ...
      }
   catch (char * Msg)
      {
      // ...
      }
   catch (...)
      {
      // ...
      }
   // other statements ...
   }
```

In this example, main calls Func, which throws an exception. When this exception occurs, the flow of program control has entered two try blocks without exiting either one; the exception thus occurs within the context of two dynamically nested try blocks. (The dynamic nesting of try blocks depends on the actual sequence of function calls that has occurred prior to the exception; for example, if Func were called from some other point in the program, the exception might take place within only a single try block.)

When an exception is thrown, the program searches for a catch handler in the following way: it first searches for a matching catch block associated with the most deeply nested try block (in the example, this would be the try block within Func). It searches the catch blocks in the order they're defined in the code, and it activates the first one that either matches the exception type or is defined with an ellipsis. Then, if it doesn't find an appropriate catch block or if the code within an activated catch block throws an exception, it searches the catch blocks associated with the *next* most deeply nested try block (in the example, the one in main). It continues in this manner until it has searched the catch blocks associated with the outermost enclosing try block. If it *doesn't* find a handler (or if an exception occurs during initialization of a catch parameter or during stack unwinding) it calls terminate, which prints an error message and terminates the program.

Handling Win32 Exceptions

In addition to exceptions generated by the throw keyword within the C++ code you've written or within C++ library functions or other software routines included in your program, exceptions can also be generated by the Win32 system code in response to hardware or software errors. These types of exceptions are known as *Win32 exceptions, structured exceptions,* or *C exceptions.* (Recall from Chapter 2 that Win32 is the underlying API, or application programming interface, that supports 32-bit console and GUI programs written for Windows.)

NOTE   The alternative names *structured exception* and *C exception* originate from the fact that when writing a C program for Win32 using Visual C++, you can handle Win32 exceptions by means of a set of built-in C keywords and structures. These keywords and structures can also be used in C++ programs; however, Microsoft recommends using the more comprehensive C++ exception-handling mechanism presented in this chapter. For more information on the C techniques for handling exceptions, see the following topic in the online help: *Visual C++ Documentation, Using Visual C++, Visual C++ Programmer's Guide, Adding Program Functionality, Details, Exception Handling Topics (SEH).*

Hardware errors that cause Win32 exceptions include attempts to divide numbers by zero as well as attempts to access invalid memory addresses (that is, addresses that haven't been properly allocated to the process). In response to certain software errors (for example, an out of memory condition), some of the Win32 API functions will generate a Win32 exception rather than simply returning an error code. For example, if you pass the Win32 API function `::HeapAlloc` the flag `HEAP_GENERATE_EXCEPTIONS`, the function will generate an exception if the allocation attempt fails. For each Win32 API function that generates an exception, the function documentation explains the circumstances under which an exception can occur. (Note that you can call Win32 API functions from console programs, which were explained in Chapter 2. You can also call them from Windows GUI programs, even if you're writing a program using the MFC; in fact, the MFC functions themselves call Win32 API functions.)

If a Win32 exception occurs and your program doesn't provide a handler for it, an error message will be displayed in a message box and the program will be terminated. For example, if a Windows console or GUI program contains the following attempt to divide an integer by zero,

```
int I = 0;
int J = 5 / I;
```

and if it *doesn't* provide a handler for the resulting Win32 exception, the message box shown in Figure 8.1 would be displayed and the program would be terminated. If the user clicks the Details >> button in this message box, detailed information on the exception is displayed, as shown in Figure 8.2.

FIGURE 8.1:

Message box that's displayed in response to a Win32 exception

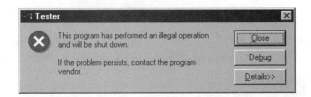

FIGURE 8.2:

The message box of Figure 8.1 after the user clicks the Details >> button

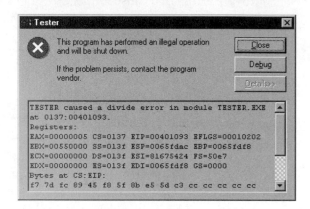

Fortunately, you can easily use the C++ exception-handling mechanism to handle Win32 exceptions as well as exceptions generated by the C++ throw keyword. You can do this in two ways. The first is to simply provide a catch block with the ellipsis syntax:

```
try
    {
    // ...
    // generate a Win32 exception:
    int I = 0;
    int J = 5 / I;
    // ...
    }
catch (...)
    {
    // will receive control in response to the Win32 exception;
    // handle exception...
    }
```

This catch block will receive control in response to any thrown exception *or* any Win32 exception that occurs in the try block. For a Win32 exception, the catch code could handle the error and, if desired, keep the program running.

(To have the message box of Figure 8.1 displayed and the program terminated, the catch code could *throw* the Win32 exception by using the throw keyword without a value.)

The problem with the first method, however, is that the catch block has no way of obtaining information on the particular exception that occurred, because it receives no parameter. The second method for handling Win32 exceptions solves this problem. To use this method, you define an *exception translator function* that has the following form:

```
void SETranslate
    (unsigned int ExCode,
    _EXCEPTION_POINTERS *PtrExPtrs)
```

(You can change the names of the function or its parameters, but the types must be the same.) You then pass the name of this function to the C++ runtime function _set_se_translator:

```
_set_se_translator (SETranslate);
```

(To call _set_se_translator, you must include the Eh.h header file.) Thereafter, whenever a Win32 exception occurs, the exception mechanism will call your exception translator function. The first parameter it passes to the translator function (ExCode) is a code for the specific exception that occurred, and the second parameter is a pointer to a block of information providing detailed information on the exception.

Table 8.1 lists some of the common Win32 exception codes that might be assigned to ExCode. If you want to use the constants for the exception codes given in the first column of this table, simply include the main Win32 header file, WINDOWS.H, in your program. For a description of the information that can be accessed through the PtrExPtrs parameter, see the documentation on the ::GetExceptionInformation Win32 API function under the following online help topic: *Platform SDK, Windows Base Services, Debugging and Error Handling, Structured Exception Handling, Structured Exception Handling Reference, Structured Exception Handling Functions.*

TABLE 8.1: Codes for Common Win32 Exceptions

Exception Code	Description of Exception
EXCEPTION_ACCESS_VIOLATION	The program attempted to access a virtual memory address that isn't properly allocated to the process.
EXCEPTION_ARRAY_BOUNDS_EXCEEDED	The program attempted to access an array element beyond the bounds of the array (array bounds checking requires hardware support).
EXCEPTION_DATATYPE_MISALIGNMENT	The program attempted to access a data item from an address that isn't on a proper boundary; for example, a 16-bit data item must be aligned on a 2-byte boundary, and a 32-bit data item must be aligned on a 4-byte boundary.
EXCEPTION_FLT_DENORMAL_OPERAND	One of the operands in a floating-point operation is too small to be represented as a floating-point value.
EXCEPTION_FLT_DIVIDE_BY_ZERO	The divisor in a floating-point division is zero.
EXCEPTION_FLT_INEXACT_RESULT	The result of a floating-point operation can't be represented exactly as a decimal fraction.
EXCEPTION_FLT_INVALID_OPERATION	A general floating-point error occurred (that is, a floating-point error other than those listed in this table).
EXCEPTION_FLT_OVERFLOW	The result of a floating-point operation is too large to be represented as a floating-point value.
EXCEPTION_FLT_STACK_CHECK	A floating-point operation caused the stack to overflow or underflow.
EXCEPTION_FLT_UNDERFLOW	The result of a floating-point operation is too small to be represented as a floating-point value.
EXCEPTION_INT_DIVIDE_BY_ZERO	The divisor in an integer operation is zero.
EXCEPTION_INT_OVERFLOW	The result of an integer operation is too large to be stored as an integer value (that is, one or more of the high-order bits were lost).
EXCEPTION_PRIV_INSTRUCTION	The program attempted to execute a machine instruction that's not permitted at the current privilege level.

NOTE   By default, exceptions generated by floating-point operations (that is, the exceptions in Table 8.1 with constants that begin with `EXCEPTION_FLT`) are disabled; if an error occurs, the operation simply yields zero or the maximum floating-point value. You can, however, enable floating-point exceptions by calling the `_controlfp` C++ runtime library function.

Your translator function can then throw a C++ exception with a value that identifies the exception and perhaps provides additional information. For example, it could throw an exception that supplies the `unsigned int` exception code, as follows:

```
void SETranslate
    (unsigned int ExCode,
    _EXCEPTION_POINTERS *PtrExPtrs)
    {
    throw ExCode;
    }
```

Finally, *if* the code that caused the original Win32 exception is contained in a `try` block, and *if* there is a `catch` block of the appropriate type (`unsigned int`, in the example), the `catch` block will be activated and can use the information in its parameter to handle the exception intelligently. The following is an example:

```
catch (unsigned int ExCode)
    {
    // ExCode contains an ID for the Win32 exception that
    // occurred; handle it appropriately ...
    }
```

Thus, an exception translator function essentially translates a Win32 exception to a C++ exception. Note that if the translator function *doesn't* explicitly throw an exception, the exception mechanism proceeds to look for a `catch (...)` handler—and terminates the program with a message box if none is found—as if you hadn't provided a translator function.

The example program ExTrans.cpp in Listing 8.3 demonstrates the use of an exception translator function.

Listing 8.3

```cpp
// ExTrans.cpp: Example program demonstrating an exception
// translator function for translating a Win32 exception to a C++
// exception
#include <windows.h>
#include <iostream.h>
#include <eh.h>

class CSExcept
{
public:
   CSExcept (unsigned int ExCode)
      {
      m_ExCode = ExCode;
      }
   unsigned int GetExCode ()
      {
      return m_ExCode;
      }

private:
   unsigned int m_ExCode;
};

void SETranslate
   (unsigned int ExCode,
   _EXCEPTION_POINTERS *PtrExPtrs)
   {
   throw CSExcept (ExCode);
   }

void main ()
   {
   char Ch;

   _set_se_translator (SETranslate);

   try
      {
      // ...
```

```
    cout << "generate 'integer divide by zero' exception? "
        "(y/n): ";
    cin >> Ch;
    if (Ch == 'y' || Ch == 'Y')
        {
        int I = 0;
        int J = 5 / I;
        }
    cout << "generate 'access violation' exception? (y/n): ";
    cin >> Ch;
    if (Ch == 'y' || Ch == 'Y')
        {
        *((char *)0) = 'x';
        }
    // other statements that may cause other exceptions...
    }
catch (CSExcept SExcept)
    {
    switch (SExcept.GetExCode ())
        {
        case EXCEPTION_INT_DIVIDE_BY_ZERO:
            cout << "'integer divide by zero' exception occurred"
                << '\n';
            break;

        case EXCEPTION_ACCESS_VIOLATION:
            cout << "'access violation' exception occurred"
                << '\n';
            break;

        default:
            cout << "unknown Win32 exception occurred" << '\n';
            throw;
            break;
        }
    }
}
```

This program installs an exception translator function named SETranslate. It then generates one of two Win32 exceptions: an *integer divide by zero* exception or an *access violation* exception (the second exception is generated by attempting to access memory at virtual address 0, which isn't allocated to the process).

When either of these Win32 exceptions occurs, the exception mechanism calls SETranslate, which throws a C++ exception with an object of the CSExcept class. The program defines CSExcept specifically for handling Win32 exceptions; its constructor stores the exception error code in the private data member m_ExCode. When the C++ exception is thrown, control passes to the catch block following the try block in which the statements causing the Win32 exception are located. The catch block receives a copy of the CSExcept object; it calls the GetExCode member function of this object to obtain the exception error code, and it uses this value to handle the exception appropriately (in this example, to simply print a descriptive message). If the catch block doesn't recognize the Win32 exception code, it prints a message and calls throw to generate default handling for the exception (that is, termination of the program with a message box describing the exception). Notice that the program includes WINDOWS.H so that it can use the exception constants EXCEPTION_INT_DIVIDE_BY_ZERO and EXCEPTION_ACCESS_VIOLATION.

TIP

As you've seen, the **new** operator normally returns 0 if it can't satisfy a memory allocation request. Rather than testing the returned value every time you invoke **new**, however, you could provide a *single* error routine in a **catch** block that handles the EXCEPTION_ACCESS_VIOLATION Win32 exception, as in the example program of Listing 8.3. Then, if **new** supplies a zero pointer, the **catch** handler will receive control as soon as the program attempts to *use* the pointer to access memory.

Summary

This chapter concludes the introduction to the C++ language with a discussion on the C++ exception-handling mechanism. The following is a summary of the main features of C++ exception handling that were covered:

- An exception is an interruption in the normal flow of program control that occurs in response to certain types of hardware or software errors.

- A software exception can be generated in C++ code by invoking the throw keyword, followed by a value that provides information on the error. The *type* of the exception is the data type of the value that follows the throw keyword (the value that's "thrown").

- To handle thrown C++ exceptions that occur within a given segment of code, you place the code within a try block and define one or more catch blocks immediately following the try block. A given catch block can be defined to handle a particular type of exception, or it can be defined to handle *any* type of exception (by using an ellipsis rather than a type declaration).

- If an exception is thrown in a try block, control will pass to the following catch block that matches the exception type, if any. The catch block can handle the error, perform clean-up tasks, and display any necessary messages; it can then resume program execution following the last catch block, terminate the program, or rethrow the exception.

- Exception handlers can be dynamically nested. The exception-handling mechanism searches for an appropriate catch handler starting from the most deeply nested try block.

- If the program *doesn't* provide a handler for a given C++ exception that's thrown, an "abnormal program termination" message is displayed and the program is terminated.

- The Win32 system can also generate an exception in response to a hardware error (for example, an attempt to address an invalid memory location) or a software error in a Win32 API function (such as ::HeapAlloc). These exceptions are known as *Win32*, *structured*, or *C* exceptions.

- Unlike a C++ thrown exception, a Win32 exception *doesn't* have an exception type. Accordingly, if a Win32 exception occurs in a try block, only an untyped catch block (that is, one defined with an . . .) will be activated.

- Rather than handling a Win32 exception in an untyped catch handler, you can define a exception translator function and install this function by calling the C++ runtime function _set_se_translator. Thereafter, if a Win32 exception occurs, the exception mechanism will call your translator function, passing it detailed information on the exception. The translator function can then use the throw keyword to throw a conventional C++ typed exception; the value that it throws can furnish the matching catch handler with exception information.

PART III

Windows GUI Programming with the MFC Library

Generating a Windows GUI Program

■ Programming for the Windows GUI

■ Creating and building the program

■ The program classes and files

■ How the program works

9

In the previous chapters you wrote basic *console* programs, which run in simple character-mode windows. In this part of the book, you'll learn how to write Windows *GUI* programs, which take full advantage of the Windows *graphical user interface*. These programs can create one or more windows that display a wide variety of user interface elements, such as menus, toolbars, status bars, list boxes, scroll bars, and so on. They can also draw graphics, display bitmaps, and render text in a wide variety of fonts.

In this chapter, you'll learn how to create a simple Windows GUI program in C++, using the AppWizard application-generating tool and Microsoft Foundation Classes (the *MFC*). The chapter begins by describing various ways to write Windows GUI programs with Microsoft Visual C++, and discusses the advantages of using AppWizard and the MFC. It then shows how to generate a basic program shell with AppWizard and how to modify the generated code. Finally, it explains how the generated files are organized and how an MFC program works.

The remaining chapters in this part of the book demonstrate how to use AppWizard and other development tools to create increasingly more advanced types of Windows GUI applications. These chapters will build on the basic skills and theoretical understanding that you gain here.

Programming for the Windows GUI

Microsoft Visual C++ provides several different pathways for writing Windows GUI programs. First, you can write GUI programs in C or C++ by directly calling the functions provided by the underlying Win32 application program interface (API), which is part of the Windows 95 and Windows NT operating systems. Using this approach, however, you must write many lines of routine code before you can begin to focus on the tasks specific to your application.

Second, you can write Windows GUI programs in C++ using the Microsoft Foundation Classes. The MFC provides a large collection of prewritten classes, as well as supporting code, which can handle many standard Windows programming tasks, such as creating windows and processing messages. You can also use the MFC to quickly add sophisticated features to your programs, such as toolbars, split window views, and OLE support. And you can use it to create ActiveX controls, which are reusable software components that can be displayed in Web browsers and other container applications (discussed in Chapter 25). The MFC can simplify your GUI programs and make your programming job considerably easier. Note that the MFC functions internally call Win32 API functions. The MFC is thus said to "wrap" the Win32 API, providing a higher-level, more portable programming interface. (In MFC programs, you're also free to directly call Win32 API functions, so you don't lose their capabilities by choosing to use the MFC.)

Third, you can write Windows GUI programs in C++ using both the MFC and the Microsoft Wizards. You can use AppWizard to generate the basic source files for a variety of different types of GUI programs. You can then use the ClassWizard tool to generate much of the routine code required to derive classes, to define member functions for processing messages or customizing the behavior of the MFC, to manage dialog boxes, and to accomplish other tasks. The code generated by the Wizards makes full use of the MFC. Note that the Wizards aren't limited to generating simple program shells, but rather can be used to produce programs containing extensive collections of advanced features, including toolbars, status windows, context-sensitive online help, OLE support, database access, and complete menus with partially or fully functional commands for opening and saving files, printing, print previewing, and performing other tasks. Once you've used the Wizards to generate the basic program source code, you can immediately begin adding code specific to the logic of your program.

Using this third approach, you benefit not only from the prewritten code in the MFC, but also from the generated source code that *uses* the MFC and handles many routine programming tasks. The MFC and the Wizards free you from much of the effort required in creating your program's visual interface, and also help ensure that this interface conforms to Microsoft's guidelines.

NOTE Using the MFC and Wizards to write your program makes it relatively easy to conform to Microsoft's Windows 95 (and later) logo requirements. For information on the logo requirements, see the following Visual C++ online help topic: *Visual C++ Documentation, Using Visual C++, Visual C++ Programmer's Guide, Adding Program Functionality, Details, Windows 95 Functionality.*

This book covers the third and highest-level pathway to writing Windows GUI applications. Not only are the MFC and Wizards the most advanced and interesting Windows GUI development tools included in Microsoft Visual C++, but they're also the newest and least understood. It's indicative of the relative simplicity of using the MFC and Wizards that the book is able to explain how to program so many features; it would take a much larger volume to teach how to program this many features using the Win32 API alone!

Creating and Building the Program

In this section you'll create a program named WinGreet, which is an example of the simplest type of program that you can generate using AppWizard. You'll first generate the program source code, then make several modifications to the generated code, and finally build and run the program.

1.   Generating the Source Code

To generate a program with AppWizard, you create a new project of the appropriate type, and then specify the desired program features in a series of dialog boxes that AppWizard displays (projects and project workspaces were described in Chapter 2). Begin by running the Microsoft Developer Studio, and then proceed as follows:

1.   Choose the File ➢ New… menu command in Developer Studio or simply press Ctrl+N. The New dialog box will appear.

2.   Open the Projects tab (if it's not already open) so that you can create a new project.

3.   In the list of project types, select the "MFC AppWizard (exe)" item. Choosing this project type will cause AppWizard to prompt you for further information and then to generate the basic C++ code for a Windows GUI program that uses the MFC. (To create a dynamic link library with AppWizard, you would choose the "MFC AppWizard (dll)" project type. Creating dynamic link libraries isn't covered in this book. For information on dynamic link libraries, see the online help topic: *Visual C++ Documentation, Using Visual C++, Visual C++ Programmer's Guide, Beginning Your Program, Creating a Win32 DLL*. The "MFC Active X ControlWizard" project type is used to create ActiveX controls, as discussed in Chapter 25.)

4.   Type the name **WinGreet** into the Project Name: text box. This will cause Visual C++ to assign the name WinGreet to the new project (as well as to the project workspace that contains this project).

5.   In the Location: text box, specify the path of the folder to contain the project files (that is, the *project folder*). If you wish, you can simply accept the default folder that is initially contained in this box (the default folder is given the same name as the project workspace, WinGreet). Click the button with the

ellipsis (…) if you want to search for a different location. If the specified project folder doesn't exist, the Developer Studio will create it (it will also create the -Res subfolder within the project folder to store several resource files, in addition to one or more output subfolders).

6. To complete the Projects tab of the New dialog box, make sure that the Win32 item is checked in the Platforms: area. Unless you've installed a cross-development edition of Visual C++, Win32 will be the only option in this area. The completed New Project Workspace dialog box is shown in Figure 9.1.

> **NOTE**
>
> Because you didn't previously open an existing project workspace, you can't select the Add To Current Workspace option. You can select only the Create New Workspace option.

FIGURE 9.1:

The completed Projects tab of the New dialog box for creating the WinGreet example program

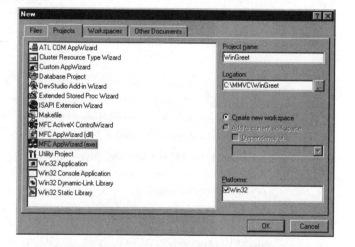

7. Click the OK button in the New dialog box. The first of the AppWizard dialog boxes, which is labeled "MFC AppWizard - Step 1," will now be displayed. In the following descriptions of the AppWizard options that need to be selected, the expression "(default)" follows the description of each option initially selected. For these options, you need only make sure that you don't change them.

8. In the Step 1 dialog box, select the Single Document application type, make sure the Document/View Architecture Support option (default) is checked, and select the English language (default). The completed dialog box is shown in Figure 9.2.

FIGURE 9.2:

The completed AppWizard Step 1 dialog box

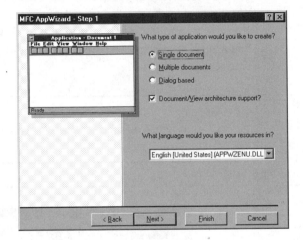

Choosing the Single Document application type causes AppWizard to generate a *single document interface* (SDI) application, which is designed to display only one document at a time. The other application types you can select are described in Chapters 16 and 17.

The Document/View Architecture Support option causes AppWizard to generate separate classes for storing and for viewing your program's data, as well as to provide code for reading and writing the data from disk. This architecture is described later in this chapter and in the following chapters. (In general, unless you're trying to minimize the size of your program, you should choose the Document/View Architecture Support option to take advantage of the added programming support it provides.)

Finally, AppWizard will use the selected language for the program menu captions and for the standard messages that the program displays.

Click the Next > button to display the Step 2 dialog box.

9. In the Step 2 dialog box, select the None item (default) to exclude database support from the program, as shown in Figure 9.3.

FIGURE 9.3:

The completed AppWizard Step 2 dialog box

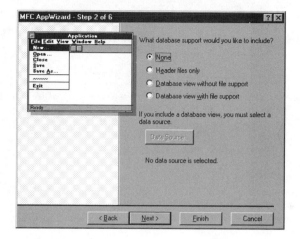

For information on using Visual C++ to develop database applications, see the following online help topics: *Visual C++ Documentation, Using Visual C++, Visual C++ Tutorials, Enroll and DAOEnrol: Database Applications,* and *Visual C++ Documentation, Using Visual C++, Visual C++ Programmer's Guide, Adding Program Functionality, Overviews, Databases: Overview.*

Note that in any of the AppWizard dialog boxes (from Step 2 on) you can click the < Back button to return to a previous step to review and possibly revise your choices. Also, you can click the Finish button to skip the remaining dialog boxes and immediately generate the program source code using the default values for all choices in the remaining dialog boxes (*don't* click this button for the current exercise). And finally, you can click the ? button in the upper-right corner and then click a control in the dialog box to obtain information on the related option.

Click the Next > button to reveal the Step 3 dialog box.

10. In the Step 3 dialog box, select the None item (default) to exclude compound document support from the program, make sure that the Automation option isn't checked to eliminate automation support, and remove the check from the ActiveX Controls option since you won't be adding any ActiveX controls to the program. Compound documents and automation are discussed in Chapter 24, and ActiveX controls in Chapter 25. The completed Step 3 dialog box is shown in Figure 9.4. Click the Next > button to display the Step 4 dialog box.

FIGURE 9.4:

The completed AppWizard
Step 3 dialog box

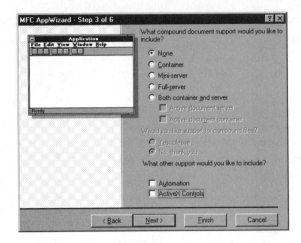

11. In the Step 4 dialog box, remove the check from each of the application features except "3D Controls" (default) and leave the value 4 (default) as the number of files you want to use in the "recent file list." You don't need to click the Advanced... button to select advanced options; rather, you'll accept the default values for these options. Figure 9.5 shows the completed Step 4 dialog box.

FIGURE 9.5:

The completed AppWizard
Step 4 dialog box

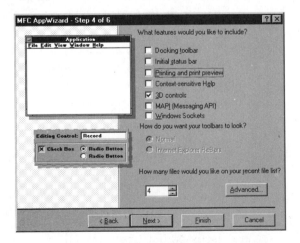

The File menu of the generated program will list the most recently opened documents; the number that you specify for the "recent file list" is the maximum number of documents that will be listed. In later chapters, you'll select additional application features in the Step 4 dialog box, and you'll set some of the advanced options as well.

Click the Next> button to display the Step 5 dialog box.

12. In the Step 5 dialog box, select the MFC Standard project-style option (default) to generate the traditional MFC user interface for your program (the Windows Explorer option implements the application as a workbook-like container). Select the "Yes, Please" option (default) to have AppWizard include comments within the source files it generates. The comments help clarify the code and clearly indicate the places where you need to insert your own code. And finally, choose the As A Statically Linked Library option for the MFC library that's used.

FIGURE 9.6:

The completed AppWizard Step 5 dialog box

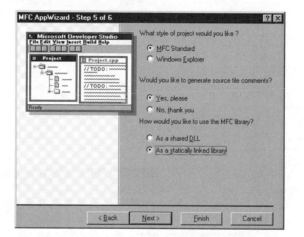

With the As A Statically Linked Library option, the MFC code is bound directly into your program's executable file. With the alternative option, As A Shared DLL, your program accesses MFC code contained in a separate dynamic link library (DLL), which can be shared by several applications (note that you'll have to select this option if you have the Standard Edition of Visual C++, which doesn't provide static MFC linking). The DLL option reduces the size of your program's executable file but requires you to distribute a separate DLL file together with your program file (as you must when you distribute a Visual Basic program). For more information on these options, see the following online help topic: *Visual C++ Documentation, Using Visual C++, Visual C++ Programmer's Guide, Adding Program Functionality, Overviews, DLLs: Overview*. The completed Step 5 dialog box is shown in Figure 9.6.

Click the Next> button to display the Step 6 dialog box.

13. The Step 6 dialog box displays information on each of the four main classes that AppWizard defines for your program, and is shown in Figure 9.7. Don't change any of this information because the remainder of the exercise assumes that you've accepted all the default values. The classes and the files in which they're defined are described later in the chapter (in the section "The Program Classes and Files"). This is the final AppWizard dialog box for collecting information; you should now click the Finish button to display the New Project Information dialog box.

FIGURE 9.7:

The completed AppWizard Step 6 dialog box

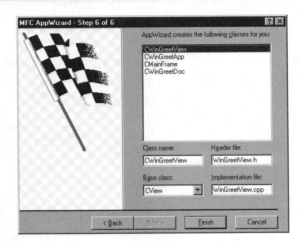

14. The New Project Information dialog box, which is shown in Figure 9.8, summarizes many of the program features that you chose in the previous dialog boxes. (If you want to change any feature, you can click the Cancel button and then go back to the appropriate dialog box to adjust the information.) Click the OK button in the New Project Information dialog box, and AppWizard will create the project folder that you specified (if necessary), generate the program source files, and open the newly created project, WinGreet. Figure 9.9 shows the FileView tab of the Visual Studio Workspace window, with the hierarchical graph fully expanded and showing all the files belonging to the WinGreet project that were generated by AppWizard.

FIGURE 9.8:

The AppWizard New Project Information dialog box for the WinGreet project

FIGURE 9.9:

The graph of the WinGreet project files in the FileView tab of the Visual Studio Workspace window

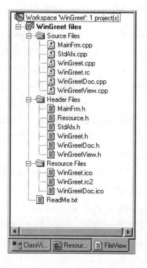

As explained in Chapter 2, the new project has two configurations: Win32 Debug (for generating the debug version of the program) and Win32 Release (for generating the final optimized version of the program). In this exercise, you won't change any project settings. If you wish to change the settings for a project, follow the instructions given in Chapter 2.

NOTE   The series of dialog boxes that AppWizard displays is tailored to the choices you make along the way. Therefore, if you generate a different program, the dialog boxes you see may not be the same as those illustrated in this chapter.

---

2.   Modifying the Source Code

The source files generated by AppWizard are sufficient for building a functional program. In other words, immediately after generating the source files with AppWizard, you could build and run the program (although it wouldn't do very much). Before building the program, however, you normally use the various Visual C++ development tools to add to the code features specific to your application.

To provide you with some practice in working with the source files, this section describes how to add code that displays the string "Greetings!" centered within the program window (if the generated code is unaltered, the program simply displays a blank window). To do this, proceed as follows:

1. Open the source file WinGreetDoc.h. The easiest way to open a source file belonging to the current project is to double-click the file name within the FileView graph. WinGreetDoc.h is the header file for the program's *document class*, which is named `CWinGreetDoc` and is derived from the MFC class `CDocument`. As you'll see later in the chapter, the document class is responsible for reading, writing, and storing the program data. In this trivial example program, the document class simply stores the fixed message string ("Greetings!"), which constitutes the program data.

NOTE   In the example programs in this part of the book, the names of data members are prefaced with an `m_` to distinguish them from parameters and other nonmember variables. (This naming convention conforms to that used by the MFC classes.)

---

2. In the `CWinGreetDoc` class definition you'll add the protected data member m_Message, which stores a pointer to the message string, and you'll add the public member function `GetMessage`, which returns a pointer to this string. To do this, enter the lines marked in **bold** within the following code:

```
class CWinGreetDoc : public CDocument
{
protected:
   char *m_Message;

public:
   char *GetMessage ()
   {
   return m_Message;
   }

protected: // create from serialization only
   CWinGreetDoc();
   DECLARE_DYNCREATE(CWinGreetDoc)

// remainder of CWinGreetDoc definition ...
```

NOTE   Some of the program lines generated by AppWizard had to be broken to fit within the margins of this book. The appearance of these lines in the book, therefore, differs slightly from what you see on the screen in your Developer Studio editor.

The code excerpt above shows the beginning of the `CWinGreetDoc` class definition, and includes the code that was generated by AppWizard, as well as the lines of code that you manually add, which are marked in bold. In the instructions given in this part of the book, all lines of code that you manually add or modify are marked in bold. Although you add or modify only the bold lines, the book typically shows a larger block of code to help you find the correct position within the generated source file to make your additions or modifications.

Listings 9.1 through 9.8, given later in the chapter, provide the full text of all the main source files for the WinGreet program, including the code that you've added.

TIP

In some of the exercises in this part of the book, the blocks of code marked in bold, which you need to add to the source files, are quite large. In these cases, you can save time and avoid errors by *copying* the new or modified code from the equivalent source files on the companion CD rather than manually typing in the lines. By doing this, you'll still gain the experience of creating the example programs step-by-step, while avoiding the tedium of typing each line.

3. Open the file WinGreetDoc.cpp, which is the implementation file for the program's document class, `CWinGreetDoc`. Within the `CWinGreetDoc` class constructor, add the statement that's marked in bold in the following code:

```
/////////////////////////////////////////////////////////////////
/////////////
// CWinGreetDoc construction/destruction

CWinGreetDoc::CWinGreetDoc()
{
    // TODO: add one-time construction code here

    m_Message = "Greetings!";
}
```

As a result of adding this line, the data member `m_Message` will automatically be assigned the address of the string "Greetings!" when an instance of the `CWinGreetDoc` class is created.

TIP

AppWizard inserts comments beginning with the word TODO at many (but not all) of the positions within the generated code where you typically add code of your own.

4. Open the file WinGreetView.cpp, which is the implementation file for the program's *view* class; this class is named `CWinGreetView` and is derived from the MFC class `CView`. As you'll see later, the view class is responsible for processing input from the user and for managing the view window, which is used for displaying the program data.

5. In the file WinGreetView.cpp, add the statements marked in bold to the CWinGreetView member function OnDraw:

```
////////////////////////////////////////////////////////////
////////////
// CWinGreetView drawing

void CWinGreetView::OnDraw(CDC* pDC)
{
    CWinGreetDoc* pDoc = GetDocument();
    ASSERT_VALID(pDoc);

    // TODO: add draw code for native data here

    RECT ClientRect;
    GetClientRect (&ClientRect);
    pDC->DrawText
       (pDoc->GetMessage (),  // obtain the string
       -1,
       &ClientRect,
       DT_CENTER | DT_VCENTER | DT_SINGLELINE);
}
```

The MFC calls the OnDraw member function of the program's view class whenever the program window needs drawing or redrawing (for example, when the window is first created, when its size is changed, or when it's uncovered after being hidden by another window). The code you added to OnDraw displays the string that's stored in the document class ("Greetings!").

OnDraw obtains a pointer to the program's document class by calling the CView member function GetDocument. It then uses this pointer to call the CWinGreetDoc member function GetMessage (which you added to the code in step 2) to obtain the message string. Although this is an elaborate method for getting a simple string, it's used here because it illustrates the typical way that the view class obtains program data from the document class, so that it can display this data.

OnDraw is passed a pointer to a *device context object* that is an instance of the MFC class CDC. A device context object is associated with a specific device (in WinGreet it's associated with the view window), and it provides a set of member functions for displaying output on that device. OnDraw uses the CDC member function DrawText to display the message string. To center the string within the view window, it calls the CWnd member function Get-ClientRect to obtain the current dimensions of the view window, and then supplies these dimensions (in a RECT structure) to DrawText, together with a set of flags that cause DrawText to center the string horizontally and vertically within the specified dimensions (DT_CENTER and DT_VCENTER). Device context objects and the DrawText function are discussed in Chapter 18.

In a full-featured application, you would of course make many more changes to the source code generated by AppWizard, typically using a variety of tools, including the resource editors and ClassWizard, which will be described in later chapters.

3. Building and Running the Program

To build the program, choose the Build ➢ Build WinGreet.exe menu command on the Build menu, or press F7, or click the Build button on the Build toolbar or Build MiniBar:

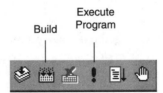

If the build process completes without error, you can run the program by choosing the Build ➢ Execute WinGreet.exe menu command, or by pressing Ctrl+F5, or by clicking the Execute Program button. The WinGreet program window is shown in Figure 9.10.

NOTE   Recall from Chapter 2 that the Developer Studio builds the program using the current active configuration. When you first create the project files using AppWizard, the active configuration is Win32 Debug. You can later change it via the Build ➢ Configurations... menu command. If you build the program using the Win32 Debug configuration, all output files are placed within the -Debug subfolder of the project folder, and if you build it using the Win32 Release configuration, all output files are placed within the -Release subfolder.

FIGURE 9.10:

The WinGreet program window

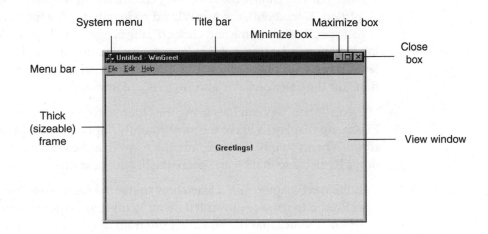

When you run the program, notice that AppWizard has created code for displaying a complete menu. The Exit command on the File menu and the About command on the Help menu are fully functional; that is, AppWizard has generated all the code needed to implement these commands. The commands on the Edit menu are nonfunctional; that is, AppWizard hasn't supplied any of the code for implementing these commands, and therefore they're disabled. You'll learn how to supply code to handle some of these commands in Chapters 10 and 11.

The commands on the File menu (other than Exit) are partially functional. That is, AppWizard has generated some of the code needed to implement the commands. If you select the Open... command, the program displays the standard Open dialog box. If you select a file in this dialog box and click OK, the name of the file is displayed in the window title bar (replacing the name "Untitled" that's displayed when the program first starts), but the contents of the file aren't actually read or displayed. If you then choose the New command, the program again displays the name "Untitled" in the title bar, but it doesn't actually initialize a new document (in Chapter 11, you'll learn how to supply code to initialize a new document).

WARNING Be careful when playing around with the WinGreet File menu commands. If you "open" an existing file via File ➢ Open... and then choose File ➢ Save, the original contents of the file will be overwritten with an empty file without warning.

Finally, if you choose the Save As... command (or the Save command with an "Untitled" document), the AppWizard code will display the Save As dialog box. If you specify a file name and click OK, the program will create an empty file having the specified name, but won't write any data to this file. In Chapter 12, you'll learn how to supply the code to perform the actual reading and writing operations for the Open..., Save, and Save As... commands.

If you "open" several files using the Open... command, you'll notice that the File menu displays a list of the most recently "opened" files (it will list up to four files). When you quit the program, the AppWizard code saves this list in the Windows Registry so that it can restore the list the next time you run the program.

In the next chapter, you'll learn how to use the resource editors of the Developer Studio to remove unwanted menu items and to design a custom icon for a program. (Notice that the WinGreet program displays the standard MFC icon, which contains the letters "MFC," for Microsoft Foundation Classes.)

The Program Classes and Files

The WinGreet program is known as a *single document interface* (or SDI) application, meaning that it displays only one document at a time. When AppWizard generates an SDI application, it derives four main classes:

- The document class
- The view class
- The main frame window class
- The application class

> **NOTE**
> In Chapter 17 you'll learn about the main classes and source files that AppWizard generates for multiple document interface (MDI) applications.

The primary program tasks are divided among these four main classes, and AppWizard creates separate source files for each class. By default, it derives the names of both the classes and the class source files from the name of the project (though, as mentioned previously, you can specify alternative names when using AppWizard to generate the program).

The WinGreet document class is named CWinGreetDoc and is derived from the MFC class CDocument. The CWinGreetDoc header file is named WinGreetDoc.h and the implementation file is named WinGreetDoc.cpp (a general description of header and implementation files was given in the section "Organizing the Source Files" in Chapter 4). The document class is responsible for storing the program data as well as for reading and writing this data to disk files. The WinGreet document class stores only a single message string and doesn't perform disk I/O.

The WinGreet view class is named CWinGreetView and is derived from the MFC class CView. The CWinGreetView header file is named WinGreetView.h, and the implementation file is named WinGreetView.cpp. The view class is responsible for displaying the program data (on the screen, printer, or other device) and for processing input from the user. This class manages the *view window*, which is used for displaying program data on the screen. The Win-Greet view class merely displays the message string within the view window.

The WinGreet main frame window class is named CMainFrame and is derived from the MFC class CFrameWnd. The CMainFrame header file is named MainFrm.h, and the implementation file is named MainFrm.cpp. The main frame window class manages the main program window, which is a *frame* window that contains a window frame, a title bar, a menu bar, and a system menu. The frame window also contains Minimize, Maximize, and Close boxes, and sometimes other user interface elements such as a toolbar or a status bar (see Figure 9.10). Note that the view window—managed by the view class—occupies the empty portion of the main frame window inside these interface elements (which is known as the *client area* of the main frame window). The view window has no visible elements except the text and graphics that the view class explicitly displays (such as the string "Greetings!" displayed by WinGreet). The view window is a *child* of the main frame window, which means—among other things—that it's always displayed on top of and within the boundaries of the client area of the main frame window.

Finally, the application class is named CWinGreetApp and is derived from the MFC class CWinApp. The CWinGreetApp header file is named WinGreet.h, and the implementation file is named WinGreet.cpp. The application class manages the program as a whole; that is, it performs general tasks that don't fall within the province of any of the other three classes, such as initializing the program and performing the final program cleanup. Every MFC Windows program must create exactly one instance of a class derived from CWinApp.

The four main classes communicate with each other and exchange data by calling each other's public member functions and by sending *messages* (messages will be explained in Chapter 10). Table 9.1 summarizes the features of the four main classes in the WinGreet program.

TABLE 9.1: The Main Program Classes and Source Files

Class	Class Name	Derived From	Header File	Implementation File	Primary Responsibilities
Document	CWinGreetDoc	CDocument	WinGreetDoc.h	WinGreetDoc.cpp	Storing program data; saving and loading program data from disk
View	CWinGreetView	CView	WinGreetView.h	WinGreetView.cpp	Displaying program data; processing user input; managing view window
Main frame window	CMainFrame	CFrameWnd	MainFrm.h	MainFrm.cpp	Managing main program window
Application	CWinGreetApp	CWinApp	WinGreet.h	WinGreet.cpp	General program tasks

AppWizard and the Developer Studio create several source and settings files in addition to the source files for the four main classes. The main additional files are briefly described in Table 9.2. (Besides these files, the Developer Studio creates the following files, which are used for storing various types of information: WinGreet.aps, WinGreet.ncb, WinGreet.opt, and WinGreet.plg.) Also, AppWizard generates a file named ReadMe.txt, which describes most of the files that it has generated for your program. Note that the set of files AppWizard creates depends on the program features you choose when generating the program; the specific files associated with various program features will be discussed when these features are introduced later in the book.

TABLE 9.2: Additional Source and Settings Files Generated by AppWizard and the Developer Studio

File	Purpose
Resource.h	Contains constant definitions for program resources. This file is maintained by the resource editors of the Developer Studio (you don't edit it directly), and it's included—indirectly—in all the main .cpp files and in the main resource-definition file (WinGreet.rc).
StdAfx.cpp and StdAfx.h	Used for generating precompiled headers.
WinGreet.clw	Stores information used by the ClassWizard tool (which is introduced in Chapter 10).
WinGreet.dsp	The WinGreet project file, which stores settings and other information for the project.
WinGreet.dsw	The WinGreet project workspace file, which stores information on the project workspace. As explained in Chapter 2, a project workspace manages one or more individual projects. To open the WinGreet project in the Developer Studio, you choose the File ➢ Open… menu command and select the WinGreet.dsw file.
WinGreet.rc	The main resource-definition file for the program, which defines the accelerator keystroke table, the "About" dialog box, the menu, the string table, and the program version information. This file is maintained by the resource editors of the Developer Studio (you *shouldn't* edit it directly), and it's processed by the Microsoft resource compiler (RC.EXE) when the program is built.
\res\WinGreet.ico	The main program icon file. Initially, this file stores the standard MFC icon; however, you can edit it using the graphics editor of the Developer Studio. This icon is displayed in the upper-left corner of the WinGreet window, on the Windows taskbar, and other places. WinGreet.rc contains an ICON statement that causes the resource compiler to include this icon in the program's resources.
\res\WinGreetDoc.ico	The document icon file. The WinGreet program doesn't display this icon (document icons are displayed in MDI programs, as explained in Chapter 17).
\res\WinGreet.rc2	This file is provided for manually defining program resources; that is, for defining them *without* using the interactive resource editors provided by the Developer Studio. Initially, it doesn't contain any definitions. If you want to define a resource manually, you can type its definition into this file. This file is included by the main resource file, WinGreet.rc, via an #include statement.

NOTE

The AppWizard-generated files listed in Tables 9.1 and 9.2 are placed in the project folder you specified when you generated the program source files (WinGreet), and in the \res subfolder within the project folder. The files listed *don't* include the output files produced when you build the program (for example, the .obj, .res, and .exe files). As mentioned before, the output files are placed in the -Debug or -Release subfolder of the project folder.

The following listings, Listings 9.1 through 9.8, provide the complete text of the header and implementation files for the four main program classes. These listings contain the code that was generated by AppWizard, plus the manual code additions described in the exercise given previously in the chapter. The files you created in the exercise should match the files below (except for the lengths of a few lines that had to be broken to make the listings fit within the book margins). Also, a complete set of these files is included in the \WinGreet companion-CD folder (which you can copy to your hard disk, as explained in Chapter 1).

NOTE

For the example programs, the book lists only the C++ files that define and implement the main classes, because these are the files that you generally work with when you develop a program (that is, these are the files that you're most likely to directly edit). The StdAfx C++ files (StdAfx.h and StdAfx.cpp) and the other source files listed in Table 9.2 are seldom viewed or directly edited, but rather are created and maintained by various development tools; they're therefore not printed in the book.

Listing 9.1

```
// WinGreet.h : main header file for the WINGREET application
//

#if !defined(AFX_WINGREET_H__E7D60DA4_9891_11D1_80FC_00C0F6A83B7F__INCLUDED_)
#define AFX_WINGREET_H__E7D60DA4_9891_11D1_80FC_00C0F6A83B7F__INCLUDED_

#if _MSC_VER > 1000
#pragma once
#endif // _MSC_VER > 1000
```

```
#ifndef __AFXWIN_H__
    #error include 'stdafx.h' before including this file for PCH
#endif

#include "resource.h"        // main symbols

/////////////////////////////////////////////////////////////////////////////
// CWinGreetApp:
// See WinGreet.cpp for the implementation of this class
//

class CWinGreetApp : public CWinApp
{
public:
    CWinGreetApp();

// Overrides
    // ClassWizard generated virtual function overrides
    //{{AFX_VIRTUAL(CWinGreetApp)
    public:
    virtual BOOL InitInstance();
    //}}AFX_VIRTUAL

// Implementation

    //{{AFX_MSG(CWinGreetApp)
    afx_msg void OnAppAbout();
        // NOTE - the ClassWizard will add and remove member functions here.
        //    DO NOT EDIT what you see in these blocks of generated code !
    //}}AFX_MSG
    DECLARE_MESSAGE_MAP()
};


/////////////////////////////////////////////////////////////////////////////

//{{AFX_INSERT_LOCATION}}
// Microsoft Visual C++ will insert additional declarations immediately before
// the previous line.

#endif
// !defined(AFX_WINGREET_H__E7D60DA4_9891_11D1_80FC_00C0F6A83B7F__INCLUDED_)
```

Listing 9.2

```cpp
// WinGreet.cpp : Defines the class behaviors for the application.
//

#include "stdafx.h"
#include "WinGreet.h"

#include "MainFrm.h"
#include "WinGreetDoc.h"
#include "WinGreetView.h"

#ifdef _DEBUG
#define new DEBUG_NEW
#undef THIS_FILE
static char THIS_FILE[] = __FILE__;
#endif

/////////////////////////////////////////////////////////////////////////////
// CWinGreetApp

BEGIN_MESSAGE_MAP(CWinGreetApp, CWinApp)
    //{{AFX_MSG_MAP(CWinGreetApp)
    ON_COMMAND(ID_APP_ABOUT, OnAppAbout)
        // NOTE - the ClassWizard will add and remove mapping macros here.
        //    DO NOT EDIT what you see in these blocks of generated code!
    //}}AFX_MSG_MAP
    // Standard file based document commands
    ON_COMMAND(ID_FILE_NEW, CWinApp::OnFileNew)
    ON_COMMAND(ID_FILE_OPEN, CWinApp::OnFileOpen)
END_MESSAGE_MAP()

/////////////////////////////////////////////////////////////////////////////
// CWinGreetApp construction

CWinGreetApp::CWinGreetApp()
{
    // TODO: add construction code here,
    // Place all significant initialization in InitInstance
}
```

```
///////////////////////////////////////////////////////////////////////
// The one and only CWinGreetApp object

CWinGreetApp theApp;

///////////////////////////////////////////////////////////////////////
// CWinGreetApp initialization

BOOL CWinGreetApp::InitInstance()
{
    // Standard initialization
    // If you are not using these features and wish to reduce the size
    //  of your final executable, you should remove from the following
    //  the specific initialization routines you do not need.

#ifdef _AFXDLL
    Enable3dControls();          // Call this when using MFC in a shared DLL
#else
    Enable3dControlsStatic();  // Call this when linking to MFC statically
#endif

    // Change the registry key under which our settings are stored.
    // You should modify this string to be something appropriate
    // such as the name of your company or organization.
    SetRegistryKey(_T("Local AppWizard-Generated Applications"));

    LoadStdProfileSettings();  // Load standard INI file options (including MRU)

    // Register the application's document templates.  Document templates
    //  serve as the connection between documents, frame windows and views.

    CSingleDocTemplate* pDocTemplate;
    pDocTemplate = new CSingleDocTemplate(
        IDR_MAINFRAME,
        RUNTIME_CLASS(CWinGreetDoc),
        RUNTIME_CLASS(CMainFrame),          // main SDI frame window
        RUNTIME_CLASS(CWinGreetView));
    AddDocTemplate(pDocTemplate);

    // Parse command line for standard shell commands, DDE, file open
    CCommandLineInfo cmdInfo;
    ParseCommandLine(cmdInfo);
```

```
    // Dispatch commands specified on the command line
    if (!ProcessShellCommand(cmdInfo))
        return FALSE;

    // The one and only window has been initialized, so show and update it.
    m_pMainWnd->ShowWindow(SW_SHOW);
    m_pMainWnd->UpdateWindow();

    return TRUE;
}


/////////////////////////////////////////////////////////////////////////////
// CAboutDlg dialog used for App About

class CAboutDlg : public CDialog
{
public:
    CAboutDlg();

// Dialog Data
    //{{AFX_DATA(CAboutDlg)
    enum { IDD = IDD_ABOUTBOX };
    //}}AFX_DATA

    // ClassWizard generated virtual function overrides
    //{{AFX_VIRTUAL(CAboutDlg)
    protected:
    virtual void DoDataExchange(CDataExchange* pDX);    // DDX/DDV support
    //}}AFX_VIRTUAL

// Implementation
protected:
    //{{AFX_MSG(CAboutDlg)
        // No message handlers
    //}}AFX_MSG
    DECLARE_MESSAGE_MAP()
};

CAboutDlg::CAboutDlg() : CDialog(CAboutDlg::IDD)
{
    //{{AFX_DATA_INIT(CAboutDlg)
    //}}AFX_DATA_INIT
}
```

```
void CAboutDlg::DoDataExchange(CDataExchange* pDX)
{
    CDialog::DoDataExchange(pDX);
    //{{AFX_DATA_MAP(CAboutDlg)
    //}}AFX_DATA_MAP
}

BEGIN_MESSAGE_MAP(CAboutDlg, CDialog)
    //{{AFX_MSG_MAP(CAboutDlg)
        // No message handlers
    //}}AFX_MSG_MAP
END_MESSAGE_MAP()

// App command to run the dialog
void CWinGreetApp::OnAppAbout()
{
    CAboutDlg aboutDlg;
    aboutDlg.DoModal();
}


/////////////////////////////////////////////////////////////////////////////
// CWinGreetApp commands
```

Listing 9.3

```
// WinGreetDoc.h : interface of the CWinGreetDoc class
//
/////////////////////////////////////////////////////////////////////////////

#if !defined(AFX_WINGREETDOC_H__E7D60DAA_9891_11D1_80FC_00C0F6A83B7F__INCLUDED_)
#define AFX_WINGREETDOC_H__E7D60DAA_9891_11D1_80FC_00C0F6A83B7F__INCLUDED_

#if _MSC_VER > 1000
#pragma once
#endif // _MSC_VER > 1000


class CWinGreetDoc : public CDocument
{
protected:
    char *m_Message;
```

```
public:
   char *GetMessage ()
   {
   return m_Message;
   }

protected: // create from serialization only
   CWinGreetDoc();
   DECLARE_DYNCREATE(CWinGreetDoc)

// Attributes
public:

// Operations
public:

// Overrides
   // ClassWizard generated virtual function overrides
   //{{AFX_VIRTUAL(CWinGreetDoc)
   public:
   virtual BOOL OnNewDocument();
   virtual void Serialize(CArchive& ar);
   //}}AFX_VIRTUAL

// Implementation
public:
   virtual ~CWinGreetDoc();
#ifdef _DEBUG
   virtual void AssertValid() const;
   virtual void Dump(CDumpContext& dc) const;
#endif

protected:

// Generated message map functions
protected:
   //{{AFX_MSG(CWinGreetDoc)
      // NOTE - the ClassWizard will add and remove member functions here.
      //    DO NOT EDIT what you see in these blocks of generated code !
   //}}AFX_MSG
   DECLARE_MESSAGE_MAP()
};
```

```
////////////////////////////////////////////////////////////////////////

//{{AFX_INSERT_LOCATION}}
// Microsoft Visual C++ will insert additional declarations immediately before
// the previous line.

#endif
// !defined(AFX_WINGREETDOC_H__E7D60DAA_9891_11D1_80FC_00C0F6A83B7F__INCLUDED_)
```

Listing 9.4

```cpp
// WinGreetDoc.cpp : implementation of the CWinGreetDoc class
//

#include "stdafx.h"
#include "WinGreet.h"

#include "WinGreetDoc.h"

#ifdef _DEBUG
#define new DEBUG_NEW
#undef THIS_FILE
static char THIS_FILE[] = __FILE__;
#endif

////////////////////////////////////////////////////////////////////////
// CWinGreetDoc

IMPLEMENT_DYNCREATE(CWinGreetDoc, CDocument)

BEGIN_MESSAGE_MAP(CWinGreetDoc, CDocument)
    //{{AFX_MSG_MAP(CWinGreetDoc)
        // NOTE - the ClassWizard will add and remove mapping macros here.
        //     DO NOT EDIT what you see in these blocks of generated code!
    //}}AFX_MSG_MAP
END_MESSAGE_MAP()

////////////////////////////////////////////////////////////////////////
// CWinGreetDoc construction/destruction

CWinGreetDoc::CWinGreetDoc()
{
    // TODO: add one-time construction code here
```

```
    m_Message = "Greetings!";
}

CWinGreetDoc::~CWinGreetDoc()
{
}

BOOL CWinGreetDoc::OnNewDocument()
{
    if (!CDocument::OnNewDocument())
        return FALSE;

    // TODO: add reinitialization code here
    // (SDI documents will reuse this document)

    return TRUE;
}



/////////////////////////////////////////////////////////////////////////
// CWinGreetDoc serialization

void CWinGreetDoc::Serialize(CArchive& ar)
{
    if (ar.IsStoring())
    {
        // TODO: add storing code here
    }
    else
    {
        // TODO: add loading code here
    }
}

/////////////////////////////////////////////////////////////////////////
// CWinGreetDoc diagnostics

#ifdef _DEBUG
void CWinGreetDoc::AssertValid() const
{
    CDocument::AssertValid();
}
```

```
void CWinGreetDoc::Dump(CDumpContext& dc) const
{
    CDocument::Dump(dc);
}
#endif //_DEBUG


/////////////////////////////////////////////////////////////////////////////
// CWinGreetDoc commands
```

Listing 9.5

```
// MainFrm.h : interface of the CMainFrame class
//
/////////////////////////////////////////////////////////////////////////////

#if !defined(AFX_MAINFRM_H__E7D60DBB_9891_11D1_80FC_00C0F6A83B7F__INCLUDED_)
#define AFX_MAINFRM_H__E7D60DBB_9891_11D1_80FC_00C0F6A83B7F__INCLUDED_

#if _MSC_VER > 1000
#pragma once
#endif // _MSC_VER > 1000

class CMainFrame : public CFrameWnd
{
protected: // create from serialization only
        CMainFrame();
        DECLARE_DYNCREATE(CMainFrame)

// Attributes
public:

// Operations
public:

// Overrides
        // ClassWizard generated virtual function overrides
        //{{AFX_VIRTUAL(CMainFrame)
        virtual BOOL PreCreateWindow(CREATESTRUCT& cs);
        //}}AFX_VIRTUAL
```

```cpp
// Implementation
public:
        virtual ~CMainFrame();
#ifdef _DEBUG
        virtual void AssertValid() const;
        virtual void Dump(CDumpContext& dc) const;
#endif

// Generated message map functions
protected:
        //{{AFX_MSG(CMainFrame)
                // NOTE - the ClassWizard will add and remove member functions here.
                //      DO NOT EDIT what you see in these blocks of generated code!
        //}}AFX_MSG
        DECLARE_MESSAGE_MAP()
};

/////////////////////////////////////////////////////////////////////////

//{{AFX_INSERT_LOCATION}}
// Microsoft Visual C++ will insert additional declarations immediately before
// the previous line.

#endif
// !defined(AFX_MAINFRM_H__E7D60DBB_9891_11D1_80FC_00C0F6A83B7F__INCLUDED_)
```

Listing 9.6

```cpp
// MainFrm.cpp : implementation of the CMainFrame class
//

#include "stdafx.h"
#include "WinGreet.h"

#include "MainFrm.h"

#ifdef _DEBUG
#define new DEBUG_NEW
#undef THIS_FILE
static char THIS_FILE[] = __FILE__;
#endif
```

```
/////////////////////////////////////////////////////////////////////////
// CMainFrame

IMPLEMENT_DYNCREATE(CMainFrame, CFrameWnd)

BEGIN_MESSAGE_MAP(CMainFrame, CFrameWnd)
    //{{AFX_MSG_MAP(CMainFrame)
        // NOTE - the ClassWizard will add and remove mapping macros here.
        //    DO NOT EDIT what you see in these blocks of generated code !
    //}}AFX_MSG_MAP
END_MESSAGE_MAP()

/////////////////////////////////////////////////////////////////////////
// CMainFrame construction/destruction

CMainFrame::CMainFrame()
{
    // TODO: add member initialization code here

}

CMainFrame::~CMainFrame()
{
}

BOOL CMainFrame::PreCreateWindow(CREATESTRUCT& cs)
{
    if( !CFrameWnd::PreCreateWindow(cs) )
        return FALSE;
    // TODO: Modify the Window class or styles here by modifying
    //   the CREATESTRUCT cs

    return TRUE;
}

/////////////////////////////////////////////////////////////////////////
// CMainFrame diagnostics

#ifdef _DEBUG
void CMainFrame::AssertValid() const
{
    CFrameWnd::AssertValid();
}
```

```
void CMainFrame::Dump(CDumpContext& dc) const
{
    CFrameWnd::Dump(dc);
}


#endif //_DEBUG


/////////////////////////////////////////////////////////////////////////////
// CMainFrame message handlers
```

Listing 9.7

```
// WinGreetView.h : interface of the CWinGreetView class
//
/////////////////////////////////////////////////////////////////////////////

#if !defined(AFX_WINGREETVIEW_H__E7D60DAC_9891_11D1_80FC_00C0F6A83B7F__INCLUDED_)
#define AFX_WINGREETVIEW_H__E7D60DAC_9891_11D1_80FC_00C0F6A83B7F__INCLUDED_

#if _MSC_VER > 1000
#pragma once
#endif // _MSC_VER > 1000

class CWinGreetView : public CView
{
protected: // create from serialization only
    CWinGreetView();
    DECLARE_DYNCREATE(CWinGreetView)

// Attributes
public:
    CWinGreetDoc* GetDocument();

// Operations
public:

// Overrides
    // ClassWizard generated virtual function overrides
    //{{AFX_VIRTUAL(CWinGreetView)
    public:
    virtual void OnDraw(CDC* pDC);  // overridden to draw this view
    virtual BOOL PreCreateWindow(CREATESTRUCT& cs);
    protected:
    //}}AFX_VIRTUAL
```

```
// Implementation
public:
   virtual ~CWinGreetView();
#ifdef _DEBUG
   virtual void AssertValid() const;
   virtual void Dump(CDumpContext& dc) const;
#endif

protected:

// Generated message map functions
protected:
   //{{AFX_MSG(CWinGreetView)
      // NOTE - the ClassWizard will add and remove member functions here.
      //    DO NOT EDIT what you see in these blocks of generated code !
   //}}AFX_MSG
   DECLARE_MESSAGE_MAP()
};

#ifndef _DEBUG  // debug version in WinGreetView.cpp
inline CWinGreetDoc* CWinGreetView::GetDocument()
   { return (CWinGreetDoc*)m_pDocument; }
#endif

/////////////////////////////////////////////////////////////////////////////

//{{AFX_INSERT_LOCATION}}
// Microsoft Visual C++ will insert additional declarations immediately before
// the previous line.

#endif
// !defined(AFX_WINGREETVIEW_H__E7D60DAC_9891_11D1_80FC_00C0F6A83B7F__INCLUDED_)
```

Listing 9.8

```
// WinGreetView.cpp : implementation of the CWinGreetView class
//

#include "stdafx.h"
#include "WinGreet.h"

#include "WinGreetDoc.h"
#include "WinGreetView.h"
```

```
#ifdef _DEBUG
#define new DEBUG_NEW
#undef THIS_FILE
static char THIS_FILE[] = __FILE__;
#endif


/////////////////////////////////////////////////////////////////////////////
// CWinGreetView

IMPLEMENT_DYNCREATE(CWinGreetView, CView)

BEGIN_MESSAGE_MAP(CWinGreetView, CView)
    //{{AFX_MSG_MAP(CWinGreetView)
        // NOTE - the ClassWizard will add and remove mapping macros here.
        //    DO NOT EDIT what you see in these blocks of generated code!
    //}}AFX_MSG_MAP
END_MESSAGE_MAP()

/////////////////////////////////////////////////////////////////////////////
// CWinGreetView construction/destruction

CWinGreetView::CWinGreetView()
{
    // TODO: add construction code here

}

CWinGreetView::~CWinGreetView()
{
}

BOOL CWinGreetView::PreCreateWindow(CREATESTRUCT& cs)
{
    // TODO: Modify the Window class or styles here by modifying
    //   the CREATESTRUCT cs

    return CView::PreCreateWindow(cs);
}
```

```
/////////////////////////////////////////////////////////////////////////
// CWinGreetView drawing

void CWinGreetView::OnDraw(CDC* pDC)
{
   CWinGreetDoc* pDoc = GetDocument();
   ASSERT_VALID(pDoc);

   // TODO: add draw code for native data here

   RECT ClientRect;
   GetClientRect (&ClientRect);
   pDC->DrawText
      (pDoc->GetMessage (),  // obtain the string
      -1,
      &ClientRect,
      DT_CENTER | DT_VCENTER | DT_SINGLELINE);
}

/////////////////////////////////////////////////////////////////////////
// CWinGreetView diagnostics

#ifdef _DEBUG
void CWinGreetView::AssertValid() const
{
   CView::AssertValid();
}

void CWinGreetView::Dump(CDumpContext& dc) const
{
   CView::Dump(dc);
}

CWinGreetDoc* CWinGreetView::GetDocument() // non-debug version is inline
{
   ASSERT(m_pDocument->IsKindOf(RUNTIME_CLASS(CWinGreetDoc)));
   return (CWinGreetDoc*)m_pDocument;
}
#endif //_DEBUG

/////////////////////////////////////////////////////////////////////////
// CWinGreetView message handlers
```

How the Program Works

If you're accustomed to procedural programming for MS-DOS or Unix, or even if you're familiar with conventional Windows GUI programming, you might be wondering how the WinGreet program works—where it first receives control, what it does next, where it exits, and so on. This section briefly describes the overall flow of control of the program, and then discusses the tasks performed by the application initialization function, InitInstance. In subsequent chapters, you'll learn how other portions of the code work (for example, Chapter 10 explains the parts of the code that handle messages, while Chapter 15 explains the code for displaying the About dialog box).

The Flow of Program Control

The following is a list of some of the significant events that occur when you run the WinGreet program. These five events were selected from the many program actions that take place, because they best help you understand how the WinGreet program works and they illustrate the purpose of the different parts of the source code:

1. The CWinApp class constructor is called.

2. The program entry function, WinMain, receives control.

3. WinMain calls the program's InitInstance function.

4. WinMain enters a loop for processing messages.

5. WinMain exits and the program terminates.

Figure 9.11 illustrates this sequence of events, and the following sections describe each event in detail.

FIGURE 9.11:

Significant events that occur when the WinGreet program is run

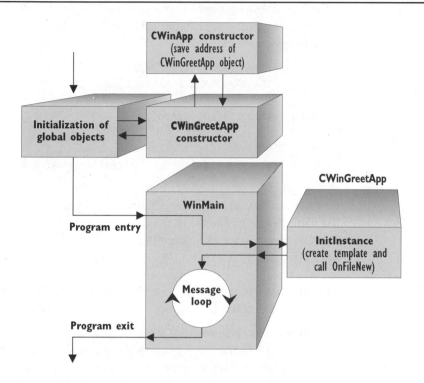

1. The *CWinApp* Constructor Is Called

As mentioned previously, an MFC application must define exactly one instance of its application class. The file WinGreet.cpp defines an instance of the WinGreet application class, CWinGreetApp, in the following global definition:

```
////////////////////////////////////////////////////////////////
///////////
// The one and only CWinGreetApp object

CWinGreetApp theApp;
```

Because the CWinGreetApp object is defined globally, the class constructor is called *before* the program entry function, WinMain, receives control. The CWinGreetApp constructor generated by AppWizard (also in WinGreet.cpp) does nothing:

```
//////////////////////////////////////////////////////////////////////
//////// CWinGreetApp construction

CWinGreetApp::CWinGreetApp()
{
   // TODO: add construction code here,
   // Place all significant initialization in InitInstance
}
```

However, as you learned in Chapter 5, such a do-nothing constructor causes the compiler to invoke the default constructor of the base class, which is CWinApp. The CWinApp constructor (supplied by the MFC) performs the following two important tasks:

- It makes sure that the program declares only *one* application object (that is, only one object belonging to CWinApp or to a class derived from it).

- It saves the address of the program's CWinGreetApp object in a global pointer declared by the MFC. It saves this address so that the MFC code can later call the WinGreetApp member functions. Calling these member functions will be described under step 3.

2. *WinMain* Receives Control

After all global objects have been created, the program entry function, WinMain, receives control. This function is defined within the MFC code; it's linked to the WinGreet program when the executable file is built. The WinMain function performs many tasks. The following steps describe the tasks that are the most important for understanding how the WinGreet program works.

3. *WinMain* Calls InitInstance

Shortly after it receives control, WinMain calls the InitInstance member function of the CWinGreetApp class. It calls this function by using the object address that the CWinApp constructor saved in step 1. InitInstance serves to initialize the application, and it will be described later in the chapter.

The MFC saves the address of the CWinGreetApp object in a CWinApp pointer, which it uses to call InitInstance. Because InitInstance is a virtual function (see Chapter 5), the overriding version of InitInstance defined within the CWinGreetApp class receives control. CWinApp defines several other virtual functions that you can override. For example, you can override the ExitInstance function to perform final clean-up tasks immediately before your application terminates. For a description of all CWinApp overridable functions, see the following online help topic: *Visual C++ Documentation, Reference, Microsoft Foundation Class Library and Templates, Microsoft Foundation Class Library, Class Library Reference, CWinApp, CWinApp Class Members*. (In this topic, see the *Overridables* section.)

4. *WinMain* Processes Messages

After completing its initialization tasks, WinMain enters a loop that calls the Windows system to obtain and dispatch all *messages* sent to objects within the WinGreet program (this loop is actually contained in a CWinApp member function named Run that's called from WinMain). Messages are explained in Chapter 10. Control remains within this loop during the remaining time that the application runs. Under Windows 95 (and later) and Windows NT, however, preemptive multitasking allows other programs to run at the same time (see Chapter 22).

5. *WinMain* Exits and the Program Terminates

When the user of the WinGreet program chooses the Exit command on the File menu or the Close command on the system menu, or clicks the Close box, the MFC code destroys the program window and calls the Win32 API function ::PostQuitMessage, which causes the message loop to exit. The WinMain function subsequently returns, causing the application to terminate.

The *InitInstance* Function

InitInstance is a member function of the application class, CWinGreetApp, and it's defined in the source file WinGreet.cpp. The MFC calls this function from WinMain, and its job is to initialize the application.

At the time `InitInstance` is called, a more traditional Windows GUI application would simply create a main program window because of the view-document programming model used by the MFC. However, the AppWizard code does something a bit more complex. It creates a *document template*, which stores information about the program's document class, its main frame window class, and its view class (don't confuse the word *template* in this context with a C++ template as described in Chapter 7). The document template also stores the identifier of the program resources used in displaying and managing a document (the menu, icon, and so on). When the program first begins running and it creates a new document, it uses the document template to create an object of the document class for storing the document, an object of the view class for creating a view window to display the document, and an object of the main frame window class to provide a main program window for framing the view window.

A document template is a C++ object; for an SDI application such as WinGreet, it's an instance of the `CSingleDocTemplate` MFC class. The following code in `InitInstance` creates the document template and stores it within the application object:

```
// Register the application's document templates. Document
// templates serve as the connection between documents, frame
// windows, and views.

CSingleDocTemplate* pDocTemplate;
pDocTemplate = new CSingleDocTemplate(
    IDR_MAINFRAME,
    RUNTIME_CLASS(CWinGreetDoc),
    RUNTIME_CLASS(CMainFrame),         // main SDI frame window
    RUNTIME_CLASS(CWinGreetView));
AddDocTemplate(pDocTemplate);
```

This code works as follows:

- It defines a pointer to a document template object, `pDocTemplate`.

- It uses the new operator to dynamically create a document template object (that is, an instance of the `CSingleDocTemplate` class), assigning the object's address to `pDocTemplate`.

- It passes four parameters to the `CSingleDocTemplate` constructor. The first parameter is the identifier of the program resources used in displaying and managing a document (namely, the accelerator table, the icon, the menu, and a descriptive string).

- The next three parameters supply information on the document class, the main frame window class, and the view class. Information on each class is obtained by calling the MFC macro RUNTIME_CLASS (which supplies a pointer to a CRuntimeClass object). This information allows the program to dynamically create an object of each class when a new document is first created.

- The template object pointer is passed to the CWinApp member function AddDocTemplate, which stores the document template within the application object so that the template will be available when a document is opened.

After creating the document template, InitInstance extracts the command line—if any—that was passed to the program when it was run, by calling the CWinApp member function ParseCommandLine:

```
// Parse command line for standard shell commands, DDE, file open
CCommandLineInfo cmdInfo;
ParseCommandLine(cmdInfo);
```

It then calls the CWinApp member function ProcessShellCommand to process the command line:

```
// Dispatch commands specified on the command line
if (!ProcessShellCommand(cmdInfo))
    return FALSE;
```

If the command line contains a file name, ProcessShellCommand attempts to open the file. The WinGreet program, however, doesn't fully implement the code for opening a file. Opening files is discussed in Chapter 12.

Normally, however, when you run WinGreet (for example, through the Developer Studio), the command line is empty. In this case ProcessShellCommand calls the CWinApp member function OnFileNew to create a new, empty document. When OnFileNew is called, the program uses the document template to create a CWinGreetDoc object, a CMainFrame object, a CWinGreetView object, and the associated main frame window and view window. The resources used for the main frame window (the menu, icon, and so on) are those identified by the resource identifier stored in the document template. Because these objects and windows are created internally by OnFileNew, you don't see within the

WinGreet code explicit definitions of the objects, nor do you see function calls for creating windows.

The `OnFileNew` function is also called whenever the user subsequently chooses the New command on the File menu. In an SDI application, however, these subsequent calls don't create new program objects or windows; rather, they reuse the existing objects and windows that were created the first time `OnFileNew` was called.

Finally, `InitInstance` calls the `ShowWindow` and `UpdateWindow` member functions of the main frame window object to make the main frame window visible on the screen and to cause the window contents to be displayed. It calls these functions by using the pointer to the main frame window object that's stored in the `CWinGreetApp` object's `m_pMainWnd` data member (which it inherits from `CWinThread`):

```
// The one and only window has been initialized, so show and
// update it.
m_pMainWnd->ShowWindow(SW_SHOW);
m_pMainWnd->UpdateWindow();
```

Other Code in *InitInstance*

`InitInstance` calls `CWinApp::Enable3dControlsStatic` (or `Enable3dControls` if you chose the shared MFC DLL, as described previously in the chapter) to cause Windows to display controls (such as check boxes) that have a three-dimensional appearance:

```
    // Standard initialization
    // If you are not using these features and wish to reduce the
    // size of your final executable, you should remove from the
    // following the specific initialization routines you do not
    // need.

#ifdef _AFXDLL
    Enable3dControls();          // Call this when using MFC in a
                                 // shared DLL
#else
    Enable3dControlsStatic();    // Call this when linking to MFC
                                 // statically
#endif
```

For more information on controls, see Chapter 15.

InitInstance also calls the CWinApp member function SetRegistryKey, which causes the program settings to be stored in the Windows Registry (rather than in an .ini file) and specifies the name of the key under which these settings are stored:

```
// Change the Registry key under which our settings are stored.
// You should modify this string to be something appropriate
// such as the name of your company or organization.
SetRegistryKey(_T("Local AppWizard-Generated Applications"));
```

To customize the name of the key under which the program settings are stored (for example, to set it to your company name), simply replace the string passed to SetRegistryKey. (Note that the macro _T converts the string to Unicode format, which SetRegistryKey requires. This format stores each character as a 16-bit value, and can be used to encode the characters in any language.)

The primary setting stored in the Registry is the list of most recently opened documents that's displayed on the program's File menu (which is also known as the MRU, or Most Recently Used, file list). InitInstance loads this document list, as well as any other program settings stored in the Registry, by calling the CWinApp::LoadStdProfileSettings function:

```
LoadStdProfileSettings(); // Load standard INI file options
                          // (including MRU)
```

If you need to perform any other application initialization tasks, the Init-Instance function is the place to add the code.

MFC Exceptions

In Chapter 8, you learned how to use the C++ exception mechanism for handling program errors that generate exceptions. The MFC fully supports standard C++ exceptions, and you can use the techniques described in Chapter 8 for handling certain types of MFC errors. Specifically, some of the MFC functions throw an exception—rather than simply returning an error code—under certain error conditions. The documentation on each MFC function that can throw an exception describes the circumstances under which it throws the exception and the *type* of the object that it throws. You can use this information to write an appropriate catch handler. The MFC functions always throw a pointer to an object of a class derived from the MFC class CException (such as CFileException and

Continued on next page

CMemoryException). When the `catch` block has finished using the exception object, it should call the object's `Delete` member function to properly delete the exception object.

For example, the following code calls the constructor of the MFC class `CFile` to create a file object and to open a file (using `CFile` to perform file I/O is discussed in Chapter 12):

```
try
    {
    CFile File ("EXISTS.NOT", CFile::modeRead);
    }
catch (CFileException *PtrFileException)
    {
    switch (PtrFileException->m_cause)
        {
        case CFileException::fileNotFound:
            AfxMessageBox ("File not found.");
            break;

        case CFileException::badPath:
            AfxMessageBox ("Bad path specification.");
            break;

        default:
            AfxMessageBox ("File open error.");
            break;
        }
    PtrFileException->Delete ();
    }
```

The `CFile` constructor attempts to open the file that's passed as the first parameter. The documentation on the constructor states that if an error occurs when opening the file, the constructor throws a `CFileException` exception; this means that the value it throws is a *pointer to* a `CFileException` object. The `CFileException` data member **m_cause** contains a code for the specific file error that occurred; the `CFileException` class defines a set of enumeration constants for the different values that can be assigned to **m_cause** (such as `CFileException::fileNotFound` and `CFileException::badPath`). Notice that the final statement in the `catch` block deletes the MFC exception object.

Continued on next page

Note also that in an MFC program, the **new** operator throws a `CMemoryException` exception if the memory allocation fails, rather than simply returning 0. Consider, for example, the following code in an MFC program:

```
try
    {
    // ...
    char *PtrBigBuffer = new char [2000000000]; // too much memory!
    // ...
    }
catch (CMemoryException *)
    {
    AfxMessageBox ("CMemoryException thrown");
    }
```

When **new** fails, rather than returning 0, it throws a `CMemoryException` exception that causes control to pass immediately to the `catch` block.

To conserve space and focus on the relevant programming techniques, the code examples in this book don't include exception handlers. In your own programs, however, you can easily provide exception handling using the techniques given in Chapter 8 together with the exception information in the documentation on the MFC functions. For additional general information on MFC exceptions, see the following online help topic: *Visual C++ Documentation*, *Using Visual C++*, *Visual C++ Programmer's Guide*, *Adding Program Functionality*, *Details*, *Exception Handling Topics (General)*, *Exception Handling Topics (MFC)*.

Summary

This chapter introduced you to the Microsoft Foundation Classes and the App-Wizard application-generating tool, by leading you through the steps for creating a simple Windows GUI program. The following are some of the general techniques and concepts that were discussed:

- A Windows *GUI* program is one that can take full advantage of the Windows graphical user interface.

- With Microsoft Visual C++, you can write a Windows GUI program using one of three basic methods: hand coding and calling the Win32 API functions, hand coding and using the MFC classes, or generating an MFC program using the Microsoft Wizards. The third approach is the easiest way to create conventional Windows programs, and it's the one discussed in this book.

- You generate the basic source code files for a Windows GUI program by creating a new project in the Developer Studio, choosing the "MFC AppWizard (.exe)" project type, and then specifying the desired program features in a series of dialog boxes that AppWizard displays.

- Once you've generated the basic program template with AppWizard, you can add your application-specific features by directly editing the source code, or by using other Visual C++ tools such as ClassWizard and the resource editors provided by the Developer Studio.

- An MFC GUI program generated using AppWizard has four main classes. The program tasks are apportioned among these classes, and each of these classes is defined in its own header file and is implemented in its own implementation file.

- The document class (derived from the MFC class CDocument) is responsible for storing the program data, as well as for saving and loading this data from disk files.

- The view class (derived from CView) manages the view window. This class is responsible for processing user input and for displaying the document within the view window and on other devices.

- The main frame window class (derived from CFrameWnd) manages the main program window. This frame window displays user interface objects such as a window frame; a menu; a title bar; Maximize, Minimize, and Close boxes; and sometimes a toolbar or a status bar. The view window is located in the blank area inside these objects.

- The application class (derived from CWinApp) manages the application as a whole and performs such general tasks as initializing the application and doing the final application clean-up.

- The program entry function, WinMain, is defined within the MFC. Among its other actions, WinMain calls the InitInstance member function of your application class, and it enters a continuous loop that processes the messages sent to the objects in your program.

- The `InitInstance` function initializes the program. This function creates and saves a document template, which stores information on the program's document, view, and main frame window classes. `InitInstance` then calls the `CWinApp` member function `OnFileNew`, which uses the document template both to create instances of these three classes and to create the main frame window and view window.

CHAPTER

TEN

10

Implementing the View

- The MiniDraw program

- The MiniEdit program

The *view* is the portion of a Microsoft Foundation Classes program that manages the view window, processes user input, and displays the document data within the view window and on other devices. As you saw in the previous chapter, when you generate a program using AppWizard, it derives a class from the MFC CView class specifically for managing the view. The view class derived by AppWizard does almost nothing itself, but rather serves as a shell for you to add your own code. In the previous chapter, you added code to the WinGreet program's view class to display a message string within the view window.

This chapter presents the first version of a simple drawing program named MiniDraw. After generating the basic shell for this program using AppWizard, you'll add code to the view class to read mouse input from the user and to draw straight lines within the view window. You'll use the ClassWizard tool to generate the functions for handling mouse input messages and for customizing the view window, and you'll use resource editors provided by the Developer Studio for modifying the program menu and designing a program icon. In later chapters, you'll create increasingly more complete versions of the MiniDraw program.

The chapter also presents the first version of a simple text editing program, MiniEdit. This program demonstrates how you can quickly create a fully functional text editor simply by deriving the program's view class from the MFC class CEditView rather than CView. In later chapters, you'll also create more advanced versions of MiniEdit.

The MiniDraw Program

In this chapter, you'll generate the first version of the MiniDraw program and implement the basic features of the program's view class. The MiniDraw program window is illustrated in Figure 10.1. MiniDraw allows you to draw straight lines within the view window. To draw a line, you place the mouse cursor at one end of the line, press the left button, drag the cursor to the other end of the line, and release the button. (Following the convention employed by the MFC and the Win32 API, this book refers to the mouse pointer as the *mouse cursor*.)

FIGURE 10.1:

The MiniDraw program
window

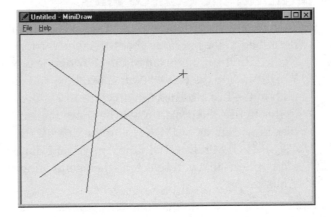

With this version of the program, all lines are erased whenever the window is redrawn (for example, when you change the window size or remove an overlapping window), or when you choose the New command on the File menu. In Chapter 11, you'll implement the basic features of the document class, which will *save* the data for each line that's drawn, allowing the program to re-create the lines whenever the window is redrawn. In later chapters, you'll add many other features to this program, such as commands for saving and loading drawings from disk, plus tools for drawing a variety of different shapes.

NOTE   Unlike the WinGreet program given in the previous chapter, MiniDraw *doesn't* implement the OnDraw function for redrawing the window, because it doesn't store the data that would be required to redraw the lines. The version of MiniDraw presented in Chapter 11, however, stores the data for the lines and implements an OnDraw function.

As with all the example programs given in this part of the book, either you can generate and modify the program source files yourself, following the step-by-step instructions given here (recommended), or you can simply load and examine the completed source files from the companion CD.

Generating the Source Files

To generate the program source files, use the AppWizard facility exactly as described in the previous chapter (in the section "1. Generating the Source Code"). In the Projects tab of the New dialog box, however, enter the name MiniDraw into the Project Name: text box, and specify the desired project folder path in the Location: text box. Figure 10.2 shows the completed Projects tab; in this figure, the project folder has been named MiniDrw1, and it has been placed within the \MMVC folder on drive C (that is, the project folder path is C:\MMVC\MiniDrw1). In the AppWizard dialog boxes, be sure to choose the *same* options that you selected when generating the WinGreet program in the previous chapter.

FIGURE 10.2:

The completed Projects tab of the New dialog box for generating the first version of the MiniDraw program

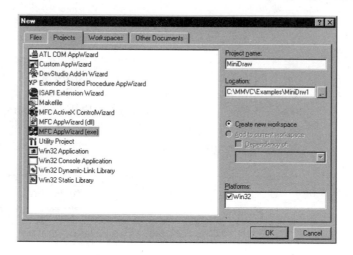

When AppWizard finishes generating the source files, it will display the names of these files within the FileView tab of the Workspace window, as shown in Figure 10.3 (in this figure, the hierarchical graph is fully expanded). Remember that if you quit the Developer Studio or close the MiniDraw project, you can later reopen the project, at any time you want to resume working on the program, by choosing the File ➢ Open Workspace… menu command and selecting the project workspace file, MiniDraw.dsw.

FIGURE 10.3:

The FileView graph displaying
the MiniDraw program
source files

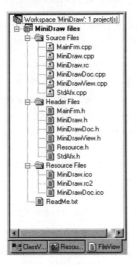

Defining and Initializing View Class Data Members

You first need to add several members to the view class: the data members
m_ClassName, m_Dragging, m_HCross, m_PointOld, and m_PointOrigin. To
do this, open the file MiniDraw.h, and add the statements marked in **bold** to
the beginning of the CMiniDrawView class definition:

```
class CMiniDrawView : public CView
{
protected:
    CString m_ClassName;
    int m_Dragging;
    HCURSOR m_HCross;
    CPoint m_PointOld;
    CPoint m_PointOrigin;

protected: // create from serialization only
    CMiniDrawView();
    DECLARE_DYNCREATE(CMiniDrawView)

// remainder of CMiniDrawView class definition ...
```

You'll see the purpose of these members in the discussions that follow.

Next, add initializations for the m_Dragging and m_HCross data members to the CMiniDrawView class constructor, which is in the file MiniDrawView.cpp:

```
//////////////////////////////////////////////////////////////////////
///////////
// CMiniDrawView construction/destruction

CMiniDrawView::CMiniDrawView()
{
   // TODO: add construction code here

   m_Dragging = 0;
   m_HCross = AfxGetApp ()->LoadStandardCursor (IDC_CROSS);
}
```

m_HCross stores a handle to the mouse cursor that the program displays when the cursor is within the view window. Calling AfxGetApp obtains a pointer to the program's application class object (the object of the class CMiniDrawApp, which is derived from CWinApp). This pointer is used to call the CWinApp member function LoadStandardCursor, which is passed the identifier IDC_CROSS so that it returns a handle to the standard cross-shaped mouse cursor. Later, you'll see how the MiniDraw program displays this cursor within the view window (in the section "The OnMouseMove Function"). Table 10.1 lists additional values that you can pass to LoadStandardCursor to obtain handles to other standard cursors. The table lists a typical use for some of the cursors; you can, however, use these cursors for other purposes.

TIP

As you edit the program source files and resources (resources are discussed later), you might want to periodically save your work. The easiest way to save all modifications you've made is to choose the File ➢ Save All menu command or click the Save All button on the Standard toolbar.

TABLE 10.1: Values Identifying Standard Windows Cursors, Which You Can Pass to the LoadStandardCursor Function

Value	Cursor
IDC_ARROW	Standard arrow cursor
IDC_CROSS	Crosshairs cursor, used for selecting
IDC_IBEAM	I-beam cursor, used within text
IDC_SIZEALL	Cursor consisting of a four-pointed arrow, used when resizing a window
IDC_SIZENESW	Two-headed arrow cursor, with ends pointing northeast and southwest
IDC_SIZENS	Two-headed arrow cursor, with ends pointing north and south
IDC_SIZENWSE	Two-headed arrow cursor, with ends pointing northwest and southeast
IDC_SIZEWE	Two-headed arrow cursor, with ends pointing west and east
IDC_UPARROW	Vertical arrow cursor
IDC_WAIT	Hourglass cursor, used when the program is performing a lengthy task

NOTE   AfxGetApp is a *global* MFC function—that is, one that's *not* a member of a class. The MFC provides a number of such global functions, which begin with the Afx prefix.

Adding Message-Handling Functions

To allow the user to draw lines within the view window with the mouse, the program must respond to mouse events that occur within this window. To process this mouse input, you must add member functions to the view class that handle the mouse *messages* sent to the view window. Before the chapter explains how to add the message-handling functions, however, the next section briefly introduces you to Windows messages.

Windows Messages

Every window in a Windows GUI program has a function associated with it known as a *window procedure*. When a significant event occurs that relates to the window, the operating system calls this function, passing it an identifier for the event that occurred, as well as any associated data required to handle the event. This process is known as *sending a message to the window*.

When you create and manage a window using an MFC class, the MFC provides the window procedure for you. (All the windows in the example programs given in this part of the book are managed by MFC classes.) The window procedure provided by the MFC performs minimal default handling for each type of message that can be sent. However, if you want to perform custom handling for a particular type of message, you can define a *message-handling function* that's a member of the class that manages the window. To define a message-handling function for a particular class, you can use the ClassWizard tool, as described shortly.

For example, when the user presses the left mouse button while the mouse cursor is within the view window, the view window receives a message that has the identifier WM_LBUTTONDOWN. To provide your own processing for this message, you can use the ClassWizard to create a member function of the program's view class that handles this message.

Command Messages   The MFC provides special handling for messages generated by *user-interface objects*. User-interface objects are standard interface elements that are supported by the MFC; they include menu commands, accelerator keystrokes, toolbar buttons, status bar indicators, and dialog bar controls. (The term *object* here doesn't refer to a C++ object. Menus are discussed in this chapter and in Chapter 11; other user-interface objects are discussed in Chapter 14.) The messages generated by user-interface objects are known as *command messages*. Whenever the user chooses a user-interface object, or whenever one of these objects needs updating, the object sends a command message to the main frame window. The MFC, however, immediately *reroutes* the message to the view object. If the view object doesn't provide a handler, the MFC reroutes the message to the document object. If the document object doesn't provide a handler, it reroutes the message to the main frame window object. If, in turn, the main frame window object doesn't provide a handler, it reroutes the message to the application object. Finally, if the application object doesn't provide a handler, the message receives minimal default processing.

Thus, the MFC *extends* the basic Windows message mechanism so that command messages can be processed not only by objects that manage windows, but also by any of the other main program objects (each of these objects belongs to a class derived—directly or indirectly—from the MFC class CCmdTarget, which provides support for the message mechanism).

The important feature of the MFC command message-routing mechanism is that the program can process a particular command message within the most appropriate class. For instance, in a program generated by AppWizard, the Exit command on the File menu is handled by the application class, because this command affects the application as a whole. In contrast, the Save command on the File menu is handled by the document class, because this class has the responsibility for storing and saving the document data. Later in the book, you'll learn how to add menu commands and other user-interface objects that generate commands, how to decide which class should handle a particular command, and how to provide the message-handling function for the command.

NOTE   For a much more detailed explanation of the MFC message-routing and -handling mechanism, see the following Visual C++ online help topic: *Visual C++ Documentation*, *Using Visual C++*, *Visual C++ Programmer's Guide*, *Adding Program Functionality*, *Details*, *Message Handling and Mapping Topics*.

The *OnLButtonDown* Function

The next task is to define a message-handling function that processes the WM_LBUTTONDOWN message. This message is sent whenever the user presses the left mouse button while the mouse cursor is within the view window. To define the function, perform the following steps:

1. Make sure that the MiniDraw project is open in the Developer Studio, and choose the View ➢ ClassWizard… menu command or press Ctrl+W. The ClassWizard dialog box will appear (labeled MFC ClassWizard).

2. In the ClassWizard dialog box, open (if necessary) the Message Maps tab, which allows you to define member functions.

3. Select the CMiniDrawView class in the Class Name: list. You choose this class name because you want to add the message-handling function to the view class.

4. Select the CMiniDrawView item in the Object IDs: list. Selecting the name of the class itself, CMiniDrawView, allows you to define a member function for handling any of the general notification messages sent to the view window. It also allows you to define a member function that overrides one of the virtual functions that CMiniDrawView inherits from CView and other MFC base classes. The other items in the Object IDs: list are identifiers for specific user-interface objects, such as menu commands. Choosing one of these items would allow you to provide a handler for a command message that originates from the object; you'll do this in Chapter 11.

5. In the Messages: list select WM_LBUTTONDOWN, which is the identifier of the message to be handled by the function you're defining. The Messages: list contains the identifier of each type of notification message that can be sent to the view window; the message identifiers are the items in all capital letters beginning with the characters WM_. You select a message identifier to define a function to handle the message. The Messages: list also contains the name of each of the virtual functions belonging to the CView class; you choose one of these to define an overriding version of the function (as you'll see in Chapter 11, in the section "Deleting the Document Data"). Notice that when you select a particular message identifier or virtual function, a brief description appears at the bottom of the ClassWizard dialog box.

6. Click the Add Function button. ClassWizard now generates the basic code for the message-handling member function, which is named OnLButtonDown. Specifically, ClassWizard adds the function declaration to the CMiniDrawView class definition within the file MiniDrawView.h, it inserts a minimal function definition into the MiniDrawView.cpp file, and it adds the function to the class message map (the message map is described in a sidebar given later in this section). Notice that the name of the message in the Messages: list is now displayed in bold to indicate that the message has a handler. Notice also that the name of the function and message are added to the Member Functions: list (in this list, an item marked with a "W" is a Windows message handler, and an item marked with a "V" is an overriding virtual function). The completed ClassWizard dialog box is shown in Figure 10.4.

FIGURE 10.4:

The completed ClassWizard dialog box for defining a WM_LBUTTONDOWN message handler

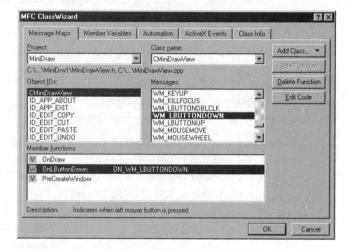

7. Click the Edit Code button. The ClassWizard dialog box will be removed. ClassWizard will open the file MiniDrawView.cpp (if it's not already open) and will display the OnLButtonDown function shell that it just generated. ClassWizard delivers you to this function so that you can add your own code.

8. Add the statements marked in bold to OnLButtonDown:

```
void CMiniDrawView::OnLButtonDown(UINT nFlags, CPoint point)
{
    // TODO: Add your message handler code here and/or call
    // default

    m_PointOrigin = point;
    m_PointOld = point;
    SetCapture ();
    m_Dragging = 1;

    RECT Rect;
    GetClientRect (&Rect);
    ClientToScreen (&Rect);
    ::ClipCursor (&Rect);

    CView::OnLButtonDown(nFlags, point);
}
```

An alternative way to use ClassWizard is through the WizardBar of the Developer Studio. If this toolbar isn't visible, you can display it by right-clicking on the menu bar or on any toolbar, and then choosing the WizardBar option on the menu that pops up. For information on using the WizardBar, see the following online help topic: *Visual C++ Documentation*, *Using Visual C++*, *Visual C++ User's Guide*, *Working with Classes*, *WizardBar*.

When the user presses the left mouse button while the cursor is over the view window, the OnLButtonDown function receives control, and the point parameter contains the current position of the mouse cursor. The code you added saves this position within the m_PointOrigin and m_PointOld data members. m_PointOrigin stores the coordinates of the point where the left button was pressed, which will be the origin of the line to be drawn. m_PointOld will be used by the other mouse message handlers to obtain the position of the mouse on the previous mouse message (as you'll see shortly).

ClassWizard adds a line of code to the OnLButtonDown function that calls the version of OnLButtonDown defined within the base class. This is routinely done so that the base class (or classes) can perform any required default message processing.

The call to the CWnd member function SetCapture *captures the mouse*, meaning that all subsequent mouse messages will be sent to the view window (until the capture is released, as explained later). Thus, the view window fully controls the mouse while the drag operation is taking place. Also, the data member m_Dragging is set to 1 to indicate to the other mouse message handlers that a drag operation is in progress.

Because CMiniDrawView is derived indirectly from the CWnd MFC class, it inherits all the many member functions of CWnd (CMiniDrawView is derived from CView, which in turn is derived from CWnd). To find out all the member functions available to a particular class, consult the class hierarchy given in the documentation on the class in the following online help topic: *Visual C++ Documentation*, *Reference*, *Microsoft Foundation Class Library and Templates*, *Microsoft Foundation Class Library*, *Class Library Reference*. Then view the documentation on each of the base classes—within the same online help topic—for a description of its member functions. When this book refers to a particular member function, it generally indicates the class in which the function is actually defined; for example, the SetCapture function is described either as "the CWnd member function SetCapture" or simply as "CWnd::SetCapture" (using the scope resolution operator to indicate the class containing the function definition).

The remaining lines of code serve to confine the mouse cursor within the view window, so that the user doesn't try to draw a line outside the boundaries of this window. The call to CWnd::GetClientRect obtains the current coordinates of the view window, and the call to CWnd::ClientToScreen converts these coordinates to *screen coordinates* (that is, coordinates with respect to the upper-left corner of the Windows screen). Finally, the call to ::ClipCursor confines the mouse cursor to the specified screen coordinates, thus keeping the cursor within the view window.

NOTE   ::ClipCursor is a function provided by the Win32 application programming interface (API), rather than by the MFC. Because it's defined as a global function, its name is prefaced with the scope resolution operator (::). Using the scope resolution operator in this way isn't actually necessary unless a global function name is hidden by a member function that has the same name. However, the book always prefaces the name of a Win32 API function with the scope resolution operator to clearly indicate that the function doesn't belong to the MFC.

The Message Map

When ClassWizard generates a message handler, in addition to declaring and defining the member function it also adds this function to an MFC contrivance known as a *message map*, which connects the function with the specific message it's intended to handle. The message map allows the MFC message mechanism to call the appropriate handler for each type of message.

The AppWizard and ClassWizard tools generate all the code necessary to implement the message map. The message map is based on a set of MFC macros. In the MiniDraw program, after you use ClassWizard to define handlers for all three mouse messages described in the chapter, the following message map macros and function declarations will be added to the **CMiniDrawView** class definition in MiniDrawView.h,

```
// Generated message map functions
protected:
    //{{AFX_MSG(CMiniDrawView)
    afx_msg void OnLButtonDown(UINT nFlags, CPoint point);
    afx_msg void OnMouseMove(UINT nFlags, CPoint point);
    afx_msg void OnLButtonUp(UINT nFlags, CPoint point);
    //}}AFX_MSG
DECLARE_MESSAGE_MAP()
```

Continued on next page

and the following corresponding macros will be added to the view implementation file, MiniDrawView.cpp:

```
BEGIN_MESSAGE_MAP(CMiniDrawView, CView)
    //{{AFX_MSG_MAP(CMiniDrawView)
    ON_WM_LBUTTONDOWN()
    ON_WM_MOUSEMOVE()
    ON_WM_LBUTTONUP()
    //}}AFX_MSG_MAP
END_MESSAGE_MAP()
```

When a message is sent to an object of a particular class, the MFC code consults the message map to determine whether the class has a handler for that message. If a handler is found, it receives control; if no handler is found, the MFC looks for a handler in the immediate base class. If it doesn't find a handler in the immediate base class, the MFC continues to search up through the class hierarchy, calling the *first* handler that it finds. If it doesn't find a handler in the hierarchy, it provides minimal default processing for the message (or, if it's a command message, it reroutes the message to the next target object in the sequence described previously).

Note that some of the MFC classes from which you derive your program classes include message handlers; therefore, even if your derived class doesn't define a handler for a particular message, a base class handler might provide appropriate processing for the message. For example, the base class for your document class, **CDocument**, provides handlers for the messages sent when the user chooses the Save, Save As..., and Close commands on the File menu (the handlers are named `OnFileSave`, `OnFileSaveAs`, and `OnFileClose`).

The *OnMouseMove* Function

Next, you'll define a function to handle the WM_MOUSEMOVE message. As the user moves the mouse cursor within the view window, this window receives a series of WM_MOUSEMOVE messages, each of which reports the current position of the cursor. To define a handler for this message, first use ClassWizard to generate the message-handling function shell. Follow the numbered steps given in the previous section; in step 5, however, choose the WM_MOUSEMOVE message in the Messages: list rather than the WM_LBUTTONDOWN message. ClassWizard will generate a member function named OnMouseMove. The completed ClassWizard dialog box (just before you click the Edit Code button) is shown in Figure 10.5.

FIGURE 10.5:

The completed ClassWizard dialog box for generating a WM_MOUSEMOVE message handler

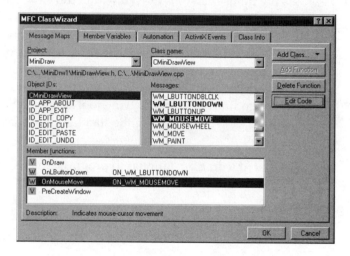

After you click the Edit Code button, enter the bold lines into the OnMouseMove function:

```
void CMiniDrawView::OnMouseMove(UINT nFlags, CPoint point)
{
   // TODO: Add your message handler code here and/or call
   // default

   ::SetCursor (m_HCross);

   if (m_Dragging)
      {
      CClientDC ClientDC (this);
      ClientDC.SetROP2 (R2_NOT);
      ClientDC.MoveTo (m_PointOrigin);
      ClientDC.LineTo (m_PointOld);
      ClientDC.MoveTo (m_PointOrigin);
      ClientDC.LineTo (point);
      m_PointOld = point;
      }

   CView::OnMouseMove(nFlags, point);
}
```

As the mouse cursor is moved within the view window, the OnMouseMove function is called at frequent intervals. The code that you added performs two main tasks. First, it calls the ::SetCursor Win32 API function to display a cross-shaped cursor rather than the standard arrow cursor. (Recall that the handle to the cross-shaped cursor was obtained by the class constructor.) Note that later versions of the MiniDraw program will display one of a variety of different cursors, depending on which drawing tool is active. (See the sidebar in this section for information on displaying the standard hourglass cursor during a lengthy operation.)

Second, if a drag operation is in progress (that is, if m_Dragging is nonzero), the code you added performs the following steps:

1. It erases the line that was drawn on the previous WM_MOUSEMOVE message (if any).

2. It draws a new line from the origin of the line (that is, the point where the left button was pressed, stored in m_PointOrigin) to the current position of the cursor (point).

3. It stores the current position of the cursor in the data member m_PointOld.

To draw within the window, OnMouseMove first creates a device context object associated with the view window. (Device context objects were introduced in Chapter 9. A device context object belonging to the MFC CClientDC class allows you to draw within the view window from a function *other* than OnDraw.) It then calls the CDC::SetROP2 function to create a drawing mode in which lines are drawn by *inverting* (reversing) the current color on the screen. Under this mode, when a line is first drawn at a particular position, it's visible; however, when a line is drawn a second time at the same position, it becomes invisible. The mouse message handlers are thus able to easily draw and erase a series of temporary lines. The lines are drawn using the CDC::MoveTo function (which specifies the position of one end of the line) and the CDC::LineTo function (which specifies the position of the other end). Device context objects are explained in Chapter 18, while the SetROP2, MoveTo, and LineTo CDC member functions are described in Chapter 19.

The overall result of the OnMouseMove function is that as the user drags the mouse cursor within the view window, a temporary line always connects the origin of the line with the current cursor position. (This line shows where the permanent line would be drawn if the user released the mouse button.)

Displaying the Hourglass

If your program performs a lengthy task (such as reading a file or drawing complex graphics), it should temporarily display the standard hourglass cursor to notify the user of the pause in normal processing. (An alternative is to perform the lengthy task using a separate thread, as explained in Chapter 22, so that normal message processing isn't interrupted.) To do this, you can call the CCmdTarget::BeginWaitCursor function immediately before beginning the lengthy process and then call CCmdTarget::EndWaitCursor after the lengthy process. You can call these two functions from any of the main program classes (that is, the document, view, main frame window, or application class), because all these classes are derived indirectly from CCmdTarget. The following is an example:

```
CCmdTarget::BeginWaitCursor ();  // display hourglass cursor

::Sleep (5000);  // pause for 5 seconds to simulate a lengthy
                 // process

EndWaitCursor ();  // restore former cursor
```

This example assumes that the code is contained within a member function of a class derived directly or indirectly from CCmdTarget (if it isn't, you could create a CCmdTarget object to use to call the functions). The example calls the Win32 API function ::Sleep to pause for five seconds, simulating a lengthy process.

The *OnLButtonUp* Function

Finally, you need to define a function to handle the WM_LBUTTONUP message, which is sent when the user releases the left mouse button. Use ClassWizard to create the basic function code in the same way you used it for the previous two messages; in the ClassWizard dialog box, however, choose the WM_LBUTTONUP identifier in the Messages: list. When the function has been generated, add code as follows to the OnLButtonUp definition in MiniDraw.cpp:

```
void CMiniDrawView::OnLButtonUp(UINT nFlags, CPoint point)
{
    // TODO: Add your message handler code here and/or call
    // default

    if (m_Dragging)
        {
        m_Dragging = 0;
```

```
    ::ReleaseCapture ();
    ::ClipCursor (NULL);
    CClientDC ClientDC (this);
    ClientDC.SetROP2 (R2_NOT);
    ClientDC.MoveTo (m_PointOrigin);
    ClientDC.LineTo (m_PointOld);
    ClientDC.SetROP2 (R2_COPYPEN);
    ClientDC.MoveTo (m_PointOrigin);
    ClientDC.LineTo (point);
    }

  CView::OnLButtonUp(nFlags, point);
}
```

If the user was dragging the mouse cursor (that is, m_Dragging is nonzero), the code that you added terminates the drag operation and draws a permanent line. Specifically, it performs the following steps:

1. It assigns 0 to m_Dragging to signal the other mouse message handlers that a drag operation is no longer in progress.

2. It calls the Win32 API function ::ReleaseCapture to end the mouse capture; as a result, mouse messages will again be sent to any window that lies under the cursor.

3. It passes NULL to the Win32 API function ::ClipCursor so that the user can again move the mouse cursor anywhere on the screen.

4. It erases the temporary line drawn by the previous WM_MOUSEMOVE message handler.

5. It draws a permanent line from the line origin to the current position of the cursor.

WM_LBUTTONDOWN is the final mouse message that you need to handle in the MiniDraw program. Table 10.2 provides a complete list of mouse notification messages. You might want to provide handlers for some of these messages in your other Windows programs.

TABLE 10.2: Mouse Notification Messages

Message	Mouse Event
WM_MOUSEMOVE	The user moved the mouse cursor to a new position within the client area.
WM_MOUSEWHEEL	The user rolled the wheel on a mouse with a wheel.
WM_LBUTTONDOWN	The user pressed the left button.
WM_RBUTTONDOWN	The user pressed the right button.
WM_LBUTTONUP	The user released the left button.
WM_RBUTTONUP	The user released the right button.
WM_LBUTTONDBLCLK	The user double-clicked the left button.
WM_RBUTTONDBLCLK	The user double-clicked the right button.

Mouse Message Parameters

The handlers for all mouse messages are passed two parameters: nFlags and point.

The nFlags parameter indicates the status of the mouse buttons, as well as the status of several keys on the keyboard, at the time the mouse event occurred. The status of each button or key is represented by a specific bit within nFlags. You can use the bit masks given in Table 10.3 to access the individual bits.

For example, the following code tests whether the Shift key was down when the mouse was moved:

```
void CMinidrawView::OnMouseMove(UINT nFlags, CPoint point)
{
    if (nFlags & MK_SHIFT)
        // then Shift key was pressed when mouse was moved
```

The parameter point is a CPoint structure that supplies the coordinates of the mouse cursor at the time the mouse event occurred. The x data member (point.x) contains the horizontal coordinate of the cursor, and the y data member (point.y) contains the vertical coordinate. The coordinates specify the position of the cursor with respect to the upper-left corner of the view window.

Continued on next page

Stated more accurately, the `point` parameter supplies the coordinates of the *hot spot* within the mouse cursor. The hot spot is a single pixel within the cursor, which is designated when the cursor is designed. The hot spot for the standard arrow cursor is at the tip of the arrow, and the hot spot for the standard cross-shaped cursor is at the point where the lines intersect.

TABLE 10.3: Bit Masks for Accessing the Bits in the **Nflags** Parameter Passed to Mouse Message Handlers

Bit Mask	Meaning of Bit
MK_CONTROL	Set if Ctrl key was down.
MK_LBUTTON	Set if left mouse button was down.
MK_MBUTTON	Set if middle mouse button was down.
MK_RBUTTON	Set if right mouse button was down.
MK_SHIFT	Set if Shift key was down.

Designing the Program Resources

In this section, you'll learn how to use the Developer Studio to customize the MiniDraw program resources—specifically, the menu and the program icon. To edit the MiniDraw resources, open the ResourceView tab in the Workspace window and expand the graph to display the names of each category of program resource (Accelerator, Dialog, Icon, Menu, String Table, and Version). The ResourceView tab, with the graph fully expanded, is shown in Figure 10.6.

To customize the MiniDraw menu, do the following:

1. Double-click the IDR_MAINFRAME identifier under the Menu branch of the ResourceView graph:

(Notice that the same identifier, IDR_MAINFRAME, is also used for the program's accelerator table and main icon.) The Developer Studio will now open the menu editor window, which displays a visual representation of the MiniDraw program menu as it was created by AppWizard. This window is shown in Figure 10.7.

FIGURE 10.6:

The ResourceView graph for the MiniDraw program

FIGURE 10.7:

The menu editor window displaying the initial MiniDraw menu

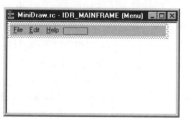

2. In the menu editor window, click on the File menu to open the pop-up menu, and delete all the items on the menu except the New command, the Exit command, and the separator between these two commands. To delete a menu item (a command or separator), simply click on the item and press the Del key. (You don't need to delete the empty box at the bottom of the menu; this is an area for you to add a new menu item, and it won't appear on the final program menu.) The completed File menu is shown in Figure 10.8.

FIGURE 10.8:

The MiniDraw menu after editing the File pop-up menu, displayed in the menu editor window

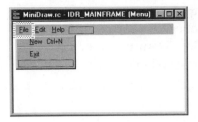

3. Click on the Edit menu and press Del to delete the entire Edit pop-up menu. Then Click OK when Visual C++ asks if you want to delete the entire menu.

4. You've now deleted all unused menu items. Remove the menu editor window by double-clicking its system menu or by clicking its Close box.

Next, if you want to design a custom program icon for the MiniDraw program (to replace the standard MFC icon), do the following:

1. Double-click the IDR_MAINFRAME identifier under the Icon branch of the ResourceView graph within the Workspace window:

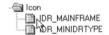

The Developer Studio will now open the graphics editor window, displaying the current program icon. Note that the icon file contains *two* versions of the icon image: a large image (32 pixels by 32 pixels) and a small image (16 pixels by 16 pixels). The small image is used where the program's "small icon" is displayed (for example, in the program's title bar or in the Explorer if the user has chosen the View ➢ Small Icons menu option). The large image is used where the program's "large icon" is displayed (for example, in the program's About dialog box or in the Explorer if the user has chosen the View ➢ Large Icons menu option).

2. To edit the large version of the icon, select the "Standard (32x32)" item in the Device: list at the top of the graphics editor window. To delete the current icon so that you can design a completely new one, just press the Del key. (For information on using the commands and tools provided by the graphics editor, see the following online help topic: *Visual C++ Documentation, Using Visual C++, Visual C++ User's Guide, Resource Editors, Graphics*

Editor.) Figure 10.9 shows the graphics editor displaying the large icon provided with the MiniDraw source files on the companion CD.

3. Display the small version of the icon by selecting the "Small (16x16)" item in the Device: list. If you wish, you can edit this image. Alternatively, you can simply delete it by choosing the Image ≻ Delete Device Image menu command. If the program doesn't include a small version of its icon, Windows will compress the large icon image as necessary (with some loss of image quality) whenever the "small icon" is displayed.

4. When you've finished editing the icon, remove the graphic-editor window by double-clicking its system menu or by clicking its Close box.

FIGURE 10.9:

The graphics editor displaying the MiniDraw icon provided on the companion CD

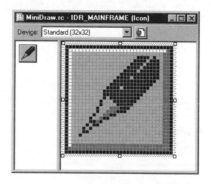

After you've made all desired changes to the program resources, save all your modifications by choosing the File ≻ Save All menu command or clicking the Save All button on the Standard toolbar. Visual C++ saves the primary resource information in the MiniDraw resource definition file, MiniDraw.rc, and it saves the icon data in the file MiniDraw.ico (which is a binary file stored in the \res subfolder of the project folder; the resource definition file contains an ICON statement that identifies this icon file). When the program is built, the Microsoft Resource Compiler program (Rc.exe) processes the resource information in these files and adds the resource data to the executable program file.

Customizing the MiniDraw Window

There are two problems with the MiniDraw program as it's currently written. First, though the WM_MOUSEMOVE message handler that you wrote displays the desired cross-shaped cursor, Windows *also* attempts to display a standard arrow cursor, because an arrow cursor is assigned to the view window when it's created by the MFC code. As a result, the cursor flickers annoyingly back and forth between these two shapes as the user moves it within the view window.

The second problem is that if the user chooses a dark "Window" color through the Windows Control Panel, the lines drawn in the view window will be invisible or at least difficult to see. When the MFC code creates the window, it assigns it a setting that causes the background to be painted using the current "Window" color set through the Control Panel. The program, however, always draws the lines in black.

You can solve both of these problems by adding code to the `CMiniDrawView` member function `PreCreateWindow`. When you generated the program, App-Wizard defined a basic function shell for `CMiniDrawView::PreCreateWindow`. This function overrides the `CView` virtual member function `PreCreateWindow`, and the MFC code calls it immediately before creating the view window.

NOTE   Because `CView::PreCreateWindow` is an important virtual function, AppWizard automatically generates an overriding version of the function in the program's view class. In Chapter 11 (in the section "Deleting the Document Data") you'll learn how to use ClassWizard to generate an overriding version of *any* of the MFC virtual functions.

To customize the MiniDraw view window, add the statements marked in bold to `PreCreateWindow` in the file MiniDrawView.cpp:

```
BOOL CMiniDrawView::PreCreateWindow(CREATESTRUCT& cs)
{
    // TODO: Modify the Window class or styles here by modifying
    //  the CREATESTRUCT cs

    m_ClassName = AfxRegisterWndClass
        (CS_HREDRAW | CS_VREDRAW,                     // class styles
        0,                                            // no cursor
        (HBRUSH)::GetStockObject (WHITE_BRUSH),       // assign white
                                                      // background brush
        0);                                           // no icon
    cs.lpszClass = m_ClassName;

    return CView::PreCreateWindow(cs);
}
```

PreCreateWindow is passed a reference to a CREATESTRUCT structure; the fields of this structure store the window features that the MFC will specify when it creates the window, such as the window coordinates, the window styles, and so on. If you assign values to one or more of the fields of this structure, the MFC will use your values rather than its default ones.

One of the CREATESTRUCT fields (lpszClass) stores the name of the *Windows window class*. The Windows window class is *not* a C++ class; rather, it's a data structure maintained by the Windows system, which stores a set of general features used when the window is created. The code you just added calls AfxRegisterWndClass to create a new Windows window class, and then assigns the class name to the lpszClass CREATESTRUCT field, so that the view window will be created using the custom features stored within this Windows window class. (Note that Afx-RegisterWndClass is a global function provided by the MFC.)

The call to AfxRegisterWndClass specifies the following features:

- The first parameter specifies the class styles CS_HREDRAW and CS_VREDRAW. These styles cause the window to be redrawn whenever the user changes the size of the window (MFC view windows are normally created with these two styles).

- The second parameter specifies the mouse cursor that Windows will automatically display within the window. This parameter is assigned 0 so that Windows *won't* attempt to display a cursor, because a cursor is explicitly displayed by the OnMouseMove function that you added. Thus, the flicker is eliminated.

- The third parameter supplies a standard white brush that will be used for painting the view window background (brushes are discussed in Chapter 19). As a result, the window background will always be white—and the black lines will always be visible—regardless of the "Window" color that the user has selected in the Control Panel.

- The last parameter specifies the window icon. Because the view window doesn't display an icon, it's assigned 0 (the program icon is assigned to the main frame window).

NOTE   The MiniDraw program displays a custom cursor by assigning *no* cursor to the window class and then displaying the desired cursor from the `OnMouseMove` message-handling function. As an alternative method, you can simply assign the desired cursor to the window by passing its handle as the second parameter to `AfxRegisterWndClass`. This alternative method, however, doesn't allow you to easily *change* cursors as the program runs. (Later versions of the MiniDraw program will change the cursor each time the user selects a new drawing tool.)

This section described the last of the changes to be made to the MiniDraw program. You can now build and run the program.

Wizard Code

In a previous sidebar ("The Message Map") you saw the code that AppWizard and Class-Wizard generated for defining the view class message map. The Wizards also generated the following code in the `CMiniDrawView` class definition in MiniDrawView.h:

```
// Overrides
    // ClassWizard generated virtual function overrides
    //{{AFX_VIRTUAL(CMiniDrawView)
    public:
    virtual void OnDraw(CDC* pDC);  // overridden to draw this view
    virtual BOOL PreCreateWindow(CREATESTRUCT& cs);
    protected:
    //}}AFX_VIRTUAL
```

This code declares the two virtual functions `OnDraw` and `PreCreateWindow` that were generated by AppWizard. Notice that the block of code for defining the message map as well as the block of code for declaring the virtual functions are surrounded by special comment lines that begin with the characters

```
//{{AFX_
```

(Later in the book, you'll see several other types of code that the Wizards place within similar comment lines.) You should never directly edit (that is, add, delete, or modify) code that is bracketed by comment lines beginning with these characters. Rather, you should make any desired changes by using ClassWizard.

Conversely, though ClassWizard may *add* code to your program outside the special comment lines (for example, definitions of member functions), it will never *delete* code that's outside the special comment lines. ClassWizard will never delete such code, because you may have modified it or added statements of your own.

Continued on next page

If you want to delete a message-handling or virtual function generated by a Wizard, you should open the ClassWizard dialog box and open the Message Maps tab. Then, select the function name in the Member Functions: list and click the Delete Function button. ClassWizard will remove the declaration and macro (if any) from the special comment-delimited section or sections of code, but it *won't* delete the function definition because it's not within a special comment-delimited section. You must delete the function definition by hand.

The MiniDraw Program Source Code

The C++ source code for the MiniDraw program is given in the following listings, Listing 10.1 through 10.8. These listings contain the code that was generated by AppWizard, plus the manual code additions described previously in the chapter. If you followed the exercises given in this section, the files you created should be the same as these listings; a complete copy of these files is also included in the \MiniDrw1 companion-CD folder.

Listing 10.1

```
// MiniDraw.h : main header file for the MINIDRAW application
//

#if !defined(AFX_MINIDRAW_H__11E83924_999A_11D1_80FC_00C0F6A83B7F__INCLUDED_)
#define AFX_MINIDRAW_H__11E83924_999A_11D1_80FC_00C0F6A83B7F__INCLUDED_

#if _MSC_VER > 1000
#pragma once
#endif // _MSC_VER > 1000

#ifndef __AFXWIN_H__
    #error include 'stdafx.h' before including this file for PCH
#endif

#include "resource.h"        // main symbols

/////////////////////////////////////////////////////////////////////////////
// CMiniDrawApp:
// See MiniDraw.cpp for the implementation of this class
//

class CMiniDrawApp : public CWinApp
```

```
{
public:
    CMiniDrawApp();

// Overrides
    // ClassWizard generated virtual function overrides
    //{{AFX_VIRTUAL(CMiniDrawApp)
    public:
    virtual BOOL InitInstance();
    //}}AFX_VIRTUAL

// Implementation

    //{{AFX_MSG(CMiniDrawApp)
    afx_msg void OnAppAbout();
        // NOTE - the ClassWizard will add and remove member functions here.
        //      DO NOT EDIT what you see in these blocks of generated code !
    //}}AFX_MSG
    DECLARE_MESSAGE_MAP()
};


/////////////////////////////////////////////////////////////////////////////

//{{AFX_INSERT_LOCATION}}
// Microsoft Visual C++ will insert additional declarations immediately before
// the previous line.

#endif
// !defined(AFX_MINIDRAW_H__11E83924_999A_11D1_80FC_00C0F6A83B7F__INCLUDED_)
```

Listing 10.2

```
// MiniDraw.cpp : Defines the class behaviors for the application.
//

#include "stdafx.h"
#include "MiniDraw.h"

#include "MainFrm.h"
#include "MiniDrawDoc.h"
#include "MiniDrawView.h"
```

```
#ifdef _DEBUG
#define new DEBUG_NEW
#undef THIS_FILE
static char THIS_FILE[] = __FILE__;
#endif

/////////////////////////////////////////////////////////////////////////////
// CMiniDrawApp

BEGIN_MESSAGE_MAP(CMiniDrawApp, CWinApp)
    //{{AFX_MSG_MAP(CMiniDrawApp)
    ON_COMMAND(ID_APP_ABOUT, OnAppAbout)
        // NOTE - the ClassWizard will add and remove mapping macros here.
        //    DO NOT EDIT what you see in these blocks of generated code!
    //}}AFX_MSG_MAP
    // Standard file based document commands
    ON_COMMAND(ID_FILE_NEW, CWinApp::OnFileNew)
    ON_COMMAND(ID_FILE_OPEN, CWinApp::OnFileOpen)
END_MESSAGE_MAP()

/////////////////////////////////////////////////////////////////////////////
// CMiniDrawApp construction

CMiniDrawApp::CMiniDrawApp()
{
    // TODO: add construction code here,
    // Place all significant initialization in InitInstance
}

/////////////////////////////////////////////////////////////////////////////
// The one and only CMiniDrawApp object

CMiniDrawApp theApp;

/////////////////////////////////////////////////////////////////////////////
// CMiniDrawApp initialization

BOOL CMiniDrawApp::InitInstance()
{
    // Standard initialization
    // If you are not using these features and wish to reduce the size
    //  of your final executable, you should remove from the following
```

```
        //  the specific initialization routines you do not need.

#ifdef _AFXDLL
    Enable3dControls();         // Call this when using MFC in a shared DLL
#else
    Enable3dControlsStatic();   // Call this when linking to MFC statically
#endif

    // Change the registry key under which our settings are stored.
    // You should modify this string to be something appropriate
    // such as the name of your company or organization.
    SetRegistryKey(_T("Local AppWizard-Generated Applications"));

    LoadStdProfileSettings();  // Load standard INI file options (including MRU)

    // Register the application's document templates.  Document templates
    //  serve as the connection between documents, frame windows and views.

    CSingleDocTemplate* pDocTemplate;
    pDocTemplate = new CSingleDocTemplate(
        IDR_MAINFRAME,
        RUNTIME_CLASS(CMiniDrawDoc),
        RUNTIME_CLASS(CMainFrame),       // main SDI frame window
        RUNTIME_CLASS(CMiniDrawView));
    AddDocTemplate(pDocTemplate);

    // Parse command line for standard shell commands, DDE, file open
    CCommandLineInfo cmdInfo;
    ParseCommandLine(cmdInfo);

    // Dispatch commands specified on the command line
    if (!ProcessShellCommand(cmdInfo))
        return FALSE;

    // The one and only window has been initialized, so show and update it.
    m_pMainWnd->ShowWindow(SW_SHOW);
    m_pMainWnd->UpdateWindow();

    return TRUE;
}
```

```
///////////////////////////////////////////////////////////////////////
// CAboutDlg dialog used for App About

class CAboutDlg : public CDialog
{
public:
   CAboutDlg();

// Dialog Data
   //{{AFX_DATA(CAboutDlg)
   enum { IDD = IDD_ABOUTBOX };
   //}}AFX_DATA

   // ClassWizard generated virtual function overrides
   //{{AFX_VIRTUAL(CAboutDlg)
   protected:
   virtual void DoDataExchange(CDataExchange* pDX);    // DDX/DDV support
   //}}AFX_VIRTUAL

// Implementation
protected:
   //{{AFX_MSG(CAboutDlg)
      // No message handlers
   //}}AFX_MSG
   DECLARE_MESSAGE_MAP()
};

CAboutDlg::CAboutDlg() : CDialog(CAboutDlg::IDD)
{
   //{{AFX_DATA_INIT(CAboutDlg)
   //}}AFX_DATA_INIT
}

void CAboutDlg::DoDataExchange(CDataExchange* pDX)
{
   CDialog::DoDataExchange(pDX);
   //{{AFX_DATA_MAP(CAboutDlg)
   //}}AFX_DATA_MAP
}

BEGIN_MESSAGE_MAP(CAboutDlg, CDialog)
   //{{AFX_MSG_MAP(CAboutDlg)
```

```
       // No message handlers
   //}}AFX_MSG_MAP
END_MESSAGE_MAP()

// App command to run the dialog
void CMiniDrawApp::OnAppAbout()
{
    CAboutDlg aboutDlg;
    aboutDlg.DoModal();
}


/////////////////////////////////////////////////////////////////////////
// CMiniDrawApp commands
```

Listing 10.3

```
// MiniDrawDoc.h : interface of the CMiniDrawDoc class
//
/////////////////////////////////////////////////////////////////////////

#if !defined(AFX_MINIDRAWDOC_H__11E8392A_999A_11D1_80FC_00C0F6A83B7F__INCLUDED_)
#define AFX_MINIDRAWDOC_H__11E8392A_999A_11D1_80FC_00C0F6A83B7F__INCLUDED_

#if _MSC_VER > 1000
#pragma once
#endif // _MSC_VER > 1000


class CMiniDrawDoc : public CDocument
{
protected: // create from serialization only
   CMiniDrawDoc();
   DECLARE_DYNCREATE(CMiniDrawDoc)

// Attributes
public:

// Operations
public:

// Overrides
```

```
    // ClassWizard generated virtual function overrides
    //{{AFX_VIRTUAL(CMiniDrawDoc)
    public:
    virtual BOOL OnNewDocument();
    virtual void Serialize(CArchive& ar);
    //}}AFX_VIRTUAL

// Implementation
public:
    virtual ~CMiniDrawDoc();
#ifdef _DEBUG
    virtual void AssertValid() const;
    virtual void Dump(CDumpContext& dc) const;
#endif

protected:

// Generated message map functions
protected:
    //{{AFX_MSG(CMiniDrawDoc)
        // NOTE - the ClassWizard will add and remove member functions here.
        //      DO NOT EDIT what you see in these blocks of generated code !
    //}}AFX_MSG
    DECLARE_MESSAGE_MAP()
};

/////////////////////////////////////////////////////////////////////////

//{{AFX_INSERT_LOCATION}}
// Microsoft Visual C++ will insert additional declarations immediately before
// the previous line.

#endif
// !defined(AFX_MINIDRAWDOC_H__11E8392A_999A_11D1_80FC_00C0F6A83B7F__INCLUDED_)
```

Listing 10.4

```
// MiniDrawDoc.cpp : implementation of the CMiniDrawDoc class
//

#include "stdafx.h"
#include "MiniDraw.h"
```

```
#include "MiniDrawDoc.h"

#ifdef _DEBUG
#define new DEBUG_NEW
#undef THIS_FILE
static char THIS_FILE[] = __FILE__;
#endif

/////////////////////////////////////////////////////////////////////////
// CMiniDrawDoc

IMPLEMENT_DYNCREATE(CMiniDrawDoc, CDocument)

BEGIN_MESSAGE_MAP(CMiniDrawDoc, CDocument)
    //{{AFX_MSG_MAP(CMiniDrawDoc)
        // NOTE - the ClassWizard will add and remove mapping macros here.
        //     DO NOT EDIT what you see in these blocks of generated code!
    //}}AFX_MSG_MAP
END_MESSAGE_MAP()

/////////////////////////////////////////////////////////////////////////
// CMiniDrawDoc construction/destruction

CMiniDrawDoc::CMiniDrawDoc()
{
    // TODO: add one-time construction code here

}

CMiniDrawDoc::~CMiniDrawDoc()
{
}

BOOL CMiniDrawDoc::OnNewDocument()
{
    if (!CDocument::OnNewDocument())
        return FALSE;

    // TODO: add reinitialization code here
    // (SDI documents will reuse this document)

    return TRUE;
}
```

```
////////////////////////////////////////////////////////////////////
// CMiniDrawDoc serialization

void CMiniDrawDoc::Serialize(CArchive& ar)
{
    if (ar.IsStoring())
    {
        // TODO: add storing code here
    }
    else
    {
        // TODO: add loading code here
    }
}


////////////////////////////////////////////////////////////////////
// CMiniDrawDoc diagnostics

#ifdef _DEBUG
void CMiniDrawDoc::AssertValid() const
{
    CDocument::AssertValid();
}

void CMiniDrawDoc::Dump(CDumpContext& dc) const
{
    CDocument::Dump(dc);
}
#endif //_DEBUG


////////////////////////////////////////////////////////////////////
// CMiniDrawDoc commands
```

Listing 10.5

```
// MainFrm.h : interface of the CMainFrame class
//
////////////////////////////////////////////////////////////////////

#if !defined(AFX_MAINFRM_H__11E83928_999A_11D1_80FC_00C0F6A83B7F__INCLUDED_)
#define AFX_MAINFRM_H__11E83928_999A_11D1_80FC_00C0F6A83B7F__INCLUDED_
```

```
#if _MSC_VER > 1000
#pragma once
#endif // _MSC_VER > 1000

class CMainFrame : public CFrameWnd
{
protected: // create from serialization only
   CMainFrame();
   DECLARE_DYNCREATE(CMainFrame)

// Attributes
public:

// Operations
public:

// Overrides
   // ClassWizard generated virtual function overrides
   //{{AFX_VIRTUAL(CMainFrame)
   virtual BOOL PreCreateWindow(CREATESTRUCT& cs);
   //}}AFX_VIRTUAL

// Implementation
public:
   virtual ~CMainFrame();
#ifdef _DEBUG
   virtual void AssertValid() const;
   virtual void Dump(CDumpContext& dc) const;
#endif

// Generated message map functions
protected:
   //{{AFX_MSG(CMainFrame)
      // NOTE - the ClassWizard will add and remove member functions here.
      //     DO NOT EDIT what you see in these blocks of generated code!
   //}}AFX_MSG
   DECLARE_MESSAGE_MAP()
};

//////////////////////////////////////////////////////////////////////

//{{AFX_INSERT_LOCATION}}
// Microsoft Visual C++ will insert additional declarations immediately before
```

```
// the previous line.

#endif
// !defined(AFX_MAINFRM_H__11E83928_999A_11D1_80FC_00C0F6A83B7F__INCLUDED_)
```

Listing 10.6

```
// MainFrm.cpp : implementation of the CMainFrame class
//

#include "stdafx.h"
#include "MiniDraw.h"

#include "MainFrm.h"

#ifdef _DEBUG
#define new DEBUG_NEW
#undef THIS_FILE
static char THIS_FILE[] = __FILE__;
#endif

/////////////////////////////////////////////////////////////////////
// CMainFrame

IMPLEMENT_DYNCREATE(CMainFrame, CFrameWnd)

BEGIN_MESSAGE_MAP(CMainFrame, CFrameWnd)
    //{{AFX_MSG_MAP(CMainFrame)
        // NOTE - the ClassWizard will add and remove mapping macros here.
        //    DO NOT EDIT what you see in these blocks of generated code !
    //}}AFX_MSG_MAP
END_MESSAGE_MAP()

/////////////////////////////////////////////////////////////////////
// CMainFrame construction/destruction

CMainFrame::CMainFrame()
{
    // TODO: add member initialization code here

}

CMainFrame::~CMainFrame()
```

```
{
}

BOOL CMainFrame::PreCreateWindow(CREATESTRUCT& cs)
{
    if( !CFrameWnd::PreCreateWindow(cs) )
        return FALSE;
    // TODO: Modify the Window class or styles here by modifying
    //   the CREATESTRUCT cs

    return TRUE;
}

/////////////////////////////////////////////////////////////////////////////
// CMainFrame diagnostics

#ifdef _DEBUG
void CMainFrame::AssertValid() const
{
    CFrameWnd::AssertValid();
}

void CMainFrame::Dump(CDumpContext& dc) const
{
    CFrameWnd::Dump(dc);
}

#endif //_DEBUG


/////////////////////////////////////////////////////////////////////////////
// CMainFrame message handlers
```

Listing 10.7

```
// MiniDrawView.h : interface of the CMiniDrawView class
//
/////////////////////////////////////////////////////////////////////////////

#if !defined(AFX_MINIDRAWVIEW_H__11E8392C_999A_11D1_80FC_00C0F6A83B7F__INCLUDED_)
#define AFX_MINIDRAWVIEW_H__11E8392C_999A_11D1_80FC_00C0F6A83B7F__INCLUDED_

#if _MSC_VER > 1000
```

```
#pragma once
#endif // _MSC_VER > 1000

class CMiniDrawView : public CView
{
protected:
    CString m_ClassName;
    int m_Dragging;
    HCURSOR m_HCross;
    CPoint m_PointOld;
    CPoint m_PointOrigin;

protected: // create from serialization only
    CMiniDrawView();
    DECLARE_DYNCREATE(CMiniDrawView)

// Attributes
public:
    CMiniDrawDoc* GetDocument();

// Operations
public:

// Overrides
    // ClassWizard generated virtual function overrides
    //{{AFX_VIRTUAL(CMiniDrawView)
    public:
    virtual void OnDraw(CDC* pDC);   // overridden to draw this view
    virtual BOOL PreCreateWindow(CREATESTRUCT& cs);
    protected:
    //}}AFX_VIRTUAL

// Implementation
public:
    virtual ~CMiniDrawView();
#ifdef _DEBUG
    virtual void AssertValid() const;
    virtual void Dump(CDumpContext& dc) const;
#endif

protected:
```

```
// Generated message map functions
protected:
    //{{AFX_MSG(CMiniDrawView)
    afx_msg void OnLButtonDown(UINT nFlags, CPoint point);
    afx_msg void OnMouseMove(UINT nFlags, CPoint point);
    afx_msg void OnLButtonUp(UINT nFlags, CPoint point);
    //}}AFX_MSG
    DECLARE_MESSAGE_MAP()
};

#ifndef _DEBUG  // debug version in MiniDrawView.cpp
inline CMiniDrawDoc* CMiniDrawView::GetDocument()
    { return (CMiniDrawDoc*)m_pDocument; }
#endif


/////////////////////////////////////////////////////////////////////////

//{{AFX_INSERT_LOCATION}}
// Microsoft Visual C++ will insert additional declarations immediately before
// the previous line.

#endif
// !defined(AFX_MINIDRAWVIEW_H__11E8392C_999A_11D1_80FC_00C0F6A83B7F__INCLUDED_)
```

Listing 10.8

```
// MiniDrawView.cpp : implementation of the CMiniDrawView class
//

#include "stdafx.h"
#include "MiniDraw.h"

#include "MiniDrawDoc.h"
#include "MiniDrawView.h"

#ifdef _DEBUG
#define new DEBUG_NEW
#undef THIS_FILE
static char THIS_FILE[] = __FILE__;
#endif
```

```
/////////////////////////////////////////////////////////////////////
// CMiniDrawView

IMPLEMENT_DYNCREATE(CMiniDrawView, CView)

BEGIN_MESSAGE_MAP(CMiniDrawView, CView)
    //{{AFX_MSG_MAP(CMiniDrawView)
    ON_WM_LBUTTONDOWN()
    ON_WM_MOUSEMOVE()
    ON_WM_LBUTTONUP()
    //}}AFX_MSG_MAP
END_MESSAGE_MAP()

/////////////////////////////////////////////////////////////////////
// CMiniDrawView construction/destruction

CMiniDrawView::CMiniDrawView()
{
    // TODO: add construction code here

    m_Dragging = 0;
    m_HCross = AfxGetApp ()->LoadStandardCursor (IDC_CROSS);
}


CMiniDrawView::~CMiniDrawView()
{
}

BOOL CMiniDrawView::PreCreateWindow(CREATESTRUCT& cs)
{
    // TODO: Modify the Window class or styles here by modifying
    //   the CREATESTRUCT cs

    m_ClassName = AfxRegisterWndClass
        (CS_HREDRAW | CS_VREDRAW,                    // class styles
        0,                                           // no cursor
        (HBRUSH)::GetStockObject (WHITE_BRUSH),      // assign white
                                                     // background brush
        0);                                          // no icon
    cs.lpszClass = m_ClassName;

    return CView::PreCreateWindow(cs);
}
```

```
/////////////////////////////////////////////////////////////////////////
// CMiniDrawView drawing

void CMiniDrawView::OnDraw(CDC* pDC)
{
    CMiniDrawDoc* pDoc = GetDocument();
    ASSERT_VALID(pDoc);

    // TODO: add draw code for native data here
}

/////////////////////////////////////////////////////////////////////////
// CMiniDrawView diagnostics

#ifdef _DEBUG
void CMiniDrawView::AssertValid() const
{
    CView::AssertValid();
}

void CMiniDrawView::Dump(CDumpContext& dc) const
{
    CView::Dump(dc);
}

CMiniDrawDoc* CMiniDrawView::GetDocument() // non-debug version is inline
{
    ASSERT(m_pDocument->IsKindOf(RUNTIME_CLASS(CMiniDrawDoc)));
    return (CMiniDrawDoc*)m_pDocument;
}
#endif //_DEBUG

/////////////////////////////////////////////////////////////////////////
// CMiniDrawView message handlers

void CMiniDrawView::OnLButtonDown(UINT nFlags, CPoint point)
{
    // TODO: Add your message handler code here and/or call default

    m_PointOrigin = point;
    m_PointOld = point;
    SetCapture ();
```

```
    m_Dragging = 1;

    RECT Rect;
    GetClientRect (&Rect);
    ClientToScreen (&Rect);
    ::ClipCursor (&Rect);

    CView::OnLButtonDown(nFlags, point);
}

void CMiniDrawView::OnMouseMove(UINT nFlags, CPoint point)
{
    // TODO: Add your message handler code here and/or call default

    ::SetCursor (m_HCross);

    if (m_Dragging)
       {
       CClientDC ClientDC (this);
       ClientDC.SetROP2 (R2_NOT);
       ClientDC.MoveTo (m_PointOrigin);
       ClientDC.LineTo (m_PointOld);
       ClientDC.MoveTo (m_PointOrigin);
       ClientDC.LineTo (point);
       m_PointOld = point;
       }

    CView::OnMouseMove(nFlags, point);
}

void CMiniDrawView::OnLButtonUp(UINT nFlags, CPoint point)
{
    // TODO: Add your message handler code here and/or call default

    if (m_Dragging)
       {
       m_Dragging = 0;
       ::ReleaseCapture ();
       ::ClipCursor (NULL);
       CClientDC ClientDC (this);
       ClientDC.SetROP2 (R2_NOT);
       ClientDC.MoveTo (m_PointOrigin);
```

```
    ClientDC.LineTo (m_PointOld);
    ClientDC.SetROP2 (R2_COPYPEN);
    ClientDC.MoveTo (m_PointOrigin);
    ClientDC.LineTo (point);
    }

  CView::OnLButtonUp(nFlags, point);
}
```

The MiniEdit Program

You can easily create a full-featured text editor by deriving your view class from the MFC CEditView class, rather than from CView. A view class derived from CEditView allows the program user to enter and edit text within the view window, and contains support for a fairly complete collection of keyboard and menu editing commands; you don't need to implement these features yourself.

In this section, you'll generate a program named MiniEdit using AppWizard. As you do so, you'll request that the view class be derived from CEditView rather than CView, thus creating an instant text editor within the view window. Next, you'll use the Developer Studio menu editor to add menu items that allow the user to access several of the editor commands. You'll also use the Developer Studio resource editors to add accelerator keystrokes and design the program icon.

The MiniEdit program window is shown in Figure 10.10. The program allows you to enter and edit text in its view window, and displays scroll bars that let you scroll through the text if it doesn't all fit within the window. The program menu includes commands for printing the text; for undoing your last editing action; for cutting, copying, and pasting text; for selecting text; and for performing search and replace operations. Also, if you click the right mouse button while the mouse cursor is within the view window, the program will display a floating menu containing most of the Edit menu commands. Versions of MiniEdit presented in subsequent chapters will add features such as commands for saving and loading text files from disk, plus a command for choosing the font.

FIGURE 10.10:

The MiniEdit program
window

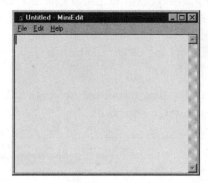

In later chapters you'll learn about several other special-purpose view classes provided by the MFC, which implement ready-to-use features. (Specifically, Chapter 13 explains CScrollView, which provides a scrolling view window, while Chapter 16 explains CFormView, which creates a scrolling view window that can be used to display a collection of controls.)

NOTE   The MFC provides the following special-purpose view classes in addition to those discussed in this book: CCtrlView, CDaoRecordView, CHtmlView, CListView, COleDBRecordView, CRecordView, CRichEditView, and CTreeView. All these classes are derived directly or indirectly from CView. You can find complete information on each of these classes in the following online help topic: *Visual C++ Documentation, Reference, Microsoft Foundation Class Library and Templates, Microsoft Foundation Class Library, Class Library Reference.*

Creating the MiniEdit Program

To create the MiniEdit program, first use AppWizard to generate the source code files in the same way you used it for the previous example programs. In the Projects tab of the New dialog box, enter the name MiniEdit into the Name: text box, and enter the project folder path into the Location: text box. In the AppWizard dialog boxes, choose the same options that you selected when generating the previous two example programs *except* that in the AppWizard Step 6 dialog box, rather than accepting all the defaults, you should do the following:

1. Select the CMiniEditView class name in the list near the top of the dialog box.

2. In the Base Class: list, select CEditView. The completed Step 6 dialog box is shown in Figure 10.11.

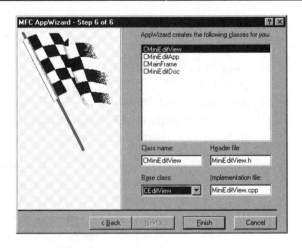

After generating the source code, open the ResourceView tab in the Developer Studio Workspace window to display the program resources:

You'll first modify the program menu, eliminating unused commands and adding new commands that invoke features provided by the CEditView class. To do this, in the ResourceView graph double-click the identifier IDR_MAINFRAME under the Menu item:

When the menu editor window opens, make the following changes:

1. Delete all items on the File menu, except the Exit command and the separator above this command.

2. Double-click the empty square at the bottom of the File menu to add a new item. The menu editor will open the Menu Item Properties dialog box. Enter the identifier ID_FILE_PRINT into the ID: box, and enter the string &Print...\tCtrl+P into the Caption: box. The new command will now appear on the File menu. (Notice that typing an & [ampersand] character before a character in the Caption: box causes the character to be underlined when it's displayed on the menu; when the menu is open, the user can type the underlined character to choose the command. Typing the \t characters inserts a tab into the caption that causes the following characters to be aligned at the right of the menu.)

3. Using the mouse, drag the new command (Print... Ctrl+P) from its current position at the bottom of the File menu to the top of the menu (above the separator that you left in place). Figure 10.12 shows the completed File menu as it appears in the menu editor.

FIGURE 10.12:

The completed File menu in the menu editor

4. Use the technique described in step 2 to add four new commands to the bottom of the Edit menu (below the existing Paste command). Table 10.4 lists the identifier and caption for each of these commands, and Figure 10.13 shows the completed Edit menu as it appears in the menu editor. After adding the Select All command, you should insert a separator. To insert a separator, simply check the Separator option in the Menu Item Properties dialog box, rather than entering an identifier and a caption.

TABLE 10.4: New Commands to Add to the Edit Menu

ID:	Caption
ID_EDIT_SELECT_ALL	Select &All
ID_EDIT_FIND	&Find...
ID_EDIT_REPEAT	Find &Next\tF3
ID_EDIT_REPLACE	&Replace...

FIGURE 10.13:

The completed Edit menu in
the menu editor

5. You can now remove the menu editor window by double-clicking its system menu or clicking its Close box.

When you add the menu commands, you must use the exact menu command identifiers given in the instructions, so that the message map defined within C-EditView will route each command message to the appropriate message-handling function (these are the standard MFC identifiers for these commands). You may have noticed that for each of the commands you added to the Edit menu, a pre-defined prompt was displayed at the bottom of the Menu Item Properties dialog box. As you'll learn in Chapter 14, if the program displays a status bar, the MFC code will print the prompt in the status bar when the menu command is highlighted.

Notice that the captions for two of the commands you added (the Print... command and the Find Next command) specify shortcut keys for executing the commands. Such shortcut keys are known as *keyboard accelerators* and must be defined using the Developer Studio accelerator editor. To define these two keyboard accelerators, do the following:

1. In the ResourceView graph, double-click the IDR_MAINFRAME identifier under the Accelerator branch of the graph:

This will open the accelerator editor window, which is shown in Figure 10.14.

FIGURE 10.14:

The accelerator editor window, displaying the MiniEdit accelerator keystrokes

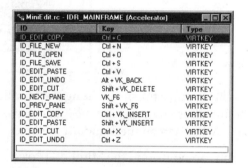

2. Double-click within the empty box at the bottom of the list of accelerator keystrokes to add a new keystroke. This will open the Accel Properties dialog box.

3. Enter the identifier ID_FILE_PRINT into the ID: text box; this is the identifier you assigned to the Print... command on the File menu.

4. Click the Next Key Typed button and then press the Ctrl+P keystroke. This will assign Ctrl+P as the accelerator keystroke for the Print... command.

5. Again, double-click within the empty box at the bottom of the list in the accelerator editor window.

6. In the Accel Properties dialog box, enter the ID_EDIT_REPEAT identifier, click the Next Key Typed button, and press F3. This will assign the F3 key as an accelerator keystroke for executing the Find Next command on the Edit menu.

7. You can now close the accelerator editor window.

Finally, you can use the graphics editor to design a custom icon for the MiniEdit program. Follow the instructions given previously for the MiniDraw program (in the section "Designing the Program Resources") to edit the IDR_MAINFRAME icon. The MiniEdit icon included with the version of the program provided on the companion CD is shown in Figure 10.15, as it appears in the graphics editor.

FIGURE 10.15:

The graphics editor displaying the MiniEdit icon included with the version of the program on the companion CD

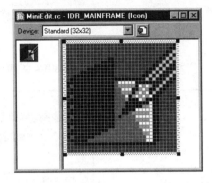

When you've finished editing the MiniEdit program resources, save all your modifications by choosing the File ≻ Save All menu command or by clicking the Save All button on the Standard toolbar.

You can now build the MiniEdit project, run the program, and experiment with its features. Notice that all the menu commands are fully functional; most of these commands are handled by code provided by the CEditView class. The MFC provides code for displaying a shortcut menu containing most of the commands on the Edit menu when you right-click within the view window. Notice, also, that if you enter text into the view window and then exit MiniEdit, the program gives you an opportunity to save your text in a disk file (this is the only way to save a file in the first version of MiniEdit; the version presented in Chapter 12 will add full support for file I/O).

The MiniEdit Program Source Code

The following listings, Listing 10.9 through 10.16, provide the C++ source code for the MiniEdit program. The files below should match the files you created in the exercise; also, a complete set of these files is included in the \MiniEdt1 companion-CD folder.

Listing 10.9

```
// MiniEdit.h : main header file for the MINIEDIT application
//

#if !defined(AFX_MINIEDIT_H__BAFB48A4_9A70_11D1_80FC_00C0F6A83B7F__INCLUDED_)
#define AFX_MINIEDIT_H__BAFB48A4_9A70_11D1_80FC_00C0F6A83B7F__INCLUDED_

#if _MSC_VER > 1000
#pragma once
#endif // _MSC_VER > 1000

#ifndef __AFXWIN_H__
    #error include 'stdafx.h' before including this file for PCH
#endif

#include "resource.h"        // main symbols

/////////////////////////////////////////////////////////////////////////////
// CMiniEditApp:
// See MiniEdit.cpp for the implementation of this class
//

class CMiniEditApp : public CWinApp
{
public:
    CMiniEditApp();

// Overrides
    // ClassWizard generated virtual function overrides
    //{{AFX_VIRTUAL(CMiniEditApp)
    public:
    virtual BOOL InitInstance();
    //}}AFX_VIRTUAL

// Implementation

    //{{AFX_MSG(CMiniEditApp)
    afx_msg void OnAppAbout();
        // NOTE - the ClassWizard will add and remove member functions here.
        //    DO NOT EDIT what you see in these blocks of generated code !
```

```
    //}}AFX_MSG
    DECLARE_MESSAGE_MAP()
};


/////////////////////////////////////////////////////////////////////////////

//{{AFX_INSERT_LOCATION}}
// Microsoft Visual C++ will insert additional declarations immediately before
// the previous line.

#endif
// !defined(AFX_MINIEDIT_H__BAFB48A4_9A70_11D1_80FC_00C0F6A83B7F__INCLUDED_)
```

Listing 10.10

```
// MiniEdit.cpp : Defines the class behaviors for the application.
//

#include "stdafx.h"
#include "MiniEdit.h"

#include "MainFrm.h"
#include "MiniEditDoc.h"
#include "MiniEditView.h"

#ifdef _DEBUG
#define new DEBUG_NEW
#undef THIS_FILE
static char THIS_FILE[] = __FILE__;
#endif

/////////////////////////////////////////////////////////////////////////////
// CMiniEditApp

BEGIN_MESSAGE_MAP(CMiniEditApp, CWinApp)
    //{{AFX_MSG_MAP(CMiniEditApp)
    ON_COMMAND(ID_APP_ABOUT, OnAppAbout)
        // NOTE - the ClassWizard will add and remove mapping macros here.
        //    DO NOT EDIT what you see in these blocks of generated code!
    //}}AFX_MSG_MAP
```

```
    // Standard file based document commands
    ON_COMMAND(ID_FILE_NEW, CWinApp::OnFileNew)
    ON_COMMAND(ID_FILE_OPEN, CWinApp::OnFileOpen)
END_MESSAGE_MAP()


/////////////////////////////////////////////////////////////////////////////
// CMiniEditApp construction

CMiniEditApp::CMiniEditApp()
{
    // TODO: add construction code here,
    // Place all significant initialization in InitInstance
}


/////////////////////////////////////////////////////////////////////////////
// The one and only CMiniEditApp object

CMiniEditApp theApp;


/////////////////////////////////////////////////////////////////////////////
// CMiniEditApp initialization

BOOL CMiniEditApp::InitInstance()
{
    // Standard initialization
    // If you are not using these features and wish to reduce the size
    //  of your final executable, you should remove from the following
    //  the specific initialization routines you do not need.

#ifdef _AFXDLL
    Enable3dControls();         // Call this when using MFC in a shared DLL
#else
    Enable3dControlsStatic();   // Call this when linking to MFC statically
#endif

    // Change the registry key under which our settings are stored.
    // You should modify this string to be something appropriate
    // such as the name of your company or organization.
    SetRegistryKey(_T("Local AppWizard-Generated Applications"));

    LoadStdProfileSettings();   // Load standard INI file options (including MRU)
```

```
// Register the application's document templates.  Document templates
//  serve as the connection between documents, frame windows and views.

CSingleDocTemplate* pDocTemplate;
pDocTemplate = new CSingleDocTemplate(
    IDR_MAINFRAME,
    RUNTIME_CLASS(CMiniEditDoc),
    RUNTIME_CLASS(CMainFrame),          // main SDI frame window
    RUNTIME_CLASS(CMiniEditView));
AddDocTemplate(pDocTemplate);

// Parse command line for standard shell commands, DDE, file open
CCommandLineInfo cmdInfo;
ParseCommandLine(cmdInfo);

// Dispatch commands specified on the command line
if (!ProcessShellCommand(cmdInfo))
    return FALSE;

// The one and only window has been initialized, so show and update it.
m_pMainWnd->ShowWindow(SW_SHOW);
m_pMainWnd->UpdateWindow();

return TRUE;
}


/////////////////////////////////////////////////////////////////////////////
// CAboutDlg dialog used for App About

class CAboutDlg : public CDialog
{
public:
    CAboutDlg();

// Dialog Data
    //{{AFX_DATA(CAboutDlg)
    enum { IDD = IDD_ABOUTBOX };
    //}}AFX_DATA
```

```
    // ClassWizard generated virtual function overrides
    //{{AFX_VIRTUAL(CAboutDlg)
    protected:
    virtual void DoDataExchange(CDataExchange* pDX);    // DDX/DDV support
    //}}AFX_VIRTUAL

// Implementation
protected:
    //{{AFX_MSG(CAboutDlg)
        // No message handlers
    //}}AFX_MSG
    DECLARE_MESSAGE_MAP()
};

CAboutDlg::CAboutDlg() : CDialog(CAboutDlg::IDD)
{
    //{{AFX_DATA_INIT(CAboutDlg)
    //}}AFX_DATA_INIT
}

void CAboutDlg::DoDataExchange(CDataExchange* pDX)
{
    CDialog::DoDataExchange(pDX);
    //{{AFX_DATA_MAP(CAboutDlg)
    //}}AFX_DATA_MAP
}

BEGIN_MESSAGE_MAP(CAboutDlg, CDialog)
    //{{AFX_MSG_MAP(CAboutDlg)
        // No message handlers
    //}}AFX_MSG_MAP
END_MESSAGE_MAP()

// App command to run the dialog
void CMiniEditApp::OnAppAbout()
{
    CAboutDlg aboutDlg;
    aboutDlg.DoModal();
}

/////////////////////////////////////////////////////////////////////////////
// CMiniEditApp commands
```

Listing 10.11

```cpp
// MiniEditDoc.h : interface of the CMiniEditDoc class
//
/////////////////////////////////////////////////////////////////////

#if !defined(AFX_MINIEDITDOC_H__BAFB48AA_9A70_11D1_80FC_00C0F6A83B7F__INCLUDED_)
#define AFX_MINIEDITDOC_H__BAFB48AA_9A70_11D1_80FC_00C0F6A83B7F__INCLUDED_

#if _MSC_VER > 1000
#pragma once
#endif // _MSC_VER > 1000


class CMiniEditDoc : public CDocument
{
protected: // create from serialization only
    CMiniEditDoc();
    DECLARE_DYNCREATE(CMiniEditDoc)

// Attributes
public:

// Operations
public:

// Overrides
    // ClassWizard generated virtual function overrides
    //{{AFX_VIRTUAL(CMiniEditDoc)
    public:
    virtual BOOL OnNewDocument();
    virtual void Serialize(CArchive& ar);
    //}}AFX_VIRTUAL

// Implementation
public:
    virtual ~CMiniEditDoc();
#ifdef _DEBUG
    virtual void AssertValid() const;
    virtual void Dump(CDumpContext& dc) const;
#endif
```

```
protected:

// Generated message map functions
protected:
    //{{AFX_MSG(CMiniEditDoc)
        // NOTE - the ClassWizard will add and remove member functions here.
        //      DO NOT EDIT what you see in these blocks of generated code !
    //}}AFX_MSG
    DECLARE_MESSAGE_MAP()
};

///////////////////////////////////////////////////////////////////////////

//{{AFX_INSERT_LOCATION}}
// Microsoft Visual C++ will insert additional declarations immediately before
// the previous line.

#endif
// !defined(AFX_MINIEDITDOC_H__BAFB48AA_9A70_11D1_80FC_00C0F6A83B7F__INCLUDED_)
```

Listing 10.12

```
// MiniEditDoc.cpp : implementation of the CMiniEditDoc class
//

#include "stdafx.h"
#include "MiniEdit.h"

#include "MiniEditDoc.h"

#ifdef _DEBUG
#define new DEBUG_NEW
#undef THIS_FILE
static char THIS_FILE[] = __FILE__;
#endif

///////////////////////////////////////////////////////////////////////////
// CMiniEditDoc

IMPLEMENT_DYNCREATE(CMiniEditDoc, CDocument)

BEGIN_MESSAGE_MAP(CMiniEditDoc, CDocument)
```

```
    //{{AFX_MSG_MAP(CMiniEditDoc)
        // NOTE - the ClassWizard will add and remove mapping macros here.
        //    DO NOT EDIT what you see in these blocks of generated code!
    //}}AFX_MSG_MAP
END_MESSAGE_MAP()


/////////////////////////////////////////////////////////////////////
// CMiniEditDoc construction/destruction

CMiniEditDoc::CMiniEditDoc()
{
    // TODO: add one-time construction code here

}

CMiniEditDoc::~CMiniEditDoc()
{
}

BOOL CMiniEditDoc::OnNewDocument()
{
    if (!CDocument::OnNewDocument())
        return FALSE;

    ((CEditView*)m_viewList.GetHead())->SetWindowText(NULL);

    // TODO: add reinitialization code here
    // (SDI documents will reuse this document)

    return TRUE;
}




/////////////////////////////////////////////////////////////////////
// CMiniEditDoc serialization

void CMiniEditDoc::Serialize(CArchive& ar)
{
    // CEditView contains an edit control which handles all serialization
    ((CEditView*)m_viewList.GetHead())->SerializeRaw(ar);
}
```

```
//////////////////////////////////////////////////////////////////////
// CMiniEditDoc diagnostics

#ifdef _DEBUG
void CMiniEditDoc::AssertValid() const
{
    CDocument::AssertValid();
}

void CMiniEditDoc::Dump(CDumpContext& dc) const
{
    CDocument::Dump(dc);
}
#endif //_DEBUG


//////////////////////////////////////////////////////////////////////
// CMiniEditDoc commands
```

Listing 10.13

```
// MainFrm.h : interface of the CMainFrame class
//
//////////////////////////////////////////////////////////////////////

#if !defined(AFX_MAINFRM_H__BAFB48A8_9A70_11D1_80FC_00C0F6A83B7F__INCLUDED_)
#define AFX_MAINFRM_H__BAFB48A8_9A70_11D1_80FC_00C0F6A83B7F__INCLUDED_

#if _MSC_VER > 1000
#pragma once
#endif // _MSC_VER > 1000

class CMainFrame : public CFrameWnd
{
protected: // create from serialization only
    CMainFrame();
    DECLARE_DYNCREATE(CMainFrame)

// Attributes
public:

// Operations
public:
```

```
// Overrides
   // ClassWizard generated virtual function overrides
   //{{AFX_VIRTUAL(CMainFrame)
   virtual BOOL PreCreateWindow(CREATESTRUCT& cs);
   //}}AFX_VIRTUAL

// Implementation
public:
   virtual ~CMainFrame();
#ifdef _DEBUG
   virtual void AssertValid() const;
   virtual void Dump(CDumpContext& dc) const;
#endif

// Generated message map functions
protected:
   //{{AFX_MSG(CMainFrame)
      // NOTE - the ClassWizard will add and remove member functions here.
      //    DO NOT EDIT what you see in these blocks of generated code!
   //}}AFX_MSG
   DECLARE_MESSAGE_MAP()
};

/////////////////////////////////////////////////////////////////////////

//{{AFX_INSERT_LOCATION}}
// Microsoft Visual C++ will insert additional declarations immediately before
// the previous line.

#endif
// !defined(AFX_MAINFRM_H__BAFB48A8_9A70_11D1_80FC_00C0F6A83B7F__INCLUDED_)
```

Listing 10.14

```
// MainFrm.cpp : implementation of the CMainFrame class
//

#include "stdafx.h"
#include "MiniEdit.h"

#include "MainFrm.h"
```

```
#ifdef _DEBUG
#define new DEBUG_NEW
#undef THIS_FILE
static char THIS_FILE[] = __FILE__;
#endif

/////////////////////////////////////////////////////////////////////////
// CMainFrame

IMPLEMENT_DYNCREATE(CMainFrame, CFrameWnd)

BEGIN_MESSAGE_MAP(CMainFrame, CFrameWnd)
    //{{AFX_MSG_MAP(CMainFrame)
        // NOTE - the ClassWizard will add and remove mapping macros here.
        //      DO NOT EDIT what you see in these blocks of generated code !
    //}}AFX_MSG_MAP
END_MESSAGE_MAP()

/////////////////////////////////////////////////////////////////////////
// CMainFrame construction/destruction

CMainFrame::CMainFrame()
{
    // TODO: add member initialization code here

}

CMainFrame::~CMainFrame()
{
}

BOOL CMainFrame::PreCreateWindow(CREATESTRUCT& cs)
{
    if( !CFrameWnd::PreCreateWindow(cs) )
        return FALSE;
    // TODO: Modify the Window class or styles here by modifying
    //   the CREATESTRUCT cs

    return TRUE;
}
```

```
/////////////////////////////////////////////////////////////////////////
// CMainFrame diagnostics

#ifdef _DEBUG
void CMainFrame::AssertValid() const
{
    CFrameWnd::AssertValid();
}

void CMainFrame::Dump(CDumpContext& dc) const
{
    CFrameWnd::Dump(dc);
}

#endif //_DEBUG

/////////////////////////////////////////////////////////////////////////
// CMainFrame message handlers
```

Listing 10.15

```
// MiniEditView.h : interface of the CMiniEditView class
//
/////////////////////////////////////////////////////////////////////////

#if !defined(AFX_MINIEDITVIEW_H__BAFB48AC_9A70_11D1_80FC_00C0F6A83B7F__INCLUDED_)
#define AFX_MINIEDITVIEW_H__BAFB48AC_9A70_11D1_80FC_00C0F6A83B7F__INCLUDED_

#if _MSC_VER > 1000
#pragma once
#endif // _MSC_VER > 1000

class CMiniEditView : public CEditView
{
protected: // create from serialization only
    CMiniEditView();
    DECLARE_DYNCREATE(CMiniEditView)

// Attributes
public:
    CMiniEditDoc* GetDocument();
```

```cpp
// Operations
public:

// Overrides
    // ClassWizard generated virtual function overrides
    //{{AFX_VIRTUAL(CMiniEditView)
    public:
    virtual void OnDraw(CDC* pDC);   // overridden to draw this view
    virtual BOOL PreCreateWindow(CREATESTRUCT& cs);
    protected:
    //}}AFX_VIRTUAL

// Implementation
public:
    virtual ~CMiniEditView();
#ifdef _DEBUG
    virtual void AssertValid() const;
    virtual void Dump(CDumpContext& dc) const;
#endif

protected:

// Generated message map functions
protected:
    //{{AFX_MSG(CMiniEditView)
        // NOTE - the ClassWizard will add and remove member functions here.
        //    DO NOT EDIT what you see in these blocks of generated code !
    //}}AFX_MSG
    DECLARE_MESSAGE_MAP()
};

#ifndef _DEBUG  // debug version in MiniEditView.cpp
inline CMiniEditDoc* CMiniEditView::GetDocument()
    { return (CMiniEditDoc*)m_pDocument; }
#endif

/////////////////////////////////////////////////////////////////////////////

//{{AFX_INSERT_LOCATION}}
// Microsoft Visual C++ will insert additional declarations immediately before
// the previous line.

#endif
// !defined(AFX_MINIEDITVIEW_H__BAFB48AC_9A70_11D1_80FC_00C0F6A83B7F__INCLUDED_)
```

Listing 10.16

```cpp
// MiniEditView.cpp : implementation of the CMiniEditView class
//

#include "stdafx.h"
#include "MiniEdit.h"

#include "MiniEditDoc.h"
#include "MiniEditView.h"

#ifdef _DEBUG
#define new DEBUG_NEW
#undef THIS_FILE
static char THIS_FILE[] = __FILE__;
#endif


/////////////////////////////////////////////////////////////////////////////
// CMiniEditView

IMPLEMENT_DYNCREATE(CMiniEditView, CEditView)

BEGIN_MESSAGE_MAP(CMiniEditView, CEditView)
    //{{AFX_MSG_MAP(CMiniEditView)
        // NOTE - the ClassWizard will add and remove mapping macros here.
        //      DO NOT EDIT what you see in these blocks of generated code!
    //}}AFX_MSG_MAP
END_MESSAGE_MAP()

/////////////////////////////////////////////////////////////////////////////
// CMiniEditView construction/destruction

CMiniEditView::CMiniEditView()
{
    // TODO: add construction code here

}

CMiniEditView::~CMiniEditView()
{
}

BOOL CMiniEditView::PreCreateWindow(CREATESTRUCT& cs)
```

```
{
    // TODO: Modify the Window class or styles here by modifying
    //   the CREATESTRUCT cs

    BOOL bPreCreated = CEditView::PreCreateWindow(cs);
    cs.style &= ~(ES_AUTOHSCROLL|WS_HSCROLL); // Enable word-wrapping

    return bPreCreated;
}

/////////////////////////////////////////////////////////////////////////////
// CMiniEditView drawing

void CMiniEditView::OnDraw(CDC* pDC)
{
    CMiniEditDoc* pDoc = GetDocument();
    ASSERT_VALID(pDoc);

    // TODO: add draw code for native data here
}

/////////////////////////////////////////////////////////////////////////////
// CMiniEditView diagnostics

#ifdef _DEBUG
void CMiniEditView::AssertValid() const
{
    CEditView::AssertValid();
}

void CMiniEditView::Dump(CDumpContext& dc) const
{
    CEditView::Dump(dc);
}

CMiniEditDoc* CMiniEditView::GetDocument() // non-debug version is inline
{
    ASSERT(m_pDocument->IsKindOf(RUNTIME_CLASS(CMiniEditDoc)));
    return (CMiniEditDoc*)m_pDocument;
}
#endif //_DEBUG

/////////////////////////////////////////////////////////////////////////////
// CMiniEditView message handlers
```

Summary

This chapter presented two example programs that showed you how to implement the view class of an MFC program. In the MiniDraw example program, the view class was derived from the general-purpose CView class, and you had to add your own code to accept user input and display output in the view window. In the MiniEdit program, however, the view class was derived from the special-purpose CEditView class, which implemented a full-featured text editor, without requiring you to add code to the view class. The following are some of the general concepts and techniques that were demonstrated:

- In an MFC program, a class object is sent *messages* to notify it of significant events. You can define a member function of a class that receives control whenever a particular type of message is sent. If you don't define a message-handling function for a particular type of message, the message will receive default processing.

- You can define a message-handling function using the ClassWizard tool, and then add your own code to the body of the function.

- Each type of message has an identifier. For example, when the user presses the left mouse button while the mouse cursor is within the view window, the view class object receives a message with the identifier WM_LBUTTONDOWN. If you want to respond to this event, you can use ClassWizard to define a WM_LBUTTONDOWN message handler as a member function of your view class.

- Windows program *resources* include menus, accelerator keystrokes, icons, and strings. (An *accelerator keystroke* is a shortcut key combination that the user can press to immediately execute a menu command.) AppWizard defines a default set of resources for a program that it generates. You can use the Developer Studio resource editors to modify program resources or add new ones.

- You can customize the view window by adding code to the PreCreate-Window virtual member function of the view class. The view-class version of this function overrides the version defined within the MFC CView class, and is called immediately before the window is created. You can assign custom window features to the fields of the CREATESTRUCT reference that Pre-CreateWindow is passed.

CHAPTER

ELEVEN

11

Implementing the Document

- Storing the graphic data

- Redrawing the window

- Adding menu commands

- Deleting the document data

- Implementing menu commands

- The MiniDraw source code

As you have seen, the document class of an MFC program is responsible for storing the document data, as well as for saving and loading this data from disk files. Also, the document class must provide public member functions that allow other classes (specifically, the view class) to obtain or modify the data, so that the user can view and edit it, and it must handle menu commands that directly affect the document data.

In this chapter, you'll build on the MiniDraw program you created in the previous chapter, by implementing the basic features of the document class. You'll first add members to the document class for storing the coordinates of each line that the user draws. You'll then modify the view class so that, in addition to drawing each line, it also stores each line within the document class object. Next, you'll implement the OnDraw member function of the view class, which will restore the lines whenever the window needs redrawing, using the data stored by the document object. (In the previous version of MiniDraw, the lines were simply erased whenever the window was redrawn, because the coordinates of the lines weren't stored by the document object.)

Finally, you'll add Undo and Delete All commands to the Edit menu. Both these commands will be handled by the document class, since they directly affect the data that it stores. The Undo command erases the most recently drawn line, and the Delete All command erases all lines in the drawing. In Chapter 12, you'll add file I/O code to the document class, so that you'll be able to save and load drawings from disk files.

In this chapter, you *won't* use AppWizard to create a new set of source files; rather, you'll use the MiniDraw files you created in the previous chapter and add various features to these files. (If you *didn't* create the files, you can obtain a copy of them from the \MiniDrw1 companion-CD folder.)

TIP   If you want to preserve the previous version of the MiniDraw program that you created in Chapter 10, *copy* all the program files into a new project folder and make all changes described in this chapter to the copies of the files.

Storing the Graphic Data

In this section, you'll make several additions to the MiniDraw source code that will allow the program to store the graphic data. To open the MiniDraw project, choose the File ➢ Open Workspace… menu command in the Developer Studio, select the folder in which you stored the MiniDraw files, and select the MiniDraw.dsw file.

After opening the project, the first step is to define a new class to store the data for each line that the user draws. Add the following definition for the CLine class (shown in **bold**) to the beginning of the document class header file, MiniDraw-Doc.h, just before the CMiniDrawDoc class definition:

```
class CLine : public CObject
{
protected:
    int m_X1, m_Y1, m_X2, m_Y2;


public:
    CLine (int X1, int Y1, int X2, int Y2)
        {
        m_X1 = X1;
        m_Y1 = Y1;
        m_X2 = X2;
        m_Y2 = Y2;
        }
    void Draw (CDC *PDC);
};

class CMiniDrawDoc : public CDocument
{
```

The CLine data members m_X1 and m_Y1 store the coordinates of one end of the line, while m_X2 and m_Y2 store the coordinates of the other end. CLine provides an inline constructor that initializes these data members. CLine also provides a member function, Draw, for drawing the line. You'll see shortly why CLine is derived from CObject.

Next, add the required members to the CMiniDrawDoc class by typing the statements marked in bold into the beginning of the CMiniDrawDoc class definition, also in MiniDrawDoc.h:

```
class CMiniDrawDoc : public CDocument
{
protected:
   CTypedPtrArray<CObArray, CLine*> m_LineArray;

public:
   void AddLine (int X1, int Y1, int X2, int Y2);
   CLine *GetLine (int Index);
   int GetNumLines ();

// remainder of CMiniDrawDoc definition ...

}
```

The new data member m_LineArray is an instance of the MFC class template CTypedPtrArray. (You might want to review the description of C++ templates in Chapter 7.) CTypedPtrArray generates a family of classes, each of which is derived from the class specified by the first template parameter (which can be either CObArray or CPtrArray), and each of which is designed to store data items of the type specified by the second template parameter. Thus, m_LineArray is an object of a class derived from CObArray, which stores pointers to CLine objects.

NOTE   In addition to CTypedPtrArray, the MFC provides the CTypedPtrList and CTypedPtrMap class templates. You can find complete information on these MFC class templates in the following Visual C++ online help topic: *Visual C++ Documentation, Reference, Microsoft Foundation Class Library and Templates, Microsoft Foundation Class Library, Class Library Reference.*

CObArray is one of the MFC general-purpose *collection* classes, which are used for storing groups of variables or objects. A CObArray instance stores a set of pointers to CObject objects (or objects of any class derived from CObject), in an array-like data structure. (CObject is the MFC class from which almost all other MFC classes are derived, directly or indirectly.) Rather than using an instance of the general-purpose CObArray class, however, MiniDraw uses the CTyped-PtrArray template to derive a class from CObArray that's designed specifically for storing CLine objects. Such a derived class allows the compiler to perform more extensive type checking, helps minimize errors, and can reduce the need for cast operations when using class objects.

To use the CTypedPtrArray (or any of the other MFC class templates), you must include the Afxtempl.h MFC header file. To make this header file available to any header or C++ source file in the MiniDraw project, you can simply include it within the standard MFC program header file, StdAfx.h, as follows:

```
#include <afxwin.h>        // MFC core and standard components
#include <afxext.h>        // MFC extensions
#include <afxdtctl.h>      // MFC support for Internet Explorer
                           // 4 Common Controls
#include <afxtempl.h>      // MFC templates
#ifndef _AFX_NO_AFXCMN_SUPPORT
#include <afxcmn.h>        // MFC support for Windows Common
                           // Controls
#endif // _AFX_NO_AFXCMN_SUPPORT
```

NOTE StdAfx.h is included at the beginning of all the project's C++ source files. StdAfx.h is also *precompiled*, meaning that this file—as well as all the header files it includes—isn't recompiled each time you modify a source file, thus saving build time. For information on precompiled headers, see the online help topic: *Visual C++ Documentation*, *Using Visual C++*, *Visual C++ Programmer's Guide*, *Compiling and Linking*, *Details*, *Creating Precompiled Header Files*.

In MiniDraw, m_LineArray is used to store a pointer to each CLine object that keeps information on a line. The member functions AddLine, GetLine, and Get-NumLines provide access to the line information stored in m_LineArray (which other classes can't access directly, because m_LineArray is protected).

Now type in the definition for the CLine::Draw function at the end of the document implementation file, MiniDrawDoc.cpp:

```
/////////////////////////////////////////////////////////////////////////
///////////
// CMiniDrawDoc commands

void CLine::Draw (CDC *PDC)
    {
    PDC->MoveTo (m_X1, m_Y1);
    PDC->LineTo (m_X2, m_Y2);
    }
```

Draw calls two CDC member functions, MoveTo and LineTo (which were introduced in Chapter 10), to draw the line at the coordinates stored in the current object.

Next, add the definitions for the AddLine, GetLine, and GetNumLines member functions of CMiniDrawDoc, also at the end of the MiniDrawDoc.cpp file:

```
void CMiniDrawDoc::AddLine (int X1, int Y1, int X2, int Y2)
   {
   CLine *PLine = new CLine (X1, Y1, X2, Y2);
   m_LineArray.Add (PLine);
   }

CLine *CMiniDrawDoc::GetLine (int Index)
   {
   if (Index < 0 || Index > m_LineArray.GetUpperBound ())
      return 0;
   return m_LineArray.GetAt (Index);
   }

int CMiniDrawDoc::GetNumLines ()
   {
   return m_LineArray.GetSize ();
   }
```

AddLine creates a new CLine object and calls the CObArray member function Add to add the object pointer to the collection of CLine pointers stored by m_LineArray.

Note that the pointers stored by m_LineArray are indexed; the first pointer added has the index 0, the second pointer added has the index 1, and so on. The GetLine function returns the pointer that has the index specified by the parameter it's passed. GetLine first checks that the index is within the valid range. (The CObArray member function GetUpperBound returns the largest valid index; that is, the index of the last pointer added.) GetLine then returns the corresponding CLine pointer, which it obtains by calling the CTypedPtrArray member function GetAt.

Finally, GetNumLines returns the number of CLine pointers currently stored by m_LineArray, which it obtains by calling the CObArray member function Get-Size. As you'll see, AddLine, GetLine, and GetNumLines are called by member functions of the view class.

The next step is to modify the OnLButtonUp member function of the view class, which is defined in the file MiniDrawView.cpp. Recall from Chapter 10 that when the user releases the left mouse button after drawing a line, this function ends the drag operation and draws the line in its final position. Add calls to GetDocument and AddLine to store the new line:

```
void CMiniDrawView::OnLButtonUp(UINT nFlags, CPoint point)
{
    // TODO: Add your message handler code here and/or call
    // default

    if (m_Dragging)
        {
        m_Dragging = 0;
        ::ReleaseCapture ();
        ::ClipCursor (NULL);
        CClientDC ClientDC (this);
        ClientDC.SetROP2 (R2_NOT);
        ClientDC.MoveTo (m_PointOrigin);
        ClientDC.LineTo (m_PointOld);
        ClientDC.SetROP2 (R2_COPYPEN);
        ClientDC.MoveTo (m_PointOrigin);
        ClientDC.LineTo (point);

        CMiniDrawDoc* PDoc = GetDocument();
        PDoc->AddLine (m_PointOrigin.x, m_PointOrigin.y, point.x,
            point.y);
        }

    CView::OnLButtonUp(nFlags, point);
}
```

As this modification illustrates, in addition to displaying the document data, the view class needs to call member functions of the document class to update the data in response to the editing actions of the user.

Redrawing the Window

Now that the program stores the data for the lines permanently within the document class object, the view class can use this data to restore the lines whenever the window is redrawn. Recall that whenever the view window needs redrawing, the system erases the window and then calls the OnDraw member function of the view class. You must add your own redrawing code to the minimal `OnDraw` function generated by AppWizard. To do this, add the lines marked in bold to the `CMiniDrawView::OnDraw` function within the MiniDrawView.cpp file:

```
//////////////////////////////////////////////////////////////////
///////////
// CMiniDrawView drawing

void CMiniDrawView::OnDraw(CDC* pDC)
{
   CMiniDrawDoc* pDoc = GetDocument();
   ASSERT_VALID(pDoc);

   // TODO: add draw code for native data here

   int Index = pDoc->GetNumLines ();
   while (Index--)
      pDoc->GetLine (Index)->Draw (pDC);
}
```

> **NOTE**
> The system actually erases only the portion of the view window that needs redrawing (for example, the portion that was covered by another window). In Chapter 13 you'll learn how to increase the efficiency of the `OnDraw` function by redrawing only the erased portion.

The code you added calls the `CMiniDrawDoc::GetNumLines` function to obtain the number of lines currently stored by the document object. For each line, it first calls the `CMiniDrawDoc::GetLine` function to obtain a pointer to the corresponding `CLine` object, and it then uses this pointer to call the `CLine::Draw` function to draw the line.

Adding Menu Commands

Because the graphic data is stored within the document object, it's now possible to add commands to the Edit menu that allow the user to modify the data. In this chapter, you'll add an Undo command for erasing the last line drawn, plus a Delete All command for erasing all lines in the drawing.

To add the Edit commands to the MiniDraw program, open the ResourceView tab in the Workspace window to display the program resources. Then, double-click the IDR_MAINFRAME identifier under the Menu branch of the graph,

to open the menu editor. In the menu editor, do the following:

1. Double-click the empty box at the right end of the menu bar. The menu editor will open the Menu Item Properties dialog box.

2. Into the Caption: text box, type &Edit. An Edit pop-up menu will now appear at the right end of the menu bar in the menu editor window. (Note that you didn't enter an identifier, because you're defining a pop-up menu item; only menu commands are assigned identifiers.)

3. Using the mouse, drag the Edit pop-up menu to the left, so that it falls between the File menu and the Help menu.

4. Double-click the empty box contained within the Edit menu (below the Edit caption), to reopen the Menu Item Properties dialog box for defining a new menu command.

5. Into the ID: box enter ID_EDIT_UNDO, and into the Caption: text box enter &Undo\tCtrl+Z. An Undo command will now appear on the Edit menu.

6. Double-click the empty box at the bottom of the Edit menu (below the Undo command), and check the Separator option in the Menu Item Properties dialog box. This will insert a separator under the Undo command.

7. Double-click the empty box at the bottom of the Edit menu, then enter ID_EDIT_CLEAR_ALL into the ID: box, and enter &Delete All into the Caption: box. This will add a Delete All command to the menu. The Edit menu is now complete and will appear as shown in Figure 11.1.

8. Close the menu editor window, and save your work by choosing the File ➤ Save All menu command in the Developer Studio or clicking the Save All button on the Standard toolbar.

FIGURE 11.1:

The completed MiniDraw
Edit menu in the Developer
Studio menu editor

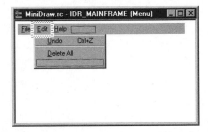

You don't need to define the Ctrl+Z accelerator for the Undo command, because AppWizard defined this accelerator when it first generated the program source code. (AppWizard also defined an Alt+Backspace accelerator keystroke for the Undo command, which is the keystroke common in older GUI programs.)

> **NOTE**
>
> When designing a menu using the menu editor, you can create cascading menus, you can arrange menu commands into columns, and you can assign a variety of initial properties to menu items (for example, you can check or disable a menu command). For an explanation of all the menu features you can implement using the menu editor, see the following online help topic: *Visual C++ Documentation*, *Using Visual C++*, *Visual C++ User's Guide*, *Resource Editors*, *Menu Editor*.

Deleting the Document Data

Whenever the user chooses the New command on the File menu, the MFC (specifically, the CWinApp member function OnFileNew) calls the virtual function CDocument::DeleteContents to delete the contents of the current document, prior to initializing a new document (in future versions of MiniDraw, the MFC code will also call DeleteContents prior to opening an existing document). You should write an overriding version of this function as a member of your document class to delete the data stored by this class.

In general, overriding a virtual function belonging to an MFC base class is a common and effective way to customize the behavior of the MFC. You can use

ClassWizard to generate the function declaration and the basic shell of the function definition for an overriding version of DeleteContents, as follows:

1. Choose the View ➤ ClassWizard... menu command or press Ctrl+W. The ClassWizard dialog box will appear.

2. Open the Message Maps tab (if necessary), which allows you to define member functions.

3. Select the CMiniDrawDoc class in the Class Name: list. You choose this class name because you want to define a virtual function belonging to the document class.

4. Select the CMiniDrawDoc item in the Object IDs: list. This will cause the Messages: list to display the names of the virtual functions defined in the CMiniDrawDoc base classes that you can override. All the items in the Messages: box are virtual functions except for the message identifiers that begin with WM_ (the name of the list, "Messages:", is thus misleading). Notice that if you select a function name in the list, a description of the function appears at the bottom of the ClassWizard dialog box.

5. In the Messages: list select DeleteContents, and click the Add Function button. The completed ClassWizard dialog box is shown in Figure 11.2.

6. Click the Edit Code button. AppWizard will now take you to the DeleteContents function shell that it has generated within the MiniDraw-Doc.cpp file.

FIGURE 11.2:

The completed ClassWizard dialog box for defining an overriding version of the DeleteContents virtual function, as a member of the MiniDraw document class

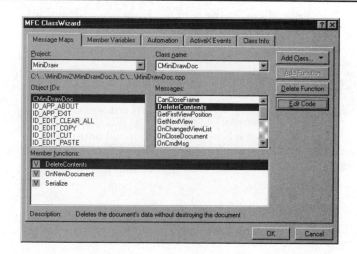

Now add the following bold lines to the ClassWizard-generated `Delete-Contents` function:

```
void CMiniDrawDoc::DeleteContents()
{
    // TODO: Add your specialized code here and/or call the base
    // class

    int Index = m_LineArray.GetSize ();
    while (Index--)
       delete m_LineArray.GetAt (Index);
    m_LineArray.RemoveAll ();

    CDocument::DeleteContents();
}
```

The code you added to `DeleteContents` first calls the `CObArray` member function `GetSize` to obtain the number of `CLine` pointers currently stored by the `m_LineArray` object. It then fetches each pointer by calling the `CTypedPtr-Array::GetAt` function and uses the C++ `delete` operator to free each corresponding `CLine` object (recall that the `CLine` objects were created using the `new` operator). Finally, it calls the `CObArray` member function `RemoveAll` to delete all the pointers currently stored by `m_LineArray`.

After calling `DeleteContents`, the MFC (indirectly) erases the view window and calls the `OnDraw` function of the view class. `OnDraw`, however, draws no lines because the lines have been deleted from the document class. The overall result is that the New command both deletes the document data and clears the view window, allowing the user to create a new drawing.

Implementing Menu Commands

You'll now use ClassWizard to implement the code for the two commands you added to the Edit menu: Delete All and Undo.

Handling the Delete All Command

To define a message handler that receives control when the user chooses the Delete All command, perform the following steps:

1. Open the ClassWizard dialog box and open the Message Maps tab.

2. In the Class Name: list, choose CMiniDrawDoc so that the Delete All message-handling function will be made a member of the document class. Recall from Chapter 10 that a command message can be handled by any of the four main program classes (the view, document, main frame window, or application class). The document class is selected to handle the Delete All command, because this command directly affects the document data (it erases it), and therefore falls within the province of the document class.

3. In the Object IDs: list, select the identifier ID_EDIT_CLEAR_ALL; recall that this is the identifier you assigned to the Delete All menu command when you designed the menu in the menu editor. As soon as you select this identifier, the Messages: list displays identifiers for the two types of messages that this menu command can send to the document class object: COMMAND and UPDATE_COMMAND_UI. The COMMAND identifier refers to the message that's sent when the user chooses the menu item; the UPDATE_COMMAND_UI identifier refers to the message that's sent when the user first opens the pop-up menu that contains the command.

   Note that COMMAND and UPDATE_COMMAND_UI refer to the two types of command messages that can be generated by a user-interface object. Chapter 10 (the section "Command Messages") described user-interface objects and explained the way that the messages generated by user-interface objects are routed through the program's main classes.

4. Select the COMMAND message in the Messages: list.

5. Click the Add Function... button to generate a message-handling function. When ClassWizard displays the Add Member Function dialog box, click the OK button to accept the default function name, OnEditClearAll, and proceed with the function generation. ClassWizard now declares the function within the CMiniDrawDoc class definition in MiniDrawDoc.h, adds a minimal function definition to MiniDrawDoc.cpp, and generates the code necessary to insert the function into the document class message map. The completed ClassWizard dialog box is shown in Figure 11.3.

FIGURE 11.3:

The ClassWizard dialog box for generating a COMMAND message handler for the Delete All menu command

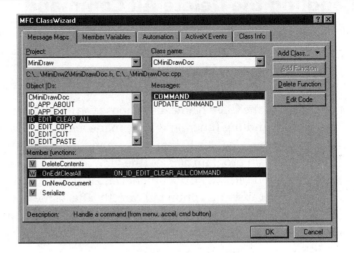

6. While the OnEditClearAll function is still selected in the Member Functions: list, click the Edit Code button in the ClassWizard dialog box. ClassWizard will open the MiniDrawDoc.cpp file (if it isn't already open) and display the OnEditClearAll function shell so that you can enter your own code for this message handler.

7. Add code as follows to OnEditClearAll:

```
void CMiniDrawDoc::OnEditClearAll()
{
    // TODO: Add your command handler code here

    DeleteContents ();
    UpdateAllViews (0);
}
```

The call to DeleteContents (which you defined previously) deletes the contents of the document. The call to the CDocument member function UpdateAll-Views then erases the current contents of the view window. (UpdateAllViews actually does more than this, as Chapter 13 will explain.)

The next step is to define a message-handling function for the UPDATE_COMMAND_UI message that's sent when the user first opens the pop-up menu containing the Delete All command (that is, the Edit menu). Because this message is sent *before* the pop-up menu becomes visible, the handler can be used to initialize the command according to the current state of the program. You'll add a handler that enables the Delete All command if the document contains one or more lines, but disables it if the document contains no lines. To do this, follow the numbered steps for using ClassWizard that were just described; in step 4, however, select the UPDATE_COMMAND_UI identifier in the Messages: list. ClassWizard will generate a function named OnUpdateEditClearAll. After clicking the Edit Code button, add code to this function as follows :

```
void CMiniDrawDoc::OnUpdateEditClearAll(CCmdUI* pCmdUI)
{
    // TODO: Add your command update UI handler code here

    pCmdUI->Enable (m_LineArray.GetSize ());
}
```

OnUpdateEditClearAll is passed a pointer to a CCmdUI object. CCmdUI is an MFC class that provides member functions for initializing menu commands (as well as other user-interface objects). The code you added calls the CCmdUI member function Enable to enable the Delete All menu command if the document contains at least one line, or to disable the command if the document contains no lines. When the command is disabled, it's displayed in gray text and the user can't choose it. Consequently, the OnEditClearAll function will never be called when the document is empty.

Initializing Menu Commands

A message-handling function that processes an UPDATE_COMMAND_UI message for a menu command is passed a pointer to a CCmdUI object, which is attached to the menu command. CCmdUI provides four member functions that you can use to initialize the menu command: Enable, SetCheck, SetRadio, and SetText.

You can pass Enable TRUE to enable the command, or FALSE to disable it:

```
virtual void Enable (BOOL bOn = TRUE);
```

You can pass SetCheck 1 to check the menu item, or 0 to uncheck it:

```
virtual void SetCheck (int nCheck = 1);
```

Normally, a menu command representing a program option is checked if the option is currently selected.

Continued on next page

You can pass SetRadio TRUE to check the menu item using a bullet, or FALSE to remove the bullet:

```
virtual void SetRadio (BOOL bOn = TRUE);
```

Usually, a bullet is used rather than a standard check mark to indicate which option is selected within a group of mutually exclusive options (for example, three menu options for choosing left, right, or centered text justification).

Finally, you can call SetText to change the menu command caption,

```
virtual void SetText (LPCTSTR lpszText);
```

where lpszText is a pointer to the new menu text. For example, if the previous action in a word processing program was to delete text, you might call SetText to set the text for the Undo command to "Undo Delete".

As you'll see in Chapter 14, you can define UPDATE_COMMAND_UI message handlers for other user interface objects, such as toolbar buttons, and can use these same four CCmdUI member functions to update these other objects. The specific action of each of these functions depends on the type of user-interface object that's being acted on.

Handling the Undo Command

The final task is to define functions to handle the Undo command on the Edit menu.

First, define a function that receives control when the user *chooses* the Undo command. To do this, use ClassWizard following the numbered steps given in the previous section. In step 3, however, choose the ID_EDIT_UNDO identifier in the Object IDs: list. ClassWizard will define a function named OnEditUndo. Add code to this function, as follows:

```
void CMiniDrawDoc::OnEditUndo()
{
    // TODO: Add your command handler code here

    int Index = m_LineArray.GetUpperBound ();
    if (Index > -1)
        {
        delete m_LineArray.GetAt (Index);
        m_LineArray.RemoveAt (Index);
        }
    UpdateAllViews (0);
}
```

The code you added first calls the CObArray member function GetUpperBound to obtain the index of the last line added to the document. It then calls CTyped-PtrArray::GetAt to obtain the pointer to the CLine object for the last line, and it uses the delete operator to delete this object. Finally, it calls UpdateAllViews, which results in erasing the view window and calling the CMiniDrawView::OnDraw function; OnDraw then redraws the lines that remain in the document. Note that if the user repeatedly chooses the Undo command, OnEditUndo keeps erasing lines, until all lines are gone.

Second, define a function to initialize the Undo menu command. To do this, use ClassWizard according to the numbered steps given in the previous section. In step 3, however, select the ID_EDIT_UNDO identifier in the Object IDs: list, and in step 4 select the UPDATE_COMMAND_UI message identifier in the Messages: list. ClassWizard will create a function named OnUpdateEditUndo. Add code to this function, as follows:

```
void CMiniDrawDoc::OnUpdateEditUndo(CCmdUI* pCmdUI)
{
    // TODO: Add your command update UI handler code here

    pCmdUI->Enable (m_LineArray.GetSize ());
}
```

This function works exactly like the OnUpdateEditClearAll function described previously. Namely, it enables the Undo command only if there's at least one line to erase.

Recall that an accelerator keystroke, Ctrl+Z, was assigned to the Undo menu command; that is, both the Undo menu command and the Ctrl+Z keyboard accelerator have the same identifier, ID_EDIT_UNDO. When the user presses the accelerator keystroke, the system first calls OnUpdateEditUndo. If OnUpdateEditUndo enables the menu command, the system then calls OnEditUndo, so that the accelerator keystroke receives the same processing as the menu command. If, however, OnUpdateEditUndo disables the menu command, the system *doesn't* call OnEditUndo. Thus, if OnUpdateEditUndo disables the menu command, the accelerator keystroke is also disabled, and OnEditUndo will never be called unless there's at least one line in the document.

This is the last change to make to the current version of MiniDraw. You can now build and run the program.

The MiniDraw Source Code

The following listings, Listings 11.1 through 11.8, are the C++ source files for the version of the MiniDraw program presented in this chapter. These files contain the code generated by AppWizard, plus all the modifications and additions you made in this chapter as well as in the previous chapter. Note that a complete copy of these files—together with the other MiniDraw source files—is contained in the \MiniDrw2 companion-CD folder.

Listing 11.1

```
// MiniDraw.h : main header file for the MINIDRAW application
//

#if !defined(AFX_MINIDRAW_H__11E83924_999A_11D1_80FC_00C0F6A83B7F__INCLUDED_)
#define AFX_MINIDRAW_H__11E83924_999A_11D1_80FC_00C0F6A83B7F__INCLUDED_

#if _MSC_VER > 1000
#pragma once
#endif // _MSC_VER > 1000

#ifndef __AFXWIN_H__
    #error include 'stdafx.h' before including this file for PCH
#endif

#include "resource.h"       // main symbols

/////////////////////////////////////////////////////////////////////////
// CMiniDrawApp:
// See MiniDraw.cpp for the implementation of this class
//

class CMiniDrawApp : public CWinApp
{
public:
    CMiniDrawApp();

// Overrides
    // ClassWizard generated virtual function overrides
    //{{AFX_VIRTUAL(CMiniDrawApp)
    public:
```

```
    virtual BOOL InitInstance();
    //}}AFX_VIRTUAL

// Implementation

    //{{AFX_MSG(CMiniDrawApp)
    afx_msg void OnAppAbout();
        // NOTE - the ClassWizard will add and remove member functions here.
        //    DO NOT EDIT what you see in these blocks of generated code !
    //}}AFX_MSG
    DECLARE_MESSAGE_MAP()
};


/////////////////////////////////////////////////////////////////////////////

//{{AFX_INSERT_LOCATION}}
// Microsoft Visual C++ will insert additional declarations immediately before
// the previous line.

#endif
// !defined(AFX_MINIDRAW_H__11E83924_999A_11D1_80FC_00C0F6A83B7F__INCLUDED_)
```

Listing 11.2

```
// MiniDraw.cpp : Defines the class behaviors for the application.
//

#include "stdafx.h"
#include "MiniDraw.h"

#include "MainFrm.h"
#include "MiniDrawDoc.h"
#include "MiniDrawView.h"

#ifdef _DEBUG
#define new DEBUG_NEW
#undef THIS_FILE
static char THIS_FILE[] = __FILE__;
#endif

/////////////////////////////////////////////////////////////////////////////
// CMiniDrawApp
```

```
BEGIN_MESSAGE_MAP(CMiniDrawApp, CWinApp)
   //{{AFX_MSG_MAP(CMiniDrawApp)
   ON_COMMAND(ID_APP_ABOUT, OnAppAbout)
       // NOTE - the ClassWizard will add and remove mapping macros here.
       //    DO NOT EDIT what you see in these blocks of generated code!
   //}}AFX_MSG_MAP
   // Standard file based document commands
   ON_COMMAND(ID_FILE_NEW, CWinApp::OnFileNew)
   ON_COMMAND(ID_FILE_OPEN, CWinApp::OnFileOpen)
END_MESSAGE_MAP()


/////////////////////////////////////////////////////////////////////////
// CMiniDrawApp construction

CMiniDrawApp::CMiniDrawApp()
{
   // TODO: add construction code here,
   // Place all significant initialization in InitInstance
}


/////////////////////////////////////////////////////////////////////////
// The one and only CMiniDrawApp object

CMiniDrawApp theApp;

/////////////////////////////////////////////////////////////////////////
// CMiniDrawApp initialization

BOOL CMiniDrawApp::InitInstance()
{
   // Standard initialization
   // If you are not using these features and wish to reduce the size
   //  of your final executable, you should remove from the following
   //  the specific initialization routines you do not need.

#ifdef _AFXDLL
   Enable3dControls();          // Call this when using MFC in a shared DLL
#else
   Enable3dControlsStatic();  // Call this when linking to MFC statically
#endif

   // Change the registry key under which our settings are stored.
   // You should modify this string to be something appropriate
```

```
    // such as the name of your company or organization.
    SetRegistryKey(_T("Local AppWizard-Generated Applications"));

    LoadStdProfileSettings();  // Load standard INI file options (including MRU)

    // Register the application's document templates.  Document templates
    //  serve as the connection between documents, frame windows and views.

    CSingleDocTemplate* pDocTemplate;
    pDocTemplate = new CSingleDocTemplate(
        IDR_MAINFRAME,
        RUNTIME_CLASS(CMiniDrawDoc),
        RUNTIME_CLASS(CMainFrame),          // main SDI frame window
        RUNTIME_CLASS(CMiniDrawView));
    AddDocTemplate(pDocTemplate);

    // Parse command line for standard shell commands, DDE, file open
    CCommandLineInfo cmdInfo;
    ParseCommandLine(cmdInfo);

    // Dispatch commands specified on the command line
    if (!ProcessShellCommand(cmdInfo))
        return FALSE;

    // The one and only window has been initialized, so show and update it.
    m_pMainWnd->ShowWindow(SW_SHOW);
    m_pMainWnd->UpdateWindow();

    return TRUE;
}


/////////////////////////////////////////////////////////////////////////////
// CAboutDlg dialog used for App About

class CAboutDlg : public CDialog
{
public:
    CAboutDlg();

// Dialog Data
    //{{AFX_DATA(CAboutDlg)
    enum { IDD = IDD_ABOUTBOX };
    //}}AFX_DATA
```

```
   // ClassWizard generated virtual function overrides
   //{{AFX_VIRTUAL(CAboutDlg)
   protected:
   virtual void DoDataExchange(CDataExchange* pDX);    // DDX/DDV support
   //}}AFX_VIRTUAL

// Implementation
protected:
   //{{AFX_MSG(CAboutDlg)
      // No message handlers
   //}}AFX_MSG
   DECLARE_MESSAGE_MAP()
};

CAboutDlg::CAboutDlg() : CDialog(CAboutDlg::IDD)
{
   //{{AFX_DATA_INIT(CAboutDlg)
   //}}AFX_DATA_INIT
}

void CAboutDlg::DoDataExchange(CDataExchange* pDX)
{
   CDialog::DoDataExchange(pDX);
   //{{AFX_DATA_MAP(CAboutDlg)
   //}}AFX_DATA_MAP
}

BEGIN_MESSAGE_MAP(CAboutDlg, CDialog)
   //{{AFX_MSG_MAP(CAboutDlg)
      // No message handlers
   //}}AFX_MSG_MAP
END_MESSAGE_MAP()

// App command to run the dialog
void CMiniDrawApp::OnAppAbout()
{
   CAboutDlg aboutDlg;
   aboutDlg.DoModal();
}


/////////////////////////////////////////////////////////////////////
// CMiniDrawApp commands
```

Listing 11.3

```cpp
// MiniDrawDoc.h : interface of the CMiniDrawDoc class
//
//////////////////////////////////////////////////////////////////////////

#if !defined(AFX_MINIDRAWDOC_H__11E8392A_999A_11D1_80FC_00C0F6A83B7F__INCLUDED_)
#define AFX_MINIDRAWDOC_H__11E8392A_999A_11D1_80FC_00C0F6A83B7F__INCLUDED_

#if _MSC_VER > 1000
#pragma once
#endif // _MSC_VER > 1000

class CLine : public CObject
{
protected:
    int m_X1, m_Y1, m_X2, m_Y2;

public:
    CLine (int X1, int Y1, int X2, int Y2)
        {
        m_X1 = X1;
        m_Y1 = Y1;
        m_X2 = X2;
        m_Y2 = Y2;
        }
    void Draw (CDC *PDC);
};

class CMiniDrawDoc : public CDocument
{
protected:
    CTypedPtrArray<CObArray, CLine*> m_LineArray;

public:
    void AddLine (int X1, int Y1, int X2, int Y2);
    CLine *GetLine (int Index);
    int GetNumLines ();

protected: // create from serialization only
    CMiniDrawDoc();
    DECLARE_DYNCREATE(CMiniDrawDoc)
```

```cpp
// Attributes
public:

// Operations
public:

// Overrides
    // ClassWizard generated virtual function overrides
    //{{AFX_VIRTUAL(CMiniDrawDoc)
    public:
    virtual BOOL OnNewDocument();
    virtual void Serialize(CArchive& ar);
    virtual void DeleteContents();
    //}}AFX_VIRTUAL

// Implementation
public:
    virtual ~CMiniDrawDoc();
#ifdef _DEBUG
    virtual void AssertValid() const;
    virtual void Dump(CDumpContext& dc) const;
#endif

protected:

// Generated message map functions
protected:
    //{{AFX_MSG(CMiniDrawDoc)
    afx_msg void OnEditClearAll();
    afx_msg void OnUpdateEditClearAll(CCmdUI* pCmdUI);
    afx_msg void OnEditUndo();
    afx_msg void OnUpdateEditUndo(CCmdUI* pCmdUI);
    //}}AFX_MSG
    DECLARE_MESSAGE_MAP()
};

/////////////////////////////////////////////////////////////////////////

//{{AFX_INSERT_LOCATION}}
// Microsoft Visual C++ will insert additional declarations immediately before
// the previous line.

#endif
// !defined(AFX_MINIDRAWDOC_H__11E8392A_999A_11D1_80FC_00C0F6A83B7F__INCLUDED_)
```

Listing 11.4

```cpp
// MiniDrawDoc.cpp : implementation of the CMiniDrawDoc class
//

#include "stdafx.h"
#include "MiniDraw.h"

#include "MiniDrawDoc.h"

#ifdef _DEBUG
#define new DEBUG_NEW
#undef THIS_FILE
static char THIS_FILE[] = __FILE__;
#endif

/////////////////////////////////////////////////////////////////////////////
// CMiniDrawDoc

IMPLEMENT_DYNCREATE(CMiniDrawDoc, CDocument)

BEGIN_MESSAGE_MAP(CMiniDrawDoc, CDocument)
    //{{AFX_MSG_MAP(CMiniDrawDoc)
    ON_COMMAND(ID_EDIT_CLEAR_ALL, OnEditClearAll)
    ON_UPDATE_COMMAND_UI(ID_EDIT_CLEAR_ALL, OnUpdateEditClearAll)
    ON_COMMAND(ID_EDIT_UNDO, OnEditUndo)
    ON_UPDATE_COMMAND_UI(ID_EDIT_UNDO, OnUpdateEditUndo)
    //}}AFX_MSG_MAP
END_MESSAGE_MAP()

/////////////////////////////////////////////////////////////////////////////
// CMiniDrawDoc construction/destruction

CMiniDrawDoc::CMiniDrawDoc()
{
    // TODO: add one-time construction code here

}

CMiniDrawDoc::~CMiniDrawDoc()
{
}
```

```
BOOL CMiniDrawDoc::OnNewDocument()
{
    if (!CDocument::OnNewDocument())
        return FALSE;

    // TODO: add reinitialization code here
    // (SDI documents will reuse this document)

    return TRUE;
}


/////////////////////////////////////////////////////////////////////////
// CMiniDrawDoc serialization

void CMiniDrawDoc::Serialize(CArchive& ar)
{
    if (ar.IsStoring())
    {
        // TODO: add storing code here
    }
    else
    {
        // TODO: add loading code here
    }
}


/////////////////////////////////////////////////////////////////////////
// CMiniDrawDoc diagnostics

#ifdef _DEBUG
void CMiniDrawDoc::AssertValid() const
{
    CDocument::AssertValid();
}

void CMiniDrawDoc::Dump(CDumpContext& dc) const
{
    CDocument::Dump(dc);
}
#endif //_DEBUG
```

```
/////////////////////////////////////////////////////////////////////////
// CMiniDrawDoc commands

void CLine::Draw (CDC *PDC)
   {
   PDC->MoveTo (m_X1, m_Y1);
   PDC->LineTo (m_X2, m_Y2);
   }

void CMiniDrawDoc::AddLine (int X1, int Y1, int X2, int Y2)
   {
   CLine *PLine = new CLine (X1, Y1, X2, Y2);
   m_LineArray.Add (PLine);
   }

CLine *CMiniDrawDoc::GetLine (int Index)
   {
   if (Index < 0 || Index > m_LineArray.GetUpperBound ())
      return 0;
   return m_LineArray.GetAt (Index);
   }

int CMiniDrawDoc::GetNumLines ()
   {
   return m_LineArray.GetSize ();
   }

void CMiniDrawDoc::DeleteContents()
{
   // TODO: Add your specialized code here and/or call the base class

   int Index = m_LineArray.GetSize ();
   while (Index--)
      delete m_LineArray.GetAt (Index);
   m_LineArray.RemoveAll ();

   CDocument::DeleteContents();
}

void CMiniDrawDoc::OnEditClearAll()
{
   // TODO: Add your command handler code here
```

```
   DeleteContents ();
   UpdateAllViews (0);
}


void CMiniDrawDoc::OnUpdateEditClearAll(CCmdUI* pCmdUI)
{
   // TODO: Add your command update UI handler code here

   pCmdUI->Enable (m_LineArray.GetSize ());
}


void CMiniDrawDoc::OnEditUndo()
{
   // TODO: Add your command handler code here

   int Index = m_LineArray.GetUpperBound ();
   if (Index > -1)
      {
      delete m_LineArray.GetAt (Index);
      m_LineArray.RemoveAt (Index);
      }
   UpdateAllViews (0);
}


void CMiniDrawDoc::OnUpdateEditUndo(CCmdUI* pCmdUI)
{
   // TODO: Add your command update UI handler code here

   pCmdUI->Enable (m_LineArray.GetSize ());
}
```

Listing 11.5

```
// MainFrm.h : interface of the CMainFrame class
//
/////////////////////////////////////////////////////////////////////////

#if !defined(AFX_MAINFRM_H__11E83928_999A_11D1_80FC_00C0F6A83B7F__INCLUDED_)
#define AFX_MAINFRM_H__11E83928_999A_11D1_80FC_00C0F6A83B7F__INCLUDED_

#if _MSC_VER > 1000
#pragma once
#endif // _MSC_VER > 1000
```

```
class CMainFrame : public CFrameWnd
{
protected: // create from serialization only
   CMainFrame();
   DECLARE_DYNCREATE(CMainFrame)

// Attributes
public:

// Operations
public:

// Overrides
   // ClassWizard generated virtual function overrides
   //{{AFX_VIRTUAL(CMainFrame)
   virtual BOOL PreCreateWindow(CREATESTRUCT& cs);
   //}}AFX_VIRTUAL

// Implementation
public:
   virtual ~CMainFrame();
#ifdef _DEBUG
   virtual void AssertValid() const;
   virtual void Dump(CDumpContext& dc) const;
#endif

// Generated message map functions
protected:
   //{{AFX_MSG(CMainFrame)
   //}}AFX_MSG
   DECLARE_MESSAGE_MAP()
};

/////////////////////////////////////////////////////////////////////////////

//{{AFX_INSERT_LOCATION}}
// Microsoft Visual C++ will insert additional declarations immediately before
// the previous line.

#endif
// !defined(AFX_MAINFRM_H__11E83928_999A_11D1_80FC_00C0F6A83B7F__INCLUDED_)
```

Listing 11.6

```cpp
// MainFrm.cpp : implementation of the CMainFrame class
//

#include "stdafx.h"
#include "MiniDraw.h"

#include "MainFrm.h"

#ifdef _DEBUG
#define new DEBUG_NEW
#undef THIS_FILE
static char THIS_FILE[] = __FILE__;
#endif

/////////////////////////////////////////////////////////////////////////////
// CMainFrame

IMPLEMENT_DYNCREATE(CMainFrame, CFrameWnd)

BEGIN_MESSAGE_MAP(CMainFrame, CFrameWnd)
    //{{AFX_MSG_MAP(CMainFrame)
    //}}AFX_MSG_MAP
END_MESSAGE_MAP()

/////////////////////////////////////////////////////////////////////////////
// CMainFrame construction/destruction

CMainFrame::CMainFrame()
{
    // TODO: add member initialization code here

}

CMainFrame::~CMainFrame()
{
}

BOOL CMainFrame::PreCreateWindow(CREATESTRUCT& cs)
{
    if( !CFrameWnd::PreCreateWindow(cs) )
        return FALSE;
    // TODO: Modify the Window class or styles here by modifying
```

```
   //  the CREATESTRUCT cs

   return TRUE;
}

//////////////////////////////////////////////////////////////////////
// CMainFrame diagnostics

#ifdef _DEBUG
void CMainFrame::AssertValid() const
{
   CFrameWnd::AssertValid();
}

void CMainFrame::Dump(CDumpContext& dc) const
{
   CFrameWnd::Dump(dc);
}

#endif //_DEBUG

//////////////////////////////////////////////////////////////////////
// CMainFrame message handlers
```

Listing 11.7

```
// MiniDrawView.h : interface of the CMiniDrawView class
//
//////////////////////////////////////////////////////////////////////

#if !defined(AFX_MINIDRAWVIEW_H__11E8392C_999A_11D1_80FC_00C0F6A83B7F__INCLUDED_)
#define AFX_MINIDRAWVIEW_H__11E8392C_999A_11D1_80FC_00C0F6A83B7F__INCLUDED_

#if _MSC_VER > 1000
#pragma once
#endif // _MSC_VER > 1000

class CMiniDrawView : public CView
{
protected:
   CString m_ClassName;
   int m_Dragging;
   HCURSOR m_HCross;
   CPoint m_PointOld;
   CPoint m_PointOrigin;
```

```
protected: // create from serialization only
   CMiniDrawView();
   DECLARE_DYNCREATE(CMiniDrawView)

// Attributes
public:
   CMiniDrawDoc* GetDocument();

// Operations
public:

// Overrides
   // ClassWizard generated virtual function overrides
   //{{AFX_VIRTUAL(CMiniDrawView)
   public:
   virtual void OnDraw(CDC* pDC);   // overridden to draw this view
   virtual BOOL PreCreateWindow(CREATESTRUCT& cs);
   protected:
   //}}AFX_VIRTUAL

// Implementation
public:
   virtual ~CMiniDrawView();
#ifdef _DEBUG
   virtual void AssertValid() const;
   virtual void Dump(CDumpContext& dc) const;
#endif

protected:

// Generated message map functions
protected:
   //{{AFX_MSG(CMiniDrawView)
   afx_msg void OnLButtonDown(UINT nFlags, CPoint point);
   afx_msg void OnMouseMove(UINT nFlags, CPoint point);
   afx_msg void OnLButtonUp(UINT nFlags, CPoint point);
   //}}AFX_MSG
   DECLARE_MESSAGE_MAP()
};
```

```
#ifndef _DEBUG  // debug version in MiniDrawView.cpp
inline CMiniDrawDoc* CMiniDrawView::GetDocument()
   { return (CMiniDrawDoc*)m_pDocument; }
#endif


/////////////////////////////////////////////////////////////////////////////

//{{AFX_INSERT_LOCATION}}
// Microsoft Visual C++ will insert additional declarations immediately before
// the previous line.

#endif
// !defined(AFX_MINIDRAWVIEW_H__11E8392C_999A_11D1_80FC_00C0F6A83B7F__INCLUDED_)
```

Listing 11.8

```
// MiniDrawView.cpp : implementation of the CMiniDrawView class
//

#include "stdafx.h"
#include "MiniDraw.h"

#include "MiniDrawDoc.h"
#include "MiniDrawView.h"

#ifdef _DEBUG
#define new DEBUG_NEW
#undef THIS_FILE
static char THIS_FILE[] = __FILE__;
#endif


/////////////////////////////////////////////////////////////////////////////
// CMiniDrawView

IMPLEMENT_DYNCREATE(CMiniDrawView, CView)

BEGIN_MESSAGE_MAP(CMiniDrawView, CView)
   //{{AFX_MSG_MAP(CMiniDrawView)
   ON_WM_LBUTTONDOWN()
```

```
   ON_WM_MOUSEMOVE()
   ON_WM_LBUTTONUP()
   //}}AFX_MSG_MAP
END_MESSAGE_MAP()


/////////////////////////////////////////////////////////////////////////////
// CMiniDrawView construction/destruction

CMiniDrawView::CMiniDrawView()
{
   // TODO: add construction code here

   m_Dragging = 0;
   m_HCross = AfxGetApp ()->LoadStandardCursor (IDC_CROSS);
}


CMiniDrawView::~CMiniDrawView()
{
}


BOOL CMiniDrawView::PreCreateWindow(CREATESTRUCT& cs)
{
   // TODO: Modify the Window class or styles here by modifying
   //   the CREATESTRUCT cs

   m_ClassName = AfxRegisterWndClass
      (CS_HREDRAW | CS_VREDRAW,                // class styles
      0,                                       // no cursor
      (HBRUSH)::GetStockObject (WHITE_BRUSH),  // assign white
                                               // background brush
      0);                                      // no icon
   cs.lpszClass = m_ClassName;

   return CView::PreCreateWindow(cs);
}


/////////////////////////////////////////////////////////////////////////////
// CMiniDrawView drawing

void CMiniDrawView::OnDraw(CDC* pDC)
{
   CMiniDrawDoc* pDoc = GetDocument();
   ASSERT_VALID(pDoc);
```

```
    // TODO: add draw code for native data here

    int Index = pDoc->GetNumLines ();
    while (Index--)
        pDoc->GetLine (Index)->Draw (pDC);

}

/////////////////////////////////////////////////////////////////////////////
// CMiniDrawView diagnostics

#ifdef _DEBUG
void CMiniDrawView::AssertValid() const
{
    CView::AssertValid();
}

void CMiniDrawView::Dump(CDumpContext& dc) const
{
    CView::Dump(dc);
}

CMiniDrawDoc* CMiniDrawView::GetDocument() // non-debug version is inline
{
    ASSERT(m_pDocument->IsKindOf(RUNTIME_CLASS(CMiniDrawDoc)));
    return (CMiniDrawDoc*)m_pDocument;
}
#endif //_DEBUG

/////////////////////////////////////////////////////////////////////////////
// CMiniDrawView message handlers

void CMiniDrawView::OnLButtonDown(UINT nFlags, CPoint point)
{
    // TODO: Add your message handler code here and/or call default

    m_PointOrigin = point;
    m_PointOld = point;
    SetCapture ();
    m_Dragging = 1;
```

```
    RECT Rect;
    GetClientRect (&Rect);
    ClientToScreen (&Rect);
    ::ClipCursor (&Rect);

    CView::OnLButtonDown(nFlags, point);
}

void CMiniDrawView::OnMouseMove(UINT nFlags, CPoint point)
{
    // TODO: Add your message handler code here and/or call default

    ::SetCursor (m_HCross);

    if (m_Dragging)
        {
        CClientDC ClientDC (this);
        ClientDC.SetROP2 (R2_NOT);
        ClientDC.MoveTo (m_PointOrigin);
        ClientDC.LineTo (m_PointOld);
        ClientDC.MoveTo (m_PointOrigin);
        ClientDC.LineTo (point);
        m_PointOld = point;
        }

    CView::OnMouseMove(nFlags, point);
}

void CMiniDrawView::OnLButtonUp(UINT nFlags, CPoint point)
{
    // TODO: Add your message handler code here and/or call default

    if (m_Dragging)
        {
        m_Dragging = 0;
        ::ReleaseCapture ();
        ::ClipCursor (NULL);
        CClientDC ClientDC (this);
        ClientDC.SetROP2 (R2_NOT);
        ClientDC.MoveTo (m_PointOrigin);
        ClientDC.LineTo (m_PointOld);
        ClientDC.SetROP2 (R2_COPYPEN);
```

```
    ClientDC.MoveTo (m_PointOrigin);
    ClientDC.LineTo (point);

    CMiniDrawDoc* PDoc = GetDocument();
    PDoc->AddLine (m_PointOrigin.x, m_PointOrigin.y, point.x, point.y);
    }

  CView::OnLButtonUp(nFlags, point);
}
```

Summary

In this chapter, you learned how to write code to perform the main duties of the document class: storing the program data, providing access to the data through public member functions, and handling menu commands that directly affect the document data. The following are some of the general techniques and concepts that were explored:

- If the document consists of discrete data items, such as graphic figures, you should define a class for storing, displaying, and performing other operations on each of these items (such as the CLine class in MiniDraw).

- The document class can conveniently store groups of variables or class objects within a member object that's an instance of one of the MFC collection classes. For example, an instance of the MFC CObArray class can store a collection of pointers to objects (which must belong to a class derived directly or indirectly from the MFC class CObject), in an array-like data structure. By using the MFC class template CTypedPtrArray you can easily derive a class from CObArray designed to work with objects of a specific class. An example is the m_LineArray member object of MiniDraw's document class; this object stores a collection of CLine pointers.

- The document class should provide public member functions that allow the view class to obtain or modify the document data. For example, the OnDraw function of the view class needs to obtain the document data so that it can redraw this data in the view window. Also, the view class must be able to change or add data to the document in response to editing actions of the user. Examples are the AddLine, GetLine, and GetNumLines member functions of MiniDraw's document class.

- A menu command that directly alters the document data, such as the Undo and Delete All commands on the MiniDraw Edit menu, should be handled by the document class. You can use ClassWizard to add to the document class a handler for a menu command message.

- You can define handlers for two types of menu command messages: a COMMAND_UPDATE_UI message, which is sent immediately before the pop-up menu containing the command is displayed; and a COMMAND message, which is sent when the user chooses the menu command.

- A COMMAND_UPDATE_UI message handler initializes the menu item, using member functions of the CCmdUI object that it's passed. If this function disables the menu item, any accelerator keystroke assigned to the menu command will also be disabled.

- A COMMAND message handler carries out the menu command.

CHAPTER
TWELVE

12

Storing Documents in Disk Files

- Adding file I/O to MiniDraw

- Adding file I/O to MiniEdit

In this chapter, you'll learn how to write the code to perform an additional important task of the document class: saving and loading the document data to and from disk files. To demonstrate the basic MFC file I/O techniques, the chapter shows you how to add code for supporting the standard File menu commands (New, Open…, Save, and Save As…) to both the MiniDraw and the MiniEdit example programs that you created previously. You'll also learn how to add the drag-and-drop feature to these programs, which allows the user to open a file by dragging a file object from a Windows folder or the Windows Explorer and dropping it in the program window.

Adding File I/O to MiniDraw

In this section you'll add Open…, Save, and Save As… commands to the MiniDraw program, as well as the code necessary to support these commands. You should add all features to the MiniDraw source files you created in Chapter 11 (or to a copy of these files). If you didn't create these files, you can obtain a copy of them from the \MiniDrw2 companion-CD folder.

Adding the File Menu Commands

After you open the MiniDraw project in the Developer Studio, open the Resource-View tab in the Workspace window to display the program resources. To modify the program menu, open the menu editor by double-clicking the IDR_MAINFRAME identifier under the Menu branch of the graph:

In the menu editor, open the MiniDraw File menu. Immediately below the existing New command on the File menu, you should now add an Open… command, a Save command, a Save As… command, a separator, and a Recent File command (in the order listed). Use the techniques described in the previous chapters. For each new command, Table 12.1 lists the identifier, the caption, and any other feature that you should select in the Menu Item Properties dialog box. Figure 12.1 shows the completed File menu as it appears in the menu editor window.

TABLE 12.1: The Properties of the Items to Be Added to the MiniDraw File Menu

ID:	Caption	Other Features
ID_FILE_OPEN	&Open...\tCtrl+O	none
ID_FILE_SAVE	&Save\tCtrl+S	none
ID_FILE_SAVE_AS	Save &As...	none
none	none	Separator
ID_FILE_MRU_FILE1	Recent File	Dimmed

FIGURE 12.1:

The completed File menu for
the MiniDraw program

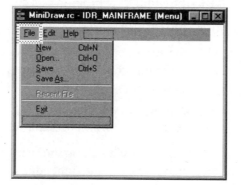

NOTE

After the program user has opened at least one file, the MFC code replaces the Recent File caption of the **ID_FILE_MRU_FILE1** menu command that you added with the name of the most recently opened file, and it also enables this command. The MFC code will add up to three more "most recently used" file commands to the File menu (you set four as the maximum number of "most recently used" file commands when you generated the program in AppWizard). The MFC code saves the names of these files in the Windows Registry, so that it can preserve the list of commands when the user quits and restarts the program.

You can now close the menu editor window. You don't need to define the keyboard accelerators for these commands, because AppWizard defined them for you when you first generated the application. (Recall that the menu generated by AppWizard included each of the commands listed in Table 12.1; in Chapter 10, however, you deleted them because they weren't needed for the first two versions of MiniDraw.)

The next step is to modify one of the MiniDraw resource strings to specify the default file extension that will be displayed in the Open and Save As dialog boxes. To do this, open the Developer Studio string editor by double-clicking the String Table item in the ResourceView hierarchical graph:

The first string listed in the string editor window has the identifier IDR_MAINFRAME. This string was created by AppWizard and contains information specific to the MiniDraw program. Its current value is as follows:

```
MiniDraw\n\nMiniDr\n\n\nMiniDraw.Document\nMiniDr Document
```

To modify the string, open the String Properties dialog box by double-clicking anywhere in the line containing the string. In the Caption: text box, modify the string so that it reads as follows:

```
MiniDraw\n\nMiniDr\nMiniDraw Files
(*.drw)\n.drw\nMiniDraw.Document\nMiniDr Document
```

(*Don't* press Enter while editing the string; the text will automatically wrap to the next line when it reaches the right edge of the text box.)

The first item you inserted (MiniDraw Files (*.drw)) is the string that the Open (or Save As) dialog box will display in the Files Of Type: (or Save As Type:) list to describe the program's *default file extension*. The second item you inserted (.drw) is the default file extension itself. When you run the MiniDraw program, if you *don't* specify a file extension when you open or save a file, the Open and Save As dialog boxes will display a list of all files with the default file extension, and the Save As dialog box will add the default file extension to the name you enter.

Specifying a Default File Extension in a New Program

The instructions just given are for adding a default file extension to an *existing* program. Alternatively, when you first create an application using AppWizard, you can specify a default file extension as follows:

1. In the AppWizard Step 4 dialog box, click the Advanced... button to open the Advanced Options dialog box, and open the Document Template Strings tab within this dialog box.

2. Enter the default file extension (without the period) into the File Extension: text box (for example, `drw`).

3. After you enter the default file extension, AppWizard will automatically enter a description of the file extension into the Filter Name: text box (for example, `MiniDraw Files` (*.drw)). This is the string that the Open (or Save As) dialog box will display in the Files Of Type: (or Save As Type:) list. If you wish, you can edit this string.

4. Click the Close button and proceed to enter the remaining information into the AppWizard dialog boxes.

Supporting the File Menu Commands

When you added the Undo and Delete All commands to the Edit menu (in the previous chapter), you had to use ClassWizard to define message handlers for these commands. You don't, however, need to define handlers for the New, Open..., Save, and Save As... commands, because the MFC classes provide handlers for you. You do, however, need to write code to *support* the MFC message handlers. (The MFC also provides handlers for the "most recently used" file commands on the File menu.)

The New menu command is handled by the `OnFileNew` member function of the `CWinApp` class (the MFC class from which the MiniDraw application class is derived). `OnFileNew` calls the version of the `DeleteContents` virtual function that you created in Chapter 11 to delete the current document contents, and then initializes a new document.

The Open... menu command is handled by the OnFileOpen member function of CWinApp. OnFileOpen displays the standard Open dialog box, which is shown in Figure 12.2. If the user selects a file and clicks the Open button, OnFileOpen proceeds to open the file for reading and then calls the Serialize member function of the document class (CMiniDrawDoc::Serialize). The Serialize function must perform the actual read operation. OnFileOpen also stores the full file path of the loaded file and displays the file name in the title bar of the main frame window. (The MFC handler for a "most recently used" file command opens the file for reading and calls Serialize, without displaying the Open dialog box.)

FIGURE 12.2:

The standard Open dialog box for opening a file

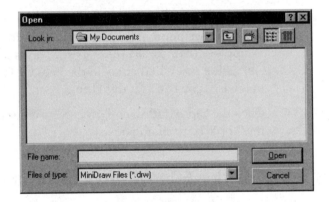

> **NOTE** If the file hasn't yet been saved, the Save As dialog box displays a default file name in the File Name: text box. This name is created by appending the default file extension (.drw for MiniDraw) to the name "Untitled".

The Save command is handled by the OnFileSave member function of the CDocument class (the MFC class from which the MiniDraw document class is derived), and the Save As... command is handled by the OnFileSaveAs member function of CDocument. OnFileSaveAs—as well as OnFileSave if the document is being saved for the first time—begins by displaying the standard Save As dialog box shown in Figure 12.3, to allow the user to specify the file name. Both OnFile-Save and OnFileSaveAs open the file for writing, and then call CMiniDrawDoc::Serialize to perform the actual write operation. These functions also store the full file path and display the file name in the title bar.

FIGURE 12.3:

The standard Save As dialog box for saving a file

NOTE

File names under Windows 95 and later and Windows NT are no longer limited to eight characters followed by a three-character extension. Under Windows 95, for example, file names can be as long as 255 characters. If you need to reserve a buffer to hold a file name, a file path, or some part of a file path, you can use one of the constants defined in the Stdlib.h C++ runtime header file to make sure that your buffer is large enough. These constants are _MAX_PATH, _MAX_DRIVE, _MAX_DIR, _MAX_FNAME, and _MAX_EXT.

Serializing the Document Data

When AppWizard generated the MiniDraw program, it defined the following minimal Serialize function as a member of the document class (in the file MiniDrawDoc.cpp):

```
//////////////////////////////////////////////////////////////////
///////////
// CMiniDrawDoc serialization

void CMiniDrawDoc::Serialize(CArchive& ar)
{
    if (ar.IsStoring())
    {
        // TODO: add storing code here
    }
    else
    {
        // TODO: add loading code here
    }
}
```

You must add your own code to this minimal definition for reading or writing the document data. To help you do this, the MFC passes Serialize a reference to an instance of the MFC class CArchive. The CArchive object is attached to the open file, and it provides a set of member functions that allow you to easily read data from this file, or write data to it.

The CArchive member function IsStoring returns TRUE if the file has been opened for writing (that is, if the user chose the Save or Save As... command), and IsStoring returns FALSE if the file has been opened for reading (that is, if the user chose the Open... command or a "most recently used" file command from the File menu). Consequently, you should place the output code within the if block and the input code within the else block.

In MiniDraw, the document class stores only a single data member, m_LineArray, which manages a set of CLine objects. Fortunately, the m_LineArray object has its own Serialize member function (which it inherits from CObArray), which you can call to read or write all the CLine objects that m_LineArray stores. As a result, you can complete the CMiniDrawDoc::Serialize function by simply adding two calls to CObArray::Serialize, as follows:

```
//////////////////////////////////////////////////////////////////
///////////
// CMiniDrawDoc serialization

void CMiniDrawDoc::Serialize(CArchive& ar)
{
   if (ar.IsStoring())
   {
      // TODO: add storing code here
      m_LineArray.Serialize (ar);
   }
   else
   {
      // TODO: add loading code here
      m_LineArray.Serialize (ar);
   }
}
```

If the data is being *written* to the file, CObArray::Serialize performs two main steps for each CLine object that it stores within the file:

1.   It writes information on the object's class to the file.

2. It calls the object's Serialize member function, which writes the object's data to the file.

If the data is being *read* from the file, CObArray::Serialize performs the following two steps for each CLine object:

1. It reads the class information from the file, dynamically creates an object of the appropriate class (that is, CLine), and saves a pointer to the object.

2. It calls the object's Serialize member function, which reads the object data from the file into the newly created object.

You must provide code that supports the serialization of the CLine objects. To do this you must first include two MFC macros, DECLARE_SERIAL and IMPLEMENT_SERIAL, in the definition of the CLine class, and you must define a default class constructor. These macros and the default constructor allow CObArray::Serialize first to store the class information in the file, and later to use this class information to dynamically create objects of the correct class (that is, the macros and constructor allow CObArray::Serialize to perform step 1 in both the lists above).

Add the DECLARE_SERIAL macro and the default constructor to the CLine class definition within MiniDrawDoc.h, as follows:

```
class CLine : public CObject
{
protected:
    int m_X1, m_Y1, m_X2, m_Y2;

    CLine ()
        {}
    DECLARE_SERIAL (CLine)

public:

// remainder of CLine definition ...

};
```

The parameter passed to DECLARE_SERIAL is simply the name of the class.

Insert the IMPLEMENT_SERIAL macro just above the CLine::Draw function definition within MiniDrawDoc.cpp:

```
////////////////////////////////////////////////////////////////
////////////
// CMiniDrawDoc commands

IMPLEMENT_SERIAL (CLine, CObject, 1)

void CLine::Draw (CDC *PDC)
    {
    PDC->MoveTo (m_X1, m_Y1);
    PDC->LineTo (m_X2, m_Y2);
    }
```

The first parameter passed to IMPLEMENT_SERIAL is the name of the class, and the second parameter is the name of its base class. The third parameter is a *schema number*, which identifies the particular version of the program. This number is stored within the data file that's written, and only a program that has specified this same number can read the file. Schema numbers thus prevent one version of a program from trying to read the data saved by another version, which might use a different data format. The current version of the MiniDraw program is assigned a schema number of 1; in later versions of the program, this number will be incremented whenever the format of the data changes. (You must not assign a version number of −1.)

The second step you must perform to support the serialization of the CLine objects is to add a Serialize member function to the CLine class, which will be called by CObArray::Serialize to read or write the data for each line. Add the Serialize declaration to the public section of the CLine class definition, in MiniDrawDoc.h:

```
public:
    CLine (int X1, int Y1, int X2, int Y2)
        {
        m_X1 = X1;
        m_Y1 = Y1;
        m_X2 = X2;
        m_Y2 = Y2;
        }
    void Draw (CDC *PDC);
    virtual void Serialize (CArchive& ar);
```

Then, add the following `Serialize` definition to the MiniDrawDoc.cpp file, immediately following the definition of `CLine::Draw`:

```
void CLine::Serialize (CArchive& ar)
  {
  if (ar.IsStoring())
     ar << m_X1 << m_Y1 << m_X2 << m_Y2;
  else
     ar >> m_X1 >> m_Y1 >> m_X2 >> m_Y2;
  }
```

NOTE A class whose objects are to be serialized, such as `CLine`, must be derived—directly or indirectly—from the MFC `CObject` class.

The `CLine::Serialize` function performs the actual reading and writing operations, rather than simply calling the `Serialize` member function of another class. `Serialize` uses the overloaded `<<` operator to write the `CLine` data members to the file, and it uses the overloaded `>>` operator to read the values of the data members from the file. Both these overloaded operators are defined by the `CArchive` class, and can be used for reading and writing a variety of data types.

Conclusion   As you can see from the file I/O code you added to MiniDraw, a class object that stores data is normally responsible for writing or reading this data to or from disk; specifically, it must provide a `Serialize` member function that writes or reads its data members to or from permanent storage in a disk file. (A general principle of object-oriented programming is that an object should operate on its own data; for example, an object should be able to draw itself, read itself, save itself, or perform other appropriate operations on its own data.) For a data member that is a class object, the `Serialize` function can call the object's `Serialize` member to have that object write or read its own data. For a data member that *isn't* an object, the `Serialize` function can use the overloaded `<<` and `>>` operators provided by `CArchive` to directly write or read the data member.

Setting the Modified Flag

The `CDocument` class maintains a *modified flag*, which indicates whether the document currently contains unsaved data. Before the MFC calls the `DeleteContents` member function of the program's document class to delete the document data, it checks this flag. (It calls `DeleteContents` before creating a new document, opening an existing document, or exiting the program.) If the modified flag is TRUE, indicating that the document contains unsaved data, it displays a message and allows the user to save the data.

CDocument sets the modified flag to FALSE whenever a document is first opened and whenever it's saved. Your responsibility is to call the CDocument: :SetModifiedFlag function to set the flag to TRUE whenever the document data is altered. To maintain the modified flag for the MiniDraw program, first add a call to SetModifiedFlag to the AddLine function in MiniDrawDoc.cpp:

```
void CMiniDrawDoc::AddLine (int X1, int Y1, int X2, int Y2)
   {
   CLine *PLine = new CLine (X1, Y1, X2, Y2);
   m_LineArray.Add (PLine);
   SetModifiedFlag ();
   }
```

Now add a call to SetModifiedFlag to the OnEditClearAll function, also in MiniDrawDoc.cpp:

```
void CMiniDrawDoc::OnEditClearAll()
{
   // TODO: Add your command handler code here

   DeleteContents ();
   UpdateAllViews (0);
   SetModifiedFlag ();
}
```

Finally, add a SetModifiedFlag call to OnEditUndo in MiniDrawDoc.cpp:

```
void CMiniDrawDoc::OnEditUndo()
{
   // TODO: Add your command handler code here

   int Index = m_LineArray.GetUpperBound ();
   if (Index > -1)
      {
      delete m_LineArray.GetAt (Index);
      m_LineArray.RemoveAt (Index);
      }
   UpdateAllViews (0);
   SetModifiedFlag ();
}
```

Because the SetModifiedFlag parameter has a default value of TRUE, you can set the modified flag to TRUE by calling the function without passing a value. To set the modified flag to FALSE, you must explicitly pass the value FALSE (though you don't normally need to do this, since CDocument handles this task for you).

Supporting Drag-and-Drop

If a program provides support for the drag-and-drop feature of Windows, the user can open a file by dragging a file object from a Windows folder (or from the Windows Explorer or other file manager that supports this feature) and dropping it in the program window.

To support the drag-and-drop feature in the MiniDraw program, you need merely to call the CWnd::DragAcceptFiles member function for the main frame window object. You should place this call within the InitInstance member function of the application class (in MiniDraw.cpp), following the call to UpdateWindow:

```
BOOL CMiniDrawApp::InitInstance()
{

   // other statements ...

   // Dispatch commands specified on the command line
   if (!ProcessShellCommand(cmdInfo))
      return FALSE;

   // The one and only window has been initialized, so show and
   // update it.
   m_pMainWnd->ShowWindow(SW_SHOW);
   m_pMainWnd->UpdateWindow();

   m_pMainWnd->DragAcceptFiles ();

   return TRUE;
}
```

The program application object contains a data member, m_pMainWnd (defined in CWinThread, the base class of CWinApp), which is a pointer that stores the address of the main frame window object. InitInstance uses this pointer to call DragAcceptFiles. The call to DragAcceptFiles must be placed *after* the call to ProcessShellCommand because it's within the call to ProcessShellCommand that the main frame window is created and m_pMainWnd is assigned its value.

As a result of calling `DragAcceptFiles`, whenever the user drops a file on the program window, the MFC automatically opens the file, creates a `CArchive` object, and calls the document object's `Serialize` function, just as if the user had chosen the Open… menu command and had selected the file. You therefore don't need to write any additional code to support the drag-and-drop feature.

Registering the MiniDraw File Type

You can add information to the Windows Registry that allows the user to open a MiniDraw file (that is, a file with the .drw file extension) by double-clicking a file object within a Windows folder or within the Windows Explorer (or other file manager that supports this feature). To do this, simply call the `CWinApp` member functions `EnableShellOpen` and `RegisterShellFileTypes` from the `InitInstance` function definition in MiniDraw.cpp, as follows:

```
BOOL CMiniDrawApp::InitInstance()
{

    // other statements ...

    AddDocTemplate(pDocTemplate);

    EnableShellOpen ();
    RegisterShellFileTypes ();

    // Parse command line for standard shell commands, DDE, file
    // open
    CCommandLineInfo cmdInfo;

    // other statements ...

}
```

These two function calls create an association—in the Windows Registry—between the MiniDraw default file extension (.drw) and the MiniDraw program. Subsequently, the object for any file with this extension will display the Mini-Draw program icon, and double-clicking the object will run the MiniDraw program—if it's not already running—and cause MiniDraw to open the file. The association will remain in the Registry permanently, unless you explicitly change it (using the Windows Explorer or by some other means).

Note that the calls to EnableShellOpen and RegisterShellFileTypes must be placed *after* the call to AddDocTemplate, which adds the document template to the application object, so that the information on the default file extension and document type will be available to the application object (recall that the default extension is included in the resource string that has the IDR_MAINFRAME identifier, and that this identifier is supplied to the template when it's created).

This completes the modifications to MiniDraw. You can now build and run the program.

The MiniDraw Source Code

The following listings, Listings 12.1 through 12.8, are the C++ source files for the latest version of the MiniDraw program. A complete copy of these files is contained in the \MiniDrw3 companion-CD folder.

Listing 12.1

```
// MiniDraw.h : main header file for the MINIDRAW application
//

#if !defined(AFX_MINIDRAW_H__11E83924_999A_11D1_80FC_00C0F6A83B7F__INCLUDED_)
#define AFX_MINIDRAW_H__11E83924_999A_11D1_80FC_00C0F6A83B7F__INCLUDED_

#if _MSC_VER > 1000
#pragma once
#endif // _MSC_VER > 1000

#ifndef __AFXWIN_H__
    #error include 'stdafx.h' before including this file for PCH
#endif

#include "resource.h"        // main symbols

/////////////////////////////////////////////////////////////////////////////
// CMiniDrawApp:
// See MiniDraw.cpp for the implementation of this class
//

class CMiniDrawApp : public CWinApp
```

```
{
public:
    CMiniDrawApp();

// Overrides
    // ClassWizard generated virtual function overrides
    //{{AFX_VIRTUAL(CMiniDrawApp)
    public:
    virtual BOOL InitInstance();
    //}}AFX_VIRTUAL

// Implementation

    //{{AFX_MSG(CMiniDrawApp)
    afx_msg void OnAppAbout();
        // NOTE - the ClassWizard will add and remove member functions here.
        //     DO NOT EDIT what you see in these blocks of generated code !
    //}}AFX_MSG
    DECLARE_MESSAGE_MAP()
};


/////////////////////////////////////////////////////////////////////////////

//{{AFX_INSERT_LOCATION}}
// Microsoft Visual C++ will insert additional declarations immediately before
// the previous line.

#endif
// !defined(AFX_MINIDRAW_H__11E83924_999A_11D1_80FC_00C0F6A83B7F__INCLUDED_)
```

Listing 12.2

```
// MiniDraw.cpp : Defines the class behaviors for the application.
//

#include "stdafx.h"
#include "MiniDraw.h"

#include "MainFrm.h"
#include "MiniDrawDoc.h"
#include "MiniDrawView.h"
```

```
#ifdef _DEBUG
#define new DEBUG_NEW
#undef THIS_FILE
static char THIS_FILE[] = __FILE__;
#endif

/////////////////////////////////////////////////////////////////////////////
// CMiniDrawApp

BEGIN_MESSAGE_MAP(CMiniDrawApp, CWinApp)
   //{{AFX_MSG_MAP(CMiniDrawApp)
   ON_COMMAND(ID_APP_ABOUT, OnAppAbout)
      // NOTE - the ClassWizard will add and remove mapping macros here.
      //    DO NOT EDIT what you see in these blocks of generated code!
   //}}AFX_MSG_MAP
   // Standard file based document commands
   ON_COMMAND(ID_FILE_NEW, CWinApp::OnFileNew)
   ON_COMMAND(ID_FILE_OPEN, CWinApp::OnFileOpen)
END_MESSAGE_MAP()

/////////////////////////////////////////////////////////////////////////////
// CMiniDrawApp construction

CMiniDrawApp::CMiniDrawApp()
{
   // TODO: add construction code here,
   // Place all significant initialization in InitInstance
}

/////////////////////////////////////////////////////////////////////////////
// The one and only CMiniDrawApp object

CMiniDrawApp theApp;

/////////////////////////////////////////////////////////////////////////////
// CMiniDrawApp initialization

BOOL CMiniDrawApp::InitInstance()
{
   // Standard initialization
   // If you are not using these features and wish to reduce the size
   //  of your final executable, you should remove from the following
   //  the specific initialization routines you do not need.
```

```
#ifdef _AFXDLL
   Enable3dControls();          // Call this when using MFC in a shared DLL
#else
   Enable3dControlsStatic();    // Call this when linking to MFC statically
#endif

   // Change the registry key under which our settings are stored.
   // You should modify this string to be something appropriate
   // such as the name of your company or organization.
   SetRegistryKey(_T("Local AppWizard-Generated Applications"));

   LoadStdProfileSettings();  // Load standard INI file options (including MRU)

   // Register the application's document templates.  Document templates
   //  serve as the connection between documents, frame windows and views.

   CSingleDocTemplate* pDocTemplate;
   pDocTemplate = new CSingleDocTemplate(
      IDR_MAINFRAME,
      RUNTIME_CLASS(CMiniDrawDoc),
      RUNTIME_CLASS(CMainFrame),         // main SDI frame window
      RUNTIME_CLASS(CMiniDrawView));
   AddDocTemplate(pDocTemplate);

   EnableShellOpen ();
   RegisterShellFileTypes ();

   // Parse command line for standard shell commands, DDE, file open
   CCommandLineInfo cmdInfo;
   ParseCommandLine(cmdInfo);

   // Dispatch commands specified on the command line
   if (!ProcessShellCommand(cmdInfo))
      return FALSE;

   // The one and only window has been initialized, so show and update it.
   m_pMainWnd->ShowWindow(SW_SHOW);
   m_pMainWnd->UpdateWindow();
```

```cpp
    m_pMainWnd->DragAcceptFiles ();

    return TRUE;
}


//////////////////////////////////////////////////////////////////////////
// CAboutDlg dialog used for App About

class CAboutDlg : public CDialog
{
public:
    CAboutDlg();

// Dialog Data
    //{{AFX_DATA(CAboutDlg)
    enum { IDD = IDD_ABOUTBOX };
    //}}AFX_DATA

    // ClassWizard generated virtual function overrides
    //{{AFX_VIRTUAL(CAboutDlg)
    protected:
    virtual void DoDataExchange(CDataExchange* pDX);    // DDX/DDV support
    //}}AFX_VIRTUAL

// Implementation
protected:
    //{{AFX_MSG(CAboutDlg)
        // No message handlers
    //}}AFX_MSG
    DECLARE_MESSAGE_MAP()
};

CAboutDlg::CAboutDlg() : CDialog(CAboutDlg::IDD)
{
    //{{AFX_DATA_INIT(CAboutDlg)
    //}}AFX_DATA_INIT
}

void CAboutDlg::DoDataExchange(CDataExchange* pDX)
{
    CDialog::DoDataExchange(pDX);
```

```
    //{{AFX_DATA_MAP(CAboutDlg)
    //}}AFX_DATA_MAP
}

BEGIN_MESSAGE_MAP(CAboutDlg, CDialog)
    //{{AFX_MSG_MAP(CAboutDlg)
        // No message handlers
    //}}AFX_MSG_MAP
END_MESSAGE_MAP()

// App command to run the dialog
void CMiniDrawApp::OnAppAbout()
{
    CAboutDlg aboutDlg;
    aboutDlg.DoModal();
}


/////////////////////////////////////////////////////////////////////////
// CMiniDrawApp commands
```

Listing 12.3

```
// MiniDrawDoc.h : interface of the CMiniDrawDoc class
//
/////////////////////////////////////////////////////////////////////////

#if !defined(AFX_MINIDRAWDOC_H__11E8392A_999A_11D1_80FC_00C0F6A83B7F__INCLUDED_)
#define AFX_MINIDRAWDOC_H__11E8392A_999A_11D1_80FC_00C0F6A83B7F__INCLUDED_

#if _MSC_VER > 1000
#pragma once
#endif // _MSC_VER > 1000

class CLine : public CObject
{
protected:
    int m_X1, m_Y1, m_X2, m_Y2;

    CLine ()
        {}
    DECLARE_SERIAL (CLine)
```

```
public:
   CLine (int X1, int Y1, int X2, int Y2)
      {
      m_X1 = X1;
      m_Y1 = Y1;
      m_X2 = X2;
      m_Y2 = Y2;
      }
   void Draw (CDC *PDC);
   virtual void Serialize (CArchive& ar);
};

class CMiniDrawDoc : public CDocument
{
protected:
   CTypedPtrArray<CObArray, CLine*> m_LineArray;

public:
   void AddLine (int X1, int Y1, int X2, int Y2);
   CLine *GetLine (int Index);
   int GetNumLines ();

protected: // create from serialization only
   CMiniDrawDoc();
   DECLARE_DYNCREATE(CMiniDrawDoc)

// Attributes
public:

// Operations
public:

// Overrides
   // ClassWizard generated virtual function overrides
   //{{AFX_VIRTUAL(CMiniDrawDoc)
   public:
   virtual BOOL OnNewDocument();
   virtual void Serialize(CArchive& ar);
   virtual void DeleteContents();
   //}}AFX_VIRTUAL
```

```
// Implementation
public:
    virtual ~CMiniDrawDoc();
#ifdef _DEBUG
    virtual void AssertValid() const;
    virtual void Dump(CDumpContext& dc) const;
#endif

protected:

// Generated message map functions
protected:
    //{{AFX_MSG(CMiniDrawDoc)
    afx_msg void OnEditClearAll();
    afx_msg void OnUpdateEditClearAll(CCmdUI* pCmdUI);
    afx_msg void OnEditUndo();
    afx_msg void OnUpdateEditUndo(CCmdUI* pCmdUI);
    //}}AFX_MSG
    DECLARE_MESSAGE_MAP()
};

//////////////////////////////////////////////////////////////////////////

//{{AFX_INSERT_LOCATION}}
// Microsoft Visual C++ will insert additional declarations immediately before
// the previous line.

#endif
// !defined(AFX_MINIDRAWDOC_H__11E8392A_999A_11D1_80FC_00C0F6A83B7F__INCLUDED_)
```

Listing 12.4

```
// MiniDrawDoc.cpp : implementation of the CMiniDrawDoc class
//

#include "stdafx.h"
#include "MiniDraw.h"

#include "MiniDrawDoc.h"

#ifdef _DEBUG
#define new DEBUG_NEW
```

```
#undef THIS_FILE
static char THIS_FILE[] = __FILE__;
#endif

/////////////////////////////////////////////////////////////////////////////
// CMiniDrawDoc

IMPLEMENT_DYNCREATE(CMiniDrawDoc, CDocument)

BEGIN_MESSAGE_MAP(CMiniDrawDoc, CDocument)
    //{{AFX_MSG_MAP(CMiniDrawDoc)
    ON_COMMAND(ID_EDIT_CLEAR_ALL, OnEditClearAll)
    ON_UPDATE_COMMAND_UI(ID_EDIT_CLEAR_ALL, OnUpdateEditClearAll)
    ON_COMMAND(ID_EDIT_UNDO, OnEditUndo)
    ON_UPDATE_COMMAND_UI(ID_EDIT_UNDO, OnUpdateEditUndo)
    //}}AFX_MSG_MAP
END_MESSAGE_MAP()

/////////////////////////////////////////////////////////////////////////////
// CMiniDrawDoc construction/destruction

CMiniDrawDoc::CMiniDrawDoc()
{
    // TODO: add one-time construction code here

}

CMiniDrawDoc::~CMiniDrawDoc()
{
}

BOOL CMiniDrawDoc::OnNewDocument()
{
    if (!CDocument::OnNewDocument())
        return FALSE;

    // TODO: add reinitialization code here
    // (SDI documents will reuse this document)

    return TRUE;
}
```

```
//////////////////////////////////////////////////////////////////////////
// CMiniDrawDoc serialization

void CMiniDrawDoc::Serialize(CArchive& ar)
{
   if (ar.IsStoring())
   {
      // TODO: add storing code here
      m_LineArray.Serialize (ar);
   }
   else
   {
      // TODO: add loading code here
      m_LineArray.Serialize (ar);
   }
}


//////////////////////////////////////////////////////////////////////////
// CMiniDrawDoc diagnostics

#ifdef _DEBUG
void CMiniDrawDoc::AssertValid() const
{
   CDocument::AssertValid();
}

void CMiniDrawDoc::Dump(CDumpContext& dc) const
{
   CDocument::Dump(dc);
}
#endif //_DEBUG


//////////////////////////////////////////////////////////////////////////
// CMiniDrawDoc commands

IMPLEMENT_SERIAL (CLine, CObject, 1)

void CLine::Draw (CDC *PDC)
   {
   PDC->MoveTo (m_X1, m_Y1);
   PDC->LineTo (m_X2, m_Y2);
   }
```

```
void CLine::Serialize (CArchive& ar)
   {
   if (ar.IsStoring())
      ar << m_X1 << m_Y1 << m_X2 << m_Y2;
   else
      ar >> m_X1 >> m_Y1 >> m_X2 >> m_Y2;
   }

void CMiniDrawDoc::AddLine (int X1, int Y1, int X2, int Y2)
   {
   CLine *PLine = new CLine (X1, Y1, X2, Y2);
   m_LineArray.Add (PLine);
   SetModifiedFlag ();
   }

CLine *CMiniDrawDoc::GetLine (int Index)
   {
   if (Index < 0 || Index > m_LineArray.GetUpperBound ())
      return 0;
   return m_LineArray.GetAt (Index);
   }

int CMiniDrawDoc::GetNumLines ()
   {
   return m_LineArray.GetSize ();
   }

void CMiniDrawDoc::DeleteContents()
{
   // TODO: Add your specialized code here and/or call the base class

   int Index = m_LineArray.GetSize ();
   while (Index--)
      delete m_LineArray.GetAt (Index);
   m_LineArray.RemoveAll ();

   CDocument::DeleteContents();
}

void CMiniDrawDoc::OnEditClearAll()
{
   // TODO: Add your command handler code here
```

```
   DeleteContents ();
   UpdateAllViews (0);
   SetModifiedFlag ();
}

void CMiniDrawDoc::OnUpdateEditClearAll(CCmdUI* pCmdUI)
{
   // TODO: Add your command update UI handler code here

   pCmdUI->Enable (m_LineArray.GetSize ());
}

void CMiniDrawDoc::OnEditUndo()
{
   // TODO: Add your command handler code here

   int Index = m_LineArray.GetUpperBound ();
   if (Index > -1)
      {
      delete m_LineArray.GetAt (Index);
      m_LineArray.RemoveAt (Index);
      }
   UpdateAllViews (0);
   SetModifiedFlag ();
}

void CMiniDrawDoc::OnUpdateEditUndo(CCmdUI* pCmdUI)
{
   // TODO: Add your command update UI handler code here

   pCmdUI->Enable (m_LineArray.GetSize ());
}
```

Listing 12.5

```
// MainFrm.h : interface of the CMainFrame class
//
/////////////////////////////////////////////////////////////////////////

#if !defined(AFX_MAINFRM_H__11E83928_999A_11D1_80FC_00C0F6A83B7F__INCLUDED_)
#define AFX_MAINFRM_H__11E83928_999A_11D1_80FC_00C0F6A83B7F__INCLUDED_
```

```
#if _MSC_VER > 1000
#pragma once
#endif // _MSC_VER > 1000

class CMainFrame : public CFrameWnd
{
protected: // create from serialization only
    CMainFrame();
    DECLARE_DYNCREATE(CMainFrame)

// Attributes
public:

// Operations
public:

// Overrides
    // ClassWizard generated virtual function overrides
    //{{AFX_VIRTUAL(CMainFrame)
    virtual BOOL PreCreateWindow(CREATESTRUCT& cs);
    //}}AFX_VIRTUAL

// Implementation
public:
    virtual ~CMainFrame();
#ifdef _DEBUG
    virtual void AssertValid() const;
    virtual void Dump(CDumpContext& dc) const;
#endif

// Generated message map functions
protected:
    //{{AFX_MSG(CMainFrame)
    //}}AFX_MSG
    DECLARE_MESSAGE_MAP()
};

/////////////////////////////////////////////////////////////////////////////

//{{AFX_INSERT_LOCATION}}
// Microsoft Visual C++ will insert additional declarations immediately before
// the previous line.
```

```
#endif
// !defined(AFX_MAINFRM_H__11E83928_999A_11D1_80FC_00C0F6A83B7F__INCLUDED_)
```

Listing 12.6

```cpp
// MainFrm.cpp : implementation of the CMainFrame class
//

#include "stdafx.h"
#include "MiniDraw.h"

#include "MainFrm.h"

#ifdef _DEBUG
#define new DEBUG_NEW
#undef THIS_FILE
static char THIS_FILE[] = __FILE__;
#endif

/////////////////////////////////////////////////////////////////////////////
// CMainFrame

IMPLEMENT_DYNCREATE(CMainFrame, CFrameWnd)

BEGIN_MESSAGE_MAP(CMainFrame, CFrameWnd)
    //{{AFX_MSG_MAP(CMainFrame)
    //}}AFX_MSG_MAP
END_MESSAGE_MAP()

/////////////////////////////////////////////////////////////////////////////
// CMainFrame construction/destruction

CMainFrame::CMainFrame()
{
    // TODO: add member initialization code here

}

CMainFrame::~CMainFrame()
{
}
```

```
BOOL CMainFrame::PreCreateWindow(CREATESTRUCT& cs)
{
    if( !CFrameWnd::PreCreateWindow(cs) )
        return FALSE;
    // TODO: Modify the Window class or styles here by modifying
    //   the CREATESTRUCT cs

    return TRUE;
}


/////////////////////////////////////////////////////////////////////////////
// CMainFrame diagnostics

#ifdef _DEBUG
void CMainFrame::AssertValid() const
{
    CFrameWnd::AssertValid();
}

void CMainFrame::Dump(CDumpContext& dc) const
{
    CFrameWnd::Dump(dc);
}

#endif //_DEBUG


/////////////////////////////////////////////////////////////////////////////
// CMainFrame message handlers
```

Listing 12.7

```
// MiniDrawView.h : interface of the CMiniDrawView class
//
/////////////////////////////////////////////////////////////////////////////

#if !defined(AFX_MINIDRAWVIEW_H__11E8392C_999A_11D1_80FC_00C0F6A83B7F__INCLUDED_)
#define AFX_MINIDRAWVIEW_H__11E8392C_999A_11D1_80FC_00C0F6A83B7F__INCLUDED_

#if _MSC_VER > 1000
#pragma once
#endif // _MSC_VER > 1000
```

```
class CMiniDrawView : public CView
{
protected:
    CString m_ClassName;
    int m_Dragging;
    HCURSOR m_HCross;
    CPoint m_PointOld;
    CPoint m_PointOrigin;

protected: // create from serialization only
    CMiniDrawView();
    DECLARE_DYNCREATE(CMiniDrawView)

// Attributes
public:
    CMiniDrawDoc* GetDocument();

// Operations
public:

// Overrides
    // ClassWizard generated virtual function overrides
    //{{AFX_VIRTUAL(CMiniDrawView)
    public:
    virtual void OnDraw(CDC* pDC);  // overridden to draw this view
    virtual BOOL PreCreateWindow(CREATESTRUCT& cs);
    protected:
    //}}AFX_VIRTUAL

// Implementation
public:
    virtual ~CMiniDrawView();
#ifdef _DEBUG
    virtual void AssertValid() const;
    virtual void Dump(CDumpContext& dc) const;
#endif

protected:

// Generated message map functions
protected:
    //{{AFX_MSG(CMiniDrawView)
    afx_msg void OnLButtonDown(UINT nFlags, CPoint point);
    afx_msg void OnMouseMove(UINT nFlags, CPoint point);
```

```
    afx_msg void OnLButtonUp(UINT nFlags, CPoint point);
    //}}AFX_MSG
    DECLARE_MESSAGE_MAP()
};


#ifndef _DEBUG  // debug version in MiniDrawView.cpp
inline CMiniDrawDoc* CMiniDrawView::GetDocument()
    { return (CMiniDrawDoc*)m_pDocument; }
#endif


/////////////////////////////////////////////////////////////////////////////

//{{AFX_INSERT_LOCATION}}
// Microsoft Visual C++ will insert additional declarations immediately before
// the previous line.

#endif
// !defined(AFX_MINIDRAWVIEW_H__11E8392C_999A_11D1_80FC_00C0F6A83B7F__INCLUDED_)
```

Listing 12.8

```cpp
// MiniDrawView.cpp : implementation of the CMiniDrawView class
//

#include "stdafx.h"
#include "MiniDraw.h"

#include "MiniDrawDoc.h"
#include "MiniDrawView.h"

#ifdef _DEBUG
#define new DEBUG_NEW
#undef THIS_FILE
static char THIS_FILE[] = __FILE__;
#endif


/////////////////////////////////////////////////////////////////////////////
// CMiniDrawView

IMPLEMENT_DYNCREATE(CMiniDrawView, CView)

BEGIN_MESSAGE_MAP(CMiniDrawView, CView)
    //{{AFX_MSG_MAP(CMiniDrawView)
```

```
    ON_WM_LBUTTONDOWN()
    ON_WM_MOUSEMOVE()
    ON_WM_LBUTTONUP()
    //}}AFX_MSG_MAP
END_MESSAGE_MAP()

/////////////////////////////////////////////////////////////////////////////
// CMiniDrawView construction/destruction

CMiniDrawView::CMiniDrawView()
{
    // TODO: add construction code here

    m_Dragging = 0;
    m_HCross = AfxGetApp ()->LoadStandardCursor (IDC_CROSS);
}


CMiniDrawView::~CMiniDrawView()
{
}


BOOL CMiniDrawView::PreCreateWindow(CREATESTRUCT& cs)
{
    // TODO: Modify the Window class or styles here by modifying
    //   the CREATESTRUCT cs

    m_ClassName = AfxRegisterWndClass
        (CS_HREDRAW | CS_VREDRAW,                  // class styles
        0,                                          // no cursor
        (HBRUSH)::GetStockObject (WHITE_BRUSH),   // assign white
                                                    // background brush
        0);                                         // no icon
    cs.lpszClass = m_ClassName;

    return CView::PreCreateWindow(cs);
}


/////////////////////////////////////////////////////////////////////////////
// CMiniDrawView drawing

void CMiniDrawView::OnDraw(CDC* pDC)
{
    CMiniDrawDoc* pDoc = GetDocument();
    ASSERT_VALID(pDoc);
```

```
    // TODO: add draw code for native data here

    int Index = pDoc->GetNumLines ();
    while (Index--)
        pDoc->GetLine (Index)->Draw (pDC);

}

///////////////////////////////////////////////////////////////////////////
// CMiniDrawView diagnostics

#ifdef _DEBUG
void CMiniDrawView::AssertValid() const
{
    CView::AssertValid();
}

void CMiniDrawView::Dump(CDumpContext& dc) const
{
    CView::Dump(dc);
}

CMiniDrawDoc* CMiniDrawView::GetDocument() // non-debug version is inline
{
    ASSERT(m_pDocument->IsKindOf(RUNTIME_CLASS(CMiniDrawDoc)));
    return (CMiniDrawDoc*)m_pDocument;
}
#endif //_DEBUG

///////////////////////////////////////////////////////////////////////////
// CMiniDrawView message handlers

void CMiniDrawView::OnLButtonDown(UINT nFlags, CPoint point)
{
    // TODO: Add your message handler code here and/or call default

    m_PointOrigin = point;
    m_PointOld = point;
    SetCapture ();
    m_Dragging = 1;
```

```
    RECT Rect;
    GetClientRect (&Rect);
    ClientToScreen (&Rect);
    ::ClipCursor (&Rect);

    CView::OnLButtonDown(nFlags, point);
}

void CMiniDrawView::OnMouseMove(UINT nFlags, CPoint point)
{
    // TODO: Add your message handler code here and/or call default

    ::SetCursor (m_HCross);

    if (m_Dragging)
        {
        CClientDC ClientDC (this);
        ClientDC.SetROP2 (R2_NOT);
        ClientDC.MoveTo (m_PointOrigin);
        ClientDC.LineTo (m_PointOld);
        ClientDC.MoveTo (m_PointOrigin);
        ClientDC.LineTo (point);
        m_PointOld = point;
        }

    CView::OnMouseMove(nFlags, point);
}

void CMiniDrawView::OnLButtonUp(UINT nFlags, CPoint point)
{
    // TODO: Add your message handler code here and/or call default

    if (m_Dragging)
        {
        m_Dragging = 0;
        ::ReleaseCapture ();
        ::ClipCursor (NULL);
        CClientDC ClientDC (this);
        ClientDC.SetROP2 (R2_NOT);
```

```
ClientDC.MoveTo (m_PointOrigin);
ClientDC.LineTo (m_PointOld);
ClientDC.SetROP2 (R2_COPYPEN);
ClientDC.MoveTo (m_PointOrigin);
ClientDC.LineTo (point);

CMiniDrawDoc* PDoc = GetDocument();
PDoc->AddLine (m_PointOrigin.x, m_PointOrigin.y, point.x, point.y);
}

CView::OnLButtonUp(nFlags, point);
}
```

Adding File I/O to MiniEdit

In this section, you'll add support for file I/O to the MiniEdit program. Specifically, you'll add New, Open…, Save, Save As…, and Recent File commands to the File menu, and you'll write the code necessary to support these commands.

You should make your modifications to the source files you created in Chapter 10. (If you didn't create these files, you can obtain a copy of them from the \MiniEdt1 companion-CD folder.)

Defining the Resources

After opening the MiniEdit project in the Developer Studio, open the Resource-View tab in the Workspace window to display the graph of the program resources.

First, open the menu editor by double-clicking the IDR_MAINFRAME identifier under the Menu branch of the graph. Use the menu editor, as described previously, to add the following commands *above* the existing Print… command on the File menu: New, Open…, Save, and Save As….

Then, *below* the Print… command, add a separator and a Recent File command. Table 12.2 lists the identifier, caption, and any other feature you need to select, for each of the menu items that you'll add. Figure 12.4 shows the completed File menu as it appears in the menu editor window.

TABLE 12.2: The Properties of the MiniEdit New File Menu Items

ID:	Caption	Other Features
ID_FILE_NEW	&New\tCtrl+N	none
ID_FILE_OPEN	&Open...\tCtrl+O	none
ID_FILE_SAVE	&Save\tCtrl+S	none
ID_FILE_SAVE_AS	Save &As...	none
none	none	Separator
ID_FILE_MRU_FILE1	Recent File	Dimmed

FIGURE 12.4:

The completed File menu for
the MiniEdit program

Next, you'll modify the MiniEdit IDR_MAINFRAME resource string to specify the
.txt default file extension, using the same technique that you employed for the
MiniDraw program (in the earlier section "Adding the File Menu Commands").
You should edit the string so that it reads as follows:

```
MiniEdit\n\nMiniEd\nMiniEdit Files
(*.txt)\n.txt\nMiniEdit.Document\nMiniEd Document
```

Adding Supporting Code

To support the menu commands, you must first define an overriding version
of the DeleteContents virtual function as a member of the document class
CMiniEditDoc. As you've seen, the MFC calls this function before creating a new

document, opening an existing document, or ending the program, and its duty is to delete the document data. To create the function declaration and a shell of the function definition, use ClassWizard as described in Chapter 11 (in the section "Deleting the Document Data"). Then add code as follows to the Delete-Contents definition generated by ClassWizard in the file MiniEditDoc.cpp:

```
///////////////////////////////////////////////////////////
///////////
// CMiniEditDoc commands

void CMiniEditDoc::DeleteContents()
{
    // TODO: Add your specialized code here and/or call the base
    // class

    POSITION Pos = GetFirstViewPosition ();
    CEditView *PCEditView = (CEditView *)GetNextView (Pos);
    if (PCEditView)
        PCEditView->SetWindowText ("");

    CDocument::DeleteContents();
}
```

Because the view class is derived from CEditView, the document text is stored internally by the view window itself. To delete this text, DeleteContents first calls the CDocument member functions GetFirstViewPosition and GetNextView to obtain a pointer to the document's view class. (As you'll learn in Chapter 13, a document can have more than one view attached to it; in this case, these two functions allow you to access *all* attached views.) GetFirstViewPosition obtains the index of the first view object (or, in the case of MiniEdit, the *only* view object). GetNewView then returns a pointer to this object and updates the parameter Pos to the index of the next view in the list, or it assigns 0 to Pos if there are no more views (as in MiniEdit). (Note that GetNextView can change Pos because it's passed as a *reference* parameter.)

NOTE   The CEditView class assigns the "EDIT" predefined Windows window class to the view window. A window belonging to this Windows window class is known as an *edit control*. The Windows code that supports an edit control not only stores the text displayed in the control, but also provides a large set of editing features.

If GetNextView returns a nonzero address for the view object, DeleteContents uses the address to call the CWnd::SetWindowText function to set the window text to the empty string, thereby deleting the document text. If, however, Get-NextView returns 0, DeleteContents proceeds without attempting to delete the document text. (When the user terminates the program, the MFC code deletes the view object and *then* calls DeleteContents; in this case, GetNextView returns zero because the view object no longer exists, and DeleteContents has no need to delete the text.)

NOTE   The size of the buffer that the CEditView window uses to store text is limited to approximately 50KB. If you try to open a file that's larger than this, the CEditView code displays a message ("Failed to open document") and doesn't read in the file. If you try to type in more than approximately this amount of text, the view window simply stops accepting characters (without issuing a warning).

Finally, to implement the drag-and-drop file opening feature, include a call to DragAcceptFiles within the InitInstance function in MiniEdit.cpp:

```
BOOL CMiniEditApp::InitInstance()
{
    // other statements ...

    m_pMainWnd->UpdateWindow();

    m_pMainWnd->DragAcceptFiles ();

    return TRUE;
}
```

For the MiniEdit program, you don't need to set the modified flag (as described for MiniDraw in the previous section), because the CEditView class handles this task for you. This is the final modification. You can now build and run the new version of MiniEdit.

NOTE

For MiniEdit, you *don't* need to add code to the `Serialize` function of the document class (as you did with the MiniDraw program), because when you base the view class on `CEditView`, AppWizard automatically adds the required code to `Serialize` for you. This code calls the `CEditView` member function `Serialize-Raw`, which reads and writes the data displayed by the view window as pure text (that is, it doesn't store class or version information in the file).

The *CArchive Read* and *Write* Functions

In this chapter, you learned how to read or write a data member that is a fundamental type by using the `CArchive` overloaded `<<` and `>>` operators. You also learned how to read or write a member object by calling the object's `Serialize` function. Additionally, `CArchive` provides the member functions `Read` and `Write`, which allow you to read or write arbitrary blocks of data. You might need to use these functions, for example, to store a structure or a text buffer.

The `CArchive::Read` function has the following form,

```
UINT Read (void* lpBuf, UINT nMax);
```

where `lpBuf` is the address of the memory location that is to receive the data, and `nMax` is the number of bytes to read.

The `CArchive::Write` function has the following form,

```
void Write (const void* lpBuf, UINT nMax);
```

where `lpBuf` is the address of the block of data you want to write, and `nMax` is the number of bytes to write. The `Write` function writes only the raw bytes from the specified location; it doesn't format the data or add class information.

Each of these functions throws an exception of type `CFileException` if it encounters an error.

For more information on the `CArchive` class and a description of all its member functions, see the following online help topic: *Visual C++ Documentation, Reference, Microsoft Foundation Class Library and Templates, Microsoft Foundation Class Library, Class Library Reference, CArchive*.

The MiniEdit Source Code

The following listings, Listings 12.9 through 12.16, provide the C++ source code for the version of MiniEdit you created in this chapter. A complete copy of these files is included in the \MiniEdt2 companion-CD folder.

Listing 12.9

```cpp
// MiniEdit.h : main header file for the MINIEDIT application
//

#if !defined(AFX_MINIEDIT_H__BAFB48A4_9A70_11D1_80FC_00C0F6A83B7F__INCLUDED_)
#define AFX_MINIEDIT_H__BAFB48A4_9A70_11D1_80FC_00C0F6A83B7F__INCLUDED_

#if _MSC_VER > 1000
#pragma once
#endif // _MSC_VER > 1000

#ifndef __AFXWIN_H__
    #error include 'stdafx.h' before including this file for PCH
#endif

#include "resource.h"        // main symbols

/////////////////////////////////////////////////////////////////////////////
// CMiniEditApp:
// See MiniEdit.cpp for the implementation of this class
//

class CMiniEditApp : public CWinApp
{
public:
    CMiniEditApp();

// Overrides
    // ClassWizard generated virtual function overrides
    //{{AFX_VIRTUAL(CMiniEditApp)
    public:
    virtual BOOL InitInstance();
    //}}AFX_VIRTUAL

// Implementation
```

```
    //{{AFX_MSG(CMiniEditApp)
    afx_msg void OnAppAbout();
        // NOTE - the ClassWizard will add and remove member functions here.
        //      DO NOT EDIT what you see in these blocks of generated code !
    //}}AFX_MSG
    DECLARE_MESSAGE_MAP()
};


///////////////////////////////////////////////////////////////////////////

//{{AFX_INSERT_LOCATION}}
// Microsoft Visual C++ will insert additional declarations immediately before
// the previous line.

#endif
// !defined(AFX_MINIEDIT_H__BAFB48A4_9A70_11D1_80FC_00C0F6A83B7F__INCLUDED_)
```

Listing 12.10

```
// MiniEdit.cpp : Defines the class behaviors for the application.
//

#include "stdafx.h"
#include "MiniEdit.h"

#include "MainFrm.h"
#include "MiniEditDoc.h"
#include "MiniEditView.h"

#ifdef _DEBUG
#define new DEBUG_NEW
#undef THIS_FILE
static char THIS_FILE[] = __FILE__;
#endif

///////////////////////////////////////////////////////////////////////////
// CMiniEditApp

BEGIN_MESSAGE_MAP(CMiniEditApp, CWinApp)
    //{{AFX_MSG_MAP(CMiniEditApp)
    ON_COMMAND(ID_APP_ABOUT, OnAppAbout)
```

```
      // NOTE - the ClassWizard will add and remove mapping macros here.
      //     DO NOT EDIT what you see in these blocks of generated code!
   //}}AFX_MSG_MAP
   // Standard file based document commands
   ON_COMMAND(ID_FILE_NEW, CWinApp::OnFileNew)
   ON_COMMAND(ID_FILE_OPEN, CWinApp::OnFileOpen)
END_MESSAGE_MAP()

/////////////////////////////////////////////////////////////////////////////
// CMiniEditApp construction

CMiniEditApp::CMiniEditApp()
{
   // TODO: add construction code here,
   // Place all significant initialization in InitInstance
}

/////////////////////////////////////////////////////////////////////////////
// The one and only CMiniEditApp object

CMiniEditApp theApp;

/////////////////////////////////////////////////////////////////////////////
// CMiniEditApp initialization

BOOL CMiniEditApp::InitInstance()
{
   // Standard initialization
   // If you are not using these features and wish to reduce the size
   //  of your final executable, you should remove from the following
   //  the specific initialization routines you do not need.

#ifdef _AFXDLL
   Enable3dControls();          // Call this when using MFC in a shared DLL
#else
   Enable3dControlsStatic();    // Call this when linking to MFC statically
#endif

   // Change the registry key under which our settings are stored.
   // You should modify this string to be something appropriate
   // such as the name of your company or organization.
   SetRegistryKey(_T("Local AppWizard-Generated Applications"));
```

```
    LoadStdProfileSettings();   // Load standard INI file options (including MRU)

    // Register the application's document templates.  Document templates
    //  serve as the connection between documents, frame windows and views.

    CSingleDocTemplate* pDocTemplate;
    pDocTemplate = new CSingleDocTemplate(
       IDR_MAINFRAME,
       RUNTIME_CLASS(CMiniEditDoc),
       RUNTIME_CLASS(CMainFrame),          // main SDI frame window
       RUNTIME_CLASS(CMiniEditView));
    AddDocTemplate(pDocTemplate);

    // Parse command line for standard shell commands, DDE, file open
    CCommandLineInfo cmdInfo;
    ParseCommandLine(cmdInfo);

    // Dispatch commands specified on the command line
    if (!ProcessShellCommand(cmdInfo))
       return FALSE;

    // The one and only window has been initialized, so show and update it.
    m_pMainWnd->ShowWindow(SW_SHOW);
    m_pMainWnd->UpdateWindow();

    m_pMainWnd->DragAcceptFiles ();

    return TRUE;
}


/////////////////////////////////////////////////////////////////////////////
// CAboutDlg dialog used for App About

class CAboutDlg : public CDialog
{
public:
   CAboutDlg();

// Dialog Data
   //{{AFX_DATA(CAboutDlg)
   enum { IDD = IDD_ABOUTBOX };
   //}}AFX_DATA
```

```
   // ClassWizard generated virtual function overrides
   //{{AFX_VIRTUAL(CAboutDlg)
   protected:
   virtual void DoDataExchange(CDataExchange* pDX);     // DDX/DDV support
   //}}AFX_VIRTUAL

// Implementation
protected:
   //{{AFX_MSG(CAboutDlg)
      // No message handlers
   //}}AFX_MSG
   DECLARE_MESSAGE_MAP()
};

CAboutDlg::CAboutDlg() : CDialog(CAboutDlg::IDD)
{
   //{{AFX_DATA_INIT(CAboutDlg)
   //}}AFX_DATA_INIT
}

void CAboutDlg::DoDataExchange(CDataExchange* pDX)
{
   CDialog::DoDataExchange(pDX);
   //{{AFX_DATA_MAP(CAboutDlg)
   //}}AFX_DATA_MAP
}

BEGIN_MESSAGE_MAP(CAboutDlg, CDialog)
   //{{AFX_MSG_MAP(CAboutDlg)
      // No message handlers
   //}}AFX_MSG_MAP
END_MESSAGE_MAP()

// App command to run the dialog
void CMiniEditApp::OnAppAbout()
{
   CAboutDlg aboutDlg;
   aboutDlg.DoModal();
}


/////////////////////////////////////////////////////////////////////////
// CMiniEditApp commands
```

Listing 12.11

```cpp
// MiniEditDoc.h : interface of the CMiniEditDoc class
//
/////////////////////////////////////////////////////////////////////////

#if !defined(AFX_MINIEDITDOC_H__BAFB48AA_9A70_11D1_80FC_00C0F6A83B7F__INCLUDED_)
#define AFX_MINIEDITDOC_H__BAFB48AA_9A70_11D1_80FC_00C0F6A83B7F__INCLUDED_

#if _MSC_VER > 1000
#pragma once
#endif // _MSC_VER > 1000


class CMiniEditDoc : public CDocument
{
protected: // create from serialization only
   CMiniEditDoc();
   DECLARE_DYNCREATE(CMiniEditDoc)

// Attributes
public:

// Operations
public:

// Overrides
   // ClassWizard generated virtual function overrides
   //{{AFX_VIRTUAL(CMiniEditDoc)
   public:
   virtual BOOL OnNewDocument();
   virtual void Serialize(CArchive& ar);
   virtual void DeleteContents();
   //}}AFX_VIRTUAL

// Implementation
public:
   virtual ~CMiniEditDoc();
#ifdef _DEBUG
   virtual void AssertValid() const;
   virtual void Dump(CDumpContext& dc) const;
#endif
```

```
protected:

// Generated message map functions
protected:
    //{{AFX_MSG(CMiniEditDoc)
        // NOTE - the ClassWizard will add and remove member functions here.
        //    DO NOT EDIT what you see in these blocks of generated code !
    //}}AFX_MSG
    DECLARE_MESSAGE_MAP()
};


/////////////////////////////////////////////////////////////////////////

//{{AFX_INSERT_LOCATION}}
// Microsoft Visual C++ will insert additional declarations immediately before
// the previous line.

#endif
// !defined(AFX_MINIEDITDOC_H__BAFB48AA_9A70_11D1_80FC_00C0F6A83B7F__INCLUDED_)
```

Listing 12.12

```
// MiniEditDoc.cpp : implementation of the CMiniEditDoc class
//

#include "stdafx.h"
#include "MiniEdit.h"

#include "MiniEditDoc.h"

#ifdef _DEBUG
#define new DEBUG_NEW
#undef THIS_FILE
static char THIS_FILE[] = __FILE__;
#endif

/////////////////////////////////////////////////////////////////////////
// CMiniEditDoc

IMPLEMENT_DYNCREATE(CMiniEditDoc, CDocument)
```

```
BEGIN_MESSAGE_MAP(CMiniEditDoc, CDocument)
    //{{AFX_MSG_MAP(CMiniEditDoc)
        // NOTE - the ClassWizard will add and remove mapping macros here.
        //     DO NOT EDIT what you see in these blocks of generated code!
    //}}AFX_MSG_MAP
END_MESSAGE_MAP()


/////////////////////////////////////////////////////////////////////////
// CMiniEditDoc construction/destruction

CMiniEditDoc::CMiniEditDoc()
{
    // TODO: add one-time construction code here

}

CMiniEditDoc::~CMiniEditDoc()
{
}

BOOL CMiniEditDoc::OnNewDocument()
{
    if (!CDocument::OnNewDocument())
        return FALSE;

    ((CEditView*)m_viewList.GetHead())->SetWindowText(NULL);

    // TODO: add reinitialization code here
    // (SDI documents will reuse this document)

    return TRUE;
}



/////////////////////////////////////////////////////////////////////////
// CMiniEditDoc serialization

void CMiniEditDoc::Serialize(CArchive& ar)
{
    // CEditView contains an edit control which handles all serialization
    ((CEditView*)m_viewList.GetHead())->SerializeRaw(ar);
}
```

```
/////////////////////////////////////////////////////////////////////
// CMiniEditDoc diagnostics

#ifdef _DEBUG
void CMiniEditDoc::AssertValid() const
{
    CDocument::AssertValid();
}

void CMiniEditDoc::Dump(CDumpContext& dc) const
{
    CDocument::Dump(dc);
}
#endif //_DEBUG


/////////////////////////////////////////////////////////////////////
// CMiniEditDoc commands

void CMiniEditDoc::DeleteContents()
{
    // TODO: Add your specialized code here and/or call the base class

    POSITION Pos = GetFirstViewPosition ();
    CEditView *PCEditView = (CEditView *)GetNextView (Pos);
    if (PCEditView)
        PCEditView->SetWindowText ("");

    CDocument::DeleteContents();
}
```

Listing 12.13

```
// MainFrm.h : interface of the CMainFrame class
//
/////////////////////////////////////////////////////////////////////

#if !defined(AFX_MAINFRM_H__BAFB48A8_9A70_11D1_80FC_00C0F6A83B7F__INCLUDED_)
#define AFX_MAINFRM_H__BAFB48A8_9A70_11D1_80FC_00C0F6A83B7F__INCLUDED_

#if _MSC_VER > 1000
#pragma once
#endif // _MSC_VER > 1000
```

```
class CMainFrame : public CFrameWnd
{
protected: // create from serialization only
    CMainFrame();
    DECLARE_DYNCREATE(CMainFrame)

// Attributes
public:

// Operations
public:

// Overrides
    // ClassWizard generated virtual function overrides
    //{{AFX_VIRTUAL(CMainFrame)
    virtual BOOL PreCreateWindow(CREATESTRUCT& cs);
    //}}AFX_VIRTUAL

// Implementation
public:
    virtual ~CMainFrame();
#ifdef _DEBUG
    virtual void AssertValid() const;
    virtual void Dump(CDumpContext& dc) const;
#endif

// Generated message map functions
protected:
    //{{AFX_MSG(CMainFrame)
        // NOTE - the ClassWizard will add and remove member functions here.
        //      DO NOT EDIT what you see in these blocks of generated code!
    //}}AFX_MSG
    DECLARE_MESSAGE_MAP()
};

/////////////////////////////////////////////////////////////////////////////

//{{AFX_INSERT_LOCATION}}
// Microsoft Visual C++ will insert additional declarations immediately before
// the previous line.

#endif
// !defined(AFX_MAINFRM_H__BAFB48A8_9A70_11D1_80FC_00C0F6A83B7F__INCLUDED_)
```

Listing 12.14

```cpp
// MainFrm.cpp : implementation of the CMainFrame class
//

#include "stdafx.h"
#include "MiniEdit.h"

#include "MainFrm.h"

#ifdef _DEBUG
#define new DEBUG_NEW
#undef THIS_FILE
static char THIS_FILE[] = __FILE__;
#endif

/////////////////////////////////////////////////////////////////////////////
// CMainFrame

IMPLEMENT_DYNCREATE(CMainFrame, CFrameWnd)

BEGIN_MESSAGE_MAP(CMainFrame, CFrameWnd)
    //{{AFX_MSG_MAP(CMainFrame)
        // NOTE - the ClassWizard will add and remove mapping macros here.
        //    DO NOT EDIT what you see in these blocks of generated code !
    //}}AFX_MSG_MAP
END_MESSAGE_MAP()

/////////////////////////////////////////////////////////////////////////////
// CMainFrame construction/destruction

CMainFrame::CMainFrame()
{
    // TODO: add member initialization code here

}

CMainFrame::~CMainFrame()
{
}

BOOL CMainFrame::PreCreateWindow(CREATESTRUCT& cs)
```

```
{
    if( !CFrameWnd::PreCreateWindow(cs) )
        return FALSE;
    // TODO: Modify the Window class or styles here by modifying
    //   the CREATESTRUCT cs

    return TRUE;
}

/////////////////////////////////////////////////////////////////////////////
// CMainFrame diagnostics

#ifdef _DEBUG
void CMainFrame::AssertValid() const
{
    CFrameWnd::AssertValid();
}

void CMainFrame::Dump(CDumpContext& dc) const
{
    CFrameWnd::Dump(dc);
}

#endif //_DEBUG

/////////////////////////////////////////////////////////////////////////////
// CMainFrame message handlers
```

Listing 12.15

```
// MiniEditView.h : interface of the CMiniEditView class
//
/////////////////////////////////////////////////////////////////////////////

#if !defined(AFX_MINIEDITVIEW_H__BAFB48AC_9A70_11D1_80FC_00C0F6A83B7F__INCLUDED_)
#define AFX_MINIEDITVIEW_H__BAFB48AC_9A70_11D1_80FC_00C0F6A83B7F__INCLUDED_

#if _MSC_VER > 1000
#pragma once
#endif // _MSC_VER > 1000

class CMiniEditView : public CEditView
```

```
{
protected: // create from serialization only
   CMiniEditView();
   DECLARE_DYNCREATE(CMiniEditView)

// Attributes
public:
   CMiniEditDoc* GetDocument();

// Operations
public:

// Overrides
   // ClassWizard generated virtual function overrides
   //{{AFX_VIRTUAL(CMiniEditView)
   public:
   virtual void OnDraw(CDC* pDC);  // overridden to draw this view
   virtual BOOL PreCreateWindow(CREATESTRUCT& cs);
   protected:
   //}}AFX_VIRTUAL

// Implementation
public:
   virtual ~CMiniEditView();
#ifdef _DEBUG
   virtual void AssertValid() const;
   virtual void Dump(CDumpContext& dc) const;
#endif

protected:

// Generated message map functions
protected:
   //{{AFX_MSG(CMiniEditView)
      // NOTE - the ClassWizard will add and remove member functions here.
      //    DO NOT EDIT what you see in these blocks of generated code !
   //}}AFX_MSG
   DECLARE_MESSAGE_MAP()
};

#ifndef _DEBUG  // debug version in MiniEditView.cpp
inline CMiniEditDoc* CMiniEditView::GetDocument()
   { return (CMiniEditDoc*)m_pDocument; }
#endif
```

```
////////////////////////////////////////////////////////////////////////

//{{AFX_INSERT_LOCATION}}
// Microsoft Visual C++ will insert additional declarations immediately before
// the previous line.

#endif
// !defined(AFX_MINIEDITVIEW_H__BAFB48AC_9A70_11D1_80FC_00C0F6A83B7F__INCLUDED_)
```

Listing 12.16

```
// MiniEditView.cpp : implementation of the CMiniEditView class
//

#include "stdafx.h"
#include "MiniEdit.h"

#include "MiniEditDoc.h"
#include "MiniEditView.h"

#ifdef _DEBUG
#define new DEBUG_NEW
#undef THIS_FILE
static char THIS_FILE[] = __FILE__;
#endif


////////////////////////////////////////////////////////////////////////
// CMiniEditView

IMPLEMENT_DYNCREATE(CMiniEditView, CEditView)

BEGIN_MESSAGE_MAP(CMiniEditView, CEditView)
    //{{AFX_MSG_MAP(CMiniEditView)
        // NOTE - the ClassWizard will add and remove mapping macros here.
        //     DO NOT EDIT what you see in these blocks of generated code!
    //}}AFX_MSG_MAP
END_MESSAGE_MAP()

////////////////////////////////////////////////////////////////////////
// CMiniEditView construction/destruction

CMiniEditView::CMiniEditView()
```

```
{
    // TODO: add construction code here

}

CMiniEditView::~CMiniEditView()
{
}

BOOL CMiniEditView::PreCreateWindow(CREATESTRUCT& cs)
{
    // TODO: Modify the Window class or styles here by modifying
    //   the CREATESTRUCT cs

    BOOL bPreCreated = CEditView::PreCreateWindow(cs);
    cs.style &= ~(ES_AUTOHSCROLL|WS_HSCROLL); // Enable word-wrapping

    return bPreCreated;
}

/////////////////////////////////////////////////////////////////////////////
// CMiniEditView drawing

void CMiniEditView::OnDraw(CDC* pDC)
{
    CMiniEditDoc* pDoc = GetDocument();
    ASSERT_VALID(pDoc);

    // TODO: add draw code for native data here
}

/////////////////////////////////////////////////////////////////////////////
// CMiniEditView diagnostics

#ifdef _DEBUG
void CMiniEditView::AssertValid() const
{
    CEditView::AssertValid();
}
```

```
void CMiniEditView::Dump(CDumpContext& dc) const
{
    CEditView::Dump(dc);
}

CMiniEditDoc* CMiniEditView::GetDocument() // non-debug version is inline
{
    ASSERT(m_pDocument->IsKindOf(RUNTIME_CLASS(CMiniEditDoc)));
    return (CMiniEditDoc*)m_pDocument;
}
#endif //_DEBUG

/////////////////////////////////////////////////////////////////////////////
// CMiniEditView message handlers
```

Other File I/O Methods

As you observed in this chapter, using the MFC file serialization mechanism provides a convenient way to read and write a document from and to a disk file in response to commands on the File menu. When you use MFC serialization with a CArchive object, you typically read an entire document sequentially from a disk file, store and process the data in your program, and then write the entire document sequentially back to a disk file. The file data is stored in a binary format and generally includes program version and class information along with the actual document data.

Alternatively, you can use one of several lower-level file I/O methods in an MFC program. These methods allow you to move a file pointer to a specific position within the file and then read or write a specific number of bytes, and they also permit you to perform a variety of other file operations. Using one of the alternative methods would be appropriate for performing file I/O that doesn't conform to the standard MFC serialization model. For example, you might want to read or write only a portion of a large file at a time, rather than attempting to store the entire file in memory. As another example, you might want to read or write simple text files.

One alternative file I/O method is to use the MFC CFile class. A CFile object is attached to a specific file, and it provides an extensive set of functions for performing general-purpose, unbuffered, binary input and output to this file. You can create your own CFile object at any time you need to perform file I/O. Also, the MFC attaches a CFile object—with an open file—to the CArchive object it passes to your document's Serialize function; you can access this CFile object by calling the CArchive::GetFile function. You can then call the CFile object's Seek, Read, Write and other member functions.

Continued on next page

Additionally, you can perform text file I/O using the `CFile` derived class `CStdioFile`, and you can read or write to blocks of memory using the `CFile` derived class `CMemFile`. For complete information on `CFile`, `CStdioFile`, and `CMemFile`, see the appropriate sections in the following online help topic: *Visual C++ Documentation, Reference Microsoft Foundation Class Library and Templates, Microsoft Foundation Class Library, Class Library Reference*.

Another alternative way to perform file I/O is to use the file I/O functions provided by the Win32 API. Unlike the 16-bit Windows 3.1 API (which included very few file functions), Win32 provides a complete set of functions for reading, writing, and managing files. Although describing these functions is beyond the scope of this book, you can find complete information in the following online help topic: *Platform SDK, Windows Base Services, Files and I/O*.

Two additional ways to perform file I/O are to use the stream or low-level file I/O functions provided by the C/C++ runtime library, or to use the file I/O functions provided by the `iostream` C++ class library. The runtime functions are described in the online help topic *Visual C++ Documentation, Reference, C/C++ Language and C++ Libraries, Standard C++ Library Reference, Files and Streams*. The file I/O functions of the `iostream` class library are discussed in *Visual C++ Documentation, Reference, C/C++ Language and C++ Libraries, iostream Library Reference*.

Summary

In this chapter, you learned how to add file I/O capability to a program's document class. The coding examples given here illustrated the following general techniques and concepts:

- The MFC classes provide message handlers for the New, Open…, Save, Save As…, and "most recently used" file commands on the File menu. You therefore don't need to use ClassWizard to define handlers for these commands. You do, however, need to write code to support the MFC message handlers.

- The MFC handlers for the Open… and Save As… commands display the standard Open and Save As dialog boxes for obtaining the file name and path from the user.

- You can edit the IDR_MAINFRAME string resource with the Developer Studio string editor to specify the default file extension that's used by the Open and Save As dialog boxes. (Alternatively, when creating a *new* program, you can specify the default file extension through the Advanced... button of the AppWizard Step 4 dialog box.)

- Before initializing a new document, opening an existing document, or terminating the program, the MFC code calls the DeleteContents member function of the document class. You should write an overriding version of this function that deletes the document data.

- The MFC handlers for the Open..., Save, Save As..., and "most recently used" file commands on the File menu open the file and then call the Serialize member function of your document class to perform the actual reading or writing of data. Serialize is also called by the MFC code that opens a file that has been dropped on the program window or has been double-clicked in a Windows folder (assuming that your program supports these features).

- AppWizard usually defines a minimal Serialize function within your document class. You should add code to this function to read or write the data stored by the document class.

- The Serialize function is passed a reference to a CArchive object that's attached to the open file and provides member functions for reading or writing data to this file.

- The Serialize function can read or write a data member that is a fundamental type by using the overloaded << and >> operators with the CArchive object.

- The Serialize function can read or write the data for a member object by calling the object's own Serialize function. If the member object belongs to a class you've defined, you must add a Serialize function to that class, which reads or writes the object's data.

- If the view class is derived from CEditView, AppWizard automatically adds the required code to Serialize for you. This code calls the CEditView member function SerializeRaw.

- You can read or write arbitrary blocks of data by calling the CArchive member functions Read or Write.

- Whenever the program data has been changed, the document class should call the CDocument member function SetModifiedFlag. Calling this function notifies the MFC that the document has changed; the MFC will subsequently give the user an opportunity to save the data before the data is deleted. If your view class is derived from CEditView, the modified flag is set automatically when the text is altered.

- You can provide support for the Windows drag-and-drop feature by placing a call to the DragAcceptFiles member function of the main frame window object within the InitInstance function (*after* the call to ProcessShellCommand).

- You can modify a program so that the user can open a file by double-clicking a Windows file object that has the program's default extension (such as .drw). To do this, call the CWinApp member functions EnableShellOpen and RegisterShellFileTypes within the InitInstance function (*after* the call to AddDocTemplate).

13

Scrolling and Splitting Views

- Adding scrolling capability

- Adding splitting capability

- Updating the views

- The MiniDraw source code

In this chapter, you'll learn how to add scrolling and splitting capabilities to the window of an MFC program. The scrolling capability allows the user to view and edit any portion of a document that's larger than the view window. The splitting capability allows the user to create more than one view of a single document, and to scroll each view independently. You'll discover that these two features are relatively easy to add to a program; almost all the work is done by the special-purpose MFC classes that support the features.

To illustrate the programming techniques, the chapter shows you how to add scrolling and splitting to the MiniDraw program. You should add the features to the MiniDraw source files you created in the previous chapter, or to a copy of these files. (If you didn't create these files, you can obtain a copy of them from the \MiniDrw3 companion-CD directory.)

Adding Scrolling Capability

In the previous version of MiniDraw, if a drawing was larger than the current size of the view window, the user could view and edit only the portion of the drawing that fit within the window. You'll now add vertical and horizontal scroll bars to the view window, as well as the code necessary to support scrolling, so that the user can view or edit any portion of a drawing that's larger than the window. The MiniDraw scroll bars that you'll add are shown in Figure 13.1.

NOTE   You don't need to add scroll bars or scrolling capability to the MiniEdit example program, because the MFC CEditView class, from which the program's view class is derived, does this task for you.

After you open the MiniDraw project, the first step is to modify the MiniDraw view class so that it's derived from CScrollView *rather than* CView. Like the CEdit-View class (which you used in the MiniEdit program to create an edit window), CScrollView is a special-purpose view class derived from the general-purpose CView class. Merely deriving the view class from CScrollView automatically adds scroll bars to the view window, and provides most of the code for supporting scrolling operations. You will, however, have to add some supporting code of your own.

The MiniDraw scroll bars

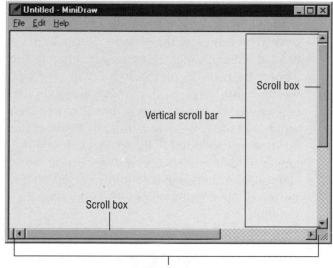

Horizontal scroll bar

To modify the view class so that it's derived from CScrollView, simply replace all occurrences of the class name CView with the class name CScrollView, within the MiniDrawView.h and MiniDrawView.cpp source files. If your files match the ones listed in the book, you'll find one occurrence of CView in MiniDrawView.h and eight occurrences in MiniDrawView.cpp.

NOTE   In this section you learned how to modify an *existing* program so that its view class is derived from CScrollView. When you're generating a *new* program, however, you can have AppWizard derive the view class from CScrollView. To do this, in the AppWizard Step 6 dialog box, select the name of the view class in the list at the top and then select the CScrollView class in the Base Class: list.

Converting Coordinates

Before you make the next change to the code, you should understand a little about the way that the CScrollView code supports scrolling. When a document is first opened, the upper-left corner of the drawing appears at the upper-left corner of the window, just as in the previous version of MiniDraw. If, however, the user scrolls the document using a scroll bar, the MFC adjusts an attribute known as the *viewport origin*.

The viewport origin determines the position of the text or graphics that you draw with respect to the window. Normally, if you draw a dot at the coordinates (0, 0), it will appear at the upper-left corner of the view window, and if you draw a dot at the coordinates (50, 100), it will appear 50 pixels from the left edge of the window and 100 pixels down from the top of the window. If, however, the user has scrolled 75 pixels down in the document using the vertical scroll bar, the MFC will adjust the viewport origin so that both of these dots will appear at *higher* positions with respect to the window. Now, a dot that's drawn at (0, 0) will no longer be visible (all output drawn outside the window is *clipped*—that is, it's simply discarded), and a dot drawn at (50, 100) will appear 25 pixels down from the top of the window. Figure 13.2 illustrates the view window before and after scrolling.

After the MFC has adjusted the viewport origin in response to a scrolling action, the MiniDraw OnDraw function redraws the lines in the view window, specifying the *same* coordinates for each line that it always specifies. However, because of the change in the viewport origin, the lines automatically appear at their proper scrolled positions. The beauty of this system is that the OnDraw function doesn't need to be altered to support scrolling; the scrolling logic is handled invisibly by the MFC.

The coordinates that you specify when you draw an object are known as the *logical coordinates*; the actual coordinates of an object within the window are known as *device coordinates*. Figure 13.3 shows the difference. All coordinates passed to MFC drawing functions (such as MoveTo and LineTo) are logical coordinates. However, certain other coordinates used by the MFC (such as the cursor position passed to mouse message handlers) are device coordinates. Before scrolling was added to the program, logical coordinates were always equal to device coordinates and the distinction was unimportant. Now that scrolling has been added to the program, however, you must make several modifications to the code to convert between these two types of coordinates.

FIGURE 13.2:

A view window before and after scrolling

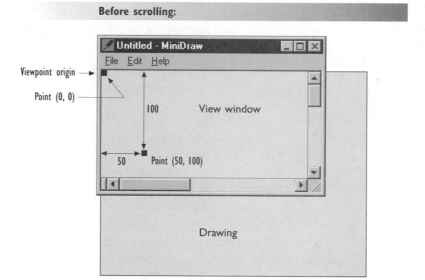

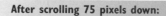

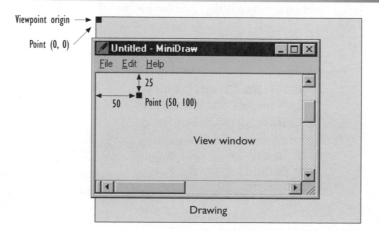

FIGURE 13.3:

Logical coordinates vs. device coordinates; in this figure, the user has scrolled down 75 pixels.

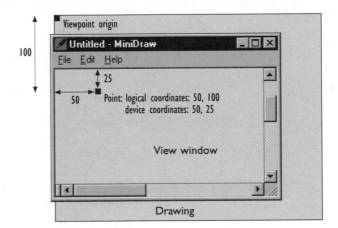

Specifically, you must convert the position of the mouse pointer (`point`) that's passed to the mouse message-handling functions from device coordinates to logical coordinates, so that the lines will be drawn at the correct positions within the drawing. To do this, first add the following code marked in bold to the `OnLButtonDown` function in the file MiniDrawView.cpp:

```
void CMiniDrawView::OnLButtonDown(UINT nFlags, CPoint point)
{
    // TODO: Add your message handler code here and/or call
    // default

    CClientDC ClientDC (this);
    OnPrepareDC (&ClientDC);
    ClientDC.DPtoLP (&point);

    m_PointOrigin = point;
    m_PointOld = point;
    SetCapture ();
    m_Dragging = 1;

    // other statements ...

}
```

To convert device coordinates to logical coordinates for a particular device, you must use a device context object that's associated with that device. Recall that a device context object manages output to a device; it stores drawing attributes and provides member functions for displaying text or graphics. The first added statement creates a device context object associated with the view window. The second statement is a call to the CScrollView member function OnPrepareDC, which adjusts the viewport origin for the device context object based on the current scrolled position of the drawing. (The viewport origin is one of the drawing attributes stored by a device context object.) Finally, the third statement is a call to the CDC member function DPtoLP, which converts the cursor position stored in point from device coordinates to logical coordinates for the device context object, using the new viewport origin that was just set. Once point has been converted to logical coordinates, the coordinates it contains can be used for drawing the line.

NOTE
The device context object that's passed to the OnDraw function has *already* had its viewport origin properly adjusted for the current scrolled position of the drawing. However, whenever you create your own device context object, you must pass it to the OnPrepareDC function to adjust the viewport origin, before you use it.

You should now modify the OnMouseMove and OnLButtonUp mouse-handling functions similarly. Both these functions already create a device context object; therefore, you need only to add the calls to OnPrepareDC and DPtoLP. The position of these statements in OnMouseMove is as follows:

```
void CMiniDrawView::OnMouseMove(UINT nFlags, CPoint point)
{
    // TODO: Add your message handler code here and/or call
    // default

    ::SetCursor (m_HCross);

    if (m_Dragging)
        {
        CClientDC ClientDC (this);
        OnPrepareDC (&ClientDC);
        ClientDC.DPtoLP (&point);

        ClientDC.SetROP2 (R2_NOT);
        ClientDC.MoveTo (m_PointOrigin);
        ClientDC.LineTo (m_PointOld);
        ClientDC.MoveTo (m_PointOrigin);
        ClientDC.LineTo (point);
        m_PointOld = point;
        }

    CScrollView::OnMouseMove(nFlags, point);
}
```

The following shows the position of the statements within OnLButtonUp:

```
void CMiniDrawView::OnLButtonUp(UINT nFlags, CPoint point)
{
    // TODO: Add your message handler code here and/or call
    // default

    if (m_Dragging)
        {
        m_Dragging = 0;
        ::ReleaseCapture ();
        ::ClipCursor (NULL);

        CClientDC ClientDC (this);
        OnPrepareDC (&ClientDC);
        ClientDC.DPtoLP (&point);

        ClientDC.SetROP2 (R2_NOT);
        ClientDC.MoveTo (m_PointOrigin);
        ClientDC.LineTo (m_PointOld);
        ClientDC.SetROP2 (R2_COPYPEN);
        ClientDC.MoveTo (m_PointOrigin);
        ClientDC.LineTo (point);

        CMiniDrawDoc* PDoc = GetDocument();
        PDoc->AddLine (m_PointOrigin.x, m_PointOrigin.y, point.x,
            point.y);
        }

    CScrollView::OnLButtonUp(nFlags, point);
}
```

Limiting the Drawing Size

When the user moves a scroll box (see Figure 13.1) to a particular position within the scroll bar, the MFC code in CScrollView must scroll to the corresponding position in the drawing. For example, if the user drags the scroll box to the bottom of the vertical scroll bar, the MFC must scroll to the bottom of the drawing; similarly, when the user drags the scroll box to the right end of the horizontal scroll bar, the MFC must scroll to the right edge of the drawing. Consequently, the MFC must know the overall *size* of the drawing.

In this section, you'll add code to MiniDraw to report the size of the drawing to the MFC. Begin by defining an overriding version of the `OnInitialUpdate` virtual function within the program's view class. Use ClassWizard to generate a function declaration and a minimal function definition, as described in Chapter 11, in the section "Deleting the Document Data." In the ClassWizard dialog box, open the Message Maps tab, select the `CMiniDrawView` class in the Class Name: and Object IDs: lists, and select the `OnInitialUpdate` virtual function in the Messages: list. After adding the function and clicking the Edit Code button, type the following code into the function definition in MiniDrawView.cpp:

```
void CMiniDrawView::OnInitialUpdate()
{
    CScrollView::OnInitialUpdate();

    // TODO: Add your specialized code here and/or call the base
    // class

    SIZE Size = {640, 480};
    SetScrollSizes (MM_TEXT, Size);
}
```

The MFC calls the `OnInitialUpdate` virtual function of the view class immediately before a new or existing document is *first* displayed in the view window.

The call to the `CScrollView` member function `SetScrollSizes` tells the MFC the size of the drawing. The horizontal and vertical dimensions of the drawing are assigned to a SIZE structure, which is passed as the second parameter. In the current version of the MiniDraw program, the drawing is simply set to a constant size: 640 pixels wide and 480 pixels high. (These dimensions were chosen—somewhat arbitrarily—to make the drawing the same size as the full Windows screen in standard VGA mode.)

TIP

A full-featured drawing program would typically allow the user to set the size of each new drawing. This would be especially important if the program prints drawings, as it would permit the user to create drawings that are the appropriate size for the printed page. After the user specifies the drawing size, the size should be stored by the document class, and when the drawing is saved in a file, the size should be saved along with the other drawing data.

NOTE   In the MiniDraw program, the document has a fixed size, and therefore the size needs to be specified only once. If an application (such as a word processor) changes the size of the document as the user enters or deletes data, it must call `SetScrollSizes` each time the size changes; this would best be done within an `OnUpdate` member function of the view class, which is called each time the document data changes, as explained later in the chapter (in the section "Redrawing Efficiently"). An example of this technique is given in Chapter 18, in the section "Supporting Scrolling."

The first parameter passed to `SetScrollSizes` indicates the *mapping mode* that you're using. Like the viewport origin, the mapping mode is a drawing attribute maintained by the device context object. The mapping mode specifies the units and coordinate system used to draw text and graphics. The MiniDraw program (as well as all the other example programs in the book) uses the MM_TEXT mapping mode. In the MM_TEXT mapping mode, all units are in pixels, horizontal coordinates increase as you go to the right, and vertical coordinates increase as you go down (see Figure 13.4). Chapter 19 briefly describes the alternative mapping modes.

FIGURE 13.4:

The MM_TEXT mapping mode

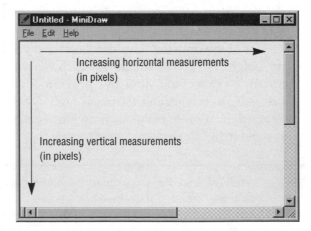

NOTE If the user clicks within a scroll bar to one side of the scroll box (but *not* on an arrow button), the view window is scrolled a distance of one *page*; by default, a page is equal to ⅒th of the document size in the direction of the scroll. If the user clicks an arrow button on a scroll bar, the view window is scrolled by one *line*; by default, a line is equal to ⅒th of a page. If you want to change the distances scrolled, you can specify the desired page and line sizes for each scroll bar as the third and fourth parameters passed to `SetScrollSizes`. See the `SetScroll-Sizes` function documentation for details.

TIP If you call `CScrollView::SetScaleToFitSize` *rather than* `SetScrollSizes` from your `OnInitialUpdate` function, the text and graphics you display in the view window will be *scaled* (that is, compressed or expanded) so that the entire document always fits within the current view window. Also, because scaling eliminates the need for scrolling, the scroll bars will be disabled. For details, see the `SetScaleToFitSize` function documentation.

Because a MiniDraw drawing has a specified size, you must add features to the program that prevent the user from drawing lines *outside* the drawing area. (As the program is currently written, if the view window is larger than the drawing, then the user could draw lines outside the drawing; scrolling wouldn't work properly with such lines.) The first step is to add code to the `OnDraw` function to draw a border at the right and bottom of the drawing area whenever the view window is redrawn; these borders show the program user the boundaries of the drawing. To do this, add the following bold lines to the `OnDraw` function in the MiniDrawView.cpp file:

```
/////////////////////////////////////////////////////////////////
///////////
// CMiniDrawView drawing

void CMiniDrawView::OnDraw(CDC* pDC)
{
    CMiniDrawDoc* pDoc = GetDocument();
    ASSERT_VALID(pDoc);

    // TODO: add draw code for native data here
```

```
CSize ScrollSize = GetTotalSize ();
pDC->MoveTo (ScrollSize.cx, 0);
pDC->LineTo (ScrollSize.cx, ScrollSize.cy);
pDC->LineTo (0, ScrollSize.cy);

int Index = pDoc->GetNumLines ();
while (Index-)
    pDoc->GetLine (Index)->Draw (pDC);
}
```

The new code first calls the CScrollView member function GetTotalSize, which returns a CSize object containing the size of the drawing (that is, the drawing size you set through the call to the SetScrollSizes function). The code then uses the dimensions contained in the CSize object to draw lines at the right and bottom edges of the drawing.

Next, you need to add code to the OnLButtonDown message handler to prevent the user from placing lines outside the drawing area. To do this, rewrite the OnLButtonDown in the MiniDrawView.cpp file, so that it's as follows (the new or changed lines are marked in bold):

```
void CMiniDrawView::OnLButtonDown(UINT nFlags, CPoint point)
{
    // TODO: Add your message handler code here and/or call
    // default

    CClientDC ClientDC (this);
    OnPrepareDC (&ClientDC);
    ClientDC.DPtoLP (&point);

    // test whether cursor is within drawing area of view window:
    CSize ScrollSize = GetTotalSize ();
    CRect ScrollRect (0, 0, ScrollSize.cx, ScrollSize.cy);
    if (!ScrollRect.PtInRect (point))
        return;

    // save cursor position, capture mouse, and set dragging flag:
    m_PointOrigin = point;
    m_PointOld = point;
    SetCapture ();
    m_Dragging = 1;
```

```
    // clip mouse cursor:
    ClientDC.LPtoDP (&ScrollRect);
    CRect ViewRect;
    GetClientRect (&ViewRect);
    CRect IntRect;
    IntRect.IntersectRect (&ScrollRect, &ViewRect);
    ClientToScreen (&IntRect);
    ::ClipCursor (&IntRect);

    CScrollView::OnLButtonDown(nFlags, point);
}
```

Because the view class received a mouse message, the mouse cursor must be within the view window; the cursor, however, may be outside the area of the drawing. To test whether the cursor is within the drawing, the added code defines the ScrollRect object, which is an instance of the MFC class CRect, and assigns this object the dimensions of the drawing (obtained by calling Get-TotalSize). The code then calls the CRect::PtInRect function for the Scroll-Rect object, passing it the coordinates of the cursor. PtInRect returns TRUE only if the cursor coordinates fall within the rectangular area stored in Scroll-Rect. If the cursor is found to be outside the drawing, the function returns immediately so that the user can't start drawing a line outside the drawing.

In addition to preventing the user from *initiating* a line outside the drawing area, OnLButtonDown must also prevent the user from *extending* a line beyond the drawing area. Accordingly, the code you added confines the cursor to the portion of the view window that's within the drawing; in other words, it restricts the cursor to the *intersection* of the drawing and the view window. (Recall that in the previous version of MiniDraw, the cursor was confined so that it could be moved *anywhere* within the view window.) To do this, the added code first calls the CDC::LPtoDP function for the ClientDC object to convert the coordinates of the drawing stored in ScrollRect from logical coordinates to device coordinates. It then defines a CRect object, ViewRect, assigning it the device coordinates of the view window (obtained by calling GetClientRect). Next, it defines another CRect object, IntRect, and calls CRect::IntersectRect for this object to assign it the coordinates of the *intersection* of the drawing area and the view window area. Finally, it calls the CWnd::ClientToScreen function to convert IntRect to screen coordinates, and it passes IntRect to the ::ClipCursor Win32 API function to confine the cursor to the intersection area. These rectangular areas are illustrated in Figure 13.5.

FIGURE 13.5:

The areas in which the mouse cursor is confined for a drawing that's smaller than the view window, and for a drawing that's larger than the view window; in both cases, the cursor is confined within the intersection of the view window and the drawing (the dark shaded area)

Drawing smaller than view window:

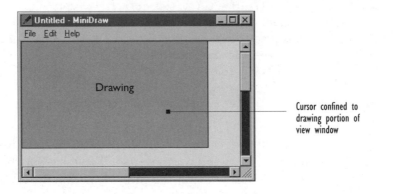

Cursor confined to drawing portion of view window

Drawing larger than view window:

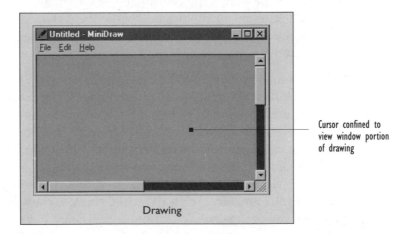

Cursor confined to view window portion of drawing

Changing the Mouse Cursor

As a final refinement, you'll now modify the program so that the mouse cursor is set to the cross shape when it's within the drawing area of the view window (to indicate that a line can be drawn) and to the standard arrow shape when it's outside the drawing area (to indicate that a line can't be drawn). To do this, add the

m_HArrow data member to the CMiniDrawView class definition in
MiniDrawView.h,

```
class CMiniDrawView : public CScrollView
{
protected:
   CString m_ClassName;
   int m_Dragging;
   HCURSOR m_HArrow;
   HCURSOR m_HCross;
   CPoint m_PointOld;
   CPoint m_PointOrigin;

// remainder of CMiniDrawView class definition ...

}
```

and initialize m_HArrow within the CMiniDrawView constructor in
MiniDrawView.cpp, as follows:

```
/////////////////////////////////////////////////////////////////
/////////////// CMiniDrawView construction/destruction

CMiniDrawView::CMiniDrawView()
{
   // TODO: add construction code here

   m_Dragging = 0;
   m_HArrow = AfxGetApp ()->LoadStandardCursor (IDC_ARROW);
   m_HCross = AfxGetApp ()->LoadStandardCursor (IDC_CROSS);
}
```

This initialization assigns m_HArrow a handle for the standard arrow-shaped
mouse cursor.

Next, in the OnMouseMove function in MiniDrawView.cpp move the declaration
of ClientDC and the calls to OnPrepareDC and DPtoLP to the beginning of the
function, and add the lines marked in bold, so that the function definition is as
follows:

```
void CMiniDrawView::OnMouseMove(UINT nFlags, CPoint point)
{
   // TODO: Add your message handler code here and/or call
   // default
```

```
    CClientDC ClientDC (this);
    OnPrepareDC (&ClientDC);
    ClientDC.DPtoLP (&point);

    CSize ScrollSize = GetTotalSize ();
    CRect ScrollRect (0, 0, ScrollSize.cx, ScrollSize.cy);
    if (ScrollRect.PtInRect (point))
        ::SetCursor (m_HCross);
    else
        ::SetCursor (m_HArrow);

    if (m_Dragging)
        {
        ClientDC.SetROP2 (R2_NOT);
        ClientDC.MoveTo (m_PointOrigin);
        ClientDC.LineTo (m_PointOld);
        ClientDC.MoveTo (m_PointOrigin);
        ClientDC.LineTo (point);
        m_PointOld = point;
        }

    CScrollView::OnMouseMove(nFlags, point);
    }
```

Rather than always displaying the cross-shaped cursor, the new version of OnMouseMove displays the cross-shaped cursor only when the cursor is within the drawing area (ScrollRect), and it displays the arrow-shaped cursor when the cursor is outside the drawing area.

Figure 13.6 illustrates the MiniDraw program when the drawing is smaller than the view window, showing the line that marks the edges of the drawing. In this figure, notice that because the drawing fits entirely within the view window, the MFC code has hidden the scroll bars. (The scroll bars will reappear if the window size is reduced so that the drawing no longer fits completely within the window.)

If you wish, you can now build and run the MiniDraw program, to test the new features you've added, before going on to the next section.

FIGURE 13.6:

The MiniDraw program with a drawing that's smaller than the view window

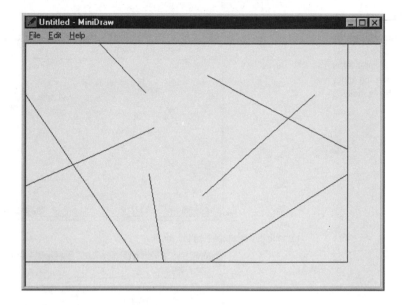

Adding Splitting Capability

In this section, you'll add a *split box* to the MiniDraw program window, which will allow the user to divide the window into two separate view windows, also known as *panes*. The border between the two panes is known as the *split bar*. The two view windows display the same drawing; however, each can be scrolled independently to display different parts of this drawing. To divide the window, the user can double-click the split box (to divide the window into two equal views) or can drag the split box to the desired position. When the window is split, a single vertical scroll bar scrolls both view windows simultaneously; however, each view has its own horizontal scroll bar so that the views can be scrolled independently in the horizontal direction. These features are illustrated in Figure 13.7.

FIGURE 13.7:

The MiniDraw program before the view window is split, immediately after it's split, and after the right pane is scrolled horizontally

Before splitting the window:

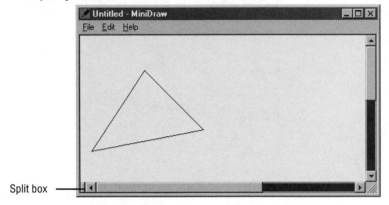

Split box

mmediately after splitting the window:

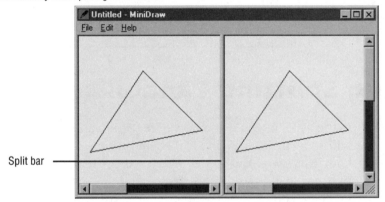

Split bar

fter scrolling the right view:

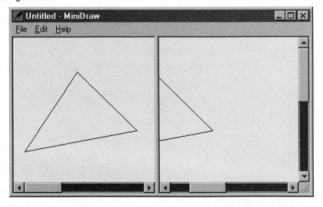

To add splitting capability to the program, you must modify the main frame window class. First, add a declaration for m_SplitterWnd to the beginning of the CMainFrame class definition in MainFrm.h, as follows:

```
class CMainFrame : public CFrameWnd
{
protected:
    CSplitterWnd m_SplitterWnd;

protected: // create from serialization only
    CMainFrame();
    DECLARE_DYNCREATE(CMainFrame)

// remainder of CMainFrame definition ...

}
```

The new member object m_SplitterWnd is an instance of the MFC class CSplitterWnd (which is derived from CWnd). This object serves to create and manage a splitter window, which is a window that can display more than one view window.

The next step is to define an overriding version of the OnCreateClient virtual function as a member of the CMainFrame class. Use ClassWizard to generate the function declaration and a minimal function definition. In the ClassWizard dialog box, open the Message Maps tab, select the CMainFrame class in the Class Name: and Object IDs: lists, and select the OnCreateClient virtual function in the Messages: list. After adding the function and clicking the Edit Code button, modify the generated function by *deleting* the call to CFrameWnd::OnCreateClient and adding the lines in bold, so that the function is as follows:

```
BOOL CMainFrame::OnCreateClient(LPCREATESTRUCT lpcs,
    CCreateContext* pContext)
{
    // TODO: Add your specialized code here and/or call the base
    // class

    return m_SplitterWnd.Create
        (this,              // parent of splitter window
        1,                  // maximum rows
        2,                  // maximum columns
        CSize (15, 15),     // minimum view window size
        pContext);          // pass on context information
}
```

The MFC calls the virtual function `OnCreateClient` when the main frame window is first created. The default version of this function (defined in `CFrameWnd`) creates a single view window that fills the client area of the main frame window. The overriding version of this function that you just defined calls the `CSplitterWnd::Create` function for the `m_SplitterWnd` object to create a splitter window *rather than* creating a view window. The splitter window itself initially creates a single view window; if the user later double-clicks the split box, the splitter window then creates another view window to provide a second view of the drawing.

The first parameter passed to `Create` specifies the parent of the splitter window; passing `this` makes the splitter window a child of the main frame window.

NOTE The splitter window is a child of the main frame window. In turn, each view window is a child of the splitter window.

The second parameter specifies the maximum number of views in the vertical direction; passing 1 means that the user *can't* divide the window with a horizontal split bar (hence, no horizontal split box appears in the window). Similarly, the third parameter specifies the maximum number of views in the horizontal direction; passing 2 means that the user can divide the window into a left and right view, as shown in Figure 13.7. You can assign only 1 or 2 to the second or third parameter; if you assigned 2 to both these parameters, the user could divide the window into four views (try it!).

The fourth parameter sets the minimum horizontal and vertical sizes of a view window; the user isn't permitted to move the split bar to a position that would create a view that has a smaller horizontal or vertical dimension. The fifth parameter passes on context information that was passed to the `OnCreateClient` function.

Adding Splitting to a New Application

In the previous section, you learned how to add splitting capability to the program window of an existing MFC application. You can also use AppWizard to add splitting capability when you're generating a *new* program. To do this, perform the following steps in the AppWizard Step 4 dialog box:

1. Click the Advanced... button. This will open the Advanced Options dialog box.

2. In the Advanced Options dialog box, open the Window Styles tab, which allows you to set advanced options that affect the main frame window.

3. Check the Use Split Window option at the top.

These steps will cause AppWizard to automatically generate the code that was described in the previous section. You can manually adjust the parameters passed to CSplitterWnd::Create (specifically, the second, third, and fourth parameters) to change the maximum number of view windows and the minimum view window size.

Updating the Views

Each view window created by the splitter window is managed by a separate view object—that is, a separate instance of the CMiniDrawView class. The MFC automatically calls CMiniDrawView::OnDraw for a view object to redraw the view window whenever some external event has invalidated the window data (for example, the user has enlarged the window or removed an overlapping window).

When the user draws a line in one view window, the other view window—if any—needs to be redrawn so that the line will appear in *both* views (provided that the second view is scrolled to the area of the drawing containing the line). The MFC, however, *doesn't* automatically call OnDraw for the second view object. Rather, after drawing a line in one view, the program must explicitly call the CDocument::UpdateAllViews function for the document object to force the MFC to call OnDraw for the other view. Accordingly, you should add the following call to UpdateAllViews to the end of the routine that draws the line in the OnLButtonUp function in MiniDrawView.cpp:

```
void CMiniDrawView::OnLButtonUp(UINT nFlags, CPoint point)
{
    // TODO: Add your message handler code here and/or call
    // default

    if (m_Dragging)
        {
        m_Dragging = 0;
        ::ReleaseCapture ();
        ::ClipCursor (NULL);

        CClientDC ClientDC (this);
        OnPrepareDC (&ClientDC);
        ClientDC.DPtoLP (&point);
```

```
ClientDC.SetROP2 (R2_NOT);
ClientDC.MoveTo (m_PointOrigin);
ClientDC.LineTo (m_PointOld);
ClientDC.SetROP2 (R2_COPYPEN);
ClientDC.MoveTo (m_PointOrigin);
ClientDC.LineTo (point);

CMiniDrawDoc* PDoc = GetDocument();
PDoc->AddLine (m_PointOrigin.x, m_PointOrigin.y, point.x,
    point.y);

PDoc->UpdateAllViews (this);
}

CScrollView::OnLButtonUp(nFlags, point);
}
```

The `UpdateAllViews` function forces the `OnDraw` function to be called for all views associated with the document, *except* the one indicated by the first parameter. In MiniDraw, passing `this` to `UpdateAllViews` results in calling the `OnDraw` function for the other view only. (The current view doesn't need redrawing because it already displays the new line.) As a result of this addition, when the user completes drawing a line in one view, it quickly appears in the other view.

NOTE   If you pass 0 to `UpdateAllViews`, *all* views will be redrawn. The MiniDraw program can have at most two views. If both a horizontal and a vertical split box were included, a single document interface program could have as many as four views of a given document. As you'll see in Chapter 17, in a multiple document interface program, there can be more than four views of a single document.

TIP   When the user splits the MiniDraw window, both view objects display the drawing in the same way. Alternatively, a program might display the document data differently in different views. For example, in a word processor, one view might display the full document text while another view displays an outline of the document. For basic information on how to do this, see the online help topic *Visual C++ Documentation; Using Visual C++; Visual C++ Programmer's Guide; Adding User Interface Features; Details; Document/View Architecture Topics; Multiple Document Types, Views, and Frame Windows*.

Redrawing Efficiently

A problem with the technique given in the previous section is that when the user draws a single line in one view, the other view is forced to re-create the entire drawing—even portions of the drawing that aren't currently visible in the view window. In this section, you'll modify the MiniDraw program so that when the user draws a line in one view, the second view redraws *only the modified and visible portion* of the drawing, thus increasing the efficiency of updating the views.

The first step is to provide a new member function of the CLine class, GetDim-Rect, which supplies the dimensions of the rectangle that bounds the line stored in the object; this rectangle represents the portion of the window that's affected when the line is drawn. Add the following GetDimRect declaration to the public section of the CLine definition in MiniDrawDoc.h,

```
class CLine : public CObject
{

// protected declarations ...

public:
    CLine (int X1, int Y1, int X2, int Y2)
      {
      m_X1 = X1;
      m_Y1 = Y1;
      m_X2 = X2;
      m_Y2 = Y2;
      }
    void Draw (CDC *PDC);
    CRect GetDimRect ();
    virtual void Serialize (CArchive& ar);
};
```

and add the following function definition to the end of the MiniDrawDoc.cpp implementation file:

```
CRect CLine::GetDimRect ()
   {
   return CRect
     (min (m_X1, m_X2),
      min (m_Y1, m_Y2),
      max (m_X1, m_X2) + 1,
      max (m_Y1, m_Y2) + 1);
   }
```

GetDimRect returns a CRect object containing the dimensions of the bounding rectangle; the min and max macros (defined in Windows.h) are used to make sure that the left field is smaller than the right field, and that the top field is smaller than the bottom field (otherwise, some of the functions that will be passed the CRect object will interpret the rectangle as empty).

The next step is to modify the AddLine member function of the document class so that it returns a pointer to the CLine object that stores the newly added line. Change the AddLine declaration (which appears in the public section of the CMiniDrawDoc definition in MiniDrawDoc.h) so that it reads as follows:

```
CLine *AddLine (int X1, int Y1, int X2, int Y2);
```

Now change the AddLine definition in MiniDrawDoc.cpp as follows:

```
CLine *CMiniDrawDoc::AddLine (int X1, int Y1, int X2, int Y2)
   {
   CLine *PLine = new CLine (X1, Y1, X2, Y2);
   m_LineArray.Add (PLine);
   SetModifiedFlag ();
   return PLine;
   }
```

Next, you should change the calls to AddLine and UpdateAllViews in the OnLButtonUp function, in MiniDrawView.cpp, to the following:

```
void CMiniDrawView::OnLButtonUp(UINT nFlags, CPoint point)
{
   // TODO: Add your message handler code here and/or call
   // default

   if (m_Dragging)
      {
      m_Dragging = 0;
      ::ReleaseCapture ();
      ::ClipCursor (NULL);

      CClientDC ClientDC (this);
      OnPrepareDC (&ClientDC);
      ClientDC.DPtoLP (&point);
```

```
ClientDC.SetROP2 (R2_NOT);
ClientDC.MoveTo (m_PointOrigin);
ClientDC.LineTo (m_PointOld);
ClientDC.SetROP2 (R2_COPYPEN);
ClientDC.MoveTo (m_PointOrigin);
ClientDC.LineTo (point);

CMiniDrawDoc* PDoc = GetDocument();
CLine *PCLine;
PCLine = PDoc->AddLine (m_PointOrigin.x, m_PointOrigin.y,
    point.x, point.y);
PDoc->UpdateAllViews (this, 0, PCLine);
}


CScrollView::OnLButtonUp(nFlags, point);
}
```

The added code saves the pointer to the new CLine object that's returned by AddLine, and then passes this pointer as the third parameter to UpdateAllViews. The UpdateAllViews member function of CDocument has the following format:

```
void UpdateAllViews (CView* pSender, LPARAM lHint = 0L,
    CObject* pHint = NULL);
```

The second and third parameters (which are optional) supply information (known as *hints*) about the modification that has been made to the document. You'll now see how this information can be used to increase the efficiency of redrawing the view windows.

The UpdateAllViews function calls the OnUpdate virtual member function for each view object, passing OnUpdate the values of the two hint parameters (lHint and pHint). The default implementation of OnUpdate (defined in CView) ignores the hint values and always causes the *entire view window* to be redrawn. To increase the efficiency of redrawing, you should now define an overriding version of OnUpdate, which uses the hint information to cause only the affected area of the view window—if any—to be redrawn. As usual, you can use ClassWizard to generate the function declaration and a minimal function definition. Open the ClassWizard dialog box and open the Message Maps tab. Then select the CMiniDrawView class in the Class Name: and Object IDs: lists, and select the OnUpdate virtual function in the

Messages: list. After adding the function and clicking the Edit Code button, enter code as follows into the function shell in MiniDrawView.cpp:

```
void CMiniDrawView::OnUpdate (CView* pSender, LPARAM lHint,
   CObject* pHint)
   {
   if (pHint != 0)
      {
      CRect InvalidRect = ((CLine *)pHint)->GetDimRect ();
      CClientDC ClientDC (this);
      OnPrepareDC (&ClientDC);
      ClientDC.LPtoDP (&InvalidRect);
      InvalidateRect (&InvalidRect);
      }
   else
      CScrollView::OnUpdate (pSender, lHint, pHint);
   }
```

If OnUpdate has been called by UpdateAllViews, the pHint parameter will contain a pointer to a CLine object. OnUpdate, however, is also called by the default implementation of the OnInitialUpdate function (which receives control just before a drawing is *first* displayed in the view window); in this case, the pHint parameter will be set to 0. OnUpdate therefore begins by testing the value of pHint.

If the pHint parameter contains a pointer to a CLine object (that is, it's nonzero), OnUpdate performs the following steps:

1. It uses the CLine pointer to call the CLine::GetDimRect function to obtain the bounding rectangle of the newly added line, which it stores in the CRect object InvalidRect.

2. It creates a device context object, ClientDC, and calls CScrollView::OnPrepareDC to adjust the object for the current scrolled position of the drawing.

3. It calls CDC::LPtoDP for the device context object to convert the coordinates in InvalidRect from logical coordinates to device coordinates.

4. It passes InvalidRect to the CWnd member function InvalidateRect. InvalidateRect *invalidates* the specified rectangular area; that is, it marks the area for redrawing. InvalidateRect also causes the view class's OnDraw function to be called. The coordinates passed to InvalidateRect must be

device coordinates. Note that if the device coordinates passed to Invalidate-Rect fall outside the view window, *no* portion of the view window is invalidated (this would happen if the view window doesn't currently display the portion of the drawing that was modified in the other view window).

> **NOTE**
>
> The total portion of the view window that has been invalidated is known as the *update region*. Calling InvalidateRect to invalidate a rectangular area adds this area to the current update region. Whenever the view window acquires a nonempty update region, as soon as any higher-priority messages have been processed, the OnDraw function is called and the update region is reset to empty. Note also that areas can be invalidated not only via the OnUpdate function, but also directly by Windows in response to an event that necessitates redrawing of the area (for example, the user's removing another window that was covering the area).

If, however, pHint doesn't contain a CLine pointer (that is, it's zero), OnUpdate calls the default implementation of OnUpdate, which invalidates the *entire* view window and causes OnDraw to be called.

The current version of the OnDraw function always attempts to redraw the entire drawing, even if only a portion of the drawing falls within the invalidated area of the view window. You will now rewrite OnDraw so that it redraws only the invalidated area, thus increasing its efficiency. The following is the new version of OnDraw:

```
///////////////////////////////////////////////////////////////
///////////
// CMiniDrawView drawing

void CMiniDrawView::OnDraw(CDC* pDC)
{
    CMiniDrawDoc* pDoc = GetDocument();
    ASSERT_VALID(pDoc);

    // TODO: add draw code for native data here

    CSize ScrollSize = GetTotalSize ();
    pDC->MoveTo (ScrollSize.cx, 0);
    pDC->LineTo (ScrollSize.cx, ScrollSize.cy);
    pDC->LineTo (0, ScrollSize.cy);
```

```
CRect ClipRect;
CRect DimRect;
CRect IntRect;
CLine *PLine;
pDC->GetClipBox (&ClipRect);

int Index = pDoc->GetNumLines ();
while (Index-)
   {
   PLine = pDoc->GetLine (Index);
   DimRect = PLine->GetDimRect ();
   if (IntRect.IntersectRect (DimRect, ClipRect))
      PLine->Draw (pDC);
   }
}
```

The new version of OnDraw calls the CDC::GetClipBox function for the device context object, to obtain the dimensions of the area that was invalidated. Before drawing each line, it calls GetDimRect for the object that stores the line to obtain the line's bounding rectangle, and it then calls IntersectRect to determine whether the bounding rectangle of the line falls within the invalidated area. (IntersectRect returns TRUE only if the two rectangles passed to it have a nonempty intersection; that is, if they overlap.) OnDraw draws the line *only* if the line's bounding rectangle is within the invalidated area.

NOTE   If you attempt to draw a portion of the drawing that falls outside the invalidated area of the view window, the output is clipped (that is, ignored). In MiniDraw, it would probably be just as efficient—or *more* efficient—to simply call functions for redrawing all the lines, because drawing lines is fast. However, a full-featured drawing or CAD program typically draws much more complex figures; in such a program, the added efficiency of redrawing only those figures that fall within the invalidated area can be significant.

The workings of the code you added in this section can be briefly summarized as follows: When the user draws a line in one view window, the view class calls UpdateAllViews for the document object, passing it a pointer to the CLine object holding the new line. UpdateAllViews then calls the OnUpdate function for the other view, passing it the CLine pointer. OnUpdate invalidates the portion of the view window bounding the new line, causing OnDraw to be called. Finally, OnDraw redraws only those lines that fall within the invalidated area (that is, it draws the new line and redraws any other lines in that area).

Note that when the view window needs repainting due to an external event (such as the user's removing an overlapping window), Windows also invalidates *only* the area of the window that needs redrawing. The new version of OnDraw then draws only the lines that fall within this area. Thus, the new OnDraw version is potentially more efficient, whether it's called in response to a newly drawn line or in response to an external event.

This completes the additions to MiniDraw. You can now build and run the program.

The MiniDraw Source Code

The following listings, Listings 13.1 through 13.8, are the C++ source files for the version of MiniDraw presented in this chapter. A complete copy of these files is contained in the \MiniDrw4 companion-CD directory.

Listing 13.1

```
// MiniDraw.h : main header file for the MINIDRAW application
//


#if !defined(AFX_MINIDRAW_H__11E83924_999A_11D1_80FC_00C0F6A83B7F__INCLUDED_)
#define AFX_MINIDRAW_H__11E83924_999A_11D1_80FC_00C0F6A83B7F__INCLUDED_

#if _MSC_VER > 1000
#pragma once
#endif // _MSC_VER > 1000

#ifndef __AFXWIN_H__
    #error include 'stdafx.h' before including this file for PCH
#endif

#include "resource.h"       // main symbols


/////////////////////////////////////////////////////////////////////
// CMiniDrawApp:
// See MiniDraw.cpp for the implementation of this class
//

class CMiniDrawApp : public CWinApp
```

```
{
public:
    CMiniDrawApp();

// Overrides
    // ClassWizard generated virtual function overrides
    //{{AFX_VIRTUAL(CMiniDrawApp)
    public:
    virtual BOOL InitInstance();
    //}}AFX_VIRTUAL

// Implementation

    //{{AFX_MSG(CMiniDrawApp)
    afx_msg void OnAppAbout();
        // NOTE - the ClassWizard will add and remove member functions here.
        //    DO NOT EDIT what you see in these blocks of generated code !
    //}}AFX_MSG
    DECLARE_MESSAGE_MAP()
};


/////////////////////////////////////////////////////////////////////////////

//{{AFX_INSERT_LOCATION}}
// Microsoft Visual C++ will insert additional declarations immediately before
// the previous line.

#endif
// !defined(AFX_MINIDRAW_H__11E83924_999A_11D1_80FC_00C0F6A83B7F__INCLUDED_)
```

Listing 13.2

```
// MiniDraw.cpp : Defines the class behaviors for the application.
//

#include "stdafx.h"
#include "MiniDraw.h"

#include "MainFrm.h"
#include "MiniDrawDoc.h"
#include "MiniDrawView.h"
```

```
#ifdef _DEBUG
#define new DEBUG_NEW
#undef THIS_FILE
static char THIS_FILE[] = __FILE__;
#endif

/////////////////////////////////////////////////////////////////////////////
// CMiniDrawApp

BEGIN_MESSAGE_MAP(CMiniDrawApp, CWinApp)
    //{{AFX_MSG_MAP(CMiniDrawApp)
    ON_COMMAND(ID_APP_ABOUT, OnAppAbout)
        // NOTE - the ClassWizard will add and remove mapping macros here.
        //    DO NOT EDIT what you see in these blocks of generated code!
    //}}AFX_MSG_MAP
    // Standard file based document commands
    ON_COMMAND(ID_FILE_NEW, CWinApp::OnFileNew)
    ON_COMMAND(ID_FILE_OPEN, CWinApp::OnFileOpen)
END_MESSAGE_MAP()

/////////////////////////////////////////////////////////////////////////////
// CMiniDrawApp construction

CMiniDrawApp::CMiniDrawApp()
{
    // TODO: add construction code here,
    // Place all significant initialization in InitInstance
}

/////////////////////////////////////////////////////////////////////////////
// The one and only CMiniDrawApp object

CMiniDrawApp theApp;

/////////////////////////////////////////////////////////////////////////////
// CMiniDrawApp initialization

BOOL CMiniDrawApp::InitInstance()
{
    // Standard initialization
    // If you are not using these features and wish to reduce the size
    //  of your final executable, you should remove from the following
    //  the specific initialization routines you do not need.
```

```
#ifdef _AFXDLL
   Enable3dControls();          // Call this when using MFC in a shared DLL
#else
   Enable3dControlsStatic();   // Call this when linking to MFC statically
#endif

   // Change the registry key under which our settings are stored.
   // You should modify this string to be something appropriate
   // such as the name of your company or organization.
   SetRegistryKey(_T("Local AppWizard-Generated Applications"));

   LoadStdProfileSettings();  // Load standard INI file options (including MRU)

   // Register the application's document templates.  Document templates
   //  serve as the connection between documents, frame windows and views.

   CSingleDocTemplate* pDocTemplate;
   pDocTemplate = new CSingleDocTemplate(
      IDR_MAINFRAME,
      RUNTIME_CLASS(CMiniDrawDoc),
      RUNTIME_CLASS(CMainFrame),        // main SDI frame window
      RUNTIME_CLASS(CMiniDrawView));
   AddDocTemplate(pDocTemplate);

   EnableShellOpen ();
   RegisterShellFileTypes ();

   // Parse command line for standard shell commands, DDE, file open
   CCommandLineInfo cmdInfo;
   ParseCommandLine(cmdInfo);

   // Dispatch commands specified on the command line
   if (!ProcessShellCommand(cmdInfo))
      return FALSE;

   // The one and only window has been initialized, so show and update it.
   m_pMainWnd->ShowWindow(SW_SHOW);
   m_pMainWnd->UpdateWindow();

   m_pMainWnd->DragAcceptFiles ();

   return TRUE;
}
```

```
///////////////////////////////////////////////////////////////////////
// CAboutDlg dialog used for App About

class CAboutDlg : public CDialog
{
public:
   CAboutDlg();

// Dialog Data
   //{{AFX_DATA(CAboutDlg)
   enum { IDD = IDD_ABOUTBOX };
   //}}AFX_DATA

   // ClassWizard generated virtual function overrides
   //{{AFX_VIRTUAL(CAboutDlg)
   protected:
   virtual void DoDataExchange(CDataExchange* pDX);    // DDX/DDV support
   //}}AFX_VIRTUAL

// Implementation
protected:
   //{{AFX_MSG(CAboutDlg)
      // No message handlers
   //}}AFX_MSG
   DECLARE_MESSAGE_MAP()
};

CAboutDlg::CAboutDlg() : CDialog(CAboutDlg::IDD)
{
   //{{AFX_DATA_INIT(CAboutDlg)
   //}}AFX_DATA_INIT
}

void CAboutDlg::DoDataExchange(CDataExchange* pDX)
{
   CDialog::DoDataExchange(pDX);
   //{{AFX_DATA_MAP(CAboutDlg)
   //}}AFX_DATA_MAP
}

BEGIN_MESSAGE_MAP(CAboutDlg, CDialog)
   //{{AFX_MSG_MAP(CAboutDlg)
```

```
      // No message handlers
   //}}AFX_MSG_MAP
END_MESSAGE_MAP()

// App command to run the dialog
void CMiniDrawApp::OnAppAbout()
{
    CAboutDlg aboutDlg;
    aboutDlg.DoModal();
}



/////////////////////////////////////////////////////////////////////
// CMiniDrawApp commands
```

Listing 13.3

```
// MiniDrawDoc.h : interface of the CMiniDrawDoc class
//
/////////////////////////////////////////////////////////////////////

#if !defined(AFX_MINIDRAWDOC_H__11E8392A_999A_11D1_80FC_00C0F6A83B7F__INCLUDED_)
#define AFX_MINIDRAWDOC_H__11E8392A_999A_11D1_80FC_00C0F6A83B7F__INCLUDED_

#if _MSC_VER > 1000
#pragma once
#endif // _MSC_VER > 1000

class CLine : public CObject
{
protected:
    int m_X1, m_Y1, m_X2, m_Y2;

    CLine ()
        {}
    DECLARE_SERIAL (CLine)

public:
    CLine (int X1, int Y1, int X2, int Y2)
        {
        m_X1 = X1;
        m_Y1 = Y1;
        m_X2 = X2;
        m_Y2 = Y2;
        }
```

```
   void Draw (CDC *PDC);
   CRect GetDimRect ();
   virtual void Serialize (CArchive& ar);
};

class CMiniDrawDoc : public CDocument
{
protected:
   CTypedPtrArray<CObArray, CLine*> m_LineArray;

public:
   CLine *AddLine (int X1, int Y1, int X2, int Y2);
   CLine *GetLine (int Index);
   int GetNumLines ();

protected: // create from serialization only
   CMiniDrawDoc();
   DECLARE_DYNCREATE(CMiniDrawDoc)

// Attributes
public:

// Operations
public:

// Overrides
   // ClassWizard generated virtual function overrides
   //{{AFX_VIRTUAL(CMiniDrawDoc)
   public:
   virtual BOOL OnNewDocument();
   virtual void Serialize(CArchive& ar);
   virtual void DeleteContents();
   //}}AFX_VIRTUAL

// Implementation
public:
   virtual ~CMiniDrawDoc();
#ifdef _DEBUG
   virtual void AssertValid() const;
   virtual void Dump(CDumpContext& dc) const;
#endif

protected:
```

```
// Generated message map functions
protected:
    //{{AFX_MSG(CMiniDrawDoc)
    afx_msg void OnEditClearAll();
    afx_msg void OnUpdateEditClearAll(CCmdUI* pCmdUI);
    afx_msg void OnEditUndo();
    afx_msg void OnUpdateEditUndo(CCmdUI* pCmdUI);
    //}}AFX_MSG
    DECLARE_MESSAGE_MAP()
};


/////////////////////////////////////////////////////////////////////////

//{{AFX_INSERT_LOCATION}}
// Microsoft Visual C++ will insert additional declarations immediately before
// the previous line.

#endif
// !defined(AFX_MINIDRAWDOC_H__11E8392A_999A_11D1_80FC_00C0F6A83B7F__INCLUDED_)
```

Listing 13.4

```
// MiniDrawDoc.cpp : implementation of the CMiniDrawDoc class
//

#include "stdafx.h"
#include "MiniDraw.h"

#include "MiniDrawDoc.h"

#ifdef _DEBUG
#define new DEBUG_NEW
#undef THIS_FILE
static char THIS_FILE[] = __FILE__;
#endif

/////////////////////////////////////////////////////////////////////////
// CMiniDrawDoc

IMPLEMENT_DYNCREATE(CMiniDrawDoc, CDocument)
```

```
BEGIN_MESSAGE_MAP(CMiniDrawDoc, CDocument)
    //{{AFX_MSG_MAP(CMiniDrawDoc)
    ON_COMMAND(ID_EDIT_CLEAR_ALL, OnEditClearAll)
    ON_UPDATE_COMMAND_UI(ID_EDIT_CLEAR_ALL, OnUpdateEditClearAll)
    ON_COMMAND(ID_EDIT_UNDO, OnEditUndo)
    ON_UPDATE_COMMAND_UI(ID_EDIT_UNDO, OnUpdateEditUndo)
    //}}AFX_MSG_MAP
END_MESSAGE_MAP()

/////////////////////////////////////////////////////////////////////////
// CMiniDrawDoc construction/destruction

CMiniDrawDoc::CMiniDrawDoc()
{
    // TODO: add one-time construction code here

}

CMiniDrawDoc::~CMiniDrawDoc()
{
}

BOOL CMiniDrawDoc::OnNewDocument()
{
    if (!CDocument::OnNewDocument())
        return FALSE;

    // TODO: add reinitialization code here
    // (SDI documents will reuse this document)

    return TRUE;
}




/////////////////////////////////////////////////////////////////////////
// CMiniDrawDoc serialization

void CMiniDrawDoc::Serialize(CArchive& ar)
{
    if (ar.IsStoring())
```

```
    {
        // TODO: add storing code here
        m_LineArray.Serialize (ar);
    }
    else
    {
        // TODO: add loading code here
        m_LineArray.Serialize (ar);
    }
}

/////////////////////////////////////////////////////////////////////////////
// CMiniDrawDoc diagnostics

#ifdef _DEBUG
void CMiniDrawDoc::AssertValid() const
{
    CDocument::AssertValid();
}

void CMiniDrawDoc::Dump(CDumpContext& dc) const
{
    CDocument::Dump(dc);
}
#endif //_DEBUG

/////////////////////////////////////////////////////////////////////////////
// CMiniDrawDoc commands

IMPLEMENT_SERIAL (CLine, CObject, 1)

void CLine::Draw (CDC *PDC)
    {
    PDC->MoveTo (m_X1, m_Y1);
    PDC->LineTo (m_X2, m_Y2);
    }

void CLine::Serialize (CArchive& ar)
    {
    if (ar.IsStoring())
        ar << m_X1 << m_Y1 << m_X2 << m_Y2;
    else
        ar >> m_X1 >> m_Y1 >> m_X2 >> m_Y2;
    }
```

```
CLine *CMiniDrawDoc::AddLine (int X1, int Y1, int X2, int Y2)
   {
   CLine *PLine = new CLine (X1, Y1, X2, Y2);
   m_LineArray.Add (PLine);
   SetModifiedFlag ();
   return PLine;
   }


CLine *CMiniDrawDoc::GetLine (int Index)
   {
   if (Index < 0 || Index > m_LineArray.GetUpperBound ())
      return 0;
   return m_LineArray.GetAt (Index);
   }


int CMiniDrawDoc::GetNumLines ()
   {
   return m_LineArray.GetSize ();
   }


void CMiniDrawDoc::DeleteContents()
{
   // TODO: Add your specialized code here and/or call the base class

   int Index = m_LineArray.GetSize ();
   while (Index--)
      delete m_LineArray.GetAt (Index);
   m_LineArray.RemoveAll ();

   CDocument::DeleteContents();
}


void CMiniDrawDoc::OnEditClearAll()
{
   // TODO: Add your command handler code here

   DeleteContents ();
   UpdateAllViews (0);
   SetModifiedFlag ();
}
```

```
void CMiniDrawDoc::OnUpdateEditClearAll(CCmdUI* pCmdUI)
{
   // TODO: Add your command update UI handler code here

   pCmdUI->Enable (m_LineArray.GetSize ());
}

void CMiniDrawDoc::OnEditUndo()
{
   // TODO: Add your command handler code here

   int Index = m_LineArray.GetUpperBound ();
   if (Index > -1)
      {
      delete m_LineArray.GetAt (Index);
      m_LineArray.RemoveAt (Index);
      }
   UpdateAllViews (0);
   SetModifiedFlag ();
}

void CMiniDrawDoc::OnUpdateEditUndo(CCmdUI* pCmdUI)
{
   // TODO: Add your command update UI handler code here

   pCmdUI->Enable (m_LineArray.GetSize ());
}

CRect CLine::GetDimRect ()
   {
   return CRect
     (min (m_X1, m_X2),
      min (m_Y1, m_Y2),
      max (m_X1, m_X2) + 1,
      max (m_Y1, m_Y2) + 1);
   }
```

Listing 13.5

```
// MainFrm.h : interface3
   virtual void Dump(CDumpContext& dc) const;
#endif
```

```
// Generated message map functions
protected:
    //{{AFX_MSG(CMainFrame)
    //}}AFX_MSG
    DECLARE_MESSAGE_MAP()
};
```

```
/////////////////////////////////////////////////////////////////////////////
```

```
//{{AFX_INSERT_LOCATION}}
// Microsoft Visual C++ will insert additional declarations immediately before
// the previous line.
```

```
#endif
// !defined(AFX_MAINFRM_H__11E83928_999A_11D1_80FC_00C0F6A83B7F__INCLUDED_)
```

Listing 13.6

```cpp
// MainFrm.cpp : implementation of the CMainFrame class
//

#include "stdafx.h"
#include "MiniDraw.h"

#include "MainFrm.h"

#ifdef _DEBUG
#define new DEBUG_NEW
#undef THIS_FILE
static char THIS_FILE[] = __FILE__;
#endif

/////////////////////////////////////////////////////////////////////////////
// CMainFrame

IMPLEMENT_DYNCREATE(CMainFrame, CFrameWnd)

BEGIN_MESSAGE_MAP(CMainFrame, CFrameWnd)
    //{{AFX_MSG_MAP(CMainFrame)
    //}}AFX_MSG_MAP
END_MESSAGE_MAP()
```

```
/////////////////////////////////////////////////////////////////////////
// CMainFrame construction/destruction

CMainFrame::CMainFrame()
{
    // TODO: add member initialization code here

}

CMainFrame::~CMainFrame()
{
}

BOOL CMainFrame::PreCreateWindow(CREATESTRUCT& cs)
{
    if( !CFrameWnd::PreCreateWindow(cs) )
        return FALSE;
    // TODO: Modify the Window class or styles here by modifying
    //   the CREATESTRUCT cs

    return TRUE;
}

/////////////////////////////////////////////////////////////////////////
// CMainFrame diagnostics

#ifdef _DEBUG
void CMainFrame::AssertValid() const
{
    CFrameWnd::AssertValid();
}

void CMainFrame::Dump(CDumpContext& dc) const
{
    CFrameWnd::Dump(dc);
}

#endif //_DEBUG
```

```
////////////////////////////////////////////////////////////////////////////
// CMainFrame message handlers


BOOL CMainFrame::OnCreateClient(LPCREATESTRUCT lpcs, CCreateContext* pContext)
{
    // TODO: Add your specialized code here and/or call the base class

    return m_SplitterWnd.Create
        (this,              // parent of splitter window
        1,                  // maximum rows
        2,                  // maximum columns
        CSize (15, 15),     // minimum view window size
        pContext);          // pass on context information
                    }
```

Listing 13.7

```
// MiniDrawView.h : interface of the CMiniDrawView class
//
////////////////////////////////////////////////////////////////////////////

#if !defined(AFX_MINIDRAWVIEW_H__11E8392C_999A_11D1_80FC_00C0F6A83B7F__INCLUDED_)
#define AFX_MINIDRAWVIEW_H__11E8392C_999A_11D1_80FC_00C0F6A83B7F__INCLUDED_

#if _MSC_VER > 1000
#pragma once
#endif // _MSC_VER > 1000

class CMiniDrawView : public CScrollView
{
protected:
    CString m_ClassName;
    int m_Dragging;
    HCURSOR m_HArrow;
    HCURSOR m_HCross;
    CPoint m_PointOld;
    CPoint m_PointOrigin;

protected: // create from serialization only
    CMiniDrawView();
    DECLARE_DYNCREATE(CMiniDrawView)
```

```
// Attributes
public:
    CMiniDrawDoc* GetDocument();

// Operations
public:

// Overrides
    // ClassWizard generated virtual function overrides
    //{{AFX_VIRTUAL(CMiniDrawView)
    public:
    virtual void OnDraw(CDC* pDC);  // overridden to draw this view
    virtual BOOL PreCreateWindow(CREATESTRUCT& cs);
    virtual void OnInitialUpdate();
    protected:
    virtual void OnUpdate(CView* pSender, LPARAM lHint, CObject* pHint);
    //}}AFX_VIRTUAL

// Implementation
public:
    virtual ~CMiniDrawView();
#ifdef _DEBUG
    virtual void AssertValid() const;
    virtual void Dump(CDumpContext& dc) const;
#endif

protected:

// Generated message map functions
protected:
    //{{AFX_MSG(CMiniDrawView)
    afx_msg void OnLButtonDown(UINT nFlags, CPoint point);
    afx_msg void OnMouseMove(UINT nFlags, CPoint point);
    afx_msg void OnLButtonUp(UINT nFlags, CPoint point);
    //}}AFX_MSG
    DECLARE_MESSAGE_MAP()
};

#ifndef _DEBUG  // debug version in MiniDrawView.cpp
inline CMiniDrawDoc* CMiniDrawView::GetDocument()
    { return (CMiniDrawDoc*)m_pDocument; }
#endif
```

```
/////////////////////////////////////////////////////////////////////////

//{{AFX_INSERT_LOCATION}}
// Microsoft Visual C++ will insert additional declarations immediately before
// the previous line.

#endif
// !defined(AFX_MINIDRAWVIEW_H__11E8392C_999A_11D1_80FC_00C0F6A83B7F__INCLUDED_)
```

Listing 13.8

```cpp
// MiniDrawView.cpp : implementation of the CMiniDrawView class
//

#include "stdafx.h"
#include "MiniDraw.h"

#include "MiniDrawDoc.h"
#include "MiniDrawView.h"

#ifdef _DEBUG
#define new DEBUG_NEW
#undef THIS_FILE
static char THIS_FILE[] = __FILE__;
#endif


/////////////////////////////////////////////////////////////////////////
// CMiniDrawView

IMPLEMENT_DYNCREATE(CMiniDrawView, CScrollView)

BEGIN_MESSAGE_MAP(CMiniDrawView, CScrollView)
    //{{AFX_MSG_MAP(CMiniDrawView)
    ON_WM_LBUTTONDOWN()
    ON_WM_MOUSEMOVE()
    ON_WM_LBUTTONUP()
    //}}AFX_MSG_MAP
END_MESSAGE_MAP()
```

```
///////////////////////////////////////////////////////////////////////
// CMiniDrawView construction/destruction

CMiniDrawView::CMiniDrawView()
{
    // TODO: add construction code here

    m_Dragging = 0;
    m_HArrow = AfxGetApp ()->LoadStandardCursor (IDC_ARROW);
    m_HCross = AfxGetApp ()->LoadStandardCursor (IDC_CROSS);
}


CMiniDrawView::~CMiniDrawView()
{
}


BOOL CMiniDrawView::PreCreateWindow(CREATESTRUCT& cs)
{
    // TODO: Modify the Window class or styles here by modifying
    //   the CREATESTRUCT cs

    m_ClassName = AfxRegisterWndClass
        (CS_HREDRAW | CS_VREDRAW,                    // class styles
        0,                                           // no cursor
        (HBRUSH)::GetStockObject (WHITE_BRUSH),      // assign white
                                                     // background brush
        0);                                          // no icon
    cs.lpszClass = m_ClassName;

    return CScrollView::PreCreateWindow(cs);
}


///////////////////////////////////////////////////////////////////////
// CMiniDrawView drawing

void CMiniDrawView::OnDraw(CDC* pDC)
{
    CMiniDrawDoc* pDoc = GetDocument();
    ASSERT_VALID(pDoc);

    // TODO: add draw code for native data here
```

```
    CSize ScrollSize = GetTotalSize ();
    pDC->MoveTo (ScrollSize.cx, 0);
    pDC->LineTo (ScrollSize.cx, ScrollSize.cy);
    pDC->LineTo (0, ScrollSize.cy);

    CRect ClipRect;
    CRect DimRect;
    CRect IntRect;
    CLine *PLine;
    pDC->GetClipBox (&ClipRect);

    int Index = pDoc->GetNumLines ();
    while (Index--)
        {
        PLine = pDoc->GetLine (Index);
        DimRect = PLine->GetDimRect ();
        if (IntRect.IntersectRect (DimRect, ClipRect))
            PLine->Draw (pDC);
        }
}


/////////////////////////////////////////////////////////////////////////
// CMiniDrawView diagnostics

#ifdef _DEBUG
void CMiniDrawView::AssertValid() const
{
    CScrollView::AssertValid();
}

void CMiniDrawView::Dump(CDumpContext& dc) const
{
    CScrollView::Dump(dc);
}

CMiniDrawDoc* CMiniDrawView::GetDocument() // non-debug version is inline
{
    ASSERT(m_pDocument->IsKindOf(RUNTIME_CLASS(CMiniDrawDoc)));
    return (CMiniDrawDoc*)m_pDocument;
}
#endif //_DEBUG
```

```
///////////////////////////////////////////////////////////////////////////
// CMiniDrawView message handlers

void CMiniDrawView::OnLButtonDown(UINT nFlags, CPoint point)
{
    // TODO: Add your message handler code here and/or call default

    CClientDC ClientDC (this);
    OnPrepareDC (&ClientDC);
    ClientDC.DPtoLP (&point);

    // test whether cursor is within drawing area of view window:
    CSize ScrollSize = GetTotalSize ();
    CRect ScrollRect (0, 0, ScrollSize.cx, ScrollSize.cy);
    if (!ScrollRect.PtInRect (point))
        return;

    // save cursor position, capture mouse, and set dragging flag:
    m_PointOrigin = point;
    m_PointOld = point;
    SetCapture ();
    m_Dragging = 1;

    // clip mouse cursor:
    ClientDC.LPtoDP (&ScrollRect);
    CRect ViewRect;
    GetClientRect (&ViewRect);
    CRect IntRect;
    IntRect.IntersectRect (&ScrollRect, &ViewRect);
    ClientToScreen (&IntRect);
    ::ClipCursor (&IntRect);

    CScrollView::OnLButtonDown(nFlags, point);
}

void CMiniDrawView::OnMouseMove(UINT nFlags, CPoint point)
{
    // TODO: Add your message handler code here and/or call default

    CClientDC ClientDC (this);
    OnPrepareDC (&ClientDC);
    ClientDC.DPtoLP (&point);
```

```
    CSize ScrollSize = GetTotalSize ();
    CRect ScrollRect (0, 0, ScrollSize.cx, ScrollSize.cy);
    if (ScrollRect.PtInRect (point))
        ::SetCursor (m_HCross);
    else
        ::SetCursor (m_HArrow);

    if (m_Dragging)
        {
        ClientDC.SetROP2 (R2_NOT);
        ClientDC.MoveTo (m_PointOrigin);
        ClientDC.LineTo (m_PointOld);
        ClientDC.MoveTo (m_PointOrigin);
        ClientDC.LineTo (point);
        m_PointOld = point;
        }

    CScrollView::OnMouseMove(nFlags, point);
}

void CMiniDrawView::OnLButtonUp(UINT nFlags, CPoint point)
{
    // TODO: Add your message handler code here and/or call default

    if (m_Dragging)
        {
        m_Dragging = 0;
        ::ReleaseCapture ();
        ::ClipCursor (NULL);

        CClientDC ClientDC (this);
        OnPrepareDC (&ClientDC);
        ClientDC.DPtoLP (&point);

        ClientDC.SetROP2 (R2_NOT);
        ClientDC.MoveTo (m_PointOrigin);
        ClientDC.LineTo (m_PointOld);
        ClientDC.SetROP2 (R2_COPYPEN);
        ClientDC.MoveTo (m_PointOrigin);
        ClientDC.LineTo (point);
```

```
      CMiniDrawDoc* PDoc = GetDocument();
      CLine *PCLine;
      PCLine = PDoc->AddLine (m_PointOrigin.x, m_PointOrigin.y,
         point.x, point.y);
      PDoc->UpdateAllViews (this, 0, PCLine);
      }

   CScrollView::OnLButtonUp(nFlags, point);
}

void CMiniDrawView::OnInitialUpdate()
{
   CScrollView::OnInitialUpdate();

   // TODO: Add your specialized code here and/or call the base class

   SIZE Size = {640, 480};
   SetScrollSizes (MM_TEXT, Size);
}

void CMiniDrawView::OnUpdate(CView* pSender, LPARAM lHint, CObject* pHint)
{
   // TODO: Add your specialized code here and/or call the base class

   if (pHint != 0)
      {
      CRect InvalidRect = ((CLine *)pHint)->GetDimRect ();
      CClientDC ClientDC (this);
      OnPrepareDC (&ClientDC);
      ClientDC.LPtoDP (&InvalidRect);
      InvalidateRect (&InvalidRect);
      }
   else
      CScrollView::OnUpdate (pSender, lHint, pHint);
}
```

Summary

In this chapter, you added scrolling and splitting capabilities to the MiniDraw program window. The following is a brief summary of the general techniques for adding scrolling:

- If you derive your view class from the MFC class CScrollView, rather than from CView, the view window will display horizontal and vertical scroll bars, and the MFC code will handle most of the logic for scrolling the document displayed in the view window. You must, however, add some supporting code of your own.

- When the user scrolls the document, the MFC adjusts the *viewport origin*, which determines the position of the text or graphics you draw with respect to the view window.

- You *don't* need to modify the OnDraw function to support scrolling. The viewport origin of the device context object passed to OnDraw has already been adjusted. You simply display text or graphics at the correct position within the document. The adjusted viewport origin automatically makes the output appear at the appropriate position with respect to the window.

- If, however, you create your own device context object, you must pass it to the CScrollView::OnPrepareDC function to adjust its viewport origin for the current scrolled position of the document, before you use the device context object.

- The coordinates you specify when you draw an object are known as *logical coordinates*; the actual coordinates of an object with respect to the window are known as *device coordinates*. Once the document has been scrolled, these two types of coordinates are no longer the same.

- The MFC sometimes uses logical coordinates (for example, when you call a drawing function), and it sometimes uses device coordinates (say, when it reports the position of the mouse cursor to a message handler). You can convert device coordinates to logical coordinates by calling CDC::DPtoLP, and you can convert logical coordinates by calling CDC::LPtoDP.

- You must call the CScrollView::SetScrollSizes function to specify the *size* of the document that's being scrolled. You typically call SetScrollSizes from an overriding version of the OnInitialUpdate function, defined as a member of your view class. OnInitialUpdate is called just before a given drawing (a new or existing one) is *first* displayed in the view window.

- If a document has a fixed size, you might need to change the logic of your program to prevent the user from attempting to add text or graphics outside the document boundaries.

The following is a summary of the general technique for adding splitting capability:

- Within the main frame window class, add a data member that is an object of the CSplitterWnd MFC class.

- Within the main frame window class, define an overriding version of the virtual function OnCreateClient, which is called when the main frame window is first created.

- From the OnCreateClient function, call the Create member function for the CSplitterWnd object to create a *splitter window*. The CSplitterWnd object automatically creates one or more view windows.

- The splitter window displays a horizontal split box, a vertical split box, or both types of split boxes. A split box allows the user to divide the program window into separate view windows, or *panes*.

- When generating a *new* program using AppWizard, you can add splitting capability by simply choosing this option through the Advanced Options dialog box, accessed through the AppWizard Step 4 dialog box.

When a document has more than a single view, a view object must update the other views whenever the user edits the data that it displays. The following are the main steps for doing this efficiently:

- When the user changes the data in a view, the view object calls the CDocument::UpdateAllViews function for the document object, passing it *hint* information that describes the modification that was made.

- UpdateAllViews calls the virtual OnUpdate member function for each view object, passing it the hint information. You should define an overriding version of this function that calls the CWnd::InvalidateRect function to invalidate the affected area of the view window. `OnUpdate` should be able to calculate the dimensions of this area from the hint information.

- `InvalidateRect` causes the `OnDraw` function of the view class to be called. `OnDraw` should call `GetClipBox` to obtain the dimensions of the invalidated area and redraw only the text and graphics that fall within this area.

Including Docking Toolbars and Status Bars

- Adding a docking toolbar and a status bar to a new program

- Adding a docking toolbar to MiniDraw

- Adding a status bar to MiniDraw

- The MiniDraw source code

In this chapter, you'll learn how to create two sophisticated user-interface elements that are supported by the Microsoft Foundation Classes: docking toolbars and status bars. A *docking toolbar* consists of a collection of custom buttons; the user can click one of these buttons to immediately execute a command or choose an option. The user can position (or "dock") the toolbar along any edge of the program window, or move it into a free-floating window. A *status bar* is usually displayed at the bottom of the main window, and is used for printing messages and showing the status of keys or program modes (for example, the Caps Lock key or the overwrite mode in a word processor).

You'll learn how to use AppWizard to create a new program that includes a preliminary docking toolbar and a preliminary status bar, and you'll learn how to modify these elements to suit the needs of your application. You'll also learn how to add a custom docking toolbar and a custom status bar to an existing MFC program; in the exercises, you'll add these features to the MiniDraw program that you created in previous chapters.

The chapter also briefly introduces two other interface elements: the *dialog bar*, which is similar to a toolbar but is based on a dialog box template and can include controls other than buttons (such as list boxes); and the *rebar control*, which is a container for toolbars and other controls that can be rearranged as in Internet Explorer. Toolbars, status bars, dialog bars, and rebar controls belong to a general category of items known as *control bars*. The MFC provides a separate class for managing each type of control bar (these classes are all derived from `CControlBar`).

Adding a Docking Toolbar and a Status Bar to a New Program

When you generate a new application using AppWizard, you can include a docking toolbar, a status bar, or both elements in the main program window by simply selecting the appropriate AppWizard options. A toolbar or a status bar generated by AppWizard contains a typical set of components. You'll probably want to modify the toolbar or status bar to match your program's actual commands and features.

In this section, you'll generate a simple AppWizard program that displays both a docking toolbar and a status bar. To create the program, follow the basic procedure that was given in Chapter 9 for generating the WinGreet program. In the Projects tab of the New dialog box, however, enter the program name Test into the Project Name: text box, and enter the desired project folder path into the Location: text box. Choose the same options described in Chapter 9 in all the AppWizard dialog boxes *except* the Step 4 dialog box; in this dialog box you should choose both the Docking Toolbar option and the Initial Status Bar option. Under the prompt "How do you want your toolbars to look?" choose the Normal option to generate a traditional docking toolbar only. (Choosing the Internet Explorer ReBars option places the toolbar, together with an empty dialog bar, within a rebar control. Rebar controls are briefly discussed in a sidebar at the end of the chapter.)

The completed Step 4 dialog box is shown in Figure 14.1. When you've generated the source files, build and run the program. Figure 14.2 shows the window of the resulting application.

FIGURE 14.1:

The AppWizard Step 4 dialog box for generating the Test program with a docking toolbar and a status bar

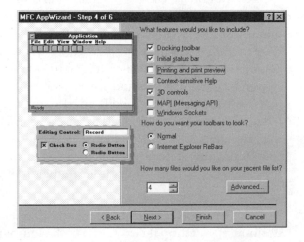

FIGURE 14.2:

The Test program window, with the toolbar in its initial position

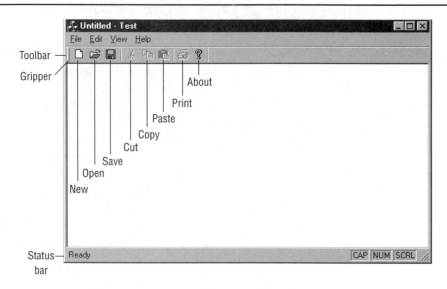

Each of the buttons displayed on the initial toolbar of the Test program—except the Print button—corresponds to a command on the program menu. Specifically, there's a button for each of the following commands: the New, Open…, and Save commands on the File menu; the Cut, Copy, and Paste commands on the Edit menu; and the About command on the Help menu. Clicking a button causes the program to perform the *same* action as choosing the corresponding menu command (as you'll see later, this is due to the fact that the button and the corresponding menu command are assigned the *same* resource identifier). Note that the Cut, Copy, Paste, and Print buttons are *disabled* (that is, they're displayed in faded tones and don't respond to the mouse). These buttons are disabled because the program doesn't initially have message-handling functions for them (the corresponding menu items are also disabled for the same reason); you must provide the handlers yourself using the techniques that will be presented later in the chapter.

Notice that you can use the mouse to drag the toolbar away from its original position. If you drop it next to one of the four window borders, the toolbar will be attached (or *docked*) to that border at the position where you drop it. If you drop the toolbar at a position *away* from a window border, the buttons will be placed within a floating window that you can move anywhere on the Windows desktop. When the toolbar is docked, to move it you must drag the gripper or one of the thin separator bars between groups of buttons. You can hide or redisplay the tool-bar or the status bar by choosing commands on the View menu.

Notice also that when you place the mouse cursor over a button, the button acquires a three-dimensional look, and a brief description of the button's function—known as a *tool tip*—appears in a small pop-up window next to the cursor. Later in the chapter you'll learn how to enable or disable tool tips and how to specify the tool-tip text.

When you place the cursor over a button, the program also displays a lengthier command prompt within the status bar. This prompt is the *same* as that displayed when the corresponding menu command is highlighted (as you'll see, the command prompt string has the same resource identifier as the menu command and button). Later in the chapter, you'll learn how to enable or disable these command prompts, and how to set their text.

In Figure 14.3 the toolbar has been placed within a floating window; this figure shows the tool tip and command prompt for the button under the mouse cursor.

FIGURE 14.3:

The Test program toolbar placed in a floating window, showing the tool tip and command prompt for the button under the mouse cursor

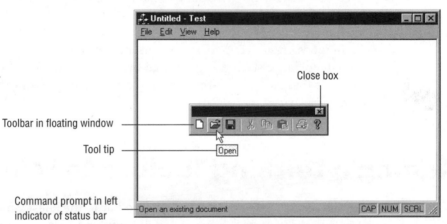

> **NOTE**   The Test program *doesn't* display a tool tip or a command prompt for the Print tool-bar button because AppWizard doesn't define a resource string for this command.

Each section of the status bar is known as an *indicator* (or *pane*). In the status bar generated by AppWizard, the prompt for a menu command or toolbar button is displayed within the left indicator. The three indicators on the right are used to display the current status of the Caps Lock, Num Lock, and Scroll Lock keys. Later in the chapter, you'll learn how to specify the prompt that's displayed for a particular toolbar button or menu command.

When you create a program, you'll probably need to modify the AppWizard-generated toolbar to suit the program. You might want to remove some of the buttons on the toolbar or add new ones. For example, if you remove a menu command, you'll most likely want to remove the corresponding button from the toolbar; and if you add a menu command, you might want to add a matching button. Note, however, that you certainly *don't* need to maintain a one-to-one correspondence between menu commands and toolbar buttons; you can have menu commands that don't have corresponding toolbar buttons, just as you can have toolbar buttons without corresponding menu commands.

Additionally, you might want to modify the status bar. For example, you could add an indicator to display the current status of a program mode, such as the overwrite mode in an editor, or the "record" mode that's active while a program records a macro. The remaining sections in this chapter show you how to add a toolbar and a status bar to an existing MFC program (a program that was initially generated *without* selecting the toolbar or status bar AppWizard option). The techniques presented in these sections, however, will also allow you to *modify* an initial toolbar or status bar generated by AppWizard. Look for the notes in these sections that provide information on modifying AppWizard-generated toolbars and status bars.

Adding a Docking Toolbar to MiniDraw

In this section, you'll add a docking toolbar to the latest version of the Mini-Draw program, which you created in Chapter 13. (If you didn't create this version of the program, you can obtain a complete set of the source files from the \MiniDrw4 companion-CD folder.) The MiniDraw program, sporting the new toolbar that you'll create, is shown in Figure 14.4; in this figure, the toolbar is in its initial position.

FIGURE 14.4:

The MiniDraw program with its new toolbar, in its initial position

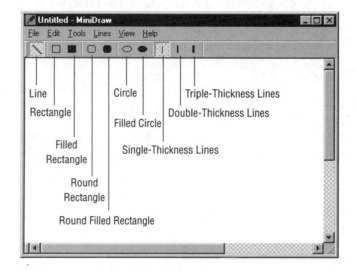

The toolbar contains 10 buttons. The first seven buttons allow the user to select a tool for drawing a particular shape; the last three buttons allow the user to choose the thickness of the lines used to draw the figures. (Note that at any time, exactly one of the first seven buttons is selected and exactly one of the last three buttons is selected.) You won't, however, add the code for drawing the different figures or using the various line thicknesses until Chapter 19. (The program in this chapter always draws simple lines, regardless of the tool selected.)

In this chapter, you'll also add menu commands that correspond to the buttons, so that the user can select a drawing tool or line thickness using either a button or a menu command.

Defining the Resources

The first phase of the project is to use the Developer Studio to define the resources for the new version of MiniDraw. To begin, open the MiniDraw project and then open the ResourceView tab of the Workspace window to display the program resources.

Designing the Toolbar Buttons

The first resource you'll design for MiniDraw is the toolbar. To do this, choose the Insert ➢ Resource… menu command or press Ctrl+R. In the Resource Type: list, choose the Toolbar item and click the New button.

Alternatively, either you can click the New Toolbar button on the Resource toolbar (to display it, right-click a toolbar and choose Resource),

or you can press Ctrl+6.

The Developer Studio will create a new toolbar and will display its identifier, IDR_TOOLBAR1, under the Toolbar node of the ResourceView graph. You should now click this name with the right mouse button,

and choose the Properties command on the pop-up menu to open the Toolbar Properties dialog box. In the ID: text box within this dialog box, enter a new identifier for the toolbar, IDR_MAINFRAME (this is the general identifier used for resources associated with the main frame window).

Notice that the Developer Studio displays the new toolbar within the toolbar editor window. This window contains three panes. The *toolbar pane* at the top displays the entire toolbar; you *select* a particular button by clicking within this pane. The *small-button pane* at the lower left displays the selected button in its actual size. The *enlarged-button pane* at the lower right displays an enlarged image of the button; you edit the selected button within this pane. While the toolbar editor window is active, the Developer Studio displays the Graphics and Colors toolbars, which you can use to create or edit the button images. Figure 14.5 shows the new toolbar in the toolbar editor.

FIGURE 14.5:

The newly created toolbar displayed within the toolbar editor

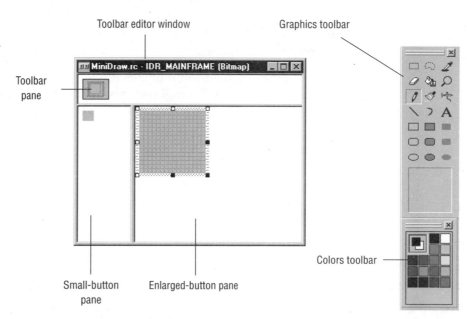

Toolbar editor window

Graphics toolbar

Toolbar pane

MiniDraw.rc - IDR_MAINFRAME (Bitmap)

Colors toolbar

Small-button pane

Enlarged-button pane

To design the toolbar buttons, do the following:

1. Design the image for the first button, working within the enlarged-button pane and using the mouse and the Graphics and Colors toolbars. The images for the toolbar belonging to the version of MiniEdit provided on the companion CD are shown in Figure 14.6. In this figure, the background color of the buttons is light gray and the foreground color is black. You can draw your own variations of these images, but keep in mind the commands that the buttons represent, as labeled in Figure 14.4. For detailed information on using the commands of the toolbar editor, see the following online help topic: *Visual C++ Documentation, Using Visual C++, Visual C++ User's Guide, Resource Editors, Toolbar Editor.*

2. Double-click within the enlarged-button pane to open the Toolbar Button Properties dialog box, and into the ID: list type the identifier for the first toolbar button, ID_TOOLS_LINE. (You don't need to enter a command description into the Prompt: box. You'll enter a prompt when you later define the corresponding menu command, which has the same identifier, ID_TOOLS_LINE, and therefore shares the same prompt.)

3. Notice that as soon as you edit the contents of the first button, a new blank button appears to its right within the toolbar pane. To design the second button, click on it within the toolbar pane, and it'll be displayed in the other two panes.

4. Repeat steps 1 through 3 for the remaining buttons. Altogether, you need to design 10 buttons. Example images for all the buttons are shown in Figure 14.6, and the button identifiers that you should assign are as follows:

```
ID_TOOLS_LINE
ID_TOOLS_RECTANGLE
ID_TOOLS_RECTFILL
ID_TOOLS_RECTROUND
ID_TOOLS_RECTROUNDFILL
ID_TOOLS_CIRCLE
ID_TOOLS_CIRCLEFILL
ID_LINE_SINGLE
ID_LINE_DOUBLEID_LINE_TRIPLE
```

FIGURE 14.6:

The toolbar buttons defined for the version of MiniDraw provided on the companion compact disc

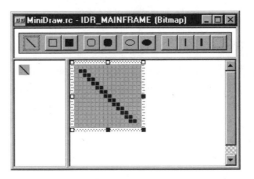

In Figure 14.6, notice that there are gaps in the toolbar following the first, third, fifth, and seventh buttons. To generate a gap, simply use the mouse within the toolbar pane to drag—toward the right—the button that follows the desired gap. These gaps will be converted to thin separator bars when the toolbar's displayed in the program window. The blank button at the right end of the toolbar shown in the toolbar pane isn't part of the actual toolbar that will be displayed by the program (as you saw, it's used to add a new button).

NOTE

You design only a *single* image for each button. The MFC automatically changes the button's appearance when the button is "pressed" (that is, when the user presses the mouse button while the cursor is over the button), when it's selected, when it's in the "indeterminate" state, or when it's disabled. These states are described later in the chapter.

TIP

If you've generated a toolbar for a *new* program using AppWizard (rather than adding one by hand to an existing program, as described in this section), you can modify the buttons by opening the toolbar editor window for the IDR_ MAINFRAME toolbar and following the general procedures given here. If you want to *remove* a button, use the mouse to drag it off the image of the toolbar in the toolbar pane.

Adding New Menu Commands

You'll now use the menu editor to add a menu command corresponding to each toolbar button, and also to add a View menu with commands for hiding or showing the toolbar. To do this, open the menu editor window for the IDR_MAINFRAME menu. To the right of the existing Edit menu, insert a Tools pop-up menu, and add to this menu the items shown in Table 14.1. Notice that for each menu command, the table includes a string that you should enter into the Prompt: text box of the Menu Item Properties dialog box. The portion of each string *before* the new-line character (\n) is the command prompt that the program displays in the status bar when the user highlights the menu command or moves the cursor over the corresponding toolbar button. The portion of each string *after* the newline is the text for the tool tip that the program displays when the user moves the cursor over the button (see Figure 14.3). Note that each string is stored as a string resource that has the same identifier as the menu command and corresponding button.

TABLE 14.1: Properties of the Tools Menu Items

ID:	Caption	Prompt	Other Features
none	&Tools	none	Popup
ID_TOOLS_LINE	&Line	Select tool to draw straight lines\nLine	none
ID_TOOLS_RECTANGLE	&Rectangle	Select tool to draw open rectangles\nRectangle	none
ID_TOOLS_RECTFILL	R&ect Fill	Select tool to draw filled rectangles\nFilled Rectangle	none
ID_TOOLS_RECTROUND	Re&ct Round	Select tool to draw open rectangles with rounded corners\nRound Rectangle	none
ID_TOOLS_RECT-ROUNDFILL	Rec&t Round Fill	Select tool to draw filled rectangles with rounded corners\nRound Filled Rectangle	none
ID_TOOLS_CIRCLE	C&ircle	Select tool to draw open circles or ellipses\nCircle	none
ID_TOOLS_CIRCLEFILL	Circle &Fill	Select tool to draw filled circles or ellipses\nFilled Circle	none

The completed Tools menu is shown in Figure 14.7. The commands on this menu correspond to the first seven toolbar buttons and allow the user to choose the current drawing tool.

Next, to the right of the Tools menu, insert a Lines pop-up menu, containing the items described in Table 14.2. The completed Lines menu is shown in Figure 14.8. The commands on this menu correspond to the last three toolbar buttons and allow the user to choose the thickness of the lines used to draw the figures.

FIGURE 14.7:

The completed Tools menu for the MiniDraw program

TABLE 14.2: Properties of the Lines Menu Items

ID:	Caption	Prompt	Other Features
none	&Lines	none	Popup
ID_LINE_SINGLE	&Single	Draw using single-thickness lines \nSingle-Thickness Lines	none
ID_LINE_DOUBLE	&Double	Draw using double-thickness lines \nDouble-Thickness Lines	none
ID_LINE_TRIPLE	&Triple	Draw using triple-thickness lines \nTriple-Thickness Lines	none

Finally, to the right of the Tools menu, insert a View pop-up menu. The menu items are described in Table 14.3 and the menu is shown in Figure 14.9. The Toolbar command on this menu allows the user to hide or display the toolbar. (Later in the chapter, you'll complete the menu by adding a command to hide or show the status bar as well.)

FIGURE 14.8:

The completed Lines menu
for the MiniDraw program

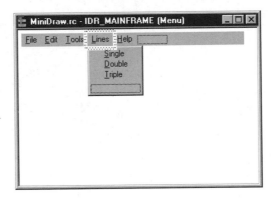

TABLE 14.3: Properties of the View Menu Items

ID:	Caption	Prompt	Other Features
none	&View	none	Popup
ID_VIEW_TOOLBAR	&Toolbar	Show or hide the toolbar	none

FIGURE 14.9:

The initial View menu for the
MiniDraw program

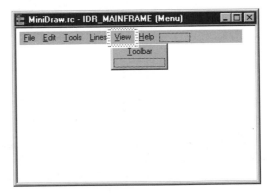

When you've completed defining the new menu items, you can save your work by choosing the File ➤ Save All menu command or clicking the Save All button on the Standard toolbar.

TIP

If you've generated a docking toolbar for a *new* program using AppWizard, and you've added one or more buttons to the toolbar bitmap, you might want to add corresponding commands to the program menu. You're not required, however, to have a menu command for each toolbar button.

Modifying the Code

In this section, you'll modify the MiniDraw code to support the toolbar you just designed. To begin, you need to define two data items. First, open the Main-Frm.h header file and declare m_ToolBar as a protected data member of the CMainFrame class:

```
class CMainFrame : public CFrameWnd
{
protected:
    CSplitterWnd m_SplitterWnd;
    CToolBar m_ToolBar;

// remainder of CMainFrame definition ...

}
```

m_ToolBar is an object of CToolBar, which is the MFC class for managing toolbars. CToolBar—as well as the classes for managing the other types of control bars discussed in this chapter—is derived from CControlBar.

The next step is to define a message-handling function within the main frame window class for the WM_CREATE message, which is sent when this window has just been created, immediately before it becomes visible. In this function, you'll create the toolbar.

Use ClassWizard to generate the function declaration and minimal definition, and to add the function to the class message map. In the ClassWizard dialog box, open the Message Maps tab and select the main frame window class, CMainFrame, in the Class Name: list. Then select CMainFrame in the Object IDs: list, select the WM_CREATE message identifier in the Messages: list, and click the Add Function button. ClassWizard will generate a message-handling function named OnCreate.

Now click the Edit Code button and add code as follows to the new OnCreate function in MainFrm.cpp:

```
int CMainFrame::OnCreate(LPCREATESTRUCT lpCreateStruct)
{
    if (CFrameWnd::OnCreate(lpCreateStruct) == -1)
        return -1;

    // TODO: Add your specialized creation code here

    if (!m_ToolBar.CreateEx
        (this,
        TBSTYLE_FLAT,
        WS_CHILD | WS_VISIBLE | CBRS_TOP | CBRS_GRIPPER
        | CBRS_TOOLTIPS | CBRS_FLYBY | CBRS_SIZE_DYNAMIC))
        return -1;

    if (!m_ToolBar.LoadToolBar(IDR_MAINFRAME))
        return -1;

    m_ToolBar.EnableDocking (CBRS_ALIGN_ANY);
    EnableDocking (CBRS_ALIGN_ANY);
    DockControlBar (&m_ToolBar);

    return 0;
}
```

The call to CToolBar::CreateEx creates the toolbar and assigns the toolbar styles. Passing this to the first parameter specifies that the main frame window is to be the toolbar's parent (the toolbar is a child window).

The second CreateEx parameter is assigned styles that are specific to toolbars. Passing TBSTYLE_FLAT creates a toolbar with flat buttons. For a description of the other styles you can assign this parameter, see the online help topic *Platform SDK, User Interface Services, Shell and Common Controls, Common Controls, Toolbar Controls, Toolbar Control Reference, Toolbar Control Constants*.

The third CreateEx parameter is assigned general control-bar styles. WS_CHILD makes the toolbar a child of the main frame window, WS_VISIBLE makes it visible, and CBRS_TOP places it initially at the top of the main frame window. CBRS_GRIPPER displays a *gripper* (a wide vertical bar) at the left end of the toolbar. The user can drag the gripper to move the toolbar (the user can also drag one of the thin separator bars within the toolbar; a gripper, however, presents a broader target and makes dragging somewhat easier).

The CBRS_TOOLTIPS style activates the tool tips feature, and the CBRS_FLYBY style causes the program to display the command prompt in the status bar when the mouse cursor is placed over a button (if the CBRS_FLYBY style isn't included, the program displays the command prompt only if the user actually presses the mouse button while the cursor is over the button). The tool tips and command prompt features were described previously (see Figure 14.3). Finally, CBRS_SIZE_DYNAMIC lets the user change the shape of the toolbar—and the arrangement of the buttons—while the toolbar is floating (*not* while it's docked), by dragging one of the toolbar edges. For information on the other styles you can assign the third CreateEx parameter, look up the constants beginning with CBRS_ in the Index tab of the online help window (the constants are described under several different topics).

The call to CToolBar::LoadToolBar loads the toolbar resource that you designed in the toolbar editor. If the call to either CreateEx or LoadToolBar returns zero, indicating an error, OnCreate returns a value of –1, which signifies that an error has occurred and causes the main frame window to be destroyed and the program to be terminated.

The final three lines of added code give the toolbar its docking capability (that is, they allow the user to change the position of the toolbar or to move the toolbar into a floating window). The first call to EnableDocking invokes the version of this function defined in CControlBar and enables docking for the toolbar itself. The second call to EnableDocking invokes the version of this function defined in CFrameWnd and enables docking for the main frame window. Passing the value CBRS_ALIGN_ANY in both calls allows the user to dock the toolbar on *any* of the four window borders. The call to CFrameWnd::DockControlBar positions the toolbar at its initial location (the upper-left border of the main frame window's client area). If you omit any of these three function calls, the toolbar will become a *standard toolbar*—that is, a nondocking toolbar that's fixed permanently at the top of the window.

Before continuing on to the next step, you might want to build the MiniDraw program to see the results of your work. If you run the program, the toolbar will be displayed and you can move it to various positions; the buttons, however, will be disabled (that is, they'll be displayed in faded tones and won't respond to the mouse), because you haven't yet defined handlers to process the button messages. For the same reason, the corresponding menu items will also be disabled. Notice that you can hide or display the toolbar through the Toolbar command on the View menu; although you didn't define message handlers for this command, the MFC provides them for you.

TIP

If you generated a docking toolbar for a *new* program, AppWizard will have defined a **CToolBar** object (named **m_wndToolBar**) and will have added the necessary code for creating and docking the toolbar. You might, however, want to change the styles specified in the call to **CToolBar::CreateEx**, to change the parameters passed in the calls to **EnableDocking**, or to eliminate the calls to **EnableDocking** and **DockControlBar** (to create a standard, nondocking toolbar).

Writing Handlers for the Button Messages

You now need to define and implement the message-handling functions that process the toolbar buttons and the corresponding menu commands.

To define the handlers, run ClassWizard and open the Message Maps tab. Select the **CMiniDrawApp** class within the Class Name: list so that the *application* class will handle the messages from the toolbar buttons and the newly added menu commands. The application class is chosen because the current drawing tool and line thickness affect the operation of the application as a whole, rather than affecting a particular document or view.

Now select the **ID_LINE_DOUBLE** identifier in the Object IDs: list, select the COMMAND message in the Messages: list, click the Add Function... button, and accept the default function name, **OnLineDouble**. Because **ID_LINE_DOUBLE** is the identifier of both the Double-Thickness Lines button and the Double command on the Lines menu, the **OnLineDouble** function will receive control when the user *either* clicks the button *or* chooses the menu command.

Next, while the **ID_LINE_DOUBLE** identifier is still selected in the Object IDs: list, select the UPDATE_COMMAND_UI message in the Messages: list, click the Add Function... button, and again accept the default function name, **OnUpdateLineDouble**. The **OnUpdateLineDouble** function receives control at regular intervals, whenever the system is idle, so that it can update the Double-Thickness Lines button. **OnUpdateLineDouble** also receives control whenever the user opens the Lines pop-up menu, so that it can initialize the Double menu command (as explained in Chapter 11).

Before adding code to the **OnLineDouble** and **OnUpdateLineDouble** functions, proceed to use ClassWizard to generate the message-handling functions for the remaining toolbar buttons (and their matching menu commands). To do this, consult Table 14.4, which describes each message-handling function that you need to define. Note that in all cases you should accept the default function name proposed by ClassWizard.

TABLE 14.4: Message-Handling Functions for the MiniDraw Toolbar Buttons

Button/Menu- Command Identifier	Message Identifier	Message-Handling Function
ID_LINE_DOUBLE	COMMAND	OnLineDouble
ID_LINE_DOUBLE	UPDATE_COMMAND_UI	OnUpdateLineDouble
ID_LINE_SINGLE	COMMAND	OnLineSingle
ID_LINE_SINGLE	UPDATE_COMMAND_UI	OnUpdateLineSingle
ID_LINE_TRIPLE	COMMAND	OnLineTriple
ID_LINE_TRIPLE	UPDATE_COMMAND_UI	OnUpdateLineTriple
ID_TOOLS_CIRCLE	COMMAND	OnToolsCircle
ID_TOOLS_CIRCLE	UPDATE_COMMAND_UI	OnUpdateToolsCircle
ID_TOOLS_CIRCLEFILL	COMMAND	OnToolsCirclefill
ID_TOOLS_CIRCLEFILL	UPDATE_COMMAND_UI	OnUpdateToolsCirclefill
ID_TOOLS_LINE	COMMAND	OnToolsLine
ID_TOOLS_LINE	UPDATE_COMMAND_UI	OnUpdateToolsLine
ID_TOOLS_RECTANGLE	COMMAND	OnToolsRectangle
ID_TOOLS_RECTANGLE	UPDATE_COMMAND_UI	OnUpdateToolsRectangle
ID_TOOLS_RECTFILL	COMMAND	OnToolsRectfill
ID_TOOLS_RECTFILL	UPDATE_COMMAND_UI	OnUpdateToolsRectfill

Continued on next page

TABLE 14.4 CONTINUED: Message-Handling Functions for the MiniDraw Toolbar Buttons

Button/Menu- Command Identifier	Message Identifier	Message-Handling Function
ID_TOOLS_RECTROUND	COMMAND	OnToolsRectround
ID_TOOLS_RECTROUND	UPDATE_COMMAND_UI	OnUpdateToolsRectround
ID_TOOLS_RECTROUNDFILL	COMMAND	OnToolsRectroundfill
ID_TOOLS_RECTROUNDFILL	UPDATE_COMMAND_UI	OnUpdateToolsRectroundfill

Also before implementing the newly defined message handlers, you need to define and initialize two new data members of the application class: m_Current-Thickness, which stores the current line thickness (1, 2, or 3), and m_Current-Tool, which stores the identifier of the currently selected tool button. Add the declarations to the beginning of the CMiniDrawApp class definition in MiniDraw.h:

```
/////////////////////////////////////////////////////////////////
///////////
// CMiniDrawApp:
// See MiniDraw.cpp for the implementation of this class
//

class CMiniDrawApp : public CWinApp
{
public:
    int m_CurrentThickness;
    UINT m_CurrentTool;
```

Add the initializations to the CMiniDrawApp constructor in MiniDraw.cpp:

```
CMiniDrawApp::CMiniDrawApp()
{
    // TODO: add construction code here,
    // Place all significant initialization in InitInstance

    m_CurrentThickness = 1;
    m_CurrentTool = ID_TOOLS_LINE;
}
```

The version of MiniDraw presented in Chapter 19 will use m_CurrentTool to determine the type of figure to generate when the user begins drawing with the mouse, and it will use m_CurrentThickness to determine the thickness of the lines to employ when generating a figure. The initializations you added will cause the program to draw simple lines, which are one pixel thick, until the user chooses another drawing tool or line thickness.

The final step is to add code to the 20 message-handling function definitions generated by ClassWizard in the file MiniDraw.cpp. You need to add only a single statement to each function, as follows:

```
////////////////////////////////////////////////////////////////////
///////////
// CMiniDrawApp commands

void CMiniDrawApp::OnLineDouble()
{
   // TODO: Add your command handler code here
   m_CurrentThickness = 2;
}

void CMiniDrawApp::OnUpdateLineDouble(CCmdUI* pCmdUI)
{
   // TODO: Add your command update UI handler code here
   pCmdUI->SetCheck (m_CurrentThickness == 2 ? 1 : 0);
}

void CMiniDrawApp::OnLineSingle()
{
   // TODO: Add your command handler code here
   m_CurrentThickness = 1;
}

void CMiniDrawApp::OnUpdateLineSingle(CCmdUI* pCmdUI)
{
   // TODO: Add your command update UI handler code here
   pCmdUI->SetCheck (m_CurrentThickness == 1 ? 1 : 0);
}

void CMiniDrawApp::OnLineTriple()
{
   // TODO: Add your command handler code here
   m_CurrentThickness = 3;
}
```

```
void CMiniDrawApp::OnUpdateLineTriple(CCmdUI* pCmdUI)
{
   // TODO: Add your command update UI handler code here
   pCmdUI->SetCheck (m_CurrentThickness == 3 ? 1 : 0);
}

void CMiniDrawApp::OnToolsCircle()
{
   // TODO: Add your command handler code here
   m_CurrentTool = ID_TOOLS_CIRCLE;
}

void CMiniDrawApp::OnUpdateToolsCircle(CCmdUI* pCmdUI)
{
   // TODO: Add your command update UI handler code here
   pCmdUI->SetCheck (m_CurrentTool == ID_TOOLS_CIRCLE ? 1 : 0);
}

void CMiniDrawApp::OnToolsCirclefill()
{
   // TODO: Add your command handler code here
   m_CurrentTool = ID_TOOLS_CIRCLEFILL;
}

void CMiniDrawApp::OnUpdateToolsCirclefill(CCmdUI* pCmdUI)
{
   // TODO: Add your command update UI handler code here
   pCmdUI->SetCheck
      (m_CurrentTool == ID_TOOLS_CIRCLEFILL ? 1 : 0);
}

void CMiniDrawApp::OnToolsLine()
{
   // TODO: Add your command handler code here
   m_CurrentTool = ID_TOOLS_LINE;
}

void CMiniDrawApp::OnUpdateToolsLine(CCmdUI* pCmdUI)
{
   // TODO: Add your command update UI handler code here
   pCmdUI->SetCheck (m_CurrentTool == ID_TOOLS_LINE ? 1 : 0);
}
```

```
void CMiniDrawApp::OnToolsRectangle()
{
   // TODO: Add your command handler code here
   m_CurrentTool = ID_TOOLS_RECTANGLE;
}

void CMiniDrawApp::OnUpdateToolsRectangle(CCmdUI* pCmdUI)
{
   // TODO: Add your command update UI handler code here
   pCmdUI->SetCheck
      (m_CurrentTool == ID_TOOLS_RECTANGLE ? 1 : 0);
}

void CMiniDrawApp::OnToolsRectfill()
{
   // TODO: Add your command handler code here
   m_CurrentTool = ID_TOOLS_RECTFILL;
}

void CMiniDrawApp::OnUpdateToolsRectfill(CCmdUI* pCmdUI)
{
   // TODO: Add your command update UI handler code here
   pCmdUI->SetCheck (m_CurrentTool == ID_TOOLS_RECTFILL ? 1 : 0);
}

void CMiniDrawApp::OnToolsRectround()
{
   // TODO: Add your command handler code here
   m_CurrentTool = ID_TOOLS_RECTROUND;
}

void CMiniDrawApp::OnUpdateToolsRectround(CCmdUI* pCmdUI)
{
   // TODO: Add your command update UI handler code here
   pCmdUI->SetCheck
      (m_CurrentTool == ID_TOOLS_RECTROUND ? 1 : 0);
}

void CMiniDrawApp::OnToolsRectroundfill()
{
   // TODO: Add your command handler code here
   m_CurrentTool = ID_TOOLS_RECTROUNDFILL;
}
```

```
void CMiniDrawApp::OnUpdateToolsRectroundfill(CCmdUI* pCmdUI)
{
    // TODO: Add your command update UI handler code here
    pCmdUI->SetCheck
        (m_CurrentTool == ID_TOOLS_RECTROUNDFILL ? 1 : 0);
}
```

To understand how these functions work, first consider OnLineDouble. This function receives control whenever the user either clicks the Double-Thickness Lines button on the toolbar or chooses the Double command on the Lines menu of the MiniDraw program. In either case, it simply sets the value of the m_Current-Thickness data member to 2.

After the m_CurrentThickness data member has been set to 2, the Double-Thickness Lines button on the toolbar should be selected and the Double menu command should be checked, so that the user can easily see which line thickness is being used. This task is performed by OnUpdateLineDouble. The OnUpdate-LineDouble function is called as soon as the program becomes idle, *and* it's called the next time the user opens the Lines pop-up menu. In either case, OnUpdate-LineDouble is passed a pointer to a CCmdUI object, and it simply calls the CCmdUI member function SetCheck, passing it a nonzero value (a nonzero value, 1, gets passed because m_CurrentThickness has been set to 2). If OnUpdateLineDouble is called at idle time, the CCmdUI object is associated with the toolbar button, and calling SetCheck selects this button. If OnUpdateLineDouble is called in response to the user's opening the Lines menu, the CCmdUI object is associated with the menu command, and calling SetCheck checks this command. Thus, SetCheck performs the appropriate action depending on the type of the user-interface object. The selected button and the checked menu item are illustrated below:

The OnUpdateLineSingle and OnUpdateLineTriple functions are also called at idle-time and the next time the user opens the Lines menu. As you can see in the code above, each of these functions passes 0 to SetCheck, thereby *deselecting* the button (if it's selected) or *unchecking* the menu command (if it's checked). Thus, the selection or check mark moves from the previously selected item to the currently selected one.

In general, whenever the user selects a particular line thickness using either the toolbar or the Lines menu, the OnLineSingle, OnLineDouble, or OnLineTriple function assigns the correct value to m_LineThickness. Also, the three functions— OnUpdateLineSingle, OnUpdateLineDouble, and OnUpdateLineTriple—ensure that the appropriate button is selected and that the other two line-thickness buttons are deselected, and they ensure that only the corresponding menu command is checked on the Lines menu.

The functions that handle the seven drawing-tool buttons (together with the corresponding commands on the Tools menu) work in an exactly analogous way to set the value of the m_CurrentTool data member, and to select the correct tool button and check the correct Tools menu command.

CCmdUI Member Functions

A CCmdUI object is passed to an UPDATE_COMMAND_UI message handler (that is, an OnUp-date... function) for *any* type of user-interface object. User-interface objects include menu commands, accelerator keystrokes, toolbar buttons, status bar indicators, and dialog bar controls. You can use the CCmdUI member functions Enable, SetCheck, SetRadio, and SetText to update any kind of user-interface object; the specific action of each of these functions (if any) depends on the type of the object. This sidebar briefly describes using these functions to update menu commands and toolbar buttons. For a complete description of the actions of these functions on other types of user-interface objects, see the following online help topic: *Visual C++ Documentation, Reference, Microsoft Foundation Class Library and Templates, Microsoft Foundation Class Library, Class Library Reference, CCmdUI*.

If you pass FALSE to Enable, it disables either a toolbar button or a menu command, by displaying the object in faint colors and preventing it from being clicked or chosen. If you pass TRUE to Enable, it restores the button or menu command to its normal state.

Continued on next page

If you pass 1 to SetCheck, it selects a toolbar button or checks a menu command; if you pass 0 to SetCheck, it deselects a toolbar button or removes the check mark from a menu command. Also, if you pass 2 to SetCheck, it sets a toolbar button to the *indeterminate* state (or simply checks a menu command). Below, you can see a normal, a disabled, a selected, and an indeterminate toolbar button:

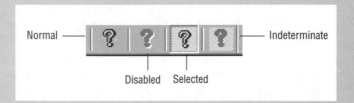

If you pass TRUE to SetRadio, it checks a menu command using a bullet rather than a check mark, or it selects a toolbar button (just like SetCheck). If you pass FALSE to SetRadio, it removes the bullet from a menu command or deselects a button.

Finally, you can call SetText to set the caption for a menu command; this function has no effect on a toolbar button.

TIP

If you've generated a docking toolbar for a *new* program using AppWizard, you must write message handlers for any of the nonimplemented toolbar commands.

If you wish, you can now build and run the MiniDraw program. Notice that the toolbar buttons and corresponding menu commands are no longer disabled and that you can select various toolbar buttons and check the corresponding menu commands.

NOTE

You don't need to write a message handler for the Toolbar command on the View menu, since the **CFrameWnd** MFC class provides a message handler—OnBarCheck—for this command. OnBarCheck calls the **CFrameWnd::Show-ControlBar** function to either hide or show the toolbar.

Adding a Status Bar to MiniDraw

To add a status bar to an MFC program, you need only to define an object of the CStatusBar class as a member of the main frame window class, define an array storing identifiers for the desired status-bar indicators, and then call two CStatusBar member functions from the OnCreate member function of the main frame window class (Create and SetIndicators). The MiniDraw program, with the new status bar that you'll add, is shown in Figure 14.10.

FIGURE 14.10:

The MiniDraw program, complete with its new status bar

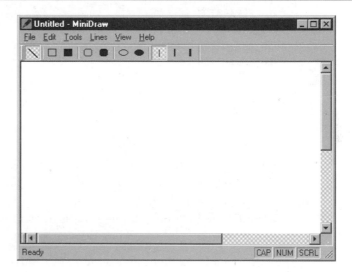

To add the status bar, begin by opening the MainFrm.h file and defining a CStatusBar object near the beginning of the CMainFrame class definition, as follows:

```
class CMainFrame : public CFrameWnd
{
protected:
    CSplitterWnd m_SplitterWnd;
    CStatusBar m_StatusBar;
    CToolBar m_ToolBar;

// remainder of CMainFrame definition ...

}
```

Next, open the MainFrm.cpp file and define the `IndicatorIDs` array as follows:

```
BEGIN_MESSAGE_MAP(CMainFrame, CFrameWnd)
    //{{AFX_MSG_MAP(CMainFrame)
    ON_WM_CREATE()
    //}}AFX_MSG_MAP
END_MESSAGE_MAP()

// IDs for status bar indicators:
static UINT IndicatorIDs [] =
    {
    ID_SEPARATOR,
    ID_INDICATOR_CAPS,
    ID_INDICATOR_NUM,
    ID_INDICATOR_SCRL,
    };


/////////////////////////////////////////////////////////////////
///////////
// CMainFrame construction/destruction
```

`IndicatorIDs` stores the identifier of each indicator that's to be displayed in the status bar. The identifier `ID_SEPARATOR` creates a blank space; because this identifier is placed first in the array, the resulting status bar will have a blank indicator at its left end. The first indicator in a status bar should be kept blank because the MFC automatically displays command prompts within this indicator.

The three remaining identifiers assigned to `IndicatorIDs` are defined by the MFC. The MFC provides message-handling functions for indicators that have these identifiers; these functions display the current status of the Caps Lock, Num Lock, and Scroll Lock keyboard keys. Note that the second, third, and fourth indicators are aligned at the right end of the status bar, while the first indicator occupies the entire remaining space at the left of the status bar.

Finally, add the code for creating the status bar to the `OnCreate` function within the MainFrm.cpp file:

```
int CMainFrame::OnCreate(LPCREATESTRUCT lpCreateStruct)
{

    // other statements...
```

```
    if (!m_StatusBar.Create (this) ||
        !m_StatusBar.SetIndicators (IndicatorIDs,
        sizeof (IndicatorIDs) / sizeof (UINT)))
        return -1;

    return 0;
}
```

The added code begins with a call to `CStatusBar::Create`, which creates the status bar. Passing the `IndicatorIDs` array to `CStatusBar::SetIndicators` then specifies the identifier of each indicator within the status bar.

The MFC provides all the message-handling functions necessary for displaying information within the status bar. You can therefore proceed to the final step: completing the View menu.

Displaying a Custom Status-Bar Indicator

The MiniDraw program status bar contains only standard indicators that are fully supported by the MFC code. If you want to add a custom indicator you must, of course, include its identifier in the array passed to `CStatusBar::SetIndicators`. You must also use the Developer Studio string editor to define a corresponding string resource that has the same identifier as the indicator. If you don't define such a string, the program will be terminated with an error message.

When the MFC displays your custom indicator, it makes it exactly wide enough to contain the corresponding resource string. However, it *doesn't* automatically display this string, because an indicator is initially disabled. To enable the indicator so that the resource string will appear, you must generate an UPDATE_COMMAND_UI message handler for the indicator (that is, an `OnUpdate...` function) and call the `CCmdUI::Enable` function from this handler (either omitting the parameter or passing TRUE). The resource string will then be visible.

If later in the program you want to change the string, you can pass the desired string to `CCmdUI::SetText`. Note, however, that the width of the indicator *won't* be adjusted to accommodate the new string. (If the new string you pass `SetText` is longer than the resource string, the new string will be truncated.)

Completing the View Menu and Building the Program

To complete the View menu, you'll add a command that allows the user to hide or show the status bar. To do this, open the IDR_MAINFRAME menu in the menu editor and add a command to the bottom of the View menu. Assign to this command the identifier ID_VIEW_STATUS_BAR, the caption &Status Bar, and the prompt Show or hide the status bar. As with the Toolbar command, you don't need to write a handler for the Status Bar command, because the MFC provides one for you. (The CFrameWnd::OnBarCheck function handles *both* the Toolbar command *and* the Status Bar command.)

Your programming job for the current version of MiniDraw is now complete, and you can build and run the program. When you run the program, notice that whenever you highlight a menu command or place the mouse cursor over a toolbar button, the MFC code displays a command prompt within the first indicator of the new status bar. Notice also that the MFC automatically displays the status of the Caps Lock, Num Lock, and Scroll Lock keys in the second, third, and fourth indicators.

Modifying Command Prompts

Recall that the text for a given command prompt is stored in a string resource that has the *same* identifier as the menu command and the corresponding toolbar button. Remember also that a string resource can store tool-tip text as well as a command prompt; in this case, the text consists of the command prompt, a newline character (\n), followed by the tool-tip text. You can modify a command prompt or tool tip for a menu command by opening the menu in the menu editor, double-clicking the command, and then editing the text in the Prompt: text box. Likewise, you can modify a command prompt or tool tip for a toolbar button by opening the toolbar in the toolbar editor, selecting the button (by clicking on it in the toolbar pane), double-clicking in the enlarged-button pane, and editing the text in the Prompt: text box.

Alternatively, you can edit the text in the string editor. For example, if the identifier of a toolbar button or menu command is ID_MYCOMMAND, you would open the String Table resource in the string editor, and then either edit the ID_MYCOMMAND string or add a string with this identifier if one doesn't already exist. (Using the string editor was described in Chapter 12, in the section "Adding the File Menu Commands.")

You can also modify the standard MFC *idle prompt*. When no menu command is highlighted, and the mouse cursor isn't on a toolbar button, the MFC displays the idle prompt in the first indicator of the status bar. By default, the idle prompt is Ready. If you want to specify a different idle prompt, edit the string with the identifier AFX_IDS_IDLEMESSAGE in the string editor. Change this string from Ready to whatever prompt you want.

The toolbar buttons and their corresponding menu commands still have no effect, other than simply changing the position of the selected button and checked menu command. The drawing tools and line widths will be implemented in the next version of MiniDraw, which you'll develop in Chapter 19.

TIP

If you've generated a status bar for a *new* program using AppWizard (by choosing the Initial Status Bar option), all code necessary for displaying the status bar described in this section will be included in your source files. If you want to change either the indicators that are included or their arrangement, you can edit the array containing the indicator identifiers, which is named `indicators` and is defined near the beginning of the MainFrm.cpp file. For information on adding a custom indicator, see the previous sidebar titled "Displaying a Custom Status-Bar Indicator."

The MiniDraw Source Code

The following listings, Listings 14.1 through 14.8, are the C++ source code listings for the version of the MiniDraw program you developed in this chapter; these files include the code for creating both the toolbar and the status bar. You'll find a complete copy of these files in the \MiniDrw5 companion-CD folder.

Listing 14.1

```
// MiniDraw.h : main header file for the MINIDRAW application
//

#if !defined(AFX_MINIDRAW_H__11E83924_999A_11D1_80FC_00C0F6A83B7F__INCLUDED_)
#define AFX_MINIDRAW_H__11E83924_999A_11D1_80FC_00C0F6A83B7F__INCLUDED_

#if _MSC_VER > 1000
#pragma once
#endif // _MSC_VER > 1000

#ifndef __AFXWIN_H__
    #error include 'stdafx.h' before including this file for PCH
#endif

#include "resource.h"        // main symbols
```

```
/////////////////////////////////////////////////////////////////////////
// CMiniDrawApp:
// See MiniDraw.cpp for the implementation of this class
//

class CMiniDrawApp : public CWinApp
{
public:
   int m_CurrentThickness;
   UINT m_CurrentTool;

public:
   CMiniDrawApp();

// Overrides
   // ClassWizard generated virtual function overrides
   //{{AFX_VIRTUAL(CMiniDrawApp)
   public:
   virtual BOOL InitInstance();
   //}}AFX_VIRTUAL

// Implementation

   //{{AFX_MSG(CMiniDrawApp)
   afx_msg void OnAppAbout();
   afx_msg void OnLineDouble();
   afx_msg void OnUpdateLineDouble(CCmdUI* pCmdUI);
   afx_msg void OnLineSingle();
   afx_msg void OnUpdateLineSingle(CCmdUI* pCmdUI);
   afx_msg void OnLineTriple();
   afx_msg void OnUpdateLineTriple(CCmdUI* pCmdUI);
   afx_msg void OnToolsCircle();
   afx_msg void OnUpdateToolsCircle(CCmdUI* pCmdUI);
   afx_msg void OnToolsCirclefill();
   afx_msg void OnUpdateToolsCirclefill(CCmdUI* pCmdUI);
   afx_msg void OnToolsLine();
   afx_msg void OnUpdateToolsLine(CCmdUI* pCmdUI);
   afx_msg void OnToolsRectangle();
   afx_msg void OnUpdateToolsRectangle(CCmdUI* pCmdUI);
   afx_msg void OnToolsRectfill();
   afx_msg void OnUpdateToolsRectfill(CCmdUI* pCmdUI);
   afx_msg void OnToolsRectround();
```

```
    afx_msg void OnUpdateToolsRectround(CCmdUI* pCmdUI);
    afx_msg void OnToolsRectroundfill();
    afx_msg void OnUpdateToolsRectroundfill(CCmdUI* pCmdUI);
    //}}AFX_MSG
    DECLARE_MESSAGE_MAP()
};


//////////////////////////////////////////////////////////////////////////

//{{AFX_INSERT_LOCATION}}
// Microsoft Visual C++ will insert additional declarations immediately before
// the previous line.

#endif
// !defined(AFX_MINIDRAW_H__11E83924_999A_11D1_80FC_00C0F6A83B7F__INCLUDED_)
```

Listing 14.2

```
// MiniDraw.cpp : Defines the class behaviors for the application.
//

#include "stdafx.h"
#include "MiniDraw.h"

#include "MainFrm.h"
#include "MiniDrawDoc.h"
#include "MiniDrawView.h"

#ifdef _DEBUG
#define new DEBUG_NEW
#undef THIS_FILE
static char THIS_FILE[] = __FILE__;
#endif

//////////////////////////////////////////////////////////////////////////
// CMiniDrawApp

BEGIN_MESSAGE_MAP(CMiniDrawApp, CWinApp)
    //{{AFX_MSG_MAP(CMiniDrawApp)
    ON_COMMAND(ID_APP_ABOUT, OnAppAbout)
    ON_COMMAND(ID_LINE_DOUBLE, OnLineDouble)
```

```
    ON_UPDATE_COMMAND_UI(ID_LINE_DOUBLE, OnUpdateLineDouble)
    ON_COMMAND(ID_LINE_SINGLE, OnLineSingle)
    ON_UPDATE_COMMAND_UI(ID_LINE_SINGLE, OnUpdateLineSingle)
    ON_COMMAND(ID_LINE_TRIPLE, OnLineTriple)
    ON_UPDATE_COMMAND_UI(ID_LINE_TRIPLE, OnUpdateLineTriple)
    ON_COMMAND(ID_TOOLS_CIRCLE, OnToolsCircle)
    ON_UPDATE_COMMAND_UI(ID_TOOLS_CIRCLE, OnUpdateToolsCircle)
    ON_COMMAND(ID_TOOLS_CIRCLEFILL, OnToolsCirclefill)
    ON_UPDATE_COMMAND_UI(ID_TOOLS_CIRCLEFILL, OnUpdateToolsCirclefill)
    ON_COMMAND(ID_TOOLS_LINE, OnToolsLine)
    ON_UPDATE_COMMAND_UI(ID_TOOLS_LINE, OnUpdateToolsLine)
    ON_COMMAND(ID_TOOLS_RECTANGLE, OnToolsRectangle)
    ON_UPDATE_COMMAND_UI(ID_TOOLS_RECTANGLE, OnUpdateToolsRectangle)
    ON_COMMAND(ID_TOOLS_RECTFILL, OnToolsRectfill)
    ON_UPDATE_COMMAND_UI(ID_TOOLS_RECTFILL, OnUpdateToolsRectfill)
    ON_COMMAND(ID_TOOLS_RECTROUND, OnToolsRectround)
    ON_UPDATE_COMMAND_UI(ID_TOOLS_RECTROUND, OnUpdateToolsRectround)
    ON_COMMAND(ID_TOOLS_RECTROUNDFILL, OnToolsRectroundfill)
    ON_UPDATE_COMMAND_UI(ID_TOOLS_RECTROUNDFILL, OnUpdateToolsRectroundfill)
    //}}AFX_MSG_MAP
    // Standard file based document commands
    ON_COMMAND(ID_FILE_NEW, CWinApp::OnFileNew)
    ON_COMMAND(ID_FILE_OPEN, CWinApp::OnFileOpen)
END_MESSAGE_MAP()


/////////////////////////////////////////////////////////////////////////
// CMiniDrawApp construction

CMiniDrawApp::CMiniDrawApp()
{
    // TODO: add construction code here,
    // Place all significant initialization in InitInstance

    m_CurrentThickness = 1;
    m_CurrentTool = ID_TOOLS_LINE;
}


/////////////////////////////////////////////////////////////////////////
// The one and only CMiniDrawApp object

CMiniDrawApp theApp;
```

```
/////////////////////////////////////////////////////////////////////////
// CMiniDrawApp initialization

BOOL CMiniDrawApp::InitInstance()
{
    // Standard initialization
    // If you are not using these features and wish to reduce the size
    //  of your final executable, you should remove from the following
    //  the specific initialization routines you do not need.

#ifdef _AFXDLL
    Enable3dControls();         // Call this when using MFC in a shared DLL
#else
    Enable3dControlsStatic();   // Call this when linking to MFC statically
#endif

    // Change the registry key under which our settings are stored.
    // You should modify this string to be something appropriate
    // such as the name of your company or organization.
    SetRegistryKey(_T("Local AppWizard-Generated Applications"));

    LoadStdProfileSettings();   // Load standard INI file options (including MRU)

    // Register the application's document templates.  Document templates
    //  serve as the connection between documents, frame windows and views.

    CSingleDocTemplate* pDocTemplate;
    pDocTemplate = new CSingleDocTemplate(
        IDR_MAINFRAME,
        RUNTIME_CLASS(CMiniDrawDoc),
        RUNTIME_CLASS(CMainFrame),       // main SDI frame window
        RUNTIME_CLASS(CMiniDrawView));
    AddDocTemplate(pDocTemplate);

    EnableShellOpen ();
    RegisterShellFileTypes ();

    // Parse command line for standard shell commands, DDE, file open
    CCommandLineInfo cmdInfo;
    ParseCommandLine(cmdInfo);
```

```
    // Dispatch commands specified on the command line
    if (!ProcessShellCommand(cmdInfo))
        return FALSE;

    // The one and only window has been initialized, so show and update it.
    m_pMainWnd->ShowWindow(SW_SHOW);
    m_pMainWnd->UpdateWindow();

    m_pMainWnd->DragAcceptFiles ();

    return TRUE;
}


/////////////////////////////////////////////////////////////////////////////
// CAboutDlg dialog used for App About

class CAboutDlg : public CDialog
{
public:
    CAboutDlg();

// Dialog Data
    //{{AFX_DATA(CAboutDlg)
    enum { IDD = IDD_ABOUTBOX };
    //}}AFX_DATA

    // ClassWizard generated virtual function overrides
    //{{AFX_VIRTUAL(CAboutDlg)
    protected:
    virtual void DoDataExchange(CDataExchange* pDX);    // DDX/DDV support
    //}}AFX_VIRTUAL

// Implementation
protected:
    //{{AFX_MSG(CAboutDlg)
        // No message handlers
    //}}AFX_MSG
    DECLARE_MESSAGE_MAP()
};
```

```
CAboutDlg::CAboutDlg() : CDialog(CAboutDlg::IDD)
{
   //{{AFX_DATA_INIT(CAboutDlg)
   //}}AFX_DATA_INIT
}

void CAboutDlg::DoDataExchange(CDataExchange* pDX)
{
   CDialog::DoDataExchange(pDX);
   //{{AFX_DATA_MAP(CAboutDlg)
   //}}AFX_DATA_MAP
}

BEGIN_MESSAGE_MAP(CAboutDlg, CDialog)
   //{{AFX_MSG_MAP(CAboutDlg)
      // No message handlers
   //}}AFX_MSG_MAP
END_MESSAGE_MAP()

// App command to run the dialog
void CMiniDrawApp::OnAppAbout()
{
   CAboutDlg aboutDlg;
   aboutDlg.DoModal();
}


/////////////////////////////////////////////////////////////////////////
// CMiniDrawApp commands

void CMiniDrawApp::OnLineDouble()
{
   // TODO: Add your command handler code here
   m_CurrentThickness = 2;
}

void CMiniDrawApp::OnUpdateLineDouble(CCmdUI* pCmdUI)
{
   // TODO: Add your command update UI handler code here
   pCmdUI->SetCheck (m_CurrentThickness == 2 ? 1 : 0);
}
```

```
void CMiniDrawApp::OnLineSingle()
{
   // TODO: Add your command handler code here
   m_CurrentThickness = 1;
}

void CMiniDrawApp::OnUpdateLineSingle(CCmdUI* pCmdUI)
{
   // TODO: Add your command update UI handler code here
   pCmdUI->SetCheck (m_CurrentThickness == 1 ? 1 : 0);
}

void CMiniDrawApp::OnLineTriple()
{
   // TODO: Add your command handler code here
   m_CurrentThickness = 3;
}

void CMiniDrawApp::OnUpdateLineTriple(CCmdUI* pCmdUI)
{
   // TODO: Add your command update UI handler code here
   pCmdUI->SetCheck (m_CurrentThickness == 3 ? 1 : 0);
}

void CMiniDrawApp::OnToolsCircle()
{
   // TODO: Add your command handler code here
   m_CurrentTool = ID_TOOLS_CIRCLE;
}

void CMiniDrawApp::OnUpdateToolsCircle(CCmdUI* pCmdUI)
{
   // TODO: Add your command update UI handler code here
   pCmdUI->SetCheck (m_CurrentTool == ID_TOOLS_CIRCLE ? 1 : 0);
}

void CMiniDrawApp::OnToolsCirclefill()
{
   // TODO: Add your command handler code here
   m_CurrentTool = ID_TOOLS_CIRCLEFILL;
}
```

```
void CMiniDrawApp::OnUpdateToolsCirclefill(CCmdUI* pCmdUI)
{
    // TODO: Add your command update UI handler code here
    pCmdUI->SetCheck
        (m_CurrentTool == ID_TOOLS_CIRCLEFILL ? 1 : 0);
}

void CMiniDrawApp::OnToolsLine()
{
    // TODO: Add your command handler code here
    m_CurrentTool = ID_TOOLS_LINE;
}

void CMiniDrawApp::OnUpdateToolsLine(CCmdUI* pCmdUI)
{
    // TODO: Add your command update UI handler code here
    pCmdUI->SetCheck (m_CurrentTool == ID_TOOLS_LINE ? 1 : 0);
}

void CMiniDrawApp::OnToolsRectangle()
{
    // TODO: Add your command handler code here
    m_CurrentTool = ID_TOOLS_RECTANGLE;
}

void CMiniDrawApp::OnUpdateToolsRectangle(CCmdUI* pCmdUI)
{
    // TODO: Add your command update UI handler code here
    pCmdUI->SetCheck
        (m_CurrentTool == ID_TOOLS_RECTANGLE ? 1 : 0);
}

void CMiniDrawApp::OnToolsRectfill()
{
    // TODO: Add your command handler code here
    m_CurrentTool = ID_TOOLS_RECTFILL;
}

void CMiniDrawApp::OnUpdateToolsRectfill(CCmdUI* pCmdUI)
{
    // TODO: Add your command update UI handler code here
    pCmdUI->SetCheck (m_CurrentTool == ID_TOOLS_RECTFILL ? 1 : 0);
}
```

```
void CMiniDrawApp::OnToolsRectround()
{
    // TODO: Add your command handler code here
    m_CurrentTool = ID_TOOLS_RECTROUND;
}

void CMiniDrawApp::OnUpdateToolsRectround(CCmdUI* pCmdUI)
{
    // TODO: Add your command update UI handler code here
    pCmdUI->SetCheck
       (m_CurrentTool == ID_TOOLS_RECTROUND ? 1 : 0);
}

void CMiniDrawApp::OnToolsRectroundfill()
{
    // TODO: Add your command handler code here
    m_CurrentTool = ID_TOOLS_RECTROUNDFILL;
}

void CMiniDrawApp::OnUpdateToolsRectroundfill(CCmdUI* pCmdUI)
{
    // TODO: Add your command update UI handler code here
    pCmdUI->SetCheck
       (m_CurrentTool == ID_TOOLS_RECTROUNDFILL ? 1 : 0);
}
```

Listing 14.3

```
// MiniDrawDoc.h : interface of the CMiniDrawDoc class
//
/////////////////////////////////////////////////////////////////////

#if !defined(AFX_MINIDRAWDOC_H__11E8392A_999A_11D1_80FC_00C0F6A83B7F__INCLUDED_)
#define AFX_MINIDRAWDOC_H__11E8392A_999A_11D1_80FC_00C0F6A83B7F__INCLUDED_

#if _MSC_VER > 1000
#pragma once
#endif // _MSC_VER > 1000

class CLine : public CObject
{
protected:
    int m_X1, m_Y1, m_X2, m_Y2;
```

```
    CLine ()
       {}
    DECLARE_SERIAL (CLine)

public:
    CLine (int X1, int Y1, int X2, int Y2)
       {
       m_X1 = X1;
       m_Y1 = Y1;
       m_X2 = X2;
       m_Y2 = Y2;
       }
    void Draw (CDC *PDC);
    CRect GetDimRect ();
    virtual void Serialize (CArchive& ar);
};

class CMiniDrawDoc : public CDocument
{
protected:
    CTypedPtrArray<CObArray, CLine*> m_LineArray;

public:
    CLine *AddLine (int X1, int Y1, int X2, int Y2);
    CLine *GetLine (int Index);
    int GetNumLines ();

protected: // create from serialization only
    CMiniDrawDoc();
    DECLARE_DYNCREATE(CMiniDrawDoc)

// Attributes
public:

// Operations
public:

// Overrides
    // ClassWizard generated virtual function overrides
    //{{AFX_VIRTUAL(CMiniDrawDoc)
    public:
    virtual BOOL OnNewDocument();
```

```
   virtual void Serialize(CArchive& ar);
   virtual void DeleteContents();
   //}}AFX_VIRTUAL

// Implementation
public:
   virtual ~CMiniDrawDoc();
#ifdef _DEBUG
   virtual void AssertValid() const;
   virtual void Dump(CDumpContext& dc) const;
#endif

protected:

// Generated message map functions
protected:
   //{{AFX_MSG(CMiniDrawDoc)
   afx_msg void OnEditClearAll();
   afx_msg void OnUpdateEditClearAll(CCmdUI* pCmdUI);
   afx_msg void OnEditUndo();
   afx_msg void OnUpdateEditUndo(CCmdUI* pCmdUI);
   //}}AFX_MSG
   DECLARE_MESSAGE_MAP()
};

/////////////////////////////////////////////////////////////////////////

//{{AFX_INSERT_LOCATION}}
// Microsoft Visual C++ will insert additional declarations immediately before
// the previous line.

#endif
// !defined(AFX_MINIDRAWDOC_H__11E8392A_999A_11D1_80FC_00C0F6A83B7F__INCLUDED_)
```

Listing 14.4

```
// MiniDrawDoc.cpp : implementation of the CMiniDrawDoc class
//

#include "stdafx.h"
#include "MiniDraw.h"

#include "MiniDrawDoc.h"
```

```
#ifdef _DEBUG
#define new DEBUG_NEW
#undef THIS_FILE
static char THIS_FILE[] = __FILE__;
#endif

/////////////////////////////////////////////////////////////////////////////
// CMiniDrawDoc

IMPLEMENT_DYNCREATE(CMiniDrawDoc, CDocument)

BEGIN_MESSAGE_MAP(CMiniDrawDoc, CDocument)
    //{{AFX_MSG_MAP(CMiniDrawDoc)
    ON_COMMAND(ID_EDIT_CLEAR_ALL, OnEditClearAll)
    ON_UPDATE_COMMAND_UI(ID_EDIT_CLEAR_ALL, OnUpdateEditClearAll)
    ON_COMMAND(ID_EDIT_UNDO, OnEditUndo)
    ON_UPDATE_COMMAND_UI(ID_EDIT_UNDO, OnUpdateEditUndo)
    //}}AFX_MSG_MAP
END_MESSAGE_MAP()

/////////////////////////////////////////////////////////////////////////////
// CMiniDrawDoc construction/destruction

CMiniDrawDoc::CMiniDrawDoc()
{
    // TODO: add one-time construction code here

}

CMiniDrawDoc::~CMiniDrawDoc()
{
}

BOOL CMiniDrawDoc::OnNewDocument()
{
    if (!CDocument::OnNewDocument())
        return FALSE;

    // TODO: add reinitialization code here
    // (SDI documents will reuse this document)

    return TRUE;
}
```

```
/////////////////////////////////////////////////////////////////////
// CMiniDrawDoc serialization

void CMiniDrawDoc::Serialize(CArchive& ar)
{
   if (ar.IsStoring())
   {
      // TODO: add storing code here
      m_LineArray.Serialize (ar);
   }
   else
   {
      // TODO: add loading code here
      m_LineArray.Serialize (ar);
   }
}

/////////////////////////////////////////////////////////////////////
// CMiniDrawDoc diagnostics

#ifdef _DEBUG
void CMiniDrawDoc::AssertValid() const
{
   CDocument::AssertValid();
}

void CMiniDrawDoc::Dump(CDumpContext& dc) const
{
   CDocument::Dump(dc);
}
#endif //_DEBUG

/////////////////////////////////////////////////////////////////////
// CMiniDrawDoc commands

IMPLEMENT_SERIAL (CLine, CObject, 1)

void CLine::Draw (CDC *PDC)
   {
   PDC->MoveTo (m_X1, m_Y1);
   PDC->LineTo (m_X2, m_Y2);
   }
```

```
void CLine::Serialize (CArchive& ar)
   {
   if (ar.IsStoring())
      ar << m_X1 << m_Y1 << m_X2 << m_Y2;
   else
      ar >> m_X1 >> m_Y1 >> m_X2 >> m_Y2;
   }

CLine *CMiniDrawDoc::AddLine (int X1, int Y1, int X2, int Y2)
   {
   CLine *PLine = new CLine (X1, Y1, X2, Y2);
   m_LineArray.Add (PLine);
   SetModifiedFlag ();
   return PLine;
   }

CLine *CMiniDrawDoc::GetLine (int Index)
   {
   if (Index < 0 || Index > m_LineArray.GetUpperBound ())
      return 0;
   return m_LineArray.GetAt (Index);
   }

int CMiniDrawDoc::GetNumLines ()
   {
   return m_LineArray.GetSize ();
   }

void CMiniDrawDoc::DeleteContents()
{
   // TODO: Add your specialized code here and/or call the base class

   int Index = m_LineArray.GetSize ();
   while (Index--)
      delete m_LineArray.GetAt (Index);
   m_LineArray.RemoveAll ();

   CDocument::DeleteContents();
}

void CMiniDrawDoc::OnEditClearAll()
{
   // TODO: Add your command handler code here
```

```
   DeleteContents ();
   UpdateAllViews (0);
   SetModifiedFlag ();
}

void CMiniDrawDoc::OnUpdateEditClearAll(CCmdUI* pCmdUI)
{
   // TODO: Add your command update UI handler code here

   pCmdUI->Enable (m_LineArray.GetSize ());
}

void CMiniDrawDoc::OnEditUndo()
{
   // TODO: Add your command handler code here

   int Index = m_LineArray.GetUpperBound ();
   if (Index > -1)
      {
      delete m_LineArray.GetAt (Index);
      m_LineArray.RemoveAt (Index);
      }
   UpdateAllViews (0);
   SetModifiedFlag ();
}

void CMiniDrawDoc::OnUpdateEditUndo(CCmdUI* pCmdUI)
{
   // TODO: Add your command update UI handler code here

   pCmdUI->Enable (m_LineArray.GetSize ());
}

CRect CLine::GetDimRect ()
   {
   return CRect
     (min (m_X1, m_X2),
      min (m_Y1, m_Y2),
      max (m_X1, m_X2) + 1,
      max (m_Y1, m_Y2) + 1);
   }
```

Listing 14.5

```cpp
// MainFrm.h : interface of the CMainFrame class
//
/////////////////////////////////////////////////////////////////////

#if !defined(AFX_MAINFRM_H__11E83928_999A_11D1_80FC_00C0F6A83B7F__INCLUDED_)
#define AFX_MAINFRM_H__11E83928_999A_11D1_80FC_00C0F6A83B7F__INCLUDED_

#if _MSC_VER > 1000
#pragma once
#endif // _MSC_VER > 1000

class CMainFrame : public CFrameWnd
{
protected:
    CSplitterWnd m_SplitterWnd;
    CStatusBar m_StatusBar;
    CToolBar m_ToolBar;

protected: // create from serialization only
    CMainFrame();
    DECLARE_DYNCREATE(CMainFrame)

// Attributes
public:

// Operations
public:

// Overrides
    // ClassWizard generated virtual function overrides
    //{{AFX_VIRTUAL(CMainFrame)
    public:
    virtual BOOL PreCreateWindow(CREATESTRUCT& cs);
    protected:
    virtual BOOL OnCreateClient(LPCREATESTRUCT lpcs, CCreateContext* pContext);
    //}}AFX_VIRTUAL
```

```
// Implementation
public:
   virtual ~CMainFrame();
#ifdef _DEBUG
   virtual void AssertValid() const;
   virtual void Dump(CDumpContext& dc) const;
#endif

// Generated message map functions
protected:
   //{{AFX_MSG(CMainFrame)
   afx_msg int OnCreate(LPCREATESTRUCT lpCreateStruct);
   //}}AFX_MSG
   DECLARE_MESSAGE_MAP()
};


/////////////////////////////////////////////////////////////////////////

//{{AFX_INSERT_LOCATION}}
// Microsoft Visual C++ will insert additional declarations immediately before
// the previous line.

#endif
// !defined(AFX_MAINFRM_H__11E83928_999A_11D1_80FC_00C0F6A83B7F__INCLUDED_)
```

Listing 14.6

```
// MainFrm.cpp : implementation of the CMainFrame class
//

#include "stdafx.h"
#include "MiniDraw.h"

#include "MainFrm.h"

#ifdef _DEBUG
#define new DEBUG_NEW
#undef THIS_FILE
static char THIS_FILE[] = __FILE__;
#endif
```

```
/////////////////////////////////////////////////////////////////////////
// CMainFrame

IMPLEMENT_DYNCREATE(CMainFrame, CFrameWnd)

BEGIN_MESSAGE_MAP(CMainFrame, CFrameWnd)
   //{{AFX_MSG_MAP(CMainFrame)
   ON_WM_CREATE()
   //}}AFX_MSG_MAP
END_MESSAGE_MAP()

// IDs for status bar indicators:
static UINT IndicatorIDs [] =
   {
   ID_SEPARATOR,
   ID_INDICATOR_CAPS,
   ID_INDICATOR_NUM,
   ID_INDICATOR_SCRL,
   };

/////////////////////////////////////////////////////////////////////////
// CMainFrame construction/destruction

CMainFrame::CMainFrame()
{
   // TODO: add member initialization code here

}

CMainFrame::~CMainFrame()
{
}

BOOL CMainFrame::PreCreateWindow(CREATESTRUCT& cs)
{
   if( !CFrameWnd::PreCreateWindow(cs) )
      return FALSE;
   // TODO: Modify the Window class or styles here by modifying
   //  the CREATESTRUCT cs

   return TRUE;
}
```

```
/////////////////////////////////////////////////////////////////////
// CMainFrame diagnostics

#ifdef _DEBUG
void CMainFrame::AssertValid() const
{
    CFrameWnd::AssertValid();
}

void CMainFrame::Dump(CDumpContext& dc) const
{
    CFrameWnd::Dump(dc);
}


#endif //_DEBUG

/////////////////////////////////////////////////////////////////////
// CMainFrame message handlers


BOOL CMainFrame::OnCreateClient(LPCREATESTRUCT lpcs, CCreateContext* pContext)
{
    // TODO: Add your specialized code here and/or call the base class

    return m_SplitterWnd.Create
        (this,              // parent of splitter window
        1,                  // maximum rows
        2,                  // maximum columns
        CSize (15, 15),     // minimum view window size
        pContext);          // pass on context information
}

int CMainFrame::OnCreate(LPCREATESTRUCT lpCreateStruct)
{
    if (CFrameWnd::OnCreate(lpCreateStruct) == -1)
        return -1;

    // TODO: Add your specialized creation code here

    if (!m_ToolBar.CreateEx
        (this,
        TBSTYLE_FLAT,
```

```
        WS_CHILD | WS_VISIBLE | CBRS_TOP | CBRS_GRIPPER
        | CBRS_TOOLTIPS | CBRS_FLYBY | CBRS_SIZE_DYNAMIC))
        return -1;

    if (!m_ToolBar.LoadToolBar(IDR_MAINFRAME))
        return -1;

    m_ToolBar.EnableDocking (CBRS_ALIGN_ANY);
    EnableDocking (CBRS_ALIGN_ANY);
    DockControlBar (&m_ToolBar);

    if (!m_StatusBar.Create (this) ||
        !m_StatusBar.SetIndicators (IndicatorIDs,
        sizeof (IndicatorIDs) / sizeof (UINT)))
        return -1;

    return 0;
}
```

Listing 14.7

```
// MiniDrawView.h : interface of the CMiniDrawView class
//
/////////////////////////////////////////////////////////////////////////

#if !defined(AFX_MINIDRAWVIEW_H__11E8392C_999A_11D1_80FC_00C0F6A83B7F__INCLUDED_)
#define AFX_MINIDRAWVIEW_H__11E8392C_999A_11D1_80FC_00C0F6A83B7F__INCLUDED_

#if _MSC_VER > 1000
#pragma once
#endif // _MSC_VER > 1000

class CMiniDrawView : public CScrollView
{
protected:
    CString m_ClassName;
    int m_Dragging;
    HCURSOR m_HArrow;
    HCURSOR m_HCross;
    CPoint m_PointOld;
    CPoint m_PointOrigin;
```

```
protected: // create from serialization only
   CMiniDrawView();
   DECLARE_DYNCREATE(CMiniDrawView)

// Attributes
public:
   CMiniDrawDoc* GetDocument();

// Operations
public:

// Overrides
   // ClassWizard generated virtual function overrides
   //{{AFX_VIRTUAL(CMiniDrawView)
   public:
   virtual void OnDraw(CDC* pDC);  // overridden to draw this view
   virtual BOOL PreCreateWindow(CREATESTRUCT& cs);
   virtual void OnInitialUpdate();
   protected:
   virtual void OnUpdate(CView* pSender, LPARAM lHint, CObject* pHint);
   //}}AFX_VIRTUAL

// Implementation
public:
   virtual ~CMiniDrawView();
#ifdef _DEBUG
   virtual void AssertValid() const;
   virtual void Dump(CDumpContext& dc) const;
#endif

protected:

// Generated message map functions
protected:
   //{{AFX_MSG(CMiniDrawView)
   afx_msg void OnLButtonDown(UINT nFlags, CPoint point);
   afx_msg void OnMouseMove(UINT nFlags, CPoint point);
   afx_msg void OnLButtonUp(UINT nFlags, CPoint point);
   //}}AFX_MSG
   DECLARE_MESSAGE_MAP()
};
```

```
#ifndef _DEBUG  // debug version in MiniDrawView.cpp
inline CMiniDrawDoc* CMiniDrawView::GetDocument()
   { return (CMiniDrawDoc*)m_pDocument; }
#endif


/////////////////////////////////////////////////////////////////////////

//{{AFX_INSERT_LOCATION}}
// Microsoft Visual C++ will insert additional declarations immediately before
// the previous line.

#endif
// !defined(AFX_MINIDRAWVIEW_H__11E8392C_999A_11D1_80FC_00C0F6A83B7F__INCLUDED_)
```

Listing 14.8

```
// MiniDrawView.cpp : implementation of the CMiniDrawView class
//

#include "stdafx.h"
#include "MiniDraw.h"

#include "MiniDrawDoc.h"
#include "MiniDrawView.h"

#ifdef _DEBUG
#define new DEBUG_NEW
#undef THIS_FILE
static char THIS_FILE[] = __FILE__;
#endif



/////////////////////////////////////////////////////////////////////////
// CMiniDrawView

IMPLEMENT_DYNCREATE(CMiniDrawView, CScrollView)

BEGIN_MESSAGE_MAP(CMiniDrawView, CScrollView)
   //{{AFX_MSG_MAP(CMiniDrawView)
   ON_WM_LBUTTONDOWN()
   ON_WM_MOUSEMOVE()
   ON_WM_LBUTTONUP()
```

```
   //}}AFX_MSG_MAP
END_MESSAGE_MAP()

/////////////////////////////////////////////////////////////////////
// CMiniDrawView construction/destruction

CMiniDrawView::CMiniDrawView()
{
   // TODO: add construction code here

   m_Dragging = 0;
   m_HArrow = AfxGetApp ()->LoadStandardCursor (IDC_ARROW);
   m_HCross = AfxGetApp ()->LoadStandardCursor (IDC_CROSS);
}

CMiniDrawView::~CMiniDrawView()
{
}

BOOL CMiniDrawView::PreCreateWindow(CREATESTRUCT& cs)
{
   // TODO: Modify the Window class or styles here by modifying
   //  the CREATESTRUCT cs

   m_ClassName = AfxRegisterWndClass
      (CS_HREDRAW | CS_VREDRAW,              // class styles
       0,                                     // no cursor
       (HBRUSH)::GetStockObject (WHITE_BRUSH), // assign white
                                              // background brush
       0);                                    // no icon
   cs.lpszClass = m_ClassName;

   return CScrollView::PreCreateWindow(cs);
}

/////////////////////////////////////////////////////////////////////
// CMiniDrawView drawing

void CMiniDrawView::OnDraw(CDC* pDC)
{
   CMiniDrawDoc* pDoc = GetDocument();
   ASSERT_VALID(pDoc);
```

```
    // TODO: add draw code for native data here

    CSize ScrollSize = GetTotalSize ();
    pDC->MoveTo (ScrollSize.cx, 0);
    pDC->LineTo (ScrollSize.cx, ScrollSize.cy);
    pDC->LineTo (0, ScrollSize.cy);

    CRect ClipRect;
    CRect DimRect;
    CRect IntRect;
    CLine *PLine;
    pDC->GetClipBox (&ClipRect);

    int Index = pDoc->GetNumLines ();
    while (Index--)
        {
        PLine = pDoc->GetLine (Index);
        DimRect = PLine->GetDimRect ();
        if (IntRect.IntersectRect (DimRect, ClipRect))
            PLine->Draw (pDC);
        }
}

/////////////////////////////////////////////////////////////////////////////
// CMiniDrawView diagnostics

#ifdef _DEBUG
void CMiniDrawView::AssertValid() const
{
    CScrollView::AssertValid();
}

void CMiniDrawView::Dump(CDumpContext& dc) const
{
    CScrollView::Dump(dc);
}

CMiniDrawDoc* CMiniDrawView::GetDocument() // non-debug version is inline
{
    ASSERT(m_pDocument->IsKindOf(RUNTIME_CLASS(CMiniDrawDoc)));
    return (CMiniDrawDoc*)m_pDocument;
}
#endif //_DEBUG
```

```
/////////////////////////////////////////////////////////////////////
// CMiniDrawView message handlers

void CMiniDrawView::OnLButtonDown(UINT nFlags, CPoint point)
{
   // TODO: Add your message handler code here and/or call default

   CClientDC ClientDC (this);
   OnPrepareDC (&ClientDC);
   ClientDC.DPtoLP (&point);

   // test whether cursor is within drawing area of view window:
   CSize ScrollSize = GetTotalSize ();
   CRect ScrollRect (0, 0, ScrollSize.cx, ScrollSize.cy);
   if (!ScrollRect.PtInRect (point))
      return;

   // save cursor position, capture mouse, and set dragging flag:
   m_PointOrigin = point;
   m_PointOld = point;
   SetCapture ();
   m_Dragging = 1;

   // clip mouse cursor:
   ClientDC.LPtoDP (&ScrollRect);
   CRect ViewRect;
   GetClientRect (&ViewRect);
   CRect IntRect;
   IntRect.IntersectRect (&ScrollRect, &ViewRect);
   ClientToScreen (&IntRect);
   ::ClipCursor (&IntRect);

   CScrollView::OnLButtonDown(nFlags, point);
}

void CMiniDrawView::OnMouseMove(UINT nFlags, CPoint point)
{
   // TODO: Add your message handler code here and/or call default
```

```
   CClientDC ClientDC (this);
   OnPrepareDC (&ClientDC);
   ClientDC.DPtoLP (&point);

   CSize ScrollSize = GetTotalSize ();
   CRect ScrollRect (0, 0, ScrollSize.cx, ScrollSize.cy);
   if (ScrollRect.PtInRect (point))
      ::SetCursor (m_HCross);
   else
      ::SetCursor (m_HArrow);

   if (m_Dragging)
      {
      ClientDC.SetROP2 (R2_NOT);
      ClientDC.MoveTo (m_PointOrigin);
      ClientDC.LineTo (m_PointOld);
      ClientDC.MoveTo (m_PointOrigin);
      ClientDC.LineTo (point);
      m_PointOld = point;
      }

   CScrollView::OnMouseMove(nFlags, point);
}

void CMiniDrawView::OnLButtonUp(UINT nFlags, CPoint point)
{
   // TODO: Add your message handler code here and/or call default

   if (m_Dragging)
      {
      m_Dragging = 0;
      ::ReleaseCapture ();
      ::ClipCursor (NULL);

      CClientDC ClientDC (this);
      OnPrepareDC (&ClientDC);
      ClientDC.DPtoLP (&point);
```

```
      ClientDC.SetROP2 (R2_NOT);
      ClientDC.MoveTo (m_PointOrigin);
      ClientDC.LineTo (m_PointOld);
      ClientDC.SetROP2 (R2_COPYPEN);
      ClientDC.MoveTo (m_PointOrigin);
      ClientDC.LineTo (point);

      CMiniDrawDoc* PDoc = GetDocument();
      CLine *PCLine;
      PCLine = PDoc->AddLine (m_PointOrigin.x, m_PointOrigin.y,
         point.x, point.y);
      PDoc->UpdateAllViews (this, 0, PCLine);
      }

   CScrollView::OnLButtonUp(nFlags, point);
}

void CMiniDrawView::OnInitialUpdate()
{
   CScrollView::OnInitialUpdate();

   // TODO: Add your specialized code here and/or call the base class

   SIZE Size = {640, 480};
   SetScrollSizes (MM_TEXT, Size);
}

void CMiniDrawView::OnUpdate(CView* pSender, LPARAM lHint, CObject* pHint)
{
   // TODO: Add your specialized code here and/or call the base class

   if (pHint != 0)
      {
      CRect InvalidRect = ((CLine *)pHint)->GetDimRect ();
      CClientDC ClientDC (this);
      OnPrepareDC (&ClientDC);
      ClientDC.LPtoDP (&InvalidRect);
      InvalidateRect (&InvalidRect);
      }
   else
      CScrollView::OnUpdate (pSender, lHint, pHint);
}
```

Dialog Bars and Rebar Controls

The MFC supports two additional user-interface elements: *dialog bars* and *rebar controls*.

A dialog bar is a hybrid between a toolbar and a dialog box. A dialog bar is managed by the MFC CDialogBar class (which is derived from CControlBar). Unlike a toolbar managed by the CToolBar class, a dialog bar is based on a dialog box template. Accordingly, you can design the bar within the dialog editor of the Developer Studio, and you can include any type of control that's available for a dialog box. The dialog editor is described in Chapter 15. A dialog bar can be placed at the top or bottom of the main frame window, or even along the left or right side of this window. As in a dialog box, the user can press the Tab and Shift+Tab keys to move among the controls. For information on dialog bars, see the following online help topic: *Visual C++ Documentation, Using Visual C++, Visual C++ Programmer's Guide, Adding User-Interface Features, Overviews, Dialog Bars: Overview*.

A rebar control is a rectangular box, usually displayed at the top of the window, that can contain one or more *bands*. Each band consists of a gripper; a text label; a bitmap; and a toolbar, a control (such as a combo box), or another type of child window. The user can rearrange the bands within the rebar control by dragging them. A rebar control can be used to display a relatively large number of controls in a small area, because the user can display individual bands as needed, partially hiding those not currently in use. Internet Explorer displays its menu bar and toolbars within a rebar control, which can be created using the CReBar or CReBarCtrl MFC class. For information, look up these two classes in the Index tab of the online help window.

If, when you generate a new application, you choose the Initial Status Bar and Internet Explorer ReBars options in the AppWizard Step 4 dialog box, AppWizard will create both an initial toolbar (the one described in the section "Adding a Docking Toolbar and a Status Bar to a New Program") and an empty dialog bar, and will place both of them within a rebar control. You can then customize any of these elements as needed.

Summary

This chapter described the techniques for adding custom docking toolbars and status bars to your MFC programs. The following are the general points discussed:

- If you're generating a new program using AppWizard, you can include an initial docking toolbar, an initial status bar, or both elements by choosing options in the AppWizard Step 4 dialog box. The docking toolbar contains buttons that allow the user to quickly execute many of the program's menu commands; the user can move the toolbar to any window edge or place the buttons within a free-floating window. The status bar displays command prompts for the menu and toolbar commands, and also shows the status of several keys.

- You'll probably need to modify the initial toolbar or status bar generated by AppWizard to make it more suitable for your particular application.

- To add a custom docking toolbar to an existing MFC program, the first step is to use the Developer Studio toolbar editor to design the image for each button in the toolbar.

- If desired, you can define menu commands corresponding to one or more of your toolbar buttons, to provide the user with an alternative way to execute the command.

- To add the toolbar, you must also define an object of the MFC CToolBar class as a member of your main frame window class, and then create and initialize the toolbar by calling the CToolBar member functions CreateEx and LoadToolBar. These functions should be called from a WM_CREATE message-handling function, OnCreate, within the main frame window class; you can generate this message handler using ClassWizard.

- To give the toolbar docking capability (that is, to allow the user to change its position), you must also call the following three functions from On-Create: CControlBar::EnableDocking, CFrameWnd::EnableDocking, and CFrameWnd::DockControlBar.

- You define message-handling functions that process the toolbar commands in the same way that you define message handlers for menu commands. In fact, a single function can handle messages from both a toolbar button and a corresponding menu command, provided that both user-interface elements have the same identifier.

- You can add a status bar to an existing MFC program by defining an instance of the CStatusBar class as a member of your main frame window class, and then calling the CStatusBar member functions Create and SetIndicators from the OnCreate message-handling function of the main frame window class. You pass SetIndicators an array that defines the identifiers and arrangement of the indicators in the status bar.

CHAPTER
FIFTEEN

Creating Custom Dialog Boxes

- Creating a modal dialog box

- Creating a modeless dialog box

- Creating a tabbed dialog box

- Common dialog boxes

In Windows programs, dialog boxes are one of the most important elements for displaying information and obtaining data from the user. In the programs you've created so far, AppWizard has generated the resources and code necessary for displaying a simple dialog box in response to the About command on the Help menu. In this chapter, you'll learn how to create dialog boxes of your own design and how to display them from your programs.

The chapter provides detailed instructions for designing and displaying a conventional *modal* dialog box, which is one that's displayed temporarily over the main program window and is removed as soon as the user has read or entered the required information. These techniques are presented by having you create an example program, FontDemo, that displays a dialog box for formatting text. The chapter then briefly explains how to display a *modeless* dialog box, which can be left open while the user continues to work in the main program window.

The chapter next explains how to create a *tabbed* dialog box, which consists of several pages of controls and displays a row of file-folder–like tabs near the top of the dialog box. The user displays the desired page by clicking the appropriate tab. You'll create a version of the FontDemo program, named TabDemo, that uses a tabbed dialog box rather than displaying all the controls at once.

NOTE For simplicity, a page and its adjoining tab in a tabbed dialog box are sometimes referred to collectively as a *tab*. For example, in discussing the Developer Studio dialog boxes, this book uses the simple expression "open the tab," rather than the more precise phrase "click the tab to open the page."

The last section introduces *common* dialog boxes, which are prewritten, standard dialog boxes provided by Windows. In the next chapter, you'll learn how to create programs in which the main window is based on a dialog box template and consists of a collection of dialog box controls.

Creating a Modal Dialog Box

In this section, you'll learn how to create and display a modal dialog box by writing an example program, FontDemo. The FontDemo program displays several lines of text within its view window, using the Windows System font (see Figure 15.1). If you choose the Format command on the Text menu, or press the Ctrl+F accelerator keystroke, FontDemo displays the Format dialog box, which allows you to change the way the lines of text in the view window are formatted (see Figure 15.2).

FIGURE 15.1:

The FontDemo program

FIGURE 15.2:

The Format dialog box

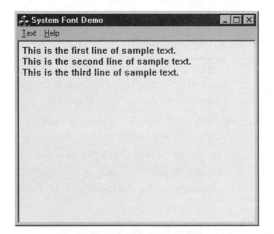

The Format dialog box allows you to specify the style of the characters (bold, italic, underlined, or any combination of these features), the line justification (left, center, or right), the pitch of the characters (variable or fixed), and the line spacing (you can enter 1, 2, or 3 for single-, double-, or triple-spaced lines). As soon as you change any feature in the Format dialog box, the text in the Sample area of this dialog box is immediately reformatted to show the currently selected combination of features. If you click the OK button, the dialog box is closed and the selected formatting features are applied to the text in the main window. If you cancel the dialog box (by clicking the Cancel button or the Close box, choosing the Close command on the system menu, or pressing Esc), the dialog box is closed but the text in the main window is left unaltered.

NOTE   The variable-pitch System font can't be displayed in bold.

While the Format dialog box is displayed, you can't activate the main program window or choose any of the menu commands in the main window. (The program beeps if you make the attempt.) You must first close the dialog box before you can resume work in the main window. Such a dialog box is known as *modal* and is the most common type of dialog box. Later in the chapter, you'll learn how to create a *modeless* dialog box, which permits you to work in the main program window while the dialog box is still displayed.

Generating the Program

You'll use AppWizard to generate the basic source code files for the FontDemo program, employing the techniques explained in Chapter 9. To do this, choose the File ➤ New... menu command. Then, in the Projects tab of the New dialog box, select the "MFC AppWizard (exe)" item in the list of project types, enter the program name—FontDemo—into the Project Name: text box, and enter the path of the desired project folder into the Location: text box. Be sure that Win32 is selected in the Platforms: list, and then click the OK button. In the AppWizard dialog boxes, choose the *same* options that you chose when generating the WinGreet program in Chapter 9.

Designing the Format Dialog Box

You'll now design the Format dialog box using the Visual C++ dialog editor. First, choose the Insert ➤ Resource... menu command or press the Ctrl+R keystroke. In the Insert Resource dialog box, select the Dialog resource type and click the New button to create a new dialog box (see Figure 15.3).

FIGURE 15.3:

The Insert Resource dialog box

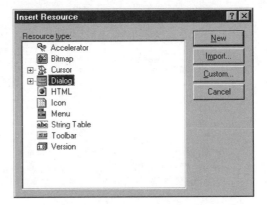

Alternatively, you can create a new dialog box by simply clicking the New Dialog button on the Resource toolbar (to display it, right-click a toolbar and choose Resource), or by pressing the Ctrl+1 keystroke.

Visual C++ will open a dialog editor window, which displays a full-sized replica of the new dialog box you're creating. Initially, the dialog box has only an OK push button and a Cancel push button. When the dialog editor is active, the Controls and Dialog toolbars will normally be displayed. (If either toolbar is missing, you can display it by right-clicking a toolbar and choosing the appropriate command from the shortcut menu.) The Controls toolbar contains a button for each type of control you can add to the dialog box, and the Dialog toolbar provides an alternative way to issue many of the menu commands used in designing a dialog box. The dialog editor is shown in Figure 15.4. Figure 15.5 shows the Controls toolbar, indicating the type of control that corresponds to each button. All the controls on this toolbar are explained in a sidebar given later in this section.

FIGURE 15.4:

The Visual C++ dialog editor, displaying the new dialog box

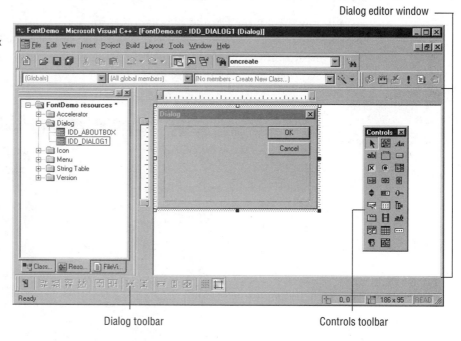

Dialog editor window

Dialog toolbar

Controls toolbar

FIGURE 15.5:

The Visual C++ Controls toolbar, indicating the type of control that can be added using each of the buttons

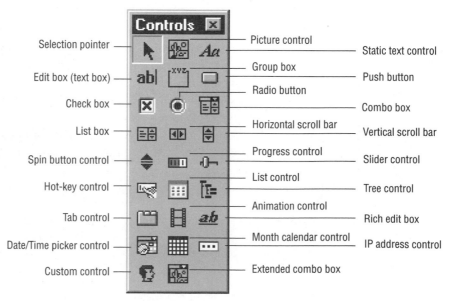

Selection pointer

Edit box (text box)

Check box

List box

Spin button control

Hot-key control

Tab control

Date/Time picker control

Custom control

Picture control

Static text control

Group box

Push button

Radio button

Combo box

Horizontal scroll bar

Vertical scroll bar

Progress control

Slider control

List control

Tree control

Animation control

Rich edit box

Month calendar control

IP address control

Extended combo box

Figure 15.6 shows the Format dialog box as it should appear when you've completed designing it in the dialog editor; this figure indicates the identifier of each control. Table 15.1 lists the properties of the dialog box itself as well as the properties of each control that you'll add. The following instructions will show you how to add the controls as well as specify the properties of the dialog box and its controls.

FIGURE 15.6:

The completed Format dialog box, indicating the identifier of each control

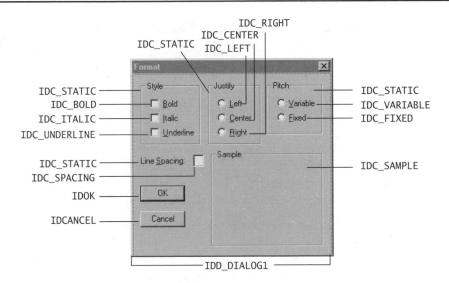

TABLE 15.1: Properties of the Format Dialog Box and Its Controls

ID:	Type of Control	Nondefault Properties You Need to Set
IDD_DIALOG1	Dialog box	Caption: Format
IDC_STATIC	Group box	Caption: Style
IDC_BOLD	Check box	Caption: &Bold
		Group
IDC_ITALIC	Check box	Caption: &Italic
IDC_UNDERLINE	Check box	Caption: &Underline
IDC_STATIC	Group box	Caption: Justify

Continued on next page

TABLE 15.1 CONTINUED: Properties of the Format Dialog Box and Its Controls

ID:	Type of Control	Nondefault Properties You Need to Set
IDC_LEFT	Radio button	Caption: &Left
		Group
		Tab Stop
IDC_CENTER	Radio button	Caption: &Center
IDC_RIGHT	Radio button	Caption: &Right
IDC_STATIC	Group box	Caption: Pitch
IDC_VARIABLE	Radio button	Caption: &Variable
		Group
		Tab Stop
IDC_FIXED	Radio button	Caption: &Fixed
IDC_STATIC	Static text control	Caption: Line &Spacing:
IDC_SPACING	Edit box (text box)	none
IDC_SAMPLE	Group box	Caption: Sample
IDOK	Push button	Caption: OK
		Default Button
IDCANCEL	Push button	Caption: Cancel

To begin, select the dialog box by clicking the selection pointer in the Controls toolbar and then clicking within the dialog box—but *not* within a control. (While following these instructions, see Figure 15.5 for the locations of the buttons on the Controls toolbar.) You can then enlarge the dialog box by dragging the lower-right corner to the desired position.

Next, set the dialog box properties by right-clicking within the dialog box—but *not* within a control—and choosing Properties on the pop-up menu, to open the Dialog Properties dialog box. Then, open the General tab, and enter the title Format into the Caption: text box. Don't change any of the other properties; the default values are acceptable. Note that for the dialog box and for each control,

Table 15.1 lists the identifier and only those additional properties that you need to *change* from their default values (the default values are the values initially displayed in the Dialog Properties dialog box).

Under Windows 95 or later, choosing the System Menu style in the Styles tab of the Dialog Properties dialog box produces two effects. First, a Close box will be displayed at the right end of the title bar (clicking the Close box has the same effect as clicking a button with the IDCANCEL identifier). Second, when the user clicks the right mouse button in the title bar, a floating system menu will appear, which allows the user to move or close the dialog box (choosing the Close command on the system menu also has the same effect as clicking a button with the IDCANCEL identifier). For a dialog box, Windows 95 or later *doesn't* display the system menu icon at the left end of the title bar, as it does for a main program window.

You should now add the dialog box controls and set their properties. To add a particular type of control, click the appropriate button within the Controls toolbar, and then click the desired target location within the dialog box; the control will initially be inserted at that position. You can then use the mouse to move or change the size of the control. To set the control's properties, right-click within the control and choose Properties on the pop-up menu to open the Properties dialog box, and then enter the control identifier and any additional nondefault properties listed for that control in Table 15.1. You can set all required properties in the General tab of the Properties dialog box, except the Default Button property for the IDOK push button, which you set in the Styles tab. (For some controls, you'll simply accept the default identifier; for others, you'll need to change the identifier to conform to Table 15.1.) If you need to delete a control you've added, select it by clicking within it and then press the Del key.

The position and size of the selected object (dialog box or control) are displayed on the status bar at the bottom of the Developer Studio window. These measurements are not in absolute units (such as pixels); rather, they're in *dialog box units*, which are scaled according to the actual size of the Windows System font at the time the program is run. As a result of using scaleable units, the text that the dialog box displays will always fit properly within the dialog box and its controls, even if the text size changes as the program is run on different computers and under various video modes (provided, of course, that the text fits properly in the original dialog box design).

Note that the & character within a control's caption causes the following character to be underlined. When the dialog box is displayed, the user can activate the control by pressing the Alt key in conjunction with the underlined character. If the control is a check box or radio button, pressing the Alt key combination will check the control. If the control is a push button, pressing the key combination will activate the button command, just as if the button had been clicked. If the control is a static text control, pressing the key combination will place the insertion point within the following edit box—that is, the edit box occurring next in the tab order (the tab order will be explained in the next section).

As you can see in Table 15.1, most of the controls are assigned unique, descriptive identifiers; these identifiers are used to reference the controls within the program source code. However, controls that *aren't* referenced by the program code don't need unique identifiers, and are left with the default identifiers proposed by the dialog editor (these are the controls with the IDC_STATIC identifier).

Assigning the OK push button the Default Button property causes the button to be displayed with a thick border, and allows the user to activate the button (thereby closing the dialog box) by simply pressing Enter. The Tab Stop and Group properties will be explained in the next section.

Using Controls

Figure 15.5 showed each type of control you can add to a dialog box.

A *picture control* displays an empty rectangular frame, a solid rectangular block, or an icon. You specify which object is displayed by setting the control's properties. A *static text control* displays a text string. It's ordinarily used to label an edit box or other type of control. A *group box* is a labeled border that can be used to group a set of related controls. Picture controls, static text controls, and group boxes don't accept user input.

An *edit box*, also known as a *text box*, allows the user to enter text and provides complete editing facilities, such as backspacing, deleting, cutting, and pasting. If you specify the Multi-line style (in the Styles tab of the Edit Properties dialog box), the user can enter multiple lines, allowing the edit box to serve as a small text editor. A *rich edit box* is an edit box in which the user can apply character and paragraph formatting to the text. An *IP address control* is an edit box that contains four separate text fields to facilitate entering a numeric Internet Protocol address (for example, 255.816.1.1).

Continued on next page

A *push button* is typically used to execute some task immediately. Normally, a *check box* is used to enable or disable an option that can be turned on or off independently of other options, and a *radio button* is used to select one of a group of mutually exclusive options.

A *list box* displays a list of items, such as file names or fonts, and allows the user to scroll through the list and select the desired item. A *list control* is a type of list box that displays a series of icons, each of which has a text label. The list items can be displayed in various ways—for example, with small icons, with large icons, or in a horizontal or vertical arrangement. An example of a list control is the right pane of the Windows Explorer.

A *tree control*, also known as a *tree-view control*, displays a hierarchical graph, such as those contained in the Workspace window of the Developer Studio or in the left pane of the Windows Explorer.

A *combo box* combines a list box with either an edit box or a static text control. A *simple* combo box consists of an edit box and a list box that's permanently displayed below it. A *dropdown* combo box consists of an edit box and a list box that appears only after the user clicks the down arrow displayed to the right of the edit box. A *drop list* combo box consists of a static text control (with a border) and a list box that appears only when the user clicks the down arrow. To specify the type of combo box, open the Styles tab in the Combo Box Properties dialog box and choose the desired type in the Type: list. An *extended combo box* is one with the ability to display images.

The two *scroll bar* controls are used for displaying horizontal or vertical scroll bars anywhere within the dialog box. These controls allow the user to adjust some quantity that varies continuously—for example, the height of a font, the intensity of a color, or the tracking speed of the mouse.

A *spin button control*, also known as an *up–down control*, consists of a pair of buttons containing arrows. It allows the user to increment or decrement a value or move some item (such as the tabs in a tabbed dialog box). The arrows can be oriented vertically or horizontally. A spin control is often used in conjunction with an edit box that accepts numeric input.

A *slider control*, sometimes known as a *trackbar*, also allows the user to change a value—for example, the hue of a color. It consists of a track containing a box that the user drags to adjust the value, plus optional tick marks. Examples can be seen in the Keyboard program of the Windows 95 Control Panel.

A *progress control* is a window that displays a series of rectangles indicating the progress of a lengthy operation, such as printing a document or saving a file. Many Windows programs, such as Microsoft Word for Windows, display a progress bar in the status bar during long operations.

Continued on next page

An *animation control* is a small window that displays a video clip in the standard Windows AVI (Audio Video Interleaved) format. You can use an animation control to entertain the user during a lengthy operation; an example is the orbiting magnifying glass displayed by the Windows 95 Find command during a file search.

A *hot-key control* is a window that allows the user to enter a key combination to be used as a program hot key. An example is the Key: box in the Accel Properties dialog box of the Developer Studio, explained in Chapter 10 (in "Creating the MiniEdit Program").

A *date/time picker control* makes it easy for the user to enter a date or a time. It consists of fields for entering each part of the date or time. If the control is used to enter a date, it includes a drop-down calendar for selecting a date; and if it's used to enter a time, it provides spin buttons for adjusting the time. A *month calendar control* permanently displays a monthly calendar, which lets the user scroll through various months and select dates.

You can use a *tab control* to add a set of tabbed pages to a dialog box. Later in the chapter (in the section "Creating a Tabbed Dialog Box"), you'll learn how to use the MFC to create a dialog box containing tabbed pages.

A *custom control* is a control that you (or a third-party supplier) have designed and programmed. With the custom control button on the Controls toolbar you can set the position and size of a custom control. The control, however, will be displayed as a simple rectangle; its actual appearance and behavior won't be manifested until the program is run. Creating custom controls is discussed in the following online help topic: *Visual C++ Documentation, Using Visual C++, Visual C++ Programmer's Guide, Adding User Interface Features, Details, Resource Editor Topics, Dialog Editor Topics for Visual C++, Using Custom Controls in the Dialog Editor*.

Finally, as you'll learn in Chapter 25, you can add a button for an ActiveX control to the Controls toolbar and then use it to add the ActiveX control to a dialog box in the same way that you work with one of the other types of controls.

Setting the Tab Order

Your next task is to set the *tab order* for the controls. In setting the tab order, you assign a sequential number to each control (that is, you assign 1 to a given control, 2 to another control, and so on). The tab order has the following effects:

- The tab order governs the order in which controls that have been assigned the Tab Stop property receive the input focus as the user presses the Tab or

Shift+Tab keystroke. Pressing Tab moves the focus to the *next* control with the Tab Stop property in the tab order, while pressing Shift+Tab moves it to the *previous* Tab Stop control in the tab order. When a particular control has the input focus, it responds to keyboard input. If the user moves the focus to a push button, pressing the spacebar executes the button command. If the user moves the focus to a check box or radio button, pressing the spacebar checks the box. If the user moves the focus to an edit box, the insertion point caret appears in the box and the text can be edited. The Tab Stop property thus allows the user to enter input into a dialog box without using the mouse.

- The tab order is also used to define *groups* of controls. If a control has the Group property, that control—as well as all controls that follow it in the tab order—belongs to a single group. If, however, a following control also has the Group property, it *doesn't* belong to the same group, but instead it starts a new group. If several radio buttons belong to the same group, whenever the user clicks a button, Windows automatically removes the check from the previously checked button within the group (provided that the buttons have the Auto property, which is enabled by default). Also, the user can press an arrow key ($\downarrow$, $\uparrow$, $\rightarrow$, $\leftarrow$) to move the check mark from radio button to radio button within a single group of radio buttons.

- If a static text control has an underlined character (that is, a character preceded with an &), pressing the Alt key in conjunction with this character moves the focus to the next edit box that follows it in the tab order. Therefore, a static text control used as a label should immediately precede the associated edit box in the tab order. The underlined character is known as a *mnemonic*.

To set the tab order, choose the Layout ➤ Tab Order menu command, or press Ctrl+D. The dialog editor will then place a number on each control indicating the current tab order (which initially matches the order in which you added the controls). To change the tab order, click the first control in the desired order, then click the second control, then the third, and so on. When you're done, the controls should have the numbers shown in Figure 15.7. Press Esc to remove the numbers.

NOTE   For more information on designing a dialog box in the dialog editor, see the following online help topic: *Visual C++ Documentation, Using Visual C++, Visual C++ User's Guide, Resource Editors, Dialog Editor.*

FIGURE 15.7:

The tab order for the Format dialog box

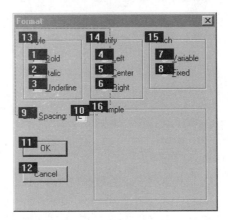

You've now finished designing the dialog box. You can save your work by choosing the File ➢ Save All menu command or clicking the Save All button on the Standard toolbar. Leave the dialog editor window open for the next step.

Creating a Class to Manage the Dialog Box

The next step is to use ClassWizard to generate a class for managing the Format dialog box that you just designed. Click in the dialog editor window to activate it (if necessary) and choose the View ➢ ClassWizard menu command or press Ctrl+W. ClassWizard will recognize that you haven't yet defined a class for the Format dialog box, and it will therefore automatically display the Adding A Class dialog box (on top of the ClassWizard dialog box). In this dialog box, choose the Create A New Class option and click OK.

ClassWizard will then open the New Class dialog box. Notice that the Format dialog box identifier, IDD_DIALOG1, is selected in the Dialog ID: list, and that CDialog is selected in the Base Class: list. Leave these values as they are. CDialog is the basic MFC class for managing dialog boxes; the new class you're generating will be derived directly from CDialog.

| NOTE | When ClassWizard generates the dialog class, it stores the identifier of the dialog resource—**IDD_DIALOG1** for the Format dialog box—within the class definition (it defines an enumerator named **IDD** that's set equal to the identifier). When a dialog class object is created, the dialog class constructor passes this identifier to the **CDialog** constructor, which stores the value. Finally, when the dialog box is displayed, the **CDialog::DoModal** function (explained later) passes this identifier to Windows so that the proper dialog template resource is used for displaying the dialog box. |

Now enter the name of the new class, CFormat, into the Name: text box. Class-Wizard will then automatically enter the file name Format.cpp into the File Name box. The CFormat implementation will be placed in Format.cpp and the CFormat definition in Format.h. If you wanted to change the file names, you'd click the Change… button. For this exercise, however, leave the default file name as well as the default values in the remaining options. The completed New Class dialog box is shown in Figure 15.8. Click the OK button to generate the source code files and remove the dialog box.

FIGURE 15.8:

The completed New Class dialog box for generating a class to manage the Format dialog box

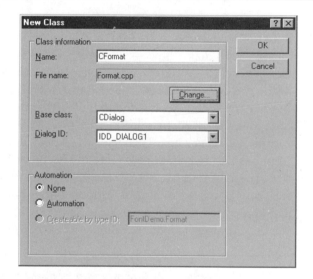

Defining Member Variables

Once the New Class dialog box is removed, you can access the main Class-Wizard dialog box. You can now use ClassWizard to add data members to the CFormat class. ClassWizard allows you to define one or more data members of the dialog class for each control contained within the dialog box. When the program is run and the dialog box is displayed, the MFC automatically transfers the value of each of these data members to its corresponding control. For example, if you've used ClassWizard to define an integer data member associated with an edit box, and if the data member contains the value 1 when the dialog box is displayed, a 1 will appear in the edit box. Also, if the user dismisses the dialog box by clicking the OK button, the value contained within each control is transferred back to its corresponding data member or members. If, however, the user *cancels* the dialog box, the control values *aren't* transferred to the data members. The type of the data member (or members) that you can define for a particular control, and the way that the exchange mechanism works, depend on the type of the control (several types of controls will be described shortly).

TIP

The MFC automatically transfers values between data members and controls when the dialog box is first opened and also when it's closed. You can force the MFC to transfer the control data to or from the data members at any time the dialog box is displayed by calling the `CWnd::UpdateData` function from a member function of the dialog class.

To define data members for FontDemo, open the Member Variables tab in the ClassWizard dialog box (see Figure 15.9). Because you just defined the `CFormat` class, this class should already be selected within the Class Name: list at the top of the dialog box (if it isn't, select it now). The Control IDs: list displays the identifier of each control you added to the Format dialog box that can be assigned a data member. Begin by selecting the IDC_BOLD identifier to define a data member for the Bold check box. Then click the Add Variable... button to display the Add Member Variable dialog box. Into the Member Variable Name: text box, enter `m_Bold` as the data member name (ClassWizard inserts the m_ portion of the name for you). Leave the default selections in the Category: and Variable Type: lists. The completed Add Member Variable dialog box is shown in Figure 15.10. Click the OK button when you're done.

FIGURE 15.9:

The Member Variables page of the ClassWizard dialog box, before defining data members

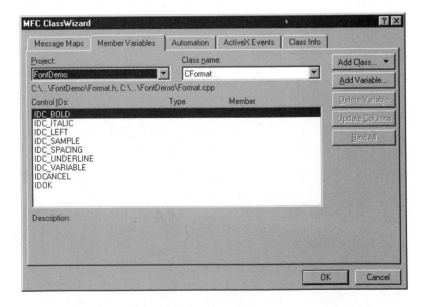

FIGURE 15.10:

The completed Add Member Variable dialog box, for defining a data member associated with the Bold check box (IDC_BOLD)

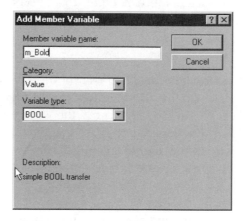

The default selection in the Category: list, Value, creates a data member of a fundamental C++ type rather than a member object. (Defining member objects will be discussed later.) The default selection in the Variable Type: list, BOOL, creates a data member that can be assigned TRUE or FALSE.

Using the same method, define a data member for the Italic check box (IDC_ ITALIC) named m_Italic, plus a data member for the Underline check box (IDC_UNDERLINE) named m_Underline.

The next step is to assign data members for the radio buttons. Rather than assigning a data member for each radio button, you assign a single data member for each *group* of radio buttons. Before the Format dialog box is displayed, the data member must be assigned the number of the radio button within the group that's to be initially checked; the number 0 indicates the *first* radio button in the group (in the tab order), the number 1 indicates the *second*, and so on. When the Format dialog box is first opened, the MFC will then check the indicated radio button (if you assign the data member –1, *no* button in the group will be checked). Likewise, when the user clicks OK, the MFC assigns the data member the number of the radio button in the group that's currently checked (or the value –1 if *no* button is checked).

Accordingly, the Control IDs: list shows only the identifier of the *first* radio button in each of the two groups, IDC_LEFT (for the group starting with the Left button) and IDC_VARIABLE (for the group starting with the Variable button). First, assign a member variable for the IDC_LEFT radio button group; in the Add Member Variable dialog box, enter the variable name m_Justify and leave the default selections in the two lists. (Notice that the Variable Type: list contains the type int; the data member is made an int so that it can store the number of the checked radio button.) Using the same method, assign a data member named m_Pitch for the IDC_VARIABLE radio button group.

Next, assign a data member for the edit box (IDC_SPACING) named m_Spacing. This time, in the Add Member Variable dialog box, leave Value selected in the Category: list but select int in the Variable Type: list rather than accepting the default selection (CString), so that the text string displayed in the edit box will be converted from and to an integer. Also, when you return to the ClassWizard dialog box, two new text boxes—labeled Minimum Value: and Maximum Value:—will be displayed at the bottom of the dialog box (see Figure 15.11, given later in this section). These text boxes allow you to enter the range of valid values for the selected data member. If you enter numbers into these text boxes, when the user clicks the OK button to dismiss the dialog box, the MFC will make sure that the value that the user has entered is within the specified range (if the value *isn't* in this range, the MFC displays a warning and keeps the dialog box open). For the IDC_SPACING control, enter 1 into the Minimum Value: box and 3 into the Maximum Value: box (so that the user can specify only single-, double-, or triple-line spacing).

Your final task is to define a member object for managing the edit box. To do this, select again the IDC_SPACING identifier in the Control IDs: list and click the Add Variable... button (you can define two data members for a single control, provided that they belong to different categories, as specified by the value you choose in the Category: list). Into the Member Variable Name: text box, enter the name m_SpacingEdit. In the Category: list, select the Control item; this will attach the IDC_SPACING edit box to a data member that's an object of the MFC CEdit class. CEdit provides a set of member functions that can be used to manage an edit box; as you'll see later, the dialog class uses one of these functions.

You've now finished defining the data members for the dialog controls. The Member Variables tab of the ClassWizard dialog box should appear as shown in Figure 15.11. Click the OK button in the ClassWizard dialog box. ClassWizard will write the code for defining the data members you specified to the header and the implementation files for the dialog class (Format.h and Format.cpp).

FIGURE 15.11:

The completed Member Variables page of the Class Wizard dialog box

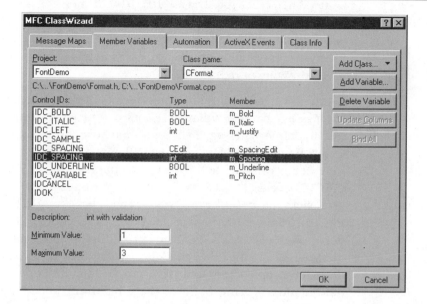

Defining Message Handlers

Like any window, a dialog box receives a variety of messages to inform it of significant events, and you must add message-handling functions to the dialog class if you want to handle any of these events. For the FontDemo program, you need to add functions for handling the messages sent when the dialog box is first opened, when the dialog box needs repainting, and when the user clicks a check box or a radio button.

To define the required message-handling functions, open the ClassWizard dialog box again, and open the Message Maps tab. The CFormat class should still be selected in the Class Name: list (if not, select it now).

To define the first two message handlers, select CFormat in the Object IDs: list. The Messages: list will now display the identifiers of the general Windows notification messages that can be sent to the dialog box. (This list doesn't include messages sent from controls.) First, select WM_INITDIALOG, and click the Add Function button to define a handler for this message; ClassWizard will create a function named OnInitDialog. The WM_INITDIALOG message is sent when the dialog box is first created, just before it's displayed. Then, select WM_PAINT in the Messages: list, and click the Add Function; ClassWizard will create a message-handling function named OnPaint. The WM_PAINT message is sent whenever the dialog box needs drawing or redrawing.

You now need to provide a message handler for each check box or radio button; the message handler will receive control whenever the user clicks the box or button. To define a message handler for the Bold check box, select IDC_BOLD in the Object IDs: list; the Messages: list will now display both types of messages that a check box can send to the dialog box (namely, BN_CLICKED and BN_DOUBLE-CLICKED). Select BN_CLICKED; this is the message that the button sends when the user clicks it to check or uncheck it. Then click the Add Function... button, and in the Add Member Function dialog box, simply click OK to accept the default function name, OnBold. Use this same procedure to define BN_CLICKED message handlers for each of the other check boxes and radio buttons; in all cases, accept the default function name. Table 15.2 lists the identifier of each check box and radio button, plus the name of the message-handling function that processes the BN_CLICKED message sent by the button.

TABLE 15.2: Handlers for the **BN_CLICKED** Messages Sent by the Check Boxes and Radio Buttons in the Format Dialog Box

Object ID:	Name of Message Handler
IDC_BOLD	OnBold
IDC_CENTER	OnCenter
IDC_FIXED	OnFixed
IDC_ITALIC	OnItalic
IDC_LEFT	OnLeft
IDC_RIGHT	OnRight
IDC_UNDERLINE	OnUnderline
IDC_VARIABLE	OnVariable

Finally, you need to define a function that receives control whenever the user changes the contents of the IDC_SPACING edit box. To do this, select IDC_SPACING in the Object IDs: list. The Messages: list will now display all the different messages that the edit box can send to the dialog box; select the EN_CHANGE message, which is sent whenever the user changes the text in the edit box. Then click the Add Function... button and accept the default function name, OnChangeSpacing. Figure 15.12 shows the ClassWizard dialog box after all member functions have been added. Because you're done defining message handlers, now click the OK button in the ClassWizard dialog box.

FIGURE 15.12:

The completed ClassWizard dialog box, after all the message-handling functions have been defined for the CFormat dialog class

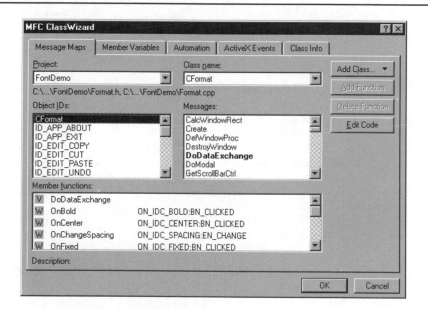

Completing the *CFormat* Code

In this section, you'll complete the coding of the CFormat class. To begin, open the file Format.h and add the following two enumerated type definitions to the beginning of the file:

```
enum {JUSTIFY_LEFT, JUSTIFY_CENTER, JUSTIFY_RIGHT};
enum {PITCH_VARIABLE, PITCH_FIXED};

//////////////////////////////////////////////////////////////////
////////////
// CFormat dialog
```

The enumerators in these definitions will be used to refer to the radio buttons. The enumerators in the first definition (which have the values 0, 1, and 2) refer to the numbers of the radio buttons in the Justify group of the Format dialog box, and the enumerators in the second definition refer to the numbers of the radio buttons in the Pitch group.

Next, add the following definition for the m_RectSample protected data member to the beginning of the CFormat class definition:

```
/////////////////////////////////////////////////////////////////
///////////
// CFormat dialog

class CFormat : public CDialog
{
protected:
   RECT m_RectSample;

// remainder of CFormat definition ...
```

Now open the file Format.cpp and add code as follows to the OnInitDialog member function:

```
BOOL CFormat::OnInitDialog()
{
   CDialog::OnInitDialog();

   // TODO: Add extra initialization here
   GetDlgItem (IDC_SAMPLE)->GetWindowRect (&m_RectSample);
   ScreenToClient (&m_RectSample);

   m_SpacingEdit.LimitText (1);

   return TRUE;  // return TRUE unless you set the focus to a
                 // control
                 // EXCEPTION: OCX Property Pages should return
                 // FALSE
}
```

As mentioned, the OnInitDialog function receives control when the Format dialog box is opened, immediately before it becomes visible. The first added statement stores the screen coordinates of the Sample group box in the data member m_RectSample. The second statement then converts the screen coordinates to client coordinates (that is, coordinates with respect to the upper-left corner of the inside of the dialog box). Data member m_RectSample will be used for displaying the sample text within the group box.

The third statement you added uses the CEdit member object, m_SpacingEdit, to call the CEdit member function LimitText. Passing LimitText a value of 1 prevents the user from entering more than one character into the IDC_SPACING edit box.

MFC Control Classes

The MFC provides a class for managing each major type of control. These classes are listed in Table 15.3 (the controls that aren't explained in this table were described in the previous sidebar, "Using Controls"). Most of these classes are derived directly from CWnd (several, however, are derived from other control classes). You can use the member functions of these classes to obtain information or perform operations on the controls within a dialog box. For example, the FontDemo program used the CEdit member function LimitText to limit the number of characters that can be entered into an edit box. Keep in mind that because each of the control classes is derived (directly or indirectly) from CWnd, the member functions you can call include those defined within CWnd, some of which might be useful for managing a control (for example, you can call CWnd::EnableWindow to disable or enable a control).

For a complete list of the member functions of a particular control class or of CWnd, see the documentation on the class in the following online help topic: *Visual C++ Documentation, Reference, Microsoft Foundation Class Library and Templates, Microsoft Foundation Class Library, Class Library Reference*.

To use one of these member functions to manage a control within a dialog box, you must create an object of the control class, which is attached to the control. There are two simple ways to do this. First, you can use ClassWizard to create a member object, such as the m_SpacingEdit member object that you defined for the FontDemo program. (In the Add Member Variable dialog box displayed by ClassWizard, select the Control item in the Category: list.) ClassWizard will create an object of the appropriate class for the type of the control (for example, it will define a CEdit object for an edit box). When the dialog box is displayed, the MFC code will automatically attach the control to the control class object, so that you can call the control class member functions to manage the control (you can call the member functions *only* while the dialog box is displayed; at other times, a control *won't* be attached to the control class object).

Continued on next page

Second, you can call the **CWnd::GetDlgItem** function for the dialog box object to obtain a pointer to a temporary object for a control within the dialog box. For example, in the FontDemo program, rather than creating a permanent member object for managing the edit box, you could call **GetDlgItem** from **OnInitDialog** to obtain a temporary object, and call **LimitText** for this object, as in the following code:

```
((CEdit *)GetDlgItem (IDC_SPACING))->LimitText (1);
```

Notice that because **GetDlgItem** returns a **CWnd** pointer, you must convert the return value to a pointer to the appropriate control class, so that you can call the member functions of that class. Because the pointer is temporary, you should use it only during processing of the current message and *not* store it for later use. (Note that **GetDlgItem** was also used for setting the value of **m_RectSample** in the code you added to **OnInitDialog** in this section.)

As an exercise in using these techniques, you might want to modify the Format dialog box in FontDemo so that the Bold push button (which has the identifier **IDC_BOLD**) is unchecked *and* disabled whenever the Variable radio button (**IDC_VARIABLE**) is checked. (Recall that the variable-pitch System font can't be displayed in bold.) The code to do this would have to be placed in the **OnInitDialog**, **OnVariable**, and **OnFixed** member functions of the **CFormat** dialog class. You could use either method explained above to obtain a **CButton** object for the Bold push button. To check or uncheck the button, call **CButton::SetCheck** for the **CButton** object; to disable or enable the button, call **CWnd::EnableWindow** for the **CButton** object.

Note, finally, that though controls are normally associated with dialog boxes, you can display them within any program window. For example, you could display one or more controls directly within the program's view window. A window that isn't a dialog box, however, doesn't have a dialog template for creating and displaying controls. Rather, you must add code to explicitly create, position, and display a control. To do this, declare an object of the appropriate MFC control class (you can make the object a member of the class that manages the window). Then call the **Create** member function of the control class to display the control, specifying the desired size, position, and other control attributes. Note that a control is a child window of the window or dialog box in which it's displayed. If your view window consists *primarily* of a collection of controls, it's best to derive the view class from **CFormView** and use a dialog template rather than creating controls individually, as explained in the next chapter.

TABLE 15.3: The MFC Classes for Managing Controls

MFC Class	Type of Control Managed
CAnimateCtrl	Animation controls
CButton	Buttons: push buttons, check boxes, radio buttons; also, group boxes
CBitmapButton	Push buttons that display bitmaps you design yourself
CComboBox	Combo boxes
CComboBoxEx	Extended combo boxes
CDateTimeCtrl	Date/Time picker controls
CEdit	Edit boxes
CHeaderCtrl	Header controls. A header control is a window placed above columns of text, which contains adjustable-width titles (the Windows Explorer displays a header control in the right pane when you display detailed file information).
CHotKeyCtrl	Hot-key controls
CIPAddressControl	IP address controls
CListBox	List boxes
CCheckListBox	Checklist boxes. A checklist box is a list box in which each item has a check box that the user can select. As an example, the Visual C++ Setup program uses checklist boxes for choosing installation components.
CDragListBox	Drag list boxes. A drag list box is a list box that allows the user to drag individual list box items in order to rearrange them.
CListCtrl	List controls
CMonthCalCtrl	Month calendar controls
COleControl	ActiveX controls (formerly known as OLE controls; hence the name of the class). An ActiveX control is a reusable software component. These custom controls can provide a wide range of services to the programs that contain them. They are discussed in Chapter 25.
CProgressCtrl	Progress controls

Continued on next page

TABLE 15.3 CONTINUED: The MFC Classes for Managing Controls

MFC Class	Type of Control Managed
CReBarCtrl	Rebar controls. These controls were explained in the sidebar "Dialog Bars and Rebar Controls" near the end of Chapter 14.
CRichEditCtrl	Rich edit boxes
CScrollBar	Scroll bars: vertical or horizontal
CSliderCtrl	Slider controls
CSpinButtonCtrl	Spin button controls
CStatic	Static text controls, picture controls, and group boxes
CStatusBarCtrl	Status bar controls. **CStatusBarCtrl** provides an *alternative* to the method for creating status bars in MFC programs that was discussed in Chapter 14.
CTabCtrl	Tab controls. **CTabCtrl** provides an *alternative* to the method for creating tabbed dialog boxes in MFC programs that's discussed later in this chapter.
CToolbarCtrl	Toolbars. **CToolbarCtrl** provides an *alternative* to the method for creating tool-bars in MFC programs that was discussed in Chapter 14.
CTooltipCtrl	Tool tips. These were discussed in Chapter 14. When you create a toolbar using the MFC method presented in Chapter 14, you can have the MFC *automatically* implement tool tips.
CTreeCtrl	Tree controls

The next step is to complete the coding of the message-handling functions that receive control whenever the user clicks a check box to check or uncheck it. First, complete the function in Format.cpp for the Bold check box as follows:

```
void CFormat::OnBold()
{
    // TODO: Add your control notification handler code here
    m_Bold = !m_Bold;
    InvalidateRect (&m_RectSample);
    UpdateWindow ();
}
```

The first statement toggles the value of the m_Bold data member between TRUE and FALSE. Thus, if the box *isn't* checked (and m_Bold is FALSE), clicking the control will check it and cause OnBold to set m_Bold to TRUE. If the box is already checked, clicking it will remove the check mark and cause OnBold to set m_Bold to FALSE.

The second added statement invalidates (that is, marks for repainting) the portion of the dialog box occupied by the Sample group box, and the third statement causes the OnPaint member function of the dialog class to be called immediately; OnPaint then displays the text using the new format (later, you'll write the code to do this).

Now complete the similar message-handling functions for the Italic and Underline check boxes as follows:

```
void CFormat::OnItalic()
{
    // TODO: Add your control notification handler code here
    m_Italic = !m_Italic;
    InvalidateRect (&m_RectSample);
    UpdateWindow ();
}

// ...

void CFormat::OnUnderline()
{
    // TODO: Add your control notification handler code here
    m_Underline = !m_Underline;
    InvalidateRect (&m_RectSample);
    UpdateWindow ();
}
```

Then, complete the message-handling functions for the radio buttons, as follows:

```
void CFormat::OnCenter()
{
    // TODO: Add your control notification handler code here
    if (IsDlgButtonChecked (IDC_CENTER))
        {
        m_Justify = JUSTIFY_CENTER;
        InvalidateRect (&m_RectSample);
        UpdateWindow ();
        }
}
```

```
void CFormat::OnFixed()
{
   // TODO: Add your control notification handler code here
   if (IsDlgButtonChecked (IDC_FIXED))
      {
      m_Pitch = PITCH_FIXED;
      InvalidateRect (&m_RectSample);
      UpdateWindow ();
      }
}

// ...

void CFormat::OnLeft()
{
   // TODO: Add your control notification handler code here
   if (IsDlgButtonChecked (IDC_LEFT))
      {
      m_Justify = JUSTIFY_LEFT;
      InvalidateRect (&m_RectSample);
      UpdateWindow ();
      }
}

void CFormat::OnRight()
{
   // TODO: Add your control notification handler code here
   if (IsDlgButtonChecked (IDC_RIGHT))
      {
      m_Justify = JUSTIFY_RIGHT;
      InvalidateRect (&m_RectSample);
      UpdateWindow ();
      }
}

// ...
```

```
void CFormat::OnVariable()
{
   // TODO: Add your control notification handler code here
   if (IsDlgButtonChecked (IDC_VARIABLE))
      {
      m_Pitch = PITCH_VARIABLE;
      InvalidateRect (&m_RectSample);
      UpdateWindow ();
      }
}
```

Each of these functions first calls CWnd::IsDlgButtonChecked to make sure that the radio button has been checked. (The message-handling function is called whenever the user clicks and thereby checks the radio button; it's also sometimes called when the user moves the focus to the button with the Tab key, *without* checking the button.) If the button is checked, the function assigns the number of the radio button to the appropriate data member (m_Justify or m_Pitch). Later, you'll see how these data members are used.

MFC Functions for Managing Dialog Boxes

A dialog class is derived from the MFC CDialog class, which in turn is derived from CWnd. Both CDialog and CWnd provide member functions for managing dialog boxes, which you can call from your dialog class. You can use these functions *in addition to* the member functions of the MFC control classes (such as CEdit) that were discussed in the previous sidebar. Some of these functions affect individual controls contained in the dialog box, others affect groups of controls, and still others affect the dialog box itself. You normally call these functions from the message-handling functions of your dialog class, which receive control while the dialog box is displayed.

The CWnd functions are listed in Table 15.4 and the CDialog functions are listed in Table 15.5. See the documentation on each of these functions for details (you can look up the documentation in the following online help topics: *Visual C++ Documentation, Reference, Microsoft Foundation Class Library and Templates, Microsoft Foundation Class Library, Class Library Reference, CWnd* and *CDialog*).

TABLE 15.4 CWnd Member Functions for Managing Dialog Box Controls

Function	Purpose
CheckDlgButton	Checks or unchecks a check box or radio button
CheckRadioButton	Checks a specified radio button and unchecks all other radio buttons within a designated set of radio buttons
DlgDirList	Adds a list of files, folders, or drives to a list box
DlgDirListComboBox	Adds a list of files, folders, or drives to the list box within a combo box
DlgDirSelect	Obtains the currently selected file, folder, or drive from a list box
DlgDirSelectComboBox	Obtains the currently selected file, folder, or drive from the list box within a combo box
GetCheckedRadioButton	Returns the identifier of the checked radio button within a designated set of radio buttons
GetDlgItem	Returns a pointer to a temporary object for a specified control
GetDlgItemInt	Returns the numeric value represented by the text in a specified control
GetDlgItemText	Obtains the text displayed within a control
GetNextDlgGroupItem	Returns a pointer to a temporary object for the next (or previous) control within a group of controls
GetNextDlgTabItem	Returns a pointer to a temporary object for the next control (in the tab order) that's assigned the Tab Stop property
IsDlgButtonChecked	Returns the checked status of a check box or radio button
SendDlgItemMessage	Sends a message to a control
SetDlgItemInt	Converts an integer to text and assigns this text to a control
SetDlgItemText	Sets the text that's displayed by a control

TABLE 15.5: CDialog Member Functions for Managing Dialog Boxes and Controls

Function	Purpose
EndDialog	Closes a modal dialog box
GetDefID	Returns the identifier of the current default push button within the dialog box
GotoDlgCtrl	Assigns the input focus to a specified control within the dialog box
MapDialogRect	Converts the coordinates of a control in dialog units to screen units
NextDlgCtrl	Assigns the input focus to the next control in the dialog box tab order
PrevDlgCtrl	Assigns the input focus to the previous control in the dialog box tab order
SetDefID	Converts the specified push button control into the default push button

Next, add code as follows to the OnChangeSpacing function, which receives control whenever the user changes the contents of the Line Spacing: edit box:

```
void CFormat::OnChangeSpacing()
{
    // TODO: Add your control notification handler code here
    int Temp;
    Temp = (int)GetDlgItemInt (IDC_SPACING);
    if (Temp > 0 && Temp < 4)
        {
        m_Spacing = Temp;
        InvalidateRect (&m_RectSample);
        UpdateWindow ();
        }
}
```

OnChangeSpacing first calls CWnd::GetDlgItemInt to obtain the contents of the edit box as an integer value. If the value is in the valid range, it then saves it in the m_Spacing data member and forces the sample text to be redrawn.

Finally, you should add the following code to the OnPaint function, which is called whenever one of the message-handling functions you wrote invalidates an area of the dialog box, or whenever the dialog box needs redrawing due to some external event (such as the user's removing an overlapping window):

```
void CFormat::OnPaint()
{
    CPaintDC dc(this); // device context for painting

    // TODO: Add your message handler code here
    CFont Font;
    LOGFONT LF;
    int LineHeight;
    CFont *PtrOldFont;
    int X, Y;

    // fill LF with the features of a standard system font:
    CFont TempFont;
    if (m_Pitch == PITCH_VARIABLE)
        TempFont.CreateStockObject (SYSTEM_FONT);
    else
        TempFont.CreateStockObject (SYSTEM_FIXED_FONT);
    TempFont.GetObject (sizeof (LOGFONT), &LF);

    // now customize lfWeight, lfItalic, and lfUnderline fields:
    if (m_Bold)
        LF.lfWeight = FW_BOLD;
    if (m_Italic)
        LF.lfItalic = 1;
    if (m_Underline)
        LF.lfUnderline = 1;

    // create and select font:
    Font.CreateFontIndirect (&LF);
    PtrOldFont = dc.SelectObject (&Font);

    // set justification:
    switch (m_Justify)
        {
        case JUSTIFY_LEFT:
            dc.SetTextAlign (TA_LEFT);
            X = m_RectSample.left + 5;
            break;
        case JUSTIFY_CENTER:
```

```
        dc.SetTextAlign (TA_CENTER);
        X = (m_RectSample.left + m_RectSample.right) / 2;
        break;
    case JUSTIFY_RIGHT:
        dc.SetTextAlign (TA_RIGHT);
        X = m_RectSample.right - 5;
        break;
    }

    // set background mode:
    dc.SetBkMode (TRANSPARENT);

    // draw lines of text:
    LineHeight = LF.lfHeight * m_Spacing;
    Y = m_RectSample.top + 15;
    dc.TextOut (X, Y, "AaBbCdDdEeFf");
    Y += LineHeight;
    dc.TextOut (X, Y, "GhHhIiJjKkLl");
    Y += LineHeight;
    dc.TextOut (X, Y, "MmNnOoPpQqRr");

    // unselect font:
    dc.SelectObject (PtrOldFont);

    // Do not call CDialog::OnPaint() for painting messages
}
```

The OnPaint function serves only to redraw the three lines of sample text within the Sample group box; it *doesn't* need to redraw the controls, because the controls redraw themselves. An explanation of the different techniques used in drawing the lines of text will be given in Chapter 18; the following is a brief summary of the steps that OnPaint performs:

- It obtains the properties of the Windows System font (the fixed-pitch or variable-pitch System font, depending on the setting of m_Pitch).

- It modifies the font properties according to the values of the m_Bold, m_Italic, and m_Underline data members, and it creates a new font with the modified properties, which will be used to draw the text.

- It sets the text justification according to the value of m_Justify.

- It calls the CDC::TextOut function to draw the text, using the member variable m_Spacing to calculate the space between each line.

NOTE

If a window class is derived from CView, the CView class provides an OnPaint message-handling function, which prepares a device context object and then calls the OnDraw member function of the view window class. However, because a dialog class *isn't* derived from CView, it must provide an OnPaint function itself if it needs to repaint the dialog box window. Note, also, that an OnPaint function must create a device context object belonging to the CPaintDC MFC class (rather than the CClientDC class, which is used for creating device context objects within other types of functions). ClassWizard adds code to the OnPaint function to create the device context object for you.

Closing the Dialog Box

The MFC class CDialog provides default message handlers that receive control when the user closes the dialog box. When the user clicks the OK button, the CDialog::OnOK function receives control; this function calls CWnd::UpdateData to validate and transfer the data from the dialog box controls to the associated data members, and then it calls CDialog::EndDialog to close the dialog box. If the user cancels the dialog box, the CDialog::OnCancel function receives control, which simply calls CDialog::End-Dialog to close the dialog box.

If your program needs to perform any final tasks before the dialog box is closed, you can use ClassWizard to define your own versions of these message-handling functions. To define your own version of OnOK, select the IDOK object identifier and select the BN_CLICKED message. To define your own version of OnCancel, select the IDCANCEL object identifier and select the BN_CLICKED message.

As an example, the following is the OnOK function definition that would be generated by ClassWizard for the CFormat dialog class:

```
void CFormat::OnOK()
{
    // TODO: Add extra validation here

    CDialog::OnOK();
}
```

Notice that ClassWizard includes a call to the CDialog version of the function, which performs the required default processing. In either an OnOK or OnCancel function generated by ClassWizard, you should add your statements *before* the call to the base class function version (CDialog::OnOK or CDialog::OnCancel).

Displaying the Dialog Box

You've now completed coding the CFormat class, which contains the code that manages the Format dialog box once it has been displayed. The next phase is to provide the code that creates the dialog class object and displays the dialog box.

Modifying the Program Menu

The first step is to provide a menu command that allows the user to open the Format dialog box. To do this, open the ResourceView tab in the Workspace window for the FontDemo project, and double-click the IDR_MAINFRAME identifier under the Menu branch of the graph. In the menu editor, perform the following steps:

1. Delete the File pop-up menu.

2. Delete the Edit pop-up menu.

3. Insert a Text pop-up menu to the left of the Help menu. The properties of this menu are given in Table 15.6.

4. Add a Format command, a separator, and an Exit command to the new Text menu. The properties of these items are also listed in Table 15.6, and the completed Text menu is shown in Figure 15.13.

TABLE 15.6: The Properties of the Text Menu Items

ID:	Caption	Other Features
none	&Text	Popup
ID_TEXT_FORMAT	&Format...\tCtrl+F	none
none	none	Separator
ID_APP_EXIT	E&xit	none

FIGURE 15.13:

The completed Text menu for
the FontDemo program

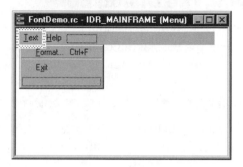

Next, add the keyboard accelerator for the Format command to the IDR_MAIN-
FRAME accelerator table. Use the method described in previous chapters, specifying the identifier of the Format command, ID_TEXT_FORMAT, and the Ctrl+F
keystroke. You're now finished defining the program resources, and you can save
your work by choosing the File ➢ Save All menu command or clicking the Save
All button on the Standard toolbar.

Adding a Menu Message Handler

Your next task is to define a message-handling function that receives control
when the user chooses the Format menu command (or presses the Ctrl+F accelerator keystroke). To do this, run ClassWizard, open the Message Maps tab, and
choose the CFontDemoDoc class name in the Class Name: list box, so that the
message-handling function will be added to the program's document class. In the
FontDemo program, the choice of class to handle the Format menu command is
somewhat arbitrary. In an actual word processing application, however, the Format command would directly affect the data stored in the document (rather than
a specific *view* of the document or the application as a whole), and therefore the
command would best be handled by the document class.

Now, select the identifier for the Format command, ID_TEXT_FORMAT, in the
Object IDs: list; select the COMMAND message in the Messages: list; and click the
Add Function... button to define the message-handling function. Accept the
default function name, OnTextFormat. Click the OK button in the ClassWizard
dialog box to close it (you'll add code to OnTextFormat later).

Modifying the Document and View Code

You'll now make the required code additions to the document and view classes for displaying the dialog box and using the data obtained from the dialog box to print the text in the program's view window. First, add the following six data member definitions to the beginning of the CFontDemoDoc class definition in the file FontDemoDoc.h:

```
class CFontDemoDoc : public CDocument
{
public:
   BOOL m_Bold;
   BOOL m_Italic;
   int m_Justify;
   int m_Pitch;
   int m_Spacing;
   BOOL m_Underline;

// remainder of CFontDemoDoc definition ...
```

These data members store the formatting features of the document; they correspond to the identically named data members of the dialog class. Next, add code to initialize these data members to the CFontDemoDoc constructor in the file Font-DemoDoc.cpp:

```
CFontDemoDoc::CFontDemoDoc()
{
   // TODO: add one-time construction code here
   m_Bold = FALSE;
   m_Italic = FALSE;
   m_Justify = JUSTIFY_LEFT;
   m_Pitch = PITCH_VARIABLE;
   m_Spacing = 1;
   m_Underline = FALSE;
}
```

These initializations will cause the text to be displayed without the bold, italic, or underlined style; in a variable-pitch font; left-justified; and with single-line spacing.

The next step is to add the code for displaying the Format dialog box to the FontDemoDoc.cpp file. At the beginning of this file, insert an `include` statement for the Format.h header file, so that the dialog class definition is available within FontDemoDoc.cpp:

```
// FontDemoDoc.cpp : implementation of the CFontDemoDoc class
//

#include "stdafx.h"
#include "FontDemo.h"

#include "FontDemoDoc.h"
#include "format.h"
```

Then add code as follows to the `OnTextFormat` function that you generated using ClassWizard:

```
/////////////////////////////////////////////////////////////////
///////////
// CFontDemoDoc commands

void CFontDemoDoc::OnTextFormat()
{
    // TODO: Add your command handler code here

    // declare a dialog class object:
    CFormat FormatDlg;

    // initialize dialog class data members:
    FormatDlg.m_Bold = m_Bold;
    FormatDlg.m_Italic = m_Italic;
    FormatDlg.m_Justify = m_Justify;
    FormatDlg.m_Pitch = m_Pitch;
    FormatDlg.m_Spacing = m_Spacing;
    FormatDlg.m_Underline = m_Underline;

    // display dialog box:
    if (FormatDlg.DoModal () == IDOK)
        {
        // save values set in dialog box:
        m_Bold = FormatDlg.m_Bold;
        m_Italic = FormatDlg.m_Italic;
        m_Justify = FormatDlg.m_Justify;
```

```
m_Pitch = FormatDlg.m_Pitch;
m_Spacing = FormatDlg.m_Spacing;
m_Underline = FormatDlg.m_Underline;

// redraw the text:
UpdateAllViews (NULL);
}
}
```

The added code first creates an instance of the CFormat dialog class. An instance of a dialog class for a modal dialog box is normally defined as a local variable (which is destroyed as soon as the function in which it's defined returns), because a modal dialog box is displayed only temporarily and is closed before the function returns.

The added code next copies the values of the document object's data members that store the formatting information to the corresponding data members of the dialog object, so that the current values of these data members will be displayed when the dialog box is first opened. (Recall that when the dialog box is first displayed, the MFC code automatically transfers the values of the dialog object's data members to the corresponding controls.)

Next, the code calls the CDialog member function DoModal, which displays the dialog box. DoModal doesn't return until the user closes the dialog box. If the user closes the dialog box by clicking the OK button, DoModal returns the value IDOK. In this case, OnTextFormat transfers the new values of the dialog object's data members back to the document object's data members, and then calls UpdateAllViews, which forces the view window to be erased and the OnDraw member function of the view class to receive control. (Recall that when the user dismisses the dialog box by clicking the OK button, the MFC code automatically validates the contents of the Line Spacing: edit box, and transfers the current contents of the controls back to the corresponding data members of the dialog object.)

If, however, the user cancels the dialog box, DoModal returns IDCANCEL. In this case, the code leaves the document object's data members unchanged. (When the user cancels the dialog box, the MFC code *doesn't* validate or transfer the contents of the controls.)

When OnDraw receives control, it redraws the lines of text in the view window, using the new formatting values stored in the document object's data members. You should now open the file FontDemoView.cpp and add the code required to perform this task. First, insert an include statement for Format.h at the beginning of the file, so that the enumerators referring to the radio buttons and corresponding styles can be used within FontDemoView.cpp:

```
// FontDemoView.cpp : implementation of the CFontDemoView class
//

#include "stdafx.h"
#include "FontDemo.h"

#include "FontDemoDoc.h"
#include "FontDemoView.h"
#include "format.h"
```

Then add the code for redrawing the lines to the OnDraw function definition, as follows:

```
///////////////////////////////////////////////////////////////
////////////
// CFontDemoView drawing

void CFontDemoView::OnDraw(CDC* pDC)
{
    CFontDemoDoc* pDoc = GetDocument();
    ASSERT_VALID(pDoc);

    // TODO: add draw code for native data here

    RECT ClientRect;
    CFont Font;
    LOGFONT LF;
    int LineHeight;
    CFont *PtrOldFont;
    int X, Y;

    // fill LF with the features of a standard system font:
    CFont TempFont;
    if (pDoc->m_Pitch == PITCH_VARIABLE)
        TempFont.CreateStockObject (SYSTEM_FONT);
    else
        TempFont.CreateStockObject (SYSTEM_FIXED_FONT);
    TempFont.GetObject (sizeof (LOGFONT), &LF);

    // now customize lfWeight, lfItalic, and lfUnderline fields:
    if (pDoc->m_Bold)
        LF.lfWeight = FW_BOLD;
```

```
if (pDoc->m_Italic)
   LF.lfItalic = 1;
if (pDoc->m_Underline)
   LF.lfUnderline = 1;

// create and select font:
Font.CreateFontIndirect (&LF);
PtrOldFont = pDC->SelectObject (&Font);

// set justification:
GetClientRect (&ClientRect);
switch (pDoc->m_Justify)
   {
   case JUSTIFY_LEFT:
      pDC->SetTextAlign (TA_LEFT);
      X = ClientRect.left + 5;
      break;
   case JUSTIFY_CENTER:
      pDC->SetTextAlign (TA_CENTER);
      X = ClientRect.right / 2;
      break;
   case JUSTIFY_RIGHT:
      pDC->SetTextAlign (TA_RIGHT);
      X = ClientRect.right - 5;
      break;
   }

// set text color and background mode:
pDC->SetTextColor (::GetSysColor (COLOR_WINDOWTEXT));
pDC->SetBkMode (TRANSPARENT);

// draw lines:
LineHeight = LF.lfHeight * pDoc->m_Spacing;
Y = 5;
pDC->TextOut (X, Y, "This is the first line of sample text.");
Y += LineHeight;
pDC->TextOut (X, Y, "This is the second line of sample "
                    "text.");
Y += LineHeight;
pDC->TextOut (X, Y, "This is the third line of sample text.");

// unselect font:
pDC->SelectObject (PtrOldFont);
}
```

This code is similar to the code you added to the OnPaint function of the dialog class. Notice, however, that rather than simply drawing the text using the default black color, it calls ::GetSysColor and CDC::SetTextColor to set the text to the "Window Font" color that the user has selected in the Display program of the Windows Control Panel (the MFC code automatically paints the window background using the "Window" color). The techniques used in OnDraw will be explained in Chapter 18.

Changing the Program Title

As the FontDemo program is written, the MFC code displays the text "Untitled - FontDemo" in the program's title bar, falsely implying that the program creates documents. To set a more appropriate title, add a call to CWnd::SetWindowText for the main frame window object near the end of the InitInstance function in FontDemo.cpp:

```
// The one and only window has been initialized, so show and
// update it.
m_pMainWnd->ShowWindow(SW_SHOW);
m_pMainWnd->UpdateWindow();

m_pMainWnd->SetWindowText ("System Font Demo");

return TRUE;
}
```

As you saw in Chapter 12, m_pMainWnd is a pointer to the main frame window object. Note that the call to SetWindowText must come *after* the call to Process-ShellCommand, which creates the main frame window.

You've now finished modifying FontDemo, and you can build and run the program.

The FontDemo Source Code

The following listings, Listings 15.1 through 15.10, contain the C++ source code for the FontDemo program you created in this chapter. Note that a copy of these files is included in the \FontDemo companion-CD folder.

Listing 15.1

```cpp
// FontDemo.h : main header file for the FONTDEMO application
//

#if !defined(AFX_FONTDEMO_H__180B6FC5_9FFD_11D1_80FC_00C0F6A83B7F__INCLUDED_)
#define AFX_FONTDEMO_H__180B6FC5_9FFD_11D1_80FC_00C0F6A83B7F__INCLUDED_

#if _MSC_VER > 1000
#pragma once
#endif // _MSC_VER > 1000

#ifndef __AFXWIN_H__
    #error include 'stdafx.h' before including this file for PCH
#endif

#include "resource.h"        // main symbols

/////////////////////////////////////////////////////////////////////////////
// CFontDemoApp:
// See FontDemo.cpp for the implementation of this class
//

class CFontDemoApp : public CWinApp
{
public:
    CFontDemoApp();

// Overrides
    // ClassWizard generated virtual function overrides
    //{{AFX_VIRTUAL(CFontDemoApp)
    public:
    virtual BOOL InitInstance();
    //}}AFX_VIRTUAL

// Implementation
    //{{AFX_MSG(CFontDemoApp)
    afx_msg void OnAppAbout();
        // NOTE - the ClassWizard will add and remove member functions here.
        //    DO NOT EDIT what you see in these blocks of generated code !
    //}}AFX_MSG
    DECLARE_MESSAGE_MAP()
};
```

```
//////////////////////////////////////////////////////////////////////////

//{{AFX_INSERT_LOCATION}}
// Microsoft Visual C++ will insert additional declarations immediately before
// the previous line.

#endif
// !defined(AFX_FONTDEMO_H__180B6FC5_9FFD_11D1_80FC_00C0F6A83B7F__INCLUDED_)
```

Listing 15.2

```
// FontDemo.cpp : Defines the class behaviors for the application.
//

#include "stdafx.h"
#include "FontDemo.h"

#include "MainFrm.h"
#include "FontDemoDoc.h"
#include "FontDemoView.h"

#ifdef _DEBUG
#define new DEBUG_NEW
#undef THIS_FILE
static char THIS_FILE[] = __FILE__;
#endif

//////////////////////////////////////////////////////////////////////////
// CFontDemoApp

BEGIN_MESSAGE_MAP(CFontDemoApp, CWinApp)
    //{{AFX_MSG_MAP(CFontDemoApp)
    ON_COMMAND(ID_APP_ABOUT, OnAppAbout)
        // NOTE - the ClassWizard will add and remove mapping macros here.
        //    DO NOT EDIT what you see in these blocks of generated code!
    //}}AFX_MSG_MAP
    // Standard file based document commands
    ON_COMMAND(ID_FILE_NEW, CWinApp::OnFileNew)
    ON_COMMAND(ID_FILE_OPEN, CWinApp::OnFileOpen)
END_MESSAGE_MAP()
```

```
//////////////////////////////////////////////////////////////////////
// CFontDemoApp construction

CFontDemoApp::CFontDemoApp()
{
    // TODO: add construction code here,
    // Place all significant initialization in InitInstance
}


//////////////////////////////////////////////////////////////////////
// The one and only CFontDemoApp object

CFontDemoApp theApp;


//////////////////////////////////////////////////////////////////////
// CFontDemoApp initialization

BOOL CFontDemoApp::InitInstance()
{
    // Standard initialization
    // If you are not using these features and wish to reduce the size
    //  of your final executable, you should remove from the following
    //  the specific initialization routines you do not need.

#ifdef _AFXDLL
    Enable3dControls();          // Call this when using MFC in a shared DLL
#else
    Enable3dControlsStatic();  // Call this when linking to MFC statically
#endif

    // Change the registry key under which our settings are stored.
    // TODO: You should modify this string to be something appropriate
    // such as the name of your company or organization.
    SetRegistryKey(_T("Local AppWizard-Generated Applications"));

    LoadStdProfileSettings();  // Load standard INI file options (including MRU)

    // Register the application's document templates.  Document templates
    //  serve as the connection between documents, frame windows and views.
```

```
   CSingleDocTemplate* pDocTemplate;
   pDocTemplate = new CSingleDocTemplate(
       IDR_MAINFRAME,
       RUNTIME_CLASS(CFontDemoDoc),
       RUNTIME_CLASS(CMainFrame),        // main SDI frame window
       RUNTIME_CLASS(CFontDemoView));
   AddDocTemplate(pDocTemplate);

   // Parse command line for standard shell commands, DDE, file open
   CCommandLineInfo cmdInfo;
   ParseCommandLine(cmdInfo);

   // Dispatch commands specified on the command line
   if (!ProcessShellCommand(cmdInfo))
       return FALSE;

   // The one and only window has been initialized, so show and update it.
   m_pMainWnd->ShowWindow(SW_SHOW);
   m_pMainWnd->UpdateWindow();

   m_pMainWnd->SetWindowText ("System Font Demo");

   return TRUE;
}


/////////////////////////////////////////////////////////////////////////////
// CAboutDlg dialog used for App About

class CAboutDlg : public CDialog
{
public:
   CAboutDlg();

// Dialog Data
   //{{AFX_DATA(CAboutDlg)
   enum { IDD = IDD_ABOUTBOX };
   //}}AFX_DATA

   // ClassWizard generated virtual function overrides
   //{{AFX_VIRTUAL(CAboutDlg)
```

```
   protected:
   virtual void DoDataExchange(CDataExchange* pDX);      // DDX/DDV support
   //}}AFX_VIRTUAL

// Implementation
protected:
   //{{AFX_MSG(CAboutDlg)
      // No message handlers
   //}}AFX_MSG
   DECLARE_MESSAGE_MAP()
};

CAboutDlg::CAboutDlg() : CDialog(CAboutDlg::IDD)
{
   //{{AFX_DATA_INIT(CAboutDlg)
   //}}AFX_DATA_INIT
}

void CAboutDlg::DoDataExchange(CDataExchange* pDX)
{
   CDialog::DoDataExchange(pDX);
   //{{AFX_DATA_MAP(CAboutDlg)
   //}}AFX_DATA_MAP
}

BEGIN_MESSAGE_MAP(CAboutDlg, CDialog)
   //{{AFX_MSG_MAP(CAboutDlg)
      // No message handlers
   //}}AFX_MSG_MAP
END_MESSAGE_MAP()

// App command to run the dialog
void CFontDemoApp::OnAppAbout()
{
   CAboutDlg aboutDlg;
   aboutDlg.DoModal();
}

/////////////////////////////////////////////////////////////////////////
// CFontDemoApp message handlers
```

Listing 15.3

```
// FontDemoDoc.h : interface of the CFontDemoDoc class
//
/////////////////////////////////////////////////////////////////////

#if !defined(AFX_FONTDEMODOC_H__180B6FCB_9FFD_11D1_80FC_00C0F6A83B7F__INCLUDED_)
#define AFX_FONTDEMODOC_H__180B6FCB_9FFD_11D1_80FC_00C0F6A83B7F__INCLUDED_

#if _MSC_VER > 1000
#pragma once
#endif // _MSC_VER > 1000


class CFontDemoDoc : public CDocument
{
public:
    BOOL m_Bold;
    BOOL m_Italic;
    int m_Justify;
    int m_Pitch;
    int m_Spacing;
    BOOL m_Underline;

protected: // create from serialization only
    CFontDemoDoc();
    DECLARE_DYNCREATE(CFontDemoDoc)

// Attributes
public:

// Operations
public:

// Overrides
    // ClassWizard generated virtual function overrides
    //{{AFX_VIRTUAL(CFontDemoDoc)
    public:
    virtual BOOL OnNewDocument();
    virtual void Serialize(CArchive& ar);
    //}}AFX_VIRTUAL
```

```
// Implementation
public:
    virtual ~CFontDemoDoc();
#ifdef _DEBUG
    virtual void AssertValid() const;
    virtual void Dump(CDumpContext& dc) const;
#endif

protected:

// Generated message map functions
protected:
    //{{AFX_MSG(CFontDemoDoc)
    afx_msg void OnTextFormat();
    //}}AFX_MSG
    DECLARE_MESSAGE_MAP()
};

//////////////////////////////////////////////////////////////////////////

//{{AFX_INSERT_LOCATION}}
// Microsoft Visual C++ will insert additional declarations immediately before
// the previous line.

#endif
// !defined(AFX_FONTDEMODOC_H__180B6FCB_9FFD_11D1_80FC_00C0F6A83B7F__INCLUDED_)
```

Listing 15.4

```
// FontDemoDoc.cpp : implementation of the CFontDemoDoc class
//

#include "stdafx.h"
#include "FontDemo.h"

#include "FontDemoDoc.h"
#include "format.h"

#ifdef _DEBUG
#define new DEBUG_NEW
#undef THIS_FILE
static char THIS_FILE[] = __FILE__;
#endif
```

```
///////////////////////////////////////////////////////////////////////
// CFontDemoDoc

IMPLEMENT_DYNCREATE(CFontDemoDoc, CDocument)

BEGIN_MESSAGE_MAP(CFontDemoDoc, CDocument)
    //{{AFX_MSG_MAP(CFontDemoDoc)
    ON_COMMAND(ID_TEXT_FORMAT, OnTextFormat)
    //}}AFX_MSG_MAP
END_MESSAGE_MAP()

///////////////////////////////////////////////////////////////////////
// CFontDemoDoc construction/destruction

CFontDemoDoc::CFontDemoDoc()
{
    // TODO: add one-time construction code here
    m_Bold = FALSE;
    m_Italic = FALSE;
    m_Justify = JUSTIFY_LEFT;
    m_Pitch = PITCH_VARIABLE;
    m_Spacing = 1;
    m_Underline = FALSE;
}

CFontDemoDoc::~CFontDemoDoc()
{
}

BOOL CFontDemoDoc::OnNewDocument()
{
    if (!CDocument::OnNewDocument())
        return FALSE;

    // TODO: add reinitialization code here
    // (SDI documents will reuse this document)

    return TRUE;
}
```

```
///////////////////////////////////////////////////////////////////////////
// CFontDemoDoc serialization

void CFontDemoDoc::Serialize(CArchive& ar)
{
   if (ar.IsStoring())
   {
      // TODO: add storing code here
   }
   else
   {
      // TODO: add loading code here
   }
}


///////////////////////////////////////////////////////////////////////////
// CFontDemoDoc diagnostics

#ifdef _DEBUG
void CFontDemoDoc::AssertValid() const
{
   CDocument::AssertValid();
}

void CFontDemoDoc::Dump(CDumpContext& dc) const
{
   CDocument::Dump(dc);
}
#endif //_DEBUG


///////////////////////////////////////////////////////////////////////////
// CFontDemoDoc commands

void CFontDemoDoc::OnTextFormat()
{
   // TODO: Add your command handler code here

   // declare a dialog class object:
   CFormat FormatDlg;

   // initialize dialog class data members:
   FormatDlg.m_Bold = m_Bold;
```

```
      FormatDlg.m_Italic = m_Italic;
      FormatDlg.m_Justify = m_Justify;
      FormatDlg.m_Pitch = m_Pitch;
      FormatDlg.m_Spacing = m_Spacing;
      FormatDlg.m_Underline = m_Underline;

      // display dialog box:
      if (FormatDlg.DoModal () == IDOK)
         {
         // save values set in dialog box:
         m_Bold = FormatDlg.m_Bold;
         m_Italic = FormatDlg.m_Italic;
         m_Justify = FormatDlg.m_Justify;
         m_Pitch = FormatDlg.m_Pitch;
         m_Spacing = FormatDlg.m_Spacing;
         m_Underline = FormatDlg.m_Underline;

         // redraw the text:
         UpdateAllViews (NULL);
         }
   }
```

Listing 15.5

```
// MainFrm.h : interface of the CMainFrame class
//
/////////////////////////////////////////////////////////////////////

#if !defined(AFX_MAINFRM_H__180B6FC9_9FFD_11D1_80FC_00C0F6A83B7F__INCLUDED_)
#define AFX_MAINFRM_H__180B6FC9_9FFD_11D1_80FC_00C0F6A83B7F__INCLUDED_

#if _MSC_VER > 1000
#pragma once
#endif // _MSC_VER > 1000

class CMainFrame : public CFrameWnd
{
```

```
protected: // create from serialization only
   CMainFrame();
   DECLARE_DYNCREATE(CMainFrame)

// Attributes
public:

// Operations
public:

// Overrides
   // ClassWizard generated virtual function overrides
   //{{AFX_VIRTUAL(CMainFrame)
   virtual BOOL PreCreateWindow(CREATESTRUCT& cs);
   //}}AFX_VIRTUAL

// Implementation
public:
   virtual ~CMainFrame();
#ifdef _DEBUG
   virtual void AssertValid() const;
   virtual void Dump(CDumpContext& dc) const;
#endif

// Generated message map functions
protected:
   //{{AFX_MSG(CMainFrame)
      // NOTE - the ClassWizard will add and remove member functions here.
      //    DO NOT EDIT what you see in these blocks of generated code!
   //}}AFX_MSG
   DECLARE_MESSAGE_MAP()
};

/////////////////////////////////////////////////////////////////////////

//{{AFX_INSERT_LOCATION}}
// Microsoft Visual C++ will insert additional declarations immediately before
// the previous line.

#endif
// !defined(AFX_MAINFRM_H__180B6FC9_9FFD_11D1_80FC_00C0F6A83B7F__INCLUDED_)
```

Listing 15.6

```cpp
// MainFrm.cpp : implementation of the CMainFrame class
//

#include "stdafx.h"
#include "FontDemo.h"

#include "MainFrm.h"

#ifdef _DEBUG
#define new DEBUG_NEW
#undef THIS_FILE
static char THIS_FILE[] = __FILE__;
#endif

/////////////////////////////////////////////////////////////////////////////
// CMainFrame

IMPLEMENT_DYNCREATE(CMainFrame, CFrameWnd)

BEGIN_MESSAGE_MAP(CMainFrame, CFrameWnd)
    //{{AFX_MSG_MAP(CMainFrame)
        // NOTE - the ClassWizard will add and remove mapping macros here.
        //    DO NOT EDIT what you see in these blocks of generated code !
    //}}AFX_MSG_MAP
END_MESSAGE_MAP()

/////////////////////////////////////////////////////////////////////////////
// CMainFrame construction/destruction

CMainFrame::CMainFrame()
{
    // TODO: add member initialization code here

}

CMainFrame::~CMainFrame()
{
}
```

```
BOOL CMainFrame::PreCreateWindow(CREATESTRUCT& cs)
{
    if( !CFrameWnd::PreCreateWindow(cs) )
        return FALSE;
    // TODO: Modify the Window class or styles here by modifying
    //   the CREATESTRUCT cs

    return TRUE;
}


/////////////////////////////////////////////////////////////////////////////
// CMainFrame diagnostics

#ifdef _DEBUG
void CMainFrame::AssertValid() const
{
    CFrameWnd::AssertValid();
}

void CMainFrame::Dump(CDumpContext& dc) const
{
    CFrameWnd::Dump(dc);
}


#endif //_DEBUG


/////////////////////////////////////////////////////////////////////////////
// CMainFrame message handlers
```

Listing 15.7

```
// FontDemoView.h : interface of the CFontDemoView class
//
/////////////////////////////////////////////////////////////////////////////

#if !defined(AFX_FONTDEMOVIEW_H__180B6FCD_9FFD_11D1_80FC_00C0F6A83B7F__INCLUDED_)
#define AFX_FONTDEMOVIEW_H__180B6FCD_9FFD_11D1_80FC_00C0F6A83B7F__INCLUDED_

#if _MSC_VER > 1000
#pragma once
#endif // _MSC_VER > 1000
```

```
class CFontDemoView : public CView
{
protected: // create from serialization only
    CFontDemoView();
    DECLARE_DYNCREATE(CFontDemoView)

// Attributes
public:
    CFontDemoDoc* GetDocument();

// Operations
public:

// Overrides
    // ClassWizard generated virtual function overrides
    //{{AFX_VIRTUAL(CFontDemoView)
    public:
    virtual void OnDraw(CDC* pDC);  // overridden to draw this view
    virtual BOOL PreCreateWindow(CREATESTRUCT& cs);
    protected:
    //}}AFX_VIRTUAL

// Implementation
public:
    virtual ~CFontDemoView();
#ifdef _DEBUG
    virtual void AssertValid() const;
    virtual void Dump(CDumpContext& dc) const;
#endif

protected:

// Generated message map functions
protected:
    //{{AFX_MSG(CFontDemoView)
        // NOTE - the ClassWizard will add and remove member functions here.
        //    DO NOT EDIT what you see in these blocks of generated code !
    //}}AFX_MSG
    DECLARE_MESSAGE_MAP()
};
```

```
#ifndef _DEBUG  // debug version in FontDemoView.cpp
inline CFontDemoDoc* CFontDemoView::GetDocument()
   { return (CFontDemoDoc*)m_pDocument; }
#endif


/////////////////////////////////////////////////////////////////////////

//{{AFX_INSERT_LOCATION}}
// Microsoft Visual C++ will insert additional declarations immediately before
// the previous line.

#endif
// !defined(AFX_FONTDEMOVIEW_H__180B6FCD_9FFD_11D1_80FC_00C0F6A83B7F__INCLUDED_)
```

Listing 15.8

```
// FontDemoView.cpp : implementation of the CFontDemoView class
//

#include "stdafx.h"
#include "FontDemo.h"

#include "FontDemoDoc.h"
#include "FontDemoView.h"
#include "format.h"

#ifdef _DEBUG
#define new DEBUG_NEW
#undef THIS_FILE
static char THIS_FILE[] = __FILE__;
#endif


/////////////////////////////////////////////////////////////////////////
// CFontDemoView

IMPLEMENT_DYNCREATE(CFontDemoView, CView)

BEGIN_MESSAGE_MAP(CFontDemoView, CView)
   //{{AFX_MSG_MAP(CFontDemoView)
      // NOTE - the ClassWizard will add and remove mapping macros here.
      //    DO NOT EDIT what you see in these blocks of generated code!
   //}}AFX_MSG_MAP
END_MESSAGE_MAP()
```

```
/////////////////////////////////////////////////////////////////////
// CFontDemoView construction/destruction

CFontDemoView::CFontDemoView()
{
   // TODO: add construction code here

}

CFontDemoView::~CFontDemoView()
{
}

BOOL CFontDemoView::PreCreateWindow(CREATESTRUCT& cs)
{
   // TODO: Modify the Window class or styles here by modifying
   //   the CREATESTRUCT cs

   return CView::PreCreateWindow(cs);
}

/////////////////////////////////////////////////////////////////////
// CFontDemoView drawing

void CFontDemoView::OnDraw(CDC* pDC)
{
   CFontDemoDoc* pDoc = GetDocument();
   ASSERT_VALID(pDoc);

   // TODO: add draw code for native data here

   RECT ClientRect;
   CFont Font;
   LOGFONT LF;
   int LineHeight;
   CFont *PtrOldFont;
   int X, Y;

   // fill LF with the features of a standard system font:
   CFont TempFont;
   if (pDoc->m_Pitch == PITCH_VARIABLE)
      TempFont.CreateStockObject (SYSTEM_FONT);
```

```
else
   TempFont.CreateStockObject (SYSTEM_FIXED_FONT);
TempFont.GetObject (sizeof (LOGFONT), &LF);

// now customize lfWeight, lfItalic, and lfUnderline fields:
if (pDoc->m_Bold)
   LF.lfWeight = FW_BOLD;
if (pDoc->m_Italic)
   LF.lfItalic = 1;
if (pDoc->m_Underline)
   LF.lfUnderline = 1;

// create and select font:
Font.CreateFontIndirect (&LF);
PtrOldFont = pDC->SelectObject (&Font);

// set justification:
GetClientRect (&ClientRect);
switch (pDoc->m_Justify)
   {
   case JUSTIFY_LEFT:
      pDC->SetTextAlign (TA_LEFT);
      X = ClientRect.left + 5;
      break;
   case JUSTIFY_CENTER:
      pDC->SetTextAlign (TA_CENTER);
      X = ClientRect.right / 2;
      break;
   case JUSTIFY_RIGHT:
      pDC->SetTextAlign (TA_RIGHT);
      X = ClientRect.right - 5;
      break;
   }

// set text color and background mode:
pDC->SetTextColor (::GetSysColor (COLOR_WINDOWTEXT));
pDC->SetBkMode (TRANSPARENT);

// draw lines:
LineHeight = LF.lfHeight * pDoc->m_Spacing;
Y = 5;
pDC->TextOut (X, Y, "This is the first line of sample text.");
```

```
   Y += LineHeight;
   pDC->TextOut (X, Y, "This is the second line of sample text.");
   Y += LineHeight;
   pDC->TextOut (X, Y, "This is the third line of sample text.");

   // unselect font:
   pDC->SelectObject (PtrOldFont);
}

/////////////////////////////////////////////////////////////////////////////
// CFontDemoView diagnostics

#ifdef _DEBUG
void CFontDemoView::AssertValid() const
{
   CView::AssertValid();
}

void CFontDemoView::Dump(CDumpContext& dc) const
{
   CView::Dump(dc);
}

CFontDemoDoc* CFontDemoView::GetDocument() // non-debug version is inline
{
   ASSERT(m_pDocument->IsKindOf(RUNTIME_CLASS(CFontDemoDoc)));
   return (CFontDemoDoc*)m_pDocument;
}
#endif //_DEBUG

/////////////////////////////////////////////////////////////////////////////
// CFontDemoView message handlers
```

Listing 15.9

```
// Format.h : header file
//

#if !defined(AFX_FORMAT_H__06955974_A0B9_11D1_80FC_00C0F6A83B7F__INCLUDED_)
#define AFX_FORMAT_H__06955974_A0B9_11D1_80FC_00C0F6A83B7F__INCLUDED_
```

```
#if _MSC_VER > 1000
#pragma once
#endif // _MSC_VER > 1000

enum {JUSTIFY_LEFT, JUSTIFY_CENTER, JUSTIFY_RIGHT};
enum {PITCH_VARIABLE, PITCH_FIXED};

/////////////////////////////////////////////////////////////////////////////
// CFormat dialog

class CFormat : public CDialog
{
protected:
   RECT m_RectSample;

// Construction
public:
   CFormat(CWnd* pParent = NULL);   // standard constructor

// Dialog Data
   //{{AFX_DATA(CFormat)
   enum { IDD = IDD_DIALOG1 };
   CEdit m_SpacingEdit;
   BOOL  m_Bold;
   BOOL  m_Italic;
   BOOL  m_Underline;
   int      m_Justify;
   int      m_Pitch;
   int      m_Spacing;
   //}}AFX_DATA


// Overrides
   // ClassWizard generated virtual function overrides
   //{{AFX_VIRTUAL(CFormat)
   protected:
   virtual void DoDataExchange(CDataExchange* pDX);    // DDX/DDV support
   //}}AFX_VIRTUAL

// Implementation
protected:
```

```
    // Generated message map functions
    //{{AFX_MSG(CFormat)
    virtual BOOL OnInitDialog();
    afx_msg void OnPaint();
    afx_msg void OnBold();
    afx_msg void OnCenter();
    afx_msg void OnFixed();
    afx_msg void OnItalic();
    afx_msg void OnLeft();
    afx_msg void OnRight();
    afx_msg void OnUnderline();
    afx_msg void OnVariable();
    afx_msg void OnChangeSpacing();
    //}}AFX_MSG
    DECLARE_MESSAGE_MAP()
};


//{{AFX_INSERT_LOCATION}}
// Microsoft Visual C++ will insert additional declarations immediately before
// the previous line.

#endif
// !defined(AFX_FORMAT_H__06955974_A0B9_11D1_80FC_00C0F6A83B7F__INCLUDED_)
```

Listing 15.10

```
// Format.cpp : implementation file
//

#include "stdafx.h"
#include "FontDemo.h"
#include "Format.h"

#ifdef _DEBUG
#define new DEBUG_NEW
#undef THIS_FILE
static char THIS_FILE[] = __FILE__;
#endif


/////////////////////////////////////////////////////////////////////////
// CFormat dialog
```

```
CFormat::CFormat(CWnd* pParent /*=NULL*/)
    : CDialog(CFormat::IDD, pParent)
{
    //{{AFX_DATA_INIT(CFormat)
    m_Bold = FALSE;
    m_Italic = FALSE;
    m_Underline = FALSE;
    m_Justify = -1;
    m_Pitch = -1;
    m_Spacing = 0;
    //}}AFX_DATA_INIT
}


void CFormat::DoDataExchange(CDataExchange* pDX)
{
    CDialog::DoDataExchange(pDX);
    //{{AFX_DATA_MAP(CFormat)
    DDX_Control(pDX, IDC_SPACING, m_SpacingEdit);
    DDX_Check(pDX, IDC_BOLD, m_Bold);
    DDX_Check(pDX, IDC_ITALIC, m_Italic);
    DDX_Check(pDX, IDC_UNDERLINE, m_Underline);
    DDX_Radio(pDX, IDC_LEFT, m_Justify);
    DDX_Radio(pDX, IDC_VARIABLE, m_Pitch);
    DDX_Text(pDX, IDC_SPACING, m_Spacing);
    DDV_MinMaxInt(pDX, m_Spacing, 1, 3);
    //}}AFX_DATA_MAP
}


BEGIN_MESSAGE_MAP(CFormat, CDialog)
    //{{AFX_MSG_MAP(CFormat)
    ON_WM_PAINT()
    ON_BN_CLICKED(IDC_BOLD, OnBold)
    ON_BN_CLICKED(IDC_CENTER, OnCenter)
    ON_BN_CLICKED(IDC_FIXED, OnFixed)
    ON_BN_CLICKED(IDC_ITALIC, OnItalic)
    ON_BN_CLICKED(IDC_LEFT, OnLeft)
    ON_BN_CLICKED(IDC_RIGHT, OnRight)
    ON_BN_CLICKED(IDC_UNDERLINE, OnUnderline)
    ON_BN_CLICKED(IDC_VARIABLE, OnVariable)
    ON_EN_CHANGE(IDC_SPACING, OnChangeSpacing)
    //}}AFX_MSG_MAP
END_MESSAGE_MAP()
```

```
//////////////////////////////////////////////////////////////////////////
// CFormat message handlers

BOOL CFormat::OnInitDialog()
{
   CDialog::OnInitDialog();

   // TODO: Add extra initialization here
   GetDlgItem (IDC_SAMPLE)->GetWindowRect (&m_RectSample);
   ScreenToClient (&m_RectSample);

   m_SpacingEdit.LimitText (1);

   return TRUE;  // return TRUE unless you set the focus to a control
                 // EXCEPTION: OCX Property Pages should return FALSE
}

void CFormat::OnPaint()
{
   CPaintDC dc(this); // device context for painting

   // TODO: Add your message handler code here
   CFont Font;
   LOGFONT LF;
   int LineHeight;
   CFont *PtrOldFont;
   int X, Y;

   // fill LF with the features of a standard system font:
   CFont TempFont;
   if (m_Pitch == PITCH_VARIABLE)
      TempFont.CreateStockObject (SYSTEM_FONT);
   else
      TempFont.CreateStockObject (SYSTEM_FIXED_FONT);
   TempFont.GetObject (sizeof (LOGFONT), &LF);

   // now customize lfWeight, lfItalic, and lfUnderline fields:
   if (m_Bold)
      LF.lfWeight = FW_BOLD;
   if (m_Italic)
      LF.lfItalic = 1;
```

```
if (m_Underline)
   LF.lfUnderline = 1;

// create and select font:
Font.CreateFontIndirect (&LF);
PtrOldFont = dc.SelectObject (&Font);

// set justification:
switch (m_Justify)
   {
   case JUSTIFY_LEFT:
      dc.SetTextAlign (TA_LEFT);
      X = m_RectSample.left + 5;
      break;
   case JUSTIFY_CENTER:
      dc.SetTextAlign (TA_CENTER);
      X = (m_RectSample.left + m_RectSample.right) / 2;
      break;
   case JUSTIFY_RIGHT:
      dc.SetTextAlign (TA_RIGHT);
      X = m_RectSample.right - 5;
      break;
   }

// set background mode:
dc.SetBkMode (TRANSPARENT);

// draw lines of text:
LineHeight = LF.lfHeight * m_Spacing;
Y = m_RectSample.top + 15;
dc.TextOut (X, Y, "AaBbCcDdEeFf");
Y += LineHeight;
dc.TextOut (X, Y, "GhHhIiJjKkLl");
Y += LineHeight;
dc.TextOut (X, Y, "MmNnOoPpQqRr");

// unselect font:
dc.SelectObject (PtrOldFont);

// Do not call CDialog::OnPaint() for painting messages
}
```

```
void CFormat::OnBold()
{
   // TODO: Add your control notification handler code here
   m_Bold = !m_Bold;
   InvalidateRect (&m_RectSample);
   UpdateWindow ();
}

void CFormat::OnCenter()
{
   // TODO: Add your control notification handler code here
   if (IsDlgButtonChecked (IDC_CENTER))
      {
      m_Justify = JUSTIFY_CENTER;
      InvalidateRect (&m_RectSample);
      UpdateWindow ();
      }
}

void CFormat::OnFixed()
{
   // TODO: Add your control notification handler code here
   if (IsDlgButtonChecked (IDC_FIXED))
      {
      m_Pitch = PITCH_FIXED;
      InvalidateRect (&m_RectSample);
      UpdateWindow ();
      }
}

void CFormat::OnItalic()
{
   // TODO: Add your control notification handler code here
   m_Italic = !m_Italic;
   InvalidateRect (&m_RectSample);
   UpdateWindow ();
}

void CFormat::OnLeft()
{
   // TODO: Add your control notification handler code here
   if (IsDlgButtonChecked (IDC_LEFT))
```

```
        {
        m_Justify = JUSTIFY_LEFT;
        InvalidateRect (&m_RectSample);
        UpdateWindow ();
        }
}

void CFormat::OnRight()
{
    // TODO: Add your control notification handler code here
    if (IsDlgButtonChecked (IDC_RIGHT))
        {
        m_Justify = JUSTIFY_RIGHT;
        InvalidateRect (&m_RectSample);
        UpdateWindow ();
        }
}

void CFormat::OnUnderline()
{
    // TODO: Add your control notification handler code here
    m_Underline = !m_Underline;
    InvalidateRect (&m_RectSample);
    UpdateWindow ();
}

void CFormat::OnVariable()
{
    // TODO: Add your control notification handler code here
    if (IsDlgButtonChecked (IDC_VARIABLE))
        {
        m_Pitch = PITCH_VARIABLE;
        InvalidateRect (&m_RectSample);
        UpdateWindow ();
        }
}

void CFormat::OnChangeSpacing()
{
    // TODO: If this is a RICHEDIT control, the control will not
    // send this notification unless you override the CDialog::OnInitDialog()
    // function and call CRichEditCtrl().SetEventMask()
```

```
// with the ENM_CHANGE flag ORed into the mask.

// TODO: Add your control notification handler code here
int Temp;
Temp = (int)GetDlgItemInt (IDC_SPACING);
if (Temp > 0 && Temp < 4)
    {
    m_Spacing = Temp;
    InvalidateRect (&m_RectSample);
    UpdateWindow ();
    }
}
```

Creating a Modeless Dialog Box

In the previous sections, you learned how to design and display *modal* dialog boxes. This section briefly introduces the techniques for displaying *modeless* dialog boxes. Although less common than modal dialog boxes, modeless dialog boxes are useful for certain purposes.

While a modal dialog box is displayed, the main program window is disabled; the user must therefore close the dialog box before continuing to work in the main window. When you display a modeless dialog box, however, the main program window *isn't* disabled. As a result, the user can continue working within the main window while the dialog box remains displayed, and the user can switch the focus back and forth between the main window and the dialog box. A modeless dialog box is thus useful for providing a secondary window that the user can employ in conjunction with the main window. For example, a spell-checking command for a word processor typically displays a modeless dialog box so that the user can make a correction in the document and then resume the spelling check, without having to close and reopen the dialog box.

As with a modal dialog box, you can design a modeless dialog box using the dialog editor of the Developer Studio, and you can use ClassWizard both to derive a class from CDialog to manage a modeless dialog box and to define data members and message-handling functions.

The following are several differences in the way you display a modeless dialog box as contrasted with the way you display a modal dialog box.

- You should declare the instance of the dialog class as a global object, or create it using the new operator, *rather* than making it a local object. This is necessary because a modeless dialog box typically remains opened after the function that displays it returns, and the object that manages the dialog box must remain in existence. If you create the object using new, be sure to use delete to destroy the object when you're done with it.

- You display a modeless dialog box by calling CDialog::Create rather than CDialog::DoModal. Unlike DoModal, the Create function returns immediately, leaving the dialog box displayed. While the dialog box is displayed, the main frame window, as well as any view windows, remains enabled; your program can continue to process input from these windows so that the user can keep working in the windows while the dialog box remains displayed.

- You close a modeless dialog box by calling the CWnd::DestroyWindow function for the dialog box object rather than calling EndDialog. You can call DestroyWindow from a member function of the dialog class or from any other function in the program.

- You should define an OnCancel message-handling function for your dialog class. If the dialog box contains an OK button (that is, a button with the IDOK identifier), you should also define an OnOK message-handling function. These functions were described in a sidebar given previously in the chapter ("Closing the Dialog Box"). For a modeless dialog box, however, the functions should call DestroyWindow to close the dialog box, and they *shouldn't* call the base class version of the message-handling function (the base class versions of OnCancel and OnOK call EndDialog, which hides the dialog box but doesn't destroy it). Note that if you've used ClassWizard to define data members of the dialog class, an OnOK function you write should call CWnd::UpdateData (passing it either TRUE or no parameter) to save and validate the contents of the controls (in a modal dialog box, this task is performed by the base class version of OnOK).

NOTE   Chapter 14 introduced a type of MFC control bar known as a *dialog bar*. A dialog bar is actually a modeless dialog box that's managed by the MFC CDialogBar class rather than CDialog.

Creating a Tabbed Dialog Box

The MFC supports tabbed dialog boxes, which are popular in recent Windows applications (including Visual C++). A tabbed dialog box allows you to display several *pages* of related controls within a single dialog box. The user accesses each page by clicking its tab within a row of file-folder–like tabs displayed near the top of the dialog box. For a tabbed dialog box, the dialog box itself is supported by an object of the MFC class `CPropertySheet`, and each page is supported by an object of the MFC class `CPropertyPage`. You use the dialog editor to design each page, as if it were a freestanding dialog box (however, as you'll see, you must choose a specific set of dialog styles).

In this section, you'll create the TabDemo program. TabDemo is similar to the previous example program, FontDemo, except that the Format dialog box is a tabbed dialog box (and, for simplicity, the dialog box doesn't display sample text). The first page in the Format dialog box (the Style page shown in Figure 15.14) contains the check boxes for choosing font styles; the second page (the Justify page shown in Figure 15.15) contains the radio buttons for selecting the text justification; and the third page (the Pitch and Spacing page shown in Figure 15.16) contains the radio buttons for choosing the pitch, as well as the edit box for setting the line spacing. (Note that the `CPropertySheet` class makes the pages at least as wide as the three buttons displayed at the bottom of the dialog box, plus a space for an optional Help button; hence, in the TabDemo program, the pages are larger than necessary to hold the controls displayed. In an actual application, however, you'd typically *not* use a tabbed dialog box unless you were displaying a greater number of controls.)

FIGURE 15.14:

The Style page of the Format dialog box

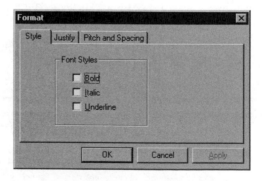

FIGURE 15.15:

The Justify page of the Format dialog box

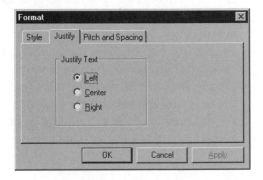

FIGURE 15.16:

The Pitch and Spacing page of the Format dialog box

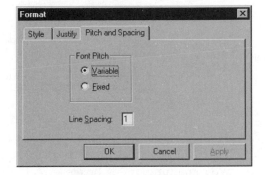

Use AppWizard to generate the basic source files for the TabDemo program, as explained in Chapter 9. In the Projects tab of the New dialog box, enter the program name, TabDemo, into the Name: text box and enter the desired project folder into the Location: text box. In the AppWizard dialog boxes, choose the same options that you chose for the WinGreet program in Chapter 9.

Once you've generated the source files, perform the following steps to customize the program:

1. To create the dialog template for the Style page, choose the Insert ➤ Resource… menu command, select the Dialog resource type, and click the New button.

2. In the dialog editor, right-click within the new dialog box and choose Properties on the menu that appears, to open the Dialog Properties dialog box. First, open the General tab and enter Style in the Caption: text box; this

caption will be displayed in the tab belonging to the page you're creating (leave all the other general properties unchanged). Then open the Styles tab, choose the Child item within the Style: list, and choose the Thin item within the Border: list. Also, set the check boxes so that only the Title Bar box is checked. The correct settings in the Styles tab are shown in Figure 15.17. Finally, open the More Styles tab and check the Disabled box; this should be the only box checked within the More Styles tab. All the settings you made are required for defining a dialog box that's going to be used as a page in a tabbed dialog box (rather than as a freestanding dialog box).

FIGURE 15.17:

The settings in the Styles tab of the Dialog Properties dialog box that are required for defining a dialog box to be used as a page of a tabbed dialog box

3. Delete the push buttons and add the controls shown in Figure 15.18. Table 15.7 describes these controls, as well as the ones you'll add to the two remaining dialog boxes.

FIGURE 15.18:

The completed dialog box for the Style page, within the dialog editor

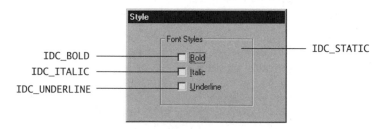

TABLE 15.7: Properties of the Controls to Be Added to the Style, Justify, and Pitch and Spacing Dialog Box Templates

ID:	Type of Control	Nondefault Properties You Need to Set
IDC_STATIC	Group box	Caption: `Font Styles`
IDC_BOLD	Check box	Caption: `&Bold`
		Group
IDC_ITALIC	Check box	Caption: `&Italic`
IDC_UNDERLINE	Check box	Caption: `&Underline`
IDC_STATIC	Group box	Caption: `Justify Text`
IDC_LEFT	Radio button	Caption: `&Left`
		Group
		Tab Stop
IDC_CENTER	Radio button	Caption: `&Center`
IDC_RIGHT	Radio button	Caption: `&Right`
IDC_STATIC	Group box	Caption: `Font Pitch`
IDC_VARIABLE	Radio button	Caption: `&Variable`
		Group
		Tab Stop
IDC_FIXED	Radio button	Caption: `&Fixed`
IDC_STATIC	Static text control	Caption: `Line &Spacing:`
IDC_SPACING	Edit box (text box)	none

4. While the dialog editor window displaying the Style dialog box is still active, run ClassWizard to create a class to manage the Style page. ClassWizard will display the Adding A Class dialog box. Choose the Create A New Class option and click OK. ClassWizard will then open the New Class dialog box. Into the Name: text box enter CStyle, and in the Base Class: list select CPropertyPage (the class that manages a page of a tabbed dialog box

must be derived from `CPropertyPage` rather than from `CDialog`). Accept all the other default options and click the OK button. The main ClassWizard dialog box will now be accessible.

5. Open the Member Variables tab of the ClassWizard dialog box to define member variables for the `CStyle` class. Following the instructions that were given for the FontDemo program (in the earlier section "Defining Member Variables"), define member variables for the Bold, Italic, and Underline check boxes. For each variable, specify the same name, category, and type as you specified for the FontDemo program.

6. Repeat steps 1 through 5 to create the second and third dialog box templates, which are for the remaining two pages. The second dialog box template (Justify) is shown in Figure 15.19 and the third (Pitch and Spacing) is shown in Figure 15.20. The properties of the controls are given in Table 15.7. The class for the Justify dialog box should be named `CJustify` and the class for the Pitch and Spacing dialog box should be named `CPitch`. For each group of radio buttons, and for the Line Spacing text box, add the same member variables that you defined for the FontDemo program.

FIGURE 15.19:

The completed dialog box for the Justify page, within the dialog editor

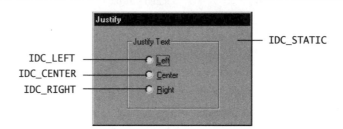

FIGURE 15.20:

The completed dialog box for the Pitch and Spacing page, within the dialog editor

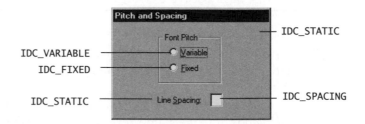

If the dialog boxes for a series of pages aren't the same size, you should normally make the *first* page the largest, because the MFC **CPropertySheet** class calculates the page size based on the size of the dialog box for the first page. (In TabDemo, however, you don't need to worry about this because all pages are smaller than the minimum page size.)

When you're laying out a series of pages for a tabbed dialog box, try to place similar groups of controls at the same position within each page. Otherwise, controls will appear to jump around as the user tabs from page to page. For example, in the first two pages of the TabDemo Format dialog box, the control groups were placed at the same position in each page.

7. Use ClassWizard to generate a **WM_INITDIALOG** message-handling function for the **CPitch** class, which will be named **OnInitDialog** (use the same technique you used for generating the **OnInitDialog** function for the **CFormat** class of the FontDemo program, explained in the earlier section "Defining Message Handlers"). Add code to the function in Pitch.cpp as follows:

```
/////////////////////////////////////////////////////////////////
///////////
// CPitch message handlers

BOOL CPitch::OnInitDialog()
{
    CPropertyPage::OnInitDialog();

    // TODO: Add extra initialization here

    m_SpacingEdit.LimitText (1);

    return TRUE;   // return TRUE unless you set the focus to a
                   // control
                   // EXCEPTION: OCX Property Pages should return
                   // FALSE
}
```

NOTE   The `OnInitDialog` function is called only the *first time* the associated page is displayed within the tabbed dialog box. It *isn't* called each time the user redisplays the page by clicking its tab.

---

8. Modify the program menu, removing the File and Edit menus and adding a Text menu with a Format and an Exit command as well as a Ctrl+F keyboard accelerator, exactly as you did for the FontDemo program (see the previous section "Modifying the Program Menu").

9. Use ClassWizard to generate a COMMAND message handler for the Format menu command, just as you did for the FontDemo program (see the section "Adding a Menu Message Handler"). Add code as follows to the resulting function, `OnTextFormat`, within TabDemoDoc.cpp:

```
//////////////////////////////////////////////////////////////////
//////////
// CTabDemoDoc commands

void CTabDemoDoc::OnTextFormat()
{
    // TODO: Add your command handler code here
    // create tabbed dialog box object:
    CPropertySheet PropertySheet ("Format");

    // create object for each page:
    CStyle StylePage;
    CJustify JustifyPage;
    CPitch PitchPage;

    // add pages to dialog box object:
    PropertySheet.AddPage (&StylePage);
    PropertySheet.AddPage (&JustifyPage);
    PropertySheet.AddPage (&PitchPage);

    // initialize page object data members:
    StylePage.m_Bold = m_Bold;
    StylePage.m_Italic = m_Italic;
    StylePage.m_Underline = m_Underline;
    JustifyPage.m_Justify = m_Justify;
    PitchPage.m_Pitch = m_Pitch;
    PitchPage.m_Spacing = m_Spacing;
```

```
            // display tabbed dialog box:
            if (PropertySheet.DoModal () == IDOK)
                {
                // save values of page object data members:
                m_Bold = StylePage.m_Bold;
                m_Italic = StylePage.m_Italic;
                m_Underline = StylePage.m_Underline;
                m_Justify = JustifyPage.m_Justify;
                m_Pitch = PitchPage.m_Pitch;
                m_Spacing = PitchPage.m_Spacing;

                // redraw the text:
                UpdateAllViews (NULL);
                }
        }
```

The added code is similar to the code for displaying the standard dialog box in FontDemo. However, rather than simply creating an instance of the dialog class, OnTextFormat first creates an instance of the MFC class CProperty-Sheet; this object displays and manages the tabbed dialog box. OnTextFormat then creates an instance of each of the CPropertyPage-derived classes you generated in ClassWizard; each of these page objects is associated with one of the dialog templates you designed, and it manages a specific page within the tabbed dialog box. Next, OnTextFormat calls AddPage for the CPropertySheet object to add each page object. Finally, it calls the CPropertySheet member function DoModal to create and display the tabbed dialog box, which will contain a page for each page object that was added.

Like CDialog, CPropertyPage provides handlers for the OK and Cancel buttons, and it validates and transfers data between the controls and the member functions of the page objects. If you want to enable the Apply button or to add a Help button and provide a handler for either of these buttons, you'll need to derive your own class from CPropertyPage. (In TabDemo, the Apply button is left permanently disabled. Microsoft's documentation states that it is proper to simply leave this button disabled rather than to try to remove it, because it's a standard part of the tabbed dialog interface.) You'll also need to derive your own class from CPropertyPage if you want to expand the size of the tabbed dialog box and add additional controls to the tabbed dialog box itself (rather than to a specific page within the tabbed dialog box). For example, you might want to include a group box where you display a sample showing the results of the dialog box options (such as the Sample group box in the Format dialog box of the FontDemo program). For information on performing these tasks, see the online help documentation on the CPropertySheet and CPropertyPage classes, as well as the following topic: *V Visual C++ Documentation, Using Visual C++, Visual C++ Programmer's Guide, Adding User Interface Features, Overviews, Property Sheets: Overview.*

10. Also in TabDemoDoc.cpp, include the header files for each of the page classes,

```
// TabDemoDoc.cpp : implementation of the CTabDemoDoc class
//

#include "stdafx.h"
#include "TabDemo.h"

#include "TabDemeDoc.h"
#include "style.h"
#include "justify.h"
#include "pitch.h"
```

and add initializations for the data members that store the formatting values:

```
/////////////////////////////////////////////////////////////////
///////////
// CTabDemoDoc construction/destruction

CTabDemoDoc::CTabDemoDoc()
{
    // TODO: add one-time construction code here
    m_Bold = FALSE;
    m_Italic = FALSE;
    m_Underline = FALSE;
    m_Justify = JUSTIFY_LEFT;
    m_Pitch = PITCH_VARIABLE;
    m_Spacing = 1;
}
```

11. In TabDemoDoc.h, define enumerators and data members as follows:

```
enum {JUSTIFY_LEFT, JUSTIFY_CENTER, JUSTIFY_RIGHT};
enum {PITCH_VARIABLE, PITCH_FIXED};

class CTabDemoDoc : public CDocument
```

```
{
public:
    BOOL m_Bold;
    BOOL m_Italic;
    BOOL m_Underline;
    int m_Justify;
    int m_Pitch;
    int m_Spacing;
```

12. In TabDemoView.cpp, add to the OnDraw function the *same* code for display-ing text in the window that you added to the OnDraw function of the Font-Demo view class (see the earlier section "Modifying the Document and View Code").

13. In TabDemo.cpp, add a call to SetWindowText to the end of the InitIn-stance function:

```
    // The one and only window has been initialized, so show and
    // update it.
    m_pMainWnd->ShowWindow(SW_SHOW);
    m_pMainWnd->UpdateWindow();

    m_pMainWnd->SetWindowText ("Tabbed Dialog Box Demo");

    return TRUE;
}
```

You can now build and run the TabDemo program.

NOTE   In this section, you learned how to display a *modal* tabbed dialog box. You can also display a *modeless* tabbed dialog box, using the techniques presented in this section combined with the special techniques discussed in the prior section "Cre-ating a Modeless Dialog Box." For additional details, see the following online help topic: *Visual C++ Documentation, Using Visual C++, Visual C++ Programmer's Guide, Adding User Interface Features, Details, Property Sheet Topics, Property Sheets: Creating a Modeless Property Sheet.*

The TabDemo Source Code

The following listings, Listings 15.11 through 15.24, are the C++ source code for the TabDemo program. A copy of these files is included in your \TabDemo companion-CD folder.

Listing 15.11

```
// TabDemo.h : main header file for the TABDEMO application
//

#if !defined(AFX_TABDEMO_H__60ECFFC5_A12D_11D1_80FC_00C0F6A83B7F__INCLUDED_)
#define AFX_TABDEMO_H__60ECFFC5_A12D_11D1_80FC_00C0F6A83B7F__INCLUDED_

#if _MSC_VER > 1000
#pragma once
#endif // _MSC_VER > 1000

#ifndef __AFXWIN_H__
    #error include 'stdafx.h' before including this file for PCH
#endif

#include "resource.h"        // main symbols

/////////////////////////////////////////////////////////////////////////
// CTabDemoApp:
// See TabDemo.cpp for the implementation of this class
//

class CTabDemoApp : public CWinApp
{
public:
    CTabDemoApp();

// Overrides
    // ClassWizard generated virtual function overrides
    //{{AFX_VIRTUAL(CTabDemoApp)
    public:
    virtual BOOL InitInstance();
    //}}AFX_VIRTUAL

// Implementation
```

```
    //{{AFX_MSG(CTabDemoApp)
    afx_msg void OnAppAbout();
        // NOTE - the ClassWizard will add and remove member functions here.
        //      DO NOT EDIT what you see in these blocks of generated code !
    //}}AFX_MSG
    DECLARE_MESSAGE_MAP()
};


//////////////////////////////////////////////////////////////////////////

//{{AFX_INSERT_LOCATION}}
// Microsoft Visual C++ will insert additional declarations immediately before
// the previous line.

#endif
// !defined(AFX_TABDEMO_H__60ECFFC5_A12D_11D1_80FC_00C0F6A83B7F__INCLUDED_)
```

Listing 15.12

```
// TabDemo.cpp : Defines the class behaviors for the application.
//

#include "stdafx.h"
#include "TabDemo.h"

#include "MainFrm.h"
#include "TabDemoDoc.h"
#include "TabDemoView.h"

#ifdef _DEBUG
#define new DEBUG_NEW
#undef THIS_FILE
static char THIS_FILE[] = __FILE__;
#endif


//////////////////////////////////////////////////////////////////////////
// CTabDemoApp

BEGIN_MESSAGE_MAP(CTabDemoApp, CWinApp)
    //{{AFX_MSG_MAP(CTabDemoApp)
    ON_COMMAND(ID_APP_ABOUT, OnAppAbout)
```

```
      // NOTE - the ClassWizard will add and remove mapping macros here.
      //    DO NOT EDIT what you see in these blocks of generated code!
   //}}AFX_MSG_MAP
   // Standard file based document commands
   ON_COMMAND(ID_FILE_NEW, CWinApp::OnFileNew)
   ON_COMMAND(ID_FILE_OPEN, CWinApp::OnFileOpen)
END_MESSAGE_MAP()


/////////////////////////////////////////////////////////////////////
// CTabDemoApp construction

CTabDemoApp::CTabDemoApp()
{
   // TODO: add construction code here,
   // Place all significant initialization in InitInstance
}


/////////////////////////////////////////////////////////////////////
// The one and only CTabDemoApp object

CTabDemoApp theApp;

/////////////////////////////////////////////////////////////////////
// CTabDemoApp initialization

BOOL CTabDemoApp::InitInstance()
{
   // Standard initialization
   // If you are not using these features and wish to reduce the size
   //  of your final executable, you should remove from the following
   //  the specific initialization routines you do not need.

#ifdef _AFXDLL
   Enable3dControls();           // Call this when using MFC in a shared DLL
#else
   Enable3dControlsStatic();  // Call this when linking to MFC statically
#endif

   // Change the registry key under which our settings are stored.
   // TODO: You should modify this string to be something appropriate
   // such as the name of your company or organization.
   SetRegistryKey(_T("Local AppWizard-Generated Applications"));
```

```
    LoadStdProfileSettings();   // Load standard INI file options (including MRU)

    // Register the application's document templates.  Document templates
    //  serve as the connection between documents, frame windows and views.

    CSingleDocTemplate* pDocTemplate;
    pDocTemplate = new CSingleDocTemplate(
        IDR_MAINFRAME,
        RUNTIME_CLASS(CTabDemoDoc),
        RUNTIME_CLASS(CMainFrame),        // main SDI frame window
        RUNTIME_CLASS(CTabDemoView));
    AddDocTemplate(pDocTemplate);

    // Parse command line for standard shell commands, DDE, file open
    CCommandLineInfo cmdInfo;
    ParseCommandLine(cmdInfo);

    // Dispatch commands specified on the command line
    if (!ProcessShellCommand(cmdInfo))
        return FALSE;

    // The one and only window has been initialized, so show and update it.
    m_pMainWnd->ShowWindow(SW_SHOW);
    m_pMainWnd->UpdateWindow();

    m_pMainWnd->SetWindowText ("Tabbed Dialog Box Demo");

    return TRUE;
}


/////////////////////////////////////////////////////////////////////////////
// CAboutDlg dialog used for App About

class CAboutDlg : public CDialog
{
public:
    CAboutDlg();

// Dialog Data
    //{{AFX_DATA(CAboutDlg)
    enum { IDD = IDD_ABOUTBOX };
    //}}AFX_DATA
```

```
   // ClassWizard generated virtual function overrides
   //{{AFX_VIRTUAL(CAboutDlg)
   protected:
   virtual void DoDataExchange(CDataExchange* pDX);      // DDX/DDV support
   //}}AFX_VIRTUAL

// Implementation
protected:
   //{{AFX_MSG(CAboutDlg)
      // No message handlers
   //}}AFX_MSG
   DECLARE_MESSAGE_MAP()
};

CAboutDlg::CAboutDlg() : CDialog(CAboutDlg::IDD)
{
   //{{AFX_DATA_INIT(CAboutDlg)
   //}}AFX_DATA_INIT
}

void CAboutDlg::DoDataExchange(CDataExchange* pDX)
{
   CDialog::DoDataExchange(pDX);
   //{{AFX_DATA_MAP(CAboutDlg)
   //}}AFX_DATA_MAP
}

BEGIN_MESSAGE_MAP(CAboutDlg, CDialog)
   //{{AFX_MSG_MAP(CAboutDlg)
      // No message handlers
   //}}AFX_MSG_MAP
END_MESSAGE_MAP()

// App command to run the dialog
void CTabDemoApp::OnAppAbout()
{
   CAboutDlg aboutDlg;
   aboutDlg.DoModal();
}

/////////////////////////////////////////////////////////////////////
// CTabDemoApp message handlers
```

Listing 15.13

```cpp
// TabDemoDoc.h : interface of the CTabDemoDoc class
//
/////////////////////////////////////////////////////////////////////

#if !defined(AFX_TABDEMODOC_H__60ECFFCB_A12D_11D1_80FC_00C0F6A83B7F__INCLUDED_)
#define AFX_TABDEMODOC_H__60ECFFCB_A12D_11D1_80FC_00C0F6A83B7F__INCLUDED_

#if _MSC_VER > 1000
#pragma once
#endif // _MSC_VER > 1000

enum {JUSTIFY_LEFT, JUSTIFY_CENTER, JUSTIFY_RIGHT};
enum {PITCH_VARIABLE, PITCH_FIXED};

class CTabDemoDoc : public CDocument
{
public:
    BOOL m_Bold;
    BOOL m_Italic;
    BOOL m_Underline;
    int m_Justify;
    int m_Pitch;
    int m_Spacing;

protected: // create from serialization only
    CTabDemoDoc();
    DECLARE_DYNCREATE(CTabDemoDoc)

// Attributes
public:

// Operations
public:

// Overrides
    // ClassWizard generated virtual function overrides
    //{{AFX_VIRTUAL(CTabDemoDoc)
    public:
    virtual BOOL OnNewDocument();
```

```
    virtual void Serialize(CArchive& ar);
    //}}AFX_VIRTUAL

// Implementation
public:
    virtual ~CTabDemoDoc();
#ifdef _DEBUG
    virtual void AssertValid() const;
    virtual void Dump(CDumpContext& dc) const;
#endif

protected:

// Generated message map functions
protected:
    //{{AFX_MSG(CTabDemoDoc)
    afx_msg void OnTextFormat();
    //}}AFX_MSG
    DECLARE_MESSAGE_MAP()
};


/////////////////////////////////////////////////////////////////////////

//{{AFX_INSERT_LOCATION}}
// Microsoft Visual C++ will insert additional declarations immediately before
// the previous line.

#endif
// !defined(AFX_TABDEMODOC_H__60ECFFCB_A12D_11D1_80FC_00C0F6A83B7F__INCLUDED_)
```

Listing 15.14

```
// TabDemoDoc.cpp : implementation of the CTabDemoDoc class
//

#include "stdafx.h"
#include "TabDemo.h"

#include "TabDemoDoc.h"
#include "style.h"
#include "justify.h"
#include "pitch.h"

#ifdef _DEBUG
#define new DEBUG_NEW
```

```
#undef THIS_FILE
static char THIS_FILE[] = __FILE__;
#endif

/////////////////////////////////////////////////////////////////////////////
// CTabDemoDoc

IMPLEMENT_DYNCREATE(CTabDemoDoc, CDocument)

BEGIN_MESSAGE_MAP(CTabDemoDoc, CDocument)
    //{{AFX_MSG_MAP(CTabDemoDoc)
    ON_COMMAND(ID_TEXT_FORMAT, OnTextFormat)
    //}}AFX_MSG_MAP
END_MESSAGE_MAP()

/////////////////////////////////////////////////////////////////////////////
// CTabDemoDoc construction/destruction

CTabDemoDoc::CTabDemoDoc()
{
    // TODO: add one-time construction code here
    m_Bold = FALSE;
    m_Italic = FALSE;
    m_Underline = FALSE;
    m_Justify = JUSTIFY_LEFT;
    m_Pitch = PITCH_VARIABLE;
    m_Spacing = 1;
}

CTabDemoDoc::~CTabDemoDoc()
{
}

BOOL CTabDemoDoc::OnNewDocument()
{
    if (!CDocument::OnNewDocument())
        return FALSE;

    // TODO: add reinitialization code here
    // (SDI documents will reuse this document)

    return TRUE;
}
```

```
///////////////////////////////////////////////////////////////////////
// CTabDemoDoc serialization

void CTabDemoDoc::Serialize(CArchive& ar)
{
   if (ar.IsStoring())
   {
      // TODO: add storing code here
   }
   else
   {
      // TODO: add loading code here
   }
}


///////////////////////////////////////////////////////////////////////
// CTabDemoDoc diagnostics

#ifdef _DEBUG
void CTabDemoDoc::AssertValid() const
{
   CDocument::AssertValid();
}

void CTabDemoDoc::Dump(CDumpContext& dc) const
{
   CDocument::Dump(dc);
}
#endif //_DEBUG


///////////////////////////////////////////////////////////////////////
// CTabDemoDoc commands

void CTabDemoDoc::OnTextFormat()
{
   // TODO: Add your command handler code here

   // create tabbed dialog box object:
   CPropertySheet PropertySheet ("Format");

   // create object for each page:
   CStyle StylePage;
```

```
    CJustify JustifyPage;
    CPitch PitchPage;

    // add pages to dialog box object:
    PropertySheet.AddPage (&StylePage);
    PropertySheet.AddPage (&JustifyPage);
    PropertySheet.AddPage (&PitchPage);

    // initialize page object data members:
    StylePage.m_Bold = m_Bold;
    StylePage.m_Italic = m_Italic;
    StylePage.m_Underline = m_Underline;
    JustifyPage.m_Justify = m_Justify;
    PitchPage.m_Pitch = m_Pitch;
    PitchPage.m_Spacing = m_Spacing;

    // display tabbed dialog box:
    if (PropertySheet.DoModal () == IDOK)
        {
        // save values of page object data members:
        m_Bold = StylePage.m_Bold;
        m_Italic = StylePage.m_Italic;
        m_Underline = StylePage.m_Underline;
        m_Justify = JustifyPage.m_Justify;
        m_Pitch = PitchPage.m_Pitch;
        m_Spacing = PitchPage.m_Spacing;

        // redraw the text:
        UpdateAllViews (NULL);
        }
}
```

Listing 15.15

```
// MainFrm.h : interface of the CMainFrame class
//
/////////////////////////////////////////////////////////////////////////////

#if !defined(AFX_MAINFRM_H__60ECFFC9_A12D_11D1_80FC_00C0F6A83B7F__INCLUDED_)
#define AFX_MAINFRM_H__60ECFFC9_A12D_11D1_80FC_00C0F6A83B7F__INCLUDED_
```

```
#if _MSC_VER > 1000
#pragma once
#endif // _MSC_VER > 1000

class CMainFrame : public CFrameWnd
{

protected: // create from serialization only
    CMainFrame();
    DECLARE_DYNCREATE(CMainFrame)

// Attributes
public:

// Operations
public:

// Overrides
    // ClassWizard generated virtual function overrides
    //{{AFX_VIRTUAL(CMainFrame)
    virtual BOOL PreCreateWindow(CREATESTRUCT& cs);
    //}}AFX_VIRTUAL

// Implementation
public:
    virtual ~CMainFrame();
#ifdef _DEBUG
    virtual void AssertValid() const;
    virtual void Dump(CDumpContext& dc) const;
#endif

// Generated message map functions
protected:
    //{{AFX_MSG(CMainFrame)
        // NOTE - the ClassWizard will add and remove member functions here.
        //    DO NOT EDIT what you see in these blocks of generated code!
    //}}AFX_MSG
    DECLARE_MESSAGE_MAP()
};

//////////////////////////////////////////////////////////////////////
```

```
//{{AFX_INSERT_LOCATION}}
// Microsoft Visual C++ will insert additional declarations immediately before
// the previous line.

#endif
// !defined(AFX_MAINFRM_H__60ECFFC9_A12D_11D1_80FC_00C0F6A83B7F__INCLUDED_)
```

Listing 15.16

```cpp
// MainFrm.cpp : implementation of the CMainFrame class
//

#include "stdafx.h"
#include "TabDemo.h"

#include "MainFrm.h"

#ifdef _DEBUG
#define new DEBUG_NEW
#undef THIS_FILE
static char THIS_FILE[] = __FILE__;
#endif

/////////////////////////////////////////////////////////////////////////////
// CMainFrame

IMPLEMENT_DYNCREATE(CMainFrame, CFrameWnd)

BEGIN_MESSAGE_MAP(CMainFrame, CFrameWnd)
    //{{AFX_MSG_MAP(CMainFrame)
        // NOTE - the ClassWizard will add and remove mapping macros here.
        //    DO NOT EDIT what you see in these blocks of generated code !
    //}}AFX_MSG_MAP
END_MESSAGE_MAP()

/////////////////////////////////////////////////////////////////////////////
// CMainFrame construction/destruction

CMainFrame::CMainFrame()
{
    // TODO: add member initialization code here

}
```

```
CMainFrame::~CMainFrame()
{
}

BOOL CMainFrame::PreCreateWindow(CREATESTRUCT& cs)
{
   if( !CFrameWnd::PreCreateWindow(cs) )
      return FALSE;
   // TODO: Modify the Window class or styles here by modifying
   //  the CREATESTRUCT cs

   return TRUE;
}

/////////////////////////////////////////////////////////////////////////////
// CMainFrame diagnostics

#ifdef _DEBUG
void CMainFrame::AssertValid() const
{
   CFrameWnd::AssertValid();
}

void CMainFrame::Dump(CDumpContext& dc) const
{
   CFrameWnd::Dump(dc);
}

#endif //_DEBUG

/////////////////////////////////////////////////////////////////////////////
// CMainFrame message handlers
```

Listing 15.17

```
// TabDemoView.h : interface of the CTabDemoView class
//
/////////////////////////////////////////////////////////////////////////////

#if !defined(AFX_TABDEMOVIEW_H__60ECFFCD_A12D_11D1_80FC_00C0F6A83B7F__INCLUDED_)
#define AFX_TABDEMOVIEW_H__60ECFFCD_A12D_11D1_80FC_00C0F6A83B7F__INCLUDED_
```

```
#if _MSC_VER > 1000
#pragma once
#endif // _MSC_VER > 1000


class CTabDemoView : public CView
{
protected: // create from serialization only
    CTabDemoView();
    DECLARE_DYNCREATE(CTabDemoView)

// Attributes
public:
    CTabDemoDoc* GetDocument();

// Operations
public:

// Overrides
    // ClassWizard generated virtual function overrides
    //{{AFX_VIRTUAL(CTabDemoView)
    public:
    virtual void OnDraw(CDC* pDC);  // overridden to draw this view
    virtual BOOL PreCreateWindow(CREATESTRUCT& cs);
    protected:
    //}}AFX_VIRTUAL

// Implementation
public:
    virtual ~CTabDemoView();
#ifdef _DEBUG
    virtual void AssertValid() const;
    virtual void Dump(CDumpContext& dc) const;
#endif

protected:

// Generated message map functions
protected:
    //{{AFX_MSG(CTabDemoView)
        // NOTE - the ClassWizard will add and remove member functions here.
        //    DO NOT EDIT what you see in these blocks of generated code !
```

```
    //}}AFX_MSG
    DECLARE_MESSAGE_MAP()
};

#ifndef _DEBUG  // debug version in TabDemoView.cpp
inline CTabDemoDoc* CTabDemoView::GetDocument()
    { return (CTabDemoDoc*)m_pDocument; }
#endif


/////////////////////////////////////////////////////////////////////////////

//{{AFX_INSERT_LOCATION}}
// Microsoft Visual C++ will insert additional declarations immediately before
// the previous line.

#endif
// !defined(AFX_TABDEMOVIEW_H__60ECFFCD_A12D_11D1_80FC_00C0F6A83B7F__INCLUDED_)
```

Listing 15.18

```
// TabDemoView.cpp : implementation of the CTabDemoView class
//

#include "stdafx.h"
#include "TabDemo.h"

#include "TabDemoDoc.h"
#include "TabDemoView.h"

#ifdef _DEBUG
#define new DEBUG_NEW
#undef THIS_FILE
static char THIS_FILE[] = __FILE__;
#endif

/////////////////////////////////////////////////////////////////////////////
// CTabDemoView

IMPLEMENT_DYNCREATE(CTabDemoView, CView)

BEGIN_MESSAGE_MAP(CTabDemoView, CView)
    //{{AFX_MSG_MAP(CTabDemoView)
```

```
        // NOTE - the ClassWizard will add and remove mapping macros here.
        //      DO NOT EDIT what you see in these blocks of generated code!
    //}}AFX_MSG_MAP
END_MESSAGE_MAP()


/////////////////////////////////////////////////////////////////////////////
// CTabDemoView construction/destruction

CTabDemoView::CTabDemoView()
{
    // TODO: add construction code here

}

CTabDemoView::~CTabDemoView()
{
}

BOOL CTabDemoView::PreCreateWindow(CREATESTRUCT& cs)
{
    // TODO: Modify the Window class or styles here by modifying
    //   the CREATESTRUCT cs

    return CView::PreCreateWindow(cs);
}


/////////////////////////////////////////////////////////////////////////////
// CTabDemoView drawing

void CTabDemoView::OnDraw(CDC* pDC)
{
    CTabDemoDoc* pDoc = GetDocument();
    ASSERT_VALID(pDoc);

    // TODO: add draw code for native data here
    RECT ClientRect;
    CFont Font;
    LOGFONT LF;
    int LineHeight;
    CFont *PtrOldFont;
    int X, Y;
```

```
// fill LF with the features of a standard system font:
CFont TempFont;
if (pDoc->m_Pitch == PITCH_VARIABLE)
   TempFont.CreateStockObject (SYSTEM_FONT);
else
   TempFont.CreateStockObject (SYSTEM_FIXED_FONT);
TempFont.GetObject (sizeof (LOGFONT), &LF);

// now customize lfWeight, lfItalic, and lfUnderline fields:
if (pDoc->m_Bold)
   LF.lfWeight = FW_BOLD;
if (pDoc->m_Italic)
   LF.lfItalic = 1;
if (pDoc->m_Underline)
   LF.lfUnderline = 1;

// create and select font:
Font.CreateFontIndirect (&LF);
PtrOldFont = pDC->SelectObject (&Font);

// set justification:
GetClientRect (&ClientRect);
switch (pDoc->m_Justify)
   {
   case JUSTIFY_LEFT:
      pDC->SetTextAlign (TA_LEFT);
      X = ClientRect.left + 5;
      break;
   case JUSTIFY_CENTER:
      pDC->SetTextAlign (TA_CENTER);
      X = ClientRect.right / 2;
      break;
   case JUSTIFY_RIGHT:
      pDC->SetTextAlign (TA_RIGHT);
      X = ClientRect.right - 5;
      break;
   }
```

```
   // set text color and background mode:
   pDC->SetTextColor (::GetSysColor (COLOR_WINDOWTEXT));
   pDC->SetBkMode (TRANSPARENT);

   // draw lines:
   LineHeight = LF.lfHeight * pDoc->m_Spacing;
   Y = 5;
   pDC->TextOut (X, Y, "This is the first line of sample text.");
   Y += LineHeight;
   pDC->TextOut (X, Y, "This is the second line of sample "
                       "text.");
   Y += LineHeight;
   pDC->TextOut (X, Y, "This is the third line of sample text.");

   // unselect font:
   pDC->SelectObject (PtrOldFont);
}

/////////////////////////////////////////////////////////////////////////////
// CTabDemoView diagnostics

#ifdef _DEBUG
void CTabDemoView::AssertValid() const
{
   CView::AssertValid();
}

void CTabDemoView::Dump(CDumpContext& dc) const
{
   CView::Dump(dc);
}

CTabDemoDoc* CTabDemoView::GetDocument() // non-debug version is inline
{
   ASSERT(m_pDocument->IsKindOf(RUNTIME_CLASS(CTabDemoDoc)));
   return (CTabDemoDoc*)m_pDocument;
}
#endif //_DEBUG

/////////////////////////////////////////////////////////////////////////////
// CTabDemoView message handlers
```

Listing 15.19

```
// Justify.h : header file
//

#if !defined(AFX_JUSTIFY_H__60ECFFD5_A12D_11D1_80FC_00C0F6A83B7F__INCLUDED_)
#define AFX_JUSTIFY_H__60ECFFD5_A12D_11D1_80FC_00C0F6A83B7F__INCLUDED_

#if _MSC_VER > 1000
#pragma once
#endif // _MSC_VER > 1000
/////////////////////////////////////////////////////////////////////////////
// CJustify dialog

class CJustify : public CPropertyPage
{
    DECLARE_DYNCREATE(CJustify)

// Construction
public:
    CJustify();
    ~CJustify();

// Dialog Data
    //{{AFX_DATA(CJustify)
    enum { IDD = IDD_DIALOG2 };
    int        m_Justify;
    //}}AFX_DATA


// Overrides
    // ClassWizard generate virtual function overrides
    //{{AFX_VIRTUAL(CJustify)
    protected:
    virtual void DoDataExchange(CDataExchange* pDX);    // DDX/DDV support
    //}}AFX_VIRTUAL

// Implementation
protected:
    // Generated message map functions
```

```cpp
	//{{AFX_MSG(CJustify)
		// NOTE: the ClassWizard will add member functions here
	//}}AFX_MSG
	DECLARE_MESSAGE_MAP()

};

//{{AFX_INSERT_LOCATION}}
// Microsoft Visual C++ will insert additional declarations immediately before
// the previous line.

#endif
// !defined(AFX_JUSTIFY_H__60ECFFD5_A12D_11D1_80FC_00C0F6A83B7F__INCLUDED_)
```

Listing 15.20

```cpp
// Justify.cpp : implementation file
//

#include "stdafx.h"
#include "TabDemo.h"
#include "Justify.h"

#ifdef _DEBUG
#define new DEBUG_NEW
#undef THIS_FILE
static char THIS_FILE[] = __FILE__;
#endif

/////////////////////////////////////////////////////////////////////////////
// CJustify property page

IMPLEMENT_DYNCREATE(CJustify, CPropertyPage)

CJustify::CJustify() : CPropertyPage(CJustify::IDD)
{
	//{{AFX_DATA_INIT(CJustify)
	m_Justify = -1;
	//}}AFX_DATA_INIT
}
```

```
CJustify::~CJustify()
{
}

void CJustify::DoDataExchange(CDataExchange* pDX)
{
    CPropertyPage::DoDataExchange(pDX);
    //{{AFX_DATA_MAP(CJustify)
    DDX_Radio(pDX, IDC_LEFT, m_Justify);
    //}}AFX_DATA_MAP
}


BEGIN_MESSAGE_MAP(CJustify, CPropertyPage)
    //{{AFX_MSG_MAP(CJustify)
        // NOTE: the ClassWizard will add message map macros here
    //}}AFX_MSG_MAP
END_MESSAGE_MAP()


/////////////////////////////////////////////////////////////////////////
// CJustify message handlers
```

Listing 15.21

```
// Pitch.h : header file
//

#if !defined(AFX_PITCH_H__60ECFFD6_A12D_11D1_80FC_00C0F6A83B7F__INCLUDED_)
#define AFX_PITCH_H__60ECFFD6_A12D_11D1_80FC_00C0F6A83B7F__INCLUDED_

#if _MSC_VER > 1000
#pragma once
#endif // _MSC_VER > 1000

/////////////////////////////////////////////////////////////////////////
// CPitch dialog

class CPitch : public CPropertyPage
{
    DECLARE_DYNCREATE(CPitch)

// Construction
```

```
public:
    CPitch();
    ~CPitch();

// Dialog Data
    //{{AFX_DATA(CPitch)
    enum { IDD = IDD_DIALOG3 };
    CEdit m_SpacingEdit;
    int       m_Pitch;
    int       m_Spacing;
    //}}AFX_DATA


// Overrides
    // ClassWizard generate virtual function overrides
    //{{AFX_VIRTUAL(CPitch)
    protected:
    virtual void DoDataExchange(CDataExchange* pDX);    // DDX/DDV support
    //}}AFX_VIRTUAL

// Implementation
protected:
    // Generated message map functions
    //{{AFX_MSG(CPitch)
    virtual BOOL OnInitDialog();
    //}}AFX_MSG
    DECLARE_MESSAGE_MAP()

};

//{{AFX_INSERT_LOCATION}}
// Microsoft Visual C++ will insert additional declarations immediately before
// the previous line.

#endif
// !defined(AFX_PITCH_H__60ECFFD6_A12D_11D1_80FC_00C0F6A83B7F__INCLUDED_)
```

Listing 15.22

```
// Pitch.cpp : implementation file
//
```

```
#include "stdafx.h"
#include "TabDemo.h"
#include "Pitch.h"

#ifdef _DEBUG
#define new DEBUG_NEW
#undef THIS_FILE
static char THIS_FILE[] = __FILE__;
#endif

/////////////////////////////////////////////////////////////////////////
// CPitch property page

IMPLEMENT_DYNCREATE(CPitch, CPropertyPage)

CPitch::CPitch() : CPropertyPage(CPitch::IDD)
{
    //{{AFX_DATA_INIT(CPitch)
    m_Pitch = -1;
    m_Spacing = 0;
    //}}AFX_DATA_INIT
}

CPitch::~CPitch()
{
}

void CPitch::DoDataExchange(CDataExchange* pDX)
{
    CPropertyPage::DoDataExchange(pDX);
    //{{AFX_DATA_MAP(CPitch)
    DDX_Control(pDX, IDC_SPACING, m_SpacingEdit);
    DDX_Radio(pDX, IDC_VARIABLE, m_Pitch);
    DDX_Text(pDX, IDC_SPACING, m_Spacing);
    DDV_MinMaxInt(pDX, m_Spacing, 1, 3);
    //}}AFX_DATA_MAP
}


BEGIN_MESSAGE_MAP(CPitch, CPropertyPage)
    //{{AFX_MSG_MAP(CPitch)
    //}}AFX_MSG_MAP
```

```
END_MESSAGE_MAP()

/////////////////////////////////////////////////////////////////////
// CPitch message handlers

BOOL CPitch::OnInitDialog()
{
    CPropertyPage::OnInitDialog();

    // TODO: Add extra initialization here

    m_SpacingEdit.LimitText (1);

    return TRUE;   // return TRUE unless you set the focus to a control
                   // EXCEPTION: OCX Property Pages should return FALSE
}
```

Listing 15.23

```
// Style.h : header file
//

#if !defined(AFX_STYLE_H__60ECFFD4_A12D_11D1_80FC_00C0F6A83B7F__INCLUDED_)
#define AFX_STYLE_H__60ECFFD4_A12D_11D1_80FC_00C0F6A83B7F__INCLUDED_

#if _MSC_VER > 1000
#pragma once
#endif // _MSC_VER > 1000

/////////////////////////////////////////////////////////////////////
// CStyle dialog

class CStyle : public CPropertyPage
{
    DECLARE_DYNCREATE(CStyle)

// Construction
public:
    CStyle();
    ~CStyle();

// Dialog Data
```

```
//{{AFX_DATA(CStyle)
enum { IDD = IDD_DIALOG1 };
BOOL    m_Bold;
BOOL    m_Italic;
BOOL    m_Underline;
//}}AFX_DATA


// Overrides
    // ClassWizard generate virtual function overrides
    //{{AFX_VIRTUAL(CStyle)
    protected:
    virtual void DoDataExchange(CDataExchange* pDX);    // DDX/DDV support
    //}}AFX_VIRTUAL

// Implementation
protected:
    // Generated message map functions
    //{{AFX_MSG(CStyle)
        // NOTE: the ClassWizard will add member functions here
    //}}AFX_MSG
    DECLARE_MESSAGE_MAP()

};

//{{AFX_INSERT_LOCATION}}
// Microsoft Visual C++ will insert additional declarations immediately before
// the previous line.

#endif // !defined(AFX_STYLE_H__60ECFFD4_A12D_11D1_80FC_00C0F6A83B7F__INCLUDED_)
```

Listing 15.24

```
// Style.cpp : implementation file
//

#include "stdafx.h"
#include "TabDemo.h"
#include "Style.h"

#ifdef _DEBUG
#define new DEBUG_NEW
```

```
#undef THIS_FILE
static char THIS_FILE[] = __FILE__;
#endif

/////////////////////////////////////////////////////////////////////////
// CStyle property page

IMPLEMENT_DYNCREATE(CStyle, CPropertyPage)

CStyle::CStyle() : CPropertyPage(CStyle::IDD)
{
    //{{AFX_DATA_INIT(CStyle)
    m_Bold = FALSE;
    m_Italic = FALSE;
    m_Underline = FALSE;
    //}}AFX_DATA_INIT
}

CStyle::~CStyle()
{
}

void CStyle::DoDataExchange(CDataExchange* pDX)
{
    CPropertyPage::DoDataExchange(pDX);
    //{{AFX_DATA_MAP(CStyle)
    DDX_Check(pDX, IDC_BOLD, m_Bold);
    DDX_Check(pDX, IDC_ITALIC, m_Italic);
    DDX_Check(pDX, IDC_UNDERLINE, m_Underline);
    //}}AFX_DATA_MAP
}


BEGIN_MESSAGE_MAP(CStyle, CPropertyPage)
    //{{AFX_MSG_MAP(CStyle)
        // NOTE: the ClassWizard will add message map macros here
    //}}AFX_MSG_MAP
END_MESSAGE_MAP()

/////////////////////////////////////////////////////////////////////////
// CStyle message handlers
```

Common Dialog Boxes

A *common dialog box* is one that's provided by Windows for performing a specific task, such as opening a file or choosing a color. The MFC provides a class for managing each type of common dialog box; these classes are summarized in Table 15.8.

TABLE 15.8: Windows Common Dialog Boxes

MFC Class	Dialog Box(es) Managed
CColorDialog	Color (for choosing a color)
CFileDialog	Open (for opening a file), Save As (for saving a file under a specified file name)
CFindReplaceDialog	Find (for finding text), Replace (for replacing text)
CFontDialog	Font (for choosing a text font)
COleDialog	This class—together with a set of classes derived from it—is designed for creating dialog boxes for OLE applications.
CPageSetupDialog	OLE Page Setup (for specifying the page setup and print margins for OLE applications)
CPrintDialog	Print (for printing a file), Print Setup (for specifying printer settings)

The MFC code uses several of these dialog boxes. The MFC code for processing the Open... and Save As... commands on the File menu uses the common dialog boxes managed by the CFileDialog class, while the code for processing the Print... and Print Setup... commands (to be described in Chapter 21) uses the common dialog boxes managed by the CPrintDialog class. Also, the CEditView MFC class uses the CFindReplaceDialog dialog box for implementing the Find... and Replace... commands on the Edit menu (as described in Chapter 10).

You can display these dialog boxes from your own code to save a great amount of programming effort. You can also customize the appearance and behavior of a common dialog box when you display it. You'll learn how to use the CFontDialog class in Chapter 18 and the CColorDialog class in Chapter 19. For further information on displaying common dialog boxes, see the documentation on the appropriate class in the following online help topic: *Visual C++ Documentation, Reference, Microsoft Foundation Class Library and Templates, Microsoft Foundation Class Library, Class Library Reference.*

Summary

In this chapter, you learned how to design, display, and manage modal dialog boxes—both conventional single-page dialog boxes as well as tabbed dialog boxes. You were also briefly introduced to modeless dialog boxes and Windows common dialog boxes. The following are the general concepts and techniques that were discussed:

- A modal dialog box is a temporary window that's opened over the main program window to display information and obtain data from the user. The user must close a modal dialog box before resuming work in the main window.

- After generating a program with AppWizard, you can design a dialog box using the dialog editor of the Developer Studio. The dialog editor displays a full-sized replica of the dialog box you're creating and includes a Controls toolbar that allows you to add controls to the dialog box.

- You can use the mouse to change the size or position of the dialog box or any of the controls contained within it. You can set the properties of the dialog box or any control by right-clicking the object, choosing Properties on the pop-up menu, and entering the desired values into the Properties dialog box. The standard controls you can add by using the Controls toolbar were shown in Figure 15.5. The different types of controls were explained in the sidebar "Using Controls."

- You can use ClassWizard to create a class (derived from CDialog) to manage the dialog box.

- You can also use ClassWizard to define data members of the dialog class. Each of these data members is associated with a particular control, and the MFC automatically transfers data between the data member and the control when the dialog box is displayed or closed.

- Finally, you can use ClassWizard to define message-handling functions for the dialog class.

- You display a modal dialog box by creating an object of the dialog class and calling the CDialog::DoModal function for that object. Control doesn't return from this call until the user has closed the dialog box.

- A modeless dialog box is one that can be left open while the user continues to work in the main program window. You can design a modeless dialog box in the dialog editor in the same way you design a modal dialog box. The way you write the dialog class and the code for displaying the modeless dialog box, however, differ from the techniques for a modal dialog box.

- A tabbed dialog box allows you to display several pages of related controls within a single dialog box.

- You must create an instance of the MFC CPropertySheet class (or a class derived from it) to manage the tabbed dialog box itself. You must also create an object of a CPropertyPage-derived class to manage each page that's to be displayed. Each page object is associated with a dialog box template you've created in the dialog editor (which defines the controls on the page), and it must be added to the CPropertySheet object by calling CPropertySheet::AddPage.

- To display the tabbed dialog box, you call the CPropertySheet::DoModal function.

- Windows provides a set of predefined common dialog boxes for performing standard tasks, such as opening files or choosing fonts.

In the next chapter, you'll learn how to create applications in which the main program window consists of a collection of controls based on a dialog box template.

CHAPTER
SIXTEEN

16

Writing Dialog-Based Applications

- Creating a simple dialog-based program

- Creating a form-view program

In each of the Windows GUI programs you've developed so far in this book, the program window contains a simple open area in which the program can freely display text and graphics. This application model is ideal for programs in which the user creates, views, and scrolls through various types of documents—for example, word processing, spreadsheet, and drawing programs.

In this chapter, you'll learn how to write *dialog-based applications*; that is, applications in which the main program window displays a collection of controls—such as edit boxes, radio buttons, and list boxes—and is based on a dialog box template you design in the Developer Studio dialog editor. This alternative application model is ideal for programs that primarily collect and display discrete items of information—for example, data entry programs, as well as many types of utilities such as file finders, phone dialers, calculators, disk utilities, and so on.

You'll learn how to create two types of dialog-based applications. First, you'll learn how to write a simple program that displays only a dialog box *without* a main frame or view window. Then, you'll learn to develop a full-featured *form-view* program, which displays a main frame window, complete with user interface objects, as well as a view window that contains a collection of controls based on a dialog template.

Learning how to use AppWizard and the Visual C++ dialog editor to create dialog-based applications affords you much of the convenience of the Microsoft Visual Basic development system, in which main program windows are interactively designed like dialog boxes. The next chapter presents another alternative application model: the multiple document interface (MDI).

Creating a Simple Dialog-Based Program

The simplest type of dialog-based program is one that *doesn't* create a main frame window or a view window, but rather simply displays a dialog box (using the basic techniques explained in Chapter 15). When generating this type of program, AppWizard creates only an application class and a dialog class. Accordingly, this application model is best for writing simple utilities and other types of programs that don't manage documents.

In the following sections, you'll create a simple dialog-based program, named DlgDemo, that allows the user to choose primary colors and then displays the result of combining these colors in an area of the dialog box. You'll first use App-Wizard to generate the basic program shell, and you'll then add custom features to the program.

Generating the DlgDemo Program in AppWizard

To generate the DlgDemo program, follow the usual procedure of choosing the File ➤ New... menu command and opening the Projects tab in the New dialog box. In the Projects tab, select the "MFC AppWizard (exe)" project type, enter the program name—DlgDemo—into the Project Name: text box, and enter the desired project folder into the Location: text box. After clicking the OK button, enter information as follows into the AppWizard Step 1 through Step 4 dialog boxes:

1. In the Step 1 dialog box, choose the Dialog Based option, as shown in Figure 16.1. Making this choice causes AppWizard to display a *different* series of "Step" dialog boxes from those displayed when you choose the Single Document option (and it shows only three more dialog boxes).

FIGURE 16.1:

The completed AppWizard Step 1 dialog box for generating the DlgDemo program

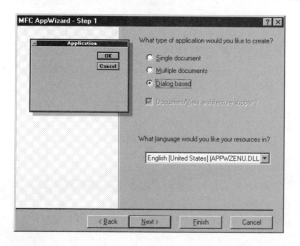

2. In the Step 2 dialog box, deselect the About Box option and the ActiveX Controls option, and enter Dialog-Based Demo into the Please Enter A Title For Your Dialog Box text box at the bottom. Leave all other options unchanged (of the other options, only 3D Controls should be selected). The completed Step 2 dialog box is shown in Figure 16.2. (The About Box and ActiveX Controls options are disabled, to simplify the program source code.

Choose About Box for other programs if you want the system menu to include a command for displaying a standard About dialog box. Choose ActiveX Controls for other programs if you want to display ActiveX controls in the dialog box, as explained in Chapter 25.)

FIGURE 16.2:

The completed AppWizard Step 2 dialog box for generating the DlgDemo program

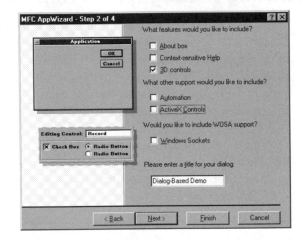

3. In the Step 3 dialog box, select the As A Statically Linked Library option, as usual. See Figure 16.3.

FIGURE 16.3:

The completed AppWizard Step 3 dialog box for generating the DlgDemo program

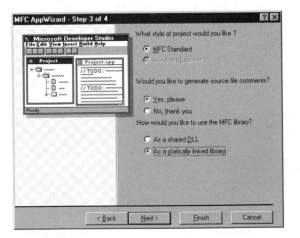

4. Make no changes to the Step 4 dialog box, which is shown in Figure 16.4. Click the Finish button in the Step 4 dialog box, and then click the OK button in the New Project Information dialog box. AppWizard will generate the program source files and will automatically open the program dialog box in the Developer Studio dialog editor.

FIGURE 16.4:

The completed AppWizard Step 4 dialog box for generating the DlgDemo program

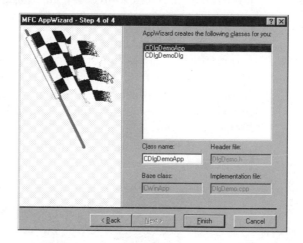

For a dialog-based application, AppWizard generates only two primary program classes: an application class and a dialog class. The application class manages the program as a whole (as usual), and it serves to display the program dialog box. The way it displays the dialog box will be explained later. For DlgDemo, the application class is named CDlgDemoApp, and it's defined in the files DlgDemo.h and DlgDemo.cpp.

The dialog class manages the program dialog box. For DlgDemo, the dialog class is named CDlgDemoDlg, and it's defined in the files DlgDemoDlg.h and DlgDemoDlg.cpp. (If you choose the About Box option, AppWiz generates another dialog class to manage the About dialog box.) Because a dialog-based application doesn't have a main frame window or a view window, AppWizard doesn't generate the corresponding classes, nor does it generate a document class.

Customizing the DlgDemo Program

You'll now customize the DlgDemo program by adding controls to the dialog box and writing code to support these controls:

1. The program dialog box should already be opened in the dialog editor. But if it isn't, open the ResourceView tab in the Workspace window, and double-click the IDD_DLGDEMO_DIALOG dialog resource.

2. In the dialog editor, right-click in the dialog box (but *not* in a control) and choose the Properties command on the pop-up menu to open the Dialog Properties dialog box. Then, open the Styles tab and choose the Minimize Box option, so that when the program is run the user will be able to minimize the dialog box. Leave the default values for the other options in the Styles tab as well as in the three other tabs, as they're appropriate for defining a dialog box that serves as the main program window. The completed Styles tab of the Dialog Properties dialog box is shown in Figure 16.5.

FIGURE 16.5:

The completed Styles tab of the Dialog Properties dialog box for designing a dialog box to be used as the main program window of an App-Wizard dialog-based program; all options in the other three tabs are left with their default values.

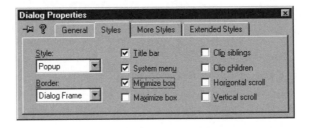

3. In the dialog box, delete the OK button and the "TODO" static text control. Also, right-click the Cancel button and choose Properties to open the Push Button Properties dialog box, and in the General tab change the button caption from Cancel to Close. (The button will be used to terminate the program; there's no action to cancel.)

4. Add the controls to the dialog box that are described in Table 16.1 and are illustrated in Figure 16.6.

T A B L E 1 6 . 1 : Properties of the Controls to Add to the DlgDemo Program Dialog Box

ID:	Type of Control	Nondefault Properties You Need to Set
IDC_STATIC	Group box	Caption: `Primary Colors`
IDC_RED	Check box	Caption: `&Red`
		Group
IDC_GREEN	Check box	Caption: `&Green`
IDC_BLUE	Check box	Caption: `&Blue`
IDC_STATIC	Group box	Caption: `Color Intensity`
IDC_DARK	Radio button	Caption: `&Dark`
		Group
		Tab Stop
IDC_LIGHT	Radio button	Caption: `&Light`
IDC_SAMPLE	Group box	Caption: `Sample`

FIGURE 16.6:

The completed DlgDemo program dialog box, as displayed in the dialog editor

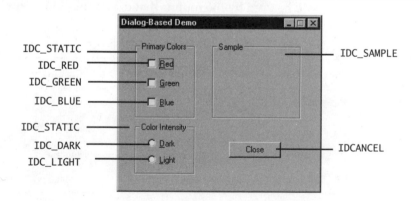

5. Choose the Layout ➢ Tab Order menu command, and click on the controls one at a time to set the tab order shown in Figure 16.7. The effect of the tab order was explained in Chapter 15.

FIGURE 16.7:

Setting the tab order for the DlgDemo program dialog box

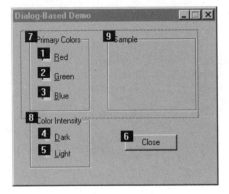

6. Use ClassWizard to define data members for several of the controls in the dialog box. To do this, run ClassWizard and open the Member Variables tab. Then, select the CDlgDemoDlg class in the Class Name: list, and add the member variables described in Table 16.2. Note that for each variable you should accept the default variable category and type. The data members will be used by the routine that draws the color sample.

TABLE 16.2: Data Members to Add to the CDlgDemoDlg Class

Control ID:	Member Variable Name	Category	Variable Type
IDC_RED	m_Red	Value	BOOL
IDC_GREEN	m_Green	Value	BOOL
IDC_BLUE	m_Blue	Value	BOOL
IDC_DARK	m_Intensity	Value	int

7. Use ClassWizard to add message handlers for several of the controls. After running ClassWizard, open the Message Maps tab. Then, add a BN_CLICKED message-handling function for each of the following controls: IDC_RED, IDC_GREEN, IDC_BLUE, IDC_DARK, and IDC_LIGHT. For each function, accept the default name.

8. Open the DlgDemoDlg.cpp source file and add code as follows to the message handlers that you just generated:

```cpp
void CDlgDemoDlg::OnRed()
{
    // TODO: Add your control notification handler code here
    m_Red = IsDlgButtonChecked (IDC_RED);
    InvalidateRect (&m_RectSample);
    UpdateWindow ();
}


void CDlgDemoDlg::OnGreen()
{
    // TODO: Add your control notification handler code here
    m_Green = IsDlgButtonChecked (IDC_GREEN);
    InvalidateRect (&m_RectSample);
    UpdateWindow ();
}


void CDlgDemoDlg::OnBlue()
{
    // TODO: Add your control notification handler code here
    m_Blue = IsDlgButtonChecked (IDC_BLUE);
    InvalidateRect (&m_RectSample);
    UpdateWindow ();
}


void CDlgDemoDlg::OnDark()
{
    // TODO: Add your control notification handler code here
    if (IsDlgButtonChecked (IDC_DARK))
        {
        m_Intensity = INT_DARK;
        InvalidateRect (&m_RectSample);
        UpdateWindow ();
        }
}


void CDlgDemoDlg::OnLight()
{
    // TODO: Add your control notification handler code here
    if (IsDlgButtonChecked (IDC_LIGHT))
```

```
        {
        m_Intensity = INT_LIGHT;
        InvalidateRect (&m_RectSample);
        UpdateWindow ();
        }
    }
```

The handler for the Red button sets the corresponding data member, m_Red, to TRUE if the button has been checked, or it sets it to FALSE if the check mark has been removed from the button. It then calls InvalidateRect and UpdateWindow to force the OnPaint function to redraw the resulting color in the Sample area, using the newly set value of m_Red. InvalidateRect and UpdateWindow were explained in Chapter 15 (in the section "Completing the CFormat Code"). The handlers for the Green and Blue buttons work the same way as the handler for the Red button. The handlers for the Dark and Light buttons set the m_Intensity data member and force repainting of the sample area only if the button has actually been checked (as explained in Chapter 15, a BN_CLICKED message handler for a radio button sometimes gets called without the button's being checked).

9. Also in the DlgDemoDlg.cpp: file, add code as follows to the dialog initialization message-handler, OnInitDialog, which was generated by AppWizard:

```
BOOL CDlgDemoDlg::OnInitDialog()
{
    CDialog::OnInitDialog();

    // Set the icon for this dialog.  The framework does this
    // automatically when the application's main window is not a
    // dialog
    SetIcon(m_hIcon, TRUE);         // Set big icon
    SetIcon(m_hIcon, FALSE);        // Set small icon

    // TODO: Add extra initialization here

    GetDlgItem (IDC_SAMPLE)->GetWindowRect (&m_RectSample);
    ScreenToClient (&m_RectSample);
    int Border = (m_RectSample.right - m_RectSample.left) / 8;
    m_RectSample.InflateRect (-Border, -Border);

    return TRUE;  // return TRUE  unless you set the focus to a
                  // control
}
```

The added code determines the coordinates of the rectangle in which the color sample will be drawn, and stores the coordinates in the CRect member object m_RectSample. This code is the same as the code you added to the FontDemo program presented in Chapter 15, except that it calls CRect::InflateRect for the m_RectSample object to reduce the size of the rectangle, so that there will be a border between the color rectangle and the outside of the Sample group box.

10. In DlgDemoDlg.cpp change the assignment of the m_Intensity data member in the dialog class constructor so that it's initialized to the value INT_LIGHT, causing the Light radio button to be checked initially:

```
CDlgDemoDlg::CDlgDemoDlg(CWnd* pParent /*=NULL*/)
   : CDialog(CDlgDemoDlg::IDD, pParent)
{
   //{{AFX_DATA_INIT(CDlgDemoDlg)
   m_Red = FALSE;
   m_Green = FALSE;
   m_Blue = FALSE;
   m_Intensity = INT_LIGHT;
   //}}AFX_DATA_INIT
   // Note that LoadIcon does not require a subsequent
   // DestroyIcon in Win32
   m_hIcon = AfxGetApp()->LoadIcon(IDR_MAINFRAME);
}
```

(Changing the value used to initialize a ClassWizard-generated data member of a dialog class is an exception to the rule against editing code within sections marked with the special ClassWizard comments.)

11. In DlgDemoDlg.cpp delete the call to CDialog::OnPaint within the else clause of the OnPaint function, and add code to the else clause as follows:

```
void CDlgDemoDlg::OnPaint()
{
   if (IsIconic())
   {
      CPaintDC dc(this); // device context for painting

      SendMessage
         (WM_ICONERASEBKGND, (WPARAM) dc.GetSafeHdc(), 0);

      // Center icon in client rectangle
```

```
            int cxIcon = GetSystemMetrics(SM_CXICON);
            int cyIcon = GetSystemMetrics(SM_CYICON);
            CRect rect;
            GetClientRect(&rect);
            int x = (rect.Width() - cxIcon + 1) / 2;
            int y = (rect.Height() - cyIcon + 1) / 2;

            // Draw the icon
            dc.DrawIcon(x, y, m_hIcon);
        }
        else
        {
            // deleted call to CDialog::OnPaint()
            COLORREF Color = RGB
              (m_Red ? (m_Intensity==INT_DARK ? 128 : 255) : 0,
               m_Green ? (m_Intensity==INT_DARK ? 128 : 255) : 0,
               m_Blue ? (m_Intensity==INT_DARK ? 128 : 255) : 0);
            CBrush Brush (Color);
            CPaintDC dc(this);
            dc.FillRect (&m_RectSample, &Brush);
        }
    }
```

The AppWizard-generated code in the if clause draws the program icon when the program window has been minimized. The code you added to the else clause paints a colored rectangle within the Sample group box. The color used to paint the rectangle is the result of combining either the light or the dark versions of the primary colors that the user has selected. See Chapter 19 for an explanation of the techniques for specifying drawing colors.

12. In the DlgDemoDlg.h file, add a definition for the m_RectSample data member and for the enumerators that indicate the selected color intensity, to the beginning of the CDlgDemoDlg class definition:

```
/////////////////////////////////////////////////////////////////
///////////
// CDlgDemoDlg dialog

class CDlgDemoDlg : public CDialog
```

```
    {
    public:
        CRect m_RectSample;

        enum {INT_DARK, INT_LIGHT};
```

The *InitInstance* Function

While you have the DlgDemo.cpp file open, observe that the AppWizard-generated `InitInstance` function of a dialog-based program performs the following main tasks (*rather than* creating a document template and calling `ProcessShellCommand` to process the command line, create a new document, and create the program windows, as in the previous example programs):

- `InitInstance` creates an object of the `CDlgDemoDlg` dialog box class.

- `InitInstance` calls the `CDialog::DoModal` function for the dialog object. `DoModal` creates and displays the dialog box based on the `IDD_DLGDEMO_DIALOG` dialog template (which is the template you edited for the DlgDemo program). After the user terminates the program by closing the dialog box, control returns from the call to `DoModal`. If your program performs some action based on the values entered into the dialog box, it can test the value returned by `DoModal` and take the appropriate steps.

- If the user cancels the dialog box, `DoModal` returns IDCANCEL.

- If, however, the user clicks a button with the IDOK identifier, `DoModal` returns IDOK. In this case, the contents of all controls have been transferred into the corresponding data members (if any have been defined using ClassWizard), and `InitInstance` can read these members as necessary.

- `InitInstance` returns FALSE so that the MFC code will terminate the program rather than proceeding to process messages (the `InitInstance` function of each of the previous example programs returned TRUE).

Building and Running DlgDemo

You can now build and run the DlgDemo program. The program window is shown in Figure 16.8.

FIGURE 16.8:

The DlgDemo program window

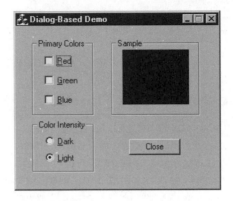

The DlgDemo Source Code

The following listings, Listings 16.1 through 16.4, contain the C++ source code for the DlgDemo program. You will find copies of these listings in your \DlgDemo companion-CD folder.

Listing 16.1

```
// DlgDemo.h : main header file for the DLGDEMO application
//

#if !defined(AFX_DLGDEMO_H__AF814125_A1F8_11D1_80FC_00C0F6A83B7F__INCLUDED_)
#define AFX_DLGDEMO_H__AF814125_A1F8_11D1_80FC_00C0F6A83B7F__INCLUDED_

#if _MSC_VER > 1000
#pragma once
#endif // _MSC_VER > 1000

#ifndef __AFXWIN_H__
    #error include 'stdafx.h' before including this file for PCH
#endif

#include "resource.h"      // main symbols

/////////////////////////////////////////////////////////////////////////////
// CDlgDemoApp:
// See DlgDemo.cpp for the implementation of this class
//
```

```
class CDlgDemoApp : public CWinApp
{
public:
    CDlgDemoApp();

// Overrides
    // ClassWizard generated virtual function overrides
    //{{AFX_VIRTUAL(CDlgDemoApp)
    public:
    virtual BOOL InitInstance();
    //}}AFX_VIRTUAL

// Implementation

    //{{AFX_MSG(CDlgDemoApp)
        // NOTE - the ClassWizard will add and remove member functions here.
        //    DO NOT EDIT what you see in these blocks of generated code !
    //}}AFX_MSG
    DECLARE_MESSAGE_MAP()
};


/////////////////////////////////////////////////////////////////////////////

//{{AFX_INSERT_LOCATION}}
// Microsoft Visual C++ will insert additional declarations immediately before
// the previous line.

#endif
// !defined(AFX_DLGDEMO_H__AF814125_A1F8_11D1_80FC_00C0F6A83B7F__INCLUDED_)
```

Listing 16.2

```
// DlgDemo.cpp : Defines the class behaviors for the application.
//

#include "stdafx.h"
#include "DlgDemo.h"
#include "DlgDemoDlg.h"

#ifdef _DEBUG
#define new DEBUG_NEW
```

```
#undef THIS_FILE
static char THIS_FILE[] = __FILE__;
#endif

/////////////////////////////////////////////////////////////////////////////
// CDlgDemoApp

BEGIN_MESSAGE_MAP(CDlgDemoApp, CWinApp)
    //{{AFX_MSG_MAP(CDlgDemoApp)
        // NOTE - the ClassWizard will add and remove mapping macros here.
        //    DO NOT EDIT what you see in these blocks of generated code!
    //}}AFX_MSG
    ON_COMMAND(ID_HELP, CWinApp::OnHelp)
END_MESSAGE_MAP()

/////////////////////////////////////////////////////////////////////////////
// CDlgDemoApp construction

CDlgDemoApp::CDlgDemoApp()
{
    // TODO: add construction code here,
    // Place all significant initialization in InitInstance
}

/////////////////////////////////////////////////////////////////////////////
// The one and only CDlgDemoApp object

CDlgDemoApp theApp;

/////////////////////////////////////////////////////////////////////////////
// CDlgDemoApp initialization

BOOL CDlgDemoApp::InitInstance()
{
    // Standard initialization
    // If you are not using these features and wish to reduce the size
    //  of your final executable, you should remove from the following
    //  the specific initialization routines you do not need.

#ifdef _AFXDLL
    Enable3dControls();           // Call this when using MFC in a shared DLL
#else
```

```
      Enable3dControlsStatic();  // Call this when linking to MFC statically
#endif

      CDlgDemoDlg dlg;
      m_pMainWnd = &dlg;
      int nResponse = dlg.DoModal();
      if (nResponse == IDOK)
      {
         // TODO: Place code here to handle when the dialog is
         //  dismissed with OK
      }
      else if (nResponse == IDCANCEL)
      {
         // TODO: Place code here to handle when the dialog is
         //  dismissed with Cancel
      }

      // Since the dialog has been closed, return FALSE so that we exit the
      //  application, rather than start the application's message pump.
      return FALSE;
}
```

Listing 16.3

```
// DlgDemoDlg.h : header file
//

#if !defined(AFX_DLGDEMODLG_H__AF814127_A1F8_11D1_80FC_00C0F6A83B7F__INCLUDED_)
#define AFX_DLGDEMODLG_H__AF814127_A1F8_11D1_80FC_00C0F6A83B7F__INCLUDED_

#if _MSC_VER > 1000
#pragma once
#endif // _MSC_VER > 1000

/////////////////////////////////////////////////////////////////////////
// CDlgDemoDlg dialog

class CDlgDemoDlg : public CDialog
{
public:
   CRect m_RectSample;

   enum {INT_DARK, INT_LIGHT};
```

```
    // Construction
public:
    CDlgDemoDlg(CWnd* pParent = NULL);   // standard constructor

// Dialog Data
    //{{AFX_DATA(CDlgDemoDlg)
    enum { IDD = IDD_DLGDEMO_DIALOG };
    BOOL  m_Red;
    BOOL  m_Green;
    BOOL  m_Blue;
    int       m_Intensity;
    //}}AFX_DATA

    // ClassWizard generated virtual function overrides
    //{{AFX_VIRTUAL(CDlgDemoDlg)
    protected:
    virtual void DoDataExchange(CDataExchange* pDX);    // DDX/DDV support
    //}}AFX_VIRTUAL

// Implementation
protected:
    HICON m_hIcon;

    // Generated message map functions
    //{{AFX_MSG(CDlgDemoDlg)
    virtual BOOL OnInitDialog();
    afx_msg void OnPaint();
    afx_msg HCURSOR OnQueryDragIcon();
    afx_msg void OnRed();
    afx_msg void OnGreen();
    afx_msg void OnBlue();
    afx_msg void OnDark();
    afx_msg void OnLight();
    //}}AFX_MSG
    DECLARE_MESSAGE_MAP()
};

//{{AFX_INSERT_LOCATION}}
// Microsoft Visual C++ will insert additional declarations immediately before
// the previous line.

#endif
// !defined(AFX_DLGDEMODLG_H__AF814127_A1F8_11D1_80FC_00C0F6A83B7F__INCLUDED_)
```

Listing 16.4

```cpp
// DlgDemoDlg.cpp : implementation file
//

#include "stdafx.h"
#include "DlgDemo.h"
#include "DlgDemoDlg.h"

#ifdef _DEBUG
#define new DEBUG_NEW
#undef THIS_FILE
static char THIS_FILE[] = __FILE__;
#endif

/////////////////////////////////////////////////////////////////////////////
// CDlgDemoDlg dialog

CDlgDemoDlg::CDlgDemoDlg(CWnd* pParent /*=NULL*/)
    : CDialog(CDlgDemoDlg::IDD, pParent)
{
    //{{AFX_DATA_INIT(CDlgDemoDlg)
    m_Red = FALSE;
    m_Green = FALSE;
    m_Blue = FALSE;
    m_Intensity = INT_LIGHT;
    //}}AFX_DATA_INIT
    // Note that LoadIcon does not require a subsequent DestroyIcon in Win32
    m_hIcon = AfxGetApp()->LoadIcon(IDR_MAINFRAME);
}

void CDlgDemoDlg::DoDataExchange(CDataExchange* pDX)
{
    CDialog::DoDataExchange(pDX);
    //{{AFX_DATA_MAP(CDlgDemoDlg)
    DDX_Check(pDX, IDC_RED, m_Red);
    DDX_Check(pDX, IDC_GREEN, m_Green);
    DDX_Check(pDX, IDC_BLUE, m_Blue);
    DDX_Radio(pDX, IDC_DARK, m_Intensity);
    //}}AFX_DATA_MAP
}
```

```
BEGIN_MESSAGE_MAP(CDlgDemoDlg, CDialog)
    //{{AFX_MSG_MAP(CDlgDemoDlg)
    ON_WM_PAINT()
    ON_WM_QUERYDRAGICON()
    ON_BN_CLICKED(IDC_RED, OnRed)
    ON_BN_CLICKED(IDC_GREEN, OnGreen)
    ON_BN_CLICKED(IDC_BLUE, OnBlue)
    ON_BN_CLICKED(IDC_DARK, OnDark)
    ON_BN_CLICKED(IDC_LIGHT, OnLight)
    //}}AFX_MSG_MAP
END_MESSAGE_MAP()

/////////////////////////////////////////////////////////////////////////////
// CDlgDemoDlg message handlers

BOOL CDlgDemoDlg::OnInitDialog()
{
    CDialog::OnInitDialog();

    // Set the icon for this dialog.  The framework does this automatically
    //  when the application's main window is not a dialog
    SetIcon(m_hIcon, TRUE);         // Set big icon
    SetIcon(m_hIcon, FALSE);        // Set small icon

    // TODO: Add extra initialization here

    GetDlgItem (IDC_SAMPLE)->GetWindowRect (&m_RectSample);
    ScreenToClient (&m_RectSample);
    int Border = (m_RectSample.right - m_RectSample.left) / 8;
    m_RectSample.InflateRect (-Border, -Border);

    return TRUE;  // return TRUE  unless you set the focus to a control
}

// If you add a minimize button to your dialog, you will need the code below
//  to draw the icon.  For MFC applications using the document/view model,
//  this is automatically done for you by the framework.

void CDlgDemoDlg::OnPaint()
{
    if (IsIconic())
```

```
    {
        CPaintDC dc(this); // device context for painting

        SendMessage(WM_ICONERASEBKGND, (WPARAM) dc.GetSafeHdc(), 0);

        // Center icon in client rectangle
        int cxIcon = GetSystemMetrics(SM_CXICON);
        int cyIcon = GetSystemMetrics(SM_CYICON);
        CRect rect;
        GetClientRect(&rect);
        int x = (rect.Width() - cxIcon + 1) / 2;
        int y = (rect.Height() - cyIcon + 1) / 2;

        // Draw the icon
        dc.DrawIcon(x, y, m_hIcon);
    }
    else
    {
        // deleted call to CDialog::OnPaint()
        COLORREF Color = RGB
            (m_Red ? (m_Intensity==INT_DARK ? 128 : 255) : 0,
             m_Green ? (m_Intensity==INT_DARK ? 128 : 255) : 0,
             m_Blue ? (m_Intensity==INT_DARK ? 128 : 255) : 0);
        CBrush Brush (Color);
        CPaintDC dc(this);
        dc.FillRect (&m_RectSample, &Brush);
    }
}

// The system calls this to obtain the cursor to display while the user drags
//   the minimized window.
HCURSOR CDlgDemoDlg::OnQueryDragIcon()
{
    return (HCURSOR) m_hIcon;
}

void CDlgDemoDlg::OnRed()
{
    // TODO: Add your control notification handler code here
    m_Red = IsDlgButtonChecked (IDC_RED);
    InvalidateRect (&m_RectSample);
    UpdateWindow ();
}
```

```
void CDlgDemoDlg::OnGreen()
{
   // TODO: Add your control notification handler code here
   m_Green = IsDlgButtonChecked (IDC_GREEN);
   InvalidateRect (&m_RectSample);
   UpdateWindow ();
}

void CDlgDemoDlg::OnBlue()
{
   // TODO: Add your control notification handler code here
   m_Blue = IsDlgButtonChecked (IDC_BLUE);
   InvalidateRect (&m_RectSample);
   UpdateWindow ();
}

void CDlgDemoDlg::OnDark()
{
   // TODO: Add your control notification handler code here
   if (IsDlgButtonChecked (IDC_DARK))
      {
      m_Intensity = INT_DARK;
      InvalidateRect (&m_RectSample);
      UpdateWindow ();
      }
}

void CDlgDemoDlg::OnLight()
{
   // TODO: Add your control notification handler code here
   if (IsDlgButtonChecked (IDC_LIGHT))
      {
      m_Intensity = INT_LIGHT;
      InvalidateRect (&m_RectSample);
      UpdateWindow ();
      }
}
```

Creating a Form-View Program

A form-view program is a full-featured program based on a dialog box. It has the same basic architecture as the MFC programs that have been presented in previous chapters; the primary difference is that the view class is derived from CFormView rather than from one of the other MFC view classes (such as CView, CScrollView, or CEditView). Because the view class is derived from CFormView, the view window displays a collection of controls, rather than a blank client area, and the layout of these controls is based on a dialog box template. Unlike a simple dialog-based program described in the previous sections, a form-view program has the following features:

- It has the four standard MFC program classes: an application class, a main frame window class, a document class, and a view class. The form-view application model is thus well suited for developing programs that store, display, and modify documents.

- The program has a standard main frame window, with standard frame window components such as a sizable border and a maximize box.

- The program can display any of the standard MFC user-interface elements—a menu, a toolbar, or a status bar—and any of the main program classes can process the messages from these elements.

- Because CFormView is derived from CScrollView (described in Chapter 13), if the controls don't all fit within the view window, the window will display a horizontal scroll bar, a vertical scroll bar, or both, and the user can use the scroll bars to access any control.

In the remaining sections of this chapter, you'll create a simple form-view program named FormDemo. The FormDemo program is similar to the DlgDemo program you created previously. However, it includes the following additional features:

- The program window has a sizable frame and a maximize box, so that the user can change the window size.

- If the user reduces the window size so that the controls aren't fully visible, the program displays scroll bars, allowing the user to scroll through the window contents.

- The program window displays a menu. Rather than choosing the color intensity with radio buttons, the intensity is selected through commands on the Options pop-up menu. There's also a Help pop-up menu with an About command.

Generating the FormDemo Program in AppWizard

Use AppWizard to generate the basic code for the FormDemo program, following the procedure given for the WinGreet program in Chapter 9. In the Projects tab of the New dialog box, choose the "MFC AppWizard (exe)" project type, enter the program name—FormDemo—into the Name: text box, and enter the project folder path into the Location: text box. In the AppWizard Step 1 dialog box choose the Single Document and the Document/View Architecture Support options as usual (for a form-view program, you *don't* choose the Dialog Based option). Enter into the AppWizard dialog boxes the same values you entered for the WinGreet Program, *except* that in the Step 6 dialog box you should do the following:

1. Select the view class, CFormDemoView, in the list at the top of the dialog box.

2. Select CFormView in the Base Class: list so that the view class will be derived from CFormView. The completed Step 6 dialog box is shown in Figure 16.9.

FIGURE 16.9:

The completed AppWizard Step 6 dialog box for generating the FormDemo form-view program

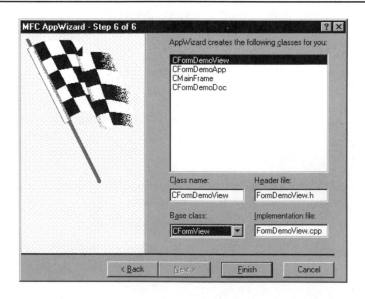

After AppWizard generates the source code files, it automatically opens the program dialog box in the Developer Studio dialog editor.

Customizing the FormDemo Program

After you've finished generating the source code files, proceed to customize the FormDemo program as follows:

1. The program dialog box should already be opened in the dialog editor. But if it isn't, open the ResourceView tab in the Workspace window and double-click the IDD_FORMDEMO_FORM dialog identifier to open the dialog editor. The IDD_FORMDEMO_FORM dialog box template was created by AppWizard and is associated with the view class; that is, the view window automatically displays the controls contained within this template. Notice that initially the template contains only a "TODO" static text control.

   You don't need to change any of the properties of the dialog box, because the properties that AppWizard initially assigns to it are appropriate for a dialog box template that's to be displayed in a form-view window. The dialog box template isn't assigned a border, a title bar, or other visible elements, because these elements are provided by the main frame window that frames the view window. (Open the Dialog Properties dialog box if you want to see its properties.)

2. Delete the existing static text control and add the controls that are described in Table 16.3 and illustrated in Figure 16.10.

TABLE 16.3: Properties of the Controls to Add to the FormDemo IDD_FORMDEMO_FORM Dialog Box

ID:	Type of Control	Nondefault Properties You Need to Set
IDC_STATIC	Group box	Caption: Primary Colors
IDC_RED	Check box	Caption: &Red
		Group
IDC_GREEN	Check box	Caption: &Green
IDC_BLUE	Check box	Caption: &Blue
IDC_SAMPLE	Group box	Caption: &Sample

FIGURE 16.10:

The completed FormDemo IDD_FORMDEMO_FORM dialog template, as displayed in the dialog editor

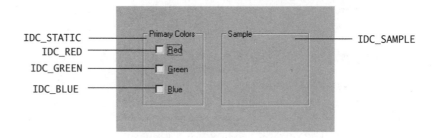

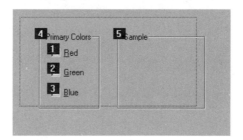

> **TIP**
>
> To save time, you can open the program dialog box that you previously created for the DlgDemo program (open DlgDemo.rc and then open the **IDD_DLGDEMO_DIALOG** resource) and copy the needed controls into the FormDemo dialog box. To copy a control, select it and use the Copy and Paste commands on the Edit menu. To select a group of controls, press Ctrl as you click on each control.

3. Set the tab order as shown in Figure 16.11.

FIGURE 16.11:

The Tab Order for the FormDemo IDD_FORMDEMO_FORM dialog template

4. Use ClassWizard to define member variables for the IDC_RED, IDC_GREEN, and IDC_BLUE check boxes. They should be members of the CFormDemoView class. For each variable you should accept the default category and variable type, and you should name the variables m_Red, m_Green, and m_Blue.

5. Open the menu editor for the IDR_MAINFRAME menu. Delete the Edit menu and change the caption for the File menu to &Options. Now delete all commands on the Options menu except the Exit command and the separator above it. Finally, above the separator, add the Light Colors command and the Dark Colors command, described in Table 16.4. The completed Options menu is shown in Figure 16.12.

TABLE 16.4: New Commands to Add to the Options Menu

ID:	Caption
ID_OPTIONS_LIGHT	&Light Colors
ID_OPTIONS_DARK	&Dark Colors

FIGURE 16.12:

The completed Options menu for the FormDemo program, as seen in the menu editor

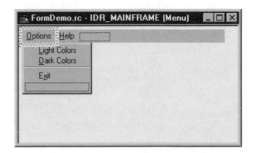

6. Run ClassWizard again, open the Message Maps tab, and choose **CForm-DemoView** in the Class Name: list. (In the FormDemo program, the messages from the menu items and buttons that you've added will be handled by the view class.) Generate a COMMAND message-handling function and an UPDATE_COMMAND_UI message-handling function for the ID_OPTIONS_DARK and ID_OPTIONS_LIGHT menu commands that you just defined. Also, define BN_CLICKED message-handling functions for the IDC_RED, IDC_GREEN, and IDC_BLUE check boxes. For all functions, accept the default names.

7. Open the FormDemoView.cpp file and add code to the five message-handling functions you just generated:

```
/////////////////////////////////////////////////////////////////
///////////
// CFormDemoView message handlers

void CFormDemoView::OnOptionsDark()
{
    // TODO: Add your command handler code here
    m_Intensity = INT_DARK;
```

```
    CClientDC ClientDC (this);
    OnPrepareDC (&ClientDC);
    CRect Rect = m_RectSample;
    ClientDC.LPtoDP (&Rect);
    InvalidateRect (&Rect);
    UpdateWindow ();
}

void CFormDemoView::OnUpdateOptionsDark(CCmdUI* pCmdUI)
{
    // TODO: Add your command update UI handler code here
    pCmdUI->SetRadio (m_Intensity == INT_DARK);
}

void CFormDemoView::OnOptionsLight()
{
    // TODO: Add your command handler code here
    m_Intensity = INT_LIGHT;

    CClientDC ClientDC (this);
    OnPrepareDC (&ClientDC);
    CRect Rect = m_RectSample;
    ClientDC.LPtoDP (&Rect);
    InvalidateRect (&Rect);
    UpdateWindow ();
}

void CFormDemoView::OnUpdateOptionsLight(CCmdUI* pCmdUI)
{
    // TODO: Add your command update UI handler code here
    pCmdUI->SetRadio (m_Intensity == INT_LIGHT);
}

void CFormDemoView::OnRed()
{
    // TODO: Add your control notification handler code here
    m_Red = IsDlgButtonChecked (IDC_RED);

    CClientDC ClientDC (this);
    OnPrepareDC (&ClientDC);
    CRect Rect = m_RectSample;
    ClientDC.LPtoDP (&Rect);
```

```
        InvalidateRect (&Rect);
        UpdateWindow ();
}

void CFormDemoView::OnGreen()
{
        // TODO: Add your control notification handler code here
        m_Green = IsDlgButtonChecked (IDC_GREEN);

        CClientDC ClientDC (this);
        OnPrepareDC (&ClientDC);
        CRect Rect = m_RectSample;
        ClientDC.LPtoDP (&Rect);
        InvalidateRect (&Rect);
        UpdateWindow ();
}

void CFormDemoView::OnBlue()
{
        // TODO: Add your control notification handler code here
        m_Blue = IsDlgButtonChecked (IDC_BLUE);

        CClientDC ClientDC (this);
        OnPrepareDC (&ClientDC);
        CRect Rect = m_RectSample;
        ClientDC.LPtoDP (&Rect);
        InvalidateRect (&Rect);
        UpdateWindow ();
}
```

The new code is similar to the code you added to the message-handling functions of the DlgDemo program. However, because the intensity options are set through menu commands rather than radio buttons, the program must provide an update handler for each command (OnUpdateOptionsDark and OnUpdateOptionsLight), to check the appropriate command. Notice that the update handlers call CCmdUI::SetRadio rather than CCmdUI::SetCheck, so that the chosen menu command is checked with a bullet rather than a conventional check mark (a bullet is normally used to indicate the selected option within a group of mutually exclusive menu options).

As in the DlgDemo program, the message handlers invalidate the rectangular area of the dialog box in which the color sample is drawn. Notice, however, that the functions first convert the coordinates of the sample area from logical coordinates to device coordinates. This step is necessary because the view window class is derived indirectly from CScrollView and—if the controls don't all fit within the view window—the user can scroll through the window contents, causing the logical coordinates of the sample area stored in m_RectSample to differ from the device coordinates (InvalidateRect must be passed device coordinates). For an explanation of this conversion, see the section "Converting Coordinates" in Chapter 13.

8. Use ClassWizard to add to the view class an overriding version of the OnDraw function. (For a form-view program, AppWizard doesn't initially include an OnDraw function.) After opening the ClassWizard dialog box, open the Message Maps tab, select the CFormDemoView class in the Class Name: and Object IDs: lists, select OnDraw in the Messages: list, and click the Add Function button. Then click the Edit Code button, and add statements as follows:

```
void CFormDemoView::OnDraw(CDC* pDC)
{
    // TODO: Add your specialized code here and/or call the base
    // class

    COLORREF Color = RGB
        (m_Red ? (m_Intensity==INT_DARK ? 128 : 255) : 0,
        m_Green ? (m_Intensity==INT_DARK ? 128 : 255) : 0,
        m_Blue ? (m_Intensity==INT_DARK ? 128 : 255) : 0);
    CBrush Brush (Color);
    pDC->FillRect (&m_RectSample, &Brush);
}
```

These statements work in the same way as the code you added to the DlgDemo program.

9. Add code as follows to the CFormView::OnInitialUpdate function in FormDemoView.cpp, which was generated by AppWizard:

```
void CFormDemoView::OnInitialUpdate()
{
    CFormView::OnInitialUpdate();
    GetParentFrame()->RecalcLayout();
    ResizeParentToFit();

    GetDlgItem (IDC_SAMPLE)->GetWindowRect (&m_RectSample);
    ScreenToClient (&m_RectSample);
```

```
    int Border = (m_RectSample.right - m_RectSample.left) / 8;
    m_RectSample.InflateRect (-Border, -Border);
}
```

As explained in Chapter 13, the OnInitialUpdate virtual function of the view class is called immediately before a new or existing document is *first* displayed in the view window.

After calling the base class version of OnInitialUpdate, the AppWizard-generated code calls the RecalcLayout function of the main frame window object to position any control bars displayed by the program (though in FormDemo there are none). The AppWizard code then calls CScroll-View::ResizeParentToFit to size the main frame window to fit the contents of the view window.

The four new statements you added are the same as those you added to the OnInitDialog function of the DlgDemo program. (You added this code to an OnInitialUpdate function rather than an OnInitDialog function because a view window isn't sent a WM_INITDIALOG message, and therefore an OnInitDialog function would never receive control.)

Note that when OnInitialUpdate is called, the view window can't yet have been scrolled; therefore, the coordinates saved in m_RectSample are the device coordinates as well as the logical coordinates of the sample area. After the window has been scrolled, the coordinates in m_RectSample are logical only.

10.   Also in the FormDemoView.cpp file, add code for initializing the m_Intensity data member to the view class constructor:

```
/////////////////////////////////////////////////////////////////
///////////
// CFormDemoView construction/destruction

CFormDemoView::CFormDemoView()
    : CFormView(CFormDemoView::IDD)
{
    //{{AFX_DATA_INIT(CFormDemoView)
    m_Red = FALSE;
    m_Green = FALSE;
    m_Blue = FALSE;
    //}}AFX_DATA_INIT
    // TODO: add construction code here

    m_Intensity = INT_LIGHT;
}
```

11. In the file FormDemoView.h, define the m_DialogBrush, m_Intensity, and m_RectSample data members of the view class, and add a definition for the INT_DARK and INT_LIGHT enumerators:

```
class CFormDemoView : public CFormView
{
public:
    CBrush m_DialogBrush;
    int m_Intensity;
    CRect m_RectSample;

    enum {INT_DARK, INT_LIGHT};
```

12. Finally, in the FormDemo.cpp file, add a call to SetWindowText at the end of the InitInstance function to set the program's title:

```
// The one and only window has been initialized, so show and
// update it.
m_pMainWnd->ShowWindow(SW_SHOW);
m_pMainWnd->UpdateWindow();

m_pMainWnd->SetWindowText ("Form-View Demo");

return TRUE;
}
```

You can now build and run the FormDemo program. Figure 16.13 shows the FormDemo window when the program is first run. Figure 16.14 shows the window after its size has been reduced so that it's smaller than the dialog template, causing the program to display scroll bars.

FIGURE 16.13:

The FormDemo window as it appears when the program is first run

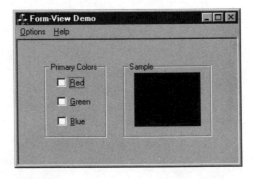

FIGURE 16.14:

The FormDemo window after
the user has made it smaller
than the size of the dialog
box template

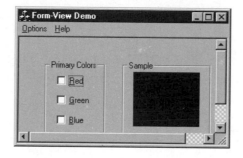

The FormDemo Source Code

Listings 16.5 through 16.12, which follow, are the C++ source listings for the
FormDemo program. You'll find complete copies of these listings in your \Form-
Demo companion-CD folder.

Listing 16.5

```
// FormDemo.h : main header file for the FORMDEMO application
//

#if !defined(AFX_FORMDEMO_H__AF814133_A1F8_11D1_80FC_00C0F6A83B7F__INCLUDED_)
#define AFX_FORMDEMO_H__AF814133_A1F8_11D1_80FC_00C0F6A83B7F__INCLUDED_

#if _MSC_VER > 1000
#pragma once
#endif // _MSC_VER > 1000

#ifndef __AFXWIN_H__
    #error include 'stdafx.h' before including this file for PCH
#endif

#include "resource.h"        // main symbols


/////////////////////////////////////////////////////////////////////////////
// CFormDemoApp:
// See FormDemo.cpp for the implementation of this class
//

class CFormDemoApp : public CWinApp
```

```
{
public:
    CFormDemoApp();

// Overrides
    // ClassWizard generated virtual function overrides
    //{{AFX_VIRTUAL(CFormDemoApp)
    public:
    virtual BOOL InitInstance();
    //}}AFX_VIRTUAL

// Implementation
    //{{AFX_MSG(CFormDemoApp)
    afx_msg void OnAppAbout();
        // NOTE - the ClassWizard will add and remove member functions here.
        //    DO NOT EDIT what you see in these blocks of generated code !
    //}}AFX_MSG
    DECLARE_MESSAGE_MAP()
};



/////////////////////////////////////////////////////////////////////////////

//{{AFX_INSERT_LOCATION}}
// Microsoft Visual C++ will insert additional declarations immediately before
// the previous line.

#endif
// !defined(AFX_FORMDEMO_H__AF814133_A1F8_11D1_80FC_00C0F6A83B7F__INCLUDED_)
```

Listing 16.6

```
// FormDemo.cpp : Defines the class behaviors for the application.
//

#include "stdafx.h"
#include "FormDemo.h"

#include "MainFrm.h"
#include "FormDemoDoc.h"
#include "FormDemoView.h"
```

```
#ifdef _DEBUG
#define new DEBUG_NEW
#undef THIS_FILE
static char THIS_FILE[] = __FILE__;
#endif

/////////////////////////////////////////////////////////////////////////////
// CFormDemoApp

BEGIN_MESSAGE_MAP(CFormDemoApp, CWinApp)
    //{{AFX_MSG_MAP(CFormDemoApp)
    ON_COMMAND(ID_APP_ABOUT, OnAppAbout)
        // NOTE - the ClassWizard will add and remove mapping macros here.
        //    DO NOT EDIT what you see in these blocks of generated code!
    //}}AFX_MSG_MAP
    // Standard file based document commands
    ON_COMMAND(ID_FILE_NEW, CWinApp::OnFileNew)
    ON_COMMAND(ID_FILE_OPEN, CWinApp::OnFileOpen)
END_MESSAGE_MAP()

/////////////////////////////////////////////////////////////////////////////
// CFormDemoApp construction

CFormDemoApp::CFormDemoApp()
{
    // TODO: add construction code here,
    // Place all significant initialization in InitInstance
}

/////////////////////////////////////////////////////////////////////////////
// The one and only CFormDemoApp object

CFormDemoApp theApp;

/////////////////////////////////////////////////////////////////////////////
// CFormDemoApp initialization

BOOL CFormDemoApp::InitInstance()
{
    // Standard initialization
    // If you are not using these features and wish to reduce the size
    //  of your final executable, you should remove from the following
```

```
    //  the specific initialization routines you do not need.

#ifdef _AFXDLL
    Enable3dControls();           // Call this when using MFC in a shared DLL
#else
    Enable3dControlsStatic();  // Call this when linking to MFC statically
#endif

    // Change the registry key under which our settings are stored.
    // TODO: You should modify this string to be something appropriate
    // such as the name of your company or organization.
    SetRegistryKey(_T("Local AppWizard-Generated Applications"));

    LoadStdProfileSettings();  // Load standard INI file options (including MRU)

    // Register the application's document templates.  Document templates
    //  serve as the connection between documents, frame windows and views.

    CSingleDocTemplate* pDocTemplate;
    pDocTemplate = new CSingleDocTemplate(
        IDR_MAINFRAME,
        RUNTIME_CLASS(CFormDemoDoc),
        RUNTIME_CLASS(CMainFrame),         // main SDI frame window
        RUNTIME_CLASS(CFormDemoView));
    AddDocTemplate(pDocTemplate);

    // Parse command line for standard shell commands, DDE, file open
    CCommandLineInfo cmdInfo;
    ParseCommandLine(cmdInfo);

    // Dispatch commands specified on the command line
    if (!ProcessShellCommand(cmdInfo))
        return FALSE;

    // The one and only window has been initialized, so show and update it.
    m_pMainWnd->ShowWindow(SW_SHOW);
    m_pMainWnd->UpdateWindow();

    m_pMainWnd->SetWindowText ("Form-View Demo");

    return TRUE;
}
```

```
/////////////////////////////////////////////////////////////////////////
// CAboutDlg dialog used for App About

class CAboutDlg : public CDialog
{
public:
   CAboutDlg();

// Dialog Data
   //{{AFX_DATA(CAboutDlg)
   enum { IDD = IDD_ABOUTBOX };
   //}}AFX_DATA

   // ClassWizard generated virtual function overrides
   //{{AFX_VIRTUAL(CAboutDlg)
   protected:
   virtual void DoDataExchange(CDataExchange* pDX);     // DDX/DDV support
   //}}AFX_VIRTUAL

// Implementation
protected:
   //{{AFX_MSG(CAboutDlg)
      // No message handlers
   //}}AFX_MSG
   DECLARE_MESSAGE_MAP()
};

CAboutDlg::CAboutDlg() : CDialog(CAboutDlg::IDD)
{
   //{{AFX_DATA_INIT(CAboutDlg)
   //}}AFX_DATA_INIT
}

void CAboutDlg::DoDataExchange(CDataExchange* pDX)
{
   CDialog::DoDataExchange(pDX);
   //{{AFX_DATA_MAP(CAboutDlg)
   //}}AFX_DATA_MAP
}

BEGIN_MESSAGE_MAP(CAboutDlg, CDialog)
   //{{AFX_MSG_MAP(CAboutDlg)
```

```
     // No message handlers
  //}}AFX_MSG_MAP
END_MESSAGE_MAP()

// App command to run the dialog
void CFormDemoApp::OnAppAbout()
{
   CAboutDlg aboutDlg;
   aboutDlg.DoModal();
}

/////////////////////////////////////////////////////////////////////////
// CFormDemoApp message handlers
```

Listing 16.7

```
// FormDemoDoc.h : interface of the CFormDemoDoc class
//
/////////////////////////////////////////////////////////////////////////

#if !defined(AFX_FORMDEMODOC_H__AF814139_A1F8_11D1_80FC_00C0F6A83B7F__INCLUDED_)
#define AFX_FORMDEMODOC_H__AF814139_A1F8_11D1_80FC_00C0F6A83B7F__INCLUDED_

#if _MSC_VER > 1000
#pragma once
#endif // _MSC_VER > 1000


class CFormDemoDoc : public CDocument
{
protected: // create from serialization only
   CFormDemoDoc();
   DECLARE_DYNCREATE(CFormDemoDoc)

// Attributes
public:

// Operations
public:

// Overrides
```

```
    // ClassWizard generated virtual function overrides
    //{{AFX_VIRTUAL(CFormDemoDoc)
    public:
    virtual BOOL OnNewDocument();
    virtual void Serialize(CArchive& ar);
    //}}AFX_VIRTUAL

// Implementation
public:
    virtual ~CFormDemoDoc();
#ifdef _DEBUG
    virtual void AssertValid() const;
    virtual void Dump(CDumpContext& dc) const;
#endif

protected:

// Generated message map functions
protected:
    //{{AFX_MSG(CFormDemoDoc)
        // NOTE - the ClassWizard will add and remove member functions here.
        //    DO NOT EDIT what you see in these blocks of generated code !
    //}}AFX_MSG
    DECLARE_MESSAGE_MAP()
};


/////////////////////////////////////////////////////////////////////////////

//{{AFX_INSERT_LOCATION}}
// Microsoft Visual C++ will insert additional declarations immediately before
// the previous line.

#endif
// !defined(AFX_FORMDEMODOC_H__AF814139_A1F8_11D1_80FC_00C0F6A83B7F__INCLUDED_)
```

Listing 16.8

```
// FormDemoDoc.cpp : implementation of the CFormDemoDoc class
//

#include "stdafx.h"
#include "FormDemo.h"
```

```
#include "FormDemoDoc.h"

#ifdef _DEBUG
#define new DEBUG_NEW
#undef THIS_FILE
static char THIS_FILE[] = __FILE__;
#endif

/////////////////////////////////////////////////////////////////////////
// CFormDemoDoc

IMPLEMENT_DYNCREATE(CFormDemoDoc, CDocument)

BEGIN_MESSAGE_MAP(CFormDemoDoc, CDocument)
    //{{AFX_MSG_MAP(CFormDemoDoc)
        // NOTE - the ClassWizard will add and remove mapping macros here.
        //    DO NOT EDIT what you see in these blocks of generated code!
    //}}AFX_MSG_MAP
END_MESSAGE_MAP()

/////////////////////////////////////////////////////////////////////////
// CFormDemoDoc construction/destruction

CFormDemoDoc::CFormDemoDoc()
{
    // TODO: add one-time construction code here

}

CFormDemoDoc::~CFormDemoDoc()
{
}

BOOL CFormDemoDoc::OnNewDocument()
{
    if (!CDocument::OnNewDocument())
        return FALSE;

    // TODO: add reinitialization code here
    // (SDI documents will reuse this document)

    return TRUE;
}
```

```
///////////////////////////////////////////////////////////////////////
// CFormDemoDoc serialization

void CFormDemoDoc::Serialize(CArchive& ar)
{
   if (ar.IsStoring())
   {
      // TODO: add storing code here
   }
   else
   {
      // TODO: add loading code here
   }
}


///////////////////////////////////////////////////////////////////////
// CFormDemoDoc diagnostics

#ifdef _DEBUG
void CFormDemoDoc::AssertValid() const
{
   CDocument::AssertValid();
}

void CFormDemoDoc::Dump(CDumpContext& dc) const
{
   CDocument::Dump(dc);
}
#endif //_DEBUG


///////////////////////////////////////////////////////////////////////
// CFormDemoDoc commands
```

Listing 16.9

```
// MainFrm.h : interface of the CMainFrame class
//
///////////////////////////////////////////////////////////////////////

#if !defined(AFX_MAINFRM_H__AF814137_A1F8_11D1_80FC_00C0F6A83B7F__INCLUDED_)
#define AFX_MAINFRM_H__AF814137_A1F8_11D1_80FC_00C0F6A83B7F__INCLUDED_
```

```cpp
#if _MSC_VER > 1000
#pragma once
#endif // _MSC_VER > 1000

class CMainFrame : public CFrameWnd
{

protected: // create from serialization only
   CMainFrame();
   DECLARE_DYNCREATE(CMainFrame)

// Attributes
public:

// Operations
public:

// Overrides
   // ClassWizard generated virtual function overrides
   //{{AFX_VIRTUAL(CMainFrame)
   virtual BOOL PreCreateWindow(CREATESTRUCT& cs);
   //}}AFX_VIRTUAL

// Implementation
public:
   virtual ~CMainFrame();
#ifdef _DEBUG
   virtual void AssertValid() const;
   virtual void Dump(CDumpContext& dc) const;
#endif

// Generated message map functions
protected:
   //{{AFX_MSG(CMainFrame)
      // NOTE - the ClassWizard will add and remove member functions here.
      //    DO NOT EDIT what you see in these blocks of generated code!
   //}}AFX_MSG
   DECLARE_MESSAGE_MAP()
};

/////////////////////////////////////////////////////////////////////////////
```

```
//{{AFX_INSERT_LOCATION}}
// Microsoft Visual C++ will insert additional declarations immediately before
// the previous line.

#endif
// !defined(AFX_MAINFRM_H__AF814137_A1F8_11D1_80FC_00C0F6A83B7F__INCLUDED_)
```

Listing 16.10

```cpp
// MainFrm.cpp : implementation of the CMainFrame class
//

#include "stdafx.h"
#include "FormDemo.h"

#include "MainFrm.h"

#ifdef _DEBUG
#define new DEBUG_NEW
#undef THIS_FILE
static char THIS_FILE[] = __FILE__;
#endif

/////////////////////////////////////////////////////////////////////////////
// CMainFrame

IMPLEMENT_DYNCREATE(CMainFrame, CFrameWnd)

BEGIN_MESSAGE_MAP(CMainFrame, CFrameWnd)
    //{{AFX_MSG_MAP(CMainFrame)
        // NOTE - the ClassWizard will add and remove mapping macros here.
        //    DO NOT EDIT what you see in these blocks of generated code !
    //}}AFX_MSG_MAP
END_MESSAGE_MAP()

/////////////////////////////////////////////////////////////////////////////
// CMainFrame construction/destruction

CMainFrame::CMainFrame()
{
    // TODO: add member initialization code here

}
```

```
CMainFrame::~CMainFrame()
{
}

BOOL CMainFrame::PreCreateWindow(CREATESTRUCT& cs)
{
    if( !CFrameWnd::PreCreateWindow(cs) )
        return FALSE;
    // TODO: Modify the Window class or styles here by modifying
    //   the CREATESTRUCT cs

    return TRUE;
}

/////////////////////////////////////////////////////////////////////////
// CMainFrame diagnostics

#ifdef _DEBUG
void CMainFrame::AssertValid() const
{
    CFrameWnd::AssertValid();
}

void CMainFrame::Dump(CDumpContext& dc) const
{
    CFrameWnd::Dump(dc);
}

#endif //_DEBUG

/////////////////////////////////////////////////////////////////////////
// CMainFrame message handlers
```

Listing 16.11

```
// FormDemoView.h : interface of the CFormDemoView class
//
/////////////////////////////////////////////////////////////////////////

#if !defined(AFX_FORMDEMOVIEW_H__AF81413B_A1F8_11D1_80FC_00C0F6A83B7F__INCLUDED_)
#define AFX_FORMDEMOVIEW_H__AF81413B_A1F8_11D1_80FC_00C0F6A83B7F__INCLUDED_
```

```cpp
#if _MSC_VER > 1000
#pragma once
#endif // _MSC_VER > 1000


class CFormDemoView : public CFormView
{
public:
    CBrush m_DialogBrush;
    int m_Intensity;
    CRect m_RectSample;

    enum {INT_DARK, INT_LIGHT};

protected: // create from serialization only
    CFormDemoView();
    DECLARE_DYNCREATE(CFormDemoView)

public:
    //{{AFX_DATA(CFormDemoView)
    enum { IDD = IDD_FORMDEMO_FORM };
    BOOL    m_Blue;
    BOOL    m_Green;
    BOOL    m_Red;
    //}}AFX_DATA

// Attributes
public:
    CFormDemoDoc* GetDocument();

// Operations
public:

// Overrides
    // ClassWizard generated virtual function overrides
    //{{AFX_VIRTUAL(CFormDemoView)
    public:
    virtual BOOL PreCreateWindow(CREATESTRUCT& cs);
    protected:
    virtual void DoDataExchange(CDataExchange* pDX);    // DDX/DDV support
    virtual void OnInitialUpdate(); // called first time after construct
    virtual void OnDraw(CDC* pDC);
```

```
    //}}AFX_VIRTUAL

// Implementation
public:
    virtual ~CFormDemoView();
#ifdef _DEBUG
    virtual void AssertValid() const;
    virtual void Dump(CDumpContext& dc) const;
#endif

protected:

// Generated message map functions
protected:
    //{{AFX_MSG(CFormDemoView)
    afx_msg void OnOptionsDark();
    afx_msg void OnUpdateOptionsDark(CCmdUI* pCmdUI);
    afx_msg void OnOptionsLight();
    afx_msg void OnUpdateOptionsLight(CCmdUI* pCmdUI);
    afx_msg void OnRed();
    afx_msg void OnGreen();
    afx_msg void OnBlue();
    //}}AFX_MSG
    DECLARE_MESSAGE_MAP()
};

#ifndef _DEBUG  // debug version in FormDemoView.cpp
inline CFormDemoDoc* CFormDemoView::GetDocument()
    { return (CFormDemoDoc*)m_pDocument; }
#endif

/////////////////////////////////////////////////////////////////////////

//{{AFX_INSERT_LOCATION}}
// Microsoft Visual C++ will insert additional declarations immediately before
// the previous line.

#endif
// !defined(AFX_FORMDEMOVIEW_H__AF81413B_A1F8_11D1_80FC_00C0F6A83B7F__INCLUDED_)
```

Listing 16.12

```cpp
// FormDemoView.cpp : implementation of the CFormDemoView class
//

#include "stdafx.h"
#include "FormDemo.h"

#include "FormDemoDoc.h"
#include "FormDemoView.h"

#ifdef _DEBUG
#define new DEBUG_NEW
#undef THIS_FILE
static char THIS_FILE[] = __FILE__;
#endif

/////////////////////////////////////////////////////////////////////////
// CFormDemoView

IMPLEMENT_DYNCREATE(CFormDemoView, CFormView)

BEGIN_MESSAGE_MAP(CFormDemoView, CFormView)
    //{{AFX_MSG_MAP(CFormDemoView)
    ON_COMMAND(ID_OPTIONS_DARK, OnOptionsDark)
    ON_UPDATE_COMMAND_UI(ID_OPTIONS_DARK, OnUpdateOptionsDark)
    ON_COMMAND(ID_OPTIONS_LIGHT, OnOptionsLight)
    ON_UPDATE_COMMAND_UI(ID_OPTIONS_LIGHT, OnUpdateOptionsLight)
    ON_BN_CLICKED(IDC_RED, OnRed)
    ON_BN_CLICKED(IDC_GREEN, OnGreen)
    ON_BN_CLICKED(IDC_BLUE, OnBlue)
    //}}AFX_MSG_MAP
END_MESSAGE_MAP()

/////////////////////////////////////////////////////////////////////////
// CFormDemoView construction/destruction

CFormDemoView::CFormDemoView()
    : CFormView(CFormDemoView::IDD)
{
    //{{AFX_DATA_INIT(CFormDemoView)
```

```
    m_Blue = FALSE;
    m_Green = FALSE;
    m_Red = FALSE;
    //}}AFX_DATA_INIT
    // TODO: add construction code here

    m_Intensity = INT_LIGHT;
}

CFormDemoView::~CFormDemoView()
{
}

void CFormDemoView::DoDataExchange(CDataExchange* pDX)
{
    CFormView::DoDataExchange(pDX);
    //{{AFX_DATA_MAP(CFormDemoView)
    DDX_Check(pDX, IDC_BLUE, m_Blue);
    DDX_Check(pDX, IDC_GREEN, m_Green);
    DDX_Check(pDX, IDC_RED, m_Red);
    //}}AFX_DATA_MAP
}

BOOL CFormDemoView::PreCreateWindow(CREATESTRUCT& cs)
{
    // TODO: Modify the Window class or styles here by modifying
    //   the CREATESTRUCT cs

    return CFormView::PreCreateWindow(cs);
}

void CFormDemoView::OnInitialUpdate()
{
    CFormView::OnInitialUpdate();
    GetParentFrame()->RecalcLayout();
    ResizeParentToFit();

    GetDlgItem (IDC_SAMPLE)->GetWindowRect (&m_RectSample);
    ScreenToClient (&m_RectSample);
    int Border = (m_RectSample.right - m_RectSample.left) / 8;
    m_RectSample.InflateRect (-Border, -Border);
}
```

```
/////////////////////////////////////////////////////////////////////////
// CFormDemoView diagnostics

#ifdef _DEBUG
void CFormDemoView::AssertValid() const
{
    CFormView::AssertValid();
}

void CFormDemoView::Dump(CDumpContext& dc) const
{
    CFormView::Dump(dc);
}

CFormDemoDoc* CFormDemoView::GetDocument() // non-debug version is inline
{
    ASSERT(m_pDocument->IsKindOf(RUNTIME_CLASS(CFormDemoDoc)));
    return (CFormDemoDoc*)m_pDocument;
}
#endif //_DEBUG

/////////////////////////////////////////////////////////////////////////
// CFormDemoView message handlers

void CFormDemoView::OnOptionsDark()
{
    // TODO: Add your command handler code here
    m_Intensity = INT_DARK;

    CClientDC ClientDC (this);
    OnPrepareDC (&ClientDC);
    CRect Rect = m_RectSample;
    ClientDC.LPtoDP (&Rect);
    InvalidateRect (&Rect);
    UpdateWindow ();
}

void CFormDemoView::OnUpdateOptionsDark(CCmdUI* pCmdUI)
{
    // TODO: Add your command update UI handler code here
    pCmdUI->SetRadio (m_Intensity == INT_DARK);
}

void CFormDemoView::OnOptionsLight()
```

```cpp
{
    // TODO: Add your command handler code here
    m_Intensity = INT_LIGHT;

    CClientDC ClientDC (this);
    OnPrepareDC (&ClientDC);
    CRect Rect = m_RectSample;
    ClientDC.LPtoDP (&Rect);
    InvalidateRect (&Rect);
    UpdateWindow ();
}

void CFormDemoView::OnUpdateOptionsLight(CCmdUI* pCmdUI)
{
    // TODO: Add your command update UI handler code here
    pCmdUI->SetRadio (m_Intensity == INT_LIGHT);
}

void CFormDemoView::OnRed()
{
    // TODO: Add your control notification handler code here
    m_Red = IsDlgButtonChecked (IDC_RED);

    CClientDC ClientDC (this);
    OnPrepareDC (&ClientDC);
    CRect Rect = m_RectSample;
    ClientDC.LPtoDP (&Rect);
    InvalidateRect (&Rect);
    UpdateWindow ();
}

void CFormDemoView::OnGreen()
{
    // TODO: Add your control notification handler code here
    m_Green = IsDlgButtonChecked (IDC_GREEN);

    CClientDC ClientDC (this);
    OnPrepareDC (&ClientDC);
    CRect Rect = m_RectSample;
    ClientDC.LPtoDP (&Rect);
    InvalidateRect (&Rect);
    UpdateWindow ();
}
```

```
void CFormDemoView::OnBlue()
{
    // TODO: Add your control notification handler code here
    m_Blue = IsDlgButtonChecked (IDC_BLUE);

    CClientDC ClientDC (this);
    OnPrepareDC (&ClientDC);
    CRect Rect = m_RectSample;
    ClientDC.LPtoDP (&Rect);
    InvalidateRect (&Rect);
    UpdateWindow ();
}

void CFormDemoView::OnDraw(CDC* pDC)
{
    // TODO: Add your specialized code here and/or call the base class

    COLORREF Color = RGB
        (m_Red ? (m_Intensity==INT_DARK ? 128 : 255) : 0,
        m_Green ? (m_Intensity==INT_DARK ? 128 : 255) : 0,
        m_Blue ? (m_Intensity==INT_DARK ? 128 : 255) : 0);
    CBrush Brush (Color);
    pDC->FillRect (&m_RectSample, &Brush);
}
```

Summary

In this chapter, you learned two different ways to create a dialog-based application—that is, a program in which the main window displays a collection of predefined Windows controls and is based on a dialog box template designed in the Visual C++ dialog editor.

The first, and easiest, way to generate a dialog-based program is to choose the Dialog Based option in the AppWizard Step 1 dialog box. The resulting program will display only a dialog box, rather than displaying a main frame window and a view window.

Generating a "dialog-based" AppWizard program is best for writing a simple utility or data entry program that doesn't need to manage documents.

To design the dialog box displayed by a "dialog-based" AppWizard program, you use the dialog editor to modify the initial dialog template that AppWizard creates. You can then use ClassWizard to add both data members and message-handling functions to the dialog class that AppWizard has created.

A second way to generate a dialog-based application is to choose the Single Document or Multiple Documents option in the Step 1 AppWizard dialog box, and then in the Step 6 dialog box choose CFormView as the base class of the program's view class. These options generate a *form-view* program.

In a form-view program, the view window displays a collection of controls, the layout of which is based on a dialog template. AppWizard generates an initial template; you must use the dialog editor to modify it for your program.

A form-view program has all the classes, windows, and user-interface elements of a regular AppWizard program, and is thus suited for developing a full-featured program that manages documents. In addition, the view window allows the user to scroll its contents if the full dialog template isn't visible.

CHAPTER

SEVENTEEN

17

Writing Multiple Document Applications

- The multiple document interface

- Generating the program

- Customizing the resources

- The MiniEdit source code

In the previous chapters in this part of the book, you learned how to write *single document interface,* or *SDI,* Windows programs. An SDI program allows the user to view and edit only one document at a time. In this chapter, you'll learn how to write *multiple document interface,* or *MDI,* programs. An MDI program allows the user to open several documents at a time; each document is viewed and edited within a separate child frame window that's contained within the application workspace of the program's main frame window.

Although managing the interface for several open documents might seem to be a difficult task, Windows and the MFC provide code that does most of the work *for* you. If your application can be written within the strictures of the standard MDI program model, you can take advantage of this code and save a great amount of programming effort. To illustrate the techniques for writing MDI programs, the chapter explains how to write an MDI version of the MiniEdit example program.

The Multiple Document Interface

When you first run the MDI version of MiniEdit, which you'll create in this chapter, the program opens a new, empty document in a child frame window (see Figure 17.1). If you then choose the New or Open… command on the File menu to create a new document or read an existing one, the newly opened document is displayed within a separate *child frame window* rather than replacing the original document as in an SDI program.

You can use the Open… and New commands to open as many documents as you wish. Figure 17.2 shows the program after several documents have been opened. To work on a particular document, you must activate its child frame window. You can activate a window by clicking in it, or by pressing—repeatedly if necessary—the Ctrl+Tab or Ctrl+F6 keystroke, which activates the *next* child frame window (or you can press Ctrl+Shift+Tab to activate the *previous* window). You can also activate a specific child frame window by choosing its title from the Window menu.

FIGURE 17.1:

The MDI version of MiniEdit when the program first starts running

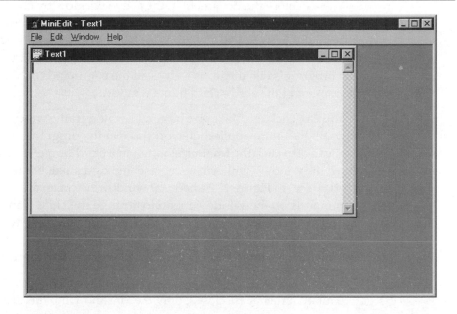

FIGURE 17.2:

The MDI version of MiniEdit after several documents have been opened (one of the child frame windows has been minimized)

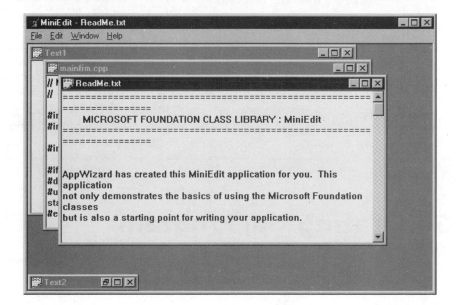

You can close the document in the active window by choosing the Close command on the program's File menu, by clicking the Close box in the upper-right corner of the document's window, or by choosing the Close command on the document window's system menu. The Save, Save As..., and Print... commands on the program's File menu, as well as all the commands on the Edit menu, affect the document in the active child frame window.

You can click the Maximize button in a child frame window to make that window fill the entire application workspace of the program's main frame window. You can also click the Minimize button in a child frame window to hide the window; the window will then be represented by a small bar within the application workspace (in Figure 17.2, the Text2 window has been minimized). You can choose commands on the Window menu to arrange the child frame windows in a cascaded (overlapping) or tiled (nonoverlapping) pattern, or to arrange the bars for any child frame windows that have been minimized (through the Arrange Icons command, so named because minimized windows are represented by icons under older versions of Windows).

If all documents are closed, only the File and Help menus are displayed, and the File menu displays only commands for opening new or existing documents or for quitting the program.

NOTE

If you use the Open... command to open a document that's already displayed in a child frame window, the program simply activates the existing child frame window rather than creating a new window. Thus, in MiniEdit, a given document can be viewed through only one child frame window at a time. As you'll see later in the chapter, however, some MDI programs allow the user to open two or more child frame windows displaying the same document, through the New Window command on the program's Window menu.

Generating the Program

To create the MDI version of MiniEdit, you'll use AppWizard to generate a *new set* of source files, using the technique described in Chapter 9 (in the section "1. Generating the Source Code"). In the Projects tab of the New dialog box, select the "MFC AppWizard (exe)" project type, enter the program name—MiniEdit—into the Name: text box, and enter the desired path for the project folder into the Location: text box. In the AppWizard dialog boxes (Step 1 through Step 6), make the same choices that you made for the WinGreet program in Chapter 9, *except* for the following options:

- In the Step 1 AppWizard dialog box, leave the Multiple Documents option selected rather than selecting the Single Document option; the completed dialog box is shown in Figure 17.3. This is all you need to do to create an MDI rather than an SDI application (this one choice, however, has a profound effect on the classes and code that AppWizard generates).

- In the Step 4 AppWizard dialog box, click the Advanced... button and open the Document Template Strings tab in the Advanced Options dialog box. Then, enter the default file extension, txt, into the File Extension: text box, enter `Text` into the Doc Type Name: text box, and enter `Text Files (*.txt)` into the Filter Name: text box. All values should match those shown in Figure 17.4.

- In the Step 6 dialog box, select the `CMiniEditView` class name in the list near the top of the dialog box, and select `CEditView` in the Base Class: list. As explained in Chapter 10 (in the section "Creating the MiniEdit Program"), a view class that's derived from `CEditView` rather than `CView` automatically provides a complete text editor within the view window.

FIGURE 17.3:

The completed AppWizard Step 1 dialog box for generating the MDI version of the MiniEdit program

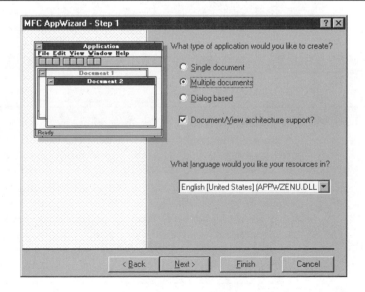

FIGURE 17.4:

The completed Advanced Options dialog box (the Document Template Strings tab)

The MiniEdit program will use the string (**Text**) that you entered into the Doc Type Name: text box of the Advanced Options dialog box to assign default names to new documents. The first new document will be named Text1, the second Text2, and so on. The program user, of course, can assign a different name when saving a file. In contrast, SDI programs simply name a new file "Untitled" (and therefore it's less important to specify a document type name when creating an SDI program). The way the program uses the default file extension you entered into the File Extension: text box was described in Chapter 12, in the section "Adding the File Menu Commands."

To simplify the code, the example programs presented in the other chapters in this book all use the SDI program model. Keep in mind, however, that you can use the MDI model with any of the types of programs presented in the other chapters (except the simple dialog-based programs described at the beginning of Chapter 16). For example, you can add a toolbar, a status bar, or a dialog bar to an MDI program, as described in Chapter 14, and you can add scrolling and splitting capability, as described in Chapter 13 (each child frame window would contain its own scroll bars and split box). Also, you can display a collection of dialog controls—based on a dialog box template—within each view window by deriving the view class from **CFormView**, as explained in Chapter 16.

The Program Classes, Files, and Code

The classes and files that AppWizard generates for an MDI program are similar to the classes and files it generates for an SDI program (which were described in the section "The Program Classes and Files" in Chapter 9). Like an SDI program, an MDI program contains an application class, a document class, a main frame window class, and a view class. There are, however, some differences in the tasks performed by these classes. Also, an MDI program employs an additional class: a *child frame window class*.

The Application Class

An MDI program's application class, like that of an SDI program, manages the program as a whole and includes an `InitInstance` member function for initializing the program. In MiniEdit, the application class is named `CMiniEditApp`; its header file is MiniEdit.h and its implementation file is MiniEdit.cpp.

The Document Class

Also like an SDI program, an MDI program's document class stores the document data and performs file I/O. An MDI program, however, creates a separate instance of this class for each open document, rather than reusing a single instance. In MiniEdit, the document class is named `CMiniEditDoc`; its header file is MiniEditDoc.h and its implementation file is MiniEditDoc.cpp.

The Main Frame Window Class

An MDI program's main frame window class, like that of an SDI program, manages the program's main frame window. However, rather than being derived directly from the `CFrameWnd` MFC class, it's derived from `CMDIFrameWnd` (which is derived from `CFrameWnd`). Also, in an MDI program, the main frame window *doesn't* contain a single view window; rather, it frames the general application workspace. Within the application workspace is a separate *child frame window* for each open document; as you'll see, each child frame window contains a separate view window.

Because the main frame window frames the general application workspace rather than a single open document, its class *isn't* included in the program's document template. (Recall from Chapter 9 that a document template stores information on the classes and resources used for displaying and managing a specific type of document.) Because the main frame window isn't automatically created when the first document is opened (as in an SDI program), the `InitInstance` function must explicitly create and display it using the following code:

```
// create main MDI Frame window
CMainFrame* pMainFrame = new CMainFrame;
if (!pMainFrame->LoadFrame(IDR_MAINFRAME))
    return FALSE;
m_pMainWnd = pMainFrame;

// ...

// The main window has been initialized, so show and update it.
pMainFrame->ShowWindow(m_nCmdShow);
pMainFrame->UpdateWindow();
```

The first statement creates an instance of the main frame window class, `CMainFrame`. The call to the `CFrameWnd` member function `LoadFrame` creates the main frame window itself, using the resources that have the `IDR_MAINFRAME` identifier (a menu, an accelerator table, a string, and an icon). Then, the window handle is stored in the `CWinApp` data member `m_pMainWnd`. Later in `InitInstance`, the call to `CWnd::ShowWindow` makes the window visible, and the call to `CWnd::Update Window` causes the client area of the window to be drawn.

In MiniEdit, the header file for the main frame window class is MainFrm.h, and the implementation file is MainFrm.cpp.

The Child Frame Window Class

In an MDI program, the child frame window class manages the child frame windows. Each child frame window contains a view window for displaying an open document. A child frame window class isn't used in an SDI program. Figure 17.5 illustrates the child frame window, as well as the other windows created in an MDI program.

In MiniEdit, the child frame window class is named `CChildFrame` and is derived from the MFC class `CMDIChildWnd` (which is derived from `CFrameWnd`; see Figure 17.6). Its header file is ChildFrm.h and its implementation file is ChildFrm.cpp.

FIGURE 17.5:

The windows in an MDI program; in this figure, there's only a single open document.

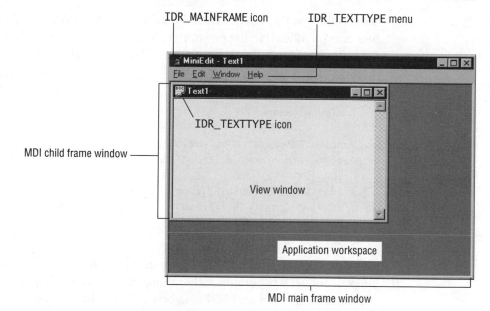

IDR_MAINFRAME icon

IDR_TEXTTYPE menu

IDR_TEXTTYPE icon

MDI child frame window

View window

Application workspace

MDI main frame window

FIGURE 17.6:

The MFC classes used for managing MDI program windows

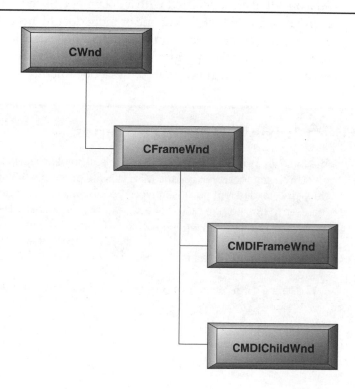

Because the CChildFrame class is used for creating and managing the child frame window that frames each document that's opened, the InitInstance function includes it in the program's document template (rather than including the main frame window class, as in an SDI program):

```
// Register the application's document templates.  Document
// templates serve as the connection between documents, frame
// windows and views.

CMultiDocTemplate* pDocTemplate;
pDocTemplate = new CMultiDocTemplate(
    IDR_TEXTTYPE,
    RUNTIME_CLASS(CMiniEditDoc),
    RUNTIME_CLASS(CChildFrame), // custom MDI child frame
    RUNTIME_CLASS(CMiniEditView));
AddDocTemplate(pDocTemplate);
```

Notice that the template belongs to the class CMultiDocTemplate, which is suitable for MDI programs, rather than the class CSingleDocTemplate, which was used in the previous SDI versions of MiniEdit. Notice, also, that the template is assigned the identifier (IDR_TEXTTYPE) of the resources—a menu, a string, and an icon—that are associated with a document. Specifically, the IDR_TEXTTYPE menu is displayed whenever one or more documents are open; the IDR_TEXT-TYPE string contains the default document file extension and a description of the type of document the program opens; and the IDR_TEXTTYPE icon is displayed in each child frame window that frames a document.

Using Multiple Document Types

The MiniEdit program manages only a single document type—namely, a plain text document. You can, however, use the MFC to write programs that allow the user to open or create several different document types. For example, a spreadsheet program might allow the user to open or create either a spreadsheet or a chart. Unfortunately, AppWizard offers little assistance in writing such a program, and a detailed example is beyond the scope of this book. The following are the basic steps for allowing a program—either SDI or MDI—to manage an additional document type:

1. Define a new document class to manage the document data.

Continued on next page

2. Define a new view class to manage the view window, receive user input, and display the document data. *Tip*: Use the existing ClassWizard generated classes as models for your new document and view classes.

3. Create a set of resources for the new document type: a menu, an accelerator table (for an SDI program), a string, and an icon. The string should have the same form as the one created by AppWizard for the original document type. Be sure to assign all these resources the *same* identifier (for example, IDR_CHARTTYPE).

4. In the `InitInstance` function of the application class, create a template object (a `CSingleDocTemplate` object for an SDI program or a `CMultiDocTemplate` object for an MDI program), specifying the identifier of the new resources, the new document and view classes, and the frame window class (a main frame window class for an SDI program or a child frame window class for an MDI program).

5. Also in `InitInstance`, call `AddDocTemplate` to add the template object to the application object (this call is *in addition to* the existing call or calls to `AddDocTemplate`).

If you've added more than one document type to the program, the New command on the File menu will display a dialog box allowing the user to choose the type of the document that's to be created. Also, the user will be able to open existing documents of any of the added types. For more information on managing several document types, see the following Visual C++ online help topic: *Visual C++ Documentation, Using Visual C++, Visual C++ Programmer's Guide, Adding Program Functionality, Details, MFC Topics (General), Document Templates and the Document/View Creation Process*.

The View Class

Finally, the view class in an MDI program is used for creating and managing the view window that displays each open document. The view window for each document occupies the client area of the document's child frame window. Because the MiniEdit view class is derived from `CEditView`, each view window serves as a text editor. In MiniEdit, the view class is named `CMiniEditView`; its header file is MiniEditView.h and its implementation file is MiniEditView.cpp.

The Generated Code

As explained in Chapter 12, when you derive the view class from `CEditView`, as you did for MiniEdit, AppWizard generates the code necessary for reading and writing text documents from and to disk files. Recall that it adds this code to the `Serialize` member function of the document class.

Also, for the MDI version of MiniEdit you *don't* need to add a `DeleteContents` member function to the document class. As explained in Chapter 12, in the SDI version you must provide a `DeleteContents` function that removes the existing text from the view window in response to the New command on the File menu. In the MDI version, however, the New command creates a *new* view window rather than reusing an existing view window; thus, the program doesn't need to remove text.

Additionally, when generating an MDI program, AppWizard automatically adds to the `InitInstance` member function of the application class a call to the `DragAcceptFiles` function, which allows the user to open a file by dragging it from a Windows folder or the Windows Explorer and dropping it on the program window. AppWizard also automatically includes within `InitInstance` calls to the `EnableShellOpen` and `RegisterShellFileTypes` functions. Usually, calling these functions permits the user to open a file by double-clicking a file object that has the program's default file extension. However, the MiniEdit default extension, .txt, is normally already registered to another program (such as the Windows Notepad.exe program); accordingly, clicking on a file with this extension runs a program other than MiniEdit (the user can change the application that's run by choosing the View ➤ Options… or View ➤ Folder Options… menu command of the Windows Explorer and opening the File Types tab). The `Drag-AcceptFiles`, `EnableShellOpen`, and `RegisterShellFileTypes` functions are discussed in Chapter 12 (in the sections "Supporting Drag-and-Drop" and "Registering the MiniDraw File Type").

Planning Ahead

In this chapter you spend quite a bit of time adding features to the MDI version of MiniEdit that are already included in the SDI version. This is necessary because you had to generate an entirely new set of source files to create an MDI program. It *isn't* possible to use App-Wizard to convert an existing SDI program to an MDI program.

In general, AppWizard can't be used to add features directly to an existing program. For example, one of the features that AppWizard supports is a program toolbar. If you generate a program without a toolbar, you *can't* run AppWizard again at a later time to add a

Continued on next page

toolbar directly to the program. To add a toolbar with AppWizard, you'd have to generate an entirely new program, and then either copy the code for the toolbar into your existing program or copy all features you've added to your existing program into the newly generated source files.

To simplify the code listings and discussions, the exercises in this book use only those AppWizard features that are required for the current version of the example program. Later exercises sometimes have you *add* AppWizard features to create more-advanced program versions. For your own applications, however, you can save much programming effort by planning ahead! When you generate an AppWizard program, you should try to include *every* feature that you anticipate needing.

Customizing the Resources

In this section you'll customize the MiniEdit program resources. You will modify the menu, add accelerator keystrokes, and provide a custom icon. To begin, make sure that the MiniEdit project is currently open, and open the ResourceView tab in the Workspace window to display the resources.

Expand the Menu branch of the ResourceView graph. Notice that because MiniEdit is now an MDI program, *two* menu identifiers appear under this branch, IDR_MAINFRAME and IDR_TEXTTYPE. IDR_MAINFRAME is the identifier of the menu that's displayed when *no* documents are open; you don't need to modify this menu. IDR_TEXTTYPE is the identifier of the menu displayed when at least one document is open. Double-click the IDR_TEXTTYPE identifier to open the menu editor for this menu.

In the menu-editor window, first open the File menu. Immediately under the existing Save As... command, add a separator and then a Print... command. Table 17.1 shows the properties of the added menu items, and Figure 17.7 shows the completed File menu.

TABLE 17.1: New Commands to Add to the File Menu

ID:	Caption	Other Features
none	none	Separator
ID_FILE_PRINT	&Print...\tCtrl+P	none

FIGURE 17.7:

The completed File menu for the MiniEdit IDR_TEXTTYPE menu

Next, open the Edit menu and, directly under the existing Paste command, add a Select All command, a separator, and Find..., Find Next, and Replace... commands. These menu items are described in Table 17.2, while the completed Edit menu is shown in Figure 17.8.

FIGURE 17.8:

The completed Edit menu for the MiniEdit program

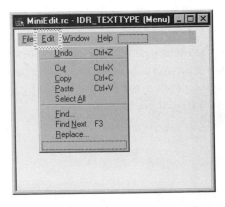

TABLE 17.2: New Commands to Add to the Edit Menu

ID:	Caption	Other Features
ID_EDIT_SELECT_ALL	Select &All	none
none	none	Separator
ID_EDIT_FIND	&Find...	none
ID_EDIT_REPEAT	Find &Next\tF3	none
ID_EDIT_REPLACE	&Replace...	none

Copying Menu Items

You can copy menu items from one program to another. Accordingly, you could copy the new File and Edit menu items from the previous version of MiniEdit (presented in Chapter 10) rather than redefining these items within the current version. Assuming that the menu-editor window for the current version of MiniEdit is open, do the following:

1. Choose the File ➤ Open... menu command in the Developer Studio.

2. In the Open dialog box select the MiniEdit.rc resource file belonging to the *previous version* of MiniEdit (if you didn't create the file, you can find a copy of it in the \MiniEdt2 companion-CD folder) and click the OK button.

3. The Developer Studio will open a resource window for the previous version of MiniEdit.

4. In the resource window for the previous MiniEdit version, double-click the **IDR_MAINFRAME** identifier under the Menu branch of the graph to open a menu-editor window for the previous version's menu.

5. Copy the desired items from the newly opened menu-editor window to the menu-editor window for the current program version. To copy a menu item—either an entire pop-up menu or an item on a pop-up menu—from one menu-editor window to the other, press the Ctrl key and then use the mouse to drag the item from the source menu to the target menu (if you drag without pressing Ctrl, the item will be *moved* rather than copied).

To finish customizing the menu, open the MiniEdit Window menu, click on the New Window command, and press the Del key to delete the command.

The New Window Command

All the code required to implement the commands on the Window menu is provided by Windows and the MFC. The New Window command on this menu creates an additional child frame window and view window for displaying the document in the currently active child window. The purpose of this command is to allow the user to view and edit a single document within more than one view window.

For the MiniEdit program, however, the New Window command is deleted for the following reason: a view window derived from `CEditView` stores the document text internally. If the program created more than one view window displaying a single document, it would be difficult to efficiently update other views each time the user made a change in one view.

In a more conventional MDI program, the document data is stored centrally within the document object. In such a program, you can allow the user to create multiple document views (through the New Window command or by using a split bar). Whenever the user makes a change in one view, the view class object can call the `UpdateAllViews` member function of the document class to update all the other views, using the techniques described in Chapter 13 (in the section "Updating the Views").

The next step is to add accelerator keystrokes for the Print... and Find Next menu commands. To do this, use the procedure that was described in Chapter 10 (in the section "Creating the MiniEdit Program"). Table 17.3 summarizes the properties of the two accelerator keystrokes that are to be defined.

TABLE 17.3: Properties of the Accelerator Keystrokes to Add to the MiniEdit Program

ID:	Key
ID_FILE_PRINT	Ctrl+P
ID_EDIT_REPEAT	F3

Finally, if you want to customize one or both of the program icons, expand the Icon branch of the ResourceView graph in the Workspace window. Notice that the identifiers for two icons appear under this branch. The IDR_MAINFRAME icon is associated with the main frame window; it's displayed in the main frame window's title bar, in the Windows task bar, and other places where a program icon is displayed. The IDR_TEXTTYPE icon is associated with each of the child frame windows; it's displayed within the title bar of each child frame window and also within each bar portraying a minimized child frame window in the application workspace. To customize one of these icons, double-click its identifier to open a graphic-editor window, select the "Standard (32x32)" size in the Device: list, and use the commands and tools provided by the Visual C++ graphics editor to create the desired pattern. As described in Chapter 10, you should also design the desired image for the "Small (16x16)" icon or simply delete it by displaying it and choosing the Image ➤ Delete Device Image menu command.

Copying an Icon

Once you've opened a graphic-editor window for an icon, rather than editing the existing icon, you can *copy* an icon into the window from another program. For example, if you created an icon for the previous version of MiniEdit, you could copy it to the current version. To copy an icon, do the following:

1. Choose the File ➤ Open... menu command in Developer Studio to open the resource file (the .rc file) for the program containing the icon you want to copy (the source icon). The resources will be displayed in a resource window.

2. Open a graphic-editor window for the source icon, and in the Device: list select the size of the icon you want to copy.

3. While the window containing the source icon is active, choose the Edit ➤ Copy... menu command, or press Ctrl+C, to copy the source icon into the Clipboard.

4. Click in the graphic-editor window for the target icon to activate it. Make sure that the appropriate icon size is selected in the Device: list (the source and target icons must be of the same size).

5. Press the Del key to delete the current icon in the target icon window.

6. Choose the Edit ➤ Paste menu command or press Ctrl+V.

You can now build and run the new version of the MiniEdit program and experiment with the program features described near the beginning of the chapter.

The MiniEdit Source Code

The following listings, Listings 17.1 through 17.10, are the C++ source code for the MDI version of MiniEdit that you created in this chapter. Complete copies of these files are included in the \MiniEdt3 companion-CD folder.

Listing 17.1

```cpp
// MiniEdit.h : main header file for the MINIEDIT application
//

#if !defined(AFX_MINIEDIT_H__349932DC_A2C4_11D1_80FC_00C0F6A83B7F__INCLUDED_)
#define AFX_MINIEDIT_H__349932DC_A2C4_11D1_80FC_00C0F6A83B7F__INCLUDED_

#if _MSC_VER > 1000
#pragma once
#endif // _MSC_VER > 1000

#ifndef __AFXWIN_H__
    #error include 'stdafx.h' before including this file for PCH
#endif

#include "resource.h"        // main symbols


/////////////////////////////////////////////////////////////////////////
// CMiniEditApp:
// See MiniEdit.cpp for the implementation of this class
//

class CMiniEditApp : public CWinApp
{
public:
    CMiniEditApp();

// Overrides
    // ClassWizard generated virtual function overrides
    //{{AFX_VIRTUAL(CMiniEditApp)
    public:
    virtual BOOL InitInstance();
    //}}AFX_VIRTUAL
```

```
// Implementation
   //{{AFX_MSG(CMiniEditApp)
   afx_msg void OnAppAbout();
      // NOTE - the ClassWizard will add and remove member functions here.
      //    DO NOT EDIT what you see in these blocks of generated code !
   //}}AFX_MSG
   DECLARE_MESSAGE_MAP()
};


/////////////////////////////////////////////////////////////////////////////

//{{AFX_INSERT_LOCATION}}
// Microsoft Visual C++ will insert additional declarations immediately before
// the previous line.

#endif
// !defined(AFX_MINIEDIT_H__349932DC_A2C4_11D1_80FC_00C0F6A83B7F__INCLUDED_)
```

Listing 17.2

```
// MiniEdit.cpp : Defines the class behaviors for the application.
//

#include "stdafx.h"
#include "MiniEdit.h"

#include "MainFrm.h"
#include "ChildFrm.h"
#include "MiniEditDoc.h"
#include "MiniEditView.h"

#ifdef _DEBUG
#define new DEBUG_NEW
#undef THIS_FILE
static char THIS_FILE[] = __FILE__;
#endif

/////////////////////////////////////////////////////////////////////////////
// CMiniEditApp

BEGIN_MESSAGE_MAP(CMiniEditApp, CWinApp)
```

```
    //{{AFX_MSG_MAP(CMiniEditApp)
    ON_COMMAND(ID_APP_ABOUT, OnAppAbout)
        // NOTE - the ClassWizard will add and remove mapping macros here.
        //      DO NOT EDIT what you see in these blocks of generated code!
    //}}AFX_MSG_MAP
    // Standard file based document commands
    ON_COMMAND(ID_FILE_NEW, CWinApp::OnFileNew)
    ON_COMMAND(ID_FILE_OPEN, CWinApp::OnFileOpen)
END_MESSAGE_MAP()

/////////////////////////////////////////////////////////////////////////
// CMiniEditApp construction

CMiniEditApp::CMiniEditApp()
{
    // TODO: add construction code here,
    // Place all significant initialization in InitInstance
}

/////////////////////////////////////////////////////////////////////////
// The one and only CMiniEditApp object

CMiniEditApp theApp;

/////////////////////////////////////////////////////////////////////////
// CMiniEditApp initialization

BOOL CMiniEditApp::InitInstance()
{
    // Standard initialization
    // If you are not using these features and wish to reduce the size
    //  of your final executable, you should remove from the following
    //  the specific initialization routines you do not need.

#ifdef _AFXDLL
    Enable3dControls();         // Call this when using MFC in a shared DLL
#else
    Enable3dControlsStatic();   // Call this when linking to MFC statically
#endif

    // Change the registry key under which our settings are stored.
    // TODO: You should modify this string to be something appropriate
    // such as the name of your company or organization.
```

```
SetRegistryKey(_T("Local AppWizard-Generated Applications"));

LoadStdProfileSettings();  // Load standard INI file options (including MRU)

// Register the application's document templates.  Document templates
//  serve as the connection between documents, frame windows and views.

CMultiDocTemplate* pDocTemplate;
pDocTemplate = new CMultiDocTemplate(
   IDR_TEXTTYPE,
   RUNTIME_CLASS(CMiniEditDoc),
   RUNTIME_CLASS(CChildFrame), // custom MDI child frame
   RUNTIME_CLASS(CMiniEditView));
AddDocTemplate(pDocTemplate);

// create main MDI Frame window
CMainFrame* pMainFrame = new CMainFrame;
if (!pMainFrame->LoadFrame(IDR_MAINFRAME))
   return FALSE;
m_pMainWnd = pMainFrame;

// Enable drag/drop open
m_pMainWnd->DragAcceptFiles();

// Enable DDE Execute open
EnableShellOpen();
RegisterShellFileTypes(TRUE);

// Parse command line for standard shell commands, DDE, file open
CCommandLineInfo cmdInfo;
ParseCommandLine(cmdInfo);

// Dispatch commands specified on the command line
if (!ProcessShellCommand(cmdInfo))
   return FALSE;

// The main window has been initialized, so show and update it.
pMainFrame->ShowWindow(m_nCmdShow);
pMainFrame->UpdateWindow();

return TRUE;
}
```

```
///////////////////////////////////////////////////////////////////////
// CAboutDlg dialog used for App About

class CAboutDlg : public CDialog
{
public:
   CAboutDlg();

// Dialog Data
   //{{AFX_DATA(CAboutDlg)
   enum { IDD = IDD_ABOUTBOX };
   //}}AFX_DATA

   // ClassWizard generated virtual function overrides
   //{{AFX_VIRTUAL(CAboutDlg)
   protected:
   virtual void DoDataExchange(CDataExchange* pDX);    // DDX/DDV support
   //}}AFX_VIRTUAL

// Implementation
protected:
   //{{AFX_MSG(CAboutDlg)
      // No message handlers
   //}}AFX_MSG
   DECLARE_MESSAGE_MAP()
};

CAboutDlg::CAboutDlg() : CDialog(CAboutDlg::IDD)
{
   //{{AFX_DATA_INIT(CAboutDlg)
   //}}AFX_DATA_INIT
}

void CAboutDlg::DoDataExchange(CDataExchange* pDX)
{
   CDialog::DoDataExchange(pDX);
   //{{AFX_DATA_MAP(CAboutDlg)
   //}}AFX_DATA_MAP
}

BEGIN_MESSAGE_MAP(CAboutDlg, CDialog)
```

```
    //{{AFX_MSG_MAP(CAboutDlg)
        // No message handlers
    //}}AFX_MSG_MAP
END_MESSAGE_MAP()

// App command to run the dialog
void CMiniEditApp::OnAppAbout()
{
    CAboutDlg aboutDlg;
    aboutDlg.DoModal();
}


/////////////////////////////////////////////////////////////////////////
// CMiniEditApp message handlers
```

Listing 17.3

```
// MiniEditDoc.h : interface of the CMiniEditDoc class
//
/////////////////////////////////////////////////////////////////////////

#if !defined(AFX_MINIEDITDOC_H__349932E4_A2C4_11D1_80FC_00C0F6A83B7F__INCLUDED_)
#define AFX_MINIEDITDOC_H__349932E4_A2C4_11D1_80FC_00C0F6A83B7F__INCLUDED_

#if _MSC_VER > 1000
#pragma once
#endif // _MSC_VER > 1000


class CMiniEditDoc : public CDocument
{
protected: // create from serialization only
    CMiniEditDoc();
    DECLARE_DYNCREATE(CMiniEditDoc)

// Attributes
public:

// Operations
public:

// Overrides
```

```
    // ClassWizard generated virtual function overrides
    //{{AFX_VIRTUAL(CMiniEditDoc)
    public:
    virtual BOOL OnNewDocument();
    virtual void Serialize(CArchive& ar);
    //}}AFX_VIRTUAL

// Implementation
public:
    virtual ~CMiniEditDoc();
#ifdef _DEBUG
    virtual void AssertValid() const;
    virtual void Dump(CDumpContext& dc) const;
#endif

protected:

// Generated message map functions
protected:
    //{{AFX_MSG(CMiniEditDoc)
        // NOTE - the ClassWizard will add and remove member functions here.
        //    DO NOT EDIT what you see in these blocks of generated code !
    //}}AFX_MSG
    DECLARE_MESSAGE_MAP()
};


/////////////////////////////////////////////////////////////////////////

//{{AFX_INSERT_LOCATION}}
// Microsoft Visual C++ will insert additional declarations immediately before
// the previous line.

#endif
// !defined(AFX_MINIEDITDOC_H__349932E4_A2C4_11D1_80FC_00C0F6A83B7F__INCLUDED_)
```

Listing 17.4

```
// MiniEditDoc.cpp : implementation of the CMiniEditDoc class
//

#include "stdafx.h"
#include "MiniEdit.h"
```

```cpp
#include "MiniEditDoc.h"

#ifdef _DEBUG
#define new DEBUG_NEW
#undef THIS_FILE
static char THIS_FILE[] = __FILE__;
#endif

/////////////////////////////////////////////////////////////////////////////
// CMiniEditDoc

IMPLEMENT_DYNCREATE(CMiniEditDoc, CDocument)

BEGIN_MESSAGE_MAP(CMiniEditDoc, CDocument)
    //{{AFX_MSG_MAP(CMiniEditDoc)
        // NOTE - the ClassWizard will add and remove mapping macros here.
        //    DO NOT EDIT what you see in these blocks of generated code!
    //}}AFX_MSG_MAP
END_MESSAGE_MAP()

/////////////////////////////////////////////////////////////////////////////
// CMiniEditDoc construction/destruction

CMiniEditDoc::CMiniEditDoc()
{
    // TODO: add one-time construction code here

}

CMiniEditDoc::~CMiniEditDoc()
{
}

BOOL CMiniEditDoc::OnNewDocument()
{
    if (!CDocument::OnNewDocument())
      return FALSE;

    // TODO: add reinitialization code here
    // (SDI documents will reuse this document)

    return TRUE;
}
```

```
/////////////////////////////////////////////////////////////////////
// CMiniEditDoc serialization

void CMiniEditDoc::Serialize(CArchive& ar)
{
    // CEditView contains an edit control which handles all serialization
    ((CEditView*)m_viewList.GetHead())->SerializeRaw(ar);
}


/////////////////////////////////////////////////////////////////////
// CMiniEditDoc diagnostics

#ifdef _DEBUG
void CMiniEditDoc::AssertValid() const
{
    CDocument::AssertValid();
}

void CMiniEditDoc::Dump(CDumpContext& dc) const
{
    CDocument::Dump(dc);
}
#endif //_DEBUG


/////////////////////////////////////////////////////////////////////
// CMiniEditDoc commands
```

Listing 17.5

```
// MainFrm.h : interface of the CMainFrame class
//
/////////////////////////////////////////////////////////////////////

#if !defined(AFX_MAINFRM_H__349932E0_A2C4_11D1_80FC_00C0F6A83B7F__INCLUDED_)
#define AFX_MAINFRM_H__349932E0_A2C4_11D1_80FC_00C0F6A83B7F__INCLUDED_

#if _MSC_VER > 1000
#pragma once
#endif // _MSC_VER > 1000
```

```cpp
class CMainFrame : public CMDIFrameWnd
{
    DECLARE_DYNAMIC(CMainFrame)
public:
    CMainFrame();

// Attributes
public:

// Operations
public:

// Overrides
    // ClassWizard generated virtual function overrides
    //{{AFX_VIRTUAL(CMainFrame)
    virtual BOOL PreCreateWindow(CREATESTRUCT& cs);
    //}}AFX_VIRTUAL

// Implementation
public:
    virtual ~CMainFrame();
#ifdef _DEBUG
    virtual void AssertValid() const;
    virtual void Dump(CDumpContext& dc) const;
#endif

// Generated message map functions
protected:
    //{{AFX_MSG(CMainFrame)
        // NOTE - the ClassWizard will add and remove member functions here.
        //      DO NOT EDIT what you see in these blocks of generated code!
    //}}AFX_MSG
    DECLARE_MESSAGE_MAP()
};

/////////////////////////////////////////////////////////////////////////

//{{AFX_INSERT_LOCATION}}
// Microsoft Visual C++ will insert additional declarations immediately before
// the previous line.

#endif
// !defined(AFX_MAINFRM_H__349932E0_A2C4_11D1_80FC_00C0F6A83B7F__INCLUDED_)
```

Listing 17.6

```cpp
// MainFrm.cpp : implementation of the CMainFrame class
//

#include "stdafx.h"
#include "MiniEdit.h"

#include "MainFrm.h"

#ifdef _DEBUG
#define new DEBUG_NEW
#undef THIS_FILE
static char THIS_FILE[] = __FILE__;
#endif

/////////////////////////////////////////////////////////////////////////
// CMainFrame

IMPLEMENT_DYNAMIC(CMainFrame, CMDIFrameWnd)

BEGIN_MESSAGE_MAP(CMainFrame, CMDIFrameWnd)
    //{{AFX_MSG_MAP(CMainFrame)
        // NOTE - the ClassWizard will add and remove mapping macros here.
        //    DO NOT EDIT what you see in these blocks of generated code !
    //}}AFX_MSG_MAP
END_MESSAGE_MAP()

/////////////////////////////////////////////////////////////////////////
// CMainFrame construction/destruction

CMainFrame::CMainFrame()
{
    // TODO: add member initialization code here

}

CMainFrame::~CMainFrame()
{
}

BOOL CMainFrame::PreCreateWindow(CREATESTRUCT& cs)
{
```

```
    if( !CMDIFrameWnd::PreCreateWindow(cs) )
        return FALSE;
    // TODO: Modify the Window class or styles here by modifying
    //   the CREATESTRUCT cs

    return TRUE;
}

/////////////////////////////////////////////////////////////////////////
// CMainFrame diagnostics

#ifdef _DEBUG
void CMainFrame::AssertValid() const
{
    CMDIFrameWnd::AssertValid();
}

void CMainFrame::Dump(CDumpContext& dc) const
{
    CMDIFrameWnd::Dump(dc);
}

#endif //_DEBUG

/////////////////////////////////////////////////////////////////////////
// CMainFrame message handlers
```

Listing 17.7

```
// MiniEditView.h : interface of the CMiniEditView class
//
/////////////////////////////////////////////////////////////////////////

#if !defined(AFX_MINIEDITVIEW_H__349932E6_A2C4_11D1_80FC_00C0F6A83B7F__INCLUDED_)
#define AFX_MINIEDITVIEW_H__349932E6_A2C4_11D1_80FC_00C0F6A83B7F__INCLUDED_

#if _MSC_VER > 1000
#pragma once
#endif // _MSC_VER > 1000


class CMiniEditView : public CEditView
{
```

```
protected: // create from serialization only
   CMiniEditView();
   DECLARE_DYNCREATE(CMiniEditView)

// Attributes
public:
   CMiniEditDoc* GetDocument();

// Operations
public:

// Overrides
   // ClassWizard generated virtual function overrides
   //{{AFX_VIRTUAL(CMiniEditView)
   public:
   virtual void OnDraw(CDC* pDC);  // overridden to draw this view
   virtual BOOL PreCreateWindow(CREATESTRUCT& cs);
   protected:
   //}}AFX_VIRTUAL

// Implementation
public:
   virtual ~CMiniEditView();
#ifdef _DEBUG
   virtual void AssertValid() const;
   virtual void Dump(CDumpContext& dc) const;
#endif

protected:

// Generated message map functions
protected:
   //{{AFX_MSG(CMiniEditView)
      // NOTE - the ClassWizard will add and remove member functions here.
      //    DO NOT EDIT what you see in these blocks of generated code !
   //}}AFX_MSG
   DECLARE_MESSAGE_MAP()
};

#ifndef _DEBUG  // debug version in MiniEditView.cpp
inline CMiniEditDoc* CMiniEditView::GetDocument()
   { return (CMiniEditDoc*)m_pDocument; }
#endif
```

```
///////////////////////////////////////////////////////////////////////

//{{AFX_INSERT_LOCATION}}
// Microsoft Visual C++ will insert additional declarations immediately before
// the previous line.

#endif
// !defined(AFX_MINIEDITVIEW_H__349932E6_A2C4_11D1_80FC_00C0F6A83B7F__INCLUDED_)
```

Listing 17.8

```
// MiniEditView.cpp : implementation of the CMiniEditView class
//

#include "stdafx.h"
#include "MiniEdit.h"

#include "MiniEditDoc.h"
#include "MiniEditView.h"

#ifdef _DEBUG
#define new DEBUG_NEW
#undef THIS_FILE
static char THIS_FILE[] = __FILE__;
#endif

///////////////////////////////////////////////////////////////////////
// CMiniEditView

IMPLEMENT_DYNCREATE(CMiniEditView, CEditView)

BEGIN_MESSAGE_MAP(CMiniEditView, CEditView)
    //{{AFX_MSG_MAP(CMiniEditView)
        // NOTE - the ClassWizard will add and remove mapping macros here.
        //      DO NOT EDIT what you see in these blocks of generated code!
    //}}AFX_MSG_MAP
END_MESSAGE_MAP()

///////////////////////////////////////////////////////////////////////
// CMiniEditView construction/destruction

CMiniEditView::CMiniEditView()
{
```

```
    // TODO: add construction code here

}

CMiniEditView::~CMiniEditView()
{
}

BOOL CMiniEditView::PreCreateWindow(CREATESTRUCT& cs)
{
    // TODO: Modify the Window class or styles here by modifying
    //   the CREATESTRUCT cs

    BOOL bPreCreated = CEditView::PreCreateWindow(cs);
    cs.style &= ~(ES_AUTOHSCROLL|WS_HSCROLL); // Enable word-wrapping

    return bPreCreated;
}

/////////////////////////////////////////////////////////////////////////
// CMiniEditView drawing

void CMiniEditView::OnDraw(CDC* pDC)
{
    CMiniEditDoc* pDoc = GetDocument();
    ASSERT_VALID(pDoc);

    // TODO: add draw code for native data here
}

/////////////////////////////////////////////////////////////////////////
// CMiniEditView diagnostics

#ifdef _DEBUG
void CMiniEditView::AssertValid() const
{
    CEditView::AssertValid();
}

void CMiniEditView::Dump(CDumpContext& dc) const
{
    CEditView::Dump(dc);
}
```

```
CMiniEditDoc* CMiniEditView::GetDocument() // non-debug version is inline
{
    ASSERT(m_pDocument->IsKindOf(RUNTIME_CLASS(CMiniEditDoc)));
    return (CMiniEditDoc*)m_pDocument;
}
#endif //_DEBUG


/////////////////////////////////////////////////////////////////////////
// CMiniEditView message handlers
```

Listing 17.9

```
// ChildFrm.h : interface of the CChildFrame class
//
/////////////////////////////////////////////////////////////////////////

#if !defined(AFX_CHILDFRM_H__349932E2_A2C4_11D1_80FC_00C0F6A83B7F__INCLUDED_)
#define AFX_CHILDFRM_H__349932E2_A2C4_11D1_80FC_00C0F6A83B7F__INCLUDED_

#if _MSC_VER > 1000
#pragma once
#endif // _MSC_VER > 1000


class CChildFrame : public CMDIChildWnd
{
    DECLARE_DYNCREATE(CChildFrame)
public:
    CChildFrame();

// Attributes
public:

// Operations
public:

// Overrides
    // ClassWizard generated virtual function overrides
    //{{AFX_VIRTUAL(CChildFrame)
    virtual BOOL PreCreateWindow(CREATESTRUCT& cs);
    //}}AFX_VIRTUAL
```

```
// Implementation
public:
    virtual ~CChildFrame();
#ifdef _DEBUG
    virtual void AssertValid() const;
    virtual void Dump(CDumpContext& dc) const;
#endif

// Generated message map functions
protected:
    //{{AFX_MSG(CChildFrame)
        // NOTE - the ClassWizard will add and remove member functions here.
        //     DO NOT EDIT what you see in these blocks of generated code!
    //}}AFX_MSG
    DECLARE_MESSAGE_MAP()
};

//////////////////////////////////////////////////////////////////////////

//{{AFX_INSERT_LOCATION}}
// Microsoft Visual C++ will insert additional declarations immediately before
// the previous line.

#endif
// !defined(AFX_CHILDFRM_H__349932E2_A2C4_11D1_80FC_00C0F6A83B7F__INCLUDED_)
```

Listing 17.10

```
// ChildFrm.cpp : implementation of the CChildFrame class
//

#include "stdafx.h"
#include "MiniEdit.h"

#include "ChildFrm.h"

#ifdef _DEBUG
#define new DEBUG_NEW
#undef THIS_FILE
static char THIS_FILE[] = __FILE__;
#endif

//////////////////////////////////////////////////////////////////////////
```

```
// CChildFrame

IMPLEMENT_DYNCREATE(CChildFrame, CMDIChildWnd)

BEGIN_MESSAGE_MAP(CChildFrame, CMDIChildWnd)
    //{{AFX_MSG_MAP(CChildFrame)
        // NOTE - the ClassWizard will add and remove mapping macros here.
        //    DO NOT EDIT what you see in these blocks of generated code !
    //}}AFX_MSG_MAP
END_MESSAGE_MAP()

/////////////////////////////////////////////////////////////////////////////
// CChildFrame construction/destruction

CChildFrame::CChildFrame()
{
    // TODO: add member initialization code here

}

CChildFrame::~CChildFrame()
{
}

BOOL CChildFrame::PreCreateWindow(CREATESTRUCT& cs)
{
    // TODO: Modify the Window class or styles here by modifying
    //   the CREATESTRUCT cs

    if( !CMDIChildWnd::PreCreateWindow(cs) )
        return FALSE;

    return TRUE;
}


/////////////////////////////////////////////////////////////////////////////
// CChildFrame diagnostics

#ifdef _DEBUG
void CChildFrame::AssertValid() const
{
    CMDIChildWnd::AssertValid();
```

```
}

void CChildFrame::Dump(CDumpContext& dc) const
{
    CMDIChildWnd::Dump(dc);
}

#endif //_DEBUG

///////////////////////////////////////////////////////////////////////////
// CChildFrame message handlers
```

Summary

In this chapter, you learned how to write programs that conform to the multiple document interface application model. The following are the general techniques and concepts that were explained:

- The programs presented in previous chapters are known as single document interface, or SDI, applications. They permit the user to open only a single document at a time.

- Multiple document interface, or MDI, programs allow the user to open several documents at once and to view and edit each document in a separate *child frame window*.

- Windows and the MFC provide most of the code for supporting the MDI interface.

- To generate an MDI program using AppWizard, simply choose the Multiple Documents option in the AppWizard Step 1 dialog box. AppWizard will create all required classes and source files.

- In an MDI program, the application, document, and view classes perform the same basic roles as in an SDI program.

- As in an SDI program, the main frame window class of an MDI program manages the program's main frame window. In an MDI program, however, the main frame window *doesn't* contain a single view window for viewing a document; rather, it contains the application workspace. The main frame window class is thus not associated with a particular document type and it's not included in the document template.

- In addition to the four classes used in an SDI program, an MDI program employs a child frame window class. This class manages the child frame window that's created for each open document. Each child frame window is displayed within the application workspace and contains a view window for displaying the document.

- An object of the child frame window class is created each time a document is opened, and the child frame window class is included in the program's document template.

- When generating a program using AppWizard, you should specify *all* features that may be required, because it's difficult to use AppWizard to "retrofit" features to an existing program.

- An MDI program has a set of resources (a menu, a string, an icon, and an accelerator) that have the identifier `IDR_MAINFRAME` and that are associated with the main frame window. The menu is displayed when *no* documents are open, and the icon is displayed in the main frame window's title bar, on the button on the Windows taskbar when the program is running, and other places that Windows displays a program's icon.

- An MDI program has another set of resources (a menu, a string, and an icon) that are associated with each child frame window used to display a document. All these resources have the same identifier; the name of this identifier is based either on the name of the program or on the document type name if you specify one when you generate the program. The menu is displayed when one or more documents are open, and the icon is displayed in the child frame window's title bar.

CHAPTER

EIGHTEEN

Performing Character I/O

- Displaying text

- Reading the keyboard

- Managing the caret

- The TextDemo source code

- The Echo source code

The programs given in previous chapters have relied primarily on standard Windows interface elements—such as title bars, menus, toolbars, status bars, edit boxes, and static text controls—for displaying information and obtaining input from the user. When you use these elements, Windows and the MFC provide the code for drawing text and for reading character input. In this chapter, you'll learn how to do the work yourself. Specifically, you'll learn how to display text directly within a view window, how to read individual characters that the user types, and how to manage the blinking *caret* that marks the position in a document where characters are inserted. These are tasks you'd need to perform if you were writing a text editor, a word processor, or one of many other types of programs.

Displaying Text

In this section, you'll create an example program named TextDemo, which demonstrates the main steps for displaying lines of text within a view window. The TextDemo program allows you to select a font by choosing the Font... command on the Options menu, which opens the Font dialog box. In that dialog box, you can select the font name (for example, Courier), the style (such as bold), the font size, font effects (strikeout or underline), as well as the text color. Once you've selected all desired font features and have closed the Font dialog box, the program displays complete information on the font; additionally, the lines of text containing this information are displayed *using* the specified font features. Figure 18.1 shows the Font dialog box after the user has chosen a set of features, while Figure 18.2 shows the resulting TextDemo program window after the user has clicked OK to close the dialog box.

FIGURE 18.1:

The Font dialog box, specifying the features of a font

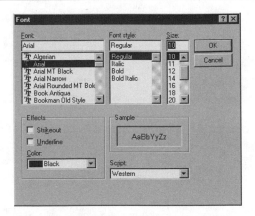

FIGURE 18.2:

The resulting TextDemo program window, after the user has clicked OK in the Font dialog box shown in Figure 18.1

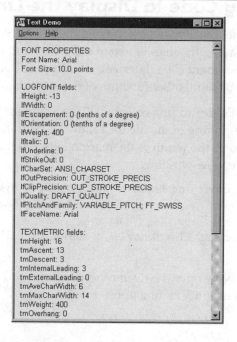

```
Text Demo                          _ □ ×
Options  Help

FONT PROPERTIES
Font Name: Arial
Font Size: 10.0 points

LOGFONT fields:
lfHeight: -13
lfWidth: 0
lfEscapement: 0 (tenths of a degree)
lfOrientation: 0 (tenths of a degree)
lfWeight: 400
lfItalic: 0
lfUnderline: 0
lfStrikeOut: 0
lfCharSet: ANSI_CHARSET
lfOutPrecision: OUT_STROKE_PRECIS
lfClipPrecision: CLIP_STROKE_PRECIS
lfQuality: DRAFT_QUALITY
lfPitchAndFamily: VARIABLE_PITCH; FF_SWISS
lfFaceName: Arial

TEXTMETRIC fields:
tmHeight: 16
tmAscent: 13
tmDescent: 3
tmInternalLeading: 3
tmExternalLeading: 0
tmAveCharWidth: 6
tmMaxCharWidth: 14
tmWeight: 400
tmOverhang: 0
```

> **NOTE**
>
> As you'll discover in Chapter 21, the basic techniques you learn here can *also* be used to display text on a printed page.

Generating the Program

Use AppWizard to generate the source files for the TextDemo program, using the techniques given in Chapter 9. In the Projects tab of the New dialog box, select the "MFC AppWizard (exe)" project type, enter the program name—TextDemo—into the Name: text box, and enter the desired project folder into the Location: text box. In the AppWizard dialog boxes (Step 1 through Step 6) enter the *same* choices that you made for the WinGreet program in Chapter 9, *except* that in the Step 6 dialog box you should do the following to add scrolling capability to the program:

1. Select the name of the view class, CTextDemoView, in the list at the top.

2. Select the CScrollView class in the Base Class: list.

Writing Code to Display the Lines

The first step in customizing the TextDemo program is to write the code for displaying the lines of text in the view window. As usual, this text is stored by the document class (later you'll see how it's generated), and it's displayed by the OnDraw member function of the view class.

Before adding code to OnDraw, open the TextDemoView.h file and enter at the beginning of the file the following definition for the constant MARGIN, which stores the width of the margin between the text and both the top and left edges of the view window:

```
const int MARGIN = 10; // margin displayed at top and left of
                       //     view window

class CTextDemoView : public CScrollView
{
```

Now open TextDemoView.cpp and add the code for displaying the lines of text to the OnDraw function:

```
/////////////////////////////////////////////////////////////////
///////////
// CTextDemoView drawing

void CTextDemoView::OnDraw(CDC* pDC)
{
    CTextDemoDoc* pDoc = GetDocument();
    ASSERT_VALID(pDoc);

    // TODO: add draw code for native data here

    // return if font has not yet been created:
    if (pDoc->m_Font.m_hObject == NULL)
        return;

    RECT ClipRect;
    int LineHeight;
    TEXTMETRIC TM;
    int Y = MARGIN;

    // select font into device context object:
    pDC->SelectObject (&pDoc->m_Font);
```

```
// obtain text metrics:
pDC->GetTextMetrics (&TM);
LineHeight = TM.tmHeight + TM.tmExternalLeading;

// set text attributes:
pDC->SetTextColor (pDoc->m_Color);
pDC->SetBkMode (TRANSPARENT);

// obtain coordinates of invalidated area:
pDC->GetClipBox (&ClipRect);

// display title line:
pDC->TextOut (MARGIN, Y, "FONT PROPERTIES");

// display text lines:
for (int Line = 0; Line < NUMLINES; ++Line)
   {
   Y += LineHeight;
   if (Y + LineHeight >= ClipRect.top && Y <= ClipRect.bottom)
      pDC->TextOut (MARGIN, Y, pDoc->m_LineTable [Line]);
   }
}
```

The code you added to OnDraw illustrates the basic steps for displaying text within a view window, which can be summarized as follows:

1. If the display code is in a function *other than* the OnDraw member function of the view class, you must obtain a device context object for the view window. (This doesn't apply to the code you just added.)

2. Select a text font, unless you want to display the text in the default System font.

3. Obtain text measurements, if needed.

4. Set any desired text attributes.

5. If you're displaying text from an OnDraw function, obtain the dimensions of the invalidated area of the view window (that is, the portion of the view window marked for repainting).

6. Call an appropriate CDC member function to display the text. (If the text is being displayed from an OnDraw function, display only the text that falls within the invalidated area.)

If the user hasn't yet chosen the Font... menu command to select a font, OnDraw returns immediately, because no text is yet available. (The text describes a font and is generated immediately after the user selects a font, as will be described later in the chapter.)

OnDraw doesn't need to do anything to accomplish step 1, because it's passed a pointer to a device context object that has already been created. Recall that to display text or graphics, you must have a device context object. A device context object is associated with a specific device (such as a window on the screen or a printer); it stores information on the font and other drawing attributes, and it provides member functions for drawing text and graphics on the associated device. If a program displays output from a function other than the OnDraw member function of the view class, it must create its own device context object. (This technique is demonstrated by the CEchoView::OnChar function in the Echo program presented later in the chapter.)

To specify the font that's used to display the text (step 2), OnDraw calls the CDC member function SelectObject:

```
pDC->SelectObject (&pDoc->m_Font);
```

SelectObject is passed the address of a font object. This object contains a complete description of the desired font. As you'll see later in the chapter, the document class initializes the font object with a font description whenever the user chooses a new font. Once the font object is selected into the device context object, all subsequent text output generated through that device context object is displayed using the font that matches the description stored in the font object (or using the closest matching font if the device lacks a font that matches exactly). Note that if you don't select a font, text is displayed in the default font, named System.

NOTE   As you'll see in Chapter 19, the CDC::SelectObject function can be used not only to select a font, but also to select various other types of objects that affect the drawing of graphics.

Once it has selected the font, OnDraw obtains the dimensions of the font characters (step 3) by calling the CDC member function GetTextMetrics:

```
TEXTMETRIC TM;

// ...
```

```
pDC->GetTextMetrics (&TM);
LineHeight = TM.tmHeight + TM.tmExternalLeading;
```

GetTextMetrics provides a complete description of the *actual* font that's used to display text on the device. This information is stored within a TEXTMETRIC structure. (As you'll see later, the TextDemo program displays the values of the fields of this structure for each font that the user chooses.) To calculate the total height of a line of text, OnDraw adds the tmHeight field of the TEXTMETRIC structure (which contains the height of the tallest letter) to the tmExternalLeading field (which contains the recommended amount of vertical space to leave between lines); it stores the result in LineHeight, which it later uses to calculate the starting position of each line. Figure 18.3 shows some of the other TEXTMETRIC fields that contain character dimensions.

FIGURE 18.3:

Text measurements provided by the CDC member function GetTextMetrics

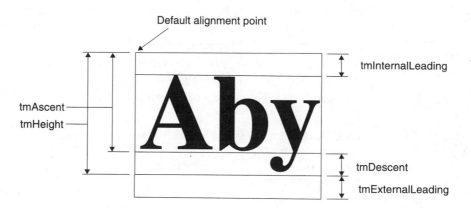

OnDraw next sets two text attributes (step 4):

```
pDC->SetTextColor (pDoc->m_Color);
pDC->SetBkMode (TRANSPARENT);
```

The call to CDC::SetTextColor sets the text to the color that the user selected when choosing the font, which is stored in the m_Color data member of the document class. If you don't specify a text color, text is displayed in black.

The call to CDC::SetBkMode sets the text background mode. The text *background* refers to the spaces surrounding the characters within the character cells. Passing TRANSPARENT to SetBkMode causes the characters to be drawn directly on top of the existing device colors, without painting the background. If you pass Set-BkMode the value OPAQUE, a text background will be drawn when the characters are displayed, overwriting the existing underlying colors on the device surface (OPAQUE is the default background mode). The default text background color used in the OPAQUE mode is white; you can set a different background color by calling CDC::SetBkColor. OnDraw specifies the TRANSPARENT mode so that the characters are drawn directly on top of the view window background color, and therefore the program doesn't need to set the text background color. (Note that the window background is painted using the "Window" system color that the user has set through the Display program of the Windows Control Panel.)

Table 18.1 summarizes the CDC functions for setting text attributes, while Table 18.2 summarizes the CDC functions for obtaining the current setting of each attribute. Note that the SetMapMode and GetMapMode functions listed in these tables set and obtain the current mapping mode, which affects the output of both text and graphics; the mapping mode will be discussed in Chapter 19 (in the section "The Mapping Mode"). For complete information on the functions in Tables 18.1 and 18.2, see the following Visual C++ online help topic: *Visual C++ Documentation, Reference, Microsoft Foundation Class Library and Templates, Microsoft Foundation Class Library, Class Library Reference, CDC.*

TABLE 18.1: CDC Member Functions for Setting Text Attributes

Function	Purpose
SetBkColor	Specifies the color used to paint the text background (the *background* refers to the areas within the character cells surrounding the letters)
SetBkMode	Enables or disables the painting of text background
SetMapMode	Sets the current mapping mode, which specifies the coordinate system and the units used to position text or graphics
SetTextAlign	Specifies the way text is aligned
SetTextCharacterExtra	Adjusts the horizontal spacing between characters to create expanded or condensed text
SetTextColor	Specifies the color used to draw the text (the letters, not the background)

TABLE 18.2: CDC Member Functions for Obtaining the Settings of Text Attributes

Function	Purpose
GetBkColor	Gets the text background color
GetBkMode	Gets the text background mode
GetMapMode	Gets the current mapping mode
GetTextAlign	Gets the text alignment style
GetTextCharacterExtra	Gets the amount of extra intercharacter spacing
GetTextColor	Gets the text color

OnDraw next obtains the dimensions of the invalidated area of the view window (step 5) by calling the CDC member function GetClipBox:

```
pDC->GetClipBox (&ClipRect);
```

Recall from Chapter 13 that the term *invalidated area* refers to the portion of a window that has been marked for drawing or redrawing, either by the program itself, or by Windows in response to some external event (such as the user's removing an overlapping window). Only output that falls within the invalidated area will appear on the screen (output that falls outside this area is *clipped*—that is, discarded).

Finally, OnDraw displays each line of text within the view window (step 6) using the CDC member function TextOut:

```
// display title line:
pDC->TextOut (MARGIN, Y, "FONT PROPERTIES");

// display text lines:
for (int Line = 0; Line < NUMLINES; ++Line)
   {
   Y += LineHeight;
   if (Y + LineHeight >= ClipRect.top && Y <= ClipRect.bottom)
      pDC->TextOut (MARGIN, Y, pDoc->m_LineTable [Line]);
   }
```

Notice that to increase efficiency, this code draws only those lines of text that fall partially or completely within the invalidated area of the view window. (When the window is redrawn, these are the only lines that need redrawing; also, Windows discards any text that a program attempts to draw outside this area.)

The first two parameters passed to TextOut specify the coordinates of the upper-left corner of the first character in the string to be displayed (that is, the coordinates of the default *alignment point* within the first character cell, as shown in Figure 18.3; note that you can change the position of the alignment point within the text string by calling CDC::SetTextAlign). The LineHeight variable is used to provide the proper vertical space between each line.

The third parameter passed to TextOut is the string that's to be displayed (or a CString object containing the string). The text for each line of text—other than the first line—is stored in the m_LineTable member of the document class; in the next section, you'll see how this text is generated.

TextOut is the simplest and most general-purpose function for displaying text. The CDC class provides several other text output functions that provide additional features. These functions are summarized in Table 18.3.

TABLE 18.3: CDC Member Functions for Displaying Text

Function	Purpose
DrawText	Draws text that's formatted within a specified rectangle—you can have this function expand tabs; align text at the left, center, or right of the formatting rectangle; or break lines between words to fit within the rectangle
ExtTextOut	Draws text within a specified rectangle—you can have this function clip text that falls outside the rectangle, fill the rectangle with the text background color, or alter the spacing between characters
GrayString	Draws dimmed text, which is usually used to indicate a disabled option or an unavailable item
TabbedTextOut	Displays text like TextOut, but expands tab characters using the specified tab stops
TextOut	Displays a string at a specified starting position

Creating the Font Object and Storing the Text

In this section, you'll add code to the TextDemo document class for displaying the Font dialog box (in response to the Font... menu command), for initializing the font object according to the user's selections in the Font dialog box, and for generating and storing the text that's to be displayed in the view window.

To create the menu command for opening the Font dialog box, open the IDR_MAINFRAME menu in the Visual C++ menu editor. First, delete the entire File and Edit pop-up menus, and then insert a new Options pop-up menu to the left of the Help menu. Table 18.4 lists the properties of the items in this menu, while Figure 18.4 shows the completed Options menu.

TABLE 18.4: The Properties of the TextDemo Options Menu Items

ID:	Caption	Other Features
none	&Options	Popup
ID_OPTIONS_FONT	&Font...	none
none	none	Separator
ID_APP_EXIT	E&xit	none

FIGURE 18.4:

The completed Options menu

You can also modify the program's icon, if you wish, by opening the IDR_MAIN-FRAME icon in the graphics editor. The icon belonging to the TextDemo program provided on the companion CD is shown in Figure 18.5 (the program includes only a Standard 32-pixel by 32-pixel icon image).

FIGURE 18.5:

The TextDemo program icon provided on the companion CD, as it appears in the Visual C++ graphics editor

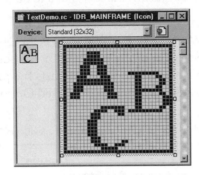

You can now save the changes you made to the program resources and close the resource editors. Next, run ClassWizard to create a handler for the Font command that you added to the TextDemo menu. In the ClassWizard dialog box, open the Message Maps tab, choose the CTextDemoDoc class in the Class Name: list, and select the ID_OPTIONS_FONT item in the Object IDs: list (the identifier of the Font menu command). Then, select the COMMAND message in the Messages: list, click the Add Function... button, and accept the default function name OnOptionsFont.

Before implementing the OnOptionsFont function, you need to open the TextDemoDoc.h header file and define several new variables. At the beginning of the file, define the constant NUMLINES, which contains the number of lines of text that will be displayed (not including the title line):

```
const int NUMLINES = 42;    // number of lines stored in document
                            // and displayed in view window

class CTextDemoDoc : public CDocument
{
```

Then add the following new data member definitions to the beginning of the CTextDemoDoc class definition:

```
class CTextDemoDoc : public CDocument
{
public:
    COLORREF m_Color;
    CString m_LineTable [NUMLINES];
    CFont m_Font;
```

m_Color stores the text color that the user selects in the Font dialog box. m_LineTable is an array of CString objects, which is used to store the lines of text displayed in the view window. m_Font is a member of the MFC CFont class and is the font object used for setting the text font.

Now open the TextDemoDoc.cpp file and add code as follows to the OnOptions-Font function you generated:

```
void CTextDemoDoc::OnOptionsFont()
{
    // TODO: Add your command handler code here

    // display Font dialog box:
    CFontDialog FontDialog;
    if (FontDialog.DoModal () != IDOK)
        return;

    // set m_Color:
    m_Color = FontDialog.GetColor ();   // get color chosen by user

    // initialize font object:
    m_Font.DeleteObject ();
    m_Font.CreateFontIndirect (&FontDialog.m_lf);

    // store values in m_LineTable:

    // store values chosen by user:
    int Num = 0;

    m_LineTable [Num++] = "Font Name: "
        + FontDialog.GetFaceName ();
```

```
m_LineTable [Num] =   "Font Size: ";
char NumBuf [18];
sprintf
   (NumBuf,"%d.%d points",
   FontDialog.GetSize () / 10,
   FontDialog.GetSize () % 10);
m_LineTable [Num++] += NumBuf;

m_LineTable [Num++] = "";

// store LOGFONT values:

m_LineTable [Num++] = "LOGFONT fields:";

m_LineTable [Num] =   "lfHeight: ";
sprintf (NumBuf,"%d",FontDialog.m_lf.lfHeight);
m_LineTable [Num++] += NumBuf;

m_LineTable [Num] =   "lfWidth: ";
sprintf (NumBuf,"%d",FontDialog.m_lf.lfWidth);
m_LineTable [Num++] += NumBuf;

m_LineTable [Num] =   "lfEscapement: ";
sprintf (NumBuf,"%d",FontDialog.m_lf.lfEscapement);
m_LineTable [Num] += NumBuf;
m_LineTable [Num++] += " (tenths of a degree)";

m_LineTable [Num] =   "lfOrientation: ";
sprintf (NumBuf,"%d",FontDialog.m_lf.lfOrientation);
m_LineTable [Num] += NumBuf;
m_LineTable [Num++] += " (tenths of a degree)";

m_LineTable [Num] =   "lfWeight: ";
sprintf (NumBuf,"%d",FontDialog.m_lf.lfWeight);
m_LineTable [Num++] += NumBuf;

m_LineTable [Num] =   "lfItalic: ";
sprintf (NumBuf,"%d",FontDialog.m_lf.lfItalic);
m_LineTable [Num++] += NumBuf;

m_LineTable [Num] =   "lfUnderline: ";
sprintf (NumBuf,"%d",FontDialog.m_lf.lfUnderline);
m_LineTable [Num++] += NumBuf;
```

```
m_LineTable [Num] =    "lfStrikeOut: ";
sprintf (NumBuf,"%d",FontDialog.m_lf.lfStrikeOut);
m_LineTable [Num++] += NumBuf;

m_LineTable [Num] = "lfCharSet: ";
switch (FontDialog.m_lf.lfCharSet)
   {
   case ANSI_CHARSET:
      m_LineTable [Num++] += "ANSI_CHARSET";
      break;

   case OEM_CHARSET:
      m_LineTable [Num++] += "OEM_CHARSET";
      break;

   case SYMBOL_CHARSET:
      m_LineTable [Num++] += "SYMBOL_CHARSET";
      break;

   default:
      m_LineTable [Num++] += "unspecified character set";
      break;
   }

m_LineTable [Num] = "lfOutPrecision: ";
switch (FontDialog.m_lf.lfOutPrecision)
   {
   case OUT_CHARACTER_PRECIS:
      m_LineTable [Num++] += "OUT_CHARACTER_PRECIS";
      break;

   case OUT_DEFAULT_PRECIS:
      m_LineTable [Num++] += "OUT_DEFAULT_PRECIS";
      break;

   case OUT_STRING_PRECIS:
      m_LineTable [Num++] += "OUT_STRING_PRECIS";
      break;

   case OUT_STROKE_PRECIS:
      m_LineTable [Num++] += "OUT_STROKE_PRECIS";
      break;
```

```
        default:
           m_LineTable [Num++] += "unspecified output precision";
           break;
        }

    m_LineTable [Num] = "lfClipPrecision: ";
    switch (FontDialog.m_lf.lfClipPrecision)
        {
        case CLIP_CHARACTER_PRECIS:
           m_LineTable [Num++] += "CLIP_CHARACTER_PRECIS";
           break;

        case CLIP_DEFAULT_PRECIS:
           m_LineTable [Num++] += "CLIP_DEFAULT_PRECIS";
           break;

        case CLIP_STROKE_PRECIS:
           m_LineTable [Num++] += "CLIP_STROKE_PRECIS";
           break;

        default:
           m_LineTable [Num++] += "unspecified clipping precision";
           break;
        }

    m_LineTable [Num] = "lfQuality: ";
    switch (FontDialog.m_lf.lfQuality)
        {
        case DEFAULT_QUALITY:
           m_LineTable [Num++] += "DEFAULT_QUALITY";
           break;

        case DRAFT_QUALITY:
           m_LineTable [Num++] += "DRAFT_QUALITY";
           break;

        case PROOF_QUALITY:
           m_LineTable [Num++] += "PROOF_QUALITY";
           break;

        default:
           m_LineTable [Num++] += "unspecified output quality";
```

```
            break;
        }

m_LineTable [Num] = "lfPitchAndFamily: ";
switch (FontDialog.m_lf.lfPitchAndFamily & 0x0003)
    {
    case DEFAULT_PITCH:
        m_LineTable [Num] += "DEFAULT_PITCH; ";
        break;

    case FIXED_PITCH:
        m_LineTable [Num] += "FIXED_PITCH; ";
        break;

    case VARIABLE_PITCH:
        m_LineTable [Num] += "VARIABLE_PITCH; ";
        break;

    default:
        m_LineTable [Num] += "unspecified pitch; ";
        break;
    }
switch (FontDialog.m_lf.lfPitchAndFamily & 0x00F0)
    {
    case FF_DECORATIVE:
        m_LineTable [Num++] += "FF_DECORATIVE";
        break;

    case FF_DONTCARE:
        m_LineTable [Num++] += "FF_DONTCARE";
        break;

    case FF_MODERN:
        m_LineTable [Num++] += "FF_MODERN";
        break;

    case FF_ROMAN:
        m_LineTable [Num++] += "FF_ROMAN";
        break;

    case FF_SCRIPT:
        m_LineTable [Num++] += "FF_SCRIPT";
        break;
```

```
        case FF_SWISS:
          m_LineTable [Num++] += "FF_SWISS";
          break;

        default:
          m_LineTable [Num++] += "unspecified family";
          break;
      }

  m_LineTable [Num] = "lfFaceName: ";
  m_LineTable [Num++] += FontDialog.m_lf.lfFaceName;

  m_LineTable [Num++] = "";

  // store TEXTMETRIC values:

  // create a device context object associated with the view
  // window:
  POSITION Pos = GetFirstViewPosition ();
  CView *PView = GetNextView (Pos);
  CClientDC ClientDC (PView);

  // select new font into device context object:
  ClientDC.SelectObject (&m_Font);
  TEXTMETRIC TM;
  ClientDC.GetTextMetrics (&TM);

  m_LineTable [Num++] = "TEXTMETRIC fields:";

  m_LineTable [Num] = "tmHeight: ";
  sprintf (NumBuf,"%d", TM.tmHeight);
  m_LineTable [Num++] += NumBuf;

  m_LineTable [Num] = "tmAscent: ";
  sprintf (NumBuf,"%d", TM.tmAscent);
  m_LineTable [Num++] += NumBuf;

  m_LineTable [Num] = "tmDescent: ";
  sprintf (NumBuf,"%d", TM.tmDescent);
  m_LineTable [Num++] += NumBuf;
```

```
m_LineTable [Num] = "tmInternalLeading: ";
sprintf (NumBuf,"%d", TM.tmInternalLeading);
m_LineTable [Num++] += NumBuf;

m_LineTable [Num] = "tmExternalLeading: ";
sprintf (NumBuf,"%d", TM.tmExternalLeading);
m_LineTable [Num++] += NumBuf;

m_LineTable [Num] = "tmAveCharWidth: ";
sprintf (NumBuf,"%d", TM.tmAveCharWidth);
m_LineTable [Num++] += NumBuf;

m_LineTable [Num] = "tmMaxCharWidth: ";
sprintf (NumBuf,"%d", TM.tmMaxCharWidth);
m_LineTable [Num++] += NumBuf;

m_LineTable [Num] = "tmWeight: ";
sprintf (NumBuf,"%d", TM.tmWeight);
m_LineTable [Num++] += NumBuf;

m_LineTable [Num] = "tmOverhang: ";
sprintf (NumBuf,"%d", TM.tmOverhang);
m_LineTable [Num++] += NumBuf;

m_LineTable [Num] = "tmDigitizedAspectX: ";
sprintf (NumBuf,"%d", TM.tmDigitizedAspectX);
m_LineTable [Num++] += NumBuf;

m_LineTable [Num] = "tmDigitizedAspectY: ";
sprintf (NumBuf,"%d", TM.tmDigitizedAspectY);
m_LineTable [Num++] += NumBuf;

m_LineTable [Num] = "tmFirstChar: ";
sprintf (NumBuf,"%d", TM.tmFirstChar);
m_LineTable [Num++] += NumBuf;

m_LineTable [Num] = "tmLastChar: ";
sprintf (NumBuf,"%d", TM.tmLastChar);
m_LineTable [Num++] += NumBuf;
```

```
m_LineTable [Num] = "tmDefaultChar: ";
sprintf (NumBuf,"%d", TM.tmDefaultChar);
m_LineTable [Num++] += NumBuf;

m_LineTable [Num] = "tmBreakChar: ";
sprintf (NumBuf,"%d", TM.tmBreakChar);
m_LineTable [Num++] += NumBuf;

m_LineTable [Num] = "tmItalic: ";
sprintf (NumBuf,"%d", TM.tmItalic);
m_LineTable [Num++] += NumBuf;

m_LineTable [Num] = "tmUnderlined: ";
sprintf (NumBuf,"%d", TM.tmUnderlined);
m_LineTable [Num++] += NumBuf;

m_LineTable [Num] = "tmStruckOut: ";
sprintf (NumBuf,"%d", TM.tmStruckOut);
m_LineTable [Num++] += NumBuf;

m_LineTable [Num++] = "tmPitchAndFamily: ";

m_LineTable [Num] = "   Pitch Info: ";
if (TM.tmPitchAndFamily & TMPF_FIXED_PITCH)
   m_LineTable [Num] += "variable pitch   ";
else
   m_LineTable [Num] += "fixed pitch    ";
if (TM.tmPitchAndFamily & TMPF_VECTOR)
   m_LineTable [Num] += "vector font    ";
if (TM.tmPitchAndFamily & TMPF_TRUETYPE)
   m_LineTable [Num] += "TrueType font    ";
if (TM.tmPitchAndFamily & TMPF_DEVICE)
   m_LineTable [Num] += "device font";
Num++;

m_LineTable [Num] = "   Family: ";
switch (TM.tmPitchAndFamily & 0x00F0)
   {
   case FF_DECORATIVE:
      m_LineTable [Num++] += "FF_DECORATIVE";
      break;
```

```
            case FF_DONTCARE:
                m_LineTable [Num++] += "FF_DONTCARE";
                break;

            case FF_MODERN:
                m_LineTable [Num++] += "FF_MODERN";
                break;

            case FF_ROMAN:
                m_LineTable [Num++] += "FF_ROMAN";
                break;

            case FF_SCRIPT:
                m_LineTable [Num++] += "FF_SCRIPT";
                break;

            case FF_SWISS:
                m_LineTable [Num++] += "FF_SWISS";
                break;

            default:
                m_LineTable [Num++] += "unknown family";
                break;
            }

    m_LineTable [Num] = "tmCharSet: ";
    switch (TM.tmCharSet)
        {
        case ANSI_CHARSET:
            m_LineTable [Num++] += "ANSI_CHARSET";
            break;

        case OEM_CHARSET:
            m_LineTable [Num++] += "OEM_CHARSET";
            break;

        case SYMBOL_CHARSET:
            m_LineTable [Num++] += "SYMBOL_CHARSET";
            break;

        default:
            m_LineTable [Num++] += "unknown character set";
```

```
        break;
    }

    // force redrawing of view window:
    UpdateAllViews (NULL);
}
```

As explained, OnOptionsFont receives control whenever the user chooses the Font... command on the Options menu. The code you added to OnOptionsFont performs the following main steps:

1. It displays the Font common dialog box.

2. It passes a font description—based on the information that the user entered into the Font dialog box—to the CFont::CreateFontIndirect function to initialize the font object (m_Font).

3. It also writes this font description to a series of strings, which are stored in m_LineTable.

4. It creates a device context object and selects the font object into the device context object.

5. It calls the GetTextMetrics member function of the device context object to obtain the features of the actual device font (GetTextMetrics copies the information to a TEXTMETRIC structure).

6. It writes descriptions of the actual font features to a series of strings, which are also stored in m_LineTable.

7. It calls UpdateAllViews to force the OnDraw function of the view class to display the lines of text contained in m_LineTable (using the new font).

The Font dialog box is one of the common dialog boxes provided by Windows (these dialog boxes were introduced in Chapter 15). The dialog box is displayed by creating a local object of the MFC CFontDialog class and then calling the DoModal member function. If the user cancels the dialog box, DoModal returns IDCANCEL, and OnOptionsFont returns immediately:

```
// display Font dialog box:
CFontDialog FontDialog;
if (FontDialog.DoModal () != IDOK)
    return;
```

The Font dialog box displayed by TextDemo allows the user to choose any of the fonts available for the Windows *screen*. You can, alternatively, have the Font dialog box display the fonts that are available for a specific printer, and you can customize the Font dialog box in various ways. For information, see the following online help topic: *Visual C++ Documentation*, *Reference*, *Microsoft Foundation Class Library and Templates*, *Microsoft Foundation Class Library*, *Class Library Reference*, *CFontDialog*.

If the user closes the dialog box by clicking the OK button, DoModal returns IDOK. In this case, OnOptionsFont proceeds to call CFontDialog member functions and access public CFontDialog data members to obtain information on the font that the user selected. Specifically, it calls CFontDialog::GetColor to obtain the value of the text color that the user chose (it saves this value in CTextDemoDoc::m_Color, which OnDraw uses to set the text color):

```
m_Color = FontDialog.GetColor ();  // get color chosen by user
```

Although it's selected in the Font dialog box, the text color *isn't* a feature of a font. Rather, it's a text attribute that must be assigned to a device context object by calling the CDC::SetTextColor function.

Also, OnOptionsFont calls CFontDialog::GetFaceName to obtain the font name that the user selected in the Font: list of the Font dialog box (for example, Arial), and it calls CFontDialog::GetSize to obtain the font size that the user selected in the Size: list. It writes both of these values to strings in m_LineTable so that they'll be displayed in the view window:

```
m_LineTable [Num++] = "Font Name: " + FontDialog.GetFaceName ();

m_LineTable [Num] =    "Font Size: ";
char NumBuf [18];
sprintf
   (NumBuf,"%d.%d points",
   FontDialog.GetSize () / 10,
   FontDialog.GetSize () % 10);
m_LineTable [Num++] += NumBuf;
```

Most importantly, OnOptionsFont obtains a complete description of the selected font from the CFontDialog::m_lf data member, which is a LOGFONT structure (a standard Windows structure). It first uses the LOGFONT structure to initialize the m_Font font object, through the following two statements:

```
m_Font.DeleteObject ();
m_Font.CreateFontIndirect (&FontDialog.m_lf);
```

The call to CFont::DeleteObject removes the existing font information from the font object in case this object was previously initialized (by a prior call to OnOptionsFont). If the font object *wasn't* previously initialized, calling Delete-Object is unnecessary but harmless. Passing the LOGFONT structure to CFont::CreateFontIndirect initializes or reinitializes the font object with a description of the newly chosen font. After the call to CreateFontIndirect, the font information is stored within the font object, and the font object is ready to be selected into a device context object so that text can be displayed using a font matching the description.

TIP

At any time after a font object has been initialized by calling CFont::Create-FontIndirect (or CFont::CreateFont), you can *obtain* the font information currently stored in the font object by calling CGdiObject::GetObject, which copies this information to a LOGFONT structure.

OnOptionsFont then writes the value of each field of the LOGFONT structure to a string within m_LineTable, so that these values will be available for displaying in the view window:

```
m_LineTable [Num++] = "LOGFONT fields:";

m_LineTable [Num] =   "lfHeight: ";
sprintf (NumBuf,"%d",FontDialog.m_lf.lfHeight);
m_LineTable [Num++] += NumBuf;

m_LineTable [Num] =   "lfWidth: ";
sprintf (NumBuf,"%d",FontDialog.m_lf.lfWidth);
m_LineTable [Num++] += NumBuf;

// and so on...
```

OnOptionsFont next creates a device context object associated with the view window, selects the newly initialized font object into this device context object, and then calls CDC::GetTextMetrics to obtain information on the actual font that will be used to display text in the window. GetTextMetrics copies this information to the fields of a TEXTMETRIC structure:

```
POSITION Pos = GetFirstViewPosition ();
CView *PView = GetNextView (Pos);
CClientDC ClientDC (PView);

// select new font into device context object:
ClientDC.SelectObject (&m_Font);
TEXTMETRIC TM;
ClientDC.GetTextMetrics (&TM);
```

As explained previously, OnDraw selects the font object into the device context object so that it can display the text using this font. OnOptionsFont, however, selects the font object merely to obtain *information* on the font (by calling GetText-Metrics). OnOptionsFont then writes the contents of each field of the TEXTMETRIC structure to m_LineTable. (The GetFirstViewPosition and GetNextView functions were explained in Chapter 12, in the section "Adding Supporting Code.")

> **NOTE**   For an explanation of each of the fields of the LOGFONT and TEXTMETRIC structures, see the following online help topic: *Platform SDK, Graphics and Multimedia Services, GDI, Fonts and Text, Font and Text Reference, Font and Text Structures*.

You may have noticed that the LOGFONT and TEXTMETRIC structures are similar and have a number of fields that store the same information. There's an important theoretical difference between these two structures, however. A LOGFONT structure is used to initialize a font object and stores a description of the *desired* font; there's no guarantee, however, that a font matching this description is actually available for any particular output device. When you select a font object into a device context, text is displayed using the actual physical font that matches the description most closely. The values that GetTextMetrics assigns the TEXTMETRIC structure describe the *actual* available font used to display text. (Because the Font dialog box allows the user to select only fonts that are actually available for the screen, the LOGFONT and TEXTMETRIC structures displayed by TextDemo match closely. In general, however, these two structures *don't* necessarily match.)

Using Stock Fonts

Displaying the Font dialog box and using a font object allows the user to choose *any* of the fonts that are available for the screen (or other device you specify before displaying the dialog box). As an alternative, you can quickly select a *stock font*, without displaying the Font dialog box or using a font object. A stock font is one of a small set of standard Windows fonts commonly used to display information on the screen. To select one of the stock fonts, you need only call the CDC member function SelectStockObject:

```
virtual CGdiObject* SelectStockObject (int nIndex);
```

The parameter **nIndex** is the index of the desired font; you can assign it one of the values described in Table 18.5. The fonts corresponding to these values are illustrated in Figure 18.6.

As an example, the following **OnDraw** function selects the fixed-pitch system font before displaying text in a window:

```
void CTextdemoView::OnDraw(CDC* pDC)
{
    CTextdemoDoc* pDoc = GetDocument();
    // TODO: add draw code here
    pDC->SelectStockObject (SYSTEM_FIXED_FONT);
    // set text attributes ...
    // display the text in the view window ...
}
```

As you'll learn in Chapter 19, you can use the **SelectStockObject** function to choose other stock items, such as the brushes and pens employed in drawing graphics.

TABLE 18.5: The Font Values You Can Assign the **nIndex** Parameter of the **SelectStockObject** Function

nIndex Value	Font Chosen
SYSTEM_FONT	The variable-pitch system font named System. This is the default font used for displaying text on the screen if you *don't* select a font into a device context object. (Early versions of Windows always used this font to draw text on title bars, menus, and other window components.)
SYSTEM_FIXED_FONT	The fixed-pitch system font named Fixedsys. This highly legible font is useful for program editors and other applications where a fixed-pitch font is desirable. It's the font used by the Windows Notepad editor.

Continued on next page

TABLE 18.5 CONTINUED: The Font Values You Can Assign the nIndex Parameter of the Select-StockObject Function

nIndex Value	Font Chosen
ANSI_VAR_FONT	A variable-pitch font that's smaller than the one specified by the SYSTEM_FONT value.
ANSI_FIXED_FONT	A fixed-pitch font that's smaller than the one specified by the SYSTEM_FIXED_FONT value.
DEVICE_DEFAULT_FONT	The default font for the device (for example, for a window it would be System, and for an HP LaserJet II printer it would be Courier).
OEM_FIXED_FONT	A fixed-pitch font, named Terminal, which matches the character set used by the underlying hardware. (Early versions of Windows always used this font for displaying text in an MS-DOS program window.)

FIGURE 18.6:

The stock fonts

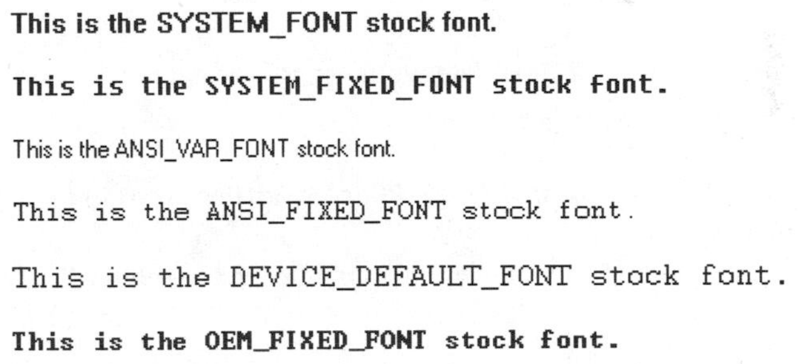

This is the SYSTEM_FONT stock font.

This is the SYSTEM_FIXED_FONT stock font.

This is the ANSI_VAR_FONT stock font.

This is the ANSI_FIXED_FONT stock font.

This is the DEVICE_DEFAULT_FONT stock font.

This is the OEM_FIXED_FONT stock font.

Supporting Scrolling

When you generated the TextDemo program in AppWizard, you specified that the view class be derived from CScrollView so that the view window would support scrolling. Scrolling is required because the lines of text might not fit completely within the view window, especially if the user selects a large font. In this section, you'll add code to report the current size of the document to the MFC scrolling code. See Chapter 13 for a general explanation of the methods for providing scrolling capability.

You'll begin by *deleting* the OnInitialUpdate virtual member function of the view class. This function was generated by AppWizard and it includes simple, default code for reporting the document size. In the TextDemo program, however, the document size changes *each time* the document class displays the Font dialog box and calls the UpdateAllViews function. Therefore, the document size must be reported in an OnUpdate virtual function (which receives control each time UpdateAllViews is called) *rather than* in an OnInitialUpdate function (which is called only once when the program first begins running). To remove the OnInitialUpdate declaration from the view class, run ClassWizard, open the Message Maps tab, choose CTextDemoView in the Class Name: list, choose On-InitialUpdate in the Member Functions: list, and click the Delete Function button. Click the Yes button when the Developer Studio asks if you want to continue. Then, open the TextDemoView.cpp file and manually delete the OnInitial-Update function definition.

To generate the code for the OnUpdate function, run ClassWizard again, open the Message Maps tab, choose CTextDemoView in the Class Name: and Object IDs: lists, choose OnUpdate in the Messages: list, and click the Add Function button. Then, click the Edit Code button and add code as follows to this function:

```
void CTextDemoView::OnUpdate (CView* pSender, LPARAM lHint, CObject*
pHint)
{
    // TODO: Add your specialized code here and/or call the base
    // class

    CTextDemoDoc* PDoc = GetDocument();

    if (PDoc->m_Font.m_hObject == NULL)  // font not yet created
        SetScrollSizes (MM_TEXT, CSize (0,0));
    else                                 // font created
        {
        CClientDC ClientDC (this);
        int LineWidth = 0;
        SIZE Size;
        TEXTMETRIC TM;

        ClientDC.SelectObject (&PDoc->m_Font);
        ClientDC.GetTextMetrics (&TM);

        for (int Line = 0; Line < NUMLINES; ++Line)
            {
            Size = ClientDC.GetTextExtent
            (PDoc->m_LineTable [Line],
            PDoc->m_LineTable [Line].GetLength ());
```

```
        if (Size.cx > LineWidth)
            LineWidth = Size.cx;
        }

    Size.cx = LineWidth + MARGIN;
    Size.cy = (TM.tmHeight + TM.tmExternalLeading)
        * (NUMLINES + 1) + MARGIN;

    SetScrollSizes (MM_TEXT, Size);
    ScrollToPosition (CPoint (0, 0));
        }

    CScrollView::OnUpdate (pSender, lHint, pHint);
    }
```

The OnUpdate virtual function is called when the view window is first created, and also whenever the CTextDemoDoc::OnOptionsFont function calls CDocument::UpdateAllViews after the user chooses a new font (OnUpdate was explained in Chapter 13). OnUpdate sets the document scroll size (that is, the total size of the body of text), which is based on the size of the new font.

To set the new document size, OnUpdate calls CScrollView::SetScrollSizes. If a font hasn't yet been selected, it specifies a zero document size to hide the scroll bars, because no text is displayed. If a font *has* been selected, OnUpdate must determine the total height and width of the text.

To calculate the height of the text, it creates a device context object for the view window, selects the font object into this device context object, and calls GetText-Metrics to obtain the measurements of the characters. The total height of the text is the height of a single line times the number of lines, plus the top margin:

```
Size.cy = (TM.tmHeight + TM.tmExternalLeading)
    * (NUMLINES + 1) + MARGIN;
```

To calculate the width of the text, it calls CDC::GetLength to obtain the width of each line. It sets the text width to the width of the widest line (which it saves in LineWidth) plus the margin:

```
Size.cx = LineWidth + MARGIN;
```

Note that the GetTextMetrics function reports the *average* width of a character (in the tmAveCharWidth TEXTMETRIC field). For a variable-pitch font, you can't use this information to obtain the width of a given character or string of characters, because the widths of the characters aren't uniform. The `GetLength` function, however, returns the actual width of a specific string of characters.

After setting the document size, `OnUpdate` calls `CScrollView::ScrollTo-Position` to scroll the view window to the beginning of the text:

```
SetScrollSizes (MM_TEXT, Size);
ScrollToPosition (CPoint (0, 0));
```

Finally, `OnUpdate` calls the `CScrollView` version of the `OnUpdate` function so that it can perform its default processing (namely, invalidating the entire view window so that it will be redrawn):

```
CScrollView::OnUpdate (pSender, lHint, pHint);
```

Modifying *InitInstance*

You should now open the TextDemo.cpp file and add the usual `SetWindowText` call to the `InitInstance` function:

```
    // The one and only window has been initialized, so show and
    // update it.
    m_pMainWnd->ShowWindow(SW_SHOW);
    m_pMainWnd->UpdateWindow();

    m_pMainWnd->SetWindowText ("Text Demo");

    return TRUE;
}
```

You can now build and run the TextDemo program, and you can use the new scroll bars to scroll through the text it displays. Leave the TextDemo project open, however, because you'll be adding features to the program in the next section.

Reading the Keyboard

You'll now learn how to read the keys that the user types while the program window is active. Like reading mouse input (described in Chapter 10), reading the keyboard is accomplished by providing an appropriate message handler in the program's view class. You'll first learn how to provide a handler for the WM_KEY-DOWN message, which is sent when *any* key (except a system key) is pressed. You'll then learn how to provide a handler for the WM_CHAR message, which is sent when a character key is typed.

Reading Keys with a *WM_KEYDOWN* Message Handler

Whenever the user presses a key, the system sends a WM_KEYDOWN message to the window that currently has the *input focus*. The input focus belongs either to the current *active window* or to a child window of the active window. (The active window is the one with a highlighted title bar, or a highlighted border if it's a dialog box.) In an MFC program generated by AppWizard, when the main frame window is active, the view window has the focus and therefore receives WM_KEYDOWN messages as keys are typed. (In an MDI program, the focus belongs to the *active* view window.) Providing a WM_KEYDOWN message handler is primarily useful for processing keys that don't generate printable characters—for example, the arrow keys and the function keys.

NOTE   If the user presses a *system key*, the focus window is sent a WM_SYSKEYDOWN message rather than a WM_KEYDOWN message. The system keys are Prt Scr, Alt, or any key pressed simultaneously with Alt. The system keys are normally processed by Windows, rather than by an application program.

To learn how to process WM_KEYDOWN messages, you'll now add a keyboard interface to the TextDemo program, which will allow the user to scroll through the text using keystrokes as well as the scroll bars. To begin, open the TextDemo project in the Developer Studio, if necessary, and then run ClassWizard. In the ClassWizard dialog box, open the Message Maps tab and choose CTextDemoView in the Class Name: list so that the message handler will be added to the view class (this is necessary because the WM_KEYDOWN messages are sent to the view window). Select CTextDemoView in the Object IDs: list, select the WM_KEYDOWN identifier in the Messages: list, and click the Add Function button. ClassWizard will add a message handler named OnKeyDown to the program's view class.

Now click the Edit Code button and add code as follows to the OnKeyDown function:

```
void CTextDemoView::OnKeyDown(UINT nChar, UINT nRepCnt, UINT
  nFlags)
{
    // TODO: Add your message handler code here and/or call
    // default

    CSize DocSize = GetTotalSize ();
    RECT ClientRect;
    GetClientRect (&ClientRect);
```

```
switch (nChar)
    {
    case VK_LEFT:      // left arrow
       if (ClientRect.right < DocSize.cx)
          SendMessage (WM_HSCROLL, SB_LINELEFT);
       break;

    case VK_RIGHT:     // right arrow
       if (ClientRect.right < DocSize.cx)
          SendMessage (WM_HSCROLL, SB_LINERIGHT);
       break;

    case VK_UP:        // up arrow
       if (ClientRect.bottom < DocSize.cy)
          SendMessage (WM_VSCROLL, SB_LINEUP);
       break;

    case VK_DOWN:      // down arrow
       if (ClientRect.bottom < DocSize.cy)
          SendMessage (WM_VSCROLL, SB_LINEDOWN);
       break;

    case VK_HOME:      // Home key
       if (::GetKeyState (VK_CONTROL) & 0x8000) // Ctrl pressed
          {
          if (ClientRect.bottom < DocSize.cy)
             SendMessage (WM_VSCROLL, SB_LEFT);
          }
       else                                     // Home key alone
          {
          if (ClientRect.right < DocSize.cx)
             SendMessage (WM_HSCROLL, SB_TOP);
          }
       break;

    case VK_END:       // End key
       if (::GetKeyState (VK_CONTROL) & 0x8000) // Ctrl pressed
          {
          if (ClientRect.bottom < DocSize.cy)
             SendMessage (WM_VSCROLL, SB_BOTTOM);
          }
       else                                     // End key alone
```

```
        {
        if (ClientRect.right < DocSize.cx)
            SendMessage (WM_HSCROLL, SB_RIGHT);
        }
    break;

    case VK_PRIOR:     // PgUp key
        if (ClientRect.bottom < DocSize.cy)
            SendMessage (WM_VSCROLL, SB_PAGEUP);
        break;

    case VK_NEXT:      // PgDn key
        if (ClientRect.bottom < DocSize.cy)
            SendMessage (WM_VSCROLL, SB_PAGEDOWN);
        break;
    }

    CScrollView::OnKeyDown(nChar, nRepCnt, nFlags);
}
```

The first parameter passed to OnKeyDown, nChar, contains a value known as a *virtual key code*, which indicates the key that was pressed. OnKeyDown uses this code to branch to the appropriate routine. Table 18.6 lists the virtual key codes for the keys that don't generate WM_CHAR messages. (Keys that generate WM_CHAR messages aren't included because, as you'll learn in the next section, they're more easily processed in a WM_CHAR message handler, where they're identified by character code.)

TABLE 18.6: Virtual Key Codes for Keys that Don't Generate WM_CHAR Messages

Value (Decimal)	Symbolic Constant	Key
12	VK_CLEAR	Numeric keypad 5 (with Num Lock off)
16	VK_SHIFT	Shift
17	VK_CONTROL	Ctrl
19	VK_PAUSE	Pause
20	VK_CAPITAL	Caps Lock
33	VK_PRIOR	PgUp

Continued on next page

TABLE 18.6 CONTINUED: Virtual Key Codes for Keys that Don't Generate WM_CHAR Messages

Value (Decimal)	Symbolic Constant	Key
34	VK_NEXT	PgDn
35	VK_END	End
36	VK_HOME	Home
37	VK_LEFT	←
38	VK_UP	↑
39	VK_RIGHT	→
40	VK_DOWN	↓
45	VK_INSERT	Insert
46	VK_DELETE	Delete
112	VK_F1	F1
113	VK_F2	F2
114	VK_F3	F3
115	VK_F4	F4
116	VK_F5	F5
117	VK_F6	F6
118	VK_F7	F7
119	VK_F8	F8
120	VK_F9	F9
121	VK_F10	F10
122	VK_F11	F11
123	VK_F12	F12
144	VK_NUMLOCK	Num Lock
145	VK_SCROLL	Scroll Lock

If the user pressed the Home key or the End key, `OnKeyDown` calls the Win32 API function `::GetKeyState` to determine whether the Ctrl key was pressed simultaneously with the Home or End key; for example:

```
case VK_HOME:        // Home key
    if (::GetKeyState (VK_CONTROL) & 0x8000)
        {
        // then Ctrl key was pressed simultaneously with the Home
        // key; process Ctrl+Home keystroke
        }
    else
        {
        // then Ctrl key was not pressed;
        // process Home key
        }
```

When calling `::GetKeyState`, you pass it the virtual code of the key you want to test. (You can obtain this code from Table 18.6.) The `::GetKeyState` function returns a value indicating the state of the specified key at the time the WM_KEY-DOWN message was generated. If the key was pressed, the high-order bit of the `::GetKeyState` return value will be set to 1 (`::GetKeyState` returns a SHORT, which is a 16-bit value); this can be tested, as in the following example:

```
if (::GetKeyState (VK_SHIFT) & 0x8000)
    // then Shift key was pressed
```

Also, if the key was toggled on at the time the WM_KEYDOWN message was generated, then the low-order bit of the `::GetKeyState` return value will be set. A key, such as Caps Lock, Num Lock, or Scroll Lock, is *toggled on* when it's in the *on* state and its indicator light on the keyboard (if it has one) is lit. The following example tests whether the Caps Lock key is toggled on:

```
if (::GetKeyState (VK_CAPITAL) & 0x0001)
    // then Caps Lock is toggled on
```

Note that `::GetKeyState` indicates whether a key was pressed or toggled on *at the time the key that generated the WM_KEYDOWN message was pressed*. It *doesn't* return the current status of the key (which might have changed by the time the message is processed). To obtain the *current* status of a key, you can call the `::GetAsync-KeyState` Win32 API function.

OnKeyDown processes each keystroke by sending one of the messages normally sent by a scroll bar when the user performs some action on the scroll bar with the mouse. The message is sent to the view window by calling the CWnd::SendMessage function. The CScrollView class provides a handler for each of these messages, which scrolls the window and adjusts the position of the scroll box, just as if the user had clicked on the scroll bar.

For example, if the user has pressed the ↓ key, OnKeyDown sends the *same* message that the vertical scroll bar sends when the user clicks within the bar below the scroll box. This message has the identifier WM_VSCROLL (indicating that it originates from the vertical scroll bar) and is sent with the code SB_LINEDOWN (indicating the specific scroll bar action):

```
case VK_DOWN:      // down arrow
   if (ClientRect.bottom < DocSize.cy)
      SendMessage (WM_VSCROLL, SB_LINEDOWN);
   break;
```

When the WM_VSCROLL message handler provided by CScrollView processes this message, it scrolls the text one line down.

Each scroll bar message is accompanied by an SB_ code indicating the specific scrolling action that occurred. Figure 18.7 shows the SB_ codes sent when the user clicks various places in the vertical or horizontal scroll bar.

FIGURE 18.7:

The SB_ codes sent with scroll bar messages when the user clicks on various positions within the vertical or horizontal scroll bar

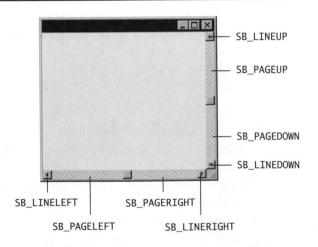

Table 18.7 lists each of the keystrokes processed by the OnKeyDown function, indicating the action that's performed in response to the keystroke and the scroll

bar message that OnKeyDown sends to the view window in order to generate this action. In this table, the term *page* refers to a scrolling distance equal to ⅒th of the document size in the direction of the scroll. The term *line* refers to a distance equal to ⅒th of a page, *not* the actual size of the text in a line. (As mentioned in Chapter 13, you can change these distances when you call CScrollView::Set-ScrollSizes.)

TABLE 18.7: Scrolling Keystrokes Processed by the OnKeyDown Function of the TextDemo Program

Keystroke	Desired Action	Message Sent to View Window
←	Scroll one "line" left	WM_HSCROLL, SB_LINELEFT
→	Scroll one "line" right	WM_HSCROLL, SB_LINERIGHT
↑	Scroll one "line" up	WM_VSCROLL, SB_LINEUP
↓	Scroll one "line" down	WM_VSCROLL, SB_LINEDOWN
Home	Scroll left as far as possible	WM_HSCROLL, SB_LEFT
Ctrl+Home	Scroll up as far as possible	WM_VSCROLL, SB_TOP
End	Scroll right as far as possible	WM_HSCROLL, SB_RIGHT
Ctrl+End	Scroll down as far as possible	WM_VSCROLL, SB_BOTTOM
PgUp	Scroll one page up	WM_VSCROLL, SB_PAGEUP
PgDn	Scroll one page down	WM_VSCROLL, SB_PAGEDOWN

Note, finally, that before sending a scroll bar message, the OnKeyDown function checks whether the corresponding scroll bar is visible. (The CScrollView code doesn't expect to receive messages from a scroll bar that's hidden, and the code doesn't work properly if such messages are sent.) The MFC hides the horizontal scroll bar if the view window is as wide as or wider than the text, and it hides the vertical scroll bar if the view window is as high as or higher than the text. To obtain the sizes of the text, OnKeyDown calls CScrollView::GetTotal-Size, and to obtain the size of the view window, it calls GetClientRect:

```
CSize DocSize = GetTotalSize ();
RECT ClientRect;
GetClientRect (&ClientRect);
```

Before sending a horizontal scroll bar message, it checks the text width as follows:

```
if (ClientRect.right < DocSize.cx)
    // then horizontal scroll bar is visible;
    // therefore send message ...
```

Likewise, before sending a vertical scroll bar message, it checks the text height as follows:

```
if (ClientRect.bottom < DocSize.cy)
    // then vertical scroll bar is visible;
    // therefore send message ...
```

This section completes the changes to TextDemo; you can now build and run the program. To avoid interrupting the current discussion, the source listings for TextDemo are placed near the end of the chapter.

Reading Keys with a *WM_CHAR* Message Handler

For most of the keys on the keyboard, when the user types the key, Windows sends a WM_CHAR message to the window with the input focus. (The keys that *don't* send WM_CHAR messages are listed in Table 18.6.) When a program allows the user to type in text, it's easiest to read the keystrokes by providing a WM_CHAR message handler. Such a handler is more convenient than a WM_KEYDOWN message handler because it's passed the standard ANSI code for the character typed, rather than a virtual key code that must be translated into a character code. The character code passed to a WM_CHAR handler can be immediately inserted into a character string for storing the text, and it can also be directly displayed in a window or on another device using a function such as CDC::TextOut.

When the user types text into a program, the program typically echoes these characters within the program window. To illustrate the basic techniques required for reading text and echoing characters, this section presents the Echo program. Echo reads characters typed by the user and displays these characters at the top of the program window. When the line reaches the right window border, the user can continue typing; the characters, however, will no longer be visible. The user can choose the Clear command on the Edit menu to erase the line, and then can type another one. Figure 18.8 illustrates the program window after the user has typed several characters.

FIGURE 18.8:

The Echo program window after the user has entered some text

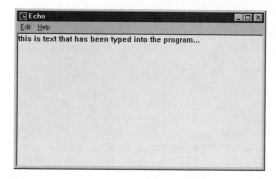

Generating the Source Code

Use AppWizard to generate the Echo program source code. In the Projects tab of the New dialog box, specify Echo as the project name, and in the AppWizard dialog boxes (Step 1 through Step 6), choose the *same* options you chose for the Win-Greet program in Chapter 9.

Modifying the Resources

After you've generated the source files, open on the ResourceView tab in the Workspace window and double-click the IDR_MAINFRAME menu identifier to open the program menu in the Visual C++ menu editor. In the menu editor, first delete the entire File menu, and then delete all the items on the Edit menu, but leave the empty Edit menu in place. Now add the items described in Table 18.8 to the Edit menu. The completed Edit menu will appear as shown in Figure 18.9.

TABLE 18.8: The Properties of the Edit Menu Items

ID:	Caption	Other Features
none	&Edit	Popup
ID_EDIT_CLEAR	&Clear	none
none	none	Separator
ID_APP_EXIT	E&xit	none

FIGURE 18.9:

The completed Edit menu, in the menu editor

You might also want to customize the program icon (IDR_MAINFRAME) in the graphics editor. The icon provided for the Echo program on the companion CD is shown in Figure 18.10 (the program includes only a standard 32-pixel by 32-pixel image).

FIGURE 18.10:

The Echo program icon provided on the companion CD, as it appears in the graphics editor

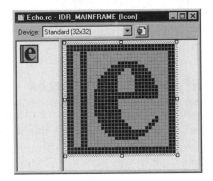

Defining the Message Handlers

You'll now define functions to handle the WM_CHAR message sent whenever the user types a character, as well as the menu message sent whenever the user chooses the Clear command on the Edit menu.

To define the message handlers, run ClassWizard. In the ClassWizard dialog box, open the Message Maps tab and choose the CEchoView class in the Class Name: list so that the message-handling functions will be added to the view class (this is necessary because the view window receives these messages).

Next, select the CEchoView class in the Object IDs: list, select WM_CHAR in the Messages: list, and click the Add Function button; ClassWizard will generate a WM_CHAR message handler named OnChar. Then choose the ID_EDIT_CLEAR item (the identifier of the Clear command) in the Object IDs: list, select the COMMAND item in the Messages: list, and click the Add Function... button. Accept the default name for the menu command handler, OnEditClear. Close the Class-Wizard dialog box by clicking the OK button.

Adding Code

You'll now add a data member to store the line of text, you'll implement the message-handling functions you just generated, and you'll add code to the OnDraw function of the view class.

First, open the EchoDoc.h file and define the public data member m_TextLine at the beginning of the CEchoDoc class definition:

```
class CEchoDoc : public CDocument
{
public:
    CString m_TextLine;

// remainder of CEchoDoc definition ...
```

This data member will be used to store the characters that the user types.

Next, open EchoView.cpp and add code as follows (again, shown in bold) to the OnChar function that you generated:

```
void CEchoView::OnChar(UINT nChar, UINT nRepCnt, UINT nFlags)
{
    // TODO: Add your message handler code here and/or call
    // default

    if (nChar < 32)
        {
        ::MessageBeep (MB_OK); // generate default sound
        return;
        }

    CEchoDoc* PDoc = GetDocument();
    PDoc->m_TextLine += nChar;

    CClientDC ClientDC (this);
    ClientDC.SetTextColor (::GetSysColor (COLOR_WINDOWTEXT));
    ClientDC.SetBkMode (TRANSPARENT);
    ClientDC.TextOut (0, 0, PDoc->m_TextLine);

    CView::OnChar(nChar, nRepCnt, nFlags);
}
```

OnChar receives control whenever the user types a character key, and the nChar parameter contains the ANSI code for the character.

Notice that if the user has typed a keystroke that generates a character code value *less than* 32, OnChar beeps and exits. Character code values less than 32 are generated by control keystrokes, such as Ctrl+A, Enter, or Tab, rather than by keys for printable characters. In general, a program either ignores control keystrokes or uses them to trigger some control action. For example, in response to the Backspace key (character code 8), a program might erase the previous character; or, in response to the Enter key (character code 13), a program might generate a new line. Some of the commonly used control keystrokes are described in Table 18.9. If you pass a character code for a control keystroke to a function such as TextOut, Windows will print a small rectangle, indicating that the code doesn't correspond to a printable character.

TABLE 18.9: Common Control Keystrokes

Keystroke	Meaning	nChar Value (Decimal)
Backspace	Backspace	8
Tab	Tab	9
Ctrl+Enter	Line feed	10
Enter	Carriage return	13
Esc	Escape	27

OnChar next adds the new character to the end of the string containing the text, using the overloaded CString += operator:

```
CEchoDoc* PDoc = GetDocument();
PDoc->m_TextLine += nChar;
```

Finally, OnChar creates a device context object for the view window and uses it to display the complete string, including the new character at the end. Even though only the character at the end is being added to the window, it's far easier to redisplay the entire string than to figure out the position of the end character and print only that character. (Determining the exact position of a character within a string is difficult for variable-pitch or italicized fonts.)

Notice that rather than setting the text to a specific color, OnChar assigns it the "Window Font" color that the user has set through the Control Panel, which it obtains by passing the value COLOR_WINDOWTEXT to the Win32 API function ::GetSysColor:

```
ClientDC.SetTextColor (::GetSysColor (COLOR_WINDOWTEXT));
```

Because OnChar doesn't set the text font, the characters are displayed in the default System font.

WARNING

Recall from Chapter 13 that if the view window supports scrolling (that is, if it's derived from CScrollView), you must pass a CClientDC device context object that you create to the CView::OnPrepareDC function *before* displaying text or graphics. OnPrepareDC adjusts the device context object for the current scrolled position of the document, so that the output will appear at the correct positions. (You don't need to call OnPrepareDC for a device context object passed to an OnDraw function, because it has *already* been adjusted.)

Although OnDraw displays the updated character string whenever the user types a character, the program must also redisplay the characters whenever the window needs redrawing. To do this, add code as follows to the OnDraw function, also in the EchoView.cpp file:

```
///////////////////////////////////////////////////////////////
///////////
// CEchoView drawing

void CEchoView::OnDraw(CDC* pDC)
{
    CEchoDoc* pDoc = GetDocument();
    ASSERT_VALID(pDoc);

    // TODO: add draw code for native data here

    pDC->SetTextColor (::GetSysColor (COLOR_WINDOWTEXT));
    pDC->SetBkMode (TRANSPARENT);
    pDC->TextOut (0, 0, pDoc->m_TextLine);
}
```

Note that rather than drawing the text itself, the OnChar function *could* call the CDocument::UpdateAllViews function to force OnDraw to display the text. However, displaying the text directly from OnChar not only is more efficient, but also avoids the annoying flicker that would occur each time the view window is repainted by OnDraw. (Flicker occurs because the invalidated area of the window is erased immediately before OnDraw is called.)

Finally, add code as follows to the OnEditClear function:

```
void CEchoView::OnEditClear()
{
    // TODO: Add your command handler code here

    CEchoDoc* PDoc = GetDocument();
    PDoc->m_TextLine.Empty ();
    PDoc->UpdateAllViews (NULL);
}
```

The added code calls the CString member function Empty to erase the characters stored in m_TextLine, setting the length of the string to zero. It then calls UpdateAllViews to cause the view window to be erased.

You can now build and run the Echo program, and you can then try typing in a line of text. Leave the Echo project open in the Developer Studio, however, because you aren't done with this program.

Managing the Caret

When you ran the Echo program, you probably noticed that it lacked something important: the familiar blinking caret marking the insertion point within the text. In this section, you'll add a caret.

To manage the caret, you must first define several new message-handling functions. The purpose of each of these functions will be explained when you add the function code. To begin, run ClassWizard, open the Message Maps tab, choose the CEchoView class in the Class Name: list, and choose CEchoView in the Object IDs: list.

You'll now define handlers for three of the Windows notification messages that are sent to the view window. First, select the WM_CREATE message in the Messages: list and click the Add Function button to create a message handler named On-Create. Then, in the same way, define handlers for the WM_KILLFOCUS and WM_SETFOCUS messages, which will be named OnKillFocus and OnSetFocus. Close the ClassWizard dialog box by clicking the OK button.

Before implementing the new message handlers, open the EchoView.h header file and add the following data member definitions to the beginning of the CEcho-View class definition:

```
class CEchoView : public CView
{
private:
    POINT m_CaretPos;
    int m_XCaret, m_YCaret;
```

m_CaretPos stores the current position of the caret, m_XCaret stores its width, and m_YCaret its height.

Now open the EchoView.cpp file and add the following initializations to the CEchoView constructor:

```
CEchoView::CEchoView()
{
    // TODO: add construction code here

    m_CaretPos.x = m_CaretPos.y = 0;
}
```

These initializations will cause the caret to appear initially at the upper-left corner of the view window.

In this same file, add the following code to the OnCreate function:

```
int CEchoView::OnCreate(LPCREATESTRUCT lpCreateStruct)
{
    if (CView::OnCreate(lpCreateStruct) == -1)
        return -1;

    // TODO: Add your specialized creation code here
```

```
        CClientDC ClientDC (this);
        TEXTMETRIC TM;

        ClientDC.GetTextMetrics (&TM);
        m_XCaret = TM.tmAveCharWidth / 3;
        m_YCaret = TM.tmHeight + TM.tmExternalLeading;

        return 0;
    }
```

The OnCreate function is called after the view window is first created, before it becomes visible. The code you added calculates and stores the size of the caret that will be displayed. Rather than setting the caret to some arbitrary width, On-Create sets the width to one-third of the average width of the characters in the default System font, which will be used to display the text. (This method ensures that the caret maintains an appropriate width, even if the size of the System font changes under various video modes.) OnCreate makes the caret height the same as the height of the characters in the System font. OnCreate obtains the average width and the height of the characters in the System font by creating a device context object and calling the familiar GetTextMetrics function.

Next, add code to the OnSetFocus function (also in Echoview.cpp), as follows:

```
void CEchoView::OnSetFocus(CWnd* pOldWnd)
{
    CView::OnSetFocus(pOldWnd);

    // TODO: Add your message handler code here

    CreateSolidCaret (m_XCaret, m_YCaret);
    SetCaretPos (m_CaretPos);
    ShowCaret ();
}
```

OnSetFocus is called whenever the view window receives the input focus—specifically, when the view window is first created and whenever the user switches to the Echo program after working in another program. OnSetFocus calls the CWnd member function CreateSolidCaret to create the caret, passing this function the caret width and height. It then calls CWnd::SetCaretPos to place the caret at the correct position. Because a newly created caret is initially invisible, it must also call CWnd::ShowCaret to make the caret appear.

Note that when the view window is created, OnSetFocus is called *after* On-Create. Therefore, it can use the caret dimensions set by OnCreate. It's easy to understand why you must create the caret before the view window is first created; however, why do you need to create it *every time* the view window receives the focus? The reason is that the caret is *destroyed* whenever the view window loses the focus, through a call to the ::DestroyCaret Win32 API function, which you should add to the OnKillFocus function:

```
void CEchoView::OnKillFocus(CWnd* pNewWnd)
{
    CView::OnKillFocus(pNewWnd);

    // TODO: Add your message handler code here

    ::DestroyCaret ();
}
```

OnKillFocus is called whenever the view window loses the input focus. DestroyCaret destroys the caret and removes the caret image from the screen. It's called because a caret should be displayed only in the window with the current input focus (in fact, only *one* caret is available in an application, even if it has several windows).

To maintain the caret, you must also modify the OnChar and OnEditClear functions. First, add the statements marked in bold to the OnChar function:

```
void CEchoView::OnChar(UINT nChar, UINT nRepCnt, UINT nFlags)
{
    // TODO: Add your message handler code here and/or call
    // default

    if (nChar < 32)
        {
        ::MessageBeep (MB_OK); // generate default sound
        return;
        }

    CEchoDoc* PDoc = GetDocument();
    PDoc->m_TextLine += nChar;
```

```
CClientDC ClientDC (this);
ClientDC.SetTextColor (::GetSysColor (COLOR_WINDOWTEXT));
ClientDC.SetBkMode (TRANSPARENT);
HideCaret ();
ClientDC.TextOut (0, 0, PDoc->m_TextLine);
CSize Size = ClientDC.GetTextExtent
    (PDoc->m_TextLine,
    PDoc->m_TextLine.GetLength ());
m_CaretPos.x = Size.cx;
SetCaretPos (m_CaretPos);
ShowCaret ();

CView::OnChar(nChar, nRepCnt, nFlags);
}
```

After the new character has been inserted at the end of the line, the added code calls GetTextExtent to determine the new length of the line, and then calls Set-CaretPos to move the caret to the end of the line (where the next character will be inserted).

Also, before drawing the text, the added code calls CWnd::HideCaret to make the caret invisible; after drawing the text and moving the caret, it calls CWnd::ShowCaret to make the caret visible again. This is done because writing to the window while the caret is visible can cause screen corruption at the position of the caret. Note that you *don't* need to hide the caret when drawing from the On-Draw function, because Windows automatically hides the caret before this function is called and restores the caret after the function returns (for the same reason, you don't need to hide a caret in the OnPaint function that draws a nonview window). Therefore, you don't need to modify OnDraw.

TIP   Calling HideCaret is cumulative; that is, if you call HideCaret more than once without calling ShowCaret, you must then call ShowCaret the same number of times to make the caret visible again.

Next, you need to add two statements to the end of the OnEditClear function:

```
void CEchoView::OnEditClear()
{
    // TODO: Add your command handler code here

    CEchoDoc* PDoc = GetDocument();
```

```
        PDoc->m_TextLine.Empty ();
        PDoc->UpdateAllViews (NULL);
        m_CaretPos.x = 0;
        SetCaretPos (m_CaretPos);
    }
```

The added statements reposition the caret at the left edge of the window after the text has been deleted in response to the Clear command on the Edit menu.

Finally, open the Echo.cpp file and add the usual `CWnd::SetWindowText` call to the `InitInstance` function:

```
        // The one and only window has been initialized, so show and
        // update it.
        m_pMainWnd->ShowWindow(SW_SHOW);
        m_pMainWnd->UpdateWindow();

        m_pMainWnd->SetWindowText ("Echo");

        return TRUE;
    }
```

You've now completed modifying Echo, and you can build and run the program. The C++ source code is given at the end of the chapter (following the source code for the TextDemo program).

The TextDemo Source Code

The following listings, Listings 18.1 through 18.8, provide the C++ source code for the TextDemo program that you created in this chapter. You'll find a copy of each of these files, as well as the other source files for the program, in your \TextDemo companion-CD folder.

Listing 18.1

```
// TextDemo.h : main header file for the TEXTDEMO application
//

#if !defined(AFX_TEXTDEMO_H__3E126285_A392_11D1_80FC_00C0F6A83B7F__INCLUDED_)
#define AFX_TEXTDEMO_H__3E126285_A392_11D1_80FC_00C0F6A83B7F__INCLUDED_
```

```
#if _MSC_VER > 1000
#pragma once
#endif // _MSC_VER > 1000

#ifndef __AFXWIN_H__
    #error include 'stdafx.h' before including this file for PCH
#endif

#include "resource.h"        // main symbols

/////////////////////////////////////////////////////////////////////////////
// CTextDemoApp:
// See TextDemo.cpp for the implementation of this class
//

class CTextDemoApp : public CWinApp
{
public:
    CTextDemoApp();

// Overrides
    // ClassWizard generated virtual function overrides
    //{{AFX_VIRTUAL(CTextDemoApp)
    public:
    virtual BOOL InitInstance();
    //}}AFX_VIRTUAL

// Implementation
    //{{AFX_MSG(CTextDemoApp)
    afx_msg void OnAppAbout();
        // NOTE - the ClassWizard will add and remove member functions here.
        //    DO NOT EDIT what you see in these blocks of generated code !
    //}}AFX_MSG
    DECLARE_MESSAGE_MAP()
};


/////////////////////////////////////////////////////////////////////////////

//{{AFX_INSERT_LOCATION}}
// Microsoft Visual C++ will insert additional declarations immediately before
// the previous line.
```

```
#endif
// !defined(AFX_TEXTDEMO_H__3E126285_A392_11D1_80FC_00C0F6A83B7F__INCLUDED_)
```

Listing 18.2

```cpp
// TextDemo.cpp : Defines the class behaviors for the application.
//

#include "stdafx.h"
#include "TextDemo.h"

#include "MainFrm.h"
#include "TextDemoDoc.h"
#include "TextDemoView.h"

#ifdef _DEBUG
#define new DEBUG_NEW
#undef THIS_FILE
static char THIS_FILE[] = __FILE__;
#endif


/////////////////////////////////////////////////////////////////////////////
// CTextDemoApp

BEGIN_MESSAGE_MAP(CTextDemoApp, CWinApp)
    //{{AFX_MSG_MAP(CTextDemoApp)
    ON_COMMAND(ID_APP_ABOUT, OnAppAbout)
        // NOTE - the ClassWizard will add and remove mapping macros here.
        //    DO NOT EDIT what you see in these blocks of generated code!
    //}}AFX_MSG_MAP
    // Standard file based document commands
    ON_COMMAND(ID_FILE_NEW, CWinApp::OnFileNew)
    ON_COMMAND(ID_FILE_OPEN, CWinApp::OnFileOpen)
END_MESSAGE_MAP()

/////////////////////////////////////////////////////////////////////////////
// CTextDemoApp construction

CTextDemoApp::CTextDemoApp()
{
    // TODO: add construction code here,
    // Place all significant initialization in InitInstance
}
```

```
/////////////////////////////////////////////////////////////////////
// The one and only CTextDemoApp object

CTextDemoApp theApp;

/////////////////////////////////////////////////////////////////////
// CTextDemoApp initialization

BOOL CTextDemoApp::InitInstance()
{
    // Standard initialization
    // If you are not using these features and wish to reduce the size
    //  of your final executable, you should remove from the following
    //  the specific initialization routines you do not need.

#ifdef _AFXDLL
    Enable3dControls();        // Call this when using MFC in a shared DLL
#else
    Enable3dControlsStatic();  // Call this when linking to MFC statically
#endif

    // Change the registry key under which our settings are stored.
    // TODO: You should modify this string to be something appropriate
    // such as the name of your company or organization.
    SetRegistryKey(_T("Local AppWizard-Generated Applications"));

    LoadStdProfileSettings();  // Load standard INI file options (including MRU)

    // Register the application's document templates.  Document templates
    //  serve as the connection between documents, frame windows and views.

    CSingleDocTemplate* pDocTemplate;
    pDocTemplate = new CSingleDocTemplate(
        IDR_MAINFRAME,
        RUNTIME_CLASS(CTextDemoDoc),
        RUNTIME_CLASS(CMainFrame),       // main SDI frame window
        RUNTIME_CLASS(CTextDemoView));
    AddDocTemplate(pDocTemplate);

    // Parse command line for standard shell commands, DDE, file open
    CCommandLineInfo cmdInfo;
    ParseCommandLine(cmdInfo);
```

```
    // Dispatch commands specified on the command line
    if (!ProcessShellCommand(cmdInfo))
        return FALSE;

    // The one and only window has been initialized, so show and update it.
    m_pMainWnd->ShowWindow(SW_SHOW);
    m_pMainWnd->UpdateWindow();

    m_pMainWnd->SetWindowText ("Text Demo");

    return TRUE;
}


/////////////////////////////////////////////////////////////////////////////
// CAboutDlg dialog used for App About

class CAboutDlg : public CDialog
{
public:
    CAboutDlg();

// Dialog Data
    //{{AFX_DATA(CAboutDlg)
    enum { IDD = IDD_ABOUTBOX };
    //}}AFX_DATA

    // ClassWizard generated virtual function overrides
    //{{AFX_VIRTUAL(CAboutDlg)
    protected:
    virtual void DoDataExchange(CDataExchange* pDX);    // DDX/DDV support
    //}}AFX_VIRTUAL

// Implementation
protected:
    //{{AFX_MSG(CAboutDlg)
        // No message handlers
    //}}AFX_MSG
    DECLARE_MESSAGE_MAP()
};

CAboutDlg::CAboutDlg() : CDialog(CAboutDlg::IDD)
{
```

```
    //{{AFX_DATA_INIT(CAboutDlg)
    //}}AFX_DATA_INIT
}

void CAboutDlg::DoDataExchange(CDataExchange* pDX)
{
    CDialog::DoDataExchange(pDX);
    //{{AFX_DATA_MAP(CAboutDlg)
    //}}AFX_DATA_MAP
}

BEGIN_MESSAGE_MAP(CAboutDlg, CDialog)
    //{{AFX_MSG_MAP(CAboutDlg)
        // No message handlers
    //}}AFX_MSG_MAP
END_MESSAGE_MAP()

// App command to run the dialog
void CTextDemoApp::OnAppAbout()
{
    CAboutDlg aboutDlg;
    aboutDlg.DoModal();
}


/////////////////////////////////////////////////////////////////////////
// CTextDemoApp message handlers
```

Listing 18.3

```
// TextDemoDoc.h : interface of the CTextDemoDoc class
//
/////////////////////////////////////////////////////////////////////////

#if !defined(AFX_TEXTDEMODOC_H__3E12628B_A392_11D1_80FC_00C0F6A83B7F__INCLUDED_)
#define AFX_TEXTDEMODOC_H__3E12628B_A392_11D1_80FC_00C0F6A83B7F__INCLUDED_

#if _MSC_VER > 1000
#pragma once
#endif // _MSC_VER > 1000

const int NUMLINES = 42;    // number of lines stored in document
                            // and displayed in view window
```

```
class CTextDemoDoc : public CDocument
{
public:
    COLORREF m_Color;
    CString m_LineTable [NUMLINES];
    CFont m_Font;

protected: // create from serialization only
    CTextDemoDoc();
    DECLARE_DYNCREATE(CTextDemoDoc)

// Attributes
public:

// Operations
public:

// Overrides
    // ClassWizard generated virtual function overrides
    //{{AFX_VIRTUAL(CTextDemoDoc)
    public:
    virtual BOOL OnNewDocument();
    virtual void Serialize(CArchive& ar);
    //}}AFX_VIRTUAL

// Implementation
public:
    virtual ~CTextDemoDoc();
#ifdef _DEBUG
    virtual void AssertValid() const;
    virtual void Dump(CDumpContext& dc) const;
#endif

protected:

// Generated message map functions
protected:
    //{{AFX_MSG(CTextDemoDoc)
    afx_msg void OnOptionsFont();
    //}}AFX_MSG
    DECLARE_MESSAGE_MAP()
};
```

```
/////////////////////////////////////////////////////////////////////////

//{{AFX_INSERT_LOCATION}}
// Microsoft Visual C++ will insert additional declarations immediately before
// the previous line.

#endif
// !defined(AFX_TEXTDEMODOC_H__3E12628B_A392_11D1_80FC_00C0F6A83B7F__INCLUDED_)
```

Listing 18.4

```cpp
// TextDemoDoc.cpp : implementation of the CTextDemoDoc class
//

#include "stdafx.h"
#include "TextDemo.h"

#include "TextDemoDoc.h"

#ifdef _DEBUG
#define new DEBUG_NEW
#undef THIS_FILE
static char THIS_FILE[] = __FILE__;
#endif

/////////////////////////////////////////////////////////////////////////
// CTextDemoDoc

IMPLEMENT_DYNCREATE(CTextDemoDoc, CDocument)

BEGIN_MESSAGE_MAP(CTextDemoDoc, CDocument)
    //{{AFX_MSG_MAP(CTextDemoDoc)
    ON_COMMAND(ID_OPTIONS_FONT, OnOptionsFont)
    //}}AFX_MSG_MAP
END_MESSAGE_MAP()

/////////////////////////////////////////////////////////////////////////
// CTextDemoDoc construction/destruction

CTextDemoDoc::CTextDemoDoc()
{
    // TODO: add one-time construction code here
```

```
}

CTextDemoDoc::~CTextDemoDoc()
{
}

BOOL CTextDemoDoc::OnNewDocument()
{
    if (!CDocument::OnNewDocument())
        return FALSE;

    // TODO: add reinitialization code here
    // (SDI documents will reuse this document)

    return TRUE;
}


/////////////////////////////////////////////////////////////////////
// CTextDemoDoc serialization

void CTextDemoDoc::Serialize(CArchive& ar)
{
    if (ar.IsStoring())
    {
        // TODO: add storing code here
    }
    else
    {
        // TODO: add loading code here
    }
}

/////////////////////////////////////////////////////////////////////
// CTextDemoDoc diagnostics

#ifdef _DEBUG
void CTextDemoDoc::AssertValid() const
{
    CDocument::AssertValid();
}
```

```
void CTextDemoDoc::Dump(CDumpContext& dc) const
{
    CDocument::Dump(dc);
}
#endif //_DEBUG

/////////////////////////////////////////////////////////////////////////////
// CTextDemoDoc commands

void CTextDemoDoc::OnOptionsFont()
{
    // TODO: Add your command handler code here

    // display Font dialog box:
    CFontDialog FontDialog;
    if (FontDialog.DoModal () != IDOK)
        return;

    // set m_Color:
    m_Color = FontDialog.GetColor ();  // get color chosen by user

    // initialize font object:
    m_Font.DeleteObject ();
    m_Font.CreateFontIndirect (&FontDialog.m_lf);

    // store values in m_LineTable:

    // store values chosen by user:
    int Num = 0;

    m_LineTable [Num++] = "Font Name: " + FontDialog.GetFaceName ();

    m_LineTable [Num] =    "Font Size: ";
    char NumBuf [18];
    sprintf
        (NumBuf,"%d.%d points",
        FontDialog.GetSize () / 10,
        FontDialog.GetSize () % 10);
    m_LineTable [Num++] += NumBuf;

    m_LineTable [Num++] = "";
```

```
// store LOGFONT values:

m_LineTable [Num++] = "LOGFONT fields:";

m_LineTable [Num] =   "lfHeight: ";
sprintf (NumBuf,"%d",FontDialog.m_lf.lfHeight);
m_LineTable [Num++] += NumBuf;

m_LineTable [Num] =   "lfWidth: ";
sprintf (NumBuf,"%d",FontDialog.m_lf.lfWidth);
m_LineTable [Num++] += NumBuf;

m_LineTable [Num] =   "lfEscapement: ";
sprintf (NumBuf,"%d",FontDialog.m_lf.lfEscapement);
m_LineTable [Num] += NumBuf;
m_LineTable [Num++] += " (tenths of a degree)";

m_LineTable [Num] =   "lfOrientation: ";
sprintf (NumBuf,"%d",FontDialog.m_lf.lfOrientation);
m_LineTable [Num] += NumBuf;
m_LineTable [Num++] += " (tenths of a degree)";

m_LineTable [Num] =   "lfWeight: ";
sprintf (NumBuf,"%d",FontDialog.m_lf.lfWeight);
m_LineTable [Num++] += NumBuf;

m_LineTable [Num] =   "lfItalic: ";
sprintf (NumBuf,"%d",FontDialog.m_lf.lfItalic);
m_LineTable [Num++] += NumBuf;

m_LineTable [Num] =   "lfUnderline: ";
sprintf (NumBuf,"%d",FontDialog.m_lf.lfUnderline);
m_LineTable [Num++] += NumBuf;

m_LineTable [Num] =   "lfStrikeOut: ";
sprintf (NumBuf,"%d",FontDialog.m_lf.lfStrikeOut);
m_LineTable [Num++] += NumBuf;

m_LineTable [Num] = "lfCharSet: ";
switch (FontDialog.m_lf.lfCharSet)
    {
    case ANSI_CHARSET:
```

```
           m_LineTable [Num++] += "ANSI_CHARSET";
           break;

        case OEM_CHARSET:
           m_LineTable [Num++] += "OEM_CHARSET";
           break;

        case SYMBOL_CHARSET:
           m_LineTable [Num++] += "SYMBOL_CHARSET";
           break;

        default:
           m_LineTable [Num++] += "unspecified character set";
           break;
        }

    m_LineTable [Num] = "lfOutPrecision: ";
    switch (FontDialog.m_lf.lfOutPrecision)
        {
        case OUT_CHARACTER_PRECIS:
           m_LineTable [Num++] += "OUT_CHARACTER_PRECIS";
           break;

        case OUT_DEFAULT_PRECIS:
           m_LineTable [Num++] += "OUT_DEFAULT_PRECIS";
           break;

        case OUT_STRING_PRECIS:
           m_LineTable [Num++] += "OUT_STRING_PRECIS";
           break;

        case OUT_STROKE_PRECIS:
           m_LineTable [Num++] += "OUT_STROKE_PRECIS";
           break;

        default:
           m_LineTable [Num++] += "unspecified output precision";
           break;
        }

    m_LineTable [Num] = "lfClipPrecision: ";
    switch (FontDialog.m_lf.lfClipPrecision)
```

```
        {
    case CLIP_CHARACTER_PRECIS:
        m_LineTable [Num++] += "CLIP_CHARACTER_PRECIS";
        break;

    case CLIP_DEFAULT_PRECIS:
        m_LineTable [Num++] += "CLIP_DEFAULT_PRECIS";
        break;

    case CLIP_STROKE_PRECIS:
        m_LineTable [Num++] += "CLIP_STROKE_PRECIS";
        break;

    default:
        m_LineTable [Num++] += "unspecified clipping precision";
        break;
    }

m_LineTable [Num] = "lfQuality: ";
switch (FontDialog.m_lf.lfQuality)
    {
    case DEFAULT_QUALITY:
        m_LineTable [Num++] += "DEFAULT_QUALITY";
        break;

    case DRAFT_QUALITY:
        m_LineTable [Num++] += "DRAFT_QUALITY";
        break;

    case PROOF_QUALITY:
        m_LineTable [Num++] += "PROOF_QUALITY";
        break;

    default:
        m_LineTable [Num++] += "unspecified output quality";
        break;
    }

m_LineTable [Num] = "lfPitchAndFamily: ";
switch (FontDialog.m_lf.lfPitchAndFamily & 0x0003)
    {
    case DEFAULT_PITCH:
```

```
      m_LineTable [Num] += "DEFAULT_PITCH; ";
      break;

   case FIXED_PITCH:
      m_LineTable [Num] += "FIXED_PITCH; ";
      break;

   case VARIABLE_PITCH:
      m_LineTable [Num] += "VARIABLE_PITCH; ";
      break;

   default:
      m_LineTable [Num] += "unspecified pitch; ";
      break;
   }
switch (FontDialog.m_lf.lfPitchAndFamily & 0x00F0)
   {
   case FF_DECORATIVE:
      m_LineTable [Num++] += "FF_DECORATIVE";
      break;

   case FF_DONTCARE:
      m_LineTable [Num++] += "FF_DONTCARE";
      break;

   case FF_MODERN:
      m_LineTable [Num++] += "FF_MODERN";
      break;

   case FF_ROMAN:
      m_LineTable [Num++] += "FF_ROMAN";
      break;

   case FF_SCRIPT:
      m_LineTable [Num++] += "FF_SCRIPT";
      break;

   case FF_SWISS:
      m_LineTable [Num++] += "FF_SWISS";
      break;
```

```
      default:
         m_LineTable [Num++] += "unspecified family";
         break;
      }

m_LineTable [Num] = "lfFaceName: ";
m_LineTable [Num++] += FontDialog.m_lf.lfFaceName;

m_LineTable [Num++] = "";

// store TEXTMETRIC values:

// create a device context object associated with the view window:
POSITION Pos = GetFirstViewPosition ();
CView *PView = GetNextView (Pos);
CClientDC ClientDC (PView);

// select new font into device context object:
ClientDC.SelectObject (&m_Font);
TEXTMETRIC TM;
ClientDC.GetTextMetrics (&TM);

m_LineTable [Num++] = "TEXTMETRIC fields:";

m_LineTable [Num] = "tmHeight: ";
sprintf (NumBuf,"%d", TM.tmHeight);
m_LineTable [Num++] += NumBuf;

m_LineTable [Num] = "tmAscent: ";
sprintf (NumBuf,"%d", TM.tmAscent);
m_LineTable [Num++] += NumBuf;

m_LineTable [Num] = "tmDescent: ";
sprintf (NumBuf,"%d", TM.tmDescent);
m_LineTable [Num++] += NumBuf;

m_LineTable [Num] = "tmInternalLeading: ";
sprintf (NumBuf,"%d", TM.tmInternalLeading);
m_LineTable [Num++] += NumBuf;
```

```
m_LineTable [Num] = "tmExternalLeading: ";
sprintf (NumBuf,"%d", TM.tmExternalLeading);
m_LineTable [Num++] += NumBuf;

m_LineTable [Num] = "tmAveCharWidth: ";
sprintf (NumBuf,"%d", TM.tmAveCharWidth);
m_LineTable [Num++] += NumBuf;

m_LineTable [Num] = "tmMaxCharWidth: ";
sprintf (NumBuf,"%d", TM.tmMaxCharWidth);
m_LineTable [Num++] += NumBuf;

m_LineTable [Num] = "tmWeight: ";
sprintf (NumBuf,"%d", TM.tmWeight);
m_LineTable [Num++] += NumBuf;

m_LineTable [Num] = "tmOverhang: ";
sprintf (NumBuf,"%d", TM.tmOverhang);
m_LineTable [Num++] += NumBuf;

m_LineTable [Num] = "tmDigitizedAspectX: ";
sprintf (NumBuf,"%d", TM.tmDigitizedAspectX);
m_LineTable [Num++] += NumBuf;

m_LineTable [Num] = "tmDigitizedAspectY: ";
sprintf (NumBuf,"%d", TM.tmDigitizedAspectY);
m_LineTable [Num++] += NumBuf;

m_LineTable [Num] = "tmFirstChar: ";
sprintf (NumBuf,"%d", TM.tmFirstChar);
m_LineTable [Num++] += NumBuf;

m_LineTable [Num] = "tmLastChar: ";
sprintf (NumBuf,"%d", TM.tmLastChar);
m_LineTable [Num++] += NumBuf;

m_LineTable [Num] = "tmDefaultChar: ";
sprintf (NumBuf,"%d", TM.tmDefaultChar);
m_LineTable [Num++] += NumBuf;

m_LineTable [Num] = "tmBreakChar: ";
sprintf (NumBuf,"%d", TM.tmBreakChar);
m_LineTable [Num++] += NumBuf;
```

```
m_LineTable [Num] = "tmItalic: ";
sprintf (NumBuf,"%d", TM.tmItalic);
m_LineTable [Num++] += NumBuf;

m_LineTable [Num] = "tmUnderlined: ";
sprintf (NumBuf,"%d", TM.tmUnderlined);
m_LineTable [Num++] += NumBuf;

m_LineTable [Num] = "tmStruckOut: ";
sprintf (NumBuf,"%d", TM.tmStruckOut);
m_LineTable [Num++] += NumBuf;

m_LineTable [Num++] = "tmPitchAndFamily: ";

m_LineTable [Num] = "   Pitch Info: ";
if (TM.tmPitchAndFamily & TMPF_FIXED_PITCH)
   m_LineTable [Num] += "variable pitch   ";
else
   m_LineTable [Num] += "fixed pitch   ";
if (TM.tmPitchAndFamily & TMPF_VECTOR)
   m_LineTable [Num] += "vector font   ";
if (TM.tmPitchAndFamily & TMPF_TRUETYPE)
   m_LineTable [Num] += "TrueType font   ";
if (TM.tmPitchAndFamily & TMPF_DEVICE)
   m_LineTable [Num] += "device font";
Num++;

m_LineTable [Num] = "   Family: ";
switch (TM.tmPitchAndFamily & 0x00F0)
   {
   case FF_DECORATIVE:
      m_LineTable [Num++] += "FF_DECORATIVE";
      break;

   case FF_DONTCARE:
      m_LineTable [Num++] += "FF_DONTCARE";
      break;

   case FF_MODERN:
      m_LineTable [Num++] += "FF_MODERN";
      break;
```

```
        case FF_ROMAN:
            m_LineTable [Num++] += "FF_ROMAN";
            break;

        case FF_SCRIPT:
            m_LineTable [Num++] += "FF_SCRIPT";
            break;

        case FF_SWISS:
            m_LineTable [Num++] += "FF_SWISS";
            break;

        default:
            m_LineTable [Num++] += "unknown family";
            break;
        }

    m_LineTable [Num] = "tmCharSet: ";
    switch (TM.tmCharSet)
        {
        case ANSI_CHARSET:
            m_LineTable [Num++] += "ANSI_CHARSET";
            break;

        case OEM_CHARSET:
            m_LineTable [Num++] += "OEM_CHARSET";
            break;

        case SYMBOL_CHARSET:
            m_LineTable [Num++] += "SYMBOL_CHARSET";
            break;

        default:
            m_LineTable [Num++] += "unknown character set";
            break;
        }

    // force redrawing of view window:
    UpdateAllViews (NULL);
}
```

Listing 18.5

```cpp
// MainFrm.h : interface of the CMainFrame class
//
/////////////////////////////////////////////////////////////////////

#if !defined(AFX_MAINFRM_H__3E126289_A392_11D1_80FC_00C0F6A83B7F__INCLUDED_)
#define AFX_MAINFRM_H__3E126289_A392_11D1_80FC_00C0F6A83B7F__INCLUDED_

#if _MSC_VER > 1000
#pragma once
#endif // _MSC_VER > 1000

class CMainFrame : public CFrameWnd
{

protected: // create from serialization only
    CMainFrame();
    DECLARE_DYNCREATE(CMainFrame)

// Attributes
public:

// Operations
public:

// Overrides
    // ClassWizard generated virtual function overrides
    //{{AFX_VIRTUAL(CMainFrame)
    virtual BOOL PreCreateWindow(CREATESTRUCT& cs);
    //}}AFX_VIRTUAL

// Implementation
public:
    virtual ~CMainFrame();
#ifdef _DEBUG
    virtual void AssertValid() const;
    virtual void Dump(CDumpContext& dc) const;
#endif
```

```
// Generated message map functions
protected:
    //{{AFX_MSG(CMainFrame)
        // NOTE - the ClassWizard will add and remove member functions here.
        //    DO NOT EDIT what you see in these blocks of generated code!
    //}}AFX_MSG
    DECLARE_MESSAGE_MAP()
};

/////////////////////////////////////////////////////////////////////

//{{AFX_INSERT_LOCATION}}
// Microsoft Visual C++ will insert additional declarations immediately before
// the previous line.

#endif
// !defined(AFX_MAINFRM_H__3E126289_A392_11D1_80FC_00C0F6A83B7F__INCLUDED_)
```

Listing 18.6

```cpp
// MainFrm.cpp : implementation of the CMainFrame class
//

#include "stdafx.h"
#include "TextDemo.h"

#include "MainFrm.h"

#ifdef _DEBUG
#define new DEBUG_NEW
#undef THIS_FILE
static char THIS_FILE[] = __FILE__;
#endif

/////////////////////////////////////////////////////////////////////
// CMainFrame

IMPLEMENT_DYNCREATE(CMainFrame, CFrameWnd)

BEGIN_MESSAGE_MAP(CMainFrame, CFrameWnd)
    //{{AFX_MSG_MAP(CMainFrame)
        // NOTE - the ClassWizard will add and remove mapping macros here.
        //    DO NOT EDIT what you see in these blocks of generated code !
```

```
   //}}AFX_MSG_MAP
END_MESSAGE_MAP()

/////////////////////////////////////////////////////////////////////
// CMainFrame construction/destruction

CMainFrame::CMainFrame()
{
   // TODO: add member initialization code here

}

CMainFrame::~CMainFrame()
{
}

BOOL CMainFrame::PreCreateWindow(CREATESTRUCT& cs)
{
   if( !CFrameWnd::PreCreateWindow(cs) )
      return FALSE;
   // TODO: Modify the Window class or styles here by modifying
   //   the CREATESTRUCT cs

   return TRUE;
}

/////////////////////////////////////////////////////////////////////
// CMainFrame diagnostics

#ifdef _DEBUG
void CMainFrame::AssertValid() const
{
   CFrameWnd::AssertValid();
}

void CMainFrame::Dump(CDumpContext& dc) const
{
   CFrameWnd::Dump(dc);
}

#endif //_DEBUG
```

```
//////////////////////////////////////////////////////////////////////
// CMainFrame message handlers
```

Listing 18.7

```cpp
// TextDemoView.h : interface of the CTextDemoView class
//
//////////////////////////////////////////////////////////////////////

#if !defined(AFX_TEXTDEMOVIEW_H__3E12628D_A392_11D1_80FC_00C0F6A83B7F__INCLUDED_)
#define AFX_TEXTDEMOVIEW_H__3E12628D_A392_11D1_80FC_00C0F6A83B7F__INCLUDED_

#if _MSC_VER > 1000
#pragma once
#endif // _MSC_VER > 1000

const int MARGIN = 10;      // margin displayed at top and left of view window

class CTextDemoView : public CScrollView
{
protected: // create from serialization only
   CTextDemoView();
   DECLARE_DYNCREATE(CTextDemoView)

// Attributes
public:
   CTextDemoDoc* GetDocument();

// Operations
public:

// Overrides
   // ClassWizard generated virtual function overrides
   //{{AFX_VIRTUAL(CTextDemoView)
   public:
   virtual void OnDraw(CDC* pDC);  // overridden to draw this view
   virtual BOOL PreCreateWindow(CREATESTRUCT& cs);
   protected:
   virtual void OnUpdate(CView* pSender, LPARAM lHint, CObject* pHint);
   //}}AFX_VIRTUAL
```

```
// Implementation
public:
    virtual ~CTextDemoView();
#ifdef _DEBUG
    virtual void AssertValid() const;
    virtual void Dump(CDumpContext& dc) const;
#endif

protected:

// Generated message map functions
protected:
    //{{AFX_MSG(CTextDemoView)
    afx_msg void OnKeyDown(UINT nChar, UINT nRepCnt, UINT nFlags);
    //}}AFX_MSG
    DECLARE_MESSAGE_MAP()
};

#ifndef _DEBUG  // debug version in TextDemoView.cpp
inline CTextDemoDoc* CTextDemoView::GetDocument()
    { return (CTextDemoDoc*)m_pDocument; }
#endif

/////////////////////////////////////////////////////////////////////////////

//{{AFX_INSERT_LOCATION}}
// Microsoft Visual C++ will insert additional declarations immediately before
// the previous line.

#endif
// !defined(AFX_TEXTDEMOVIEW_H__3E12628D_A392_11D1_80FC_00C0F6A83B7F__INCLUDED_)
```

Listing 18.8

```
// TextDemoView.cpp : implementation of the CTextDemoView class
//

#include "stdafx.h"
#include "TextDemo.h"

#include "TextDemoDoc.h"
#include "TextDemoView.h"
```

```
#ifdef _DEBUG
#define new DEBUG_NEW
#undef THIS_FILE
static char THIS_FILE[] = __FILE__;
#endif

/////////////////////////////////////////////////////////////////////////////
// CTextDemoView

IMPLEMENT_DYNCREATE(CTextDemoView, CScrollView)

BEGIN_MESSAGE_MAP(CTextDemoView, CScrollView)
    //{{AFX_MSG_MAP(CTextDemoView)
    ON_WM_KEYDOWN()
    //}}AFX_MSG_MAP
END_MESSAGE_MAP()

/////////////////////////////////////////////////////////////////////////////
// CTextDemoView construction/destruction

CTextDemoView::CTextDemoView()
{
    // TODO: add construction code here

}

CTextDemoView::~CTextDemoView()
{
}

BOOL CTextDemoView::PreCreateWindow(CREATESTRUCT& cs)
{
    // TODO: Modify the Window class or styles here by modifying
    //   the CREATESTRUCT cs

    return CScrollView::PreCreateWindow(cs);
}

/////////////////////////////////////////////////////////////////////////////
// CTextDemoView drawing

void CTextDemoView::OnDraw(CDC* pDC)
```

```
{
   CTextDemoDoc* pDoc = GetDocument();
   ASSERT_VALID(pDoc);

   // TODO: add draw code for native data here

   // return if font has not yet been created:
   if (pDoc->m_Font.m_hObject == NULL)
      return;

   RECT ClipRect;
   int LineHeight;
   TEXTMETRIC TM;
   int Y = MARGIN;

   // select font into device context object:
   pDC->SelectObject (&pDoc->m_Font);

   // obtain text metrics:
   pDC->GetTextMetrics (&TM);
   LineHeight = TM.tmHeight + TM.tmExternalLeading;

   // set text attributes:
   pDC->SetTextColor (pDoc->m_Color);
   pDC->SetBkMode (TRANSPARENT);

   // obtain coordinates of invalidated area:
   pDC->GetClipBox (&ClipRect);

   // display title line:
   pDC->TextOut (MARGIN, Y, "FONT PROPERTIES");

   // display text lines:
   for (int Line = 0; Line < NUMLINES; ++Line)
      {
      Y += LineHeight;
      if (Y + LineHeight >= ClipRect.top && Y <= ClipRect.bottom)
         pDC->TextOut (MARGIN, Y, pDoc->m_LineTable [Line]);
      }
}

//////////////////////////////////////////////////////////////////////////
```

```
// CTextDemoView diagnostics

#ifdef _DEBUG
void CTextDemoView::AssertValid() const
{
   CScrollView::AssertValid();
}

void CTextDemoView::Dump(CDumpContext& dc) const
{
   CScrollView::Dump(dc);
}

CTextDemoDoc* CTextDemoView::GetDocument() // non-debug version is inline
{
   ASSERT(m_pDocument->IsKindOf(RUNTIME_CLASS(CTextDemoDoc)));
   return (CTextDemoDoc*)m_pDocument;
}
#endif //_DEBUG

/////////////////////////////////////////////////////////////////////////
// CTextDemoView message handlers

void CTextDemoView::OnUpdate(CView* pSender, LPARAM lHint, CObject* pHint)
{
   // TODO: Add your specialized code here and/or call the base class

   CTextDemoDoc* PDoc = GetDocument();

   if (PDoc->m_Font.m_hObject == NULL)  // font not yet created
      SetScrollSizes (MM_TEXT, CSize (0,0));
   else                                 // font created
      {
      CClientDC ClientDC (this);
      int LineWidth = 0;
      SIZE Size;
      TEXTMETRIC TM;

      ClientDC.SelectObject (&PDoc->m_Font);
      ClientDC.GetTextMetrics (&TM);
```

```
        for (int Line = 0; Line < NUMLINES; ++Line)
            {
            Size = ClientDC.GetTextExtent
            (PDoc->m_LineTable [Line],
            PDoc->m_LineTable [Line].GetLength ());
            if (Size.cx > LineWidth)
                LineWidth = Size.cx;
            }

        Size.cx = LineWidth + MARGIN;
        Size.cy = (TM.tmHeight + TM.tmExternalLeading) * (NUMLINES + 1) + MARGIN;

        SetScrollSizes (MM_TEXT, Size);
        ScrollToPosition (CPoint (0, 0));
        }

    CScrollView::OnUpdate (pSender, lHint, pHint);
}

void CTextDemoView::OnKeyDown(UINT nChar, UINT nRepCnt, UINT nFlags)
{
    // TODO: Add your message handler code here and/or call default

    CSize DocSize = GetTotalSize ();
    RECT ClientRect;
    GetClientRect (&ClientRect);

    switch (nChar)
        {
        case VK_LEFT:     // left arrow
            if (ClientRect.right < DocSize.cx)
                SendMessage (WM_HSCROLL, SB_LINELEFT);
            break;

        case VK_RIGHT:     // right arrow
            if (ClientRect.right < DocSize.cx)
                SendMessage (WM_HSCROLL, SB_LINERIGHT);
            break;

        case VK_UP:        // up arrow
            if (ClientRect.bottom < DocSize.cy)
```

```
         SendMessage (WM_VSCROLL, SB_LINEUP);
      break;

   case VK_DOWN:      // down arrow
      if (ClientRect.bottom < DocSize.cy)
         SendMessage (WM_VSCROLL, SB_LINEDOWN);
      break;

   case VK_HOME:      // Home key
      if (::GetKeyState (VK_CONTROL) & 0x8000)  // Ctrl pressed
         {
         if (ClientRect.bottom < DocSize.cy)
            SendMessage (WM_VSCROLL, SB_TOP);
         }
      else                                      // Home key alone
         {
         if (ClientRect.right < DocSize.cx)
            SendMessage (WM_HSCROLL, SB_LEFT);
         }
      break;

   case VK_END:       // End key
      if (::GetKeyState (VK_CONTROL) & 0x8000)  // Ctrl pressed
         {
         if (ClientRect.bottom < DocSize.cy)
            SendMessage (WM_VSCROLL, SB_BOTTOM);
         }
      else                                      // End key alone
         {
         if (ClientRect.right < DocSize.cx)
            SendMessage (WM_HSCROLL, SB_RIGHT);
         }
      break;

   case VK_PRIOR:     // PgUp key
      if (ClientRect.bottom < DocSize.cy)
         SendMessage (WM_VSCROLL, SB_PAGEUP);
      break;

   case VK_NEXT:      // PgDn key
      if (ClientRect.bottom < DocSize.cy)
         SendMessage (WM_VSCROLL, SB_PAGEDOWN);
```

```
        break;
    }

    CScrollView::OnKeyDown(nChar, nRepCnt, nFlags);
}
```

The Echo Source Code

The following listings, Listings 18.9 through 18.16, contain the C++ source code for the Echo program given in this chapter. A set of these files is contained in the \Echo companion-CD folder.

Listing 18.9

```cpp
// Echo.h : main header file for the ECHO application
//

#if !defined(AFX_ECHO_H__3E126298_A392_11D1_80FC_00C0F6A83B7F__INCLUDED_)
#define AFX_ECHO_H__3E126298_A392_11D1_80FC_00C0F6A83B7F__INCLUDED_

#if _MSC_VER > 1000
#pragma once
#endif // _MSC_VER > 1000

#ifndef __AFXWIN_H__
    #error include 'stdafx.h' before including this file for PCH
#endif

#include "resource.h"        // main symbols

/////////////////////////////////////////////////////////////////////
// CEchoApp:
// See Echo.cpp for the implementation of this class
//

class CEchoApp : public CWinApp
{
public:
    CEchoApp();
```

```
// Overrides
    // ClassWizard generated virtual function overrides
    //{{AFX_VIRTUAL(CEchoApp)
    public:
    virtual BOOL InitInstance();
    //}}AFX_VIRTUAL

// Implementation
    //{{AFX_MSG(CEchoApp)
    afx_msg void OnAppAbout();
        // NOTE - the ClassWizard will add and remove member functions here.
        //      DO NOT EDIT what you see in these blocks of generated code !
    //}}AFX_MSG
    DECLARE_MESSAGE_MAP()
};


/////////////////////////////////////////////////////////////////////////////

//{{AFX_INSERT_LOCATION}}
// Microsoft Visual C++ will insert additional declarations immediately before
// the previous line.

#endif
// !defined(AFX_ECHO_H__3E126298_A392_11D1_80FC_00C0F6A83B7F__INCLUDED_)
```

Listing 18.10

```
// Echo.cpp : Defines the class behaviors for the application.
//

#include "stdafx.h"
#include "Echo.h"

#include "MainFrm.h"
#include "EchoDoc.h"
#include "EchoView.h"

#ifdef _DEBUG
#define new DEBUG_NEW
#undef THIS_FILE
static char THIS_FILE[] = __FILE__;
#endif
```

```
/////////////////////////////////////////////////////////////////////////
// CEchoApp

BEGIN_MESSAGE_MAP(CEchoApp, CWinApp)
    //{{AFX_MSG_MAP(CEchoApp)
    ON_COMMAND(ID_APP_ABOUT, OnAppAbout)
        // NOTE - the ClassWizard will add and remove mapping macros here.
        //      DO NOT EDIT what you see in these blocks of generated code!
    //}}AFX_MSG_MAP
    // Standard file based document commands
    ON_COMMAND(ID_FILE_NEW, CWinApp::OnFileNew)
    ON_COMMAND(ID_FILE_OPEN, CWinApp::OnFileOpen)
END_MESSAGE_MAP()

/////////////////////////////////////////////////////////////////////////
// CEchoApp construction

CEchoApp::CEchoApp()
{
    // TODO: add construction code here,
    // Place all significant initialization in InitInstance
}

/////////////////////////////////////////////////////////////////////////
// The one and only CEchoApp object

CEchoApp theApp;

/////////////////////////////////////////////////////////////////////////
// CEchoApp initialization

BOOL CEchoApp::InitInstance()
{
    // Standard initialization
    // If you are not using these features and wish to reduce the size
    //  of your final executable, you should remove from the following
    //  the specific initialization routines you do not need.

#ifdef _AFXDLL
    Enable3dControls();         // Call this when using MFC in a shared DLL
#else
    Enable3dControlsStatic();   // Call this when linking to MFC statically
#endif
```

```
    // Change the registry key under which our settings are stored.
    // TODO: You should modify this string to be something appropriate
    // such as the name of your company or organization.
    SetRegistryKey(_T("Local AppWizard-Generated Applications"));

    LoadStdProfileSettings();  // Load standard INI file options (including MRU)

    // Register the application's document templates.  Document templates
    //  serve as the connection between documents, frame windows and views.

    CSingleDocTemplate* pDocTemplate;
    pDocTemplate = new CSingleDocTemplate(
        IDR_MAINFRAME,
        RUNTIME_CLASS(CEchoDoc),
        RUNTIME_CLASS(CMainFrame),        // main SDI frame window
        RUNTIME_CLASS(CEchoView));
    AddDocTemplate(pDocTemplate);

    // Parse command line for standard shell commands, DDE, file open
    CCommandLineInfo cmdInfo;
    ParseCommandLine(cmdInfo);

    // Dispatch commands specified on the command line
    if (!ProcessShellCommand(cmdInfo))
        return FALSE;

    // The one and only window has been initialized, so show and update it.
    m_pMainWnd->ShowWindow(SW_SHOW);
    m_pMainWnd->UpdateWindow();

    m_pMainWnd->SetWindowText ("Echo");

    return TRUE;
}


/////////////////////////////////////////////////////////////////////////////
// CAboutDlg dialog used for App About

class CAboutDlg : public CDialog
{
```

```
public:
   CAboutDlg();

// Dialog Data
   //{{AFX_DATA(CAboutDlg)
   enum { IDD = IDD_ABOUTBOX };
   //}}AFX_DATA

   // ClassWizard generated virtual function overrides
   //{{AFX_VIRTUAL(CAboutDlg)
   protected:
   virtual void DoDataExchange(CDataExchange* pDX);    // DDX/DDV support
   //}}AFX_VIRTUAL

// Implementation
protected:
   //{{AFX_MSG(CAboutDlg)
      // No message handlers
   //}}AFX_MSG
   DECLARE_MESSAGE_MAP()
};

CAboutDlg::CAboutDlg() : CDialog(CAboutDlg::IDD)
{
   //{{AFX_DATA_INIT(CAboutDlg)
   //}}AFX_DATA_INIT
}

void CAboutDlg::DoDataExchange(CDataExchange* pDX)
{
   CDialog::DoDataExchange(pDX);
   //{{AFX_DATA_MAP(CAboutDlg)
   //}}AFX_DATA_MAP
}

BEGIN_MESSAGE_MAP(CAboutDlg, CDialog)
   //{{AFX_MSG_MAP(CAboutDlg)
      // No message handlers
   //}}AFX_MSG_MAP
END_MESSAGE_MAP()
```

```
// App command to run the dialog
void CEchoApp::OnAppAbout()
{
    CAboutDlg aboutDlg;
    aboutDlg.DoModal();
}


/////////////////////////////////////////////////////////////////////////
// CEchoApp message handlers
```

Listing 18.11

```
// EchoDoc.h : interface of the CEchoDoc class
//
/////////////////////////////////////////////////////////////////////////

#if !defined(AFX_ECHODOC_H__3E12629E_A392_11D1_80FC_00C0F6A83B7F__INCLUDED_)
#define AFX_ECHODOC_H__3E12629E_A392_11D1_80FC_00C0F6A83B7F__INCLUDED_

#if _MSC_VER > 1000
#pragma once
#endif // _MSC_VER > 1000


class CEchoDoc : public CDocument
{
public:
    CString m_TextLine;

protected: // create from serialization only
    CEchoDoc();
    DECLARE_DYNCREATE(CEchoDoc)

// Attributes
public:

// Operations
public:

// Overrides
    // ClassWizard generated virtual function overrides
```

```
    //{{AFX_VIRTUAL(CEchoDoc)
    public:
    virtual BOOL OnNewDocument();
    virtual void Serialize(CArchive& ar);
    //}}AFX_VIRTUAL

// Implementation
public:
    virtual ~CEchoDoc();
#ifdef _DEBUG
    virtual void AssertValid() const;
    virtual void Dump(CDumpContext& dc) const;
#endif

protected:

// Generated message map functions
protected:
    //{{AFX_MSG(CEchoDoc)
        // NOTE - the ClassWizard will add and remove member functions here.
        //     DO NOT EDIT what you see in these blocks of generated code !
    //}}AFX_MSG
    DECLARE_MESSAGE_MAP()
};

/////////////////////////////////////////////////////////////////////////

//{{AFX_INSERT_LOCATION}}
// Microsoft Visual C++ will insert additional declarations immediately before
// the previous line.

#endif
// !defined(AFX_ECHODOC_H__3E12629E_A392_11D1_80FC_00C0F6A83B7F__INCLUDED_)
```

Listing 18.12

```
// EchoDoc.cpp : implementation of the CEchoDoc class
//

#include "stdafx.h"
#include "Echo.h"
```

```
#include "EchoDoc.h"

#ifdef _DEBUG
#define new DEBUG_NEW
#undef THIS_FILE
static char THIS_FILE[] = __FILE__;
#endif

/////////////////////////////////////////////////////////////////////////
// CEchoDoc

IMPLEMENT_DYNCREATE(CEchoDoc, CDocument)

BEGIN_MESSAGE_MAP(CEchoDoc, CDocument)
    //{{AFX_MSG_MAP(CEchoDoc)
        // NOTE - the ClassWizard will add and remove mapping macros here.
        //    DO NOT EDIT what you see in these blocks of generated code!
    //}}AFX_MSG_MAP
END_MESSAGE_MAP()

/////////////////////////////////////////////////////////////////////////
// CEchoDoc construction/destruction

CEchoDoc::CEchoDoc()
{
    // TODO: add one-time construction code here

}

CEchoDoc::~CEchoDoc()
{
}

BOOL CEchoDoc::OnNewDocument()
{
    if (!CDocument::OnNewDocument())
        return FALSE;

    // TODO: add reinitialization code here
    // (SDI documents will reuse this document)

    return TRUE;
}
```

```
/////////////////////////////////////////////////////////////////////////
// CEchoDoc serialization

void CEchoDoc::Serialize(CArchive& ar)
{
   if (ar.IsStoring())
   {
      // TODO: add storing code here
   }
   else
   {
      // TODO: add loading code here
   }
}


/////////////////////////////////////////////////////////////////////////
// CEchoDoc diagnostics

#ifdef _DEBUG
void CEchoDoc::AssertValid() const
{
   CDocument::AssertValid();
}

void CEchoDoc::Dump(CDumpContext& dc) const
{
   CDocument::Dump(dc);
}
#endif //_DEBUG


/////////////////////////////////////////////////////////////////////////
// CEchoDoc commands
```

Listing 18.13

```
// MainFrm.h : interface of the CMainFrame class
//
/////////////////////////////////////////////////////////////////////////

#if !defined(AFX_MAINFRM_H__3E12629C_A392_11D1_80FC_00C0F6A83B7F__INCLUDED_)
#define AFX_MAINFRM_H__3E12629C_A392_11D1_80FC_00C0F6A83B7F__INCLUDED_
```

```
#if _MSC_VER > 1000
#pragma once
#endif // _MSC_VER > 1000

class CMainFrame : public CFrameWnd
{

protected: // create from serialization only
   CMainFrame();
   DECLARE_DYNCREATE(CMainFrame)

// Attributes
public:

// Operations
public:

// Overrides
   // ClassWizard generated virtual function overrides
   //{{AFX_VIRTUAL(CMainFrame)
   virtual BOOL PreCreateWindow(CREATESTRUCT& cs);
   //}}AFX_VIRTUAL

// Implementation
public:
   virtual ~CMainFrame();
#ifdef _DEBUG
   virtual void AssertValid() const;
   virtual void Dump(CDumpContext& dc) const;
#endif

// Generated message map functions
protected:
   //{{AFX_MSG(CMainFrame)
      // NOTE - the ClassWizard will add and remove member functions here.
      //    DO NOT EDIT what you see in these blocks of generated code!
   //}}AFX_MSG
   DECLARE_MESSAGE_MAP()
};
```

```
//////////////////////////////////////////////////////////////////////////

//{{AFX_INSERT_LOCATION}}
// Microsoft Visual C++ will insert additional declarations immediately before
// the previous line.

#endif
// !defined(AFX_MAINFRM_H__3E12629C_A392_11D1_80FC_00C0F6A83B7F__INCLUDED_)
```

Listing 18.14

```cpp
// MainFrm.cpp : implementation of the CMainFrame class
//

#include "stdafx.h"
#include "Echo.h"

#include "MainFrm.h"

#ifdef _DEBUG
#define new DEBUG_NEW
#undef THIS_FILE
static char THIS_FILE[] = __FILE__;
#endif

//////////////////////////////////////////////////////////////////////////
// CMainFrame

IMPLEMENT_DYNCREATE(CMainFrame, CFrameWnd)

BEGIN_MESSAGE_MAP(CMainFrame, CFrameWnd)
    //{{AFX_MSG_MAP(CMainFrame)
        // NOTE - the ClassWizard will add and remove mapping macros here.
        //     DO NOT EDIT what you see in these blocks of generated code !
    //}}AFX_MSG_MAP
END_MESSAGE_MAP()

//////////////////////////////////////////////////////////////////////////
// CMainFrame construction/destruction
```

```
CMainFrame::CMainFrame()
{
   // TODO: add member initialization code here

}

CMainFrame::~CMainFrame()
{
}

BOOL CMainFrame::PreCreateWindow(CREATESTRUCT& cs)
{
   if( !CFrameWnd::PreCreateWindow(cs) )
      return FALSE;
   // TODO: Modify the Window class or styles here by modifying
   //  the CREATESTRUCT cs

   return TRUE;
}

/////////////////////////////////////////////////////////////////////////////
// CMainFrame diagnostics

#ifdef _DEBUG
void CMainFrame::AssertValid() const
{
   CFrameWnd::AssertValid();
}

void CMainFrame::Dump(CDumpContext& dc) const
{
   CFrameWnd::Dump(dc);
}

#endif //_DEBUG

/////////////////////////////////////////////////////////////////////////////
// CMainFrame message handlers
```

Listing 18.15

```cpp
// EchoView.h : interface of the CEchoView class
//
/////////////////////////////////////////////////////////////////////

#if !defined(AFX_ECHOVIEW_H__3E1262A0_A392_11D1_80FC_00C0F6A83B7F__INCLUDED_)
#define AFX_ECHOVIEW_H__3E1262A0_A392_11D1_80FC_00C0F6A83B7F__INCLUDED_

#if _MSC_VER > 1000
#pragma once
#endif // _MSC_VER > 1000


class CEchoView : public CView
{
private:
    POINT m_CaretPos;
    int m_XCaret, m_YCaret;

protected: // create from serialization only
    CEchoView();
    DECLARE_DYNCREATE(CEchoView)

// Attributes
public:
    CEchoDoc* GetDocument();

// Operations
public:

// Overrides
    // ClassWizard generated virtual function overrides
    //{{AFX_VIRTUAL(CEchoView)
    public:
    virtual void OnDraw(CDC* pDC);  // overridden to draw this view
    virtual BOOL PreCreateWindow(CREATESTRUCT& cs);
    protected:
    //}}AFX_VIRTUAL
```

```
// Implementation
public:
    virtual ~CEchoView();
#ifdef _DEBUG
    virtual void AssertValid() const;
    virtual void Dump(CDumpContext& dc) const;
#endif

protected:

// Generated message map functions
protected:
    //{{AFX_MSG(CEchoView)
    afx_msg void OnChar(UINT nChar, UINT nRepCnt, UINT nFlags);
    afx_msg void OnEditClear();
    afx_msg int OnCreate(LPCREATESTRUCT lpCreateStruct);
    afx_msg void OnKillFocus(CWnd* pNewWnd);
    afx_msg void OnSetFocus(CWnd* pOldWnd);
    //}}AFX_MSG
    DECLARE_MESSAGE_MAP()
};

#ifndef _DEBUG  // debug version in EchoView.cpp
inline CEchoDoc* CEchoView::GetDocument()
    { return (CEchoDoc*)m_pDocument; }
#endif

/////////////////////////////////////////////////////////////////////////////

//{{AFX_INSERT_LOCATION}}
// Microsoft Visual C++ will insert additional declarations immediately before
// the previous line.

#endif
// !defined(AFX_ECHOVIEW_H__3E1262A0_A392_11D1_80FC_00C0F6A83B7F__INCLUDED_)
```

Listing 18.16

```
// EchoView.cpp : implementation of the CEchoView class
//

#include "stdafx.h"
#include "Echo.h"
```

```
#include "EchoDoc.h"
#include "EchoView.h"

#ifdef _DEBUG
#define new DEBUG_NEW
#undef THIS_FILE
static char THIS_FILE[] = __FILE__;
#endif

/////////////////////////////////////////////////////////////////////////////
// CEchoView

IMPLEMENT_DYNCREATE(CEchoView, CView)

BEGIN_MESSAGE_MAP(CEchoView, CView)
    //{{AFX_MSG_MAP(CEchoView)
    ON_WM_CHAR()
    ON_COMMAND(ID_EDIT_CLEAR, OnEditClear)
    ON_WM_CREATE()
    ON_WM_KILLFOCUS()
    ON_WM_SETFOCUS()
    //}}AFX_MSG_MAP
END_MESSAGE_MAP()

/////////////////////////////////////////////////////////////////////////////
// CEchoView construction/destruction

CEchoView::CEchoView()
{
    // TODO: add construction code here

    m_CaretPos.x = m_CaretPos.y = 0;
}

CEchoView::~CEchoView()
{
}

BOOL CEchoView::PreCreateWindow(CREATESTRUCT& cs)
{
    // TODO: Modify the Window class or styles here by modifying
    //  the CREATESTRUCT cs
```

```
   return CView::PreCreateWindow(cs);
}


/////////////////////////////////////////////////////////////////////////////
// CEchoView drawing

void CEchoView::OnDraw(CDC* pDC)
{
   CEchoDoc* pDoc = GetDocument();
   ASSERT_VALID(pDoc);

   // TODO: add draw code for native data here

   pDC->SetTextColor (::GetSysColor (COLOR_WINDOWTEXT));
   pDC->SetBkMode (TRANSPARENT);
   pDC->TextOut (0, 0, pDoc->m_TextLine);
}


/////////////////////////////////////////////////////////////////////////////
// CEchoView diagnostics

#ifdef _DEBUG
void CEchoView::AssertValid() const
{
   CView::AssertValid();
}

void CEchoView::Dump(CDumpContext& dc) const
{
   CView::Dump(dc);
}

CEchoDoc* CEchoView::GetDocument() // non-debug version is inline
{
   ASSERT(m_pDocument->IsKindOf(RUNTIME_CLASS(CEchoDoc)));
   return (CEchoDoc*)m_pDocument;
}
#endif //_DEBUG


/////////////////////////////////////////////////////////////////////////////
// CEchoView message handlers
```

```cpp
void CEchoView::OnChar(UINT nChar, UINT nRepCnt, UINT nFlags)
{
    // TODO: Add your message handler code here and/or call default

    if (nChar < 32)
        {
        ::MessageBeep (MB_OK); // generate default sound
        return;
        }

    CEchoDoc* PDoc = GetDocument();
    PDoc->m_TextLine += nChar;

    CClientDC ClientDC (this);
    ClientDC.SetTextColor (::GetSysColor (COLOR_WINDOWTEXT));
    ClientDC.SetBkMode (TRANSPARENT);
    HideCaret ();
    ClientDC.TextOut (0, 0, PDoc->m_TextLine);
    CSize Size = ClientDC.GetTextExtent
        (PDoc->m_TextLine,
        PDoc->m_TextLine.GetLength ());
    m_CaretPos.x = Size.cx;
    SetCaretPos (m_CaretPos);
    ShowCaret ();

    CView::OnChar(nChar, nRepCnt, nFlags);
}

void CEchoView::OnEditClear()
{
    // TODO: Add your command handler code here

    CEchoDoc* PDoc = GetDocument();
    PDoc->m_TextLine.Empty ();
    PDoc->UpdateAllViews (NULL);
    m_CaretPos.x = 0;
    SetCaretPos (m_CaretPos);
}

int CEchoView::OnCreate(LPCREATESTRUCT lpCreateStruct)
{
    if (CView::OnCreate(lpCreateStruct) == -1)
```

```
        return -1;

    // TODO: Add your specialized creation code here

    CClientDC ClientDC (this);
    TEXTMETRIC TM;

    ClientDC.GetTextMetrics (&TM);
    m_XCaret = TM.tmAveCharWidth / 3;
    m_YCaret = TM.tmHeight + TM.tmExternalLeading;

    return 0;
}

void CEchoView::OnKillFocus(CWnd* pNewWnd)
{
    CView::OnKillFocus(pNewWnd);

    // TODO: Add your message handler code here

    ::DestroyCaret ();
}

void CEchoView::OnSetFocus(CWnd* pOldWnd)
{
    CView::OnSetFocus(pOldWnd);

    // TODO: Add your message handler code here

    CreateSolidCaret (m_XCaret, m_YCaret);
    SetCaretPos (m_CaretPos);
    ShowCaret ();
}
```

Summary

In this chapter, you learned how to display lines of text in the view window, how to read character and noncharacter keys from the keyboard, and how to display and manage a caret for marking the text insertion point. The following are some of the general facts and techniques that were covered:

- The first step in displaying text in a window is to obtain a device context object. If you're displaying text from an OnDraw function, you can use the device context object whose address is passed to the function.

- If you don't want to display text using the default System font, the second step in displaying text is to select an alternative font by calling CDC::Select-Object (to select a font described in a CFont object) or CDC::Select-StockObject (to select a stock font).

- The third step is to call CDC::GetTextMetrics if you need to obtain the size or other features of the characters in the selected font.

- The fourth step is to set any text attributes you'd like to change from their default values. To do this, you call CDC member functions, such as SetText-Color (for setting the text color) or SetTextCharacterExtra (for changing the character spacing).

- If you're displaying text from an OnDraw function, the fifth step is to call CDC::GetClipBox to obtain the dimensions of the invalidated area, so that you can increase the program's efficiency by displaying text only within the area of the window that needs redrawing.

- The sixth and final step is to display the text using a CDC function such as TextOut or DrawText. In an OnDraw function, display only the text that falls partially or completely within the invalidated area of the view window.

- You can have the user choose a font by displaying the Font common dialog box. To display this dialog box, you create an object of the MFC CFontDialog class and then call the DoModal member function. After DoModal returns, you can obtain a complete description of the selected font by accessing data members and calling member functions of the CFontDialog object.

- You can use the font information supplied by the CFontDialog object to initialize a font object (which is an instance of the MFC CFont class). The font object can then be selected into a device context object to begin displaying text using the font.

- You can read the keyboard by providing a handler for the WM_KEYDOWN message, which is sent when any key (except a system key) is pressed. The handler is passed a virtual key code identifying the key. A WM_KEYDOWN message handler is especially suitable for processing noncharacter keys, such as Home, End, an arrow key, or a function key.

- The most convenient way to read character keys (that is, keys corresponding to printable characters) is to provide a WM_CHAR message handler, which is passed the actual ANSI code for the character typed.

- To create and display a caret in a window, you should call CWnd::CreateSolidCaret and CWnd::ShowCaret within a WM_SETFOCUS message handler, which receives control whenever the window obtains the input focus.

- You should call ::DestroyCaret to destroy the caret within a WM_KILLFOCUS message handler, which is called whenever the window loses the input focus. The reason for destroying the caret is that a caret should be displayed only in the window that currently has the input focus.

- You can move the caret to the desired position by calling CWnd::SetCaretPos.

- Before drawing in a window containing a caret—from a function other than OnDraw or OnPaint—you must first call CWnd::HideCaret to hide the caret, and then call CWnd::ShowCaret to restore the caret after the drawing is completed.

- In an MFC program generated by AppWizard, a WM_KEYDOWN, WM_CHAR, WM_SETFOCUS, or WM_KILLFOCUS message-handling function should normally be made a member of the view class, because these messages are sent to the view window.

Using Drawing Functions

- Creating the device context object

- Selecting drawing tools

- Setting drawing attributes

- Drawing the graphics

- The MiniDraw program

In this chapter and in the following one (Chapter 20), you'll learn how to create and manipulate graphic images using two different approaches. In this chapter, you'll learn how to call Windows drawing functions to create graphic images at program runtime; these functions are well suited for generating drawings composed of individual geometric shapes, such as straight lines, arcs, and rectangles. In Chapter 20, you'll learn how to create and display bitmaps, which store the actual pixel values used to produce an image on a device; bitmaps are well suited for creating more complex drawings, which are not easily divided into separate geometric shapes. The techniques presented in these two chapters are closely related. As you'll learn, you can use drawing functions to change the pattern of pixels within a bitmap, and you can use bit operations to manipulate images created with drawing functions (for example, moving or stretching an image).

This chapter explains how to use the graphics-drawing functions provided by Windows and the MFC. These functions, used in conjunction with the bitmap techniques that will be given in Chapter 20, provide a complete set of tools for creating graphic images within a view window or on another device such as a printer (Chapter 21 describes the special techniques required for displaying graphics or text on a printer). The first four sections in the chapter explain the basic steps for drawing:

1. Create a device context object.

2. Select drawing tools into the device context object.

3. Set drawing attributes for the device context object.

4. Call member functions for the device context object to draw the graphics.

In the final section of the chapter, you'll develop a version of the MiniDraw program that draws a variety of different figures and illustrates many of the techniques presented in the chapter.

Creating the Device Context Object

As you've seen, to display text or graphics, you must have a device context object associated with the window or device that's to receive the output. When you're drawing graphics, the device context object stores the drawing tools you've selected and the attributes you've set, and provides a collection of member functions for drawing points, lines, rectangles, and other figures.

To display graphics from the OnDraw member function of the view class, you can simply use the device context object whose address is passed to the function, as in the following example:

```
void CMyView::OnDraw(CDC* pDC)
   {
   // display graphics using 'pDC->'


   }
```

The OnDraw function is called whenever the view window needs drawing or redrawing, and, if the view class supports scrolling (that is, the view class is derived from CScrollView), the device context object that's passed to it has already been adjusted for the current scrolled position of the document.

If your program displays graphics within a window *other than* a view window (such as a dialog box), the window class must provide a WM_PAINT message handler, named OnPaint, to draw or redraw the graphics. OnPaint must create a device context object that's derived from the CPaintDC MFC class, as shown in the following example:

```
void CMyDialog::OnPaint()
   {
   CPaintDC PaintDC (this);

   // display graphics using 'PaintDC' ...
   }
```

For an example of an OnPaint function for a dialog box, see the section "Completing the CFormat Code" in Chapter 15.

NOTE   Like any other type of window, a view window is sent a WM_PAINT message when it needs drawing or redrawing. However, the CView class provides an OnPaint function for you, which creates and prepares a device context object and then passes the object to your OnDraw function. Only a window class that *isn't* derived from CView must provide its own OnPaint function that does all the work of drawing the contents of the window.

To display graphics—in either a view or a nonview window—from a function *other than* an OnDraw or OnPaint message handler, you must create a device context object that's a member of the MFC CClientDC class. Also, if the function draws in a view window that supports scrolling, before using the object you must call the CScrollView::OnPrepareDC function to adjust it for the current scrolled position of the document. The following is an example:

```
void CMyView::OtherFunction ()
    {
    CClientDC ClientDC (this);

    // IF DISPLAYING GRAPHICS IN A VIEW WINDOW THAT SUPPORTS
    // SCROLLING:
    OnPrepareDC (&ClientDC);

    // display graphics using 'ClientDC' ...
    }
```

> **TIP**
>
> To display text or graphics *outside* the client area of a window, you can create an object of the **CWindowDC** class.

The drawing functions discussed in this chapter are all members of the CDC device context class. Because CDC is the base class for all the other device context classes, these functions can be called using any type of device context object.

This chapter focuses on drawing graphics within a window (primarily a view window). However, the functions and techniques that it presents are largely device-independent and can be used to display graphics on other types of devices, such as printers or plotters. Chapter 21 explains the special techniques required for displaying graphics on printers.

Selecting Drawing Tools

Windows provides two tools that affect the way the CDC drawing functions work: the *pen* and the *brush*. The current pen affects the way that lines are drawn; it affects straight or curved lines (drawn, for example, using the LineTo or Arc function), as well as the borders drawn around closed figures (such as rectangles and ellipses). The current brush affects the way that the interiors of closed figures are drawn. As you'll see, a closed figure consists of two separate elements: a border and an interior.

NOTE

Although termed *drawing tools* in this section, pens and brushes belong to a category of items known as Windows *graphic objects* or *GDI objects* (the term *object* refers to a Windows data structure and not a C++ object; *GDI* stands for *Graphical Device Interface*). Other graphic objects are fonts, bitmaps, regions, paths, and palettes. Fonts were discussed in Chapter 18 and bitmaps will be discussed in Chapter 20. Although regions, paths, and palettes are also related to the drawing of graphics, discussing them is beyond the scope of the book. For general discussions on regions, paths, and palettes, see the following Visual C++ online help topic: *Platform SDK, Graphics and Multimedia Services, GDI* (palettes are discussed under the subtopic *Colors*). For information on using regions and palettes in MFC programs, see the following topics: *Visual C++ Documentation, Reference, Microsoft Foundation Class Library and Templates, Microsoft Foundation Class Library, Class Library Reference, CRgn* and *CPalette*. For information on using paths with MFC, see *Visual C++ Documentation, Reference, Microsoft Foundation Class Library and Templates, Microsoft Foundation Class Library, Class Library Reference, CDC, CDC Class Members* and look under the heading *Path Functions*.

When you first create a device context object, it has a default pen and a default brush. The default pen draws a solid black line that has a width of 1 pixel (regardless of the current mapping mode; mapping modes are explained later in the chapter). The default brush fills the interior of closed figures with solid white. For each of these two tools, Table 19.1 lists the drawing functions affected by the tool and gives the identifier of the tool that's selected by default. (This is the identifier that you'd pass to the SelectStockObject function if you wanted to select the tool, as described in the next section.) The table includes only those drawing functions discussed in this chapter.

TABLE 19.1: The Drawing Tools

Drawing Tool	Default Tool	Drawing Functions It Affects
Pen	BLACK_PEN	Arc
		Chord
		Ellipse

Continued on next page

TABLE 19.1 CONTINUED: The Drawing Tools

Drawing Tool	Default Tool	Drawing Functions It Affects
Pen	BLACK_PEN	Arc
		LineTo
		Pie
		PolyBezier
		PolyBezierTo
		Polygon
		Polyline
		PolylineTo
		PolyPolygon
		PolyPolyline
		Rectangle
		RoundRect
Brush	WHITE_BRUSH	Chord
		Ellipse
		ExtFloodFill
		FloodFill
		Pie
		Polygon
		PolyPolygon
		Rectangle
		RoundRect

To change the current pen or brush, either you can select a stock pen or brush, or you can create a custom pen or brush and then select it into the device context object. Once you select a particular pen or brush, it will be used in the drawing of all subsequent graphics, until you explicitly select a different pen or brush.

Selecting Stock Drawing Tools

To select a stock pen or brush, you can simply call the CDC member function SelectStockObject:

```
CGdiObject* SelectStockObject (int nIndex);
```

The parameter nIndex is a code for the particular stock object you want to select into the device context object. The nIndex values for selecting stock pens and brushes are listed in Table 19.2. (As explained in Chapter 18, you can also call SelectStockObject to select a stock font.)

TABLE 19.2: Values Passed to SelectStockObject for Selecting Stock Pens and Brushes

Value	Stock Object
BLACK_BRUSH	Black brush
DKGRAY_BRUSH	Dark-gray brush
GRAY_BRUSH	Medium-gray brush
LTGRAY_BRUSH	Light-gray brush
NULL_BRUSH	Null brush (interior not filled)
WHITE_BRUSH	White brush (the default brush)
BLACK_PEN	Black pen (the default pen)
NULL_PEN	Null pen (no line or border drawn)
WHITE_PEN	White pen

For example, the following code would select a white pen and a medium-gray brush:

```
void CMyView::OnDraw(CDC* pDC)
   {
   pDC->SelectStockObject (WHITE_PEN);
   pDC->SelectStockObject (GRAY_BRUSH);

   // call other graphics functions and draw graphics ...
```

```
    // (lines and borders will be white, interiors of closed
    // figures will be medium-gray)
}
```

If you select the NULL_PEN stock pen, *no* line will be drawn; this choice isn't very useful. Likewise, if you select the NULL_BRUSH stock brush, the interior of a closed figure won't be filled; this tool is useful for drawing a figure such as a rectangle that consists of only a border, leaving the existing screen graphics on the inside of the border unchanged. The MiniDraw program given at the end of the chapter selects NULL_BRUSH when drawing closed figures that aren't filled.

NOTE   The stock pens draw solid lines that are exactly 1 pixel wide, regardless of the current mapping mode. The stock brushes draw solid colors (rather than patterns, which will be described later).

Creating Custom Drawing Tools

You can create a custom pen or brush by performing the following steps:

1. Create an instance of the CPen class for a pen, or the CBrush class for a brush.

2. Call the appropriate CPen or CBrush member function to initialize the pen or brush.

3. Select the pen or brush object into the device context object, saving the pointer to the former pen or brush object.

4. Call drawing functions to produce the graphic output.

5. Select the old pen or brush back into the device context object.

To create a temporary pen or brush, you can declare the instance of the CPen or CBrush class as a local object within the function that generates the graphics output. (This method is demonstrated by the example code at the end of this section.) If, however, you're going to use a given pen or brush repeatedly throughout the course of the program, it would be more efficient to declare the object as a data member of the view class (or whatever class manages the output window).

To initialize a pen, you can call the CPen member function CreatePen:

```
BOOL CreatePen (int nPenStyle, int nWidth, COLORREF crColor);
```

The nPenStyle parameter specifies the style of line that the pen will draw; the values you can assign nPenStyle—and the resulting lines—are shown in Figure 19.1. Assigning the PS_NULL style creates a pen that's the same as the NULL_PEN stock pen. The PS_INSIDEFRAME style causes the pen to draw a border around a closed figure entirely within the figure's bounding rectangle. (The bounding rectangle and the effect of the PS_INSIDEFRAME style are explained later.) The styles PS_DASH, PS_DOT, PS_DASHDOT, and PS_DASHDOTDOT are effective only if the pen has a width of 1 (if the pen is wider than 1, these styles will generate solid lines).

FIGURE 19.1

Values you can assign the nPenStyle parameter of CreatePen to initialize a pen

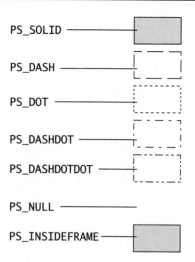

The nWidth parameter specifies the width of the line that the pen draws, in *logical units* (that is, the units used in the current mapping mode). If you assign a width value of 0, the line will be exactly 1 pixel wide regardless of the current mapping mode (just like the lines drawn by the default and stock pens).

The crColor parameter specifies the color of the line. It's easiest to specify a color by using the Win32 RGB macro:

```
COLORREF RGB(bRed, bGreen, bBlue)
```

The bRed, bGreen, and bBlue parameters indicate the relative intensities of the red, green, and blue components of the color; each parameter may be assigned a value in the range from 0 to 255. Table 19.3 gives the values you'd pass to the RGB macro to specify the pure colors available in the original 16-color VGA graphics mode.

TABLE 19.3: Values You Pass to the RGB Macro to Generate the Colors Available in 16-Color Video Mode

VGA Color	bRed, bGreen, and bBlue RGB Values
Dark red	128, 0, 0
Light red	255, 0, 0
Dark green	0, 128, 0
Light green	0, 255, 0
Dark blue	0, 0, 128
Light blue	0, 0, 255
Dark yellow	128, 128, 0
Light yellow	255, 255, 0
Dark cyan	0, 128, 128
Light cyan	0, 255, 255
Dark magenta	128, 0, 128
Light magenta	255, 0, 255
Black	0, 0, 0
Dark gray	128, 128, 128
Light gray	192, 192, 192
White	255, 255, 255

Note that you can assign a pen only a *pure* color. A pure color is a color that's generated by the video hardware and *doesn't* have to be simulated by mixing pixels of different colors (which is known as *dithering*). If you assign a color value that doesn't correspond to one of the pure colors, the line will be drawn using the closest pure color. There is, however, one exception to this rule: if the pen has the PS_INSIDEFRAME style and a width greater than 1, Windows will use a dithered color if the color value you assign doesn't correspond to a pure color.

NOTE   The **CPen** class provides a more advanced version of the **CreatePen** function that takes five parameters. Under Windows NT, this function version allows you to specify the way the ends of wide pens are drawn and joined together, and permits you to create pens that have a custom style. However, most of these features aren't supported by Windows 95. Note also that rather than calling **CPen::CreatePen**, you can initialize the pen object when you create it, by passing appropriate parameters to the **CPen** constructor. For information on the advanced version of the **CreatePen** function and the **CPen** constructors, see the following online help topic: *Visual C++ Documentation, Reference, Microsoft Foundation Class Library and Templates, Microsoft Foundation Class Library, Class Library Reference, CPen*.

You can initialize a brush so that it fills the inside of figures with a single, uniform color by calling the CBrush member function CreateSolidBrush,

```
BOOL CreateSolidBrush (COLORREF crColor);
```

where the crColor parameter specifies the fill color. You can specify any color value; if the value you assign doesn't correspond to a pure color under the current video mode, Windows will generate a dithered color.

Alternatively, you can initialize a brush to fill the inside of figures with a hatched pattern by calling the CBrush member function CreateHatchBrush:

```
BOOL CreateHatchBrush (int nIndex, COLORREF crColor);
```

The parameter nIndex specifies the desired pattern; the values you can assign nIndex—and the resulting patterns—are shown in Figure 19.2. The crColor parameter specifies the color of the hatch lines.

Finally, you can initialize a brush that fills figures with a custom pattern by calling the CBrush member function CreatePatternBrush:

```
BOOL CreatePatternBrush (CBitmap* pBitmap);
```

The pBitmap parameter is a pointer to a bitmap object. When a figure is drawn using the brush, the interior is completely filled with copies of the bitmap, placed side-by-side. You can create and initialize the bitmap object using one of the methods explained in Chapter 20. You should give the bitmap a size of 8 pixels by 8 pixels. (If the bitmap is monochrome, Windows will draw it using the current text and text-background colors.)

FIGURE 19.2:

Values you can assign the nIndex parameter of CreateHatchBrush to initialize a hatched brush

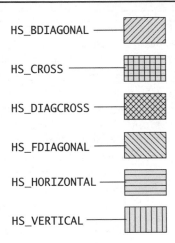

HS_BDIAGONAL ————

HS_CROSS ————

HS_DIAGCROSS ————

HS_FDIAGONAL ————

HS_HORIZONTAL ————

HS_VERTICAL ————

NOTE As with a pen object, you can initialize a brush object at the time you create it by passing appropriate parameters to the **CBrush** constructor. For information on this method, see the following online help topic: *Visual C++ Documentation, Reference, Microsoft Foundation Class Library and Templates, Microsoft Foundation Class Library, Class Library Reference, CBrush.*

Once you've initialized the pen or brush, you must select it into the device context object using the CDC member function SelectObject. To select a pen, you call the following version of SelectObject,

```
CPen* SelectObject (CPen* pPen);
```

where pPen is a pointer to the pen object. SelectObject returns a pointer to the *previous* pen object selected into the device context object (if you haven't previously selected a pen, this will be a temporary object for the default pen).

To select a brush, you call the following version of SelectObject,

```
CBrush* SelectObject (CBrush* pBrush);
```

where pBrush is a pointer to the brush object. SelectObject returns a pointer to the previously selected brush (if you haven't previously selected a brush, this will be a temporary object for the default brush).

When calling SelectObject to select either a pen or a brush, you should save the pointer that's returned. Then, after you've finished calling graphics functions to display output using the pen or brush (as described later in the chapter), you should *remove* the pen or brush from the device context by calling SelectObject again to select the previous object back into the device context object.

TIP

You should remove the pen or brush from the device context object so that the device context object isn't left with an invalid handle after the pen or brush object is destroyed. (When you initialize a pen or brush, Windows supplies a handle that's stored within the pen or brush object; when you select the pen or brush object, the device context object also stores this handle. When either the pen or the brush object goes out of scope, or is otherwise destroyed, the object destructor destroys the handle.) You don't need to perform this step, however, if you're certain that the device context object will be destroyed *before* the pen or brush object is destroyed.

The following example OnDraw function illustrates the steps that have been explained in this section:

```
void CMyView::OnDraw(CDC* pDC)
   {
   CBrush Brush;             // declare brush object
   CPen Pen;                 // declare pen object
   CBrush *PtrOldBrush;      // stores pointer to previous brush
   CPen *PtrOldPen;          // stores pointer to previous pen

   // initialize solid, 3-pixel wide, blue pen:
   Pen.CreatePen (PS_SOLID, 3, RGB (0, 0, 255));

   // initialize solid, yellow brush:
   Brush.CreateSolidBrush (RGB (255, 255, 0));

   // select pen into device context object:
   PtrOldPen = pDC->SelectObject (&Pen);

   // select brush into device context object:
   PtrOldBrush = pDC->SelectObject (&Brush);

   // set any required drawing attributes ...

   // call drawing functions to create graphics output ...
   // (lines and borders will be blue, interiors of closed
   // figures will be yellow)
```

```
// remove new pen and brush from device context object:
pDC->SelectObject (PtrOldPen);
pDC->SelectObject (PtrOldBrush);
}
```

Setting Drawing Attributes

When you first create a device context object, it has a default set of attributes that affect the way the graphics-drawing functions work. The CDC class provides member functions for changing these attributes and also for obtaining the current values of the attributes. Table 19.4 describes the drawing attributes that are most relevant for the techniques discussed in this chapter. (It doesn't include all of them; also, the lists of affected drawing functions include only the functions presented in the chapter.)

TABLE 19.4: Important Drawing Attributes

Drawing Attribute	Default Value	Function Used to Set (Get) Value	Drawing Function(s) Affected
Arc drawing direction	Counterclockwise	SetArcDirection (GetArcDirection)	Arc
			Chord
			Ellipse
			Pie
Background color	White	SetBkColor (GetBkColor)	(same functions as Drawing Mode)
Background mode	OPAQUE	SetBkMode (GetBkMode)	(same functions as Drawing Mode)
Brush origin	0, 0 (screen coordinates)	SetBrushOrg (GetBrushOrg)	Chord
			Ellipse
			Pie
			Polygon

Continued on next page

TABLE 19.4 CONTINUED: Important Drawing Attributes

Drawing Attribute	Default Value	Function Used to Set (Get) Value	Drawing Function(s) Affected
			PolyPolygon
			Rectangle
			RoundRect
Current position	0, 0 (client coordinates)	MoveTo (GetCurrent-Position)	LineTo
			PolyBezierTo
			PolylineTo
Drawing mode	R2_COPYPEN	SetROP2 (GetROP2)	Arc
			Chord
			Ellipse
			LineTo
			Pie
			PolyBezier
			PolyBezierTo
			Polygon
			Polyline
			PolylineTo
			PolyPolygon
			PolyPolyline
			Rectangle
			RoundRect
Mapping mode	MM_TEXT	SetMapMode (GetMapMode)	All drawing functions
Polygon-filling mode	ALTERNATE	SetPolyFillMode (GetPolyFillMode)	Polygon
			PolyPolygon

The first column in Table 19.4 gives the attribute, while the second column gives the default value of this attribute in a newly created device context object. The third column gives the CDC member function for changing the setting of the attribute and the function for obtaining the current setting, and the fourth column lists the drawing function or functions affected by the attribute. Note that attributes affecting only the display of text were described in Chapter 18 (Tables 18.1 and 18.2).

The mapping mode attribute is explained in the next section, and each of the other attributes is explained in the discussion on the function or functions that it affects, later in the chapter.

The Mapping Mode

The current mapping mode affects all the graphics and text drawing functions. The mapping mode defines the units—as well as the directions of increasing coordinate values—that are used to display graphics and text. It affects the way that Windows interprets all coordinate values that you pass to graphics output functions as well as all other functions that accept *logical coordinates*. The current mapping mode, however, *doesn't* affect functions that are passed *device coordinates*. The basic distinction between logical coordinates and device coordinates was explained in Chapter 13, in the section "Converting Coordinates."

Device coordinates specify the position of an object by giving the horizontal and vertical distances of the object *in pixels* (also known as *device units*) from the upper-left corner of the client area of the window (or the upper-left corner of the printable area of a page). Horizontal coordinates increase as you move right, and vertical coordinates increase as you move down. For device coordinates, the *origin* (that is, the point 0, 0) is always at the upper-left corner.

Under the default mapping mode (which has the identifier MM_TEXT), logical coordinates are also given in pixels, with horizontal coordinates increasing as you move right and vertical coordinates increasing as you move down, as shown in Figure 19.3. (In the default MM_TEXT mapping mode, logical coordinates are the same as device coordinates, *unless* the program has moved the relative position of the origin of the logical coordinate system, as discussed later.)

Creating an alternative mapping mode can change both the logical units and the directions of increasing logical coordinates. To designate an alternative mapping mode, you call the CDC member function SetMapMode,

```
virtual int SetMapMode (int nMapMode);
```

where nMapMode is an index that specifies the new mapping mode. Table 19.5 lists each of the values you can assign nMapMode, and for each value it gives the size of a logical unit in the resulting mapping mode.

TABLE 19.5: The Mapping Modes

Value Assigned to SetMapMode nMapMode Parameter	Size of Logical Unit
MM_ANISOTROPIC	(you define)
MM_HIENGLISH	0.001 inch
MM_HIMETRIC	0.01 millimeter
MM_ISOTROPIC	(you define)
MM_ LOENGLISH	0.01 inch
MM_LOMETRIC	0.1 millimeter
MM_TEXT (default mapping mode)	1 device unit (pixel)
MM_TWIPS	$\frac{1}{1440}$ inch ($\frac{1}{20}$ point)

For the MM_HIENGLISH, MM_HIMETRIC, MM_LOENGLISH, MM_LOMETRIC, and MM_TWIPS mapping modes, horizontal coordinates increase as you move right, and vertical coordinates increase *as you move up* (unlike the default mapping mode). Figure 19.3 illustrates the directions of increasing coordinates for the default MM_TEXT mapping mode, and Figure 19.4 illustrates the directions of increasing coordinates for the alternative mapping modes MM_HIENGLISH, MM_HIMETRIC, MM_LO-ENGLISH, MM_LOMETRIC, and MM_TWIPS.

Note that the MM_ANISOMETRIC or MM_ISOMETRIC mapping mode allows you to specify both the size of the logical units and the directions of increasing coordinates, thereby creating a custom mapping mode. For the MM_ISOMETRIC mode, the vertical and horizontal units are made the same size, but for the MM_ANISOMETRIC mode, they can be different sizes. To specify these sizes, you use the CDC member functions SetWindowExt and SetViewportExt.

FIGURE 19.3:

Directions of increasing coordinates for the default MM_TEXT mapping mode

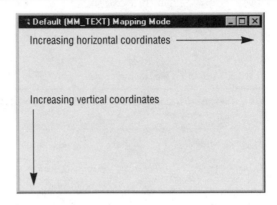

FIGURE 19.4:

Directions of increasing coordinates for the MM_HIENGLISH, MM_HIMETRIC, MM_LOENGLISH, MM_LOMETRIC, and MM_TWIPS alternative mapping modes

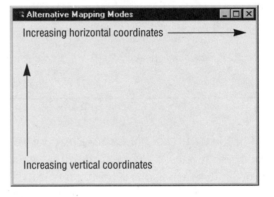

Under all mapping modes, the origin of the logical coordinate system (that is, the point at logical coordinates 0, 0) is initially at the upper-left corner of the client area of the window. If, however, the view window class is derived from CScrollView (explained in Chapter 13), the MFC will adjust the relative position of the logical origin as the user scrolls the document (it does this by changing an attribute known as the *viewport origin*). Recall from Chapter 13 that for a CScroll-View-derived view window class, you must pass the identifier of the mapping mode you're using when you call CScrollView::SetScrollSizes to set the scrolling size. Also, as you'll learn in Chapter 21, an MFC program typically alters the viewport origin in order to print a given page in a multiple-page document.

TIP

You must supply logical coordinates when calling any of the text display functions given in Chapter 18, the graphics-drawing functions given in this chapter, or the bit-operation functions (such as `BitBlt`) given in Chapter 20. However, many Windows functions and notification messages use device coordinates; for example, the `CWnd::GetClientRect` and `CWnd::MoveWindow` functions and the `WM_MOUSEMOVE` message. If you're using the default mapping mode and your view window *doesn't* support scrolling, you needn't be concerned about the type of coordinates used by a particular function or message, because logical coordinates will be the same as device coordinates. If, however, your view class supports scrolling or you're using an alternative mapping mode, you must pay attention to the type of coordinates employed (which should be indicated in the documentation on the function or message). Recall from Chapter 13 that you can convert logical coordinates to device coordinates by calling the **CDC** member function **LPtoDP**, and you can convert device coordinates to logical coordinates by calling the **CDC** member function **DPtoLP**.

NOTE

This section discussed device and logical *coordinates*; a coordinate value indicates the location of a point on a display surface. Occasionally, however, you'll use simple *measurement* values; a measurement value indicates the size of some item. Measurement values can be in *logical units*, that is, the units defined by the current mapping mode—for example, the pen width you pass to `CPen::CreatePen` or the graphic block sizes you pass to `CDC::BitBlt` (discussed in Chapter 20). Measurement values can also be in device units, that is, pixels—for example, the scroll amount you pass to `CWnd::ScrollWindow` or the window size reported by the `WM_SIZE` message. The function or message documentation should tell which units are used.

An important advantage of using one of the alternative mapping modes (that is, MM_HIENGLISH, MM_HIMETRIC, MM_LOENGLISH, MM_LOMETRIC, or MM_TWIPS; also MM_ANISOMETRIC or MM_ISOMETRIC if you define the units properly) is that the size of an image you draw isn't dependent on the device on which you draw it. In contrast, with the default mapping mode, MM_TEXT, the image size depends on the device resolution. Accordingly, the alternative mapping modes are useful for programs that conform to the WYSIWYG principle (What You See Is What You Get)—specifically, programs in which the size of an object on the screen is the same as its size on any printer or other output device. For the sake of clarity, however, the example programs given in the remainder of the book continue to use the default mapping mode.

NOTE   For information on defining and using the alternative mapping modes, see the documentation on the CDC member function SetMapMode, as well as the other CDC mapping functions. For a complete list of the mapping functions, see the online help topic: *Visual C++ Documentation, Reference, Microsoft Foundation Class Library and Templates, Microsoft Foundation Class Library, Class Library Reference, CDC, CDC Class Members* and look under the heading *Mapping Functions*. Also, for a general discussion on mapping modes, see the following topic: *Platform SDK, Graphics and Multimedia Services, GDI, Coordinate Spaces and Transformations*.

Drawing the Graphics

After you've created the device context object and have selected all desired drawing tools and attributes, you're finally ready to start drawing graphics. The CDC class provides member functions for drawing points, straight lines, curves, and closed figures.

For all these functions, the position of the figure is specified in logical coordinates. Whenever a pair of coordinates specifying a point is passed to a function, *the horizontal coordinate is passed before the vertical coordinate*. The horizontal coordinate is often referred to as the x coordinate, and the vertical coordinate as the y coordinate.

The coordinate parameters passed to all drawing function are int values. Because the size of an int is 32 bits, it can store values in the range from –2147483648 to +2147483647. For Windows NT programs, you can pass coordinate values within this full range. For Windows 95 programs, however, you can pass coordinate values only within the range from –32768 to +32767 (which represents the storage range of a 16-bit integer; Windows 95 truncates the int values to 16 bits).

All the drawing functions discussed throughout the remainder of the chapter are members of the CDC class. You can look up details on the functions that are discussed, as well as those that are only briefly mentioned, in the following online help topic: *Visual C++ Documentation, Reference, Microsoft Foundation Class Library and Templates, Microsoft Foundation Class Library, Class Library Reference, CDC.*

Drawing Points

You can color a single pixel by calling the CDC member function SetPixelV, as in the following example:

```
pDC->SetPixelV (10, 15, RGB (255, 0, 0));
```

NOTE
The SetPixelV example, as well as the example calls in the following sections, assumes that **pDC** is a pointer to a valid device context object—either one passed to an OnDraw function or one that you've explicitly defined.

The first two parameters specify the horizontal and vertical logical coordinates of the pixel, and the third parameter specifies the pixel color. If the color you specify doesn't match one of the pure colors that are available under the current video mode, SetPixelV will use the closest pure color. (Obviously, it can't use a dithered color for a single pixel!)

TIP
If you need to obtain the current color value of the point you're setting, you can call the slightly slower function **CDC::SetPixel**, rather than calling SetPixelV. SetPixel sets the pixel to the specified color and returns its former color. Also, you can simply *obtain* the current color value of any pixel by calling **CDC::Get-Pixel**.

NOTE
The MFC provides alternative versions of most of the drawing functions, which allow you to specify the coordinates by passing an appropriate structure, rather than by passing individual horizontal and vertical coordinates. For example, you can pass a single **POINT** structure to the **SetPixelV** function in place of the first two parameters. For the syntax of the alternative function versions, see the function documentation.

The Mandel Program

The program presented in this section, named Mandel, demonstrates the use of the SetPixelV function, as well as several other graphics drawing techniques.

When you run this program, it immediately begins drawing a fractal pattern (specifically, the Mandelbrot set), which completely fills the client area of the view window. If you change the size of the window, or if you remove an overlapping window, Mandel erases the invalidated area of the view window and begins redrawing the entire pattern. (On a slower machine, the pattern can take quite a while to generate; therefore, be careful that you don't cause the program to start redrawing the pattern before it's complete.) Figure 19.5 shows the program window after a complete fractal pattern has been drawn.

FIGURE 19.5:

The Mandel program with a complete fractal pattern

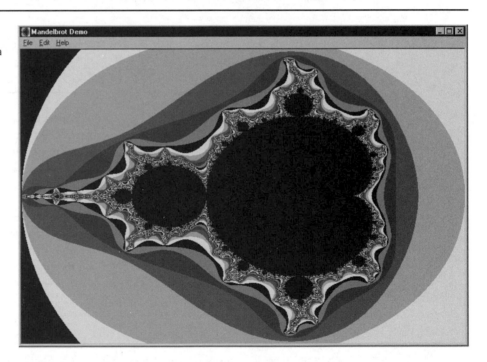

Use AppWizard to generate the basic source files for the Mandel program. Create a new AppWizard project named Mandel, and in the AppWizard Step 1 through Step 6 dialog boxes, enter the same options that you specified for the WinGreet program in Chapter 9.

After you've produced the source files, begin customizing the program by using ClassWizard to generate an overriding version of the OnIdle virtual member function of the application class. To do this, run ClassWizard, open the Message Maps tab, and choose CMandelApp in the Class Name: and Object IDs: lists. Then select OnIdle in the Messages: list and click the Add Function button.

Finally, click the Edit Code button and in the OnIdle function, *delete* the return keyword from in front of the call to CWinApp::OnIdle, and add the statements marked in bold:

```
BOOL CMandelApp::OnIdle(LONG lCount)
{
    // TODO: Add your specialized code here and/or call the base
    // class

    CWinApp::OnIdle(lCount); // remove the 'return' from this
                             // statement!

    CMandelView *PView =
        (CMandelView *)((CFrameWnd *)m_pMainWnd)->GetActiveView ();
    PView->DrawCol ();
    return TRUE;
}
```

The OnIdle function is called periodically whenever the program is idle—that is, whenever it isn't processing a message (it's called from the main message loop within the MFC code). OnIdle first calls the base class version of OnIdle to perform any required default idle-time processing. The code you added to OnIdle then calls the CFrameWnd::GetActiveView function to obtain a pointer to the view object. (The m_pMainWnd data member of the application class stores the address of the main frame window object, and is used to call GetActiveView.) Next, it calls the DrawCol member function of the view class (which you'll define later) to draw a single column of the fractal pattern. Finally, OnIdle returns TRUE so that the MFC code will continue to call it periodically (if OnIdle returns FALSE, the MFC won't call it again until the program receives the next message).

Because drawing the fractal pattern can take a long time (the required time varies *greatly* depending on the hardware), the Mandel program *doesn't* draw the complete figure from the OnDraw function. Doing so would block message processing by the Mandel program during the entire time the pattern is being drawn, preventing the user from choosing menu commands or exiting the program. (A message-handling function, such as OnDraw, must return control before the next message can be processed.) Rather, Mandel draws only a *single column* of pixels within the pattern each time the OnIdle function is called. After drawing this column, OnIdle returns, allowing any pending messages to be processed. The next time OnIdle receives control, it draws the next column. This process continues until the pattern is complete.

NOTE   While drawing the fractal pattern, the Mandel program alternately draws the next column of the pattern and then checks for a pending message, processing the message if one is available. Chapter 22 presents an alternative version of Mandel, which uses a simpler and more efficient method for performing a lengthy graphics operation by starting a separate thread of control, which is dedicated to drawing the entire graphic pattern, while the primary thread continues to process messages.

The next step is to add to the view class a message handler for the WM_SIZE message, which will be explained later. To do this, run ClassWizard, open the Message Maps tab, and select the CMandelView class in the Class Name: list. Then select CMandelView in the Object IDs: list, select WM_SIZE in the Messages: list, and click the Add Function button to create a handler named OnSize.

Next, open the MandelView.h file and add the following member declarations marked in bold to the beginning of the CMandelView class definition:

```
class CMandelView : public CView
{
private:
    int m_Col;
    int m_ColMax;
    float m_CR;
    float m_DCI;
    float m_DCR;
    int m_RowMax;

public:
    void DrawCol ();

// remainder of CMandelView class definition ...
```

m_Col is used to store the number of the next column of pixels within the fractal pattern that's to be drawn. m_ColMax and m_RowMax store the numbers of the last row and column in the view window. (These values depend on the size of the view window; later, you'll see how they're set.) m_CR, m_DCI, and m_DCR are variables used in generating the fractal pattern, and DrawCol is the function that draws each column of the pattern.

Now open MandelView.cpp and add the definitions marked in bold type to the beginning of the file:

```
// MandelView.cpp : implementation of the CMandelView class
//
```

```
#include "stdafx.h"
#include "Mandel.h"

#include "MandelDoc.h"
#include "MandelView.h"

#ifdef _DEBUG
#define new DEBUG_NEW
#undef THIS_FILE
static char THIS_FILE[] = __FILE__;
#endif

// define Mandelbrot set constants:
#define CIMAX 1.2
#define CIMIN -1.2
#define CRMAX 1.0
#define CRMIN -2.0
#define NMAX 128

// colors used to create Mandelbrot pattern:
DWORD ColorTable [6] =
   {0x0000ff, // red
    0x00ff00, // green
    0xff0000, // blue
    0x00ffff, // yellow
    0xffff00, // cyan
    0xff00ff}; // magenta
```

The constants and the ColorTable array are used in generating the fractal pattern. Leave the MandelView.cpp file open, because you'll make several additional modifications to this file.

Add the following initialization to the CMandelView constructor,

```
CMandelView::CMandelView()
{
    // TODO: add construction code here
    m_Col = 0;
}
```

and enter the following definition of the DrawCol function at the end of the file:

```
void CMandelView::DrawCol ()
{
    CClientDC ClientDC (this);
```

```
float CI;
int ColorVal;
float I;
float ISqr;
float R;
int Row;
float RSqr;

if (m_Col >= m_ColMax || GetParentFrame ()->IsIconic ())
    return;

CI = (float)CIMAX;
for (Row = 0; Row < m_RowMax; ++Row)
    {
    R = (float)0.0;
    I = (float)0.0;
    RSqr = (float)0.0;
    ISqr = (float)0.0;
    ColorVal = 0;
    while (ColorVal < NMAX && RSqr + ISqr < 4)
        {
        ++ColorVal;
        RSqr = R * R;
        ISqr = I * I;
        I *= R;
        I += I + CI;
        R = RSqr - ISqr + m_CR;
        }
    ClientDC.SetPixelV (m_Col, Row, ColorTable [ColorVal % 6]);
    CI -= m_DCI;
    }
m_Col++;
m_CR += m_DCR;
}
```

Each time DrawCol is called, it draws the next column of pixels within the fractal
pattern, moving from left to right. DrawCol creates a CClientDC device context
object, and then uses the Mandelbrot equation to calculate a color value for each
pixel in the current column. To color each pixel, it calls the CDC member function
SetPixelV. A description of the method for calculating the color value of each
pixel in the Mandelbrot set is beyond the scope of the current discussion; for an
explanation, see one of the many books and articles on fractals (for example,

Fractal Programming and Ray Tracing with C++ by Roger Stevens, IDG Books Worldwide). Notice that DrawCol returns immediately without drawing a column if the main frame window has been minimized—that is, if CWnd::IsIconic returns TRUE (the address of the main frame window object used to call this function is obtained by calling CWnd::GetParentFrame).

Note that the fractal pattern fills the entire view window; accordingly, the values of several of the data members used in its creation depend on the current view window size. These members must be set in response to the WM_SIZE message, which is sent when the window is first created and whenever it changes in size. To set the data members, add the following code to the handler you generated for this message, OnSize, in MandelView.cpp:

```
void CMandelView::OnSize(UINT nType, int cx, int cy)
{
    CView::OnSize(nType, cx, cy);

    // TODO: Add your message handler code here

    if (cx <= 1 || cy <= 1) // avoid divide-by-zero
        return;

    m_ColMax = cx;
    m_RowMax = cy;

    m_DCR = (float)((CRMAX - CRMIN) / (m_ColMax-1));
    m_DCI = (float)((CIMAX - CIMIN) / (m_RowMax-1));
}
```

The cx and cy parameters passed to OnSize contain the current dimensions of the view window in device units (pixels).

After OnSize is called, the view window is erased, and then the OnDraw function is called to repaint the window. OnDraw is also called when the view window needs redrawing for any other reason (such as the user's removing an overlapping window). OnDraw doesn't draw the image itself; rather, it simply resets the column back to 0 so that DrawCol begins redrawing the fractal pattern—a column at a time—starting with the first column. Complete the OnDraw definition as follows:

```
/////////////////////////////////////////////////////////////////
////////////
// CMandelView drawing
```

```
void CMandelView::OnDraw(CDC* pDC)
{
    CMandelDoc* pDoc = GetDocument();
    ASSERT_VALID(pDoc);

    // TODO: add draw code for native data here

    m_Col = 0;
    m_CR = (float)CRMIN;
}
```

If you wish, you can now customize the program icon, following the instructions given previously. Figure 19.6 shows the icon for the Mandel program provided on the companion CD.

FIGURE 19.6:

The Mandel program icon provided on the companion CD, as it appears in the Visual C++ graphics editor

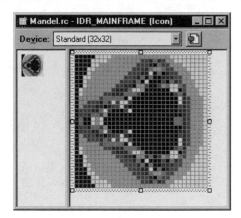

Finally, open the Mandel.cpp file and add the usual SetWindowText call to InitInstance:

```
    // The one and only window has been initialized, so show and
    // update it.
    m_pMainWnd->ShowWindow(SW_SHOW);
    m_pMainWnd->UpdateWindow();

    m_pMainWnd->SetWindowText ("Mandelbrot Demo");

    return TRUE;
}
```

You can now build and run the Mandel program.

The Mandel Program Source Code   The following listings, Listing 19.1 through Listing 19.8, provide the C++ source code for the Mandel program. A copy of these files is contained in the \Mandel companion-CD folder.

Listing 19.1

```cpp
// Mandel.h : main header file for the MANDEL application
//

#if !defined(AFX_MANDEL_H__A3F5D265_A63C_11D1_80FC_00C0F6A83B7F__INCLUDED_)
#define AFX_MANDEL_H__A3F5D265_A63C_11D1_80FC_00C0F6A83B7F__INCLUDED_

#if _MSC_VER > 1000
#pragma once
#endif // _MSC_VER > 1000

#ifndef __AFXWIN_H__
    #error include 'stdafx.h' before including this file for PCH
#endif

#include "resource.h"        // main symbols

/////////////////////////////////////////////////////////////////////////
// CMandelApp:
// See Mandel.cpp for the implementation of this class
//

class CMandelApp : public CWinApp
{
public:
    CMandelApp();

// Overrides
    // ClassWizard generated virtual function overrides
    //{{AFX_VIRTUAL(CMandelApp)
    public:
    virtual BOOL InitInstance();
    virtual BOOL OnIdle(LONG lCount);
    //}}AFX_VIRTUAL

// Implementation
    //{{AFX_MSG(CMandelApp)
```

```
    afx_msg void OnAppAbout();
        // NOTE - the ClassWizard will add and remove member functions here.
        //    DO NOT EDIT what you see in these blocks of generated code !
    //}}AFX_MSG
    DECLARE_MESSAGE_MAP()
};


/////////////////////////////////////////////////////////////////////////////

//{{AFX_INSERT_LOCATION}}
// Microsoft Visual C++ will insert additional declarations immediately before
// the previous line.

#endif
// !defined(AFX_MANDEL_H__A3F5D265_A63C_11D1_80FC_00C0F6A83B7F__INCLUDED_)
```

Listing 19.2

```
// Mandel.cpp : Defines the class behaviors for the application.
//

#include "stdafx.h"
#include "Mandel.h"

#include "MainFrm.h"
#include "MandelDoc.h"
#include "MandelView.h"

#ifdef _DEBUG
#define new DEBUG_NEW
#undef THIS_FILE
static char THIS_FILE[] = __FILE__;
#endif

/////////////////////////////////////////////////////////////////////////////
// CMandelApp

BEGIN_MESSAGE_MAP(CMandelApp, CWinApp)
    //{{AFX_MSG_MAP(CMandelApp)
    ON_COMMAND(ID_APP_ABOUT, OnAppAbout)
```

```
    // NOTE - the ClassWizard will add and remove mapping macros here.
    //     DO NOT EDIT what you see in these blocks of generated code!
  //}}AFX_MSG_MAP
  // Standard file based document commands
  ON_COMMAND(ID_FILE_NEW, CWinApp::OnFileNew)
  ON_COMMAND(ID_FILE_OPEN, CWinApp::OnFileOpen)
END_MESSAGE_MAP()

/////////////////////////////////////////////////////////////////////////////
// CMandelApp construction

CMandelApp::CMandelApp()
{
  // TODO: add construction code here,
  // Place all significant initialization in InitInstance
}

/////////////////////////////////////////////////////////////////////////////
// The one and only CMandelApp object

CMandelApp theApp;

/////////////////////////////////////////////////////////////////////////////
// CMandelApp initialization

BOOL CMandelApp::InitInstance()
{
   // Standard initialization
  // If you are not using these features and wish to reduce the size
  //  of your final executable, you should remove from the following
  //  the specific initialization routines you do not need.

#ifdef _AFXDLL
  Enable3dControls();        // Call this when using MFC in a shared DLL
#else
  Enable3dControlsStatic();  // Call this when linking to MFC statically
#endif

  // Change the registry key under which our settings are stored.
  // TODO: You should modify this string to be something appropriate
  // such as the name of your company or organization.
  SetRegistryKey(_T("Local AppWizard-Generated Applications"));
```

```
LoadStdProfileSettings();  // Load standard INI file options (including MRU)

// Register the application's document templates.  Document templates
//  serve as the connection between documents, frame windows and views.

CSingleDocTemplate* pDocTemplate;
pDocTemplate = new CSingleDocTemplate(
    IDR_MAINFRAME,
    RUNTIME_CLASS(CMandelDoc),
    RUNTIME_CLASS(CMainFrame),        // main SDI frame window
    RUNTIME_CLASS(CMandelView));
AddDocTemplate(pDocTemplate);

// Parse command line for standard shell commands, DDE, file open
CCommandLineInfo cmdInfo;
ParseCommandLine(cmdInfo);

// Dispatch commands specified on the command line
if (!ProcessShellCommand(cmdInfo))
    return FALSE;

// The one and only window has been initialized, so show and update it.
m_pMainWnd->ShowWindow(SW_SHOW);
m_pMainWnd->UpdateWindow();

m_pMainWnd->SetWindowText ("Mandelbrot Demo");

    return TRUE;
}


/////////////////////////////////////////////////////////////////////////
// CAboutDlg dialog used for App About

class CAboutDlg : public CDialog
{
public:
    CAboutDlg();

// Dialog Data
    //{{AFX_DATA(CAboutDlg)
    enum { IDD = IDD_ABOUTBOX };
    //}}AFX_DATA
```

```
    // ClassWizard generated virtual function overrides
    //{{AFX_VIRTUAL(CAboutDlg)
    protected:
    virtual void DoDataExchange(CDataExchange* pDX);     // DDX/DDV support
    //}}AFX_VIRTUAL

// Implementation
protected:
    //{{AFX_MSG(CAboutDlg)
        // No message handlers
    //}}AFX_MSG
    DECLARE_MESSAGE_MAP()
};

CAboutDlg::CAboutDlg() : CDialog(CAboutDlg::IDD)
{
    //{{AFX_DATA_INIT(CAboutDlg)
    //}}AFX_DATA_INIT
}

void CAboutDlg::DoDataExchange(CDataExchange* pDX)
{
    CDialog::DoDataExchange(pDX);
    //{{AFX_DATA_MAP(CAboutDlg)
    //}}AFX_DATA_MAP
}

BEGIN_MESSAGE_MAP(CAboutDlg, CDialog)
    //{{AFX_MSG_MAP(CAboutDlg)
        // No message handlers
    //}}AFX_MSG_MAP
END_MESSAGE_MAP()

// App command to run the dialog
void CMandelApp::OnAppAbout()
{
    CAboutDlg aboutDlg;
    aboutDlg.DoModal();
}

/////////////////////////////////////////////////////////////////////////
// CMandelApp message handlers
```

```
BOOL CMandelApp::OnIdle(LONG lCount)
{
    // TODO: Add your specialized code here and/or call the base class

    CWinApp::OnIdle(lCount);

    CMandelView *PView =
        (CMandelView *)((CFrameWnd *)m_pMainWnd)->GetActiveView ();
    PView->DrawCol ();
    return TRUE;
}
```

Listing 19.3

```
// MandelDoc.h : interface of the CMandelDoc class
//
/////////////////////////////////////////////////////////////////////

#if !defined(AFX_MANDELDOC_H__A3F5D26B_A63C_11D1_80FC_00C0F6A83B7F__INCLUDED_)
#define AFX_MANDELDOC_H__A3F5D26B_A63C_11D1_80FC_00C0F6A83B7F__INCLUDED_

#if _MSC_VER > 1000
#pragma once
#endif // _MSC_VER > 1000


class CMandelDoc : public CDocument
{
protected: // create from serialization only
    CMandelDoc();
    DECLARE_DYNCREATE(CMandelDoc)

// Attributes
public:

// Operations
public:

// Overrides
    // ClassWizard generated virtual function overrides
    //{{AFX_VIRTUAL(CMandelDoc)
    public:
```

```
   virtual BOOL OnNewDocument();
   virtual void Serialize(CArchive& ar);
   //}}AFX_VIRTUAL

// Implementation
public:
   virtual ~CMandelDoc();
#ifdef _DEBUG
   virtual void AssertValid() const;
   virtual void Dump(CDumpContext& dc) const;
#endif

protected:

// Generated message map functions
protected:
   //{{AFX_MSG(CMandelDoc)
      // NOTE - the ClassWizard will add and remove member functions here.
      //    DO NOT EDIT what you see in these blocks of generated code !
   //}}AFX_MSG
   DECLARE_MESSAGE_MAP()
};

/////////////////////////////////////////////////////////////////////////////

//{{AFX_INSERT_LOCATION}}
// Microsoft Visual C++ will insert additional declarations immediately before
// the previous line.

#endif
// !defined(AFX_MANDELDOC_H__A3F5D26B_A63C_11D1_80FC_00C0F6A83B7F__INCLUDED_)
```

Listing 19.4

```
// MandelDoc.cpp : implementation of the CMandelDoc class
//

#include "stdafx.h"
#include "Mandel.h"

#include "MandelDoc.h"
```

```
#ifdef _DEBUG
#define new DEBUG_NEW
#undef THIS_FILE
static char THIS_FILE[] = __FILE__;
#endif

/////////////////////////////////////////////////////////////////////////
// CMandelDoc

IMPLEMENT_DYNCREATE(CMandelDoc, CDocument)

BEGIN_MESSAGE_MAP(CMandelDoc, CDocument)
    //{{AFX_MSG_MAP(CMandelDoc)
        // NOTE - the ClassWizard will add and remove mapping macros here.
        //    DO NOT EDIT what you see in these blocks of generated code!
    //}}AFX_MSG_MAP
END_MESSAGE_MAP()

/////////////////////////////////////////////////////////////////////////
// CMandelDoc construction/destruction

CMandelDoc::CMandelDoc()
{
    // TODO: add one-time construction code here

}

CMandelDoc::~CMandelDoc()
{
}

BOOL CMandelDoc::OnNewDocument()
{
    if (!CDocument::OnNewDocument())
        return FALSE;

    // TODO: add reinitialization code here
    // (SDI documents will reuse this document)

    return TRUE;
}
```

```
/////////////////////////////////////////////////////////////////////////
// CMandelDoc serialization

void CMandelDoc::Serialize(CArchive& ar)
{
   if (ar.IsStoring())
   {
      // TODO: add storing code here
   }
   else
   {
      // TODO: add loading code here
   }
}


/////////////////////////////////////////////////////////////////////////
// CMandelDoc diagnostics

#ifdef _DEBUG
void CMandelDoc::AssertValid() const
{
   CDocument::AssertValid();
}

void CMandelDoc::Dump(CDumpContext& dc) const
{
   CDocument::Dump(dc);
}
#endif //_DEBUG


/////////////////////////////////////////////////////////////////////////
// CMandelDoc commands
```

Listing 19.5

```
// MainFrm.h : interface of the CMainFrame class
//
/////////////////////////////////////////////////////////////////////////

#if !defined(AFX_MAINFRM_H__A3F5D269_A63C_11D1_80FC_00C0F6A83B7F__INCLUDED_)
#define AFX_MAINFRM_H__A3F5D269_A63C_11D1_80FC_00C0F6A83B7F__INCLUDED_
```

```
#if _MSC_VER > 1000
#pragma once
#endif // _MSC_VER > 1000

class CMainFrame : public CFrameWnd
{

protected: // create from serialization only
   CMainFrame();
   DECLARE_DYNCREATE(CMainFrame)

// Attributes
public:

// Operations
public:

// Overrides
   // ClassWizard generated virtual function overrides
   //{{AFX_VIRTUAL(CMainFrame)
   virtual BOOL PreCreateWindow(CREATESTRUCT& cs);
   //}}AFX_VIRTUAL

// Implementation
public:
   virtual ~CMainFrame();
#ifdef _DEBUG
   virtual void AssertValid() const;
   virtual void Dump(CDumpContext& dc) const;
#endif

// Generated message map functions
protected:
   //{{AFX_MSG(CMainFrame)
      // NOTE - the ClassWizard will add and remove member functions here.
      //    DO NOT EDIT what you see in these blocks of generated code!
   //}}AFX_MSG
   DECLARE_MESSAGE_MAP()
};

/////////////////////////////////////////////////////////////////////

//{{AFX_INSERT_LOCATION}}
```

```
// Microsoft Visual C++ will insert additional declarations immediately before
// the previous line.

#endif
// !defined(AFX_MAINFRM_H__A3F5D269_A63C_11D1_80FC_00C0F6A83B7F__INCLUDED_)
```

Listing 19.6

```cpp
// MainFrm.cpp : implementation of the CMainFrame class
//

#include "stdafx.h"
#include "Mandel.h"

#include "MainFrm.h"

#ifdef _DEBUG
#define new DEBUG_NEW
#undef THIS_FILE
static char THIS_FILE[] = __FILE__;
#endif


/////////////////////////////////////////////////////////////////////////////
// CMainFrame

IMPLEMENT_DYNCREATE(CMainFrame, CFrameWnd)

BEGIN_MESSAGE_MAP(CMainFrame, CFrameWnd)
    //{{AFX_MSG_MAP(CMainFrame)
        // NOTE - the ClassWizard will add and remove mapping macros here.
        //    DO NOT EDIT what you see in these blocks of generated code !
    //}}AFX_MSG_MAP
END_MESSAGE_MAP()

/////////////////////////////////////////////////////////////////////////////
// CMainFrame construction/destruction

CMainFrame::CMainFrame()
{
    // TODO: add member initialization code here

}
```

```
CMainFrame::~CMainFrame()
{
}

BOOL CMainFrame::PreCreateWindow(CREATESTRUCT& cs)
{
   if( !CFrameWnd::PreCreateWindow(cs) )
      return FALSE;
   // TODO: Modify the Window class or styles here by modifying
   //   the CREATESTRUCT cs

   return TRUE;
}

/////////////////////////////////////////////////////////////////////////
// CMainFrame diagnostics

#ifdef _DEBUG
void CMainFrame::AssertValid() const
{
   CFrameWnd::AssertValid();
}

void CMainFrame::Dump(CDumpContext& dc) const
{
   CFrameWnd::Dump(dc);
}

#endif //_DEBUG

/////////////////////////////////////////////////////////////////////////
// CMainFrame message handlers
```

Listing 19.7

```
// MandelView.h : interface of the CMandelView class
//
/////////////////////////////////////////////////////////////////////////

#if !defined(AFX_MANDELVIEW_H__A3F5D26D_A63C_11D1_80FC_00C0F6A83B7F__INCLUDED_)
#define AFX_MANDELVIEW_H__A3F5D26D_A63C_11D1_80FC_00C0F6A83B7F__INCLUDED_
```

```cpp
#if _MSC_VER > 1000
#pragma once
#endif // _MSC_VER > 1000


class CMandelView : public CView
{
private:
    int m_Col;
    int m_ColMax;
    float m_CR;
    float m_DCI;
    float m_DCR;
    int m_RowMax;

public:
    void DrawCol ();

protected: // create from serialization only
    CMandelView();
    DECLARE_DYNCREATE(CMandelView)

// Attributes
public:
    CMandelDoc* GetDocument();

// Operations
public:

// Overrides
    // ClassWizard generated virtual function overrides
    //{{AFX_VIRTUAL(CMandelView)
    public:
    virtual void OnDraw(CDC* pDC);  // overridden to draw this view
    virtual BOOL PreCreateWindow(CREATESTRUCT& cs);
    protected:
    //}}AFX_VIRTUAL

// Implementation
public:
```

```
   virtual ~CMandelView();
#ifdef _DEBUG
   virtual void AssertValid() const;
   virtual void Dump(CDumpContext& dc) const;
#endif

protected:

// Generated message map functions
protected:
   //{{AFX_MSG(CMandelView)
   afx_msg void OnSize(UINT nType, int cx, int cy);
   //}}AFX_MSG
   DECLARE_MESSAGE_MAP()
};

#ifndef _DEBUG  // debug version in MandelView.cpp
inline CMandelDoc* CMandelView::GetDocument()
   { return (CMandelDoc*)m_pDocument; }
#endif

/////////////////////////////////////////////////////////////////////////////

//{{AFX_INSERT_LOCATION}}
// Microsoft Visual C++ will insert additional declarations immediately before
// the previous line.

#endif
// !defined(AFX_MANDELVIEW_H__A3F5D26D_A63C_11D1_80FC_00C0F6A83B7F__INCLUDED_)
```

Listing 19.8

```
// MandelView.cpp : implementation of the CMandelView class
//

#include "stdafx.h"
#include "Mandel.h"

#include "MandelDoc.h"
#include "MandelView.h"

#ifdef _DEBUG
#define new DEBUG_NEW
```

```
#undef THIS_FILE
static char THIS_FILE[] = __FILE__;
#endif

// define Mandelbrot set constants:
#define CIMAX 1.2
#define CIMIN -1.2
#define CRMAX 1.0
#define CRMIN -2.0
#define NMAX 128

// colors used to create Mandelbrot pattern:
DWORD ColorTable [6] =
   {0x0000ff, // red
   0x00ff00,  // green
   0xff0000,  // blue
   0x00ffff,  // yellow
   0xffff00,  // cyan
   0xff00ff}; // magenta

//////////////////////////////////////////////////////////////////////
// CMandelView

IMPLEMENT_DYNCREATE(CMandelView, CView)

BEGIN_MESSAGE_MAP(CMandelView, CView)
   //{{AFX_MSG_MAP(CMandelView)
   ON_WM_SIZE()
   //}}AFX_MSG_MAP
END_MESSAGE_MAP()

//////////////////////////////////////////////////////////////////////
// CMandelView construction/destruction

CMandelView::CMandelView()
{
   // TODO: add construction code here
   m_Col = 0;
}

CMandelView::~CMandelView()
{
}
```

```
BOOL CMandelView::PreCreateWindow(CREATESTRUCT& cs)
{
    // TODO: Modify the Window class or styles here by modifying
    //   the CREATESTRUCT cs

    return CView::PreCreateWindow(cs);
}

/////////////////////////////////////////////////////////////////////
// CMandelView drawing

void CMandelView::OnDraw(CDC* pDC)
{
    CMandelDoc* pDoc = GetDocument();
    ASSERT_VALID(pDoc);

    // TODO: add draw code for native data here
    m_Col = 0;
    m_CR = (float)CRMIN;
}

/////////////////////////////////////////////////////////////////////
// CMandelView diagnostics

#ifdef _DEBUG
void CMandelView::AssertValid() const
{
    CView::AssertValid();
}

void CMandelView::Dump(CDumpContext& dc) const
{
    CView::Dump(dc);
}

CMandelDoc* CMandelView::GetDocument() // non-debug version is inline
{
    ASSERT(m_pDocument->IsKindOf(RUNTIME_CLASS(CMandelDoc)));
    return (CMandelDoc*)m_pDocument;
}
#endif //_DEBUG

/////////////////////////////////////////////////////////////////////
```

```cpp
// CMandelView message handlers

void CMandelView::OnSize(UINT nType, int cx, int cy)
{
    CView::OnSize(nType, cx, cy);

    // TODO: Add your message handler code here

    if (cx <= 1 || cy <= 1) // avoid divide-by-zero
        return;

    m_ColMax = cx;
    m_RowMax = cy;

    m_DCR = (float)((CRMAX - CRMIN) / (m_ColMax-1));
    m_DCI = (float)((CIMAX - CIMIN) / (m_RowMax-1));
}

void CMandelView::DrawCol ()
{
    CClientDC ClientDC (this);
    float CI;
    int ColorVal;
    float I;
    float ISqr;
    float R;
    int Row;
    float RSqr;

    if (m_Col >= m_ColMax || GetParentFrame ()->IsIconic ())
        return;

    CI = (float)CIMAX;
    for (Row = 0; Row < m_RowMax; ++Row)
        {
        R = (float)0.0;
        I = (float)0.0;
        RSqr = (float)0.0;
        ISqr = (float)0.0;
        ColorVal = 0;
        while (ColorVal < NMAX && RSqr + ISqr < 4)
            {
            ++ColorVal;
```

```
        RSqr = R * R;
        ISqr = I * I;
        I *= R;
        I += I + CI;
        R = RSqr - ISqr + m_CR;
        }
     ClientDC.SetPixelV (m_Col, Row, ColorTable [ColorVal % 6]);
     CI -= m_DCI;
     }
  m_Col++;
  m_CR += m_DCR;
}
```

Drawing Straight Lines and Curves

In the following sections you'll learn how to draw single straight lines, sets of straight lines, regular curves that are sections of ellipses, and irregular curves. You'll then learn about the drawing and background modes that affect straight lines and curves.

Straight Lines

To draw a straight line, you first call CDC::MoveTo to specify the starting point of the line, and then call CDC::LineTo to specify the ending point and to generate the line. For example, the following code draws a line from the point (5, 15) to the point (25, 40):

```
pDC->MoveTo (5, 15);
pDC->LineTo (25, 40);
```

The parameters you pass to the MoveTo function specify the horizontal and vertical coordinates of the new *current position*. The LineTo function draws a line from the current position to the end point specified by the parameters you pass it. LineTo also resets the current position to the specified end point. Consequently, if you're drawing a series of connected lines, you need to call MoveTo only before the first call to LineTo. For example, the following code draws a connected series of lines that form a "W":

```
pDC->MoveTo (50, 50);
pDC->LineTo (100, 150);
pDC->LineTo (150, 100);
```

```
pDC->LineTo (200, 150);
pDC->LineTo (250, 50);
```

> **NOTE**
>
> When a device context object is first created, the current position is at the logical coordinates (0, 0).

Alternatively, you can draw a series of connected lines by calling the CDC::Polyline function. For example, the following code draws the same series of connected lines as the previous example:

```
POINT Points [5];

Points [0].x = 50;
Points [0].y = 50;
Points [1].x = 100;
Points [1].y = 150;
Points [2].x = 150;
Points [2].y = 100;
Points [3].x = 200;
Points [3].y = 150;
Points [4].x = 250;
Points [4].y = 50;

pDC->Polyline (Points, 5);
```

The first parameter passed to Polyline is a pointer to an array of POINT structures giving the points to be connected, and the second parameter indicates the total number of points.

> **NOTE**
>
> The Polyline function neither uses nor resets the current position. In contrast, the CDC::PolylineTo function begins by drawing a line from the current position to the first specified point, and it also resets the current position to the last specified point. Also, you can call the CDC::PolyPolyline function to draw multiple disjointed sets of connected line segments—the lines within each set are connected but the sets aren't connected to each other. Like Polyline, PolyPolyline neither uses nor resets the current position. Finally, if any of these functions is used to draw a closed figure, the figure *isn't* automatically filled with color, in contrast to the closed figure functions that will be discussed in the section "Drawing Closed Figures."

Regular Curves

You can draw a regular curved line—that is, one that's a segment of an ellipse—by calling the CDC::Arc function, which has the following form:

```
BOOL Arc
    (int x1, int y1,    // u-l corner of bounding rectangle
     int x2, int y2,    // l-r corner of bounding rectangle
     int x3, int y3,    // starting point for arc
     int x4, int y4 );  // ending point for arc
```

Notice that Arc is passed four pairs of coordinates. The first pair of coordinates specifies the upper-left corner of the rectangle that bounds the ellipse (the arc will be a segment of this ellipse), while the second pair of coordinates specifies the lower-right corner of the bounding rectangle. The third pair of coordinates indicates the starting point of the arc, and the fourth pair of coordinates gives the ending point of the arc. By default, the arc extends from the starting point in a counterclockwise direction to the ending point. You can, however, call the CDC::SetArcDirection function to change the drawing direction to clockwise. The Arc function neither uses nor updates the current position.

Note that the specified starting point doesn't actually have to be on the ellipse; rather, it can be anywhere along a line that originates at the center of the bounding rectangle and passes through the desired starting point on the ellipse. The same is true of the specified ending point. The coordinates you specify—together with the resulting arc—are illustrated in Figure 19.7.

FIGURE 19.7:

The coordinates passed
to the Arc function

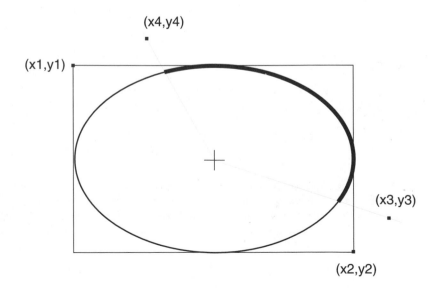

Irregular Curves

You can draw an irregular curve—that is, a curve that *isn't* a section of an ellipse—by calling the CDC::PolyBezier function, which has the following form:

```
BOOL PolyBezier
    (const POINT* lpPoints,  // pointer to array of POINT
                             // structures
    int nCount);             // number of POINT structures in
                             // array
```

PolyBezier draws a series of connected curves, each of which is known as a *Bézier spline*. First, consider drawing a single spline. To do this, the array you pass as the first parameter must contain four POINT structures; the first point is the starting point of the curve, the second and third points are control points that specify the shape of the curve, and the fourth point is the ending point of the curve. For example, the following code draws the single spline shown in Figure 19.8:

```
// Draw a curve consisting of a single spline:
POINT Points [4];

Points [0].x = 25;  Points [0].y = 25;
Points [1].x = 35;  Points [1].y = 170;
Points [2].x = 130; Points [2].y = 20;
Points [3].x = 150; Points [3].y = 150;

pDC->PolyBezier (Points, 4);
```

FIGURE 19.8:

A curve consisting of a single spline, as drawn by the example code

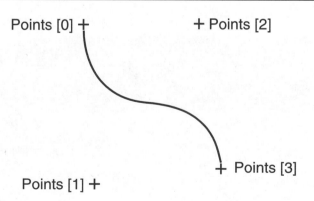

To add another spline to the curve, you need add only *three* more points to the array; the first and second added points are the control points for the new spline, and the third added point is the ending point of the new spline. The starting point for the new spline is the same as the ending point of the first spline. For example, the following code draws a curve consisting of two connected splines (the first spline is the same as the one drawn by the previous code), as shown in Figure 19.9:

```
// Draw a curve consisting of two splines:
POINT Points [7];

Points [0].x = 25;  Points [0].y = 25;
Points [1].x = 35;  Points [1].y = 170;
Points [2].x = 130; Points [2].y = 20;
Points [3].x = 150; Points [3].y = 150;
Points [4].x = 170; Points [4].y = 280;
Points [5].x = 250; Points [5].y = 115;
Points [6].x = 250; Points [6].y = 225;

pDC->PolyBezier (HWinDC, Points, 7);
```

FIGURE 19.9:

A curve consisting of two connected splines, as drawn by the example code

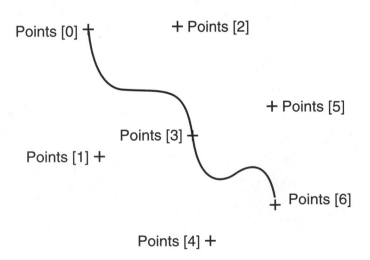

In general, the number of POINT elements in the array (which is the number you assign to the nCount parameter) must be three times the number of splines you want to draw plus 1. Because the ending point of a given spline is used as the starting point of the next spline, the individual splines drawn by a call to PolyBezier are always connected. However, to make a *smooth* transition from one spline to the next, you should make sure that the last control point of the first spline, the ending point of the first spline (which is also the starting point of the second spline), and the first control point of the second spline all lie within a single line. For example, the transition between the two splines in Figure 19.9 is smooth because the points `Points [2]`, `Points [3]`, and `Points [4]` are collinear.

`PolyBezier` neither uses nor updates the current position. In contrast, the alternative function `CDC::PolyBezierTo` uses and updates the current position.

The Drawing Mode for Lines

The style, thickness, and color of lines drawn using any of the functions described in the previous sections are determined by the pen that's currently selected into the device context object. (In this discussion, the term *line* refers to either a straight line or a curve.) The drawing of lines is also affected by the current *drawing mode*. The drawing mode specifies the way that Windows combines the color of the pen with the current colors on the display device. The final color of each pixel within a line depends on the current color of the pixel, the color of the pen, and the drawing mode. Under the default drawing mode, Windows simply copies the pen color to the display; thus, if the pen is red, each pixel within a line that's drawn will always be colored red regardless of its current color. You can change the drawing mode by calling the `CDC` member function `SetRop2`:

```
int SetROP2 (int nDrawMode);
```

The `nDrawMode` parameter specifies the desired drawing mode. There are 16 possible drawing modes; the most common ones are listed in Table 19.6. (See the documentation on this function for a description of the more esoteric drawing modes.) For each drawing mode, the table describes the resulting color of each pixel in a line that's drawn using the mode. The value `R2_COPYPEN` specifies the default drawing mode.

If you choose the `R2_NOT` drawing mode, a line will be drawn by inverting the existing screen colors. This method of drawing has several advantages. First, the line will be visible over almost any screen color; you can thus use the `R2_NOT` mode to draw a visible line within an area containing mixed colors. Also, if you draw the same line a second time, the line will automatically be erased and the existing screen colors restored; thus, you can use this mode for drawing selection rectangles, for creating animation, and for other purposes.

Choosing the `R2_NOP` mode is equivalent to selecting both a `NULL` pen and a `NULL` brush.

TABLE 19.6:   Useful Drawing Modes You Can Set by Calling SetROP2

nDrawMode Parameter Value	Effect on Each Pixel of Figures Drawn
RC_COPYPEN (default mode)	The pixel is the pen color.
RC_NOTCOPYPEN	The pixel is the inverse of the pen color.
R2_NOT	The pixel is the inverse of its former color.
R2_BLACK	The pixel is always black.
R2_WHITE	The pixel is always white.
R2_NOP	The pixel is unchanged.

NOTE   The drawing mode *also* affects the drawing of the borders and interiors of closed figures, which are discussed in the next section, in the same way it affects the drawing of lines.

The Background Mode and Color for Nonsolid Lines

When you draw a nonsolid line (that is, a line drawn using a pen with the PS_DASH, PS_DOT, PS_DASHDOT, or PS_DASHDOTDOT style), the color used to fill the gaps in the line depends on the current background mode and background color. Recall from Chapter 18 that you set the background mode by calling CDC::SetBkMode:

```
int SetBkMode (int nBkMode);
```

If you assign nBkMode the value OPAQUE (the default value), gaps within lines will be filled with the current background color. If you assign it the value TRANSPARENT, the gaps won't be filled (the existing colors on the display surface will be unchanged). As you learned, you set the background color by calling CDC::SetBkColor:

```
virtual COLORREF SetBkColor (COLORREF crColor);
```

NOTE   Chapter 18 discussed the effect of the background mode and color on drawing text. As you'll see later in the chapter, the background mode and color also affect the borders drawn around closed figures with nonsolid pens, as well as the interiors of closed figures drawn with hatched brushes.

Drawing Closed Figures

The following CDC member functions draw closed figures—that is, figures that completely enclose one or more areas on the display surface:

- Rectangle

- RoundRect

- Ellipse

- Chord

- Pie

- Polygon

- PolyPolygon

To draw a simple rectangle, call the CDC::Rectangle function, as in the following example:

```
pDC->Rectangle (25, 50, 175, 225);
```

The upper-left corner of the rectangle drawn by this call would be at the position (25, 50), and the lower-right corner would be at (175, 225).

You can draw a rectangle with rounded corners by calling the CDC::RoundRect function:

```
BOOL RoundRect
    (int x1, int y1,     // u-l corner of rectangle
     int x2, int y2,     // l-r corner of rectangle
     int x3, int y3);    // dimensions of rectangle bounding corner
                         // ellipse
```

The first pair of coordinates passed to RoundRect specifies the position of the upper-left corner of the rectangle, and the second pair of coordinates specifies the position of the lower-right corner. The third pair of coordinates gives the width and height of the rectangle bounding the ellipse used to draw the rounded corners. These parameters are illustrated in Figure 19.10.

To draw a circle or ellipse, call the CDC::Ellipse function:

```
BOOL Ellipse
    (int x1, int y1,     // u-l corner of bounding rectangle
     int x2, int y2 );   // l-r corner of bounding rectangle
```

FIGURE 19.10:

The coordinates passed to the RoundRect function

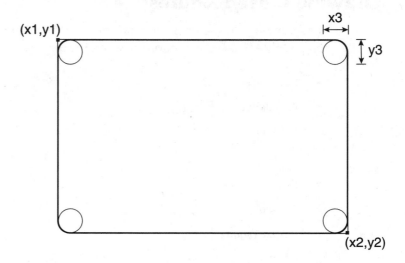

The first pair of coordinates specifies the position of the upper-left corner of the rectangle bounding the ellipse, and the second pair specifies the position of the lower-right corner of the bounding rectangle. See Figure 19.11.

FIGURE 19.11:

The coordinates passed to the Ellipse function

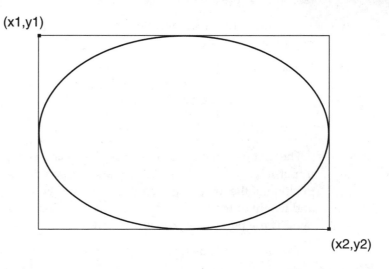

You can draw a chord by calling the CDC::Chord function:

```
BOOL Chord
    (int x1, int y1,      // u-l corner of bounding rectangle
     int x2, int y2,      // l-r corner of bounding rectangle
     int x3, int y3,      // starting point for chord
     int x4, int y4 );    // ending point for chord
```

A chord is a figure formed by the intersection of an ellipse and a line segment. The first two pairs of coordinates you pass to Chord specify the rectangle bounding the ellipse. The third pair of coordinates specifies the starting point of the chord, and the fourth pair of coordinates specifies the ending point of the chord. As with the Arc function, the chord is drawn from the starting point to the ending point in a counterclockwise direction (unless you call SetArcDirection to change the direction), and the specified starting and ending points don't need to be on the ellipse. These coordinates are illustrated in Figure 19.12.

FIGURE 19.12:

The coordinates passed to the Chord function

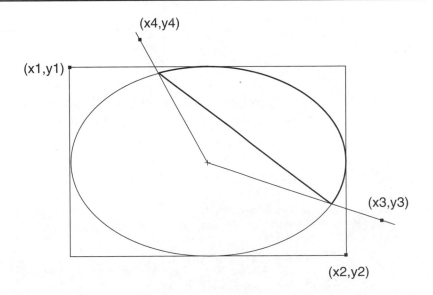

To draw a pie-shaped figure, you can call the CDC::Pie function:

```
BOOL Pie
    (int x1, int y1,      // u-l corner of bounding rectangle
     int x2, int y2,      // l-r corner of bounding rectangle
     int x3, int y3,      // starting point for pie
     int x4, int y4 );    // ending point for pie
```

The coordinates passed to the Pie function work the same way as those passed to the Arc and Chord functions. They're illustrated in Figure 19.13.

FIGURE 19.13:

The coordinates passed to the Pie function

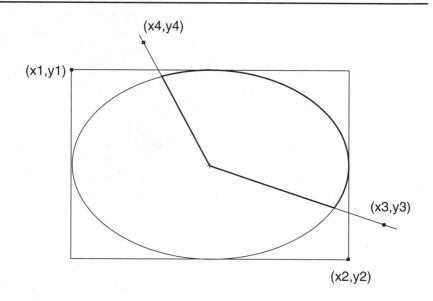

The CDC::Polygon function draws a polygon, which consists of two or more vertices connected by lines. For example, the following code draws a triangle:

```
POINT Points [3];

Points [0].x = 20;
Points [0].y = 10;
Points [1].x = 30;
Points [1].y = 30;
Points [2].x = 10;
Points [2].y = 30;


pDC->Polygon (Points, 3);
```

The first parameter passed to Polygon is a pointer to an array of POINT structures; the members of this array specify the coordinates of the vertices. The second parameter specifies the number of vertices to be connected. Unlike the Polyline function discussed in the previous section, the Polygon function always creates a closed figure (unless you supply only two vertices); to close the figure, it draws a line—if necessary—from the last vertex specified to the first vertex. In the above example, `Polygon` would connect the first point (`Points [0]`) to the second point, the second point to the third, and the third point to the first, making a closed triangle. In contrast, if passed the same array of points `Polyline` would connect only the first point to the second and the second point to the third.

You can draw several separate polygons, in a single function call, by calling the `CDC` member function `CDC::PolyPolygon`. You can also call the `CDC::SetPoly-FillMode` function to change the polygon filling mode, which affects the way complex polygons are filled. For details, see the documentation on these two functions.

For each of the closed figures discussed in this section, the borders are drawn using the current pen, and the interiors are filled using the current brush. Note that if you draw a closed figure with a pen that's been assigned the `PS_INSIDE-FRAME` style, the border is drawn entirely within the bounding rectangle. Note, also, that if you want to draw a closed figure *without* filling the interior (that is, you want to leave the current graphics inside the border undisturbed), you can call `CDC::SelectStockObject` to select the `NULL_BRUSH` stock object before drawing the figure.

The current drawing mode—set by calling `SetROP2`—affects the way that *both* the border *and* the interior of a closed figure are drawn, in the same way that it affects the drawing of lines, which was described previously (in the section "The Drawing Mode for Lines").

The background mode and background color, set by calling `CDC::SetBkMode` and `CDC::SetBkColor`, affect closed figures in two ways. First, if you've selected a non-solid pen (that is, one created with the `PS_DASH`, `PS_DOT`, `PS_DASHDOT`, or `PS_DASH-DOTDOT` style), the background mode and color control the drawing of the gaps in figure borders; namely, in the `OPAQUE` mode gaps are filled with the background color, and in the `TRANSPARENT` mode gaps are not filled. Second, if you're using a hatched brush (that is, a brush created by calling `CreateHatchBrush`), the background mode and color control the painting of the spaces between the hatch lines; that is, in the `OPAQUE` mode the spaces are painted using the background color, and in the `TRANSPARENT` mode the spaces aren't painted.

NOTE   If you're using a patterned brush—that is, one created by calling either **Create-HatchBrush** or **CreatePatternBrush**—you can call the **CDC** member function **SetBrushOrg** to adjust the alignment of the fill pattern.

Other Drawing Functions.

Table 19.7 lists several additional drawing functions that you might find useful. All these functions are members of the CDC class.

TABLE 19.7: Some Additional Drawing Functions

Function	Purpose
DrawFocusRect	Draws a rectangular border using a dotted line, without filling the interior; the border is drawn by inverting the existing screen colors, so that calling this function a second time with the same coordinates erases the border
DrawIcon	Draws an icon
ExtFloodFill	Fills an area on the display surface that's bounded by a given color, using the current brush; you can optionally fill an area that consists of a specified color
FillRect	Fills a rectangular area using a specified brush, without drawing a border
FloodFill	Fills an area on the display surface that's bounded by a given color, using the current brush
FrameRect	Draws a rectangular border using a specified brush, without filling the interior
InvertRect	Inverts the existing colors within a rectangular area on the display surface
PolyDraw	Draws figures consisting of a combination of straight and curved lines (that is, straight line segments and Bézier splines)

The MiniDraw Program

This section presents a new version of the MiniDraw program, which adds the following features (see Figure 19.14):

- The user can draw a variety of different shapes, the particular shape depending on the drawing tool that's selected. A drawing tool is selected by clicking a button on the toolbar or by choosing a command on the Tools menu.

- The user can specify the thickness of the lines used for drawing figures (single, double, or triple) by clicking a toolbar button or choosing a command on the Options menu.

The user can select the color of the figures drawn by choosing a command on the Options menu.

FIGURE 19.14:

The MiniDraw program window

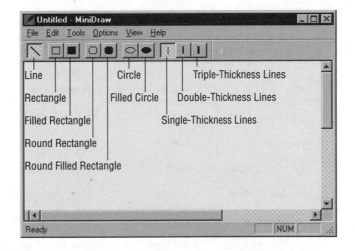

The code that you'll add to the MiniDraw program demonstrates not only many of the methods for drawing graphics that were presented in this chapter, but also several of the techniques for designing class hierarchies and using polymorphism that were explained in Chapter 5.

You'll make all changes to the MiniDraw source files that you created in Chapter 14 (or a copy of the files). If necessary, you can obtain a copy of these files from the \MiniDrw5 companion-CD folder. The first step is to customize the program menu. To do this, open the MiniDraw project in the Developer Studio, open the ResourceView tab in the Workspace window, and open the IDR_MAINFRAME menu in the menu editor. Now delete the entire Lines pop-up menu, and replace it with an Options pop-up menu, which contains two cascading pop-up submenus. Table 19.8 lists the properties of the new menu items, and Figure 19.15 shows the finished result.

TABLE 19.8: The Properties of the MiniDraw Options Menu Items

The Options pop-up menu and the items it contains

ID:	Caption	Other Features
none	&Options	Popup
none	&Color	Popup
none	&Line Thickness	Popup

The items on the Color pop-up submenu

ID:	Caption	Prompt	Other Features
ID_COLOR_BLACK	&Black	Draw using black	none
ID_COLOR_WHITE	&White	Draw using white	none
ID_COLOR_RED	&Red	Draw using red	none
ID_COLOR_GREEN	&Green	Draw using green	none
ID_COLOR_BLUE	B&lue	Draw using blue	none
ID_COLOR_YELLOW	&Yellow	Draw using yellow	none
ID_COLOR_CYAN	&Cyan	Draw using cyan	none
ID_COLOR_MAGENTA	&Magenta	Draw using magenta	none
ID_COLOR_CUSTOM	C&ustom...	Select a custom drawing color	none

The items on the Line Thickness pop-up submenu

ID:	Caption	Prompt	Other Features
ID_LINE_SINGLE	&Single	Draw using single-thickness lines\nSingle-Thickness Lines	none
ID_LINE_DOUBLE	&Double	Draw using double-thickness lines\nDouble-Thickness Lines	none
ID_LINE_TRIPLE	&Triple	Draw using triple-thickness lines\nTriple-Thickness Lines	none

FIGURE 19.15:

The completed Options
menu of the MiniDraw pro-
gram in the menu editor

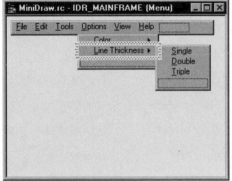

The next step is to use ClassWizard to generate handlers for the new menu
commands you added. In the ClassWizard dialog box, open the Message Maps
tab and select the CMiniDrawApp class in the Class Name: list. You'll now define
both a COMMAND message handler and an UPDATE_COMMAND_UI message handler for
each of the commands on the Color pop-up menu. In all cases, accept the default
function name. For each of these message handlers, Table 19.9 lists the command
identifier (which you select in the Object IDs: list), the message identifier (which
you select in the Messages: list), and the default name of the message-handling
function. When you're done, close the ClassWizard dialog box by clicking the
OK button.

TABLE 19.9: Message-Handling Functions for the Color Menu Commands

Object ID:	Message	Function Name
ID_COLOR_BLACK	COMMAND	OnColorBlack
ID_COLOR_BLACK	UPDATE_COMMAND_UI	OnUpdateColorBlack
ID_COLOR_BLUE	COMMAND	OnColorBlue
ID_COLOR_BLUE	UPDATE_COMMAND_UI	OnUpdateColorBlue
ID_COLOR_CUSTOM	COMMAND	OnColorCustom
ID_COLOR_CUSTOM	UPDATE_COMMAND_UI	OnUpdateColorCustom
ID_COLOR_CYAN	COMMAND	OnColorCyan
ID_COLOR_CYAN	UPDATE_COMMAND_UI	OnUpdateColorCyan
ID_COLOR_GREEN	COMMAND	OnColorGreen
ID_COLOR_GREEN	UPDATE_COMMAND_UI	OnUpdateColorGreen
ID_COLOR_MAGENTA	COMMAND	OnColorMagenta
ID_COLOR_MAGENTA	UPDATE_COMMAND_UI	OnUpdateColorMagenta
ID_COLOR_RED	COMMAND	OnColorRed
ID_COLOR_RED	UPDATE_COMMAND_UI	OnUpdateColorRed
ID_COLOR_WHITE	COMMAND	OnColorWhite
ID_COLOR_WHITE	UPDATE_COMMAND_UI	OnUpdateColorWhite
ID_COLOR_YELLOW	COMMAND	OnColorYellow
ID_COLOR_YELLOW	UPDATE_COMMAND_UI	OnUpdateColorYellow

Next, open the MiniDraw.h file and add definitions for two new data members to the beginning of the CMiniDrawApp class definition:

```
class CMiniDrawApp : public CWinApp
{
public:
    COLORREF m_CurrentColor;
    int m_CurrentThickness;
    UINT m_CurrentTool;
    UINT m_IdxColorCmd;
```

The m_CurrentColor function stores the value of the color that's currently used to draw figures, and m_IdxColorCmd stores the identifier of the command on the Color menu that was chosen to obtain that color. To initialize these data members, open the MiniDraw.cpp file and add the statements marked in bold to the CMiniDrawApp constructor:

```
CMiniDrawApp::CMiniDrawApp()
{
    // TODO: add construction code here,
    // Place all significant initialization in InitInstance

    m_CurrentColor = RGB (0,0,0);
    m_CurrentThickness = 1;
    m_CurrentTool = ID_TOOLS_LINE;
    m_IdxColorCmd = ID_COLOR_BLACK;
}
```

These initializations set the initial drawing color to black.

Also in MiniDraw.cpp, add code to the handlers you just generated for the new menu commands, as follows:

```
void CMiniDrawApp::OnColorBlack()
{
    // TODO: Add your command handler code here
    m_CurrentColor = RGB (0,0,0);
    m_IdxColorCmd = ID_COLOR_BLACK;
}

void CMiniDrawApp::OnUpdateColorBlack(CCmdUI* pCmdUI)
{
    // TODO: Add your command update UI handler code here
    pCmdUI->SetCheck (m_IdxColorCmd == ID_COLOR_BLACK ? 1 : 0);
}

void CMiniDrawApp::OnColorBlue()
{
    // TODO: Add your command handler code here
    m_CurrentColor = RGB (0,0,255);
    m_IdxColorCmd = ID_COLOR_BLUE;
}

void CMiniDrawApp::OnUpdateColorBlue(CCmdUI* pCmdUI)
{
    // TODO: Add your command update UI handler code here
```

```
      pCmdUI->SetCheck (m_IdxColorCmd == ID_COLOR_BLUE ? 1 : 0);
}

void CMiniDrawApp::OnColorCustom()
{
   // TODO: Add your command handler code here
   CColorDialog ColorDialog;

   if (ColorDialog.DoModal () == IDOK)
      {
      m_CurrentColor = ColorDialog.GetColor ();
      m_IdxColorCmd = ID_COLOR_CUSTOM;
      }
}

void CMiniDrawApp::OnUpdateColorCustom(CCmdUI* pCmdUI)
{
   // TODO: Add your command update UI handler code here
   pCmdUI->SetCheck (m_IdxColorCmd == ID_COLOR_CUSTOM ? 1 : 0);
}

void CMiniDrawApp::OnColorCyan()
{
   // TODO: Add your command handler code here
   m_CurrentColor = RGB (0,255,255);
   m_IdxColorCmd = ID_COLOR_CYAN;
}

void CMiniDrawApp::OnUpdateColorCyan(CCmdUI* pCmdUI)
{
   // TODO: Add your command update UI handler code here
   pCmdUI->SetCheck (m_IdxColorCmd == ID_COLOR_CYAN ? 1 : 0);
}

void CMiniDrawApp::OnColorGreen()
{
   // TODO: Add your command handler code here
   m_CurrentColor = RGB (0,255,0);
   m_IdxColorCmd = ID_COLOR_GREEN;
}

void CMiniDrawApp::OnUpdateColorGreen(CCmdUI* pCmdUI)
```

```
   {
      // TODO: Add your command update UI handler code here
      pCmdUI->SetCheck (m_IdxColorCmd == ID_COLOR_GREEN ? 1 : 0);
   }

void CMiniDrawApp::OnColorMagenta()
   {
      // TODO: Add your command handler code here
      m_CurrentColor = RGB (255,0,255);
      m_IdxColorCmd = ID_COLOR_MAGENTA;
   }

void CMiniDrawApp::OnUpdateColorMagenta(CCmdUI* pCmdUI)
   {
      // TODO: Add your command update UI handler code here
      pCmdUI->SetCheck (m_IdxColorCmd == ID_COLOR_MAGENTA ? 1 : 0);
   }

void CMiniDrawApp::OnColorRed()
   {
      // TODO: Add your command handler code here
      m_CurrentColor = RGB (255,0,0);
      m_IdxColorCmd = ID_COLOR_RED;
   }

void CMiniDrawApp::OnUpdateColorRed(CCmdUI* pCmdUI)
   {
      // TODO: Add your command update UI handler code here
      pCmdUI->SetCheck (m_IdxColorCmd == ID_COLOR_RED ? 1 : 0);
   }

void CMiniDrawApp::OnColorWhite()
   {
      // TODO: Add your command handler code here
      m_CurrentColor = RGB (255,255,255);
      m_IdxColorCmd = ID_COLOR_WHITE;
   }

void CMiniDrawApp::OnUpdateColorWhite(CCmdUI* pCmdUI)
   {
      // TODO: Add your command update UI handler code here
      pCmdUI->SetCheck (m_IdxColorCmd == ID_COLOR_WHITE ? 1 : 0);
```

```
    }

    void CMiniDrawApp::OnColorYellow()
    {
        // TODO: Add your command handler code here
        m_CurrentColor = RGB (255,255,0);
        m_IdxColorCmd = ID_COLOR_YELLOW;
    }

    void CMiniDrawApp::OnUpdateColorYellow(CCmdUI* pCmdUI)
    {
        // TODO: Add your command update UI handler code here
        pCmdUI->SetCheck (m_IdxColorCmd == ID_COLOR_YELLOW ? 1 : 0);
    }
```

These menu message handlers work exactly like the ones you added to the program in Chapter 14 for the toolbar buttons; for an explanation, see the section "Writing Handlers for the Button Messages" in Chapter 14. Notice that the On-ColorCustom function, which receives control when the user chooses the Custom… command on the Color menu, displays the Color common dialog box, to allow the user to select a custom color. This dialog box is shown in Figure 19.16. The technique for displaying a common dialog box was discussed in Chapter 18, in the section "Creating the Font Object and Storing the Text."

FIGURE 19.16:

The Color common dialog box displayed by the MiniDraw program

Defining Classes for the Figures

Your next task is to open the MiniDrawDoc.h header file for the document class and *erase* the current CLine definition. Then, add the following class definitions:

```cpp
// class hierarchy for figures:

class CFigure : public CObject
{
protected:
   COLORREF m_Color;
   DWORD m_X1, m_Y1, m_X2, m_Y2;

   CFigure () {}
   DECLARE_SERIAL (CFigure)


public:
   virtual void Draw (CDC *PDC) {}
   CRect GetDimRect ();
   virtual void Serialize (CArchive& ar);
};

class CLine : public CFigure
{
protected:
   DWORD m_Thickness;
   CLine () {}
   DECLARE_SERIAL (CLine)


public:
   CLine (int X1, int Y1, int X2, int Y2, COLORREF Color,
      int Thickness);
   virtual void Draw (CDC *PDC);
   virtual void Serialize (CArchive& ar);
};

class CRectangle : public CFigure
{
protected:
   DWORD m_Thickness;
```

```
      CRectangle () {}
      DECLARE_SERIAL (CRectangle)


public:
   CRectangle (int X1, int Y1, int X2, int Y2, COLORREF Color,
      int Thickness);
   virtual void Draw (CDC *PDC);
   virtual void Serialize (CArchive& ar);
};

class CRectFill : public CFigure
{
protected:
   CRectFill () {}
   DECLARE_SERIAL (CRectFill)


public:
   CRectFill (int X1, int Y1, int X2, int Y2, COLORREF Color);
   virtual void Draw (CDC *PDC);
};

class CRectRound : public CFigure
{
protected:
   DWORD m_Thickness;

   CRectRound () {}
   DECLARE_SERIAL (CRectRound)

public:
   CRectRound (int X1, int Y1, int X2, int Y2, COLORREF Color,
      int Thickness);
   virtual void Draw (CDC *PDC);
   virtual void Serialize (CArchive& ar);
};

class CRectRoundFill : public CFigure
{
protected:
   CRectRoundFill () {}
   DECLARE_SERIAL (CRectRoundFill)
```

```
public:
   CRectRoundFill (int X1, int Y1, int X2, int Y2,
     COLORREF Color);
   virtual void Draw (CDC *PDC);
};


class CCircle : public CFigure
{
protected:
   DWORD m_Thickness;

   CCircle () {}
   DECLARE_SERIAL (CCircle)

public:
   CCircle (int X1, int Y1, int X2, int Y2, COLORREF Color,
       int Thickness);
   virtual void Draw (CDC *PDC);
   virtual void Serialize (CArchive& ar);
};


class CCircleFill : public CFigure
{
protected:
   CCircleFill () {}
   DECLARE_SERIAL (CCircleFill)

public:
   CCircleFill (int X1, int Y1, int X2, int Y2, COLORREF Color);
   virtual void Draw (CDC *PDC);
};
```

Notice that in the hierarchy of classes you just defined, there's a single base class, CFigure (derived from CObject), plus a class derived from CFigure for each type of figure that the program can draw. This hierarchy is shown in Figure 19.17. In general, CFigure provides data members and member functions used for *all* types of figures, and the derived class for each figure adds members used for that particular type of figure.

Specifically, CFigure contains the data member for storing the figure color (m_Color) because all types of figures have a color. Likewise, CFigure contains four data members for storing coordinates (m_X1, m_Y1, m_X2, m_Y2) because the position and size of all types of figures are specified using four coordinates. In contrast, only lines and open figures have a line thickness (filled figures don't); therefore, a data member for storing the thickness (m_Thickness) is provided only within the classes for open figures and lines. Each derived class provides its own constructor for initializing the data members.

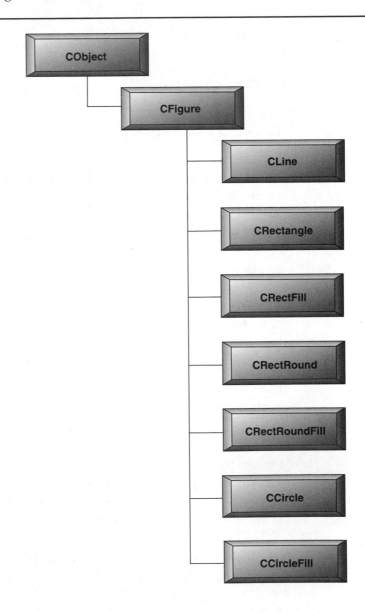

CFigure also provides a member function that calculates the dimensions of the rectangle that bounds the figure (GetDimRect), because a single routine works for any type of figure. Additionally, CFigure provides a virtual Serialize member function for reading and writing the CFigure data members from and to the disk. The classes that don't have an m_Thickness member can simply rely on the CFigure::Serialize function. However, each of the classes that has an m_Thickness data member must provide its own Serialize function to read and write the value of m_Thickness (as you'll see, each of these Serialize functions also explicitly calls the CFigure::Serialize function to read or write the data members defined in CFigure).

Finally, CFigure provides a virtual member function, Draw, which does nothing itself:

```
virtual void Draw (CDC *PDC) {}
```

Defining this function, however, allows the program to use a single CFigure pointer to call the Draw function for each type of figure. The class for each type of figure provides an overriding version of the Draw function, which performs the actual drawing using a routine that's appropriate for the specific type of figure. As you'll see, this use of polymorphism greatly simplifies the code in the view class that manages the drawing of the figures. For an explanation of class derivation, inheritance, virtual functions, and polymorphism, see Chapter 5.

TIP

For readers familiar with C++, note that you could—but are certainly not required to—define the CFigure::Draw function as a *pure virtual function*, making CFigure an *abstract* base class. Because pure virtual functions aren't covered in Part II of this book, however, Draw was simply made an ordinary virtual function.

Next, open the MiniDrawDoc.cpp file and *erase* the CLine implementation code; namely, *erase* the line

```
IMPLEMENT_SERIAL (CLine, CObject, 1)  // delete this line
```

as well as the implementations of the functions CLine::Draw, CLine::Serialize, and CLine::GetDimRect. Then, add the following code for implementing the member functions of the figure classes, at the end of the file:

```
// implementation of figure classes:

IMPLEMENT_SERIAL (CFigure, CObject, 2)
```

```
CRect CFigure::GetDimRect ()
   {
   return CRect
     (min (m_X1, m_X2),
      min (m_Y1, m_Y2),
      max (m_X1, m_X2) + 1,
      max (m_Y1, m_Y2) + 1);
   }

void CFigure::Serialize (CArchive& ar)
   {
   if (ar.IsStoring ())
      ar << m_X1 << m_Y1 << m_X2 << m_Y2 << m_Color;
   else
      ar >> m_X1 >> m_Y1 >> m_X2 >> m_Y2 >> m_Color;
   }

IMPLEMENT_SERIAL (CLine, CFigure, 2)

CLine::CLine (int X1, int Y1, int X2, int Y2, COLORREF Color,
   int Thickness)
   {
   m_X1 = X1;
   m_Y1 = Y1;
   m_X2 = X2;
   m_Y2 = Y2;
   m_Color = Color;
   m_Thickness = Thickness;
   }

void CLine::Serialize (CArchive& ar)
   {
   CFigure::Serialize (ar);
   if (ar.IsStoring ())
      ar << m_Thickness;
   else
      ar >> m_Thickness;
   }

void CLine::Draw (CDC *PDC)
   {
   CPen Pen, *POldPen;
```

```
   // select pen/brush:
   Pen.CreatePen (PS_SOLID, m_Thickness, m_Color);
   POldPen = PDC->SelectObject (&Pen);

   // draw figure:
   PDC->MoveTo (m_X1, m_Y1);
   PDC->LineTo (m_X2, m_Y2);

   // remove pen/brush:
   PDC->SelectObject (POldPen);
   }

IMPLEMENT_SERIAL (CRectangle, CFigure, 2)

CRectangle::CRectangle (int X1, int Y1, int X2, int Y2,
   COLORREF Color, int Thickness)
   {
   m_X1 = X1;
   m_Y1 = Y1;
   m_X2 = X2;
   m_Y2 = Y2;
   m_Color = Color;
   m_Thickness = Thickness;
   }

void CRectangle::Serialize (CArchive& ar)
   {
   CFigure::Serialize (ar);
   if (ar.IsStoring ())
      ar << m_Thickness;
   else
      ar >> m_Thickness;
   }

void CRectangle::Draw (CDC *PDC)
   {
   CPen Pen, *POldPen;

   // select pen/brush:
   Pen.CreatePen (PS_INSIDEFRAME, m_Thickness, m_Color);
   POldPen = PDC->SelectObject (&Pen);
   PDC->SelectStockObject (NULL_BRUSH);
```

```
    // draw figure:
    PDC->Rectangle (m_X1, m_Y1, m_X2, m_Y2);

    // remove pen/brush:
    PDC->SelectObject (POldPen);
    }

IMPLEMENT_SERIAL (CRectFill, CFigure, 2)

CRectFill::CRectFill (int X1, int Y1, int X2, int Y2,
    COLORREF Color)
    {
    m_X1 = min (X1, X2);
    m_Y1 = min (Y1, Y2);
    m_X2 = max (X1, X2);
    m_Y2 = max (Y1, Y2);
    m_Color = Color;
    }

void CRectFill::Draw (CDC *PDC)
    {
    CBrush Brush, *POldBrush;
    CPen Pen, *POldPen;

    // select pen/brush:
    Pen.CreatePen (PS_INSIDEFRAME, 1, m_Color);
    POldPen = PDC->SelectObject (&Pen);
    Brush.CreateSolidBrush (m_Color);
    POldBrush = PDC->SelectObject (&Brush);

    // draw figure:
    PDC->Rectangle (m_X1, m_Y1, m_X2, m_Y2);

    // remove pen/brush:
    PDC->SelectObject (POldPen);
    PDC->SelectObject (POldBrush);
    }

IMPLEMENT_SERIAL (CRectRound, CFigure, 2)

CRectRound::CRectRound (int X1, int Y1, int X2, int Y2,
    COLORREF Color, int Thickness)
    {
```

```
      m_X1 = min (X1, X2);
      m_Y1 = min (Y1, Y2);
      m_X2 = max (X1, X2);
      m_Y2 = max (Y1, Y2);
      m_Color = Color;
      m_Thickness = Thickness;
      }

void CRectRound::Serialize (CArchive& ar)
      {
      CFigure::Serialize (ar);
      if (ar.IsStoring ())
         ar << m_Thickness;
      else
         ar >> m_Thickness;
      }

void CRectRound::Draw (CDC *PDC)
      {
      CPen Pen, *POldPen;

      // select pen/brush:
      Pen.CreatePen (PS_INSIDEFRAME, m_Thickness, m_Color);
      POldPen = PDC->SelectObject (&Pen);
      PDC->SelectStockObject (NULL_BRUSH);

      // draw figure:
      int SizeRound = (m_X2 - m_X1 + m_Y2 - m_Y1) / 6;
      PDC->RoundRect (m_X1, m_Y1, m_X2, m_Y2, SizeRound, SizeRound);

      // remove pen/brush:
      PDC->SelectObject (POldPen);
      }

IMPLEMENT_SERIAL (CRectRoundFill, CFigure, 2)

CRectRoundFill::CRectRoundFill (int X1, int Y1, int X2, int Y2,
   COLORREF Color)
      {
      m_X1 = min (X1, X2);
      m_Y1 = min (Y1, Y2);
      m_X2 = max (X1, X2);
      m_Y2 = max (Y1, Y2);
```

```
      m_Color = Color;
      }

void CRectRoundFill::Draw (CDC *PDC)
   {
   CBrush Brush, *POldBrush;
   CPen Pen, *POldPen;

   // select pen/brush:
   Pen.CreatePen (PS_INSIDEFRAME, 1, m_Color);
   POldPen = PDC->SelectObject (&Pen);
   Brush.CreateSolidBrush (m_Color);
   POldBrush = PDC->SelectObject (&Brush);

   // draw figure:
   int SizeRound = (m_X2 - m_X1 + m_Y2 - m_Y1) / 6;
   PDC->RoundRect (m_X1, m_Y1, m_X2, m_Y2, SizeRound, SizeRound);

   // remove pen/brush:
   PDC->SelectObject (POldPen);
   PDC->SelectObject (POldBrush);
   }

IMPLEMENT_SERIAL (CCircle, CFigure, 2)

CCircle::CCircle (int X1, int Y1, int X2, int Y2,
   COLORREF Color, int Thickness)
   {
   m_X1 = min (X1, X2);
   m_Y1 = min (Y1, Y2);
   m_X2 = max (X1, X2);
   m_Y2 = max (Y1, Y2);
   m_Color = Color;
   m_Thickness = Thickness;
   }

void CCircle::Serialize (CArchive& ar)
   {
   CFigure::Serialize (ar);
   if (ar.IsStoring ())
      ar << m_Thickness;
   else
```

```
    ar >> m_Thickness;
    }

void CCircle::Draw (CDC *PDC)
    {
    CPen Pen, *POldPen;

    // select pen/brush:
    Pen.CreatePen (PS_INSIDEFRAME, m_Thickness, m_Color);
    POldPen = PDC->SelectObject (&Pen);
    PDC->SelectStockObject (NULL_BRUSH);

    // draw figure:
    PDC->Ellipse (m_X1, m_Y1, m_X2, m_Y2);

    // remove pen/brush:
    PDC->SelectObject (POldPen);
    }

IMPLEMENT_SERIAL (CCircleFill, CFigure, 2)

CCircleFill::CCircleFill (int X1, int Y1, int X2, int Y2,
    COLORREF Color)
    {
    m_X1 = min (X1, X2);
    m_Y1 = min (Y1, Y2);
    m_X2 = max (X1, X2);
    m_Y2 = max (Y1, Y2);
    m_Color = Color;
    }

void CCircleFill::Draw (CDC *PDC)
    {
    CBrush Brush, *POldBrush;
    CPen Pen, *POldPen;

    // select pen/brush:
    Pen.CreatePen (PS_INSIDEFRAME, 1, m_Color);
    POldPen = PDC->SelectObject (&Pen);
    Brush.CreateSolidBrush (m_Color);
    POldBrush = PDC->SelectObject (&Brush);
```

```
// draw figure:
PDC->Ellipse (m_X1, m_Y1, m_X2, m_Y2);

// remove pen/brush:
PDC->SelectObject (POldPen);
PDC->SelectObject (POldBrush);
}
```

Each of the Draw functions uses the techniques that were described in this chapter to draw the appropriate figure. Notice that the Draw function for each class that draws an open figure selects the NULL_BRUSH stock object so that the interior of the figure isn't painted. Notice, also, that the Draw functions for closed figures initialize the pen using the PS_INSIDEFRAME style so that the figure will lie completely within the bounding rectangle that the user drags within the view window. Notice, finally, that the two classes that draw rounded rectangles (CRectRound and CRectRoundFill) calculate the size of the ellipse for drawing the rounded corners as follows:

```
int SizeRound = (m_X2 - m_X1 + m_Y2 - m_Y1) / 6;
PDC->RoundRect (m_X1, m_Y1, m_X2, m_Y2, SizeRound, SizeRound);
```

This calculation makes the rounded corners circular and makes the width of the circle used for the corners equal to one-third the average length of the sides of the rectangle.

Other Code Modifications

In this section you'll make a variety of changes to the code to support the drawing of different types of figures. First, in MiniDrawDoc.h, erase the declarations for the AddLine and GetLine member functions from the CMiniDrawDoc class. Also, change the name of the CMiniDrawDoc::GetNumLines function to CMiniDrawDoc::GetNumFigs, and the name of m_LineArray to m_FigArray (these members are now used for figures of all types, not just lines). Also, change the pointer type stored in CTypedPtrArray from CLine to CFigure. Finally, add declarations for the AddFigure and GetFigure member functions. The changes are as follows:

```
class CMiniDrawDoc : public CDocument
{
protected:
  CTypedPtrArray<CObArray, CFigure*> m_FigArray;

public:
  // erased AddLine and GetLine declarations
```

```
void AddFigure (CFigure *PFigure);
CFigure *GetFigure (int Index);
int GetNumFigs ();  // changed name from GetNumLines
```

```
// remainder of CMiniDrawDoc definition ...
```

Likewise, in the MiniDrawDoc.cpp file, erase the implementations for
CMiniDrawDoc::AddLine and CMiniDrawDoc::GetLine, change the name of GetNum-
Lines to the new name GetNumFigs, and add the following implementations for
the new AddFigure and GetFigure member functions:

```
// erased CMiniDrawDoc::AddLine and CMiniDrawDoc::GetLine
```

```
void CMiniDrawDoc::AddFigure (CFigure *PFigure)
  {
  m_FigArray.Add (PFigure);
  SetModifiedFlag ();
  }
```

```
CFigure *CMiniDrawDoc::GetFigure (int Index)
  {
  if (Index < 0 || Index > m_FigArray.GetUpperBound ())
     return 0;
  return (CFigure *)m_FigArray.GetAt (Index);
  }
```

```
int CMiniDrawDoc::GetNumFigs ()  // name changed from GetNumLines
  {
  return m_FigArray.GetSize ();
  }
```

The new functions work with any type of figure; they add or obtain CFigure
object pointers rather than CLine object pointers. Also, unlike the former AddLine
function, AddFigure doesn't invoke new to create the object; this task is now performed by the view class.

Also in MiniDrawDoc.cpp, replace all occurrences of the object name m_Line-
Array with the new name, m_FigArray (there should be 11 occurrences).

Next, in the MiniDrawView.h file, add a definition for the m_PenDotted data
member to the beginning of the CMiniDrawView class definition:

```
class CMiniDrawView : public CScrollView
{
protected:
```

```
CString m_ClassName;
int m_Dragging;
HCURSOR m_HArrow;
HCURSOR m_HCross;
CPen m_PenDotted;
CPoint m_PointOld;
CPoint m_PointOrigin;
```

Then, in the MiniDrawView.cpp file, add the following m_PenDotted initialization to the CMiniDrawView constructor:

```
CMiniDrawView::CMiniDrawView()
{
   // TODO: add construction code here

   m_Dragging = 0;
   m_HArrow = AfxGetApp ()->LoadStandardCursor (IDC_ARROW);
   m_HCross = AfxGetApp ()->LoadStandardCursor (IDC_CROSS);
   m_PenDotted.CreatePen (PS_DOT, 1, RGB (0,0,0));
}
```

m_PenDotted will be used to draw dotted temporary lines (rather than solid lines) when the user drags the mouse pointer to draw a figure. All the remaining changes are also made within the MiniDrawView.cpp file.

Modify the OnMouseMove function as follows:

```
void CMiniDrawView::OnMouseMove(UINT nFlags, CPoint point)
{
   // TODO: Add your message handler code here and/or call
   // default

   CClientDC ClientDC (this);
   OnPrepareDC (&ClientDC);
   ClientDC.DPtoLP (&point);

   if (!m_Dragging)
      {
      CSize ScrollSize = GetTotalSize ();
      CRect ScrollRect (0, 0, ScrollSize.cx, ScrollSize.cy);
      if (ScrollRect.PtInRect (point))
         ::SetCursor (m_HCross);
      else
         ::SetCursor (m_HArrow);
```

```
      return;
      }

ClientDC.SetROP2 (R2_NOT);
ClientDC.SelectObject (&m_PenDotted);
ClientDC.SetBkMode (TRANSPARENT);
ClientDC.SelectStockObject (NULL_BRUSH);

switch ((((CMiniDrawApp *)AfxGetApp ())->m_CurrentTool)
   {
   case ID_TOOLS_LINE:
      ClientDC.MoveTo (m_PointOrigin);
      ClientDC.LineTo (m_PointOld);
      ClientDC.MoveTo (m_PointOrigin);
      ClientDC.LineTo (point);
      break;

   case ID_TOOLS_RECTANGLE:
   case ID_TOOLS_RECTFILL:
      ClientDC.Rectangle (m_PointOrigin.x, m_PointOrigin.y,
                          m_PointOld.x, m_PointOld.y);
      ClientDC.Rectangle (m_PointOrigin.x, m_PointOrigin.y,
                          point.x, point.y);
      break;

   case ID_TOOLS_RECTROUND:
   case ID_TOOLS_RECTROUNDFILL:
      {
      int SizeRound = (abs (m_PointOld.x - m_PointOrigin.x) +
         abs (m_PointOld.y - m_PointOrigin.y)) / 6;
      ClientDC.RoundRect (m_PointOrigin.x, m_PointOrigin.y,
                          m_PointOld.x, m_PointOld.y,
      SizeRound, SizeRound);
      SizeRound = (abs (point.x - m_PointOrigin.x) +
                  abs (point.y - m_PointOrigin.y)) / 6;
      ClientDC.RoundRect (m_PointOrigin.x, m_PointOrigin.y,
                          point.x, point.y,
                          SizeRound, SizeRound);
      break;
      }

   case ID_TOOLS_CIRCLE:
```

```
    case ID_TOOLS_CIRCLEFILL:
        ClientDC.Ellipse (m_PointOrigin.x, m_PointOrigin.y,
                          m_PointOld.x, m_PointOld.y);
        ClientDC.Ellipse (m_PointOrigin.x, m_PointOrigin.y,
                          point.x, point.y);
        break;
    }

m_PointOld = point;

CScrollView::OnMouseMove(nFlags, point);
}
```

The new code you added erases the previous temporary figure and then redraws a new temporary figure at the current mouse position (the temporary figure marks the position where the permanent figure would be drawn if the user released the mouse button). The code begins by selecting the required drawing tools and setting the required drawing attributes. It then branches to the appropriate drawing routine for the currently selected drawing tool.

You now need to modify the OnLButtonUp function, as follows:

```
void CMiniDrawView::OnLButtonUp(UINT nFlags, CPoint point)
{
    // TODO: Add your message handler code here and/or call
    // default

    if (!m_Dragging)
        return;

    m_Dragging = 0;
    ::ReleaseCapture ();
    ::ClipCursor (NULL);

    CClientDC ClientDC (this);
    OnPrepareDC (&ClientDC);
    ClientDC.DPtoLP (&point);
    ClientDC.SetROP2 (R2_NOT);
    ClientDC.SelectObject (&m_PenDotted);
    ClientDC.SetBkMode (TRANSPARENT);
    ClientDC.SelectStockObject (NULL_BRUSH);

    CMiniDrawApp *PApp = (CMiniDrawApp *)AfxGetApp ();
```

```
CFigure *PFigure;

switch (PApp->m_CurrentTool)
    {
    case ID_TOOLS_LINE:
        ClientDC.MoveTo (m_PointOrigin);
        ClientDC.LineTo (m_PointOld);
        PFigure = new CLine
            (m_PointOrigin.x, m_PointOrigin.y,
            point.x, point.y,
            PApp->m_CurrentColor,
            PApp->m_CurrentThickness);
        break;

    case ID_TOOLS_RECTANGLE:
        ClientDC.Rectangle (m_PointOrigin.x, m_PointOrigin.y,
                            m_PointOld.x, m_PointOld.y);
        PFigure = new CRectangle
            (m_PointOrigin.x, m_PointOrigin.y,
            point.x, point.y,
            PApp->m_CurrentColor,
            PApp->m_CurrentThickness);
        break;

    case ID_TOOLS_RECTFILL:
        ClientDC.Rectangle (m_PointOrigin.x, m_PointOrigin.y,
                            m_PointOld.x, m_PointOld.y);
        PFigure = new CRectFill
            (m_PointOrigin.x, m_PointOrigin.y,
            point.x, point.y,
            PApp->m_CurrentColor);
        break;

    case ID_TOOLS_RECTROUND:
        {
        int SizeRound = (abs (m_PointOld.x - m_PointOrigin.x) +
            abs (m_PointOld.y - m_PointOrigin.y)) / 6;
        ClientDC.RoundRect (m_PointOrigin.x, m_PointOrigin.y,
                            m_PointOld.x, m_PointOld.y,
                            SizeRound, SizeRound);
        PFigure = new CRectRound
            (m_PointOrigin.x, m_PointOrigin.y,
```

```
                   point.x, point.y,
                   PApp->m_CurrentColor,
                   PApp->m_CurrentThickness);
               break;
               }

       case ID_TOOLS_RECTROUNDFILL:
           {
           int SizeRound = (abs (m_PointOld.x - m_PointOrigin.x) +
               abs (m_PointOld.y - m_PointOrigin.y)) / 6;
           ClientDC.RoundRect (m_PointOrigin.x, m_PointOrigin.y,
                               m_PointOld.x, m_PointOld.y,
           SizeRound, SizeRound);
           PFigure = new CRectRoundFill
               (m_PointOrigin.x, m_PointOrigin.y,
               point.x, point.y,
               PApp->m_CurrentColor);
           break;
           }

       case ID_TOOLS_CIRCLE:
           ClientDC.Ellipse (m_PointOrigin.x, m_PointOrigin.y,
                             m_PointOld.x, m_PointOld.y);
           PFigure = new CCircle
               (m_PointOrigin.x, m_PointOrigin.y,
               point.x, point.y,
               PApp->m_CurrentColor,
               PApp->m_CurrentThickness);
           break;

       case ID_TOOLS_CIRCLEFILL:
           ClientDC.Ellipse (m_PointOrigin.x, m_PointOrigin.y,
                             m_PointOld.x, m_PointOld.y);
           PFigure = new CCircleFill
               (m_PointOrigin.x, m_PointOrigin.y,
               point.x, point.y,
               PApp->m_CurrentColor);
           break;
       }

   ClientDC.SetROP2 (R2_COPYPEN);
   PFigure->Draw (&ClientDC);
```

```
      CMiniDrawDoc* PDoc = GetDocument ();
      PDoc->AddFigure (PFigure);

      PDoc->UpdateAllViews (this, 0, PFigure);

      CScrollView::OnLButtonUp(nFlags, point);
   }
```

The new code begins by selecting the required drawing tools and setting the required drawing attributes. It then branches to a routine that's appropriate for the current drawing tool. Each routine erases the temporary figure and then creates an object of the correct class to store and draw the new permanent figure, assigning the object's address to PFigure. After the switch statement, OnLButtonUp then calls SetROP2 to restore the default drawing mode and uses the PFigure pointer to call the Draw function to draw the permanent figure; because Draw is a virtual function, this call automatically invokes the appropriate version of Draw for the current type of figure. Finally, the new code calls CMiniDrawDoc::AddFigure to store the figure within the document class, and it calls UpdateAllViews to force redrawing of the other view window (in case two views are open).

Finally, you need to change several lines within the OnDraw function:

```
void CMiniDrawView::OnDraw(CDC* pDC)
{
   CMiniDrawDoc* pDoc = GetDocument();
   ASSERT_VALID(pDoc);

   // TODO: add draw code for native data here

   CSize ScrollSize = GetTotalSize ();
   pDC->MoveTo (ScrollSize.cx, 0);
   pDC->LineTo (ScrollSize.cx, ScrollSize.cy);
   pDC->LineTo (0, ScrollSize.cy);

   CRect ClipRect;
   CRect DimRect;
   CRect IntRect;
   CFigure *PFigure;   // changed from 'CLine *PLine'

   pDC->GetClipBox (&ClipRect);

   int NumFigs = pDoc->GetNumFigs ();
   for (int Index = 0; Index < NumFigs; ++Index)
      {
```

```
                    PFigure = pDoc->GetFigure (Index);
                    DimRect = PFigure->GetDimRect ();
                    if (IntRect.IntersectRect (DimRect, ClipRect))
                       PFigure->Draw (pDC);
                    }
            }
```

The modified code uses the new CFigure class rather than CLine. It also draws the figures in the same order in which they were added (the previous version drew them in the opposite order), so that the figures will overlap in the order in which they were drawn.

The modifications to MiniDraw are now complete, and you can build and run the program.

The MiniDraw Source Code

Listings 19.9 through 19.16 contain the C++ source code for the version of the MiniDraw program that you created in this chapter. A copy of these files can be obtained from the \MiniDrw6 companion-CD folder.

Listing 19.9

```
// MiniDraw.h : main header file for the MINIDRAW application
//

#if !defined(AFX_MINIDRAW_H__11E83924_999A_11D1_80FC_00C0F6A83B7F__INCLUDED_)
#define AFX_MINIDRAW_H__11E83924_999A_11D1_80FC_00C0F6A83B7F__INCLUDED_

#if _MSC_VER > 1000
#pragma once
#endif // _MSC_VER > 1000

#ifndef __AFXWIN_H__
   #error include 'stdafx.h' before including this file for PCH
#endif

#include "resource.h"       // main symbols


/////////////////////////////////////////////////////////////////////////
// CMiniDrawApp:
// See MiniDraw.cpp for the implementation of this class
//
```

```
class CMiniDrawApp : public CWinApp
{
public:
    COLORREF m_CurrentColor;
    int m_CurrentThickness;
    UINT m_CurrentTool;
    UINT m_IdxColorCmd;

public:
    CMiniDrawApp();

// Overrides
    // ClassWizard generated virtual function overrides
    //{{AFX_VIRTUAL(CMiniDrawApp)
    public:
    virtual BOOL InitInstance();
    //}}AFX_VIRTUAL

// Implementation

    //{{AFX_MSG(CMiniDrawApp)
    afx_msg void OnAppAbout();
    afx_msg void OnLineDouble();
    afx_msg void OnUpdateLineDouble(CCmdUI* pCmdUI);
    afx_msg void OnLineSingle();
    afx_msg void OnUpdateLineSingle(CCmdUI* pCmdUI);
    afx_msg void OnLineTriple();
    afx_msg void OnUpdateLineTriple(CCmdUI* pCmdUI);
    afx_msg void OnToolsCircle();
    afx_msg void OnUpdateToolsCircle(CCmdUI* pCmdUI);
    afx_msg void OnToolsCirclefill();
    afx_msg void OnUpdateToolsCirclefill(CCmdUI* pCmdUI);
    afx_msg void OnToolsLine();
    afx_msg void OnUpdateToolsLine(CCmdUI* pCmdUI);
    afx_msg void OnToolsRectangle();
    afx_msg void OnUpdateToolsRectangle(CCmdUI* pCmdUI);
    afx_msg void OnToolsRectfill();
    afx_msg void OnUpdateToolsRectfill(CCmdUI* pCmdUI);
    afx_msg void OnToolsRectround();
    afx_msg void OnUpdateToolsRectround(CCmdUI* pCmdUI);
    afx_msg void OnToolsRectroundfill();
    afx_msg void OnUpdateToolsRectroundfill(CCmdUI* pCmdUI);
    afx_msg void OnColorBlack();
```

```
    afx_msg void OnUpdateColorBlack(CCmdUI* pCmdUI);
    afx_msg void OnColorBlue();
    afx_msg void OnUpdateColorBlue(CCmdUI* pCmdUI);
    afx_msg void OnColorCustom();
    afx_msg void OnUpdateColorCustom(CCmdUI* pCmdUI);
    afx_msg void OnColorCyan();
    afx_msg void OnUpdateColorCyan(CCmdUI* pCmdUI);
    afx_msg void OnColorGreen();
    afx_msg void OnUpdateColorGreen(CCmdUI* pCmdUI);
    afx_msg void OnColorMagenta();
    afx_msg void OnUpdateColorMagenta(CCmdUI* pCmdUI);
    afx_msg void OnColorRed();
    afx_msg void OnUpdateColorRed(CCmdUI* pCmdUI);
    afx_msg void OnColorWhite();
    afx_msg void OnUpdateColorWhite(CCmdUI* pCmdUI);
    afx_msg void OnColorYellow();
    afx_msg void OnUpdateColorYellow(CCmdUI* pCmdUI);
    //}}AFX_MSG
    DECLARE_MESSAGE_MAP()
};


/////////////////////////////////////////////////////////////////////////

//{{AFX_INSERT_LOCATION}}
// Microsoft Visual C++ will insert additional declarations immediately before
// the previous line.

#endif
// !defined(AFX_MINIDRAW_H__11E83924_999A_11D1_80FC_00C0F6A83B7F__INCLUDED_)
```

Listing 19.10

```
// MiniDraw.cpp : Defines the class behaviors for the application.
//

#include "stdafx.h"
#include "MiniDraw.h"

#include "MainFrm.h"
#include "MiniDrawDoc.h"
#include "MiniDrawView.h"
```

```
#ifdef _DEBUG
#define new DEBUG_NEW
#undef THIS_FILE
static char THIS_FILE[] = __FILE__;
#endif

/////////////////////////////////////////////////////////////////////////////
// CMiniDrawApp

BEGIN_MESSAGE_MAP(CMiniDrawApp, CWinApp)
   //{{AFX_MSG_MAP(CMiniDrawApp)
   ON_COMMAND(ID_APP_ABOUT, OnAppAbout)
   ON_COMMAND(ID_LINE_DOUBLE, OnLineDouble)
   ON_UPDATE_COMMAND_UI(ID_LINE_DOUBLE, OnUpdateLineDouble)
   ON_COMMAND(ID_LINE_SINGLE, OnLineSingle)
   ON_UPDATE_COMMAND_UI(ID_LINE_SINGLE, OnUpdateLineSingle)
   ON_COMMAND(ID_LINE_TRIPLE, OnLineTriple)
   ON_UPDATE_COMMAND_UI(ID_LINE_TRIPLE, OnUpdateLineTriple)
   ON_COMMAND(ID_TOOLS_CIRCLE, OnToolsCircle)
   ON_UPDATE_COMMAND_UI(ID_TOOLS_CIRCLE, OnUpdateToolsCircle)
   ON_COMMAND(ID_TOOLS_CIRCLEFILL, OnToolsCirclefill)
   ON_UPDATE_COMMAND_UI(ID_TOOLS_CIRCLEFILL, OnUpdateToolsCirclefill)
   ON_COMMAND(ID_TOOLS_LINE, OnToolsLine)
   ON_UPDATE_COMMAND_UI(ID_TOOLS_LINE, OnUpdateToolsLine)
   ON_COMMAND(ID_TOOLS_RECTANGLE, OnToolsRectangle)
   ON_UPDATE_COMMAND_UI(ID_TOOLS_RECTANGLE, OnUpdateToolsRectangle)
   ON_COMMAND(ID_TOOLS_RECTFILL, OnToolsRectfill)
   ON_UPDATE_COMMAND_UI(ID_TOOLS_RECTFILL, OnUpdateToolsRectfill)
   ON_COMMAND(ID_TOOLS_RECTROUND, OnToolsRectround)
   ON_UPDATE_COMMAND_UI(ID_TOOLS_RECTROUND, OnUpdateToolsRectround)
   ON_COMMAND(ID_TOOLS_RECTROUNDFILL, OnToolsRectroundfill)
   ON_UPDATE_COMMAND_UI(ID_TOOLS_RECTROUNDFILL, OnUpdateToolsRectroundfill)
   ON_COMMAND(ID_COLOR_BLACK, OnColorBlack)
   ON_UPDATE_COMMAND_UI(ID_COLOR_BLACK, OnUpdateColorBlack)
   ON_COMMAND(ID_COLOR_BLUE, OnColorBlue)
   ON_UPDATE_COMMAND_UI(ID_COLOR_BLUE, OnUpdateColorBlue)
   ON_COMMAND(ID_COLOR_CUSTOM, OnColorCustom)
   ON_UPDATE_COMMAND_UI(ID_COLOR_CUSTOM, OnUpdateColorCustom)
   ON_COMMAND(ID_COLOR_CYAN, OnColorCyan)
   ON_UPDATE_COMMAND_UI(ID_COLOR_CYAN, OnUpdateColorCyan)
   ON_COMMAND(ID_COLOR_GREEN, OnColorGreen)
```

```
    ON_UPDATE_COMMAND_UI(ID_COLOR_GREEN, OnUpdateColorGreen)
    ON_COMMAND(ID_COLOR_MAGENTA, OnColorMagenta)
    ON_UPDATE_COMMAND_UI(ID_COLOR_MAGENTA, OnUpdateColorMagenta)
    ON_COMMAND(ID_COLOR_RED, OnColorRed)
    ON_UPDATE_COMMAND_UI(ID_COLOR_RED, OnUpdateColorRed)
    ON_COMMAND(ID_COLOR_WHITE, OnColorWhite)
    ON_UPDATE_COMMAND_UI(ID_COLOR_WHITE, OnUpdateColorWhite)
    ON_COMMAND(ID_COLOR_YELLOW, OnColorYellow)
    ON_UPDATE_COMMAND_UI(ID_COLOR_YELLOW, OnUpdateColorYellow)
    //}}AFX_MSG_MAP
    // Standard file based document commands
    ON_COMMAND(ID_FILE_NEW, CWinApp::OnFileNew)
    ON_COMMAND(ID_FILE_OPEN, CWinApp::OnFileOpen)
END_MESSAGE_MAP()


/////////////////////////////////////////////////////////////////////////
// CMiniDrawApp construction

CMiniDrawApp::CMiniDrawApp()
{
    // TODO: add construction code here,
    // Place all significant initialization in InitInstance

    m_CurrentColor = RGB (0,0,0);
    m_CurrentThickness = 1;
    m_CurrentTool = ID_TOOLS_LINE;
    m_IdxColorCmd = ID_COLOR_BLACK;
}


/////////////////////////////////////////////////////////////////////////
// The one and only CMiniDrawApp object

CMiniDrawApp theApp;

/////////////////////////////////////////////////////////////////////////
// CMiniDrawApp initialization

BOOL CMiniDrawApp::InitInstance()
{
    // Standard initialization
    // If you are not using these features and wish to reduce the size
    //  of your final executable, you should remove from the following
    //  the specific initialization routines you do not need.
```

```
#ifdef _AFXDLL
    Enable3dControls();        // Call this when using MFC in a shared DLL
#else
    Enable3dControlsStatic();  // Call this when linking to MFC statically
#endif

    // Change the registry key under which our settings are stored.
    // You should modify this string to be something appropriate
    // such as the name of your company or organization.
    SetRegistryKey(_T("Local AppWizard-Generated Applications"));

    LoadStdProfileSettings();  // Load standard INI file options (including MRU)

    // Register the application's document templates.  Document templates
    //  serve as the connection between documents, frame windows and views.

    CSingleDocTemplate* pDocTemplate;
    pDocTemplate = new CSingleDocTemplate(
        IDR_MAINFRAME,
        RUNTIME_CLASS(CMiniDrawDoc),
        RUNTIME_CLASS(CMainFrame),        // main SDI frame window
        RUNTIME_CLASS(CMiniDrawView));
    AddDocTemplate(pDocTemplate);

    EnableShellOpen ();
    RegisterShellFileTypes ();

    // Parse command line for standard shell commands, DDE, file open
    CCommandLineInfo cmdInfo;
    ParseCommandLine(cmdInfo);

    // Dispatch commands specified on the command line
    if (!ProcessShellCommand(cmdInfo))
        return FALSE;

    // The one and only window has been initialized, so show and update it.
    m_pMainWnd->ShowWindow(SW_SHOW);
    m_pMainWnd->UpdateWindow();

    m_pMainWnd->DragAcceptFiles ();

    return TRUE;
}
```

```
/////////////////////////////////////////////////////////////////////////
// CAboutDlg dialog used for App About

class CAboutDlg : public CDialog
{
public:
   CAboutDlg();

// Dialog Data
   //{{AFX_DATA(CAboutDlg)
   enum { IDD = IDD_ABOUTBOX };
   //}}AFX_DATA

   // ClassWizard generated virtual function overrides
   //{{AFX_VIRTUAL(CAboutDlg)
   protected:
   virtual void DoDataExchange(CDataExchange* pDX);    // DDX/DDV support
   //}}AFX_VIRTUAL

// Implementation
protected:
   //{{AFX_MSG(CAboutDlg)
      // No message handlers
   //}}AFX_MSG
   DECLARE_MESSAGE_MAP()
};

CAboutDlg::CAboutDlg() : CDialog(CAboutDlg::IDD)
{
   //{{AFX_DATA_INIT(CAboutDlg)
   //}}AFX_DATA_INIT
}

void CAboutDlg::DoDataExchange(CDataExchange* pDX)
{
   CDialog::DoDataExchange(pDX);
   //{{AFX_DATA_MAP(CAboutDlg)
   //}}AFX_DATA_MAP
}

BEGIN_MESSAGE_MAP(CAboutDlg, CDialog)
   //{{AFX_MSG_MAP(CAboutDlg)
      // No message handlers
```

```
    //}}AFX_MSG_MAP
END_MESSAGE_MAP()

// App command to run the dialog
void CMiniDrawApp::OnAppAbout()
{
    CAboutDlg aboutDlg;
    aboutDlg.DoModal();
}


/////////////////////////////////////////////////////////////////////////////
// CMiniDrawApp commands

void CMiniDrawApp::OnLineDouble()
{
    // TODO: Add your command handler code here
    m_CurrentThickness = 2;
}

void CMiniDrawApp::OnUpdateLineDouble(CCmdUI* pCmdUI)
{
    // TODO: Add your command update UI handler code here
    pCmdUI->SetCheck (m_CurrentThickness == 2 ? 1 : 0);
}

void CMiniDrawApp::OnLineSingle()
{
    // TODO: Add your command handler code here
    m_CurrentThickness = 1;
}

void CMiniDrawApp::OnUpdateLineSingle(CCmdUI* pCmdUI)
{
    // TODO: Add your command update UI handler code here
    pCmdUI->SetCheck (m_CurrentThickness == 1 ? 1 : 0);
}

void CMiniDrawApp::OnLineTriple()
{
    // TODO: Add your command handler code here
    m_CurrentThickness = 3;
}
```

```
void CMiniDrawApp::OnUpdateLineTriple(CCmdUI* pCmdUI)
{
    // TODO: Add your command update UI handler code here
    pCmdUI->SetCheck (m_CurrentThickness == 3 ? 1 : 0);
}

void CMiniDrawApp::OnToolsCircle()
{
    // TODO: Add your command handler code here
    m_CurrentTool = ID_TOOLS_CIRCLE;
}

void CMiniDrawApp::OnUpdateToolsCircle(CCmdUI* pCmdUI)
{
    // TODO: Add your command update UI handler code here
    pCmdUI->SetCheck (m_CurrentTool == ID_TOOLS_CIRCLE ? 1 : 0);
}

void CMiniDrawApp::OnToolsCirclefill()
{
    // TODO: Add your command handler code here
    m_CurrentTool = ID_TOOLS_CIRCLEFILL;
}

void CMiniDrawApp::OnUpdateToolsCirclefill(CCmdUI* pCmdUI)
{
    // TODO: Add your command update UI handler code here
    pCmdUI->SetCheck
        (m_CurrentTool == ID_TOOLS_CIRCLEFILL ? 1 : 0);
}

void CMiniDrawApp::OnToolsLine()
{
    // TODO: Add your command handler code here
    m_CurrentTool = ID_TOOLS_LINE;
}

void CMiniDrawApp::OnUpdateToolsLine(CCmdUI* pCmdUI)
{
    // TODO: Add your command update UI handler code here
    pCmdUI->SetCheck (m_CurrentTool == ID_TOOLS_LINE ? 1 : 0);
}
```

```
void CMiniDrawApp::OnToolsRectangle()
{
    // TODO: Add your command handler code here
    m_CurrentTool = ID_TOOLS_RECTANGLE;
}

void CMiniDrawApp::OnUpdateToolsRectangle(CCmdUI* pCmdUI)
{
    // TODO: Add your command update UI handler code here
    pCmdUI->SetCheck
        (m_CurrentTool == ID_TOOLS_RECTANGLE ? 1 : 0);
}

void CMiniDrawApp::OnToolsRectfill()
{
    // TODO: Add your command handler code here
    m_CurrentTool = ID_TOOLS_RECTFILL;
}

void CMiniDrawApp::OnUpdateToolsRectfill(CCmdUI* pCmdUI)
{
    // TODO: Add your command update UI handler code here
    pCmdUI->SetCheck (m_CurrentTool == ID_TOOLS_RECTFILL ? 1 : 0);
}

void CMiniDrawApp::OnToolsRectround()
{
    // TODO: Add your command handler code here
    m_CurrentTool = ID_TOOLS_RECTROUND;
}

void CMiniDrawApp::OnUpdateToolsRectround(CCmdUI* pCmdUI)
{
    // TODO: Add your command update UI handler code here
    pCmdUI->SetCheck
        (m_CurrentTool == ID_TOOLS_RECTROUND ? 1 : 0);
}

void CMiniDrawApp::OnToolsRectroundfill()
{
    // TODO: Add your command handler code here
    m_CurrentTool = ID_TOOLS_RECTROUNDFILL;
}
```

```
void CMiniDrawApp::OnUpdateToolsRectroundfill(CCmdUI* pCmdUI)
{
   // TODO: Add your command update UI handler code here
   pCmdUI->SetCheck
      (m_CurrentTool == ID_TOOLS_RECTROUNDFILL ? 1 : 0);
}

void CMiniDrawApp::OnColorBlack()
{
   // TODO: Add your command handler code here
   m_CurrentColor = RGB (0,0,0);
   m_IdxColorCmd = ID_COLOR_BLACK;
}

void CMiniDrawApp::OnUpdateColorBlack(CCmdUI* pCmdUI)
{
   // TODO: Add your command update UI handler code here
   pCmdUI->SetCheck (m_IdxColorCmd == ID_COLOR_BLACK ? 1 : 0);
}

void CMiniDrawApp::OnColorBlue()
{
   // TODO: Add your command handler code here
   m_CurrentColor = RGB (0,0,255);
   m_IdxColorCmd = ID_COLOR_BLUE;
}

void CMiniDrawApp::OnUpdateColorBlue(CCmdUI* pCmdUI)
{
   // TODO: Add your command update UI handler code here
   pCmdUI->SetCheck (m_IdxColorCmd == ID_COLOR_BLUE ? 1 : 0);
}

void CMiniDrawApp::OnColorCustom()
{
   // TODO: Add your command handler code here
   CColorDialog ColorDialog;

   if (ColorDialog.DoModal () == IDOK)
      {
      m_CurrentColor = ColorDialog.GetColor ();
      m_IdxColorCmd = ID_COLOR_CUSTOM;
      }
}
```

```
void CMiniDrawApp::OnUpdateColorCustom(CCmdUI* pCmdUI)
{
    // TODO: Add your command update UI handler code here
    pCmdUI->SetCheck (m_IdxColorCmd == ID_COLOR_CUSTOM ? 1 : 0);
}

void CMiniDrawApp::OnColorCyan()
{
    // TODO: Add your command handler code here
    m_CurrentColor = RGB (0,255,255);
    m_IdxColorCmd = ID_COLOR_CYAN;
}

void CMiniDrawApp::OnUpdateColorCyan(CCmdUI* pCmdUI)
{
    // TODO: Add your command update UI handler code here
    pCmdUI->SetCheck (m_IdxColorCmd == ID_COLOR_CYAN ? 1 : 0);
}

void CMiniDrawApp::OnColorGreen()
{
    // TODO: Add your command handler code here
    m_CurrentColor = RGB (0,255,0);
    m_IdxColorCmd = ID_COLOR_GREEN;
}

void CMiniDrawApp::OnUpdateColorGreen(CCmdUI* pCmdUI)
{
    // TODO: Add your command update UI handler code here
    pCmdUI->SetCheck (m_IdxColorCmd == ID_COLOR_GREEN ? 1 : 0);
}

void CMiniDrawApp::OnColorMagenta()
{
    // TODO: Add your command handler code here
    m_CurrentColor = RGB (255,0,255);
    m_IdxColorCmd = ID_COLOR_MAGENTA;
}

void CMiniDrawApp::OnUpdateColorMagenta(CCmdUI* pCmdUI)
{
    // TODO: Add your command update UI handler code here
    pCmdUI->SetCheck (m_IdxColorCmd == ID_COLOR_MAGENTA ? 1 : 0);
```

```
}

void CMiniDrawApp::OnColorRed()
{
    // TODO: Add your command handler code here
    m_CurrentColor = RGB (255,0,0);
    m_IdxColorCmd = ID_COLOR_RED;
}

void CMiniDrawApp::OnUpdateColorRed(CCmdUI* pCmdUI)
{
    // TODO: Add your command update UI handler code here
    pCmdUI->SetCheck (m_IdxColorCmd == ID_COLOR_RED ? 1 : 0);
}

void CMiniDrawApp::OnColorWhite()
{
    // TODO: Add your command handler code here
    m_CurrentColor = RGB (255,255,255);
    m_IdxColorCmd = ID_COLOR_WHITE;
}

void CMiniDrawApp::OnUpdateColorWhite(CCmdUI* pCmdUI)
{
    // TODO: Add your command update UI handler code here
    pCmdUI->SetCheck (m_IdxColorCmd == ID_COLOR_WHITE ? 1 : 0);
}

void CMiniDrawApp::OnColorYellow()
{
    // TODO: Add your command handler code here
    m_CurrentColor = RGB (255,255,0);
    m_IdxColorCmd = ID_COLOR_YELLOW;
}

void CMiniDrawApp::OnUpdateColorYellow(CCmdUI* pCmdUI)
{
    // TODO: Add your command update UI handler code here
    pCmdUI->SetCheck (m_IdxColorCmd == ID_COLOR_YELLOW ? 1 : 0);
}
```

Listing 19.11

```cpp
// MiniDrawDoc.h : interface of the CMiniDrawDoc class
//
/////////////////////////////////////////////////////////////////////

#if !defined(AFX_MINIDRAWDOC_H__11E8392A_999A_11D1_80FC_00C0F6A83B7F__INCLUDED_)
#define AFX_MINIDRAWDOC_H__11E8392A_999A_11D1_80FC_00C0F6A83B7F__INCLUDED_

#if _MSC_VER > 1000
#pragma once
#endif // _MSC_VER > 1000

// class hierarchy for figures:

class CFigure : public CObject
{
protected:
    COLORREF m_Color;
    DWORD m_X1, m_Y1, m_X2, m_Y2;

    CFigure () {}
    DECLARE_SERIAL (CFigure)

public:
    virtual void Draw (CDC *PDC) {}
    CRect GetDimRect ();
    virtual void Serialize (CArchive& ar);
};

class CLine : public CFigure
{
protected:
    DWORD m_Thickness;
    CLine () {}
    DECLARE_SERIAL (CLine)

public:
    CLine (int X1, int Y1, int X2, int Y2, COLORREF Color, int Thickness);
    virtual void Draw (CDC *PDC);
    virtual void Serialize (CArchive& ar);
```

```
};

class CRectangle : public CFigure
{
protected:
   DWORD m_Thickness;

   CRectangle () {}
   DECLARE_SERIAL (CRectangle)

public:
   CRectangle (int X1, int Y1, int X2, int Y2, COLORREF Color, int Thickness);
   virtual void Draw (CDC *PDC);
   virtual void Serialize (CArchive& ar);
};

class CRectFill : public CFigure
{
protected:
   CRectFill () {}
   DECLARE_SERIAL (CRectFill)

public:
   CRectFill (int X1, int Y1, int X2, int Y2, COLORREF Color);
   virtual void Draw (CDC *PDC);
};

class CRectRound : public CFigure
{
protected:
   DWORD m_Thickness;

   CRectRound () {}
   DECLARE_SERIAL (CRectRound)

public:
   CRectRound (int X1, int Y1, int X2, int Y2, COLORREF Color, int Thickness);
   virtual void Draw (CDC *PDC);
   virtual void Serialize (CArchive& ar);
};

class CRectRoundFill : public CFigure
```

```
{
protected:
   CRectRoundFill () {}
   DECLARE_SERIAL (CRectRoundFill)

public:
   CRectRoundFill (int X1, int Y1, int X2, int Y2, COLORREF Color);
   virtual void Draw (CDC *PDC);
};

class CCircle : public CFigure
{
protected:
   DWORD m_Thickness;

   CCircle () {}
   DECLARE_SERIAL (CCircle)

public:
   CCircle (int X1, int Y1, int X2, int Y2, COLORREF Color, int Thickness);
   virtual void Draw (CDC *PDC);
   virtual void Serialize (CArchive& ar);
};

class CCircleFill : public CFigure
{
protected:
   CCircleFill () {}
   DECLARE_SERIAL (CCircleFill)

public:
   CCircleFill (int X1, int Y1, int X2, int Y2, COLORREF Color);
   virtual void Draw (CDC *PDC);
};

class CMiniDrawDoc : public CDocument
{
protected:
   CTypedPtrArray<CObArray, CFigure*> m_FigArray;

public:
   void AddFigure (CFigure *PFigure);
```

```
    CFigure *GetFigure (int Index);
    int GetNumFigs ();

protected: // create from serialization only
    CMiniDrawDoc();
    DECLARE_DYNCREATE(CMiniDrawDoc)

// Attributes
public:

// Operations
public:

// Overrides
    // ClassWizard generated virtual function overrides
    //{{AFX_VIRTUAL(CMiniDrawDoc)
    public:
    virtual BOOL OnNewDocument();
    virtual void Serialize(CArchive& ar);
    virtual void DeleteContents();
    //}}AFX_VIRTUAL

// Implementation
public:
    virtual ~CMiniDrawDoc();
#ifdef _DEBUG
    virtual void AssertValid() const;
    virtual void Dump(CDumpContext& dc) const;
#endif

protected:

// Generated message map functions
protected:
    //{{AFX_MSG(CMiniDrawDoc)
    afx_msg void OnEditClearAll();
    afx_msg void OnUpdateEditClearAll(CCmdUI* pCmdUI);
    afx_msg void OnEditUndo();
    afx_msg void OnUpdateEditUndo(CCmdUI* pCmdUI);
    //}}AFX_MSG
    DECLARE_MESSAGE_MAP()
};
```

```
//////////////////////////////////////////////////////////////////////

//{{AFX_INSERT_LOCATION}}
// Microsoft Visual C++ will insert additional declarations immediately before
// the previous line.

#endif
// !defined(AFX_MINIDRAWDOC_H__11E8392A_999A_11D1_80FC_00C0F6A83B7F__INCLUDED_)
```

Listing 19.12

```cpp
// MiniDrawDoc.cpp : implementation of the CMiniDrawDoc class
//

#include "stdafx.h"
#include "MiniDraw.h"

#include "MiniDrawDoc.h"

#ifdef _DEBUG
#define new DEBUG_NEW
#undef THIS_FILE
static char THIS_FILE[] = __FILE__;
#endif

//////////////////////////////////////////////////////////////////////
// CMiniDrawDoc

IMPLEMENT_DYNCREATE(CMiniDrawDoc, CDocument)

BEGIN_MESSAGE_MAP(CMiniDrawDoc, CDocument)
    //{{AFX_MSG_MAP(CMiniDrawDoc)
    ON_COMMAND(ID_EDIT_CLEAR_ALL, OnEditClearAll)
    ON_UPDATE_COMMAND_UI(ID_EDIT_CLEAR_ALL, OnUpdateEditClearAll)
    ON_COMMAND(ID_EDIT_UNDO, OnEditUndo)
    ON_UPDATE_COMMAND_UI(ID_EDIT_UNDO, OnUpdateEditUndo)
    //}}AFX_MSG_MAP
END_MESSAGE_MAP()

//////////////////////////////////////////////////////////////////////
// CMiniDrawDoc construction/destruction
```

```
CMiniDrawDoc::CMiniDrawDoc()
{
   // TODO: add one-time construction code here

}

CMiniDrawDoc::~CMiniDrawDoc()
{
}

BOOL CMiniDrawDoc::OnNewDocument()
{
   if (!CDocument::OnNewDocument())
      return FALSE;

   // TODO: add reinitialization code here
   // (SDI documents will reuse this document)

   return TRUE;
}




/////////////////////////////////////////////////////////////////////
// CMiniDrawDoc serialization

void CMiniDrawDoc::Serialize(CArchive& ar)
{
   if (ar.IsStoring())
   {
      // TODO: add storing code here
      m_FigArray.Serialize (ar);
   }
   else
   {
      // TODO: add loading code here
      m_FigArray.Serialize (ar);
   }
}

/////////////////////////////////////////////////////////////////////
// CMiniDrawDoc diagnostics
```

```
#ifdef _DEBUG
void CMiniDrawDoc::AssertValid() const
{
    CDocument::AssertValid();
}

void CMiniDrawDoc::Dump(CDumpContext& dc) const
{
    CDocument::Dump(dc);
}
#endif //_DEBUG

/////////////////////////////////////////////////////////////////////////////
// CMiniDrawDoc commands

void CMiniDrawDoc::AddFigure (CFigure *PFigure)
    {
    m_FigArray.Add (PFigure);
    SetModifiedFlag ();
    }

CFigure *CMiniDrawDoc::GetFigure (int Index)
    {
    if (Index < 0 || Index > m_FigArray.GetUpperBound ())
        return 0;
    return (CFigure *)m_FigArray.GetAt (Index);
    }

int CMiniDrawDoc::GetNumFigs ()
    {
    return m_FigArray.GetSize ();
    }

void CMiniDrawDoc::DeleteContents()
{
    // TODO: Add your specialized code here and/or call the base class

    int Index = m_FigArray.GetSize ();
    while (Index--)
        delete m_FigArray.GetAt (Index);
    m_FigArray.RemoveAll ();

    CDocument::DeleteContents();
```

```
}

void CMiniDrawDoc::OnEditClearAll()
{
   // TODO: Add your command handler code here

   DeleteContents ();
   UpdateAllViews (0);
   SetModifiedFlag ();
}

void CMiniDrawDoc::OnUpdateEditClearAll(CCmdUI* pCmdUI)
{
   // TODO: Add your command update UI handler code here

   pCmdUI->Enable (m_FigArray.GetSize ());
}

void CMiniDrawDoc::OnEditUndo()
{
   // TODO: Add your command handler code here

   int Index = m_FigArray.GetUpperBound ();
   if (Index > -1)
      {
      delete m_FigArray.GetAt (Index);
      m_FigArray.RemoveAt (Index);
      }
   UpdateAllViews (0);
   SetModifiedFlag ();
}

void CMiniDrawDoc::OnUpdateEditUndo(CCmdUI* pCmdUI)
{
   // TODO: Add your command update UI handler code here

   pCmdUI->Enable (m_FigArray.GetSize ());
}

// implementation of figure classes:

IMPLEMENT_SERIAL (CFigure, CObject, 2)

CRect CFigure::GetDimRect ()
```

```
    {
    return CRect
      (min (m_X1, m_X2),
       min (m_Y1, m_Y2),
       max (m_X1, m_X2) + 1,
       max (m_Y1, m_Y2) + 1);
    }

void CFigure::Serialize (CArchive& ar)
    {
    if (ar.IsStoring ())
        ar << m_X1 << m_Y1 << m_X2 << m_Y2 << m_Color;
    else
        ar >> m_X1 >> m_Y1 >> m_X2 >> m_Y2 >> m_Color;
    }

IMPLEMENT_SERIAL (CLine, CFigure, 2)

CLine::CLine (int X1, int Y1, int X2, int Y2, COLORREF Color, int Thickness)
    {
    m_X1 = X1;
    m_Y1 = Y1;
    m_X2 = X2;
    m_Y2 = Y2;
    m_Color = Color;
    m_Thickness = Thickness;
    }

void CLine::Serialize (CArchive& ar)
    {
    CFigure::Serialize (ar);
    if (ar.IsStoring ())
        ar << m_Thickness;
    else
        ar >> m_Thickness;
    }

void CLine::Draw (CDC *PDC)
    {
    CPen Pen, *POldPen;

    // select pen/brush:
    Pen.CreatePen (PS_SOLID, m_Thickness, m_Color);
    POldPen = PDC->SelectObject (&Pen);
```

```
    // draw figure:
    PDC->MoveTo (m_X1, m_Y1);
    PDC->LineTo (m_X2, m_Y2);

    // remove pen/brush:
    PDC->SelectObject (POldPen);
    }

IMPLEMENT_SERIAL (CRectangle, CFigure, 2)

CRectangle::CRectangle (int X1, int Y1, int X2, int Y2,
    COLORREF Color, int Thickness)
    {
    m_X1 = X1;
    m_Y1 = Y1;
    m_X2 = X2;
    m_Y2 = Y2;
    m_Color = Color;
    m_Thickness = Thickness;
    }

void CRectangle::Serialize (CArchive& ar)
    {
    CFigure::Serialize (ar);
    if (ar.IsStoring ())
        ar << m_Thickness;
    else
        ar >> m_Thickness;
    }

void CRectangle::Draw (CDC *PDC)
    {
    CPen Pen, *POldPen;

    // select pen/brush:
    Pen.CreatePen (PS_INSIDEFRAME, m_Thickness, m_Color);
    POldPen = PDC->SelectObject (&Pen);
    PDC->SelectStockObject (NULL_BRUSH);

    // draw figure:
    PDC->Rectangle (m_X1, m_Y1, m_X2, m_Y2);
```

```
    // remove pen/brush:
    PDC->SelectObject (POldPen);
    }

IMPLEMENT_SERIAL (CRectFill, CFigure, 2)

CRectFill::CRectFill (int X1, int Y1, int X2, int Y2, COLORREF Color)
    {
    m_X1 = min (X1, X2);
    m_Y1 = min (Y1, Y2);
    m_X2 = max (X1, X2);
    m_Y2 = max (Y1, Y2);
    m_Color = Color;
    }

void CRectFill::Draw (CDC *PDC)
    {
    CBrush Brush, *POldBrush;
    CPen Pen, *POldPen;

    // select pen/brush:
    Pen.CreatePen (PS_INSIDEFRAME, 1, m_Color);
    POldPen = PDC->SelectObject (&Pen);
    Brush.CreateSolidBrush (m_Color);
    POldBrush = PDC->SelectObject (&Brush);

    // draw figure:
    PDC->Rectangle (m_X1, m_Y1, m_X2, m_Y2);

    // remove pen/brush:
    PDC->SelectObject (POldPen);
    PDC->SelectObject (POldBrush);
    }

IMPLEMENT_SERIAL (CRectRound, CFigure, 2)

CRectRound::CRectRound (int X1, int Y1, int X2, int Y2,
    COLORREF Color, int Thickness)
    {
    m_X1 = min (X1, X2);
    m_Y1 = min (Y1, Y2);
    m_X2 = max (X1, X2);
    m_Y2 = max (Y1, Y2);
```

```
    m_Color = Color;
    m_Thickness = Thickness;
    }

void CRectRound::Serialize (CArchive& ar)
    {
    CFigure::Serialize (ar);
    if (ar.IsStoring ())
        ar << m_Thickness;
    else
        ar >> m_Thickness;
    }

void CRectRound::Draw (CDC *PDC)
    {
    CPen Pen, *POldPen;

    // select pen/brush:
    Pen.CreatePen (PS_INSIDEFRAME, m_Thickness, m_Color);
    POldPen = PDC->SelectObject (&Pen);
    PDC->SelectStockObject (NULL_BRUSH);

    // draw figure:
    int SizeRound = (m_X2 - m_X1 + m_Y2 - m_Y1) / 6;
    PDC->RoundRect (m_X1, m_Y1, m_X2, m_Y2, SizeRound, SizeRound);

    // remove pen/brush:
    PDC->SelectObject (POldPen);
    }

IMPLEMENT_SERIAL (CRectRoundFill, CFigure, 2)

CRectRoundFill::CRectRoundFill (int X1, int Y1, int X2, int Y2, COLORREF Color)
    {
    m_X1 = min (X1, X2);
    m_Y1 = min (Y1, Y2);
    m_X2 = max (X1, X2);
    m_Y2 = max (Y1, Y2);
    m_Color = Color;
    }

void CRectRoundFill::Draw (CDC *PDC)
    {
```

```
   CBrush Brush, *POldBrush;
   CPen Pen, *POldPen;

   // select pen/brush:
   Pen.CreatePen (PS_INSIDEFRAME, 1, m_Color);
   POldPen = PDC->SelectObject (&Pen);
   Brush.CreateSolidBrush (m_Color);
   POldBrush = PDC->SelectObject (&Brush);

   // draw figure:
   int SizeRound = (m_X2 - m_X1 + m_Y2 - m_Y1) / 6;
   PDC->RoundRect (m_X1, m_Y1, m_X2, m_Y2, SizeRound, SizeRound);

   // remove pen/brush:
   PDC->SelectObject (POldPen);
   PDC->SelectObject (POldBrush);
   }

IMPLEMENT_SERIAL (CCircle, CFigure, 2)

CCircle::CCircle (int X1, int Y1, int X2, int Y2,
   COLORREF Color, int Thickness)
   {
   m_X1 = min (X1, X2);
   m_Y1 = min (Y1, Y2);
   m_X2 = max (X1, X2);
   m_Y2 = max (Y1, Y2);
   m_Color = Color;
   m_Thickness = Thickness;
   }

void CCircle::Serialize (CArchive& ar)
   {
   CFigure::Serialize (ar);
   if (ar.IsStoring ())
      ar << m_Thickness;
   else
      ar >> m_Thickness;
   }

void CCircle::Draw (CDC *PDC)
   {
   CPen Pen, *POldPen;
```

```
    // select pen/brush:
    Pen.CreatePen (PS_INSIDEFRAME, m_Thickness, m_Color);
    POldPen = PDC->SelectObject (&Pen);
    PDC->SelectStockObject (NULL_BRUSH);

    // draw figure:
    PDC->Ellipse (m_X1, m_Y1, m_X2, m_Y2);

    // remove pen/brush:
    PDC->SelectObject (POldPen);
    }

IMPLEMENT_SERIAL (CCircleFill, CFigure, 2)

CCircleFill::CCircleFill (int X1, int Y1, int X2, int Y2, COLORREF Color)
    {
    m_X1 = min (X1, X2);
    m_Y1 = min (Y1, Y2);
    m_X2 = max (X1, X2);
    m_Y2 = max (Y1, Y2);
    m_Color = Color;
    }

void CCircleFill::Draw (CDC *PDC)
    {
    CBrush Brush, *POldBrush;
    CPen Pen, *POldPen;

    // select pen/brush:
    Pen.CreatePen (PS_INSIDEFRAME, 1, m_Color);
    POldPen = PDC->SelectObject (&Pen);
    Brush.CreateSolidBrush (m_Color);
    POldBrush = PDC->SelectObject (&Brush);

    // draw figure:
    PDC->Ellipse (m_X1, m_Y1, m_X2, m_Y2);

    // remove pen/brush:
    PDC->SelectObject (POldPen);
    PDC->SelectObject (POldBrush);
    }
```

Listing 19.13

```
// MainFrm.h : interface of the CMainFrame class
//
/////////////////////////////////////////////////////////////////////

#if !defined(AFX_MAINFRM_H__11E83928_999A_11D1_80FC_00C0F6A83B7F__INCLUDED_)
#define AFX_MAINFRM_H__11E83928_999A_11D1_80FC_00C0F6A83B7F__INCLUDED_

#if _MSC_VER > 1000
#pragma once
#endif // _MSC_VER > 1000

class CMainFrame : public CFrameWnd
{
protected:
    CSplitterWnd m_SplitterWnd;
    CStatusBar m_StatusBar;
    CToolBar m_ToolBar;

protected: // create from serialization only
    CMainFrame();
    DECLARE_DYNCREATE(CMainFrame)

// Attributes
public:

// Operations
public:

// Overrides
    // ClassWizard generated virtual function overrides
    //{{AFX_VIRTUAL(CMainFrame)
    public:
    virtual BOOL PreCreateWindow(CREATESTRUCT& cs);
    protected:
    virtual BOOL OnCreateClient(LPCREATESTRUCT lpcs, CCreateContext* pContext);
    //}}AFX_VIRTUAL

// Implementation
public:
    virtual ~CMainFrame();
```

```
#ifdef _DEBUG
   virtual void AssertValid() const;
   virtual void Dump(CDumpContext& dc) const;
#endif

// Generated message map functions
protected:
   //{{AFX_MSG(CMainFrame)
   afx_msg int OnCreate(LPCREATESTRUCT lpCreateStruct);
   //}}AFX_MSG
   DECLARE_MESSAGE_MAP()
};

/////////////////////////////////////////////////////////////////////////////

//{{AFX_INSERT_LOCATION}}
// Microsoft Visual C++ will insert additional declarations immediately before
// the previous line.

#endif
// !defined(AFX_MAINFRM_H__11E83928_999A_11D1_80FC_00C0F6A83B7F__INCLUDED_)
```

Listing 19.14

```
// MainFrm.cpp : implementation of the CMainFrame class
//

#include "stdafx.h"
#include "MiniDraw.h"

#include "MainFrm.h"

#ifdef _DEBUG
#define new DEBUG_NEW
#undef THIS_FILE
static char THIS_FILE[] = __FILE__;
#endif

/////////////////////////////////////////////////////////////////////////////
// CMainFrame

IMPLEMENT_DYNCREATE(CMainFrame, CFrameWnd)
```

```
BEGIN_MESSAGE_MAP(CMainFrame, CFrameWnd)
    //{{AFX_MSG_MAP(CMainFrame)
    ON_WM_CREATE()
    //}}AFX_MSG_MAP
END_MESSAGE_MAP()

// IDs for status bar indicators:
static UINT IndicatorIDs [] =
    {
    ID_SEPARATOR,
    ID_INDICATOR_CAPS,
    ID_INDICATOR_NUM,
    ID_INDICATOR_SCRL,
    };

/////////////////////////////////////////////////////////////////////////////
// CMainFrame construction/destruction

CMainFrame::CMainFrame()
{
    // TODO: add member initialization code here

}

CMainFrame::~CMainFrame()
{
}

BOOL CMainFrame::PreCreateWindow(CREATESTRUCT& cs)
{
    if( !CFrameWnd::PreCreateWindow(cs) )
        return FALSE;
    // TODO: Modify the Window class or styles here by modifying
    //   the CREATESTRUCT cs

    return TRUE;
}

/////////////////////////////////////////////////////////////////////////////
// CMainFrame diagnostics

#ifdef _DEBUG
```

```
void CMainFrame::AssertValid() const
{
    CFrameWnd::AssertValid();
}

void CMainFrame::Dump(CDumpContext& dc) const
{
    CFrameWnd::Dump(dc);
}

#endif //_DEBUG

/////////////////////////////////////////////////////////////////////////
// CMainFrame message handlers


BOOL CMainFrame::OnCreateClient(LPCREATESTRUCT lpcs, CCreateContext* pContext)
{
    // TODO: Add your specialized code here and/or call the base class

    return m_SplitterWnd.Create
        (this,              // parent of splitter window
        1,                  // maximum rows
        2,                  // maximum columns
        CSize (15, 15),     // minimum view window size
        pContext);          // pass on context information
}

int CMainFrame::OnCreate(LPCREATESTRUCT lpCreateStruct)
{
    if (CFrameWnd::OnCreate(lpCreateStruct) == -1)
        return -1;

    // TODO: Add your specialized creation code here

    if (!m_ToolBar.CreateEx
        (this,
        TBSTYLE_FLAT,
        WS_CHILD | WS_VISIBLE | CBRS_TOP | CBRS_GRIPPER
        | CBRS_TOOLTIPS | CBRS_FLYBY | CBRS_SIZE_DYNAMIC))
        return -1;

    if (!m_ToolBar.LoadToolBar(IDR_MAINFRAME))
        return -1;
```

```
    m_ToolBar.EnableDocking (CBRS_ALIGN_ANY);
    EnableDocking (CBRS_ALIGN_ANY);
    DockControlBar (&m_ToolBar);

    if (!m_StatusBar.Create (this) ||
        !m_StatusBar.SetIndicators (IndicatorIDs,
        sizeof (IndicatorIDs) / sizeof (UINT)))
        return -1;

    return 0;
}
```

Listing 19.15

```cpp
// MiniDrawView.h : interface of the CMiniDrawView class
//
/////////////////////////////////////////////////////////////////////////////

#if !defined(AFX_MINIDRAWVIEW_H__11E8392C_999A_11D1_80FC_00C0F6A83B7F__INCLUDED_)
#define AFX_MINIDRAWVIEW_H__11E8392C_999A_11D1_80FC_00C0F6A83B7F__INCLUDED_

#if _MSC_VER > 1000
#pragma once
#endif // _MSC_VER > 1000

class CMiniDrawView : public CScrollView
{
protected:
    CString m_ClassName;
    int m_Dragging;
    HCURSOR m_HArrow;
    HCURSOR m_HCross;
    CPen m_PenDotted;
    CPoint m_PointOld;
    CPoint m_PointOrigin;

protected: // create from serialization only
    CMiniDrawView();
    DECLARE_DYNCREATE(CMiniDrawView)

// Attributes
```

```
public:
    CMiniDrawDoc* GetDocument();

// Operations
public:

// Overrides
    // ClassWizard generated virtual function overrides
    //{{AFX_VIRTUAL(CMiniDrawView)
    public:
    virtual void OnDraw(CDC* pDC);   // overridden to draw this view
    virtual BOOL PreCreateWindow(CREATESTRUCT& cs);
    virtual void OnInitialUpdate();
    protected:
    virtual void OnUpdate(CView* pSender, LPARAM lHint, CObject* pHint);
    //}}AFX_VIRTUAL

// Implementation
public:
    virtual ~CMiniDrawView();
#ifdef _DEBUG
    virtual void AssertValid() const;
    virtual void Dump(CDumpContext& dc) const;
#endif

protected:

// Generated message map functions
protected:
    //{{AFX_MSG(CMiniDrawView)
    afx_msg void OnLButtonDown(UINT nFlags, CPoint point);
    afx_msg void OnMouseMove(UINT nFlags, CPoint point);
    afx_msg void OnLButtonUp(UINT nFlags, CPoint point);
    //}}AFX_MSG
    DECLARE_MESSAGE_MAP()
};

#ifndef _DEBUG  // debug version in MiniDrawView.cpp
inline CMiniDrawDoc* CMiniDrawView::GetDocument()
    { return (CMiniDrawDoc*)m_pDocument; }
#endif

/////////////////////////////////////////////////////////////////////////
```

```
//{{AFX_INSERT_LOCATION}}
// Microsoft Visual C++ will insert additional declarations immediately before
// the previous line.

#endif
// !defined(AFX_MINIDRAWVIEW_H__11E8392C_999A_11D1_80FC_00C0F6A83B7F__INCLUDED_)
```

Listing 19.16

```cpp
// MiniDrawView.cpp : implementation of the CMiniDrawView class
//

#include "stdafx.h"
#include "MiniDraw.h"

#include "MiniDrawDoc.h"
#include "MiniDrawView.h"

#ifdef _DEBUG
#define new DEBUG_NEW
#undef THIS_FILE
static char THIS_FILE[] = __FILE__;
#endif


/////////////////////////////////////////////////////////////////////////////
// CMiniDrawView

IMPLEMENT_DYNCREATE(CMiniDrawView, CScrollView)

BEGIN_MESSAGE_MAP(CMiniDrawView, CScrollView)
	//{{AFX_MSG_MAP(CMiniDrawView)
	ON_WM_LBUTTONDOWN()
	ON_WM_MOUSEMOVE()
	ON_WM_LBUTTONUP()
	//}}AFX_MSG_MAP
END_MESSAGE_MAP()

/////////////////////////////////////////////////////////////////////////////
// CMiniDrawView construction/destruction

CMiniDrawView::CMiniDrawView()
```

```
{
    // TODO: add construction code here

    m_Dragging = 0;
    m_HArrow = AfxGetApp ()->LoadStandardCursor (IDC_ARROW);
    m_HCross = AfxGetApp ()->LoadStandardCursor (IDC_CROSS);
    m_PenDotted.CreatePen (PS_DOT, 1, RGB (0,0,0));
}

CMiniDrawView::~CMiniDrawView()
{
}

BOOL CMiniDrawView::PreCreateWindow(CREATESTRUCT& cs)
{
    // TODO: Modify the Window class or styles here by modifying
    //  the CREATESTRUCT cs

    m_ClassName = AfxRegisterWndClass
        (CS_HREDRAW | CS_VREDRAW,              // class styles
        0,                                     // no cursor
        (HBRUSH)::GetStockObject (WHITE_BRUSH), // assign white
                                               // background brush
        0);                                    // no icon
    cs.lpszClass = m_ClassName;

    return CScrollView::PreCreateWindow(cs);
}

/////////////////////////////////////////////////////////////////////
// CMiniDrawView drawing

void CMiniDrawView::OnDraw(CDC* pDC)
{
    CMiniDrawDoc* pDoc = GetDocument();
    ASSERT_VALID(pDoc);

    // TODO: add draw code for native data here

    CSize ScrollSize = GetTotalSize ();
    pDC->MoveTo (ScrollSize.cx, 0);
    pDC->LineTo (ScrollSize.cx, ScrollSize.cy);
    pDC->LineTo (0, ScrollSize.cy);
```

```
   CRect ClipRect;
   CRect DimRect;
   CRect IntRect;
   CFigure *PFigure;

   pDC->GetClipBox (&ClipRect);

   int NumFigs = pDoc->GetNumFigs ();
   for (int Index = 0; Index < NumFigs; ++Index)
      {
      PFigure = pDoc->GetFigure (Index);
      DimRect = PFigure->GetDimRect ();
      if (IntRect.IntersectRect (DimRect, ClipRect))
         PFigure->Draw (pDC);
      }
}

/////////////////////////////////////////////////////////////////////////
// CMiniDrawView diagnostics

#ifdef _DEBUG
void CMiniDrawView::AssertValid() const
{
   CScrollView::AssertValid();
}

void CMiniDrawView::Dump(CDumpContext& dc) const
{
   CScrollView::Dump(dc);
}

CMiniDrawDoc* CMiniDrawView::GetDocument() // non-debug version is inline
{
   ASSERT(m_pDocument->IsKindOf(RUNTIME_CLASS(CMiniDrawDoc)));
   return (CMiniDrawDoc*)m_pDocument;
}
#endif //_DEBUG

/////////////////////////////////////////////////////////////////////////
// CMiniDrawView message handlers

void CMiniDrawView::OnLButtonDown(UINT nFlags, CPoint point)
{
```

```
   // TODO: Add your message handler code here and/or call default

   CClientDC ClientDC (this);
   OnPrepareDC (&ClientDC);
   ClientDC.DPtoLP (&point);

   // test whether cursor is within drawing area of view window:
   CSize ScrollSize = GetTotalSize ();
   CRect ScrollRect (0, 0, ScrollSize.cx, ScrollSize.cy);
   if (!ScrollRect.PtInRect (point))
      return;

   // save cursor position, capture mouse, and set dragging flag:
   m_PointOrigin = point;
   m_PointOld = point;
   SetCapture ();
   m_Dragging = 1;

   // clip mouse cursor:
   ClientDC.LPtoDP (&ScrollRect);
   CRect ViewRect;
   GetClientRect (&ViewRect);
   CRect IntRect;
   IntRect.IntersectRect (&ScrollRect, &ViewRect);
   ClientToScreen (&IntRect);
   ::ClipCursor (&IntRect);

   CScrollView::OnLButtonDown(nFlags, point);
}

void CMiniDrawView::OnMouseMove(UINT nFlags, CPoint point)
{
   // TODO: Add your message handler code here and/or call default

   CClientDC ClientDC (this);
   OnPrepareDC (&ClientDC);
   ClientDC.DPtoLP (&point);

   if (!m_Dragging)
      {
      CSize ScrollSize = GetTotalSize ();
      CRect ScrollRect (0, 0, ScrollSize.cx, ScrollSize.cy);
      if (ScrollRect.PtInRect (point))
```

```
      ::SetCursor (m_HCross);
   else
      ::SetCursor (m_HArrow);
   return;
   }

ClientDC.SetROP2 (R2_NOT);
ClientDC.SelectObject (&m_PenDotted);
ClientDC.SetBkMode (TRANSPARENT);
ClientDC.SelectStockObject (NULL_BRUSH);

switch ((((CMiniDrawApp *)AfxGetApp ())->m_CurrentTool)
   {
   case ID_TOOLS_LINE:
      ClientDC.MoveTo (m_PointOrigin);
      ClientDC.LineTo (m_PointOld);
      ClientDC.MoveTo (m_PointOrigin);
      ClientDC.LineTo (point);
      break;

   case ID_TOOLS_RECTANGLE:
   case ID_TOOLS_RECTFILL:
      ClientDC.Rectangle (m_PointOrigin.x, m_PointOrigin.y,
                          m_PointOld.x, m_PointOld.y);
      ClientDC.Rectangle (m_PointOrigin.x, m_PointOrigin.y,
                          point.x, point.y);
      break;

   case ID_TOOLS_RECTROUND:
   case ID_TOOLS_RECTROUNDFILL:
      {
      int SizeRound = (abs (m_PointOld.x - m_PointOrigin.x) +
                       abs (m_PointOld.y - m_PointOrigin.y)) / 6;
      ClientDC.RoundRect (m_PointOrigin.x, m_PointOrigin.y,
                          m_PointOld.x, m_PointOld.y,
      SizeRound, SizeRound);
      SizeRound = (abs (point.x - m_PointOrigin.x) +
                   abs (point.y - m_PointOrigin.y)) / 6;
      ClientDC.RoundRect (m_PointOrigin.x, m_PointOrigin.y,
                          point.x, point.y,
                          SizeRound, SizeRound);
      break;
      }
```

```
      case ID_TOOLS_CIRCLE:
      case ID_TOOLS_CIRCLEFILL:
         ClientDC.Ellipse (m_PointOrigin.x, m_PointOrigin.y,
                           m_PointOld.x, m_PointOld.y);
         ClientDC.Ellipse (m_PointOrigin.x, m_PointOrigin.y,
                           point.x, point.y);
         break;
      }

   m_PointOld = point;

   CScrollView::OnMouseMove(nFlags, point);
}

void CMiniDrawView::OnLButtonUp(UINT nFlags, CPoint point)
{
   // TODO: Add your message handler code here and/or call default

   if (!m_Dragging)
      return;

   m_Dragging = 0;
   ::ReleaseCapture ();
   ::ClipCursor (NULL);

   CClientDC ClientDC (this);
   OnPrepareDC (&ClientDC);
   ClientDC.DPtoLP (&point);
   ClientDC.SetROP2 (R2_NOT);
   ClientDC.SelectObject (&m_PenDotted);
   ClientDC.SetBkMode (TRANSPARENT);
   ClientDC.SelectStockObject (NULL_BRUSH);

   CMiniDrawApp *PApp = (CMiniDrawApp *)AfxGetApp ();
   CFigure *PFigure;

   switch (PApp->m_CurrentTool)
      {
      case ID_TOOLS_LINE:
         ClientDC.MoveTo (m_PointOrigin);
         ClientDC.LineTo (m_PointOld);
         PFigure = new CLine
            (m_PointOrigin.x, m_PointOrigin.y,
```

```
                    point.x, point.y,
                    PApp->m_CurrentColor,
                    PApp->m_CurrentThickness);
            break;

case ID_TOOLS_RECTANGLE:
    ClientDC.Rectangle (m_PointOrigin.x, m_PointOrigin.y,
                        m_PointOld.x, m_PointOld.y);
    PFigure = new CRectangle
        (m_PointOrigin.x, m_PointOrigin.y,
        point.x, point.y,
        PApp->m_CurrentColor,
        PApp->m_CurrentThickness);
    break;

case ID_TOOLS_RECTFILL:
    ClientDC.Rectangle (m_PointOrigin.x, m_PointOrigin.y,
                        m_PointOld.x, m_PointOld.y);
    PFigure = new CRectFill
        (m_PointOrigin.x, m_PointOrigin.y,
        point.x, point.y,
        PApp->m_CurrentColor);
    break;

case ID_TOOLS_RECTROUND:
    {
    int SizeRound = (abs (m_PointOld.x - m_PointOrigin.x) +
        abs (m_PointOld.y - m_PointOrigin.y)) / 6;
    ClientDC.RoundRect (m_PointOrigin.x, m_PointOrigin.y,
                        m_PointOld.x, m_PointOld.y,
                        SizeRound, SizeRound);
    PFigure = new CRectRound
        (m_PointOrigin.x, m_PointOrigin.y,
        point.x, point.y,
        PApp->m_CurrentColor,
        PApp->m_CurrentThickness);
    break;
    }

case ID_TOOLS_RECTROUNDFILL:
    {
    int SizeRound = (abs (m_PointOld.x - m_PointOrigin.x) +
                    abs (m_PointOld.y - m_PointOrigin.y)) / 6;
```

```
        ClientDC.RoundRect (m_PointOrigin.x, m_PointOrigin.y,
                            m_PointOld.x, m_PointOld.y,
        SizeRound, SizeRound);
        PFigure = new CRectRoundFill
            (m_PointOrigin.x, m_PointOrigin.y,
            point.x, point.y,
            PApp->m_CurrentColor);
        break;
        }

    case ID_TOOLS_CIRCLE:
        ClientDC.Ellipse (m_PointOrigin.x, m_PointOrigin.y,
                          m_PointOld.x, m_PointOld.y);
        PFigure = new CCircle
            (m_PointOrigin.x, m_PointOrigin.y,
            point.x, point.y,
            PApp->m_CurrentColor,
            PApp->m_CurrentThickness);
        break;

    case ID_TOOLS_CIRCLEFILL:
        ClientDC.Ellipse (m_PointOrigin.x, m_PointOrigin.y,
                          m_PointOld.x, m_PointOld.y);
        PFigure = new CCircleFill
            (m_PointOrigin.x, m_PointOrigin.y,
            point.x, point.y,
            PApp->m_CurrentColor);
        break;
        }

    ClientDC.SetROP2 (R2_COPYPEN);
    PFigure->Draw (&ClientDC);

    CMiniDrawDoc* PDoc = GetDocument();
    PDoc->AddFigure (PFigure);

    PDoc->UpdateAllViews (this, 0, PFigure);

    CScrollView::OnLButtonUp(nFlags, point);
}

void CMiniDrawView::OnInitialUpdate()
{
```

```
    CScrollView::OnInitialUpdate();

    // TODO: Add your specialized code here and/or call the base class

    SIZE Size = {640, 480};
    SetScrollSizes (MM_TEXT, Size);
}

void CMiniDrawView::OnUpdate(CView* pSender, LPARAM lHint, CObject* pHint)
{
    // TODO: Add your specialized code here and/or call the base class

    if (pHint != 0)
        {
        CRect InvalidRect = ((CLine *)pHint)->GetDimRect ();
        CClientDC ClientDC (this);
        OnPrepareDC (&ClientDC);
        ClientDC.LPtoDP (&InvalidRect);
        InvalidateRect (&InvalidRect);
        }
    else
        CScrollView::OnUpdate (pSender, lHint, pHint);
}
```

Summary

In this chapter you learned how to draw figures by using member functions of the CDC class. The following is a brief summary of the main steps for drawing graphics:

- First, create a device context object. If you're drawing from an OnDraw member function of the view class, you can simply use the device context object that's passed to the function. If you're drawing from an OnPaint message handler for a nonview window, you must create an instance of the CPaintDC class. If you're drawing from any other type of function, you must create an instance of the CClientDC class and—if you're drawing in a view window that supports scrolling—pass the object to the CScrollView::OnPrepareDC function before using it.

- Next, select a pen for drawing lines and the borders of closed figures, and select a brush for filling the interiors of closed figures.

- You can select a stock pen or brush by calling `CDC::SelectStockObject`.

- You can select a custom pen or brush by creating a `CPen` or `CBrush` object, calling the appropriate member function to initialize the pen or brush, and then calling `CDC::SelectObject` to select the pen or brush into the device context object. Save the handle of the previously selected object, which is returned by `SelectObject`.

- Then, use the `CDC` member functions listed in Table 19.4 to set any desired drawing attributes, such as the mapping mode that determines the units and the directions of positive coordinate values used to draw graphics.

- Draw the graphics by calling member functions of the `CDC` class. This class provides functions for coloring individual pixels, for drawing straight or curved lines, and for drawing closed figures such as rectangles and ellipses.

- If you created and selected a custom pen or brush, remove it from the device context object by calling `SelectObject` to select the previous pen or brush object.

In the next chapter, you'll learn how to create graphics by using bitmaps, as well as how to use bit operations to quickly transfer or modify blocks of graphic data.

CHAPTER

TWENTY

Using Bitmaps
and Bit Operations

- Creating a bitmap

- Performing bit operations

- Displaying icons

- The BitDemo program

A Windows *bitmap* is a data structure that stores an exact representation of a graphic image in memory or in a file. A bitmap stores the color of every pixel required to generate the image on a specific device, such as a monitor or printer. Bitmaps allow you to store, manipulate, and display detailed graphic images in your programs. In this chapter, you'll learn how to create bitmaps and how to display them on devices. You'll also learn how to take advantage of the versatile and efficient bit-operation functions that Windows provides for transferring and modifying blocks of graphic data. At the end of the chapter you'll create an example program named BitDemo, which demonstrates the techniques for displaying a bitmap in a view window.

Creating a Bitmap

Creating a bitmap allows you to display a graphic image on the screen or on a device such as a printer; to provide a custom image for a push button, menu command, or other interface element; and to work with graphics in other ways.

The MFC provides a class, CBitmap, for managing bitmaps. The first step in creating a bitmap, therefore, is to declare an instance of this class, as in the following example:

```
CBitmap m_Bitmap;
```

A bitmap object is typically declared as a data member of one of the main program classes, such as the view class.

Once you've declared a CBitmap object, you must call an appropriate CBitmap member function to initialize the object. In this chapter, you'll learn how to initialize a CBitmap object either by calling the LoadBitmap member function to load the bitmap data from a program resource, or by calling the CreateCompatible-Bitmap member function to produce a blank bitmap in which you can draw the desired image at program runtime.

NOTE   In addition to the two methods described in this chapter, Windows provides several other ways to initialize a bitmap object. For example, you can call the `CBitmap::LoadOEMBitmap` function to load a predefined bitmap supplied by Windows, you can call `CBitmap::CreateBitmap` to create a bitmap conforming to a specific structure, or you can call `CGdiObject::Attach` to initialize a bitmap object using a Windows bitmap handle (`CGdiObject` is the base class of `CBitmap`). For general information, see the documentation on the `CBitmap` class in the following Visual C++ online help topic: *Visual C++ Documentation, Reference, Microsoft Foundation Class Library and Templates, Microsoft Foundation Class Library, Class Library Reference, CBitmap.*

Loading a Bitmap from a Resource

Including a bitmap as a program resource gives you the advantage that you can design the bitmap using an interactive bitmap editing program, such as the Visual C++ graphics editor or a separate drawing program such as Windows 95 Paint. This method, therefore, is especially useful for creating relatively complex or nongeometric images, which are not easily generated with drawing functions.

The first step is to open the project for the program in which you want to use the bitmap. (If you don't open a project, the bitmap resource will be placed in a freestanding resource [.rc] file.)

To design a bitmap using the Visual C++ graphics editor, choose the Insert ➤ Resource... menu command (or press Ctrl+R), and select the Bitmap resource type in the Insert Resource dialog box. (Alternatively, you can simply click the New Bitmap button on the Resource toolbar or press Ctrl+5.) Visual C++ will then open a window for the new bitmap in the graphics editor, which is similar to the toolbar editor you used in Chapter 14. You can then design the desired bitmap image.

When you create a new bitmap, Visual C++ will assign it a default identifier (IDB_BITMAP1 for the first bitmap you create, IDB_BITMAP2 for the second, and so on). If you wish, you can assign a different identifier by double-clicking in the bitmap window, opening the General tab in the Bitmap Properties dialog box, and entering the new identifier into the ID: text box. Whether you accept the default identifier or assign your own, remember the identifier, because you'll need to use it when you write the code to load the bitmap at program runtime.

TIP	Rather than designing a new bitmap, you can copy graphics into the Clipboard from another program (any program that allows you to copy graphics in bitmap format), and then paste the graphics into the Visual C++ graphics editor (by choosing the Edit ➤ Paste menu command or pressing Ctrl+V).

Alternatively, you can design a bitmap in a separate drawing program and save it in a file. You can use any program that saves files in bitmap format (the file will normally have the .bmp or .dib extension); an example of such a program is the Windows 95 Paint utility. Or, you can simply use a bitmap file that you've obtained from some other source (perhaps one you've downloaded from the Internet). To use the bitmap in your program, choose the Insert ➤ Resource... menu command in the Developer Studio, click the Import... button in the Insert Resource dialog box, and then select the name of the file you saved from the other program. The imported bitmap will be displayed in the Visual C++ graphics editor; if you wish, you can edit it, change its size, or assign it a different identifier.

Whether you design the bitmap in the Visual C++ graphics editor or import it from a bitmap file, the bitmap will be incorporated within the program's resources. (If a project wasn't open when you created or imported the bitmap, the bitmap will be included in a freestanding resource [.rc] file. You can add the bitmap to a project by opening the resource file and copying the bitmap resource into the project.) At program runtime, you can then load the bitmap and use it to initialize a bitmap object. To do this, call the CBitmap member function LoadBitmap, as in the following example:

```
class CProgView : public CView  // the program's view class
{
// ...
   CBitmap m_Bitmap;
   void LoadBitmapImage ();
// ...
};

// ...
```

```
void CProgView::LoadBitmapImage ()
  {
  // ...

  m_Bitmap.LoadBitmap (IDB_BITMAP1);

  // ...
  }
```

The parameter passed to LoadBitmap is the identifier that was assigned to the bitmap when you created it in the graphics editor or imported it from a bitmap file.

NOTE   The steps for designing a bitmap in the Visual C++ graphics editor and using this bitmap to initialize a bitmap object are described in the tutorial exercise for creating the BitDemo program, given near the end of the chapter.

Creating a Bitmap Using Drawing Functions

Rather than designing the bitmap in an editor, you can initialize a blank bitmap at program runtime and use the MFC drawing functions to draw the desired pattern within the bitmap. The following is a summary of the required steps:

1. Initialize a blank bitmap.

2. Create a memory device context object.

3. Select the bitmap into the memory device context object.

4. Draw the desired image within the bitmap, by calling CDC drawing functions for the memory device context object.

To initialize a blank bitmap, you can call the function CreateCompatible-Bitmap, as in the following example:

```
class CProgView : public CView  // the program's view class
  {
  // ...
    CBitmap m_Bitmap;
    void DrawBitmapImage ();
  // ...
  };
```

```
// ...

void CProgView::DrawBitmapImage ()
    {
    CClientDC ClientDC (this); // create view window device
                               // context object

    m_Bitmap.CreateCompatibleBitmap (&ClientDC, 32, 32);

    // ...
    }
```

The first parameter passed to CreateCompatibleBitmap is the address of a device context object; the bitmap will be made compatible with the device associated with this object. The term *compatible* means that the graphic data in the bitmap will be structured in the same way that graphic data is structured by the device; as a result of the compatibility, you'll be able to transfer graphics readily between the bitmap and the device. To create a bitmap that will be displayed on the screen, you should pass the address of a device context object for the screen (usually, a CClientDC or CPaintDC device context object that you've explicitly created for a window, or the device context object for the view window that's passed to the OnDraw member function of the view class).

NOTE   When you call CBitmap::LoadBitmap to load a bitmap, as described in the previous section, the bitmap is automatically made compatible with the screen.

The second parameter passed to CreateCompatibleBitmap is the width of the bitmap, and the third parameter is the height; both of these dimensions are in pixels.

When you call CreateCompatibleBitmap, Windows reserves a block of memory for the bitmap. The pixel values stored within this bitmap are initially undefined; you must use drawing functions to create the desired background and image. Before you can draw within the bitmap, however, you need to create a device context object that's associated with the bitmap (just as you must have a device context object to send output to a device such as the screen). Windows provides a special type of device context object for accessing a bitmap, which is known as a *memory device context object*. To create a memory device context object, you declare an instance of the CDC class and then call the CDC member function `CreateCompatibleDC`, as in the following example:

```
void CProgView::DrawBitmapImage ()
    {
    CClientDC ClientDC (this);// view window device context object
    CDC MemDC;                 // memory device contect object

    m_Bitmap.CreateCompatibleBitmap (&ClientDC, 32, 32);

    MemDC.CreateCompatibleDC (&ClientDC);

    // ...
    }
```

The parameter passed to `CreateCompatibleDC` is the address of a device context object; the resulting memory device context will be made compatible with the device that's associated with this device context object. The device context object you pass must be associated with the *same* device as the object passed to `CreateCompatibleBitmap`; in other words, both the bitmap and the memory device context object that's used to access the bitmap must be compatible with the same device. (In these examples, both the bitmap and the memory device context object are compatible with the screen.)

TIP

If you pass NULL to `CreateCompatibleDC`, the function will initialize a memory device context object that's compatible with the screen.

Next, you must call the CDC member function `SelectObject` to select the bitmap object into the memory device context object; the following is an example:

```
MemDC.SelectObject (&m_Bitmap);
```

The parameter passed to `SelectObject` is the address of the bitmap object.

You can now draw the desired background and image within the bitmap by calling CDC drawing functions for the memory device context object. You can display text or graphics within the bitmap using the functions discussed in Chapters 18 and 19, just as if you were drawing within a window. You can also use any of the bit operations that will be discussed later in the chapter (for instance, the PatBlt function is useful for painting the background color within a bitmap). For example, the following code paints a white background and then draws a circle within the bitmap that's selected into the MemDC memory device context object:

```
// paint white background:
MemDC.PatBlt (0, 0, 32, 32, WHITENESS);

// draw a circle:
MemDC.Ellipse (2, 2, 30, 30);
```

This example assumes that the bitmap was given a size of 32 pixels by 32 pixels (in the call to CreateCompatibleBitmap).

The following code illustrates all the steps discussed in this section; it initializes a bitmap and then draws an image within it:

```
class CProgView : public CView  // the program's view class
{
// ...
   CBitmap m_Bitmap;
   void DrawBitmapImage ();
// ...
};

// ...

void CProgView::DrawBitmapImage ()
{
   CClientDC ClientDC (this);// view window device context object
   CDC MemDC;                 // memory device context object

   // initialize a blank bitmap:
   m_Bitmap.CreateCompatibleBitmap (&ClientDC, 32, 32);

   // initialize the memory device context object:
   MemDC.CreateCompatibleDC (&ClientDC);

   // select the bitmap object into the memory dc object:
   MemDC.SelectObject (&m_Bitmap);

   // use CDC member functions to draw within bitmap:
```

```
    // draw white background:
    MemDC.PatBlt (0, 0, 32, 32, WHITENESS);

    // draw circle:
    MemDC.Ellipse (2, 2, 30, 30);

    // call other drawing functions ...
    }
```

Usually, a bitmap object is declared as a data member of one of the main program classes (such as the view class), and therefore it typically persists throughout the entire course of the program. If, however, the bitmap object is destroyed *before* the memory device context object is destroyed, you should first remove it from the memory device context object. This is done as explained in Chapter 19 (for a drawing tool). Namely, when calling `SelectObject`, save the pointer to the default bitmap that's returned (the default bitmap for a newly created memory device context object is a monochrome bitmap consisting of a single pixel). When you've finished accessing the bitmap, call `SelectObject` again to select the default bitmap back into the device context object.

Displaying a Bitmap

After you've created and initialized a bitmap object, using either of the two methods presented, you can display the bitmap directly within a window or on another device. Neither the Win32 API nor the MFC provides a function that you can call to simply display a bitmap on a device. However, you can write your own function to perform this task; the following is an example:

```
void DisplayBitmap (CDC *PDC, CBitmap *PBitmap, int X, int Y)
    {
    BITMAP BM;
    CDC MemDC;

    MemDC.CreateCompatibleDC (NULL);
    MemDC.SelectObject (PBitmap);
    PBitmap->GetObject (sizeof (BM), &BM);
    PDC->BitBlt
        (X,             // logical horizontal coordinate of
                        // destination;
        Y,              // logical vertical coordinate of destination;
```

```
        BM.bmWidth,    // width of block to transfer (in logical
                       // units);
        BM.bmHeight,   // height of block to transfer (in logical
                       // units);
        &MemDC,        // source dc for graphic data;
        0,             // logical horizontal coordinate of block
                       // within source;
        0,             // logical vertical coordinate of block within
                       // source;
        SRCCOPY);      // code for type of transfer
    }
```

The `DisplayBitmap` function displays a bitmap on the device associated with the device context object passed as the first parameter. The second parameter supplies the address of the bitmap object, which must have been initialized using one of the techniques discussed in the chapter and *must be compatible with the screen*. The last two parameters specify the horizontal and vertical coordinates of the position within the target device where the upper-left corner of the bitmap is to be positioned.

`DisplayBitmap` first creates a memory device context object that's compatible with the screen and selects the bitmap into this object, so that it can access the contents of the bitmap. It then calls the `CGdiObject` member function `GetObject`, which fills the fields of a `BITMAP` structure with information on the bitmap; `DisplayBitmap` obtains the size of the bitmap from the `bmWidth` and `bmHeight` fields of this structure. It next calls the `CDC` member function `BitBlt`, which transfers the graphic data contained in the bitmap directly to the target device.

The first two parameters passed to `BitBlt` specify the upper-left corner of the destination location, and the third and fourth parameters specify the width and height of the block of data to be transferred; `DisplayBitmap` transfers the entire bitmap by passing the bitmap width and height obtained from the `bmWidth` and `bmHeight` fields of the `BITMAP` structure. The fifth parameter (`&MemDC`) is the address of the device context object that's the source of the graphic data; `Display-Bitmap` specifies the memory device context object associated with the bitmap. The sixth and seventh parameters specify the upper-left corner of the block of graphic data to be transferred from the source device context object; because `DisplayBitmap` transfers the entire bitmap, it specifies the coordinates (0, 0). The last parameter is a code that indicates how the graphic data is to be transferred; the value SRCCOPY indicates that it should be copied without modification. The `BitBlt` function is one of the bit-operation functions described in the next section.

NOTE The `DisplayBitmap` function assumes that the device context object for the target device uses the default **MM_TEXT** mapping mode. If the target device context object uses an alternative mapping mode, the bitmap will be expanded or compressed as it's copied.

The following code illustrates how the `DisplayBitmap` function could be used to display a bitmap within the view window at logical coordinates (0, 0):

```
void CProgView::OnDraw(CDC* pDC)
{
    DisplayBitmap (pDC, &m_Bitmap, 0, 0);

}
```

This example assumes that `m_Bitmap` is a `CBitmap` object that has been defined as a member of the view class (`CProgView`), and that it has been initialized—and made compatible with the screen—using one of the methods discussed previously. The BitDemo program given at the end of the chapter demonstrates an alternative way to display a bitmap in the view window.

`DisplayBitmap` can also be used to *print* a bitmap, by passing it a device context object associated with a printer. Depending on the particular printer, the bitmap colors may be changed to black-and-white, or rendered in shades of gray. See Chapter 21 for a description of printing techniques.

Other Ways to Use a Bitmap

An initialized bitmap object can be used for a variety of purposes in an MFC program, in addition to its use for displaying a bitmapped image on a device. For example, you can use an initialized bitmap object to:

- Create a custom push button control, by means of the MFC `CBitmap-Button` class; a custom push button is labeled with a bitmapped image rather than text

- Display a custom check mark next to a menu command, by calling the `CMenu::SetMenuItemBitmaps` function (you can obtain a temporary `CMenu` object attached to the main program menu by calling the `CWnd::GetMenu` function for the main frame window object)

- Design a custom menu label, by calling the `CMenu::AppendMenu` function or one of several similar `CMenu` member functions and specifying a bitmap rather than a text label

- Fill areas with a custom pattern by calling `CBrush::CreatePatternBrush` to create a brush, as described in Chapter 19

When performing any of these tasks, you must supply a `CBitmap` object that has been initialized using one of the methods discussed in the chapter. For information on any of these four ways of using bitmaps, see the documentation on the class or member function mentioned in the list above in the following online help topic: *Visual C++ Documentation, Reference, Microsoft Foundation Class Library and Templates, Microsoft Foundation Class Library, Class Library Reference*.

Performing Bit Operations

The `CDC` class provides three versatile and efficient functions for transferring blocks of graphic data: `PatBlt`, `BitBlt`, and `StretchBlt`. You can use these functions when creating drawings; you can also use them for copying blocks of graphic data, and for modifying graphic data in simple or complex ways (for example, inverting colors or flipping images). Previously in the chapter, you saw how to use the `PatBlt` function to paint the background color in a bitmap, and you saw how to use `BitBlt` to transfer the graphic data from a bitmap to a window or other device. In general, you can use these functions to copy graphic data from one position to another on the display surface of a single device, or to copy graphic data from one device to another or between a device and a bitmap.

TIP   You can freely use the bit-operation functions with a device context object associated with the screen, or with a memory device context object that's compatible with the screen. These functions, however, might not be supported by other types of devices, such as certain printers or plotters. To determine whether a particular device supports the bit-operation functions, you can pass the value **RASTERCAPS** to the `CDC::GetDeviceCaps` function for the device context object that's associated with the device. See the documentation on this function for an explanation of the information that `GetDeviceCaps` returns.

PatBlt

You can use the CDC member function PatBlt to paint a rectangular area using the current brush. (See Chapter 19 for a description of the current brush.) In the context of bit operations, the current brush is usually referred to as the current *pattern*. Although you can also fill an area using the current pattern by calling the CDC::FillRect function, the PatBlt function is more versatile. PatBlt has the following syntax:

```
BOOL PatBlt
    (int x, int y,             // logical coordinates of upper-left
                               // corner of area to fill;
    int nWidth, int nHeight,   // dimensions of area to fill in
                               // logical units;
    DWORD dwRop);              // raster-operation code
```

The first two parameters specify the logical coordinates of the upper-left corner of the rectangular area that's to be painted, while the second two parameters specify the width and height of this area in logical units.

> **NOTE**
>
> Specifying a raster-operation code when calling a bit-operation function is similar to setting the drawing mode, as explained in Chapter 19. The drawing mode, however, affects lines and the interiors of closed figures created using drawing commands; it doesn't affect the outcome of the bit operations discussed here.

The last parameter, dwRop, is the *raster-operation code*. The raster-operation code is what gives PatBlt (as well as the other bit-operation functions) its versatility; it specifies the way that each pixel within the pattern is combined with the current pixel at the destination location, to derive the final destination pixel color. The raster-operation codes that you can pass to PatBlt are listed in Table 20.1. For each code, this table provides a Boolean expression (using C++ syntax) that describes the resulting color of each pixel within the area that's filled; in these expressions, D refers to the destination pixel and P refers to the pattern pixel.

TABLE 20.1: The Raster-Operation Codes You Can Pass to PatBlt

Raster-Operation Code	Boolean Expression	Description of Result on Destination Area
BLACKNESS	D = 0	Each pixel is set to black.
DSTINVERT	D = ~D	The color of each pixel is inverted.
PATCOPY	D = P	Each pixel is set to the color of the pattern pixel.
PATINVERT	D = D ^ P	The color of each pixel is the result of combining the destination pixel and the pattern pixel using the Boolean XOR operator.
WHITENESS	D = 1	Each pixel is set to white.

NOTE Windows actually performs the specified raster operation on *each bit* that's used to encode the pixel's color. For a monochrome device, only one bit is used for each pixel; for a color device, however, several bits are used for each pixel. For example, when the color of a pixel is inverted (D = ~D), Windows inverts *each bit* used to encode the color; the exact resulting color depends on the way that colors are represented by the device associated with the device context object.

For example, the following OnDraw function paints the entire view window using the current pattern, completely replacing the current window contents:

```
void CProgView::OnDraw(CDC* pDC)
{
   RECT Rect;
   GetClientRect (&Rect);

   pDC->PatBlt
      (Rect.left,
       Rect.top,
       Rect.right - Rect.left,
       Rect.bottom - Rect.top,
       PATCOPY);
}
```

BitBlt

The CDC member function BitBlt allows you to transfer a block of graphic data from one location to another. The source and destination locations can be within the same device (or bitmap) or within different devices (or bitmaps). BitBlt has the following syntax:

```
BOOL BitBlt
    (int x, int y,              // logical coordinates of upper-left
                                // corner of destination block;
     int nWidth, int nHeight,   // dimensions of block in logical
                                // units;
     CDC* pSrcDC,               // source device context object;
     int xSrc, int ySrc,        // logical coordinates of upper-left
                                // corner of block within source;
     DWORD dwRop);              // raster-operation code
```

The first two parameters specify the logical coordinates of the upper-left corner of the destination location for the transfer, and the second two parameters specify the dimensions of the block of graphic data that's to be transferred, in logical units. The fifth parameter (pSrcDC) is a pointer to the source device context object, and the sixth and seventh parameters (xSrc and ySrc) specify the logical coordinates of the upper-left corner of the block within the source device. The last parameter (dwRop) is the raster-operation code.

BitBlt copies the block of graphic data *from* the device associated with the context object indicated by the fifth parameter *to* the device associated with the device context object for which the function is called. For example, the following call transfers a block of graphic data *from* a bitmap (selected into the memory device context object MemDC) *to* a view window (associated with the device context object *pDC):

```
pDC->BitBlt (X, Y, Width, Height, &MemDC, 0, 0, SRCCOPY);
```

When BitBlt paints the destination area, the final color of each pixel depends on the current pixel color, the color of the corresponding pixel within the source device, *and* the color of the corresponding pixel within the current pattern (that is, the brush currently selected into the *destination* device context object). The way that BitBlt combines these color values depends on the raster-operation code that you assign to the dwRop parameter. Because the raster-operation code passed to BitBlt affects the way the colors from *three* different pixels are combined, there are many more possible codes that you can specify than there are for PatBlt. (The raster-operation code passed to PatBlt affects the way only *two* pixels are combined.)

In fact, there are 256 different raster-operation codes that you can pass to `Bit-Blt`! Some of the more common ones are described in Table 20.2; for a complete list of these codes, see the following online help topic: *Platform SDK, Graphics and Multimedia Services, GDI, Raster Operation Codes*. In the Boolean expressions given in Table 20.2, the symbol D refers to the destination pixel, S refers to the source pixel, and P refers to the pattern pixel. As with the `PatBlt` function, `BitBlt` performs the specified operation on *each bit* used to encode the pixel's color.

TABLE 20.2: Common Raster-Operation Codes You Can Pass to `BitBlt` or `StretchBlt`

Raster-Operation Code	Boolean Expression	Description of Result on Destination Area
MERGECOPY	D = P & S	The color of each pixel is the result of combining the pattern pixel and the source pixel using the Boolean AND operator.
MERGEPAINT	D = ~S | D	The color of each pixel is the result of combining the inverted source pixel and the destination pixel using the Boolean OR operator.
NOTSRCCOPY	D = ~S	Each pixel is set to the inverse of the source pixel color.
NOTSRCERASE	D = ~(D | S)	The color of each pixel is the result of combining the destination pixel and the source pixel using the Boolean OR operator and then inverting the result.
PATPAINT	D = ~S | P | D	The color of each pixel is the result of combining the inverse of the source pixel, the pattern pixel, and the destination pixel, using the Boolean OR operator.
SRCAND	D = D & S	The color of each pixel is the result of combining the destination pixel and the source pixel using the Boolean AND operator.
SRCCOPY	D = S	Each pixel is set to the color of the source pixel.
SRCERASE	D = ~D & S	The color of each pixel is the result of combining the inverse of the destination pixel and the source pixel using the Boolean AND operator.
SRCINVERT	D = D ^ S	The color of each pixel is the result of combining the destination pixel and the source pixel using the Boolean XOR operator.
SRCPAINT	D = D | S	The color of each pixel is the result of combining the destination pixel and the source pixel using the Boolean OR operator.

Using *BitBlt* for Animation

You already saw how to use BitBlt, in conjunction with the SRCCOPY raster-operation code, to simply copy a block of graphic data from one location to another (see the DisplayBitmap function, given in the section "Displaying a Bitmap"). In this section, you'll learn how to use several of the other raster-operation codes to perform animation.

When writing games or other types of applications, you sometimes need to move a small drawing across the window (you might move it in response to movements of the mouse, or move it automatically using a Windows timer). If the drawing is rectangular, you can simply call BitBlt with the SRCCOPY raster-operation code to display a bitmap containing the drawing at each new drawing location in the window. You can also use this method to display the drawing if the window has a uniform background color, regardless of the shape of the drawing. (In the source bitmap, simply paint the area surrounding the drawing using the window background color, so that this portion of the bitmap will be invisible when copied to the window.)

Commonly, however, you need to animate a nonrectangular drawing within a window that contains various colors; an example would be moving a drawing of a chess piece within a window containing a chess board pattern. The problem is that the BitBlt function always transfers a *rectangular* block of graphics, and the pixels surrounding the drawing in the source bitmap would overwrite the existing pixels on the screen (thus, the chess piece would have an undesirable rectangular "aura" around it).

The solution to this problem is to create two source bitmaps: a *mask* bitmap and an *image* bitmap. In the mask bitmap, the drawing is colored black and the background is painted white. In the image bitmap, the drawing is given its normal colors and the background is painted black. Figure 20.1 illustrates mask and image bitmaps for a drawing of a cube.

FIGURE 20.1:

Mask and image bitmaps for a drawing of a cube

Mask bitmap   Image bitmap

To display the drawing at a particular location within the window, you use *two* calls to BitBlt. In the first call, you transfer the mask bitmap using the SRCAND raster-operation code, and in the second call, you transfer the image bitmap using the SRCINVERT raster-operation code, as in the following example function:

```
void CProgView::DisplayDrawing (int X, int Y)
{
    CClientDC ClientDC (this);
    CDC MemDC;
    MemDC.CreateCompatibleDC (&ClientDC);

    // transfer mask bitmap:
    MemDC.SelectObject (&m_MaskBitmap);
    ClientDC.BitBlt
        (X, Y,
        BMWIDTH, BMHEIGHT,
        &MemDC,
        0, 0,
        SRCAND);

    // transfer image bitmap:
    MemDC.SelectObject (&m_ImageBitmap);
    ClientDC.BitBlt
        (X, Y,
        BMWIDTH, BMHEIGHT,
        &MemDC,
        0, 0,
        SRCINVERT);
}
```

This example assumes that the program has already created and initialized two screen-compatible bitmap objects—m_MaskBitmap for the mask bitmap and m_ImageBitmap for the image bitmap—and that the program has defined the constants BMWIDTH and BMHEIGHT equal to the width and height of these bitmaps.

The first call to BitBlt displays the drawing in black, without disturbing the existing graphics in the window surrounding the drawing. The second call to BitBlt then transfers a colored version of the drawing to the window, again without disturbing the existing graphics surrounding the drawing. The overall result is that a nonrectangular drawing is displayed within the window, and the drawing is surrounded by the original window graphics. This two-step process is illustrated in Figure 20.2.

FIGURE 20.2:

The two-step process for displaying a nonrectangular drawing over existing background graphics

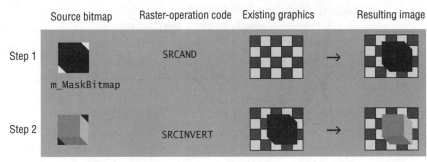

> **NOTE**
>
> In a typical application, you'd also need to save and restore the window graphics at each location where you temporarily display the moving drawing. You can do this by using another bitmap that has the same size as the mask and image bitmaps. You could use `BitBlt` with the `SRCCOPY` raster-operation code first to copy the graphics from the screen to this bitmap (before the drawing is displayed), and then to copy the graphics from the bitmap back to the screen (after the drawing is displayed).

StretchBlt

The most versatile of the three bit-operation functions discussed in this chapter is `StretchBlt`. The `StretchBlt` function allows you to perform all the operations that are possible using `BitBlt`; in addition, it permits you to *change the size* of the block of graphic data, or to flip the block (horizontally, vertically, or in both directions) as it's transferred. `StretchBlt` has the following syntax:

```
BOOL StretchBlt
    (int x, int y,              // logical coordinates of upper-left
                                // corner of destination block;
        int nWidth, int nHeight, // dimensions of destination block in
                                // logical units;
        CDC* pSrcDC,            // source device context object;
        int xSrc, int ySrc,     // logical coordinates of upper-left
                                // corner of block within source;
        int nSrcWidth, int nSrcHeight, // dimensions of source block
                                    // in logical units;
        DWORD dwRop);           // raster-operation code
```

StretchBlt allows you to specify the size of both the source block *and* the destination block (recall that BitBlt allows you to specify only a single block size). If the destination size (nWidth, nHeight) is smaller than the source size (nSrcWidth, nSrcHeight), the image is compressed; if the destination size is larger than the source size, the image is expanded. If nWidth and nSrcWidth are given different signs (one positive, the other negative), the destination image will be a mirror image—in the horizontal direction—of the source image. Likewise, if nHeight and nSrcHeight are given different signs, the destination image will be a mirror image—in the vertical direction—of the source image. The BitDemo program, presented later in the chapter, shows how to use StretchBlt to display a bitmap so that it always fills the entire view window.

TIP
You can call the CDC member function CDC::SetStretchBltMode to fine-tune the way that StretchBlt processes eliminated pixels when a block of graphic data is compressed.

Displaying Icons

An icon is a special form of bitmap. An icon differs from a standard bitmap in two primary ways. First, a bitmap file or resource contains only a single image. An icon file or resource, however, may contain one or more images. For example, it might contain a 16-pixel by 16-pixel 16-color image, a 32-pixel by 32-pixel 16-color image, and a 32-pixel by 32-pixel 2-color (monochrome) image. When the icon is displayed, the system uses the image that's most appropriate for the current video mode and the desired image size (in Windows Explorer, for example, you can choose to display either small or large icon images).

Second, when you design an icon using the Visual C++ graphics editor or another icon designer, as an alternative to assigning a specific color to a given pixel, you can assign it the *screen color* or the *inverse screen color*. When Windows displays the icon, the color of the existing pixel at the position of each screen-colored pixel is left unaltered; screen-colored portions of the icon are thus transparent. Likewise, the color of the existing pixel at the position of each inverse screen-colored pixel is inverted; inverse screen-colored portions of the icon are thus visible over almost any colored background.

You've already seen the following two ways for using icons:

- You can create a custom icon for a main program window (Chapter 10), or for a child window in an MDI program (Chapter 17), which will be displayed in the program's title bar and other locations.

- You can display an icon within a dialog box (Chapter 15).

This section completes the discussion on icons by describing how to display an icon at any position within a program window.

The first step is to open the project in which you want to use the icon and design the icon with the Visual C++ graphics editor, as explained in Chapter 10. If the icon is assigned the IDR_MAINFRAME identifier (or the identifier of a program document type in an MDI program), it's automatically assigned to the main frame window (or child frame window) and it's displayed in the window title bar. If you don't want the icon you are designing to be assigned to a window, make sure that it has a different identifier. (Visual C++ assigns the default identifiers IDI_ICON1, IDI_ICON2, and so on to the new icons you create or import.)

TIP

As with a bitmap, rather than designing an icon within the Visual C++ graphics editor, you can *import* an icon from an .ico file that you've created using a separate icon-editing program or that you've obtained from another source. If you want, you can then edit the icon or change its identifier in the Visual C++ graphics editor. To import an icon file, choose the Insert ➤ Resource... menu command in the Developer Studio, click the Import... button in the Insert Resource dialog box, and then select the .ico file in the Import Resource dialog box.

The icon you create or import will be stored in an .ico file and will be incorporated into the program's resources when the program is built. (The program's resource [.rc] file contains an ICON statement that causes the icon defined in the file to be included in the program's resources.) Before displaying the icon in a window at program runtime, the program must call the CWinApp member function LoadIcon to load the icon from the resources and to obtain a handle to it, as in the following code:

```
HICON HIcon;

HIcon = AfxGetApp ()->LoadIcon (IDI_ICON1);
```

In this example, IDI_ICON1 is the identifier that was assigned to the icon when it was created or imported into the Visual C++ project. Notice that the **AfxGetApp** function is called to obtain a pointer to the program's application object, which is used to call **LoadIcon**. If the icon resource includes more than one image (for example, a 32-pixel by 32-pixel 16-color image and a 32-pixel by 32-pixel 2-color [monochrome] image), Windows will automatically load the image that's most appropriate for the current video mode.

TIP

Rather than calling **LoadIcon** to load a custom icon from the program's resources, you can call the **CWinApp** member function **LoadStandardIcon** or **LoadOEMIcon** to obtain a handle to a predefined icon provided by Windows. For details, see the documentation on these two functions under the following online help topic: *Visual C++ Documentation, Reference, Microsoft Foundation Class Library and Templates, Microsoft Foundation Class Library, Class Library Reference, CWinApp.*

Finally, to display the icon within a window, call the **CDC** member function **DrawIcon**:

```
BOOL DrawIcon (int x, int y, HICON hIcon);
```

The parameters x and y specify the coordinates of the upper-left corner of the position where the icon is to be displayed, and the hIcon parameter is the handle to the icon obtained from **LoadIcon** (or **LoadStandardIcon** or **LoadOEMIcon**).

As an example, the following function loads and displays an icon, which was created or imported into the project, at the center of the view window:

```
void CProgView::DisplayIcon ()
    {
    CClientDC ClientDC (this);
    HICON HIcon;
    int IconHeight;
    int IconWidth;
    RECT Rect;
```

```
HIcon = AfxGetApp ()->LoadIcon (IDI_ICON1);

GetClientRect (&Rect);
IconWidth = ::GetSystemMetrics (SM_CXICON);
IconHeight = ::GetSystemMetrics (SM_CYICON);
ClientDC.DrawIcon
    (Rect.right / 2 - IconWidth / 2,
    Rect.bottom / 2 - IconHeight / 2,
    HIcon);
}
```

Notice that this function calls the Win32 API function `::GetSystemMetrics` to obtain the dimensions of the icon; this information is used to calculate the position of the icon's upper-left corner. (Note that the dimensions of an icon image loaded by `LoadIcon` are always equal to the current values of the SM_CXICON and SM_CYICON system metrics. If the icon resource doesn't have an image that matches these dimensions, `LoadIcon` scales an image to make it match.)

The BitDemo Program

In this section, you'll create a program named BitDemo, which illustrates the techniques for designing a bitmap in Visual C++ and for displaying a bitmap in the program's view window. The BitDemo program displays a checkerboard, which fills the view window. As you change the size of the window, the checkerboard pattern is stretched or compressed as necessary so that it always completely fills the window (see Figure 20.3).

Use AppWizard to generate the BitDemo program source files, assigning the project name BitDemo and, in the Projects tab of the New dialog box and in the AppWizard Step 1 through Step 6 dialog boxes, choosing the *same* options you chose for the WinGreet program in Chapter 9.

FIGURE 20.3:

The BitDemo program window, showing that the checkerboard pattern always fills the window regardless of the window's size or proportions

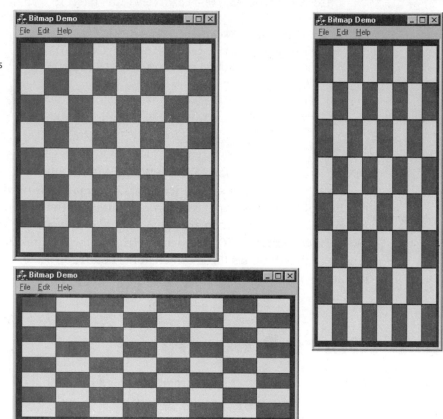

Designing the Bitmap

Once the source files have been generated, begin by designing the bitmap that the program displays. To do this, choose the Insert ➢ Resource… menu command and select the Bitmap resource type in the Insert Resource dialog box. When you click the New button, Visual C++ will display a new blank bitmap in the graphics editor, and it will assign this bitmap the default identifier IDB_BITMAP1, which you shouldn't change. Now use the graphics editor tools and commands to create the bitmap pattern. The bitmap that was designed for the version of Bit-Demo on the companion CD is shown in Figure 20.4.

FIGURE 20.4:

The IDB_BITMAP1 bitmap provided for the BitDemo program on the companion CD, as it appears in the Visual C++ graphics editor

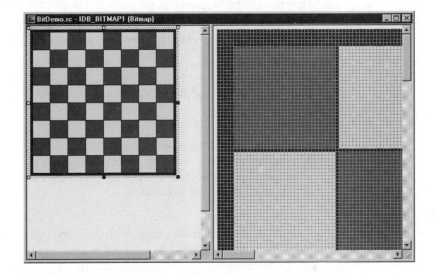

As an alternative method, you can design the bitmap in the Window 95 Paint program or in any other drawing program that saves drawings in bitmap format. When you've completed the drawing, save it in a .bmp or .dib file and return to Visual C++. You can then import the bitmap into the BitDemo program by choosing the Insert ➤ Resource... menu command in the Developer Studio, clicking the Import... button in the Insert Resource dialog box, and then selecting the name of the file in which you saved the bitmap. Whether you create the bitmap in Visual C++ or import it from a file, make sure that it has the identifier IDB_BITMAP1.

Modifying the Code

To display the bitmap, you need to modify the program's view class. In Bit-DemoView.h, define the following data members at the beginning of the CBit-DemoView class definition:

```
class CBitDemoView : public CView
{
protected:
   CBitmap m_Bitmap;
   int m_BitmapHeight;
   int m_BitmapWidth;
```

m_Bitmap is the bitmap object, while m_BitmapHeight and m_BitmapWidth store the dimensions of the bitmap. Next, in BitDemoView.cpp, initialize these data members within the class constructor, as follows:

```
CBitDemoView::CBitDemoView()
{
    // TODO: add construction code here
    BITMAP BM;

    m_Bitmap.LoadBitmap (IDB_BITMAP1);
    m_Bitmap.GetObject (sizeof (BM), &BM);
    m_BitmapWidth = BM.bmWidth;
    m_BitmapHeight = BM.bmHeight;
}
```

The call to CBitmap::LoadBitmap initializes the bitmap object by loading the bitmap you created in the graphics editor or imported into the program. The dimensions of the bitmap are then obtained by calling CBitmap::GetObject, which returns information on the attached bitmap.

Finally, add code as follows to the OnDraw function in BitDemoView.cpp to display the bitmap:

```
/////////////////////////////////////////////////////////////
///////////
// CBitDemoView drawing

void CBitDemoView::OnDraw(CDC* pDC)
{
    CBitDemoDoc* pDoc = GetDocument();
    ASSERT_VALID(pDoc);

    // TODO: add draw code for native data here
    CDC MemDC;
    RECT ClientRect;

    // create memory device context object and select bitmap
    // object into it:
    MemDC.CreateCompatibleDC (NULL);
    MemDC.SelectObject (&m_Bitmap);

    // get current dimensions of view window:
    GetClientRect (&ClientRect);
```

```
// display bitmap, stretching it to fit view window:
pDC->StretchBlt
   (0,                    // coordinates of upper-left corner of
    0,                    // destination rectangle;
    ClientRect.right,     // width of destination rectangle;
    ClientRect.bottom,    // height of destination rectangle;
    &MemDC,               // source device context object;
    0,                    // coordinates of upper-left corner of
    0,                    // source rectangle;
    m_BitmapWidth,        // width of source rectangle;
    m_BitmapHeight,       // height of source rectangle;
    SRCCOPY);             // raster-operation code
}
```

OnDraw displays the bitmap in the same way as the example function Display-
Bitmap, given previously in the chapter (in the section "Displaying a Bitmap").
However, rather than using BitBlt to transfer the bitmap in its original size, it
uses StretchBlt to copy the bitmap to the view window and to compress or
expand the bitmap as necessary so that it fits exactly within the window.

Finally, add the usual SetWindowText call to the InitInstance function in Bit-
Demo.cpp:

```
// The one and only window has been initialized, so show and
// update it.
m_pMainWnd->ShowWindow(SW_SHOW);
m_pMainWnd->UpdateWindow();

m_pMainWnd->SetWindowText ("Bitmap Demo");

return TRUE;
}
```

You can now build and run the BitDemo program.

The BitDemo Source Code

Listings 20.1 through 20.8, which follow, contain the C++ source code for the Bit-
Demo program. A copy of these files can be found in the \BitDemo companion-
CD folder.

Listing 20.1

```
// BitDemo.h : main header file for the BITDEMO application
//

#if !defined(AFX_BITDEMO_H__0955F7ED_A77B_11D1_80FC_00C0F6A83B7F__INCLUDED_)
#define AFX_BITDEMO_H__0955F7ED_A77B_11D1_80FC_00C0F6A83B7F__INCLUDED_

#if _MSC_VER > 1000
#pragma once
#endif // _MSC_VER > 1000

#ifndef __AFXWIN_H__
    #error include 'stdafx.h' before including this file for PCH
#endif

#include "resource.h"        // main symbols

/////////////////////////////////////////////////////////////////////////
// CBitDemoApp:
// See BitDemo.cpp for the implementation of this class
//

class CBitDemoApp : public CWinApp
{
public:
    CBitDemoApp();

// Overrides
    // ClassWizard generated virtual function overrides
    //{{AFX_VIRTUAL(CBitDemoApp)
    public:
    virtual BOOL InitInstance();
    //}}AFX_VIRTUAL

// Implementation
    //{{AFX_MSG(CBitDemoApp)
    afx_msg void OnAppAbout();
        // NOTE - the ClassWizard will add and remove member functions here.
        //    DO NOT EDIT what you see in these blocks of generated code !
    //}}AFX_MSG
```

```
    DECLARE_MESSAGE_MAP()
};


//////////////////////////////////////////////////////////////////////////

//{{AFX_INSERT_LOCATION}}
// Microsoft Visual C++ will insert additional declarations immediately before
// the previous line.

#endif
// !defined(AFX_BITDEMO_H__0955F7ED_A77B_11D1_80FC_00C0F6A83B7F__INCLUDED_)
```

Listing 20.2

```cpp
// BitDemo.cpp : Defines the class behaviors for the application.
//

#include "stdafx.h"
#include "BitDemo.h"

#include "MainFrm.h"
#include "BitDemoDoc.h"
#include "BitDemoView.h"

#ifdef _DEBUG
#define new DEBUG_NEW
#undef THIS_FILE
static char THIS_FILE[] = __FILE__;
#endif


//////////////////////////////////////////////////////////////////////////
// CBitDemoApp

BEGIN_MESSAGE_MAP(CBitDemoApp, CWinApp)
    //{{AFX_MSG_MAP(CBitDemoApp)
    ON_COMMAND(ID_APP_ABOUT, OnAppAbout)
        // NOTE - the ClassWizard will add and remove mapping macros here.
        //    DO NOT EDIT what you see in these blocks of generated code!
    //}}AFX_MSG_MAP
    // Standard file based document commands
    ON_COMMAND(ID_FILE_NEW, CWinApp::OnFileNew)
```

```
   ON_COMMAND(ID_FILE_OPEN, CWinApp::OnFileOpen)
END_MESSAGE_MAP()

/////////////////////////////////////////////////////////////////////////
// CBitDemoApp construction

CBitDemoApp::CBitDemoApp()
{
   // TODO: add construction code here,
   // Place all significant initialization in InitInstance
}

/////////////////////////////////////////////////////////////////////////
// The one and only CBitDemoApp object

CBitDemoApp theApp;

/////////////////////////////////////////////////////////////////////////
// CBitDemoApp initialization

BOOL CBitDemoApp::InitInstance()
{
   // Standard initialization
   // If you are not using these features and wish to reduce the size
   //  of your final executable, you should remove from the following
   //  the specific initialization routines you do not need.

#ifdef _AFXDLL
   Enable3dControls();          // Call this when using MFC in a shared DLL
#else
   Enable3dControlsStatic();    // Call this when linking to MFC statically
#endif

   // Change the registry key under which our settings are stored.
   // TODO: You should modify this string to be something appropriate
   // such as the name of your company or organization.
   SetRegistryKey(_T("Local AppWizard-Generated Applications"));

   LoadStdProfileSettings();  // Load standard INI file options (including MRU)

   // Register the application's document templates.  Document templates
   //  serve as the connection between documents, frame windows and views.
```

```
    CSingleDocTemplate* pDocTemplate;
    pDocTemplate = new CSingleDocTemplate(
        IDR_MAINFRAME,
        RUNTIME_CLASS(CBitDemoDoc),
        RUNTIME_CLASS(CMainFrame),          // main SDI frame window
        RUNTIME_CLASS(CBitDemoView));
    AddDocTemplate(pDocTemplate);

    // Parse command line for standard shell commands, DDE, file open
    CCommandLineInfo cmdInfo;
    ParseCommandLine(cmdInfo);

    // Dispatch commands specified on the command line
    if (!ProcessShellCommand(cmdInfo))
        return FALSE;

    // The one and only window has been initialized, so show and update it.
    m_pMainWnd->ShowWindow(SW_SHOW);
    m_pMainWnd->UpdateWindow();

    m_pMainWnd->SetWindowText ("Bitmap Demo");

    return TRUE;
}


/////////////////////////////////////////////////////////////////////////
// CAboutDlg dialog used for App About

class CAboutDlg : public CDialog
{
public:
    CAboutDlg();

// Dialog Data
    //{{AFX_DATA(CAboutDlg)
    enum { IDD = IDD_ABOUTBOX };
    //}}AFX_DATA

    // ClassWizard generated virtual function overrides
    //{{AFX_VIRTUAL(CAboutDlg)
    protected:
```

```
    virtual void DoDataExchange(CDataExchange* pDX);    // DDX/DDV support
    //}}AFX_VIRTUAL

// Implementation
protected:
    //{{AFX_MSG(CAboutDlg)
        // No message handlers
    //}}AFX_MSG
    DECLARE_MESSAGE_MAP()
};

CAboutDlg::CAboutDlg() : CDialog(CAboutDlg::IDD)
{
    //{{AFX_DATA_INIT(CAboutDlg)
    //}}AFX_DATA_INIT
}

void CAboutDlg::DoDataExchange(CDataExchange* pDX)
{
    CDialog::DoDataExchange(pDX);
    //{{AFX_DATA_MAP(CAboutDlg)
    //}}AFX_DATA_MAP
}

BEGIN_MESSAGE_MAP(CAboutDlg, CDialog)
    //{{AFX_MSG_MAP(CAboutDlg)
        // No message handlers
    //}}AFX_MSG_MAP
END_MESSAGE_MAP()

// App command to run the dialog
void CBitDemoApp::OnAppAbout()
{
    CAboutDlg aboutDlg;
    aboutDlg.DoModal();
}

/////////////////////////////////////////////////////////////////////////
// CBitDemoApp message handlers
```

Listing 20.3

```
// BitDemoDoc.h : interface of the CBitDemoDoc class
//
/////////////////////////////////////////////////////////////////////////

#if !defined(AFX_BITDEMODOC_H__0955F7F3_A77B_11D1_80FC_00C0F6A83B7F__INCLUDED_)
#define AFX_BITDEMODOC_H__0955F7F3_A77B_11D1_80FC_00C0F6A83B7F__INCLUDED_

#if _MSC_VER > 1000
#pragma once
#endif // _MSC_VER > 1000


class CBitDemoDoc : public CDocument
{
protected: // create from serialization only
   CBitDemoDoc();
   DECLARE_DYNCREATE(CBitDemoDoc)

// Attributes
public:

// Operations
public:

// Overrides
   // ClassWizard generated virtual function overrides
   //{{AFX_VIRTUAL(CBitDemoDoc)
   public:
   virtual BOOL OnNewDocument();
   virtual void Serialize(CArchive& ar);
   //}}AFX_VIRTUAL

// Implementation
public:
   virtual ~CBitDemoDoc();
#ifdef _DEBUG
   virtual void AssertValid() const;
   virtual void Dump(CDumpContext& dc) const;
#endif
```

```
protected:

// Generated message map functions
protected:
    //{{AFX_MSG(CBitDemoDoc)
        // NOTE - the ClassWizard will add and remove member functions here.
        //    DO NOT EDIT what you see in these blocks of generated code !
    //}}AFX_MSG
    DECLARE_MESSAGE_MAP()
};


///////////////////////////////////////////////////////////////////////////

//{{AFX_INSERT_LOCATION}}
// Microsoft Visual C++ will insert additional declarations immediately before
// the previous line.

#endif
// !defined(AFX_BITDEMODOC_H__0955F7F3_A77B_11D1_80FC_00C0F6A83B7F__INCLUDED_)
```

Listing 20.4

```
// BitDemoDoc.cpp : implementation of the CBitDemoDoc class
//

#include "stdafx.h"
#include "BitDemo.h"

#include "BitDemoDoc.h"

#ifdef _DEBUG
#define new DEBUG_NEW
#undef THIS_FILE
static char THIS_FILE[] = __FILE__;
#endif


///////////////////////////////////////////////////////////////////////////
// CBitDemoDoc

IMPLEMENT_DYNCREATE(CBitDemoDoc, CDocument)

BEGIN_MESSAGE_MAP(CBitDemoDoc, CDocument)
```

```
    //{{AFX_MSG_MAP(CBitDemoDoc)
        // NOTE - the ClassWizard will add and remove mapping macros here.
        //      DO NOT EDIT what you see in these blocks of generated code!
    //}}AFX_MSG_MAP
END_MESSAGE_MAP()


/////////////////////////////////////////////////////////////////////////
// CBitDemoDoc construction/destruction

CBitDemoDoc::CBitDemoDoc()
{
    // TODO: add one-time construction code here

}

CBitDemoDoc::~CBitDemoDoc()
{
}

BOOL CBitDemoDoc::OnNewDocument()
{
    if (!CDocument::OnNewDocument())
        return FALSE;

    // TODO: add reinitialization code here
    // (SDI documents will reuse this document)

    return TRUE;
}




/////////////////////////////////////////////////////////////////////////
// CBitDemoDoc serialization

void CBitDemoDoc::Serialize(CArchive& ar)
{
    if (ar.IsStoring())
    {
        // TODO: add storing code here
    }
    else
```

```
   {
       // TODO: add loading code here
   }
}

/////////////////////////////////////////////////////////////////////
// CBitDemoDoc diagnostics

#ifdef _DEBUG
void CBitDemoDoc::AssertValid() const
{
   CDocument::AssertValid();
}

void CBitDemoDoc::Dump(CDumpContext& dc) const
{
   CDocument::Dump(dc);
}
#endif //_DEBUG


/////////////////////////////////////////////////////////////////////
// CBitDemoDoc commands
```

Listing 20.5

```
// MainFrm.h : interface of the CMainFrame class
//
/////////////////////////////////////////////////////////////////////

#if !defined(AFX_MAINFRM_H__0955F7F1_A77B_11D1_80FC_00C0F6A83B7F__INCLUDED_)
#define AFX_MAINFRM_H__0955F7F1_A77B_11D1_80FC_00C0F6A83B7F__INCLUDED_

#if _MSC_VER > 1000
#pragma once
#endif // _MSC_VER > 1000

class CMainFrame : public CFrameWnd
{
```

```cpp
protected: // create from serialization only
    CMainFrame();
    DECLARE_DYNCREATE(CMainFrame)

// Attributes
public:

// Operations
public:

// Overrides
    // ClassWizard generated virtual function overrides
    //{{AFX_VIRTUAL(CMainFrame)
    virtual BOOL PreCreateWindow(CREATESTRUCT& cs);
    //}}AFX_VIRTUAL

// Implementation
public:
    virtual ~CMainFrame();
#ifdef _DEBUG
    virtual void AssertValid() const;
    virtual void Dump(CDumpContext& dc) const;
#endif

// Generated message map functions
protected:
    //{{AFX_MSG(CMainFrame)
        // NOTE - the ClassWizard will add and remove member functions here.
        //      DO NOT EDIT what you see in these blocks of generated code!
    //}}AFX_MSG
    DECLARE_MESSAGE_MAP()
};

/////////////////////////////////////////////////////////////////////////////

//{{AFX_INSERT_LOCATION}}
// Microsoft Visual C++ will insert additional declarations immediately before
// the previous line.

#endif
// !defined(AFX_MAINFRM_H__0955F7F1_A77B_11D1_80FC_00C0F6A83B7F__INCLUDED_)
```

Listing 20.6

```cpp
// MainFrm.cpp : implementation of the CMainFrame class
//

#include "stdafx.h"
#include "BitDemo.h"

#include "MainFrm.h"

#ifdef _DEBUG
#define new DEBUG_NEW
#undef THIS_FILE
static char THIS_FILE[] = __FILE__;
#endif

/////////////////////////////////////////////////////////////////////////
// CMainFrame

IMPLEMENT_DYNCREATE(CMainFrame, CFrameWnd)

BEGIN_MESSAGE_MAP(CMainFrame, CFrameWnd)
    //{{AFX_MSG_MAP(CMainFrame)
        // NOTE - the ClassWizard will add and remove mapping macros here.
        //    DO NOT EDIT what you see in these blocks of generated code !
    //}}AFX_MSG_MAP
END_MESSAGE_MAP()

/////////////////////////////////////////////////////////////////////////
// CMainFrame construction/destruction

CMainFrame::CMainFrame()
{
    // TODO: add member initialization code here

}

CMainFrame::~CMainFrame()
{
}
```

```
BOOL CMainFrame::PreCreateWindow(CREATESTRUCT& cs)
{
    if( !CFrameWnd::PreCreateWindow(cs) )
        return FALSE;
    // TODO: Modify the Window class or styles here by modifying
    //   the CREATESTRUCT cs

    return TRUE;
}


/////////////////////////////////////////////////////////////////////////
// CMainFrame diagnostics

#ifdef _DEBUG
void CMainFrame::AssertValid() const
{
    CFrameWnd::AssertValid();
}

void CMainFrame::Dump(CDumpContext& dc) const
{
    CFrameWnd::Dump(dc);
}

#endif //_DEBUG


/////////////////////////////////////////////////////////////////////////
// CMainFrame message handlers
```

Listing 20.7

```
// BitDemoView.h : interface of the CBitDemoView class
//
/////////////////////////////////////////////////////////////////////////

#if !defined(AFX_BITDEMOVIEW_H__0955F7F5_A77B_11D1_80FC_00C0F6A83B7F__INCLUDED_)
#define AFX_BITDEMOVIEW_H__0955F7F5_A77B_11D1_80FC_00C0F6A83B7F__INCLUDED_

#if _MSC_VER > 1000
#pragma once
#endif // _MSC_VER > 1000
```

```
class CBitDemoView : public CView
{
protected:
    CBitmap m_Bitmap;
    int m_BitmapHeight;
    int m_BitmapWidth;

protected: // create from serialization only
    CBitDemoView();
    DECLARE_DYNCREATE(CBitDemoView)

// Attributes
public:
    CBitDemoDoc* GetDocument();

// Operations
public:

// Overrides
    // ClassWizard generated virtual function overrides
    //{{AFX_VIRTUAL(CBitDemoView)
    public:
    virtual void OnDraw(CDC* pDC);  // overridden to draw this view
    virtual BOOL PreCreateWindow(CREATESTRUCT& cs);
    protected:
    //}}AFX_VIRTUAL

// Implementation
public:
    virtual ~CBitDemoView();
#ifdef _DEBUG
    virtual void AssertValid() const;
    virtual void Dump(CDumpContext& dc) const;
#endif

protected:

// Generated message map functions
protected:
    //{{AFX_MSG(CBitDemoView)
        // NOTE - the ClassWizard will add and remove member functions here.
        //    DO NOT EDIT what you see in these blocks of generated code !
```

```
    //}}AFX_MSG
    DECLARE_MESSAGE_MAP()
};

#ifndef _DEBUG  // debug version in BitDemoView.cpp
inline CBitDemoDoc* CBitDemoView::GetDocument()
    { return (CBitDemoDoc*)m_pDocument; }
#endif

/////////////////////////////////////////////////////////////////////////////

//{{AFX_INSERT_LOCATION}}
// Microsoft Visual C++ will insert additional declarations immediately before
// the previous line.

#endif
// !defined(AFX_BITDEMOVIEW_H__0955F7F5_A77B_11D1_80FC_00C0F6A83B7F__INCLUDED_)
```

Listing 20.8

```
// BitDemoView.cpp : implementation of the CBitDemoView class
//

#include "stdafx.h"
#include "BitDemo.h"

#include "BitDemoDoc.h"
#include "BitDemoView.h"

#ifdef _DEBUG
#define new DEBUG_NEW
#undef THIS_FILE
static char THIS_FILE[] = __FILE__;
#endif

/////////////////////////////////////////////////////////////////////////////
// CBitDemoView

IMPLEMENT_DYNCREATE(CBitDemoView, CView)

BEGIN_MESSAGE_MAP(CBitDemoView, CView)
    //{{AFX_MSG_MAP(CBitDemoView)
```

```
      // NOTE - the ClassWizard will add and remove mapping macros here.
      //     DO NOT EDIT what you see in these blocks of generated code!
   //}}AFX_MSG_MAP
END_MESSAGE_MAP()


/////////////////////////////////////////////////////////////////////////////
// CBitDemoView construction/destruction

CBitDemoView::CBitDemoView()
{
   // TODO: add construction code here
   BITMAP BM;

   m_Bitmap.LoadBitmap (IDB_BITMAP1);
   m_Bitmap.GetObject (sizeof (BM), &BM);
   m_BitmapWidth = BM.bmWidth;
   m_BitmapHeight = BM.bmHeight;
}


CBitDemoView::~CBitDemoView()
{
}


BOOL CBitDemoView::PreCreateWindow(CREATESTRUCT& cs)
{
   // TODO: Modify the Window class or styles here by modifying
   //  the CREATESTRUCT cs

   return CView::PreCreateWindow(cs);
}


/////////////////////////////////////////////////////////////////////////////
// CBitDemoView drawing

void CBitDemoView::OnDraw(CDC* pDC)
{
   CBitDemoDoc* pDoc = GetDocument();
   ASSERT_VALID(pDoc);

   // TODO: add draw code for native data here
   CDC MemDC;
   RECT ClientRect;

   // create memory device context object and select bitmap
```

```
    // object into it:
    MemDC.CreateCompatibleDC (NULL);
    MemDC.SelectObject (&m_Bitmap);

    // get current dimensions of view window:
    GetClientRect (&ClientRect);

    // display bitmap, stretching it to fit view window:
    pDC->StretchBlt
        (0,                   // coordinates of upper-left corner of
        0,                    // destination rectangle;
        ClientRect.right,     // width of destination rectangle;
        ClientRect.bottom,    // height of destination rectangle;
        &MemDC,               // source device context object;
        0,                    // coordinates of upper-left corner of
        0,                    // source rectangle;
        m_BitmapWidth,        // width of source rectangle;
        m_BitmapHeight,       // height of source rectangle;
        SRCCOPY);             // raster-operation code
}


/////////////////////////////////////////////////////////////////////////
// CBitDemoView diagnostics

#ifdef _DEBUG
void CBitDemoView::AssertValid() const
{
    CView::AssertValid();
}

void CBitDemoView::Dump(CDumpContext& dc) const
{
    CView::Dump(dc);
}

CBitDemoDoc* CBitDemoView::GetDocument() // non-debug version is inline
{
    ASSERT(m_pDocument->IsKindOf(RUNTIME_CLASS(CBitDemoDoc)));
    return (CBitDemoDoc*)m_pDocument;
}
#endif //_DEBUG


/////////////////////////////////////////////////////////////////////////
// CBitDemoView message handlers
```

Summary

In this chapter, you learned how to create and display bitmaps, as well as how to use bit-operation functions to transfer and manipulate blocks of graphic data. This chapter completes the discussion on the basic methods for displaying textual and graphic data within program windows. The following is a summary of some of the important concepts and methods discussed:

- A bitmap stores—in memory or in a file—an exact representation of an image by recording the state of every pixel used to create the image on a particular device.

- To create a bitmap, you first declare an instance of the MFC CBitmap class, and then call an appropriate CBitmap member function to initialize the object.

- You can initialize a bitmap object by calling CBitmap::LoadBitmap to load the bitmap data from a program resource. To use this method, you must have designed the bitmap in the Visual C++ graphics editor or imported the bitmap from a bitmap file obtained elsewhere.

- Alternatively, you can initialize a blank bitmap by calling the CBitmap::CreateCompatibleBitmap function, specifying the desired bitmap size. You can then draw the image you want within this bitmap by selecting the bitmap object into a memory device context object, and then using any of the drawing functions provided by the CDC class.

- You can display a bitmap within a window or on another device by selecting the bitmap into a memory device context object, and then using the CDC::BitBlt function to transfer the data from the bitmap to a window or other device.

- You can call the CDC::PatBlt function to paint a rectangular area using the current pattern (that is, the brush currently selected into the device context object). You pass PatBlt a raster-operation code that specifies the way the pixels in the pattern are to be combined with the pixels in the destination area.

- You can call the CDC::BitBlt function to transfer a block of graphics from one location to another location that's in the same device or in a different device. The raster-operation code you pass to BitBlt specifies the way that the pixels within the source device, within the current pattern, and within the destination device are to be combined.

- The `CDC::StretchBlt` function provides all the features of the `BitBlt` function, but also allows you to change the size of the block of graphics, or to flip the block horizontally or vertically, as it's transferred.

CHAPTER
TWENTY-ONE

Printing and Print Previewing

- Basic printing and print previewing

- Advanced printing

- The MiniDraw source code

In this chapter, you'll learn how to print text and graphics, as well as how to provide a print preview feature that allows the user to view the printed appearance of a document before sending it to the printer. Specifically, you'll learn how to implement the standard Print…, Print Preview, and Print Setup… commands on a program's File menu. Fortunately, because of Window's device-independent output model, you can use the techniques you've already learned for displaying text and graphics on the printed page. The chapter focuses on the tasks unique to printing—selecting and setting up the printer, dividing the document into pages, and performing other steps necessary for managing a print job.

The chapter first explains how to provide basic printing support, which allows the program to print or preview a single page. It then presents the more advanced techniques required to print or preview the pages of a document that won't fit on a single page. To illustrate the techniques, the chapter shows you how to add printing and print previewing support to the MiniDraw example program.

Basic Printing and Print Previewing

When you generate a new program using AppWizard, you can include basic printing and print previewing support in the program by selecting the Printing And Print Preview option in the AppWizard Step 4 dialog box, as shown in Figure 21.1. Selecting this option adds Print…, Print Preview, and Print Setup… commands to the program's File menu. As it's implemented by AppWizard, the Print… command prints as much of the document as will fit on a single page (any portion of the document that doesn't fit on a single page is ignored). Likewise, the Print Preview command displays the printed appearance of a single document page. As you'll see, both the Print… command and the Print Preview command call your OnDraw function to generate the actual text and graphics output. The Print Setup… command displays the Print Setup common dialog box, which allows the user to select a printer and to specify printer settings.

In this section, you'll add each of these printing features to the MiniDraw program. When you finish these steps, the MiniDraw program will have the same level of printer support that it would have if you had chosen the Printing And Print Preview option when you first generated the program using AppWizard. You'll add each feature to the version of MiniDraw you created in Chapter 19. (If you didn't create this version, you can obtain a complete copy of the program source files from the \MiniDrw6 companion-CD folder.)

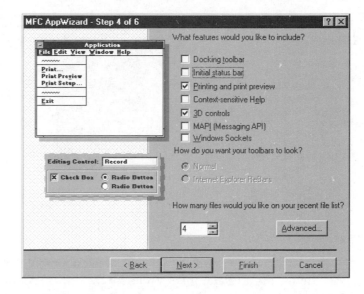

FIGURE 21.1:

Adding "Printing and print preview" support in the App-Wizard Step 4 dialog box

Modifying the Resources

To begin modifying the program resources, open the MiniDraw project, open the ResourceView tab in the Workspace window to display the program resources, and open the IDR_MAINFRAME menu in the menu editor. Immediately below the existing Save As... command on the File menu, add a separator, a Print... command, a Print Preview command, and a Print Setup... command. The properties of each of these menu items is shown in Table 21.1, and the completed File menu is shown in Figure 21.2.

TABLE 21.1: The Properties of the New File Menu Items

ID:	Caption	Prompt	Other Features
none	none	none	Separator
ID_FILE_PRINT	&Print...\tCtrl+P	Print the document	none
ID_FILE_PRINT_PREVIEW	Print Pre&view	Display full pages	none
ID_FILE_PRINT_SETUP	P&rint Setup...	Change the printer and printing options	none

The completed File menu

Next, open the IDR_MAINFRAME accelerator table in the accelerator editor to define the accelerator keystroke for the Print... command (Ctrl+P). Using the technique described previously (Chapter 10, in the section "Creating the Mini-Edit Program"), add an accelerator with the ID_FILE_PRINT identifier and the Ctrl+P keystroke.

You now need to include some additional predefined resources in the Mini-Draw resource definition file. To do this, choose the View ➤ Resource Includes... menu command in the Developer Studio. In the Resource Includes dialog box, add the following line to the end of the text within the Compile-Time Directives: text box:

```
#include "afxprint.rc"
```

The completed Resource Includes dialog box is shown in Figure 21.3. Click OK, and then click OK again when the Developer Studio asks you to confirm your action. Adding this new line causes the resource compiler to include the resource definitions contained in the resource script Afxprint.rc, which is provided by Visual C++. This script defines several resources that are used to support the program's Print... and Print Preview commands (such as the Printing dialog box that's displayed while printing is in progress).

FIGURE 21.3:

The completed Resource
Includes dialog box

Modifying the Code

The first code modification is to set up the handler for the new Print Setup...
command you added to the File menu. You don't need to write the handler
yourself because the CWinApp class provides one for you, which is named
OnFilePrintSetup. The MFC code, however, hasn't added this command to
the message map (thus, the function currently *won't* receive control when the
user chooses the Print Setup... command); you must therefore manually add
it to the message map for the MiniDraw application class. To do this, open the
MiniDraw.cpp file and add the entry marked in bold directly to the message-
map definition:

```
///////////////////////////////////////////////////////////////
///////////
// CMiniDrawApp

BEGIN_MESSAGE_MAP(CMiniDrawApp, CWinApp)
    //{{AFX_MSG_MAP(CMiniDrawApp)

    // ClassWizard message map entries ...

    //}}AFX_MSG_MAP
    // Standard file based document commands
```

```
ON_COMMAND(ID_FILE_NEW, CWinApp::OnFileNew)
ON_COMMAND(ID_FILE_OPEN, CWinApp::OnFileOpen)
ON_COMMAND(ID_FILE_PRINT_SETUP, CWinApp::OnFilePrintSetup)
END_MESSAGE_MAP()
```

The new message-map entry causes the `CWinApp::OnFilePrintSetup` function to be called whenever the user chooses the Print Setup... command. `OnFilePrintSetup` displays the Print Setup common dialog box, which allows the user to choose a printer and to set a variety of printing options. This is all you need to do to support the Print Setup... command!

Similarly, the `CView` class provides message-handling functions for the standard Print... and Print Preview menu commands. You must activate these message-handling functions by adding them to the message map for the MiniDraw view class. To do this, open the MiniDrawView.cpp file and add the following two entries to the end of the message map:

```
BEGIN_MESSAGE_MAP(CMiniDrawView, CScrollView)
    //{{AFX_MSG_MAP(CMiniDrawView)
    ON_WM_LBUTTONDOWN()
    ON_WM_MOUSEMOVE()
    ON_WM_LBUTTONUP()
    //}}AFX_MSG_MAP
    ON_COMMAND(ID_FILE_PRINT, CView::OnFilePrint)
    ON_COMMAND(ID_FILE_PRINT_PREVIEW, CView::OnFilePrintPreview)
END_MESSAGE_MAP()
```

Both the `CView::OnFilePrint` function and the `CView::OnFilePrintPreview` function conduct a print operation; `OnFilePrint`, however, sends the output to the actual printer, while `OnFilePrintPreview` sends the output to a print preview window that's displayed on top of the normal program window and shows a replica of either one or two printed pages. In the course of conducting the print job, both of these functions call a series of virtual functions that are defined within the `CView` class. The `CView` implementation of these virtual functions provides limited default print processing. As you'll see later in the chapter, you can define overriding versions of one or more of these functions to enhance the printing capabilities of the program.

To provide basic printing and print previewing support, however, you *must* override only the `CView::OnPreparePrinting` virtual function; the MFC calls this function before either printing or previewing the document. To provide an overriding version of the `OnPreparePrinting` function for MiniDraw, run Class-Wizard, open the Message Maps tab, select `CMiniDrawView` in the Class Name: and

Object IDs: lists, choose OnPreparePrinting in the Messages: lists, and click the Add Function button. Then, click the Edit Code button and, in the OnPreparePrinting function, *erase* the call to the base class version of OnPreparePrinting and add a call to CView::DoPreparePrinting:

```
BOOL CMiniDrawView::OnPreparePrinting(CPrintInfo* pInfo)
{
    // TODO: Add your specialized code here and/or call the base
    // class

    return DoPreparePrinting (pInfo);   // erase call to
        // CScrollView::OnPreparePrinting(pInfo);
}
```

The DoPreparePrinting function creates a device context object that's associated with the printer. If the document is being *printed*, DoPreparePrinting first displays the Print common dialog box, which allows the user to set several printing options and to choose a specific printer; it then creates a device context object that's associated with the chosen printer and is assigned the selected printer settings. If, however, the document is being *previewed*, DoPreparePrinting creates a device context object that's associated with the current default Windows printer and that's assigned the default printer settings, without displaying the Print dialog box. (If a device context object is associated with a printer, it stores printer settings *in addition to* storing the drawing attributes and drawing tools that were described in the previous chapters.) Note that you *must* provide an OnPreparePrinting function, because the default version of this function defined in CView does *nothing* and would therefore cause the MFC to attempt to print or preview the document without a valid device context object.

NOTE   A pointer to a CPrintInfo object is passed to all the virtual printing functions. This object contains information on the print job and provides both member functions and data members that the virtual printing functions in your program can use to obtain or change printer settings. For instance, if you know the number of printed pages in the document, you can call the CPrintInfo::SetMaxPage function from your OnPreparePrinting function (*before* the call to DoPreparePrinting) to specify the number of printed pages. If the document is being printed, this number will then be displayed in the Print dialog box (in the To: text box). If the document is being previewed, supplying this number will cause the MFC to display a scroll bar in the preview window, allowing the user to scroll through the document pages (the MFC must know the total number of pages so that it can properly position the scroll box within the scroll bar).

After the MFC calls `OnPreparePrinting` to prepare the device context object for printing or previewing, it passes this object to the `OnDraw` member function of the view class. Because the device context object is associated with the *printer* rather than the view window, the graphics output appears on the printed page (or in the print preview window), rather than within the view window. It's possible for a single drawing routine within `OnDraw` to display output either in a view window or on the printer because the CDC member functions that it calls are largely device-independent.

NOTE   Whether the document is being printed or previewed, the MFC prepares a device context object associated with the *printer*, and passes this object to `OnDraw`. If the document is being previewed, however, the MFC code in the device context object reroutes the actual output to the print preview window, using a separate device context that's associated with the preview window and has been assigned settings to make it *simulate* the appearance of the printed page.

You can now build and run the new version of the MiniDraw program. If you choose the Print Setup... command on the program's File menu, the Print Setup dialog box is displayed (see Figure 21.4), which allows you to choose the printer that's to receive printed output (if you've installed more than one printer in Windows) and to specify several printer settings; clicking the Properties button in the Print Setup dialog box allows you to access all available printer settings (the specific settings displayed depend on the chosen printer).

FIGURE 21.4:

The Print Setup dialog box

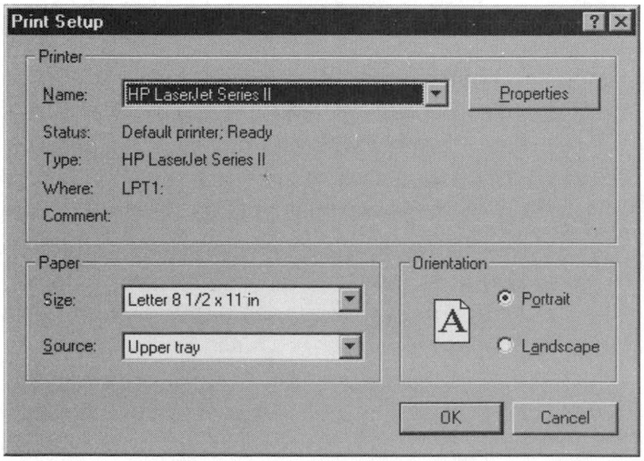

If you choose the Print... command, the program opens the Print dialog box (see Figure 21.5). In the Print dialog box, you can choose the printer that's to receive the output, and you can specify several printing options (the printing range and number of copies). Clicking the Properties button in the Print dialog box allows you to modify any of the available printer settings immediately before printing the drawing (these are the same options displayed by clicking the Properties button in the Print Setup dialog box). Unless the drawing is printed too quickly, you'll see a Printing dialog box during printing; you can click the Cancel button in this dialog box to stop the print job. (If you do this before the Windows Print Manager begins to send output to the printer, nothing will be printed.)

FIGURE 21.5:

The Print dialog box

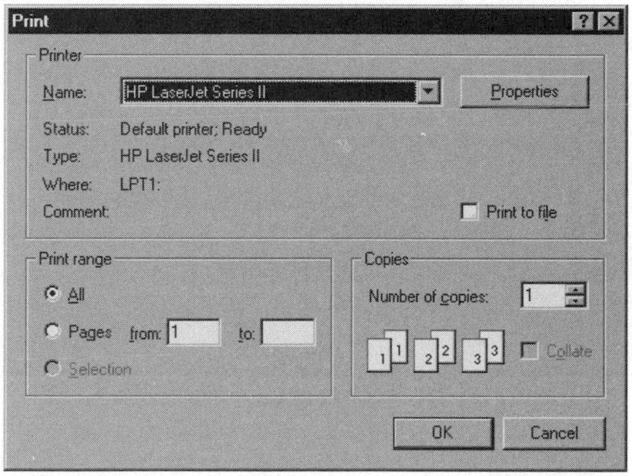

Finally, if you choose the Print Preview menu command, the program displays the print preview window, which contains an image of the entire printed page, scaled to fit within the program window. The print preview window allows you to judge the appearance of the page layout, although it doesn't permit editing the drawing; to edit, you must click the Close button to return to the normal view window. (The print preview window displayed by the final MiniDraw version is shown later in the chapter, in Figure 21.8.)

Adding Printing Support to a *CEditView* View Window

If the view class in your program is derived from CEditView (discussed in Chapter 10 and used for the MiniEdit program), the MFC and Windows itself provide much of the code required to support printing. Even if you haven't chosen the Printing And Print Preview option in AppWizard, you can implement the Print..., Print Preview, and Print Setup... commands with little programming effort.

To implement the Print... command, merely add the command to the File menu (assigning it the identifier ID_FILE_PRINT), without making any further coding changes. The resulting Print command will print the entire text document even if it requires more than one page.

To implement the Print Preview command, add the command to the File menu (assigning it the identifier ID_FILE_PRINT_PREVIEW), add the include statement for Afxprint.rc, and add the ON_COMMAND macro to the message map for the view class, as described in this section.

To implement the Print... or Print Preview command, you *don't* need to provide an OnPreparePrinting function.

The procedure for implementing the Print Setup... command is the same as that described in this section for the MiniDraw program.

Advanced Printing

With the printing support that you've added so far, MiniDraw prints or previews only the portion of the drawing that fits on a single printed page; the portion of the drawing (if any) that doesn't fit on this page is ignored. In this section, you'll enhance the program so that it will always print the entire drawing; any parts of the drawing that don't fit on a single page will be printed on additional pages. As you'll see, this enhancement is accomplished by overriding several other virtual print functions called during the print job.

Also, the current version of the OnDraw function always prints a border at the right and bottom of the drawing. This border, however, serves only to mark the boundaries of the drawing within the view window; it shouldn't appear on the printed copy of the drawing. In this section, you'll modify the OnDraw command so that it prints the borders only if the output is being sent to the view window.

Changing the Drawing Size

Recall from Chapter 13 that the MiniDraw program sets the drawing size to 640 by 480 pixels. For most printers, a drawing of this size easily fits on a single page. To demonstrate the techniques for printing multiple pages, you should first modify the MiniDraw program so that the drawing is *larger* than the typical size of a printed page. To do this, first define constant integers for the drawing width and height, at the beginning of the MiniDrawView.h file, as follows:

```
const int DRAWWIDTH  = 4000;  // drawing width
const int DRAWHEIGHT = 6000;  // drawing height

class CMiniDrawView : public CScrollView
{
```

Then, in the OnInitialUpdate function in the MiniDrawView.cpp file, use these constants rather than the numeric values (640 and 480):

```
void CMiniDrawView::OnInitialUpdate()
{
   // TODO: Add your specialized code here and/or call the base
   // class

   SIZE Size = {DRAWWIDTH, DRAWHEIGHT};
   SetScrollSizes (MM_TEXT, Size);
}
```

Using the constants DRAWHEIGHT and DRAWWIDTH rather than fixed numeric values will make it easy to change the size of the drawing if desired. The OnInitial-Update function was explained in Chapter 13 (in the section "Limiting the Drawing Size").

Because you changed the drawing size, you should also change the schema number used for serializing the document, so that the user can't inadvertently read a file created by a previous version (or—when using a previous version of the program—try to read a file created by the current version). To do this, open the file MiniDrawDoc.cpp and change the schema number from 2 to 3 in each occurrence of the IMPLEMENT_SERIAL macro (you should find eight occurrences). For example, you should change the macro

```
IMPLEMENT_SERIAL (CFigure, CObject, 2)
```

to

```
IMPLEMENT_SERIAL (CFigure, CObject, 3)
```

Schema numbers were explained in Chapter 12 (in the section "Serializing the Document Data").

TIP   A full-featured drawing program would typically allow the user to set the size of each drawing, perhaps through a command on the program's Options menu. When the drawing is saved in a disk file, the drawing size would have to be saved along with the data for the individual figures.

Overriding Virtual Printing Functions

As mentioned, when the MFC prints or previews a document, it calls a series of virtual functions defined within the CView class to perform various printing tasks. To enhance the printing process, you can define overriding versions of one or more of these functions within your view class, and add code to these functions to perform the desired tasks. Figure 21.6 illustrates the overall printing and print previewing processes and shows where each of the virtual functions is called within the procedure. Note that the process passes through the loop shown in this figure once for each page that's to be printed.

FIGURE 21.6:

The printing and print pre-viewing processes, and the CView virtual functions that are called

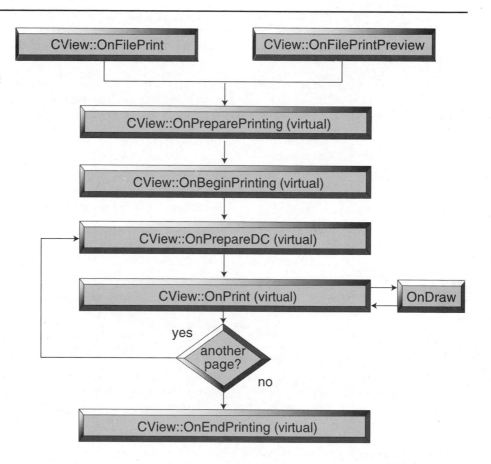

Table 21.2 lists the virtual functions and describes the tasks that you might perform from each one. For details, see the documentation on each of these functions. Note that because the MFC calls the virtual functions when either printing or previewing a document, the overriding functions you define will affect *both* printing *and* print previewing.

TABLE 21.2: The CView Virtual Printing Functions

Function Name	Possible Tasks Performed by Overriding Version of Function
OnPreparePrinting	Call CPrintInfo member functions (such as CPrintInfo::SetMax-Page to set length of document) or set CPrintInfo data members to affect Print dialog box or print preview operation; then call DoPrepare-Printing to create the device context object used for printing or pre-viewing (note that you *must* override OnPreparePrinting and call DoPreparePrinting).
OnBeginPrinting	Allocate any fonts, pens, brushes, and other objects used exclusively for printing; calculate and set length of document based on device context object; store any required information on device context object (this is the first virtual function that has access to the device context object).
OnPrepareDC	Set text or drawing attributes for printing current page; modify viewport origin to print current page; if document length has *not* been set, termi-nate print loop at end of document (by assigning FALSE to CPrint-Info::m_bContinuePrinting).
OnPrint	Call OnDraw to perform output; before calling OnDraw, select any fonts or other objects allocated by OnBeginPrinting; after calling OnDraw, deselect objects; print headers or footers that appear only in *printed* ver-sion of document; if printed output looks different from screen output, print it here *rather* than calling OnDraw.
OnEndPrinting	Delete any objects allocated by OnBeginPrinting (by calling CGdi-Object::DeleteObject).

NOTE
If you've written Windows printing code without using the MFC, you'll be happy to know that the MFC provides all the code necessary for displaying the Printing dialog box while the document is being printed, which allows the user to cancel the print job. It also provides a function that processes program messages during printing, so that the user can issue program commands (for example, clicking the Cancel button in the Printing dialog box); this function is known as an *abort procedure*.

You've already provided an overriding version of the OnPreparePrinting function (which is the only virtual printing function that *must* be overridden). To implement multiple-page printing, you'll now generate overriding versions of the OnBeginPrinting and OnPrepareDC virtual functions. Before defining these functions, however, you need to add several data members to the view class.

Open the MiniDrawView.h file, and add the data member definitions marked in bold to the `CMiniDrawView` class definition:

```
class CMiniDrawView : public CScrollView
{
protected:
    CString m_ClassName;
    int m_Dragging;
    HCURSOR m_HArrow;
    HCURSOR m_HCross;
    int m_NumCols, m_NumRows;
    int m_PageHeight, m_PageWidth;
    CPen m_PenDotted;
    CPoint m_PointOld;
    CPoint m_PointOrigin;
```

The data members m_NumCols and m_NumRows will be used to store the numbers of pages in the horizontal and vertical directions that are required to print the entire drawing, while m_PageHeight and m_PageWidth will be used to store the dimensions of the printed page.

To override the `OnBeginPrinting` virtual function, run ClassWizard, open the Message Maps: tab, choose `CMiniDrawView` in the Class Name: and Object IDs: lists, select `OnBeginPrinting` in the Messages: list, and click the Add Function button. In the same way, generate an overriding version of the `OnPrepareDC` virtual function.

Now open the MiniDrawView.cpp file and add the code as follows to the On-BeginPrinting function that you generated:

```
void CMiniDrawView::OnBeginPrinting(CDC* pDC, CPrintInfo* pInfo)
{
    // TODO: Add your specialized code here and/or call the base
    // class

    m_PageHeight = pDC->GetDeviceCaps (VERTRES);
    m_PageWidth = pDC->GetDeviceCaps (HORZRES);

    m_NumRows = DRAWHEIGHT / m_PageHeight  + (DRAWHEIGHT %
        m_PageHeight > 0);
    m_NumCols = DRAWWIDTH / m_PageWidth  + (DRAWWIDTH %
        m_PageWidth > 0);
    pInfo->SetMinPage (1);
```

```
        pInfo->SetMaxPage (m_NumRows * m_NumCols);

        CScrollView::OnBeginPrinting(pDC, pInfo);
    }
```

As shown in Figure 21.6, the OnBeginPrinting virtual function is called once at the beginning of the print job, *after* the device context object for the printer has been created but *before* the printing process enters the loop for printing each page. OnBeginPrinting is the first of the virtual printing functions that has access to the device context object.

The code you added to OnBeginPrinting first uses the device context object to call the CDC member function GetDeviceCaps in order to obtain the dimensions of the printable area of the page. When passed VERTRES, GetDeviceCaps returns the height of the printable area of the page in pixels (which is saved in m_PageHeight), and when passed HORZRES, it returns the width of the printable area in pixels (which is saved in m_PageWidth).

OnBeginPrinting then uses the dimensions of the printed page and the dimensions of the drawing to calculate the number of pages that will be required to print the entire drawing. First, it calculates the number of pages required in the vertical direction and saves the result in m_NumRows; it then calculates the number of pages required in the horizontal direction and saves the result in m_NumCols. (Notice that the expressions used to calculate the numbers of pages both use the % operator to round the number of pages *up* to the nearest whole number.) The *total* number of pages required to print the entire drawing is m_NumRows * m_NumCols.

Finally, OnBeginPrinting reports the total number of pages to the MFC. It calls CPrintInfo::SetMinPage to specify the number of the first page (1), and it calls CPrintInfo::SetMaxPage to specify the number of the last page (m_NumRows * m_NumCols). The MFC printing code will print the specified number of pages; that is, it will call the OnPrepareDC and OnPrint virtual functions (which are shown in the print loop in Figure 21.6) once for each specified page.

NOTE In the Print dialog box, the user can specify a limited range of pages *within* the range of pages that you indicate using the SetMinPage and SetMaxPage functions; in this case, the MFC prints the limited range. Note, also, that if you *don't* call SetMaxPage to set the maximum number of pages, you must define an OnPrepareDC function (described next), which manually terminates the printing loop by assigning FALSE to CPrintInfo::m_bContinuePrinting when the last page has been printed.

Also in MiniDrawView.cpp, you should add code as follows to the OnPrepareDC function that you generated:

```
void CMiniDrawView::OnPrepareDC(CDC* pDC, CPrintInfo* pInfo)
{
    // TODO: Add your specialized code here and/or call the base
    // class

    CScrollView::OnPrepareDC(pDC, pInfo);

    if (pInfo == NULL)
        return;

    int CurRow = pInfo->m_nCurPage / m_NumCols +
        (pInfo->m_nCurPage % m_NumCols > 0);
    int CurCol = (pInfo->m_nCurPage - 1) % m_NumCols + 1;

    pDC->SetViewportOrg
        (-m_PageWidth * (CurCol - 1),
        -m_PageHeight * (CurRow - 1));
}
```

As you can see in Figure 21.6, the MFC calls OnPrepareDC before printing each page in the document, and its primary duty is to prepare the device context object for printing the current page. As explained in Chapter 13, the MFC *also* calls On-PrepareDC immediately before calling OnDraw to redraw the view window; in this case, its duty is to adjust the viewport origin for the current scrolled position of the document (provided that the view class is derived from CScrollView and therefore supports scrolling).

If OnPrepareDC has been called prior to redrawing the view window, the call to CScrollView::OnPrepareDC at the beginning of the function will adjust the device context object for the current scrolled position, if necessary. Also, if the view window is being drawn, pInfo will equal NULL, and OnPrepareDC will then exit.

If OnPrepareDC has been called prior to printing a page, the call to OnPrepare-DC will make no changes to the device context object. However, pInfo will contain the address of a CPrintInfo object (providing print information), and the code you added will adjust the device context object so that the OnDraw function will print the *next* portion of the drawing on the current page.

The code you added to OnPrepareDC adjusts the device context object using the *same* method employed by the CScrollView class when a document is scrolled in the view window; namely, it adjusts the viewport origin (see the explanation of the viewport origin in the section "Converting Coordinates" near the beginning of Chapter 13). Before each new page is printed, OnPrepareDC adjusts the viewport origin to shift the positions of the figures relative to the page so that the *next portion* of the document will be printed when OnDraw is called.

When the first page is printed, the viewport origin is set to 0, 0 (the default value) so that the upper-left portion of the document is printed. When the next page is printed, OnPrepareDC subtracts the width of a page from the horizontal setting of the viewport origin so that the next portion of the drawing to the right is printed. It continues in this way to print the entire document, row by row, as shown in Figure 21.7.

FIGURE 21.7:

The order in which portions of the drawing are printed on subsequent pages

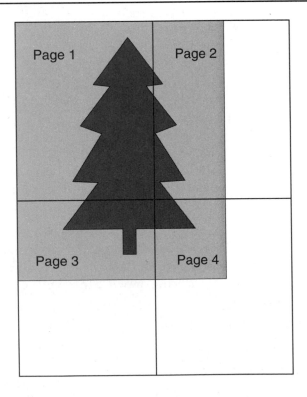

Note that the m_nCurPage data member of the CPrintInfo object that's passed to OnPrepareDC contains the number of the current page that's being printed. OnPrepareDC uses this value—together with the m_NumCols data member set by OnBeginPrinting—to calculate the row (CurRow) and column (CurCol) position of the portion of the drawing that's to be printed on the current page. It then uses CurRow and CurCol—as well as the page dimensions stored in m_PageWidth and m_PageHeight—to calculate the new coordinates of the viewport origin, which it passes to the CDC member function SetViewportOrg.

Modifying the *OnDraw* Function

As you can see in Figure 21.6, after calling OnPrepareDC, the MFC calls the On-Print virtual function. The default implementation of this function simply calls the OnDraw member function of your view class, passing it the device context object that was created by OnPreparePrinting and prepared by OnPrepareDC.

Because this device context object is associated with the printer, the output generated by OnDraw is automatically sent to the printer (or print preview window) rather than the view window. Also, because the viewport origin of the device context object has been adjusted (by OnPrepareDC), OnDraw automatically prints the correct portion of the drawing (that is, the portion that's to appear on the current page).

NOTE   The portion of the drawing that coincides with the physical printer page, and is therefore printed, depends on the current coordinates of the viewport origin that were set by OnPrepareDC. The other portions of the drawing are *clipped* (that is, they're discarded because they fall outside the boundaries of the physical page). The OnDraw function, however, doesn't waste time calling drawing functions for any figure that's completely outside the page. The call to GetClipBox returns the logical coordinates of the area of the drawing that will appear on the physical page; OnDraw *doesn't* call CFigure::Draw for any figure that falls completely outside this area.

In general, the code in OnDraw should be device-independent, because this function is used to send output to a variety of target devices. However, the On-Draw function in MiniDraw needs to print borders *only* if it's sending output to the view window. To prevent drawing borders when the output is being sent to a printer, place the code for drawing the lines within an `if` block, as follows:

```
void CMiniDrawView::OnDraw(CDC* pDC)
{
    CMiniDrawDoc* pDoc = GetDocument();
    ASSERT_VALID(pDoc);

    // TODO: add draw code for native data here

    if (pDC->GetDeviceCaps (TECHNOLOGY) == DT_RASDISPLAY)
        {
        CSize ScrollSize = GetTotalSize ();
        pDC->MoveTo (ScrollSize.cx, 0);
        pDC->LineTo (ScrollSize.cx, ScrollSize.cy);
        pDC->LineTo (0, ScrollSize.cy);
        }

    // remainder of OnDraw ...
```

When GetDeviceCaps is passed the index TECHNOLOGY, it returns a code indicating the type of device that's associated with the device context object. The code DT_RASDISPLAY indicates that the device is the screen; if OnDraw receives this code, it knows that the output is being sent to the view window (rather than the printer or the print preview window), and it proceeds to draw the borders. In general, you can use this technique whenever you need to customize the output generated by OnDraw for a particular target device. (See the GetDeviceCaps documentation in the online help for a description of the other codes it can return when it's passed the TECHNOLOGY index.)

The *GetDeviceCaps* Function

GetDeviceCaps is a useful CDC member function that you can call to help manage the print job once you've obtained a device context object for the printer. Typically, you'd call this function from an OnBeginPrinting, OnPrepareDC, or OnPrint virtual printing function that you've defined, or from the standard OnDraw member function of the view class.

You've already seen how to use GetDeviceCaps to determine the type of the output device (by passing TECHNOLOGY), and how to obtain the size of the printable area of the page in *pixels* (by passing HORZRES and VERTRES). Alternatively, you can obtain the width

Continued on next page

of the printable area in *millimeters* by passing the index HORZSIZE and the height in millimeters by passing VERTSIZE. Note that GetDeviceCaps returns the dimensions of the portion of the page on which you can actually print; because many printers (notably, laser printers) can't print all the way to the edge of the page, the dimensions returned by GetDeviceCaps are typically smaller than the physical page size.

When displaying data in a window, you generally assume that the display device is capable of performing all the basic drawing and bitmap operations discussed in Chapters 19 and 20. A printer or plotter, however, might not support all these operations. You can call GetDeviceCaps to determine whether the associated printer is capable of supporting the specific operations you want to perform. To find out whether the printer can perform the bitmap operations described in Chapter 20, you can pass GetDeviceCaps the index RASTERCAPS. If the return code includes the value RC_BITBLT, then the device supports the PatBlt and BitBlt functions; if the return code includes the value RC_STRETCHBLT, then the device supports the StretchBlt function. The following code shows how you'd test for bitmap operation capabilities:

```
int Caps;

Caps = pDC->GetDeviceCaps (RASTERCAPS);

if (Caps & RC_BITBLT)
   // then you can call 'PatBlt' or 'BitBlt'

if (Caps & RC_STRETCHBLT)
   // then you can call 'StretchBlt'
```

You can also determine the graphics drawing capabilities of the printer by passing GetDeviceCaps the index CURVECAPS (to determine its curve-drawing capabilities), LINECAPS (to determine its straight-line–drawing capabilities), or POLYGONALCAPS (to determine its capabilities for drawing rectangles and other polygons). For a complete description of the information that's returned when you pass any of these indexes, as well as the information you can obtain by passing other indexes to GetDeviceCaps, see the following online help topic: *Visual C++ Documentation, Reference, Microsoft Foundation Class Library and Templates, Microsoft Foundation Class Library, Class Library Reference, CDC, Member Functions, CDC::GetDeviceCaps.*

You can now build and run the MiniDraw program. The drawing will be much larger than in the previous version of the program, and you'll have to use the scroll bars to access various portions of it. When you choose the Print… command, *all* pages of the drawing will be printed (on a LaserJet Series II printer at a

300-pixel by 300-pixel resolution and with the Portrait orientation, the drawing will require four pages). When you choose the Print Preview command on the File menu, you'll be able to view *all* the pages required to print the drawing. The print preview window is shown in Figure 21.8.

FIGURE 21.8:

The print preview window in the final version of the MiniDraw program

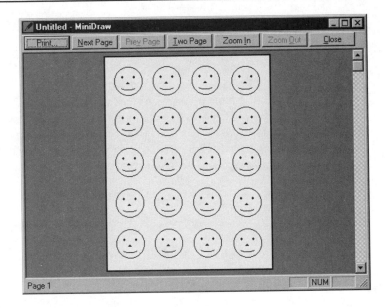

The MiniDraw Source Code

Listings 21.1 through 21.8 contain the C++ source code for the latest (and final) version of the MiniDraw program. You'll find a copy of these files in the \MiniDrw7 companion-CD folder.

Listing 21.1

```
// MiniDraw.h : main header file for the MINIDRAW application
//

#if !defined(AFX_MINIDRAW_H__11E83924_999A_11D1_80FC_00C0F6A83B7F__INCLUDED_)
#define AFX_MINIDRAW_H__11E83924_999A_11D1_80FC_00C0F6A83B7F__INCLUDED_

#if _MSC_VER > 1000
#pragma once
```

```
#endif // _MSC_VER > 1000

#ifndef __AFXWIN_H__
    #error include 'stdafx.h' before including this file for PCH
#endif

#include "resource.h"         // main symbols

/////////////////////////////////////////////////////////////////////////////
// CMiniDrawApp:
// See MiniDraw.cpp for the implementation of this class
//

class CMiniDrawApp : public CWinApp
{
public:
    COLORREF m_CurrentColor;
    int m_CurrentThickness;
    UINT m_CurrentTool;
    UINT m_IdxColorCmd;

public:
    CMiniDrawApp();

// Overrides
    // ClassWizard generated virtual function overrides
    //{{AFX_VIRTUAL(CMiniDrawApp)
    public:
    virtual BOOL InitInstance();
    //}}AFX_VIRTUAL

// Implementation

    //{{AFX_MSG(CMiniDrawApp)
    afx_msg void OnAppAbout();
    afx_msg void OnLineDouble();
    afx_msg void OnUpdateLineDouble(CCmdUI* pCmdUI);
    afx_msg void OnLineSingle();
    afx_msg void OnUpdateLineSingle(CCmdUI* pCmdUI);
    afx_msg void OnLineTriple();
    afx_msg void OnUpdateLineTriple(CCmdUI* pCmdUI);
    afx_msg void OnToolsCircle();
    afx_msg void OnUpdateToolsCircle(CCmdUI* pCmdUI);
    afx_msg void OnToolsCirclefill();
```

```
    afx_msg void OnUpdateToolsCirclefill(CCmdUI* pCmdUI);
    afx_msg void OnToolsLine();
    afx_msg void OnUpdateToolsLine(CCmdUI* pCmdUI);
    afx_msg void OnToolsRectangle();
    afx_msg void OnUpdateToolsRectangle(CCmdUI* pCmdUI);
    afx_msg void OnToolsRectfill();
    afx_msg void OnUpdateToolsRectfill(CCmdUI* pCmdUI);
    afx_msg void OnToolsRectround();
    afx_msg void OnUpdateToolsRectround(CCmdUI* pCmdUI);
    afx_msg void OnToolsRectroundfill();
    afx_msg void OnUpdateToolsRectroundfill(CCmdUI* pCmdUI);
    afx_msg void OnColorBlack();
    afx_msg void OnUpdateColorBlack(CCmdUI* pCmdUI);
    afx_msg void OnColorBlue();
    afx_msg void OnUpdateColorBlue(CCmdUI* pCmdUI);
    afx_msg void OnColorCustom();
    afx_msg void OnUpdateColorCustom(CCmdUI* pCmdUI);
    afx_msg void OnColorCyan();
    afx_msg void OnUpdateColorCyan(CCmdUI* pCmdUI);
    afx_msg void OnColorGreen();
    afx_msg void OnUpdateColorGreen(CCmdUI* pCmdUI);
    afx_msg void OnColorMagenta();
    afx_msg void OnUpdateColorMagenta(CCmdUI* pCmdUI);
    afx_msg void OnColorRed();
    afx_msg void OnUpdateColorRed(CCmdUI* pCmdUI);
    afx_msg void OnColorWhite();
    afx_msg void OnUpdateColorWhite(CCmdUI* pCmdUI);
    afx_msg void OnColorYellow();
    afx_msg void OnUpdateColorYellow(CCmdUI* pCmdUI);
    //}}AFX_MSG
    DECLARE_MESSAGE_MAP()
};


/////////////////////////////////////////////////////////////////////

//{{AFX_INSERT_LOCATION}}
// Microsoft Visual C++ will insert additional declarations immediately before
// the previous line.

#endif
// !defined(AFX_MINIDRAW_H__11E83924_999A_11D1_80FC_00C0F6A83B7F__INCLUDED_)
```

Listing 21.2

```cpp
// MiniDraw.cpp : Defines the class behaviors for the application.
//

#include "stdafx.h"
#include "MiniDraw.h"

#include "MainFrm.h"
#include "MiniDrawDoc.h"
#include "MiniDrawView.h"

#ifdef _DEBUG
#define new DEBUG_NEW
#undef THIS_FILE
static char THIS_FILE[] = __FILE__;
#endif

/////////////////////////////////////////////////////////////////////////////
// CMiniDrawApp

BEGIN_MESSAGE_MAP(CMiniDrawApp, CWinApp)
    //{{AFX_MSG_MAP(CMiniDrawApp)
    ON_COMMAND(ID_APP_ABOUT, OnAppAbout)
    ON_COMMAND(ID_LINE_DOUBLE, OnLineDouble)
    ON_UPDATE_COMMAND_UI(ID_LINE_DOUBLE, OnUpdateLineDouble)
    ON_COMMAND(ID_LINE_SINGLE, OnLineSingle)
    ON_UPDATE_COMMAND_UI(ID_LINE_SINGLE, OnUpdateLineSingle)
    ON_COMMAND(ID_LINE_TRIPLE, OnLineTriple)
    ON_UPDATE_COMMAND_UI(ID_LINE_TRIPLE, OnUpdateLineTriple)
    ON_COMMAND(ID_TOOLS_CIRCLE, OnToolsCircle)
    ON_UPDATE_COMMAND_UI(ID_TOOLS_CIRCLE, OnUpdateToolsCircle)
    ON_COMMAND(ID_TOOLS_CIRCLEFILL, OnToolsCirclefill)
    ON_UPDATE_COMMAND_UI(ID_TOOLS_CIRCLEFILL, OnUpdateToolsCirclefill)
    ON_COMMAND(ID_TOOLS_LINE, OnToolsLine)
    ON_UPDATE_COMMAND_UI(ID_TOOLS_LINE, OnUpdateToolsLine)
    ON_COMMAND(ID_TOOLS_RECTANGLE, OnToolsRectangle)
    ON_UPDATE_COMMAND_UI(ID_TOOLS_RECTANGLE, OnUpdateToolsRectangle)
    ON_COMMAND(ID_TOOLS_RECTFILL, OnToolsRectfill)
    ON_UPDATE_COMMAND_UI(ID_TOOLS_RECTFILL, OnUpdateToolsRectfill)
    ON_COMMAND(ID_TOOLS_RECTROUND, OnToolsRectround)
```

```
    ON_UPDATE_COMMAND_UI(ID_TOOLS_RECTROUND, OnUpdateToolsRectround)
    ON_COMMAND(ID_TOOLS_RECTROUNDFILL, OnToolsRectroundfill)
    ON_UPDATE_COMMAND_UI(ID_TOOLS_RECTROUNDFILL, OnUpdateToolsRectroundfill)
    ON_COMMAND(ID_COLOR_BLACK, OnColorBlack)
    ON_UPDATE_COMMAND_UI(ID_COLOR_BLACK, OnUpdateColorBlack)
    ON_COMMAND(ID_COLOR_BLUE, OnColorBlue)
    ON_UPDATE_COMMAND_UI(ID_COLOR_BLUE, OnUpdateColorBlue)
    ON_COMMAND(ID_COLOR_CUSTOM, OnColorCustom)
    ON_UPDATE_COMMAND_UI(ID_COLOR_CUSTOM, OnUpdateColorCustom)
    ON_COMMAND(ID_COLOR_CYAN, OnColorCyan)
    ON_UPDATE_COMMAND_UI(ID_COLOR_CYAN, OnUpdateColorCyan)
    ON_COMMAND(ID_COLOR_GREEN, OnColorGreen)
    ON_UPDATE_COMMAND_UI(ID_COLOR_GREEN, OnUpdateColorGreen)
    ON_COMMAND(ID_COLOR_MAGENTA, OnColorMagenta)
    ON_UPDATE_COMMAND_UI(ID_COLOR_MAGENTA, OnUpdateColorMagenta)
    ON_COMMAND(ID_COLOR_RED, OnColorRed)
    ON_UPDATE_COMMAND_UI(ID_COLOR_RED, OnUpdateColorRed)
    ON_COMMAND(ID_COLOR_WHITE, OnColorWhite)
    ON_UPDATE_COMMAND_UI(ID_COLOR_WHITE, OnUpdateColorWhite)
    ON_COMMAND(ID_COLOR_YELLOW, OnColorYellow)
    ON_UPDATE_COMMAND_UI(ID_COLOR_YELLOW, OnUpdateColorYellow)
    //}}AFX_MSG_MAP
    // Standard file based document commands
    ON_COMMAND(ID_FILE_NEW, CWinApp::OnFileNew)
    ON_COMMAND(ID_FILE_OPEN, CWinApp::OnFileOpen)
    ON_COMMAND(ID_FILE_PRINT_SETUP, CWinApp::OnFilePrintSetup)
END_MESSAGE_MAP()

/////////////////////////////////////////////////////////////////////////////
// CMiniDrawApp construction

CMiniDrawApp::CMiniDrawApp()
{
    // TODO: add construction code here,
    // Place all significant initialization in InitInstance

    m_CurrentColor = RGB (0,0,0);
    m_CurrentThickness = 1;
    m_CurrentTool = ID_TOOLS_LINE;
    m_IdxColorCmd = ID_COLOR_BLACK;
}
```

```
/////////////////////////////////////////////////////////////////////////
// The one and only CMiniDrawApp object

CMiniDrawApp theApp;

/////////////////////////////////////////////////////////////////////////
// CMiniDrawApp initialization

BOOL CMiniDrawApp::InitInstance()
{
    // Standard initialization
    // If you are not using these features and wish to reduce the size
    //  of your final executable, you should remove from the following
    //  the specific initialization routines you do not need.

#ifdef _AFXDLL
    Enable3dControls();         // Call this when using MFC in a shared DLL
#else
    Enable3dControlsStatic();   // Call this when linking to MFC statically
#endif

    // Change the registry key under which our settings are stored.
    // You should modify this string to be something appropriate
    // such as the name of your company or organization.
    SetRegistryKey(_T("Local AppWizard-Generated Applications"));

    LoadStdProfileSettings();   // Load standard INI file options (including MRU)

    // Register the application's document templates.  Document templates
    //  serve as the connection between documents, frame windows and views.

    CSingleDocTemplate* pDocTemplate;
    pDocTemplate = new CSingleDocTemplate(
        IDR_MAINFRAME,
        RUNTIME_CLASS(CMiniDrawDoc),
        RUNTIME_CLASS(CMainFrame),        // main SDI frame window
        RUNTIME_CLASS(CMiniDrawView));
    AddDocTemplate(pDocTemplate);

    EnableShellOpen ();
    RegisterShellFileTypes ();
```

```
// Parse command line for standard shell commands, DDE, file open
CCommandLineInfo cmdInfo;
ParseCommandLine(cmdInfo);

// Dispatch commands specified on the command line
if (!ProcessShellCommand(cmdInfo))
   return FALSE;

// The one and only window has been initialized, so show and update it.
m_pMainWnd->ShowWindow(SW_SHOW);
m_pMainWnd->UpdateWindow();

m_pMainWnd->DragAcceptFiles ();

return TRUE;
}


/////////////////////////////////////////////////////////////////////////////
// CAboutDlg dialog used for App About

class CAboutDlg : public CDialog
{
public:
   CAboutDlg();

// Dialog Data
   //{{AFX_DATA(CAboutDlg)
   enum { IDD = IDD_ABOUTBOX };
   //}}AFX_DATA

   // ClassWizard generated virtual function overrides
   //{{AFX_VIRTUAL(CAboutDlg)
   protected:
   virtual void DoDataExchange(CDataExchange* pDX);    // DDX/DDV support
   //}}AFX_VIRTUAL

// Implementation
protected:
   //{{AFX_MSG(CAboutDlg)
      // No message handlers
   //}}AFX_MSG
```

```
    DECLARE_MESSAGE_MAP()
};

CAboutDlg::CAboutDlg() : CDialog(CAboutDlg::IDD)
{
    //{{AFX_DATA_INIT(CAboutDlg)
    //}}AFX_DATA_INIT
}

void CAboutDlg::DoDataExchange(CDataExchange* pDX)
{
    CDialog::DoDataExchange(pDX);
    //{{AFX_DATA_MAP(CAboutDlg)
    //}}AFX_DATA_MAP
}

BEGIN_MESSAGE_MAP(CAboutDlg, CDialog)
    //{{AFX_MSG_MAP(CAboutDlg)
        // No message handlers
    //}}AFX_MSG_MAP
END_MESSAGE_MAP()

// App command to run the dialog
void CMiniDrawApp::OnAppAbout()
{
    CAboutDlg aboutDlg;
    aboutDlg.DoModal();
}


/////////////////////////////////////////////////////////////////////
// CMiniDrawApp commands

void CMiniDrawApp::OnLineDouble()
{
    // TODO: Add your command handler code here
    m_CurrentThickness = 2;
}

void CMiniDrawApp::OnUpdateLineDouble(CCmdUI* pCmdUI)
{
    // TODO: Add your command update UI handler code here
```

```
   pCmdUI->SetCheck (m_CurrentThickness == 2 ? 1 : 0);
}

void CMiniDrawApp::OnLineSingle()
{
   // TODO: Add your command handler code here
   m_CurrentThickness = 1;
}

void CMiniDrawApp::OnUpdateLineSingle(CCmdUI* pCmdUI)
{
   // TODO: Add your command update UI handler code here
   pCmdUI->SetCheck (m_CurrentThickness == 1 ? 1 : 0);
}

void CMiniDrawApp::OnLineTriple()
{
   // TODO: Add your command handler code here
   m_CurrentThickness = 3;
}

void CMiniDrawApp::OnUpdateLineTriple(CCmdUI* pCmdUI)
{
   // TODO: Add your command update UI handler code here
   pCmdUI->SetCheck (m_CurrentThickness == 3 ? 1 : 0);
}

void CMiniDrawApp::OnToolsCircle()
{
   // TODO: Add your command handler code here
   m_CurrentTool = ID_TOOLS_CIRCLE;
}

void CMiniDrawApp::OnUpdateToolsCircle(CCmdUI* pCmdUI)
{
   // TODO: Add your command update UI handler code here
   pCmdUI->SetCheck (m_CurrentTool == ID_TOOLS_CIRCLE ? 1 : 0);
}

void CMiniDrawApp::OnToolsCirclefill()
{
   // TODO: Add your command handler code here
```

```
   m_CurrentTool = ID_TOOLS_CIRCLEFILL;
}

void CMiniDrawApp::OnUpdateToolsCirclefill(CCmdUI* pCmdUI)
{
   // TODO: Add your command update UI handler code here
   pCmdUI->SetCheck
      (m_CurrentTool == ID_TOOLS_CIRCLEFILL ? 1 : 0);
}

void CMiniDrawApp::OnToolsLine()
{
   // TODO: Add your command handler code here
   m_CurrentTool = ID_TOOLS_LINE;
}

void CMiniDrawApp::OnUpdateToolsLine(CCmdUI* pCmdUI)
{
   // TODO: Add your command update UI handler code here
   pCmdUI->SetCheck (m_CurrentTool == ID_TOOLS_LINE ? 1 : 0);
}

void CMiniDrawApp::OnToolsRectangle()
{
   // TODO: Add your command handler code here
   m_CurrentTool = ID_TOOLS_RECTANGLE;
}

void CMiniDrawApp::OnUpdateToolsRectangle(CCmdUI* pCmdUI)
{
   // TODO: Add your command update UI handler code here
   pCmdUI->SetCheck
      (m_CurrentTool == ID_TOOLS_RECTANGLE ? 1 : 0);
}

void CMiniDrawApp::OnToolsRectfill()
{
   // TODO: Add your command handler code here
   m_CurrentTool = ID_TOOLS_RECTFILL;
}
```

```
void CMiniDrawApp::OnUpdateToolsRectfill(CCmdUI* pCmdUI)
{
    // TODO: Add your command update UI handler code here
    pCmdUI->SetCheck (m_CurrentTool == ID_TOOLS_RECTFILL ? 1 : 0);
}

void CMiniDrawApp::OnToolsRectround()
{
    // TODO: Add your command handler code here
    m_CurrentTool = ID_TOOLS_RECTROUND;
}

void CMiniDrawApp::OnUpdateToolsRectround(CCmdUI* pCmdUI)
{
    // TODO: Add your command update UI handler code here
    pCmdUI->SetCheck
        (m_CurrentTool == ID_TOOLS_RECTROUND ? 1 : 0);
}

void CMiniDrawApp::OnToolsRectroundfill()
{
    // TODO: Add your command handler code here
    m_CurrentTool = ID_TOOLS_RECTROUNDFILL;
}

void CMiniDrawApp::OnUpdateToolsRectroundfill(CCmdUI* pCmdUI)
{
    // TODO: Add your command update UI handler code here
    pCmdUI->SetCheck
        (m_CurrentTool == ID_TOOLS_RECTROUNDFILL ? 1 : 0);
}

void CMiniDrawApp::OnColorBlack()
{
    // TODO: Add your command handler code here
    m_CurrentColor = RGB (0,0,0);
    m_IdxColorCmd = ID_COLOR_BLACK;
}

void CMiniDrawApp::OnUpdateColorBlack(CCmdUI* pCmdUI)
{
    // TODO: Add your command update UI handler code here
    pCmdUI->SetCheck (m_IdxColorCmd == ID_COLOR_BLACK ? 1 : 0);
}
```

```cpp
void CMiniDrawApp::OnColorBlue()
{
   // TODO: Add your command handler code here
   m_CurrentColor = RGB (0,0,255);
   m_IdxColorCmd = ID_COLOR_BLUE;
}

void CMiniDrawApp::OnUpdateColorBlue(CCmdUI* pCmdUI)
{
   // TODO: Add your command update UI handler code here
   pCmdUI->SetCheck (m_IdxColorCmd == ID_COLOR_BLUE ? 1 : 0);
}

void CMiniDrawApp::OnColorCustom()
{
   // TODO: Add your command handler code here
   CColorDialog ColorDialog;

   if (ColorDialog.DoModal () == IDOK)
      {
      m_CurrentColor = ColorDialog.GetColor ();
      m_IdxColorCmd = ID_COLOR_CUSTOM;
      }
}

void CMiniDrawApp::OnUpdateColorCustom(CCmdUI* pCmdUI)
{
   // TODO: Add your command update UI handler code here
   pCmdUI->SetCheck (m_IdxColorCmd == ID_COLOR_CUSTOM ? 1 : 0);
}

void CMiniDrawApp::OnColorCyan()
{
   // TODO: Add your command handler code here
   m_CurrentColor = RGB (0,255,255);
   m_IdxColorCmd = ID_COLOR_CYAN;
}

void CMiniDrawApp::OnUpdateColorCyan(CCmdUI* pCmdUI)
{
   // TODO: Add your command update UI handler code here
   pCmdUI->SetCheck (m_IdxColorCmd == ID_COLOR_CYAN ? 1 : 0);
}
```

```
void CMiniDrawApp::OnColorGreen()
{
   // TODO: Add your command handler code here
   m_CurrentColor = RGB (0,255,0);
   m_IdxColorCmd = ID_COLOR_GREEN;
}

void CMiniDrawApp::OnUpdateColorGreen(CCmdUI* pCmdUI)
{
   // TODO: Add your command update UI handler code here
   pCmdUI->SetCheck (m_IdxColorCmd == ID_COLOR_GREEN ? 1 : 0);
}

void CMiniDrawApp::OnColorMagenta()
{
   // TODO: Add your command handler code here
   m_CurrentColor = RGB (255,0,255);
   m_IdxColorCmd = ID_COLOR_MAGENTA;
}

void CMiniDrawApp::OnUpdateColorMagenta(CCmdUI* pCmdUI)
{
   // TODO: Add your command update UI handler code here
   pCmdUI->SetCheck (m_IdxColorCmd == ID_COLOR_MAGENTA ? 1 : 0);
}

void CMiniDrawApp::OnColorRed()
{
   // TODO: Add your command handler code here
   m_CurrentColor = RGB (255,0,0);
   m_IdxColorCmd • ID_COLOR_RED;
}

void CMiniDrawApp::OnUpdateColorRed(CCmdUI* pCmdUI)
{
   // TODO: Add your command update UI handler code here
   pCmdUI->SetCheck (m_IdxColorCmd == ID_COLOR_RED ? 1 : 0);
}

void CMiniDrawApp::OnColorWhite()
{
   // TODO: Add your command handler code here
```

```
      m_CurrentColor = RGB (255,255,255);
      m_IdxColorCmd = ID_COLOR_WHITE;
}

void CMiniDrawApp::OnUpdateColorWhite(CCmdUI* pCmdUI)
{
      // TODO: Add your command update UI handler code here
      pCmdUI->SetCheck (m_IdxColorCmd == ID_COLOR_WHITE ? 1 : 0);
}

void CMiniDrawApp::OnColorYellow()
{
      // TODO: Add your command handler code here
      m_CurrentColor = RGB (255,255,0);
      m_IdxColorCmd = ID_COLOR_YELLOW;
}

void CMiniDrawApp::OnUpdateColorYellow(CCmdUI* pCmdUI)
{
      // TODO: Add your command update UI handler code here
      pCmdUI->SetCheck (m_IdxColorCmd == ID_COLOR_YELLOW ? 1 : 0);
}
```

Listing 21.3

```
// MiniDrawDoc.h : interface of the CMiniDrawDoc class
//
/////////////////////////////////////////////////////////////////////////

#if !defined(AFX_MINIDRAWDOC_H__11E8392A_999A_11D1_80FC_00C0F6A83B7F__INCLUDED_)
#define AFX_MINIDRAWDOC_H__11E8392A_999A_11D1_80FC_00C0F6A83B7F__INCLUDED_

#if _MSC_VER > 1000
#pragma once
#endif // _MSC_VER > 1000

// class hierarchy for figures:

class CFigure : public CObject
{
protected:
      COLORREF m_Color;
      DWORD m_X1, m_Y1, m_X2, m_Y2;
```

```
   CFigure () {}
   DECLARE_SERIAL (CFigure)

public:
   virtual void Draw (CDC *PDC) {}
   CRect GetDimRect ();
   virtual void Serialize (CArchive& ar);
};

class CLine : public CFigure
{
protected:
   DWORD m_Thickness;
   CLine () {}
   DECLARE_SERIAL (CLine)

public:
   CLine (int X1, int Y1, int X2, int Y2, COLORREF Color, int Thickness);
   virtual void Draw (CDC *PDC);
   virtual void Serialize (CArchive& ar);
};

class CRectangle : public CFigure
{
protected:
   DWORD m_Thickness;

   CRectangle () {}
   DECLARE_SERIAL (CRectangle)

public:
   CRectangle (int X1, int Y1, int X2, int Y2, COLORREF Color, int Thickness);
   virtual void Draw (CDC *PDC);
   virtual void Serialize (CArchive& ar);
};

class CRectFill : public CFigure
{
protected:
   CRectFill () {}
   DECLARE_SERIAL (CRectFill)
```

```
public:
   CRectFill (int X1, int Y1, int X2, int Y2, COLORREF Color);
   virtual void Draw (CDC *PDC);
};

class CRectRound : public CFigure
{
protected:
   DWORD m_Thickness;

   CRectRound () {}
   DECLARE_SERIAL (CRectRound)

public:
   CRectRound (int X1, int Y1, int X2, int Y2, COLORREF Color, int Thickness);
   virtual void Draw (CDC *PDC);
   virtual void Serialize (CArchive& ar);
};

class CRectRoundFill : public CFigure
{
protected:
   CRectRoundFill () {}
   DECLARE_SERIAL (CRectRoundFill)

public:
   CRectRoundFill (int X1, int Y1, int X2, int Y2, COLORREF Color);
   virtual void Draw (CDC *PDC);
};

class CCircle : public CFigure
{
protected:
   DWORD m_Thickness;

   CCircle () {}
   DECLARE_SERIAL (CCircle)

public:
   CCircle (int X1, int Y1, int X2, int Y2, COLORREF Color, int Thickness);
   virtual void Draw (CDC *PDC);
   virtual void Serialize (CArchive& ar);
};
```

```
class CCircleFill : public CFigure
{
protected:
   CCircleFill () {}
   DECLARE_SERIAL (CCircleFill)

public:
   CCircleFill (int X1, int Y1, int X2, int Y2, COLORREF Color);
   virtual void Draw (CDC *PDC);
};

class CMiniDrawDoc : public CDocument
{
protected:
   CTypedPtrArray<CObArray, CFigure*> m_FigArray;

public:
   void AddFigure (CFigure *PFigure);
   CFigure *GetFigure (int Index);
   int GetNumFigs ();

protected: // create from serialization only
   CMiniDrawDoc();
   DECLARE_DYNCREATE(CMiniDrawDoc)

// Attributes
public:

// Operations
public:

// Overrides
   // ClassWizard generated virtual function overrides
   //{{AFX_VIRTUAL(CMiniDrawDoc)
   public:
   virtual BOOL OnNewDocument();
   virtual void Serialize(CArchive& ar);
   virtual void DeleteContents();
   //}}AFX_VIRTUAL
```

```cpp
// Implementation
public:
    virtual ~CMiniDrawDoc();
#ifdef _DEBUG
    virtual void AssertValid() const;
    virtual void Dump(CDumpContext& dc) const;
#endif

protected:

// Generated message map functions
protected:
    //{{AFX_MSG(CMiniDrawDoc)
    afx_msg void OnEditClearAll();
    afx_msg void OnUpdateEditClearAll(CCmdUI* pCmdUI);
    afx_msg void OnEditUndo();
    afx_msg void OnUpdateEditUndo(CCmdUI* pCmdUI);
    //}}AFX_MSG
    DECLARE_MESSAGE_MAP()
};

/////////////////////////////////////////////////////////////////////////////

//{{AFX_INSERT_LOCATION}}
// Microsoft Visual C++ will insert additional declarations immediately before
// the previous line.

#endif
// !defined(AFX_MINIDRAWDOC_H__11E8392A_999A_11D1_80FC_00C0F6A83B7F__INCLUDED_)
```

Listing 21.4

```cpp
// MiniDrawDoc.cpp : implementation of the CMiniDrawDoc class
//

#include "stdafx.h"
#include "MiniDraw.h"

#include "MiniDrawDoc.h"
```

```
#ifdef _DEBUG
#define new DEBUG_NEW
#undef THIS_FILE
static char THIS_FILE[] = __FILE__;
#endif

/////////////////////////////////////////////////////////////////////////////
// CMiniDrawDoc

IMPLEMENT_DYNCREATE(CMiniDrawDoc, CDocument)

BEGIN_MESSAGE_MAP(CMiniDrawDoc, CDocument)
    //{{AFX_MSG_MAP(CMiniDrawDoc)
    ON_COMMAND(ID_EDIT_CLEAR_ALL, OnEditClearAll)
    ON_UPDATE_COMMAND_UI(ID_EDIT_CLEAR_ALL, OnUpdateEditClearAll)
    ON_COMMAND(ID_EDIT_UNDO, OnEditUndo)
    ON_UPDATE_COMMAND_UI(ID_EDIT_UNDO, OnUpdateEditUndo)
    //}}AFX_MSG_MAP
END_MESSAGE_MAP()

/////////////////////////////////////////////////////////////////////////////
// CMiniDrawDoc construction/destruction

CMiniDrawDoc::CMiniDrawDoc()
{
    // TODO: add one-time construction code here

}

CMiniDrawDoc::~CMiniDrawDoc()
{
}

BOOL CMiniDrawDoc::OnNewDocument()
{
    if (!CDocument::OnNewDocument())
        return FALSE;

    // TODO: add reinitialization code here
    // (SDI documents will reuse this document)

    return TRUE;
}
```

```
/////////////////////////////////////////////////////////////////////
// CMiniDrawDoc serialization

void CMiniDrawDoc::Serialize(CArchive& ar)
{
   if (ar.IsStoring())
   {
      // TODO: add storing code here
      m_FigArray.Serialize (ar);
   }
   else
   {
      // TODO: add loading code here
      m_FigArray.Serialize (ar);
   }
}


/////////////////////////////////////////////////////////////////////
// CMiniDrawDoc diagnostics

#ifdef _DEBUG
void CMiniDrawDoc::AssertValid() const
{
   CDocument::AssertValid();
}

void CMiniDrawDoc::Dump(CDumpContext& dc) const
{
   CDocument::Dump(dc);
}
#endif //_DEBUG


/////////////////////////////////////////////////////////////////////
// CMiniDrawDoc commands

void CMiniDrawDoc::AddFigure (CFigure *PFigure)
   {
   m_FigArray.Add (PFigure);
   SetModifiedFlag ();
   }

CFigure *CMiniDrawDoc::GetFigure (int Index)
```

```
   {
   if (Index < 0 || Index > m_FigArray.GetUpperBound ())
      return 0;
   return (CFigure *)m_FigArray.GetAt (Index);
   }

int CMiniDrawDoc::GetNumFigs ()
   {
   return m_FigArray.GetSize ();
   }

void CMiniDrawDoc::DeleteContents()
{
   // TODO: Add your specialized code here and/or call the base class

   int Index = m_FigArray.GetSize ();
   while (Index--)
      delete m_FigArray.GetAt (Index);
   m_FigArray.RemoveAll ();

   CDocument::DeleteContents();
}

void CMiniDrawDoc::OnEditClearAll()
{
   // TODO: Add your command handler code here

   DeleteContents ();
   UpdateAllViews (0);
   SetModifiedFlag ();
}

void CMiniDrawDoc::OnUpdateEditClearAll(CCmdUI* pCmdUI)
{
   // TODO: Add your command update UI handler code here

   pCmdUI->Enable (m_FigArray.GetSize ());
}

void CMiniDrawDoc::OnEditUndo()
{
   // TODO: Add your command handler code here
```

```
   int Index = m_FigArray.GetUpperBound ();
   if (Index > -1)
      {
      delete m_FigArray.GetAt (Index);
      m_FigArray.RemoveAt (Index);
      }
   UpdateAllViews (0);
   SetModifiedFlag ();
}

void CMiniDrawDoc::OnUpdateEditUndo(CCmdUI* pCmdUI)
{
   // TODO: Add your command update UI handler code here

   pCmdUI->Enable (m_FigArray.GetSize ());
}

// implementation of figure classes:

IMPLEMENT_SERIAL (CFigure, CObject, 3)

CRect CFigure::GetDimRect ()
   {
   return CRect
     (min (m_X1, m_X2),
      min (m_Y1, m_Y2),
      max (m_X1, m_X2) + 1,
      max (m_Y1, m_Y2) + 1);
   }

void CFigure::Serialize (CArchive& ar)
   {
   if (ar.IsStoring ())
      ar << m_X1 << m_Y1 << m_X2 << m_Y2 << m_Color;
   else
      ar >> m_X1 >> m_Y1 >> m_X2 >> m_Y2 >> m_Color;
   }

IMPLEMENT_SERIAL (CLine, CFigure, 3)
```

```
CLine::CLine (int X1, int Y1, int X2, int Y2, COLORREF Color, int Thickness)
    {
    m_X1 = X1;
    m_Y1 = Y1;
    m_X2 = X2;
    m_Y2 = Y2;
    m_Color = Color;
    m_Thickness = Thickness;
    }

void CLine::Serialize (CArchive& ar)
    {
    CFigure::Serialize (ar);
    if (ar.IsStoring ())
        ar << m_Thickness;
    else
        ar >> m_Thickness;
    }

void CLine::Draw (CDC *PDC)
    {
    CPen Pen, *POldPen;

    // select pen/brush:
    Pen.CreatePen (PS_SOLID, m_Thickness, m_Color);
    POldPen = PDC->SelectObject (&Pen);

    // draw figure:
    PDC->MoveTo (m_X1, m_Y1);
    PDC->LineTo (m_X2, m_Y2);

    // remove pen/brush:
    PDC->SelectObject (POldPen);
    }

IMPLEMENT_SERIAL (CRectangle, CFigure, 3)

CRectangle::CRectangle (int X1, int Y1, int X2, int Y2,
    COLORREF Color, int Thickness)
    {
    m_X1 = X1;
    m_Y1 = Y1;
```

```
   m_X2 = X2;
   m_Y2 = Y2;
   m_Color = Color;
   m_Thickness = Thickness;
   }

void CRectangle::Serialize (CArchive& ar)
   {
   CFigure::Serialize (ar);
   if (ar.IsStoring ())
      ar << m_Thickness;
   else
      ar >> m_Thickness;
   }

void CRectangle::Draw (CDC *PDC)
   {
   CPen Pen, *POldPen;

   // select pen/brush:
   Pen.CreatePen (PS_INSIDEFRAME, m_Thickness, m_Color);
   POldPen = PDC->SelectObject (&Pen);
   PDC->SelectStockObject (NULL_BRUSH);

   // draw figure:
   PDC->Rectangle (m_X1, m_Y1, m_X2, m_Y2);

   // remove pen/brush:
   PDC->SelectObject (POldPen);
   }

IMPLEMENT_SERIAL (CRectFill, CFigure, 3)

CRectFill::CRectFill (int X1, int Y1, int X2, int Y2, COLORREF Color)
   {
   m_X1 = min (X1, X2);
   m_Y1 = min (Y1, Y2);
   m_X2 = max (X1, X2);
   m_Y2 = max (Y1, Y2);
   m_Color = Color;
   }
```

```
void CRectFill::Draw (CDC *PDC)
   {
   CBrush Brush, *POldBrush;
   CPen Pen, *POldPen;

   // select pen/brush:
   Pen.CreatePen (PS_INSIDEFRAME, 1, m_Color);
   POldPen = PDC->SelectObject (&Pen);
   Brush.CreateSolidBrush (m_Color);
   POldBrush = PDC->SelectObject (&Brush);

   // draw figure:
   PDC->Rectangle (m_X1, m_Y1, m_X2, m_Y2);

   // remove pen/brush:
   PDC->SelectObject (POldPen);
   PDC->SelectObject (POldBrush);
   }

IMPLEMENT_SERIAL (CRectRound, CFigure, 3)

CRectRound::CRectRound (int X1, int Y1, int X2, int Y2,
   COLORREF Color, int Thickness)
   {
   m_X1 = min (X1, X2);
   m_Y1 = min (Y1, Y2);
   m_X2 = max (X1, X2);
   m_Y2 = max (Y1, Y2);
   m_Color = Color;
   m_Thickness = Thickness;
   }

void CRectRound::Serialize (CArchive& ar)
   {
   CFigure::Serialize (ar);
   if (ar.IsStoring ())
      ar << m_Thickness;
   else
      ar >> m_Thickness;
   }
```

```
void CRectRound::Draw (CDC *PDC)
   {
   CPen Pen, *POldPen;

   // select pen/brush:
   Pen.CreatePen (PS_INSIDEFRAME, m_Thickness, m_Color);
   POldPen = PDC->SelectObject (&Pen);
   PDC->SelectStockObject (NULL_BRUSH);

   // draw figure:
   int SizeRound = (m_X2 - m_X1 + m_Y2 - m_Y1) / 6;
   PDC->RoundRect (m_X1, m_Y1, m_X2, m_Y2, SizeRound, SizeRound);

   // remove pen/brush:
   PDC->SelectObject (POldPen);
   }

IMPLEMENT_SERIAL (CRectRoundFill, CFigure, 3)

CRectRoundFill::CRectRoundFill (int X1, int Y1, int X2, int Y2, COLORREF Color)
   {
   m_X1 = min (X1, X2);
   m_Y1 = min (Y1, Y2);
   m_X2 = max (X1, X2);
   m_Y2 = max (Y1, Y2);
   m_Color = Color;
   }

void CRectRoundFill::Draw (CDC *PDC)
   {
   CBrush Brush, *POldBrush;
   CPen Pen, *POldPen;

   // select pen/brush:
   Pen.CreatePen (PS_INSIDEFRAME, 1, m_Color);
   POldPen = PDC->SelectObject (&Pen);
   Brush.CreateSolidBrush (m_Color);
   POldBrush = PDC->SelectObject (&Brush);

   // draw figure:
   int SizeRound = (m_X2 - m_X1 + m_Y2 - m_Y1) / 6;
   PDC->RoundRect (m_X1, m_Y1, m_X2, m_Y2, SizeRound, SizeRound);
```

```
    // remove pen/brush:
    PDC->SelectObject (POldPen);
    PDC->SelectObject (POldBrush);
    }

IMPLEMENT_SERIAL (CCircle, CFigure, 3)

CCircle::CCircle (int X1, int Y1, int X2, int Y2,
    COLORREF Color, int Thickness)
    {
    m_X1 = min (X1, X2);
    m_Y1 = min (Y1, Y2);
    m_X2 = max (X1, X2);
    m_Y2 = max (Y1, Y2);
    m_Color = Color;
    m_Thickness = Thickness;
    }

void CCircle::Serialize (CArchive& ar)
    {
    CFigure::Serialize (ar);
    if (ar.IsStoring ())
        ar << m_Thickness;
    else
        ar >> m_Thickness;
    }

void CCircle::Draw (CDC *PDC)
    {
    CPen Pen, *POldPen;

    // select pen/brush:
    Pen.CreatePen (PS_INSIDEFRAME, m_Thickness, m_Color);
    POldPen = PDC->SelectObject (&Pen);
    PDC->SelectStockObject (NULL_BRUSH);

    // draw figure:
    PDC->Ellipse (m_X1, m_Y1, m_X2, m_Y2);

    // remove pen/brush:
    PDC->SelectObject (POldPen);
    }
```

```
IMPLEMENT_SERIAL (CCircleFill, CFigure, 3)

CCircleFill::CCircleFill (int X1, int Y1, int X2, int Y2, COLORREF Color)
   {
   m_X1 = min (X1, X2);
   m_Y1 = min (Y1, Y2);
   m_X2 = max (X1, X2);
   m_Y2 = max (Y1, Y2);
   m_Color = Color;
   }

void CCircleFill::Draw (CDC *PDC)
   {
   CBrush Brush, *POldBrush;
   CPen Pen, *POldPen;

   // select pen/brush:
   Pen.CreatePen (PS_INSIDEFRAME, 1, m_Color);
   POldPen = PDC->SelectObject (&Pen);
   Brush.CreateSolidBrush (m_Color);
   POldBrush = PDC->SelectObject (&Brush);

   // draw figure:
   PDC->Ellipse (m_X1, m_Y1, m_X2, m_Y2);

   // remove pen/brush:
   PDC->SelectObject (POldPen);
   PDC->SelectObject (POldBrush);
   }
```

Listing 21.5

```
// MainFrm.h : interface of the CMainFrame class
//
/////////////////////////////////////////////////////////////////////////////

#if !defined(AFX_MAINFRM_H__11E83928_999A_11D1_80FC_00C0F6A83B7F__INCLUDED_)
#define AFX_MAINFRM_H__11E83928_999A_11D1_80FC_00C0F6A83B7F__INCLUDED_

#if _MSC_VER > 1000
#pragma once
#endif // _MSC_VER > 1000
```

```cpp
class CMainFrame : public CFrameWnd
{
protected:
    CSplitterWnd m_SplitterWnd;
    CStatusBar m_StatusBar;
    CToolBar m_ToolBar;

protected: // create from serialization only
    CMainFrame();
    DECLARE_DYNCREATE(CMainFrame)

// Attributes
public:

// Operations
public:

// Overrides
    // ClassWizard generated virtual function overrides
    //{{AFX_VIRTUAL(CMainFrame)
    public:
    virtual BOOL PreCreateWindow(CREATESTRUCT& cs);
    protected:
    virtual BOOL OnCreateClient(LPCREATESTRUCT lpcs, CCreateContext* pContext);
    //}}AFX_VIRTUAL

// Implementation
public:
    virtual ~CMainFrame();
#ifdef _DEBUG
    virtual void AssertValid() const;
    virtual void Dump(CDumpContext& dc) const;
#endif

// Generated message map functions
protected:
    //{{AFX_MSG(CMainFrame)
    afx_msg int OnCreate(LPCREATESTRUCT lpCreateStruct);
    //}}AFX_MSG
    DECLARE_MESSAGE_MAP()
};
```

```
//////////////////////////////////////////////////////////////////////

//{{AFX_INSERT_LOCATION}}
// Microsoft Visual C++ will insert additional declarations immediately before
// the previous line.

#endif
// !defined(AFX_MAINFRM_H__11E83928_999A_11D1_80FC_00C0F6A83B7F__INCLUDED_)
```

Listing 21.6

```cpp
// MainFrm.cpp : implementation of the CMainFrame class
//

#include "stdafx.h"
#include "MiniDraw.h"

#include "MainFrm.h"

#ifdef _DEBUG
#define new DEBUG_NEW
#undef THIS_FILE
static char THIS_FILE[] = __FILE__;
#endif

//////////////////////////////////////////////////////////////////////
// CMainFrame

IMPLEMENT_DYNCREATE(CMainFrame, CFrameWnd)

BEGIN_MESSAGE_MAP(CMainFrame, CFrameWnd)
    //{{AFX_MSG_MAP(CMainFrame)
    ON_WM_CREATE()
    //}}AFX_MSG_MAP
END_MESSAGE_MAP()

// IDs for status bar indicators:
static UINT IndicatorIDs [] =
    {
    ID_SEPARATOR,
    ID_INDICATOR_CAPS,
    ID_INDICATOR_NUM,
```

```
    ID_INDICATOR_SCRL,
    };

/////////////////////////////////////////////////////////////////////////
// CMainFrame construction/destruction

CMainFrame::CMainFrame()
{
    // TODO: add member initialization code here

}

CMainFrame::~CMainFrame()
{
}

BOOL CMainFrame::PreCreateWindow(CREATESTRUCT& cs)
{
    if( !CFrameWnd::PreCreateWindow(cs) )
        return FALSE;
    // TODO: Modify the Window class or styles here by modifying
    //   the CREATESTRUCT cs

    return TRUE;
}

/////////////////////////////////////////////////////////////////////////
// CMainFrame diagnostics

#ifdef _DEBUG
void CMainFrame::AssertValid() const
{
    CFrameWnd::AssertValid();
}

void CMainFrame::Dump(CDumpContext& dc) const
{
    CFrameWnd::Dump(dc);
}

#endif //_DEBUG
```

```
/////////////////////////////////////////////////////////////////////////
// CMainFrame message handlers


BOOL CMainFrame::OnCreateClient(LPCREATESTRUCT lpcs, CCreateContext* pContext)
{
    // TODO: Add your specialized code here and/or call the base class

    return m_SplitterWnd.Create
        (this,               // parent of splitter window
        1,                   // maximum rows
        2,                   // maximum columns
        CSize (15, 15),      // minimum view window size
        pContext);           // pass on context information
}

int CMainFrame::OnCreate(LPCREATESTRUCT lpCreateStruct)
{
    if (CFrameWnd::OnCreate(lpCreateStruct) == -1)
        return -1;

    // TODO: Add your specialized creation code here

    if (!m_ToolBar.CreateEx
        (this,
        TBSTYLE_FLAT,
        WS_CHILD | WS_VISIBLE | CBRS_TOP | CBRS_GRIPPER
        | CBRS_TOOLTIPS | CBRS_FLYBY | CBRS_SIZE_DYNAMIC))
        return -1;

    if (!m_ToolBar.LoadToolBar(IDR_MAINFRAME))
        return -1;

    m_ToolBar.EnableDocking (CBRS_ALIGN_ANY);
    EnableDocking (CBRS_ALIGN_ANY);
    DockControlBar (&m_ToolBar);

    if (!m_StatusBar.Create (this) ||
        !m_StatusBar.SetIndicators (IndicatorIDs,
        sizeof (IndicatorIDs) / sizeof (UINT)))
        return -1;

    return 0;
}
```

Listing 21.7

```cpp
// MiniDrawView.h : interface of the CMiniDrawView class
//
/////////////////////////////////////////////////////////////////////

#if !defined(AFX_MINIDRAWVIEW_H__11E8392C_999A_11D1_80FC_00C0F6A83B7F__INCLUDED_)
#define AFX_MINIDRAWVIEW_H__11E8392C_999A_11D1_80FC_00C0F6A83B7F__INCLUDED_

#if _MSC_VER > 1000
#pragma once
#endif // _MSC_VER > 1000

const int DRAWWIDTH  = 4000;  // drawing width
const int DRAWHEIGHT = 6000;  // drawing height

class CMiniDrawView : public CScrollView
{
protected:
    CString m_ClassName;
    int m_Dragging;
    HCURSOR m_HArrow;
    HCURSOR m_HCross;
    int m_NumCols, m_NumRows;
    int m_PageHeight, m_PageWidth;
    CPen m_PenDotted;
    CPoint m_PointOld;
    CPoint m_PointOrigin;

protected: // create from serialization only
    CMiniDrawView();
    DECLARE_DYNCREATE(CMiniDrawView)

// Attributes
public:
    CMiniDrawDoc* GetDocument();

// Operations
public:

// Overrides
```

```
    // ClassWizard generated virtual function overrides
    //{{AFX_VIRTUAL(CMiniDrawView)
    public:
    virtual void OnDraw(CDC* pDC);  // overridden to draw this view
    virtual BOOL PreCreateWindow(CREATESTRUCT& cs);
    virtual void OnInitialUpdate();
    virtual void OnPrepareDC(CDC* pDC, CPrintInfo* pInfo = NULL);
    protected:
    virtual void OnUpdate(CView* pSender, LPARAM lHint, CObject* pHint);
    virtual BOOL OnPreparePrinting(CPrintInfo* pInfo);
    virtual void OnBeginPrinting(CDC* pDC, CPrintInfo* pInfo);
    //}}AFX_VIRTUAL

// Implementation
public:
    virtual ~CMiniDrawView();
#ifdef _DEBUG
    virtual void AssertValid() const;
    virtual void Dump(CDumpContext& dc) const;
#endif

protected:

// Generated message map functions
protected:
    //{{AFX_MSG(CMiniDrawView)
    afx_msg void OnLButtonDown(UINT nFlags, CPoint point);
    afx_msg void OnMouseMove(UINT nFlags, CPoint point);
    afx_msg void OnLButtonUp(UINT nFlags, CPoint point);
    //}}AFX_MSG
    DECLARE_MESSAGE_MAP()
};

#ifndef _DEBUG  // debug version in MiniDrawView.cpp
inline CMiniDrawDoc* CMiniDrawView::GetDocument()
    { return (CMiniDrawDoc*)m_pDocument; }
#endif

/////////////////////////////////////////////////////////////////////////

//{{AFX_INSERT_LOCATION}}
// Microsoft Visual C++ will insert additional declarations immediately before
```

```
// the previous line.

#endif
// !defined(AFX_MINIDRAWVIEW_H__11E8392C_999A_11D1_80FC_00C0F6A83B7F__INCLUDED_)
```

Listing 21.8

```cpp
// MiniDrawView.cpp : implementation of the CMiniDrawView class
//

#include "stdafx.h"
#include "MiniDraw.h"

#include "MiniDrawDoc.h"
#include "MiniDrawView.h"

#ifdef _DEBUG
#define new DEBUG_NEW
#undef THIS_FILE
static char THIS_FILE[] = __FILE__;
#endif


/////////////////////////////////////////////////////////////////////////////
// CMiniDrawView

IMPLEMENT_DYNCREATE(CMiniDrawView, CScrollView)

BEGIN_MESSAGE_MAP(CMiniDrawView, CScrollView)
    //{{AFX_MSG_MAP(CMiniDrawView)
    ON_WM_LBUTTONDOWN()
    ON_WM_MOUSEMOVE()
    ON_WM_LBUTTONUP()
    //}}AFX_MSG_MAP
    ON_COMMAND(ID_FILE_PRINT, CView::OnFilePrint)
    ON_COMMAND(ID_FILE_PRINT_PREVIEW, CView::OnFilePrintPreview)
END_MESSAGE_MAP()

/////////////////////////////////////////////////////////////////////////////
// CMiniDrawView construction/destruction

CMiniDrawView::CMiniDrawView()
```

```
{
   // TODO: add construction code here

   m_Dragging = 0;
   m_HArrow = AfxGetApp ()->LoadStandardCursor (IDC_ARROW);
   m_HCross = AfxGetApp ()->LoadStandardCursor (IDC_CROSS);
   m_PenDotted.CreatePen (PS_DOT, 1, RGB (0,0,0));
}

CMiniDrawView::~CMiniDrawView()
{
}

BOOL CMiniDrawView::PreCreateWindow(CREATESTRUCT& cs)
{
   // TODO: Modify the Window class or styles here by modifying
   //   the CREATESTRUCT cs

   m_ClassName = AfxRegisterWndClass
      (CS_HREDRAW | CS_VREDRAW,                // class styles
       0,                                      // no cursor
       (HBRUSH)::GetStockObject (WHITE_BRUSH), // assign white
                                               // background brush
       0);                                     // no icon
   cs.lpszClass = m_ClassName;

   return CScrollView::PreCreateWindow(cs);
}

/////////////////////////////////////////////////////////////////////////
// CMiniDrawView drawing

void CMiniDrawView::OnDraw(CDC* pDC)
{
   CMiniDrawDoc* pDoc = GetDocument();
   ASSERT_VALID(pDoc);

   // TODO: add draw code for native data here

   if (pDC->GetDeviceCaps (TECHNOLOGY) == DT_RASDISPLAY)
      {
      CSize ScrollSize = GetTotalSize ();
```

```
      pDC->MoveTo (ScrollSize.cx, 0);
      pDC->LineTo (ScrollSize.cx, ScrollSize.cy);
      pDC->LineTo (0, ScrollSize.cy);
      }

   CRect ClipRect;
   CRect DimRect;
   CRect IntRect;
   CFigure *PFigure;

   pDC->GetClipBox (&ClipRect);

   int NumFigs = pDoc->GetNumFigs ();
   for (int Index = 0; Index < NumFigs; ++Index)
      {
      PFigure = pDoc->GetFigure (Index);
      DimRect = PFigure->GetDimRect ();
      if (IntRect.IntersectRect (DimRect, ClipRect))
         PFigure->Draw (pDC);
      }
}

///////////////////////////////////////////////////////////////////////
// CMiniDrawView diagnostics

#ifdef _DEBUG
void CMiniDrawView::AssertValid() const
{
   CScrollView::AssertValid();
}

void CMiniDrawView::Dump(CDumpContext& dc) const
{
   CScrollView::Dump(dc);
}

CMiniDrawDoc* CMiniDrawView::GetDocument() // non-debug version is inline
{
   ASSERT(m_pDocument->IsKindOf(RUNTIME_CLASS(CMiniDrawDoc)));
   return (CMiniDrawDoc*)m_pDocument;
}
#endif //_DEBUG
```

```
//////////////////////////////////////////////////////////////////////////////
// CMiniDrawView message handlers

void CMiniDrawView::OnLButtonDown(UINT nFlags, CPoint point)
{
    // TODO: Add your message handler code here and/or call default

    CClientDC ClientDC (this);
    OnPrepareDC (&ClientDC);
    ClientDC.DPtoLP (&point);

    // test whether cursor is within drawing area of view window:
    CSize ScrollSize = GetTotalSize ();
    CRect ScrollRect (0, 0, ScrollSize.cx, ScrollSize.cy);
    if (!ScrollRect.PtInRect (point))
        return;

    // save cursor position, capture mouse, and set dragging flag:
    m_PointOrigin = point;
    m_PointOld = point;
    SetCapture ();
    m_Dragging = 1;

    // clip mouse cursor:
    ClientDC.LPtoDP (&ScrollRect);
    CRect ViewRect;
    GetClientRect (&ViewRect);
    CRect IntRect;
    IntRect.IntersectRect (&ScrollRect, &ViewRect);
    ClientToScreen (&IntRect);
    ::ClipCursor (&IntRect);

    CScrollView::OnLButtonDown(nFlags, point);
}

void CMiniDrawView::OnMouseMove(UINT nFlags, CPoint point)
{
    // TODO: Add your message handler code here and/or call default

    CClientDC ClientDC (this);
    OnPrepareDC (&ClientDC);
    ClientDC.DPtoLP (&point);
```

```
if (!m_Dragging)
    {
    CSize ScrollSize = GetTotalSize ();
    CRect ScrollRect (0, 0, ScrollSize.cx, ScrollSize.cy);
    if (ScrollRect.PtInRect (point))
        ::SetCursor (m_HCross);
    else
        ::SetCursor (m_HArrow);
    return;
    }

ClientDC.SetROP2 (R2_NOT);
ClientDC.SelectObject (&m_PenDotted);
ClientDC.SetBkMode (TRANSPARENT);
ClientDC.SelectStockObject (NULL_BRUSH);

switch ((((CMiniDrawApp *)AfxGetApp ())->m_CurrentTool)
    {
    case ID_TOOLS_LINE:
        ClientDC.MoveTo (m_PointOrigin);
        ClientDC.LineTo (m_PointOld);
        ClientDC.MoveTo (m_PointOrigin);
        ClientDC.LineTo (point);
        break;

    case ID_TOOLS_RECTANGLE:
    case ID_TOOLS_RECTFILL:
        ClientDC.Rectangle (m_PointOrigin.x, m_PointOrigin.y,
                            m_PointOld.x, m_PointOld.y);
        ClientDC.Rectangle (m_PointOrigin.x, m_PointOrigin.y,
                            point.x, point.y);
        break;

    case ID_TOOLS_RECTROUND:
    case ID_TOOLS_RECTROUNDFILL:
        {
        int SizeRound = (abs (m_PointOld.x - m_PointOrigin.x) +
                         abs (m_PointOld.y - m_PointOrigin.y)) / 6;
        ClientDC.RoundRect (m_PointOrigin.x, m_PointOrigin.y,
                            m_PointOld.x, m_PointOld.y,
        SizeRound, SizeRound);
        SizeRound = (abs (point.x - m_PointOrigin.x) +
```

```
                            abs (point.y - m_PointOrigin.y)) / 6;
              ClientDC.RoundRect (m_PointOrigin.x, m_PointOrigin.y,
                                  point.x, point.y,
                                  SizeRound, SizeRound);
              break;
              }

          case ID_TOOLS_CIRCLE:
          case ID_TOOLS_CIRCLEFILL:
              ClientDC.Ellipse (m_PointOrigin.x, m_PointOrigin.y,
                                m_PointOld.x, m_PointOld.y);
              ClientDC.Ellipse (m_PointOrigin.x, m_PointOrigin.y,
                                point.x, point.y);
              break;
          }

      m_PointOld = point;

      CScrollView::OnMouseMove(nFlags, point);
}

void CMiniDrawView::OnLButtonUp(UINT nFlags, CPoint point)
{
      // TODO: Add your message handler code here and/or call default

      if (!m_Dragging)
         return;

      m_Dragging = 0;
      ::ReleaseCapture ();
      ::ClipCursor (NULL);

      CClientDC ClientDC (this);
      OnPrepareDC (&ClientDC);
      ClientDC.DPtoLP (&point);
      ClientDC.SetROP2 (R2_NOT);
      ClientDC.SelectObject (&m_PenDotted);
      ClientDC.SetBkMode (TRANSPARENT);
      ClientDC.SelectStockObject (NULL_BRUSH);

      CMiniDrawApp *PApp = (CMiniDrawApp *)AfxGetApp ();
      CFigure *PFigure;
```

```
switch (PApp->m_CurrentTool)
   {
   case ID_TOOLS_LINE:
      ClientDC.MoveTo (m_PointOrigin);
      ClientDC.LineTo (m_PointOld);
      PFigure = new CLine
         (m_PointOrigin.x, m_PointOrigin.y,
         point.x, point.y,
         PApp->m_CurrentColor,
         PApp->m_CurrentThickness);
      break;

   case ID_TOOLS_RECTANGLE:
      ClientDC.Rectangle (m_PointOrigin.x, m_PointOrigin.y,
                          m_PointOld.x, m_PointOld.y);
      PFigure = new CRectangle
         (m_PointOrigin.x, m_PointOrigin.y,
         point.x, point.y,
         PApp->m_CurrentColor,
         PApp->m_CurrentThickness);
      break;

   case ID_TOOLS_RECTFILL:
      ClientDC.Rectangle (m_PointOrigin.x, m_PointOrigin.y,
                          m_PointOld.x, m_PointOld.y);
      PFigure = new CRectFill
         (m_PointOrigin.x, m_PointOrigin.y,
         point.x, point.y,
         PApp->m_CurrentColor);
      break;

   case ID_TOOLS_RECTROUND:
      {
      int SizeRound = (abs (m_PointOld.x - m_PointOrigin.x) +
         abs (m_PointOld.y - m_PointOrigin.y)) / 6;
      ClientDC.RoundRect (m_PointOrigin.x, m_PointOrigin.y,
                          m_PointOld.x, m_PointOld.y,
                          SizeRound, SizeRound);
      PFigure = new CRectRound
         (m_PointOrigin.x, m_PointOrigin.y,
         point.x, point.y,
         PApp->m_CurrentColor,
```

```
            PApp->m_CurrentThickness);
        break;
        }

    case ID_TOOLS_RECTROUNDFILL:
        {
        int SizeRound = (abs (m_PointOld.x - m_PointOrigin.x) +
                         abs (m_PointOld.y - m_PointOrigin.y)) / 6;
        ClientDC.RoundRect (m_PointOrigin.x, m_PointOrigin.y,
                            m_PointOld.x, m_PointOld.y,
        SizeRound, SizeRound);
        PFigure = new CRectRoundFill
            (m_PointOrigin.x, m_PointOrigin.y,
            point.x, point.y,
            PApp->m_CurrentColor);
        break;
        }

    case ID_TOOLS_CIRCLE:
        ClientDC.Ellipse (m_PointOrigin.x, m_PointOrigin.y,
                          m_PointOld.x, m_PointOld.y);
        PFigure = new CCircle
            (m_PointOrigin.x, m_PointOrigin.y,
            point.x, point.y,
            PApp->m_CurrentColor,
            PApp->m_CurrentThickness);
        break;

    case ID_TOOLS_CIRCLEFILL:
        ClientDC.Ellipse (m_PointOrigin.x, m_PointOrigin.y,
                          m_PointOld.x, m_PointOld.y);
        PFigure = new CCircleFill
            (m_PointOrigin.x, m_PointOrigin.y,
            point.x, point.y,
            PApp->m_CurrentColor);
        break;
    }

ClientDC.SetROP2 (R2_COPYPEN);
PFigure->Draw (&ClientDC);

CMiniDrawDoc* PDoc = GetDocument();
PDoc->AddFigure (PFigure);
```

```
   PDoc->UpdateAllViews (this, 0, PFigure);

   CScrollView::OnLButtonUp(nFlags, point);
}

void CMiniDrawView::OnInitialUpdate()
{
   CScrollView::OnInitialUpdate();

   // TODO: Add your specialized code here and/or call the base class

   SIZE Size = {DRAWWIDTH, DRAWHEIGHT};
   SetScrollSizes (MM_TEXT, Size);
}

void CMiniDrawView::OnUpdate(CView* pSender, LPARAM lHint, CObject* pHint)
{
   // TODO: Add your specialized code here and/or call the base class

   if (pHint != 0)
      {
      CRect InvalidRect = ((CLine *)pHint)->GetDimRect ();
      CClientDC ClientDC (this);
      OnPrepareDC (&ClientDC);
      ClientDC.LPtoDP (&InvalidRect);
      InvalidateRect (&InvalidRect);
      }
   else
      CScrollView::OnUpdate (pSender, lHint, pHint);
}

BOOL CMiniDrawView::OnPreparePrinting(CPrintInfo* pInfo)
{
   // TODO: call DoPreparePrinting to invoke the Print dialog box

   return DoPreparePrinting (pInfo);
}

void CMiniDrawView::OnBeginPrinting(CDC* pDC, CPrintInfo* pInfo)
{
   // TODO: Add your specialized code here and/or call the base class
```

```
    m_PageHeight = pDC->GetDeviceCaps (VERTRES);
    m_PageWidth = pDC->GetDeviceCaps (HORZRES);

    m_NumRows = DRAWHEIGHT / m_PageHeight  + (DRAWHEIGHT % m_PageHeight > 0);
    m_NumCols = DRAWWIDTH / m_PageWidth  + (DRAWWIDTH % m_PageWidth > 0);
    pInfo->SetMinPage (1);
    pInfo->SetMaxPage (m_NumRows * m_NumCols);

    CScrollView::OnBeginPrinting(pDC, pInfo);
}

void CMiniDrawView::OnPrepareDC(CDC* pDC, CPrintInfo* pInfo)
{
    // TODO: Add your specialized code here and/or call the base class

    CScrollView::OnPrepareDC(pDC, pInfo);

    if (pInfo == NULL)
        return;

    int CurRow = pInfo->m_nCurPage / m_NumCols +
        (pInfo->m_nCurPage % m_NumCols > 0);
    int CurCol = (pInfo->m_nCurPage - 1) % m_NumCols + 1;

    pDC->SetViewportOrg
        (-m_PageWidth * (CurCol - 1),
        -m_PageHeight * (CurRow - 1));
}
```

Using Alternative Mapping Modes

Chapter 19 (in the section "The Mapping Mode") described the *mapping mode*, which is maintained by the device context object and affects the output of both text and graphics. Although using the default MM_TEXT mapping mode simplifies writing a program, in this mode the sizes of text and graphic images that the program displays *vary* depending on the resolution of the output device. (Recall that in the MM_TEXT mapping mode all coordinates are specified in pixels; the number of pixels per physical inch *varies* according to the device resolution.) In the MM_TEXT mode, not only are the sizes of the images on the printer different from their sizes on the screen, but also the sizes vary from one printer to another. Furthermore, on a laser printer or other high-resolution printer, the printed image sizes are quite small compared to their sizes on the screen.

Continued on next page

To produce images that are the *same* size regardless of the output device, you can use one of the alternative mapping modes: `MM_HIENGLISH`, `MM_HIMETRIC`, `MM_LOENGLISH`, `MM_LOMETRIC`, or `MM_TWIPS`. In each of these mapping modes, coordinates are specified in standard units of measurement (inches, millimeters, and so on), rather than in device-dependent pixels. (You could also employ one of the user-defined mapping modes, `MM_ANISOTROPIC` and `MM_ISOTROPIC`, provided that you set the units properly.) Using an alternative mapping mode changes the logic of the display code; a detailed discussion on the use of these mapping modes is beyond the scope of the book. For information, see the online help topic: *Visual C++ Documentation, Reference, Microsoft Foundation Class Library and Templates, Microsoft Foundation Class Library, Class Library Reference, CDC, CDC Class Members* and look under the heading *Mapping Functions*. Also, for a *general* discussion on mapping modes, see the following topic: *Platform SDK, Graphics and Multimedia Services, GDI, Coordinate Spaces and Transformations*.

Summary

In this chapter, you learned how to provide the code to support the standard Print…, Print Preview, and Print Setup… commands on the File menu. The following is a summary of the main concepts and techniques that were presented:

- If you're creating a new program using AppWizard, you can include Print…, Print Preview, and Print Setup… commands on the program's File menu by selecting the Printing And Print Preview option in the AppWizard Step 4 dialog box. The initial code that AppWizard generates, however, will print or preview only as much of a document as will fit on a single page.

- You can also add Print…, Print Preview, and Print Setup… commands to an existing program, and you can modify the program code to support these commands. In the menu editor, you should add the print commands to the program's File menu. Also, you must choose the View ➢ Resource Includes… menu command and specify the prewritten file Afxprint.rc, so that the resources defined in this file (which are used for printing) are included in the program.

- To process the Print Setup... command, you must add a message-map entry to the application class, which invokes the `CWinApp::OnFilePrintSetup` function.

- To process the Print... and Print Preview commands, you must add message-map entries to the view class, which invoke the `CView::OnFilePrint` and `CView::OnFilePrintPreview` functions.

- When the `OnFilePrint` and `OnFilePrintPreview` functions conduct the print or print preview job, they call a series of virtual functions defined within the `CView` class. You *must* provide an overriding version of the `OnPreparePrinting` virtual function; your function must call `CView::DoPreparePrinting` to create a device context object for printing or previewing.

- If your program is to print more than one page, you should call the `CPrintInfo` member functions `SetMinPage` and `SetMaxPage` to specify the numbers of the first and last pages. You normally call these functions in an overriding version of the `OnBeginPrinting` virtual function, which is the first virtual function that has access to the device context object.

- To support multiple-page printing, you should also provide an overriding version of the `OnPrepareDC` virtual function, which is called before each page is printed. Your function should adjust the viewport origin so that the program's `OnDraw` function will print the portion of the document that's to appear on the current page.

- After calling `OnPrepareDC`, the MFC calls the `OnPrint` virtual function; the default version of this function simply calls `OnDraw` to display output on the current page.

- The device-independent code in `OnDraw` serves to display output on a variety of devices. To customize the output for a specific device, you can pass the index TECHNOLOGY to the `GetDeviceCaps` function to determine the type of the target device.

Using Multiple Threads

- Creating and managing secondary threads

- Synchronizing threads

- A multithreading version of the Mandel program

The term *thread* refers to the execution of a sequence of program instructions. All the programs presented in the book so far run with a single thread, which is known as the *primary thread*. A program written for Windows 95 or later or for Windows NT, however, can start one or more *secondary threads*, each thread independently executing a series of instructions within the program code. From the viewpoint of the user or application programmer, the threads in a program run simultaneously. The operating system typically achieves this apparent simultaneity by rapidly switching control from thread to thread (if the computer has more than one processor, however, the system can execute threads literally simultaneously). When a program must perform more than one task at a given time (as do many applications), being able to assign each task to a separate thread not only can make the program more efficient, but also can simplify the job of developing it.

In this chapter, you'll first learn how to create and manage secondary threads in an MFC program. You'll then learn how to use the mechanisms provided by the Win32 API to synchronize the activities of the separate threads. Finally, you'll create a multithreading version of the Mandel program that was presented in Chapter 19. In the next chapter, you'll learn how to divide programming tasks among separate *processes* and how to communicate among these processes (a *process* is started whenever a program is run).

Creating and Managing Secondary Threads

Multithreading is especially useful in a Windows GUI program, where the primary program thread can be dedicated to processing messages so that the program can respond quickly to commands and other events. A secondary thread can be used to perform any lengthy task that would block program message processing if performed by the primary thread—for example, drawing complex graphics, recalculating a spreadsheet, executing a disk operation, or communicating with a serial port. Starting a separate program thread is relatively quick and consumes little memory (compared with starting a separate process, as described in the next chapter). Also, all the threads within a program run within the same memory space and own the same set of Windows resources; consequently, they can easily share memory variables and Windows objects such as windows, pens, memory allocations, device contexts, and so on (as you'll see later in the chapter, however, there are some limitations in sharing MFC objects).

NOTE   Many of the techniques discussed in this chapter are illustrated in the MandelMT program presented near the end of the chapter.

You can freely use multithreading in an MFC program, provided that you start and manage new threads using the techniques described in this chapter. First, you must make sure that the Use Run-Time Library: project setting has an appropriate value for multithreading. A new project has an appropriate setting by default, but if you've changed it, you must reset it as follows: choose the Project ➢ Settings... menu command, select the name of the project in the hierarchical list, open the C/C++ tab, and select the Code Generation item in the Category: list. For the release project configuration, choose the Multithreaded or the Multithreaded DLL option in the Use Run-Time Library: list; for the debug configuration, choose Debug Multithreaded or Debug Multithreaded DLL in this list. (Recall that you select the configuration in the Settings For: list of the Project Settings dialog box.)

To start a new thread in your program, you call the global MFC function AfxBeginThread, which has the following form:

```
CWinThread* AfxBeginThread
    (AFX_THREADPROC pfnThreadProc,
    LPVOID pParam,
    int nPriority = THREAD_PRIORITY_NORMAL,
    UINT nStackSize = 0,
    DWORD dwCreateFlags = 0,
    LPSECURITY_ATTRIBUTES lpSecurityAttrs = NULL);
```

NOTE   The AfxBeginThread MFC function initializes the MFC library so that it can be used in a multithreading program. AfxBeginThread then calls the C++ runtime library _beginthreadex function, which initializes the runtime library for multithreading and ultimately calls the Win32 API function ::CreateThread to start the thread. Consequently, if you use AfxBeginThread to start secondary threads in an MFC program, you're free to use the MFC classes, the C++ runtime library functions, and the Win32 API functions. In an MFC program, you must *not* start a new thread by directly calling either the _beginthread or _beginthreadex runtime library function or the ::CreateThread Win32 API function.

`AfxBeginThread` starts the new thread running and returns control promptly; afterward, both the new thread and the thread that called `AfxBeginThread` run simultaneously. The first parameter, `pfnThreadProc`, specifies the thread function; the new thread begins by executing this function. The thread function can, of course, call other functions, and when the thread function returns, the new thread is terminated. The `pParam` parameter specifies the value that's to be passed to the thread function. You must define the thread function so that it has the following form:

```
UINT ThreadFunction (LPVOID pParam);
```

(You can use any name for the function or its parameter. The function return type and parameter type, however, must match those shown.)

Notice that the thread function returns a UINT value; this value is known as the *exit code*, and later you'll see how other threads can read it. Normally, the thread function returns the value 0 to indicate a normal exit; however, you can use any return value convention you wish, because the value is read and interpreted only by your own code. (You must not, however, return the special value STILL_ACTIVE, which equals 0x00000103L and is used to indicate that the thread is still running, as described later.)

TIP

You can supply information to the new thread through the `pParam` pointer that's passed to the thread function. This pointer can contain the address of a simple value, such as an `int`, or the address of a structure containing any amount of information. Likewise, the thread can pass information back to the original thread (in addition to the exit code it returns) by assigning a value or values to the data item pointed to by the `pParam` parameter (to do this successfully, the two threads might need to synchronize their actions; synchronizing threads is discussed later).

The last four `AfxBeginThread` parameters have default values, which you can generally accept. The `nPriority` parameter specifies the *priority* of the new thread. In simple terms, the priority of a thread determines how frequently the thread is allowed to run as the operating system switches control from thread to thread. If the thread must perform its task quickly and respond to events efficiently, you should assign it a relatively high priority. Conversely, if a thread performs a less important task, which can be accomplished during the times that other threads are inactive, you should assign it a relatively low priority. The default value THREAD_PRIORITY_NORMAL assigns the thread an average priority and is suitable for most purposes. For a list of the different priority values you can assign, see the following Visual C++ online help topic: *Platform SDK, Windows Base Services, Executables, Processes and Threads, Process and Thread Reference, Process and Thread Functions, SetThreadPriority.*

If the dwCreateFlags parameter is assigned 0 (the default value), the new thread begins running immediately. If it's assigned CREATE_SUSPENDED, the new thread won't start running until you call the CWinThread::ResumeThread function, which is described later. You almost always assign the default values to the nStackSize and lpSecurityAttrs parameters, which specify the thread's stack size and security attributes.

The following example code starts a new thread, which executes Thread-Function (plus any functions ThreadFunction calls):

```
UINT ThreadFunction (LPVOID pParam)
{

    // statements and function calls to be executed by
    // the new thread ...

    return 0;  // terminate the thread and return 0 exit code
}

// ...

void SomeFunction (void)
{
    // ...

    int Code = 1;
    CWinThread *PWinThread;
    PWinThread = AfxBeginThread (ThreadFunction, &Code);

    // ...
}
```

Terminating a Thread

You can terminate a new thread you've started in one of two ways. First, you can simply have the thread return from the thread function (ThreadFunction in the example above), passing back the desired exit code. This is the most orderly way to end a thread—the stack used by the thread will be deallocated and all automatic data objects that the thread has created will be properly destroyed (that is, destructors for automatic objects will be called).

Second, the thread can call the MFC function AfxEndThread, passing it the desired exit code:

```
void AfxEndThread (UINT nExitCode);
```

Calling AfxEndThread is a convenient way to immediately end a thread from within a nested function (rather than having to return to the original thread function). Using this method, the thread stack will be deallocated, but destructors for automatic objects created by the thread *won't* be called.

Note that both these ways of stopping a thread must be performed by the thread itself. If you want to terminate a thread from *another* thread, the Microsoft documentation recommends having the other thread signal the thread that's to be ended, requesting it to terminate itself. Later in the chapter, you'll see a variety of ways to set up communication between threads. (The documentation recommends against having a thread in an MFC program call the Win32 API function ::TerminateThread to terminate another thread.)

Managing the Thread

AfxBeginThread returns a pointer to a CWinThread object that you can use to manage the new thread. You can call the CWinThread member function Suspend-Thread to temporarily stop the thread from running:

```
PWinThread->SuspendThread ();
```

(The examples in this section assume that PWinThread contains the CWinThread pointer returned by AfxBeginThread.)

You can call CWinThread::ResumeThread to start the thread running again:

```
PWinThread->ResumeThread ();
```

You'd also call ResumeThread to start a thread that was created in the suspended state by assigning CREATE_SUSPENDED to the dwCreateFlags AfxBegin-Thread parameter.

You can change the thread's priority from the level it was initially assigned in the `AfxBeginThread` call by calling `CWinThread::SetThreadPriority`. For example, the following code raises a thread's priority from the default level:

```
PWinThread->SetThreadPriority (THREAD_PRIORITY_ABOVE_NORMAL);
```

You can *obtain* the thread's current priority level by calling `CWinThread::Get-ThreadPriority`.

Also, you can call the Win32 API function `::GetExitCodeThread` to determine whether the thread is still running and, if it has stopped running, to obtain its exit code (that is, the value it returned from the thread function or passed to `Afx-EndThread`). You must assign the first `::GetExitCodeThread` parameter the Windows handle for the thread, which is stored in the `CWinThread` data member `m_hThread`:

```
DWORD ExitCode;

::GetExitCodeThread
    (PWinThread->m_hThread,   // Windows handle for thread;
    &ExitCode);               // address of DWORD variable to
                              // receive exit code

if (ExitCode == STILL_ACTIVE)
    // thread is still running...
else
    // thread has terminated and ExitCode contains its exit code
```

`::GetExitCodeThread` assigns a value to the DWORD variable whose address you pass as the second parameter. If the thread is still running, it assigns this variable the value STILL_ACTIVE; if the thread has terminated, it assigns the variable the thread's exit code. (This is the reason that when a thread exits it must *not* return the value STILL_ACTIVE, which equals 0x00000103L.)

A serious problem exists, however, with using the techniques for managing a thread that have been presented in this section: normally, when the thread terminates, the `CWinThread` object supplied by `AfxBeginThread` is *automatically destroyed*. If you attempt to access a `CWinThread` member after the thread has exited, the program will generate a protection fault; yet, ironically, you need to access a `CWinThread` member (namely, `m_HThread`) to determine whether the thread has exited. The solution to this problem is to *prevent* the MFC from automatically destroying the CWinThread object on thread termination. This can be done by assigning FALSE to the CWinThread data member m_bAutoDelete, as in the following example:

```
PWinThread = AfxBeginThread
    (ThreadFunction,
    &Code
    THREAD_PRIORITY_NORMAL,
    0,
    CREATE_SUSPENDED);
PWinThread->m_bAutoDelete = FALSE;
PWinThread->ResumeThread ();
```

The thread is started in the suspended state to make sure that the m_bAutoDelete data member can be set to FALSE *before* the thread exits. With m_bAutoDelete set to FALSE, the CWinThread object will exist even after the thread has exited, and the program can freely call ::GetExitCodeThread to determine whether the thread has stopped, as well as to obtain its exit code. (If the thread has exited, calling a CWinThread member function such as SuspendThread will have no effect, but at least won't generate a protection fault!) When you're done using the thread object, you should explicitly delete it:

```
delete PWinThread;
```

MFC Limitations

Because threads running in a given process share the same memory space, they can generally share global or dynamically allocated variables and objects. There are, however, two limitations in the sharing of MFC objects (that is, instances of MFC classes).

First, two threads shouldn't attempt to access the same MFC object simultaneously. For example, two threads can share a single CString object, provided that they don't attempt to manipulate the object—by calling a CString member function—at the same time. To prevent separate threads from simultaneously accessing an MFC object, you can use one of the synchronization methods discussed in the next section. (Two threads *can* simultaneously access *separate* objects even if they belong to the same MFC class—for example, two distinct CString objects.)

Second, an object of any of the following MFC classes—or an object of a class derived from one of these—should be accessed only by the thread that created the object:

CWnd
CDC
CMenu
CGdiObject

These classes have a common feature—each of them stores a Windows handle for some underlying item; for example, a CWnd object stores a handle to a window (which is kept in the object's m_hWnd data member). If a given thread has created an object of one of these classes, but you want to access the underlying item from a second thread, you should pass the second thread the Windows handle, and the second thread should create its own object. For example, if a thread has created a CWnd object for managing a window and you want to draw in this window from a second thread, rather than passing the second thread the CWnd object, you should pass it the window handle stored in the object's m_hWnd data member. The second thread can then call the CWnd member function FromHandle to create its own CWnd object for drawing in the window. This technique is demonstrated by the MandelMT program.

NOTE   The secondary threads described in this chapter are known as *worker threads*. A worker thread typically performs a background or secondary task, while the main thread continues to process messages. Alternatively, you can call a second version of the AfxBeginThread function (which takes a CRuntimeClass pointer as its first parameter) to create a *user-interface* thread. A user-interface thread is designed to create one or more additional windows and to process the messages sent to these windows. To call the alternative version of AfxBeginThread, you must derive a class from CWinThread to manage the thread, and you must define as a member of this class an overriding version of the CWinThread virtual member function InitInstance. Your InitInstance function should create any windows displayed by the thread and perform any required initialization tasks. (This InitInstance function is similar to the one belonging to the application class. Note that the application class, which is derived indirectly from CWinThread, manages the *primary* program thread. The primary program thread is a user-interface thread.) For information on creating user-interface threads, see the following online help topic: *Visual C++ Documentation, Using Visual C++, Visual C++ Programmer's Guide, Adding Program Functionality, Details, Multithreading Topics, Multithreading with C++ and MFC, Multithreading: Creating User-Interface Threads*. Also, see the documentation on the CWinThread class and the AfxBeginThread function.

Synchronizing Threads

For 32-bit programs running under Windows 95 or later or under Windows NT, multithreading is *preemptive*, meaning that a given thread can be interrupted—and another thread can receive control—between any two machine instructions, and you can't predict when a thread will be interrupted. Also, the threads run *asynchronously*, meaning that when one thread executes a particular instruction, you can't predict—nor should you try to predict—which instruction another thread is currently executing.

These features of multithreading can cause problems when two or more threads access a shared resource, such as a global variable. (In the following discussions, the term *resource* is used in a broad sense to indicate an item owned by the process; it can refer, for example, to a variable, a C++ object, a memory allocation, a graphics object, or a hardware device.) Consider, for instance, that two threads execute a block of code, which increments a global counter and then prints out the new counter value:

```
// declared globally:
int Count = 0;

// ...

// function that is executed by two threads:
void SharedFunction ()
   {
   // ...
   ++Count;
   cout << Count << '\n';
   // ...
   }
```

If this function is called repeatedly, the expected result would be to print a series of consecutive integer values starting with 1. However, because the code is executed by two threads, the following scenario could occur:

1. The first thread increments Count.

2. The first thread is preempted and the second thread receives control.

3. The second thread increments Count and prints the new value.

4. The first thread again receives control. It then prints the same value just printed by the second thread; the value it *should* have printed is skipped.

To prevent this type of error, the separate threads need to synchronize their actions. There are many other situations in which threads might need to be synchronized. First, there are other kinds of resources that might not allow simultaneous access by multiple threads—for example, objects of MFC classes (as mentioned previously), graphics objects, nonsharable files, and nonsharable hardware devices. Also, you might need to synchronize the actions of a *producer thread* and a *consumer thread*; for example, if one thread (the producer) writes characters to a buffer and another thread (the consumer) reads and removes characters from the buffer, the reading thread might need to wait until the writing thread has added a character, and the writing thread might need to wait until the reading thread has removed a character.

Fortunately, the Win32 API provides a variety of *synchronization objects* that you can use to synchronize the actions of separate threads (in this context, the term *object* doesn't refer to a C++ object). Using these objects, you can perform various types of synchronization: you can prevent more than one thread from accessing a resource at the same time, you can *limit* the number of threads that can simultaneously access a resource, or you can perform other types of signaling between threads.

NOTE   The MFC provides a set of classes for managing synchronization objects, which you can use rather than calling the Win32 API functions discussed in this chapter and in Chapter 23. However, the features of these classes are less comprehensive than those of the Win32 API functions, and they don't permit some of the programming techniques described in this book, such as waiting for the termination of a thread or process. The following are the MFC synchronization classes: `CSync-Object`, `CSemaphore`, `CCriticalSection`, `CMutex`, `CEvent`, `CSingleLock`, `CMultiLock`. For a general discussion on using these classes, see the following topic in the online help: *Visual C++ Documentation, Using Visual C++, Visual C++ Programmer's Guide, Adding Program Functionality, Details, Multithreading Topics, Multithreading with C++ and MFC, Multithreading: How to Use the Synchronization Classes*.

One of the simplest and most typical of the synchronization objects is the *mutex*. The name of this synchronization object derives from the expression *mutual exclusion*. It's used for limiting access to a given resource to a *single* thread at a time.

To use a mutex, the first step is to call the Win32 API function ::CreateMutex to create a mutex synchronization object (any thread in the program can do this). The following is an example:

```
HANDLE HMutex;  // mutex handle declared globally so that all
                // threads can access it

// ...

void SomeFunction ()
{
// ...
   HMutex = ::CreateMutex
      (NULL,   // assign default security attributes; handle not
               // inheritable;
       FALSE,  // mutex initially signaled;
       NULL);  // no name assigned to mutex
// ...
}
```

The first parameter specifies the security attributes of the mutex; passing NULL assigns it default security attributes and makes the mutex handle noninheritable (inheritance of handles is discussed in Chapter 23). The second parameter specifies the initial state of the mutex; passing FALSE creates a mutex that's initially signaled (if you pass TRUE, the mutex will initially be nonsignaled; these two states will be explained shortly). The third parameter specifies the mutex name; passing NULL creates a mutex without a name (assigning a name allows you to access the mutex from another process, as explained in Chapter 23). ::Create-Mutex returns a handle, which the threads in the program use for referring to the mutex.

The next step is to add a call to the ::WaitForSingleObject Win32 API function to the beginning of any block of code that accesses the resource you want to protect, and to add a call to the ::ReleaseMutex Win32 API function to the end of each of these blocks. For example, you could prevent more than one thread from simultaneously accessing the global counter in the example just given, as follows:

```
::WaitForSingleObject
   (HMutex,    // mutex handle
    INFINITE); // wait as long as necessary
++Count;
cout << Count << '\n';
::ReleaseMutex (HMutex);
```

These function calls work as follows: a mutex (as well as any other synchronization object) is in one of two states—*signaled* or *nonsignaled*. Usually, a newly created mutex is signaled (though you can create it in the nonsignaled state). You can think of signaled as meaning to "go ahead." If the mutex in the example is signaled when a thread calls ::WaitForSingleObject, this function changes the mutex to the nonsignaled state and returns immediately. The thread proceeds to execute the protected block of code and then calls ::ReleaseMutex, which sets the mutex back to signaled. If the mutex is nonsignaled when a thread calls ::WaitForSingleObject (because another thread is currently executing the protected block of code), ::WaitForSingleObject first *waits* until the mutex becomes signaled and then sets the mutex to nonsignaled and returns. The overall result is that only one thread at a time can execute the protected block of code. Note that when a synchronization object is nonsignaled, it's also said to be *owned* by the thread that caused it to become nonsignaled.

In the example, if *several* blocks of code manipulated Count, you'd have to bracket each block with calls to ::WaitForSingleObject and ::ReleaseMutex, specifying the same mutex in every call. In this case, if a thread is currently executing *any* of the blocks of code, no other thread can execute any of the blocks.

The first parameter passed to ::WaitForSingleObject and ::ReleaseMutex is the mutex handle returned by ::CreateMutex. The second ::WaitForSingleObject parameter is the time-out period in milliseconds. After waiting for the specified time-out period, ::WaitForSingleObject will return even if the mutex hasn't become signaled. Most programs, however, assign this parameter the special value INFINITE, which causes ::WaitForSingleObject to wait as long as necessary for the mutex to become signaled.

TIP

You can call the Win32 API function ::WaitForMultipleObjects to wait for *several* different mutexes or other synchronization objects. You can either wait until *any* of the synchronization objects is signaled, or wait until *all* objects are signaled. Note that ::WaitForSingleObject and ::WaitForMultipleObjects are general functions that allow you to wait for any of the synchronization objects, as well as for other Windows objects that will be explained later.

If your program has finished using a mutex, it can call the Win32 API function ::CloseHandle to close the mutex handle. The following call would close the mutex handle used in the previous examples:

```
::CloseHandle (HMutex);
```

If you don't call `::CloseHandle`, the system will automatically close the handle when the program exits. When *all* handles for a given object have been closed, the system releases the object and frees the memory it consumes. (Chapter 23 will discuss opening more than one handle for a single object.)

NOTE   One of the advantages of using a synchronization object is that while a thread is waiting for an object to become signaled, the thread is *blocked*. When a thread is blocked, the operating system doesn't run it and it therefore doesn't needlessly consume processor time that can be used by other threads.

Other Synchronization Objects

The other Win32 synchronization objects are critical sections, semaphores, and events. A *critical section* performs the same task as a mutex, though you must call an entirely different set of Win32 functions; a critical section can be slightly more efficient than a mutex, but you can't use it for synchronizing threads in different processes (all the other synchronization objects can be shared among separate processes). A *semaphore* is similar to a mutex, except that rather than allowing only a *single* thread to access a resource at a given time, it allows *several* threads to simultaneously access a resource; you specify the maximum number of threads allowed when you create the semaphore. An *event* is a versatile synchronization object that permits one thread to signal one or more other threads in a variety of ways. Table 22.1 lists the Win32 synchronization objects; for each object, it briefly describes the object's purpose and gives the Win32 API functions that you use to create and manage the object.

TABLE 22.1: The Win32 Synchronization Objects

Synchronization Object	Primary Purpose of Object	Win32 API Functions Used to Create and Manage Object

Mutex	Prevents more than *one* thread from simultaneously accessing a shared resource	`::CreateMutex`
		`::WaitForSingleObject`
		`::WaitForMultipleObjects`
		`::ReleaseMutex`
		`::CloseHandle`

Continued on next page

TABLE 22.1 CONTINUED: The Win32 Synchronization Objects

Synchronization Object	Primary Purpose of Object	Win32 API Functions Used to Create and Manage Object

Critical section	Prevents more than *one* thread from simultaneously accessing a shared resource; efficient, but can't be shared among processes	`::InitializeCriticalSection`
		`::EnterCriticalSection`
		`::LeaveCriticalSection`
		`::DeleteCriticalSection`

Semaphore	Limits the number of threads that can simultaneously access a shared resource	`::CreateSemaphore`
		`::WaitForSingleObject`
		`::WaitForMultipleObjects`
		`::ReleaseSemaphore`
		`::CloseHandle`

Event	Allows a thread to signal one or more other threads in a variety of ways	`::CreateEvent`
		`::SetEvent`
		`::PulseEvent`
		`::ResetEvent`
		`::WaitForSingleObject`
		`::WaitForMultipleObjects`
		`::CloseHandle`

Other Types of Synchronization

When calling `::WaitForSingleObject` or `::WaitForMultipleObjects`, in addition to waiting for the synchronization objects discussed previously, you can wait for several other types of Windows objects (in this context, the term *object* refers to a Windows item represented by a handle, *not* a C++ class instance). Table 22.2 lists these additional objects; for each object it gives the function or data member from which you obtain the object handle, and it describes the event that causes the object to become signaled. To wait for the object to become signaled, you simply pass the object's handle to `::WaitForSingleObject` or `::WaitForMultiple-Objects`. For example, the MandelMT program given in the next section passes a thread's handle to `::WaitForSingleObject` to wait for the thread to terminate. For more information, see the documentation on `::WaitForSingleObject` and on the function used to obtain the object's handle.

TABLE 22.2: Additional Windows Objects You Can Wait for When Calling `WaitForSingleObject` or `WaitForMultipleObjects`

Windows Object	Function or Data Member for Obtaining Object Handle	Event that Causes Object to Become Signaled
Thread	`CWinThread::m_hThread`	Thread terminates
Process	`::CreateProcess` or `::OpenProcess`	Process terminates
Console input	`::CreateFile` or `::GetStdHandle`	Console input becomes available
Change notification	`::FindFirstChangeNotification`	Change occurs in specified file folder

A thread can call several additional Win32 API functions to wait for various occurrences. First, by calling `::MsgWaitForMultipleObjects` a thread can wait *either* for one or more objects to become signaled *or* for one or more specified messages to be received. Also, a thread can call `::Sleep` to wait for a specified number of milliseconds. Note that when a thread is waiting during a call to `::MsgWaitForMultipleObjects` or `::Sleep`, it's blocked and doesn't consume processor time (just as it's blocked during a call to `::WaitForSingleObject` or `::WaitForMultipleObjects`).

Finally, threads might be able to signal each other or synchronize their activities using a simple global variable. For an example, see the use of the `StopDraw` global flag in the MandelMT program.

A Multithreading Version of the Mandel Program

Recall that in the Mandel program presented in Chapter 19, the primary program thread draws a single column of the fractal pattern, then processes any incoming messages, then draws another column, then processes messages, and so on. This procedure allows the program to respond to messages *while* the pattern is being drawn (which can take a long time). The multithreading version of Mandel, called MandelMT, that's presented in this section should convince you that when a program must perform more than one task at a time, it's more efficient and easier to assign each main task to a separate thread. In MandelMT, the primary thread is dedicated to processing messages, while a secondary thread is dedicated to drawing the fractal pattern. MandelMT is more responsive than Mandel because the primary thread can immediately process an incoming message without having to wait until the current column of the pattern is completed. Mandel-MT is also simpler, because the code executed by each thread performs only its specialized task without having to switch among different jobs; for example, the fractal drawing routine simply draws the entire pattern without having to save its state and return after drawing each column.

You'll also learn, however, that multithreading in the Windows environment can induce some program complications that you must handle. For example, you must prevent a secondary thread from drawing in a window while the primary thread is moving or sizing the window. Also, separate threads can't freely share MFC objects, as discussed previously.

To create the MandelMT program, you'll use AppWizard to generate a *new* set of source files rather than modifying the Mandel source files (keep in mind, however, that you can copy code from Mandel into MandelMT). When you use AppWizard to generate the source files, name the project Mandel MT, and in the Projects tab of the New dialog box and in the AppWizard Step 1 through Step 6 dialog boxes make the *same* choices that you specified for the WinGreet program in Chapter 9.

After generating the source files, open MandelMTView.h and define the m_PDraw-Thread data member of the view class:

```
class CMandelMTView : public CView
{
public:
    CWinThread *m_PDrawThread;
```

m_PDrawThread is used to store the address of the object that manages the secondary thread.

Next, open the MandelMTView.cpp file and add code to the view class constructor for initializing m_PDrawThread:

```
CMandelMTView::CMandelMTView()
{
    // TODO: add construction code here

    m_PDrawThread = 0;
}
```

Also, add code so that the view class destructor destroys the thread object:

```
CMandelMTView::~CMandelMTView()
{
    delete m_PDrawThread;
}
```

At the beginning of MandelMTView.cpp, add definitions as follows:

```
// MandelMTView.cpp : implementation of the CMandelMTView class
//

#include "stdafx.h"
#include "MandelMT.h"

#include "MandelMTDoc.h"
#include "MandelMTView.h"

#ifdef _DEBUG
#define new DEBUG_NEW
#undef THIS_FILE
static char THIS_FILE[] = __FILE__;
#endif

// Mandelbrot set constants:
#define CIMAX 1.2
#define CIMIN -1.2
#define CRMAX 1.0
#define CRMIN -2.0
#define NMAX 128

// Global variables for communicating among threads:
int ColMax;
int RowMax;
BOOL StopDraw;
```

The Mandelbrot set constants (CIMAX, and so on) are the same as those you defined in Mandel. ColMax and RowMax store the current dimensions of the view window; in MandelMT, they're made global variables rather than data members of the view class so that both threads can freely access them (recall the limitations discussed previously on accessing an MFC object from multiple threads). Stop-Draw is a flag that the primary thread uses to signal the secondary thread to exit immediately without finishing the drawing of the current pattern.

Next, implement a message handler for the WM_SIZE function. To do this, run ClassWizard, open the Message Maps tab, select CMandelMTView in both the Class

Name: and Object IDs: lists, and select WM_SIZE in the Messages: list. Then, click the Add Function button, click the Edit Code button, and add code as follows to OnSize:

```
void CMandelMTView::OnSize(UINT nType, int cx, int cy)
{
    CView::OnSize(nType, cx, cy);

    // TODO: Add your message handler code here

    if (cx <= 1 || cy <= 1)
        return;

    ColMax = cx;
    RowMax = cy;
}
```

As explained in Chapter 19, the OnSize function receives control when the window is first created and whenever its size changes. It sets the global variables, RowMax and ColMax, that the drawing routine uses to determine the total size of the view window.

Also in MandelMTView.cpp, add code as follows to the OnDraw function:

```
void CMandelMTView::OnDraw(CDC* pDC)
{
    CMandelMTDoc* pDoc = GetDocument();
    ASSERT_VALID(pDoc);

    // TODO: add draw code for native data here

    if (m_PDrawThread)
        {
        StopDraw = TRUE;
        m_PDrawThread->ResumeThread ();
        ::WaitForSingleObject
            (m_PDrawThread->m_hThread,  // drawing thread handle
            INFINITE);                  // wait as long as necessary
        delete m_PDrawThread;
        }

    m_PDrawThread = AfxBeginThread
        (DrawFractal,
```

```
        &m_hWnd,
        THREAD_PRIORITY_BELOW_NORMAL,
        0,
        CREATE_SUSPENDED);
    m_PDrawThread->m_bAutoDelete = FALSE;
    StopDraw = FALSE;
    m_PDrawThread->ResumeThread ();
}
```

Rather than drawing the fractal pattern itself, OnDraw starts a secondary thread and then returns control quickly, so that the program can continue to process messages while the secondary thread draws the fractal pattern, running in the background.

If a secondary thread was started previously (indicated by a nonzero value in the pointer to the thread object, m_PDrawThread), OnDraw begins by *stopping* the thread and deleting the thread object. To stop the thread, it performs the following steps:

1. It sets the global flag StopDraw to TRUE. As you'll see, the secondary thread function tests this flag and terminates itself if it's TRUE.

2. It calls ResumeThread for the thread object to restart the thread *in case it has been suspended*; later, you'll see how the thread can become suspended.

3. It calls ::WaitForSingleObject to wait until the thread has terminated itself.

4. Once the thread has stopped running, it deletes the thread object—that is, the CWinThread object whose address is stored in m_PDrawThread.

Note that if the thread has already stopped running (as you'll see, it automatically stops running after it has completed drawing the pattern), steps 1, 2, and 3 are unnecessary but harmless.

Once it has stopped any existing drawing thread, OnDraw creates a *new* thread to draw or redraw the entire fractal pattern using the current view window dimensions. When it calls AfxBeginThread, OnDraw assigns the first parameter the address of the secondary thread function, DrawFractal, which you'll define shortly. It assigns the second parameter the handle of the view window, so that the secondary thread can draw within this window. It assigns the third parameter the value THREAD_PRIORITY_BELOW_NORMAL so that the drawing thread will have a lower priority than the primary thread. This is done to help ensure both that the primary thread can respond quickly to messages and that the second-ary thread draws only when the primary thread isn't busy.

OnDraw assigns the fifth AfxBeginThread parameter the value CREATE_SUSPENDED, so that it can assign FALSE to the m_bAutoDelete data member of the thread object before the thread starts running. As explained previously (in the section "Managing the Thread"), m_bAutoDelete is assigned FALSE so that the thread object won't destroy itself when the thread stops running (the program needs to access the thread object whether or not the thread is still run-ning). Finally, OnDraw resets the StopDraw flag to FALSE and calls ResumeThread to start the thread running.

Now, just above the OnDraw function in MandelMTView.cpp, add the following definition for the drawing thread function, DrawFractal:

```
/////////////////////////////////////////////////////////////////////////////
///////////
// CMandelMTView drawing

UINT DrawFractal (LPVOID PHWndView)
{
    float CI;
    CClientDC ClientDC (CWnd::FromHandle (*(HWND *)PHWndView));
    int Col;
    static DWORD ColorTable [6] =
        {0x0000ff, // red
        0x00ff00, // green
        0xff0000, // blue
        0x00ffff, // yellow
        0xffff00, // cyan
        0xff00ff}; // magenta
    int ColorVal;
    float CR = (float)CRMIN;
    float DCI = (float)((CIMAX - CIMIN) / (RowMax-1));
    float DCR = (float)((CRMAX - CRMIN) / (ColMax-1));
    float I;
    float ISqr;
    float R;
    int Row;
    float RSqr;
```

```
for (Col = 0; Col < ColMax; ++Col)
    {
    if (StopDraw)
        break;

    CI = (float)CIMAX;

    for (Row = 0; Row < RowMax; ++Row)
        {
        R = (float)0.0;
        I = (float)0.0;
        RSqr = (float)0.0;
        ISqr = (float)0.0;
        ColorVal = 0;
        while (ColorVal < NMAX && RSqr + ISqr < 4)
            {
            ++ColorVal;
            RSqr = R * R;
            ISqr = I * I;
            I *= R;
            I += I + CI;
            R = RSqr - ISqr + CR;
            }
        ClientDC.SetPixelV
            (Col, Row, ColorTable [ColorVal % 6]);
        CI -= DCI;
        }

    CR += DCR;
    }

return (0);
}
```

The DrawFractal function is executed by the secondary program thread. It works very much like CMandelView::DrawCol in the Mandel program. However, rather than returning after drawing each column of the fractal pattern, it returns *either* when the entire pattern has been drawn *or* when the primary program thread has set the StopDraw flag to TRUE. When DrawFractal returns, the secondary thread is terminated.

Also, because `DrawFractal` isn't a member function of the program's view class, when it creates a device context object, it can't simply pass the `this` pointer to the `CClientDC` constructor. Rather, it passes the handle of the view window (contained in the `DrawFractal` parameter) to the static `CWnd::FromHandle` function to obtain a pointer to a new, temporary object for the view window. It then passes this pointer to the `CClientDC` constructor:

```
CClientDC ClientDC (CWnd::FromHandle (*(HWND *)PHWndView));
```

(Note that `OnDraw` passes `DrawThread` the Windows *handle* for the view window rather than passing a pointer to the program's view window *object* because of the warnings in the Microsoft documentation about sharing `CWnd`-derived objects among separate program threads, as discussed in the earlier section "MFC Limitations.")

The MandelMT program is almost complete; however, there's one problem in the way that it's written: if the user moves the program window while the pattern is being drawn, the secondary thread will continue drawing in the window while the main thread (within the system code) conducts the move operation. However, during the move, the system *discards* any output sent to the window. As a result, when the move operation is ended, the pattern will have a gap in it (you might want to build and run the program now to see this for yourself).

NOTE   In some versions of the Windows desktop, the user can select the Show Window Contents While Dragging option (this option is set by choosing the Start ➤ Settings ➤ Folder Options… menu command on the Windows taskbar and opening the View tab). If this option is selected, graphics written to the MandelMT window while it's being moved will be displayed normally, and no gap will appear in the pattern.

A solution to the problem is to *suspend* the secondary thread while the system code moves the window. Windows moves the window only in response to a `WM_SYSCOMMAND` message; accordingly, you can provide a handler for this message, which suspends the thread, passes control to the default message handler, and then resumes the thread. To do this, run ClassWizard, open the Class Info tab, choose the `CMainFrame` item in the Class Name: list, and choose the Window item in the Message Filter: list. This step allows you to define handlers for a larger set of messages, including `WM_SYSCOMMAND`. Then, open the Message Maps tab, choose CMainFrame in the Object IDs: list, choose WM_SYSCOMMAND in the Messages: list, and click the Add Function button. Click the Edit Code button, and finally add code as follows to the OnSysCommand function in MainFrm.cpp:

```
////////////////////////////////////////////////////////////////////
////////////
// CMainFrame message handlers

void CMainFrame::OnSysCommand(UINT nID, LPARAM lParam)
{
    // TODO: Add your message handler code here and/or call
    // default

    CWinThread *PDrawThread =
        ((CMandelMTView *)GetActiveView ())->m_PDrawThread;

    if (PDrawThread)
        PDrawThread->SuspendThread ();

    CFrameWnd::OnSysCommand(nID, lParam);

    if (PDrawThread && PDrawThread->m_hThread != NULL)
        PDrawThread->ResumeThread ();
}
```

Also in MainFrm.cpp, you must add include statements for two program header files so that OnSysCommand can access the view class definition:

```
// MainFrm.cpp : implementation of the CMainFrame class
//

#include "stdafx.h"
#include "MandelMT.h"

#include "MainFrm.h"
#include "MandelMTDoc.h"
#include "MandelMTView.h"
```

Before building the program, you might want to remove the unneeded commands from the program menu and define a custom icon. Finally, add the usual SetWindowText call to the InitInstance function in MandelMT.cpp:

```
// The one and only window has been initialized, so show and
// update it.
```

```
       m_pMainWnd->ShowWindow(SW_SHOW);
       m_pMainWnd->UpdateWindow();

       m_pMainWnd->SetWindowText ("Multithreading Mandelbrot Demo");

       return TRUE;
   }
```

The MandelMT Source Code

The following listings, Listings 22.1 through 22.8, contain the C++ source code for MandelMT, the multithreading version of the Mandel program. You'll find a copy of these files in your \MandelMT companion-CD folder.

Listing 22.1

```
// MandelMT.h : main header file for the MANDELMT application
//

#if !defined(AFX_MANDELMT_H__3DD7B0E5_A9DC_11D1_80FC_00C0F6A83B7F__INCLUDED_)
#define AFX_MANDELMT_H__3DD7B0E5_A9DC_11D1_80FC_00C0F6A83B7F__INCLUDED_

#if _MSC_VER > 1000
#pragma once
#endif // _MSC_VER > 1000

#ifndef __AFXWIN_H__
    #error include 'stdafx.h' before including this file for PCH
#endif

#include "resource.h"       // main symbols

/////////////////////////////////////////////////////////////////////////
// CMandelMTApp:
// See MandelMT.cpp for the implementation of this class
//

class CMandelMTApp : public CWinApp
{
public:
    CMandelMTApp();
```

```
// Overrides
   // ClassWizard generated virtual function overrides
   //{{AFX_VIRTUAL(CMandelMTApp)
   public:
   virtual BOOL InitInstance();
   //}}AFX_VIRTUAL

// Implementation
   //{{AFX_MSG(CMandelMTApp)
   afx_msg void OnAppAbout();
      // NOTE - the ClassWizard will add and remove member functions here.
      //    DO NOT EDIT what you see in these blocks of generated code !
   //}}AFX_MSG
   DECLARE_MESSAGE_MAP()
};


/////////////////////////////////////////////////////////////////////////////

//{{AFX_INSERT_LOCATION}}
// Microsoft Visual C++ will insert additional declarations immediately before
// the previous line.

#endif
// !defined(AFX_MANDELMT_H__3DD7B0E5_A9DC_11D1_80FC_00C0F6A83B7F__INCLUDED_)
```

Listing 22.2

```
// MandelMT.cpp : Defines the class behaviors for the application.
//

#include "stdafx.h"
#include "MandelMT.h"

#include "MainFrm.h"
#include "MandelMTDoc.h"
#include "MandelMTView.h"

#ifdef _DEBUG
#define new DEBUG_NEW
#undef THIS_FILE
static char THIS_FILE[] = __FILE__;
#endif
```

```
/////////////////////////////////////////////////////////////////////////
// CMandelMTApp

BEGIN_MESSAGE_MAP(CMandelMTApp, CWinApp)
    //{{AFX_MSG_MAP(CMandelMTApp)
    ON_COMMAND(ID_APP_ABOUT, OnAppAbout)
        // NOTE - the ClassWizard will add and remove mapping macros here.
        //    DO NOT EDIT what you see in these blocks of generated code!
    //}}AFX_MSG_MAP
    // Standard file based document commands
    ON_COMMAND(ID_FILE_NEW, CWinApp::OnFileNew)
    ON_COMMAND(ID_FILE_OPEN, CWinApp::OnFileOpen)
END_MESSAGE_MAP()

/////////////////////////////////////////////////////////////////////////
// CMandelMTApp construction

CMandelMTApp::CMandelMTApp()
{
    // TODO: add construction code here,
    // Place all significant initialization in InitInstance
}

/////////////////////////////////////////////////////////////////////////
// The one and only CMandelMTApp object

CMandelMTApp theApp;

/////////////////////////////////////////////////////////////////////////
// CMandelMTApp initialization

BOOL CMandelMTApp::InitInstance()
{
    // Standard initialization
    // If you are not using these features and wish to reduce the size
    //  of your final executable, you should remove from the following
    //  the specific initialization routines you do not need.

#ifdef _AFXDLL
    Enable3dControls();         // Call this when using MFC in a shared DLL
#else
    Enable3dControlsStatic();   // Call this when linking to MFC statically
#endif
```

```
// Change the registry key under which our settings are stored.
// TODO: You should modify this string to be something appropriate
// such as the name of your company or organization.
SetRegistryKey(_T("Local AppWizard-Generated Applications"));

LoadStdProfileSettings();  // Load standard INI file options (including MRU)

// Register the application's document templates.  Document templates
//  serve as the connection between documents, frame windows and views.

CSingleDocTemplate* pDocTemplate;
pDocTemplate = new CSingleDocTemplate(
    IDR_MAINFRAME,
    RUNTIME_CLASS(CMandelMTDoc),
    RUNTIME_CLASS(CMainFrame),          // main SDI frame window
    RUNTIME_CLASS(CMandelMTView));
AddDocTemplate(pDocTemplate);

// Parse command line for standard shell commands, DDE, file open
CCommandLineInfo cmdInfo;
ParseCommandLine(cmdInfo);

// Dispatch commands specified on the command line
if (!ProcessShellCommand(cmdInfo))
    return FALSE;

// The one and only window has been initialized, so show and update it.
m_pMainWnd->ShowWindow(SW_SHOW);
m_pMainWnd->UpdateWindow();

m_pMainWnd->SetWindowText ("Multithreading Mandelbrot Demo");

    return TRUE;
}


/////////////////////////////////////////////////////////////////////////////
// CAboutDlg dialog used for App About

class CAboutDlg : public CDialog
{
public:
    CAboutDlg();
```

```cpp
// Dialog Data
    //{{AFX_DATA(CAboutDlg)
    enum { IDD = IDD_ABOUTBOX };
    //}}AFX_DATA

    // ClassWizard generated virtual function overrides
    //{{AFX_VIRTUAL(CAboutDlg)
    protected:
    virtual void DoDataExchange(CDataExchange* pDX);    // DDX/DDV support
    //}}AFX_VIRTUAL

// Implementation
protected:
    //{{AFX_MSG(CAboutDlg)
        // No message handlers
    //}}AFX_MSG
    DECLARE_MESSAGE_MAP()
};

CAboutDlg::CAboutDlg() : CDialog(CAboutDlg::IDD)
{
    //{{AFX_DATA_INIT(CAboutDlg)
    //}}AFX_DATA_INIT
}

void CAboutDlg::DoDataExchange(CDataExchange* pDX)
{
    CDialog::DoDataExchange(pDX);
    //{{AFX_DATA_MAP(CAboutDlg)
    //}}AFX_DATA_MAP
}

BEGIN_MESSAGE_MAP(CAboutDlg, CDialog)
    //{{AFX_MSG_MAP(CAboutDlg)
        // No message handlers
    //}}AFX_MSG_MAP
END_MESSAGE_MAP()

// App command to run the dialog
void CMandelMTApp::OnAppAbout()
{
    CAboutDlg aboutDlg;
```

```
      aboutDlg.DoModal();
}


/////////////////////////////////////////////////////////////////////
// CMandelMTApp message handlers
```

Listing 22.3

```
// MandelMTDoc.h : interface of the CMandelMTDoc class
//
/////////////////////////////////////////////////////////////////////

#if !defined(AFX_MANDELMTDOC_H__3DD7B0EB_A9DC_11D1_80FC_00C0F6A83B7F__INCLUDED_)
#define AFX_MANDELMTDOC_H__3DD7B0EB_A9DC_11D1_80FC_00C0F6A83B7F__INCLUDED_

#if _MSC_VER > 1000
#pragma once
#endif // _MSC_VER > 1000


class CMandelMTDoc : public CDocument
{
protected: // create from serialization only
   CMandelMTDoc();
   DECLARE_DYNCREATE(CMandelMTDoc)

// Attributes
public:

// Operations
public:

// Overrides
   // ClassWizard generated virtual function overrides
   //{{AFX_VIRTUAL(CMandelMTDoc)
   public:
   virtual BOOL OnNewDocument();
   virtual void Serialize(CArchive& ar);
   //}}AFX_VIRTUAL
```

```
// Implementation
public:
   virtual ~CMandelMTDoc();
#ifdef _DEBUG
   virtual void AssertValid() const;
   virtual void Dump(CDumpContext& dc) const;
#endif

protected:

// Generated message map functions
protected:
   //{{AFX_MSG(CMandelMTDoc)
      // NOTE - the ClassWizard will add and remove member functions here.
      //    DO NOT EDIT what you see in these blocks of generated code !
   //}}AFX_MSG
   DECLARE_MESSAGE_MAP()
};

/////////////////////////////////////////////////////////////////////////////

//{{AFX_INSERT_LOCATION}}
// Microsoft Visual C++ will insert additional declarations immediately before
// the previous line.

#endif
// !defined(AFX_MANDELMTDOC_H__3DD7B0EB_A9DC_11D1_80FC_00C0F6A83B7F__INCLUDED_)
```

Listing 22.4

```
// MandelMTDoc.cpp : implementation of the CMandelMTDoc class
//

#include "stdafx.h"
#include "MandelMT.h"

#include "MandelMTDoc.h"

#ifdef _DEBUG
#define new DEBUG_NEW
#undef THIS_FILE
static char THIS_FILE[] = __FILE__;
#endif
```

```
///////////////////////////////////////////////////////////////////////
// CMandelMTDoc

IMPLEMENT_DYNCREATE(CMandelMTDoc, CDocument)

BEGIN_MESSAGE_MAP(CMandelMTDoc, CDocument)
   //{{AFX_MSG_MAP(CMandelMTDoc)
      // NOTE - the ClassWizard will add and remove mapping macros here.
      //    DO NOT EDIT what you see in these blocks of generated code!
   //}}AFX_MSG_MAP
END_MESSAGE_MAP()

///////////////////////////////////////////////////////////////////////
// CMandelMTDoc construction/destruction

CMandelMTDoc::CMandelMTDoc()
{
   // TODO: add one-time construction code here

}

CMandelMTDoc::~CMandelMTDoc()
{
}

BOOL CMandelMTDoc::OnNewDocument()
{
   if (!CDocument::OnNewDocument())
      return FALSE;

   // TODO: add reinitialization code here
   // (SDI documents will reuse this document)

   return TRUE;
}



///////////////////////////////////////////////////////////////////////
// CMandelMTDoc serialization

void CMandelMTDoc::Serialize(CArchive& ar)
```

```
{
    if (ar.IsStoring())
    {
        // TODO: add storing code here
    }
    else
    {
        // TODO: add loading code here
    }
}


/////////////////////////////////////////////////////////////////////////
// CMandelMTDoc diagnostics

#ifdef _DEBUG
void CMandelMTDoc::AssertValid() const
{
    CDocument::AssertValid();
}

void CMandelMTDoc::Dump(CDumpContext& dc) const
{
    CDocument::Dump(dc);
}
#endif //_DEBUG


/////////////////////////////////////////////////////////////////////////
// CMandelMTDoc commands
```

Listing 22.5

```
// MainFrm.h : interface of the CMainFrame class
//
/////////////////////////////////////////////////////////////////////////

#if !defined(AFX_MAINFRM_H__3DD7B0E9_A9DC_11D1_80FC_00C0F6A83B7F__INCLUDED_)
#define AFX_MAINFRM_H__3DD7B0E9_A9DC_11D1_80FC_00C0F6A83B7F__INCLUDED_

#if _MSC_VER > 1000
#pragma once
#endif // _MSC_VER > 1000
```

```
class CMainFrame : public CFrameWnd
{

protected: // create from serialization only
    CMainFrame();
    DECLARE_DYNCREATE(CMainFrame)

// Attributes
public:

// Operations
public:

// Overrides
    // ClassWizard generated virtual function overrides
    //{{AFX_VIRTUAL(CMainFrame)
    virtual BOOL PreCreateWindow(CREATESTRUCT& cs);
    //}}AFX_VIRTUAL

// Implementation
public:
    virtual ~CMainFrame();
#ifdef _DEBUG
    virtual void AssertValid() const;
    virtual void Dump(CDumpContext& dc) const;
#endif

// Generated message map functions
protected:
    //{{AFX_MSG(CMainFrame)
    afx_msg void OnSysCommand(UINT nID, LPARAM lParam);
    //}}AFX_MSG
    DECLARE_MESSAGE_MAP()
};

/////////////////////////////////////////////////////////////////////

//{{AFX_INSERT_LOCATION}}
// Microsoft Visual C++ will insert additional declarations immediately before
// the previous line.

#endif
// !defined(AFX_MAINFRM_H__3DD7B0E9_A9DC_11D1_80FC_00C0F6A83B7F__INCLUDED_)
```

Listing 22.6

```cpp
// MainFrm.cpp : implementation of the CMainFrame class
//

#include "stdafx.h"
#include "MandelMT.h"

#include "MainFrm.h"
#include "MandelMTDoc.h"
#include "MandelMTView.h"

#ifdef _DEBUG
#define new DEBUG_NEW
#undef THIS_FILE
static char THIS_FILE[] = __FILE__;
#endif


/////////////////////////////////////////////////////////////////////////
// CMainFrame

IMPLEMENT_DYNCREATE(CMainFrame, CFrameWnd)

BEGIN_MESSAGE_MAP(CMainFrame, CFrameWnd)
    //{{AFX_MSG_MAP(CMainFrame)
    ON_WM_SYSCOMMAND()
    //}}AFX_MSG_MAP
END_MESSAGE_MAP()

/////////////////////////////////////////////////////////////////////////
// CMainFrame construction/destruction

CMainFrame::CMainFrame()
{
    // TODO: add member initialization code here

}

CMainFrame::~CMainFrame()
{
}
```

```
BOOL CMainFrame::PreCreateWindow(CREATESTRUCT& cs)
{
   if( !CFrameWnd::PreCreateWindow(cs) )
      return FALSE;
   // TODO: Modify the Window class or styles here by modifying
   //  the CREATESTRUCT cs

   return TRUE;
}

/////////////////////////////////////////////////////////////////////////////
// CMainFrame diagnostics

#ifdef _DEBUG
void CMainFrame::AssertValid() const
{
   CFrameWnd::AssertValid();
}

void CMainFrame::Dump(CDumpContext& dc) const
{
   CFrameWnd::Dump(dc);
}

#endif //_DEBUG

/////////////////////////////////////////////////////////////////////////////
// CMainFrame message handlers


void CMainFrame::OnSysCommand(UINT nID, LPARAM lParam)
{
   // TODO: Add your message handler code here and/or call default

   CWinThread *PDrawThread = ((CMandelMTView *)GetActiveView ())->m_PDrawThread;

   if (PDrawThread)
      PDrawThread->SuspendThread ();

   CFrameWnd::OnSysCommand(nID, lParam);

   if (PDrawThread && PDrawThread->m_hThread != NULL)
      PDrawThread->ResumeThread ();
}
```

Listing 22.7

```cpp
// MandelMTView.h : interface of the CMandelMTView class
//
/////////////////////////////////////////////////////////////////////

#if !defined(AFX_MANDELMTVIEW_H__3DD7B0ED_A9DC_11D1_80FC_00C0F6A83B7F__INCLUDED_)
#define AFX_MANDELMTVIEW_H__3DD7B0ED_A9DC_11D1_80FC_00C0F6A83B7F__INCLUDED_

#if _MSC_VER > 1000
#pragma once
#endif // _MSC_VER > 1000


class CMandelMTView : public CView
{
public:
   CWinThread *m_PDrawThread;

protected: // create from serialization only
   CMandelMTView();
   DECLARE_DYNCREATE(CMandelMTView)

// Attributes
public:
   CMandelMTDoc* GetDocument();

// Operations
public:

// Overrides
   // ClassWizard generated virtual function overrides
   //{{AFX_VIRTUAL(CMandelMTView)
   public:
   virtual void OnDraw(CDC* pDC);  // overridden to draw this view
   virtual BOOL PreCreateWindow(CREATESTRUCT& cs);
   protected:
   //}}AFX_VIRTUAL

// Implementation
public:
   virtual ~CMandelMTView();
```

```
#ifdef _DEBUG
   virtual void AssertValid() const;
   virtual void Dump(CDumpContext& dc) const;
#endif

protected:

// Generated message map functions
protected:
   //{{AFX_MSG(CMandelMTView)
   afx_msg void OnSize(UINT nType, int cx, int cy);
   //}}AFX_MSG
   DECLARE_MESSAGE_MAP()
};

#ifndef _DEBUG  // debug version in MandelMTView.cpp
inline CMandelMTDoc* CMandelMTView::GetDocument()
   { return (CMandelMTDoc*)m_pDocument; }
#endif


/////////////////////////////////////////////////////////////////////////////

//{{AFX_INSERT_LOCATION}}
// Microsoft Visual C++ will insert additional declarations immediately before
// the previous line.

#endif
// !defined(AFX_MANDELMTVIEW_H__3DD7B0ED_A9DC_11D1_80FC_00C0F6A83B7F__INCLUDED_)
```

Listing 22.8

```
// MandelMTView.cpp : implementation of the CMandelMTView class
//

#include "stdafx.h"
#include "MandelMT.h"

#include "MandelMTDoc.h"
#include "MandelMTView.h"

#ifdef _DEBUG
#define new DEBUG_NEW
```

```
#undef THIS_FILE
static char THIS_FILE[] = __FILE__;
#endif

// Mandelbrot set constants:
#define CIMAX 1.2
#define CIMIN -1.2
#define CRMAX 1.0
#define CRMIN -2.0
#define NMAX 128

// Global variables for communicating among threads:
int ColMax;
int RowMax;
BOOL StopDraw;

/////////////////////////////////////////////////////////////////////////
// CMandelMTView

IMPLEMENT_DYNCREATE(CMandelMTView, CView)

BEGIN_MESSAGE_MAP(CMandelMTView, CView)
    //{{AFX_MSG_MAP(CMandelMTView)
    ON_WM_SIZE()
    //}}AFX_MSG_MAP
END_MESSAGE_MAP()

/////////////////////////////////////////////////////////////////////////
// CMandelMTView construction/destruction

CMandelMTView::CMandelMTView()
{
    // TODO: add construction code here

    m_PDrawThread = 0;
}

CMandelMTView::~CMandelMTView()
{
    delete m_PDrawThread;
}
```

```cpp
BOOL CMandelMTView::PreCreateWindow(CREATESTRUCT& cs)
{
    // TODO: Modify the Window class or styles here by modifying
    //  the CREATESTRUCT cs

    return CView::PreCreateWindow(cs);
}

/////////////////////////////////////////////////////////////////////////////
// CMandelMTView drawing

UINT DrawFractal (LPVOID PHWndView)
{
    float CI;
    CClientDC ClientDC (CWnd::FromHandle (*(HWND *)PHWndView));
    int Col;
    static DWORD ColorTable [6] =
        {0x0000ff, // red
        0x00ff00,  // green
        0xff0000,  // blue
        0x00ffff,  // yellow
        0xffff00,  // cyan
        0xff00ff}; // magenta
    int ColorVal;
    float CR = (float)CRMIN;
    float DCI = (float)((CIMAX - CIMIN) / (RowMax-1));
    float DCR = (float)((CRMAX - CRMIN) / (ColMax-1));
    float I;
    float ISqr;
    float R;
    int Row;
    float RSqr;

    for (Col = 0; Col < ColMax; ++Col)
        {
        if (StopDraw)
            break;

        CI = (float)CIMAX;

        for (Row = 0; Row < RowMax; ++Row)
            {
            R = (float)0.0;
```

```
        I = (float)0.0;
        RSqr = (float)0.0;
        ISqr = (float)0.0;
        ColorVal = 0;
        while (ColorVal < NMAX && RSqr + ISqr < 4)
            {
            ++ColorVal;
            RSqr = R * R;
            ISqr = I * I;
            I *= R;
            I += I + CI;
            R = RSqr - ISqr + CR;
            }
        ClientDC.SetPixelV (Col, Row, ColorTable [ColorVal % 6]);
        CI -= DCI;
        }

    CR += DCR;
    }

    return (0);
}

void CMandelMTView::OnDraw(CDC* pDC)
{
    CMandelMTDoc* pDoc = GetDocument();
    ASSERT_VALID(pDoc);

    // TODO: add draw code for native data here

    if (m_PDrawThread)
        {
        StopDraw = TRUE;
        m_PDrawThread->ResumeThread ();
        ::WaitForSingleObject
            (m_PDrawThread->m_hThread,    // drawing thread handle
            INFINITE);                    // wait as long as necessary
        delete m_PDrawThread;
        }

    m_PDrawThread = AfxBeginThread
        (DrawFractal,
```

```
        &m_hWnd,
        THREAD_PRIORITY_BELOW_NORMAL,
        0,
        CREATE_SUSPENDED);
    m_PDrawThread->m_bAutoDelete = FALSE;
    StopDraw = FALSE;
    m_PDrawThread->ResumeThread ();
}

/////////////////////////////////////////////////////////////////////////////
// CMandelMTView diagnostics

#ifdef _DEBUG
void CMandelMTView::AssertValid() const
{
    CView::AssertValid();
}

void CMandelMTView::Dump(CDumpContext& dc) const
{
    CView::Dump(dc);
}

CMandelMTDoc* CMandelMTView::GetDocument() // non-debug version is inline
{
    ASSERT(m_pDocument->IsKindOf(RUNTIME_CLASS(CMandelMTDoc)));
    return (CMandelMTDoc*)m_pDocument;
}
#endif //_DEBUG

/////////////////////////////////////////////////////////////////////////////
// CMandelMTView message handlers

void CMandelMTView::OnSize(UINT nType, int cx, int cy)
{
    CView::OnSize(nType, cx, cy);

    // TODO: Add your message handler code here
}
```

```
    if (cx <= 1 || cy <= 1)
        return;

    ColMax = cx;
    RowMax = cy;
}
```

Summary

In this chapter, you learned how to start and manage secondary threads of execution in an MFC program, as well as how to synchronize the activities of these threads. The following is a summary of the principal facts and techniques that were discussed:

- A *thread* is the execution of a sequence of program instructions. All programs begin running a *primary thread*. A program can then start one or more *secondary threads*, each of which runs independently and can perform a specialized task.

- Starting a new thread involves relatively little time or memory overhead, and all threads within the same program can share program resources, such as global or static data items, memory allocations, windows, and open files.

- To start a new thread in an MFC program, call the MFC global function AfxBeginThread, assigning the first two parameters the address of the function that the thread is to execute (the *thread function*) and the value of the parameter that's to be passed to this function. The remaining AfxBeginThread parameters have default values, which you can often accept. AfxBeginThread returns control quickly; after its return, the calling thread and the new thread run simultaneously.

- A secondary thread is terminated when it returns from the thread function or when it calls the MFC global function AfxEndThread.

- The call to AfxBeginThread returns a pointer to a CWinThread object. You can use the members of this object to suspend or resume the thread, to change the thread's priority, and to manage the thread in other ways.

- You sometimes need to synchronize the activities of separate threads—for example, when they manipulate a shared resource such as a global variable.

- The Win32 API provides a set of objects for synchronizing threads; these are mutexes, critical sections, semaphores, and events.

- You can use a mutex or critical section to prevent more than one thread from accessing a shared resource at a given time.

- You can use a semaphore to prevent more than a specified number of threads from accessing a shared resource at a given time.

- You can use an event to cause one thread to signal one or more additional threads in a variety of ways.

- You can also synchronize thread actions by calling the `::WaitForSingle-Object`, `::WaitForMultipleObjects`, or `::MsgWaitForMultipleObjects` Win32 API function to wait for a thread or process to end, or to wait for one of several other occurrences.

- A thread can suspend itself for a specified number of milliseconds by calling the Win32 API function `::Sleep`.

- If any of the Win32 synchronization functions forces a thread to wait, the thread stops running and *doesn't* consume processor time while waiting.

CHAPTER

TWENTY-THREE

23

Communicating Among Processes

- Starting new processes

- Synchronizing processes and obtaining handles to shared objects

- Exchanging data through pipes

- Sharing memory

- Using the Clipboard

Whenever you run an executable program file, you create a new *process*. A process can be defined as a running instance of a program. The two terms *program* and *process* have similar meanings; however, *program* connotes a thing—namely, the executable file or its source code—while *process* connotes an occurrence— namely, what happens when you run the program.

In the previous chapter, you learned how to create and manage multiple threads of execution within a single process. In this chapter, you'll learn how to create, manage, and communicate among multiple processes. You'll first learn how to start a new process from a program and how to control or wait for a process. The chapter then explains how to use synchronization objects to coordinate the activities of threads within separate processes and how to share Windows handles among processes. Next, you'll learn how to use two mechanisms for exchanging any type of data among processes: pipes and shared memory.

The techniques for synchronizing processes and for exchanging data through pipes and shared memory are especially useful for suites of programs that are designed to work together. In the final section of the chapter, you'll learn how to exchange data through the Windows Clipboard, which allows even unrelated applications to perform simple transfers of data in standard formats. In Chapter 24, you'll learn how to use the more versatile mechanisms provided by the OLE protocol, which allows you to transfer data among widely diverse programs in a virtually unlimited variety of formats.

Starting New Processes

In the previous chapter, you learned how to make an application more efficient and easier to program by assigning different tasks to separate threads of execution. In some cases, you might want to divide an application into separate *processes* rather than separate threads within a single process. The code for each process would be contained in a separate executable file. Starting a separate process is slower and consumes more system resources than starting a separate thread, and exchanging information between separate processes is more difficult than exchanging information between threads in a single process. However, because each process runs in its own address space, separate processes are less likely to interfere with each other than separate threads. Also, using separate processes allows you to develop suites of closely related programs, or to divide a large application into separate modules. For example, the payroll module for an accounting package could be developed and shipped in a separate executable file, and it could be run as a separate process.

When an application consists of separate processes, one process (typically the main program module) can start one or more additional processes. Accordingly, the user needs to run only the main executable program file, and doesn't need to manually run the executable file for each additional process. For example, in a multiprocess accounting application, if the user chooses a payroll command, the program can run the executable file for the payroll module.

To run an executable file, thereby starting a new process, a program can call the Win32 API function ::CreateProcess, which has the following form:

```
BOOL CreateProcess
    (LPCTSTR lpszImageName,              // path of executable file;
    LPTSTR lpszCommandLine,              // command line;
    LPSECURITY_ATTRIBUTES lpsaProcess,  // process security
                                        // attributes;
    LPSECURITY_ATTRIBUTES lpsaThread,   // thread security
                                        // attributes;
    BOOL fInheritHandles,               // does new process inherit
                                        // handles?;
    DWORD fdwCreate,                    // process creation flags;
    LPVOID lpvEnvironment,              // environment block for
                                        // new process;
    LPCTSTR lpszCurDir,                 // current folder for
                                        // new process;
    LPSTARTUPINFO lpsiStartInfo,        // specifies features of
                                        // window for new process;
    LPPROCESS_INFORMATION lppiProcInfo); // receives information
                                        // on new process
```

The process that calls ::CreateProcess is known as the *parent,* and the new process that's started is known as the *child.* The ::CreateProcess function can be used to run any type of program supported by the operating system—for example, a 32-bit Windows GUI program, a 32-bit Windows console program, a 16-bit Windows 3.1 program, or a 16-bit MS-DOS program.

As an example, the following call would run the program Payroll.exe as a separate process:

```
STARTUPINFO StartupInfo;
memset (&StartupInfo, 0, sizeof (STARTUPINFO));// use default
                                              // window features
StartupInfo.cb = sizeof (STARTUPINFO);  // this field must be
                                        // filled in

PROCESS_INFORMATION ProcessInfo;
```

```
::CreateProcess
    ("PAYROLL.EXE",   // run "PAYROLL.EXE" executable file
    NULL,             // no command line specified
    NULL,             // default process security attributes
    NULL,             // default thread security attributes
    FALSE,            // process does not inherit handles
    0,                // no creation flags (use defaults)
    NULL,             // use environment of calling process
    NULL,             // same current folder as calling process
    &StartupInfo,     // specifies features of process window
    &ProcessInfo);    // receives information on process
```

In this example, because the first parameter specifies only the simple name of the executable file, this file must be located in the current folder. Also, because the example assigns NULL to the second parameter, the command line passed to the child process consists of only the executable file name, Payroll.exe. (You can use the second parameter to pass command-line arguments to the child process. The child process can access the command line either by calling the ::GetCommand-Line Win32 API function or through the lpCmdLine parameter passed to the Win-Main function of a Windows GUI program.) The example passes default values for the third through the ninth parameters. The tenth and final parameter specifies the address of an uninitialized PROCESS_INFORMATION structure, Process-Info; ::CreateProcess assigns this structure the handles and identifiers of the child process and its primary thread.

TIP　　After a parent process has called ::CreateProcess to start a child process, it can call the ::WaitForInputIdle Win32 API function to wait until the child process has completed its initialization tasks (such as creating the program window) and has no pending messages. For example, if a parent process needs to send messages to the child process's window, it could call this function to wait until the child process has completed creating its window.

::CreateProcess returns control promptly; thereafter, the child and parent processes run simultaneously. Like any process, the child process stops running when it returns from its starting function (WinMain for a Windows GUI program) or when it calls the Win32 API function ::ExitProcess. The value that the child process returns or assigns to ::ExitProcess is known as its *exit code*. The parent process (or any other process that has a valid handle for the child process, as discussed later) can obtain this code by calling the ::GetExitCodeProcess Win32 API function, as in the following example:

```
DWORD ExitCode;

::GetExitCodeProcess
    (ProcessInfo.hProcess,  // process handle supplied by
                            // CreateProcess;
     &ExitCode);            // address of DWORD variable to
                            // receive exit code

if (ExitCode == STILL_ACTIVE)
    // process is still running ...
else
    // process has terminated and ExitCode contains its exit code ...
```

This example assumes that ProcessInfo is the PROCESS_INFORMATION structure that was filled in by the call to ::CreateProcess. Notice that if the process is still running, ::GetExitCodeProcess supplies the special value STILL_ACTIVE rather than the exit code.

Also, a program can pass the child process's handle to the ::WaitForSingle-Object Win32 API function (described in Chapter 22) to *wait* until the child process has exited.

A program can pass the child process handle to a variety of other Win32 API functions to manage the child process. For example, it can pass the handle to ::SetPriorityClass to change the process priority or to ::TerminateProcess to immediately stop the process.

Note that a process handle is valid even after the process exits. When a program has finished using a process handle, it can close it by passing it to the ::Close-Handle Win32 API function (if a program doesn't close a handle, it will be closed automatically when the program exits). When *all* handles to a given process have been closed, Windows releases the process information that it maintains.

Note that once the parent process has started the child process, there's no special relationship between the two processes. For example, when the parent process terminates, Windows *doesn't* automatically terminate any child processes that it has started. Also, *any* process—not just the parent process—can call a Win32 API function (such as ::WaitForInputIdle, ::GetExitCodeProcess, ::WaitForSingle-Object, ::SetPriorityClass, or ::TerminateProcess) to control or wait for the child process, provided that it has a handle for this process. Each process, however, must obtain its *own* handle for the child process, using one of the methods for sharing handles that are discussed in the next section.

Synchronizing Processes and Obtaining Handles to Shared Objects

In Chapter 22, you learned how to use the four types of Win32 synchronization objects to synchronize the actions of separate threads within a single process. You can also use three of these synchronization object types—namely mutexes, semaphores, and events—to synchronize the actions of threads within *separate processes*. Recall that when you use a synchronization object, you must pass its handle to the appropriate Win32 API function. In general, however, a Windows handle that has been obtained by one process (for example, a mutex handle obtained by calling ::CreateMutex) can't be used by another process. Rather, each process must obtain its *own* handle to the object (an exception is a handle that is *inherited* by a child process, as explained in a sidebar given later).

The easiest way for separate processes to obtain handles to the same synchronization object is to assign a name to the object, which is used by each process that shares the object. For example, a process could create a mutex and assign it a name as follows:

```
// in first process:
HMutex = ::CreateMutex
    (NULL,  // assign default security attributes; handle not
            // inheritable;
    FALSE,  // mutex initially signaled;
    "Acme Accounting Mutex");  // mutex name
```

(In this example and in the following examples, HMutex is assumed to be a global HANDLE variable.) A second process could obtain a handle to the *same* mutex by making an identical function call, specifying the same mutex name:

```
// in second process:
HMutex = ::CreateMutex
    (NULL,  // assign default security attributes; handle not
            // inheritable;
    FALSE,  // mutex initially signaled;
    "Acme Accounting Mutex");  // mutex name
```

If the mutex doesn't exist when a process calls ::CreateMutex, this function creates the object and returns a handle that can be used by the current process. If, however, the mutex already exists, ::CreateMutex simply returns a new handle—which can be used by the current process—to the *same* object. Be sure, therefore, to assign the mutex a name that's not likely to be used by someone else's program, and be sure the name you assign to each API function matches exactly, including the case of each letter. See the documentation on `::CreateMutex` for additional details.

Likewise, several processes can share a single semaphore or event by assigning a name when calling `::CreateSemaphore` or `::CreateEvent`. Once two or more processes have obtained handles to a single synchronization object, the object can be used in the same way it's used by separate threads within one process, as described in Chapter 22. For example, a mutex can be used to prevent more than one process from accessing a shared memory location at a given time (shared memory is discussed later in the chapter).

Another way to share handles for named synchronization objects is to call the appropriate Win32 `::Open...` function. For example, if one process has already created a mutex through the following call,

```
// in first process:
HMutex = ::CreateMutex
    (NULL,  // assign default security attributes; handle not
            // inheritable;
    FALSE,  // mutex initially signaled;
    "Acme Accounting Mutex");  // mutex name
```

another process could obtain a handle to the same mutex by calling `::OpenMutex`, as follows:

```
// in second process:
HMutex = ::OpenMutex
    (MUTEX_ALL_ACCESS,  // access flag: allow maximum access;
    FALSE,              // inherit flag: mutex handle not
                        // inheritable;
    "Acme Accounting Mutex");  // mutex name
```

Note that if another process hasn't already created a mutex with a matching name, `::OpenMutex` fails and returns NULL. Therefore, when using this method to share a mutex, you must make sure that the process that calls `::CreateMutex` does so before the other process calls `::OpenMutex` (in contrast, if both processes obtain a handle by calling `::OpenMutex`, they can do so in either order). In the same way, a process can obtain a handle to an existing semaphore or event by calling `::OpenSemaphore` or `::OpenEvent`.

Synchronization objects (as well as file-mapping objects, which will be discussed later) share the same name space. That is, if the name you pass to a `::Create...` or `::Open...` function matches the name of a different type of synchronization (or file-mapping) object, an error results.

Also, a process can obtain a handle to any other process, even if it didn't create that process, by calling the `::OpenProcess` Win32 API function. `::Open-Process`, however, must be passed the process *identifier* rather than a name (unlike synchronization objects, processes can't be assigned names), as in the following example:

```
HANDLE HProcess;
DWORD IDPproces;

// get process ID and assign it to IDProcess ...

HProcess = ::OpenProcess
   (PROCESS_ALL_ACCESS,  // access flag: allow maximum access;
    FALSE,               // inherit flag: process handle not
                         // inheritable;
    IDProcess);          // identifier of process
```

In this example, the program must somehow obtain the identifier of the process for which it wants a handle (though a program can know an object *name* in advance, it must obtain an object *identifier* at runtime). It could obtain this handle from the parent of the process—or from the process itself—using some form of interprocess data sharing, such as a pipe or a shared memory block (both of which will be discussed later in the chapter). The parent can obtain the handle from the `dwProcessId` field of the `LPPROCESS_INFORMATION` structure that's filled in by `::CreateProcess`, and the process itself can get its own identifier by calling the Win32 API function `::GetCurrentProcessId`.

Once the program obtains a handle to the process, it can use this handle to call any of the Win32 API functions that control or wait for processes, which were discussed in the previous section.

Inherited and Duplicated Handles

In addition to using the `::Create...` and `::Open...` functions as discussed in this section, two other ways are available to share Windows handles among different processes.

First, a child process can *inherit* one or more handles from its parent process. To have a child inherit a handle, the parent must specify that the particular handle is to be *inheritable* when it creates or opens the object (in the examples in Chapters 22 and 23, the handles *aren't* made inheritable). For example, if it creates a mutex, it must assign TRUE to the **bInheritHandle** field of the SECURITY_ATTRIBUTES structure:

```
SECURITY_ATTRIBUTES Security =
    {sizeof (SECURITY_ATTRIBUTES),
    NULL,   // assign default security;
    TRUE};  // MAKE HANDLE INHERITABLE


HMutex = ::CreateMutex
    (&Security,  // specify security and handle
                 // inheritance;
    FALSE,       // mutex initially signaled;
    NULL);       // no name assigned to mutex
```

Also, when the parent creates the child process, it must assign TRUE to the fifth `::CreateProcess` parameter (`fInheritHandles`), which causes the child process to inherit any *inheritable* handle owned by the parent. Finally, the parent must provide the actual handle value to the child; this can be done using an appropriate form of interprocess communication such as a pipe (I) or a shared memory block.

Second, if a process has a handle to a particular object, it can call the Win32 API function `::DuplicateHandle` to generate a *new* handle to the same object that can be used by *any* specified process, including the current process.

In general, these two methods for sharing handles are less convenient than using the `::Create...` and `::Open...` functions because you must exchange information (handles or identifiers) between processes at runtime. You can, however, use these two methods to share a wider variety of handle types. Specifically, you can share handles for the following Windows objects: synchronization objects, threads, processes, pipes, file-mapping objects, and any object created with the `::CreateFile` Win32 API function. Handles to the following Windows objects *can't* be shared between processes: memory allocations, graphics objects, and windows (such objects are always private to the process that owns them).

In this section, you learned how to create multiple handles for a single object, such as a synchronization object or a process. Keep in mind that the Windows object isn't destroyed until *all* its handles have been closed; a handle can be closed by an explicit call to the Win32 API function `::CloseHandle` or by the process that owns the handle exiting.

Exchanging Data Through Pipes

A *pipe* is a mechanism that allows one process to send data to another process. Although Win32 provides both *named* and *anonymous* pipes, Windows 95 supports only anonymous pipes.

Most commonly, an anonymous pipe is used to exchange data between a parent and a child process (or among child processes). The parent process creates the pipe by calling the Win32 API function `::CreatePipe`, which supplies two handles— one for writing to the pipe and one for reading from the pipe. When the parent calls `::CreatePipe`, it must make the pipe handles inheritable. Before creating the child process, the parent can make the read or write handle available to the child process by calling the Win32 API function `::SetStdHandle`, which modifies the standard input, standard output, or standard error handle for both the parent and the child. If the parent wants to send data *to* the child, it should use `::SetStd-Handle` to assign the pipe's read handle to the standard input handle. If, however, the parent wants to receive data *from* the child, it should use `::SetStdHandle` to assign the pipe's write handle to the standard output handle.

Next, the parent calls `::CreateProcess` to create the child process; in doing so, it must permit handle inheritance. If the parent is sending data *to* the child, the parent can use the Win32 API function `::WriteFile` to write data to the pipe (passing this function the pipe's write handle). The child can call the `::GetStdHandle` Win32 API function to obtain the pipe's read handle (which is the standard input handle), and then pass this handle to the Win32 API function `::ReadFile` to read the data from the pipe.

If the parent receives data *from* the child, the child can call `::GetStdHandle` to obtain the pipe's write handle (which is the standard output handle), and then pass this handle to `::WriteFile` to write the data to the pipe. The parent can then call `::ReadFile` to obtain the data from the pipe (passing this function the pipe's read handle).

For more information on pipes, see the documentation on the Win32 API functions that were mentioned, as well as the following online help topic: *Platform SDK, Windows Base Services, Interprocess Communication, Pipes.*

NOTE   Win32 provides another mechanism for interprocess communication, known as a *mailslot*. A process (known as a *mailslot client*) can send a message to a specific mailslot, which is identified by name. The message will be received by any other process (known as a *mailslot server*) that has created a mailslot with that name. Mailslots are convenient because they allow a process to broadcast a message to an entire group of other processes; the sending process, however, doesn't receive any confirmation that the message has been received. In contrast, a pipe allows a process to send data to only a single other process, but permits the sending process to verify that the message has been received. For information on mailslots, see the following Visual C++ online help topic: *Platform SDK, Windows Base Services, Interprocess Communication, Mailslots.*

Sharing Memory

Normally, a Windows process can't read or modify the data—that is, the variables, objects, or memory allocations—belonging to another process. Using Win32 *file mapping*, however, two or more processes can access a single shared block of memory. In general, file mapping allows one or more processes to access a disk file by reading or writing to a copy (or *mapping*) of that file within memory. However, when file mapping is used simply to allow processes to share a memory block, you don't need to open or create a disk file (rather, as with any block of memory, the operating system will swap the memory as necessary to its own paging file).

The following are the basic steps required for two processes to allocate and access a shared block of memory using file mapping. First, *each* process calls the `::CreateFileMapping` Win32 API function, as in the following example:

```
// code within BOTH processes:
HANDLE HFileMapping;

HFileMapping = ::CreateFileMapping
    ((HANDLE)0xFFFFFFFF,            // no new file (use system
                                    // paging file);
```

```
(LPSECURITY_ATTRIBUTES) NULL,    // default security and handle
                                 // not inheritable;
PAGE_READWRITE,                  // allow read-write access;
0,                               // high-order 32-bits of maximum
                                 // size: 0;
1024,                            // low-order 32-bits of maximum
                                 // size: 1 K;
"MyFileMappingObject");          // name of file mapping object
```

The first call to ::CreateFileMapping (in one process) creates a *file-mapping object* and returns a handle to it. The second call to ::CreateFileMapping (in the other process) returns a new handle, valid within the current process, to the existing file-mapping object. The example calls specify that the shared memory block will have a maximum size of 1KB. As a result of these calls, both processes obtain a handle to the same Windows file-mapping object.

Second, each process calls the ::MapViewOfFile Win32 API function to allocate a block of memory known as a *file view*, passing the handle of the file-mapping object and specifying the *same* name ("MyFileMappingObject") and size (1,024 bytes) that were given in the call to ::CreateFileMapping. The following is an example:

```
// code within BOTH processes:
char *PtrSharedMemory;

PtrSharedMemory = (char *)::MapViewOfFile
    (HFileMapping,        // handle of file-mapping object;
    FILE_MAP_ALL_ACCESS,  // allow read-write access;
    0,                    // high order 32-bits of offset of
                          // shared block: 0;
    0,                    // low-order 32-bits of offset of shared
                          // block: 0;
    1024);                // 1 K bytes in shared block
```

The first call to ::MapViewOfFile (in one process) allocates a block of memory and returns a pointer to it. The second call to ::MapViewOfFile (in the other process) returns a pointer to the *same* block of memory. Each process can now use its pointer to access the shared memory block, in the same way it accesses any memory allocation. Because both processes have access to the *same* data, they may need to use Win32 synchronization objects to synchronize their access to this data.

Finally, when the processes have finished using the shared memory block, they should each call the Win32 API function ::UnmapViewOfFile to eliminate the file view and then call Win32 API function ::CloseFile to close the handles to the file-mapping object.

Using the Clipboard

In the following sections, you'll learn how to use the Windows Clipboard to transfer data within your program and to exchange data with other programs. The first section describes the commands that your program should provide if it makes use of the Clipboard. The following sections then explain how to use the Clipboard to transfer plain text, graphic images in bitmap format, and data that conforms to a custom format.

The Clipboard Commands

If your program makes use of the Windows Clipboard facilities, it should generally include Cut, Copy, and Paste commands on its Edit menu. If you use App-Wizard to generate your program, AppWizard will add Cut, Copy, and Paste commands to the initial Edit menu. (In many of the example programs given in this book, you've been instructed to remove these menu commands because the program hasn't used them.) Table 23.1 lists the properties of these menu commands as they're defined by AppWizard and as they'd appear in the Visual C++ menu editor, while Figure 23.1 illustrates the initial Edit menu generated by App-Wizard, showing the Cut, Copy, and Paste commands.

TABLE 23.1: The Properties of the Cut, Copy, and Paste Menu Commands Generated by AppWizard

ID:	Caption	Prompt	Other Features
ID_EDIT_CUT	Cu&t\tCtrl+X	Cut the selection and put it on the Clipboard\nCut	none
ID_EDIT_COPY	&Copy\tCtrl+C	Copy the selection and put it on the Clipboard\nCopy	none
ID_EDIT_PASTE	&Paste\tCtrl+V	Insert Clipboard contents\nPaste	none

FIGURE 23.1:

The initial Edit menu generated by AppWizard, showing the Cut, Copy, and Paste commands

AppWizard also defines two accelerator keystrokes for each of the Cut, Copy, and Paste menu commands. One accelerator keystroke conforms to the older keystroke convention, and the other keystroke conforms to the newer convention. The user can thus use *either* the older *or* the newer keystroke to activate a given command. Note that the menu captions display the keystrokes conforming to the newer convention. These accelerator keystrokes are described in Table 23.2.

TABLE 23.2: Accelerator Keystrokes for the Cut, Copy, and Paste Commands Generated by AppWizard

Menu Command	ID: of Menu Command and Accelerator	Keystroke for Older Convention	Keystroke for Newer Convention
Cut	ID_EDIT_CUT	Shift+Del	Ctrl+X
Copy	ID_EDIT_COPY	Ctrl+Ins	Ctrl+C
Paste	ID_EDIT_PASTE	Shift+Ins	Ctrl+V

AppWizard doesn't, however, provide handlers for the Cut, Copy, and Paste commands. Therefore, these menu commands are initially disabled, as you can see in Figure 23.1. As usual, you can define message-handling functions for these commands using ClassWizard. You should normally add these message handlers to the program's view class, which is responsible for the command interface that allows the user to edit the document displayed in the view window. Also, for each of the Cut, Copy, and Paste commands, you should provide both a COMMAND handler and an UPDATE_COMMAND_UI handler. The UPDATE_COMMAND_UI handler receives control when the user first opens the Edit menu, and either enables or disables the command based on the current state of the Clipboard or the view window. The COMMAND handler receives control when the user chooses the command and it carries out the Clipboard operation. Table 23.3 lists the default names of the handlers that ClassWizard generates for these commands.

TABLE 23.3: The Default Message-Handling Functions that ClassWizard Defines for the Cut, Copy, and Paste Menu Commands

Command	ID:	Message Type	Message-Handling Function
Cut	ID_EDIT_CUT	COMMAND	OnEditCut
Cut	ID_EDIT_CUT	UPDATE_COMMAND_UI	OnUpdateEditCut
Copy	ID_EDIT_COPY	COMMAND	OnEditCopy
Copy	ID_EDIT_COPY	UPDATE_COMMAND_UI	OnUpdateEditCopy
Paste	ID_EDIT_PASTE	COMMAND	OnEditPaste
Paste	ID_EDIT_PASTE	UPDATE_COMMAND_UI	OnUpdateEditPaste

NOTE

If you choose the Docking Toolbar option in AppWizard (in the Step 4 dialog box), AppWizard will add toolbar buttons for the Cut, Copy, and Paste commands. Like the corresponding menu commands, these buttons will be disabled unless you define message handlers. Because the buttons are assigned the *same* identifiers as the corresponding menu commands, you need to define only a single set of message handlers for processing either the Edit menu commands or the corresponding toolbar buttons.

The COMMAND handlers for the Cut and Copy commands should transfer the selected data (text or graphics) into the Clipboard. In addition, the Cut COMMAND handler should delete the selected data from the document. The UPDATE_COMMAND_UI handlers for the Cut and Copy commands should enable the command only if the user has selected document data within the view window.

TIP

You might also include a Delete or Clear command on the Edit menu for deleting the selected data *without* copying it to the Clipboard. Although it doesn't use the Clipboard, a Delete or Clear command is normally grouped together with the Clipboard commands on the Edit menu.

After the data has been transferred to the Clipboard, the user can paste it into another position within the same document, into another document in the same program, or into a document in another program. The receiving program can be a 32-bit Windows GUI or console program, or a 16-bit Windows 3.1 or MS-DOS program (you can paste only textual data into console or MS-DOS programs).

The COMMAND handler for the Paste command should insert the contents of the Clipboard into the current document. The data might have been obtained from the current document, from another document within the same program, or from another program (a Windows GUI or console program, a 16-bit Windows 3.1 program, or a 16-bit MS-DOS program). The textual or graphic data is generally inserted at the position of the caret that marks the text insertion point in the view window (for example, in a word processing application). Alternatively, the program might insert *graphic* data at an arbitrary location within the view window, and select the data so that the user can move it to the desired position (this might be done in a drawing program).

The UPDATE_COMMAND_UI handler for the Paste command should enable the command only if the Clipboard contains data in the appropriate format. The technique for testing for specific formats is discussed later in the chapter.

The way that the COMMAND and UPDATE_COMMAND_UI handlers work depends on the format of the data that's being transferred. Details are given in the following sections.

Using the Clipboard to Transfer Text

In this section, you'll learn how to use the Clipboard to transfer plain text (that is, text consisting of a simple stream of printable ANSI characters without embedded formatting codes, such as the text displayed by the Windows Notepad editor). To transfer text containing proprietary formatting codes (for example, the formatted text displayed in a word processor), you can use the techniques given later in the chapter, in the section "Using the Clipboard to Transfer Registered Data Formats." You'll first learn how to transfer text to the Clipboard, and then learn how to obtain text from the Clipboard.

NOTE   If you derive your program's view class from the MFC CEditView class (which provides text editing as discussed in Chapter 10), you don't need to write any code to support the Cut, Copy, and Paste commands for transferring view-window text. You need only make sure that the program's Edit menu includes Cut, Copy, and Paste commands, and that these commands have the identifiers given in Table 23.1. The CEditView class provides a full set of message handlers for these commands.

Adding Text to the Clipboard

Text is transferred to the Clipboard in response to the Cut or Copy command. The UPDATE_COMMAND_UI message handlers for these commands should enable the command only if the user has selected a block of text, as shown in the following examples:

```
void CProgView::OnUpdateEditCut(CCmdUI* pCmdUI)
{
    // TODO: Add your command update UI handler code here
    pCmdUI->Enable (m_IsSelection);
}

void CProgView::OnUpdateEditCopy(CCmdUI* pCmdUI)
{
    // TODO: Add your command update UI handler code here
    pCmdUI->Enable (m_IsSelection);
}
```

These examples assume that m_IsSelection is a BOOL data member of your view class that's set to TRUE only when a block of text is selected.

The COMMAND message handlers for the Cut and Copy commands must add the selected block of text to the Clipboard. The following are the general steps for doing this:

1. Call the ::GlobalAlloc Win32 API function to allocate a block of memory that's large enough to hold the text that's to be inserted into the Clipboard.

2. Call the ::GlobalLock Win32 API function to lock the memory block and obtain a pointer to it.

3. Copy the text into the allocated memory block.

4. Call the ::GlobalUnlock Win32 API function to unlock the allocated memory.

5. Call the CWnd member function OpenClipboard to open the Clipboard.

6. Call the ::EmptyClipboard Win32 API function to remove the current Clipboard contents.

7. Call the ::SetClipboardData Win32 API function to supply the handle of the allocated memory block to the Clipboard.

8. Call the ::CloseClipboard Win32 API function to close the Clipboard.

9. The COMMAND handler for the *Cut* command should remove the selected data from the document.

The text you add to the Clipboard using the procedure discussed in this section must conform to the standard Clipboard text format, which has the following three characteristics:

- The text consists of a simple stream of printable ANSI characters, without embedded formatting or control codes.

- Each line is terminated with a carriage-return and a linefeed character.

- The entire block of text is terminated with a single NULL character.

If the text stored in your program doesn't conform to this format, you can convert it into the proper format as you copy it to the Clipboard.

When you add text to the Clipboard, the Windows Clipboard facility doesn't store the data for you. Rather, you must explicitly allocate a memory block, copy the text to this block, and then supply the *handle* for this memory allocation to the Clipboard. The Clipboard stores only the handle (and supplies an appropriate handle to any program that wants to access the data in the Clipboard).

Accordingly, the first step in adding text to the Clipboard is to allocate a memory block from the program's heap by calling the Win32 API function ::GlobalAlloc:

```
HGLOBAL GlobalAlloc
    (UINT uFlags,     // allocation attributes
     DWORD dwBytes); // number of bytes to allocate
```

You assign the first parameter, uFlags, one or more flags describing the block of memory. When you allocate a memory block that's to be supplied to the Clipboard, you must specify the flags GMEM_MOVEABLE and GMEM_DDESHARE. Also, if you include the flag GMEM_ZEROINIT, the block of memory will be initialized with all zeros. See the documentation on the ::GlobalAlloc function for an explanation of all the flags you can assign (in the Visual C++ online help topic: *Platform SDK, Windows Base Services, General Library, Memory Management, Memory Management Reference, Memory Management Functions*).

The second parameter, dwBytes, specifies the desired size of the memory block in bytes. When you specify the memory block size, be sure to allow room for the

NULL character that must terminate the text. If successful, `::GlobalAlloc` returns the handle of the memory block; if, however, it can't allocate the requested memory, it returns NULL.

Assume, for example, that the text you want to add to the Clipboard is contained within the character array `Buffer`, and that this text is properly formatted and is NULL terminated. You could then allocate memory as follows:

```
HGLOBAL HMem;

HMem = ::GlobalAlloc
    (GMEM_MOVEABLE | GMEM_DDESHARE,
    strlen (Buffer) + 1);
if (HMem == NULL)
    {
    AfxMessageBox ("Error copying data to the Clipboard.");
    return;
    }
```

Before you can access the block of allocated memory, you must call the Win32 API function `::GlobalLock`,

```
LPVOID GlobalLock (HGLOBAL hglbMem);
```

where `hglbMem` is the handle obtained from `::GlobalAlloc`. If successful, `::GlobalLock` returns a pointer to the beginning of the memory block; if an error occurs, it returns NULL. The following code obtains a pointer to the memory allocated in the previous example:

```
char *PMem;

PMem = (char *)::GlobalLock (HMem);
if (PMem == NULL)
    {
    ::GlobalFree (HMem);
    AfxMessageBox ("Error copying data to the Clipboard.");
    return;
    }
```

In this example, notice that if the call to `::GlobalLock` fails, the memory block is released before the function exits by passing the memory handle to the Win32 API function `::GlobalFree`.

Next, you need to copy the text that you want to add to the Clipboard into the allocated memory block. To do this, you might use the Win32 API function `::lstrcpy`, as in the following example:

```
::lstrcpy (PMem, Buffer);
```

The `::lstrcpy` function copies a NULL-terminated string from the location given by the second parameter to the location given by the first parameter. If the text you want to add to the Clipboard doesn't conform to the standard text format, or doesn't contain a NULL termination, you can write your own copy routine to perform the necessary conversion as the data is copied.

Next, you must prepare the allocated memory handle so that it can be passed to the Clipboard, by calling the Win32 API function `::GlobalUnlock`, as in the following example:

```
::GlobalUnlock (HMem);
```

Before you can access the Clipboard, you must open it by calling the `CWnd` member function `OpenClipboard`:

```
BOOL OpenClipboard ();
```

`OpenClipboard` returns TRUE if successful. If, however, another program has already opened the Clipboard and hasn't yet closed it, `OpenClipboard` returns FALSE; in this case, you can't complete the Clipboard operation. The following is an example:

```
if (!OpenClipboard ())
    {
    ::GlobalFree (HMem);
    AfxMessageBox ("Clipboard not available.");
    }
```

(Because `OpenClipboard` is a member function of `CWnd`, this example assumes that the code is within a member function of a class derived from `CWnd`, such as a program's view class.)

After opening the Clipboard, you must remove the current Clipboard contents by calling the Win32 API function `::EmptyClipboard`:

```
BOOL EmptyClipboard (VOID);
```

You can now add your text to the Clipboard by calling the Win32 API function `::SetClipboardData`:

```
HANDLE SetClipboardData (UINT uFormat, HANDLE hData);
```

The first parameter, uFormat, specifies the format of the data you're adding to the Clipboard; to add text, you pass the value CF_TEXT. (See the documentation on this function for a description of the other standard formats you can specify.) The second parameter, hData, is the handle to the memory allocation that contains the data. The following is an example:

```
::SetClipboardData (CF_TEXT, HMem);
```

After calling ::SetClipboardData, you must *not* use the memory handle (specifically, you must *not* attempt to read or write to the memory, nor call ::GlobalFree to free the memory block; the handle now belongs to Windows, which will automatically free the memory block when appropriate). To avoid the temptation to use the handle, you might set the variable containing the handle to NULL immediately after calling ::SetClipboardData. If you need to access the memory block after calling ::SetClipboardData, you must use the standard procedure for obtaining Clipboard data in response to the Paste command, which is described in the next section.

NOTE   If you use the ::GlobalAlloc function to obtain a block of memory that you *don't* pass to the Clipboard, you must call ::GlobalUnlock (if you previously called ::GlobalLock) and then call ::GlobalFree when you've finished using the memory.

Finally, you must close the Clipboard by calling the Win32 API function ::CloseClipboard:

```
BOOL CloseClipboard (VOID);
```

Because only one program can have the Clipboard open at a given time, you should close the Clipboard as soon as possible.

The following is an example of a COMMAND message-handling function for the Copy command (defined as a member function of the view class), which illustrates all the steps discussed in this section:

```
char Buffer [] = "Sample text to be copied to the Clipboard.";

void CProgView::OnEditCopy()
{
    // TODO: Add your command handler code here
```

```
HGLOBAL HMem;
char *PMem;

// 1. allocate memory block:
HMem = (char *)::GlobalAlloc
    (GMEM_MOVEABLE | GMEM_DDESHARE,
    strlen (Buffer) + 1);
if (HMem == NULL)
    {
    AfxMessageBox ("Error copying data to the Clipboard.");
    return;
    }

// 2. lock allocated memory and obtain a pointer:
PMem = (char *)::GlobalLock (HMem);
if (PMem == NULL)
    {
    ::GlobalFree (HMem);
    AfxMessageBox ("Error copying data to the Clipboard.");
    return;
    }

// 3. copy selected text into allocated memory block:
::lstrcpy (PMem, Buffer);

// 4. unlock allocated memory:
::GlobalUnlock (HMem);

// 5. open Clipboard:
if (!OpenClipboard ())
    {
    ::GlobalFree (HMem);
    AfxMessageBox ("Error copying data to the Clipboard.");
    return;
    }

// 6. remove current Clipboard contents:
::EmptyClipboard ();

// 7. supply the memory handle to the Clipboard:
::SetClipboardData (CF_TEXT, HMem);
HMem = 0;
```

```
    // 8. close Clipboard:
    ::CloseClipboard ();
}
```

Notice that Buffer is a global character array containing a sample NULL-terminated string to be copied to the Clipboard. In an actual application, Buffer would contain the currently selected text, terminated with a NULL.

The COMMAND message handler that processes the Cut command (OnEditCut) could call OnEditCopy and then proceed to remove the selected text from the document.

Obtaining Text from the Clipboard

If your program allows the user to paste only standard text from the Clipboard, the UPDATE_COMMAND_UI message-handling function for the Paste command should enable the command only if the Clipboard currently contains text. To determine whether the Clipboard contains data that conforms to a specific format, you can call the Win32 API function ::IsClipboardFormatAvailable:

```
BOOL IsClipboardFormatAvailable (UINT uFormat);
```

The parameter uFormat specifies the desired format. The following is an example of an UPDATE_COMMAND_UI message-handling function that enables or disables the Paste command, depending on whether or not the Clipboard contains text:

```
void CProgView::OnUpdateEditPaste(CCmdUI* pCmdUI)
{
    // TODO: Add your command update UI handler code here

    pCmdUI->Enable (::IsClipboardFormatAvailable (CF_TEXT));
}
```

TIP The Clipboard may contain data in more than one format at a given time. To determine *all* formats currently available, you can call the Win32 API function ::EnumClipboardFormats. To determine the *best* format available—according to a priority list of formats that you specify—you can call the Win32 API function ::GetPriorityClipboardFormat.

The COMMAND message handler for the Paste command needs to obtain the text from the Clipboard and then insert the text into the document. In the following procedures and examples, the Paste command handler allocates a temporary buffer and copies the Clipboard text into this buffer; after the Clipboard is closed, the program can process this text as necessary, add it to the document, and then free the buffer. Alternatively, a program could copy the text directly from the Clipboard into whatever data structure stores the document text, provided that it can perform this operation quickly so that the Clipboard isn't left open for an undue length of time.

The following is a general procedure that can be used to obtain text from the Clipboard in response to the Paste command:

1. Call CWnd::OpenClipboard to open the Clipboard.

2. Call the Win32 API function ::GetClipboardData to obtain a handle to the block of memory holding the Clipboard text.

3. Allocate a temporary buffer to store a copy of the Clipboard text.

4. Call ::GlobalLock to lock the Clipboard memory and to obtain a pointer to this memory.

5. Copy the text from the Clipboard memory to the temporary buffer.

6. Call ::GlobalUnlock to unlock the Clipboard memory.

7. Call ::CloseClipboard to close the Clipboard.

8. After the program has finished processing the text in the temporary buffer and adding the text to the document, free the buffer.

After you've opened the Clipboard, you can obtain a handle to the block of Clipboard memory holding the text by calling the ::GetClipboardData Win32 API function, as in the following example:

```
HANDLE HClipText;

HClipText = ::GetClipboardData (CF_TEXT);
if (HClipText == NULL)
    {
    ::CloseClipboard ();
    AfxMessageBox ("Error obtaining text from Clipboard.");
    return;
    }
```

The parameter you pass to ::GetClipboardData specifies the desired data format. If the Clipboard doesn't contain data in the specified format, it returns NULL.

(This might happen if another process removes the data from the Clipboard after your program has enabled the Paste command but before it has opened the Clipboard.) If you request data in the CF_TEXT format, but the Clipboard contains only one of the *other* text formats (CF_OEMTEXT or CF_UNICODETEXT), Windows will automatically convert the text to the CF_TEXT format.

The handle you obtain by calling ::GetClipboardData remains valid only until you call ::CloseClipboard. You can read or copy the data from the associated memory block, but you must *not* alter the data or call ::GlobalFree to free the memory block. (This block must remain unaltered and available so that the Clipboard can supply the data in response to subsequent requests by your program or other programs.)

After you've successfully obtained a handle to the memory block containing the Clipboard text, you can allocate a temporary buffer to hold a copy of the text. Call the Win32 API function ::GlobalSize to determine the size of the Clipboard's memory block. As an example, the following code uses the C++ new operator to allocate a temporary buffer that's large enough to hold the text from the Clipboard:

```
char *PTempBuffer = new char [::GlobalSize (HClipText)];
if (PTempBuffer == 0)
    {
    ::CloseClipboard ();
    AfxMessageBox ("Out of memory!");
    return;
    }
```

In this example, HClipText is the memory handle that was returned by ::GetClipboardData.

Before you can access the Clipboard memory, you must call ::GlobalLock to obtain a pointer to the memory block:

```
char *PClipText;

PClipText = (char *)::GlobalLock (HClipText);
if (PClipText == NULL)
    {
    ::CloseClipboard ();
    delete [] PTempBuffer;
    AfxMessageBox ("Error obtaining text from Clipboard.");
    return;
    }
```

You can now read or copy the Clipboard data; you should do so as quickly as possible and then close the Clipboard. Before closing the Clipboard, be sure to call ::GlobalUnlock to unlock the Clipboard memory:

```
::GlobalUnlock (HClipText);
::CloseClipboard ();
```

After calling ::CloseClipboard, you *can't* use the handle to the memory that was obtained from the Clipboard. If the program has copied the Clipboard text into a temporary buffer, it can now process the text at its leisure and delete the buffer when it's done:

```
delete [] PTempBuffer;
```

The following is an example of a COMMAND message-handling function (defined as a member of the view class) that obtains text from the Clipboard in response to the Paste command:

```
void CProgView::OnEditPaste()
{
    // TODO: Add your command handler code here

    HANDLE HClipText;
    char *PClipText;
    char *PTempBuffer;

    // 1. open Clipboard:
    if (!OpenClipboard ())
        {
        AfxMessageBox ("Could not open Clipboard.");
        return;
        }

    // 2. obtain handle to Clipboard data:
    HClipText = ::GetClipboardData (CF_TEXT);
    if (HClipText == NULL)
        {
        ::CloseClipboard ();
        AfxMessageBox ("Error obtaining text from Clipboard.");
        return;
        }
```

```
// 3. allocate a temporary buffer to store text from Clipboard:
PTempBuffer = new char [::GlobalSize (HClipText)];
if (PTempBuffer == 0)
    {
    ::CloseClipboard ();
    AfxMessageBox ("Out of memory!");
    return;
    }

// 4. lock handle to Clipboard text and obtain pointer:
PClipText = (char *)::GlobalLock (HClipText);
if (PClipText == NULL)
    {
    ::CloseClipboard ();
    delete [] PTempBuffer;
    AfxMessageBox ("Error obtaining text from Clipboard.");
    return;
    }

// 5. copy text from Clipboard:
::lstrcpy (PTempBuffer, PClipText);

// 6. unlock Clipboard memory block:
::GlobalUnlock (HClipText);

// 7. close Clipboard:
::CloseClipboard ();

// 8. insert text into document and free temporary buffer:
InsertText (PTempBuffer);
delete [] PTempBuffer;
}
```

This example assumes that the function InsertText inserts into the current document the text from the NULL-terminated buffer that's passed to it.

Using the Clipboard to Transfer Graphics

You can transfer graphic information within a program or among separate programs by using the Clipboard to exchange bitmaps. In this section you'll learn how to add a bitmap to the Clipboard and how to obtain a bitmap from the Clipboard. The procedures you learn here will be useful for developing drawing programs, word processors, or other programs that display graphics in bitmap format.

Adding a Bitmap to the Clipboard

As with a block of text, a bitmap is transferred to the Clipboard in response to the Cut or Copy command. The UPDATE_COMMAND_UI message handlers for these commands should enable the command only if the user has selected a bitmap, as in the following examples:

```
void CProgView::OnUpdateEditCut(CCmdUI* pCmdUI)
{
    // TODO: Add your command update UI handler code here
    pCmdUI->Enable (m_IsSelection);
}

void CProgView::OnUpdateEditCopy(CCmdUI* pCmdUI)
{
    // TODO: Add your command update UI handler code here
    pCmdUI->Enable (m_IsSelection);
}
```

These examples assume that m_IsSelection is a BOOL data member of the view class that's set to TRUE only when a bitmap is selected (or, if the program also permits the user to transfer text to the Clipboard, that m_IsSelection is set to TRUE if *either* text *or* a bitmap is selected).

The bitmap should be added to the Clipboard by the COMMAND message handlers for the Cut and Copy commands. The following is the general procedure for doing this:

1. Call CWnd::OpenClipboard to open the Clipboard.

2. Call ::EmptyClipboard to remove the current Clipboard contents.

3. Call ::SetClipboardData, passing this function the code CF_BITMAP as the first parameter, and the handle of the bitmap you want to place in the Clipboard as the second parameter. (As you saw in Chapter 20, there are several different ways to create a bitmap and obtain a bitmap handle. The example code that follows creates an empty bitmap and copies data into it.)

4. Call ::CloseClipboard to close the Clipboard.

5. The COMMAND message handler for the Cut command should remove the graphic data from the document.

As an example, the following COMMAND message handler for the Copy command creates a bitmap that contains the current contents of the view window. It then adds this bitmap to the Clipboard.

```
void CProgView::OnEditCopy()
{
    // TODO: Add your command handler code here

    CBitmap BitmapClip;
    CClientDC ClientDC (this);
    CDC MemDC;
    RECT Rect;

    // create an empty bitmap:
    GetClientRect (&Rect);
    BitmapClip.CreateCompatibleBitmap
        (&ClientDC,
        Rect.right - Rect.left,
        Rect.bottom - Rect.top);

    // create a memory DC object and select bitmap into it:
    MemDC.CreateCompatibleDC (&ClientDC);
    MemDC.SelectObject (&BitmapClip);

    // copy contents of view window into bitmap:
    MemDC.BitBlt
        (0,
        0,
        Rect.right - Rect.left,
        Rect.bottom - Rect.top,
        &ClientDC,
        0,
        0,
        SRCCOPY);

    // 1. open Clipboard:
    if (!OpenClipboard ())
        return;
```

```
    // 2. remove current Clipboard contents:
    ::EmptyClipboard ();

    // 3. give bitmap handle to Clipboard:
    ::SetClipboardData (CF_BITMAP, BitmapClip.m_hObject);

    // prevent bitmap from being destroyed:
    BitmapClip.Detach ();

    // 4. close Clipboard:
    ::CloseClipboard ();
}
```

The example OnEditCopy function begins by calling the CBitmap member function CreateCompatibleBitmap to create an empty bitmap the size of the entire view window. It then creates a memory device context and selects the new bitmap into it. Next, it calls the CDC member function BitBlt to copy the contents of the view window to the bitmap (that is, it copies whatever text or graphics happen to be displayed in the view window).

NOTE   See Chapter 20 for information on creating bitmaps and on calling functions for performing bit operations (such as BitBlt).

OnEditCopy calls ::SetClipboardData to add the bitmap to the opened Clipboard. It assigns the first parameter the value CF_BITMAP to specify the bitmap format, and it assigns the second parameter BitmapClip.m_hObject, which contains the handle of the bitmap (m_hObject is a data member that the CBitmap class inherits from CGdiObject).

After calling ::SetClipboardData to supply the bitmap to the Clipboard, you must *not* use or destroy the bitmap. Accordingly, the example OnEditCopy function calls the CGdiObject member function Detach to remove the bitmap handle from the BitmapClip object. If this step wasn't performed, the CBitmap destructor would automatically destroy the bitmap when the BitmapClip object goes out of scope (which happens when the OnEditCopy function returns).

NOTE   If the program also supports copying text to the Clipboard, the OnEditCopy function would have to determine the format of the selected data and switch to an appropriate routine.

Obtaining a Bitmap from the Clipboard

Your UPDATE_COMMAND_UI message-handling function for the Paste command can pass the flag CF_BITMAP to the ::IsClipboardFormatAvailable function to determine whether the Clipboard currently contains data in the bitmap format. It can then use this information to enable or disable the Paste command, as in the following example:

```
void CProgView::OnUpdateEditPaste(CCmdUI* pCmdUI)
{
    // TODO: Add your command update UI handler code here

    pCmdUI->Enable (::IsClipboardFormatAvailable (CF_BITMAP));
}
```

(If the program supports the pasting of text as well as bitmaps, the OnUpdateEdit-Paste function should also test for the CF_TEXT format, which was described previously.)

The COMMAND message handler for the Paste command should obtain the bitmap from the Clipboard. The following is the general procedure for doing this:

1. Call OpenClipboard to open the Clipboard.

2. Pass the value CF_BITMAP to the function ::GetClipboardData to obtain a handle to the bitmap.

3. Use the bitmap handle to copy or display the bitmap, but *don't* alter the bitmap contents.

4. Call ::CloseClipboard to close the Clipboard.

As an example, the following COMMAND message handler for the Paste command obtains a bitmap from the Clipboard and displays it within the view window (the upper-left corner of the bitmap is placed at the upper-left corner of the window):

```
void CProgView::OnEditPaste()
{
    // TODO: Add your command handler code here

    CClientDC ClientDC (this);
    CBitmap BitmapClip;
    BITMAP BitmapClipInfo;
    HANDLE HBitmapClip;
    CDC MemDC;
```

```
// 1. open Clipboard:
if (!OpenClipboard ())
   return;

// 2. obtain bitmap handle from Clipboard:
HBitmapClip = ::GetClipboardData (CF_BITMAP);
if (HBitmapClip == NULL)
   {
   ::CloseClipboard ();
   return;
   }

// 3. use bitmap handle to display bitmap:

// initialize bitmap object using handle from Clipboard:
BitmapClip.Attach (HBitmapClip);

// get information on bitmap:
BitmapClip.GetObject (sizeof (BITMAP), &BitmapClipInfo);

// create a memory device context and select bitmap into it:
MemDC.CreateCompatibleDC (&ClientDC);
MemDC.SelectObject (&BitmapClip);

// copy bitmap contents to client area:
ClientDC.BitBlt
   (0,
   0,
   BitmapClipInfo.bmWidth,
   BitmapClipInfo.bmHeight,
   &MemDC,
   0,
   0,
   SRCCOPY);

// remove the bitmap handle from the bitmap object:
BitmapClip.Detach ();

// 4. close Clipboard:
   ::CloseClipboard ();
}
```

The OnEditPaste function declares a CBitmap object, BitmapClip, to manage the bitmap that's obtained from the Clipboard. After it calls ::GetClipboard-Data to get the bitmap handle, it passes the handle to the CGdiObject member function Attach to initialize the bitmap object with the bitmap from the Clipboard. It then calls the CGdiObject member function GetObject to obtain information on this bitmap. (The information is written to the fields of the BITMAP structure BitmapClipInfo.)

Next, OnEditPaste creates a memory device context, selects the bitmap into it, and calls BitBlt to copy the bitmap to the client area of the window. The width and height of the bitmap are obtained from the bmWidth and bmHeight fields of the BITMAP structure.

NOTE
If the bitmap is larger than the view window, Windows automatically clips the portion that falls outside this window.

Before closing the Clipboard, OnPaste calls Detach to remove the bitmap handle from the BitmapClip object. (As with the example OnEditCopy function given in the previous section, this is done to prevent the CBitmap destructor from destroying the bitmap that belongs to the Clipboard.) After calling ::CloseClipboard, the program must *not* use the bitmap handle.

NOTE
If the program also supports the pasting of text, OnEditPaste must test for *both* the CF_BITMAP *and* the CF_TEXT formats, and then branch to an appropriate routine according to the format that's found. (::GetClipboardData will return NULL if the specified format isn't contained in the Clipboard.) If the Clipboard contains data in *both* formats, the program would have to choose one.

Using the Clipboard to Transfer Registered Data Formats

The standard Clipboard formats are described in the documentation on the ::SetClipboardData function. The data you want to transfer, however, might not conform to one of these formats. For example, if you're writing a word processor, you might store formatted text using your own custom format (the text characters might be stored along with embedded codes indicating fonts and other text features). You can, however, still use the Clipboard to transfer your data by calling the ::RegisterClipboardFormat Win32 API function to register your custom data format:

```
UINT RegisterClipboardFormat (LPCTSTR lpszFormat);
```

You can pass any name you want to ::RegisterClipboardFormat, and the function will return a format identifier. You can then use the other Clipboard functions to transfer the formatted text, using the same techniques employed for transferring plain text; however, rather than specifying the CF_TEXT format identifier, you specify the format identifier returned from ::RegisterClipboard-Format. For example, if you register a custom text format as follows,

```
UINT TextFormat;

TextFormat = ::RegisterClipboardFormat ("MyAppText");
```

you could add text that conforms to this format to the Clipboard, using the following call:

```
::SetClipboardData (TextFormat, HMyText);
```

In this call, HMyText is a handle to a block of memory allocated by ::Global-Alloc, which contains the formatted text. Similarly, you could pass Text-Format—rather than CF_TEXT—to the ::IsClipboardFormatAvailable and ::GetClipboardData functions.

NOTE   If a custom format has already been registered under the specified name, ::RegisterClipboardFormat returns an identifier for the *same* format rather than registering a new one. This means that *several* programs can exchange data with the Clipboard using the registered format, provided that each program knows the format name and can interpret the data. Also, because of this feature, you should try to choose a unique name to avoid *unintentionally* sharing a registered format with another program!

You can add *several* blocks of data to the Clipboard, provided that each block has a different format. Whenever you add data to the Clipboard in a registered format, you should, if possible, *also* add an equivalent block of data that conforms to a standard format. Doing so allows programs that don't understand your custom format to access or display the data. For example, when you add custom-formatted text to the Clipboard, you should also add plain text:

```
::SetClipboardData (TextFormat, HFormattedText);
::SetClipboardData (CF_TEXT, HPlainText);
```

In this example, HFormattedText is a handle to a block of text in your custom format, HPlainText is a handle to a block of text that conforms to the standard Clipboard text format, and TextFormat is the index of the custom format returned by ::RegisterClipboardFormat.

In general, you should add as many formats as possible so that your data can be accessed by the widest possible range of Windows programs. Obviously, some formats provide more information than others; in the example above, the custom formatted text contains more information than the plain text.

TIP   Windows programs commonly call ::EnumClipboardFormats to enumerate available Clipboard formats and use the *first* format that they can understand. Because ::EnumClipboardFormats reports formats in the order in which they were added to the Clipboard, your program should add a format that contains more information *before* adding one that contains less information. As a result, other programs will tend to use your most information-rich data formats.

Summary

In this chapter, you learned how to write code to start and manage new processes. You also learned several ways to communicate and coordinate activities among separate processes: using synchronization objects, sending data through pipes, sharing blocks of memory, and exchanging data with the Clipboard. The following are some of the chapter highlights:

- A new process is created whenever a program is run. As an alternative to having the user run a program, one program—known as the *parent*—can call the Win32 API function ::CreateProcess to run another program—known as the *child*.

- ::CreateProcess supplies a handle for the child process. The parent can pass this handle to one of several Win32 API functions: ::GetExitCode-Process to obtain the process exit code, ::WaitForSingleObject to wait until the process has exited, ::SetPriorityClass to change the process's priority, or ::TerminateProcess to stop the process.

- You can use mutexes, semaphores, or events to synchronize the activities of separate processes. To do so, each process must obtain its own handle to the synchronization object.

- Separate processes can obtain handles to a shared synchronization object by assigning a name to the object when calling the ::Create... function (::CreateMutex, ::CreateSemaphore, or ::CreateEvent) or the ::Open... function (::OpenMutex, ::OpenSemaphore, or ::OpenEvent).

- A program can obtain a handle to another process—even if it's not the parent of that process—by passing the process identifier to ::OpenProcess.

- An *anonymous pipe* is a mechanism that allows two processes—typically a parent and a child—to exchange information in a way that's similar to reading or writing to disk files.

- Processes can also exchange information by using shared memory. To allocate a block of shared memory, both processes call the ::Create-FileMapping and ::MapViewOfFile functions.

- Programs can use the Windows Clipboard facility to perform simple data exchanges. In using the Clipboard, the data must conform either to a standard format (for example, text or a bitmap) or to a registered custom format that the receiving program understands.

- A program normally provides access to the Clipboard by including Cut, Copy, and Paste commands on the Edit menu.

- You can exchange textual information by adding a block of text to the Clipboard in response to the Cut or Copy command, and by obtaining text from the Clipboard in response to the Paste command.

- You add text to the Clipboard by calling ::GlobalAlloc to allocate a block of memory, copying the text to this block, and then supplying the handle of the allocated memory to the Clipboard.

- You obtain text from the Clipboard by requesting a handle to the block of memory that contains the text. You can then use this handle to read or copy the text into a private memory area within your program.

- You can exchange graphics information by adding a bitmap to the Clipboard or obtaining a bitmap from the Clipboard.

- To add a bitmap, you supply the bitmap handle to the Clipboard.

- To obtain a bitmap from the Clipboard, you request the bitmap handle and then display or make a private copy of the bitmap within your program.

- You can exchange data that doesn't conform to one of the standard Clipboard formats by calling `::RegisterClipboardFormat` to register your own format. You then follow the procedures for exchanging text with the Clipboard; however, rather than passing the index for the text format, you pass the index returned by `::RegisterClipboardFormat`.

- You can call the `::IsClipboardFormatAvailable` function to determine whether the Clipboard currently contains data conforming to a specific format.

CHAPTER

TWENTY-FOUR

24

Using OLE

- Embedding, linking, and automation

- Creating a server

- Creating a container

In the previous chapter, you learned how to use the Windows Clipboard to perform simple data transfers from one program to another. When you use the Clipboard, the receiving program must be able to display and possibly modify the data, and therefore the data must normally conform to one of a relatively small set of standard formats understood by a wide range of programs. Furthermore, if the receiving program can't edit the data (for example, a word processor might be able to display but not edit a bitmap), to change the data the user must manually switch to the source program, edit or perhaps re-create the data, and then perform the copy and paste operation all over again.

OLE, which stands for *object linking and embedding*, is a method for exchanging data among programs that overcomes these limitations. With OLE, after a block of data has been added to a document in the receiving program, it maintains a tie to the source program that originally created it. The receiving program doesn't need to understand the data format because the source program and the OLE mechanism are responsible for displaying and editing the data. When the user edits the data, the source program automatically runs and makes its editing commands available. With OLE, therefore, a program can transfer data in *any* format to *any* program that's capable of receiving OLE data. Also, to modify the data in the receiving program, the user doesn't need to manually run—or even remember the name of—the source program. (Of course, the source program must still be installed on the user's computer.)

With OLE, the user of a program such as a word processor can create a single document that contains blocks of data from a variety of source programs. Such a document is known as a *compound document*. Once the data has been assembled, the user can focus on the document itself, without keeping track of the various source programs. OLE thus fosters a *document-centered*, rather than an application-centered, approach to using a computer.

As you might expect, the convenience that OLE provides for the user comes at the cost of great complexity for the programmer. This chapter offers only a brief introduction to OLE programming, which could easily form the topic of several large volumes. The chapter focuses on using the OLE code that's provided by the MFC and the Visual C++ Wizards, rather than on manually writing complex OLE routines. The chapter begins with an overview of three basic OLE mechanisms: embedding, linking, and automation. In the next section, you'll create a simple OLE *server*, a program that's the source of OLE data. Then, you'll create a simple OLE *container*, a program that can receive OLE data. The sections on creating a server and container describe the code that the Wizards and the MFC provide, as well as the code you must add yourself.

Embedding, Linking, and Automation

An OLE server or container can support *object embedding* (the E of OLE), *object linking* (the L of OLE), and *automation*. Of these three mechanisms, object embedding is the most common and is the one you'll learn to program in this chapter. The term *object* (the O of OLE) refers to the block of data created by the server and displayed in the container.

In object embedding, the container application stores the object data as part of the container document in which the item has been inserted. The user can embed an object in one of two ways. First, the user can copy or cut a block of data from a document in the server program, and then paste the data into a document in the container program. Typically, if the data *isn't* in a format that's native to the container program, the Paste command on the container's Edit menu automatically embeds the data rather than performing a simple static Clipboard transfer as described in the previous chapter. Commonly, a container's Edit menu also includes a Paste Special command that allows the user to explicitly embed the data (or to transfer the data using any other available method). Although the data originates from a document in the server, once it's embedded in the container it *isn't* linked with the original server document; that is, the container maintains a *separate copy* of the data, and modifying or deleting the original server document won't affect it. As a variation on this transfer method, the user can normally *drag and drop* the data directly from the server document window to the container document window.

Second, to embed an object, the user can choose the Insert New Object… command on the Edit menu of the container program (this command might be located on a different menu and given a slightly different name). This command displays a dialog box listing the various types of objects that can be embedded (each OLE server program that has been installed registers one or more object types in the Windows Registry; these types are listed in the dialog box). When the user chooses an object type, the OLE mechanism automatically runs the server program, allowing the user to employ the server's commands to create the object data. The second method is useful for creating a new block of embedded data rather than embedding an existing block of data. The server and container you'll create later in the chapter support this method of object embedding.

Once an object has been embedded, there are two ways in which the user can edit the object. First, the user can edit the object *in place*. With in-place editing, the object remains displayed within the container's window. However, the server program temporarily merges its menu commands (and possibly its toolbar buttons) with those of the container and makes its keystroke commands available, thereby offering its editing facilities so that the user can edit the object. To initiate in-place editing, the user usually double-clicks within the object, or selects the object and then chooses the Edit command on the Object submenu of the container's Edit menu. (The Object submenu on the Edit menu is labeled according to the type of the selected embedded object; for example, if the object is a bitmap generated by the Windows Paint program, the submenu will be labeled "Bitmap Image Object.")

Second, the user can edit an embedded object within the server program's window. This is known as *fully-opened* editing because the server fully opens its own window rather than taking over the container's window. To initiate fully-opened editing, the user normally selects the object and chooses the Open command on the Object submenu of the container's Edit menu. The server and container you'll create later in the chapter offer both these modes of object editing, and you will have an opportunity to experiment with object embedding after you generate the programs.

In object *linking*, the data for the object is stored by the *server* program rather than by the container program. The server stores the data within one of its documents; this data can constitute part or all of the server document. The container stores a *link* to the data in the original document as part of its document, rather than storing the actual object data. To insert a linked object, the user copies the desired data from a document within the server, and then issues the Paste Link command on the container's Edit menu (in some programs, the user inserts the object by choosing the Paste Special... command on the Edit menu and then selecting the Paste Link option). The linked object will then be displayed within the container document. To edit the object, the user usually double-clicks within the object in the container window; alternatively, the user can edit the object by selecting it and then choosing the Open or Edit command on the Object submenu of the container's Edit menu. The user can also manually run the server program and open the source document. Regardless of the method used to initiate editing, editing is always performed within the server's window—that is, in fully-opened rather than in-place mode.

Object linking is more cumbersome than object embedding because editing the object requires opening *two* documents (the container document containing the object link and the server document containing the object data), and an object can't be edited in place. Linking, however, allows you to create and maintain a master document in a server program, and have one or more linked objects within other programs updated automatically. For example, you could create and maintain a spreadsheet in a spreadsheet program, and then use object linking to insert part or all of the spreadsheet into one or more documents in other programs. Whenever you changed the original spreadsheet, all linked objects could be automatically updated. (In contrast, if part or all of the spreadsheet were copied and *embedded* into another program, the embedded object couldn't be automatically updated to match the source, because it constitutes a separate copy of the original data.)

A third mechanism related to OLE is *automation*. Using automation, a program—known as an *automation server*—can share some of its facilities with another program—known as an *automation client*. For example, a Web browser program could offer its facilities to other programs through automation; another program might use these facilities to display a Web page or download a file via FTP. Specifically, a client can modify some of the server's data items—known as *properties*—or call some of the server's functions—known as *methods*.

This mechanism is termed *automation* because it allows a client program to automate a task using the features of one or more other programs. With automation, programmers can use software objects provided by other programs rather than writing their own routines, and they can make separate programs work together. Furthermore, an automation client program can provide a macro language that allows the program user to control other applications and automate multiple-program tasks (for example, a user of Microsoft Word can write a macro to control Word, Excel, and other applications in the Microsoft Office suite). The MFC supports both automation clients and servers, while the Visual C++ Wizards help you generate automation code. For information on automation, see the Visual C++ online help topic: *Visual C++ Documentation, Using Visual C++, Visual C++ Programmer's Guide, Adding Program Functionality, Overviews, Automation: Overview.*

Creating a Server

In this section you'll create a simple OLE server program, ServDemo. The ServDemo program is based on the third version of the MiniDraw program presented in Chapter 12, and it allows you to create drawings consisting of straight lines and to save these drawings in disk files. Unlike MiniDraw, however, ServDemo also permits OLE container programs to embed its drawings in their documents. ServDemo supports both methods for editing embedded objects: in-place editing and fully-opened editing. ServDemo doesn't support linking, and objects may be embedded only through the Insert New Object… command on the container's Edit menu (not by copying and pasting or by using drag-and-drop).

You'll first use AppWizard to generate a program shell that supports the basic features of an OLE server. You'll then add application-specific code to implement the drawing capabilities of MiniDraw as well as additional OLE features. Later in the chapter, you'll create a simple container program that you can use to test ServDemo.

Generating the Server Code in AppWizard

Begin by using AppWizard to generate the program source code, as explained in Chapter 9. Name the project ServDemo, and, in the Projects tab of the New dialog box as well as in the AppWizard Step 1 through Step 6 dialog boxes, choose the same options you chose in Chapter 9, *except* for the following:

- In the Step 3 dialog box, choose the Full-Server option, uncheck the ActiveX Controls option, and leave all other options unchanged, as shown in Figure 24.1.

- In the Step 4 dialog box, click the Advanced… button, and in the Document Template Strings tab enter srv into the File Extension: text box. As explained in Chapter 12, this specifies the default file extension for the documents that the program saves.

Selecting the Full-Server option in the Step 3 dialog box generates a program that can run *either* as a stand-alone application (like all the previous programs in this book) *or* as an OLE server to create or edit embedded or linked items (though ServDemo won't support linking). Choosing the Mini-Server option generates a program that can run only as an OLE server to create or edit embedded items (it can't run as a stand-alone program, nor can it support linked items). Selecting the Container option generates an OLE container program; you'll choose this option when you create the ContDemo example container program later in the chapter. The Both Container And Server option creates a program that's *both* an OLE container *and* a full OLE server.

NOTE   The general literature on OLE typically uses the term *object* to refer to a block of embedded or linked OLE data. However, the MFC documentation and the remainder of this chapter use the term *item* rather than *object*, to avoid confusion with C++ objects (particularly those that manage OLE items).

FIGURE 24.1

The completed AppWizard
Step 3 dialog box for
generating the ServDemo
program

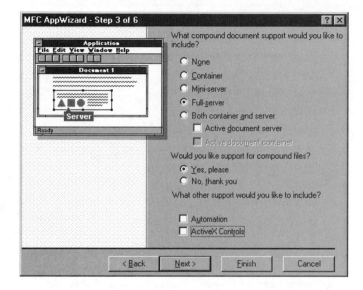

After you've generated the ServDemo source files, you'll notice that choosing the Full-Server option results in quite a few changes to the classes and code that AppWizard generates. AppWizard creates two new classes, a server item class (CServDemoSrvrItem) and an in-place editing class (CInPlaceFrame), and it makes a number of additions and modifications to the standard MFC program classes. These changes are necessary to make the program an OLE server, and they're described in the following sections.

The Application Class

When generating an OLE server, AppWizard makes several additions to the standard InitInstance member function of the application class. First, it adds a call to the global MFC function AfxOleInit to the beginning of InitInstance:

```
if (!AfxOleInit())
{
    AfxMessageBox(IDP_OLE_INIT_FAILED);
    return FALSE;
}
```

This function call initializes the MFC OLE libraries.

> **NOTE**
>
> AppWizard includes the file Afxole.h within the precompiled header file, StdAfx.h. Afxole.h contains definitions for the MFC OLE classes.

Also, after the document template has been created, AppWizard adds a call to `CSingleDocTemplate::SetServerInfo`:

```
pDocTemplate->SetServerInfo(
    IDR_SRVR_EMBEDDED, IDR_SRVR_INPLACE,
    RUNTIME_CLASS(CInPlaceFrame));
```

This function call specifies both the identifier of the menu that ServDemo displays when it's run as an OLE server to edit an OLE item in the fully-opened mode (IDR_SRVR_EMBEDDED) and the identifier of the menu that it displays when it's run as a server to create or edit an OLE item in the in-place mode (IDR_SRVR_INPLACE); these identifiers also specify the corresponding accelerator resources. These menus will be described later. The call to `SetServerInfo` also specifies the class that manages the frame window that surrounds an OLE item when it's edited in-place (CInPlaceFrame, which will be described later).

AppWizard also defines a new member of the application class, `m_server`, which is an instance of the `COleTemplateServer` class and is known as a *template server object*. This object creates a new document object, using the information that's stored in the document template, whenever the program is run as an OLE server. AppWizard adds a call to `COleTemplateServer::ConnectTemplate`, which provides `m_server` with the address of the document template:

```
m_server.ConnectTemplate(clsid, pDocTemplate, TRUE);
```

The first parameter specifies an identifier for the type of document that the server supports. The server program can choose its own identifier; AppWizard generates the following one for ServDemo:

```
// This identifier was generated to be statistically unique for
// your app. You may change it if you prefer to choose a specific
// identifier.

// {03A2EC83-ABBE-11D1-80FC-00C0F6A83B7F}
static const CLSID clsid =
{ 0x3a2ec83, 0xabbe, 0x11d1,
    { 0x80, 0xfc, 0x0, 0xc0, 0xf6, 0xa8, 0x3b, 0x7f } };
```

The second parameter to `ConnectTemplate` is a pointer to the document template. Assigning TRUE to the third parameter indicates that a new instance of the server is run each time a container calls on the server to create or edit an embedded item. Passing TRUE is necessary for an SDI program, because such a program is designed to handle only one document at a time. Each time ServDemo is run, either as a stand-alone program or as an OLE server, a new instance is started; thus, several copies of the program can be running at the same time.

Specifying the Full-Server option also causes AppWizard to add calls to the EnableShellOpen and RegisterShellFileTypes functions, which were explained in Chapter 12 (in the section "Registering the MiniDraw File Type"):

```
// Enable DDE Execute open
EnableShellOpen();
RegisterShellFileTypes();
```

If ServDemo is being run as an OLE server, the new AppWizard-generated code calls the static function COleTemplateServer::RegisterAll to register the server with the OLE libraries, in preparation for editing the embedded item:

```
// Check to see if launched as OLE server
if (cmdInfo.m_bRunEmbedded || cmdInfo.m_bRunAutomated)
{
    // Register all OLE server (factories) as running.  This
    // enables the OLE libraries to create objects from other
    // applications.
    COleTemplateServer::RegisterAll();

    // Application was run with /Embedding or /Automation.  Don't
    // show the main window in this case.
    return TRUE;
}
```

If ServDemo is being run as an OLE server, the template server and OLE libraries automatically create a document for managing the embedded item data. In this case, therefore, InitInstance returns immediately *without* proceeding to call the usual function for creating or opening a document, ProcessShell-Command, which is appropriate only when the program is run as a stand-alone application.

The next added feature is a call to COleTemplateServer::UpdateRegistry:

```
// When a server application is launched stand-alone, it is a
// good idea to update the system registry in case it has been
// damaged.
m_server.UpdateRegistry(OAT_INPLACE_SERVER);
```

This function call registers the server with the Windows Registry. Registering the server enters information into the Registry on the program and the type of embedded item that it supports. A server must be registered before it can be used to create an embedded item; you can do this in one of the following two ways:

- Simply run the server program once as a stand-alone program, so that the UpdateRegistry function is called.

- In the Windows Explorer (or in a folder window), double-click the file ServDemo.reg, which is located in the ServDemo project folder. This file was created by AppWizard and it contains registration information for ServDemo. Double-clicking the file name runs the Windows Registry Editor program (RegEdit.exe), which enters the ServDemo registration information into the Registry.

Although a server needs to be registered only once, ServDemo registers itself every time it's run as a stand-alone program, in case the Registry is damaged or the folder path of the executable program file has changed.

AppWizard makes one final change to the InitInstance function in response to the Full-Server option (though this change isn't directly related to OLE): InitInstance calls CWnd::DragAcceptFiles to enable drag-and-drop file opening as explained in Chapter 12 (in the section "Supporting Drag-and-Drop").

The Document Class

The program document class, CServDemoDoc, is derived from the MFC COle-ServerDoc class rather than from CDocument. COleServerDoc provides the usual features required to manage a normal document when the program is run as a stand-alone application, *plus* the features needed to manage the document when the program is run as an OLE server to create or edit an embedded OLE item (in this case the document consists of the data for the item).

Also, the document class overrides the COleServerDoc::OnGetEmbeddedItem virtual function. This function is called whenever the program is run as an OLE server. Its job is to create an object of the CServDemoSrvrItem class, which will be described in the next section:

```
COleServerItem* CServDemoDoc::OnGetEmbeddedItem()
{
    // OnGetEmbeddedItem is called by the framework to get the
    // COleServerItem that is associated with the document.  It is
```

```
    // only called when necessary.

    CServDemoSrvrItem* pItem = new CServDemoSrvrItem(this);
    ASSERT_VALID(pItem);
    return pItem;
}
```

The Server Item Class

In response to the Full-Server option, AppWizard creates a new class, CServ-DemoSrvrItem, which is derived from the MFC class COleServerItem. This class provides *additional* support for the document when the program is run as an OLE server to create or edit an embedded item. As you saw in the previous section, when the program is run as a server the system calls CServDemoDoc::OnGet-EmbeddedItem, which creates a CServDemoSrvrItem object that's associated with the document object. CServDemoSrvrItem is defined and implemented in its own set of files—SrvrItem.h and SrvrItem.cpp.

The CServDemoSrvrItem::OnDraw function is called whenever the *container* program needs to draw an embedded item in its view window. The container is responsible for drawing an item in its view window when the item is *inactive*—that is, when it's not being edited by the server. The container must also draw the representation of the item in its own window when the item is being edited in the server's window in the fully-opened mode (keep in mind that during fully-opened editing, the item is visible in both the server and container window). Rather than drawing directly in the container's window, however, CServDemo-SrvrItem::OnDraw generates a metafile that stores the drawing commands needed to draw the item. The container then causes this metafile to be played within its view window. (A Windows *metafile* stores text and graphics by recording the actual output commands used to generate the text and graphics. When a metafile is *played*, these commands are executed and the output appears on the specified device.) AppWizard provides a partial implementation of CServDemo-SrvrItem::OnDraw; later in the chapter, you'll add application-specific code to it.

In contrast, the OnDraw member function of the *view* class is called to draw the document in the view window when the program is run in stand-alone mode (as with the previous programs in the book). The view class OnDraw function is also called when the *server* needs to draw an embedded item in its view window. The server is responsible for drawing an item in its view window when the item is *active*—that is, when it's being edited (in either in-place or fully-opened mode).

Note that whenever the program is run as an OLE server, it creates a view object for displaying the item, as well as an application, document, and frame window object. The drawing code within these two OnDraw functions is normally quite similar; later in the chapter, however, you'll learn about some differences.

The CServDemoSrvrItem::OnGetExtent function returns the size of the OLE embedded item when the size is requested by the container program. The App-Wizard-generated implementation of this function simply returns a hard-coded size (specifically, it returns a size of 3,000 by 3,000 HIMETRIC units; a HIMETRIC unit is equal to 0.01 millimeter).

The In-Place Frame Window Class

AppWizard also creates the new class CInPlaceFrame, which is derived from the MFC class COleIPFrameWnd. When ServDemo is run as a stand-alone program, or when it's run as a server in the fully-opened mode, the view window is framed with a standard main frame window, which is managed as usual by the main frame window class, CFrameWnd. If, however, ServDemo is run as a server in the in-place mode, the view window is framed with a special in-place frame window, which is managed by an instance of the CInPlaceFrame class. CInPlaceFrame is defined and implemented in the files IpFrame.h and IpFrame.cpp.

AppWizard defines the m_wndResizeBar data member of the CInPlaceFrame class; m_wndResizeBar is an instance of the MFC class COleResizeBar. App-Wizard provides an implementation of the CInPlaceFrame::OnCreate function, which calls the Create function for the m_wndResizeBar object to add a border to the in-place frame window. This border displays sizing handles that the user can drag to change the size of the embedded item.

The in-place frame window is displayed only while the embedded item is being edited by the server. A container program typically displays its own border around an inactive embedded item when the item is selected; this border can also have sizing handles that allow the user to change the item's size (the simple container program you'll create later, however, doesn't display a border or permit sizing of the item when it's inactive).

The View Class

AppWizard adds the OnCancelEditSrvr function to the ServDemo view class. This function receives control when the user presses the Esc key while an OLE embedded item is being edited in the in-place mode. It calls the `COleServer-Doc::OnDeactivateUI` function to terminate the in-place editing session:

```
// The following command handler provides the standard keyboard
//  user interface to cancel an in-place editing session.  Here,
//  the server (not the container) causes the deactivation.
void CServDemoView::OnCancelEditSrvr()
{
    GetDocument()->OnDeactivateUI(FALSE);
}
```

The Esc key is defined as an accelerator keystroke (with the identifier ID_CANCEL_EDIT_SRVR) within the accelerator table that's loaded during in-place editing (that is, the IDR_SRVR_INPLACE accelerator table). AppWizard adds `OnCancelEditSrvr` to the message map so that it's called in response to this accelerator keystroke (this is an example of an accelerator keystroke that doesn't correspond to a menu command).

The Resources

AppWizard includes the file Afxolesv.rc within the program resource file. Afxolesv.rc defines several resources used by the MFC's OLE server classes.

AppWizard defines a separate menu and corresponding accelerator table for each of the three modes in which ServDemo can be run. The IDR_MAINFRAME menu and accelerator table are used when the program is run in stand-alone mode. The IDR_SRVR_EMBEDDED menu and accelerator table are used when the program is run as an OLE server in the fully-opened mode. Finally, the IDR_SRVR_INPLACE menu and accelerator table are used when the program is run as an in-place server. Later in the chapter you'll modify each of these menus and learn about the purpose of the various menu items.

Adding the Application-Specific Server Code

Once you've generated the basic source code files for an OLE server using App-Wizard, the next step is to add the application-specific code. The goal of the ServDemo program is to allow the user to create simple drawings consisting of straight-line segments, either as normal documents edited in stand-alone mode or as embedded items in a container program. To add these drawing capabilities, you need to perform the *same* modifications and add the *same* code to ServDemo that you added to the MiniDraw program in Chapters 10, 11, and 12. To do this, follow all the instructions given in these chapters for creating the MiniDraw program, with the following exceptions:

- Substitute the appropriate class and file names. For example, rather than modifying the CMiniDrawDoc document class in the MiniDrawDoc.h file, you'd modify the CServDemoDoc document class in the ServDemoDoc.h file.

- In Chapter 10, you delete several items on the File menu only to add them back in Chapter 12; to save time, you can just leave all items on the File menu in place. Also, in Chapter 10, you delete the Edit menu and then add back a modified version of the Edit menu in Chapter 11; you can just leave the Edit menu unchanged until Chapter 11.

- If you wish, you can skip customizing the program icon as described in Chapter 10.

- You don't need to modify the IDR_MAINFRAME string resource to specify the default file extension, as described in Chapter 12. You already specified the default file extension when you generated the ServDemo program in AppWizard.

- You don't need to add code to InitInstance as described in Chapter 12. AppWizard already added the required calls to DragAcceptFiles, Enable-ShellOpen, and RegisterShellFileTypes.

You can of course save time by copying code from the MiniDraw source files into the ServDemo files.

Adding OLE Support

Now that you've finished implementing the drawing capabilities of ServDemo, you'll add several features to the program for supporting OLE.

The first step is to modify the two OLE-specific menus. To begin, open the IDR_SRVR_EMBEDDED menu in the Visual C++ menu editor. This is the menu that's displayed when ServDemo run as an OLE server in the fully-opened mode. Notice that the commands on the File menu (see Figure 24.2) are different from those that AppWizard assigns to a normal program menu that's displayed when the program is run in stand-alone mode (that is, the IDR_MAINFRAME menu). The menu commands reflect the fact that when the program is running as a server, it doesn't open or create new documents (it edits only the embedded item); hence, the usual New and Open... commands aren't present. Also, rather than saving a document in a disk file, the server copies the updated document data back to the container program; therefore, the usual Save command is replaced with an Update command that performs this copy operation. The server, however, does allow the user to save a separate *copy* of the embedded item in a disk file; this task is performed in response to the Save Copy As... command on the server File menu, which is equivalent to the usual Save As... command (the server program can later open this document when it's run in stand-alone mode). Note finally that, when the server is running, the MFC code modifies the wording of the Update and Exit commands to indicate the name of the document containing the embedded item. For example, if the document containing the embedded item in the container program were named House.con, the captions for these commands would be as shown in Figure 24.3.

FIGURE 24.2:

The File pop-up menu of the ServDemo IDR_ SRVR_EMBEDDED menu as it appears in the Visual C++ menu editor

FIGURE 24.3:

The File pop-up menu of the ServDemo IDR_ SRVR_EMBEDDED menu as it appears at runtime, while the program is performing fully-opened editing of an embedded item contained in a document named House.con

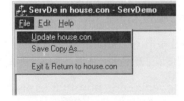

You don't need to make any modifications to the File menu. You should, however, make the Edit menu the *same* as the Edit menu for the IDR_MAINFRAME

stand-alone menu. (To do this, you can first delete the IDR_SRVR_EMBEDDED Edit pop-up menu. Then, hold down Ctrl and drag the Edit menu from the IDR_MAIN-FRAME menu bar and drop it on the IDR_SRVR_EMBEDDED menu bar.) The final Edit menu is shown in Figure 24.4.

FIGURE 24.4:

The modified Edit pop-up menu of the IDR_SRVR_EMBEDDED menu

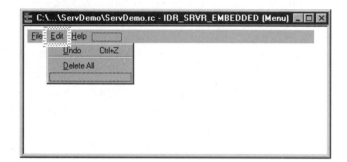

Next, open the IDR_SRVR_INPLACE menu in the menu editor (shown in Figure 24.5). This is the menu that's displayed when ServDemo is performing in-place editing of an OLE embedded item. This menu *doesn't* have a File pop-up menu, because during in-place editing the container program is responsible for executing file commands and displays its own File menu. During in-place editing, the system *merges* the server and the container menus, so that both programs can display appropriate pop-up menus. The resulting merged menu consists of the following pop-up menus, going from left to right:

- All pop-up menus on the container's in-place menu before the double separator on this menu (for the ContDemo example container you'll create later, this would be only the File pop-up menu)

- All pop-up menus on the server's in-place menu before the double separator (for ServDemo, this would be only the Edit pop-up menu; see Figure 24.5)

- The remaining pop-up menus on the container's in-place menu, if any (Cont-Demo has *no* remaining pop-up menus to the right of the double separator)

- The remaining pop-up menus on the server's in-place menu (for ServDemo, this would be the Help pop-up menu)

The result of merging the ServDemo in-place menu with the in-place menu of the ContDemo program (which you'll create later) is given later in the chapter, in Figure 24.8.

FIGURE 24.5:

The ServDemo IDR_
SRVR_INPLACE menu,
as it appears in the Visual
C++ menu editor

You should now modify the Edit pop-up menu on the IDR_SRVR_INPLACE
menu so that it's the same as the Edit pop-up menus on the IDR_MAINFRAME and
IDR_SRVR_EMBEDDED menus.

The next step is to open the ServDemoDoc.h file and add definitions for the
GetMaxX and GetMaxY functions to the public section of the CLine class definition:

```cpp
class CLine : public CObject
{
protected:
    int m_X1, m_Y1, m_X2, m_Y2;

    CLine ()
        {}
    DECLARE_SERIAL (CLine)

public:
    CLine (int X1, int Y1, int X2, int Y2)
        {
        m_X1 = X1;
        m_Y1 = Y1;
        m_X2 = X2;
        m_Y2 = Y2;
        }
    void Draw (CDC *PDC);
    int GetMaxX ()
        {
        return m_X1 > m_X2 ? m_X1 : m_X2;
        }
    int GetMaxY ()
        {
        return m_Y1 > m_Y2 ? m_Y1 : m_Y2;
        }
```

```
    virtual void Serialize (CArchive& ar);
};
```

These functions will be used in the new GetDocSize function that you'll add to the document class.

While you still have the ServDemoDoc.h file open, add a declaration for GetDocSize to the document class, CServDemoDoc, as follows:

```
class CServDemoDoc : public COleServerDoc
{
protected:
    CTypedPtrArray<CObArray, CLine*> m_LineArray;

public:
    void AddLine (int X1, int Y1, int X2, int Y2);
    CSize GetDocSize ();
    CLine *GetLine (int Index);
    int GetNumLines ();
```

Now open ServDemoDoc.cpp and insert the definition for the GetDocSize method, between the existing AddLine and GetLine function definitions:

```
void CServDemoDoc::AddLine (int X1, int Y1, int X2, int Y2)
    {
    CLine *PLine = new CLine (X1, Y1, X2, Y2);
    m_LineArray.Add (PLine);
    SetModifiedFlag ();
    }

CSize CServDemoDoc::GetDocSize ()
    {
    int XMax = 1, YMax = 1;
    int X, Y;

    int Index = m_LineArray.GetSize ();
    while (Index--)
        {
        X = m_LineArray.GetAt (Index)->GetMaxX ();
        XMax = X > XMax ? X : XMax;
        Y = m_LineArray.GetAt (Index)->GetMaxY ();
        YMax = Y > YMax ? Y : YMax;
        }
    return CSize (XMax, YMax);
    }
```

```
CLine *CServDemoDoc::GetLine (int Index)
    {
```

GetDocSize returns the current size of the drawing. It derives the size by examining all the lines in the drawing and saving the maximum *x* and the maximum *y* end-point coordinates. As explained shortly, GetDocSize is called by the CServ-DemoSrvrItem::OnDraw function to obtain the current drawing size.

You now need to modify the view class so that it calls the COleServerDoc::UpdateAllItems function each time the contents of the document change or the size of the view window changes. If ServDemo is editing an embedded item, UpdateAllItems notifies the OLE libraries that the contents or size of the embedded item has changed, and it forces the OLE code to call the OnDraw member function of the CServDemoSrvrItem class, which re-creates the metafile that's used to draw the inactive embedded item in the container window. As a result, if you're editing an embedded drawing item in the fully-opened mode, each time you make a change to the drawing, the change will immediately appear on the representation of the item within the container window. (If ServDemo is running in stand-alone mode, calling UpdateAllItems does nothing.)

All changes in the size or content of the document are accompanied by a call to either the OnLButtonUp or the OnDraw member function of the view class; therefore, you need to add calls to UpdateAllItems only to these two functions in the ServDemoView.cpp file. First, add a call to UpdateAllItems to OnLButtonUp:

```
void CServDemoView::OnLButtonUp(UINT nFlags, CPoint point)
{
    // TODO: Add your message handler code here and/or call
    // default

    if (m_Dragging)
        {
        m_Dragging = 0;
        ::ReleaseCapture ();
        ::ClipCursor (NULL);
        CClientDC ClientDC (this);
        ClientDC.SetROP2 (R2_NOT);
        ClientDC.MoveTo (m_PointOrigin);
        ClientDC.LineTo (m_PointOld);
        ClientDC.SetROP2 (R2_COPYPEN);
        ClientDC.MoveTo (m_PointOrigin);
        ClientDC.LineTo (point);
```

```
        CServDemoDoc* PDoc = GetDocument();
        PDoc->AddLine
            (m_PointOrigin.x, m_PointOrigin.y, point.x, point.y);
        PDoc->UpdateAllItems (0);
        }

    CView::OnLButtonUp(nFlags, point);
}
```

Then, add a call to `CServDemoView::UpdateAllItems` to `OnDraw`:

```
void CServDemoView::OnDraw(CDC* pDC)
{
    CServDemoDoc* pDoc = GetDocument();
    ASSERT_VALID(pDoc);

    // TODO: add draw code for native data here

    int Index = pDoc->GetNumLines ();
    while (Index-)
        pDoc->GetLine (Index)->Draw (pDC);

    pDoc->UpdateAllItems (0);
}
```

The next job is to add code as follows to the `OnDraw` member function of the `CServDemoSrvrItem` class in SrvrItem.cpp:

```
BOOL CServDemoSrvrItem::OnDraw(CDC* pDC, CSize& rSize)
{
    // Remove this if you use rSize
    UNREFERENCED_PARAMETER(rSize);

    CServDemoDoc* pDoc = GetDocument();
    ASSERT_VALID(pDoc);

    // TODO: set mapping mode and extent
    //   (The extent is usually the same as the size returned from
    //   OnGetExtent)
    pDC->SetMapMode(MM_ANISOTROPIC);
    pDC->SetWindowOrg(0,0);

    // modify the AppWizard-generated call to SetWindowExtent:
    pDC->SetWindowExt (pDoc->GetDocSize ());

    // TODO: add drawing code here.  Optionally, fill in the
```

```
        // HIMETRIC extent. All drawing takes place in the metafile
        // device context (pDC).

        // same code as in CServDemoView::OnDraw:
        int Index = pDoc->GetNumLines ();
        while (Index--)
          pDoc->GetLine (Index)->Draw (pDC);

        return TRUE;
   }
```

Note that the call to SetWindowExt shown in this code *replaces* the AppWizard-generated call to SetWindowExt.

As explained previously, CServDemoSrvrItem::OnDraw creates the metafile that's used to draw the inactive embedded item within the container window. The AppWizard-generated code begins by setting the mapping mode to MM_ANISOTROPIC (this mapping mode allows the OLE mechanism to easily scale the embedded item so that it fits exactly within the area allotted to it within the container window; mapping modes were explained in Chapter 19). Next, the code calls CDC::SetWindowExt, which specifies the total horizontal and vertical size of the metafile in logical units. The AppWizard-generated call to SetWindowExt specified an arbitrary size of 3,000 by 3,000 logical units. You modified the call so that the function is passed the actual logical size of the embedded item (obtained by calling the newly added CServDemoDoc::GetDocSize function); as a result, the entire drawing will be scaled to fit exactly within the borders around the embedded item in the container window. The remainder of the added code is the same as the drawing code in the OnDraw member function of the view class.

You can now build the ServDemo program. You can run the program in stand-alone mode, and it should function just like the third version of MiniDraw you created in Chapter 12. If you have an OLE container program, you can also run ServDemo as a server in either in-place or fully-opened mode, using the commands that were described previously in the chapter (in the section "Embedding, Linking, and Automation"). In the second main section of this chapter ("Creating a Container"), you'll create a container program that you can use to test ServDemo.

The ServDemo Source Code

Listings 24.1 through 24.12, which follow, contain the C++ source code for the ServDemo program that you just created. You'll find a copy of these files in your \ServDemo companion-CD folder.

Listing 24.1

```
// ServDemo.h : main header file for the SERVDEMO application
//

#if !defined(AFX_SERVDEMO_H__03A2EC86_ABBE_11D1_80FC_00C0F6A83B7F__INCLUDED_)
#define AFX_SERVDEMO_H__03A2EC86_ABBE_11D1_80FC_00C0F6A83B7F__INCLUDED_

#if _MSC_VER > 1000
#pragma once
#endif // _MSC_VER > 1000

#ifndef __AFXWIN_H__
    #error include 'stdafx.h' before including this file for PCH
#endif

#include "resource.h"        // main symbols

/////////////////////////////////////////////////////////////////////////////
// CServDemoApp:
// See ServDemo.cpp for the implementation of this class
//

class CServDemoApp : public CWinApp
{
public:
    CServDemoApp();

// Overrides
    // ClassWizard generated virtual function overrides
    //{{AFX_VIRTUAL(CServDemoApp)
    public:
    virtual BOOL InitInstance();
    //}}AFX_VIRTUAL

// Implementation
    COleTemplateServer m_server;
        // Server object for document creation
    //{{AFX_MSG(CServDemoApp)
    afx_msg void OnAppAbout();
        // NOTE - the ClassWizard will add and remove member functions here.
        //    DO NOT EDIT what you see in these blocks of generated code !
```

```
    //}}AFX_MSG
    DECLARE_MESSAGE_MAP()
};


/////////////////////////////////////////////////////////////////////////////

//{{AFX_INSERT_LOCATION}}
// Microsoft Visual C++ will insert additional declarations immediately before
// the previous line.

#endif
// !defined(AFX_SERVDEMO_H__03A2EC86_ABBE_11D1_80FC_00C0F6A83B7F__INCLUDED_)
```

Listing 24.2

```
// ServDemo.cpp : Defines the class behaviors for the application.
//

#include "stdafx.h"
#include "ServDemo.h"

#include "MainFrm.h"
#include "IpFrame.h"
#include "ServDemoDoc.h"
#include "ServDemoView.h"

#ifdef _DEBUG
#define new DEBUG_NEW
#undef THIS_FILE
static char THIS_FILE[] = __FILE__;
#endif


/////////////////////////////////////////////////////////////////////////////
// CServDemoApp

BEGIN_MESSAGE_MAP(CServDemoApp, CWinApp)
    //{{AFX_MSG_MAP(CServDemoApp)
    ON_COMMAND(ID_APP_ABOUT, OnAppAbout)
        // NOTE - the ClassWizard will add and remove mapping macros here.
        //    DO NOT EDIT what you see in these blocks of generated code!
    //}}AFX_MSG_MAP
    // Standard file based document commands
```

```
   ON_COMMAND(ID_FILE_NEW, CWinApp::OnFileNew)
   ON_COMMAND(ID_FILE_OPEN, CWinApp::OnFileOpen)
END_MESSAGE_MAP()

/////////////////////////////////////////////////////////////////////
// CServDemoApp construction

CServDemoApp::CServDemoApp()
{
   // TODO: add construction code here,
   // Place all significant initialization in InitInstance
}

/////////////////////////////////////////////////////////////////////
// The one and only CServDemoApp object

CServDemoApp theApp;

// This identifier was generated to be statistically unique for your app.
// You may change it if you prefer to choose a specific identifier.

// {03A2EC83-ABBE-11D1-80FC-00C0F6A83B7F}
static const CLSID clsid =
{ 0x3a2ec83, 0xabbe, 0x11d1, { 0x80, 0xfc, 0x0, 0xc0, 0xf6, 0xa8, 0x3b, 0x7f } };

/////////////////////////////////////////////////////////////////////
// CServDemoApp initialization

BOOL CServDemoApp::InitInstance()
{
   // Initialize OLE libraries
   if (!AfxOleInit())
   {
      AfxMessageBox(IDP_OLE_INIT_FAILED);
      return FALSE;
   }

   // Standard initialization
   // If you are not using these features and wish to reduce the size
   //  of your final executable, you should remove from the following
   //  the specific initialization routines you do not need.

#ifdef _AFXDLL
```

```
   Enable3dControls();          // Call this when using MFC in a shared DLL
#else
   Enable3dControlsStatic();   // Call this when linking to MFC statically
#endif

   // Change the registry key under which our settings are stored.
   // TODO: You should modify this string to be something appropriate
   // such as the name of your company or organization.
   SetRegistryKey(_T("Local AppWizard-Generated Applications"));

   LoadStdProfileSettings();   // Load standard INI file options (including MRU)

   // Register the application's document templates.  Document templates
   //  serve as the connection between documents, frame windows and views.

   CSingleDocTemplate* pDocTemplate;
   pDocTemplate = new CSingleDocTemplate(
      IDR_MAINFRAME,
      RUNTIME_CLASS(CServDemoDoc),
      RUNTIME_CLASS(CMainFrame),        // main SDI frame window
      RUNTIME_CLASS(CServDemoView));
   pDocTemplate->SetServerInfo(
      IDR_SRVR_EMBEDDED, IDR_SRVR_INPLACE,
      RUNTIME_CLASS(CInPlaceFrame));
   AddDocTemplate(pDocTemplate);

   // Connect the COleTemplateServer to the document template.
   //  The COleTemplateServer creates new documents on behalf
   //  of requesting OLE containers by using information
   //  specified in the document template.
   m_server.ConnectTemplate(clsid, pDocTemplate, TRUE);
      // Note: SDI applications register server objects only if /Embedding
      //  or /Automation is present on the command line.

   // Enable DDE Execute open
   EnableShellOpen();
   RegisterShellFileTypes(TRUE);

   // Parse command line for standard shell commands, DDE, file open
   CCommandLineInfo cmdInfo;
   ParseCommandLine(cmdInfo);

   // Check to see if launched as OLE server
```

```
    if (cmdInfo.m_bRunEmbedded || cmdInfo.m_bRunAutomated)
    {
        // Register all OLE server (factories) as running.  This enables the
        //  OLE libraries to create objects from other applications.
        COleTemplateServer::RegisterAll();

        // Application was run with /Embedding or /Automation.  Don't show the
        //  main window in this case.
        return TRUE;
    }

    // When a server application is launched stand-alone, it is a good idea
    //  to update the system registry in case it has been damaged.
    m_server.UpdateRegistry(OAT_INPLACE_SERVER);

    // Dispatch commands specified on the command line
    if (!ProcessShellCommand(cmdInfo))
        return FALSE;

    // The one and only window has been initialized, so show and update it.
    m_pMainWnd->ShowWindow(SW_SHOW);
    m_pMainWnd->UpdateWindow();

    // Enable drag/drop open
    m_pMainWnd->DragAcceptFiles();

    return TRUE;
}


/////////////////////////////////////////////////////////////////////////
// CAboutDlg dialog used for App About

class CAboutDlg : public CDialog
{
public:
    CAboutDlg();

// Dialog Data
    //{{AFX_DATA(CAboutDlg)
    enum { IDD = IDD_ABOUTBOX };
    //}}AFX_DATA
```

```
    // ClassWizard generated virtual function overrides
    //{{AFX_VIRTUAL(CAboutDlg)
    protected:
    virtual void DoDataExchange(CDataExchange* pDX);    // DDX/DDV support
    //}}AFX_VIRTUAL

// Implementation
protected:
    //{{AFX_MSG(CAboutDlg)
        // No message handlers
    //}}AFX_MSG
    DECLARE_MESSAGE_MAP()
};

CAboutDlg::CAboutDlg() : CDialog(CAboutDlg::IDD)
{
    //{{AFX_DATA_INIT(CAboutDlg)
    //}}AFX_DATA_INIT
}

void CAboutDlg::DoDataExchange(CDataExchange* pDX)
{
    CDialog::DoDataExchange(pDX);
    //{{AFX_DATA_MAP(CAboutDlg)
    //}}AFX_DATA_MAP
}

BEGIN_MESSAGE_MAP(CAboutDlg, CDialog)
    //{{AFX_MSG_MAP(CAboutDlg)
        // No message handlers
    //}}AFX_MSG_MAP
END_MESSAGE_MAP()

// App command to run the dialog
void CServDemoApp::OnAppAbout()
{
    CAboutDlg aboutDlg;
    aboutDlg.DoModal();
}

/////////////////////////////////////////////////////////////////////////////
// CServDemoApp message handlers
```

Listing 24.3

```
// ServDemoDoc.h : interface of the CServDemoDoc class
//
/////////////////////////////////////////////////////////////////////

#if !defined(AFX_SERVDEMODOC_H__03A2EC8C_ABBE_11D1_80FC_00C0F6A83B7F__INCLUDED_)
#define AFX_SERVDEMODOC_H__03A2EC8C_ABBE_11D1_80FC_00C0F6A83B7F__INCLUDED_

#if _MSC_VER > 1000
#pragma once
#endif // _MSC_VER > 1000

class CLine : public CObject
{
protected:
   int m_X1, m_Y1, m_X2, m_Y2;

   CLine ()
      {}
   DECLARE_SERIAL (CLine)

public:
   CLine (int X1, int Y1, int X2, int Y2)
      {
      m_X1 = X1;
      m_Y1 = Y1;
      m_X2 = X2;
      m_Y2 = Y2;
      }
   void Draw (CDC *PDC);
   int GetMaxX ()
      {
      return m_X1 > m_X2 ? m_X1 : m_X2;
      }
   int GetMaxY ()
      {
      return m_Y1 > m_Y2 ? m_Y1 : m_Y2;
      }
   virtual void Serialize (CArchive& ar);
};
```

```
class CServDemoSrvrItem;

class CServDemoDoc : public COleServerDoc
{
protected:
    CTypedPtrArray<CObArray, CLine*> m_LineArray;

public:
    void AddLine (int X1, int Y1, int X2, int Y2);
    CSize GetDocSize ();
    CLine *GetLine (int Index);
    int GetNumLines ();

protected: // create from serialization only
    CServDemoDoc();
    DECLARE_DYNCREATE(CServDemoDoc)

// Attributes
public:
    CServDemoSrvrItem* GetEmbeddedItem()
        { return (CServDemoSrvrItem*)COleServerDoc::GetEmbeddedItem(); }

// Operations
public:

// Overrides
    // ClassWizard generated virtual function overrides
    //{{AFX_VIRTUAL(CServDemoDoc)
    public:
    virtual BOOL OnNewDocument();
    virtual void Serialize(CArchive& ar);
    virtual void DeleteContents();
    protected:
    virtual COleServerItem* OnGetEmbeddedItem();
    //}}AFX_VIRTUAL

// Implementation
public:
    virtual ~CServDemoDoc();
#ifdef _DEBUG
    virtual void AssertValid() const;
    virtual void Dump(CDumpContext& dc) const;
#endif
```

```
protected:

// Generated message map functions
protected:
    //{{AFX_MSG(CServDemoDoc)
    afx_msg void OnEditClearAll();
    afx_msg void OnUpdateEditClearAll(CCmdUI* pCmdUI);
    afx_msg void OnEditUndo();
    afx_msg void OnUpdateEditUndo(CCmdUI* pCmdUI);
    //}}AFX_MSG
    DECLARE_MESSAGE_MAP()
};

/////////////////////////////////////////////////////////////////////////

//{{AFX_INSERT_LOCATION}}
// Microsoft Visual C++ will insert additional declarations immediately before
// the previous line.

#endif
// !defined(AFX_SERVDEMODOC_H__03A2EC8C_ABBE_11D1_80FC_00C0F6A83B7F__INCLUDED_)
```

Listing 24.4

```
// ServDemoDoc.cpp : implementation of the CServDemoDoc class
//

#include "stdafx.h"
#include "ServDemo.h"

#include "ServDemoDoc.h"
#include "SrvrItem.h"

#ifdef _DEBUG
#define new DEBUG_NEW
#undef THIS_FILE
static char THIS_FILE[] = __FILE__;
#endif

/////////////////////////////////////////////////////////////////////////
// CServDemoDoc
```

```
IMPLEMENT_DYNCREATE(CServDemoDoc, COleServerDoc)

BEGIN_MESSAGE_MAP(CServDemoDoc, COleServerDoc)
   //{{AFX_MSG_MAP(CServDemoDoc)
   ON_COMMAND(ID_EDIT_CLEAR_ALL, OnEditClearAll)
   ON_UPDATE_COMMAND_UI(ID_EDIT_CLEAR_ALL, OnUpdateEditClearAll)
   ON_COMMAND(ID_EDIT_UNDO, OnEditUndo)
   ON_UPDATE_COMMAND_UI(ID_EDIT_UNDO, OnUpdateEditUndo)
   //}}AFX_MSG_MAP
END_MESSAGE_MAP()

/////////////////////////////////////////////////////////////////////////////
// CServDemoDoc construction/destruction

CServDemoDoc::CServDemoDoc()
{
   // Use OLE compound files
   EnableCompoundFile();

   // TODO: add one-time construction code here

}

CServDemoDoc::~CServDemoDoc()
{
}

BOOL CServDemoDoc::OnNewDocument()
{
   if (!COleServerDoc::OnNewDocument())
      return FALSE;

   // TODO: add reinitialization code here
   // (SDI documents will reuse this document)

   return TRUE;
}

/////////////////////////////////////////////////////////////////////////////
// CServDemoDoc server implementation

COleServerItem* CServDemoDoc::OnGetEmbeddedItem()
{
```

```
   // OnGetEmbeddedItem is called by the framework to get the COleServerItem
   //  that is associated with the document.  It is only called when necessary.

   CServDemoSrvrItem* pItem = new CServDemoSrvrItem(this);
   ASSERT_VALID(pItem);
   return pItem;
}



/////////////////////////////////////////////////////////////////////////////
// CServDemoDoc serialization

void CServDemoDoc::Serialize(CArchive& ar)
{
   if (ar.IsStoring())
   {
      // TODO: add storing code here
      m_LineArray.Serialize (ar);
   }
   else
   {
      // TODO: add loading code here
      m_LineArray.Serialize (ar);
   }
}

/////////////////////////////////////////////////////////////////////////////
// CServDemoDoc diagnostics

#ifdef _DEBUG
void CServDemoDoc::AssertValid() const
{
   COleServerDoc::AssertValid();
}

void CServDemoDoc::Dump(CDumpContext& dc) const
{
   COleServerDoc::Dump(dc);
}
#endif //_DEBUG

/////////////////////////////////////////////////////////////////////
```

```
// CServDemoDoc commands

IMPLEMENT_SERIAL (CLine, CObject, 1)

void CLine::Draw (CDC *PDC)
   {
   PDC->MoveTo (m_X1, m_Y1);
   PDC->LineTo (m_X2, m_Y2);
   }

void CLine::Serialize (CArchive& ar)
   {
   if (ar.IsStoring())
      ar << m_X1 << m_Y1 << m_X2 << m_Y2;
   else
      ar >> m_X1 >> m_Y1 >> m_X2 >> m_Y2;
   }

void CServDemoDoc::AddLine (int X1, int Y1, int X2, int Y2)
   {
   CLine *PLine = new CLine (X1, Y1, X2, Y2);
   m_LineArray.Add (PLine);
   SetModifiedFlag ();
   }

CSize CServDemoDoc::GetDocSize ()
   {
   int XMax = 1, YMax = 1;
   int X, Y;

   int Index = m_LineArray.GetSize ();
   while (Index--)
      {
      X = m_LineArray.GetAt (Index)->GetMaxX ();
      XMax = X > XMax ? X : XMax;
      Y = m_LineArray.GetAt (Index)->GetMaxY ();
      YMax = Y > YMax ? Y : YMax;
      }
   return CSize (XMax, YMax);
   }

CLine *CServDemoDoc::GetLine (int Index)
   {
```

```
    if (Index < 0 || Index > m_LineArray.GetUpperBound ())
        return 0;
    return m_LineArray.GetAt (Index);
    }

int CServDemoDoc::GetNumLines ()
    {
    return m_LineArray.GetSize ();
    }

void CServDemoDoc::DeleteContents ()
{
    // TODO: Add your specialized code here and/or call the base class

    int Index = m_LineArray.GetSize ();
    while (Index--)
        delete m_LineArray.GetAt (Index);
    m_LineArray.RemoveAll ();

    COleServerDoc::DeleteContents();
}

void CServDemoDoc::OnEditClearAll()
{
    // TODO: Add your command handler code here

    DeleteContents ();
    UpdateAllViews (0);
    SetModifiedFlag ();
}

void CServDemoDoc::OnUpdateEditClearAll(CCmdUI* pCmdUI)
{
    // TODO: Add your command update UI handler code here

    pCmdUI->Enable (m_LineArray.GetSize ());
}

void CServDemoDoc::OnEditUndo()
{
    // TODO: Add your command handler code here
```

```
   int Index = m_LineArray.GetUpperBound ();
   if (Index > -1)
      {
      delete m_LineArray.GetAt (Index);
      m_LineArray.RemoveAt (Index);
      }
   UpdateAllViews (0);
   SetModifiedFlag ();
}


void CServDemoDoc::OnUpdateEditUndo(CCmdUI* pCmdUI)
{
   // TODO: Add your command update UI handler code here

   pCmdUI->Enable (m_LineArray.GetSize ());
}
```

Listing 24.5

```
// MainFrm.h : interface of the CMainFrame class
//
/////////////////////////////////////////////////////////////////////////

#if !defined(AFX_MAINFRM_H__03A2EC8A_ABBE_11D1_80FC_00C0F6A83B7F__INCLUDED_)
#define AFX_MAINFRM_H__03A2EC8A_ABBE_11D1_80FC_00C0F6A83B7F__INCLUDED_

#if _MSC_VER > 1000
#pragma once
#endif // _MSC_VER > 1000

class CMainFrame : public CFrameWnd
{

protected: // create from serialization only
   CMainFrame();
   DECLARE_DYNCREATE(CMainFrame)

// Attributes
public:

// Operations
public:
```

```
// Overrides
    // ClassWizard generated virtual function overrides
    //{{AFX_VIRTUAL(CMainFrame)
    virtual BOOL PreCreateWindow(CREATESTRUCT& cs);
    //}}AFX_VIRTUAL

// Implementation
public:
    virtual ~CMainFrame();
#ifdef _DEBUG
    virtual void AssertValid() const;
    virtual void Dump(CDumpContext& dc) const;
#endif

// Generated message map functions
protected:
    //{{AFX_MSG(CMainFrame)
        // NOTE - the ClassWizard will add and remove member functions here.
        //      DO NOT EDIT what you see in these blocks of generated code!
    //}}AFX_MSG
    DECLARE_MESSAGE_MAP()
};

/////////////////////////////////////////////////////////////////////////

//{{AFX_INSERT_LOCATION}}
// Microsoft Visual C++ will insert additional declarations immediately before
// the previous line.

#endif
// !defined(AFX_MAINFRM_H__03A2EC8A_ABBE_11D1_80FC_00C0F6A83B7F__INCLUDED_)
```

Listing 24.6

```
// MainFrm.cpp : implementation of the CMainFrame class
//

#include "stdafx.h"
#include "ServDemo.h"

#include "MainFrm.h"

#ifdef _DEBUG
```

```
#define new DEBUG_NEW
#undef THIS_FILE
static char THIS_FILE[] = __FILE__;
#endif

/////////////////////////////////////////////////////////////////////////////
// CMainFrame

IMPLEMENT_DYNCREATE(CMainFrame, CFrameWnd)

BEGIN_MESSAGE_MAP(CMainFrame, CFrameWnd)
    //{{AFX_MSG_MAP(CMainFrame)
        // NOTE - the ClassWizard will add and remove mapping macros here.
        //      DO NOT EDIT what you see in these blocks of generated code !
    //}}AFX_MSG_MAP
END_MESSAGE_MAP()

/////////////////////////////////////////////////////////////////////////////
// CMainFrame construction/destruction

CMainFrame::CMainFrame()
{
    // TODO: add member initialization code here

}

CMainFrame::~CMainFrame()
{
}

BOOL CMainFrame::PreCreateWindow(CREATESTRUCT& cs)
{
    if( !CFrameWnd::PreCreateWindow(cs) )
        return FALSE;
    // TODO: Modify the Window class or styles here by modifying
    //  the CREATESTRUCT cs

    return TRUE;
}

/////////////////////////////////////////////////////////////////////////////
// CMainFrame diagnostics
```

```
#ifdef _DEBUG
void CMainFrame::AssertValid() const
{
    CFrameWnd::AssertValid();
}

void CMainFrame::Dump(CDumpContext& dc) const
{
    CFrameWnd::Dump(dc);
}


#endif //_DEBUG


/////////////////////////////////////////////////////////////////////
// CMainFrame message handlers
```

Listing 24.7

```
// ServDemoView.h : interface of the CServDemoView class
//
/////////////////////////////////////////////////////////////////////

#if !defined(AFX_SERVDEMOVIEW_H__03A2EC8E_ABBE_11D1_80FC_00C0F6A83B7F__INCLUDED_)
#define AFX_SERVDEMOVIEW_H__03A2EC8E_ABBE_11D1_80FC_00C0F6A83B7F__INCLUDED_

#if _MSC_VER > 1000
#pragma once
#endif // _MSC_VER > 1000


class CServDemoView : public CView
{
protected:
    CString m_ClassName;
    int m_Dragging;
    HCURSOR m_HCross;
    CPoint m_PointOld;
    CPoint m_PointOrigin;

protected: // create from serialization only
    CServDemoView();
    DECLARE_DYNCREATE(CServDemoView)
```

```cpp
// Attributes
public:
   CServDemoDoc* GetDocument();

// Operations
public:

// Overrides
   // ClassWizard generated virtual function overrides
   //{{AFX_VIRTUAL(CServDemoView)
   public:
   virtual void OnDraw(CDC* pDC);  // overridden to draw this view
   virtual BOOL PreCreateWindow(CREATESTRUCT& cs);
   protected:
   //}}AFX_VIRTUAL

// Implementation
public:
   virtual ~CServDemoView();
#ifdef _DEBUG
   virtual void AssertValid() const;
   virtual void Dump(CDumpContext& dc) const;
#endif

protected:

// Generated message map functions
protected:
   //{{AFX_MSG(CServDemoView)
   afx_msg void OnCancelEditSrvr();
   afx_msg void OnLButtonDown(UINT nFlags, CPoint point);
   afx_msg void OnMouseMove(UINT nFlags, CPoint point);
   afx_msg void OnLButtonUp(UINT nFlags, CPoint point);
   //}}AFX_MSG
   DECLARE_MESSAGE_MAP()
};

#ifndef _DEBUG  // debug version in ServDemoView.cpp
inline CServDemoDoc* CServDemoView::GetDocument()
   { return (CServDemoDoc*)m_pDocument; }
#endif

/////////////////////////////////////////////////////////////////////
```

```
//{{AFX_INSERT_LOCATION}}
// Microsoft Visual C++ will insert additional declarations immediately before
// the previous line.

#endif
// !defined(AFX_SERVDEMOVIEW_H__03A2EC8E_ABBE_11D1_80FC_00C0F6A83B7F__INCLUDED_)
```

Listing 24.8

```cpp
// ServDemoView.cpp : implementation of the CServDemoView class
//

#include "stdafx.h"
#include "ServDemo.h"

#include "ServDemoDoc.h"
#include "ServDemoView.h"

#ifdef _DEBUG
#define new DEBUG_NEW
#undef THIS_FILE
static char THIS_FILE[] = __FILE__;
#endif

/////////////////////////////////////////////////////////////////////////////
// CServDemoView

IMPLEMENT_DYNCREATE(CServDemoView, CView)

BEGIN_MESSAGE_MAP(CServDemoView, CView)
    //{{AFX_MSG_MAP(CServDemoView)
    ON_COMMAND(ID_CANCEL_EDIT_SRVR, OnCancelEditSrvr)
    ON_WM_LBUTTONDOWN()
    ON_WM_MOUSEMOVE()
    ON_WM_LBUTTONUP()
    //}}AFX_MSG_MAP
END_MESSAGE_MAP()

/////////////////////////////////////////////////////////////////////////////
// CServDemoView construction/destruction

CServDemoView::CServDemoView()
{
```

```
   // TODO: add construction code here
   m_Dragging = 0;
   m_HCross = AfxGetApp ()->LoadStandardCursor (IDC_CROSS);
}

CServDemoView::~CServDemoView()
{
}

BOOL CServDemoView::PreCreateWindow(CREATESTRUCT& cs)
{
   // TODO: Modify the Window class or styles here by modifying
   //   the CREATESTRUCT cs

   m_ClassName = AfxRegisterWndClass
      (CS_HREDRAW | CS_VREDRAW,                   // class styles
       0,                                          // no cursor
       (HBRUSH)::GetStockObject (WHITE_BRUSH), // assign white
                                                   // background brush
       0);                                         // no icon
   cs.lpszClass = m_ClassName;

   return CView::PreCreateWindow(cs);
}

/////////////////////////////////////////////////////////////////////////
// CServDemoView drawing

void CServDemoView::OnDraw(CDC* pDC)
{
   CServDemoDoc* pDoc = GetDocument();
   ASSERT_VALID(pDoc);

   // TODO: add draw code for native data here

   int Index = pDoc->GetNumLines ();
   while (Index--)
      pDoc->GetLine (Index)->Draw (pDC);

   pDoc->UpdateAllItems (0);
}

/////////////////////////////////////////////////////////////////////////
```

```cpp
// OLE Server support

// The following command handler provides the standard keyboard
//  user interface to cancel an in-place editing session.  Here,
//  the server (not the container) causes the deactivation.
void CServDemoView::OnCancelEditSrvr()
{
    GetDocument()->OnDeactivateUI(FALSE);
}


/////////////////////////////////////////////////////////////////////////////
// CServDemoView diagnostics

#ifdef _DEBUG
void CServDemoView::AssertValid() const
{
    CView::AssertValid();
}

void CServDemoView::Dump(CDumpContext& dc) const
{
    CView::Dump(dc);
}

CServDemoDoc* CServDemoView::GetDocument() // non-debug version is inline
{
    ASSERT(m_pDocument->IsKindOf(RUNTIME_CLASS(CServDemoDoc)));
    return (CServDemoDoc*)m_pDocument;
}
#endif //_DEBUG

/////////////////////////////////////////////////////////////////////////////
// CServDemoView message handlers

void CServDemoView::OnLButtonDown(UINT nFlags, CPoint point)
{
    // TODO: Add your message handler code here and/or call default

    m_PointOrigin = point;
    m_PointOld = point;
    SetCapture ();
    m_Dragging = 1;
```

```
    RECT Rect;
    GetClientRect (&Rect);
    ClientToScreen (&Rect);
    ::ClipCursor (&Rect);

    CView::OnLButtonDown(nFlags, point);
}

void CServDemoView::OnMouseMove(UINT nFlags, CPoint point)
{
    // TODO: Add your message handler code here and/or call default

    ::SetCursor (m_HCross);

    if (m_Dragging)
        {
        CClientDC ClientDC (this);
        ClientDC.SetROP2 (R2_NOT);
        ClientDC.MoveTo (m_PointOrigin);
        ClientDC.LineTo (m_PointOld);
        ClientDC.MoveTo (m_PointOrigin);
        ClientDC.LineTo (point);
        m_PointOld = point;
        }

    CView::OnMouseMove(nFlags, point);
}

void CServDemoView::OnLButtonUp(UINT nFlags, CPoint point)
{
    // TODO: Add your message handler code here and/or call default

    if (m_Dragging)
        {
        m_Dragging = 0;
        ::ReleaseCapture ();
        ::ClipCursor (NULL);
        CClientDC ClientDC (this);
        ClientDC.SetROP2 (R2_NOT);
        ClientDC.MoveTo (m_PointOrigin);
        ClientDC.LineTo (m_PointOld);
        ClientDC.SetROP2 (R2_COPYPEN);
        ClientDC.MoveTo (m_PointOrigin);
```

```
    ClientDC.LineTo (point);

    CServDemoDoc* PDoc = GetDocument();
    PDoc->AddLine (m_PointOrigin.x, m_PointOrigin.y, point.x,
        point.y);
    PDoc->UpdateAllItems (0);
    }

  CView::OnLButtonUp(nFlags, point);
}
```

Listing 24.9

```cpp
// IpFrame.h : interface of the CInPlaceFrame class
//

#if !defined(AFX_IPFRAME_H__03A2EC93_ABBE_11D1_80FC_00C0F6A83B7F__INCLUDED_)
#define AFX_IPFRAME_H__03A2EC93_ABBE_11D1_80FC_00C0F6A83B7F__INCLUDED_

#if _MSC_VER > 1000
#pragma once
#endif // _MSC_VER > 1000

class CInPlaceFrame : public COleIPFrameWnd
{
    DECLARE_DYNCREATE(CInPlaceFrame)
public:
    CInPlaceFrame();

// Attributes
public:

// Operations
public:

// Overrides
    // ClassWizard generated virtual function overrides
    //{{AFX_VIRTUAL(CInPlaceFrame)
    virtual BOOL PreCreateWindow(CREATESTRUCT& cs);
    //}}AFX_VIRTUAL

// Implementation
```

```
public:
   virtual ~CInPlaceFrame();
#ifdef _DEBUG
   virtual void AssertValid() const;
   virtual void Dump(CDumpContext& dc) const;
#endif

protected:
   COleDropTarget m_dropTarget;
   COleResizeBar  m_wndResizeBar;

// Generated message map functions
protected:
   //{{AFX_MSG(CInPlaceFrame)
   afx_msg int OnCreate(LPCREATESTRUCT lpCreateStruct);
      // NOTE - the ClassWizard will add and remove member functions here.
      //    DO NOT EDIT what you see in these blocks of generated code!
   //}}AFX_MSG
   DECLARE_MESSAGE_MAP()
};

/////////////////////////////////////////////////////////////////////////////

//{{AFX_INSERT_LOCATION}}
// Microsoft Visual C++ will insert additional declarations immediately before
// the previous line.

#endif
// !defined(AFX_IPFRAME_H__03A2EC93_ABBE_11D1_80FC_00C0F6A83B7F__INCLUDED_)
```

Listing 24.10

```
// IpFrame.cpp : implementation of the CInPlaceFrame class
//

#include "stdafx.h"
#include "ServDemo.h"

#include "IpFrame.h"

#ifdef _DEBUG
#define new DEBUG_NEW
```

```
#undef THIS_FILE
static char THIS_FILE[] = __FILE__;
#endif

/////////////////////////////////////////////////////////////////////////
// CInPlaceFrame

IMPLEMENT_DYNCREATE(CInPlaceFrame, COleIPFrameWnd)

BEGIN_MESSAGE_MAP(CInPlaceFrame, COleIPFrameWnd)
    //{{AFX_MSG_MAP(CInPlaceFrame)
    ON_WM_CREATE()
    //}}AFX_MSG_MAP
END_MESSAGE_MAP()

/////////////////////////////////////////////////////////////////////////
// CInPlaceFrame construction/destruction

CInPlaceFrame::CInPlaceFrame()
{
}

CInPlaceFrame::~CInPlaceFrame()
{
}

int CInPlaceFrame::OnCreate(LPCREATESTRUCT lpCreateStruct)
{
    if (COleIPFrameWnd::OnCreate(lpCreateStruct) == -1)
        return -1;

    // CResizeBar implements in-place resizing.
    if (!m_wndResizeBar.Create(this))
    {
        TRACE0("Failed to create resize bar\n");
        return -1;       // fail to create
    }

    // By default, it is a good idea to register a drop-target that does
    //  nothing with your frame window.  This prevents drops from
    //  "falling through" to a container that supports drag-drop.
    m_dropTarget.Register(this);
```

```
    return 0;
}

BOOL CInPlaceFrame::PreCreateWindow(CREATESTRUCT& cs)
{
    // TODO: Modify the Window class or styles here by modifying
    //   the CREATESTRUCT cs

    return COleIPFrameWnd::PreCreateWindow(cs);
}

///////////////////////////////////////////////////////////////////////
// CInPlaceFrame diagnostics

#ifdef _DEBUG
void CInPlaceFrame::AssertValid() const
{
    COleIPFrameWnd::AssertValid();
}

void CInPlaceFrame::Dump(CDumpContext& dc) const
{
    COleIPFrameWnd::Dump(dc);
}
#endif //_DEBUG

///////////////////////////////////////////////////////////////////////
// CInPlaceFrame commands
```

Listing 24.11

```
// SrvrItem.h : interface of the CServDemoSrvrItem class
//

#if !defined(AFX_SRVRITEM_H__03A2EC91_ABBE_11D1_80FC_00C0F6A83B7F__INCLUDED_)
#define AFX_SRVRITEM_H__03A2EC91_ABBE_11D1_80FC_00C0F6A83B7F__INCLUDED_

#if _MSC_VER > 1000
#pragma once
#endif // _MSC_VER > 1000

class CServDemoSrvrItem : public COleServerItem
{
```

```
   DECLARE_DYNAMIC(CServDemoSrvrItem)

// Constructors
public:
   CServDemoSrvrItem(CServDemoDoc* pContainerDoc);

// Attributes
   CServDemoDoc* GetDocument() const
      { return (CServDemoDoc*)COleServerItem::GetDocument(); }

// Overrides
   // ClassWizard generated virtual function overrides
   //{{AFX_VIRTUAL(CServDemoSrvrItem)
   public:
   virtual BOOL OnDraw(CDC* pDC, CSize& rSize);
   virtual BOOL OnGetExtent(DVASPECT dwDrawAspect, CSize& rSize);
   //}}AFX_VIRTUAL

// Implementation
public:
   ~CServDemoSrvrItem();
#ifdef _DEBUG
   virtual void AssertValid() const;
   virtual void Dump(CDumpContext& dc) const;
#endif

protected:
   virtual void Serialize(CArchive& ar);    // overridden for document i/o
};

/////////////////////////////////////////////////////////////////////////

//{{AFX_INSERT_LOCATION}}
// Microsoft Visual C++ will insert additional declarations immediately before
// the previous line.

#endif
// !defined(AFX_SRVRITEM_H__03A2EC91_ABBE_11D1_80FC_00C0F6A83B7F__INCLUDED_)
```

Listing 24.12

```
// SrvrItem.cpp : implementation of the CServDemoSrvrItem class
//
```

```
#include "stdafx.h"
#include "ServDemo.h"

#include "ServDemoDoc.h"
#include "SrvrItem.h"

#ifdef _DEBUG
#define new DEBUG_NEW
#undef THIS_FILE
static char THIS_FILE[] = __FILE__;
#endif

/////////////////////////////////////////////////////////////////////////////
// CServDemoSrvrItem implementation

IMPLEMENT_DYNAMIC(CServDemoSrvrItem, COleServerItem)

CServDemoSrvrItem::CServDemoSrvrItem(CServDemoDoc* pContainerDoc)
   : COleServerItem(pContainerDoc, TRUE)
{
   // TODO: add one-time construction code here
   //  (eg, adding additional clipboard formats to the item's data source)
}

CServDemoSrvrItem::~CServDemoSrvrItem()
{
   // TODO: add cleanup code here
}

void CServDemoSrvrItem::Serialize(CArchive& ar)
{
   // CServDemoSrvrItem::Serialize will be called by the framework if
   //  the item is copied to the clipboard.  This can happen automatically
   //  through the OLE callback OnGetClipboardData.  A good default for
   //  the embedded item is simply to delegate to the document's Serialize
   //  function.  If you support links, then you will want to serialize
   //  just a portion of the document.

   if (!IsLinkedItem())
   {
      CServDemoDoc* pDoc = GetDocument();
      ASSERT_VALID(pDoc);
      pDoc->Serialize(ar);
```

```
    }
}

BOOL CServDemoSrvrItem::OnGetExtent(DVASPECT dwDrawAspect, CSize& rSize)
{
    // Most applications, like this one, only handle drawing the content
    //  aspect of the item.  If you wish to support other aspects, such
    //  as DVASPECT_THUMBNAIL (by overriding OnDrawEx), then this
    //  implementation of OnGetExtent should be modified to handle the
    //  additional aspect(s).

    if (dwDrawAspect != DVASPECT_CONTENT)
        return COleServerItem::OnGetExtent(dwDrawAspect, rSize);

    // CServDemoSrvrItem::OnGetExtent is called to get the extent in
    //  HIMETRIC units of the entire item.  The default implementation
    //  here simply returns a hard-coded number of units.

    CServDemoDoc* pDoc = GetDocument();
    ASSERT_VALID(pDoc);

    // TODO: replace this arbitrary size

    rSize = CSize(3000, 3000);    // 3000 x 3000 HIMETRIC units

    return TRUE;
}

BOOL CServDemoSrvrItem::OnDraw(CDC* pDC, CSize& rSize)
{
    // Remove this if you use rSize
    UNREFERENCED_PARAMETER(rSize);

    CServDemoDoc* pDoc = GetDocument();
    ASSERT_VALID(pDoc);

    // TODO: set mapping mode and extent
    // (The extent is usually the same as the size returned from OnGetExtent)
    pDC->SetMapMode(MM_ANISOTROPIC);
    pDC->SetWindowOrg(0,0);

    // modify the AppWizard-generated call to SetWindowExt:
    pDC->SetWindowExt (pDoc->GetDocSize ());
```

```
    // TODO: add drawing code here.  Optionally, fill in the HIMETRIC extent.
    //  All drawing takes place in the metafile device context (pDC).

    // same code as in CServDemoView::OnDraw:
    int Index = pDoc->GetNumLines ();
    while (Index--)
        pDoc->GetLine (Index)->Draw (pDC);

    return TRUE;
}


/////////////////////////////////////////////////////////////////////////////
// CServDemoSrvrItem diagnostics

#ifdef _DEBUG
void CServDemoSrvrItem::AssertValid() const
{
    COleServerItem::AssertValid();
}

void CServDemoSrvrItem::Dump(CDumpContext& dc) const
{
    COleServerItem::Dump(dc);
}
#endif


/////////////////////////////////////////////////////////////////////////////
```

Creating a Container

You'll now use AppWizard to generate a simple OLE container program named ContDemo. You won't need to add any application-specific code, because the program as it's generated by AppWizard is adequate for testing the OLE server that you created previously in the chapter.

Create a new program using AppWizard, assigning it the name ContDemo. In the Projects tab of the New dialog box and the AppWizard Step 1 through Step 6 dialog boxes, you should make all the same choices that you made when generating WinGreet in Chapter 9, *except* that you should choose the Container option in the Step 3 dialog box, as shown in Figure 24.6.

FIGURE 24.6:

The completed AppWizard
Step 3 dialog box for generating the ContDemo OLE
container program

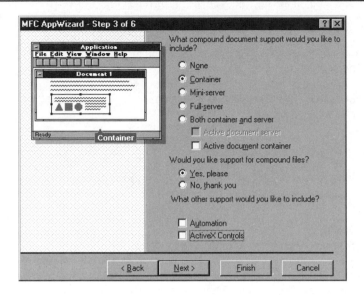

The following sections discuss the main changes that AppWizard makes to the usual program code in order to make ContDemo an OLE container. The chapter then describes how the program works and explains some of the features you might add to a full-featured container application.

The Application Class

As with a server application, AppWizard adds an `AfxOleInit` call to the `Init-Instance` member function of the ContDemo application class to initialize the MFC OLE libraries:

```
// Initialize OLE libraries
if (!AfxOleInit())
{
    AfxMessageBox(IDP_OLE_INIT_FAILED);
    return FALSE;
}
```

AppWizard also inserts a call to `CSingleDocTemplate::SetContainerInfo` into the `InitInstance` code after the document template has been created:

```
pDocTemplate->SetContainerInfo(IDR_CNTR_INPLACE);
```

The call to SetContainerInfo specifies the identifier of the menu—and accompanying accelerator resource—that ContDemo displays while an embedded OLE item is being edited in place. Recall that this menu is *merged* with the menu that the server program displays during in-place editing. (SetContainer-Info is similar to the SetServerInfo function that's called for a server, as described previously.)

The Document Class

The ContDemo document class is derived from the MFC class COleDocument rather than from the usual CDocument class. COleDocument provides the basic support required to manage documents in OLE container or server programs. (Recall that a server's document class is derived from COleServerDoc, which is derived indirectly from COleDocument).

The document object in an OLE container manages the storage of the embedded item or items, as well as the native document data (such as the text for a word processor program; note, however, that the ContDemo program stores only embedded items and *not* native data). As you'll see in the next section, the data for each embedded item is stored within an object of the CContDemoCntrItem class (derived from COleClientItem), which is managed by the document class.

At the end of the Serialize member function of the document class, App-Wizard adds a call to the COleDocument::Serialize function, which serializes the embedded items currently stored in the document (by calling the Serialize function of each CContDemoCntrItem that stores an embedded item):

```
void CContDemoDoc::Serialize(CArchive& ar)
{
    if (ar.IsStoring())
    {
        // TODO: add storing code here
    }
    else
    {
        // TODO: add loading code here
    }

    // Calling the base class COleDocument enables serialization
    //  of the container document's COleClientItem objects.
    COleDocument::Serialize(ar);
}
```

The Container Item Class

AppWizard creates a new class, CContDemoCntrItem, which is derived from the MFC COleClientItem class and is implemented in the files CntrItem.h and CntrItem.cpp. Whenever a new OLE item is embedded in the program, the view class (as described in the next section) creates an object of this class to store and manage the embedded item. Each CContDemoCntrItem object is associated with the document object, which maintains a list of these objects.

AppWizard provides overriding implementations of several of the virtual member functions of the COleClientItem class. The remainder of this section discusses those AppWizard-generated virtual functions that perform some action other than merely calling the base-class function version.

The CContDemoCntrItem::OnChange virtual function receives control whenever the server changes the item during in-place or fully-opened editing. The AppWizard-implemented version of this function calls the base-class version of this function, and then calls CDocument::UpdateAllViews (explained in Chapter 13) so the OnDraw member function of the view class will redraw the item:

```
void CContDemoCntrItem::OnChange(OLE_NOTIFICATION nCode,
    DWORD dwParam)
{
    ASSERT_VALID(this);

    COleClientItem::OnChange(nCode, dwParam);

    // When an item is being edited (either in-place or fully
    // open) it sends OnChange notifications for changes in the
    // state of the item or visual appearance of its content.

    // TODO: invalidate the item by calling UpdateAllViews
    //   (with hints appropriate to your application)

    GetDocument()->UpdateAllViews(NULL);
        // for now just update ALL views/no hints
}
```

Whenever an embedded item is edited in-place, the OLE code calls the CContDemoCntrItem::OnGetItemPosition virtual function to obtain the size and position of the item. This function must supply the current size and position of the embedded item in device units, relative to the client area of the container's view window. The AppWizard-generated implementation of this function simply supplies a constant size:

```
void CContDemoCntrItem::OnGetItemPosition(CRect& rPosition)
{
    ASSERT_VALID(this);

    // During in-place activation,
    // CContDemoCntrItem::OnGetItemPosition will be called to
    // determine the location of this item.  The default
    // implementation created from AppWizard simply returns a
    // hard-coded rectangle.  Usually, this rectangle would
    // reflect the current position of the item relative to the
    // view used for activation. You can obtain the view by
    // calling CContDemoCntrItem::GetActiveView.

    // TODO: return correct rectangle (in pixels) in rPosition

    rPosition.SetRect(10, 10, 210, 210);
}
```

A container program *must* implement OnGetItemPosition, because the base-class version does nothing.

Finally, the OnDeactivateUI function is called when the user deactivates the embedded item (in ContDemo, by pressing Esc). The AppWizard-generated function implementation calls the base-class version of this function and then calls COleClientItem::Deactivate to deactivate the embedded item and free the resources that it consumes:

```
void CContDemoCntrItem::OnDeactivateUI(BOOL bUndoable)
{
    COleClientItem::OnDeactivateUI(bUndoable);

    // Hide the object if it is not an outside-in object
    DWORD dwMisc = 0;
    m_lpObject->GetMiscStatus(GetDrawAspect(), &dwMisc);
    if (dwMisc & OLEMISC_INSIDEOUT)
        DoVerb(OLEIVERB_HIDE, NULL);
}
```

The View Class

AppWizard makes quite a few changes to the view class of an OLE container. This section discusses several of the important changes.

To begin, it defines a new public data member of the view class, m_pSelection:

```
CContDemoCntrItem* m_pSelection;
```

m_pSelection is initialized to NULL in CContDemoView::OnInitialUpdate, and whenever the user embeds an OLE item it's set to the address of the CContDemoCntrItem object that manages the new item (this is done in the CContDemoView::OnInsertObject function, described later). Thus, in ContDemo, m_pSelection always points to the most recently embedded item or equals NULL if no item has been embedded. In a full-featured container program, you'd normally use m_pSelection to point to the currently *selected* item or set it to NULL if no item is selected.

The AppWizard implementation of the CContDemoView::OnDraw function draws only the most recently embedded item, if any, by using the address in m_pSelection to call the COleClientItem::Draw function (this function draws the item by playing the metafile that was created by the server program, as explained previously). In a full-featured container program, OnDraw would typically draw *all* visible embedded items and the container's native data as well.

AppWizard adds a handler to the view class for the Insert New Object... command on the container program's Edit menu. This handler is named OnInsertObject and performs the following main actions:

- It displays the Insert Object common dialog box, which allows the user to choose a type of embedded item to insert.

- After the dialog box has been closed, it creates a CContDemoCntrItem object to manage the new embedded item. The CContDemoCntrItem constructor is passed the address of the program's document object.

- It initializes the CContDemoCntrItem object using information from the dialog box object, based on the choices the user made in the dialog box.

- It activates the item for in-place editing.

- It assigns m_pSelection the address of the CContDemoCntrItem object for the new embedded item.

AppWizard also adds to the view class a handler for the Esc key, which is one of the IDR_CNTR_INPLACE accelerator keystrokes that are in effect during in-place editing. This function is named OnCancelEditCntr, and it calls the COleClient-Item::Close function to inactivate the item undergoing in-place editing (if any). OnCancelEditCntr works in conjunction with the OnCancelEditSrvr member function of the server's view class, which was described previously.

The Resources

AppWizard includes the file Afxolecl.rc within the program resource file. Afxolecl.rc defines several resources used by the OLE container classes of the MFC.

AppWizard defines a separate menu and corresponding accelerator table for each of the two modes in which ContDemo can be run. The IDR_MAINFRAME menu and accelerator table are used when no embedded item is active. This menu contains the normal commands that AppWizard defines for a non-OLE program *plus* several commands on the Edit pop-up menu that are specific to an OLE container. The container-specific commands are Paste Special…, Insert New Object…, and Links…, plus a space for the Object submenu (initially labeled "<<OLE VERBS GO HERE>>"). Of the container-specific commands, the AppWizard code implements only the Insert New Object… command and the commands on the Object submenu.

The IDR_CNTR_INPLACE menu and accelerator table are used when an embedded item is being edited in place. The IDR_CNTR_INPLACE menu as it appears in the Visual C++ menu editor is shown in Figure 24.7. As described previously, during in-place editing the server's in-place menu is merged with the container's in-place menu. For example, if the ContDemo program contains an active embedded item generated by the ServDemo program, the merged menu would appear as shown in Figure 24.8 (the ServDemo in-place menu, as it appears in the menu editor, is shown in Figure 24.5).

NOTE   For some reason, the IDR_CNTR_INPLACE menu is initially displayed by the menu editor in the View As Popup mode, which displays the File pop-up menu and the two separators all on a single pop-up menu. To view the IDR_CNTR_INPLACE menu in the conventional mode, in which the items are displayed on a menu bar, right-click anywhere in the menu editor window and click the View As Popup option to deselect it.

FIGURE 24.7:

The ContDemo
IDR_CNTR_INPLACE
menu as it appears in the
Visual C++ menu editor

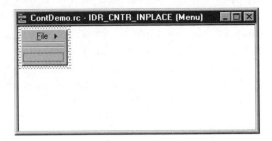

FIGURE 24.8:

The merged menu that
would be displayed during
in-place editing of a
ServDemo-created embed-
ded item within the Cont-
Demo program; the
separate menus, as they
appear in the Visual C++
menu editor, are shown in
Figures 24.5 and 24.7.

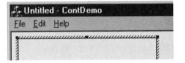

Building and Running ContDemo

You can now build and run the ContDemo program. If you haven't yet run
ServDemo in stand-alone mode, you should do so now, so that it will register
the ServeDemo object type. You can quit ServDemo; it doesn't need to be running
to embed an object in ContDemo.

After running ContDemo, embed an OLE item by choosing the Insert New
Object… command on the Edit menu. The program will now display the Insert
Object dialog box, which allows you to choose the type of item you want to
embed. The Object Type: list shows each of the item types that have been registered by the OLE server programs installed on your system. You can embed *any*
of these item types (an advantage of OLE is that a container can embed any available item type, present or future, without the need to understand the data).

For now, choose the ServDe Document item type, which is the item type registered by the ServDemo program, so that you can test both ContDemo and ServDemo. The completed Insert Object dialog box is shown in Figure 24.9.

FIGURE 24.9:

The completed Insert Object dialog box for inserting an embedded item created by the ServDemo program

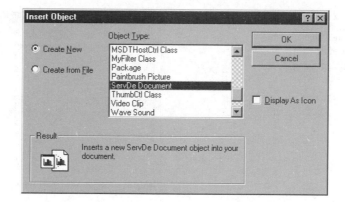

When you click the OK button in the Insert Object dialog box, a new, blank ServDemo item is embedded and is displayed in the upper-left corner of the container window. The item is automatically activated in-place—that is, the ServDemo program is run as a server in the in-place mode. Notice that Serv-Demo's in-place pop-up menus (the Edit and Help menus) are merged with ContDemo's in-place pop-up menu (File), so that you can choose the Serv-Demo drawing commands. Notice also that the item is surrounded by a border containing handles that allow you to change the size of the drawing (for now, leave the size unchanged). This border, as well as the view window inside of it, is created by the ServDemo program. If the server program had defined an in-place toolbar, it would also be displayed at this time (replacing any toolbar that the container displays).

NOTE

A full-featured server and container would also allow you to embed an item by copying a block of data from a document in the server and then issuing the Paste or Paste Special... command on the container's Edit menu, or by dragging the data from the server's window and dropping it on the container's window. ServDemo and ContDemo, however, *don't* support these methods of embedding.

Now use the mouse to draw a figure within the item. Notice that the ServDemo program displays a cross-shaped cursor when the cursor is within the item's view window. Figure 24.10 shows a completed drawing.

FIGURE 24.10:

Drawing a figure within a ServDemo embedded item, using ServDemo's drawing facilities

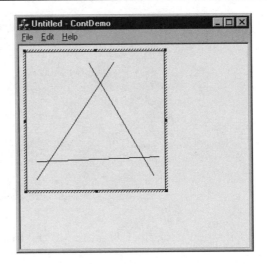

When you've finished drawing the figure, press Esc to deactivate the item (usually, a full-featured container would also allow you to deactivate the item by clicking in its view window outside the item). The ServDemo program will stop running, the menu bar will be restored to ContDemo's normal menu, and the inactive item will be displayed by ContDemo within its window. ContDemo doesn't draw a border around the inactive item, and the size of the inactive item remains fixed. (A full-featured container program would typically allow you to select an inactive embedded item by clicking within it; it would then surround the item with a border containing sizing handles that would allow you to change the item's size. Also, you'd usually be able to drag the entire item to a new location within the container document. Of course, in a full-featured container the embedded item or items would be displayed along with the native document data.)

Now reactivate the item in-place by opening the ServDe Object submenu on the Edit menu and choosing the Edit command. (Typically, a full-featured container program would also allow you to activate an item in-place by double-clicking within the item.) This time, use the sizing handles to increase the size of the drawing and add one or more lines to the newly exposed area of the drawing. When you press Esc to end the in-place editing session, notice that the lines within the drawing shrink in size. This happens because the inactive embedded item retains its original size in the container, and the larger drawing must be compressed to fit within this size.

Next, edit the item in the fully-opened mode by opening the ServDe Object submenu on the Edit menu, and choosing the Open command. This time, ServDemo runs and displays the item within a separate window. If the ContDemo program window is visible on your screen while you edit the drawing in ServDemo, you'll notice that any editing change you make in ServDemo is immediately shown in the representation of the drawing in ContDemo.

When you're done editing the item, choose the Exit & Return To Untitled command on the ServDemo File menu. The ServDemo window will now be closed and the edited inactive item will be displayed in ContDemo. (Note that when ServDemo is running in the fully opened mode, you can choose the Save Copy As... command on its File menu to save a *copy* of the embedded item as a ServDemo document on disk. To open this document, you'd have to run ServDemo as a stand-alone program.)

The ContDemo Source Code

The following listings, Listings 24.13 through 24.22, are the C++ source code for the ContDemo program. A copy of these files is contained in the \ContDemo companion-CD folder.

Listing 24.13

```
// ContDemo.h : main header file for the CONTDEMO application
//

#if !defined(AFX_CONTDEMO_H__726A17A5_AC7D_11D1_80FC_00C0F6A83B7F__INCLUDED_)
#define AFX_CONTDEMO_H__726A17A5_AC7D_11D1_80FC_00C0F6A83B7F__INCLUDED_

#if _MSC_VER > 1000
#pragma once
#endif // _MSC_VER > 1000

#ifndef __AFXWIN_H__
    #error include 'stdafx.h' before including this file for PCH
#endif
```

```
#include "resource.h"        // main symbols

/////////////////////////////////////////////////////////////////////
// CContDemoApp:
// See ContDemo.cpp for the implementation of this class
//

class CContDemoApp : public CWinApp
{
public:
    CContDemoApp();

// Overrides
    // ClassWizard generated virtual function overrides
    //{{AFX_VIRTUAL(CContDemoApp)
    public:
    virtual BOOL InitInstance();
    //}}AFX_VIRTUAL

// Implementation
    //{{AFX_MSG(CContDemoApp)
    afx_msg void OnAppAbout();
        // NOTE - the ClassWizard will add and remove member functions here.
        //    DO NOT EDIT what you see in these blocks of generated code !
    //}}AFX_MSG
    DECLARE_MESSAGE_MAP()
};


/////////////////////////////////////////////////////////////////////

//{{AFX_INSERT_LOCATION}}
// Microsoft Visual C++ will insert additional declarations immediately before
// the previous line.

#endif
// !defined(AFX_CONTDEMO_H__726A17A5_AC7D_11D1_80FC_00C0F6A83B7F__INCLUDED_)
```

Listing 24.14

```
// ContDemo.cpp : Defines the class behaviors for the application.
//
```

```
#include "stdafx.h"
#include "ContDemo.h"

#include "MainFrm.h"
#include "ContDemoDoc.h"
#include "ContDemoView.h"

#ifdef _DEBUG
#define new DEBUG_NEW
#undef THIS_FILE
static char THIS_FILE[] = __FILE__;
#endif

/////////////////////////////////////////////////////////////////////////////
// CContDemoApp

BEGIN_MESSAGE_MAP(CContDemoApp, CWinApp)
   //{{AFX_MSG_MAP(CContDemoApp)
   ON_COMMAND(ID_APP_ABOUT, OnAppAbout)
      // NOTE - the ClassWizard will add and remove mapping macros here.
      //    DO NOT EDIT what you see in these blocks of generated code!
   //}}AFX_MSG_MAP
   // Standard file based document commands
   ON_COMMAND(ID_FILE_NEW, CWinApp::OnFileNew)
   ON_COMMAND(ID_FILE_OPEN, CWinApp::OnFileOpen)
END_MESSAGE_MAP()

/////////////////////////////////////////////////////////////////////////////
// CContDemoApp construction

CContDemoApp::CContDemoApp()
{
   // TODO: add construction code here,
   // Place all significant initialization in InitInstance
}

/////////////////////////////////////////////////////////////////////////////
// The one and only CContDemoApp object

CContDemoApp theApp;

/////////////////////////////////////////////////////////////////////////////
// CContDemoApp initialization
```

```
BOOL CContDemoApp::InitInstance()
{
    // Initialize OLE libraries
    if (!AfxOleInit())
    {
        AfxMessageBox(IDP_OLE_INIT_FAILED);
        return FALSE;
    }

    // Standard initialization
    // If you are not using these features and wish to reduce the size
    //  of your final executable, you should remove from the following
    //  the specific initialization routines you do not need.

#ifdef _AFXDLL
    Enable3dControls();         // Call this when using MFC in a shared DLL
#else
    Enable3dControlsStatic();   // Call this when linking to MFC statically
#endif

    // Change the registry key under which our settings are stored.
    // TODO: You should modify this string to be something appropriate
    // such as the name of your company or organization.
    SetRegistryKey(_T("Local AppWizard-Generated Applications"));

    LoadStdProfileSettings();   // Load standard INI file options (including MRU)

    // Register the application's document templates.  Document templates
    //  serve as the connection between documents, frame windows and views.

    CSingleDocTemplate* pDocTemplate;
    pDocTemplate = new CSingleDocTemplate(
        IDR_MAINFRAME,
        RUNTIME_CLASS(CContDemoDoc),
        RUNTIME_CLASS(CMainFrame),       // main SDI frame window
        RUNTIME_CLASS(CContDemoView));
    pDocTemplate->SetContainerInfo(IDR_CNTR_INPLACE);
    AddDocTemplate(pDocTemplate);

    // Parse command line for standard shell commands, DDE, file open
    CCommandLineInfo cmdInfo;
    ParseCommandLine(cmdInfo);
```

```
    // Dispatch commands specified on the command line
    if (!ProcessShellCommand(cmdInfo))
        return FALSE;

    // The one and only window has been initialized, so show and update it.
    m_pMainWnd->ShowWindow(SW_SHOW);
    m_pMainWnd->UpdateWindow();

    return TRUE;
}


/////////////////////////////////////////////////////////////////////////////
// CAboutDlg dialog used for App About

class CAboutDlg : public CDialog
{
public:
    CAboutDlg();

// Dialog Data
    //{{AFX_DATA(CAboutDlg)
    enum { IDD = IDD_ABOUTBOX };
    //}}AFX_DATA

    // ClassWizard generated virtual function overrides
    //{{AFX_VIRTUAL(CAboutDlg)
    protected:
    virtual void DoDataExchange(CDataExchange* pDX);    // DDX/DDV support
    //}}AFX_VIRTUAL

// Implementation
protected:
    //{{AFX_MSG(CAboutDlg)
        // No message handlers
    //}}AFX_MSG
    DECLARE_MESSAGE_MAP()
};

CAboutDlg::CAboutDlg() : CDialog(CAboutDlg::IDD)
{
    //{{AFX_DATA_INIT(CAboutDlg)
    //}}AFX_DATA_INIT
```

```
}

void CAboutDlg::DoDataExchange(CDataExchange* pDX)
{
    CDialog::DoDataExchange(pDX);
    //{{AFX_DATA_MAP(CAboutDlg)
    //}}AFX_DATA_MAP
}

BEGIN_MESSAGE_MAP(CAboutDlg, CDialog)
    //{{AFX_MSG_MAP(CAboutDlg)
        // No message handlers
    //}}AFX_MSG_MAP
END_MESSAGE_MAP()

// App command to run the dialog
void CContDemoApp::OnAppAbout()
{
    CAboutDlg aboutDlg;
    aboutDlg.DoModal();
}

/////////////////////////////////////////////////////////////////////////
// CContDemoApp message handlers
```

Listing 24.15

```
// ContDemoDoc.h : interface of the CContDemoDoc class
//
/////////////////////////////////////////////////////////////////////////

#if !defined(AFX_CONTDEMODOC_H__726A17AB_AC7D_11D1_80FC_00C0F6A83B7F__INCLUDED_)
#define AFX_CONTDEMODOC_H__726A17AB_AC7D_11D1_80FC_00C0F6A83B7F__INCLUDED_

#if _MSC_VER > 1000
#pragma once
#endif // _MSC_VER > 1000


class CContDemoDoc : public COleDocument
{
protected: // create from serialization only
    CContDemoDoc();
```

```
    DECLARE_DYNCREATE(CContDemoDoc)

// Attributes
public:

// Operations
public:

// Overrides
    // ClassWizard generated virtual function overrides
    //{{AFX_VIRTUAL(CContDemoDoc)
    public:
    virtual BOOL OnNewDocument();
    virtual void Serialize(CArchive& ar);
    //}}AFX_VIRTUAL

// Implementation
public:
    virtual ~CContDemoDoc();
#ifdef _DEBUG
    virtual void AssertValid() const;
    virtual void Dump(CDumpContext& dc) const;
#endif

protected:

// Generated message map functions
protected:
    //{{AFX_MSG(CContDemoDoc)
        // NOTE - the ClassWizard will add and remove member functions here.
        //      DO NOT EDIT what you see in these blocks of generated code !
    //}}AFX_MSG
    DECLARE_MESSAGE_MAP()
};

/////////////////////////////////////////////////////////////////////////////

//{{AFX_INSERT_LOCATION}}
// Microsoft Visual C++ will insert additional declarations immediately before
// the previous line.

#endif
// !defined(AFX_CONTDEMODOC_H__726A17AB_AC7D_11D1_80FC_00C0F6A83B7F__INCLUDED_)
```

Listing 24.16

```cpp
// ContDemoDoc.cpp : implementation of the CContDemoDoc class
//

#include "stdafx.h"
#include "ContDemo.h"

#include "ContDemoDoc.h"
#include "CntrItem.h"

#ifdef _DEBUG
#define new DEBUG_NEW
#undef THIS_FILE
static char THIS_FILE[] = __FILE__;
#endif

/////////////////////////////////////////////////////////////////////////////
// CContDemoDoc

IMPLEMENT_DYNCREATE(CContDemoDoc, COleDocument)

BEGIN_MESSAGE_MAP(CContDemoDoc, COleDocument)
    //{{AFX_MSG_MAP(CContDemoDoc)
        // NOTE - the ClassWizard will add and remove mapping macros here.
        //    DO NOT EDIT what you see in these blocks of generated code!
    //}}AFX_MSG_MAP
    // Enable default OLE container implementation
    ON_UPDATE_COMMAND_UI(ID_EDIT_PASTE, COleDocument::OnUpdatePasteMenu)
    ON_UPDATE_COMMAND_UI(ID_EDIT_PASTE_LINK, COleDocument::OnUpdatePasteLinkMenu)
    ON_UPDATE_COMMAND_UI(ID_OLE_EDIT_CONVERT, COleDocument::OnUpdateObjectVerbMenu)
    ON_COMMAND(ID_OLE_EDIT_CONVERT, COleDocument::OnEditConvert)
    ON_UPDATE_COMMAND_UI(ID_OLE_EDIT_LINKS, COleDocument::OnUpdateEditLinksMenu)
    ON_COMMAND(ID_OLE_EDIT_LINKS, COleDocument::OnEditLinks)
    ON_UPDATE_COMMAND_UI_RANGE(ID_OLE_VERB_FIRST, ID_OLE_VERB_LAST, COleDocument::OnUpdateObjectVerbMenu)
END_MESSAGE_MAP()

/////////////////////////////////////////////////////////////////////////////
// CContDemoDoc construction/destruction

CContDemoDoc::CContDemoDoc()
```

```
{
    // Use OLE compound files
    EnableCompoundFile();

    // TODO: add one-time construction code here

}

CContDemoDoc::~CContDemoDoc()
{
}

BOOL CContDemoDoc::OnNewDocument()
{
    if (!COleDocument::OnNewDocument())
        return FALSE;

    // TODO: add reinitialization code here
    // (SDI documents will reuse this document)

    return TRUE;
}



/////////////////////////////////////////////////////////////////////////
// CContDemoDoc serialization

void CContDemoDoc::Serialize(CArchive& ar)
{
    if (ar.IsStoring())
    {
        // TODO: add storing code here
    }
    else
    {
        // TODO: add loading code here
    }

    // Calling the base class COleDocument enables serialization
    //  of the container document's COleClientItem objects.
    COleDocument::Serialize(ar);
```

```
}

///////////////////////////////////////////////////////////////////////
// CContDemoDoc diagnostics

#ifdef _DEBUG
void CContDemoDoc::AssertValid() const
{
    COleDocument::AssertValid();
}

void CContDemoDoc::Dump(CDumpContext& dc) const
{
    COleDocument::Dump(dc);
}
#endif //_DEBUG


///////////////////////////////////////////////////////////////////////
// CContDemoDoc commands
```

Listing 24.17

```
// MainFrm.h : interface of the CMainFrame class
//
///////////////////////////////////////////////////////////////////////

#if !defined(AFX_MAINFRM_H__726A17A9_AC7D_11D1_80FC_00C0F6A83B7F__INCLUDED_)
#define AFX_MAINFRM_H__726A17A9_AC7D_11D1_80FC_00C0F6A83B7F__INCLUDED_

#if _MSC_VER > 1000
#pragma once
#endif // _MSC_VER > 1000

class CMainFrame : public CFrameWnd
{

protected: // create from serialization only
    CMainFrame();
    DECLARE_DYNCREATE(CMainFrame)

// Attributes
public:
```

```
// Operations
public:

// Overrides
    // ClassWizard generated virtual function overrides
    //{{AFX_VIRTUAL(CMainFrame)
    virtual BOOL PreCreateWindow(CREATESTRUCT& cs);
    //}}AFX_VIRTUAL

// Implementation
public:
    virtual ~CMainFrame();
#ifdef _DEBUG
    virtual void AssertValid() const;
    virtual void Dump(CDumpContext& dc) const;
#endif

// Generated message map functions
protected:
    //{{AFX_MSG(CMainFrame)
        // NOTE - the ClassWizard will add and remove member functions here.
        //      DO NOT EDIT what you see in these blocks of generated code!
    //}}AFX_MSG
    DECLARE_MESSAGE_MAP()
};

///////////////////////////////////////////////////////////////////////

//{{AFX_INSERT_LOCATION}}
// Microsoft Visual C++ will insert additional declarations immediately before
// the previous line.

#endif
// !defined(AFX_MAINFRM_H__726A17A9_AC7D_11D1_80FC_00C0F6A83B7F__INCLUDED_)
```

Listing 24.18

```
// MainFrm.cpp : implementation of the CMainFrame class
//

#include "stdafx.h"
#include "ContDemo.h"
```

```
#include "MainFrm.h"

#ifdef _DEBUG
#define new DEBUG_NEW
#undef THIS_FILE
static char THIS_FILE[] = __FILE__;
#endif

/////////////////////////////////////////////////////////////////////////
// CMainFrame

IMPLEMENT_DYNCREATE(CMainFrame, CFrameWnd)

BEGIN_MESSAGE_MAP(CMainFrame, CFrameWnd)
   //{{AFX_MSG_MAP(CMainFrame)
      // NOTE - the ClassWizard will add and remove mapping macros here.
      //    DO NOT EDIT what you see in these blocks of generated code !
   //}}AFX_MSG_MAP
END_MESSAGE_MAP()

/////////////////////////////////////////////////////////////////////////
// CMainFrame construction/destruction

CMainFrame::CMainFrame()
{
   // TODO: add member initialization code here

}

CMainFrame::~CMainFrame()
{
}

BOOL CMainFrame::PreCreateWindow(CREATESTRUCT& cs)
{
   if( !CFrameWnd::PreCreateWindow(cs) )
      return FALSE;
   // TODO: Modify the Window class or styles here by modifying
   //   the CREATESTRUCT cs

   return TRUE;
}
```

```
/////////////////////////////////////////////////////////////////////////
// CMainFrame diagnostics

#ifdef _DEBUG
void CMainFrame::AssertValid() const
{
    CFrameWnd::AssertValid();
}

void CMainFrame::Dump(CDumpContext& dc) const
{
    CFrameWnd::Dump(dc);
}

#endif //_DEBUG


/////////////////////////////////////////////////////////////////////////
// CMainFrame message handlers
```

Listing 24.19

```
// ContDemoView.h : interface of the CContDemoView class
//
/////////////////////////////////////////////////////////////////////////

#if !defined(AFX_CONTDEMOVIEW_H__726A17AD_AC7D_11D1_80FC_00C0F6A83B7F__INCLUDED_)
#define AFX_CONTDEMOVIEW_H__726A17AD_AC7D_11D1_80FC_00C0F6A83B7F__INCLUDED_

#if _MSC_VER > 1000
#pragma once
#endif // _MSC_VER > 1000

class CContDemoCntrItem;

class CContDemoView : public CView
{
protected: // create from serialization only
    CContDemoView();
    DECLARE_DYNCREATE(CContDemoView)

// Attributes
public:
    CContDemoDoc* GetDocument();
```

```
    // m_pSelection holds the selection to the current CContDemoCntrItem.
    // For many applications, such a member variable isn't adequate to
    //  represent a selection, such as a multiple selection or a selection
    //  of objects that are not CContDemoCntrItem objects.  This selection
    //  mechanism is provided just to help you get started.

    // TODO: replace this selection mechanism with one appropriate to your app.
    CContDemoCntrItem* m_pSelection;

// Operations
public:

// Overrides
    // ClassWizard generated virtual function overrides
    //{{AFX_VIRTUAL(CContDemoView)
    public:
    virtual void OnDraw(CDC* pDC);  // overridden to draw this view
    virtual BOOL PreCreateWindow(CREATESTRUCT& cs);
    protected:
    virtual void OnInitialUpdate(); // called first time after construct
    virtual BOOL IsSelected(const CObject* pDocItem) const;// Container support
    //}}AFX_VIRTUAL

// Implementation
public:
    virtual ~CContDemoView();
#ifdef _DEBUG
    virtual void AssertValid() const;
    virtual void Dump(CDumpContext& dc) const;
#endif

protected:

// Generated message map functions
protected:
    //{{AFX_MSG(CContDemoView)
        // NOTE - the ClassWizard will add and remove member functions here.
        //    DO NOT EDIT what you see in these blocks of generated code !
    afx_msg void OnDestroy();
    afx_msg void OnSetFocus(CWnd* pOldWnd);
    afx_msg void OnSize(UINT nType, int cx, int cy);
    afx_msg void OnInsertObject();
    afx_msg void OnCancelEditCntr();
```

```
   //}}AFX_MSG
   DECLARE_MESSAGE_MAP()
};

#ifndef _DEBUG  // debug version in ContDemoView.cpp
inline CContDemoDoc* CContDemoView::GetDocument()
   { return (CContDemoDoc*)m_pDocument; }
#endif

/////////////////////////////////////////////////////////////////////////////

//{{AFX_INSERT_LOCATION}}
// Microsoft Visual C++ will insert additional declarations immediately before
// the previous line.

#endif
// !defined(AFX_CONTDEMOVIEW_H__726A17AD_AC7D_11D1_80FC_00C0F6A83B7F__INCLUDED_)
```

Listing 24.20

```
// ContDemoView.cpp : implementation of the CContDemoView class
//

#include "stdafx.h"
#include "ContDemo.h"

#include "ContDemoDoc.h"
#include "CntrItem.h"
#include "ContDemoView.h"

#ifdef _DEBUG
#define new DEBUG_NEW
#undef THIS_FILE
static char THIS_FILE[] = __FILE__;
#endif

/////////////////////////////////////////////////////////////////////////////
// CContDemoView

IMPLEMENT_DYNCREATE(CContDemoView, CView)

BEGIN_MESSAGE_MAP(CContDemoView, CView)
   //{{AFX_MSG_MAP(CContDemoView)
```

```
        // NOTE - the ClassWizard will add and remove mapping macros here.
        //    DO NOT EDIT what you see in these blocks of generated code!
    ON_WM_DESTROY()
    ON_WM_SETFOCUS()
    ON_WM_SIZE()
    ON_COMMAND(ID_OLE_INSERT_NEW, OnInsertObject)
    ON_COMMAND(ID_CANCEL_EDIT_CNTR, OnCancelEditCntr)
    //}}AFX_MSG_MAP
END_MESSAGE_MAP()


/////////////////////////////////////////////////////////////////////////////
// CContDemoView construction/destruction

CContDemoView::CContDemoView()
{
    m_pSelection = NULL;
    // TODO: add construction code here

}


CContDemoView::~CContDemoView()
{
}

BOOL CContDemoView::PreCreateWindow(CREATESTRUCT& cs)
{
    // TODO: Modify the Window class or styles here by modifying
    //   the CREATESTRUCT cs

    return CView::PreCreateWindow(cs);
}


/////////////////////////////////////////////////////////////////////////////
// CContDemoView drawing

void CContDemoView::OnDraw(CDC* pDC)
{
    CContDemoDoc* pDoc = GetDocument();
    ASSERT_VALID(pDoc);

    // TODO: add draw code for native data here
    // TODO: also draw all OLE items in the document
```

```
   // Draw the selection at an arbitrary position.  This code should be
   //  removed once your real drawing code is implemented.  This position
   //  corresponds exactly to the rectangle returned by CContDemoCntrItem,
   //  to give the effect of in-place editing.

   // TODO: remove this code when final draw code is complete.

   if (m_pSelection == NULL)
   {
      POSITION pos = pDoc->GetStartPosition();
      m_pSelection = (CContDemoCntrItem*)pDoc->GetNextClientItem(pos);
   }
   if (m_pSelection != NULL)
      m_pSelection->Draw(pDC, CRect(10, 10, 210, 210));
}

void CContDemoView::OnInitialUpdate()
{
   CView::OnInitialUpdate();


   // TODO: remove this code when final selection model code is written
   m_pSelection = NULL;     // initialize selection

}

void CContDemoView::OnDestroy()
{
   // Deactivate the item on destruction; this is important
   // when a splitter view is being used.
   CView::OnDestroy();
   COleClientItem* pActiveItem = GetDocument()->GetInPlaceActiveItem(this);
   if (pActiveItem != NULL && pActiveItem->GetActiveView() == this)
   {
      pActiveItem->Deactivate();
      ASSERT(GetDocument()->GetInPlaceActiveItem(this) == NULL);
   }
}


/////////////////////////////////////////////////////////////////////////////
// OLE Client support and commands
```

```
BOOL CContDemoView::IsSelected(const CObject* pDocItem) const
{
    // The implementation below is adequate if your selection consists of
    //   only CContDemoCntrItem objects.  To handle different selection
    //   mechanisms, the implementation here should be replaced.

    // TODO: implement this function that tests for a selected OLE client item

    return pDocItem == m_pSelection;
}

void CContDemoView::OnInsertObject()
{
    // Invoke the standard Insert Object dialog box to obtain information
    //   for new CContDemoCntrItem object.
    COleInsertDialog dlg;
    if (dlg.DoModal() != IDOK)
        return;

    BeginWaitCursor();

    CContDemoCntrItem* pItem = NULL;
    TRY
    {
        // Create new item connected to this document.
        CContDemoDoc* pDoc = GetDocument();
        ASSERT_VALID(pDoc);
        pItem = new CContDemoCntrItem(pDoc);
        ASSERT_VALID(pItem);

        // Initialize the item from the dialog data.
        if (!dlg.CreateItem(pItem))
            AfxThrowMemoryException();  // any exception will do
        ASSERT_VALID(pItem);

        // If item created from class list (not from file) then launch
        //   the server to edit the item.
        if (dlg.GetSelectionType() == COleInsertDialog::createNewItem)
            pItem->DoVerb(OLEIVERB_SHOW, this);

        ASSERT_VALID(pItem);

        // As an arbitrary user interface design, this sets the selection
```

```
        //  to the last item inserted.

        // TODO: reimplement selection as appropriate for your application

        m_pSelection = pItem;    // set selection to last inserted item
        pDoc->UpdateAllViews(NULL);
    }
    CATCH(CException, e)
    {
        if (pItem != NULL)
        {
            ASSERT_VALID(pItem);
            pItem->Delete();
        }
        AfxMessageBox(IDP_FAILED_TO_CREATE);
    }
    END_CATCH

    EndWaitCursor();
}


// The following command handler provides the standard keyboard
//  user interface to cancel an in-place editing session.  Here,
//  the container (not the server) causes the deactivation.
void CContDemoView::OnCancelEditCntr()
{
    // Close any in-place active item on this view.
    COleClientItem* pActiveItem = GetDocument()->GetInPlaceActiveItem(this);
    if (pActiveItem != NULL)
    {
        pActiveItem->Close();
    }
    ASSERT(GetDocument()->GetInPlaceActiveItem(this) == NULL);
}


// Special handling of OnSetFocus and OnSize are required for a container
//  when an object is being edited in-place.
void CContDemoView::OnSetFocus(CWnd* pOldWnd)
{
    COleClientItem* pActiveItem = GetDocument()->GetInPlaceActiveItem(this);
    if (pActiveItem != NULL &&
        pActiveItem->GetItemState() == COleClientItem::activeUIState)
    {
```

```
        // need to set focus to this item if it is in the same view
        CWnd* pWnd = pActiveItem->GetInPlaceWindow();
        if (pWnd != NULL)
        {
            pWnd->SetFocus();   // don't call the base class
            return;
        }
    }

    CView::OnSetFocus(pOldWnd);
}

void CContDemoView::OnSize(UINT nType, int cx, int cy)
{
    CView::OnSize(nType, cx, cy);
    COleClientItem* pActiveItem = GetDocument()->GetInPlaceActiveItem(this);
    if (pActiveItem != NULL)
        pActiveItem->SetItemRects();
}

/////////////////////////////////////////////////////////////////////////////
// CContDemoView diagnostics

#ifdef _DEBUG
void CContDemoView::AssertValid() const
{
    CView::AssertValid();
}

void CContDemoView::Dump(CDumpContext& dc) const
{
    CView::Dump(dc);
}

CContDemoDoc* CContDemoView::GetDocument() // non-debug version is inline
{
    ASSERT(m_pDocument->IsKindOf(RUNTIME_CLASS(CContDemoDoc)));
    return (CContDemoDoc*)m_pDocument;
}
#endif //_DEBUG

/////////////////////////////////////////////////////////////////////////////
// CContDemoView message handlers
```

Listing 24.21

```
// CntrItem.h : interface of the CContDemoCntrItem class
//

#if !defined(AFX_CNTRITEM_H__726A17AF_AC7D_11D1_80FC_00C0F6A83B7F__INCLUDED_)
#define AFX_CNTRITEM_H__726A17AF_AC7D_11D1_80FC_00C0F6A83B7F__INCLUDED_

#if _MSC_VER > 1000
#pragma once
#endif // _MSC_VER > 1000

class CContDemoDoc;
class CContDemoView;

class CContDemoCntrItem : public COleClientItem
{
    DECLARE_SERIAL(CContDemoCntrItem)

// Constructors
public:
    CContDemoCntrItem(CContDemoDoc* pContainer = NULL);
        // Note: pContainer is allowed to be NULL to enable IMPLEMENT_SERIALIZE.
        //  IMPLEMENT_SERIALIZE requires the class have a constructor with
        //  zero arguments.  Normally, OLE items are constructed with a
        //  non-NULL document pointer.

// Attributes
public:
    CContDemoDoc* GetDocument()
        { return (CContDemoDoc*)COleClientItem::GetDocument(); }
    CContDemoView* GetActiveView()
        { return (CContDemoView*)COleClientItem::GetActiveView(); }

    // ClassWizard generated virtual function overrides
    //{{AFX_VIRTUAL(CContDemoCntrItem)
    public:
    virtual void OnChange(OLE_NOTIFICATION wNotification, DWORD dwParam);
    virtual void OnActivate();
    protected:
    virtual void OnGetItemPosition(CRect& rPosition);
    virtual void OnDeactivateUI(BOOL bUndoable);
    virtual BOOL OnChangeItemPosition(const CRect& rectPos);
    //}}AFX_VIRTUAL
```

```
// Implementation
public:
    ~CContDemoCntrItem();
#ifdef _DEBUG
    virtual void AssertValid() const;
    virtual void Dump(CDumpContext& dc) const;
#endif
    virtual void Serialize(CArchive& ar);
};


//////////////////////////////////////////////////////////////////////////

//{{AFX_INSERT_LOCATION}}
// Microsoft Visual C++ will insert additional declarations immediately before
// the previous line.

#endif
// !defined(AFX_CNTRITEM_H__726A17AF_AC7D_11D1_80FC_00C0F6A83B7F__INCLUDED_)
```

Listing 24.22

```
// CntrItem.cpp : implementation of the CContDemoCntrItem class
//

#include "stdafx.h"
#include "ContDemo.h"

#include "ContDemoDoc.h"
#include "ContDemoView.h"
#include "CntrItem.h"

#ifdef _DEBUG
#define new DEBUG_NEW
#undef THIS_FILE
static char THIS_FILE[] = __FILE__;
#endif

//////////////////////////////////////////////////////////////////////////
// CContDemoCntrItem implementation

IMPLEMENT_SERIAL(CContDemoCntrItem, COleClientItem, 0)

CContDemoCntrItem::CContDemoCntrItem(CContDemoDoc* pContainer)
```

```
    : COleClientItem(pContainer)
{
    // TODO: add one-time construction code here

}

CContDemoCntrItem::~CContDemoCntrItem()
{
    // TODO: add cleanup code here

}

void CContDemoCntrItem::OnChange(OLE_NOTIFICATION nCode, DWORD dwParam)
{
    ASSERT_VALID(this);

    COleClientItem::OnChange(nCode, dwParam);

    // When an item is being edited (either in-place or fully open)
    //  it sends OnChange notifications for changes in the state of the
    //  item or visual appearance of its content.

    // TODO: invalidate the item by calling UpdateAllViews
    //  (with hints appropriate to your application)

    GetDocument()->UpdateAllViews(NULL);
        // for now just update ALL views/no hints
}

BOOL CContDemoCntrItem::OnChangeItemPosition(const CRect& rectPos)
{
    ASSERT_VALID(this);

    // During in-place activation CContDemoCntrItem::OnChangeItemPosition
    //  is called by the server to change the position of the in-place
    //  window.  Usually, this is a result of the data in the server
    //  document changing such that the extent has changed or as a result
    //  of in-place resizing.
    //
    // The default here is to call the base class, which will call
    //  COleClientItem::SetItemRects to move the item
    //  to the new position.
```

```
    if (!COleClientItem::OnChangeItemPosition(rectPos))
       return FALSE;

    // TODO: update any cache you may have of the item's rectangle/extent

    return TRUE;
}


void CContDemoCntrItem::OnGetItemPosition(CRect& rPosition)
{
    ASSERT_VALID(this);

    // During in-place activation, CContDemoCntrItem::OnGetItemPosition
    //  will be called to determine the location of this item.  The default
    //  implementation created from AppWizard simply returns a hard-coded
    //  rectangle.  Usually, this rectangle would reflect the current
    //  position of the item relative to the view used for activation.
    //  You can obtain the view by calling CContDemoCntrItem::GetActiveView.

    // TODO: return correct rectangle (in pixels) in rPosition

    rPosition.SetRect(10, 10, 210, 210);
}


void CContDemoCntrItem::OnActivate()
{
    // Allow only one inplace activate item per frame
    CContDemoView* pView = GetActiveView();
    ASSERT_VALID(pView);
    COleClientItem* pItem = GetDocument()->GetInPlaceActiveItem(pView);
    if (pItem != NULL && pItem != this)
        pItem->Close();

    COleClientItem::OnActivate();
}


void CContDemoCntrItem::OnDeactivateUI(BOOL bUndoable)
{
    COleClientItem::OnDeactivateUI(bUndoable);

    // Hide the object if it is not an outside-in object
    DWORD dwMisc = 0;
    m_lpObject->GetMiscStatus(GetDrawAspect(), &dwMisc);
```

```cpp
    if (dwMisc & OLEMISC_INSIDEOUT)
        DoVerb(OLEIVERB_HIDE, NULL);
}

void CContDemoCntrItem::Serialize(CArchive& ar)
{
    ASSERT_VALID(this);

    // Call base class first to read in COleClientItem data.
    // Since this sets up the m_pDocument pointer returned from
    //  CContDemoCntrItem::GetDocument, it is a good idea to call
    //  the base class Serialize first.
    COleClientItem::Serialize(ar);

    // now store/retrieve data specific to CContDemoCntrItem
    if (ar.IsStoring())
    {
        // TODO: add storing code here
    }
    else
    {
        // TODO: add loading code here
    }
}

/////////////////////////////////////////////////////////////////////////////
// CContDemoCntrItem diagnostics

#ifdef _DEBUG
void CContDemoCntrItem::AssertValid() const
{
    COleClientItem::AssertValid();
}

void CContDemoCntrItem::Dump(CDumpContext& dc) const
{
    COleClientItem::Dump(dc);
}
#endif

/////////////////////////////////////////////////////////////////////////////
```

Summary

This chapter provided a concise introduction to programming and using some of the basic mechanisms provided by OLE. The following is a summary of the facts and techniques that were discussed:

- OLE, which stands for *object linking and embedding,* is a versatile set of mechanisms that allow a program to incorporate into its documents data from a wide variety of other programs and also to use the facilities of other programs.

- An OLE *server* is a program that creates, provides, and edits blocks of OLE data known as *objects* or *items*. An OLE *container* is a program that receives OLE items and inserts them into its documents.

- In OLE *embedding* the container stores the data for an OLE item as an integral part of the container document in which it has inserted the item. In OLE *linking* the server stores the data for an OLE item as part of a server document.

- With both embedding and linking, the server and the OLE libraries are responsible for displaying and editing the data. With embedding, the document can be edited within the container's window (*in-place* editing), or within the server's window (*fully-opened* editing). With linking, the document can only be edited in the fully-opened mode.

- *Automation* is a mechanism related to OLE that allows an *automation client* program to control and use facilities provided by an *automation server* program.

- The MFC and Visual C++ Wizards allow you to create programs using OLE embedding, linking, and automation.

- To create the basic source code for an OLE server, generate the program with AppWizard, and in the Step 3 dialog box choose the Full-Server, Mini-Server, or Both Container And Server option.

- The Full-Server option generates a program that can run as a stand-alone application or as an OLE server for embedded or linked items. The Mini-Server option generates a program that can run only as a server for creating or editing embedded items. The Both Container And Server option generates a program that can function *both* as a full OLE server *and* as an OLE container.

- When you choose the Full-Server option, AppWizard generates two additional program classes for managing the OLE item and the border that surrounds the item during in-place editing. It also adds to the standard program classes much of the code required for an OLE server.

- When creating a server, you typically add application-specific code to enhance the OLE features of the program, as well as code for implementing the program's native capabilities (such as drawing for a drawing program).

- To create the basic source code for an OLE container, generate the program with AppWizard, and in the Step 3 dialog box choose either the Container or the Both Container And Server option.

- When generating a container, AppWizard creates a new class to manage embedded or linked items, and also makes many changes to the standard program classes.

- As with a server, you must then add code to enhance the OLE capabilities of a container program, as well as the code to create, edit, and save documents.

Creating and Using ActiveX Controls

- Creating an ActiveX control

- Creating an ActiveX control container program

An ActiveX control is a portable software module that performs a specific task or set of tasks. For example, an ActiveX control might display a calendar, run a multimedia presentation, generate a chart, conduct an Internet chat session, or serve as a form for reading and writing information in a database. ActiveX controls are similar to the standard Windows controls—such as push buttons and list boxes—that you can display in dialog boxes and other windows. However, you can create ActiveX controls yourself, download them from the Internet, or obtain them from other sources. And they can perform a virtually unlimited variety of functions.

NOTE   ActiveX controls were formerly known as OLE *controls* or *OCXs* (because of the .ocx extension on the file used to store an ActiveX control). Many old-timers still call them OCXs.

The code and resources for an ActiveX control are stored in a single file, which has the .ocx extension. Once you develop or obtain an ActiveX control, you can incorporate it in a Visual C++ program, in a Visual Basic program, in a Visual J++ program, in a Web page on the Internet or an intranet, in an Access database application, or in any program that has been written as an ActiveX control container.

The beauty of an ActiveX control is that you can "plug" it into any container application regardless of the computer language used for that application, and yet the container can interact intimately with the control almost as if it were a part of its own code. ActiveX controls provide three primary mechanisms for interacting with container applications: properties, methods, and events. A *property* is an attribute of the control, such as its background color, that the container can read or modify. A *method* is a function provided by the control that the container can call; a method, for example, might display an About dialog box giving information on the control. An *event* is an occurrence within the control, such as the user's clicking the control, that causes the control to notify the container (the control does this by calling a function within the container that has been designated to handle the specific event).

This chapter provides a brief introduction to the world of ActiveX controls—a topic that could easily fill several volumes. In the first part of the chapter, you'll create a simple ActiveX control, which demonstrates the basic techniques for defining properties, methods, and events. In the second part of the chapter, you'll create a custom ActiveX control container application that's designed specifically for displaying and manipulating the ActiveX control you created in the first part.

> **NOTE**
> For more detailed information on ActiveX controls, see the Visual C++ online help topic: *Visual C++ Documentation, Using Visual C++, Visual C++ Programmer's Guide, Adding User Interface Features, Overviews, ActiveX Controls: Overview.*

Creating an ActiveX Control

In this part of the chapter, you'll create a simple ActiveX control named AXCtrl, which displays a picture. When the user clicks the control, it switches between two versions of the picture (analogous to the way a standard control such as a check box changes its state when it's clicked).

The control provides properties that allow the container to change the control's background color (the color of the picture "mat"), and to add or remove the frame around the picture. The control provides a method that the container can call to display an About dialog box showing information on the control. And the control defines an event that notifies the container each time the user clicks the control. If you can't wait to see what the control looks like, go to Figure 25.15 (near the end of the chapter), which shows the control within a container application.

Generating the Source Code Files

To generate the source code files for the AXCtrl ActiveX control, perform the following steps:

1. Choose the File ➤ New… menu command in Visual C++ and open the Projects tab in the New dialog box.

2. In the list of project types, select the MFC ActiveX ControlWizard item.

3. Enter AXCtrl into the Project Name: text box, and enter the path of the folder where you want to store the project files into the Location: text box.

4. Make sure that the Create New Workspace option and the Win32 platform are both selected.

5. Click the OK button. Visual C++ will now run the ControlWizard, which displays two dialog boxes that let you select options and then generates the source code files for the ActiveX control. ControlWizard is analogous to AppWizard for generating an application.

6. In the ControlWizard Step 1 dialog box (see Figure 25.1), just click the Finish button to select all the default ControlWizard options.

FIGURE 25.1:

The ControlWizard Step 1 dialog box, showing the default options that you should accept

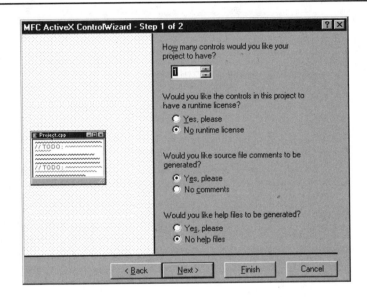

The options in the ControlWizard Step 1 and Step 2 dialog boxes allow you to create more than one ActiveX control in a single project, to optimize your ActiveX controls in various ways, and to adapt the controls for specialized purposes.

7. Click the OK button in the New Project Information dialog box.

Customizing the ActiveX Control Program

In the following sections, you'll customize the program resources, write the code to display the pictures, and add a message handler. These techniques *aren't* unique to creating ActiveX controls, and they've all been covered in previous chapters, so the instructions will be brief.

Creating the Bitmaps That Are Displayed in the Control

The two pictures displayed in the ActiveX control are generated using bitmaps. To create the first bitmap, choose the Insert ➤ Resource... menu command to open the Insert Resource dialog box, select Bitmap in the Resource Type list, and click the New button. Then draw the desired image in the Visual C++ graphics editor. Be sure to retain the default bitmap identifier, IDB_BITMAP1, and make the bitmap approximately 130 to 150 pixels in width and height (you can adjust the size of the bitmap by dragging the sizing handle in the lower-right corner).

Now create the second bitmap the same way. Retain the default identifier, IDB_BITMAP2, and make the bitmap the same size as the first one. The bitmaps for the version of the AXCtrl program provided on the companion CD—as they appear in the Visual C++ graphics editor—are shown in Figures 25.2 and 25.3. (These bitmaps measure 140 pixels by 140 pixels.)

FIGURE 25.2:

The IDB_BITMAP1 bitmap in the AXCtrl program provided on the companion CD

FIGURE 25.3:

The IDB_BITMAP2 bitmap in the AXCtrl program provided on the companion CD

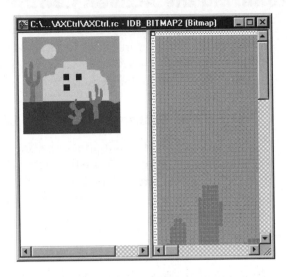

| TIP | Rather than creating new bitmaps in the Visual C++ graphics editor, you can import the bitmaps from .bmp files (for example, you could use the two bitmaps shown in Figures 25.2 and 25.3 by importing the files Night.bmp and Day.bmp from the \AXCtrl companion-CD folder). To import a bitmap file, choose the Insert ➤ Resource... menu command, click the Import... button, and then select the .bmp file. |

Optional: Modifying the Program Bitmap and Icon

If you wish, you can customize the program bitmap, which has the IDB_AXCTRL resource identifier. This bitmap will be displayed in the Visual C++ Controls tool-bar (along with the bitmaps for the standard Windows controls) when you design a dialog box in a container program that incorporates the AXCtrl control. The default version of the bitmap contains the letters OCX.

You can also customize the program icon, IDI_ABOUTDLL, which is displayed in the About dialog box. Note that the AXCtrl program on the companion CD uses the default versions of both these resources.

Creating and Displaying the Bitmaps

The next step is to add the code to create and display the bitmaps within the control. For an explanation of these techniques, see Chapter 20.

Begin by adding declarations for three member functions near the beginning of the CAXCtrlCtrl class definition in the AXCtrlCtl.h source file:

```
class CAXCtrlCtrl : public COleControl
{
    DECLARE_DYNCREATE(CAXCtrlCtrl)

public:
    CBitmap *m_CurrentBitmap, m_BitmapNight, m_BitmapDay;
```

CAXCtrlCtrl is the class that manages the ActiveX control. The m_Bitmap-Night and m_BitmapDay members will be used to manage the two bitmaps displayed in the control, and m_CurrentBitmap will serve as a pointer to the object for the currently displayed bitmap. Next, add code to the CAXCtrlCtrl constructor in AXCtrlCtl.cpp for loading the bitmaps from the bitmap resources and for initializing m_CurrentBitmap:

```
CAXCtrlCtrl::CAXCtrlCtrl()
{
    InitializeIIDs(&IID_DAXCtrl, &IID_DAXCtrlEvents);

    // TODO: Initialize your control's instance data here.

    m_BitmapNight.LoadBitmap (IDB_BITMAP1);
    m_BitmapDay.LoadBitmap (IDB_BITMAP2);
    m_CurrentBitmap = &m_BitmapNight; // initially display the
                                      // "night" bitmap
}
```

Whenever the control needs drawing or redrawing, the OnDraw member function of the control class (CAXCtrlCtrl) is called. You'll now modify the OnDraw definition in AXCtrlCtl.cpp, so that the function displays the current bitmap within the control. First, *remove* the call to the Ellipse function (the initial

ControlWizard-generated code paints a white background and draws an ellipse). Then, add code as follows:

```
void CAXCtrlCtrl::OnDraw
    (CDC* pdc, const CRect& rcBounds, const CRect& rcInvalid)
{
    // TODO: Replace the following code with your own drawing
    // code.
    pdc->FillRect
        (rcBounds,
        Brush::FromHandle((HBRUSH)GetStockObject(WHITE_BRUSH)));

    BITMAP BM;
    CDC MemDC;

    MemDC.CreateCompatibleDC (NULL);
    MemDC.SelectObject (*m_CurrentBitmap);
    m_CurrentBitmap->GetObject (sizeof (BM), &BM);
    pdc->BitBlt
        ((rcBounds.right  - BM.bmWidth)  / 2,
        ( rcBounds.bottom - BM.bmHeight) / 2,
        BM.bmWidth,
        BM.bmHeight,
        &MemDC,
        0,
        0,
        SRCCOPY);
}
```

Note that the `rcBounds` parameter passed to `OnDraw` contains the current dimensions of the control, while the `rcInvalid` parameter contains the coordinates of the current invalid area within the control (that is, the area marked for redrawing). Drawing from the `OnDraw` function of an ActiveX control class is just like drawing from the `OnDraw` function of a view window class, as described in previous chapters.

Adding a Click Message Handler

Your next task is to define a message-handling function that receives control whenever the user clicks the control while it's displayed within a container. To do this, run ClassWizard and open the Message Maps tab. Select the name of the class that manages the control, `CAXCtrlCtrl`, in the Class Name: and Object

IDs: lists. Select the WM_LBUTTONUP Windows message identifier in the Messages: list. Then, click the Add Function button, click the Edit Code button, and add code as follows to the OnLButtonUp function generated by ClassWizard:

```
void CAXCtrlCtrl::OnLButtonUp(UINT nFlags, CPoint point)
{
    // TODO: Add your message handler code here and/or call
    // default

    if (m_CurrentBitmap == &m_BitmapNight)
       m_CurrentBitmap = &m_BitmapDay;
    else
       m_CurrentBitmap = &m_BitmapNight;

    InvalidateControl ();

    COleControl::OnLButtonUp(nFlags, point);
}
```

OnLButtonUp is called when the user clicks on the control, after the mouse button is released. The added code changes m_CurrentBitmap so that it points to the other of the two bitmaps. It then calls InvalidateControl to force the OnDraw function to be called, which redraws the control using the new bitmap.

Defining Properties

You'll now begin learning techniques that are unique to developing ActiveX controls. First, you'll define two properties: the BackColor stock property, which lets a container application change the control's background color, and the ShowFrame custom property, which lets a container add or remove the frame from around the picture in the control.

Defining the BackColor Stock Property

The BackColor property that you'll define is a *stock* property, meaning that it's one of a set of common properties (including Caption, Font, and others) that the Microsoft Foundation Classes code stores and initializes for you. The MFC code also performs the appropriate action when the value of a stock property is changed. You need only enable the property and provide the code to use the property value.

To enable the BackColor property, run ClassWizard and open the Automation tab. Make sure that the control class, CAXCtrlCtrl, is selected in the Class Name: list and click the Add Property... button. In the Add Property dialog box select the BackColor stock property from the External Name: list and make sure the Stock option is selected in the Implementation area. The completed dialog box is shown in Figure 25.4. Click OK to return to the Automation tab of ClassWizard (leave ClassWizard running so that you can define the next property).

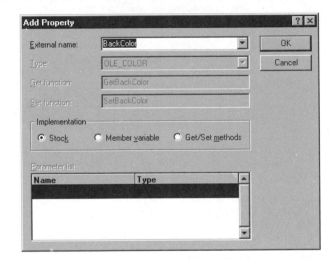

The MFC code stores the value of the BackColor property, and initializes it to the background color of the container window or dialog box in which the control is displayed. The MFC also invalidates the control—thereby forcing the OnDraw function to redraw it—whenever the value of the property is changed, either by the container or by the control program itself. The only thing the MFC doesn't do is use the color contained in the property to paint the control background. Later, you'll add the code to do this to the OnDraw method.

Defining the ShowFrame Custom Property

The ShowFrame property that you'll define is a *custom* property, meaning that it's a property you devise yourself, assigning it a name and providing most of the supporting code.

To define the ShowFrame property, once again click the Add Property… button in the Automation tab of the ClassWizard dialog box to open the Add Property dialog box. Then, type ShowFrame into the External Name: box, select BOOL in the Type: list, and make sure that the Member Variable option is selected in the Implementation area. Leave the name m_showFrame in the Variable Name: text box and the name OnShowFrameChanged in the Notification Function: text box.

These choices create a custom property that has the name ShowFrame and the data type BOOL (that is, it can be set to either TRUE or FALSE). The property value will be stored in a BOOL variable named m_showFrame, which ClassWizard defines as a member of the control class (CAXCtrlCtrl). Whenever the container changes the value of the property, the MFC code will assign the new value to m_show-Frame and will call the CAXCtrlCtrl::OnShowFrameChanged notification function. ClassWizard defines the basic shell for this function; later, you'll add code to it.

The completed Add Property dialog box is shown in Figure 25.5. When you're done entering the values, click the OK button to return to the Automation tab of the ClassWizard dialog box, which will show both properties you defined, as you can see in Figure 25.6. Now click OK to close ClassWizard.

FIGURE 25.5:

The completed Add Property dialog box for defining the ShowFrame custom property

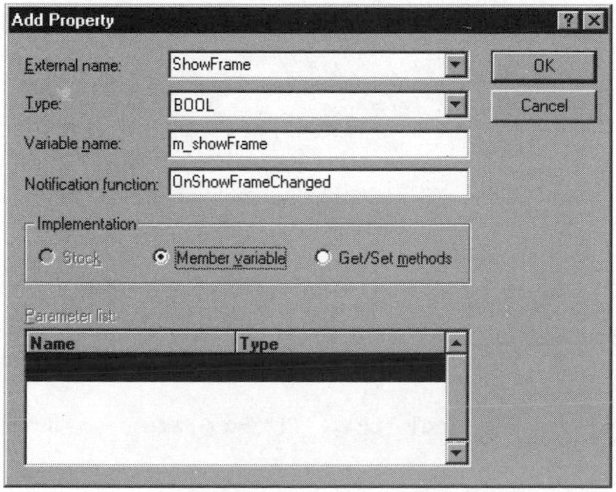

FIGURE 25.6:

The Automation tab after both properties have been defined

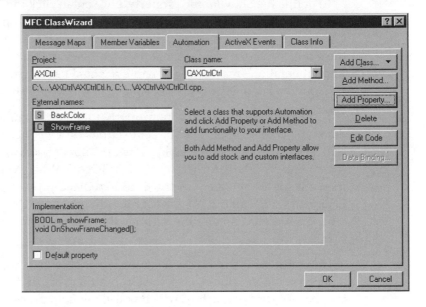

Because ShowFrame is a custom property, you need to explicitly initialize its value. Do this by adding a call to the global MFC function PX_Bool to the CAX-CtrlCtrl::DoPropExchange function in AXCtrlCtl.cpp:

```
///////////////////////////////////////////////////////////////////
///////////
// CAXCtrlCtrl::DoPropExchange - Persistence support

void CAXCtrlCtrl::DoPropExchange(CPropExchange* pPX)
{
    ExchangeVersion(pPX, MAKELONG(_wVerMinor, _wVerMajor));
    COleControl::DoPropExchange(pPX);

    // TODO: Call PX_ functions for each persistent custom
    // property.
    PX_Bool (pPX, _T("ShowFrame"), m_showFrame, FALSE);
}
```

This call initializes both the ShowFrame property and the m_showFrame member variable to FALSE.

Finally, add a call to COleControl::InvalidateControl to the notification function, CAXCtrlCtrl::OnShowFrameChanged, in CAXCtrlCtl.cpp:

```
void CAXCtrlCtrl::OnShowFrameChanged()
{
    // TODO: Add notification handler code

    InvalidateControl ();

    SetModifiedFlag();
}
```

Whenever the container changes the ShowFrame property, OnShowFrameChanged receives control. The call to InvalidateControl forces the CAXCtrlCtrl::OnDraw function to be called, which redraws the ActiveX control with or without the frame, according to the value of the ShowFrame property.

Modifying the OnDraw Function

You now need to modify the CAXCtrlCtrl::OnDraw function in the AXCtrlCtl.cpp file so that it uses the current values of the two new properties when it draws the control. See Chapter 19 for an explanation of the drawing techniques.

First, *remove* the existing call to FillRect. Then, add code as follows:

```
void CAXCtrlCtrl::OnDraw(CDC* pdc, const CRect& rcBounds, const
    CRect& rcInvalid)
{
    // TODO: Replace the following code with your own drawing
    // code.

    CBrush Brush (TranslateColor (GetBackColor ()));
    pdc->FillRect (rcBounds, &Brush);

    BITMAP BM;
    CDC MemDC;

    MemDC.CreateCompatibleDC (NULL);
    MemDC.SelectObject (*m_CurrentBitmap);
    m_CurrentBitmap->GetObject (sizeof (BM), &BM);
    pdc->BitBlt
        ((rcBounds.right  - BM.bmWidth) / 2,
        ( rcBounds.bottom - BM.bmHeight) / 2,
        BM.bmWidth,
```

```
            BM.bmHeight,
            &MemDC,
            0,
            0,
            SRCCOPY);

    if (m_showFrame)
        {
        CBrush *pOldBrush =
            (CBrush *)pdc->SelectStockObject (NULL_BRUSH);
        CPen Pen (PS_SOLID | PS_INSIDEFRAME, 10, RGB (0,0,0));
        CPen *pOldPen = pdc->SelectObject (&Pen);

        pdc->Rectangle (rcBounds);

        pdc->SelectObject (pOldPen);
        pdc->SelectObject (pOldBrush);
        }
    }
```

The first two added statements draw the control background using the color currently assigned to the BackColor property, which is obtained by calling the `COleControl::GetBackColor` function. `GetBackColor` returns an `OLE_COLOR` value, which conforms to the format used to represent a color in an ActiveX control. The call to `TranslateColor` converts the returned value to a `COLORREF` value, which conforms to the format used to represent a color in a Windows program. (Note that you can *set* the BackColor property by passing an `OLE_COLOR` value to `COleControl::GetBackColor`.)

The second block of code you added draws a border around the periphery of the control *if* the ShowFrame property—whose value is stored in `m_showFrame`—is currently set to TRUE.

Modifying the Property Pages

An ActiveX control program can also include one or more *property pages*. Each property page is defined like a dialog box and contains a collection of controls for setting the values of the ActiveX control's properties. As you'll see later in the chapter, when you design a container program for an ActiveX control using Visual C++, you can use the property pages to assign initial values to the control's properties. Each property page is displayed as a tab in the Properties dialog box shown by the Visual C++ dialog editor.

The ActiveX control project initially contains a single default property page, which is defined in the IDD_PROPPAGE_AXCTRL dialog resource. The original version of this property page contains only a static text control with a "TODO" message. You'll replace this control with a check box that can be used to change the ShowFrame property. To do this, open the IDD_PROPPAGE_AXCTRL dialog resource in the Visual C++ dialog editor. First, delete the existing static text control with the "TODO" message. Then, add a check box control, assigning it the identifier IDC_SHOWFRAME and the caption "Display a frame around the picture." The completed dialog resource is shown in Figure 25.7.

FIGURE 25.7:

The completed IDD_ PROPPAGE_AXCTRL dialog resource, which defines the layout of the ActiveX control's default property page

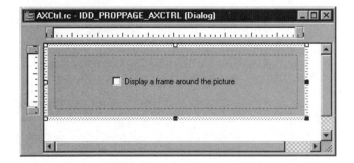

Next, you must link the new check box control to the ShowFrame property by doing the following:

1. Run ClassWizard and open the Member Variables tab.

2. In the Class Name list, select the name of the class that manages the default property page, CAXCtrlPropPage. The identifier of the check box, IDC_ SHOWFRAME, will already be selected in the Control IDs: list because it's the only control contained in the default property page.

3. Click the Add Variable... button to open the Add Member Variable dialog box.

4. Enter m_ShowFrame into the Member Variable Name: text box. Leave Value selected in the Category: list. Leave BOOL selected in the Variable Type: list. And type ShowFrame into the Optional Property Name: text box. The completed dialog box is shown in Figure 25.8. Click the OK button when you're done, to return to the ClassWizard dialog box, which should now appear as shown in Figure 25.9.

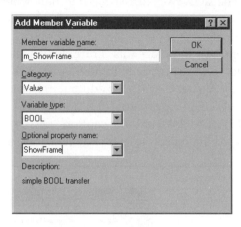

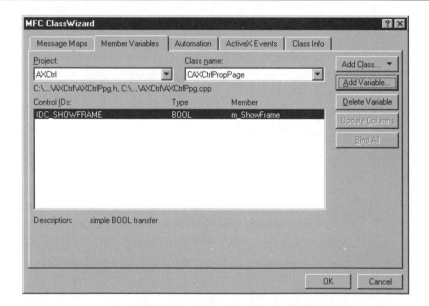

5. Click the OK button to remove the ClassWizard dialog box.

Because you initialized the ShowFrame property to FALSE (following the
instructions in the section "Defining the ShowFrame Custom Property"), the
check box—which is now linked to the ShowFrame property—will initially
be unchecked when the property page is displayed during development of a
container.

The final step is to add a second property page to the program. You'll add the stock Color property page, which can be used to set the value of the BackColor property when you design a container. To add this property page, open the file AXCtrlCtl.cpp and modify the property-page table (which defines all the property pages provided by the control), as shown here:

```
//////////////////////////////////////////////////////////////////
///////////
// Property pages

// TODO: Add more property pages as needed.  Remember to increase
// the count!
BEGIN_PROPPAGEIDS(CAXCtrlCtrl, 2)
    PROPPAGEID(CAXCtrlPropPage::guid)
    PROPPAGEID(CLSID_CColorPropPage)
END_PROPPAGEIDS(CAXCtrlCtrl)
```

You need to change the number passed to the BEGIN_PROPPAGEIDS macro from 1 to 2, and then add a new call to the PROPPAGEID macro. (The first PROPPAGEID call in this table adds the default property page that you just modified.) The stock Color property page will be automatically linked to the BackColor property; therefore, you don't need to link it manually, as you did with the check box in the default property page.

Defining Methods

The AXCtrl project already contains a method named AboutBox, which was defined by ControlWizard. When a container program calls this method, the control displays an "About" dialog box (which is defined in the IDD_ABOUTBOX_ AXCTRL dialog resource).

In this exercise, you won't define any additional methods. If you wish to add a method to some other ActiveX control that you're developing, run ClassWizard, open the Automation tab, select the name of the control class (CAXCtrlCtrl for AXCtrl) in the Class Name: list, and click the Add Method... button. Then, specify the name, return type, and parameters (if any) for the method. Like a property, the method can be either stock or custom.

Defining Events

Once an event has been defined, an ActiveX control program can call the associated Fire... function (for example, FireClick or FireModified) to notify the container program that the event has occurred. Calling the Fire... function is known as *firing an event*. As you'll see later, firing an event causes an event-handling function in the container to be called if one has been defined for that event.

Like a property or a method, an event can be either stock or custom. For a stock event, the MFC provides the `Fire`... function as well as the code that calls this function at the appropriate times. For a custom event, ClassWizard generates a new `Fire`... function, and you must write the code to call this function when you want to fire the event.

You'll now define a stock event for the AXCtrl program, which notifies the container whenever the user clicks the control:

1. Run ClassWizard and open the ActiveX Events tab.

2. Click the Add Event... button to open the Add Event dialog box.

3. Select the Click stock event in the External Name: list. The *external name* is the name used by a container program to reference the event. Notice that `FireClick` is displayed in the Internal Name: text box. The *internal name* is the name of the function that the control program calls to fire the event. (For a stock event, you can't change the internal name.)

4. Make sure the Stock option is enabled in the Implementation area. The completed dialog box is shown in Figure 25.10. Click the OK button to return to the ClassWizard dialog box, which will list the Click event you just defined.

FIGURE 25.10:

The completed Add Event dialog box for defining the Click stock event

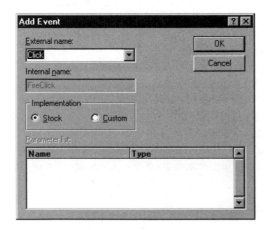

5. Click OK in the ClassWizard dialog box.

The FireClick function is defined within the COleControl class. The MFC code automatically calls this function to fire the Click event whenever the user clicks on the control. You therefore don't need to add any calls to FireClick to your program code (though you could do so if you wanted to fire the event at additional times).

Building the Control

You can now click the Build button to build the AXCtrl ActiveX control. This will generate the ActiveX control file, AXCtrl.ocx, and will automatically register the control on your system so that it can be accessed by container programs. In the next part of the chapter, you'll write a container program to display the control.

If you ship an ActiveX control to other users (perhaps together with a container program that displays it), you should provide an installation program that registers the control on the user's system. For information on doing this, see the following Visual C++ online help topic: *Visual C++ Documentation, Using Visual C++, Visual C++ Programmer's Guide, Adding User Interface Features, Details, ActiveX Control Topics, ActiveX Controls, ActiveX Controls: Distributing ActiveX Controls.*

TIP

As you develop an ActiveX control, you can periodically test its features by displaying it within the Test Container program provided with Visual C++. If you've included the Test Container in your Visual C++ installation, you can run it by choosing the Tools ➤ ActiveX Control Test Container menu command. For information, see the online help topic: *Visual C++ Documentation, Using Visual C++, Visual C++ Programmer's Guide, Debugging, Debugging Specific Types of Applications, Debugging an ActiveX Control, Test Container.*

The AXCtrl Source Code

The listings below, Listings 25.1 through 25.6, are the C++ source code files for the AXCtrl ActiveX control program. You'll find a copy of these files in the \AXCtrl folder on the companion CD.

Listing 25.1

```
// AXCtrl.h : main header file for AXCTRL.DLL

#if !defined(AFX_AXCTRL_H__CC31D28C_B1B1_11D1_80FC_00C0F6A83B7F__INCLUDED_)
#define AFX_AXCTRL_H__CC31D28C_B1B1_11D1_80FC_00C0F6A83B7F__INCLUDED_

#if _MSC_VER > 1000
#pragma once
#endif // _MSC_VER > 1000

#if !defined( __AFXCTL_H__ )
   #error include 'afxctl.h' before including this file
#endif

#include "resource.h"        // main symbols

/////////////////////////////////////////////////////////////////////////////
// CAXCtrlApp : See AXCtrl.cpp for implementation.

class CAXCtrlApp : public COleControlModule
{
public:
   BOOL InitInstance();
   int ExitInstance();
};

extern const GUID CDECL _tlid;
extern const WORD _wVerMajor;
extern const WORD _wVerMinor;

//{{AFX_INSERT_LOCATION}}
// Microsoft Visual C++ will insert additional declarations immediately before
// the previous line.

#endif // !defined(AFX_AXCTRL_H__CC31D28C_B1B1_11D1_80FC_00C0F6A83B7F__INCLUDED)
```

Listing 25.2

```
// AXCtrl.cpp : Implementation of CAXCtrlApp and DLL registration.

#include "stdafx.h"
#include "AXCtrl.h"
```

```
#ifdef _DEBUG
#define new DEBUG_NEW
#undef THIS_FILE
static char THIS_FILE[] = __FILE__;
#endif


CAXCtrlApp NEAR theApp;

const GUID CDECL BASED_CODE _tlid =
    {0xcc31d283, 0xb1b1, 0x11d1, {0x80, 0xfc, 0, 0xc0, 0xf6, 0xa8, 0x3b, 0x7f }};
const WORD _wVerMajor = 1;
const WORD _wVerMinor = 0;


/////////////////////////////////////////////////////////////////////////////
// CAXCtrlApp::InitInstance - DLL initialization

BOOL CAXCtrlApp::InitInstance()
{
   BOOL bInit = COleControlModule::InitInstance();

   if (bInit)
   {
       // TODO: Add your own module initialization code here.
   }

   return bInit;
}


/////////////////////////////////////////////////////////////////////////////
// CAXCtrlApp::ExitInstance - DLL termination

int CAXCtrlApp::ExitInstance()
{
   // TODO: Add your own module termination code here.

   return COleControlModule::ExitInstance();
}
```

```
/////////////////////////////////////////////////////////////////////////////
// DllRegisterServer - Adds entries to the system registry

STDAPI DllRegisterServer(void)
{
    AFX_MANAGE_STATE(_afxModuleAddrThis);

    if (!AfxOleRegisterTypeLib(AfxGetInstanceHandle(), _tlid))
        return ResultFromScode(SELFREG_E_TYPELIB);

    if (!COleObjectFactoryEx::UpdateRegistryAll(TRUE))
        return ResultFromScode(SELFREG_E_CLASS);

    return NOERROR;
}


/////////////////////////////////////////////////////////////////////////////
// DllUnregisterServer - Removes entries from the system registry

STDAPI DllUnregisterServer(void)
{
    AFX_MANAGE_STATE(_afxModuleAddrThis);

    if (!AfxOleUnregisterTypeLib(_tlid, _wVerMajor, _wVerMinor))
        return ResultFromScode(SELFREG_E_TYPELIB);

    if (!COleObjectFactoryEx::UpdateRegistryAll(FALSE))
        return ResultFromScode(SELFREG_E_CLASS);

    return NOERROR;
}
```

Listing 25.3

```
// AXCtrlCtl.h : Declaration of the CAXCtrlCtrl ActiveX Control class.

#if !defined(AFX_AXCTRLCTL_H__CC31D294_B1B1_11D1_80FC_00C0F6A83B7F__INCLUDED_)
#define AFX_AXCTRLCTL_H__CC31D294_B1B1_11D1_80FC_00C0F6A83B7F__INCLUDED_

#if _MSC_VER > 1000
#pragma once
#endif // _MSC_VER > 1000
```

```
//////////////////////////////////////////////////////////////////////
// CAXCtrlCtrl : See AXCtrlCtl.cpp for implementation.

class CAXCtrlCtrl : public COleControl
{
   DECLARE_DYNCREATE(CAXCtrlCtrl)

public:
   CBitmap *m_CurrentBitmap, m_BitmapNight, m_BitmapDay;

// Constructor
public:
   CAXCtrlCtrl();

// Overrides
   // ClassWizard generated virtual function overrides
   //{{AFX_VIRTUAL(CAXCtrlCtrl)
   public:
   virtual void OnDraw(CDC* pdc, const CRect& rcBounds, const CRect& rcInvalid);
   virtual void DoPropExchange(CPropExchange* pPX);
   virtual void OnResetState();
   //}}AFX_VIRTUAL

// Implementation
protected:
   ~CAXCtrlCtrl();

   DECLARE_OLECREATE_EX(CAXCtrlCtrl)    // Class factory and guid
   DECLARE_OLETYPELIB(CAXCtrlCtrl)      // GetTypeInfo
   DECLARE_PROPPAGEIDS(CAXCtrlCtrl)     // Property page IDs
   DECLARE_OLECTLTYPE(CAXCtrlCtrl)      // Type name and misc status

// Message maps
   //{{AFX_MSG(CAXCtrlCtrl)
   afx_msg void OnLButtonUp(UINT nFlags, CPoint point);
   //}}AFX_MSG
   DECLARE_MESSAGE_MAP()

// Dispatch maps
   //{{AFX_DISPATCH(CAXCtrlCtrl)
   BOOL m_showFrame;
   afx_msg void OnShowFrameChanged();
```

```
    //}}AFX_DISPATCH
    DECLARE_DISPATCH_MAP()

    afx_msg void AboutBox();

// Event maps
    //{{AFX_EVENT(CAXCtrlCtrl)
    //}}AFX_EVENT
    DECLARE_EVENT_MAP()

// Dispatch and event IDs
public:
    enum {
    //{{AFX_DISP_ID(CAXCtrlCtrl)
    dispidShowFrame = 1L,
    //}}AFX_DISP_ID
    };
};

//{{AFX_INSERT_LOCATION}}
// Microsoft Visual C++ will insert additional declarations immediately before
// the previous line.

#endif
// !defined(AFX_AXCTRLCTL_H__CC31D294_B1B1_11D1_80FC_00C0F6A83B7F__INCLUDED)
```

Listing 25.4

```
// AXCtrlCtl.cpp : Implementation of the CAXCtrlCtrl ActiveX Control class.

#include "stdafx.h"
#include "AXCtrl.h"
#include "AXCtrlCtl.h"
#include "AXCtrlPpg.h"


#ifdef _DEBUG
#define new DEBUG_NEW
#undef THIS_FILE
static char THIS_FILE[] = __FILE__;
#endif


IMPLEMENT_DYNCREATE(CAXCtrlCtrl, COleControl)
```

```
/////////////////////////////////////////////////////////////////////
// Message map

BEGIN_MESSAGE_MAP(CAXCtrlCtrl, COleControl)
   //{{AFX_MSG_MAP(CAXCtrlCtrl)
   ON_WM_LBUTTONUP()
   //}}AFX_MSG_MAP
   ON_OLEVERB(AFX_IDS_VERB_PROPERTIES, OnProperties)
END_MESSAGE_MAP()


/////////////////////////////////////////////////////////////////////
// Dispatch map

BEGIN_DISPATCH_MAP(CAXCtrlCtrl, COleControl)
   //{{AFX_DISPATCH_MAP(CAXCtrlCtrl)
   DISP_PROPERTY_NOTIFY(CAXCtrlCtrl, "ShowFrame", m_showFrame, OnShowFrameChanged,
VT_BOOL)
   DISP_STOCKPROP_BACKCOLOR()
   //}}AFX_DISPATCH_MAP
   DISP_FUNCTION_ID(CAXCtrlCtrl, "AboutBox", DISPID_ABOUTBOX, AboutBox, VT_EMPTY,
      VTS_NONE)
END_DISPATCH_MAP()


/////////////////////////////////////////////////////////////////////
// Event map

BEGIN_EVENT_MAP(CAXCtrlCtrl, COleControl)
   //{{AFX_EVENT_MAP(CAXCtrlCtrl)
   EVENT_STOCK_CLICK()
   //}}AFX_EVENT_MAP
END_EVENT_MAP()



/////////////////////////////////////////////////////////////////////
// Property pages

// TODO: Add more property pages as needed.  Remember to increase the count!
BEGIN_PROPPAGEIDS(CAXCtrlCtrl, 2)
   PROPPAGEID(CAXCtrlPropPage::guid)
   PROPPAGEID(CLSID_CColorPropPage)
END_PROPPAGEIDS(CAXCtrlCtrl)
```

```
//////////////////////////////////////////////////////////////////////
// Initialize class factory and guid

IMPLEMENT_OLECREATE_EX(CAXCtrlCtrl, "AXCTRL.AXCtrlCtrl.1",
    0xcc31d286, 0xb1b1, 0x11d1, 0x80, 0xfc, 0, 0xc0, 0xf6, 0xa8, 0x3b, 0x7f)


//////////////////////////////////////////////////////////////////////
// Type library ID and version

IMPLEMENT_OLETYPELIB(CAXCtrlCtrl, _tlid, _wVerMajor, _wVerMinor)


//////////////////////////////////////////////////////////////////////
// Interface IDs

const IID BASED_CODE IID_DAXCtrl =
    {0xcc31d284, 0xb1b1, 0x11d1, {0x80, 0xfc, 0, 0xc0, 0xf6, 0xa8, 0x3b, 0x7f}};
const IID BASED_CODE IID_DAXCtrlEvents =
    {0xcc31d285, 0xb1b1, 0x11d1, {0x80, 0xfc, 0, 0xc0, 0xf6, 0xa8, 0x3b, 0x7f}};


//////////////////////////////////////////////////////////////////////
// Control type information

static const DWORD BASED_CODE _dwAXCtrlOleMisc =
    OLEMISC_ACTIVATEWHENVISIBLE |
    OLEMISC_SETCLIENTSITEFIRST |
    OLEMISC_INSIDEOUT |
    OLEMISC_CANTLINKINSIDE |
    OLEMISC_RECOMPOSEONRESIZE;

IMPLEMENT_OLECTLTYPE(CAXCtrlCtrl, IDS_AXCTRL, _dwAXCtrlOleMisc)


//////////////////////////////////////////////////////////////////////
// CAXCtrlCtrl::CAXCtrlCtrlFactory::UpdateRegistry -
// Adds or removes system registry entries for CAXCtrlCtrl

BOOL CAXCtrlCtrl::CAXCtrlCtrlFactory::UpdateRegistry(BOOL bRegister)
{
    // TODO: Verify that your control follows apartment-model threading rules.
    // Refer to MFC TechNote 64 for more information.
```

```
    // If your control does not conform to the apartment-model rules, then
    // you must modify the code below, changing the 6th parameter from
    // afxRegApartmentThreading to 0.

    if (bRegister)
        return AfxOleRegisterControlClass(
            AfxGetInstanceHandle(),
            m_clsid,
            m_lpszProgID,
            IDS_AXCTRL,
            IDB_AXCTRL,
            afxRegApartmentThreading,
            _dwAXCtrlOleMisc,
            _tlid,
            _wVerMajor,
            _wVerMinor);
    else
        return AfxOleUnregisterClass(m_clsid, m_lpszProgID);
}


/////////////////////////////////////////////////////////////////////////////
// CAXCtrlCtrl::CAXCtrlCtrl - Constructor

CAXCtrlCtrl::CAXCtrlCtrl()
{
    InitializeIIDs(&IID_DAXCtrl, &IID_DAXCtrlEvents);

    // TODO: Initialize your control's instance data here.

    m_BitmapNight.LoadBitmap (IDB_BITMAP1);
    m_BitmapDay.LoadBitmap (IDB_BITMAP2);
    m_CurrentBitmap = &m_BitmapNight; // initially display the "night" bitmap
}


/////////////////////////////////////////////////////////////////////////////
// CAXCtrlCtrl::~CAXCtrlCtrl - Destructor

CAXCtrlCtrl::~CAXCtrlCtrl()
{
    // TODO: Cleanup your control's instance data here.
}
```

```
//////////////////////////////////////////////////////////////////////
// CAXCtrlCtrl::OnDraw - Drawing function

void CAXCtrlCtrl::OnDraw(CDC* pdc, const CRect& rcBounds, const CRect& rcInvalid)
{
    // TODO: Replace the following code with your own drawing code.

    CBrush Brush (TranslateColor (GetBackColor ()));
    pdc->FillRect (rcBounds, &Brush);

    BITMAP BM;
    CDC MemDC;

    MemDC.CreateCompatibleDC (NULL);
    MemDC.SelectObject (*m_CurrentBitmap);
    m_CurrentBitmap->GetObject (sizeof (BM), &BM);
    pdc->BitBlt
        ((rcBounds.right  - BM.bmWidth)  / 2,
        ( rcBounds.bottom - BM.bmHeight) / 2,
        BM.bmWidth,
        BM.bmHeight,
        &MemDC,
        0,
        0,
        SRCCOPY);

    if (m_showFrame)
        {
        CBrush *pOldBrush = (CBrush *)pdc->SelectStockObject (NULL_BRUSH);
        CPen Pen (PS_SOLID | PS_INSIDEFRAME, 10, RGB (0,0,0));
        CPen *pOldPen = pdc->SelectObject (&Pen);

        pdc->Rectangle (rcBounds);

        pdc->SelectObject (pOldPen);
        pdc->SelectObject (pOldBrush);
        }
}


//////////////////////////////////////////////////////////////////////
// CAXCtrlCtrl::DoPropExchange - Persistence support
```

```
void CAXCtrlCtrl::DoPropExchange(CPropExchange* pPX)
{
    ExchangeVersion(pPX, MAKELONG(_wVerMinor, _wVerMajor));
    COleControl::DoPropExchange(pPX);

    // TODO: Call PX_ functions for each persistent custom property.
    PX_Bool (pPX, _T("ShowFrame"), m_showFrame, FALSE);
}


/////////////////////////////////////////////////////////////////////////////
// CAXCtrlCtrl::OnResetState - Reset control to default state

void CAXCtrlCtrl::OnResetState()
{
    COleControl::OnResetState();  // Resets defaults found in DoPropExchange

    // TODO: Reset any other control state here.
}


/////////////////////////////////////////////////////////////////////////////
// CAXCtrlCtrl::AboutBox - Display an "About" box to the user

void CAXCtrlCtrl::AboutBox()
{
    CDialog dlgAbout(IDD_ABOUTBOX_AXCTRL);
    dlgAbout.DoModal();
}


/////////////////////////////////////////////////////////////////////////////
// CAXCtrlCtrl message handlers

void CAXCtrlCtrl::OnLButtonUp(UINT nFlags, CPoint point)
{
    // TODO: Add your message handler code here and/or call default

    if (m_CurrentBitmap == &m_BitmapNight)
        m_CurrentBitmap = &m_BitmapDay;
    else
        m_CurrentBitmap = &m_BitmapNight;
```

```
    InvalidateControl ();

    COleControl::OnLButtonUp(nFlags, point);
}

void CAXCtrlCtrl::OnShowFrameChanged()
{
    // TODO: Add notification handler code

    InvalidateControl ();

    SetModifiedFlag();
}
```

Listing 25.5

```
// AXCtrlPpg.h : Declaration of the CAXCtrlPropPage property page class.

#if !defined(AFX_AXCTRLPPG_H__CC31D296_B1B1_11D1_80FC_00C0F6A83B7F__INCLUDED_)
#define AFX_AXCTRLPPG_H__CC31D296_B1B1_11D1_80FC_00C0F6A83B7F__INCLUDED_

#if _MSC_VER > 1000
#pragma once
#endif // _MSC_VER > 1000


/////////////////////////////////////////////////////////////////////
// CAXCtrlPropPage : See AXCtrlPpg.cpp.cpp for implementation.

class CAXCtrlPropPage : public COlePropertyPage
{
    DECLARE_DYNCREATE(CAXCtrlPropPage)
    DECLARE_OLECREATE_EX(CAXCtrlPropPage)

// Constructor
public:
    CAXCtrlPropPage();

// Dialog Data
    //{{AFX_DATA(CAXCtrlPropPage)
    enum { IDD = IDD_PROPPAGE_AXCTRL };
    BOOL   m_ShowFrame;
    //}}AFX_DATA
```

```
// Implementation
protected:
    virtual void DoDataExchange(CDataExchange* pDX);     // DDX/DDV support

// Message maps
protected:
    //{{AFX_MSG(CAXCtrlPropPage)
        // NOTE - ClassWizard will add and remove member functions here.
        //     DO NOT EDIT what you see in these blocks of generated code !
    //}}AFX_MSG
    DECLARE_MESSAGE_MAP()

};

//{{AFX_INSERT_LOCATION}}
// Microsoft Visual C++ will insert additional declarations immediately before
// the previous line.

#endif
// !defined(AFX_AXCTRLPPG_H__CC31D296_B1B1_11D1_80FC_00C0F6A83B7F__INCLUDED)
```

Listing 25.6

```
// AXCtrlPpg.cpp : Implementation of the CAXCtrlPropPage property page class.

#include "stdafx.h"
#include "AXCtrl.h"
#include "AXCtrlPpg.h"

#ifdef _DEBUG
#define new DEBUG_NEW
#undef THIS_FILE
static char THIS_FILE[] = __FILE__;
#endif


IMPLEMENT_DYNCREATE(CAXCtrlPropPage, COlePropertyPage)


/////////////////////////////////////////////////////////////////////////////
// Message map
```

```
BEGIN_MESSAGE_MAP(CAXCtrlPropPage, COlePropertyPage)
   //{{AFX_MSG_MAP(CAXCtrlPropPage)
   // NOTE - ClassWizard will add and remove message map entries
   //     DO NOT EDIT what you see in these blocks of generated code !
   //}}AFX_MSG_MAP
END_MESSAGE_MAP()


/////////////////////////////////////////////////////////////////////////
// Initialize class factory and guid

IMPLEMENT_OLECREATE_EX(CAXCtrlPropPage, "AXCTRL.AXCtrlPropPage.1",
   0xcc31d287, 0xb1b1, 0x11d1, 0x80, 0xfc, 0, 0xc0, 0xf6, 0xa8, 0x3b, 0x7f)


/////////////////////////////////////////////////////////////////////////
// CAXCtrlPropPage::CAXCtrlPropPageFactory::UpdateRegistry -
// Adds or removes system registry entries for CAXCtrlPropPage

BOOL CAXCtrlPropPage::CAXCtrlPropPageFactory::UpdateRegistry(BOOL bRegister)
{
   if (bRegister)
      return AfxOleRegisterPropertyPageClass(AfxGetInstanceHandle(),
         m_clsid, IDS_AXCTRL_PPG);
   else
      return AfxOleUnregisterClass(m_clsid, NULL);
}


/////////////////////////////////////////////////////////////////////////
// CAXCtrlPropPage::CAXCtrlPropPage - Constructor

CAXCtrlPropPage::CAXCtrlPropPage() :
   COlePropertyPage(IDD, IDS_AXCTRL_PPG_CAPTION)
{
   //{{AFX_DATA_INIT(CAXCtrlPropPage)
   m_ShowFrame = FALSE;
   //}}AFX_DATA_INIT
}
```

```
/////////////////////////////////////////////////////////////////////////
// CAXCtrlPropPage::DoDataExchange - Moves data between page and properties

void CAXCtrlPropPage::DoDataExchange(CDataExchange* pDX)
{
    //{{AFX_DATA_MAP(CAXCtrlPropPage)
    DDP_Check(pDX, IDC_SHOWFRAME, m_ShowFrame, _T("ShowFrame") );
    DDX_Check(pDX, IDC_SHOWFRAME, m_ShowFrame);
    //}}AFX_DATA_MAP
    DDP_PostProcessing(pDX);
}


/////////////////////////////////////////////////////////////////////////
// CAXCtrlPropPage message handlers
```

Creating an ActiveX Control Container Program

In this part of the chapter, you'll use AppWizard and other Visual C++ tools to create an ActiveX control container program, AXCont, that's designed specifically to display and interact with the ActiveX control you created in the first part of the chapter. AXCont is a dialog-based program that displays the ActiveX control, gets and sets its properties (BackColor and ShowFrame), calls its method (AboutBox), and beeps in response to its event (Click).

Generating the Source Code Files

To create the AXCont source code files, follow the instructions for generating a dialog-based program that were given in Chapter 16 (in the section "Generating the DlgDemo Program in AppWizard"), *except* for the following:

1. In the Projects tab of the New dialog box, enter AXCont into the Project Name: box and enter the desired project folder into the Location: text box.

2. In the AppWizard Step 2 dialog box, deselect the About Box option (as before), but leave the ActiveX Controls option selected and enter ActiveX Control Container Demo into the Please Enter A Title For Your Dialog: text box at the bottom. The completed Step 2 dialog box is shown in Figure 25.11.

FIGURE 25.11:

The completed AppWizard Step 2 dialog box for creating the AXCont dialog-based container program

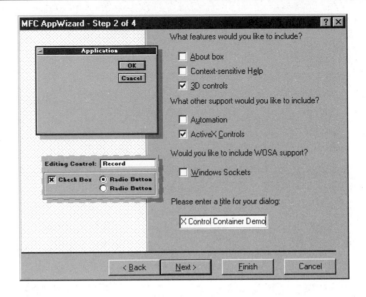

You can display an ActiveX control in an MFC program that you generated *without* choosing the ActiveX Controls option in AppWizard. To do this, you must add the function call `AfxEnableControlContainer();` to the program's `InitInstance` function and add the statement #include `<Afxdisp.h>` to the project's StdAfx.h header file.

Adding the ActiveX Control to the Project

Before you can display the AXCtrl ActiveX control in your container application, you must add the control to the project. Adding the control generates a "wrapper class" (named `CAXCtrl`) that allows the program to interact with the control, and also appends a button for the control to the Controls toolbar of the dialog editor so that you can easily add the control to a dialog box.

Here are the steps for adding the ActiveX control:

1.   Choose the Project ➤ Add to Project ➤ Components And Controls... menu command, which will open the Components And Controls Gallery dialog box.

2. In the Components And Controls Gallery dialog box, make sure that the Gallery folder is selected in the Look In: list and double-click the Registered ActiveX Controls item in the main list box. This will display a list of all ActiveX controls that have been installed and registered on your computer.

3. Select the name of the ActiveX control that you created in the first part of the chapter, AXCtrl Control. See Figure 25.12.

FIGURE 25.12:

Adding the AXCtrl Control ActiveX control to the project through the Components And Controls Gallery dialog box

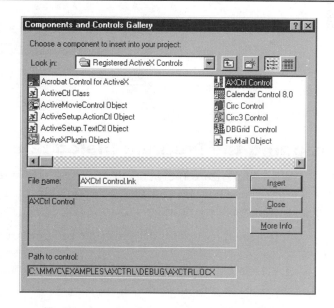

4. Click the Insert button and then click OK in the message box that asks whether you want to insert the component. Visual C++ then displays the Confirm Classes dialog box, which lists and lets you edit the names of the wrapper class for the ActiveX control and the files in which the class is defined. See Figure 25.13.

5. Click the OK button to accept the default class and file names.

6. Click the Close button in the Components And Controls Gallery dialog box.

FIGURE 25.13:

The dialog box for confirming classes

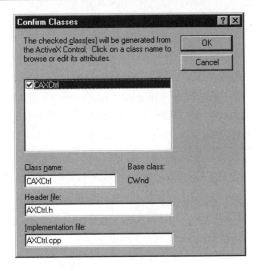

Designing the Program Dialog Box

When AppWizard first generates the AXCont source files, it opens the main program dialog box, IDD_AXCONT_DIALOG, in the dialog editor. If this resource isn't still open, open it now.

Here are the steps for designing the program dialog box:

1. Delete the existing static text control with the "TODO" message and delete the OK push button.

2. Change the Caption property of the Cancel push button to Close and add an About push button and a Frame push button. Table 25.1 lists the properties of all three buttons.

TABLE 25.1: Properties of the Push Button Controls to Be Included in the Dialog Box Displayed by the AXCont Program

ID:	Nondefault Properties You Need to Set
IDC_ABOUT	Caption: About
IDC_FRAME	Caption: Frame
IDC_CANCEL	Caption: Close

3. Add the ActiveX control to the dialog box by clicking on the OCX button at the bottom of the Controls toolbar and then clicking on the desired position within the dialog box.

   The OCX button was added to the Controls toolbar when you added the ActiveX control to the project in the previous section. You can insert the ActiveX control into the dialog box and adjust its size and position just like a standard Windows control.

4. Modify the properties of the ActiveX control by right-clicking it and choosing the Properties command. Notice that the AXCtrl Control Properties dialog box includes the two property pages that you added or modified when you created the control: the Color property page and the default property page.

5. Open the Color property page by clicking the Color tab and then click the red button to set the background color of the control to red. This modifies the control's BackColor property. Recall that the MFC code in the control program initializes this property to the current background color of the containing dialog box, which in this case is light-gray. The color you set in the Color tab at design time overrides the initial setting made by the control program.

6. Open the control program's default property page by clicking the Control tab, and check the Display A Frame Around The Picture check box. This sets the ShowFrame property of the control to TRUE, causing a black frame to be drawn around the control. Recall that in the control program you initialized this property to FALSE. The setting you make in the Control tab at design time overrides the initial value set by the control program.

7. Leave all other properties, including the dialog box identifier (IDC_AXCTRLCTRL1), with their default values. The final dialog box is shown in Figure 25.14.

FIGURE 25.14:

The completed main dialog box for the AXCont program

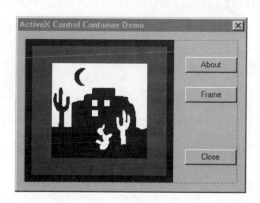

Attaching the ActiveX Control to a Wrapper Class Object

You now need to attach the ActiveX control in the dialog box to an instance of the wrapper class that was generated when you added the control to the project (in the section "Adding the ActiveX Control to the Project"). This will allow the code in the dialog box class to use functions of the wrapper class both to change the control's properties and to call its method. Here are the steps:

1. Run ClassWizard and open the Member Variables tab.

2. Select the dialog box class, CAXContDlg, in the Class Name: list so that the wrapper class object will be a member of the dialog box class.

3. Select the identifier of the ActiveX control, IDC_AXCTRLCTRL1, in the Control IDs: list.

4. Click the Add Variable... button to open the Add Member Variable dialog box.

5. Enter m_AXCtrl into the Member Variable Name: text box; this will be the name of the wrapper-class object. Leave Control selected in the Category: list, which indicates that the member variable is to be an instance of a wrapper class. And leave the name of the wrapper class, CAXCtrl, selected in the Variable Type: list (it's the only choice in the list because only one wrapper class was generated).

6. Click OK when you've finished entering information into the Add Member Variable dialog box, but leave the ClassWizard dialog box open for the task you'll perform in the next section.

Defining Message Handlers for the Push Buttons

The next task is to define message handlers for the About and Frame push buttons displayed in the program dialog box. (You don't need to define a handler for the Close button, because the MFC provides one for you.) These are the steps:

1. Open the Message Maps tab in the ClassWizard dialog box.

2. Select the dialog box class, CAXContDlg, in the Class Name: list.

3. Define a message-handling function that receives control when the Frame button is clicked by selecting the button's identifier, IDC_FRAME, in the Object IDs: list, selecting BN_CLICKED in the Messages: list, clicking the Add Function... button, and accepting the default function name, On-Frame. Then click the Edit Code button and add code as follows to the OnFrame function in AXContDlg.cpp:

```
void CAXContDlg::OnFrame()
{
    // TODO: Add your control notification handler code here

    m_AXCtrl.SetShowFrame (!m_AXCtrl.GetShowFrame ());
}
```

The added code simply toggles the ShowFrame property on and off. It uses the GetShowFrame and SetShowFrame functions of the control wrapper class to get and set the property.

4. In the same way, use ClassWizard to define a BN_CLICKED message handler for the About button (IDC_ABOUT), and add code to this handler as follows:

```
void CAXContDlg::OnAbout()
{
    // TODO: Add your control notification handler code here

    m_AXCtrl.AboutBox ();
}
```

The added statement calls the AboutBox function of the control wrapper class to invoke the AboutBox method, which displays the About dialog box.

Adding a Click Event Handler

Your final job is to define a function to handle the ActiveX control's Click event. This function will receive control each time the user clicks the control and the control fires the Click event. These are the steps:

1. Run ClassWizard and open the Message Maps tab.

2. Select the dialog box class, CAXContDlg, in the Class Name: list.

3. Select the identifier of the ActiveX control, IDC_AXCTRLCTRL1, in the Control IDs: list.

4. Select the name of the event that's to be handled, Click, in the Messages: list. (There are no other items in the list because Click is the only event that the control program fires.)

5. Click the Add Function... button and accept the default function name, OnClickAxctrlctrl1.

6. Click the Edit Code button and add code as follows to the function definition that ClassWizard generates:

```
void CAXContDlg::OnClickAxctrlctrl1()
{
    // TODO: Add your control notification handler code here

    ::MessageBeep (MB_OK);
}
```

The added line generates the default system sound.

Building and Testing AXCont

You can now build and run the AXCont program and test all its features. Whenever you click on the control, the control program switches between the day and night version of the picture and fires the Click event; in response to this event, the container program beeps. The program window is shown in Figure 25.15.

FIGURE 25.15:

The AXCont program window, as it appears when the program first starts

The AXCont Source Code

The C++ source code for the AXCont program is given in Listings 25.7 through 25.12, below. The \AXCont companion-CD folder contains a copy of these files.

Listing 25.7

```cpp
// AXCont.h : main header file for the AXCONT application
//

#if !defined(AFX_AXCONT_H__8B0C9E05_B276_11D1_80FC_00C0F6A83B7F__INCLUDED_)
#define AFX_AXCONT_H__8B0C9E05_B276_11D1_80FC_00C0F6A83B7F__INCLUDED_

#if _MSC_VER > 1000
#pragma once
#endif // _MSC_VER > 1000

#ifndef __AFXWIN_H__
    #error include 'stdafx.h' before including this file for PCH
#endif

#include "resource.h"        // main symbols

/////////////////////////////////////////////////////////////////////////////
// CAXContApp:
// See AXCont.cpp for the implementation of this class
//

class CAXContApp : public CWinApp
{
public:
    CAXContApp();

// Overrides
    // ClassWizard generated virtual function overrides
    //{{AFX_VIRTUAL(CAXContApp)
    public:
    virtual BOOL InitInstance();
    //}}AFX_VIRTUAL

// Implementation
```

```
    //{{AFX_MSG(CAXContApp)
        // NOTE - the ClassWizard will add and remove member functions here.
        //      DO NOT EDIT what you see in these blocks of generated code !
    //}}AFX_MSG
    DECLARE_MESSAGE_MAP()
};



//////////////////////////////////////////////////////////////////////

//{{AFX_INSERT_LOCATION}}
// Microsoft Visual C++ will insert additional declarations immediately before
// the previous line.

#endif // !defined(AFX_AXCONT_H__8B0C9E05_B276_11D1_80FC_00C0F6A83B7F__INCLUDED_)
```

Listing 25.8

```
// AXCont.cpp : Defines the class behaviors for the application.
//

#include "stdafx.h"
#include "AXCont.h"
#include "AXContDlg.h"

#ifdef _DEBUG
#define new DEBUG_NEW
#undef THIS_FILE
static char THIS_FILE[] = __FILE__;
#endif

//////////////////////////////////////////////////////////////////////
// CAXContApp

BEGIN_MESSAGE_MAP(CAXContApp, CWinApp)
    //{{AFX_MSG_MAP(CAXContApp)
        // NOTE - the ClassWizard will add and remove mapping macros here.
        //      DO NOT EDIT what you see in these blocks of generated code!
    //}}AFX_MSG
    ON_COMMAND(ID_HELP, CWinApp::OnHelp)
END_MESSAGE_MAP()
```

```
///////////////////////////////////////////////////////////////////////
// CAXContApp construction

CAXContApp::CAXContApp()
{
    // TODO: add construction code here,
    // Place all significant initialization in InitInstance
}

///////////////////////////////////////////////////////////////////////
// The one and only CAXContApp object

CAXContApp theApp;

///////////////////////////////////////////////////////////////////////
// CAXContApp initialization

BOOL CAXContApp::InitInstance()
{
    AfxEnableControlContainer();

    // Standard initialization
    // If you are not using these features and wish to reduce the size
    //  of your final executable, you should remove from the following
    //  the specific initialization routines you do not need.

#ifdef _AFXDLL
    Enable3dControls();          // Call this when using MFC in a shared DLL
#else
    Enable3dControlsStatic();   // Call this when linking to MFC statically
#endif

    CAXContDlg dlg;
    m_pMainWnd = &dlg;
    int nResponse = dlg.DoModal();
    if (nResponse == IDOK)
    {
        // TODO: Place code here to handle when the dialog is
        //   dismissed with OK
    }
    else if (nResponse == IDCANCEL)
    {
```

```
    // TODO: Place code here to handle when the dialog is
    //  dismissed with Cancel
  }

  // Since the dialog has been closed, return FALSE so that we exit the
  //  application, rather than start the application's message pump.
  return FALSE;
}
```

Listing 25.9

```cpp
// AXContDlg.h : header file
//
//{{AFX_INCLUDES()
#include "axctrl.h"
//}}AFX_INCLUDES

#if !defined(AFX_AXCONTDLG_H__8B0C9E07_B276_11D1_80FC_00C0F6A83B7F__INCLUDED_)
#define AFX_AXCONTDLG_H__8B0C9E07_B276_11D1_80FC_00C0F6A83B7F__INCLUDED_

#if _MSC_VER > 1000
#pragma once
#endif // _MSC_VER > 1000


/////////////////////////////////////////////////////////////////////
// CAXContDlg dialog

class CAXContDlg : public CDialog
{
// Construction
public:
  CAXContDlg(CWnd* pParent = NULL);   // standard constructor

// Dialog Data
  //{{AFX_DATA(CAXContDlg)
  enum { IDD = IDD_AXCONT_DIALOG };
  CAXCtrl  m_AXCtrl;
  //}}AFX_DATA

  // ClassWizard generated virtual function overrides
  //{{AFX_VIRTUAL(CAXContDlg)
  protected:
```

```
    virtual void DoDataExchange(CDataExchange* pDX);    // DDX/DDV support
    //}}AFX_VIRTUAL

// Implementation
protected:
    HICON m_hIcon;

    // Generated message map functions
    //{{AFX_MSG(CAXContDlg)
    virtual BOOL OnInitDialog();
    afx_msg void OnPaint();
    afx_msg HCURSOR OnQueryDragIcon();
    afx_msg void OnFrame();
    afx_msg void OnAbout();
    afx_msg void OnClickAxctrlctrl1();
    DECLARE_EVENTSINK_MAP()
    //}}AFX_MSG
    DECLARE_MESSAGE_MAP()
};

//{{AFX_INSERT_LOCATION}}
// Microsoft Visual C++ will insert additional declarations immediately before
// the previous line.

#endif
// !defined(AFX_AXCONTDLG_H__8B0C9E07_B276_11D1_80FC_00C0F6A83B7F__INCLUDED_)
```

Listing 25.10

```
// AXContDlg.cpp : implementation file
//

#include "stdafx.h"
#include "AXCont.h"
#include "AXContDlg.h"

#ifdef _DEBUG
#define new DEBUG_NEW
#undef THIS_FILE
static char THIS_FILE[] = __FILE__;
#endif
```

```
//////////////////////////////////////////////////////////////////////
// CAXContDlg dialog

CAXContDlg::CAXContDlg(CWnd* pParent /*=NULL*/)
    : CDialog(CAXContDlg::IDD, pParent)
{
    //{{AFX_DATA_INIT(CAXContDlg)
        // NOTE: the ClassWizard will add member initialization here
    //}}AFX_DATA_INIT
    // Note that LoadIcon does not require a subsequent DestroyIcon in Win32
    m_hIcon = AfxGetApp()->LoadIcon(IDR_MAINFRAME);
}

void CAXContDlg::DoDataExchange(CDataExchange* pDX)
{
    CDialog::DoDataExchange(pDX);
    //{{AFX_DATA_MAP(CAXContDlg)
    DDX_Control(pDX, IDC_AXCTRLCTRL1, m_AXCtrl);
    //}}AFX_DATA_MAP
}

BEGIN_MESSAGE_MAP(CAXContDlg, CDialog)
    //{{AFX_MSG_MAP(CAXContDlg)
    ON_WM_PAINT()
    ON_WM_QUERYDRAGICON()
    ON_BN_CLICKED(IDC_FRAME, OnFrame)
    ON_BN_CLICKED(IDC_ABOUT, OnAbout)
    //}}AFX_MSG_MAP
END_MESSAGE_MAP()

//////////////////////////////////////////////////////////////////////
// CAXContDlg message handlers

BOOL CAXContDlg::OnInitDialog()
{
    CDialog::OnInitDialog();

    // Set the icon for this dialog.  The framework does this automatically
    //  when the application's main window is not a dialog
    SetIcon(m_hIcon, TRUE);         // Set big icon
    SetIcon(m_hIcon, FALSE);        // Set small icon
```

```
    // TODO: Add extra initialization here

    return TRUE;  // return TRUE  unless you set the focus to a control
}

// If you add a minimize button to your dialog, you will need the code below
//  to draw the icon.  For MFC applications using the document/view model,
//  this is automatically done for you by the framework.

void CAXContDlg::OnPaint()
{
    if (IsIconic())
    {
        CPaintDC dc(this); // device context for painting

        SendMessage(WM_ICONERASEBKGND, (WPARAM) dc.GetSafeHdc(), 0);

        // Center icon in client rectangle
        int cxIcon = GetSystemMetrics(SM_CXICON);
        int cyIcon = GetSystemMetrics(SM_CYICON);
        CRect rect;
        GetClientRect(&rect);
        int x = (rect.Width() - cxIcon + 1) / 2;
        int y = (rect.Height() - cyIcon + 1) / 2;

        // Draw the icon
        dc.DrawIcon(x, y, m_hIcon);
    }
    else
    {
        CDialog::OnPaint();
    }
}

// The system calls this to obtain the cursor to display while the user drags
//  the minimized window.
HCURSOR CAXContDlg::OnQueryDragIcon()
{
    return (HCURSOR) m_hIcon;
}

void CAXContDlg::OnFrame()
```

```
{
    // TODO: Add your control notification handler code here

    m_AXCtrl.SetShowFrame (!m_AXCtrl.GetShowFrame ());
}

void CAXContDlg::OnAbout()
{
    // TODO: Add your control notification handler code here

    m_AXCtrl.AboutBox ();
}

BEGIN_EVENTSINK_MAP(CAXContDlg, CDialog)
    //{{AFX_EVENTSINK_MAP(CAXContDlg)
    ON_EVENT(CAXContDlg, IDC_AXCTRLCTRL1, -600 /* Click */, OnClickAxctrlctrl1, VTS_NONE)
    //}}AFX_EVENTSINK_MAP
END_EVENTSINK_MAP()

void CAXContDlg::OnClickAxctrlctrl1()
{
    // TODO: Add your control notification handler code here

    ::MessageBeep (MB_OK);
}
```

Listing 25.11

```
///////////////////////////////////////////////////////////////////////
// AXCtrl.h wrapper class

#if !defined(AFX_AXCTRL_H__8B0C9E0F_B276_11D1_80FC_00C0F6A83B7F__INCLUDED_)
#define AFX_AXCTRL_H__8B0C9E0F_B276_11D1_80FC_00C0F6A83B7F__INCLUDED_

#if _MSC_VER > 1000
#pragma once
#endif // _MSC_VER > 1000
// Machine generated IDispatch wrapper class(es) created by Microsoft Visual C++

// NOTE: Do not modify the contents of this file.  If this class is regenerated
// by Microsoft Visual C++, your modifications will be overwritten.
```

```
class CAXCtrl : public CWnd
{
protected:
   DECLARE_DYNCREATE(CAXCtrl)
public:
   CLSID const& GetClsid()
   {
      static CLSID const clsid
         = { 0xcc31d286, 0xb1b1, 0x11d1, { 0x80, 0xfc, 0x0, 0xc0, 0xf6, 0xa8,
            0x3b, 0x7f } };
      return clsid;
   }
   virtual BOOL Create(LPCTSTR lpszClassName,
      LPCTSTR lpszWindowName, DWORD dwStyle,
      const RECT& rect,
      CWnd* pParentWnd, UINT nID,
      CCreateContext* pContext = NULL)
   { return CreateControl(GetClsid(), lpszWindowName, dwStyle, rect, pParentWnd,
      nID); }

    BOOL Create(LPCTSTR lpszWindowName, DWORD dwStyle,
      const RECT& rect, CWnd* pParentWnd, UINT nID,
      CFile* pPersist = NULL, BOOL bStorage = FALSE,
      BSTR bstrLicKey = NULL)
   { return CreateControl(GetClsid(), lpszWindowName, dwStyle, rect, pParentWnd,
      nID, pPersist, bStorage, bstrLicKey); }

// Attributes
public:
   OLE_COLOR GetBackColor();
   void SetBackColor(OLE_COLOR);
   BOOL GetShowFrame();
   void SetShowFrame(BOOL);

// Operations
public:
   void AboutBox();
};


//{{AFX_INSERT_LOCATION}}
// Microsoft Visual C++ will insert additional declarations immediately before
// the previous line.

#endif // !defined(AFX_AXCTRL_H__8B0C9E0F_B276_11D1_80FC_00C0F6A83B7F__INCLUDED_)
```

Listing 25.12

```cpp
////////////////////////////////////////////////////////////////////////
// AXCtrl.cpp
// Machine generated IDispatch wrapper class(es) created by Microsoft Visual C++

// NOTE: Do not modify the contents of this file.  If this class is regenerated
// by Microsoft Visual C++, your modifications will be overwritten.

#include "stdafx.h"
#include "axctrl.h"


IMPLEMENT_DYNCREATE(CAXCtrl, CWnd)


////////////////////////////////////////////////////////////////////////
// CAXCtrl properties

OLE_COLOR CAXCtrl::GetBackColor()
{
   OLE_COLOR result;
   GetProperty(DISPID_BACKCOLOR, VT_I4, (void*)&result);
   return result;
}

void CAXCtrl::SetBackColor(OLE_COLOR propVal)
{
   SetProperty(DISPID_BACKCOLOR, VT_I4, propVal);
}

BOOL CAXCtrl::GetShowFrame()
{
   BOOL result;
   GetProperty(0x1, VT_BOOL, (void*)&result);
   return result;
}

void CAXCtrl::SetShowFrame(BOOL propVal)
{
   SetProperty(0x1, VT_BOOL, propVal);
}
```

```
/////////////////////////////////////////////////////////////////////////
// CAXCtrl operations

void CAXCtrl::AboutBox()
{
    InvokeHelper(0xfffffdd8, DISPATCH_METHOD, VT_EMPTY, NULL, NULL);
}
```

Summary

In this chapter you learned how to use Visual C++ both to create an ActiveX control and to create a container application that can display and interact with an ActiveX control. Here are some of the highlights:

- An ActiveX control is a portable software module that can be plugged into any ActiveX control container program.

- A container program displays an ActiveX control as an integral part of its interface and interacts with it through properties, methods, and events.

- A *property* is an attribute of the control that the container can read or modify.

- A *method* is a function provided by the control that the container can call.

- An *event* is an occurrence within the control that causes the control to notify the container by calling a function within the container that has been defined to handle that event.

- You can quickly create an ActiveX control that's based on the MFC by selecting the MFC ActiveX ControlWizard project type in the Projects tab of the New dialog box. Selecting this option runs ControlWizard, which lets you choose options and then generates the basic source code files for the ActiveX control.

- You can use ClassWizard to define properties, methods, and events for an ActiveX control program. Each of these items comes in two varieties: stock and custom. The MFC provides most of the code to support a stock item, while you have to write your own supporting code for a custom item.

- You can also include in an ActiveX control one or more *property pages*, which contain controls that let you set the initial values of control properties when you design a container program.

- When you build an ActiveX control, Visual C++ generates the .ocx file that contains the control's code and resources, and also registers the control on your computer system so that it can be accessed by container programs.

- Any program you create with AppWizard (by choosing the "MFC App-Wizard (.exe)" item in the Projects tab of the New dialog box) can serve as an ActiveX control container, provided that you select the ActiveX Controls option in the AppWizard Step 2 dialog box.

- To include an ActiveX control in a container program, you need to generate a wrapper class and to add a button for the control to the Controls toolbar of the dialog editor. You do this by choosing the Project ➢ Add to Project ➢ Components And Controls... menu command and selecting the name of the control.

- You add an ActiveX control to a dialog box by clicking the button for the control in the Controls toolbar and then using the same techniques used to add and customize a standard Windows control.

- You can use ClassWizard to attach an ActiveX control to an object of the control's wrapper class. The dialog class can then call member functions of the wrapper class to get or set control properties or to call control methods.

- You can also use ClassWizard to define a member function of the dialog class that gets called when the ActiveX control fires a specific event.

INDEX

Note to the Reader: Throughout this index **boldfaced** page numbers indicate primary discussions of a topic. *Italicized* page numbers indicate illustrations.

SYMBOLS

& (ampersands)
    for dialog box controls, 572, 575
    for menu items, 325
    for reference types, 65–66
<> (angle brackets)
    for class templates, 191–192
    for function templates, 185–186
* (asterisks)
    for comments, 56
    as operator, overloading, 162
: (colons)
    for member initializer lists, 104
    for scope resolution operator, 60
, (commas), 104
{} (curly brackets)
    for arrays, 179
    for blocks, 57
. (dot operators) for member access, 94
… (ellipses)
    with catch statements, 206, 218
    for project folders, 18
= (equal signs) operator
    overloading, **164–168**
    with reference types, 66

> (greater than signs), 397
< (less than signs)
    as insertion operator, 28–29, 397
    for serializing objects, 397
- (minus signs), overloading, 162
() (parentheses)
    for catch statements, 203
    for constructors, 102
    for member initializer lists, 104
+ (plus signs), overloading, **154–162**, **175–176**
/ (slashes)
    for comments, 56
    as operator, overloading, 162
[] (square brackets) for arrays, 83, 111
~ (tildes) for destructors, 108

A

abort procedures, 1052
About command
    toolbar button for, 504, *504*
    for WinGreet, 245
About method, 1295
AboutBox function
    in CAXCtrl, 1329
    in CAXCtrlCtrl, 1307

B

(

E

F

G

H

J

K

L

N

O

P

U

V

W

X

Y

Using the Companion CD

The Mastering Visual C++ 6 companion CD contains all the source code and executable files for the example programs provided in this book. You can use these files to save typing when working through the exercises given in the book, to explore the features of the example programs, and to experiment with additional programming techniques. You can also use them as a basis for creating your own programs. For more information, see the section "Using the Companion CD" in Chapter 1, as well as the file Readme.txt in the root folder of the CD.

Program Name	File name
AXCont—An ActiveX control container program that displays the AXCtrl ActiveX control	AXCont.exe
AXCtrl—An example ActiveX control	AXCtrl.ocx
BitDemo—A program that illustrates the techniques for designing, displaying, and manipulating bitmaps	BitDemo.exe
ContDemo—A basic OLE container program (can be used to embed drawings created by the ServDemo program)	ContDemo.exe
Cpp—A folder (not a program) that contains all the code listings from Part II of the book	
DlgDemo—A simple dialog-based program	DlgDemo.exe
Echo—A program that illustrates the basic techniques for reading characters from the keyboard and echoing them in a window	Echo.exe
FontDemo—A program that displays and exchanges information with a modal dialog box	FontDemo.exe
FormDemo—A form-view program, which is a full-featured program based on a dialog box	FormDemo.exe
Greet—A simple console (that is, character-mode) program	Greet.exe
Mandel—A program that generates a fractal pattern to illustrate the techniques for drawing points, as well as several other graphics drawing techniques	Mandel.exe
MandelMT—A multithreaded version of the Mandel program	MandelMT.exe
MiniDraw 1 (MiniDrw1 folder)—The first version of the MiniDraw program, a simple drawing application that illustrates the techniques for creating a full-featured MFC Windows program and for drawing graphics. This version lets you draw only straight lines.	MiniDraw.exe
MiniDraw 2 (MiniDrw2 folder)—The second version of the MiniDraw program, which stores the drawn lines and adds undo and delete commands	MiniDraw.exe
MiniDraw 3 (MiniDrw3 folder)—The third version of the MiniDraw program, which adds file I/O	MiniDraw.exe
MiniDraw 4 (MiniDrw4 folder)—The fourth version of the MiniDraw program, which adds scrolling capability, as well as a split box that allows you to divide the window into two panes	MiniDraw.exe
MiniDraw 5 (MiniDrw5 folder)—The fifth version of the MiniDraw program, which adds a docking toolbar and a status bar to the program interface	MiniDraw.exe
MiniDraw 6 (MiniDrw6 folder)—The sixth version of the MiniDraw program, which adds new shapes to the figures that you can draw (lines, rectangles, rounded rectangles, and circles) and lets you adjust the line thickness and choose the drawing color	MiniDraw.exe
MiniDraw 7 (MiniDrw7 folder)—The seventh and final version of the MiniDraw program, which adds printing and print previewing	MiniDraw.exe
MiniEdit 1 (MiniEdt1 folder)—The first version of the MiniEdit program, which illustrates the techniques for creating a text editor. This version provides the basic text editing commands.	MiniEdit.exe
MiniEdit 2 (MiniEdt2 folder)—The second version of the MiniEdit program, which adds file I/O	MiniEdit.exe
MiniEdit 3 (MiniEdt3 folder)—An MDI (multiple document interface) version of the MiniEdit program, which lets open and edit several text files simultaneously	MiniEdit.exe
ServDemo—A basic OLE server program, which is based on the MiniDraw program and allows OLE container programs (such as ContDemo) to embed drawings	ServDemo.exe
TabDemo—A program that displays a tabbed dialog box	TabDemo.exe
TextDemo—A program that demonstrates the main steps for choosing fonts and displaying lines of text in a window	TextDemo.exe
WinGreet—A basic MFC Windows application	WinGreet.exe